THE OXFORD
DICTIONARY OF
MODERN
QUOTATIONS

THE OXFORD DICTIONARY OF
MODERN
QUOTATIONS

Edited by

TONY AUGARDE

Oxford   New York

OXFORD UNIVERSITY PRESS

1991

Oxford University Press, Walton Street, Oxford OX2 6DP
Oxford New York Toronto
Delhi Bombay Calcutta Madras Karachi
Petaling Jaya Singapore Hong Kong Tokyo
Nairobi Dar es Salaam Cape Town
Melbourne Auckland
and associated companies in
Berlin Ibadan

Oxford is a trade mark of Oxford University Press

British Library Cataloguing in Publication Data
Data available

Library of Congress Cataloging in Publication Data
The Oxford dictionary of modern quotations / edited by Tony Augarde.
p. cm
Includes index.
ISBN 0–19–866141–X
1. Quotations. I. Augarde, Tony
PN6080.094 1991
080—dc20 90–26588
CIP

Typeset by Latimer Trend & Co Limited, Plymouth
Printed in the United States of America

Preface

THIS is a completely new dictionary, containing about 5,000 quotations.

What is a 'quotation'? It is a saying or piece of writing that strikes people as so true or memorable that they quote it (or allude to it) in speech or writing. Often they will quote it directly, introducing it with a phrase like 'As —— says' but equally often they will assume that the reader or listener already knows the quotation, and they will simply allude to it without mentioning its source (as in the headline 'A rosé is a rosé is a rosé', referring obliquely to a line by Gertrude Stein).

This dictionary has been compiled from extensive evidence of the quotations that are actually used in this way. The dictionary includes the commonest quotations which were found in a collection of more than 200,000 citations assembled by combing books, magazines, and newspapers. For example, our collections contained more than thirty examples each for Edward Heath's 'unacceptable face of capitalism' and Marshall McLuhan's 'The medium is the message', so both these quotations had to be included.

As a result, this book is not—like many quotations dictionaries—a subjective anthology of the editor's favourite quotations, but an objective selection of the quotations which are most widely known and used. Popularity and familiarity are the main criteria for inclusion, although no reader is likely to be familiar with all the quotations in this dictionary.

The book can be used for reference or for browsing: to trace the source of a particular quotation or to find an appropriate saying for a special need.

The quotations are drawn from novels, plays, poems, essays, speeches, films, radio and television broadcasts, songs, advertisements, and even book titles. It is difficult to draw the line between quotations and similar sayings like proverbs, catch-phrases, and idioms. For example, some quotations (like 'The opera ain't over till the fat lady sings') become proverbial. These are usually included if they can be traced to a particular originator. However, we have generally omitted phrases like 'agonizing reappraisal' which are covered adequately in the *Oxford English Dictionary*. Catch-phrases are included if there is evidence that they are widely remembered or used.

We have taken care to verify all the quotations in original or authoritative sources—something which few other quotations dictionaries have tried to do. We have corrected many errors found in other dictionaries, and we have traced the true origins of such phrases as 'There ain't no such thing as a free lunch' and 'Shaken and not stirred'.

The quotations are arranged in alphabetical order of authors, with anonymous quotations in the middle of 'A'. Under each author, the quotations are listed in alphabetical order of the titles of their sources. The anonymous quotations are arranged in alphabetical order of their first words. Foreign quotations are, wherever possible, given in the original language as well as in translation.

Authors are cited under the names by which they are best known: for example, Graham Greene (not Henry Graham Greene); F. Scott Fitzgerald (not Francis Scott Key Fitzgerald); George Orwell (not Eric Blair); W. C. Fields (not William Claude Dukenfield). Authors' dates of birth and death are given when ascertainable. The actual writers of the words are credited for quotations from songs, film-scripts, etc.

The references after each quotation are designed to be as helpful as possible, enabling the reader to trace quotations in their original sources if desired.

The index has been carefully prepared—with ingenious computer assistance—to help the reader to trace quotations from their most important keywords. Each reference includes not only the page and the number of the quotation on the page but also the first few letters of the author's name. The index includes references to book-titles which have become well known as quotations in their own right.

One difficulty in a dictionary of modern quotations is to decide what the word 'modern' means. In this dictionary it means 'twentieth-century'. Quotations are eligible if they originated from someone who was still alive after 1900. Where an author (like George Bernard Shaw, who died in 1950) said memorable things before and after 1900, these are all included.

This dictionary could not have been compiled without the work of many people, most notably Paula Clifford, Angela Partington, Fiona Mullan, Penelope Newsome, Julia Cresswell, Michael McKinley, Charles McCreery, Heidi Abbey, Jean Harker, Elizabeth Knowles, George Chowdharay-Best, Tracey Ward, and Ernest Trehern. I am also very grateful to the OUP Dictionary Department's team of checkers, who verified the quotations at libraries in Oxford, London, Washington, New York, and elsewhere. James Howes deserves credit for his work in computerizing the index.

The Editor is responsible for any errors, which he will be grateful to have drawn to his attention. As the quotation from Simeon Strunsky reminds us, 'Famous remarks are very seldom quoted correctly', but we have endeavoured to make this book more accurate, authoritative, and helpful than any other dictionary of modern quotations.

TONY AUGARDE

Contents

How to Use this Dictionary

The arrangement is alphabetical by the names of authors: usually the names by which each person is best known. So look under *Maya Angelou*, not *Maya Johnson*; *Princess Anne*, not *HRH The Princess Royal*; *Lord Beaverbrook*, not *William Maxwell Aitken*; *Irving Berlin*, not *Israel Balin*; *Greta Garbo*, not *Greta Lovisa Gustafsson*.

Anonymous quotations are all together, starting on page 5. They are arranged in alphabetical order of their first significant word.

Under each author, quotations are arranged by the alphabetical order of the titles of the works from which they come, even if those works were not written by the person who is being quoted. Poems are usually cited from the first book in which they appeared.

Quotations by foreign authors are, where possible, given in the original language and also in an English translation.

A reference is given after each quotation to its original source or to an authoritative record of its use. The reference usually consists of either (*a*) a book-title with its date of publication and a reference to where the quotation occurs in the book; or (*b*) the title of a newspaper or magazine with its date of publication. The reference is preceded by 'In' if the quotation comes from a secondary source: for example if a writer is quoted by another author in a newspaper article, or if a book refers to a saying but does not indicate where or when it was made.

EXAMPLES

Here are some typical entries, with notes to clarify the meaning of each part.

> *Charlie Chaplin (Sir Charles Spencer Chaplin)* 1889–1977
>
> **8** All I need to make a comedy is a park, a policeman and a pretty girl.
> *My Autobiography* (1964) ch. 10

Charlie Chaplin is the name by which this person is best known but *Sir Charles Spencer Chaplin* is the name which would appear in reference books such as *Who's Who*.

Charlie Chaplin was born in 1889 and died in 1977. The number '8' indicates that this is the eighth quotation on the page (page 49). The quotation comes from the tenth chapter of Chaplin's autobiography, which was published in 1964.

Martin Luther King 1929–1968

11 Injustice anywhere is a threat to justice everywhere.
Letter from Birmingham Jail, Alabama, 16 Apr. 1963, in
Atlantic Monthly Aug. 1963, p. 78

Martin Luther King wrote these words in a letter that he sent from Birmingham Jail on 16 April 1963. The letter was published later that year on page 78 of the August issue of the *Atlantic Monthly*.

Dorothy Parker 1893–1967

14 One more drink and I'd have been under the host.
In Howard Teichmann *George S. Kaufman* (1972) p. 68

Dorothy Parker must have said this before she died in 1967 but the earliest reliable source we can find is a 1972 book by Howard Teichmann. 'In' signals the fact that the quotation is cited from a secondary source.

INDEX

If you remember part of a quotation and want to know the rest of it, or who said it, you can trace it by means of the index.

The index lists the most significant words from each quotation. These keywords are listed alphabetically in the index, each with a section of the text to show the context of every keyword. These sections are listed in strict alphabetical order under each keyword. Foreign keywords are included in their alphabetical place.

The references show the first few letters of the author's name, followed by the page and item numbers (e.g. 163:15 refers to the fifteenth quotation on page 163).

As an example, suppose that you want to verify a quotation which you remember contains the line 'to purify the dialect of the tribe'. If you decide that *tribe* is a significant word and refer to it in the index, you will find this entry:

tribe: To purify the dialect of the t.   ELIOT 74:19

This will lead you to the poem by T. S. Eliot which is the nineteenth quotation on page 74.

THE OXFORD
DICTIONARY OF
MODERN
QUOTATIONS

Quotations

Bud Abbott 1895–1974 and *Lou Costello* (*Louis Francis Cristillo*) 1906–1959

1 ABBOTT: Now, on the St Louis team we have Who's on first, What's on second, I Don't Know is on third.
COSTELLO: That's what I want to find out.
Naughty Nineties (1945 film), in R. J. Anobile *Who's On First?* (1973) p. 224

Dannie Abse 1923–

2 I know the colour rose, and it is lovely,
But not when it ripens in a tumour;
And healing greens, leaves and grass, so springlike,
In limbs that fester are not springlike.
A Small Desperation (1968) 'Pathology of Colours'

3 So in the simple blessing of a rainbow,
In the bevelled edge of a sunlit mirror,
I have seen visible, Death's artifact
Like a soldier's ribbon on a tunic tacked.
A Small Desperation (1968) 'Pathology of Colours'

4 That Greek one then is my hero, who watched the bath water rise above his navel and rushed out naked, 'I found it, I found it' into the street in all his shining, and forgot that others would only stare at his genitals.
Walking under Water (1952) 'Letter to Alex Comfort'

Goodman Ace 1899–1982

5 Jane and I got mixed up with a television show—or as we call it back east here, TV—a clever contraction derived from the words Terrible Vaudeville. However, it is our latest medium—we call it a medium because nothing's well done. It was discovered, I suppose you've heard, by a man named Fulton Berle, and it has already revolutionized social grace by cutting down parlour conversation to two sentences: 'What's on television?' and 'Good night'.
Letter to Groucho Marx, in *The Groucho Letters* (1967) p. 114

Dean Acheson 1893–1971

6 The first requirement of a statesman is that he be dull. This is not always easy to achieve.
In *Observer* 21 June 1970

7 I will undoubtedly have to seek what is happily known as gainful employment, which I am glad to say does not describe holding public office.
In *Time* 22 Dec. 1952

8 Great Britain has lost an empire and has not yet found a role.
Speech at the Military Academy, West Point, 5 Dec. 1962, in *Vital Speeches* 1 Jan. 1963, p. 163

9 A memorandum is written not to inform the reader but to protect the writer.
In *Wall Street Journal* 8 Sept. 1977

J. R. Ackerley 1896–1967

10 I was born in 1896 and my parents were married in 1919.
My Father and Myself (1968) ch. 1

Douglas Adams 1952–

11 Don't panic.
Hitch Hiker's Guide to the Galaxy (1979) preface

12 'Life,' said Marvin, 'don't talk to me about Life.'
Hitch Hiker's Guide to the Galaxy (1979) ch. 11

13 And of course I've got this terrible pain in all the diodes down my left hand side.
Hitch Hiker's Guide to the Galaxy (1979) ch. 13

14 The Answer to the Great Question Of. . . . Life, the Universe and Everything. . . . Is. . . . Forty-two.
Hitch Hiker's Guide to the Galaxy (1979) ch. 27

15 'The first ten million years were the worst,' said Marvin, 'and the second ten million years, they were the worst too. The third ten million I didn't enjoy at all. After that I went into a bit of a decline.'
Restaurant at the End of the Universe (1980) ch. 18

Frank Adams and *Will M. Hough*

16 I wonder who's kissing her now.
Title of song (1909)

Franklin P. Adams 1881–1960

17 When the political columnists say 'Every thinking man' they mean themselves, and when candidates appeal to 'Every intelligent voter' they mean everybody who is going to vote for them.
Nods and Becks (1944) p. 3

18 Years ago we discovered the exact point, the dead centre of middle age. It occurs when you are too young to take up golf and too old to rush up to the net.
Nods and Becks (1944) p. 53

19 The trouble with this country is that there are too many politicians who believe, with a conviction based on experience, that you can fool all of the people all of the time.
Nods and Becks (1944) p. 74

20 Elections are won by men and women chiefly because most people vote against somebody rather than for somebody.
Nods and Becks (1944) p. 206

Henry Brooks Adams 1838–1918

1 Politics, as a practice, whatever its professions, has always been the systematic organization of hatreds.
Education of Henry Adams (1907) ch. 1

2 A friend in power is a friend lost.
Education of Henry Adams (1907) ch. 7

3 Chaos often breeds life, when order breeds habit.
Education of Henry Adams (1907) ch. 16

4 One friend in a lifetime is much; two are many; three are hardly possible. Friendship needs a certain parallelism of life, a community of thought, a rivalry of aim.
Education of Henry Adams (1907) ch. 20

5 What one knows is, in youth, of little moment; they know enough who know how to learn.
Education of Henry Adams (1907) ch. 21

6 Practical politics consists in ignoring facts.
Education of Henry Adams (1907) ch. 22

7 Some day science may have the existence of mankind in its power, and the human race commit suicide, by blowing up the world.
Letter 11 Apr. 1862, in *Letters of Henry Adams* (1982) vol. 1, p. 290

Harold Adamson 1906–1980

8 Comin' in on a wing and a pray'r.
Title of song (1943)

George Ade 1866–1944

9 'Whom are you?' he asked, for he had attended business college.
Chicago Record 16 Mar. 1898, 'The Steel Box'

10 Anybody can Win, unless there happens to be a Second Entry.
Fables in Slang (1900) p. 133

11 After being Turned Down by numerous Publishers, he had decided to write for posterity.
Fables in Slang (1900) p. 158

12 If it were not for the presents, an elopement would be preferable.
Forty Modern Fables (1901) p. 218

13 R-E-M-O-R-S-E!
Those dry Martinis did the work for me;
Last night at twelve I felt immense,
Today I feel like thirty cents.
My eyes are bleared, my coppers hot,
I'll try to eat, but I cannot.
It is no time for mirth and laughter,
The cold, gray dawn of the morning after.
Sultan of Sulu (1903) act 2, p. 63

Konrad Adenauer 1876–1967

14 A thick skin is a gift from God.
In *New York Times* 30 Dec. 1959, p. 5

Alfred Adler 1870–1937

15 It is always easier to fight for one's principles than to live up to them.
In Phyllis Bottome *Alfred Adler* (1939) p. 76

16 The truth is often a terrible weapon of aggression. It is possible to lie, and even to murder, for the truth.
Problems of Neurosis (1929) ch. 2

Polly Adler 1900–1962

17 A house is not a home.
Title of book (1954)

AE (A.E., Æ) (George William Russell) 1867–1935

18 In ancient shadows and twilights
Where childhood had strayed,
The world's great sorrows were born
And its heroes were made.
In the lost boyhood of Judas
Christ was betrayed.
Vale and Other Poems (1931) 'Germinal'

Herbert Agar 1897–1980

19 The truth which makes men free is for the most part the truth which men prefer not to hear.
Time for Greatness (1942) ch. 7

James Agate 1877–1947

20 I don't know very much, but what I do know I know better than anybody, and I don't want to argue about it. I know what I think about an actor or an actress, and am not interested in what anybody else thinks. My mind is not a bed to be made and re-made.
Ego 6 (1944) 9 June 1943

Spiro T. Agnew 1918–

21 I didn't say I wouldn't go into ghetto areas. I've been in many of them and to some extent I would have to say this: If you've seen one city slum you've seen them all.
In *Detroit Free Press* 19 Oct. 1968

22 A spirit of national masochism prevails, encouraged by an effete corps of impudent snobs who characterize themselves as intellectuals.
Speech in New Orleans, 19 Oct. 1969, in *Frankly Speaking* (1970) ch. 3

Max Aitken

See LORD BEAVERBROOK

Zoë Akins 1886–1958

23 The Greeks had a word for it.
Title of play (1930)

Alain (Émile-Auguste Chartier) 1868–1951

1 *Rien n'est plus dangereux qu'une idée, quand on n'a qu'une idée.*

Nothing is more dangerous than an idea, when you have only one idea.
Propos sur la religion (Remarks on Religion, 1938) no. 74

Edward Albee 1928–

2 Who's afraid of Virginia Woolf?
Title of play (1962). Cf. Frank E. Churchill

3 I have a fine sense of the ridiculous, but no sense of humour.
Who's Afraid of Virginia Woolf? (1962) act 1

Richard Aldington 1892–1962

4 Patriotism is a lively sense of collective responsibility. Nationalism is a silly cock crowing on its own dunghill.
Colonel's Daughter (1931) pt. 1, ch. 6

Brian Aldiss 1925–

5 Keep violence in the mind
Where it belongs.
Barefoot in the Head (1969) (last lines of concluding poem 'Charteris')

Nelson Algren 1909–

6 Never play cards with a man called Doc. Never eat at a place called Mom's. Never sleep with a woman whose troubles are worse than your own.
In *Newsweek* 2 July 1956

7 A walk on the wild side.
Title of novel (1956)

8 I got a glimpse into the uses of a certain kind of criticism this past summer at a writers' conference into how the avocation of assessing the failures of better men can be turned into a comfortable livelihood, providing you back it up with a Ph.D. I saw how it was possible to gain a chair of literature on no qualification other than persistence in nipping the heels of Hemingway, Faulkner, and Steinbeck. I know, of course, that there are true critics, one or two. For the rest all I can say is, Deal around me.
In Malcolm Cowley (ed.) *Writers at Work* (1958) 1st Ser. p. 222

Muhammad Ali (Cassius Clay) 1942–

9 Float like a butterfly, sting like a bee.
Catch-phrase used from c.1964, in G. Sullivan *Cassius Clay Story* (1964) ch. 8

10 I'm the greatest.
Catch-phrase used from 1962, in *Louisville Times* 16 Nov. 1962

Fred Allen (John Florence Sullivan) 1894–1956

11 California is a fine place to live—if you happen to be an orange.
American Magazine Dec. 1945, p. 120

12 Hollywood is a place where people from Iowa mistake each other for stars.
In Maurice Zolotow *No People like Show People* (1951) ch. 8

13 Committee—a group of men who individually can do nothing but as a group decide that nothing can be done.
In Laurence J. Peter *Quotations for our Time* (1978) p. 120

Woody Allen (Allen Stewart Konigsberg) 1935–

14 It's not that I'm afraid to die. I just don't want to be there when it happens.
Death (1975) p. 63

15 Is sex dirty? Only if it's done right.
Everything You Always Wanted to Know about Sex (1972 film)

16 If it turns out that there is a God, I don't think that he's evil. But the worst that you can say about him is that basically he's an underachiever.
Love and Death (1975 film)

17 The lion and the calf shall lie down together but the calf won't get much sleep.
New Republic 31 Aug. 1974 'The Scrolls'

18 Not only is there no God, but try getting a plumber on weekends.
New Yorker 27 Dec. 1969 'My Philosophy'

19 If only God would give me some clear sign! Like making a large deposit in my name at a Swiss bank.
New Yorker 5 Nov. 1973 'Selections from the Allen Notebooks'

20 On bisexuality: It immediately doubles your chances for a date on Saturday night.
New York Times 1 Dec. 1975, p. 33

21 More than any other time in history, mankind faces a crossroads. One path leads to despair and utter hopelessness. The other, to total extinction. Let us pray we have the wisdom to choose correctly.
Side Effects (1980) 'My Speech to the Graduates'

22 Take the money and run.
Title of film (1968)

23 On the plus side, death is one of the few things that can be done as easily lying down.
Without Feathers (1976) 'Early Essays'

24 Money is better than poverty, if only for financial reasons.
Without Feathers (1976) 'Early Essays'

25 My one regret in life is that I am not someone else.
Epigraph to Eric Lax *Woody Allen and his Comedy* (1975)

26 And my parents finally realize that I'm kidnapped and they snap into action immediately: They rent out my room.
In Eric Lax *Woody Allen and his Comedy* (1975) ch. 1

1 I don't want to achieve immortality through my work. . . . I want to achieve it through not dying.
  In Eric Lax *Woody Allen and his Comedy* (1975) ch. 12

2 It was partially my fault that we got divorced. . . . I tended to place my wife under a pedestal.
  At night-club in Chicago, Mar. 1964, recorded on *Woody Allen Volume Two* (Colpix CP 488) side 1, band 6

3 I must say . . . a fast word about oral contraception. I asked a girl to go to bed with me and she said 'no'.
  At night-club in Washington, Apr. 1965, recorded on *Woody Allen Volume Two* (Colpix CP 488) side 4, band 6

Woody Allen
(*Allen Stewart Konigsberg*) 1935–
and *Marshall Brickman* 1941–

4 That [sex] was the most fun I ever had without laughing.
  Annie Hall (1977 film)

5 Don't knock masturbation. It's sex with someone I love.
  Annie Hall (1977 film)

6 I feel that life is—is divided up into the horrible and the miserable.
  Annie Hall (1977 film)

7 My brain? It's my second favourite organ.
  Sleeper (1973 film)

8 I'm not the heroic type, really. I was beaten up by Quakers.
  Sleeper (1973 film)

Margery Allingham 1904–1966

9 Once sex rears its ugly 'ead it's time to steer clear.
  Flowers for the Judge (1936) ch. 4

Joseph Alsop

10 Gratitude, like love, is never a dependable international emotion.
  In *Observer* 30 Nov. 1952

Robert Altman 1922–

11 After all, what's a cult? It just means not enough people to make a minority.
  In *Guardian* 11 Apr. 1981

Leo Amery 1873–1955

12 I will quote certain other words. I do it with great reluctance, because I am speaking of those who are old friends and associates of mine, but they are words which, I think, are applicable to the present situation. This is what Cromwell said to the Long Parliament when he thought it was no longer fit to conduct the affairs of the nation: 'You have sat too long here for any good you have been doing. Depart, I say, and let us have done with you. In the name of God, go.'
  Hansard 7 May 1940, col. 1150. Cf. *Oxford Dictionary of Quotations* (1979) 169:26

13 Speak for England.
  Said to Arthur Greenwood in House of Commons, 2 Sept. 1939, in L. Amery *My Political Life* (1955) vol. 3, p. 324

14 For twenty years he [H. H. Asquith] has held a season-ticket on the line of least resistance and has gone wherever the train of events has carried him, lucidly justifying his position at whatever point he has happened to find himself.
  Quarterly Review July 1914, p. 276

Kingsley Amis 1922–

15 The delusion that there are thousands of young people about who are capable of benefiting from university training, but have somehow failed to find their way there, is . . . a necessary component of the expansionist case. . . . More will mean worse.
  Encounter July 1960

16 The point about white Burgundies is that I hate them myself. I take whatever my wine supplier will let me have at a good price (which I would never dream of doing with any other drinkable). I enjoyed seeing those glasses of Chablis or Pouilly Fuissé, so closely resembling a blend of cold chalk soup and alum cordial with an additive or two to bring it to the colour of children's pee, being peered and sniffed at, rolled round the shrinking tongue and forced down somehow by parties of young technology dons from Cambridge or junior television producers and their girls.
  The Green Man (1969) ch. 1

17 Dixon . . . tried to flail his features into some sort of response to humour. Mentally, however, he was making a different face and promising himself he'd make it actually when next alone. He'd draw his lower lip in under his top teeth and by degrees retract his chin as far as possible, all this while dilating his eyes and nostrils. By these means he would, he was confident, cause a deep dangerous flush to suffuse his face.
  Lucky Jim (1953) ch. 1

18 Alun's life was coming to consist more and more exclusively of being told at dictation speed what he knew.
  The Old Devils (1986) ch. 7

19 Outside every fat man there was an even fatter man trying to close in.
  One Fat Englishman (1963) ch. 3. See also Cyril Connolly 59:12 and George Orwell 164:11

20 He was of the faith chiefly in the sense that the church he currently did not attend was Catholic.
  One Fat Englishman (1963) ch. 8

Maxwell Anderson 1888–1959

21 But it's a long, long while
  From May to December;
  And the days grow short
  When you reach September.
  September Song (1938 song; music by Kurt Weill)

Maxwell Anderson 1888–1959 and Lawrence Stallings 1894–1968

1 What price glory?
Title of play (1924)

Robert Anderson 1917–

2 All you're supposed to do is every once in a while give the boys a little tea and sympathy.
Tea and Sympathy (1957) act 1

James Anderton 1932–

3 God works in mysterious ways. Given my love of God and my belief in God and in Jesus Christ, I have to accept that I may well be used by God in this way [as a prophet].
In radio interview, 18 Jan. 1987, in *Daily Telegraph* 19 Jan. 1987

4 Everywhere I go I see increasing evidence of people swirling about in a human cesspit of their own making.
Speech at seminar on AIDS, 11 Dec. 1986, in *Guardian* 12 Dec. 1986

Sir Norman Angell 1872–1967

5 The great illusion.
Title of book (1910), first published as 'Europe's optical illusion' (1909), on the futility of war

Maya Angelou (Maya Johnson) 1928-

6 I know why the caged bird sings.
Title of book (1969), taken from the last line of 'Sympathy' by Paul Laurence Dunbar in *Lyrics of Hearthside* (1899). Cf. *Oxford Dictionary of Quotations* (1979) 567:10

Paul Anka 1941–

7 And now the end is near
And so I face the final curtain,
My friend, I'll say it clear,
I'll state my case of which I'm certain.
I've lived a life that's full, I've travelled each and ev'ry highway
And more, much more than this. I did it my way.
My Way (1969 song; music by Claude François and Jacques Revaux)

Princess Anne (HRH the Princess Royal) 1950–

8 It could be said that the Aids pandemic is a classic own-goal scored by the human race against itself.
In *Daily Telegraph* 27 Jan. 1988

Anonymous

9 Access—your flexible friend.
Advertising slogan for Access credit cards, 1981 onwards, in Nigel Rees *Slogans* (1982) p. 91

10 All the way with LBJ.
US Democratic Party campaign slogan, in *Washington Post* 4 June 1960

11 American Express? . . . That'll do nicely, sir.
Advertisement for American Express credit card, 1970s, in F. Jenkins *Advertising* (1985) ch. 1

12 *Arbeit macht frei.*

Work liberates.
Words inscribed on the gates of Dachau concentration camp, 1933

13 Australians wouldn't give a XXXX for anything else.
Advertisement for Castlemaine lager, 1986 onwards, in Philip Kleinman *The Saatchi and Saatchi Story* (1987) ch. 5

14 Ban the bomb.
US anti-nuclear slogan, 1953 onwards, adopted by the Campaign for Nuclear Disarmament

15 A bayonet is a weapon with a worker at each end.
British pacifist slogan (1940)

16 The best defence against the atom bomb is not to be there when it goes off.
Contributor to *British Army Journal*, in *Observer* 20 Feb. 1949

17 Better red than dead.
Slogan of nuclear disarmament campaigners, late 1950s

18 Bigamy is having one husband too many. Monogamy is the same.
In Erica Jong *Fear of Flying* (1973) ch. 1 (epigraph)

19 A bigger bang for a buck.
Description of Charles E. Wilson's defence policy, in *Newsweek* 22 Mar. 1954

20 Black is beautiful.
Slogan of American civil rights campaigners in the mid-1960s, cited in *Newsweek* 11 July 1966

21 Burn, baby, burn.
Black extremist slogan used in Los Angeles riots, August 1965, in *Los Angeles Times* 15 Aug 1965, p. 1

22 The butler did it!
In Nigel Rees *Sayings of the Century* (1984) p. 45 (as a solution for detective stories. Rees cannot trace the origin of the phrase, but he quotes a correspondent who recalls hearing it at a cinema *c*.1916)

23 A camel is a horse designed by a committee.
In *Financial Times* 31 Jan. 1976

24 Can't act. Slightly bald. Also dances.
Studio official's comment on Fred Astaire, in Bob Thomas *Astaire* (1985) ch. 3

25 Can you tell Stork from butter?
Advertisement for Stork margarine, from *c*.1956

26 Careless talk costs lives.
World War II publicity slogan, in J. Darracott and B. Loftus *Second World War Posters* (1972) p. 28

27 Coughs and sneezes spread diseases. Trap the germs in your handkerchief.
1942 health slogan, in J. Darracott and B. Loftus *Second World War Posters* (1972) p. 19

28 [Death is] nature's way of telling you to slow down.
Newsweek, 25 Apr. 1960, p. 70

1 Do not fold, spindle or mutilate in any way.

1950s instruction on punched cards, found in various forms *c*.1935 onwards

2 Don't ask a man to drink and drive.

UK road safety slogan, from 1964

3 Don't die of ignorance.

Slogan used in AIDS publicity campaign, 1987: see *The Times* 9 and 13 Jan. 1987

4 *Ein Reich, ein Volk, ein Führer.*

One realm, one people, one leader.

Nazi Party slogan, early 1930s

5 Even your closest friends won't tell you.

US advertisement for Listerine mouthwash, in *Woman's Home Companion* Nov. 1923, p. 63

6 Every picture tells a story.

Advertisement for Doan's Backache Kidney Pills, in *Daily Mail* 26 Feb. 1904

7 Expletive deleted.

Submission of Recorded Presidential Conversations to the Committee on the Judiciary of the House of Representatives by President Richard M. Nixon 30 Apr. 1974, app. 1, p. 2

8 Faster than a speeding bullet! More powerful than a locomotive! Able to leap tall buildings at a single bound! Look! Up in the sky! It's a bird! It's a plane! It's Superman! Yes, it's Superman! Strange visitor from another planet, who came to earth with powers and abilities far beyond those of mortal men. Superman! Who can change the course of mighty rivers, bend steel with his bare hands, and who—disguised as Clark Kent, mild-mannered reporter for a great metropolitan newspaper—fights a never ending battle for truth, justice and the American way!

Preamble to *Superman*, US radio show, 1940 onwards

9 The following is a copy of Orders issued by the German Emperor on August 19th: 'It is my Royal and Imperial command that you concentrate your energies for the immediate present upon one single purpose, and that is that you address all your skill and all the valour of my soldiers to exterminate first, the treacherous English, walk over General French's contemptible little army. . . . '

Annexe to B.E.F. [British Expeditionary Force] Routine Orders of 24 September 1914, in Arthur Ponsonby *Falsehood in Wartime* (1928) ch. 10 (although this is often attributed to Kaiser Wilhelm II, it was most probably fabricated by the British)

10 Frankie and Albert were lovers, O Lordy, how they could love.
Swore to be true to each other, true as the stars above;
He was her man, but he done her wrong.

'Frankie and Albert' in John Huston *Frankie and Johnny* (1930) p. 95 (St Louis ballad later better known as 'Frankie and Johnny')

11 Full of Eastern promise.

Advertising slogan for Fry's Turkish Delight, 1950s onwards

12 God gave Noah the rainbow sign,
No more water, the fire next time.

Home in that Rock (Negro spiritual). Cf. James Baldwin 16:14

13 God is not dead but alive and well and working on a much less ambitious project.

Graffito quoted in *Guardian* 26 Nov. 1975

14 Gotcha!

Headline on the sinking of the *General Belgrano*, in *Sun* 4 May 1982

15 Go to work on an egg.

Advertising slogan for the British Egg Marketing Board, from 1957; perhaps written by Fay Weldon or Mary Gowing: see Nigel Rees *Slogans* (1982) p. 133

16 The Governments of the States parties to this Constitution on behalf of their peoples declare, that since wars begin in the minds of men, it is in the minds of men that the defences of peace must be constructed.

Constitution of the United Nations Educational, Scientific and Cultural Organisation (1945), in *UK Parliamentary Papers 1945–6* vol. 26

17 The hands that do dishes can be soft as your face, with mild green Fairy Liquid.

Advertising slogan for Procter & Gamble's washing-up liquid

18 Hark the herald angels sing
Mrs Simpson's pinched our king.

1936 children's rhyme quoted in letter from Clement Attlee, 26 Dec. 1938, in Kenneth Harris *Attlee* (1982) ch. 11

19 Have you heard? The Prime Minister [Lloyd George] has resigned and Northcliffe has sent for the King.

1919 saying in Hamilton Fyfe *Northcliffe, an Intimate Biography* (1930) ch. 16

20 Here we go, here we go, here we go.

Song sung by football supporters etc., 1980s

21 His [W. S. Gilbert's] foe was folly and his weapon wit.

Inscription on memorial to Gilbert on the Victoria Embankment, London, 1915

22 I don't like the family Stein!
There is Gert, there is Ep, there is Ein.
Gert's writings are punk,
Ep's statues are junk,
Nor can anyone understand Ein.

In R. Graves and A. Hodge *The Long Weekend* (1940) ch. 12 (rhyme current in the USA in the 1920s)

23 If it moves, salute it; if it doesn't move, pick it up; and if you can't pick it up, paint it.

1940s saying, in Paul Dickson *The Official Rules* (1978) p. 21

24 If you want to get ahead, get a hat.

Advertising slogan for the Hat Council, UK, 1965

25 *Ils ne passeront pas.*

They shall not pass.

Slogan used by French army at defence of Verdun in 1916; variously attributed to Marshal Pétain and to General Robert Nivelle. Cf. Dolores Ibarruri 109:18

26 I'm backing Britain.

Slogan coined by workers at the Colt factory, Surbiton, Surrey and subsequently used in a national campaign, in *The Times* 1 Jan. 1968

27 I'm worried about Jim.

Frequent line in *Mrs Dale's Diary*, BBC radio series 1948–69: see Denis Gifford *The Golden Age of Radio* (1985) p. 179 (where the line is given as 'I'm a little worried about Jim')

28 The iron lady.

In *Sunday Times* 25 Jan. 1976 (name given to Margaret Thatcher, then Leader of the Opposition, by the Soviet defence ministry newspaper *Red Star*, which accused her of trying to revive the cold war)

1 Is your journey *really* necessary?

1939 slogan (coined to discourage Civil Servants from going home for Christmas), in Norman Longmate *How We Lived Then* (1971) ch. 25

2 It became necessary to destroy the town to save it.

Comment by unidentified United States Army Major in Associated Press Report, *New York Times* 8 Feb. 1968 [the town referred to is Ben Tre, Vietnam]

3 It's for you-hoo!

Slogan for British Telecom television advertisements, 1985 onwards

4 It's that man again . . . ! At the head of a cavalcade of seven black motor cars Hitler swept out of his Berlin Chancellery last night on a mystery journey.

Headline in *Daily Express* 2 May 1939 [the abbreviation ITMA was used as title of a BBC radio show from 19 Sept. 1939]

5 It will play in Peoria.

In *New York Times* 9 June 1973 (catch-phrase of the Nixon administration)

6 *Je suis Marxiste—tendance Groucho.*

I am a Marxist—of the Groucho tendency.

Slogan used at Nanterre in Paris, 1968

7 Just when you thought it was safe to go back in the water.

Advertisement for *Jaws 2* (1978 film)

8 Kentucky Fried Chicken. . . . '*It's finger lickin' good.*'

American Restaurant Magazine June 1958

9 King's Moll Reno'd in Wolsey's Home Town.

In Frances Donaldson *Edward VIII* (1974) ch. 7 (American newspaper headline referring to Mrs Simpson's divorce proceedings in Ipswich)

10 Labour isn't working.

In Philip Kleinman *The Saatchi and Saatchi Story* (1987) ch. 2 (British Conservative Party slogan, 1978–9, on poster showing a long queue outside an unemployment office)

11 LBJ, LBJ, how many kids have you killed today?

In Jacquin Sanders *The Draft and the Vietnam War* (1966) ch. 3 (anti-Vietnam marching slogan)

12 Let's get out of these wet clothes and into a dry Martini.

Line coined in 1920s by press agent for Robert Benchley (and often attributed to Benchley), in Howard Teichmann *Smart Alec* (1976) ch. 9. Cf. Mae West 225:10

13 Let the train take the strain.

British Rail advertising slogan, 1970 onwards

14 Let your fingers do the walking.

1960s advertisement for Bell system Telephone Directory Yellow Pages, in Harold S. Sharp *Advertising Slogans of America* (1984) p. 44

15 Liberty is always unfinished business.

Title of 36th Annual Report of the American Civil Liberties Union, 1 July 1955–30 June 1956

16 Life is a sexually transmitted disease.

In D. J. Enright (ed.) *Faber Book of Fevers and Frets* (1989) (graffito in the London Underground)

17 Life's better with the Conservatives. Don't let Labour ruin it.

In David Butler and Richard Rose *British General Election of 1959* (1960) ch. 3 (Conservative Party election slogan)

18 Lloyd George knows my father,
My father knows Lloyd George.

Comic song consisting of these two lines sung over and over again to the tune of *Onward, Christian Soldiers*, perhaps originally by Tommy Rhys Roberts (1910–75); sometimes with 'knew' instead of 'knows'

19 Lousy but loyal.

London East End slogan at George V's Jubilee (1935), in Nigel Rees *Slogans* (1982)

20 Mademoiselle from Armenteers,
Hasn't been kissed for forty years,
Hinky, dinky, parley-voo.

Song of World War I, variously ascribed to Edward Rowland and Harry Carlton

21 Make do and mend.

Wartime slogan, 1940s

22 Make love not war.

Student slogan, 1960s

23 The man from Del Monte says 'Yes'.

Advertising slogan for tinned fruit, 1985

24 The man you love to hate.

Billing for Erich von Stroheim in the film *The Heart of Humanity* (1918), in Peter Noble *Hollywood Scapegoat* (1950) ch. 2

25 Mother may I go and bathe?
Yes, my darling daughter.
Hang your clothes on yonder tree,
But don't go near the water.

In Iona and Peter Opie *Oxford Dictionary of Nursery Rhymes* (1951) p. 314. Cf. Walter de la Mare 66:20

26 The nearest thing to death in life
Is David Patrick Maxwell Fyfe,
Though underneath that gloomy shell
He does himself extremely well.

In E. Grierson *Confessions of a Country Magistrate* (1972) p. 35 (rhyme about Sir David Maxwell Fyfe, said to have been current on the Northern circuit in the late 1930s)

27 *Nil carborundum illegitimi.*

Mock-Latin proverb translated as 'Don't let the bastards grind you down'; often simply 'nil carborundum' or 'illegitimi non carborundum'

28 No manager ever got fired for buying IBM.

IBM advertising slogan

29 Nice one, Cyril.

1972 television advertising campaign for Wonderloaf; taken up by supporters of Cyril Knowles, Tottenham Hotspur footballer; the Spurs team later made a record featuring the line

30 No more Latin, no more French,
No more sitting on a hard board bench.

Rhyme used by children at the end of school term: see Iona and Peter Opie *Lore and Language of Schoolchildren* (1959) ch. 13; also found with variants such as: No more Latin, no more Greek, No more cares to make me squeak

31 Nostalgia isn't what it used to be.

Graffito, used as title of book by Simone Signoret

32 Not so much a programme, more a way of life!

Title of BBC television series, 1964

1 O Death, where is thy sting-a-ling-a-ling,
O grave, thy victory?
The bells of Hell go ting-a-ling-a-ling
For you but not for me.
> *For You But Not For Me* (song of World War I) in S. Louis
> Guiraud (ed.) *Songs That Won the War* (1930). Cf.
> 1 Corinthians 15:55

2 Once again we stop the mighty roar of London's traffic
and from the great crowds we bring you some of the
interesting people who have come by land, sea and air
to be *in town tonight*.
> *In Town Tonight* (BBC radio series, 1933–60) introductory
> words

3 Power to the people.
> Slogan of the Black Panther movement, *c.*1968 onwards, in
> *Black Panther* 14 Sept. 1968

4 *Puella Rigensis ridebat*
Quam tigris in tergo vehebat;
Externa profecta,
Interna revecta,
Risusque cum tigre manebat.

There was a young lady of Riga
Who went for a ride on a tiger;
They returned from the ride
With the lady inside,
And a smile on the face of the tiger.
> In R. L. Green (ed.) *A Century of Humorous Verse* (1959)
> p. 285

5 The [*or* A] quick brown fox jumps over the lazy dog.
> Sentence used by typists etc. to ensure that all letters of the
> alphabet are printing properly: see R. Hunter Middleton's
> introduction to *The Quick Brown Fox* (1945) by Richard H.
> Templeton Jr.

6 The rabbit has a charming face:
Its private life is a disgrace.
I really dare not name to you
The awful things that rabbits do.
> *The Rabbit*, in *The Week-End Book* (1925) p. 171

7 See the happy moron,
He doesn't give a damn,
I wish I were a moron,
My God! perhaps I am!
> *Eugenics Review* July 1929

8 She was poor but she was honest
Victim of a rich man's game.
First he loved her, than he left her,
And she lost her maiden name.

See her on the bridge at midnight,
Saying 'Farewell, blighted love.'
Then a scream, a splash and goodness,
What is she a-doin' of?

It's the same the whole world over,
It's the poor wot gets the blame,
It's the rich wot gets the gravy.
Ain't it all a bleedin shame?
> *She was Poor but she was Honest* (song sung by British soldiers
> in World War I)

9 Shome mishtake, shurely?
> Catch-phrase in *Private Eye* magazine, 1980s

10 Snap! Crackle! Pop!
> Slogan for Kellogg's Rice Krispies, from *c.*1928

11 So farewell then. . . .
> Frequent opening of poems by 'E. J. Thribb' in *Private Eye*
> magazine, 1970s onwards, usually as an obituary

12 Some television programmes are so much chewing gum
for the eyes.
> John Mason Brown, quoting a friend of his young son, in
> interview 28 July 1955, in James Beasley Simpson *Best
> Quotes of '50, '55, '56* (1957) p. 233

13 Sticks nix hick pix.
> *Variety* 17 July 1935 (headline on lack of interest for farm
> dramas in rural areas)

14 Stop-look-and-listen.
> Safety slogan current in the US from 1912

15 Take me to your leader.
> Catch-phrase from science-fiction stories

16 Tell Sid.
> Advertising slogan for the privatization of British Gas, 1986,
> in Philip Kleinman *The Saatchi and Saatchi Story* (1987)
> ch. 11

17 There is one thing stronger than all the armies in the
world; and that is an idea whose time has come.
> *Nation* 15 Apr. 1943. Cf. *Oxford Dictionary of Quotations*
> (1979) 267:11

18 There is so much good in the worst of us,
And so much bad in the best of us,
That it hardly becomes [*or* behooves] any of us
To talk about the rest of us.
> Attributed to many authors, especially Edward Wallis Hoch
> (1849–1945) because printed in the *Marion Record* (Kansas)
> which he owned, but disclaimed by him

19 There was a faith-healer of Deal
Who said, 'Although pain isn't real,
If I sit on a pin
And it punctures my skin,
I dislike what I fancy I feel.'
> *The Week-End Book* (1925) p. 158

20 They [Jacob Epstein's] sculptures for the former BMA
building in the Strand] are a form of statuary which no
careful father would wish his daughter, or no
discerning young man his fiancée, to see.
> *Evening Standard* 19 June 1908

21 They come as a boon and a blessing to men,
The Pickwick, the Owl, and the Waverley pen.
> Advertisement by MacNiven and H. Cameron Ltd., *c.*1920

22 [This film] is so cryptic as to be almost meaningless. If
there is a meaning, it is doubtless objectionable.
> The British Board of Film Censors, banning Jean Cocteau's
> film *The Seashell and the Clergyman* (1929), in J. C. Robertson
> *Hidden Cinema* (1989) ch. 1

23 Though I yield to no one in my admiration for Mr
Coolidge, I do wish he did not look as if he had been
weaned on a pickle.
> Anonymous remark reported in Alice Roosevelt Longworth
> *Crowded Hours* (1933) ch. 21

24 To err is human but to really foul things up requires
a computer.
> *Farmers' Almanac for 1978* (1977) 'Capsules of Wisdom'

25 Top people take The Times.
> Advertising slogan for *The Times* newspaper from Jan. 1959:
> see I. McDonald *History of The Times* (1984) vol. 5, ch. 16

1 *Tous les êtres humains naissent libres et égaux en dignité et en droits.*

All human beings are born free and equal in dignity and rights.
  Universal Declaration of Human Rights (1948) Article 1 (modified from a draft by René Cassin)

2 Ulster says no.
  Slogan coined in response to the Anglo-Irish Agreement of 15 Nov. 1985, in *Irish Times* 25 Nov. 1985

3 *Vorsprung durch Technik.*

Progress through technology.
  Advertising slogan for Audi cars, from 1986

4 Vote early. Vote often.
  Chicago (and Irish) election proverb, in David Frost and Michael Shea *Mid-Atlantic Companion* (1986) p. 95

5 Wall St. lays an egg.
  Variety 30 Oct. 1929 (headline on the Wall Street Crash)

6 War will cease when men refuse to fight.
  Pacifist slogan, from *c.*1936 (often 'Wars will cease . . . '): see *Birmingham Gazette* 21 Nov. 1936, p. 3, and *Peace News* 15 Oct. 1938, p. 12

7 We are the Ovaltineys,
  Little [*or* Happy] girls and boys.
  We are the Ovaltineys (song promoting the drink Ovaltine, from *c.*1935)

8 The weekend starts here.
  Catch-phrase of *Ready, Steady, Go*, British television series, *c.*1963

9 We're number two. We try harder.
  Advertising slogan for Avis car rentals

10 We're here
  Because
  We're here
  Because
  We're here
  Because we're here.
  In John Brophy and Eric Partridge *Songs and Slang of the British Soldier 1914–18* (1930) p. 33 (sung to the tune of *Auld Lang Syne*)

11 We shall not be moved.
  Title of song (1931)

12 We shall not pretend that there is nothing in his long career which those who respect and admire him would wish otherwise.
  The Times 23 Jan. 1901 (leading article on the accession of Edward VII)

13 We shall overcome,
  We shall overcome,
  We shall overcome some day.
  Oh, deep in my heart
  I do believe
  We shall overcome some day.
  We Shall Overcome (song derived from several sources, notably the singers Zilphia Horton and Pete Seeger)

14 Who dares wins.
  Motto on badge of British Special Air Service regiment, from 1942 (see J. L. Collins *Elite Forces: the SAS* (1986) introduction)

15 Whose finger do you want on the trigger?
  Daily Mirror 21 Sept. 1951

16 Winston is back.
  Board of Admiralty signal to the Fleet on Winston Churchill's reappointment as First Sea Lord, 3 Sept. 1939, in Martin Gilbert *Winston S. Churchill* (1976) vol. 5, ch. 53

17 Would you like to sin
  With Elinor Glyn
  On a tiger-skin?
  Or would you prefer
  To err
  With her
  On some other fur?
  In A. Glyn *Elinor Glyn* (1955) bk. 2

Jean Anouilh 1910–1987

18 *Dieu est avec tout le monde. . . . Et, en fin de compte, il est toujours avec ceux qui ont beaucoup d'argent et de grosses armées.*

God is on everyone's side. . . . And, in the last analysis, he is on the side with plenty of money and large armies.
  L'Alouette (The Lark, 1953) p. 120

19 *Il y a l'amour bien sûr. Et puis il y a la vie, son ennemie.*

There is love of course. And then there's life, its enemy.
  Ardèle (1949) p. 8

20 *Vous savez bien que l'amour, c'est avant tout le don de soi!*

You know very well that love is, above all, the gift of oneself!
  Ardèle (1949) p. 79

21 *C'est très jolie la vie, mais cela n'a pas de forme. L'art a pour objet de lui en donner une précisément et de faire par tous les artifices possibles—plus vrai que le vrai.*

Life is very nice, but it has no shape. The object of art is actually to give it some and to do it by every artifice possible—truer than the truth.
  La Répétition (The Rehearsal, 1950) act 2

Guillaume Apollinaire 1880–1918

22 *Sous le pont Mirabeau coule la Seine.*
  Et nos amours, faut-il qu'il m'en souvienne?
  La joie venait toujours après la peine.
  Vienne la nuit, sonne l'heure,
  Les jours s'en vont, je demeure.

Under Mirabeau Bridge flows the Seine.
  And our loves, must I remember them?
  Joy always comes after pain.
  Let night come, ring out the hour,
  The days go by, I remain.
  Les Soirées de Paris Feb. 1912 'Le Pont Mirabeau'

23 *Les souvenirs sont cors de chasse*
  Dont meurt le bruit parmi le vent.

Memories are hunting horns
  Whose sound dies on the wind.
  Les Soirées de Paris Sept. 1912 'Cors de Chasse'

Sir Edward Appleton 1892–1965

1 I do not mind what language an opera is sung in so long as it is a language I don't understand.
   In *Observer* 28 Aug. 1955

Louis Aragon 1897–1982

2 *O mois des floraisons mois des métamorphoses*
   Mai qui fut sans nuage et Juin poignardé
   Je n'oublierai jamais les lilas ni les roses
   Ni ceux que le printemps dans ses plis a gardé.

   O month of flowerings, month of metamorphoses,
   May without cloud and June that was stabbed,
   I shall never forget the lilac and the roses
   Nor those whom spring has kept in its folds.
   Le Crève-Cœur (Heartbreak, 1940) 'Les lilas et les roses'

Hannah Arendt 1906–1975

3 Under conditions of tyranny it is far easier to act than to think.
   In W. H. Auden *A Certain World* (1970) p. 369

4 It was as though in those last minutes he [Eichmann] was summing up the lessons that this long course in human wickedness had taught us—the lesson of the fearsome, word-and-thought-defying banality of evil.
   Eichmann in Jerusalem: a Report on the Banality of Evil (1963) ch. 15

5 It is well known that the most radical revolutionary will become a conservative on the day after the revolution.
   New Yorker 12 Sept. 1970, p. 88

G. D. Armour 1864–1949

6 Look here, Steward, if this is coffee, I want tea; but if this is tea, then I wish for coffee.
   Punch 23 July 1902 (cartoon caption)

Harry Armstrong 1879–1951

7 There's an old mill by the stream, Nellie Dean,
   Where we used to sit and dream, Nellie Dean.
   And the waters as they flow
   Seem to murmur sweet and low,
   'You're my heart's desire; I love you, Nellie Dean.'
   Nellie Dean (1905 song)

Louis Armstrong 1901–1971

8 All music is folk music, I ain't never heard no horse sing a song.
   In *New York Times* 7 July 1971, p. 41

9 If you still have to ask ... shame on you.
   Habitual reply when asked what jazz is, in Max Jones et al. *Salute to Satchmo* (1970) p. 25

Neil Armstrong 1930–

10 That's one small step for a man, one giant leap for mankind.
   In *New York Times* 31 July 1969, p. 20

Sir Robert Armstrong 1927–

11 It [a letter] contains a misleading impression, not a lie. It was being economical with the truth.
   In Supreme Court, New South Wales, 18 Nov. 1986, in *Daily Telegraph* 19 Nov. 1986. Cf. Edmund Burke's *Two letters on Proposals for Peace* (1796) pt. 1, p. 137: Falsehood and delusion are allowed in no case whatsoever: But, as in the exercise of all the virtues, there is an economy of truth.

Raymond Aron 1905–

12 *La pensée politique, en France, est rétrospective ou utopique.*

   Political thought, in France, is retrospective or utopian.
   L'opium des intellectuels (The opium of the intellectuals, 1955) ch. 1

George Asaf 1880–1951

13 What's the use of worrying?
   It never was worth while,
   So, pack up your troubles in your old kit-bag,
   And smile, smile, smile.
   Pack up your Troubles (1915 song; music by Felix Powell)

Dame Peggy Ashcroft 1907–

14 It seems silly that more people should see me in 'Jewel in the Crown' than in all my years in the theatre.
   In *Observer* 18 Mar. 1984

Daisy Ashford 1881–1972

15 Mr Salteena was an elderly man of 42 and was fond of asking peaple to stay with him.
   Young Visiters (1919) ch. 1

16 I do hope I shall enjoy myself with you. I am fond of digging in the garden and I am parshial to ladies if they are nice I suppose it is my nature. I am not quite a gentleman but you would hardly notice it but can't be helped anyhow.
   Young Visiters (1919) ch. 1

17 You look rather rash my dear your colors dont quite match your face.
   Young Visiters (1919) ch. 2

18 My own room is next the bath room said Bernard it is decorated dark red as I have somber tastes. The bath room has got a tip up bason and a hose thing for washing your head.
   Young Visiters (1919) ch. 2

19 Bernard always had a few prayers in the hall and some whiskey afterwards as he was rarther pious but Mr Salteena was not very addicted to prayers so he marched up to bed.
   Young Visiters (1919) ch. 3

20 It was a sumpshous spot all done up in gold with plenty of looking glasses.
   Young Visiters (1919) ch. 5

21 Oh I see said the Earl but my own idear is that these things are as piffle before the wind.
   Young Visiters (1919) ch. 5

1 The bearer of this letter is an old friend of mine not quite the right side of the blanket as they say in fact he is the son of a first rate butcher but his mother was a decent family called Hyssopps of the Glen so you see he is not so bad and is desireus of being the correct article.

Young Visiters (1919) ch. 5

2 Ethel patted her hair and looked very sneery.

Young Visiters (1919) ch. 8

3 My life will be sour grapes and ashes without you.

Young Visiters (1919) ch. 8

4 Oh Bernard muttered Ethel this is so sudden. No no cried Bernard and taking the bull by both horns he kissed her violently on her dainty face. My bride to be he murmered several times.

Young Visiters (1919) ch. 9

Isaac Asimov 1920–

5 The three fundamental Rules of Robotics. . . . One, a robot may not injure a human being, or, through inaction, allow a human being to come to harm. . . . Two . . . a robot must obey the orders given it by human beings except where such orders would conflict with the First Law . . . three, a robot must protect its own existence as long as such protection does not conflict with the First or Second Laws.

I, Robot (1950) 'Runaround'

Elizabeth Asquith (Princess Antoine Bibesco) 1897–1945

6 Kitchener is a great poster.

In Margot Asquith *More Memories* (1933) ch. 6

Herbert Henry Asquith (Earl of Oxford and Asquith) 1852–1928

7 We had better wait and see.

Hansard 3 Mar. 1910, col. 972 (expression used in various forms when answering questions on the Finance Bill)

8 Happily there seems to be no reason why we should be anything more than spectators [of the approaching war].

Letters to Venetia Stanley (1982) 24 July 1914

9 Youth would be an ideal state if it came a little later in life.

In *Observer* 15 Apr. 1923

10 [The War Office kept three sets of figures:] one to mislead the public, another to mislead the Cabinet, and the third to mislead itself.

In Alistair Horne *Price of Glory* (1962) ch. 2

11 We shall never sheath the sword which we have not lightly drawn until Belgium recovers in full measure all and more than all that she has sacrificed, until France is adequately secured against the menace of aggression, until the rights of the smaller nationalities of Europe are placed upon an unassailable foundation, and until the military domination of Prussia is wholly and finally destroyed.

Speech at the Guildhall, 9 Nov. 1914, in *The Times* 10 Nov. 1914

12 It is fitting that we should have buried the Unknown Prime Minister [Bonar Law] by the side of the Unknown Soldier.

In Robert Blake *The Unknown Prime Minister* (1955) p. 531

Margot Asquith (Countess of Oxford and Asquith) 1864–1945

13 It [10 Downing Street] is an inconvenient house with three poor staircases, and after living there a few weeks I made up my mind that owing to the impossibility of circulation I could only entertain my Liberal friends at dinner or at garden parties.

Autobiography (1922) vol. 2, ch. 5

14 Ettie [Lady Desborough] is an ox: she will be made into Bovril when she dies.

In Jeanne Mackenzie *Children of the Souls* (1986) ch. 4

15 Jean Harlow kept calling Margot Asquith by her first name, or kept trying to: she pronounced it Mar*got*. Finally Margot set her right. 'No, no, Jean. The *t* is silent, as in *Harlow*.'

T. S. Matthews *Great Tom* (1973) ch. 7

16 The King [George V] told me he would never have died if it had not been for that fool Dawson of Penn.

In letter from Mark Bonham Carter to Kenneth Rose 23 Oct. 1978, quoted in Kenneth Rose *King George V* (1983) ch. 9

17 Lord Birkenhead is very clever but sometimes his brains go to his head.

In *Listener* 11 June 1953 'Margot Oxford: a Personal Impression' by Lady Violet Bonham Carter

18 She [Lady Desborough] tells enough white lies to ice a wedding cake.

In *Listener* 11 June 1953 'Margot Oxford: a Personal Impression' by Lady Violet Bonham Carter

19 He [Lloyd George?] can't see a belt without hitting below it.

In *Listener* 11 June 1953 'Margot Oxford: a Personal Impression' by Lady Violet Bonham Carter

Raymond Asquith 1878–1916

20 The sun like a Bishop's bottom
Rosy and round and hot
Looked down upon us who shot 'em
And down on the devils we shot.
And the stink of the damned dead niggers
Went up to the Lord high God
But we stuck to our starboard triggers
Though we yawned like dying cod.

Letter, 4 Mar. 1900, in J. Jolliffe *Raymond Asquith Life and Letters* (1980) p. 64

Nancy Astor (Viscountess Astor) 1879–1964

21 One reason why I don't drink is because I wish to know when I am having a good time.

In *Christian Herald* June 1960, p. 31

22 I married beneath me, all women do.

In *Dictionary of National Biography 1961–1970* (1981) p. 43

23 After a heated argument on some trivial matter Nancy . . . shouted, 'If I were your wife I would put poison in your coffee!' Whereupon Winston [Churchill] with equal heat and sincerity answered, 'And if I were your husband I would drink it.'

> Consuelo Vanderbilt Balsan *Glitter and Gold* (1952) ch. 7

1 Jakie, is it my birthday or am I dying?

> In J. Grigg *Nancy Astor* (1980) p. 184

Brooks Atkinson 1894–1984

2 After each war there is a little less democracy to save.

> *Once Around the Sun* (1951) 7 Jan.

3 In every age 'the good old days' were a myth. No one ever thought they were good at the time. For every age has consisted of crises that seemed intolerable to the people who lived through them.

> *Once Around the Sun* (1951) 8 Feb.

4 There is a good deal of solemn cant about the common interests of capital and labour. As matters stand, their only common interest is that of cutting each other's throat.

> *Once Around the Sun* (1951) 7 Sept.

E. L. Atkinson 1882–1929 and Apsley Cherry-Garrard 1882–1959

5 Hereabouts died a very gallant gentleman, Captain L. E. G. Oates of the Inniskilling Dragoons. In March 1912, returning from the Pole, he walked willingly to his death in a blizzard to try and save his comrades, beset by hardships.

> Epitaph on cairn erected in the Antarctic, 15 Nov. 1912, in Apsley Cherry-Garrard *Worst Journey in the World* (1922) p. 487

Clement Attlee 1883–1967

6 Few thought he was even a starter
There were many who thought themselves smarter
But he ended PM
CH and OM
An earl and a knight of the garter.

> Letter to Tom Attlee, 8 Apr.1956, in Kenneth Harris *Attlee* (1982) p. 545 (describing himself)

7 I should be a sad subject for any publicity expert. I have none of the qualities which create publicity.

> In Harold Nicolson *Diary* (1968) 14 Jan. 1949

8 I think the British have the distinction above all other nations of being able to put new wine into old bottles without bursting them.

> *Hansard* 24 Oct. 1950, col. 2705

9 The voice we heard was that of Mr Churchill but the mind was that of Lord Beaverbrook.

> Speech on radio, 5 June 1945, in Francis Williams *Prime Minister Remembers* (1961) ch. 6

10 I remember he [Winston Churchill] complained once in Opposition that a matter had been brought up several times in Cabinet and I had to say, 'I must remind the Right Honourable Gentleman that a monologue is not a decision.'

> In Francis Williams *Prime Minister Remembers* (1961) ch. 7

11 You have no right whatever to speak on behalf of the Government. Foreign Affairs are in the capable hands of

Ernest Bevin. . . . I can assure you there is widespread resentment in the Party at your activities and a period of silence on your part would be welcome.

> Letter to Harold Laski, 20 Aug. 1945, in Francis Williams *Prime Minister Remembers* (1961) ch. 11

12 [Russian Communism is] the illegitimate child of Karl Marx and Catherine the Great.

> Speech at Aarhus University, 11 Apr. 1956, in *The Times* 12 Apr. 1956

13 Democracy means government by discussion, but it is only effective if you can stop people talking.

> Speech at Oxford, 14 June 1957, in *The Times* 15 June 1957

W. H. Auden 1907–1973

14 Some thirty inches from my nose
The frontier of my Person goes,
And all the untilled air between
Is private *pagus* or demesne.
Stranger, unless with bedroom eyes
I beckon you to fraternize,
Beware of rudely crossing it:
I have no gun, but I can spit.

> *About the House* (1966) 'Prologue: the Birth of Architecture'

15 Sob, heavy world,
Sob as you spin
Mantled in mist, remote from the happy.

> *Age of Anxiety* (1947) p. 104

16 I'll love you, dear, I'll love you
Till China and Africa meet
And the river jumps over the mountain
And the salmon sing in the street.

I'll love you till the ocean
Is folded and hung up to dry
And the seven stars go squawking
Like geese about the sky.

> *Another Time* (1940) 'As I Walked Out One Evening'

17 O plunge your hands in water,
Plunge them in up to the wrist;
Stare, stare in the basin
And wonder what you've missed.

The glacier knocks in the cupboard,
The desert sighs in the bed,
And the crack in the tea-cup opens
A lane to the land of the dead.

> *Another Time* (1940) 'As I Walked Out One Evening'

18 Perfection, of a kind, was what he was after,
And the poetry he invented was easy to understand;
He knew human folly like the back of his hand,
And was greatly interested in armies and fleets;
When he laughed, respectable senators burst with laughter,
And when he cried the little children died in the streets.

> *Another Time* (1940) 'Epitaph on a Tyrant'

19 To us he is no more a person
Now but a whole climate of opinion.

> *Another Time* (1940) 'In Memory of Sigmund Freud'

20 He disappeared in the dead of winter:
The brooks were frozen, the airports almost deserted,
And snow disfigured the public statues;
The mercury sank in the mouth of the dying day.

What instruments we have agree
The day of his death was a dark cold day.
   Another Time (1940) 'In Memory of W. B. Yeats'

1 You were silly like us: your gift survived it all;
The parish of rich women, physical decay,
Yourself; mad Ireland hurt you into poetry.
Now Ireland has her madness and her weather still,
For poetry makes nothing happen: it survives
In the valley of its saying where executives
Would never want to tamper; it flows south
From ranches of isolation and the busy griefs,
Raw towns that we believe and die in; it survives,
A way of happening, a mouth.
   Another Time (1940) 'In Memory of W. B. Yeats'

2 Earth, receive an honoured guest;
William Yeats is laid to rest:
Let the Irish vessel lie
Emptied of its poetry.
   Another Time (1940) 'In Memory of W. B. Yeats'

3 In the nightmare of the dark
All the dogs of Europe bark,
And the living nations wait,
Each sequestered in its hate;

Intellectual disgrace
Stares from every human face,
And the seas of pity lie
Locked and frozen in each eye.
   Another Time (1940) 'In Memory of W. B. Yeats'

4 In the deserts of the heart
Let the healing fountain start,
In the prison of his days
Teach the free man how to praise.
   Another Time (1940) 'In Memory of W. B. Yeats'

5 About suffering they were never wrong,
The Old Masters: how well they understood
Its human position; how it takes place
While someone else is eating or opening a window or
   just walking dully along.
   Another Time (1940) 'Musée des Beaux Arts'

6 They never forgot
That even the dreadful martyrdom must run its course
Anyhow in a corner, some untidy spot
Where the dogs go on with their doggy life and the
   torturer's horse
Scratches its innocent behind on a tree.
   Another Time (1940) 'Musée des Beaux Arts'

7 Lay your sleeping head, my love,
Human on my faithless arm;
Time and fevers burn away
Individual beauty from
Thoughtful children, and the grave
Proves the child ephemeral:
But in my arms till break of day
Let the living creature lie,
Mortal, guilty, but to me
The entirely beautiful.
   Another Time (1940) no. 18, p. 43

8 I and the public know
What all schoolchildren learn,
Those to whom evil is done
Do evil in return.
   Another Time (1940) 'September 1, 1939'

9 All I have is a voice
To undo the folded lie,
The romantic lie in the brain
Of the sensual man-in-the-street
And the lie of Authority
Whose buildings grope the sky:
There is no such thing as the State
And no one exists alone;
Hunger allows no choice
To the citizen or the police;
We must love one another or die.
   Another Time (1940) 'September 1, 1939'

10 Our researchers into Public Opinion are content
That he held the proper opinions for the time of year;
When there was peace, he was for peace; when there
   was war, he went.
   Another Time (1940) 'The Unknown Citizen'

11 Was he free? Was he happy? The question is absurd:
Had anything been wrong, we should certainly have
   heard.
   Another Time (1940) 'The Unknown Citizen'

12 All sin tends to be addictive, and the terminal point of
addiction is what is called damnation.
   A Certain World (1970) 'Hell'

13 Of course, Behaviourism 'works'. So does torture. Give
me a no-nonsense, down-to-earth behaviourist, a few
drugs, and simple electrical appliances, and in six
months I will have him reciting the Athanasian Creed
in public.
   A Certain World (1970) 'Behaviourism'

14 A poet's hope: to be,
like some valley cheese,
local, but prized elsewhere.
   Collected Poems (1976) p. 639

15 It is a sad fact about our culture that a poet can earn
much more money writing or talking about his art than
he can by practising it.
   Dyer's Hand (1963) foreword

16 Between the ages of twenty and forty we are engaged in
the process of discovering who we are, which involves
learning the difference between accidental limitations
which it is our duty to outgrow and the necessary
limitations of our nature beyond which we cannot
trespass with impunity.
   Dyer's Hand (1963) 'Reading'

17 Some books are undeservedly forgotten; none are
undeservedly remembered.
   Dyer's Hand (1963) 'Reading'

18 One cannot review a bad book without showing off.
   Dyer's Hand (1963) 'Reading'

19 No poet or novelist wishes he were the only one who
ever lived, but most of them wish they were the only
one alive, and quite a number fondly believe their wish
has been granted.
   Dyer's Hand (1963) 'Writing'

20 It takes little talent to see clearly what lies under one's
nose, a good deal of it to know in which direction to
point that organ.
   Dyer's Hand (1963) 'Writing'

1 The true men of action in our time, those who transform the world, are not the politicians and statesmen, but the scientists. Unfortunately poetry cannot celebrate them, because their deeds are concerned with things, not persons, and are, therefore, speechless. When I find myself in the company of scientists, I feel like a shabby curate who has strayed by mistake into a drawing room full of dukes.
  Dyer's Hand (1963) 'The Poet and the City'

2 The image of myself which I try to create in my own mind in order that I may love myself is very different from the image which I try to create in the minds of others in order that they may love me.
  Dyer's Hand (1963) 'Hic et Ille'

3 Almost all of our relationships begin and most of them continue as forms of mutual exploitation, a mental or physical barter, to be terminated when one or both parties run out of goods.
  Dyer's Hand (1963) 'Hic et Ille'

4 Man is a history-making creature who can neither repeat his past nor leave it behind.
  Dyer's Hand (1963) 'D. H. Lawrence'

5 Among those whom I like or admire, I can find no common denominator, but among those whom I love, I can: all of them make me laugh.
  Dyer's Hand (1963) 'Notes on the Comic'

6 At Dirty Dick's and Sloppy Joe's
  We drank our liquor straight,
  Some went upstairs with Margery,
  And some, alas, with Kate.
    For the Time Being (1944) 'The Sea and the Mirror'—'Master and Boatswain'

7 My Dear One is mine as mirrors are lonely.
    For the Time Being (1944) 'The Sea and the Mirror'—'Miranda'

8 The desires of the heart are as crooked as corkscrews
  Not to be born is the best for man
  The second best is a formal order
  The dance's pattern, dance while you can.
  Dance, dance, for the figure is easy
  The tune is catching and will not stop
  Dance till the stars come down with the rafters
  Dance, dance, dance till you drop.
    Letter from Iceland (1937, by Auden and MacNeice) 'Letter to William Coldstream, Esq.'

9 And make us as Newton was, who in his garden watching
  The apple falling towards England, became aware
  Between himself and her of an eternal tie.
    Look, Stranger! (1936) no. 1

10 Out on the lawn I lie in bed,
  Vega conspicuous overhead.
    Look, Stranger! (1936) no. 2

11 Let the florid music praise,
  The flute and the trumpet,
  Beauty's conquest of your face:
  In that land of flesh and bone,
  Where from citadels on high
  Her imperial standards fly,
  Let the hot sun
  Shine on, shine on.
    Look, Stranger! (1936) no. 4

12 Look, stranger, at this island now
  The leaping light for your delight discovers,
  Stand stable here
  And silent be,
  That through the channels of the ear
  May wander like a river
  The swaying sound of the sea.
    Look, Stranger! (1936) no. 5

13 O what is that sound which so thrills the ear
  Down in the valley drumming, drumming?
  Only the scarlet soldiers, dear,
  The soldiers coming.
    Look, Stranger! (1936) no. 6

14 O it's broken the lock and splintered the door,
  O it's the gate where they're turning, turning;
  Their boots are heavy on the floor
  And their eyes are burning.
    Look, Stranger! (1936) no. 6

15 A shilling life will give you all the facts.
    Look, Stranger! (1936) no. 13

16 August for the people and their favourite islands.
  Daily the steamers sidle up to meet
  The effusive welcome of the pier.
    Look, Stranger! (1936) no. 30

17 Geniuses are the luckiest of mortals because what they must do is the same as what they most want to do.
    In Dag Hammarskjöld *Markings* (1964) foreword

18 I see it often since you've been away:
  The island, the veranda, and the fruit;
  The tiny steamer breaking from the bay;
  The literary mornings with its hoot;
  Our ugly comic servant; and then you,
  Lovely and willing every afternoon.
    New Verse Oct. 1933, p. 15

19 At the far end of the enormous room
  An orchestra is playing to the rich.
    New Verse Oct. 1933, p. 15

20 To the man-in-the-street, who, I'm sorry to say,
  Is a keen observer of life,
  The word 'Intellectual' suggests straight away
  A man who's untrue to his wife.
    New Year Letter (1961) note to line 1277

21 This is the Night Mail crossing the Border,
  Bringing the cheque and the postal order,
  Letters for the rich, letters for the poor,
  The shop at the corner, the girl next door.
  Pulling up Beattock, a steady climb:
  The gradient's against her, but she's on time.
  Past cotton-grass and moorland border,
  Shovelling white steam over her shoulder.
    Night Mail (1936) in *Collected Shorter Poems* (1966)

22 Letters of thanks, letters from banks,
  Letters of joy from girl and boy,
  Receipted bills and invitations
  To inspect new stock or to visit relations,
  And applications for situations,
  And timid lovers' declarations,
  And gossip, gossip from all the nations.
    Night Mail (1936) in *Collected Shorter Poems* (1966)

23 Altogether elsewhere, vast
  Herds of reindeer move across

Miles and miles of golden moss,
Silently and very fast.
> *Nones* (1951) 'The Fall of Rome'

1 Private faces in public places
Are wiser and nicer
Than public faces in private places.
> *Orators* (1932) dedication

2 Sir, no man's enemy, forgiving all
But will his negative inversion, be prodigal:
Send to us power and light, a sovereign touch
Curing the intolerable neutral itch,
The exhaustion of weaning, the liar's quinsy,
And the distortions of ingrown virginity.
> *Poems* (1930) 'Sir, No Man's Enemy'

3 Harrow the house of the dead; look shining at
New styles of architecture, a change of heart.
> *Poems* (1930) 'Sir, No Man's Enemy'

4 Let us honour if we can
The vertical man
Though we value none
But the horizontal one.
> *Poems* (1930) 'To Christopher Isherwood'

5 To ask the hard question is simple.
> *Poems* (1933) no. 27

6 This great society is going smash;
They cannot fool us with how fast they go,
How much they cost each other and the gods!
A culture is no better than its woods.
> *Shield of Achilles* (1955) 'Bucolics'

7 To save your world you asked this man to die:
Would this man, could he see you now, ask why?
> *Shield of Achilles* (1955) 'Epitaph for the Unknown Soldier'

8 Out of the air a voice without a face
Proved by statistics that some cause was just
In tones as dry and level as the place.
> *Shield of Achilles* (1955) 'The Shield of Achilles'

9 Tomorrow for the young the poets exploding like
bombs,
The walks by the lake, the weeks of perfect
communion;
Tomorrow the bicycle races
Through the suburbs on summer evenings. But today
the struggle.
> *Spain* (1937) p. 11

10 The stars are dead. The animals will not look:
We are left alone with our day, and the time is short,
and
History to the defeated
May say Alas but cannot help nor pardon.
> *Spain* (1937) p. 12

11 In a garden shady this holy lady
With reverent cadence and subtle psalm,
Like a black swan as death came on
Poured forth her song in perfect calm:
And by ocean's margin this innocent virgin
Constructed an organ to enlarge her prayer,
And notes tremendous from her great engine
Thundered out on the Roman air.

Blonde Aphrodite rose up excited,
Moved to delight by the melody,

White as an orchid she rode quite naked
In an oyster shell on top of the sea.
> *Three Songs for St Cecilia's Day* (1941). Dedicated to Benjamin Britten, and set to music by Britten as *Hymn to St Cecilia*, op. 27 (1942)

12 Blessed Cecilia, appear in visions
To all musicians, appear and inspire:
Translated Daughter, come down and startle
Composing mortals with immortal fire.
> *Three Songs for St Cecilia's Day* (1941)

13 No opera plot can be sensible, for in sensible situations people do not sing. An opera plot must be, in both senses of the word, a melodrama.
> *Times Literary Supplement* 2 Nov. 1967, p. 1038

14 Your cameraman might enjoy himself because my face looks like a wedding-cake left out in the rain.
> In Humphrey Carpenter *W. H. Auden* (1981) pt. 2, ch. 6

15 You [Stephen Spender] are so infinitely capable of being humiliated. Art is born of humiliation.
> In Stephen Spender *World Within World* (1951) ch. 2

W. H. Auden 1907–1973 and Christopher Isherwood 1904–1986

16 Happy the hare at morning, for she cannot read
The Hunter's waking thoughts.
> *Dog beneath the Skin* (1935) chorus following act 2, sc. 2

Tex Avery (Fred Avery) 1907–1980

17 What's up, Doc?
> Catch-phrase in Bugs Bunny cartoons, from *c*.1940

Earl of Avon

See SIR ANTHONY EDEN

Revd W. Awdry 1911–

18 You've a lot to learn about trucks, little Thomas. They are silly things and must be kept in their place. After pushing them about here for a few weeks you'll know almost as much about them as Edward. Then you'll be a Really Useful Engine.
> *Thomas the Tank Engine* (1946) p. 46

Alan Ayckbourn 1939–

19 My mother used to say, Delia, if S-E-X ever rears its ugly head, close your eyes before you see the rest of it.
> *Bedroom Farce* (1978) act 2

20 This place, you tell them you're interested in the arts, you get messages of sympathy.
> *Chorus of Disapproval* (1986) act 2

21 Do you realize, Mrs Foster, the hours I've put into that woman? When I met her, you know, she was nothing. Nothing at all. With my own hands I have built her up. Encouraging her to join the public library and make use of her non-fiction tickets.
> *How the Other Half Loves* (1972) act 2, sc. 1

22 I only wanted to make you happy.
> *Round and Round the Garden* (1975) act 2, sc. 2

1 If you gave Ruth a rose, she'd peel all the petals off to make sure there weren't any greenfly. And when she'd done that, she'd turn round and say, do you call that a rose? Look at it, it's all in bits.
Table Manners (1975) act 1, sc. 2

2 I always feel with Norman that I have him on loan from somewhere. Like one of his library books.
Table Manners (1975) act 2, sc. 1

A. J. Ayer 1910–1989

3 No moral system can rest solely on authority.
Humanist Outlook (1968) introduction

4 It seems that I have spent my entire time trying to make life more rational and that it was all wasted effort.
In *Observer* 17 Aug. 1986

Pam Ayres 1947–

5 I am a bunny rabbit,
Sitting in me hutch,
I like to sit up this end,
I don't care for that end, much,
I'm glad tomorrow's Thursday,
'Cause with a bit of luck,
As far as I remember,
That's the day they pass the buck.
Some of Me Poetry (1976) 'The Bunny Poem'

6 Oh, I wish I'd looked after me teeth,
And spotted the perils beneath,
All the toffees I chewed,
And the sweet sticky food,
Oh, I wish I'd looked after me teeth.
Some of Me Poetry (1976) 'Oh, I wish I'd looked after me teeth'

7 I might have been a farmyard hen,
Scratchin' in the sun,
There might have been a crowd of chicks,
After me to run,
There might have been a cockerel fine,
To pay us his respects,
Instead of sittin' here,
Till someone comes and wrings our necks.

I see the Time and Motion clock,
Is sayin' nearly noon,
I 'spec me squirt of water,
Will come flyin' at me soon,
And then me spray of pellets,
Will nearly break me leg,
And I'll bite the wire nettin'
And lay one more bloody egg.
Some of Me Poetry (1976) 'The Battery Hen'

8 Medicinal discovery,
It moves in mighty leaps,
It leapt straight past the common cold
And gave it us for keeps.
Now I'm not a fussy woman,
There's no malice in me eye
But I wish that they could cure
the common cold. That's all. Goodbye.
Some of Me Poetry (1976) 'Oh no, I got a cold'

Robert Baden-Powell (Baron Baden-Powell) 1857–1941

9 The scouts' motto is founded on my initials, it is: BE PREPARED, which means, you are always to be in a state of readiness in mind and body to do your DUTY.
Scouting for Boys (1908) pt. 1

Joan Baez 1941–

10 The only thing that's been a worse flop than the organization of non-violence has been the organization of violence.
Daybreak (1970) 'What Would You Do If?'

Sydney D. Bailey 1916–

11 It has been said that this Minister [the Lord Privy Seal] is neither a Lord, nor a privy, nor a seal.
British Parliamentary Democracy (ed. 3, 1971) ch. 8

Bruce Bairnsfather 1888–1959

12 Well, if you knows of a better 'ole, go to it.
Fragments from France (1915) p. 1

Hylda Baker 1908–1986

13 She knows, you know!
Catch-phrase used in comedy act, about her friend Cynthia

James Baldwin 1924–1987

14 Money, it turned out, was exactly like sex, you thought of nothing else if you didn't have it and thought of other things if you did.
Esquire May 1961 'Black Boy looks at the White Boy'

15 The fire next time.
Title of book (1963). Cf. Anonymous 6:12

16 At the root of the American Negro problem is the necessity of the American white man to find a way of living with the Negro in order to be able to live with himself.
Harper's Magazine Oct. 1953 'Stranger in a Village'

17 If the concept of God has any validity or any use, it can only be to make us larger, freer, and more loving. If God cannot do this, then it is time we got rid of Him.
New Yorker 17 Nov. 1962 'Down at the Cross'

18 If they take you in the morning, they will be coming for us that night.
New York Review of Books 7 Jan. 1971 'Open Letter to my Sister, Angela Davis'

19 It comes as a great shock around the age of 5, 6 or 7 to discover that the flag to which you have pledged allegiance, along with everybody else, has not pledged allegiance to you. It comes as a great shock to see Gary Cooper killing off the Indians and, although you are rooting for Gary Cooper, that the Indians are you.
Speech at Cambridge University, 17 Feb. 1965, in *New York Times Magazine* 7 March 1965, p. 32

20 The situation of our youth is not mysterious. Children have never been very good at listening to their elders,

but they have never failed to imitate them. They must,
they have no other models.

> Nobody Knows My Name (1961) 'Fifth Avenue, Uptown:
> a letter from Harlem'

1 Anyone who has ever struggled with poverty knows
how extremely expensive it is to be poor.

> Nobody Knows My Name (1961) 'Fifth Avenue, Uptown: a
> letter from Harlem'

2 Freedom is not something that anybody can be given;
freedom is something people take and people are as free
as they want to be.

> Nobody Knows My Name (1961) 'Notes for a Hypothetical
> Novel'

Stanley Baldwin (Earl Baldwin of Bewdley) 1867–1947

3 Do not run up your nose dead against the Pope or the
NUM!

> In Lord Butler Art of Memory (1982) p. 110

4 You will find in politics that you are much exposed to
the attribution of false motive. Never complain and
never explain.

> In Harold Nicolson Diary (1967) 21 July 1943

5 They [parliament] are a lot of hard-faced men who look
as if they had done very well out of the war.

> In J. M. Keynes Economic Consequences of the Peace (1919)
> ch. 5

6 A platitude is simply a truth repeated until people get
tired of hearing it.

> Hansard 29 May 1924, col. 727

7 I think it is well also for the man in the street to realize
that there is no power on earth that can protect him
from being bombed. Whatever people may tell him, the
bomber will always get through. The only defence is in
offence, which means that you have to kill more
women and children more quickly than the enemy if
you want to save yourselves.

> Hansard 10 Nov. 1932, col. 632

8 Let us never forget this; since the day of the air, the old
frontiers are gone. When you think of the defence of
England you no longer think of the chalk cliffs of Dover;
you think of the Rhine. That is where our frontier lies.

> Hansard 30 July 1934, col. 2339

9 I shall be but a short time tonight. I have seldom spoken
with greater regret, for my lips are not yet unsealed.
Were these troubles over I would make a case, and
I guarantee that not a man would go into the lobby
against us.

> Hansard 10 Dec. 1935, col. 856

10 I put before the whole House my own views with an
appalling frankness. . . . Supposing I had gone to the
country and said that Germany was rearming and that
we must rearm, does anybody think that this pacific
democracy would have rallied to that cry at that
moment? I cannot think of anything that would have
made the loss of the election from my point of view
more certain.

> Hansard 12 Nov. 1936, col. 1144

11 There are three classes which need sanctuary

more than others—birds, wild flowers, and Prime
Ministers.

> In Observer 24 May 1925

12 Then comes Winston with his hundred-horse-power
mind and what can I do?

> In G. M. Young Stanley Baldwin (1952) ch. 11

13 The intelligent are to the intelligentsia what
a gentleman is to a gent.

> In G. M. Young Stanley Baldwin (1952) ch. 13

14 'Safety first' does not mean a smug self-satisfaction
with everything as it is. It is a warning to all persons
who are going to cross a road in dangerous
circumstances.

> The Times 21 May 1929

15 Had the employers of past generations all of them dealt
fairly with their men there would have been no unions.

> Speech in Birmingham, 14 Jan. 1931, in The Times 15 Jan.
> 1931

Arthur James Balfour (Earl of Balfour) 1848–1930

16 His Majesty's Government view with favour the
establishment in Palestine of a national home for the
Jewish people, and will use their best endeavours to
facilitate the achievement of this object, it being
clearly understood that nothing shall be done which
may prejudice the civil and religious rights of existing
non-Jewish communities in Palestine, or the rights
and political status enjoyed by Jews in any other
country.

> Letter to Lord Rothschild 2 Nov. 1917, in K. Young
> A. J. Balfour (1963) p. 478

17 Frank Harris . . . said . . . 'The fact is, Mr Balfour, all the
faults of the age come from Christianity and
journalism.' To which Arthur replied . . . 'Christianity,
of course . . . but why journalism?'

> Margot Asquith Autobiography (1920) vol. 1, ch. 10

18 I never forgive but I always forget.

> In R. Blake Conservative Party (1970) ch. 7

19 I thought he [Churchill] was a young man of promise,
but it appears he is a young man of promises.

> In Winston Churchill My Early Life (1930) ch. 17

20 Biography should be written by an acute enemy.

> In Observer 30 Jan. 1927

21 It is unfortunate, considering that enthusiasm moves
the world, that so few enthusiasts can be trusted to
speak the truth.

> Letter to Mrs Drew, 19 May 1891, in Some Hawarden Letters
> (1917) ch. 7

Whitney Balliett 1926–

22 Critics are biased, and so are readers. (Indeed, a critic
is a bundle of biases held loosely together by a sense of
taste.) But intelligent readers soon discover how to
allow for the windage of their own and a critic's
prejudices.

> Dinosaurs in the Morning (1962) introductory note

23 The sound of surprise.

> Title of book on jazz (1959)

Pierre Balmain 1914–1982

1 The trick of wearing mink is to look as though you were wearing a cloth coat. The trick of wearing a cloth coat is to look as though you are wearing mink.
In Observer 25 Dec. 1955

Tallulah Bankhead 1903–1968

2 I'm as pure as the driven slush.
Quoted by Maurice Zolotow in Saturday Evening Post 12 Apr. 1947

3 There is less in this than meets the eye.
In Alexander Woollcott Shouts and Murmurs (1922) ch. 4 (describing a revival of Maeterlinck's play 'Aglavaine and Selysette')

4 Cocaine habit-forming? Of course not. I ought to know. I've been using it for years.
Tallulah (1952) ch. 4

Nancy Banks-Smith

5 In my experience, if you have to keep the lavatory door shut by extending your left leg, it's modern architecture.
Guardian 20 Feb. 1979

6 I'm still suffering from the big dénouement in [Jeffrey Archer's book] Not A Penny More when 'the three stood motionless like sheep in the stare of a python.' The whole thing keeps me awake at night. Here are these sheep, gambolling about in the Welsh jungle, when up pops a python. A python, what's more, who thinks he's a cobra.
Guardian 26 Mar. 1990

Imamu Amiri Baraka (Everett LeRoi Jones) 1934–

7 A rich man told me recently that a liberal is a man who tells other people what to do with their money.
Kulchur Spring 1962 'Tokenism'

8 A man is either free or he is not. There cannot be any apprenticeship for freedom.
Kulchur Spring 1962 'Tokenism'

9 God has been replaced, as he has all over the West, with respectability and airconditioning.
Midstream (1963) p. 39

W. N. P. Barbellion (Bruce Frederick Cummings) 1889–1919

10 Give me the man who will surrender the whole world for a moss or a caterpillar, and impracticable visions for a simple human delight. Yes, that shall be my practice. I prefer Richard Jefferies to Swedenborg and Oscar Wilde to Thomas à Kempis.
Enjoying Life and Other Literary Remains (1919) 'Crying for the Moon'

11 Am writing an essay on the life-history of insects and have abandoned the idea of writing on 'How Cats Spend their Time'.
Journal of a Disappointed Man (1919) 3 Jan. 1903

12 I can remember wondering as a child if I were a young Macaulay or Ruskin and secretly deciding that I was. My infant mind even was bitter with those who insisted on regarding me as a normal child and not as a prodigy.
Journal of a Disappointed Man (1919) 23 Oct. 1910

Maurice Baring 1874–1945

13 In Mozart and Salieri we see the contrast between the genius which does what it must and the talent which does what it can.
Outline of Russian Literature (1914) ch. 3

Ronnie Barker 1929–

14 The marvellous thing about a joke with a double meaning is that it can only mean one thing.
Sauce (1977) 'Daddie's Sauce'

Frederick R. Barnard

15 One picture is worth ten thousand words.
Printers' Ink 10 Mar. 1927

Clive Barnes 1927–

16 This [Oh, Calcutta!] is the kind of show to give pornography a dirty name.
New York Times 18 June 1969, p. 33

Julian Barnes 1946–

17 What does this journey seem like to those who aren't British—as they head towards the land of embarrassment and breakfast?
Flaubert's Parrot (1984) ch. 7

18 The writer must be universal in sympathy and an outcast by nature: only then can he see clearly.
Flaubert's Parrot (1984) ch. 10

19 Do not imagine that Art is something which is designed to give gentle uplift and self-confidence. Art is not a *brassière*. At least, not in the English sense. But do not forget that *brassière* is the French for life-jacket.
Flaubert's Parrot (1984) ch. 10

20 Books say: she did this because. Life says: she did this. Books are where things are explained to you; life is where things aren't. I'm not surprised some people prefer books. Books make sense of life. The only problem is that the lives they make sense of are other people's lives, never your own.
Flaubert's Parrot (1984) ch. 13

Peter Barnes 1931–

21 CLAIRE: How do you know you're . . . God?
EARL OF GURNEY: Simple. When I pray to Him I find I'm talking to myself.
The Ruling Class (1969) act 1, sc. 4

Sir J. M. Barrie 1860–1937

22 I'm not young enough to know everything.
The Admirable Crichton (performed 1902, pubd. 1914) act 1

1 His lordship may compel us to be equal upstairs, but there will never be equality in the servants' hall.
The Admirable Crichton (performed 1902, pubd. 1914) act 1

2 It's my deserts; I'm a second eleven sort of chap.
The Admirable Crichton (performed 1902, pubd. 1914) act 3

3 Times have changed since a certain author was executed for murdering his publisher. They say that when the author was on the scaffold he said goodbye to the minister and to the reporters, and then he saw some publishers sitting in the front row below, and to them he did not say goodbye. He said instead, 'I'll see you later.'
Speech at Aldine Club, New York, 5 Nov. 1896, in *Critic* 14 Nov. 1896

4 The life of every man is a diary in which he means to write one story, and writes another; and his humblest hour is when he compares the volume as it is with what he vowed to make it.
The Little Minister (1891) vol. 1, ch. 1

5 It's grand, and you canna expect to be baith grand and comfortable.
The Little Minister (1891) vol. 1, ch. 10

6 I loathe entering upon explanations to anybody about anything.
My Lady Nicotine (1890) ch. 14

7 When the first baby laughed for the first time, the laugh broke into a thousand pieces and they all went skipping about, and that was the beginning of fairies.
Peter Pan (1928) act 1

8 Every time a child says 'I don't believe in fairies' there is a little fairy somewhere that falls down dead.
Peter Pan (1928) act 1

9 To die will be an awfully big adventure.
Peter Pan (1928) act 3. Cf. Charles Frohman

10 Do you believe in fairies? Say quick that you believe! If you believe, clap your hands!
Peter Pan (1928) act 4

11 That is ever the way. 'Tis all jealousy to the bride and good wishes to the corpse.
Quality Street (performed 1901, pubd. 1913) act 1

12 The printing press is either the greatest blessing or the greatest curse of modern times, one sometimes forgets which.
Sentimental Tommy (1896) ch. 5

13 Someone said that God gave us memory so that we might have roses in December.
Rectorial Address at St Andrew's, 3 May 1922, in *The Times* 4 May 1922

14 Never ascribe to an opponent motives meaner than your own.
Rectorial Address at St Andrew's, 3 May 1922, in *The Times* 4 May 1922

15 Courage is the thing. All goes if courage goes!
Rectorial Address at St Andrews, 3 May 1922, in *The Times* 4 May 1922

16 For several days after my first book was published I carried it about in my pocket, and took surreptitious peeps at it to make sure that the ink had not faded.
Speech at the Critics' Circle in London, 26 May 1922, in *The Times* 27 May 1922

17 Have you ever noticed, Harry, that many jewels make women either incredibly fat or incredibly thin?
The Twelve-Pound Look and Other Plays (1921) p. 27

18 One's religion is whatever he is most interested in, and yours is Success.
The Twelve-Pound Look and Other Plays (1921) p. 28

19 Oh the gladness of her gladness when she's glad,
And the sadness of her sadness when she's sad,
But the gladness of her gladness
And the sadness of her sadness
Are as nothing, Charles,
To the badness of her badness when she's bad.
Rosalind in *The Twelve-Pound Look and Other Plays* (1921) p. 113

20 Charm . . . it's a sort of bloom on a woman. If you have it, you don't need to have anything else; and if you don't have it, it doesn't much matter what else you have. Some women, the few, have charm for all; and most have charm for one. But some have charm for none.
What Every Woman Knows (1918) act 1

21 A young Scotsman of your ability let loose upon the world with £300, what could he not do? It's almost appalling to think of; especially if he went among the English.
What Every Woman Knows (1918) act 1

22 My lady, there are few more impressive sights in the world than a Scotsman on the make.
What Every Woman Knows (1918) act 2

23 You've forgotten the grandest moral attribute of a Scotsman, Maggie, that he'll do nothing which might damage his career.
What Every Woman Knows (1918) act 2

24 The tragedy of a man who has found himself out.
What Every Woman Knows (1918) act 4

25 Every man who is high up loves to think that he has done it all himself; and the wife smiles, and lets it go at that. It's our only joke. Every woman knows that.
What Every Woman Knows (1918) act 4

Ethel Barrymore 1879–1959

26 For an actress to be a success, she must have the face of a Venus, the brains of a Minerva, the grace of Terpsichore, the memory of a Macaulay, the figure of Juno, and the hide of a rhinoceros.
In George Jean Nathan *The Theatre in the Fifties* (1953) p. 30

John Barrymore 1882–1942

27 He [Barrymore] would quote from Genesis the text which says, 'It is not good for man to be alone,' and then add, 'But O my God, what a relief.'
Alma Power-Waters *John Barrymore* (1941) ch. 13

28 My only regret in the theatre is that I could never sit out front and watch me.
In Eddie Cantor *The Way I See It* (1959) ch. 2

29 Die? I should say not, old fellow. No Barrymore would allow such a conventional thing to happen to him.
In Lionel Barrymore *We Barrymores* (1951) ch. 26

Lionel Bart 1930–

See FRANK NORMAN

Karl Barth 1886–1968

1 *Die Menschen aber waren nie gut, sind es nicht und werden es auch nie sein.*

Men have never been good, they are not good and they never will be good.
> *Christliche Gemeinde* (Christian Community, 1948) p. 36

2 Whether the angels play only Bach in praising God I am not quite sure; I am sure, however, that en famille they play Mozart.
> In *New York Times* 11 Dec. 1968, p. 42

Roland Barthes 1915–1980

3 *Ce que le public réclame, c'est l'image de la passion, non la passion elle-même.*

What the public wants is the image of passion, not passion itself.
> *Esprit* (1952) vol. 20, pt. 10, p. 412 'Le monde où l'on catche' (The world of wrestling)

4 *Je crois que l'automobile est aujourd'hui l'équivalent assez exact des grandes cathédrales gothiques : je veux dire une grande création d'époque, conçue passionnément par des artistes inconnus, consommée dans son image, sinon dans son usage, par un peuple entier qui s'approprie en elle un objet parfaitement magique.*

I think that cars today are almost the exact equivalent of the great Gothic cathedrals: I mean the supreme creation of an era, conceived with passion by unknown artists, and consumed in image if not in usage by a whole population which appropriates them as a purely magical object.
> *Mythologies* (1957) 'La nouvelle Citroën' (The new Citroën)

Bernard Baruch 1870–1965

5 To me old age is always fifteen years older than I am.
> In *Newsweek* 29 Aug. 1955

6 Vote for the man who promises least; he'll be the least disappointing.
> In Meyer Berger *New York* (1960)

7 Let us not be deceived—we are today in the midst of a cold war.
> Speech to South Carolina Legislature 16 Apr. 1947, in *New York Times* 17 Apr. 1947, p. 21

8 A political leader must keep looking over his shoulder all the time to see if the boys are still there. If they aren't still there, he's no longer a political leader.
> In *New York Times* 21 June 1965, p. 16

9 You can talk about capitalism and communism and all that sort of thing, but the important thing is the struggle everybody is engaged in to get better living conditions, and they are not interested too much in forms of government.
> In *The Times* 20 Aug. 1964

Jacques Barzun 1907–

10 If it were possible to talk to the unborn, one could never explain to them how it feels to be alive, for life is washed in the speechless real.
> *The House of Intellect* (1959) ch. 6

11 Art distils sensation and embodies it with enhanced meaning in memorable form—or else it is not art.
> *The House of Intellect* (1959) ch. 6

L. Frank Baum 1856–1919

12 The road to the City of Emeralds is paved with yellow brick.
> *Wonderful Wizard of Oz* (1900) ch. 2

Vicki Baum 1888–1960

13 *Verheiratet sein verlangt immer und überall die feinsten Kunst der Unaufrichtigkeit zwischen Mensch und Mensch.*

Marriage always demands the finest arts of insincerity possible between two human beings.
> *Zwischenfall in Lohwinckel* (1930) p. 140, translated by Margaret Goldsmith as *Results of an Accident* (1931) p. 140

Sir Arnold Bax 1883–1953

14 A sympathetic Scot summed it all up very neatly in the remark, 'You should make a point of trying every experience once, excepting incest and folk-dancing.'
> *Farewell, My Youth* (1943) p. 17

Sir Beverley Baxter 1891–1964

15 Beaverbrook is so pleased to be in the Government that he is like the town tart who has finally married the Mayor!
> In Sir Henry Channon *Chips: the Diaries* (1967) 12 June 1940

Beachcomber

See J. B. MORTON

David, First Earl Beatty 1871–1936

16 There seems to be something wrong with our bloody ships today [at the Battle of Jutland].
> In S. Roskill *Beatty* (1980) ch. 8

17 The German flag will be hauled down at sunset to-day (Thursday) and will not be hoisted again without permission.
> Signal to the Fleet, 21 Nov. 1918, in *The Times* 22 Nov. 1918

Lord Beaverbrook (William Maxwell Aitken, first Baron Beaverbrook) 1879–1964

18 I ran the paper [*Daily Express*] purely for propaganda, and with no other purpose.
> Evidence to Royal Commission on the Press, 18 Mar. 1948, in A. J. P. Taylor *Beaverbrook* (1972) ch. 23

1 This is my final word. It is time for me to become an apprentice once more. I have not settled in which direction. But somewhere, sometime soon.

Speech at Dorchester Hotel, 25 May 1964, in A. J. P. Taylor Beaverbrook (1972) ch. 25

2 The Flying Scotsman is no less splendid a sight when it travels north to Edinburgh than when it travels south to London. Mr Baldwin denouncing sanctions was as dignified as Mr Baldwin imposing them. At times it seemed that there were two Mr Baldwins on the stage, a prudent Mr Baldwin, who scented the danger in foolish projects, and a reckless Mr Baldwin, who plunged into them head down, eyes shut. But there was, in fact, only one Mr Baldwin, a well-meaning man of indifferent judgement, who, whether he did right or wrong, was always sustained by a belief that he was acting for the best.

Daily Express 29 May 1937

3 The Daily Express declares that Great Britain will not be involved in a European war this year or next year either.

Daily Express 19 Sept. 1938

4 He [Lloyd George] did not seem to care which way he travelled providing he was in the driver's seat.

Decline and Fall of Lloyd George (1963) ch. 7

5 Now who is responsible for this work of development on which so much depends? To whom must the praise be given? To the boys in the back rooms. They do not sit in the limelight. But they are the men who do the work.

Listener 27 Mar. 1941. Cf. Frank Loesser

6 With the publication of his [Earl Haig's] Private Papers in 1952, he committed suicide 25 years after his death.

Men and Power (1956) p. xviii

7 Churchill on top of the wave has in him the stuff of which tyrants are made.

Politicians and the War (1932) vol. 2, ch. 6

Carl Becker 1873–1945

8 The significance of man is that he is that part of the universe that asks the question, What is the significance of Man? He alone can stand apart imaginatively and, regarding himself and the universe in their eternal aspects, pronounce a judgment: The significance of man is that he is insignificant and is aware of it.

Progress and Power (1936) ch. 3

Samuel Beckett 1906–1989

9 It is suicide to be abroad. But what is it to be at home, Mr Tyler, what is it to be at home? A lingering dissolution.

All That Fall (1957) p. 10

10 We could have saved sixpence. We have saved fivepence. (*Pause*) But at what cost?

All That Fall (1957) p. 25

11 CLOV: Do you believe in the life to come?
HAMM: Mine was always that.

Endgame (1958) p. 35

12 Personally I have no bone to pick with graveyards, I take the air there willingly, perhaps more willingly than elsewhere, when take the air I must.

First Love (1973) p. 8

13 If I had the use of my body I would throw it out of the window.

Malone Dies (1958) p. 44

14 Where I am, I don't know, I'll never know, in the silence you don't know, you must go on, I can't go on, I'll go on.

The Unnamable (1959) p. 418

15 Nothing to be done.

Waiting for Godot (1955) act 1

16 One of the thieves was saved. (*Pause*) It's a reasonable percentage.

Waiting for Godot (1955) act 1

17 ESTRAGON: Charming spot. Inspiring prospects. Let's go.
VLADIMIR: We can't.
ESTRAGON: Why not?
VLADIMIR: We're waiting for Godot.

Waiting for Godot (1955) act 1

18 Nothing happens, nobody comes, nobody goes, it's awful!

Waiting for Godot (1955) act 1

19 He can't think without his hat.

Waiting for Godot (1955) act 1

20 VLADIMIR: That passed the time.
ESTRAGON: It would have passed in any case.
VLADIMIR: Yes, but not so rapidly.

Waiting for Godot (1955) act 1

21 We always find something, eh, Didi, to give us the impression that we exist?

Waiting for Godot (1955) act 2

22 We are not saints, but we have kept our appointment. How many people can boast as much?

Waiting for Godot (1955) act 2

23 We all are born mad. Some remain so.

Waiting for Godot (1955) act 2

24 They give birth astride of a grave, the light gleams an instant, then it's night once more.

Waiting for Godot (1955) act 2

25 The air is full of our cries. (*He listens.*) But habit is a great deadener.

Waiting for Godot (1955) act 2

Harry Bedford and Terry Sullivan

26 I'm a bit of a ruin that Cromwell knock'd about a bit.

It's a Bit of a Ruin that Cromwell Knocked about a Bit (1920 song; written for Marie Lloyd)

Sir Thomas Beecham 1879–1961

27 A musicologist is a man who can read music but can't hear it.

In H. Proctor-Gregg Beecham Remembered (1976) pt. 2, p. 154

1 There are two golden rules for an orchestra: start together and finish together. The public doesn't give a damn what goes on in between.

> In Harold Atkins and Archie Newman *Beecham Stories* (1978) p. 27

2 [The harpsichord] sounds like two skeletons copulating on a corrugated tin roof.

> In Harold Atkins and Archie Newman *Beecham Stories* (1978) p. 34

3 In the first movement alone, of the Seventh Symphony [by Bruckner], I took note of six pregnancies and at least four miscarriages.

> In Harold Atkins and Archie Newman *Beecham Stories* (1978) p. 50

4 [Herbert von Karajan is] a kind of musical Malcolm Sargent.

> In Harold Atkins and Archie Newman *Beecham Stories* (1978) p. 61

5 I am not the greatest conductor in this country. On the other hand I'm better than any damned foreigner.

> In *Daily Express* 9 Mar. 1961

6 Musicians did not like the piece [Strauss's *Elektra*] at all. One eminent British composer on leaving the theatre was asked what he thought of it. 'Words fail me,' he replied, 'and I'm going home at once to play the chord of C major twenty times over to satisfy myself that it still exists.'

> *Mingled Chime* (1944) ch. 18

7 The plain fact is that music *per se* means nothing; it is sheer sound, and the interpreter can do no more with it than his own capacities, mental and spiritual, will allow, and the same applies to the listener.

> *Mingled Chime* (1944) ch. 33

8 The English may not like music, but they absolutely love the noise it makes.

> In *New York Herald Tribune* 9 Mar. 1961

9 Good music is that which penetrates the ear with facility and quits the memory with difficulty.

> Speech, *c*.1950, in *New York Times* 9 Mar. 1961

10 All the arts in America are a gigantic racket run by unscrupulous men for unhealthy women.

> In *Observer* 5 May 1946

11 Hark! the herald angels sing!
Beecham's Pills are just the thing,
Two for a woman, one for a child . . .
Peace on earth and mercy mild!

> In Neville Cardus *Sir Thomas Beecham* (1961) p. 23

12 At a rehearsal I let the orchestra play as they like. At the concert I make them play as *I* like.

> In Neville Cardus *Sir Thomas Beecham* (1961) p. 111

13 Dear old Elgar—he is furious with me for drastically cutting his A flat symphony—it's a very long work, the musical equivalent of the Towers of St Pancras Station—neo-Gothic, you know.

> In Neville Cardus *Sir Thomas Beecham* (1961) p. 113

14 I am entirely with you in your obvious reluctance to rehearse on a morning as chilly and dismal as this—but please do try to keep in touch with us from time to time.

> In Neville Cardus *Sir Thomas Beecham* (1961) p. 113

15 Why do we have to have all these third-rate foreign conductors around—when we have so many second-rate ones of our own?

> In L. Ayre *Wit of Music* (1966) p. 70

Sir Max Beerbohm 1872–1956

16 I have known no man of genius who had not to pay, in some affliction or defect either physical or spiritual, for what the gods had given him.

> *And Even Now* (1920) 'No. 2, The Pines'

17 One might well say that mankind is divisible into two great classes: hosts and guests.

> *And Even Now* (1920) 'Hosts and Guests'

18 I maintain that though you would often in the fifteenth century have heard the snobbish Roman say, in a would-be off-hand tone, 'I am dining with the Borgias tonight,' no Roman ever was able to say, 'I dined last night with the Borgias.'

> *And Even Now* (1920) 'Hosts and Guests'

19 They so very indubitably *are*, you know!

> *Christmas Garland* (1912) 'Mote in the Middle Distance'

20 Of course he [William Morris] was a wonderful all-round man, but the act of walking round him has always tired me.

> Letter to S. N. Behrman *c*.1953, in *Conversations with Max* (1960) ch. 2

21 A swear-word in a rustic slum
A simple swear-word is to some,
To Masefield something more.

> *Fifty Caricatures* (1912) no. 12

22 Not that I had any special reason for hating school! Strange as it may seem to my readers, I was not unpopular there. I was a modest, good-humoured boy. It is Oxford that has made me insufferable.

> *More* (1899) 'Going Back to School'

23 Undergraduates owe their happiness chiefly to the consciousness that they are no longer at school. The nonsense which was knocked out of them at school is all put gently back at Oxford or Cambridge.

> *More* (1899) 'Going Back to School'

24 I have the satiric temperament: when I am laughing at anyone I am generally rather amusing, but when I am praising anyone, I am always deadly dull.

> *Saturday Review* 28 May 1898

25 The only tribute a French translator can pay Shakespeare is not to translate him—even to please Sarah [Bernhardt].

> *Saturday Review* 17 June 1899

26 'I'm afraid I found [the British Museum] rather a depressing place. It—it seemed to sap one's vitality.' 'It does. That's why I go there. The lower one's vitality, the more sensitive one is to great art.'

> *Seven Men* (1919) 'Enoch Soames'

27 Enter Michael Angelo. Andrea del Sarto appears for a moment at a window. Pippa passes.

> *Seven Men* (1919) ' Savonarola Brown' act 3

28 Most women are not so young as they are painted.

> *Yellow Book* (1894) vol. 1, p. 67

1 'After all,' as a pretty girl once said to me, 'women are a sex by themselves, so to speak.'
Yellow Book (1894) vol. 1, p. 70

2 Fate wrote her [Queen Caroline of Brunswick] a most tremendous tragedy, and she played it in tights.
Yellow Book (1894) vol. 3, p. 260

3 There is always something rather absurd about the past.
Yellow Book (1895) vol. 4, p. 282

4 To give an accurate and exhaustive account of the period would need a far less brilliant pen than mine.
Yellow Book (1895) vol. 4, p. 283

5 None, it is said, of all who revelled with the Regent, was half so wicked as Lord George Hell.
Yellow Book (1896) vol. 11, p. 11 ' Happy Hypocrite' ch. 1

6 The fading signals and grey eternal walls of that antique station, which, familiar to them and insignificant, does yet whisper to the tourist the last enchantments of the Middle Age.
Zuleika Dobson (1911) ch. 1

7 Zuleika, on a desert island, would have spent most of her time in looking for a man's footprint.
Zuleika Dobson (1911) ch. 2

8 The dullard's envy of brilliant men is always assuaged by the suspicion that they will come to a bad end.
Zuleika Dobson (1911) ch. 4

9 Women who love the same man have a kind of bitter freemasonry.
Zuleika Dobson (1911) ch. 4

10 You will find that the woman who is really kind to dogs is always one who has failed to inspire sympathy in men.
Zuleika Dobson (1911) ch. 6

11 Beauty and the lust for learning have yet to be allied.
Zuleika Dobson (1911) ch. 7

12 You will think me lamentably crude: my experience of life has been drawn from life itself.
Zuleika Dobson (1911) ch. 7

13 He held, too, in his enlightened way, that Americans have a perfect right to exist. But he did often find himself wishing Mr Rhodes had not enabled them to exercise that right in Oxford.
Zuleika Dobson (1911) ch. 8

14 She was one of the people who say 'I don't know anything about music really, but I know what I like.'
Zuleika Dobson (1911) ch. 9. Cf. Henry James 112:3

15 You cannot make a man by standing a sheep on its hind-legs. But by standing a flock of sheep in that position you can make a crowd of men.
Zuleika Dobson (1911) ch. 9

16 Deeply regret inform your grace last night two black owls came and perched on battlements remained there through night hooting at dawn flew away none knows whither awaiting instructions Jellings.
Zuleika Dobson (1911) ch. 14

17 Prepare vault for funeral Monday Dorset.
Zuleika Dobson (1911) ch. 14

18 The Socratic manner is not a game at which two can play. Please answer my question, to the best of your ability.
Zuleika Dobson (1911) ch. 15

19 Byron!—he would be all forgotten today if he had lived to be a florid old gentleman with iron-grey whiskers, writing very long, very able letters to *The Times* about the Repeal of the Corn Laws.
Zuleika Dobson (1911) ch. 18

Brendan Behan 1923–1964

20 He was born an Englishman and remained one for years.
Hostage (1958) act 1

21 PAT: He was an Anglo-Irishman.
MEG: In the blessed name of God what's that?
PAT: A Protestant with a horse.
Hostage (1958) act 1

22 Meanwhile I'll sing that famous old song, 'The Hound that Caught the Pubic Hare'.
Hostage (1958) act 1

23 When I came back to Dublin, I was courtmartialled in my absence and sentenced to death in my absence, so I said they could shoot me in my absence.
Hostage (1958) act 1

24 SOLDIER: What's a mixed infant?
TERESA: A little boy or girl under five years old. They were called mixed infants because until that time the boys and girls were mixed together.
SOLDIER: I wish I'd been a mixed infant.
Hostage (1958) act 2

25 I am a sociable worker. Have you your testament?
Hostage (1958) act 2

26 Go on, abuse me—your own husband that took you off the streets on a Sunday morning, when there wasn't a pub open in the city.
Hostage (1958) act 2

27 We're here because we're queer
Because we're queer because we're here.
Hostage (1958) act 3

28 There's no such thing as bad publicity except your own obituary.
In Dominic Behan *My Brother Brendan* (1965) p. 158

John Hay Beith

See IAN HAY

Clive Bell 1881–1964

29 One account . . . given me by a very good artist, is that what he tries to express in a picture is 'a passionate apprehension of form'.
Art (1914) pt. 1, ch. 3

30 It would follow that 'significant form' was form behind which we catch a sense of ultimate reality.
Art (1914) pt. 1, ch. 3

31 Art and Religion are, then, two roads by which men escape from circumstance to ecstasy. Between aesthetic

and religious rapture there is a family alliance. Art
and Religion are means to similar states of mind.

Art (1914) pt. 2, ch. 1

1 I will try to account for the degree of my aesthetic
emotion. That, I conceive, is the function of the critic.

Art (1914) pt. 3 ch. 3

2 Only reason can convince us of those three
fundamental truths without a recogniton of which
there can be no effective liberty: that what we believe is
not necessarily true; that what we like is not
necessarily good; and that all questions are open.

Civilization (1928) ch. 5

Henry Bellamann

3 '*Randy*—where—where's the rest of me?' His voice
rose to a sharp wail.

King's Row (1940) pt. 5, ch. 1 (also used in the 1941 film of
the book, where the line was spoken by Ronald Reagan)

Hilaire Belloc 1870–1953

4 Child! do not throw this book about;
Refrain from the unholy pleasure
Of cutting all the pictures out!
Preserve it as your chiefest treasure.

Bad Child's Book of Beasts (1896) dedication

5 I call you bad, my little child,
Upon the title page,
Because a manner rude and wild
Is common at your age.

Bad Child's Book of Beasts (1896) introduction

6 Who take their manners from the Ape,
Their habits from the Bear,
Indulge in loud unseemly jape,
And never brush their hair.

Bad Child's Book of Beasts (1896) introduction

7 Mothers of large families (who claim to common sense)
Will find a Tiger well repay the trouble and expense.

Bad Child's Book of Beasts (1896) 'The Tiger'

8 I shoot the Hippopotamus
With bullets made of platinum,
Because if I use leaden ones
His hide is sure to flatten 'em.

Bad Child's Book of Beasts (1896) 'The Hippopotamus'

9 When people call this beast to mind,
They marvel more and more
At such a little tail behind,
So large a trunk before.

Bad Child's Book of Beasts (1896) 'The Elephant'

10 And always keep a-hold of Nurse
For fear of finding something worse.

Cautionary Tales (1907) 'Jim'

11 The Chief Defect of Henry King
Was chewing little bits of String.

Cautionary Tales (1907) 'Henry King'

12 Physicians of the Utmost Fame
Were called at once; but when they came
They answered, as they took their Fees,
'There is no Cure for this Disease.'

Cautionary Tales (1907) 'Henry King'

13 'Oh, my Friends, be warned by me,
That Breakfast, Dinner, Lunch, and Tea
Are all the Human Frame requires . . .
With that, the Wretched Child expires.

Cautionary Tales (1907) 'Henry King'

14 Matilda told such Dreadful Lies,
It made one Gasp and Stretch one's Eyes;
Her Aunt, who, from her Earliest Youth,
Had kept a Strict Regard for Truth,
Attempted to Believe Matilda:
The effort very nearly killed her.

Cautionary Tales (1907) 'Matilda'

15 It happened that a few Weeks later
Her Aunt was off to the Theatre
To see that Interesting Play
The Second Mrs Tanqueray.

Cautionary Tales (1907) 'Matilda'

16 For every time She shouted 'Fire!'
They only answered 'Little Liar!'
And therefore when her Aunt returned,
Matilda, and the House, were Burned.

Cautionary Tales (1907) 'Matilda'

17 In my opinion, Butlers ought
To know their place, and not to play
The Old Retainer night and day.

Cautionary Tales (1907) 'Lord Lundy'

18 Sir! you have disappointed us!
We had intended you to be
The next Prime Minister but three:
The stocks were sold; the Press was squared;
The Middle Class was quite prepared.
But as it is! . . . My language fails!
Go out and govern New South Wales!

Cautionary Tales (1907) 'Lord Lundy'

19 A Trick that everyone abhors
In Little Girls is slamming Doors.

Cautionary Tales (1907) 'Rebecca'

20 She was not really bad at heart,
But only rather rude and wild:
She was an aggravating child.

Cautionary Tales (1907) 'Rebecca'

21 The nicest child I ever knew
Was Charles Augustus Fortescue.
He never lost his cap, or tore
His stockings or his pinafore:
In eating Bread he made no Crumbs,
He was extremely fond of sums.

Cautionary Tales (1907) 'Charles Augustus Fortescue'

22 The pleasure politicians take in their limelight pleases
me with a sort of pleasure I get when I see a child's eyes
gleam over a new toy.

Conversation with a Cat (1931) ch. 17

23 Gentlemen, I am a Catholic. As far as possible, I go to
Mass every day. This is a rosary. As far as possible,
I kneel down and tell these beads every day. If you
reject me on account of my religion, I shall thank God
that He has spared me the indignity of being your
representative.

Speech to voters of South Salford, 1906, in R. Speaight *Life of
Hilaire Belloc* (1957) ch. 10

1 I always like to associate with a lot of priests because it makes me understand anti-clerical things so well.
   Letter to E. S. P. Haynes, 9 Nov. 1909, in R. Speaight *Life of Hilaire Belloc* (1957) ch. 17

2 Whatever happens we have got
   The Maxim Gun, and they have not.
   Modern Traveller (1898) pt. 6

3 I had an Aunt in Yucatan
   Who bought a Python from a man
   And kept it for a pet.
   She died, because she never knew
   These simple little rules and few;—
   The Snake is living yet.
   More Beasts for Worse Children (1897) 'The Python'

4 The Llama is a woolly sort of fleecy hairy goat,
   With an indolent expression and an undulating throat
   Like an unsuccessful literary man.
   More Beasts for Worse Children (1897) 'The Llama'

5 The Microbe is so very small
   You cannot make him out at all.
   More Beasts for Worse Children (1897) 'The Microbe'

6 Oh! let us never, never doubt
   What nobody is sure about!
   More Beasts for Worse Children (1897) 'The Microbe'

7 Lord Finchley tried to mend the Electric Light
   Himself. It struck him dead: And serve him right!
   It is the business of the wealthy man
   To give employment to the artisan.
   More Peers (1911) 'Lord Finchley'

8 Lord Hippo suffered fearful loss
   By putting money on a horse
   Which he believed, if it were pressed,
   Would run far faster than the rest.
   More Peers (1911) 'Lord Hippo'

9 Like many of the Upper Class
   He liked the Sound of Broken Glass.
   New Cautionary Tales (1930) 'About John'. Cf. Evelyn Waugh 222:19

10 Birds in their little nests agree
   With Chinamen, but not with me.
   New Cautionary Tales (1930) 'On Food'

11 It is the best of all trades, to make songs, and the second best to sing them.
   On Everything (1909) 'On Song'

12 Is there no Latin word for Tea? Upon my soul, if I had known that I would have let the vulgar stuff alone.
   On Nothing (1908) 'On Tea'

13 Strong brother in God and last companion, Wine.
   Short Talks with the Dead (1926) 'Heroic Poem upon Wine'

14 Sally is gone that was so kindly
   Sally is gone from Ha'nacker Hill.
   Sonnets and Verse (1923) 'Ha'nacker Mill'

15 Do you remember an Inn,
   Miranda?
   Do you remember an Inn?
   And the tedding and the spreading
   Of the straw for a bedding,
   And the fleas that tease in the High Pyrenees
   And the wine that tasted of the tar?
   Sonnets and Verse (1923) 'Tarantella'

16 When I am dead, I hope it may be said:
   'His sins were scarlet, but his books were read.'
   Sonnets and Verse (1923) 'On His Books'

17 The Devil, having nothing else to do,
   Went off to tempt My Lady Poltagrue.
   My Lady, tempted by a private whim,
   To his extreme annoyance, tempted him.
   Sonnets and Verse (1923) 'On Lady Poltagrue'

18 Of this bad world the loveliest and the best
   Has smiled and said 'Good Night', and gone to rest.
   Sonnets and Verse (1923) 'On a Dead Hostess'

19 The accursed power which stands on Privilege
   (And goes with Women, and Champagne, and Bridge)
   Broke—and Democracy resumed her reign:
   (Which goes with Bridge, and Women and Champagne).
   Sonnets and Verse (1923) 'On a Great Election'

20 Lady, when your lovely head
   Droops to sink among the Dead,
   And the quiet places keep
   You that so divinely sleep;
   Then the dead shall blessèd be
   With a new solemnity,
   For such Beauty, so descending,
   Pledges them that Death is ending,
   Sleep your fill—but when you wake
   Dawn shall over Lethe break.
   Sonnets and Verse (1923) 'On a Sleeping Friend'

21 I'm tired of Love: I'm still more tired of Rhyme.
   But Money gives me pleasure all the time.
   Sonnets and Verse (1923) 'Fatigued'

22 Pale Ebenezer thought it wrong to fight,
   But Roaring Bill (who killed him) thought it right.
   Sonnets and Verse (ed. 2, 1938) 'The Pacifist'

23 I am a sundial, and I make a botch
   Of what is done much better by a watch.
   Sonnets and Verse (ed. 2, 1938) 'On a Sundial'

24 From the towns all Inns have been driven: from the villages most. . . . Change your hearts or you will lose your Inns and you will deserve to have lost them. But when you have lost your Inns drown your empty selves, for you will have lost the last of England.
   This and That (1912) 'On Inns'

25 When I am living in the Midlands
   That are sodden and unkind,
   I light my lamp in the evening:
   My work is left behind;
   And the great hills of the South Country
   Come back into my mind.
   Verses (1910) 'The South Country'

26 If I ever become a rich man,
   Or if ever I grow to be old,
   I will build a house with deep thatch
   To shelter me from the cold,
   And there shall the Sussex songs be sung
   And the story of Sussex told.

   I will hold my house in the high wood
   Within a walk of the sea,
   And the men that were boys when I was a boy
   Shall sit and drink with me.
   Verses (1910) 'The South Country'

1 Of Courtesy, it is much less
Than Courage of Heart or Holiness,
Yet in my Walks it seems to me
That the Grace of God is in Courtesy.
Verses (1910) 'Courtesy'

2 Balliol made me, Balliol fed me,
Whatever I had she gave me again:
And the best of Balliol loved and led me.
God be with you, Balliol men.
Verses (1910) 'To the Balliol Men Still in Africa'

3 From quiet homes and first beginning,
Out to the undiscovered ends,
There's nothing worth the wear of winning,
But laughter and the love of friends.
Verses (1910) 'Dedicatory Ode'

4 Remote and ineffectual Don
That dared attack my Chesterton.
Verses (1910) 'Lines to a Don'

5 Don different from those regal Dons!
With hearts of gold and lungs of bronze,
Who shout and bang and roar and bawl
The Absolute across the hall,
Or sail in amply billowing gown
Enormous through the Sacred Town,
Bearing from College to their homes
Deep cargoes of gigantic tomes;
Dons admirable! Dons of Might!
Uprising on my inward sight
Compact of ancient tales, and port
And sleep—and learning of a sort.
Verses (1910) 'Lines to a Don'

6 A smell of burning fills the startled Air—
The Electrician is no longer there!
Verses (1910) 'Newdigate Poem'

7 I said to Heart, 'How goes it ?' Heart replied:
'Right as a Ribstone Pippin!' But it lied.
Verses (1910) 'The False Heart'

8 The Moon on the one hand, the Dawn on the other;
The Moon is my sister, the Dawn is my brother.
The Moon on my Left and the Dawn on my right.
My Brother, good morning: my Sister good night.
Verses and Sonnets (1896) 'The Early Morning'

Saul Bellow 1915–

9 If I am out of my mind, it's all right with me, thought
Moses Herzog.
Herzog (1961) p. 1 (opening sentence)

10 The idea, anyway, was to ward off trouble. But now the
moronic inferno had caught up with me. My elegant
car . . . was mutilated.
Humboldt's Gift (1975) p. 35

11 The only real distinction at this dangerous moment in
human history and cosmic development has nothing to
do with medals and ribbons. Not to fall asleep is
distinguished. Everything else is mere popcorn.
Humboldt's Gift (1975) p. 283

12 I feel that art has something to do with the
achievement of stillness in the midst of chaos.
A stillness which characterizes prayer, too, and the eye

of the storm. I think that art has something to do with
an arrest of attention in the midst of distraction.
In George Plimpton *Writers at Work* (1967) 3rd series,
p. 190

Robert Benchley 1889–1945

13 I haven't been abroad in so long that I almost speak
English without an accent now.
After 1903—What? (1938) p. 241

14 On a summer vacation trip Benchley arrived in Venice
and immediately wired a friend: 'STREETS FLOODED.
PLEASE ADVISE.'
In R. E. Drennan *Algonquin Wits* (1968) p. 45

15 I do most of my work sitting down; that's where
I shine.
In R. E. Drennan *Algonquin Wits* (1968) p. 55

16 My only solution for the problem of habitual accidents
and, so far, nobody has asked me for my solution, is to
stay in bed all day. Even then, there is always the
chance that you will fall out.
Chips off the old Benchley (1949) 'Safety Second'

17 I had just dozed off into a stupor when I heard what
I thought was myself talking to myself. I didn't pay
much attention to it, as I knew practically everything
I would have to say to myself, and wasn't particularly
interested.
Chips off the old Benchley (1949) 'First Pigeon of Spring '

18 A great many people have come up to me and asked
how I manage to get so much work done and still keep
looking so dissipated.
Chips off the old Benchley (1949) 'How to get things Done'

19 The biggest obstacle to professional writing is the
necessity for changing a typewriter ribbon.
Chips off the old Benchley (1949) 'Learn to Write'

20 Bob Benchley was one of the few writers I knew who
always laughed at other writers' lines. I always laughed
at one of his. When he returned for his twenty-fifth
homecoming at Harvard [in 1937], he stated to
underclassmen, 'I feel as I always have, except for an
occasional heart attack.'
Groucho Marx *Grouchophile* (1976) p. 204

21 The surest way to make a monkey of a man is to quote
him.
My Ten Years in a Quandary (1936) p. 204

22 Tell us your phobias and we will tell you what you are
afraid of.
My Ten Years in a Quandary (1936) p. 295

23 He [Benchley] came out of a night club one evening
and, tapping a uniformed figure on the shoulder, said,
'Get me a cab.' The uniformed figure turned around
furiously and informed him that he was not a doorman
but a rear admiral. 'O.K.,' said Benchley, 'Get me
a battleship.'
New Yorker 5 Jan. 1946

24 The famous office that Benchley and Dorothy Parker
shared in the Metropolitan Opera House . . . was
a cramped triangle stolen from a hallway. 'One square
foot less and it would be adulterous,' said Benchley.
New Yorker 5 Jan. 1946

1 In America there are two classes of travel—first class, and with children.
   Pluck and Luck (1925) p. 6

2 Often Daddy sat up very late working on a case of Scotch.
   Pluck and Luck (1925) p. 198

3 A friend told him that the particular drink he was drinking was slow poison, and he replied, 'So who's in a hurry?'
   Nathaniel Benchley *Robert Benchley* (1955) ch. 1

4 It took me fifteen years to discover that I had no talent for writing, but I couldn't give it up because by that time I was too famous.
   In Nathaniel Benchley *Robert Benchley* (1955) ch. 1
   See also: MAE WEST

Julien Benda 1867–1956

5 *La trahison des clercs.*

   The treachery of the intellectuals.
   Title of book (1927)

Stephen Vincent Benét 1898–1943

6 We thought we were done with these things but we were wrong.
   We thought, because we had power, we had wisdom.
   Atlantic Monthly Sept. 1935 'Litany for Dictatorships'

7 I have fallen in love with American names,
   The sharp, gaunt names that never get fat,
   The snakeskin-titles of mining-claims,
   The plumed war-bonnet of Medicine Hat,
   Tucson and Deadwood and Lost Mule Flat.
   Yale Review (1927) vol. 17, p. 63 'American Names'

8 I shall not rest quiet in Montparnasse.
   I shall not lie easy at Winchelsea.
   You may bury my body in Sussex grass,
   You may bury my tongue at Champmédy.
   I shall not be there, I shall rise and pass.
   Bury my heart at Wounded Knee.
   Yale Review (1927) vol. 17, p. 64 'American Names'

William Rose Benét 1886–1950

9 Blake saw a treefull of angels at Peckham Rye,
   And his hands could lay hold on the tiger's terrible heart.
   Blake knew how deep is Hell, and Heaven how high,
   And could build the universe from one tiny part.
   Burglar of Zodiac (1918) 'Mad Blake'

Tony Benn 1925–

10 A holy war with atom bombs could end the human family for ever. I say this as a socialist whose political commitment owes much more to the teachings of Jesus—without the mysteries within which they are presented—than to the writings of Marx whose analysis seems to lack an understanding of the deeper needs of humanity.
   Arguments for Democracy (1981) ch. 7

11 The distortion of the Marxist idea that developed in Russia was as great, and of the same character, as the distortion of the Christian teaching at the time of the Inquisition. But it is as wholly wrong to blame Marx for what was done in his name, as it is to blame Jesus for what was done in his.
   In Alan Freeman *The Benn Heresy* (1982) p. 172

12 In developing our industrial strategy for the period ahead, we have the benefit of much experience. Almost everything has been tried at least once.
   Hansard 13 Mar. 1974, col. 197

13 Broadcasting is really too important to be left to the broadcasters.
   In Anthony Sampson *The New Anatomy of Britain* (1971) ch. 24

14 It is arguable that what has really happened has amounted to such a breakdown in the social contract, upon which parliamentary democracy by universal suffrage was based, that that contract now needs to be re-negotiated on a basis that shares power much more widely, before it can win general assent again.
   The New Politics (1970) ch. 4

15 The British House of Lords is the British Outer Mongolia for retired politicians.
   In *Observer* 4 Feb. 1962

16 We thought we could put the economy right in five years. We were wrong. It will probably take ten.
   Speech at Bristol, 18 Apr. 1968 , in *The Times* 19 Apr. 1968

George Bennard 1873–1958

17 I will cling to the old rugged cross,
   And exchange it some day for a crown.
   The Old Rugged Cross (1913 hymn)

Alan Bennett 1934–

18 Life, you know, is rather like opening a tin of sardines. We are all of us looking for the key. And, I wonder, how many of you here tonight have wasted years of your lives looking behind the kitchen dressers of this life for that key. I know I have. Others think they've found the key, don't they? They roll back the lid of the sardine tin of life, they reveal the sardines, the riches of life, therein, and they get them out, they enjoy them. But, you know, there's always a little bit in the corner you can't get out. I wonder—I wonder, is there a little bit in the corner of your life? I know there is in mine.
   Beyond the Fringe (1961 revue) 'Take a Pew', in Roger Wilmut *Complete Beyond the Fringe* (1987) p. 104

19 I have never understood this liking for war. It panders to instincts already catered for within the scope of any respectable domestic establishment.
   Forty Years On (1969) act 1

20 We started off trying to set up a small anarchist community, but people wouldn't obey the rules.
   Getting On (1972) act 1

21 One of the few lessons I have learned in life is that there is invariably something odd about women who wear ankle socks.
   Old Country (1978) act 1

1 We were put to Dickens as children but it never quite
took. That unremitting humanity soon had me
cheesed off.
   Old Country (1978) act 2

Arnold Bennett 1867–1931

2 I place it upon record frankly—the Clayhanger trilogy
is good . . . .The scene, for instance, where Darius
Clayhanger dies that lingering death could scarcely be
bettered . . . .And why? . . . Because I took infinite
pains over it. All the time my father was dying, I was
at the bedside making copious notes. You can't just
slap these things down. You have to take trouble.
   Overheard conversation with Hugh Walpole *c*.1926, in P. G.
   Wodehouse and Guy Bolton *Bring on the Girls* (1954) ch. 15

3 His opinion of himself, having once risen, remained at
'set fair'.
   The Card (1911) ch. 1

4 'Ye can call it influenza if ye like,' said Mrs Machin.
'There was no influenza in my young days. We called
a cold a cold.'
   The Card (1911) ch. 8

5 'And yet,' demanded Councillor Barlow, 'what's he
done? Has he ever done a day's work in his life? What
great cause is he identified with?' 'He's identified,' said
the first speaker, 'with the great cause of cheering us all
up.'
   The Card (1911) ch. 12

6 My general impression is that Englishmen act better
than Frenchmen, and Frenchwomen better than
Englishwomen.
   Cupid and Commonsense (1909) preface

7 Good taste is better than bad taste, but bad taste is
better than no taste, and men without individuality
have no taste—at any rate no taste that they can
impose on their publics.
   Evening Standard 21 Aug. 1930

8 'Bah!' she said. 'With people like you, love only means
one thing.' 'No,' he replied. 'It means twenty things,
but it doesn't mean nineteen.'
   Journal (1932) 20 Nov. 1904

9 A test of a first-rate work, and a test of your sincerity in
calling it a first-rate work, is that you finish it.
   Things that have Interested Me (1921) 'Finishing Books'

10 In the meantime alcohol produces a delightful social
atmosphere that nothing else can produce.
   Things that have Interested Me (1921) 'For and Against
   Prohibition'

11 Seventy minutes had passed before Mr Lloyd George
arrived at his proper theme. He spoke for a hundred and
seventeen minutes, in which period he was detected
only once in the use of an argument.
   Things that have Interested Me (1921) 'After the March
   Offensive.'

12 Pessimism, when you get used to it, is just as agreeable
as optimism. Indeed, I think it must be more agreeable,
must have a more real savour, than optimism—from
the way in which pessimists abandon themselves to it.
   Things that have Interested Me (1921) 'Slump in Pessimism'

13 The price of justice is eternal publicity.
   Things that have Interested Me (2nd series, 1923) 'Secret
   Trials'

14 A cause may be inconvenient, but it's magnificent. It's
like champagne or high heels, and one must be
prepared to suffer for it.
   The Title (1918) act 1

15 Examine the Honours List and you can instantly tell
how the Government feels in its inside. When the
Honours List is full of rascals, millionaires,
and—er—chumps, you may be quite sure that the
Government is dangerously ill.
   The Title (1918) act 1

16 Being a husband is a whole-time job. That is why so
many husbands fail. They cannot give their entire
attention to it.
   The Title (1918) act 1

17 Journalists say a thing that they know isn't true, in the
hope that if they keep on saying it long enough it will
be true.
   The Title (1918) act 2

18 Literature's always a good card to play for Honours. It
makes people think that Cabinet ministers are educated.
   The Title (1918) act 3

Ada Benson and Fred Fisher 1875–1942

19 Your feet's too big,
Don't want you 'cause your feet's too big,
Mad at you 'cause your feet's too big,
Hates you 'cause your feet's too big.
   Your Feet's Too Big (1936 song)

A. C. Benson 1862–1925

20 I don't like authority, at least I don't like other
people's authority.
   Excerpts from Letters to M. E. A. (1926) p. 41

21 Land of Hope and Glory, Mother of the Free,
How shall we extol thee who are born of thee?
Wider still and wider shall thy bounds be set;
God who made thee mighty, make thee mightier yet.
   Land of Hope and Glory (1902 song; music by Sir Edward
   Elgar)

Stella Benson 1892–1933

22 Call no man foe, but never love a stranger.
   This is the End (1917) p. 63

Edmund Clerihew Bentley 1875–1956

23 When their lordships asked Bacon
How many bribes he had taken
He had at least the grace
To get very red in the face.
   Baseless Biography (1939) 'Bacon'

24 The Art of Biography
Is different from Geography.
Geography is about Maps,
But Biography is about Chaps.
   Biography for Beginners (1905) introd.

1 Sir Christopher Wren
Said, 'I am going to dine with some men.
If anybody calls
Say I am designing St Paul's.'
   Biography for Beginners (1905) 'Sir Christopher Wren'

2 Sir Humphrey Davy
Abominated gravy.
He lived in the odium
Of having discovered Sodium.
   Biography for Beginners (1905) 'Sir Humphrey Davy'

3 John Stuart Mill,
By a mighty effort of will,
Overcame his natural bonhomie
And wrote 'Principles of Political Economy'.
   Biography for Beginners (1905) 'John Stuart Mill'

4 What I like about Clive
Is that he is no longer alive.
There is a great deal to be said
For being dead.
   Biography for Beginners (1905) 'Clive'

5 Edward the Confessor
Slept under the dresser.
When that began to pall,
He slept in the hall.
   Biography for Beginners (1905) 'Edward the Confessor'

6 Chapman & Hall
Swore not at all.
Mr Chapman's yea was yea,
And Mr Hall's nay was nay.
   Biography for Beginners (1905) 'Chapman & Hall'

7 George the Third
Ought never to have occurred.
One can only wonder
At so grotesque a blunder.
   More Biography (1929) 'George the Third'

Eric Bentley 1916–

8 The theatre of farce is the theatre of the human body
but of that body in a state as far from the natural as
the voice of Chaliapin is from my voice or yours. It is
a theatre in which, though the marionettes are men,
the men are supermarionettes. It is the theatre of the
surrealist body.
   Life of Drama (1964) ch. 7

9 Ours is the age of substitutes: instead of language, we
have jargon; instead of principles, slogans; and, instead
of genuine ideas, Bright Ideas.
   New Republic 29 Dec. 1952

Nikolai Berdyaev 1874–1948

10 Утопии осуществимы, они осуществимее того, что
представлялось «реальной политикой» и что было
лишь рационалистическим расчетом кабинетных
людей. Жизнь движется к утопиям. И
открывается, быть может, новое столетие
мечтаний интеллигенции и культурного слоя о
том, как избежать утопий, как вернуться к не
утопическому обществу, к менее «совершенному»
и более свободному обществу.

Utopias are realizable, they are more realizable than
what has been presented as 'realist politics' and what
has simply been the calculated rationalism of armchair
politicians. Life is moving towards utopias. But
perhaps a new age is opening up before us, in which
the intelligentsia and the cultured classes will dream of
ways to avoid utopias and to return to a non-utopian
society, to a less 'perfect', a freer society.
   Novoe srednevekov'e (New Middle Ages, 1924) p. 122

Lord Charles Beresford 1846–1919

11 On one occasion, when at the eleventh hour he
[Beresford] had been summoned to dine with the then
Prince of Wales, he is said to have telegraphed back:
'Very sorry can't come. Lie follows by post.' This story
has been told of several other people, but Lord Charles
was the real originator.
   Ralph Nevill *World of Fashion 1837–1922* (1923) ch. 5.
   Cf. Marcel Proust 176:5

Henri Bergson 1859–1941

12 *La fonction essentielle de l'univers, qui est une machine à
faire des dieux.*

The essential function of the universe, which is
a machine for making gods.
   Les Deux sources de la morale et de la religion (The Two Sources
   of Morality and Religion, 1932) ch. 4

Irving Berlin (Israel Baline) 1888–1989

13 Come on and hear,
Come on and hear,
Alexander's ragtime band,
Come on and hear,
Come on and hear,
It's the best band in the land.
   Alexander's Ragtime Band (1911 song)

14 Anything you can do, I can do better,
I can do anything better than you.
   Anything You Can Do (1946 song)

15 God bless America,
Land that I love,
Stand beside her and guide her
Thru the night with a light from above.
From the mountains to the prairies,
To the oceans white with foam,
God bless America,
My home sweet home.
   God Bless America (1939 song)

16 Oh! how I hate to get up in the morning,
Oh! how I'd love to remain in bed;
For the hardest blow of all,
Is to hear the bugler call,
You've got to get up, you've got to get up,
You've got to get up this morning!
   Oh! How I Hate to Get Up in the Morning (1918 song)

17 A pretty girl is like a melody
That haunts you night and day.
   A Pretty Girl is like a Melody (1919 song)

18 The song is ended (but the melody lingers on).
   Title of song (1927)

1 There's no business like show business.
   Title of song (1946)

2 I'm puttin' on my top hat,
   Tyin' up my white tie,
   Brushin' off my tails.
   Top Hat, White Tie and Tails (1935 song)

3 I'm dreaming of a white Christmas,
   Just like the ones I used to know,
   Where the tree-tops glisten
   And children listen
   To hear sleigh bells in the snow.
   White Christmas (1942 song)

Sir Isaiah Berlin 1909–

4 There exists a great chasm between those, on one side,
   who relate everything to a single central vision . . .
   and, on the other side, those who pursue many ends,
   often unrelated and even contradictory. . . . The first
   kind of intellectual and artistic personality belongs to
   the hedgehogs, the second to the foxes.
   Hedgehog and Fox (1953) ch. 1

5 Rousseau was the first militant lowbrow.
   Observer 9 Nov. 1952

6 Liberty is liberty, not equality or fairness or justice or
   human happiness or a quiet conscience.
   Two Concepts of Liberty (1958) p. 10

Georges Bernanos 1888–1948

7 *Le désir de la prière est déjà une prière.*

   The wish for prayer is a prayer in itself.
   Journal d'un curé de campagne (Diary of a Country Priest,
   1936) ch. 2

8 *L'enfer, madame, c'est de ne plus aimer.*

   Hell, madam, is to love no more.
   Journal d'un curé de campagne (Diary of a Country Priest,
   1936) ch. 2

Jeffrey Bernard

9 When people say, 'You're breaking my heart,' they do
   in fact usually mean that you're breaking their
   genitals.
   Spectator 31 May 1986

Eric Berne 1910–1970

10 The sombre picture presented in Parts I and II of this
   book, in which human life is mainly a process of filling
   in time until the arrival of death, or Santa Claus, with
   very little choice, if any, of what kind of business one
   is going to transact during the long wait, is
   a commonplace but not the final answer.
   Games People Play (1964) ch. 18

11 Games people play: the psychology of human
   relationships.
   Title of book (1964)

Carl Bernstein 1944–
and Bob Woodward 1943–

12 All the President's men.
   Title of book (1974)

Chuck Berry 1931–

13 Roll over, Beethoven, and tell Tchaikovsky the news.
   Roll Over, Beethoven (1956 song)

John Berryman 1914–1972

14 Blossomed Sarah, and I
   blossom. Is that thing alive? I hear a famisht howl.
   Partisan Review (1953) vol. 20, p. 494 'Homage to Mistress
   Bradstreet'

15 We must travel in the direction of our fear.
   Poems (1942) 'A Point of Age'

16 Life, friends, is boring. We must not say so.
   77 Dream Songs (1964) no. 14

17 And moreover my mother taught me as a boy
   (repeatedly) 'Ever to confess you're bored
   means you have no

   Inner Resources.' I conclude now I have no
   inner resources, because I am heavy bored.
   77 Dream Songs (1964) no. 14

18 I seldom go to films. They are too exciting,
   said the Honourable Possum.
   77 Dream Songs (1964) no. 53

Pierre Berton 1920–

19 [Definition of a Canadian:] Somebody who knows how
   to make love in a canoe.
   Toronto Star, Canadian Mag. 22 Dec. 1973

Theobald von Bethmann Hollweg 1856–1921

20 He [Bethmann Hollweg] said that the step taken by
   His Majesty's Government was terrible to a degree, just
   for a word 'neutrality'—a word which in wartime had
   so often been disregarded—just for a scrap of paper,
   Great Britain was going to make war on a kindred
   nation who desired nothing better than to be friends
   with her.
   Report by Sir E. Goschen to Sir Edward Grey, in *British
   Documents on Origins of the War 1898–1914* (1926) vol. 11,
   p. 351

Sir John Betjeman 1906–1984

21 He sipped at a weak hock and seltzer
   As he gazed at the London skies
   Through the Nottingham lace of the curtains
   Or was it his bees-winged eyes?

   He rose, and he put down The Yellow Book.
   He staggered—and, terrible-eyed,
   He brushed past the palms on the staircase
   And was helped to a hansom outside.
   Continual Dew (1937) 'Arrest of Oscar Wilde at the Cadogan
   Hotel'

1 Come, friendly bombs, and fall on Slough!
   It isn't fit for humans now,
   There isn't grass to graze a cow.
   Swarm over, Death!
   Continual Dew (1937) 'Slough'

2 Rime Intrinsica, Fontmell Magna, Sturminster Newton
   and Melbury Bubb,
   Whist upon whist upon whist upon whist drive, in
   Institute, Legion and Social Club.
   Horny hands that hold the aces which this morning
   held the plough—
   While Tranter Reuben, T. S. Eliot, H. G. Wells and
   Edith Sitwell lie in Mellstock churchyard now.
   Continual Dew (1937) 'Dorset'

3 Spirits of well-shot woodcock, partridge, snipe
   Flutter and bear him up the Norfolk sky:
   In that red house in a red mahogany book-case
   The stamp collection waits with mounts long dry.
   Continual Dew (1937) 'Death of King George V'

4 And girls in slacks remember Dad,
   And oafish louts remember Mum,
   And sleepless children's hearts are glad,
   And Christmas-morning bells say 'Come!'
   Even to shining ones who dwell
   Safe in the Dorchester Hotel.

   And is it true? And is it true,
   This most tremendous tale of all,
   Seen in a stained-glass window's hue,
   A Baby in an ox's stall?
   The Maker of the stars and sea
   Become a Child on earth for me?
   Few Late Chrysanthemums (1954) 'Christmas'

5 In the licorice fields at Pontefract
   My love and I did meet
   And many a burdened licorice bush
   Was blooming round our feet;
   Red hair she had and golden skin,
   Her sulky lips were shaped for sin,
   Her sturdy legs were flannel-slack'd,
   The strongest legs in Pontefract.
   Few Late Chrysanthemums (1954) 'The Licorice Fields at
   Pontefract'

6 In the Garden City Café with its murals on the wall
   Before a talk on 'Sex and Civics' I meditated on the Fall.
   Few Late Chrysanthemums (1954) 'Huxley Hall'

7 Gaily into Ruislip Gardens
   Runs the red electric train,
   With a thousand Ta's and Pardon's
   Daintily alights Elaine;
   Hurries down the concrete station
   With a frown of concentration,
   Out into the outskirt's edges
   Where a few surviving hedges
   Keep alive our lost Elysium—rural Middlesex again.
   Few Late Chrysanthemums (1954) 'Middlesex'

8 There was sun enough for lazing upon beaches,
   There was fun enough for far into the night.
   But I'm dying now and done for,
   What on earth was all the fun for?
   For God's sake keep that sunlight out of sight.
   Few Late Chrysanthemums (1954) 'Sun and Fun'

9 It's awf'lly bad luck on Diana,
   Her ponies have swallowed their bits;
   She fished down their throats with a spanner
   And frightened them all into fits.
   Few Late Chrysanthemums (1954) 'Hunter Trials'

10 Oh wasn't it naughty of Smudges?
    Oh, Mummy, I'm sick with disgust.
    She threw me in front of the Judges
    And my silly old collarbone's bust.
    Few Late Chrysanthemums (1954) 'Hunter Trials'

11 Phone for the fish-knives, Norman
    As Cook is a little unnerved;
    You kiddies have crumpled the serviettes
    And I must have things daintily served.
    Few Late Chrysanthemums (1954) 'How to get on in Society'

12 Milk and then just as it comes dear?
    I'm afraid the preserve's full of stones;
    Beg pardon, I'm soiling the doileys
    With afternoon tea-cakes and scones.
    Few Late Chrysanthemums (1954) 'How to get on in Society'

13 Ghastly good taste, or a depressing story of the rise and
    fall of English architecture.
    Title of book (1933)

14 Oh! Chintzy, Chintzy cheeriness,
    Half dead and half alive!
    Mount Zion (1931) 'Death in Leamington'

15 The Church's Restoration
    In eighteen-eighty-three
    Has left for contemplation
    Not what there used to be.
    Mount Zion (1931) 'Hymn'

16 Sing on, with hymns uproarious,
    Ye humble and aloof,
    Look up! and oh how glorious
    He has restored the roof!
    Mount Zion (1931) 'Hymn'

17 Broad of Church and 'broad of Mind',
    Broad before and broad behind,
    A keen ecclesiologist,
    A rather dirty Wykehamist.
    Mount Zion (1931) 'The Wykehamist'

18 Oh shall I see the Thames again?
    The prow-promoted gems again,
    As beefy ATS
    Without their hats
    Come shooting through the bridge?
    And 'cheerioh' or 'cheeri-bye'
    Across the waste of waters die
    And low the mists of evening lie
    And lightly skims the midge.
    New Bats in Old Belfries (1945) 'Henley-on-Thames'

19 Rumbling under blackened girders, Midland, bound for
    Cricklewood,
    Puffed its sulphur to the sunset where that Land of
    Laundries stood.
    Rumble under, thunder over, train and tram alternate
    go.
    Shake the floor and smudge the ledger, Charrington,
    Sells, Dale and Co.,
    Nuts and nuggets in the window, trucks along the lines
    below.
    New Bats in Old Belfries (1945) 'Parliament Hill Fields'

1 Miss J. Hunter Dunn, Miss J. Hunter Dunn,
Furnish'd and burnish'd by Aldershot sun,
What strenuous singles we played after tea,
We in the tournament—you against me.

Love-thirty, love-forty, oh! weakness of joy,
The speed of a swallow, the grace of a boy,
With carefullest carelessness, gaily you won,
I am weak from your loveliness, Joan Hunter Dunn.

Miss Joan Hunter Dunn, Miss Joan Hunter Dunn,
How mad I am, sad I am, glad that you won.
The warm-handled racket is back in its press,
But my shock-headed victor, she loves me no less.
New Bats in Old Belfries (1945) 'Subaltern's Love-Song'

2 The scent of the conifers, sound of the bath,
The view from my bedroom of moss-dappled path,
As I struggle with double-end evening tie,
For we dance at the Golf Club, my victor and I.
New Bats in Old Belfries (1945) 'Subaltern's Love-Song'

3 By roads 'not adopted', by woodlanded ways,
She drove to the club in the late summer haze,
Into nine-o'clock Camberley, heavy with bells
And mushroomy, pine-woody, evergreen smells.

Miss Joan Hunter Dunn, Miss Joan Hunter Dunn,
I can hear from the car park the dance has begun.
Oh! full Surrey twilight! importunate band!
Oh! strongly adorable tennis-girl's hand!
New Bats in Old Belfries (1945) 'Subaltern's Love-Song'

4 We sat in the car park till twenty to one
And now I'm engaged to Miss Joan Hunter Dunn.
New Bats in Old Belfries (1945) 'Subaltern's Love-Song'

5 Belbroughton Road is bonny, and pinkly bursts the
    spray
Of prunus and forsythia across the public way,
For a full spring-tide of blossom seethed and departed
    hence,
Leaving land-locked pools of jonquils by sunny garden
    fence.

And a constant sound of flushing runneth from
    windows where
The toothbrush too is airing in this new North Oxford
    air.
New Bats in Old Belfries (1945) 'May-Day Song for North
Oxford'

6 Bells are booming down the bohreens,
White the mist along the grass.
Now the Julias, Maeves and Maureens
Move between the fields to Mass.
New Bats in Old Belfries (1945) 'Ireland with Emily'

7 The gas was on in the Institute,
The flare was up in the gymn,
A man was running a mineral line,
A lass was singing a hymn,
When Captain Webb the Dawley man,
Captain Webb from Dawley,
Came swimming along in the old canal
That carries the bricks to Lewley.
Old Lights for New Chancels (1940) 'A Shropshire Lad'

8 Pam, I adore you, Pam, you great big mountainous
    sports girl,
Whizzing them over the net, full of the strength of five:

That old Malvernian brother, you zephyr and khaki
    shorts girl,
Although he's playing for Woking,
Can't stand up to your wonderful backhand drive.
Old Lights for New Chancels (1940) 'Pot Pourri from a Surrey
Garden'

9 Think of what our Nation stands for,
Books from Boots' and country lanes,
Free speech, free passes, class distinction,
Democracy and proper drains.
Lord, put beneath Thy special care
One-eighty-nine Cadogan Square.
Old Lights for New Chancels (1940) 'In Westminster Abbey'

10 The dread of beatings! Dread of being late!
And, greatest dread of all, the dread of games!
Summoned by Bells (1960) ch. 7

11 Balkan Sobranies in a wooden box,
The college arms upon the lid; Tokay
And sherry in the cupboard; on the shelves
The University Statutes bound in blue,
Crome Yellow, *Prancing Nigger*, Blunden, Keats.
Summoned by Bells (1960) ch. 9

12 As one more solemn of our number said:
'Spiritually I was at Eton, John.'
Summoned by Bells (1960) ch. 9

Aneurin Bevan 1897–1960

13 He [Winston Churchill] is a man suffering from
petrified adolescence.
In Vincent Brome *Aneurin Bevan* (1953) ch. 11

14 Listening to a speech by Chamberlain is like paying
a visit to Woolworth's: everything in its place and
nothing above sixpence.
In Michael Foot *Aneurin Bevan* (1962) vol. 1, ch. 8

15 I know that the right kind of leader for the Labour
Party is a desiccated calculating machine who must not
in any way permit himself to be swayed by indignation.
If he sees suffering, privation or injustice he must not
allow it to move him, for that would be evidence of the
lack of proper education or of absence of self-control.
He must speak in calm and objective accents and talk
about a dying child in the same way as he would about
the pieces inside an internal combustion engine.
In Michael Foot *Aneurin Bevan* (1973) vol. 2, ch. 11

16 Damn it all, you can't have the crown of thorns and the
thirty pieces of silver.
In Michael Foot *Aneurin Bevan* (1973) vol. 2, ch. 13

17 This island is made mainly of coal and surrounded by
fish. Only an organizing genius could produce
a shortage of coal and fish at the same time.
Speech at Blackpool 24 May 1945, in *Daily Herald* 25 May
1945

18 I do not think Winston Churchill wants war, but the
trouble with him is that he doesn't even know how to
avoid it. He does not talk the language of the 20th
century but that of the 18th. He is still fighting
Blenheim all over again. His only answer to a difficult
situation is send a gun-boat.
Speech at Scarborough 2 Oct. 1951, in *Daily Herald* 3 Oct.
1951

1 If you carry this resolution you will send Britain's Foreign Secretary naked into the conference chamber.
Speech at Brighton, in *Daily Herald* 4 Oct. 1957

2 The worst thing I can say about democracy is that it has tolerated the Right Honourable Gentleman [Neville Chamberlain] for four and a half years.
Hansard 23 July 1929, col. 1191

3 Why read the crystal when he can read the book?
Hansard 29 Sept. 1949, col. 319

4 I am not going to spend any time whatsoever in attacking the Foreign Secretary. Quite honestly, I am beginning to feel extremely sorry for him. If we complain about the tune, there is no reason to attack the monkey when the organ grinder is present.
Hansard 16 May 1957, col. 680

5 We know what happens to people who stay in the middle of the road. They get run down.
In *Observer* 6 Dec. 1953

6 The language of priorities is the religion of Socialism.
Speech at Labour Party Conference in Blackpool, 8 June 1949, in *Report of 48th Annual Conference* (1949) p. 172

7 No amount of cajolery, and no attempts at ethical or social seduction, can eradicate from my heart a deep burning hatred for the Tory Party that inflicted those bitter experiences on me. So far as I am concerned they are lower than vermin. They condemned millions of first-class people to semi-starvation.
Speech at Manchester, 4 July 1948, in *The Times* 5 July 1948

8 I read the newspapers avidly. It is my one form of continuous fiction.
The Times 29 Mar. 1960

William Henry Beveridge (First Baron Beveridge) 1879–1963

9 Ignorance is an evil weed, which dictators may cultivate among their dupes, but which no democracy can afford among its citizens.
Full Employment in a Free Society (1944) pt. 7

10 The object of government in peace and in war is not the glory of rulers or of races, but the happiness of the common man.
Social Insurance and Allied Services (1942) pt. 7

11 The state is or can be master of money, but in a free society it is master of very little else.
Voluntary Action (1948) ch. 12

Ernest Bevin 1881–1951

12 If you open that Pandora's Box [the Council of Europe], you never know what Trojan 'orses will jump out.
In Sir Roderick Barclay *Ernest Bevin and Foreign Office* (1975) ch. 3

13 A Ministerial colleague with whom Ernie [Bevin] was almost always on bad terms was Nye Bevan. There was a well-known occasion when the latter had incurred Ernie's displeasure, and one of those present, seeking to excuse Nye, observed that he was sometimes his own

worst enemy. 'Not while I'm alive 'e aint!' retorted Ernie.
Sir Roderick Barclay *Ernest Bevin and Foreign Office* (1975) ch. 4

14 There never has been a war yet which, if the facts had been put calmly before the ordinary folk, could not have been prevented. . . . The common man, I think, is the great protection against war.
Hansard 23 Nov. 1945, col. 786

15 The most conservative man in this world is the British Trade Unionist when you want to change him.
Speech, 8 Sept. 1927, in *Report of Proceedings of the Trades Union Congress* (1927) p. 298

16 I didn't ought never to have done it. It was you, Willie, what put me up to it.
To Lord Strang, after officially recognizing Communist China, in C. Parrott *Serpent and Nightingale* (1977) ch. 3

17 My policy is to be able to take a ticket at Victoria Station and go anywhere I damn well please.
In *Spectator* 20 Apr. 1951, p. 514

Georges Bidault 1899–1983

18 The weak have one weapon: the errors of those who think they are strong.
In *Observer* 15 July 1962

Ambrose Bierce 1842–?1914

19 Acquaintance, n. A person whom we know well enough to borrow from, but not well enough to lend to. A degree of friendship called slight when its object is poor or obscure, and intimate when he is rich or famous.
Cynic's Word Book (1906) p. 12

20 Admiration, n. Our polite recognition of another's resemblance to ourselves.
Cynic's Word Book (1906) p. 13

21 Advice, n. The smallest current coin.
Cynic's Word Book (1906) p. 14

22 Alliance, n. In international politics, the union of two thieves who have their hands so deeply inserted in each other's pocket that they cannot separately plunder a third.
Cynic's Word Book (1906) p. 16

23 Ambition, n. An overmastering desire to be vilified by enemies while living and made ridiculous by friends when dead.
Cynic's Word Book (1906) p. 17

24 Applause, n. The echo of a platitude.
Cynic's Word Book (1906) p. 19

25 Auctioneer, n. The man who proclaims with a hammer that he has picked a pocket with his tongue.
Cynic's Word Book (1906) p. 24

26 Battle, n. A method of untying with the teeth a political knot that would not yield to the tongue.
Cynic's Word Book (1906) p. 30

27 Bore, n. A person who talks when you wish him to listen.
Cynic's Word Book (1906) p. 37

1 Brain, n. An apparatus with which we think that we think.
Cynic's Word Book (1906) p. 39

2 Calamity, n. . . . Calamities are of two kinds: misfortune to ourselves, and good fortune to others.
Cynic's Word Book (1906) p. 41

3 Conservative, n. A statesman who is enamoured of existing evils, as distinguished from the Liberal, who wishes to replace them with others.
Cynic's Word Book (1906) p. 56

4 Cynic, n. A blackguard whose faulty vision sees things as they are, not as they ought to be.
Cynic's Word Book (1906) p. 63

5 Education, n. That which discloses to the wise and disguises from the foolish their lack of understanding.
Cynic's Word Book (1906) p. 86

6 Egotist, n. A person of low taste, more interested in himself than in me.
Cynic's Word Book (1906) p. 86

7 Future, n. That period of time in which our affairs prosper, our friends are true, and our happiness is assured.
Cynic's Word Book (1906) p. 129

8 History, n. An account, mostly false, of events, mostly unimportant, which are brought about by rulers, mostly knaves, and soldiers, mostly fools.
Cynic's Word Book (1906) p. 161

9 Marriage, n. The state or condition of a community consisting of a master, a mistress and two slaves, making in all, two.
Devil's Dictionary (1911) p. 213

10 Noise, n. A stench in the ear. . . . The chief product and authenticating sign of civilization.
Devil's Dictionary (1911) p. 228

11 Patience, n. A minor form of despair, disguised as a virtue.
Devil's Dictionary (1911) p. 248

12 Peace, n. In international affairs, a period of cheating between two periods of fighting.
Devil's Dictionary (1911) p. 248

13 Prejudice, n. A vagrant opinion without visible means of support.
Devil's Dictionary (1911) p. 264

14 Saint, n. A dead sinner revised and edited.
Devil's Dictionary (1911) p. 306

15 Destiny, n. A tyrant's authority for crime and a fool's excuse for failure.
Enlarged Devil's Dictionary (1967) p. 64

Laurence Binyon 1869–1943

16 Now is the time for the burning of the leaves.
Horizon Oct. 1942, 'The Ruins'

17 With proud thanksgiving, a mother for her children,
England mourns for her dead across the sea.
Flesh of her flesh they were, spirit of her spirit,
Fallen in the cause of the free.
The Times 21 Sept. 1914, 'For the Fallen'

18 They shall grow not old, as we that are left grow old.
Age shall not weary them, nor the years condemn.
At the going down of the sun and in the morning
We will remember them.
The Times 21 Sept. 1914, 'For the Fallen'

Nigel Birch (Baron Rhyl) 1906–1981

19 My God! They've shot our fox! [said 13 Nov. 1947, when hearing of the resignation of Hugh Dalton, Chancellor of the Exchequer in the Labour Government].
In Harold Macmillan *Tides of Fortune* (1969) ch. 3

John Bird

20 That was the week that was.
Title of BBC television series, 1962–3: see Ned Sherrin *A Small Thing—Like an Earthquake* (1983) p. 62

Earl of Birkenhead

See F. E. SMITH

Lord Birkett (William Norman Birkett, Baron Birkett) 1883–1962

21 I do not object to people looking at their watches when I am speaking. But I strongly object when they start shaking them to make certain they are still going.
In *Observer* 30 Oct. 1960

Eric Blair

See GEORGE ORWELL

Eubie Blake (James Hubert Blake) 1883–1983

22 If I'd known I was gonna live this long [100 years], I'd have taken better care of myself.
In *Observer* 13 Feb. 1983

Lesley Blanch 1907–

23 She was an Amazon. Her whole life was spent riding at breakneck speed towards the wilder shores of love.
The Wilder Shores of Love (1954) pt. 2, ch. 1

Alan Bleasdale 1946–

24 YOSSER HUGHES: Gizza job. . . . I can do that.
Boys from the Blackstuff (1985) p. 7 (often quoted as 'Gissa job')

Karen Blixen

See ISAK DINESEN

Edmund Blunden 1896–1974

25 Dance on this ball-floor thin and wan,
Use him as though you love him;

Court him, elude him, reel and pass,
And let him hate you through the glass.
  Masks of Time (1925) 'Midnight Skaters'

1 I have been young, and now am not too old;
And I have seen the righteous forsaken,
His health, his honour and his quality taken.
This is not what we were formerly told.
  Near and Far (1929) 'Report on Experience'

2 This was my country and it may be yet,
But something flew between me and the sun.
  Retreat (1928) 'The Resignation'

3 I am for the woods against the world,
But are the woods for me?
  To Themis (1931) 'The Kiss'

Alfred Blunt (Bishop of Bradford) 1879–1957

4 The benefit of the King's Coronation depends, under
God, upon two elements: First, on the faith, prayer,
and self-dedication of the King himself, and on that it
would be improper for me to say anything except to
commend him, and ask you to commend him, to
God's grace, which he will so abundantly need . . . if
he is to do his duty faithfully. We hope that he is
aware of his need. Some of us wish that he gave more
positive signs of his awareness.
  Speech to Bradford Diocesan Conference, 1 Dec. 1936, in *The
  Times* 2 Dec. 1936

Wilfrid Scawen Blunt 1840–1922

5 To the Grafton Gallery to look at . . . the
Post-Impressionist pictures sent over from Paris. . . .
The drawing is on the level of that of an untaught
child of seven or eight years old, the sense of colour
that of a tea-tray painter, the method that of
a schoolboy who wipes his fingers on a slate after
spitting on them. . . . These are not works of art at all,
unless throwing a handful of mud against a wall may
be called one. They are the works of idleness and
impotent stupidity, a pornographic show.
  My Diaries (1920) 15 Nov. 1910

6 I like the hunting of the hare
Better than that of the fox.
  New Pilgrimage (1889) 'The Old Squire'

Ronald Blythe 1922–

7 As for the British churchman, he goes to church as he
goes to the bathroom, with the minimum of fuss and
with no explanation if he can help it.
  Age of Illusion (1963) ch. 12

8 An industrial worker would sooner have a £5 note but
a countryman must have praise.
  Akenfield (1969) ch. 5

Enid Blyton 1897–1968

9 Five go off in a caravan.
  Title of children's story (1946)

10 The naughtiest girl in the school.
  Title of children's story (1940)

Louise Bogan 1897–1970

11 Women have no wilderness in them,
They are provident instead,
Content in the tight hot cell of their hearts
To eat dusty bread.
  Body of this Death (1923) 'Women'

Humphrey Bogart 1899–1957

12 Contrary to legend, as a juvenile I never said 'Tennis,
anyone?' just as I never said 'Drop the gun, Louie' as
a heavy.
  In Ezra Goodman *Bogey: the Good-Bad Guy* (1965) ch. 4. Cf.
  George Bernard Shaw 199:4

See also JULIUS J. EPSTEIN *et al.*

John B. Bogart 1848–1921

13 When a dog bites a man, that is not news, because it
happens so often. But if a man bites a dog, that is
news.
  In F. M. O'Brien *Story of the Sun* (1918) ch. 10 (the
  quotation is often attributed to Charles A. Dana)

Niels Bohr 1885–1962

14 One of the favourite maxims of my father was the
distinction between the two sorts of truths, profound
truths recognized by the fact that the opposite is also
a profound truth, in contrast to trivialities where
opposites are obviously absurd.
  In S. Rozental *Niels Bohr* (1967) p. 328

Alan Bold 1943–

15 They mattered more than they should have. It is so
In Scotland, land of the omnipotent No.
  Perpetual Motion Machine (1969) 'A Memory of Death'

Robert Bolt 1924–

16 Morality's *not* practical. Morality's a gesture.
A complicated gesture learned from books.
  A Man for All Seasons (1960) act 2

Andrew Bonar Law 1858–1923

17 If, therefore, war should ever come between these two
countries [Great Britain and Germany], which Heaven
forbid! it will not, I think, be due to irresistible natural
laws; it will be due to the want of human wisdom.
  Hansard 27 Nov. 1911, col. 167

18 If I am a great man, then all great men are frauds.
  In Lord Beaverbrook *Politicians and the War* (1932) vol. 2,
  ch. 4

Carrie Jacobs Bond 1862–1946

19 When you come to the end of a perfect day,
And you sit alone with your thought,

While the chimes ring out with a carol gay
For the joy that the day has brought,
Do you think what the end of a perfect day
Can mean to a tired heart,
When the sun goes down with a flaming ray,
And the dear friends have to part?

Well, this is the end of a perfect day,
Near the end of a journey, too;
But it leaves a thought that is big and strong,
With a wish that is kind and true.
For mem'ry has painted this perfect day
With colours that never fade,
And we find, at the end of a perfect day,
The soul of a friend we've made.

A Perfect Day (1910 song)

Sir David Bone 1874–1959

1 It's 'Damn you, Jack—I'm all right!' with you chaps.

Brassbounder (1910) ch. 3

Dietrich Bonhoeffer 1906–1945

2 *Es ist der Vorzug und das Wesen der Starken, dass sie die grossen Entscheidungsfragen stellen und zu ihnen klar Stellung nehmen können. Die Schwachen müssen sich immer zwischen Alternativen entscheiden, die nicht die ihren sind.*

It is the nature, and the advantage, of strong people that they can bring out the crucial questions and form a clear opinion about them. The weak always have to decide between alternatives that are not their own.

Widerstand und Ergebung (Resistance and Submission, 1951)

3 *Jesus nur 'für andere da ist'. . . . Gott in Menschengestalt! . . . nicht die griechische Gott-Menschgestalt des 'Menschen an sich', sondern 'der Mensch für andere', darum der Gekreuzigte.*

Jesus is there only for others. . . . God in human form! not . . . in the Greek divine-human form of 'man in himself', but 'the man for others', and therefore the crucified.

Widerstand und Ergebung (Resistance and Submission, 1951)

Sonny Bono (Salvatore Bono) 1953–

4 The beat goes on.

Title of song (1966)

Daniel J. Boorstin 1914–

5 The celebrity is a person who is known for his well-knownness.

The Image (1961) ch. 2

6 A bestseller was a book which somehow sold well simply because it was selling well.

The Image (1961) ch. 4

James H. Boren 1925–

7 Guidelines for bureaucrats: (1) When in charge, ponder. (2) When in trouble, delegate. (3) When in doubt, mumble.

In *New York Times* 8 Nov. 1970, p. 45

Jorge Luis Borges 1899–1986

8 *El original es infiel a la traducción.*

The original is unfaithful to the translation [Henley's translation of Beckford's *Vathek*].

Sobre el 'Vathek' de William Beckford (1943) in *Obras Completas* (1974) p. 730

9 *Para uno de esos gnósticos, el visible universo era una ilusión ó (mas precisamente) un sofisma. Los espejos y la paternidad son abominables porque lo multiplican y lo divulgan.*

For one of those gnostics, the visible universe was an illusion or, more precisely, a sophism. Mirrors and fatherhood are abominable because they multiply it and extend it.

Tlön, Uqbar, Orbis, Tertius (1941) in *Obras Completas* (1974) p. 431

10 The Falklands thing [the Falklands War of 1982] was a fight between two bald men over a comb.

In *Time* 14 Feb. 1983

Max Born 1882–1970

11 The human race has today the means for annihilating itself—either in a fit of complete lunacy, i.e., in a big war, by a brief fit of destruction, or by careless handling of atomic technology, through a slow process of poisoning and of deterioration in its genetic structure.

Bulletin of Atomic Scientists (1957) vol. 13, p. 186

John Collins Bossidy 1860–1928

12 And this is good old Boston,
The home of the bean and the cod,
Where the Lowells talk to the Cabots
And the Cabots talk only to God.

Verse spoken at Holy Cross College alumni dinner in Boston, Mass., 1910, in *Springfield Sunday Republican* 14 Dec. 1924

Gordon Bottomley 1874–1948

13 When you destroy a blade of grass
You poison England at her roots:
Remember no man's foot can pass
Where evermore no green life shoots.

Chambers of Imagery (1912) 'To Ironfounders and Others'

14 Your worship is your furnaces,
Which, like old idols, lost obscenes,
Have molten bowels; your vision is
Machines for making more machines.

Chambers of Imagery (1912) 'To Ironfounders and Others'

Horatio Bottomley 1860–1933

15 During his incarceration at the Scrubbs [1922–3], Bottomley was largely employed in the making of mail-bags. It was while he was so engaged one afternoon that a prison visitor . . . saw him busily stitching away. 'Ah, Bottomley,' he remarked brightly, 'sewing?' 'No,' grunted the old man without looking up, 'reaping.'

In S.T. Felstead *Horatio Bottomley* (1936) ch. 16

1 Gentlemen: I have not had your advantages. What poor education I have received has been gained in the University of Life.

    Speech at Oxford Union, 2 Dec. 1920, in Beverley Nichols *25* (1926) ch. 7

Sir Harold Edwin Boulton 1859–1935

2 When Adam and Eve were dispossessed
Of the garden hard by Heaven,
They planted another one down in the west,
'Twas Devon, glorious Devon!

    Lyrics and other Poems (1902) 'Glorious Devon'

3 Speed, bonnie boat, like a bird on the wing,
'Onward,' the sailors cry;
Carry the lad that's born to be king,
Over the sea to Skye.

    National Songs and Some Ballads (1908) 'Skye Boat Song'

Elizabeth Bowen 1899–1973

4 Experience isn't interesting till it begins to repeat itself—in fact, till it does that, it hardly *is* experience.

    Death of the Heart (1938) pt. 1, ch. 1

5 In fact, it is about five o'clock in an evening that the first hour of spring strikes—autumn arrives in the early morning, but spring at the close of a winter day.

    Death of the Heart (1938) pt. 2, ch. 1

6 Some people are moulded by their admirations, others by their hostilities.

    Death of the Heart (1938) pt. 2, ch. 2

7 The heart may think it knows better: the senses know that absence blots people out. We have really no absent friends.

    Death of the Heart (1938) pt. 2, ch. 2

8 Elizabeth Bowen said that she [Edith Sitwell] looked like 'a high altar on the move'.

    V. Glendinning *Edith Sitwell* (1981) ch. 25

9 I suppose art is the only thing that can go on mattering once it has stopped hurting.

    Heat of the Day (1949) ch. 16

10 There is no end to the violations committed by children on children, quietly talking alone.

    House in Paris (1935) pt. 1, ch. 2

11 Nobody speaks the truth when there's something they must have.

    House in Paris (1935) pt. 1, ch. 5

12 Meetings that do not come off keep a character of their own. They stay as they were projected.

    House in Paris (1935) pt. 2, ch. 1

13 Fate is not an eagle, it creeps like a rat.

    House in Paris (1935) pt. 2, ch. 2

14 Jealousy is no more than feeling alone against smiling enemies.

    House in Paris (1935) pt. 2, ch. 8

15 My failing to have a nice ear for vowel sounds, and the Anglo-Irish slurred, hurried way of speaking made me take the words 'Ireland' and 'island' to be synonymous.

Thus, all other countries quite surrounded by water took (it appeared) their generic name from ours.

    Seven Winters (1942) p. 12

David Bowie (David Jones) 1947–

16 Ground control to Major Tom.

    Space Oddity (1969 song)

Sir Maurice Bowra 1898–1971

17 There is also that story, perhaps apocryphal, of Maurice [Bowra]'s decision to get married. When he announced that he had at last chosen a girl, a friend remonstrated: 'But you can't marry anyone as plain as that.' Maurice answered: 'My dear fellow, buggers can't be choosers.'

    Francis King in Hugh Lloyd-Jones *Maurice Bowra: a Celebration* (1974) p. 150

18 I'm a man more dined against than dining.

    In John Betjeman *Summoned by Bells* (1960) ch. 9

Charles Boyer 1898–1978

19 Come with me to the Casbah.

    Catch-phrase often attributed to Boyer, but L. Swindell *Charles Boyer* (1983) ch. 7 says: *Algiers* . . . is the picture in which Charles Boyer did *not* say 'Come wiz me to zee Casbah' to Hedy Lamarr. . . . Boyer and Lamarr were *in* the Casbah in most of their *Algiers* scenes, and they *did* have an important scene in which they were not in the Casbah, but the dialogue was nowhere close.

Lord Brabazon (Baron Brabazon of Tara) 1884–1964

20 I take the view, and always have, that if you cannot say what you are going to say in twenty minutes you ought to go away and write a book about it.

    Hansard (Lords) 21 June 1955, col. 207

Charles Brackett 1892–1969, Billy Wilder 1906– , and D. M. Marshman Jr.

21 JOE GILLIS: You used to be in pictures. You used to be big.
NORMA DESMOND: I am big. It's the pictures that got small.

    Sunset Boulevard (1950 film)

22 All right, Mr de Mille, I'm ready for my close-up now.

    Sunset Boulevard (1950 film)

Charles Brackett 1892–1969, Billy Wilder 1906– , and Walter Reisch 1903–1983

23 IRANOFF: What a charming idea for Moscow to surprise us with a lady Comrade.
KOPALSKI: If we had known we would have greeted you with flowers.
IRANOFF: Ahh—yes.

NINOTCHKA: Don't make an issue of my womanhood.
Ninotchka (1939 film)

1 NINOTCHKA: Why should you carry other people's bags?
PORTER: Well, that's my business, Madame.
NINOTCHKA: That's no business. That's social injustice.
PORTER: That depends on the tip.
Ninotchka (1939 film)

F. H. Bradley 1846–1924

2 The propriety of some persons seems to consist in having improper thoughts about their neighbours.
Aphorisms (1930) no. 9

3 True penitence condemns to silence. What a man is ready to recall he would be willing to repeat.
Aphorisms (1930) no. 10

4 The secret of happiness is to admire without desiring. And that is not happiness.
Aphorisms (1930) no. 33

5 Metaphysics is the finding of bad reasons for what we believe upon instinct; but to find these reasons is no less an instinct.
Appearance and Reality (1893) preface

6 Of Optimism I have said that 'The world is the best of all possible worlds, and everything in it is a necessary evil.'
Appearance and Reality (1893) preface

7 That the glory of this world . . . is appearance leaves the world more glorious, if we feel it is a show of some fuller splendour; but the sensuous curtain is a deception . . . if it hides some colourless movement of atoms, some . . . unearthly ballet of bloodless categories.
Principles of Logic (1883) bk. 3, pt. 2, ch. 4

Omar Bradley 1893–1981

8 The way to win an atomic war is to make certain it never starts.
Speech to Boston Chamber of Commerce, 10 Nov. 1948, in *Collected Writings* (1967) vol. 1, p. 588

9 We have grasped the mystery of the atom and rejected the Sermon on the Mount.
Speech to Boston Chamber of Commerce, 10 Nov. 1948, in *Collected Writings* (1967) vol. 1, p. 588

10 Red China is not the powerful nation seeking to dominate the world. Frankly, in the opinion of the Joint Chiefs of Staff, this strategy would involve us in the wrong war, at the wrong place, at the wrong time, and with the wrong enemy.
US Cong. Senate Comm. on Armed Services (1951) vol. 2, p. 732

Caryl Brahms (Doris Caroline Abrahams) 1901–1982 and S. J. Simon (Simon Jasha Skidelsky)

11 The suffragettes were triumphant. Woman's place was in the gaol.
No Nightingales (1944) pt. 6, ch. 37

John Braine 1922–

12 Room at the top.
Title of novel (1957). Cf. *Oxford Dictionary of Quotations* (1979) 566:9

Ernest Bramah (Ernest Bramah Smith) 1868–1942

13 It is a mark of insincerity of purpose to spend one's time in looking for the sacred Emperor in the low-class tea-shops.
Wallet of Kai Lung (1900) p. 6

14 In his countenance this person read an expression of no-encouragement towards his venture.
Wallet of Kai Lung (1900) p. 224

15 The whole narrative is permeated with the odour of joss-sticks and honourable high-mindedness.
Wallet of Kai Lung (1900) p. 330

Georges Braque 1882–1963

16 *L'Art est fait pour troubler, la Science rassure.*

Art is meant to disturb, science reassures.
Le Jour et la nuit: Cahiers 1917–52 (Day and Night, Notebooks, 1952) p. 11

17 *La vérité existe; on n'invente que le mensonge.*

Truth exists; only lies are invented.
Le Jour et la nuit: Cahiers 1917–52 (Day and Night, Notebooks, 1952) p. 20

John Bratby 1928–

18 A real art student wears coloured socks, has a fringe and a beard, wears dirty jeans and an equally dirty seaman's pullover, carries a sketch-book, is despised by the rest of society, and loafs in a coffee bar.
Breakdown (1960) ch. 8

Irving Brecher 1914–

19 I'll bet your father spent the first year of your life throwing rocks at the stork.
(Marx Brothers) *At the Circus* (1939 film)

20 Time wounds all heals.
Marx Brothers Go West (1940 film)

Bertolt Brecht 1898–1956

21 *Und der Haifisch, der hat Zähne*
Und die trägt er im Gesicht
Und Macheath, der hat ein Messer
Doch das Messer sieht man nicht.

Oh, the shark has pretty teeth, dear,
And he shows them pearly white.
Just a jack-knife has Macheath, dear
And he keeps it out of sight.
Dreigroschenoper (Threepenny Opera, 1928) prologue

22 *Erst kommt das Fressen, dann kommt die Moral.*

Food comes first, then morals.
Dreigroschenoper (Threepenny Opera, 1928) act 2, sc. 3

1 *Was ist ein Einbruch in eine Bank gegen die Gründung einer Bank?*

What is robbing a bank compared with founding a bank?
  Dreigroschenoper (Threepenny Opera, 1928) act 3, sc. 3

2 ANDREA: *Unglücklich das Land, das keine Helden hat!* ...
  GALILEI: *Nein. Unglücklich das Land, das Helden nötig hat.*

  ANDREA: Unhappy the land that has no heroes! ...
  GALILEO: No. Unhappy the land that needs heroes.
  Leben des Galilei (Life of Galileo, 1939) sc. 13

3 *Man merkts, hier ist zu lang kein Krieg gewesen. Wo soll da Moral herkommen, frag ich? Frieden, das ist nur Schlamperei, erst der Krieg schafft Ordnung.*

One observes, they have gone too long without a war here. What is the moral, I ask? Peace is nothing but slovenliness, only war creates order.
  Mutter Courage (Mother Courage, 1939) sc. 1

4 *Weil ich ihm nicht trau, wir sind befreundet.*

Because I don't trust him, we are friends.
  Mutter Courage (Mother Courage, 1939) sc. 3

5 *Die schönsten Plän sind schon zuschanden geworden durch die Kleinlichkeit von denen, wo sie ausführen sollten, denn die Kaiser selber können ja nix machen.*

The finest plans are always ruined by the littleness of those who ought to carry them out, for the Emperor himself can actually do nothing.
  Mutter Courage (Mother Courage, 1939) sc. 6

6 *Der Krieg findet immer einen Ausweg.*

War always finds a way.
  Mutter Courage (Mother Courage, 1939) sc. 6

7 *Sagen Sie mir nicht, dass Friede ausgebrochen ist, wo ich eben neue Vorräte eingekauft hab.*

Don't tell me peace has broken out, when I've just bought some new supplies.
  Mutter Courage (Mother Courage, 1939) sc. 8

Gerald Brenan 1894–

8 Those who have some means think that the most important thing in the world is love. The poor know that it is money.
  Thoughts in a Dry Season (1978) p. 22

9 Religions are kept alive by heresies, which are really sudden explosions of faith. Dead religions do not produce them.
  Thoughts in a Dry Season (1978) p. 45

Aristide Briand 1862–1932

10 *Les hautes parties contractantes déclarent solennellement* ... *qu'elles condamnent le recours à la guerre* ... *et y renoncent en tant qu'instrument de politique nationale dans leurs relations mutuelles* ... *le règlement ou la solution de tous les différends ou conflits—de quelque nature ou de quelque origine qu'ils puissent être—qui pourront surgir entre elles ne devra jamais être cherché que par des moyens pacifiques.*

The high contracting powers solemnly declare ... that they condemn recourse to war and renounce it ... as an instrument of their national policy towards each other. ... The settlement or the solution of all disputes or conflicts of whatever nature or of whatever origin they may be which may arise ... shall never be sought by either side except by pacific means.
  Draft, 20 June 1927, which became part of the Kellogg Pact, 1928, in *Le Temps* 13 Apr. 1928

Vera Brittain 1893–1970

11 Politics are usually the executive expression of human immaturity.
  Rebel Passion (1964) ch. 1

David Broder 1929–

12 Anybody that wants the presidency so much that he'll spend two years organizing and campaigning for it is not to be trusted with the office.
  Washington Post 18 July 1973, p. A 25

Jacob Bronowski 1908–1974

13 We have to understand that the world can only be grasped by action, not by contemplation. The hand is more important than the eye. ... The hand is the cutting edge of the mind.
  Ascent of Man (1973) ch. 3

14 That is the essence of science: ask an impertinent question, and you are on the way to a pertinent answer.
  Ascent of Man (1973) ch. 4

15 The wish to hurt, the momentary intoxication with pain, is the loophole through which the pervert climbs into the minds of ordinary men.
  Face of Violence (1954) ch. 5

16 The world is made of people who never quite get into the first team and who just miss the prizes at the flower show.
  Face of Violence (1954) ch. 6

17 Man masters nature not by force but by understanding. This is why science has succeeded where magic failed: because it has looked for no spell to cast on nature.
  Universities Quarterly (1956) vol. 10, no. 3, p. 252

Rupert Brooke 1887–1915

18 Breathless, we flung us on the windy hill,
Laughed in the sun, and kissed the lovely grass.
  Cambridge Review 8 Dec. 1910, 'Sonnet'

19 Then, the cool kindliness of sheets, that soon
Smooth away trouble; and the rough male kiss
Of blankets; grainy wood; live hair that is
Shining and free; blue-massing clouds; the keen
Unpassioned beauty of a great machine;
The benison of hot water; furs to touch;
The good smell of old clothes.
  New Numbers no. 3 (1914) 'The Great Lover'

1 Now, God be thanked Who has matched us with His
    hour,
And caught our youth, and wakened us from sleeping,
With hand made sure, clear eye, and sharpened power,
To turn, as swimmers into cleanness leaping,
Glad from a world grown old and cold and weary,
Leave the sick hearts that honour could not move,
And half-men, and their dirty songs and dreary,
And all the little emptiness of love!
Oh! we, who have known shame, we have found
    release there,
Where there's no ill, no grief, but sleep has mending,
Naught broken save this body, lost but breath;
Nothing to shake the laughing heart's long peace there
But only agony, and that has ending;
And the worst friend and enemy is but Death.
    New Numbers no. 4 (1914) 'Peace'

2 War knows no power. Safe shall be my going,
Secretly armed against all death's endeavour;
Safe though all safety's lost; safe where men fall;
And if these poor limbs die, safest of all.
    New Numbers no. 4 (1914) 'Safety'

3 Blow out, you bugles, over the rich Dead!
There's none of these so lonely and poor of old,
But, dying, has made us rarer gifts than gold.
These laid the world away; poured out the red
Sweet wine of youth; gave up the years to be
Of work and joy, and that unhoped serene,
That men call age; and those that would have been,
Their sons, they gave, their immortality.
    New Numbers no. 4 (1914) 'The Dead'

4 Honour has come back, as a king, to earth,
And paid his subjects with a royal wage;
And Nobleness walks in our ways again;
And we have come into our heritage.
    New Numbers no. 4 (1914) 'The Dead'

5 If I should die, think only this of me:
That there's some corner of a foreign field
That is for ever England. There shall be
In that rich earth a richer dust concealed;
A dust whom England bore, shaped, made aware,
Gave, once, her flowers to love, her ways to roam,
A body of England's, breathing English air,
Washed by the rivers, blest by suns of home.
And think, this heart, all evil shed away,
A pulse in the eternal mind, no less
Gives somewhere back the thoughts by England given;
Her sights and sounds; dreams happy as her day;
And laughter, learnt of friends; and gentleness,
In hearts at peace, under an English heaven.
    New Numbers no. 4 (1914) 'The Soldier'

6 Fish say, they have their Stream and Pond;
But is there anything Beyond?
    1914 and Other Poems (1915) 'Heaven'

7 But somewhere, beyond Space and Time
Is wetter water, slimier slime!
    1914 and Other Poems (1915) 'Heaven'

8 Oh! never fly conceals a hook,
Fish say, in the Eternal Brook,
But more than mundane weeds are there,
And mud, celestially fair;
Fat caterpillars drift around,
And Paradisal grubs are found;

Unfading moths, immortal flies,
And the worm that never dies.
And in that Heaven of all their wish,
There shall be no more land, say fish.
    1914 and Other Poems (1915) 'Heaven'

9 But there's wisdom in women, of more than they have
    known,
And thoughts go blowing through them, are wiser than
    their own.
    1914 and Other Poems (1915) 'There's Wisdom in Women'

10 Just now the lilac is in bloom,
All before my little room.
    1914 and Other Poems (1915) 'The Old Vicarage,
    Grantchester'

11 Here tulips bloom as they are told;
Unkempt about those hedges blows
An English unofficial rose;
And there the unregulated sun
Slopes down to rest when day is done,
And wakes a vague unpunctual star,
A slippered Hesper; and there are
Meads towards Haslingfield and Coton
Where *das Betreten*'s not *verboten*.
εἴθε γενοίμην.... would I were
In Grantchester, in Grantchester!
    1914 and Other Poems (1915) 'The Old Vicarage,
    Grantchester'

12 And in that garden, black and white,
Creep whispers through the grass all night;
And spectral dance, before the dawn,
A hundred Vicars down the lawn;
Curates, long dust, will come and go
On lissom, clerical, printless toe;
And oft between the boughs is seen
The sly shade of a Rural Dean.
    1914 and Other Poems (1915) 'The Old Vicarage,
    Grantchester'

13 God! I will pack, and take a train,
And get me to England once again!
For England's the one land, I know,
Where men with Splendid Hearts may go;
And Cambridgeshire, of all England,
The shire for Men who Understand;
And of *that* district I prefer
The lovely hamlet Grantchester.
For Cambridge people rarely smile,
Being urban, squat, and packed with guile.
    1914 and Other Poems (1915) 'The Old Vicarage,
    Grantchester'

14 They love the Good; they worship Truth;
They laugh uproariously in youth;
(And when they get to feeling old,
They up and shoot themselves, I'm told).
    1914 and Other Poems (1915) 'The Old Vicarage,
    Grantchester'

15 Oh, is the water sweet and cool,
Gentle and brown, above the pool?
And laughs the immortal river still
Under the mill, under the mill?
Say, is there Beauty yet to find?
And Certainty? and Quiet kind?
Deep meadows yet, for to forget
The lies, and truths, and pain? ... oh! yet

Stands the Church clock at ten to three?
And is there honey still for tea?
> *1914 and Other Poems* (1915) 'The Old Vicarage,
> Grantchester'

Anita Brookner 1938–

1 Good women always think it is their fault when
someone else is being offensive. Bad women never take
the blame for anything.
> *Hotel du Lac* (1984) ch. 7

2 Blanche Vernon occupied her time most usefully in
keeping feelings at bay.
> *Misalliance* (1986) ch. 1

Mel Brooks 1926–

3 That's it baby, when you got it, flaunt it.
> *The Producers* (1968 film)

Heywood Broun 1888–1939

4 Free speech is about as good a cause as the world has
ever known. But, like the poor, it is always with us
and gets shoved aside in favour of things which seem
at some given moment more vital. . . . Everybody
favours free speech in the slack moments when no
axes are being ground.
> *New York World* 23 Oct. 1926, p. 13

5 Just as every conviction begins as a whim so does every
emancipator serve his apprenticeship as a crank.
A fanatic is a great leader who is just entering the
room.
> *New York World* 6 Feb. 1928, p. 11

6 Men build bridges and throw railroads across deserts,
and yet they contend successfully that the job of sewing
on a button is beyond them. Accordingly, they don't
have to sew buttons.
> *Seeing Things at Night* (1921) 'Holding a Baby'

7 Posterity is as likely to be wrong as anybody else.
> *Sitting on the World* (1924) 'The Last Review'

H. Rap Brown 1943–

8 I say violence is necessary. It is as American as cherry
pie.
> Speech at Washington, 27 July 1967, in *Washington Post*
> 28 July 1967, p. A7

Helen Gurley Brown 1922–

9 Sex and the single girl.
> Title of book (1962)

Ivor Brown 1891–1974

10 For nearly a century after his death, Shakespeare
remained more a theme for criticism by the few than
a subject of adulation by the many.
> *Shakespeare* (1949) ch. 1

John Mason Brown 1900–1969

11 Tallulah Bankhead barged down the Nile last night as
Cleopatra—and sank.
> *New York Post* 11 Nov. 1937, p. 18

Lew Brown (Louis Brownstein) 1893–1958

12 Life is just a bowl of cherries.
> Title of song (1931; music by Ray Henderson)

Nacio Herb Brown 1896–1964

See ARTHUR FREED

Cecil Browne

13 But not so odd
As those who choose
A Jewish God,
But spurn the Jews.
> Reply to verse by William Norman Ewer: see 78:4

Sir Frederick Browning 1896–1965

14 I think we might be going a bridge too far.
> Expressing reservations about the Arnhem 'Market Garden'
> operation to Field Marshal Montgomery on 10 Sept. 1944, in
> R. E. Urquhart *Arnhem* (1958) p. 4

Lenny Bruce (Leonard Alfred Schneider) 1925–1966

15 The liberals can understand everything but people
who don't understand them.
> In John Cohen *Essential Lenny Bruce* (1970) p. 59

Anita Bryant 1940–

16 If homosexuality were the normal way, God would
have made Adam and Bruce.
> In *New York Times* 5 June 1977, p. 22

Martin Buber 1878–1965

17 *Der Mensch wird am Du zum Ich.*

Through the Thou a person becomes I.
> *Ich und Du* (I and Thou, 1923) in *Werke* (1962) vol. 1, p. 97

John Buchan (Baron Tweedsmuir) 1875–1940

18 To live for a time close to great minds is the best kind
of education.
> *Memory Hold-the-Door* (1940) ch. 2

19 'Back to Glasgow to do some work for the cause,' I said
lightly. 'Just so,' he said, with a grin. 'It's a great life if
you don't weaken.'
> *Mr Standfast* (1919) ch. 5

20 An atheist is man who has no invisible means of
support.
> In H. E. Fosdick *On Being a Real Person* (1943) ch. 10

Frank Buchman 1878–1961

1 I thank heaven for a man like Adolf Hitler, who built a front line of defence against the anti-Christ of Communism.

    New York World-Telegram 26 Aug. 1936

2 Suppose everybody cared enough, everybody shared enough, wouldn't everybody have enough? There is enough in the world for everyone's need, but not enough for everyone's greed.

    Remaking the World (1947) p. 56

Gene Buck (Edward Eugene Buck) 1885–1957 and Herman Ruby 1891–1959

3 That Shakespearian rag,—
Most intelligent, very elegant.

    That Shakespearian Rag (1912 song; music by David Stamper). Cf. T. S. Eliot 76:21

Richard Buckle 1916–

4 John Lennon, Paul McCartney and George Harrison are the greatest composers since Beethoven, with Paul McCartney way out in front.

    Sunday Times 29 Dec. 1963

Arthur Buller 1874–1944

5 There was a young lady named Bright,
Whose speed was far faster than light;
She set out one day
In a relative way
And returned on the previous night.

    Punch 19 Dec. 1923, 'Relativity'

Ivor Bulmer-Thomas 1905–

6 If he [Harold Wilson] ever went to school without any boots it was because he was too big for them.

    Speech at Conservative Party Conference, in *Manchester Guardian* 13 Oct. 1949

Luis Buñuel 1900–1983

7 *Le charme discret de la bourgeoisie.*

The discreet charm of the bourgeoisie.

    Title of film (1972)

8 *Grâce à Dieu, je suis toujours athée.*

Thanks to God, I am still an atheist.

    In *Le Monde* 16 Dec. 1959

Anthony Burgess 1917–

9 Who ever heard of a clockwork orange? Then I read a malenky bit out loud in a sort of very high type preaching goloss: 'The attempt to impose upon man, a creature of growth and capable of sweetness, to ooze juicily at the last round the bearded lips of God, to attempt to impose, I say, laws and conditions appropriate to a mechanical creation, against this I raise my sword-pen.'

    A Clockwork Orange (1962) p. 21

10 It was the afternoon of my eighty-first birthday, and I was in bed with my catamite when Ali announced that the archbishop had come to see me.

    Earthly Powers (1980) p. 7

11 He said it was artificial respiration, but now I find I am to have his child.

    Inside Mr Enderby (1963) pt. 1, ch. 4

12 The possession of a book becomes a substitute for reading it.

    New York Times Book Review 4 Dec. 1966, p. 74

Johnny Burke 1908–1964

13 Every time it rains, it rains
Pennies from heaven.
Don't you know each cloud contains
Pennies from heaven?
You'll find your fortune falling
All over town
Be sure that your umbrella
Is upside down.

    Pennies from Heaven (1936 song; music by Arthur Johnston)

14 Like Webster's Dictionary, we're Morocco bound.

    The Road to Morocco (1942 song from film *The Road to Morocco*; music by James van Heusen)

John Burns 1858–1943

15 'What have you in the Mississippi?' he [John Burns] asked an American who had spoken disparagingly of the Thames. The American replied that there was water—miles and miles of it. 'Ah, but you see, the Thames is liquid history,' said Burns.

    Daily Mail 25 Jan. 1943

William S. Burroughs 1914–

16 I think there are innumerable gods. What we on earth call God is a little tribal God who has made an awful mess. Certainly forces operating through human consciousness control events.

    Paris Review Fall 1965

Benjamin Hapgood Burt 1880–1950

17 One evening in October, when I was one-third sober,
An' taking home a 'load' with manly pride;
My poor feet began to stutter, so I lay down in the gutter,
And a pig came up an' lay down by my side;
Then we sang 'It's all fair weather when good fellows get together,'
Till a lady passing by was heard to say:
'You can tell a man who "boozes" by the company he chooses'
And the pig got up and slowly walked away.

    The Pig Got Up and Slowly Walked Away (1933 song)

Nat Burton

18 There'll be bluebirds over the white cliffs of Dover,
Tomorrow, just you wait and see.

    White Cliffs of Dover (1941 song; music by Walter Kent)

R. A. Butler (*Baron Butler of Saffron Walden*) 1902–1982

1 Politics is the Art of the Possible. That is what these pages show I have tried to achieve—not more—and that is what I have called my book.
   The Art of the Possible (1971) p. xi. Cf. Bismarck's 'Die Politik ist die Lehre vom Möglichen', *Oxford Dictionary of Quotations* (1979) 84:20

2 REPORTER: Mr Butler, would you say that this [Anthony Eden] is the best Prime Minister we have? R. A. BUTLER: Yes.
   Interview at London Airport, 8 Jan. 1956, in R. A. Butler *The Art of the Possible* (1971) ch. 9

Ralph Butler and Noel Gay (*Richard Moxon Armitage*) 1898–1954

3 The sun has got his hat on
Hip hip hip hooray!
The sun has got his hat on
And he's coming out today.
   The Sun Has Got His Hat On (1932 song)

Samuel Butler 1835–1902

4 Yet meet we shall, and part, and meet again
Where dead men meet, on lips of living men.
   Athenaeum 4 Jan. 1902, 'Μέλλοντα ταῦτα'

5 It has been said that the love of money is the root of all evil. The want of money is so quite as truly.
   Erewhon (1872) ch. 20

6 It has been said that though God cannot alter the past, historians can; it is perhaps because they can be useful to Him in this respect that He tolerates their existence.
   Erewhon Revisited (1901) ch. 14

7 Life is like playing a violin solo in public and learning the instrument as one goes on.
   Speech at the Somerville Club, 27 Feb. 1895, in R. A. Streatfield *Essays on Life, Art and Science* (1904) p. 69

8 An honest God's the noblest work of man.
   Further Extracts from Notebooks (1934) p. 26. Cf. *Oxford Dictionary of Quotations* (1979) 270:17 and 379:24

9 A lawyer's dream of heaven: every man reclaimed his own property at the resurrection, and each tried to recover it from all his forefathers.
   Further Extracts from Notebooks (1934) p. 27

10 The three most important things a man has are, briefly, his private parts, his money, and his religious opinions.
   Further Extracts from Notebooks (1934) p. 93

11 The course of true anything never does run smooth.
   Further Extracts from Notebooks (1934) p. 260

12 Conscience is thoroughly well-bred and soon leaves off talking to those who do not wish to hear it.
   Further Extracts from Notebooks (1934) p. 279

13 I heard a man say that brigands demand your money *or* your life, whereas women require both.
   Further Extracts from Notebooks (1934) p. 315

14 It was very good of God to let Carlyle and Mrs Carlyle marry one another and so make only two people miserable instead of four, besides being very amusing.
   Letters between Samuel Butler and Miss E. M. A. Savage 1871–1885 (1935) 21 Nov. 1884

15 The most perfect humour and irony is generally quite unconscious.
   Life and Habit (1877) ch. 2

16 It has, I believe, been often remarked that a hen is only an egg's way of making another egg.
   Life and Habit (1877) ch. 8

17 Life is one long process of getting tired.
   Notebooks (1912) ch. 1

18 Life is the art of drawing sufficient conclusions from insufficient premises.
   Notebooks (1912) ch. 1

19 All progress is based upon a universal innate desire on the part of every organism to live beyond its income.
   Notebooks (1912) ch. 1

20 The healthy stomach is nothing if not conservative. Few radicals have good digestions.
   Notebooks (1912) ch. 6

21 Always eat grapes downwards—that is, always eat the best grape first; in this way there will be none better left on the bunch, and each grape will seem good down to the last. If you eat the other way, you will not have a good grape in the lot. Besides you will be tempting providence to kill you before you come to the best.
   Notebooks (1912) ch. 7

22 How thankful we ought to be that Wordsworth was only a poet and not a musician. Fancy a symphony by Wordsworth! Fancy having to sit it out! And fancy what it would have been if he had written fugues!
   Notebooks (1912) ch. 8

23 The history of art is the history of revivals.
   Notebooks (1912) ch. 8

24 Genius . . . has been defined as a supreme capacity for taking trouble. . . . It might be more fitly described as a supreme capacity for getting its possessors into trouble of all kinds and keeping them therein so long as the genius remains.
   Notebooks (1912) ch. 11

25 An apology for the Devil: It must be remembered that we have only heard one side of the case. God has written all the books.
   Notebooks (1912) ch. 14

26 The great pleasure of a dog is that you may make a fool of yourself with him and not only will he not scold you, but he will make a fool of himself too.
   Notebooks (1912) ch. 14

27 A definition is the enclosing a wilderness of idea within a wall of words.
   Notebooks (1912) ch. 14

28 To live is like to love—all reason is against it, and all healthy instinct for it.
   Notebooks (1912) ch. 14

29 The public buys its opinions as it buys its meat, or takes in its milk, on the principle that it is cheaper to do this

than to keep a cow. So it is, but the milk is more likely
to be watered.

Notebooks (1912) ch. 17

1 I do not mind lying, but I hate inaccuracy.

Notebooks (1912) ch. 19

2 Stowed away in a Montreal lumber room
The Discobolus standeth and turneth his face to the
wall;
Dusty, cobweb-covered, maimed, and set at naught,
Beauty crieth in an attic, and no man regardeth.
O God! O Montreal!

Spectator 18 May 1878, 'Psalm of Montreal'

3 I do not like books. I believe I have the smallest library
of any literary man in London, and I have no wish to
increase it. I keep my books at the British Museum and
at Mudie's, and it makes me very angry if any one gives
me one for my private library.

Universal Review Dec. 1890, 'Ramblings in Cheapside'

4 Adversity, if a man is set down to it by degrees, is more
supportable with equanimity by most people than any
great prosperity arrived at in a single lifetime.

Way of All Flesh (1903) ch. 5

5 They would have been equally horrified at hearing the
Christian religion doubted, and at seeing it practised.

Way of All Flesh (1903) ch. 15

6 All animals, except man, know that the principal
business of life is to enjoy it—and they do enjoy it as
much as man and other circumstances will allow.

Way of All Flesh (1903) ch. 19

7 The advantage of doing one's praising for oneself is that
one can lay it on so thick and exactly in the right
places.

Way of All Flesh (1903) ch. 34

8 Young as he was, his instinct told him that the best liar
is he who makes the smallest amount of lying go the
longest way.

Way of All Flesh (1903) ch. 39

9 Beyond a haricot vein in one of my legs, I'm as young
as ever I was. Old indeed! There's many a good tune
played on an old fiddle!

Way of All Flesh (1903) ch. 61

10 'Tis better to have loved and lost than never to have
lost at all.

Way of All Flesh (1903) ch. 67. Cf. Tennyson in *Oxford
Dictionary of Quotations* (1979) 536:16

Max Bygraves 1922–

See ERIC SYKES *and* MAX BYGRAVES

James Branch Cabell 1879–1958

11 The optimist proclaims that we live in the best of all
possible worlds; and the pessimist fears this is true.

Silver Stallion (1926) bk. 4, ch. 26

Irving Caesar 1895–

12 Picture you upon my knee,
Just tea for two and two for tea.

Tea for Two (1925 song; music by Vincent Youmans)

John Cage 1912–

13   I have nothing to say
                        and I am saying it   and that is
poetry.

Silence (1961) 'Lecture on nothing'

James Cagney 1899–1986

14 Frank Gorshin—oh, Frankie, just in passing: I never
said [in any film] 'Mmm, you dirty rat!' What
I actually did say was 'Judy! Judy! Judy!'

Speech at American Film Institute banquet, 13 Mar. 1974,
in *Cagney by Cagney* (1976) ch. 14

Sammy Cahn (Samuel Cohen) 1913–

15 Love and marriage, love and marriage,
Go together like a horse and carriage,
This I tell ya, brother,
Ya can't have one without the other.

Love and Marriage (1955 song; music by James Van Heusen)

16 It's that second time you hear your love song sung,
Makes you think perhaps, that
Love like youth is wasted on the young.

The Second Time Around (1960 song; music by James Van
Heusen)

James M. Cain 1892–1977

17 The postman always rings twice.

Title of novel (1934) and play (1936)

Michael Caine (Maurice Joseph Micklewhite) 1933–

18 Not many people know that.

Title of book (1984)

Sir Joseph Cairns 1920–

19 The betrayal of Ulster, the cynical and entirely
undemocratic banishment of its properly elected
Parliament and a relegation to the status of a fuzzy
wuzzy colony is, I hope, a last betrayal contemplated
by Downing Street because it is the last that Ulster will
countenance.

Speech on retiring as Lord Mayor of Belfast, 31 May 1972, in
Daily Telegraph 1 June 1972

Charles Calhoun 1897–1972

20 Shake, rattle and roll.

Title of song (1954)

James Callaghan (*Leonard James Callaghan, Baron Callaghan of Cardiff*) 1912–

1 We say that what Britain needs is a new social contract. That is what this document [*Labour's Programme for Britain*] is about.
  Speech at Labour Party Annual Conference, 2 Oct. 1972, in *Conference Report* (1972) p. 115

2 A lie can be half-way around the world before truth has got his boots on.
  Hansard 1 Nov. 1976, col. 976

3 I don't think other people in the world would share the view there is mounting chaos.
  In interview at London Airport, 10 Jan. 1979, in the *Sun* 11 Jan. 1979; the *Sun* headlined its report:'Crisis? What Crisis?'

Joseph Campbell (*Seosamh MacCathmhaoil*) 1879–1944

4 As a white candle
  In a holy place,
  So is the beauty
  Of an agéd face.
  Irishry (1913) 'Old Woman'

Mrs Patrick Campbell (*Beatrice Stella Campbell*) 1865–1940

5 Oh dear me—its too late to do anything but *accept* you and *love* you—but when you were quite a little boy somebody ought to have said 'hush' just once!
  Letter to G. B. Shaw, 1 Nov. 1912, cited in Alan Dent *Bernard Shaw and Mrs Patrick Campbell* (1952) p. 52

6 A popular anecdote describes a well known actor-manager [Sir Herbert Beerbohm Tree] as saying one day at rehearsal to an actress of distinguished beauty [Mrs Patrick Campbell], 'Let us give Shaw a beefsteak and put some red blood into him.' 'For heaven's sake, don't,' she exclaimed: 'he is bad enough as it is; but if you give him meat no woman in London will be safe.'
  G. B. Shaw in Frank Harris *Contemporary Portraits* (1919) p. 331

7 It doesn't matter what you do in the bedroom as long as you don't do it in the street and frighten the horses.
  In Daphne Fielding *Duchess of Jermyn Street* (1964) ch. 2

8 Tallulah [Bankhead] is always skating on thin ice. Everyone wants to be there when it breaks.
  In *The Times* 13 Dec. 1968

9 It was Mrs Campbell, for instance, who, on a celebrated occasion, threw her companion into a flurry by describing her recent marriage as 'the deep, deep peace of the double-bed after the hurly-burly of the chaise-longue.'
  Alexander Woollcott *While Rome Burns* (1934) 'The First Mrs Tanqueray'

Roy Campbell 1901–1957

10 Of all the clever people round me here
  I most delight in Me—
  Mine is the only voice I care to hear,
  And mine the only face I like to see.
  Adamastor (1930) 'Home Thoughts in Bloomsbury'

11 You praise the firm restraint with which they write—
  I'm with you there, of course:
  They use the snaffle and the curb all right,
  But where's the bloody horse?
  Adamastor (1930) 'On Some South African Novelists'

12 I hate 'Humanity' and all such abstracts: but I love *people*. Lovers of 'Humanity' generally hate *people and children*, and keep parrots or puppy dogs.
  Light on a Dark Horse (1951) ch. 13

13 Translations (like wives) are seldom strictly faithful if they are in the least attractive.
  Poetry Review June-July 1949

14 Giraffes!—a People
  Who live between the earth and skies,
  Each in his lone religious steeple,
  Keeping a light-house with his eyes.
  Talking Bronco (1946) 'Dreaming Spires'

15 South Africa, renowned both far and wide
  For politics and little else beside.
  The Wayzgoose (1928) p. 7

Sir Henry Campbell-Bannerman 1836–1908

16 There is a phrase which seems in itself somewhat self-evident, which is often used to account for a good deal—that 'war is war'. But when you come to ask about it, then you are told that the war now going on is not war. [Laughter] When is a war not a war? When it is carried on by methods of barbarism in South Africa.
  Speech to National Reform Union, 14 June 1901, in *Daily News* 15 June 1901

17 Good government could never be a substitute for government by the people themselves.
  Speech at Stirling, 23 Nov. 1905, in *Daily News* 24 Nov. 1905

Albert Camus 1913–1960

18 *Intellectuel = celui qui se dédouble.*

  An intellectual is someone whose mind watches itself.
  Carnets, 1935–42 (Notebooks, 1962) p. 41

19 *La politique et le sort des hommes sont formés par des hommes sans idéal et sans grandeur. Ceux qui ont une grandeur en eux ne font pas de politique.*

  Politics and the fate of mankind are formed by men without ideals and without greatness. Those who have greatness within them do not go in for politics.
  Carnets, 1935–42 (Notebooks, 1962) p. 99

20 *Vous savez ce qu'est le charme: une manière de s'entendre répondre oui sans avoir posé aucune question claire.*

  You know what charm is: a way of getting the answer yes without having asked any clear question.
  La Chute (The Fall, 1956) p. 62

1 *Nous sommes tous des cas exceptionnels. Nous voulons tous faire appel de quelque chose! Chacun exige d'être innocent, à tout prix, même si, pour cela, il faut accuser le genre humain et le ciel.*

We are all special cases. We all want to appeal to something! Everyone insists on his innocence, at all costs, even if it means accusing the rest of the human race and heaven.
   La Chute (The Fall, 1956) p. 95

2 *C'est si vrai que nous nous confions rarement à ceux qui sont meilleurs que nous.*

It is very true that we seldom confide in those who are better than ourselves.
   La Chute (The Fall, 1956) p. 97

3 *Je vais vous dire un grand secret, mon cher. N'attendez pas le jugement dernier. Il a lieu tous les jours.*

I'll tell you a great secret, my friend. Don't wait for the last judgement. It happens every day.
   La Chute (The Fall, 1956) p. 129

4 *Aujourd'hui, maman est morte. Ou peut-être hier, je ne sais pas.*

Mother died today. Or perhaps it was yesterday, I don't know.
   L'Étranger (The Outsider, 1944) p. 9

5 *Qu'est-ce qu'un homme révolté ? Un homme qui dit non.*

What is a rebel? A man who says no.
   L'Homme révolté (The Rebel, 1951) p. 25

6 *Toutes les révolutions modernes ont abouti à un renforcement de l'État.*

All modern revolutions have ended in a reinforcement of the State.
   L'Homme révolté (The Rebel, 1951) p. 221

7 *Tout révolutionnaire finit en oppresseur ou en hérétique.*

Every revolutionary ends as an oppressor or a heretic.
   L'Homme révolté (The Rebel, 1951) p. 306

8 *La lutte elle-même vers les sommets suffit à remplir un cœur d'homme. Il faut imaginer Sisyphe heureux.*

The struggle itself towards the heights is enough to fill a human heart. One must imagine that Sisyphus is happy.
   Le Mythe de Sisyphe (The Myth of Sisyphus, 1942) p. 168

Elias Canetti 1905–

9 *Alles was man vergessen hat, schreit im Traum um Hilfe.*

All the things one has forgotten scream for help in dreams.
   Die Provinz der Menschen (The Human Province, 1973) p. 269

Hughie Cannon 1877–1912

10 Won't you come home Bill Bailey, won't you come home?
   Bill Bailey, Won't You Please Come Home (1902 song)

John R. Caples 1900–

11 They laughed when I sat down at the piano. But when I started to play!
   Advertisement for US School of Music, in *Physical Culture* Dec. 1925, p. 95

Al Capone 1899–1947

12 Don't you get the idea I'm one of these goddam radicals. Don't get the idea I'm knocking the American system.
   Interview, c.1929, in Claud Cockburn *In Time of Trouble* (1956) ch. 16

13 Once in the racket you're always in it.
   Philadelphia Public Ledger 18 May 1929

Truman Capote 1924–1984

14 Mr Capote . . . commented on the difficulty he had reading the Beat novels. He had tried but he had been unable to finish any one of them. . . . 'None of these people have anything interesting to say,' he observed, 'and none of them can write, not even Mr Kerouac.' What they do, he added, 'isn't writing at all—it's typing.'
   Report of television discussion, in *New Republic* 9 Feb. 1959

15 Venice is like eating an entire box of chocolate liqueurs in one go.
   In *Observer* 26 Nov. 1961

16 Other voices, other rooms.
   Title of novel (1948)

Al Capp 1909–1979

17 [Abstract art is] a product of the untalented, sold by the unprincipled to the utterly bewildered.
   In *National Observer* 1 July 1963

Ethna Carbery (Anna MacManus) 1866–1902

18 Oh, Kathaleen Ní Houlihan, your road's a thorny way,
   And 'tis a faithful soul would walk the flints with you for aye,
   Would walk the sharp and cruel flints until his locks grew grey.
   Four Winds Of Eirinn (1902) 'Passing of the Gael'

Hoagy Carmichael (Hoagland Howard Carmichael) 1899–1981

See STUART GORRELL

Stokely Carmichael 1941– and Charles Vernon Hamilton 1929–

19 The adoption of the concept of Black Power is one of the most legitimate and healthy developments in American politics and race relations in our time. . . . It is a call for black people in this country to unite, to recognize their heritage, to build a sense of

community. It is a call for black people to begin to define their own goals, to lead their own organizations and to support those organizations. It is a call to reject the racist institutions and values of this society.
Black Power (1967) ch. 2

Dale Carnegie 1888–1955

1 How to win friends and influence people.
Title of book (1936)

J. L. Carr

2 'I've never been spoken to like this before in all my thirty years' experience,' she wails. '*You* have not had thirty years' experience, Mrs Grindle-Jones,' he says witheringly. '*You* have had one year's experience 30 times.'
Harpole Report (1972) p. 128

Edward Carson (Baron Carson) 1854–1935

3 My only great qualification for being put at the head of the Navy is that I am very much at sea.
In Ian Colvin *Life of Lord Carson* (1936) vol. 3, ch. 23

Jimmy Carter 1924–

4 We should live our lives as though Christ were coming this afternoon.
Speech to Bible class at Plains, Georgia, March 1976, in *Boston Sunday Herald Advertiser* 11 Apr. 1976

5 I'm Jimmy Carter, and I'm going to be your next president.
Said to the son of a campaign supporter, Nov. 1975, in *I'll Never Lie to You* (1976) ch. 1

6 I've looked on a lot of women with lust. I've committed adultery in my heart many times. This is something that God recognizes I will do—and I have done it—and God forgives me for it.
Playboy Nov. 1976

Sydney Carter 1915–

7 I danced in the morning
When the world was begun
And I danced in the moon
And the stars and the sun
And I came down from heaven
And I danced on the earth—
At Bethlehem I had my birth.
Dance then wherever you may be,
I am the Lord of the Dance, said he,
And I'll lead you all, wherever you may be
And I'll lead you all in the dance, said he.
Nine Carols or Ballads (1967) 'Lord of the Dance'

8 It's God they ought to crucify
Instead of you and me,
I said to the carpenter
A-hanging on the tree.
Nine Carols or Ballads (1967) 'Friday Morning'

Pablo Casals 1876–1973

9 It [the cello] is like a beautiful woman who has not grown older, but younger with time, more slender, more supple, more graceful.
In *Time* 29 Apr. 1957

Ted Castle (Baron Castle of Islington) 1907–1979

10 In place of strife.
Title of Labour Government's White Paper, 17 Jan. 1969, suggested by Castle to his wife, Barbara Castle (Secretary of State for Employment): see Barbara Castle *Diaries* (1984) 15 Jan. 1969

Harry Castling and C. W. Murphy

11 Let's all go down the Strand!
Let's all go down the Strand!
I'll be leader, you can march behind
Come with me, and see what we can find
Let's all go down the Strand!
Let's All Go Down the Strand! (1909 song)

Fidel Castro 1926–

12 *La historia me absolvéra.*

History will absolve me.
Title of pamphlet (1953)

Willa Cather 1873–1947

13 Religion and art spring from the same root and are close kin. Economics and art are strangers.
Commonweal 17 Apr. 1936

14 The history of every country begins in the heart of a man or a woman.
O Pioneers! (1913) pt. 1, ch. 5

15 I like trees because they seem more resigned to the way they have to live than other things do.
O Pioneers! (1913) pt. 2, ch. 8

Mr Justice Caulfield (Sir Bernard Caulfield) 1914–

16 Remember Mary Archer in the witness box. Your vision of her will probably never disappear. Has she elegance? Has she fragrance? Would she have—without the strain of this trial—a radiance?
Summing up of court case between Jeffrey Archer and the *News of the World*, July 1987, in *The Times* 24 July 1987

Charles Causley 1917–

17 O are you the boy
Who would wait on the quay
With the silver penny
And the apricot tree?
Farewell, Aggie Weston (1951) 'Nursery Rhyme of Innocence and Experience'

18 Timothy Winters comes to school
With eyes as wide as a football-pool,

Ears like bombs and teeth like splinters:
A blitz of a boy is Timothy Winters.
Union Street (1957) 'Timothy Winters'

Constantine Cavafy 1863–1933

1 Τί περιμένουμε στὴν ἀγορά συναθροισμένοι;
Εἶναι οἱ βάρβαροι νά φθάσουν σήμερα.

What are we all waiting for, gathered together like
this on the public square?
The Barbarians are coming today.
Περιμενοντας τους βαρβαρους (Waiting for the Barbarians,
1904) in *Poems* (1963)

2 Καινούριους τόπους δὲν θὰ βρεῖς, δὲν θάβρεις ἄλλες
θάλασσες,
Ἡ πόλις θὰ σὲ ἀκολουθεῖ.

You will find no new places, no other seas,
The town will follow you.
Ποιηματα (Poems, 1911) 'Ἡ Πόλις' ('The Town')

Edith Cavell 1865–1915

3 They have all been very kind to me here. But this
I would say, standing, as I do, in view of God and
eternity, I realize that patriotism is not enough. I must
have no hatred or bitterness towards anyone.
Words spoken in prison the night before her execution, in
The Times 23 Oct. 1915

Lord David Cecil 1902–1986

4 The primary object of a student of literature is to be
delighted. His duty is to enjoy himself: his efforts
should be directed to developing his faculty of
appreciation.
Reading as one of the Fine Arts (1949) p. 4

Patrick Reginald Chalmers 1872–1942

5 What's lost upon the roundabouts we pulls up on the
swings!
Green Days and Blue Days (1912) 'Roundabouts and Swings'

Joseph Chamberlain 1836–1914

6 In politics, there is no use looking beyond the next
fortnight.
In letter from A. J. Balfour to 3rd Marquess of Salisbury,
24 Mar. 1886, in A. J. Balfour *Chapters of Autobiography*
(1930) ch. 16

7 It is said that the City is the centre of the world's
finance, that the fate of our manufactures therefore is
a secondary consideration; that, provided that the City
of London remains, as it is at present, the
clearing-house of the world, any other nation may be
its workshop. Now I ask you, gentlemen, whether . . .
that is not a very short-sighted view.
Speech at the Guildhall, 19 Jan. 1904, in *The Times* 20 Jan.
1904

8 In the great revolution which separated the United
States from Great Britain the greatest man that that

revolution produced . . . was Alexander Hamilton . . .
he left a precious legacy to his countrymen when he
disclosed to them the secrets of union and when he said
to them, 'Learn to think continentally.' And, my
fellow-citizens, if I may venture to give you a message,
now I would say to you, 'Learn to think Imperially.'
Speech at the Guildhall, 19 Jan. 1904, in *The Times* 20 Jan.
1904

9 The day of small nations has long passed away. The
day of Empires has come.
Speech at Birmingham, 12 May 1904, in *The Times* 13 May
1904

10 We are not downhearted. The only trouble is we cannot
understand what is happening to our neighbours.
Speech at Smethwick, 18 Jan. 1906, in *The Times* 19 Jan.
1906

Neville Chamberlain 1869–1940

11 In war, whichever side may call itself the victor, there
are no winners, but all are losers.
Speech at Kettering, 3 July 1938, in *The Times* 4 July 1938

12 How horrible, fantastic, incredible it is that we should
be digging trenches and trying on gas-masks here
because of a quarrel in a far away country
[Czechoslovakia] between people of whom we know
nothing.
Broadcast speech, 27 Sept. 1938, in *The Times* 28 Sept. 1938

13 This morning I had another talk with the German
Chancellor, Herr Hitler, and here is the paper which
bears his name upon it as well as mine. . . . 'We regard
the agreement signed last night and the Anglo-German
Naval Agreement, as symbolic of the desire of our two
peoples never to go to war with one another again.'
Speech at Heston Airport, 30 Sept. 1938, in *The Times* 1 Oct.
1938

14 My good friends, this is the second time in our history
that there has come back from Germany to Downing
Street peace with honour. I believe it is peace for our
time. We thank you from the bottom of our hearts. And
now I recommend you to go home and sleep quietly in
your beds.
Speech from window of 10 Downing Street, 30 Sept. 1938,
in *The Times* 1 Oct. 1938

15 This morning, the British Ambassador in Berlin handed
the German government a final Note stating that,
unless we heard from them by eleven o'clock that they
were prepared at once to withdraw their troops from
Poland, a state of war would exist between us. I have to
tell you now that no such undertaking has been
received, and that consequently this country is at war
with Germany.
Radio broadcast, 3 Sept. 1939, in *The Times* 4 Sept. 1939

16 Whatever may be the reason—whether it was that
Hitler thought he might get away with what he had got
without fighting for it, or whether it was that after all
the preparations were not sufficiently
complete—however, one thing is certain—he missed
the bus.
Speech at Central Hall, Westminster, 4 Apr. 1940, in *The
Times* 5 Apr. 1940

Harry Champion 1866–1942

See CHARLES COLLINS, E. A. SHEPPARD, and FRED TERRY

Raymond Chandler 1888–1959

1 Down these mean streets a man must go who is not himself mean, who is neither tarnished nor afraid.
Atlantic Monthly Dec. 1944 'The Simple Art of Murder'

2 It was about eleven o'clock in the morning, mid October, with the sun not shining and a look of hard wet rain in the clearness of the foothills. I was wearing my powder-blue suit, with dark blue shirt, tie and display handkerchief, black brogues, black wool socks with dark blue clocks on them. I was neat, clean, shaved and sober, and I didn't care who knew it.
The Big Sleep (1939) ch. 1

3 It was a blonde. A blonde to make a bishop kick a hole in a stained glass window.
Farewell, My Lovely (1940) ch. 13

4 Would you convey my compliments to the purist who reads your proofs and tell him or her that I write in a sort of broken-down patois which is something like the way a Swiss waiter talks, and that when I split an infinitive, God damn it, I split it so it will stay split.
Letter to Edward Weeks, 18 Jan. 1947, in F. MacShane *Life of Raymond Chandler* (1976) ch. 7

5 A big hard-boiled city with no more personality than a paper cup.
The Little Sister (1949) ch. 26 (of Los Angeles)

6 If my books had been any worse, I should not have been invited to Hollywood, and if they had been any better, I should not have come.
Letter to Charles W. Morton, 12 Dec. 1945, in Dorothy Gardiner and Katherine S. Walker *Raymond Chandler Speaking* (1962) p. 126

Coco Chanel 1883–1971

7 Youth is something very new: twenty years ago no one mentioned it.
In Marcel Haedrich *Coco Chanel, Her Life, Her Secrets* (1971) ch. 1

Charlie Chaplin (Sir Charles Spencer Chaplin) 1889–1977

8 All I need to make a comedy is a park, a policeman and a pretty girl.
My Autobiography (1964) ch. 10

Arthur Chapman 1873–1935

9 Out where the handclasp's a little stronger,
Out where the smile dwells a little longer,
That's where the West begins.
Out Where the West Begins (1916) p. 1

Graham Chapman 1941–89, John Cleese 1939– , Terry Gilliam 1940– , Eric Idle 1943– , Terry Jones 1942– , and Michael Palin 1943–

10 I'm a lumberjack
And I'm OK
I sleep all night
And I work all day.
Monty Python's Big Red Book (1971)

11 And now for something completely different.
Catch-phrase popularized in *Monty Python's Flying Circus* (BBC TV programme, 1969–74)

12 Your wife interested in . . . *photographs*? Eh? Know what I mean—*photographs*? He asked him knowingly . . . nudge nudge, snap snap, grin grin, wink wink, say no more.
Monty Python's Flying Circus (BBC TV programme, 1969), in Roger Wilmut *From Fringe to Flying Circus* (1980) ch. 11

13 CUSTOMER: I wish to complain about this parrot what I purchased not half an hour ago from this very boutique.
SHOPKEEPER: Oh yes, the Norwegian Blue—what's wrong with it?
CUSTOMER: I'll tell you what's wrong with it—it's dead that's what's wrong with it.
SHOPKEEPER: No, no—it's resting. . . . It's probably pining for the fiords. . . .
CUSTOMER: It's not pining—it's passed on! This parrot is no more! It has ceased to be! It's expired and gone to meet its maker! This is a late parrot! It's a stiff! Bereft of life it rests in peace—if you hadn't nailed it to the perch it would be pushing up the daisies! It's rung down the curtain and joined the choir invisible! THIS IS AN EX–PARROT!
Monty Python's Flying Circus (BBC TV programme, 1969), in Roger Wilmut *From Fringe to Flying Circus* (1980) ch. 11

14 Nobody expects the Spanish Inquisition! Our chief weapon is surprise—surprise and fear . . . fear and surprise . . . our two weapons are fear and surprise—and ruthless efficiency . . . our *three* weapons are fear and surprise and ruthless efficiency and an almost fanatical devotion to the Pope . . . our *four* . . . no. . . . *Amongst* our weapons—amongst our weaponry—are such elements as fear, surprise. . . . I'll come in again.
Monty Python's Flying Circus (BBC TV programme, 1970), in Roger Wilmut *From Fringe to Flying Circus* (1980) ch. 11

Prince Charles (Charles Philip Arthur George, Prince of Wales) 1948–

15 I have not the slightest hesitation in making the observation that much of British management doesn't seem to understand the importance of the human factor.
Speech to Parliamentary and Scientific Committee, 21 Feb. 1979, in *Daily Telegraph* 22 Feb. 1979

16 I just come and talk to the plants, really—very important to talk to them, they respond I find.
Television interview, 21 Sept. 1986, in *Daily Telegraph* 22 Sept. 1986

1 We do need a sense of urgency in our outlook in the regeneration of industry and enterprise, because otherwise what really worries me is that we are going to end up as a fourth-rate country and I don't want to see that.

   Speech at Edinburgh, 26 Nov. 1985, in *Scotsman* 27 Nov. 1985

2 Instead of designing an extension to the elegant façade of the National Gallery which complements it . . . it looks as if we may be presented with a kind of vast municipal fire station. . . . I would understand better this type of high-tech approach if you demolished the whole of Trafalgar Square and started again . . . but what is proposed is like a monstrous carbuncle on the face of a much-loved and elegant friend.

   Speech to Royal Institute of British Architects, 30 May 1984, in *The Times* 31 May 1984. Cf. Countess Spencer

Apsley Cherry-Garrard 1882–1959

See E. L. ATKINSON

G. K. Chesterton 1874–1936

3 An adventure is only an inconvenience rightly considered. An inconvenience is only an adventure wrongly considered.

   All Things Considered (1908) 'On Running after one's Hat'

4 No animal ever invented anything so bad as drunkenness—or so good as drink.

   All Things Considered (1908) 'Wine When it is Red'

5 Of those days the tale is told that I once sent a telegram to my wife in London, which ran: 'Am in Market Harborough. Where ought I to be?' I cannot remember whether this story is true; but it is not unlikely, or, I think, unreasonable.

   Autobiography (1936) ch. 16

6 They died to save their country and they only saved the world.

   Ballad of St Barbara and Other Verses (1922) 'English Graves'

7 Before the gods that made the gods
Had seen their sunrise pass,
The White Horse of the White Horse Vale
Was cut out of the grass.

   Ballad of the White Horse (1911) bk. 1, p. 1

8 I tell you naught for your comfort,
Yea, naught for your desire,
Save that the sky grows darker yet
And the sea rises higher.

   Ballad of the White Horse (1911) bk. 1, p. 18

9 For the great Gaels of Ireland
Are the men that God made mad,
For all their wars are merry,
And all their songs are sad.

   Ballad of the White Horse (1911) bk. 2, p. 35

10 The thing on the blind side of the heart,
On the wrong side of the door,
The green plant groweth, menacing
Almighty lovers in the Spring;
There is always a forgotten thing,
And love is not secure.

   Ballad of the White Horse (1911) bk. 3, p. 52

11 Literature is a luxury; fiction is a necessity.

   Defendant (1901) 'Defence of Penny Dreadfuls'

12 All slang is metaphor, and all metaphor is poetry.

   Defendant (1901) 'Defence of Slang'

13 'My country, right or wrong', is a thing that no patriot would think of saying except in a desperate case. It is like saying, 'My mother, drunk or sober'.

   Defendant (1901) 'Defence of Patriotism'

14 And Noah he often said to his wife when he sat down to dine,
'I don't care where the water goes if it doesn't get into the wine.'

   Flying Inn (1914) ch. 5 'Wine and Water'

15 God made the wicked Grocer
For a mystery and a sign,
That men might shun the awful shops
And go to inns to dine.

   Flying Inn (1914) ch. 6 'Song against Grocers'

16 He keeps a lady in a cage
Most cruelly all day,
And makes her count and calls her 'Miss'
Until she fades away.

   Flying Inn (1914) ch. 6 'Song against Grocers'

17 The folk that live in Liverpool, their heart is in their boots;
They go to hell like lambs, they do, because the hooter hoots.

   Flying Inn (1914) ch. 7 'Me Heart'

18 They haven't got no noses,
The fallen sons of Eve.

   Flying Inn (1914) ch. 15 'Song of Quoodle'

19 And goodness only knowses
The Noselessness of Man.

   Flying Inn (1914) ch. 15 'Song of Quoodle'

20 The rich are the scum of the earth in every country.

   Flying Inn (1914) ch. 15

21 Tea, although an Oriental,
Is a gentleman at least;
Cocoa is a cad and coward,
Cocoa is a vulgar beast.

   Flying Inn (1914) ch. 18 'Song of Right and Wrong'

22 Before the Roman came to Rye or out to Severn strode,
The rolling English drunkard made the rolling English road.
A reeling road, a rolling road, that rambles round the shire,
And after him the parson ran, the sexton and the squire;
A merry road, a mazy road, and such as we did tread
The night we went to Birmingham by way of Beachy Head.

   Flying Inn (1914) ch. 21 'Rolling English Road'

23 For there is good news yet to hear and fine things to be seen,
Before we go to Paradise by way of Kensal Green.

   Flying Inn (1914) ch. 21 'Rolling English Road'

24 Ten thousand women marched through the streets of London [in support of women's suffrage] saying: 'We will not be dictated to,' and then went off to become stenographers.

   In M. Ffinch *G. K. Chesterton* (1986) ch. 11

1 The word 'orthodoxy' not only no longer means being right; it practically means being wrong.
   Heretics (1905) ch. 1

2 There is no such thing on earth as an uninteresting subject; the only thing that can exist is an uninterested person.
   Heretics (1905) ch. 3

3 The artistic temperament is a disease that afflicts amateurs. It is a disease which arises from men not having sufficient power of expression to utter and get rid of the element of art in their being.
   Heretics (1905) ch. 17

4 Bigotry may be roughly defined as the anger of men who have no opinions.
   Heretics (1905) ch. 20

5 After the first silence the small man said to the other: 'Where does a wise man hide a pebble?'
   And the tall man answered in a low voice: 'On the beach.'
   The small man nodded, and after a short silence said: 'Where does a wise man hide a leaf?'
   And the other answered: 'In the forest.'
   Innocence of Father Brown (1911) 'The Sign of the Broken Sword'

6 Thieves respect property. They merely wish the property to become their property that they may more perfectly respect it.
   Man who was Thursday (1908) ch. 4

7 The human race, to which so many of my readers belong, has been playing at children's games from the beginning, and will probably do it till the end, which is a nuisance for the few people who grow up.
   Napoleon of Notting Hill (1904) bk. 1, ch. 1

8 Why do you rush through the fields in trains,
   Guessing so much and so much.
   Why do you flash through the flowery meads,
   Fat-head poet that nobody reads;
   And why do you know such a frightful lot
   About people in gloves and such?
   New Poems (1933) 'The Fat White Woman Speaks' (an answer to Frances Cornford, see 61:8)

9 Democracy means government by the uneducated, while aristocracy means government by the badly educated.
   New York Times 1 Feb. 1931, pt. 5, p. 1

10 The men who really believe in themselves are all in lunatic asylums.
   Orthodoxy (1908) ch. 2

11 Poets do not go mad; but chess-players do. Mathematicians go mad, and cashiers; but creative artists very seldom. I am not, as will be seen, in any sense attacking logic: I only say that this danger does lie in logic, not in imagination.
   Orthodoxy (1908) ch. 2

12 Mr Shaw is (I suspect) the only man on earth who has never written any poetry.
   Orthodoxy (1908) ch. 3

13 Tradition may be defined as an extension of the franchise. Tradition means giving votes to the most obscure of all classes, our ancestors. It is the democracy of the dead. Tradition refuses to submit to the small and arrogant oligarchy of those who merely happen to be walking about. All democrats object to men being disqualified by the accident of birth; tradition objects to their being disqualified by the accident of death. Democracy tells us not to neglect a good man's opinion, even if he is our groom; tradition asks us not to neglect a good man's opinion, even if he is our father.
   Orthodoxy (1908) ch. 4

14 All conservatism is based upon the idea that if you leave things alone you leave them as they are. But you do not. If you leave a thing alone you leave it to a torrent of change.
   Orthodoxy (1908) ch. 7

15 Angels can fly because they take themselves lightly.
   Orthodoxy (1908) ch. 7

16 White founts falling in the Courts of the sun,
   And the Soldan of Byzantium is smiling as they run.
   Poems (1915) 'Lepanto'

17 Strong gongs groaning as the guns boom far,
   Don John of Austria is going to the war,
   Stiff flags straining in the night-blasts cold
   In the gloom black-purple, in the glint old-gold,
   Torchlight crimson on the copper kettle-drums,
   Then the tuckets, then the trumpets, then the cannon, and he comes.
   Poems (1915) 'Lepanto'

18 From all that terror teaches,
   From lies of tongue and pen,
   From all the easy speeches
   That comfort cruel men,
   From sale and profanation
   Of honour and the sword,
   From sleep and from damnation,
   Deliver us, good Lord!
   Poems (1915) 'A Hymn'

19 Are they clinging to their crosses, F. E. Smith?
   Poems (1915) 'Antichrist'

20 Talk about the pews and steeples
   And the Cash that goes therewith!
   But the souls of Christian peoples . . .
   Chuck it, Smith!
   Poems (1915) 'Antichrist'

21 The souls most fed with Shakespeare's flame
   Still sat unconquered in a ring,
   Remembering him like anything.
   Poems (1915) 'Shakespeare Memorial'

22 John Grubby, who was short and stout
   And troubled with religious doubt,
   Refused about the age of three
   To sit upon the curate's knee.
   Poems (1915) 'New Freethinker'

23 And I dream of the days when work was scrappy,
   And rare in our pockets the mark of the mint,
   When we were angry and poor and happy,
   And proud of seeing our names in print.
   Poems (1915) 'Song of Defeat'

24 Smile at us, pay us, pass us; but do not quite forget.
   For we are the people of England, that never have spoken yet.
   Poems (1915) 'The Secret People'

1 We only know the last sad squires ride slowly towards the
  sea,
  And a new people takes the land: and still it is not we.
    Poems (1915) 'The Secret People'

2 They spoke of Progress spiring round,
  Of Light and Mrs Humphry Ward—
  It is not true to say I frowned,
  Or ran about the room and roared;
  I might have simply sat and snored—
  I rose politely in the club
  And said,'I feel a little bored.
  Will someone take me to a pub?'
    Poems (1915) 'Ballade of an Anti-Puritan'

3 The gallows in my garden, people say,
  Is new and neat and adequately tall.
  I tie the noose on in a knowing way
  As one that knots his necktie for a ball;
  But just as all the neighbours—on the wall—
  Are drawing a long breath to shout 'Hurray!'
  The strangest whim has seized me. . . . After all
  I think I will not hang myself today.
    Poems (1915) 'Ballade of Suicide'

4 It isn't that they can't see the solution. It is that they can't
  see the problem.
    Scandal of Father Brown (1935) 'Point of a Pin'

5 Lying in bed would be an altogether perfect and supreme
  experience if only one had a coloured pencil long enough
  to draw on the ceiling.
    Tremendous Trifles (1909) 'On Lying in Bed'

6 Hardy went down to botanize in the swamp, while
  Meredith climbed towards the sun. Meredith became, at
  his best, a sort of daintily dressed Walt Whitman: Hardy
  became a sort of village atheist brooding and blaspheming
  over the village idiot.
    Victorian Age in Literature (1912) ch. 2

7 He [Tennyson] could not think up to the height of his own
  towering style.
    Victorian Age in Literature (1912) ch. 3

8 The Christian ideal has not been tried and found wanting.
  It has been found difficult; and left untried.
    What's Wrong with the World (1910) pt. 1, ch. 5

9 She was maintaining the prime truth of woman, the
  universal mother: that if a thing is worth doing, it is
  worth doing badly.
    What's Wrong with the World (1910) pt. 4, ch. 14

10 When fishes flew and forests walked
  And figs grew upon thorn,
  Some moment when the moon was blood
  Then surely I was born.

  With monstrous head and sickening cry
  And ears like errant wings,
  The devil's walking parody
  On all four-footed things.
    Wild Knight and Other Poems (1900) 'The Donkey'

11 Fools! For I also had my hour;
  One far fierce hour and sweet:
  There was a shout about my ears,
  And palms before my feet.
    Wild Knight and Other Poems (1900) 'The Donkey'

12 But Higgins is a Heathen,
  And to lecture rooms is forced,
  Where his aunts, who are not married,
  Demand to be divorced.
    Wine, Water and Song (1915) 'Song of the Strange Ascetic'

13 To be clever enough to get all that money, one must be
  stupid enough to want it.
    Wisdom of Father Brown (1914) 'Paradise of Thieves'

14 Journalism largely consists in saying 'Lord Jones
  Dead' to people who never knew that Lord Jones was
  alive.
    Wisdom of Father Brown (1914) 'The Purple Wig'

Maurice Chevalier 1888–1972

15 On his seventy-second birthday in 1960, he [Chevalier]
  was asked what he felt about the advancing years.
  'Considering the alternative,' he said, 'it's not too bad at
  all.'
    Michael Freedland *Maurice Chevalier* (1981) ch. 20

Erskine Childers 1870–1922

16 The riddle of the sands.
    Title of novel (1903)

17 The [firing] squad took up their positions across the prison
  yard. 'Come closer, boys,' Childers called out to them. 'It
  will be easier for you.'
    Burke Wilkinson *Zeal of Convert* (1976) ch. 26

Charles Chilton 1914–

See JOAN LITTLEWOOD

Noam Chomsky 1928–

18 As soon as questions of will or decision or reason or
  choice of action arise, human science is at a loss.
    Television interview, 30 Mar. 1978, in *Listener* 6 Apr. 1978

19 The notion 'grammatical' cannot be identified with
  'meaningful' or 'significant' in any semantic sense.
  Sentences (1) and (2) are equally nonsensical, but . . .
  only the former is grammatical.
    (1) Colourless green ideas sleep furiously.
    (2) Furiously sleep ideas green colourless.
    Syntactic Structures (1957) ch. 2

Dame Agatha Christie 1890–1976

20 One is left with the horrible feeling now that war settles
  nothing; that to *win* a war is as disastrous as to lose one!
    Autobiography (1977) pt. 10

21 'This affair must all be unravelled from within.' He
  [Hercule Poirot] tapped his forehead. 'These little grey
  cells. It is "up to them"—as you say over here.'
    The Mysterious Affair at Styles (1920) ch. 10

1 Trust the train, Mademoiselle, for it is *le bon Dieu* who drives it.

> *The Mystery of the Blue Train* (1928) ch. 36

Frank E. Churchill 1901–1942

2 Who's afraid of the big bad wolf?

> Title of song (1933; probably written in collaboration with Ann Ronell)

Sir Winston Churchill 1874–1965

3 In defeat unbeatable: in victory unbearable.

> In Edward Marsh *Ambrosia and Small Beer* (1964) ch. 5 (describing Viscount Montgomery)

4 After the war one quip which went the rounds of Westminster was attributed to Churchill himself. 'An empty taxi arrived at 10 Downing Street, and when the door was opened [Clement] Attlee got out.' When [John] Colville repeated this, and its attribution, to Churchill he obviously did not like it. His face set hard, and 'after an awful pause' he said: 'Mr Attlee is an honourable and gallant gentleman, and a faithful colleague who served his country well at the time of her greatest need. I should be obliged if you would make it clear whenever an occasion arises that I would never make such a remark about him, and that I strongly disapprove of anybody who does.'

> Kenneth Harris *Attlee* (1982) ch. 16

5 Always remember, Clemmie, that I have taken more out of alcohol than alcohol has taken out of me.

> In Quentin Reynolds *By Quentin Reynolds* (1964) ch. 11

6 [Clement Attlee is] a modest man who has a good deal to be modest about.

> In *Chicago Sunday Tribune Magazine of Books* 27 June 1954

7 QUESTION: What are the desirable qualifications for any young man who wishes to become a politician?
MR CHURCHILL: It is the ability to foretell what is going to happen tomorrow, next week, next month, and next year. And to have the ability afterwards to explain why it didn't happen.

> In B. Adler *Churchill Wit* (1965) p. 4

8 The British people have taken for themselves this motto—'Business carried on as usual during alterations on the map of Europe'. They expect the navy, on which they have lavished so much care and expense, to make that good, and that is what, upon the whole, we are actually achieving at the present time.

> Speech at the Guildhall, 9 Nov. 1914, in *Complete Speeches* (1974) vol. 3, p. 2341

9 Here is the answer which I will give to President Roosevelt. . . . We shall not fail or falter; we shall not weaken or tire. Neither the sudden shock of battle nor the long-drawn trials of vigilance and exertion will wear us down. Give us the tools and we will finish the job.

> Speech on radio, 9 Feb. 1941, in *Complete Speeches* (1974) vol. 6, p. 6350

10 The people of London with one voice would say to Hitler: 'You have committed every crime under the sun. . . . We will have no truce or parley with you,

or the grisly gang who work your wicked will. You do your worst—and we will do our best.'

> Speech at County Hall, London, 14 July 1941, in *Complete Speeches* (1974) vol. 6, p. 6451

11 Do not let us speak of darker days; let us rather speak of sterner days. These are not dark days: these are great days—the greatest days our country has ever lived; and we must all thank God that we have been allowed, each of us according to our stations, to play a part in making these days memorable in the history of our race.

> Speech at Harrow School, 29 Oct. 1941, in *Complete Speeches* (1974) vol. 6, p. 6500

12 It becomes still more difficult to reconcile Japanese action with prudence or even with sanity. What kind of a people do they think we are?

> Speech to US Congress, 26 Dec. 1941, in *Complete Speeches* (1974) vol. 6, p. 6540

13 When I warned them [the French Government] that Britain would fight on alone whatever they did, their generals told their Prime Minister and his divided Cabinet, 'In three weeks England will have her neck wrung like a chicken.' Some chicken! Some neck!

> Speech to Canadian Parliament, 30 Dec. 1941, in *Complete Speeches* (1974) vol. 6, p. 6544

14 There is no finer investment for any community than putting milk into babies. Healthy citizens are the greatest asset any country can have.

> Speech on radio, 21 Mar. 1943, in *Complete Speeches* (1974) vol. 7, p. 6761

15 From Stettin in the Baltic to Trieste in the Adriatic an iron curtain has descended across the Continent.

> Speech at Westminster College, Fulton, Missouri, 5 Mar. 1946, in *Complete Speeches* (1974) vol. 7, p. 7290

16 Somebody said, 'One never hears of Baldwin nowadays—he might as well be dead.' 'No,' said Winston, 'not dead. But the candle in that great turnip has gone out.'

> Harold Nicolson *Diary* 17 Aug. 1950, in *Diaries and Letters* (1968) p. 193

17 Now this is not the end. It is not even the beginning of the end. But it is, perhaps, the end of the beginning.

> Speech at the Mansion House, London, 10 Nov. 1942, in *End of the Beginning* (1943) p. 214

18 We mean to hold our own. I have not become the King's First Minister in order to preside over the liquidation of the British Empire.

> Speech in London, 10 Nov. 1942, in *End of the Beginning* (1943) p. 215

19 Once he [Churchill] said to me, 'Alfred, if you met Picasso coming down the street, would you join with me in kicking his something something something?' I said, 'Yes, sir, I would.'

> Sir Alfred Munnings in speech at Royal Academy, 28 Apr. 1949, in *The Finish* (1952) ch. 22

20 Don't talk to me about naval tradition. It's nothing but rum, sodomy and the lash.

> In Sir Peter Gretton *Former Naval Person* (1968) ch. 1

21 A labour contract into which men enter voluntarily for a limited and for a brief period, under which they are paid wages which they consider adequate, under which they are not bought or sold and from which they can obtain relief . . . on payment of £17.10s, the cost of their passage, may not be a healthy or proper contract, but it cannot in the opinion of His Majesty's Government be classified as slavery in the extreme acceptance of the word without some risk of terminological inexactitude.

Hansard 22 Feb. 1906, col. 555

1 He [Lord Charles Beresford] is one of those orators of whom it was well said, 'Before they get up, they do not know what they are going to say; when they are speaking, they do not know what they are saying; and when they have sat down, they do not know what they have said.'

Hansard 20 Dec. 1912, col. 1893

2 The whole map of Europe has been changed. The position of countries has been violently altered. The modes of thought of men, the whole outlook on affairs, the grouping of parties, all have encountered violent and tremendous changes in the deluge of the world, but as the deluge subsides and the waters fall short we see the dreary steeples of Fermanagh and Tyrone emerging once again. The integrity of their quarrel is one of the few institutions that has been unaltered in the cataclysm which has swept the world.

Hansard 16 Feb. 1922, col. 1270

3 I decline utterly to be impartial as between the fire brigade and the fire.

Hansard 7 July 1926, col. 2216 (replying to complaints of his bias in editing the *British Gazette* during the General Strike)

4 I remember, when I was a child, being taken to the celebrated Barnum's circus, which contained an exhibition of freaks and monstrosities, but the exhibit on the programme which I most desired to see was the one described as 'The Boneless Wonder'. My parents judged that that spectacle would be too revolting and demoralizing for my youthful eyes, and I have waited 50 years to see the boneless wonder [Ramsay Macdonald] sitting on the Treasury Bench.

Hansard 28 Jan. 1931, col. 1021

5 So they [the Government] go on in strange paradox, decided only to be undecided, resolved to be irresolute, adamant for drift, solid for fluidity, all-powerful to be impotent.

Hansard 12 Nov. 1936, col. 1107

6 The utmost he [Neville Chamberlain] has been able to gain for Czechoslovakia and in the matters which were in dispute has been that the German dictator, instead of snatching his victuals from the table, has been content to have them served to him course by course.

Hansard 5 Oct. 1938, col. 361

7 I would say to the House, as I said to those who have joined this Government: 'I have nothing to offer but blood, toil, tears and sweat.'

Hansard 13 May 1940, col. 1502

8 You ask, what is our policy? I will say: It is to wage war, by sea, land and air, with all our might and with all the strength that God can give us; to wage war against a monstrous tyranny, never surpassed in the dark, lamentable catalogue of human crime. That is our policy. You ask, what is our aim? I can answer in

one word: Victory, victory at all costs, victory in spite of all terror; victory, however long and hard the road may be; for without victory, there is no survival.

Hansard 13 May 1940, col. 1502

9 At this time I feel entitled to claim the aid of all, and I say, 'Come then, let us go forward together with our united strength.'

Hansard 13 May 1940, col. 1502

10 Even though large tracts of Europe and many old and famous States have fallen or may fall into the grip of the Gestapo and all the odious apparatus of Nazi rule, we shall not flag or fail. We shall go on to the end. We shall fight in France, we shall fight on the seas and oceans, we shall fight with growing confidence and growing strength in the air, we shall defend our island, whatever the cost may be. We shall fight on the beaches, we shall fight on the landing grounds, we shall fight in the fields and in the streets, we shall fight in the hills; we shall never surrender, and even if, which I do not for a moment believe, this island or a large part of it were subjugated and starving, then our Empire beyond the seas, armed and guarded by the British Fleet, would carry on the struggle, until, in God's good time, the new world, with all its power and might, steps forth to the rescue and the liberation of the old.

Hansard 4 June 1940, col. 796

11 What General Weygand called the 'Battle of France' is over. I expect that the Battle of Britain is about to begin. Upon this battle depends the survival of Christian civilization. Upon it depends our own British life and the long continuity of our institutions and our Empire. The whole fury and might of the enemy must very soon be turned on us. Hitler knows that he will have to break us in this island or lose the war. If we can stand up to him all Europe may be free and the life of the world may move forward into broad, sunlit uplands; but if we fail then the whole world, including the United States, and all that we have known and cared for, will sink into the abyss of a new dark age made more sinister, and perhaps more prolonged, by the lights of a perverted science. Let us therefore brace ourselves to our duty, and so bear ourselves that, if the British Commonwealth and its Empire lasts for a thousand years, men will still say, 'This was their finest hour.'

Hansard 18 June 1940, col. 60

12 The gratitude of every home in our Island, in our Empire, and indeed throughout the world, except in the abodes of the guilty, goes out to the British airmen who, undaunted by odds, unwearied in their constant challenge and mortal danger, are turning the tide of world war by their prowess and by their devotion. Never in the field of human conflict was so much owed by so many to so few.

Hansard 20 Aug. 1940, col. 1166

13 The British nation is unique in this respect. They are the only people who like to be told how bad things are, who like to be told the worst.

Hansard 10 June 1941, col. 152

14 We make this wide encircling movement in the Mediterranean, having for its primary object the recovery of the command of that vital sea, but also

having for its object the exposure of the under-belly of the Axis, especially Italy, to heavy attack.

> *Hansard* 11 Nov. 1942, col. 28 (often misquoted as 'the soft under-belly of the Axis')

1 He [President Roosevelt] devised the extraordinary measure of assistance called Lend-Lease, which will stand forth as the most unselfish and unsordid financial act of any country in all history.

> *Hansard* 17 Apr. 1945, col. 76

2 Unless the right hon. Gentleman [Mr Bevan] changes his policy and methods and moves without the slightest delay, he will be as great a curse to this country in time of peace, as he was a squalid nuisance in time of war.

> *Hansard* 6 Dec. 1945, col. 2544

3 Many forms of Government have been tried, and will be tried in this world of sin and woe. No one pretends that democracy is perfect or all-wise. Indeed, it has been said that democracy is the worst form of Government except all those other forms that have been tried from time to time.

> *Hansard* 11 Nov. 1947, col. 206

4 I cannot forecast to you the action of Russia. It is a riddle wrapped in a mystery inside an enigma: but perhaps there is a key. That key is Russian national interest.

> Radio talk, 1 Oct. 1939, in *Into Battle* (1941) p. 131

5 *Nous attendons l'invasion promise de longue date. Les poissons aussi.*

We are waiting for the long-promised invasion. So are the fishes.

> Radio broadcast to the French people, 21 Oct. 1940, in *Into Battle* (1941) p. 298

6 Shortly after returning from his tour of the Near East, Anthony Eden submitted a long-winded report to the Prime Minister on his experiences and impressions. Churchill, it is told, returned it to his War Minister with a note saying: 'As far as I can see you have used every cliché except "God is Love" and "Please adjust your dress before leaving".'

> *Life* 9 Dec. 1940 (when this story was repeated in the Daily Mirror, Churchill denied that it was true)

7 I wrote my name at the top of the page. I wrote down the number of the question '1'. After much reflection I put a bracket round it thus '(1)'. But thereafter I could not think of anything connected with it that was either relevant or true. ... It was from these slender indications of scholarship that Mr Welldon drew the conclusion that I was worthy to pass into Harrow. It is very much to his credit.

> *My Early Life* (1930) ch. 2

8 By being so long in the lowest form [at Harrow] I gained an immense advantage over the cleverer boys. They all went on to learn Latin and Greek. ... But I was taught English. ... Thus I got into my bones the essential structure of the ordinary British sentence—which is a noble thing. ... Naturally I am biased in favour of boys learning English. I would make them all learn English: and then I would let the clever ones learn Latin as an honour, and Greek as a treat.

> *My Early Life* (1930) ch. 2

9 Headmasters have powers at their disposal with which Prime Ministers have never yet been invested.

> *My Early Life* (1930) ch. 2

10 So they told me how Mr Gladstone read Homer for fun, which I thought served him right.

> *My Early Life* (1930) ch. 2

11 It is a good thing for an uneducated man to read books of quotations.

> *My Early Life* (1930) ch. 9

12 To jaw-jaw is always better than to war-war.

> Speech at White House, 26 June 1954, in *New York Times* 27 June 1954, p. 1

13 I am prepared to meet my Maker. Whether my Maker is prepared for the great ordeal of meeting me is another matter.

> At news conference in Washington, 1954, in *New York Times* 25 Jan. 1965 (Suppl.) p. 7

14 The empires of the future are the empires of the mind.

> Speech at Harvard, 6 Sept. 1943, in *Onwards to Victory* (1944) p. 238

15 It is said that Mr Winston Churchill once made this marginal comment against a sentence that clumsily avoided a prepositional ending: 'This is the sort of English up with which I will not put.'

> Ernest Gowers *Plain Words* (1948) ch. 9

16 Moral of the Work. In war: resolution. In defeat: defiance. In victory: magnanimity. In peace: goodwill.

> *Second World War* (1948) vol. 1, epigraph (Sir Edward Marsh in *A Number of People* (1939) p. 152, says that this motto occurred to Churchill shortly after the First World War)

17 One day President Roosevelt told me that he was asking publicly for suggestions about what the war should be called. I said at once 'The Unnecessary War'.

> *Second World War* (1948) vol. 1, p. viii

18 I felt as if I were walking with destiny, and that all my past life had been but a preparation for this hour and this trial. Eleven years in the political wilderness had freed me from ordinary Party antagonisms. My warnings over the last six years had been so numerous, so detailed, and were now so terribly vindicated, that no one could gainsay me. I could not be reproached either for making the war or with want of preparation for it. I thought I knew a good deal about it all, and I was sure I should not fail. Therefore, although impatient for the morning, I slept soundly and had no need for cheering dreams. Facts are better than dreams.

> *Second World War* (1948) vol. 1, p. 526

19 No one can guarantee success in war, but only deserve it.

> Letter to Lord Wavell, 26 Nov. 1940, in *Second World War* (1949) vol. 2, ch. 27

20 It may almost be said, 'Before Alamein we never had a victory. After Alamein we never had a defeat.'

> *Second World War* (1951) vol. 4, ch. 33

21 Dictators ride to and fro upon tigers which they dare not dismount. And the tigers are getting hungry.

> Letter, 11 Nov. 1937, in *Step by Step* (1939) p. 186. Cf. the proverb 'He who rides a tiger is afraid to dismount' (see *Concise Oxford Dictionary of Proverbs* under *rides*)

1 You must rank me and my colleagues as strong partisans of national compulsory insurance for all classes for all purposes from the cradle to the grave.
Radio broadcast, 21 Mar. 1943, in *The Times* 22 Mar. 1943

2 I have never accepted what many people have kindly said—namely, that I inspired the nation. . . . It was the nation and the race dwelling all round the globe that had the lion's heart. I had the luck to be called upon to give the roar. I also hope that I sometimes suggested to the lion the right place to use his claws.
Speech at Westminster Hall, 30 Nov. 1954, in *The Times* 1 Dec. 1954

3 Mr Attlee, whom Churchill once playfully described as a 'sheep in sheep's clothing'.
Lord Home *Way the Wind Blows* (1976) ch. 6. Cf. Sir Edmund Gosse

4 Take away that pudding—it has no theme.
In Lord Home *Way the Wind Blows* (1976) ch. 16

5 We are all worms. But I do believe that I am a glow-worm.
In Violet Bonham-Carter *Winston Churchill as I Knew Him* (1965) ch. 1

6 Jellicoe was the only man on either side who could lose the war in an afternoon.
World Crisis (1927) pt. 1, ch. 5

Count Galeazzo Ciano 1903–1944

7 *La vittoria trova cento padri, e nessuno vuole riconoscere l'insuccesso.*

Victory has a hundred fathers, but defeat is an orphan.
Diary 9 Sept. 1942 (1946) vol. 2, p. 196

Brian Clark 1932–

8 Whose life is it anyway?
Title of play (1977)

Kenneth Clark (Baron Clark) 1903–1983

9 Perrault's façade [of the Louvre] reflects the triumph of an authoritarian state, and of those logical solutions that Colbert, the great administrator of the seventeenth century, was imposing on politics, economics and every department of contemporary life, including, above all, the arts. This gives French Classical architecture a certain inhumanity. It was the work not of craftsmen, but of wonderfully gifted civil servants.
Civilization (1969) ch. 9

Arthur C. Clarke 1917–

10 If an elderly but distinguished scientist says that something is possible he is almost certainly right, but if he says that it is impossible he is very probably wrong.
In *New Yorker* 9 Aug. 1969

Grant Clarke 1891–1931 and Edgar Leslie 1885–1976

11 He'd have to get under, get out and get under And fix up his automobile.
He'd Have to Get Under—Get Out and Get Under (1913 song; music by Maurice Abrahams)

Eldridge Cleaver 1935–

12 What we're saying today is that you're either part of the solution or you're part of the problem.
Speech in San Francisco, 1968, in R. Scheer *Eldridge Cleaver, Post Prison Writings and Speeches* (1969) p. xxxii

John Cleese 1939–

See GRAHAM CHAPMAN *et al.*

John Cleese 1939– and Connie Booth

13 They're Germans. Don't mention the war.
Fawlty Towers 'The Germans' (BBC TV programme, 1975), in *Complete Fawlty Towers* (1988) p. 153

14 So Harry says, 'You don't like me any more. Why not?' And he says, 'Because you've got so terribly pretentious.' And Harry says, 'Pretentious? *Moi?*'
Fawlty Towers 'The Psychiatrist' (BBC TV programme, 1979), in *Complete Fawlty Towers* (1988) p. 190

Sarah Norcliffe Cleghorn 1876–1959

15 The golf-links lie so near the mill
That almost every day
The labouring children can look out
And watch the men at play.
New York Tribune 23 Jan. 1914 'For Some Must Watch, While—'

Georges Clemenceau 1841–1929

16 *La guerre, c'est une chose trop grave pour la confier à des militaires.*

War is too serious a matter to entrust to military men.
Attributed to Clemenceau e.g. in Hampden Jackson *Clemenceau and the Third Republic* (1946) p. 228, but also attributed to Briand and Talleyrand

17 *Politique intérieure, je fais la guerre; politique extérieure, je fais toujours la guerre. Je fais toujours la guerre .*

My home policy: I wage war; my foreign policy: I wage war. All the time I wage war.
Speech to French Chamber of Deputies, 8 Mar. 1918, in *Discours de Guerre* (War Speeches, 1968) p. 172

18 *Il est plus facile de faire la guerre que la paix.*

It is easier to make war than to make peace.
Speech at Verdun, 20 July 1919, in *Discours de Paix* (Peace Speeches, 1938) p. 122

Harlan Cleveland 1918–

19 In 1950 he [Harlan Cleveland] invented the phrase, so thrashed to death in later years, 'the revolution of rising expectations'.
Arthur Schlesinger *Thousand Days* (1965) ch. 16

Richard Cobb 1917–

1 In an operation of this kind one would not go for a Proust or a Joyce—not that I would know about that, never having read either.
   Speech at Booker Prize awards in London, 18 Oct. 1984, in *The Times* 19 Oct. 1984

Claud Cockburn 1904–

2 Small earthquake in Chile. Not many dead.
   In Time of Trouble (1956) ch. 10 (the words with which Cockburn claims to have won a competition at *The Times* for the dullest headline)

Jean Cocteau 1889–1963

3 *Le tact dans l'audace c'est de savoir jusqu'où on peut aller trop loin.*

   Being tactful in audacity is knowing how far one can go too far.
   Le Coq et l'Arlequin (1918) in *Le Rappel à l'ordre* (Recall to Order, 1926) p. 2

4 *Le pire drame pour un poète, c'est d'être admiré par malentendu.*

   The worst tragedy for a poet is to be admired through being misunderstood.
   Le Coq et l'Arlequin (1918) in *Le Rappel à l'ordre* (Recall to Order, 1926) p. 20

5 *S'il faut choisir un crucifié, la foule sauve toujours Barabbas.*

   If it has to choose who is to be crucified, the crowd will always save Barabbas.
   Le Coq et l'Arlequin (1918) in *Le Rappel à l'ordre* (Recall to Order, 1926) p. 39

6 *L'Histoire est un alliage de réel et de mensonge. Le réel de l'Histoire devient un mensonge. L'irréel de la fable devient vérité .*

   History is a combination of reality and lies. The reality of History becomes a lie. The unreality of the fable becomes the truth.
   Journal d'un inconnu (Diary of an Unknown Man, 1953) p. 143

7 *Vivre est une chute horizontale.*

   Life is a horizontal fall.
   Opium (1930) p. 37

8 *Quand j'ai écrit que Victor Hugo était un fou qui se croyait Victor Hugo, je ne plaisantais pas.*

   When I wrote that Victor Hugo was a madman who thought he was Victor Hugo, I was not joking.
   Opium (1930) p. 77

Lenore Coffee ?1897–1984

9 What a dump!
   Beyond the Forest (1949 film; line spoken by Bette Davis, entering a room)

George M. Cohan 1878–1942

10 It was Cohan who first said to a newspaperman (who wanted some information about *Broadway Jones* in 1912), 'I don't care what you say about me, as long as you say *something* about me, and as long as you spell my name right.'
   John McCabe *George M. Cohan* (1973) ch. 13

11 Give my regards to Broadway,
   Remember me to Herald Square,
   Tell all the gang at Forty-Second Street
   That I will soon be there.
   Give My Regards to Broadway (1904 song)

12 Over there, over there,
   Send the word, send the word over there
   That the Yanks are coming, the Yanks are coming,
   The drums rum-tumming everywhere.
   So prepare, say a prayer,
   Send the word, send the word to beware.
   We'll be over, we're coming over
   And we won't come back till it's over, over there.
   Over There (1917 song)

13 I'm a Yankee Doodle Dandy,
   A Yankee Doodle, do or die;
   A real live nephew of my Uncle Sam's,
   Born on the fourth of July.
   I've got a Yankee Doodle sweetheart,
   She's my Yankee Doodle joy.
   Yankee Doodle came to London,
   Just to ride the ponies;
   I am the Yankee Doodle Boy.
   Yankee Doodle Boy (1904 song)

Desmond Coke 1879–1931

14 His blade struck the water a full second before any other: the lad had started well. Nor did he flag as the race wore on: as the others tired, he seemed to grow more fresh, until at length, as the boats began to near the winning-post, his oar was dipping into the water nearly twice as often as any other.
   Sandford of Merton (1903) ch. 12 (often misquoted as 'All rowed fast, but none so fast as stroke')

Colette (Sidonie-Gabrielle Colette) 1873–1954

15 *Il découvrait . . . le monde des émotions qu'on nomme, à la légère, physiques.*

   He was discovering . . . the world of the emotions that are so lightly called physical.
   Le Blé en herbe (Ripening Seed, 1923) p. 161

16 *Quand elle lève ses paupières, on dirait qu'elle se déshabille.*

   When she raises her eyelids, it is as if she is undressing.
   Claudine s'en va (Claudine Goes Away, 1931) p. 59

17 *Ne porte jamais de bijoux artistiques, ça déconsidère complètement une femme.*

   Don't ever wear artistic jewellery; it wrecks a woman's reputation.
   Gigi (1944) p. 40

R. G. Collingwood 1889–1943

1 Perfect freedom is reserved for the man who lives by his own work and in that work does what he wants to do.
Speculum Mentis (1924) p. 25

Charles Collins and Fred W. Leigh

2 My old man said, 'Follow the van,
Don't dilly-dally on the way!'
Off went the cart with the home packed in it,
I walked behind with my old cock linnet.
But I dillied and dallied, dallied and dillied,
Lost the van and don't know where to roam.
You can't trust the 'specials' like the old time 'coppers'
When you can't find your way home.
Don't Dilly-Dally on the Way (1919 song; made famous by Marie Lloyd)

Charles Collins and Fred Murray

3 Boiled beef and carrots.
Title of song (1910; made famous by Harry Champion)

Charles Collins, E. A. Sheppard, and Fred Terry

4 Any old iron, any old iron,
Any any old old iron?
You look neat
Talk about a treat,
You look dapper from your napper to your feet.
Dressed in style, brand new tile,
And your father's old green tie on,
But I wouldn't give you tuppence for your old watch chain;
Old iron, old iron?
Any Old Iron (1911 song; made famous by Harry Champion; the second line is often sung as 'Any any any old iron?')

John Churton Collins 1848–1908

5 To ask advice is in nine cases out of ten to tout for flattery.
In L. C. Collins *Life of John Churton Collins* (1912) p. 316

Michael Collins 1890–1922

6 Think—what I have got for Ireland? Something which she has wanted these past seven hundred years. Will anyone be satisfied at the bargain? Will anyone? I tell you this—early this morning I signed my death warrant. I thought at the time how odd, how ridiculous—a bullet may just as well have done the job five years ago.
Letter, 6 Dec. 1921, in T. R. Dwyer *Michael Collins and the Treaty* (1981) ch. 4

Betty Comden 1919– and Adolph Green 1915–

7 New York, New York,—a helluva town,
The Bronx is up but the Battery's down,

And people ride in a hole in the ground:
New York, New York,—It's a helluva town.
New York, New York (1945 song; music by Leonard Bernstein)

8 The party's over.
Title of song (1956; music by Jule Styne)

Dame Ivy Compton-Burnett 1884–1969

9 'Well, of course, people are only human,' said Dudley to his brother, as they walked to the house behind the women. 'But it really does not seem much for them to be.'
A Family and a Fortune (1939) ch. 2

10 There are different kinds of wrong. The people sinned against are not always the best.
The Mighty and their Fall (1961) ch. 7

11 There is more difference within the sexes than between them.
Mother and Son (1955) ch. 10

12 As regards plots I find real life no help at all. Real life seems to have no plots.
In R. Lehmann et al. *Orion I* (1945) p. 25

Billy Connolly 1942–

13 Marriage is a wonderful invention; but, then again, so is a bicycle repair kit.
In Duncan Campbell *Billy Connolly* (1976) p. 92

Cyril Connolly 1903–1974

14 Literature is the art of writing something that will be read twice; journalism what will be read once.
Enemies of Promise (1938) ch. 3

15 As repressed sadists are supposed to become policemen or butchers, so those with an irrational fear of life become publishers.
Enemies of Promise (1938) ch. 10

16 Whom the gods wish to destroy they first call promising.
Enemies of Promise (1938) ch. 13

17 There is no more sombre enemy of good art than the pram in the hall.
Enemies of Promise (1938) ch. 14

18 All charming people have something to conceal, usually their total dependence on the appreciation of others.
Enemies of Promise (1938) ch. 16

19 I have called this style the Mandarin style, since it is beloved by literary pundits, by those who would make the written word as unlike as possible to the spoken one. It is the style of those writers whose tendency is to make their language convey more than they mean or more than they feel, it is the style of most artists and all humbugs.
Enemies of Promise (1938) ch. 20

1 In the eighteenth century he [Alec Douglas-Home] would have become Prime Minister before he was thirty; as it was he appeared honourably ineligible for the struggle of life.
Enemies of Promise (1938) ch. 23

2 Were I to deduce any system from my feelings on leaving Eton, it might be called *The Theory of Permanent Adolescence.*
Enemies of Promise (1938) ch. 24

3 It is closing time in the gardens of the West and from now on an artist will be judged only by the resonance of his solitude or the quality of his despair.
Horizon Dec. 1949—Jan. 1950, p. 362

4 Better to write for yourself and have no public, than to write for the public and have no self.
New Statesman 25 Feb. 1933

5 Destroy him as you will, the bourgeois always bounces up—execute him, expropriate him, starve him out *en masse*, and he reappears in your children.
In *Observer* 7 Mar. 1937

6 He [George Orwell] could not blow his nose without moralising on the state of the handkerchief industry.
Sunday Times 29 Sept. 1968

7 The more books we read, the sooner we perceive that the only function of a writer is to produce a masterpiece. No other task is of any consequence.
Unquiet Grave (1944) pt. 1

8 There is no fury like a woman looking for a new lover.
Unquiet Grave (1944) pt. 1. Cf. *Oxford Dictionary of Quotations* (1979) 160:15

9 In the sex-war thoughtlessness is the weapon of the male, vindictiveness of the female.
Unquiet Grave (1944) pt. 1

10 Life is a maze in which we take the wrong turning before we have learnt to walk.
Unquiet Grave (1944) pt. 1

11 The civilization of one epoch becomes the manure of the next. Everything over-ripens in the same way. The disasters of the world are due to its inhabitants not being able to grow old simultaneously.
Unquiet Grave (1944) pt. 2

12 Imprisoned in every fat man a thin one is wildly signalling to be let out.
Unquiet Grave (1944) pt. 2. See also George Orwell 164:11

13 The true index of a man's character is the health of his wife.
Unquiet Grave (1944) pt. 2

14 We are all serving a life-sentence in the dungeon of self.
Unquiet Grave (1944) pt. 2

15 Peeling off the kilometres to the tune of 'Blue Skies', sizzling down the long black liquid reaches of Nationale Sept, the plane trees going sha-sha-sha through the open window, the windscreen yellowing with crushed midges, she with the Michelin beside me, a handkerchief binding her hair.
Unquiet Grave (1944) pt. 3

16 Our memories are card-indexes consulted, and then put back in disorder by authorities whom we do not control.
Unquiet Grave (1944) pt. 3

James Connolly 1868–1916

17 The worker is the slave of capitalist society, the female worker is the slave of that slave.
Re-conquest of Ireland (1915) p. 38

Joseph Conrad (*Teodor Josef Konrad Korzeniowski*) 1857–1924

18 In plucking the fruit of memory one runs the risk of spoiling its bloom.
Arrow of Gold (author's note, 1920, to 1924 Uniform Edition) p. viii

19 The conquest of the earth, which mostly means the taking it away from those who have a different complexion or slightly flatter noses than ourselves, is not a pretty thing when you look into it.
Heart of Darkness ch. 1, in *Youth* (1902)

20 We live, as we dream—alone.
Heart of Darkness ch. 1, in *Youth* (1902)

21 Exterminate all the brutes!
Heart of Darkness ch. 2, in *Youth* (1902)

22 He [Kurtz] cried in a whisper at some image, at some vision,—he cried out twice, a cry that was no more than a breath—'The horror! The horror!'
Heart of Darkness ch. 3, in *Youth* (1902)

23 Mistah Kurtz—he dead.
Heart of Darkness ch. 3, in *Youth* (1902)

24 A man that is born falls into a dream like a man who falls into the sea. If he tries to climb out into the air as inexperienced people endeavour to do, he drowns—*nicht wahr?* . . . No! I tell you! The way is to the destructive element submit yourself, and with the exertions of your hands and feet in the water make the deep, deep sea keep you up. . . . In the destructive element immerse. . . . That was the way. To follow the dream, and again to follow the dream—and so—*ewig*—*usque ad finem.*
Lord Jim (1900) ch. 20

25 You shall judge of a man by his foes as well as by his friends.
Lord Jim (1900) ch. 34

26 Any work that aspires, however humbly, to the condition of art should carry its justification in every line.
The Nigger of the Narcissus, author's note, in *New Review* Dec. 1897

27 Action is consolatory. It is the enemy of thought and the friend of flattering illusions.
Nostromo (1904) pt. 1, ch. 6

28 It's only those who do nothing that make no mistakes, I suppose.
Outcast of the Islands (1896) pt. 3, ch. 2

29 The terrorist and the policeman both come from the same basket.
Secret Agent (1907) ch. 4

1 All ambitions are lawful except those which climb upwards on the miseries or credulities of mankind.

> *Some Reminiscences* (1912; in USA entitled 'A Personal Record') p. 19

2 The scrupulous and the just, the noble, humane, and devoted natures; the unselfish and the intelligent may begin a movement—but it passes away from them. They are not the leaders of a revolution. They are its victims.

> *Under Western Eyes* (1911) pt. 2, ch. 3

3 A belief in a supernatural source of evil is not necessary; men alone are quite capable of every wickedness.

> *Under Western Eyes* (1911) pt. 2, ch. 4

4 I remember my youth and the feeling that will never come back any more—the feeling that I could last for ever, outlast the sea, the earth, and all men; the deceitful feeling that lures us on to joys, to perils, to love, to vain effort—to death; the triumphant conviction of strength, the heat of life in the handful of dust, the glow in the heart that with every year grows dim, grows cold, grows small, and expires—and expires, too soon, too soon—before life itself.

> *Youth* (1902) p. 41

Shirley Conran 1932–

5 OUR MOTTO: *Life is too short to stuff a mushroom.*

> *Superwoman* (1975) p. 15

6 First things first, second things never.

> *Superwoman* (1975) p. 157

A. J. Cook 1885–1931

7 Not a penny off the pay, not a second on the day.

> Speech at York, 3 Apr. 1926, in *The Times* 5 Apr. 1926 (referring to miners' slogan)

Dan Cook

8 The opera ain't over 'til the fat lady sings.

> In *Washington Post* 3 June 1978

Peter Cook 1937–

9 I have recently been travelling round the world—on your behalf, and at your expense—visiting some of the chaps with whom I hope to be shaping your future. I went first to Germany, and there I spoke with the German Foreign Minister, Herr ... Herr and there, and we exchanged many frank words in our respective languages.

> *Beyond the Fringe* (1961 revue) 'TVPM', in Roger Wilmut *Complete Beyond the Fringe* (1987) p. 54

10 Yes, I could have been a judge but I never had the Latin, never had the Latin for the judging, I just never had sufficient of it to get through the rigorous judging exams. They're noted for their rigour. People come staggering out saying, 'My God, what a rigorous exam'—and so I became a miner instead.

> *Beyond the Fringe* (1961 revue) 'Sitting on the Bench', in Roger Wilmut *Complete Beyond the Fringe* (1987) p. 97

Calvin Coolidge 1872–1933

11 Shortly after Mr Coolidge had gone to the White House, Mrs Coolidge was unable to go to church with him one Sunday. At lunch she asked what the sermon was about. 'Sins,' he said. 'Well, what did he say about sin?' 'He was against it.'

> John H. McKee *Coolidge: Wit and Wisdom* (1933) p. 4 (but Edward C. Lathem's *Meet Calvin Coolidge* (1960) p. 151 quotes Mrs Coolidge as saying that this was one of 'the stories which might reasonably be attributed to him [Coolidge] but which did not originate with him')

12 Mr Coolidge ... interrupted a discussion of cancellation of the war debts with: 'Well, they hired the money, didn't they?'

> John H. McKee *Coolidge: Wit and Wisdom* (1933) p. 118

13 There is no right to strike against the public safety by anybody, anywhere, any time.

> Telegram to Samuel Gompers, 14 Sept. 1919, in *Have Faith in Massachusetts* (1919) p. 223

14 Civilization and profits go hand in hand.

> Speech in New York, 27 Nov. 1920, in *New York Times* 28 Nov. 1920, p. 20

15 The chief business of the American people is business.

> Speech in Washington, 17 Jan. 1925, in *New York Times* 18 Jan. 1925, p. 19

16 I do not choose to run for President in nineteen twenty-eight.

> Statement issued at Rapid City, South Dakota, 2 Aug. 1927, in *New York Times* 3 Aug. 1927, p. 1

Ananda Coomaraswamy 1877–1947

17 The artist is not a special kind of man, but every man is a special kind of artist.

> *Transformation of Nature in Art* (1934) ch. 2

Alfred Duff Cooper (Viscount Norwich) 1890–1954

18 I really did enjoy Belvoir you know. ... You must I think have enjoyed it too, with your two stout lovers frowning at one another across the hearth rug, while your small, but perfectly formed one kept the party in a roar.

> Letter to Lady Diana Manners, Oct. 1914, in Artemis Cooper *Durable Fire* (1983) p. 17

Tommy Cooper 1921–1984

19 Just like that!

> Title of autobiography (1975), from his catch-phrase.

Wendy Cope 1945–

20 I used to think all poets were Byronic—
Mad, bad and dangerous to know.
And then I met a few. Yes it's ironic—
I used to think all poets were Byronic.
They're mostly wicked as a ginless tonic
And wild as pension plans.

> *Making Cocoa for Kingsley Amis* (1986) 'Triolet'. Cf. *Oxford Dictionary of Quotations* (1979) 306:25

1 It's nice to meet serious people
And hear them explain their views:
Your concern for the rights of women
Is especially welcome news.

I'm sure you'd never exploit one;
I expect you'd rather be dead;
I'm thoroughly convinced of it—
Now can we go to bed?

Making Cocoa for Kingsley Amis (1986) 'From June to December'

2 There are so many kinds of awful men—
One can't avoid them all. She often said
She'd never make the same mistake again:
She always made a new mistake instead.

Making Cocoa for Kingsley Amis (1986) 'Rondeau Redoublé'

3 It was a dream I had last week
And some kind of record seemed vital.
I knew it wouldn't be much of a poem
But I love the title.

Making Cocoa for Kingsley Amis (1986) title-poem

Aaron Copland 1900–1990

4 The whole problem can be stated quite simply by asking, 'Is there a meaning to music?' My answer to that would be, 'Yes.' And 'Can you state in so many words what the meaning is?' My answer to that would be, 'No.'

What to Listen for in Music (1939) ch. 2

Bernard Cornfeld 1927–

5 Do you sincerely want to be rich?

Question often asked by Cornfeld of salesmen in the 1960s, in Charles Raw et al. *Do You Sincerely Want to be Rich?* (1971) p. 67

Frances Cornford 1886–1960

6 Whoso maintains that I am humbled now
(Who wait the Awful Day) is still a liar;
I hope to meet my Maker brow to brow
And find my own the higher.

Collected Poems (1954) 'Epitaph for a Reviewer'

7 A young Apollo, golden-haired,
Stands dreaming on the verge of strife,
Magnificently unprepared
For the long littleness of life.

Poems (1910) 'Youth'

8 O why do you walk through the fields in gloves,
Missing so much and so much?
O fat white woman whom nobody loves,
Why do you walk through the fields in gloves,
When the grass is soft as the breast of doves
And shivering-sweet to the touch?
O why do you walk through the fields in gloves,
Missing so much and so much?

Poems (1910) 'To a Fat Lady seen from the Train'. Cf. G. K. Chesterton 51:8

9 How long ago Hector took off his plume,
Not wanting that his little son should cry,
Then kissed his sad Andromache goodbye—
And now we three in Euston waiting-room.

Travelling Home (1948) 'Parting in Wartime'

Francis Macdonald Cornford 1874–1943

10 If you persist to the threshold of old age—your fiftieth year, let us say—you will be a powerful person yourself, with an accretion of peculiarities which other people will have to study in order to square you. The toes you will have trodden on by this time will be as sands on the sea-shore; and from far below you will mount the roar of a ruthless multitude of young men in a hurry. You may perhaps grow to be aware what they are in a hurry to do. They are in a hurry to get you out of the way.

Microcosmographia Academica (1908) p. 2

11 Every public action, which is not customary, either is wrong, or, if it is right, is a dangerous precedent. It follows that nothing should ever be done for the first time.

Microcosmographia Academica (1908) p. 28

Baron Pierre de Coubertin 1863–1937

12 *L'important dans la vie ce n'est point le triomphe mais le combat; l'essentiel ce n'est pas d'avoir vaincu mais de s'être bien battu.*

The important thing in life is not the victory but the contest; the essential thing is not to have won but to be well beaten.

Speech at government banquet in London, 24 July 1908, in T. A. Cook *Fourth Olympiad* (1909) p. 793

Émile Coué 1857–1926

13 *Tous les jours, à tous points de vue, je vais de mieux en mieux.*

Every day, in every way, I am getting better and better.

De la suggestion et de ses applications (On Suggestion and its Applications, 1915) p. 17 (Coué advised his patients to repeat this phrase 15 to 20 times, morning and evening)

Noël Coward 1899–1973

14 Let's drink to the spirit of gallantry and courage that made a strange Heaven out of unbelievable Hell, and let's drink to the hope that one day this country of ours, which we love so much, will find dignity and greatness and peace again.

Cavalcade (1932) act 3

15 Dance, dance, dance, little lady!
Dance, dance, dance, little lady!
Leave tomorrow behind.

Dance, Little Lady (1928 song)

16 Don't let's be beastly to the Germans
When our Victory is ultimately won.

Don't Let's Be Beastly to the Germans (1943 song)

17 I believe that since my life began
The most I've had is just
A talent to amuse.
Heigho, if love were all!

If Love Were All (1929 song)

18 I'll see you again,
Whenever Spring breaks through again.

I'll See You Again (1929 song)

1 Dear 338171 (May I call you 338?)
  Letter to T. E. Lawrence, 25 Aug. 1930, in D. Garnett (ed.)
  Letters of T. E. Lawrence (1938) p. 696

2 London Pride has been handed down to us.
  London Pride is a flower that's free.
  London Pride means our own dear town to us,
  And our pride it for ever will be.
  London Pride (1941 song)

3 Mad about the boy,
  It's pretty funny but I'm mad about the boy.
  He has a gay appeal
  That makes me feel
  There may be something sad about the boy.
  Mad about the Boy (1932 song)

4 Mad dogs and Englishmen
  Go out in the midday sun.
  The Japanese don't care to,
  The Chinese wouldn't dare to,
  The Hindus and Argentines sleep firmly from twelve to
    one,
  But Englishmen detest a siesta.
  In the Philippines, there are lovely screens
  To protect you from the glare;
  In the Malay states, they have hats like plates
  Which the Britishers won't wear.
  At twelve noon, the natives swoon,
  And no further work is done;
  But mad dogs and Englishmen go out in the midday
    sun.
  Mad Dogs and Englishmen (1931 song)

5 Don't put your daughter on the stage, Mrs
    Worthington,
  Don't put your daughter on the stage.
  Mrs Worthington (1935 song)

6 Poor little rich girl
  You're a bewitched girl,
  Better beware!
  Poor Little Rich Girl (1925 song)

7 Extraordinary how potent cheap music is.
  Private Lives (1930) act 1 (in a gramophone recording also
  made in 1930, Gertrude Lawrence spoke the line as 'Strange
  how potent cheap music is')

8 AMANDA: I've been brought up to believe that it's
    beyond the pale, for a man to strike a woman.
  ELYOT: A very poor tradition. Certain women should be
    struck regularly, like gongs.
  Private Lives (1930) act 3

9 Someday I'll find you,
  Moonlight behind you,
  True to the dream I am dreaming.
  Someday I'll Find You (1930 song)

10 Dear Mrs A.,
   Hooray, hooray,
   At last you are deflowered.
   On this as every other day
   I love you—Noel Coward.
   *Telegram to Gertrude Lawrence, 5 July 1940 (the day after
   her wedding), in Gertrude Lawrence A Star Danced* (1945)
   p. 201

11 The Stately Homes of England,
   How beautiful they stand,
   To prove the upper classes

Have still the upper hand;
Though the fact that they have to be rebuilt
And frequently mortgaged to the hilt
Is inclined to take the gilt
Off the gingerbread,
And certainly damps the fun
Of the eldest son.
The Stately Homes of England (1938 song). Cf. *Oxford
Dictionary of Quotations* (1979) 244:21

12 Tho' the pipes that supply the bathroom burst
   And the lavatory makes you fear the worst,
   It was used by Charles the First
   Quite informally,
   And later by George the Fourth
   On a journey North.
   The Stately Homes of England (1938 song)

13 The Stately Homes of England,
   Tho' rather in the lurch,
   Provide a lot of chances
   For Psychical Research—
   There's the ghost of a crazy younger son
   Who murdered, in thirteen fifty-one,
   An extremely rowdy Nun
   Who resented it,
   And people who come to call
   Meet her in the hall.
   The Stately Homes of England (1938 song)

Hart Crane 1899–1932

14 Cowslip and shad-blow, flaked like tethered foam
   Around bared teeth of stallions, bloomed that spring
   When first I read thy lines, rife as the loam
   Of prairies, yet like breakers cliffward leaping!
   ... My hand
   in yours,
   Walt Whitman—
   so—
   The Bridge (1930) pt. 4

15 O Sleepless as the river under thee,
   Vaulting the sea, the prairies' dreaming sod,
   Unto us lowliest sometime sweep, descend
   And of the curveship lend a myth to God.
   Dial June 1927, p. 490 'To Brooklyn Bridge'

16 You who desired so much—in vain to ask—
   Yet fed your hunger like an endless task,
   Dared dignify the labor, bless the quest—
   Achieved that stillness ultimately best,

   Being, of all, least sought for: Emily, hear!
   Nation 29 June 1927, p. 718 'To Emily Dickinson'

James Creelman 1901–1941 and Ruth Rose

17 Oh no, it wasn't the aeroplanes. It was Beauty killed
   the Beast.
   King Kong (1933 film; final words)

Bishop Mandell Creighton 1843–1901

18 No people do so much harm as those who go about
   doing good.
   In Louise Creighton Life (1904) vol. 2, p. 503

Quentin Crisp 1908–

1 There was no need to do any housework at all. After the first four years the dirt doesn't get any worse.
Naked Civil Servant (1968) ch. 15

2 I became one of the stately homos of England.
Naked Civil Servant (1968) ch. 24

3 An autobiography is an obituary in serial form with the last instalment missing.
Naked Civil Servant (1968) ch. 29

Julian Critchley 1930–

4 The only safe pleasure for a parliamentarian is a bag of boiled sweets.
Listener 10 June 1982

5 She [Margaret Thatcher] has been beastly to the Bank of England, has demanded that the BBC 'set its house in order' and tends to believe the worst of the Foreign and Commonwealth Office. She cannot see an institution without hitting it with her handbag.
The Times 21 June 1982

Richmal Crompton (Richmal Crompton Lamburn) 1890–1969

6 'If anyone trith to hang me,' said Violet Elizabeth complacently, 'I'll thcream and thcream and thcream till I'm thick. I can.'
Still—William (1925) ch. 8

Bing Crosby (Harry Lillis Crosby) 1903–1977

7 Half joking, he [Crosby] asked that his epitaph read, 'He was an average guy who could carry a tune.'
Newsweek 24 Oct. 1977, p. 102

Bing Crosby 1903–1977, Roy Turk 1892–1934, and Fred Ahlert 1892–1933

8 Where the blue of the night
Meets the gold of the day,
Someone waits for me.
Where the Blue of the Night (1931 song)

Richard Crossman 1907–1974

9 The Civil Service is profoundly deferential—'Yes, Minister! No, Minister! If you wish it, Minister!'
Diary, 22 Oct. 1964, in *Diaries of a Cabinet Minister* (1975) vol. 1, p. 21

Aleister Crowley 1875–1947

10 Do what thou wilt shall be the whole of the Law.
Book of the Law (1909) l. 40. Cf. *Oxford Dictionary of Quotations* (1979) 403:28

Leslie Crowther 1933–

11 Come on down!
Catch-phrase in 'The Price is Right', ITV programme, 1984 onwards.

Robert Crumb 1943–

12 Keep on truckin'.
Catch-phrase used in cartoons from *c*.1972

Bruce Frederick Cummings

See W. N. P. Barbellion

e. e. cummings 1894–1962

13 anyone lived in a pretty how town
(with up so floating many bells down)
spring summer autumn winter
he sang his didn't he danced his did.
50 Poems (1949) no. 29

14 Humanity i love you because
when you're hard up you pawn your
intelligence to buy a drink.
XLI Poems (1925) 'La Guerre', no. 2

15 'next to of course god america i
love you land of the pilgrims' and so forth oh
say can you see by the dawn's early my
country 'tis of centuries come and go
and are no more what of it we should worry
in every language even deafanddumb
thy sons acclaim your glorious name by gorry
by jingo by gee by gosh by gum
why talk of beauty what could be more beautiful than these heroic happy dead
who rushed like lions to the roaring slaughter
they did not stop to think they died instead
then shall the voices of liberty be mute?

He spoke. And drank rapidly a glass of water.
is 5 (1926) p. 62

16 Buffalo Bill's
defunct
who used to
ride a watersmooth-silver
stallion
and break onetwothreefourfive pigeons-
justlikethat
Jesus
he was a handsome man
and what i want to know is
how do you like your blueeyed boy
Mister Death.
Tulips and Chimneys (1923) 'Portraits' no. 8

17 the Cambridge ladies who live in furnished souls
are unbeautiful and have comfortable minds.
Tulips and Chimneys (1923) 'Sonnets-Realities' no. 1

18 (i do not know what it is about you that closes
and opens; only something in me understands
the voice of your eyes is deeper than all noses)
nobody, not even the rain, has such small hands.
W (1931) 'somewhere I have never travelled'

1 a politician is an arse upon
which everyone has sat except a man.
1 × 1 (1944) no. 10

2 pity this busy monster, manunkind,
not. Progress is a comfortable disease.
1 × 1 (1944) no. 14

3 We doctors know
a hopeless case if—listen: there's a hell
of a good universe next door; let's go.
1 × 1 (1944) no. 14

William Thomas Cummings 1903–1945

4 There are no atheists in the foxholes.
In Carlos P. Romulo *I Saw the Fall of the Philippines* (1943) ch. 15

Will Cuppy 1884–1949

5 The Dodo never had a chance. He seems to have been invented for the sole purpose of becoming extinct and that was all he was good for.
How to Become Extinct (1941) p. 163

Edwina Currie 1946–

6 Good Christian people who wouldn't dream of misbehaving will not catch Aids. My message to the businessmen of this country when they go abroad on business is that there is one thing above all they can take with them to stop them catching Aids—and that is the wife.
Speech at Runcorn, 12 Feb. 1987, in *Guardian* 13 Feb. 1987

7 We have problems here of high smoking and alcoholism. Some of these problems are things we can tackle by impressing on people the need to look after themselves better. That is something which is taken more seriously down South. . . . I honestly don't think the problem has anything to do with poverty. . . . The problem very often for people is, I think, just ignorance and failing to realise that they do have some control over their lives.
Speech at Newcastle upon Tyne, 23 Sept. 1986, in *Guardian* 24 Sept. 1986

Michael Curtiz 1888–1962

8 Bring on the empty horses!
In David Niven *Bring on the Empty Horses* (1975) ch. 6 (said while Curtiz was directing the 1936 film, *The Charge of the Light Brigade*)

Lord Curzon (George Nathaniel Curzon, Marquess Curzon of Kedleston) 1859–1925

9 Not even a public figure. A man of no experience. And of the utmost insignificance.
In Harold Nicolson *Curzon: the Last Phase* (1934) ch. 12 (said of Stanley Baldwin on his being appointed Prime Minister in 1923)

10 The Domestic Bursar of Balliol (according to his own story) sent Curzon a specimen menu [for a luncheon for Queen Mary in 1921], beginning with soup. The menu

came back with one sentence written across the corner in Curzon's large and old-fashioned hand: 'Gentlemen do not take soup at luncheon.'
E. L. Woodward *Short Journey* (1942) ch. 7

11 Dear me, I never knew that the lower classes had such white skins.
In K. Rose *Superior Person* (1969) ch. 12 (words supposedly said by Curzon when watching troops bathing during the First World War)

Paul Daniels 1938–

12 You're going to like this . . . not a lot . . . but you'll like it!
Catch-phrase used in his conjuring act, especially on television from 1981 onwards

Charles Brace Darrow 1889–1967

13 Go to jail. Go directly to jail. Do not pass go. Do not collect £200.
Instructions on 'Community Chest' card in the game 'Monopoly', invented by Darrow in 1931

Clarence Darrow 1857–1938

14 When I was a boy I was told that anybody could become President. I'm beginning to believe it.
In Irving Stone *Clarence Darrow for the Defence* (1941) ch. 6

15 I do not consider it an insult, but rather a compliment to be called an agnostic. I do not pretend to know where many ignorant men are sure—that is all that agnosticism means.
Speech at trial of John Thomas Scopes, 15 July 1925, in *The World's Most Famous Court Trial* (1925) ch. 4

Sir Francis Darwin 1848–1925

16 In science the credit goes to the man who convinces the world, not to the man to whom the idea first occurs.
Eugenics Review Apr. 1914, 'Francis Galton'

Jules Dassin 1911–

17 Ποτέ τήν Κυριακή.

Never on Sunday.
Title of film (1959)

Worton David and Lawrence Wright

18 Not tonight, Josephine.
Title of song (1915; popularized by Florrie Forde)

Jack Davies and Ken Annakin

19 Those magnificent men in their flying machines, or How I flew from London to Paris in 25 hours and 11 minutes.
Title of film (1965)

W. H. Davies 1871–1940

20 A rainbow and a cuckoo's song
May never come together again;

May never come
This side the tomb.
  Bird of Paradise (1914) 'A Great Time'

1 And hear the pleasant cuckoo, loud and long—
The simple bird that thinks two notes a song.
  Child Lovers (1916) 'April's Charms'

2 Girls scream,
Boys shout;
Dogs bark,
School's out.
  Complete Poems (1963) 'School's Out'

3 It was the Rainbow gave thee birth,
And left thee all her lovely hues.
  Farewell to Poesy (1910) 'Kingfisher'

4 Sweet Stay-at-Home, sweet Well-content,
Thou knowest of no strange continent:
Thou hast not felt thy bosom keep
A gentle motion with the deep;
Thou hast not sailed in Indian Seas,
Where scent comes forth in every breeze.
  Foliage (1913) 'Sweet Stay-At-Home'

5 What is this life if, full of care,
We have no time to stand and stare.
  Songs of Joy (1911) 'Leisure'

Bette Davis (Ruth Elizabeth Davis) 1908–1989

See LENORE COFFEE, JOSEPH L. MANKIEWICZ, and OLIVE HIGGINS PROUTY

Lord Dawson of Penn (Bertrand Edward Dawson, Viscount Dawson of Penn) 1864–1945

6 The King's life is moving peacefully towards its close.
  Bulletin on George V, 20 Jan. 1936, in *History Today* Dec. 1986, p. 28

C. Day-Lewis 1904–1972

7 Do not expect again a phoenix hour,
The triple-towered sky, the dove complaining,
Sudden the rain of gold and heart's first ease
Traced under trees by the eldritch light of sundown.
  Collected Poems, 1929–33 (1935) 'From Feathers to Iron'

8 Hurry! We burn
For Rome so near us, for the phoenix moment
When we have thrown off this traveller's trance,
And mother-naked and ageless-ancient
Wake in her warm nest of renaissance.
  Italian Visit (1953) 'Flight to Italy'

9 Tempt me no more; for I
Have known the lightning's hour,
The poet's inward pride,
The certainty of power.
  Magnetic Mountain (1933) pt. 3, no. 24

10 You that love England, who have an ear for her music,
The slow movement of clouds in benediction,

Clear arias of light thrilling over her uplands,
Over the chords of summer sustained peacefully.
  Magnetic Mountain (1933) pt. 4, no. 32

11 It is the logic of our times,
No subject for immortal verse—
That we who lived by honest dreams
Defend the bad against the worse.
  Word over All (1943) 'Where are the War Poets?'

Simone de Beauvoir 1908–1986

12 *On ne naît pas femme: on le devient. Aucun destin biologique, psychique, économique ne définit la figure que revêt au sein de la société la femelle humaine.*

One is not born a woman: one becomes a woman. No biological, psychological or economic destiny can determine how the human female will appear in society.
  Le deuxième sexe (The Second Sex, 1949) vol. 2, pt. 1, ch. 1

Edward de Bono 1933–

13 Unhappiness is best defined as the difference between our talents and our expectations.
  In *Observer* 12 June 1977

Eugene Victor Debs 1855–1926

14 I said then, I say now, that while there is a lower class, I am in it; while there is a criminal element, I am of it; while there is a soul in prison, I am not free.
  Speech at trial in Cleveland, Ohio, 14 Sept. 1918, in *Liberator* Nov. 1918, p. 12

15 When great changes occur in history, when great principles are involved, as a rule the majority are wrong. The minority are right.
  Speech at Federal Court, Cleveland, Ohio, 11 Sept. 1918, in *Speeches* (1928) p. 66

Edgar Degas 1834–1917

16 *L'art, c'est le vice. On ne l'épouse pas légitimement, on le viole.*

Art is vice. You don't marry it legitimately, you rape it.
  In Paul Lafond *Degas* (1918) p. 140

Charles de Gaulle 1890–1970

17 *Les traités, voyez-vous, sont comme les jeunes filles et comme les roses: ça dure ce que ça dure.*

Treaties, you see, are like girls and roses: they last while they last.
  Speech at Elysée Palace, 2 July 1963, in André Passeron *De Gaulle parle 1962–6* (1966) p. 340

18 *Vive Le Québec Libre.*

Long Live Free Quebec.
  Speech in Montreal, 24 July 1967, in *Discours et messages* (1970) p. 192

19 *La France a perdu une bataille! Mais la France n'a pas perdu la guerre!*

France has lost a battle. But France has not lost the war!

> Proclamation, 18 June 1940, in *Discours, messages et déclarations du Général de Gaulle* (1941)

1 *Comment voulez-vous gouverner un pays qui a deux cent quarante-six variétés de fromage?*

How can you govern a country which has 246 varieties of cheese?

> In Ernest Mignon *Les Mots du Général* (1962) p. 57

2 *Comme un homme politique ne croit jamais ce qu'il dit, il est tout étonné quand il est cru sur parole.*

Since a politician never believes what he says, he is quite surprised to be taken at his word.

> In Ernest Mignon *Les Mots du Général* (1962) p. 67

3 I reviewed a book of his after the war. I said, 'General de Gaulle is a very good soldier and a very bad politician.' So he wrote back to me and said, 'I have come to the conclusion that politics are too serious a matter to be left to the politicians.'

> Clement Attlee *Prime Minister Remembers* (1961) ch. 4

J. de Knight (James E. Myers) 1919– and M. Freedman 1893–1962

4 (We're gonna) rock around the clock.

> Title of song (1953)

Walter de la Mare 1873–1956

5 Oh, no man knows
Through what wild centuries
Roves back the rose.

> *The Listeners and Other Poems* (1912) 'All That's Past'

6 Softly along the road of evening,
In a twilight dim with rose,
Wrinkled with age, and drenched with dew,
Old Nod, the shepherd, goes.

> *The Listeners and Other Poems* (1912) 'Nod'

7 He is crazed with the spell of far Arabia,
They have stolen his wits away.

> *The Listeners and Other Poems* (1912) 'Arabia'

8 'Is there anybody there?' said the Traveller,
Knocking on the moonlit door;
And his horse in the silence champed the grasses
Of the forest's ferny floor.

> *The Listeners and Other Poems* (1912) 'The Listeners'

9 'Tell them I came, and no one answered,
That I kept my word,' he said.

> *The Listeners and Other Poems* (1912) 'The Listeners'

10 Here lies a most beautiful lady,
Light of step and heart was she;
I think she was the most beautiful lady
That ever was in the West Country.
But beauty vanishes; beauty passes;
However rare—rare it be;
And when I crumble, who will remember
This lady of the West Country?

> *The Listeners and Other Poems* (1912) 'Epitaph'

11 A face peered. All the grey night
In chaos of vacancy shone;
Nought but vast Sorrow was there—
The sweet cheat gone.

> *Motley and Other Poems* (1918) 'The Ghost'

12 Look thy last on all things lovely,
Every hour. Let no night
Seal thy sense in deathly slumber
Till to delight
Thou have paid thy utmost blessing;
Since that all things thou wouldst praise
Beauty took from those who loved them
In other days.

> *Motley and Other Poems* (1918) 'Fare Well'

13 Ann, Ann!
Come! quick as you can!
There's a fish that *talks*
In the frying-pan.

> *Peacock Pie* (1913) 'Alas, Alack'

14 Three jolly gentlemen,
In coats of red,
Rode their horses
Up to bed.

> *Peacock Pie* (1913) 'The Huntsmen'

15 It's a very odd thing—
As odd as can be—
That whatever Miss T eats
Turns into Miss T.

> *Peacock Pie* (1913) 'Miss T'

16 Three jolly Farmers
Once bet a pound
Each dance the others would
Off the ground.

> *Peacock Pie* (1913) 'Off the Ground'

17 Slowly, silently, now the moon
Walks the night in her silver shoon.

> *Peacock Pie* (1913) 'Silver'

18 What is the world, O soldiers?
It is I:
I, this incessant snow,
This northern sky;
Soldiers, this solitude
Through which we go
Is I.

> *Poems* (1906) 'Napoleon'

19 Hi! handsome hunting man
Fire your little gun.
Bang! Now the animal
Is dead and dumb and done.
Nevermore to peep again, creep again, leap again,
Eat or sleep or drink again, Oh, what fun!

> *Poems for Children* (1930) 'Hi!'

20 'Holiday tasks always remind me, my dear, of the young lady who wanted to go out to swim:
Mother may I go out to swim?
Yes, my darling daughter.
Fold your clothes up neat and trim,
And don't go near the water.'
'The rhyme I know,' said Laetitia, 'is, Hang your clothes on a hickory limb.'

'That's all very well,' said her uncle, 'but just you show me one!'
  The Scarecrow (1945) p. 11. Cf. Anonymous 7:25

Shelagh Delaney 1939–

1 Women never have young minds. They are born three thousand years old.
  A Taste of Honey (1959) act 1, sc. 2

Jack Dempsey 1895–1983

2 Honey, I just forgot to duck.
  Comment to his wife Estelle after losing his World Heavyweight title, 23 Sept. 1926, in J. and B. P. Dempsey *Dempsey* (1977) p. 202 (after someone tried to assassinate Ronald Reagan in 1981, Reagan told his wife: 'Honey, I forgot to duck')

Nigel Dennis 1912–

3 I am a well-to-do, revered and powerful figure. That Establishment which we call England has taken me in: I am become her Fortieth Article. I sit upon her Boards, I dominate her stage, her museums, her dances and her costumes; I have an honoured voice in her elected House. To her—and her alone—I bend the knee, and in return for my homage she is gently blind to my small failings, asking only that I indulge them privately.
  Cards of Identity (1955) pt. 2, p. 230

Buddy De Sylva (George Gard De Sylva) 1895–1950 and Lew Brown 1893–1958

4 The moon belongs to everyone,
  The best things in life are free,
  The stars belong to everyone,
  They gleam there for you and me.
  The Best Things in Life are Free (1927 song; music by Ray Henderson)

Peter De Vries 1910–

5 You can make a sordid thing sound like a brilliant drawing-room comedy. Probably a fear we have of facing up to the real issues. Could you say we were guilty of Noel Cowardice?
  Comfort me with Apples (1956) ch. 15

6 It is the final proof of God's omnipotence that he need not exist in order to save us.
  Mackerel Plaza (1958) ch. 1

7 Who of us is mature enough for offspring before the offspring themselves arrive? The value of marriage is not that adults produce children but that children produce adults.
  Tunnel of Love (1954) ch. 8

Lord Dewar 1864–1930

8 Lord Dewar . . . made the famous epigram about there being only two classes of pedestrians in these days of reckless motor traffic—the quick, and the dead.
  George Robey *Looking Back on Life* (1933) ch. 28

Sergei Diaghilev 1872–1929

9 *Étonne-moi.*

Astonish me.
  In *Journals of Jean Cocteau* (1957) ch. 1

Paul Dickson 1939–

10 Rowe's Rule: the odds are five to six that the light at the end of the tunnel is the headlight of an oncoming train.
  Washingtonian Nov. 1978. Cf. Robert Lowell 139:21

Joan Didion 1934–

11 That is one last thing to remember: *writers are always selling somebody out.*
  Slouching towards Bethlehem (1968) p. xvi

Howard Dietz

12 *Ars gratia artis.*

Art for art's sake.
  Motto of Metro-Goldwyn-Mayer film studios: see Bosley Crowthier *The Lion's Share* (1957) p. 64

William Dillon

13 I want a girl (just like the girl that married dear old dad).
  Title of song (1911; music by Harry von Tilzer)

Ernest Dimnet

14 Architecture, of all the arts, is the one which acts the most slowly, but the most surely, on the soul.
  What We Live By (1932) pt. 2, ch. 12

Isak Dinesen (Karen Blixen) 1885–1962

15 Out of Africa.
  English title of her novel *Den Afrikanske Farm* (1937). Cf. Pliny the Elder's *Historia Naturalis* bk. 8, sec. 6: *Semper aliquid novi Africam adferre.* Always bringing something new out of Africa.

16 What is man, when you come to think upon him, but a minutely set, ingenious machine for turning, with infinite artfulness, the red wine of Shiraz into urine?
  Seven Gothic Tales (1934) p. 275

Mort Dixon 1892–1956

17 Bye bye blackbird.
  Title of song (1926; music by Ray Henderson)

18 I'm looking over a four leaf clover
  That I overlooked before.
  I'm Looking Over a Four Leaf Clover (1927 song; music by Harry Woods)

Milovan Djilas 1911–

19 The Party line is that there is no Party line.
  Comment on reforms of Yugoslavian Communist Party, Nov. 1952, in Fitzroy Maclean *Disputed Barricade* (1957) caption facing p. 416

Austin Dobson (Henry Austin Dobson)
1840–1921

1 Fame is a food that dead men eat,—
I have no stomach for such meat.
Century Nov. 1906, 'Fame is a Food'

2 I intended an Ode,
And it turned to a Sonnet.
It began *à la mode*,
I intended an Ode;
But Rose crossed the road
In her latest new bonnet;
I intended an Ode;
And it turned to a Sonnet.
Graphic 23 May 1874, 'Rose-Leaves'

3 The ladies of St James's!
They're painted to the eyes;
Their white it stays for ever,
Their red it never dies:
But Phyllida, my Phyllida!
Her colour comes and goes;
It trembles to a lily,—
It wavers to a rose.
Harper's Jan. 1883, 'Ladies of St James's'

4 Time goes, you say? Ah no!
Alas, Time stays, we go.
Proverbs in Porcelain (1877) 'Paradox of Time'

Ken Dodd 1931–

5 The trouble with [Sigmund] Freud is that he never
played the Glasgow Empire Saturday night.
In *The Times* 7 Aug. 1965

J. P. Donleavy 1926–

6 But Jesus, when you don't have any money, the
problem is food. When you have money, it's sex.
When you have both it's health, you worry about
getting rupture or something. If everything is simply
jake then you're frightened of death.
Ginger Man (1955) ch. 5

7 When I die I want to decompose in a barrel of porter
and have it served in all the pubs in Dublin. I wonder
would they know it was me?
Ginger Man (1955) ch. 31

Sir Reginald Dorman-Smith 1899–1977

8 Half a million more allotments properly worked will
provide potatoes and vegetables that will feed another
million adults and $1\frac{1}{2}$ million children for eight
months out of 12. The matter is not one that can
wait. So—let's get going. Let 'Dig for Victory' be the
motto of every one with a garden and of every
able-bodied man and woman capable of digging an
allotment in their spare time.
Radio broadcast, 3 Oct. 1939, in *The Times* 4 Oct. 1939

Keith Douglas 1920–1944

9 And all my endeavours are unlucky explorers
come back, abandoning the expedition;

the specimens, the lilies of ambition
still spring in their climate, still unpicked:
but time, time is all I lacked
to find them, as the great collectors before me.
Alamein to Zem Zem (1946) 'On Return from Egypt, 1943–4'

10 Remember me when I am dead
And simplify me when I'm dead.
Collected Poems (1966) 'Simplify me when I'm Dead' (1941)

11 But she would weep to see today
how on his skin the swart flies move;
the dust upon the paper eye
and the burst stomach like a cave.

For here the lover and killer are mingled
who had one body and one heart.
And death, who had the soldier singled
has done the lover mortal hurt.
Collected Poems (1966) 'Vergissmeinnicht, 1943'

12 If at times my eyes are lenses
through which the brain explores
constellations of feeling
my ears yielding like swinging doors
admit princes to the corridors
into the mind, do not envy me.
I have a beast on my back.
Collected Poems (1966) 'Bête Noire' (1944)

Norman Douglas 1868–1952

13 To find a friend one must close one eye. To keep
him—two.
Almanac (1941) p. 77

14 The bishop was feeling rather sea-sick. Confoundedly
sea-sick, in fact.
South Wind (1917) ch. 1

15 You can tell the ideals of a nation by its advertisements.
South Wind (1917) ch. 6

16 Many a man who thinks to found a home discovers that
he has merely opened a tavern for his friends.
South Wind (1917) ch. 20

Sir Alec Douglas-Home

See LORD HOME

Caroline Douglas-Home 1937–

17 He [Lord Home] is used to dealing with estate workers.
I cannot see how anyone can say he is out of touch.
Comment on her father becoming Prime Minister, in *Daily
Herald* 21 Oct. 1963

Sir Arthur Conan Doyle 1859–1930

18 To Sherlock Holmes she [Irene Adler] is always *the*
woman. I have seldom heard him mention her under
any other name. In his eyes she eclipses and
predominates the whole of her sex.
Adventures of Sherlock Holmes (1892) 'Scandal in Bohemia'

19 You see, but you do not observe.
Adventures of Sherlock Holmes (1892) 'Scandal in Bohemia'

1 It is quite a three-pipe problem, and I beg that you won't speak to me for fifty minutes.
Adventures of Sherlock Holmes (1892) 'Red-Headed League'

2 It has long been an axiom of mine that the little things are infinitely the most important.
Adventures of Sherlock Holmes (1892) 'Case of Identity'

3 The case has, in some respects, been not entirely devoid of interest.
Adventures of Sherlock Holmes (1892) 'Case of Identity'

4 Singularity is almost invariably a clue. The more featureless and commonplace a crime is, the more difficult is it to bring it home.
Adventures of Sherlock Holmes (1892) 'Boscombe Valley Mystery'

5 A man should keep his little brain attic stocked with all the furniture that he is likely to use, and the rest he can put away in the lumber room of his library, where he can get it if he wants it.
Adventures of Sherlock Holmes (1892) 'Five Orange Pips'

6 It is my belief, Watson, founded upon my experience, that the lowest and vilest alleys in London do not present a more dreadful record of sin than does the smiling and beautiful countryside.
Adventures of Sherlock Holmes (1892) 'Copper Beeches'

7 Matilda Briggs . . . was a ship which is associated with the giant rat of Sumatra, a story for which the world is not yet prepared.
Case-Book of Sherlock Holmes (1927) 'Sussex Vampire'

8 But here, unless I am mistaken, is our client.
His Last Bow (1917) 'Wisteria Lodge'

9 All other men are specialists, but his specialism is omniscience.
His Last Bow (1917) 'Bruce-Partington Plans'

10 'I [Sherlock Holmes] followed you.' 'I saw no one.' 'That is what you may expect to see when I follow you.'
His Last Bow (1917) 'Devil's Foot'

11 Good old Watson! You are the one fixed point in a changing age.
His Last Bow (1917) title story

12 They were the footprints of a gigantic hound!
Hound of the Baskervilles (1902) ch. 2

13 A long shot, Watson; a very long shot!
Memoirs of Sherlock Holmes (1894) 'Silver Blaze'

14 'Is there any other point to which you would wish to draw my attention?'
'To the curious incident of the dog in the night-time.'
'The dog did nothing in the night-time.'
'That was the curious incident,' remarked Sherlock Holmes.
Memoirs of Sherlock Holmes (1894) 'Silver Blaze'

15 'Excellent,' I [Dr Watson] cried. 'Elementary,' said he [Sherlock Holmes].
Memoirs of Sherlock Holmes (1894) 'The Crooked Man'
('Elementary' is often expanded into 'Elementary, my dear Watson' but the longer phrase is not found in any book by Conan Doyle, although a review of the film *The Return of Sherlock Holmes* in New York Times 19 Oct. 1929, p. 22, says: In the final scene Dr Watson is there with his 'Amazing Holmes', and Holmes comes forth with his 'Elementary, my dear Watson, elementary'.)

16 Ex-Professor Moriarty of mathematical celebrity . . . is the Napoleon of crime, Watson.
Memoirs of Sherlock Holmes (1894) 'The Final Problem'

17 You mentioned your name as if I should recognise it, but I assure you that, beyond the obvious facts that you are a bachelor, a solicitor, a Freemason, and an asthmatic, I know nothing whatever about you.
Return of Sherlock Holmes (1905) 'The Norwood Builder'

18 Now, Watson, the fair sex is your department.
Return of Sherlock Holmes (1905) 'The Second Stain'

19 Detection is, or ought to be, an exact science, and should be treated in the same cold and unemotional manner. You have attempted to tinge it with romanticism, which produces much the same effect as if you worked a love-story or an elopement into the fifth proposition of Euclid.
Sign of Four (1890) ch. 1

20 Yes, I have been guilty of several monographs. . . . Here . . . is one 'Upon the Distinction between the Ashes of the Various Tobaccos'. In it I enumerate a hundred and forty forms of cigar, cigarette and pipe tobacco.
Sign of Four (1890) ch. 1

21 In an experience of women that extends over many nations and three separate continents, I have never looked upon a face which gave a clearer promise of a refined and sensitive nature.
Sign of Four (1890) ch. 2

22 How often have I said to you that when you have eliminated the impossible, whatever remains, *however improbable*, must be the truth?
Sign of Four (1890) ch. 6

23 You know my methods. Apply them.
Sign of Four (1890) ch. 6

24 'It is the unofficial force—the Baker Street irregulars.' As he spoke, there came a swift pattering of naked feet upon the stairs, a clatter of high voices, and in rushed a dozen dirty and ragged little street Arabs.
Sign of Four (1890) ch. 8

25 London, that great cesspool into which all the loungers and idlers of the Empire are irresistibly drained.
Study in Scarlet (1888) ch. 1

26 It is a capital mistake to theorize before you have all the evidence. It biases the judgement.
Study in Scarlet (1888) ch. 3

27 Where there is no imagination there is no horror.
Study in Scarlet (1888) ch. 5

28 It is a mistake to confound strangeness with mystery. The most commonplace crime is often the most mysterious, because it presents no new or special features from which deductions may be drawn.
Study in Scarlet (1888) ch. 7

29 'I am inclined to think—' said I [Dr Watson]. 'I should do so,' Sherlock Holmes remarked, impatiently.
Valley of Fear (1915) ch. 1

30 The vocabulary of 'Bradshaw' is nervous and terse, but limited. The selection of words would hardly lend itself to the sending of general messages.
Valley of Fear (1915) ch. 1

1 Mediocrity knows nothing higher than itself, but talent instantly recognizes genius.
   Valley of Fear (1915) ch. 1

2 What of the bow?
   The bow was made in England,
   Of true wood, of yew wood,
   The wood of English bows.
   White Company (1891) 'Song of the Bow'

Maurice Drake

3 Beanz meanz Heinz.
   Advertising slogan for Heinz baked beans *c.*1967, in Nigel Rees *Slogans* (1982) p. 131

William A. Drake 1899–

See GRETA GARBO

John Drinkwater 1882–1937

4 In the corridors under there is nothing but sleep.
   And stiller than ever on orchard boughs they keep
   Tryst with the moon, and deep is the silence, deep
   On moon-washed apples of wonder.
   Tides (1917) 'Moonlit Apples'

Alexander Dubček 1921–

5 *Proto vedení strany klade takový důraz na to, aby . . . naše země hospodářsky a kulturně nezaostávala a hlavně abychom ve službách lidu dělali takovou politiku, aby socialismus neztrácel svou lidskou tvář.*

That is why the leadership of the country has put such emphasis on ensuring that . . . our land did not lag behind economically and culturally, and, most important, why in the service of the people we followed a policy so that socialism would not lose its human face.
   In *Rudé Právo* 19 July 1968

Al Dubin 1891–1945

6 Tiptoe through the tulips.
   Title of song (1929; music by Joseph Burke)

W. E. B. DuBois 1868–1963

7 One thing alone I charge you. As you live, believe in life! Always human beings will live and progress to greater, broader and fuller life.
   The only possible death is to lose belief in this truth simply because the great end comes slowly, because time is long.
   Last message (written 26 June, 1957) read at his funeral, 1963, in *Journal of Negro History* Apr. 1964

8 The problem of the twentieth century is the problem of the colour line—the relation of the darker to the lighter races of men in Asia and Africa, in America and the islands of the sea.
   Souls of Black Folk (1903) ch. 2

Georges Duhamel 1884–1966

9 *Je respecte trop l'idée de Dieu pour la rendre responsable d'un monde aussi absurde.*

I have too much respect for the idea of God to make it responsible for such an absurd world.
   Le désert de Bièvres (1937) in *Chronique des Pasquier* (1948) vol. 5, p. 249

Raoul Duke

See HUNTER S. THOMPSON

John Foster Dulles 1888–1959

10 You have to take chances for peace, just as you must take chances in war. Some say that we were brought to the verge of war. Of course we were brought to the verge of war. The ability to get to the verge without getting into the war is the necessary art. If you cannot master it, you inevitably get into war. If you try to run away from it, if you are scared to go to the brink, you are lost. We've had to look it square in the face—on the question of enlarging the Korean war, on the question of getting into the Indochina war, on the question of Formosa. We walked to the brink and we looked it in the face.
   In *Life* 16 Jan. 1956

11 If . . . the European Defence Community should not become effective; if France and Germany remain apart. . . . That would compel an agonizing reappraisal of basic United States policy.
   Speech to NATO Council in Paris, 14 Dec. 1953, in *New York Times* 15 Dec. 1953, p. 14

Dame Daphne du Maurier 1907–1989

12 Last night I dreamt I went to Manderley again.
   Rebecca (1938) ch. 1 (opening sentence)

Isadora Duncan 1878–1927

13 *Adieu, mes amis. Je vais à la gloire.*

Farewell, my friends. I am going to glory.
   Last words before her scarf caught in a car wheel and broke her neck, in Mary Desti *Isadora Duncan's End* (1929) ch. 25

Ian Dunlop

14 The shock of the new: seven historic exhibitions of modern art.
   Title of book (1972)

Jimmy Durante 1893–1980

15 Everybody wants to get inta the act!
   Catch-phrase, in W. Cahn *Good Night, Mrs Calabash* (1963) p. 95

Leo Durocher 1906–

16 I called off his players' names as they came marching up the steps behind him, 'Walker, Cooper, Mize,

Marshall, Kerr, Gordon, Thomson. Take a look at them. All nice guys. They'll finish last. Nice guys. Finish last.'

Said on 6 July 1946, in *Nice Guys Finish Last* (1975) pt. 1, p. 14 (generally quoted as 'Nice guys finish last')

Ian Dury

1 Sex and drugs and rock and roll.

Title of song (1977; music by Chaz Jankel)

2 I could be the catalyst that sparks the revolution.
I could be an inmate in a long term institution
I could lean to wild extremes I could do or die,
I could yawn and be withdrawn and watch them gallop by,
What a waste, what a waste, what a waste, what a waste.

What a Waste (1978 song; music by Chaz Jankel)

Lillian K. Dykstra

3 He [Thomas Dewey] is just about the nastiest little man I've ever known. He struts sitting down.

Letter to Franz Dykstra, 8 July 1952, in James T. Patterson *Mr Republican* (1972) ch. 35

Bob Dylan (Robert Zimmerman) 1941–

4 How many roads must a man walk down
Before you can call him a man? . . .
The answer, my friend, is blowin' in the wind,
The answer is blowin' in the wind.

Blowin' in the Wind (1962 song)

5 Don't think twice, it's all right.

Title of song (1963)

6 I saw ten thousand talkers whose tongues were all broken,
I saw guns and sharp swords, in the hands of young children,
And it's a hard, and it's a hard, it's a hard, it's a hard,
And it's a hard rain's a gonna fall.

A Hard Rain's A Gonna Fall (1963 song)

7 Money doesn't talk, it swears.

It's Alright, Ma (1965 song)

8 How does it feel
To be on your own
With no direction home
Like a complete unknown
Like a rolling stone?

Like a Rolling Stone (1965 song)

9 She knows there's no success like failure
And that failure's no success at all.

Love Minus Zero/No Limit (1965 song)

10 I ain't gonna work on Maggie's Farm no more.

Maggie's Farm (1965 song)

11 Hey! Mr Tambourine Man, play a song for me.
I'm not sleepy and there is no place I'm going to.

Mr Tambourine Man (1965 song)

12 'Equality,' I spoke the word
As if a wedding vow

Ah, but I was so much older then,
I'm younger than that now.

My Back Pages (1964 song)

13 Don't follow leaders
Watch the parkin' meters.

Subterranean Homesick Blues (1965 song)

14 Come mothers and fathers,
Throughout the land
And don't criticize
What you can't understand.
Your sons and your daughters
Are beyond your command
Your old road is
Rapidly agin'
Please get out of the new one
If you can't lend your hand
For the times they are a-changin'!

The Times They Are A-Changing (1964 song)

15 But I can't think for you
You'll have to decide,
Whether Judas Iscariot
Had God on his side.

With God on our Side (1963 song)

Stephen T. Early 1889–1951

16 I received a card the other day from Steve Early which said, 'Don't Worry Me—I am an 8 Ulcer Man on 4 Ulcer Pay.'

William Hillman *Mr President; the First Publication from the Personal Diaries, Private Letters, Papers and Revealing Interviews of Harry S. Truman* (1952) pt. 5, p. 222

Clint Eastwood 1930–

See HARRY JULIAN FINK, RITA M. FINK, and DEAN RIESNER

Abba Eban 1915–

17 History teaches us that men and nations behave wisely once they have exhausted all other alternatives.

Speech in London, 16 Dec. 1970, in *The Times* 17 Dec. 1970

Sir Anthony Eden (Earl of Avon) 1897–1977

18 We are in an armed conflict; that is the phrase I have used. There has been no declaration of war.

Hansard 1 Nov. 1956, col. 1641

Clarissa Eden (Countess of Avon) 1920–

19 For the past few weeks I have really felt as if the Suez Canal was flowing through my drawing room.

Speech at Gateshead, 20 Nov. 1956, in *Gateshead Post* 23 Nov. 1956

Marriott Edgar 1880–1951

20 There's a famous seaside place called Blackpool,
That's noted for fresh air and fun,
And Mr and Mrs Ramsbottom
Went there with young Albert, their son.

A grand little lad was young Albert,
All dressed in his best; quite a swell
With a stick with an 'orse's 'ead 'andle,
The finest that Woolworth's could sell.

They didn't think much to the Ocean:
The waves, they were fiddlin' and small,
There was no wrecks and nobody drownded,
Fact, nothing to laugh at at all.

The Lion and Albert (1932) in *Albert, 'Arold and Others*
(1937)—monologue recorded by Stanley Holloway in 1932

1 The Magistrate gave his opinion
That no one was really to blame
And he said that he hoped the Ramsbottoms
Would have further sons to their name.

At that Mother got proper blazing,
'And thank you, sir, kindly,' said she.
'What, waste all our lives raising children
To feed ruddy Lions? Not me!'

The Lion and Albert (1932) in *Albert, 'Arold and Others* (1937)

Duke of Edinburgh 1921–

See PRINCE PHILIP, DUKE OF EDINBURGH

Thomas Alva Edison 1847–1931

2 Genius is one per cent inspiration, ninety-nine per
cent perspiration.

Harper's Monthly Magazine Sept. 1932 (quoted by M. A.
Rosanoff as having been said by Edison *c*.1903)

John Maxwell Edmonds 1875–1958

3 When you go home, tell them of us and say,
'For your tomorrows these gave their today.'

Inscriptions Suggested for War Memorials (1919)

King Edward VII 1841–1910

4 That's the fourth time that infernal noise has roused
me.

Said to his secretary 'Fritz' Ponsonby at the first performance
of 'The Wreckers', an opera by Dame Ethel Smyth, quoted in
H. Atkins and A. Newman *Beecham Stories* (1978) p. 43

5 I thought everyone must know that a *short* jacket is
always worn with a silk hat at a private view in the
morning.

In Sir P. Magnus *Edward VII* (1964) ch. 19 (said to Sir
Frederick Ponsonby, who had proposed to accompany him in
a tail-coat)

6 Because a man has a black face and a different religion
from our own, there is no reason why he should be
treated as a brute.

Letter to Lord Granville, 30 Nov. 1875, in Sir Sydney Lee
King Edward VII (1925) vol. 1, ch. 21

King Edward VIII (Duke of Windsor) 1894–1972

7 The thing that impresses me most about America is
the way parents obey their children.

Look 5 Mar. 1957

8 At long last I am able to say a few words of my own.
I have never wanted to withhold anything, but until

now it has not been constitutionally possible for me to
speak. A few hours ago I discharged my last duty as
King and Emperor, and now that I have been succeeded
by my brother, the Duke of York, my first words must
be to declare allegiance to him. This I do with all my
heart. You all know the reasons which have impelled
me to renounce the throne. But I want you to
understand that in making up my mind I did not forget
the country or the Empire which as Prince of Wales,
and lately as King, I have for twenty-five years tried to
serve. But you must believe me when I tell you that
I have found it impossible to carry the heavy burden of
responsibility and to discharge my duties as King as
I would wish to do without the help and support of the
woman I love. . . .

This decision has been made less difficult to me by the
sure knowledge that my brother, with his long training
in the public affairs of this country and with his fine
qualities, will be able to take my place forthwith,
without interruption or injury to the life and progress of
the Empire. And he has one matchless blessing, enjoyed
by so many of you and not bestowed on me—a happy
home with his wife and children. . . .

I now quit altogether public affairs, and I lay down
my burden. . . . God bless you all. God save the King.

Broadcast, 11 Dec. 1936, in *The Times* 12 Dec. 1936

9 These works [the derelict Dowlais Iron and Steel Works]
brought all these people here. Something should be
done to get them at work again.

Spoken to Charles Keen, 18 Nov. 1936, in *Western Mail*
19 Nov. 1936

John Ehrlichman 1925–

10 I think we ought to let him [Patrick Gray] hang there.
Let him twist slowly, slowly in the wind.

Telephone conversation with John Dean, 7 or 8 Mar. 1973,
in *Washington Post* 27 July 1973, p. A27 (regarding Patrick
Gray's nomination as Director of the FBI)

Albert Einstein 1879–1955

11 Nationalism is an infantile sickness. It is the measles of
the human race.

In Helen Dukas and Banesh Hoffman *Albert Einstein, the
Human Side* (1979) p. 38

12 I am an absolute pacifist. . . . It is an instinctive feeling.
It is a feeling that possesses me, because the murder of
men is disgusting.

Interview with Paul Hutchinson, in *Christian Century*
28 Aug. 1929

13 *Raffiniert ist der Herrgott, aber boshaft ist er nicht.*

God is subtle but he is not malicious.

Remark made during a week at Princeton beginning 9 May
1921, later carved above the fireplace of the Common Room
of Fine Hall (the Mathematical Institute), Princeton
University – in R. W. Clark *Einstein* (1973) ch. 14

14 *Jedenfalls bin ich überzeugt, dass der nicht würfelt.*

At any rate, I am convinced that *He* [God] does not play
dice.

Letter to Max Born, 4 Dec. 1926, in *Einstein und Born
Briefwechsel* (1969) p. 130 (often quoted as *Gott würfelt nicht*
God does not play dice, e.g. in B. Hoffmann *Albert Einstein*
(1973) ch. 10)

1 If my theory of relativity is proven correct, Germany will claim me as a German and France will declare that I am a citizen of the world. Should my theory prove untrue, France will say that I am a German and Germany will declare that I am a Jew.

> Address at the Sorbonne, Paris, ?early Dec. 1929, in *New York Times* 16 Feb. 1930

2 The unleashed power of the atom has changed everything save our modes of thinking and we thus drift toward unparalleled catastrophe.

> Telegram sent to prominent Americans, 24 May 1946, in *New York Times* 25 May 1946

3 If *A* is a success in life, then *A* equals *x* plus *y* plus *z*. Work is *x*; *y* is play; and *z* is keeping your mouth shut.

> In *Observer* 15 Jan. 1950

4 If I would be a young man again and had to decide how to make my living, I would not try to become a scientist or scholar or teacher. I would rather choose to be a plumber or a peddler in the hope to find that modest degree of independence still available under present circumstances.

> *Reporter* 18 Nov. 1954

5 Science without religion is lame, religion without science is blind.

> *Science, Philosophy and Religion: a Symposium* (1941) ch. 13

Dwight D. Eisenhower 1890–1969

6 This conjunction of an immense military establishment and a large arms industry is new in the American experience. . . . We recognize the imperative need for this development. Yet we must not fail to comprehend its grave implications. . . . In the councils of government, we must guard against the acquisition of unwarranted influence, whether sought or unsought, by the military-industrial complex. The potential for the disastrous rise of misplaced power exists and will persist.

> Farewell broadcast, 17 Jan. 1961, in *New York Times* 18 Jan. 1961

7 Every gun that is made, every warship launched, every rocket fired signifies, in the final sense, a theft from those who hunger and are not fed, those who are cold and are not clothed. This world in arms is not spending money alone. It is spending the sweat of its laborers, the genius of its scientists, the hopes of its children.

> Speech in Washington, 16 Apr. 1953, in *Public Papers of Presidents 1953* (1960) p. 182

8 You have broader considerations that might follow what you might call the 'falling domino' principle. You have a row of dominoes set up. You knock over the first one, and what will happen to the last one is that it will go over very quickly. So you have the beginning of a disintegration that would have the most profound influences.

> Speech at press conference, 7 Apr. 1954, in *Public Papers of Presidents 1954* (1960) p. 383

9 I think that people want peace so much that one of these days governments had better get out of the way and let them have it.

> Broadcast discussion, 31 Aug. 1959, in *Public Papers of Presidents 1959* (1960) p. 625

T. S. Eliot 1888–1965

10 Where are the eagles and the trumpets?

> Buried beneath some snow-deep Alps.
> Over buttered scones and crumpets
> Weeping, weeping multitudes
> Droop in a hundred A.B.C.'s.
>
> *Ara Vus Prec* (1920) 'Cooking Egg'

11 Here I am, an old man in a dry month
Being read to by a boy, waiting for rain.

> *Ara Vus Prec* (1920) 'Gerontion'

12 After such knowledge, what forgiveness? Think now
History has many cunning passages, contrived corridors
And issues, deceives with whispering ambitions,
Guides us by vanities.

> *Ara Vus Prec* (1920) 'Gerontion'

13 Tenants of the house,
Thoughts of a dry brain in a dry season.

> *Ara Vus Prec* (1920) 'Gerontion'

14 A cold coming we had of it,
Just the worst time of the year
For a journey, and such a long journey:
The ways deep and the weather sharp,
The very dead of winter.

> *Ariel Poems* (1927) 'Journey of the Magi'

15 But set down
This set down
This: were we led all that way for
Birth or Death? There was a Birth, certainly,
We had evidence and no doubt. I had seen birth and death
But had thought they were different; this Birth was
Hard and bitter agony for us, like Death, our death.
We returned to our places, these Kingdoms,
But no longer at ease here, in the old dispensation,
With an alien people clutching their gods.
I should be glad of another death.

> *Ariel Poems* (1927) 'Journey of the Magi'

16 Because I do not hope to turn again
Because I do not hope
Because I do not hope to turn.

> *Ash-Wednesday* (1930) pt. 1

17 Because these wings are no longer wings to fly
But merely vans to beat the air
The air which is now thoroughly small and dry
Smaller and dryer than the will
Teach us to care and not to care
Teach us to sit still.

> *Ash-Wednesday* (1930) pt. 1

18 Lady, three white leopards sat under a juniper-tree
In the cool of the day.

> *Ash-Wednesday* (1930) pt. 2

19 You've missed the point completely, Julia:
There *were* no tigers. *That* was the point.

> *Cocktail Party* (1950) act 1, sc. 1

20 What is hell?
Hell is oneself,
Hell is alone, the other figures in it

Merely projections. There is nothing to escape from
And nothing to escape to. One is always alone.
  Cocktail Party (1950) act 1, sc. 3

1 How unpleasant to meet Mr Eliot!
With his features of clerical cut,
And his brow so grim
And his mouth so prim
And his conversation, so nicely
Restricted to What Precisely
And If and Perhaps and But.
  Collected Poems (1936) 'Five-Finger Exercises'

2 Time present and time past
Are both perhaps present in time future,
And time future contained in time past.
  Collected Poems (1936) 'Burnt Norton' pt. 1

3 Footfalls echo in the memory
Down the passage which we did not take
Towards the door we never opened
Into the rose-garden. My words echo
Thus, in your mind.
  Collected Poems (1936) 'Burnt Norton' pt. 1

4 Human kind
Cannot bear very much reality.
  Collected Poems (1936) 'Burnt Norton' pt. 1.

5 At the still point of the turning world. Neither flesh nor
  fleshless;
Neither from nor towards; at the still point, there the
  dance is,
But neither arrest nor movement.
  Collected Poems (1936) 'Burnt Norton' pt. 2

6 Words strain,
Crack and sometimes break, under the burden,
Under the tension, slip, slide, perish,
Decay with imprecision, will not stay in place,
Will not stay still.
  Collected Poems (1936) 'Burnt Norton' pt. 5

7 I do not know much about gods; but I think that the river
Is a strong brown god—sullen, untamed and intractable.
  Dry Salvages (1941) pt. 1

8 In my beginning is my end.
  East Coker (1940) pt. 1

9 That was a way of putting it—not very satisfactory:
A periphrastic study in a worn-out poetical fashion,
Leaving one still with the intolerable wrestle
With words and meanings. The poetry does not matter.
  East Coker (1940) pt. 2

10 The houses are all gone under the sea.
The dancers are all gone under the hill.
  East Coker (1940) pt. 2

11 O dark dark dark. They all go into the dark,
The vacant interstellar spaces, the vacant into the
  vacant.
  East Coker (1940) pt. 3

12 The wounded surgeon plies the steel
That questions the distempered part;
Beneath the bleeding hands we feel
The sharp compassion of the healer's art
Resolving the enigma of the fever chart.
  East Coker (1940) pt. 4

13 Each venture
Is a new beginning, a raid on the inarticulate

With shabby equipment always deteriorating
In the general mess of imprecision of feeling.
  East Coker (1940) pt. 5

14 Success is relative:
It is what we can make of the mess we have made of
  things.
  Family Reunion (1939) pt. 2, sc. 3

15 Agatha! Mary! come!
The clock has stopped in the dark!
  Family Reunion (1939) pt. 2, sc. 3

16 Round and round the circle
Completing the charm
So the knot be unknotted
The cross be uncrossed
The crooked be made straight
And the curse be ended.
  Family Reunion (1939) pt. 2, sc. 3

17 And what the dead had no speech for, when living,
They can tell you, being dead: the communication
Of the dead is tongued with fire beyond the language of
  the living.
  Little Gidding (1942) pt. 1

18 Ash on an old man's sleeve
Is all the ash the burnt roses leave.
Dust in the air suspended
Marks the place where a story ended.
Dust inbreathed was a house—
The wall, the wainscot and the mouse.
The death of hope and despair,
This is the death of air.
  Little Gidding (1942) pt. 2

19 Since our concern was speech, and speech impelled us
To purify the dialect of the tribe
And urge the mind to aftersight and foresight.
  Little Gidding (1942) pt. 2

20 We shall not cease from exploration
And the end of all our exploring
Will be to arrive where we started
And know the place for the first time.
  Little Gidding (1942) pt. 5

21 What we call the beginning is often the end
And to make an end is to make a beginning.
The end is where we start from.
  Little Gidding (1942) pt. 5

22 A people without history
Is not redeemed from time, for history is a pattern
Of timeless moments. So, while the light fails
On a winter's afternoon, in a secluded chapel
History is now and England.
  Little Gidding (1942) pt. 5

23 A condition of complete simplicity
(Costing not less than everything)
And all shall be well and
All manner of thing shall be well
When the tongues of flame are in-folded
Into the crowned knot of fire
And the fire and the rose are one.
  Little Gidding (1942) pt. 5

24 Yet we have gone on living,
Living and partly living.
  Murder in the Cathedral (1935) pt. 1

1 The last temptation is the greatest treason:
To do the right deed for the wrong reason.
Murder in the Cathedral (1935) pt. 1

2 Clear the air! clean the sky! wash the wind! take the
stone from stone, take the skin from the arm, take the
muscle from bone, and wash them.
Murder in the Cathedral (1935) pt. 2

3 Culture may even be described simply as that which
makes life worth living.
Notes Towards a Definition of Culture (1948) ch. 1

4 Macavity, Macavity, there's no one like Macavity,
There never was a Cat of such deceitfulness and
suavity.
He always has an alibi, and one or two to spare:
At whatever time the deed took place—MACAVITY
WASN'T THERE!
And they say that all the Cats whose wicked deeds are
widely known
(I might mention Mungojerrie, I might mention
Griddlebone)
Are nothing more than agents for the Cat who all the
time
Just controls their operations: the Napoleon of Crime!
Old Possum's Book of Practical Cats (1939) 'Macavity: the
Mystery Cat'. Cf. Conan Doyle 69:16

5 The host with someone indistinct
Converses at the door apart,
The nightingales are singing near
The Convent of the Sacred Heart,

And sang within the bloody wood
When Agamemnon cried aloud
And let their liquid siftings fall
To stain the stiff dishonoured shroud.
Poems (1919) 'Sweeney among the Nightingales'

6 The hippopotamus's day
Is passed in sleep; at night he hunts;
God works in a mysterious way—
The Church can feed and sleep at once.
Poems (1919) 'The Hippopotamus'

7 Polyphiloprogenitive
The sapient sutlers of the Lord
Drift across window-panes
In the beginning was the Word.
Poems (1919) 'Mr Eliot's Sunday Morning Service'

8 Webster was much possessed by death
And saw the skull beneath the skin;
And breastless creatures underground
Leaned backward with a lipless grin.
Poems (1919) 'Whispers of Immortality'

9 Grishkin is nice: her Russian eye
Is underlined for emphasis;
Uncorseted, her friendly bust
Gives promise of pneumatic bliss.
Poems (1919) 'Whispers of Immortality'

10 We are the hollow men
We are the stuffed men
Leaning together
Headpiece filled with straw. Alas!
Poems 1909–1925 (1925) 'The Hollow Men'

11 *Here we go round the prickly pear*
Prickly pear prickly pear
Here we go round the prickly pear
At five o'clock in the morning.

Between the idea
And the reality
Between the motion
And the act
Falls the Shadow.
Poems 1909–1925 (1925) 'The Hollow Men'

12 This is the way the world ends
Not with a bang but a whimper.
Poems 1909–1925 (1925) 'The Hollow Men'

13 Let us go then, you and I,
When the evening is spread out against the sky
Like a patient etherized upon a table.
Prufrock (1917) 'Love Song of J. Alfred Prufrock'

14 In the room the women come and go
Talking of Michelangelo.

The yellow fog that rubs its back upon the
window-panes.
The yellow smoke that rubs its muzzle on the
window-panes.
Licked its tongue into the corners of the evening.
Prufrock (1917) 'Love Song of J. Alfred Prufrock'

15 I have measured out my life with coffee spoons.
Prufrock (1917) 'Love Song of J. Alfred Prufrock'

16 I should have been a pair of ragged claws
Scuttling across the floors of silent seas.
Prufrock (1917) 'Love Song of J. Alfred Prufrock'

17 I have seen the moment of my greatness flicker,
And I have seen the eternal Footman hold my coat, and
snicker,
And in short, I was afraid.
Prufrock (1917) 'Love Song of J. Alfred Prufrock'

18 No! I am not Prince Hamlet, nor was meant to be;
Am an attendant lord, one that will do
To swell a progress, start a scene or two,
Advise the prince.
Prufrock (1917) 'Love Song of J. Alfred Prufrock'

19 I grow old . . . I grow old . . .
I shall wear the bottoms of my trousers rolled.

Shall I part my hair behind? Do I dare to eat a peach?
I shall wear white flannel trousers, and walk upon the
beach.
I have heard the mermaids singing, each to each.

I do not think that they will sing to me.
Prufrock (1917) 'Love Song of J. Alfred Prufrock'

20 The winter evening settles down
With smell of steaks in passageways.
Six o'clock.
The burnt-out ends of smoky days.
Prufrock (1917) 'Preludes'

21 Every street lamp that I pass
Beats like a fatalistic drum,
And through the spaces of the dark
Midnight shakes the memory
As a madman shakes a dead geranium.
Prufrock (1917) 'Rhapsody on a Windy Night'

1 I am aware of the damp souls of housemaids
  Sprouting despondently at area gates.
  Prufrock (1917) 'Morning at the Window'

2 Stand on the highest pavement of the stair—
  Lean on a garden urn—
  Weave, weave the sunlight in your hair.
  Prufrock (1917) 'La Figlia Che Piange'

3 Sometimes these cogitations still amaze
  The troubled midnight and the noon's repose.
  Prufrock (1917) 'La Figlia Che Piange'

4 Where is the Life we have lost in living?
  Where is the wisdom we have lost in knowledge?
  Where is the knowledge we have lost in information?
  The Rock (1934) pt. 1

5 And the wind shall say: 'Here were decent godless
    people:
  Their only monument the asphalt road
  And a thousand lost golf balls.'
  The Rock (1934) pt. 1

6 Poetry is not a turning loose of emotion, but an escape
  from emotion; it is not the expression of personality but
  an escape from personality. But, of course, only those
  who have personality and emotions know what it
  means to want to escape from these things.
  Sacred Wood (1920) 'Tradition and Individual Talent'

7 The only way of expressing emotion in the form of a₁t is
  by finding an 'objective correlative'; in other words,
  a set of objects, a situation, a chain of events which
  shall be the formula of that *particular* emotion; such
  that when the external facts, which must terminate in
  sensory experience, are given, the emotion is
  immediately evoked.
  Sacred Wood (1920) 'Hamlet and his Problems'

8 Immature poets imitate; mature poets steal.
  Sacred Wood (1920) 'Philip Massinger'

9 Birth, and copulation, and death.
  That's all the facts when you come to brass tacks:
  Birth, and copulation, and death.
  I've been born, and once is enough.
  Sweeney Agonistes (1932) p. 24

10 In the seventeenth century a dissociation of sensibility
   set in, from which we have never recovered; and this
   dissociation, as is natural, was due to the influence of
   the two most powerful poets of the century, Milton and
   Dryden.
   Times Literary Supplement 20 Oct. 1921

11 We can only say that it appears likely that poets in our
   civilization, as it exists at present, must be *difficult*.
   Times Literary Supplement 20 Oct. 1921

12 Stone, bronze, stone, steel, stone, oakleaves, horses'
     heels
   Over the paving.
   Triumphal March (1931)

13 April is the cruellest month, breeding
   Lilacs out of the dead land, mixing
   Memory and desire, stirring
   Dull roots with spring rain.
   Winter kept us warm, covering

Earth in forgetful snow, feeding
A little life with dried tubers.
  Waste Land (1922) pt. 1

14 I read, much of the night, and go south in the winter.
   Waste Land (1922) pt. 1

15 And I will show you something different from either
   Your shadow at morning striding behind you
   Or your shadow at evening rising to meet you;
   I will show you fear in a handful of dust.
   Waste Land (1922) pt. 1. Cf. Joseph Conrad 60:4

16 Madame Sosostris, famous clairvoyante,
   Had a bad cold, nevertheless
   Is known to be the wisest woman in Europe,
   With a wicked pack of cards.
   Waste Land (1922) pt. 1

17 Unreal City,
   Under the brown fog of a winter dawn,
   A crowd flowed over London Bridge, so many,
   I had not thought death had undone so many.
   Sighs, short and infrequent, were exhaled,
   And each man fixed his eyes before his feet
   Flowed up the hill and down King William Street,
   To where Saint Mary Woolnoth kept the hours
   With a dead sound on the final stroke of nine.
   Waste Land (1922) pt. 1

18 The Chair she sat in, like a burnished throne,
   Glowed on the marble.
   Waste Land (1922) pt. 2 (cf. Shakespeare's *Antony and Cleopatra* act 2, sc. 2, l. 199)

19 And still she cried, and still the world pursues,
   'Jug Jug' to dirty ears.
   Waste Land (1922) pt. 2

20 I think we are in rats' alley
   Where the dead men lost their bones.
   Waste Land (1922) pt. 2

21 O O O O that Shakespeherian Rag—
   It's so elegant
   So intelligent.
   Waste Land (1922) pt. 2. Cf. Gene Buck and Herman Ruby

22 Hurry up please it's time.
   Waste Land (1922) pt. 2

23 But at my back from time to time I hear
   The sound of horns and motors, which shall bring
   Sweeney to Mrs Porter in the spring.
   O the moon shone bright on Mrs Porter
   And on her daughter
   They wash their feet in soda water.
   Waste Land (1922) pt. 3. Cf. *Oxford Dictionary of Quotations* (1979) 332:19

24 At the violet hour, when the eyes and back
   Turn upward from the desk, when the human engine
     waits
   Like a taxi throbbing waiting,
   I, Tiresias, though blind, throbbing between two lives,
   Old man with wrinkled female breasts, can see
   At the violet hour, the evening hour that strives
   Homeward, and brings the sailor home from sea,
   The typist home at teatime, clears her breakfast, lights
   Her stove, and lays out food in tins.
   Waste Land (1922) pt. 3

1 I Tiresias, old man with wrinkled dugs
Perceived the scene, and foretold the rest—
I too awaited the expected guest.
He, the young man carbuncular, arrives,
A small house agent's clerk, with one bold stare,
One of the low on whom assurance sits
As a silk hat on a Bradford millionaire.
Waste Land (1922) pt. 3

2 When lovely woman stoops to folly and
Paces about her room again, alone,
She smoothes her hair with automatic hand,
And puts a record on the gramophone.
Waste Land (1922) pt. 3

3 Phlebas the Phoenician, a fortnight dead,
Forgot the cry of gulls, and the deep sea swell
And the profit and loss.
Waste Land (1922) pt. 4

4 Who is the third who walks always beside you?
When I count, there are only you and I together
But when I look ahead up the white road
There is always another one walking beside you.
Waste Land (1922) pt. 5

5 A woman drew her long black hair out tight
And fiddled whisper music on those strings
And bats with baby faces in the violet light
Whistled.
Waste Land (1922) pt. 5

6 These fragments I have shored against my ruins.
Waste Land (1922) pt. 5

Queen Elizabeth II 1926–

7 I declare before you all that my whole life, whether it
be long or short, shall be devoted to your service and
the service of our great Imperial family to which we
all belong.
Broadcast speech (as Princess Elizabeth) to the
Commonwealth from Cape Town, 21 Apr. 1947, in *The
Times* 22 Apr. 1947

8 I think everybody really will concede that on this, of all
days, I should begin my speech with the words 'My
husband and I'.
Speech at Guildhall on her 25th wedding anniversary,
20 Nov. 1972, in *The Times* 21 Nov. 1972

Queen Elizabeth, the Queen Mother 1900–

9 I'm glad we've been bombed. It makes me feel I can
look the East End in the face.
Said to a policeman, 13 Sept. 1940, in John
Wheeler-Bennett *King George VI* (1958) pt. 3, ch. 6

Alf Ellerton

10 Belgium put the kibosh on the Kaiser.
Title of song (1914)

Havelock Ellis (Henry Havelock Ellis) 1859–1939

11 It is certainly strange to observe . . . how many people
seem to feel vain of their own unqualified optimism

when the place where optimism most flourishes is the
lunatic asylum.
Dance of Life (1923) ch. 3

12 The sanitary and mechanical age we are now entering
makes up for the mercy it grants to our sense of smell
by the ferocity with which it assails our sense of
hearing. As usual, what we call 'Progress' is the
exchange of one Nuisance for another Nuisance.
Impressions and Comments (1914) 31 July 1912

13 Every artist writes his own autobiography.
New Spirit (1890) 'Tolstoi'

Paul Eluard 1895–1952

14 *Adieu tristesse*
Bonjour tristesse
Tu es inscrite dans les lignes du plafond.

Farewell sadness
Good-day sadness
You are inscribed in the lines of the ceiling.
La vie immédiate (1930) 'A peine défigurée', in *Œuvres
complètes* (1968) vol. 1, p. 365

Sir William Empson 1906–1984

15 Slowly the poison the whole blood stream fills.
It is not the effort nor the failure tires.
The waste remains, the waste remains and kills.
Poems (1935) 'Missing Dates'

16 Seven types of ambiguity.
Title of book (1930)

Julius J. Epstein 1909– , Philip G. Epstein 1909–1952, and Howard Koch 1902–

17 Of all the gin joints in all the towns in all the world,
she walks into mine.
Casablanca (1942 film), words spoken by Humphrey Bogart

18 If she can stand it, I can. Play it!
Casablanca (1942 film), words spoken by Humphrey Bogart,
often misquoted as 'Play it again, Sam' (earlier in the film,
Ingrid Bergman says: 'Play it, Sam. Play *As Time Goes By*.')

19 Here's looking at you, kid.
Casablanca (1942 film), words spoken by Humphrey Bogart

20 Major Strasser has been shot. Round up the usual
suspects.
Casablanca (1942 film), words spoken by Claude Rains

Susan Ertz 1894–1985

21 Someone has somewhere commented on the fact that
millions long for immortality who don't know what to
do with themselves on a rainy Sunday afternoon.
Anger in the Sky (1943) p. 137

Dudley Erwin 1917–1984

22 Mr Dudley Erwin, former Air Minister [in Australia],
claimed last night that the secretary of Mr John

Gorton, the Prime Minster, had cost him his job in the reshuffled Government announced earlier this week. At first Mr Erwin said he was dropped because of a 'political manoeuvre'. Later, when asked to explain what this meant, he said: 'It wiggles, it's shapely and its name is Ainsley Gotto.'

> *The Times* 14 Nov. 1969

Howard Estabrook and Harry Behn

1 Excuse me while I slip into something more comfortable.

> *Hell's Angels* (1930 film), words spoken by Jean Harlow

Gavin Ewart 1916–

2 Miss Twye was soaping her breasts in the bath
When she heard behind her a meaning laugh
And to her amazement she discovered
A wicked man in the bathroom cupboard.

> *Poems and Songs* (1939) 'Miss Twye'

William Norman Ewer 1885–1976

3 I gave my life for freedom—This I know:
For those who bade me fight had told me so.

> *Five Souls and Other Verses* (1917) 'Five Souls'

4 How odd
Of God
To choose
The Jews.

> In *Week-End Book* (1924) p. 117 (for the reply, see Cecil Browne)

Clifton Fadiman 1904–

5 Provided it be well and truly made there is really for the confirmed turophile no such thing as a *bad* cheese. A cheese may disappoint. It may be dull, it may be naive, it may be oversophisticated. Yet it remains cheese, milk's leap toward immortality.

> *Any Number Can Play* (1957) p. 105

6 On November 17 . . . I encountered the mama of dada [Gertrude Stein] again (something called *Portraits and Prayers*) and as usual withdrew worsted.

> *Party of One* (1955) p. 90

Eleanor Farjeon 1881–1965

7 Morning has broken
Like the first morning,
Blackbird has spoken
Like the first bird.
Praise for the singing!
Praise for the morning!
Praise for them, springing
Fresh from the Lord!

> *Children's Bells* (1957) 'A Morning Song (for the First Day of Spring)'

8 King's Cross!
What shall we do?
His Purple Robe
Is rent in two!

Out of his Crown
He's torn the gems!
He's thrown his Sceptre
Into the Thames!
The Court is shaking
In its shoe—
King's Cross!
What shall we do?
Leave him alone
For a minute or two.

> *Nursery Rhymes of London Town* (1916) 'King's Cross'

King Farouk of Egypt 1920–1965

9 The whole world is in revolt. Soon there will be only five Kings left—the King of England, the King of Spades, the King of Clubs, the King of Hearts and the King of Diamonds.

> Said to Lord Boyd-Orr at a conference in Cairo, 1948, in Lord Boyd-Orr *As I Recall* (1966) ch. 21

William Faulkner 1897–1962

10 The long summer.

> *The Hamlet* (1940), title of bk. 3. Cf. Irving Ravetch and Harriet Frank

11 The writer's only responsibility is to his art. He will be completely ruthless if he is a good one. He has a dream. It anguishes him so much he must get rid of it. He has no peace until then. Everything goes by the board: honor, pride, decency, security, happiness, all, to get the book written. If a writer has to rob his mother, he will not hesitate; the *Ode on a Grecian Urn* is worth any number of old ladies.

> In *Paris Review* Spring 1956, p. 30

12 He [the writer] must teach himself that the basest of all things is to be afraid and, teaching himself that, forget it forever, leaving no room in his workshop for anything but the old verities and truths of the heart, the old universal truths lacking which any story is ephemeral and doomed—love and honor and pity and pride and compassion and sacrifice.

> Nobel Prize speech, 1950, in *Les Prix Nobel en 1950* (1951) p. 71

13 I believe man will not merely endure, he will prevail. He is immortal, not because he, alone among creatures, has an inexhaustible voice but because he has a soul, a spirit capable of compassion and sacrifice and endurance.

> Nobel Prize speech, 1950, in *Les Prix Nobel en 1950* (1951) p. 71

14 There is no such thing . . . as bad whiskey. Some whiskeys just happen to be better than others. But a man shouldn't fool with booze until he's fifty; then he's a damn fool if he doesn't.

> In James M. Webb and A. Wigfall Green *William Faulkner of Oxford* (1965) p. 110

George Fearon 1901–1972

15 In my capacity as Press Representative for the English Stage Company I had read John Osborne's play [*Look Back in Anger*]. When I met the author I ventured to prophesy that his generation would praise his play

while mine would, in general, dislike it. I then told him jokingly that Sloane Square might well become a bloody battleground. 'If this happens,' I told him, 'you would become known as the Angry Young Man.' In fact, we decided then and there that henceforth he was to be known as that.

Daily Telegraph 2 Oct. 1957

James Fenton 1949–

1 It is not what they built. It is what they knocked down.
It is not the houses. It is the spaces between the houses.
It is not the streets that exist. It is the streets that no longer exist.

German Requiem (1981) p. 1

Edna Ferber 1887–1968

2 Mother knows best.
Title of story (1927)

3 Being an old maid is like death by drowning, a really delightful sensation after you cease to struggle.
In R. E. Drennan *Wit's End* (1973)

Kathleen Ferrier 1912–1953

4 Enid and I visited her just before the end to be greeted by her with smiling affection. She tired quickly and gently sent us away by murmuring, 'Now I'll have eine kleine Pause.' Those were the last words we heard her utter.
Gerald Moore *Am I Too Loud?* (1962) ch. 19

Eric Field

5 Towards the end of July 1914, I . . . received a surprise call from Colonel Strachey, the A.A.G. (Recruiting). He swore me to secrecy, told me that war was imminent and that the moment it broke out we should have to start advertising at once. . . . That night I worked out a draft schedule and wrote an advertisement headed 'Your King and Country need you' with the inevitable Coat of Arms at the top.
Advertising (1959) ch. 2

Dorothy Fields 1905–1974

6 The minute you walked in the joint,
I could see you were a man of distinction,
A real big spender.
Good looking, so refined,
Say, wouldn't you like to know what's going on in my mind?
So let me get right to the point.
I don't pop my cork for every guy I see.
Hey! big spender, spend a little time with me.
Big Spender (1966 song; music by Cy Coleman)

7 A fine romance with no kisses.
A fine romance, my friend, this is.
We should be like a couple of hot tomatoes,
But you're as cold as yesterday's mashed potatoes.
A Fine Romance (1936 song; music by Jerome Kern)

8 I can't give you anything but love (baby).
Title of song (1928; music by Jimmy McHugh)

9 Grab your coat, and get your hat,
Leave your worry on the doorstep,
Just direct your feet
To the sunny side of the street.
On the Sunny Side of the Street (1930 song; music by Jimmy McHugh)

Dame Gracie Fields (Grace Stansfield) 1898–1979

See JIMMY HARPER *et al.*

W. C. Fields (William Claude Dukenfield) 1880–1946

10 Some weasel took the cork out of my lunch.
You Can't Cheat an Honest Man (1939 film), in William K. Everson *Art of W. C. Fields* (1968) p. 167

11 Never give a sucker an even break.
In *Collier's* 28 Nov. 1925. It was W. C. Fields's catch-phrase, and he is said to have used it in the musical comedy *Poppy* (1923), although it does not occur in the libretto. It was used as the title of a W. C. Fields film in 1941.

12 Last week, I went to Philadelphia, but it was closed.
In Richard J. Anobile *Godfrey Daniels* (1975) p. 6

13 I was in love with a beautiful blonde once, dear. She drove me to drink. That's the one thing I'm indebted to her for.
Never Give a Sucker an Even Break (1941 film), in Richard J. Anobile *Flask of Fields* (1972) p. 219

14 I always keep a supply of stimulant handy in case I see a snake—which I also keep handy.
In Corey Ford *Time of Laughter* (1970) p. 182

15 Here lies W. C. Fields. I would rather be living in Philadelphia.
Suggested epitaph for himself, in *Vanity Fair* June 1925

16 Fifteen years ago, I made the line 'It ain't a fit night out for man or beast' a by-word by using it in my sketch in Earl Carroll's *Vanities*. Later on, I used it as a title for a moving picture I did for Mack Sennett. I do not claim to be the originator of this line as it was probably used long before I was born in some old melodrama.
Letter, 8 Feb. 1944, in R. J. Fields (ed.) *W. C. Fields by Himself* (1974) pt. 2 (also used by Fields in his 1933 film *The Fatal Glass of Beer*)

17 Hell, I never vote *for* anybody. I always vote *against*.
In Robert Lewis Taylor *W. C. Fields: His Follies and Fortunes* (1950) p. 228

Harry Julian Fink, Rita M. Fink, and Dean Riesner

18 Go ahead, make my day.
Dirty Harry (1971 film; words spoken by Clint Eastwood)

Ronald Firbank 1886–1926

19 'O! help me, heaven,' she prayed, 'to be decorative and to do right!'
Flower Beneath the Foot (1923) ch. 2

1 Looking back, I remember the average curate at home as something between a eunuch and a snigger.
  Flower Beneath the Foot (1923) ch. 4

2 There was a pause—just long enough for an angel to pass, flying slowly.
  Vainglory (1915) ch. 6

3 All millionaires love a baked apple.
  Vainglory (1915) ch. 13

4 'I know of no joy,' she airily began, 'greater than a cool white dress after the sweetness of confession.'
  Valmouth (1919) ch. 4

Fred Fisher 1875–1942

See ADA BENSON

H. A. L. Fisher 1856–1940

5 One intellectual excitement has, however, been denied me. Men wiser and more learned than I have discerned in history a plot, a rhythm, a predetermined pattern. These harmonies are concealed from me. I can see only one emergency following upon another as wave follows upon wave, only one great fact with respect to which, since it is unique, there can be no generalizations, only one safe rule for the historian: that he should recognize in the development of human destinies the play of the contingent and the unforeseen.
  History of Europe (1935) p. vii

John Arbuthnot Fisher (Baron Fisher) 1841–1920

6 The essence of war is violence. Moderation in war is imbecility.
  Lecture notes 1899–1902, in R. H. Bacon *Life of Lord Fisher* (1929) vol. 1, ch. 7

7 Yours till Hell freezes.
  Letter to George Lambert, 5 Apr. 1909, in A. J. Marder *Fear God and Dread Nought* (1956) vol. 2, pt. 1, ch. 2.
  Cf. F. Ponsonby *Reflections of Three Reigns* (1951) p. 131: Once an officer in India wrote to me and ended his letter 'Yours till Hell freezes'. I used this forcible expression in a letter to Fisher, and he adopted it instead of 'Yours sincerely' and used it a great deal.

8 You must be ruthless, relentless, and remorseless! Sack the lot!
  Letter to *The Times* 2 Sept. 1919

9 This letter is not to argue with your leading article of September 2. (It's only d—d fools who argue!)
  Never contradict
  Never explain
  Never apologize
  (Those are the secrets of a happy life!)
  Letter to *The Times*, 5 Sept.1919

Marve Fisher

10 I want an old-fashioned house
  With an old-fashioned fence
  And an old-fashioned millionaire.
  Old-Fashioned Girl (1954 song; popularized by Eartha Kitt)

Albert H. Fitz

11 You are my honey, honeysuckle, I am the bee.
  The Honeysuckle and the Bee (1901 song; music by William H. Penn)

F. Scott Fitzgerald 1896–1940

12 Let me tell you about the very rich. They are different from you and me.
  All Sad Young Men (1926) 'Rich Boy' (Ernest Hemingway's rejoinder in his story 'The Snows of Kilimanjaro'—in *Esquire* Aug. 1936—was: 'Yes, they have more money')

13 The beautiful and damned.
  Title of novel (1922)

14 No grand idea was ever born in a conference, but a lot of foolish ideas have died there.
  Note-Books E, in Edmund Wilson *Crack-Up* (1945)

15 Show me a hero and I will write you a tragedy.
  Note-Books E, in Edmund Wilson *Crack-Up* (1945)

16 The test of a first-rate intelligence is the ability to hold two opposed ideas in the mind at the same time, and still retain the ability to function.
  Esquire Feb. 1936, 'The Crack-Up'

17 In a real dark night of the soul it is always three o'clock in the morning, day after day.
  Esquire Mar. 1936, 'Handle with Care'

18 In my younger and more vulnerable years my father gave me some advice I've been turning over in my mind ever since.
  Great Gatsby (1925) ch. 1

19 In his blue gardens, men and girls came and went like moths among the whisperings and the champagne and the stars.
  Great Gatsby (1925) ch. 3

20 Her voice is full of money.
  Great Gatsby (1925) ch. 7

21 Gatsby believed in the green light, the orgastic future that year by year recedes before us. It eluded us then, but that's no matter—to-morrow we will run faster, stretch out our arms farther. . . . And one fine morning—
  So we beat on, boats against the current, borne back ceaselessly into the past.
  Great Gatsby (1925) ch. 9

22 There are no second acts in American lives.
  In Edmund Wilson *Last Tycoon* (1949) 'Hollywood, etc. Notes'

23 She had once been a Catholic, but discovering that priests were infinitely more attentive when she was in process of losing or regaining faith in Mother Church, she maintained an enchantingly wavering attitude.
  This Side of Paradise (1921) bk. 1, ch. 1

Zelda Fitzgerald 1900–1948

24 Ernest, don't you think Al Jolson is greater than Jesus?
  In Ernest Hemingway *Moveable Feast* (1964) ch. 18. Cf. John Lennon 135:2

Robert Fitzsimmons 1862–1917

1 You know the old saying, 'The bigger they are, the further they have to fall.'
  In *Brooklyn Daily Eagle* 11 Aug. 1900

Bud Flanagan (Chaim Reeven Weintrop) 1896–1968

2 Underneath the Arches,
  I dream my dreams away,
  Underneath the Arches,
  On cobble-stones I lay.
  Underneath the Arches (1932 song; additional words by Reg Connelly)

Michael Flanders 1922–1975 and Donald Swann 1923–

3 I'm a gnu
  A gnother gnu.
  The Gnu (1956 song)

4 Mud! Mud! Glorious mud!
  Nothing quite like it for cooling the blood.
  So, follow me, follow,
  Down to the hollow,
  And there let us wallow
  In glorious mud.
  Hippopotamus Song (1952)

5 I don't eat people,
  I won't eat people,
  I don't eat people,
  Eating people is wrong!
  The Reluctant Cannibal (1956 song)

James Elroy Flecker 1884–1915

6 We who with songs beguile your pilgrimage
  And swear that beauty lives though lilies die,
  We Poets of the proud old lineage
  Who sing to find your hearts, we know not why,—
  What shall we tell you? Tales, marvellous tales
  Of ships and stars and isles where good men rest.
  Golden Journey to Samarkand (1913) 'Prologue'

7 When the great markets by the sea shut fast
  All that calm Sunday that goes on and on:
  When even lovers find their peace at last,
  And earth is but a star, that once had shone.
  Golden Journey to Samarkand (1913) 'Prologue'

8 Sweet to ride forth at evening from the wells,
  When shadows pass gigantic on the sand,
  And softly through the silence beat the bells
  Along the Golden Road to Samarkand.
  Golden Journey to Samarkand (1913) p. 8

9 For lust of knowing what should not be known,
  We take the Golden Road to Samarkand.
  Golden Journey to Samarkand (1913) p. 8

10 How splendid in the morning glows the lily; with what grace he throws
  His supplication to the rose.
  Golden Journey to Samarkand (1913) 'Yasmin'

11 And some to Meccah turn to pray, and I toward thy bed, Yasmin.
  Golden Journey to Samarkand (1913) 'Yasmin'

12 For one night or the other night
  Will come the Gardener in white, and gathered flowers are dead, Yasmin.
  Golden Journey to Samarkand (1913) 'Yasmin'

13 The dragon-green, the luminous, the dark, the serpent-haunted sea.
  Golden Journey to Samarkand (1913) 'Gates of Damascus'

14 A ship, an isle, a sickle moon—
  With few but with how splendid stars
  The mirrors of the sea are strewn
  Between their silver bars!
  Golden Journey to Samarkand (1913) 'A Ship, an Isle, and a Sickle Moon'

15 For pines are gossip pines the wide world through
  And full of runic tales to sigh or sing.
  Golden Journey to Samarkand (1913) 'Brumana'

16 Half to forget the wandering and pain,
  Half to remember days that have gone by,
  And dream and dream that I am home again!
  Golden Journey to Samarkand (1913) 'Brumana'

17 Noon strikes on England, noon on Oxford town,
  Beauty she was statue cold—there's blood upon her gown:
  Noon of my dreams, O noon!
  Proud and godly kings had built her, long ago,
  With her towers and tombs and statues all arow,
  With her fair and floral air and the love that lingers there,
  And the streets where the great men go.
  Golden Journey to Samarkand (1913) 'Dying Patriot'

18 West of these out to seas colder than the Hebrides I must go
  Where the fleet of stars is anchored and the young Star captains glow.
  Golden Journey to Samarkand (1913) 'Dying Patriot'

19 I have seen old ships sail like swans asleep
  Beyond the village which men still call Tyre,
  With leaden age o'ercargoed, dipping deep
  For Famagusta and the hidden sun
  That rings black Cyprus with a lake of fire.
  Old Ships (1915) title poem

20 And with great lies about his wooden horse
  Set the crew laughing, and forgot his course.
  Old Ships (1915) title poem

21 It was so old a ship—who knows, who knows?
  —And yet so beautiful, I watched in vain
  To see the mast burst open with a rose,
  And the whole deck put on its leaves again.
  Old Ships (1915) title poem

22 How shall we conquer? Like a wind
  That falls at eve our fancies blow,
  And old Maeonides the blind
  Said it three thousand years ago.
  36 Poems (1910) 'To a Poet a Thousand Years Hence'

23 O friend unseen, unborn, unknown,
  Student of our sweet English tongue,

Read out my words at night, alone:
I was a poet, I was young.
36 Poems (1910) 'To a Poet a Thousand Years Hence'

Ian Fleming 1908–1964

1 Bond said, 'And I would like a medium Vodka dry
Martini—with a slice of lemon peel. Shaken and not
stirred, please. I would prefer Russian or Polish vodka.'
Dr No (1958) ch. 14

2 From Russia with love.
Title of novel (1957)

3 Live and let die.
Title of novel (1954)

Robert, Marquis de Flers 1872–1927 and Arman de Caillavet 1869–1915

4 *Démocratie est le nom que nous donnons au peuple toutes
les fois que nous avons besoin de lui.*

Democracy is the name we give the people whenever
we need them.
L'habit vert act 1, sc. 12, in *La petite illustration série théâtre*
31 May 1913

Dario Fo 1926–

5 *Non si paga, non si paga.*

We won't pay, we won't pay.
Title of play (1975; translated by Lino Pertile in 1978 as 'We
Can't Pay? We Won't Pay!' and performed in London in
1981 as '*Can't Pay? Won't Pay!*')

Marshal Ferdinand Foch 1851–1929

6 *Mon centre cède, ma droite recule, situation excellente,
j'attaque.*

My centre is giving way, my right is retreating,
situation excellent, I am attacking.
Message sent during the first Battle of the Marne, Sept.
1914, in R. Recouly *Foch* (1919) ch. 6

7 *Ce n'est pas un traité de paix, c'est un armistice de vingt
ans.*

This [the treaty signed at Versailles in 1919] is not
a peace treaty, it is an armistice for twenty years.
In Paul Reynaud *Mémoires* (1963) vol. 2, p. 457

J. Foley

8 Old soldiers never die,
They simply fade away.
Old Soldiers Never Die (1920 song; copyrighted by J. Foley
but perhaps a 'folk-song' from the First World War)

Michael Foot 1913–

9 A speech from Ernest Bevin on a major occasion had
all the horrific fascination of a public execution. If the
mind was left immune, eyes and ears and emotions
were riveted.
Aneurin Bevan (1962) vol. 1, ch. 13

10 Think of it! A second Chamber selected by the Whips.
A seraglio of eunuchs.
Hansard 3 Feb. 1969, col. 88

11 It is not necessary that every time he [Norman Tebbit]
rises he should give his famous imitation of a semi-
house-trained polecat.
Hansard 2 Mar. 1978, col. 668

Anna Ford 1943–

12 Let's face it, there are no plain women on television.
In *Observer* 23 Sept. 1979

Gerald Ford 1909–

13 I believe that truth is the glue that holds Government
together, not only our Government, but civilization
itself.
Speech, 9 Aug. 1974, in G. J. Lankevich *Gerald R. Ford*
(1977)

14 My fellow Americans, our long national nightmare is
over. Our Constitution works; our great Republic is
a Government of laws and not of men. Here the people
rule.
Speech, 9 Aug. 1974, in G. J. Lankevich *Gerald R. Ford*
(1977)

15 There is no Soviet domination of Eastern Europe and
there never will be under a Ford administration.
In television debate with Jimmy Carter, 6 Oct. 1976, in
S. Kraus *Great Debates* (1979) p. 482

16 If the Government is big enough to give you everything
you want, it is big enough to take away everything you
have.
In John F. Parker *If Elected* (1960) p. 193

17 I am a Ford, not a Lincoln. My addresses will never be
as eloquent as Lincoln's. But I will do my best to equal
his brevity and plain speaking.
Speech on taking vice-presidential oath, 6 Dec. 1973, in
Washington Post 7 Dec. 1973

Henry Ford 1863–1947

18 History is more or less bunk. It's tradition. We don't
want tradition. We want to live in the present and the
only history that is worth a tinker's damn is the
history we make today.
Chicago Tribune 25 May 1916 (interview with Charles N.
Wheeler)

19 People can have the Model T in any colour—so long as
it's black.
In Allan Nevins *Ford* (1957) vol. 2, ch. 15

Lena Guilbert Ford 1870–1916

20 Keep the Home-fires burning,
While your hearts are yearning,
Though your lads are far away
They dream of Home.
There's a silver lining
Through the dark cloud shining;
Turn the dark cloud inside out,
Till the boys come Home.
'*Till the Boys Come Home!* (1914 song; music by Ivor
Novello)

Howell Forgy 1908–1983

1 Lieutenant Forgy . . . said that on Dec. 7 he was at Pearl Harbor directing preparations for church services aboard his ship . . . when general quarters were sounded as the Japanese attacked. He reported to his battle station. The power was off on a powder hoist, he said, and so Lieutenant Edwin Woodhead formed a line of sailors to pass the ammunition by hand to the deck. The chaplain moved along the line, encouraging the passers and repeating, 'Praise the Lord and pass the ammunition.'

New York Times 1 Nov. 1942. Cf. Frank Loesser's 1942 song *Praise the Lord and Pass the Ammunition.*

E. M. Forster 1879–1970

2 They [public schoolboys] go forth into a world that is not entirely composed of public-school men or even of Anglo-Saxons, but of men who are as various as the sands of the sea; into a world of whose richness and subtlety they have no conception. They go forth into it with well-developed bodies, fairly developed minds, and undeveloped hearts.

Abinger Harvest (1936) 'Notes on English Character'

3 It is not that the Englishman can't feel—it is that he is afraid to feel. He has been taught at his public school that feeling is bad form. He must not express great joy or sorrow, or even open his mouth too wide when he talks—his pipe might fall out if he did.

Abinger Harvest (1936) 'Notes on English Character'

4 Everything must be like something, so what is this like?

Abinger Harvest (1936) 'Doll Souse'

5 American women shoot the hippopotamus with eyebrows made of platinum.

Abinger Harvest (1936) 'Mickey and Minnie'. Cf. 24:8

6 It is frivolous stuff, and how rare, how precious is frivolity! How few writers can prostitute all their powers! They are always implying 'I am capable of higher things.'

Abinger Harvest (1936) 'Ronald Firbank'

7 The historian must have a third quality as well: some conception of how men who are not historians behave. Otherwise he will move in a world of the dead.

Abinger Harvest (1936) 'Captain Edward Gibbon'

8 Yes—oh dear yes—the novel tells a story.

Aspects of the Novel (1927) ch. 2

9 That old lady in the anecdote . . . was not so much angry as contemptuous. . . . 'How can I tell what I think till I see what I say?'

Aspects of the Novel (1927) ch. 5. Cf. Graham Wallas 222:8

10 I am only touching on one aspect of *Ulysses*: it is of course far more than a fantasy—it is a dogged attempt to cover the universe with mud, an inverted Victorianism, an attempt to make crossness and dirt succeed where sweetness and light failed, a simplification of the human character in the interests of Hell.

Aspects of the Novel (1927) ch. 6

11 Long books, when read, are usually overpraised, because the reader wishes to convince others and himself that he has not wasted his time.

Note from commonplace book, in O. Stallybrass (ed.) *Aspects of the Novel and Related Writings* (1974) p. 129

12 Like many others who have lived long in a great capital, she had strong feelings about the various railway termini. They are our gates to the glorious and the unknown. Through them we pass out into adventure and sunshine, to them, alas! we return.

Howards End (1910) ch. 2

13 It will be generally admitted that Beethoven's Fifth Symphony is the most sublime noise that has ever penetrated into the ear of man.

Howards End (1910) ch. 5

14 The music [the scherzo of Beethoven's 5th Symphony] started with a goblin walking quietly over the universe, from end to end. Others followed him. They were not aggressive creatures; it was that that made them so terrible to Helen. They merely observed in passing that there was no such thing as splendour or heroism in the world. After the interlude of elephants dancing, they returned and made the observation for a second time. Helen could not contradict them, for, once at all events, she had felt the same, and had seen the reliable walls of youth collapse. Panic and emptiness! The goblins were right.

Howards End (1910) ch. 5

15 All men are equal—all men, that is to say, who possess umbrellas.

Howards End (1910) ch. 6

16 Personal relations are the important thing for ever and ever, and not this outer life of telegrams and anger.

Howards End (1910) ch. 19

17 She would only point out the salvation that was latent in his own soul, and in the soul of every man. Only connect! That was the whole of her sermon. Only connect the prose and the passion, and both will be exalted, and human love will be seen at its height. Live in fragments no longer. Only connect, and the beast and the monk, robbed of the isolation that is life to either, will die.

Howards End (1910) ch. 22 (the title-page also has 'Only connect . . . ')

18 Death destroys a man: the idea of Death saves him.

Howards End (1910) ch. 27 (chapter 41 has 'Death destroys a man, but the idea of death saves him')

19 'I don't think I understand people very well. I only know whether I like or dislike them.'
'Then you are an Oriental.'

Passage to India (1924) ch. 2

20 The so-called white races are really pinko-grey.

Passage to India (1924) ch. 7

21 The echo in a Marabar cave is not like these, it is entirely devoid of distinction. Whatever is said, the same monotonous noise replies, and quivers up and down the walls until it is absorbed into the roof. 'Boum' is the sound as far as the human alphabet can express it, or 'bou-oum', or 'ou-boum',—utterly dull. Hope, politeness, the blowing of a nose, the squeak of a boot, all produce 'boum'.

Passage to India (1924) ch. 14

1 The echo began in some indescribable way to undermine her hold on life. Coming at a moment when she chanced to be fatigued, it had managed to murmur, 'Pathos, piety, courage—they exist, but are identical, and so is filth. Everything exists, nothing has value.'
Passage to India (1924) ch. 14

2 The inscriptions which the poets of the State had composed were hung where they could not be read, or had twitched their drawing-pins out of the stucco, and one of them (composed in English to indicate His universality) consisted, by an unfortunate slip of the draughtsman, of the words, 'God si Love.'
God si Love. Is this the first message of India?
Passage to India (1924) ch. 33

3 A room with a view.
Title of novel (1908)

4 The traveller who has gone to Italy to study the tactile values of Giotto, or the corruption of the Papacy, may return remembering nothing but the blue sky and the men and women under it.
Room with a View (1908) ch. 2

5 I hate the idea of causes, and if I had to choose between betraying my country and betraying my friend, I hope I should have the guts to betray my country.
Two Cheers for Democracy (1951) 'What I Believe'

6 So Two cheers for Democracy: one because it admits variety and two because it permits criticism. Two cheers are quite enough: there is no occasion to give three. Only Love the Beloved Republic deserves that.
Two Cheers for Democracy (1951) 'What I Believe' ('Love, the Beloved Republic' is a phrase from Swinburne's poem *Hertha*)

7 Think before you speak is criticism's motto; speak before you think creation's.
Two Cheers for Democracy (1951) 'Raison d'être of Criticism'

8 I suggest that the only books that influence us are those for which we are ready, and which have gone a little farther down our particular path than we have yet got ourselves.
Two Cheers for Democracy (1951) 'Books That Influenced Me'

9 Creative writers are always greater than the causes that they represent.
Two Cheers for Democracy (1951) 'Gide and George'

Bruce Forsyth 1928–

10 Didn't she [*or* he *or* they] do well?
Catch-phrase in 'The Generation Game' on BBC Television, 1973 onwards

11 Nice to see you—to see you, nice.
Catch-phrase in 'The Generation Game' on BBC Television, 1973 onwards

12 I'm in charge.
Catch-phrase in 'Sunday Night at the London Palladium' on ITV, 1958 onwards

Harry Emerson Fosdick 1878–1969

13 I renounce war for its consequences, for the lies it lives on and propagates, for the undying hatred it arouses, for the dictatorships it puts in the place of democracy,

for the starvation that stalks after it. I renounce war and never again, directly or indirectly, will I sanction or support another.
Sermon in New York on Armistice Day 1933, in *Secret of Victorious Living* (1934) p. 97

Anatole France (Jacques-Anatole-François Thibault) 1844–1924

14 *Dans tout État policé, la richesse est chose sacrée; dans les démocraties elle est la seule chose sacrée.*

In every well-governed state, wealth is a sacred thing; in democracies it is the only sacred thing.
L'Île des pingouins (Penguin Island, 1908) pt. 6, ch. 2

15 *Ils [les pauvres] y doivent travailler devant la majestueuse égalité des lois, qui interdit au riche comme au pauvre de coucher sous les ponts, de mendier dans les rues et de voler du pain.*

They [the poor] have to labour in the face of the majestic equality of the law, which forbids the rich as well as the poor to sleep under bridges, to beg in the streets, and to steal bread.
Le Lys rouge (The Red Lily, 1894) ch. 7

16 *Le bon critique est celui qui raconte les aventures de son âme au milieu des chefs-d'œuvre.*

The good critic is he who relates the adventures of his soul among masterpieces.
La Vie littéraire (The Literary Life, 1888) dedicatory letter

Georges Franju 1912–

See JEAN-LUC GODARD

Sir James George Frazer 1854–1941

17 The awe and dread with which the untutored savage contemplates his mother-in-law are amongst the most familiar facts of anthropology.
The Golden Bough (ed. 2, 1900) vol. 1, p. 288

Stan Freberg 1926–

18 It's too loud, man. . . . It's too shrill, man, it's too piercing.
Banana Boat (Day-O) (1957 record; lines spoken by Peter Leeds)

19 Excuse me, you ain't any kin to the snare drummer, are you?
Yellow Rose of Texas (1955 record; words spoken to a loud banjo-player)

Arthur Freed 1894–1973

20 Singin' in the rain.
Title of song (1929; music by Nacio Herb Brown)

Ralph Freed

1 I like New York in June,
How about you?

How About You (1941 song; music by Burton Lane)

Cliff Freeman

2 Where's the beef?

Advertising slogan for Wendy's Hamburgers in campaign
launched 9 Jan. 1984 (taken up by Walter Mondale in
a televised debate with Gary Hart from Atlanta, 11 March
1984: 'When I hear your new ideas I'm reminded of that ad,
"Where's the beef?"')

John Freeman 1880–1929

3 It was the lovely moon—she lifted
Slowly her white brow among
Bronze cloud–waves that ebbed and drifted
Faintly, faintlier afar.

Stone Trees (1916) 'It Was the Lovely Moon'

Marilyn French 1929–

4 Whatever they may be in public life, whatever their
relations with men, in their relations with women, all
men are rapists, and that's all they are. They rape us
with their eyes, their laws, and their codes.

The Women's Room (1977) bk. 5, ch. 19

Sigmund Freud 1856–1939

5 *Die Anatomie ist das Schicksal.*

Anatomy is destiny.

Gesammelte Schriften (Collected Writings, 1924) vol. 5,
p. 210

6 *'Itzig, wohin reit'st Du?' 'Weiss ich, frag das Pferd.'*

'Itzig, where are you riding to?' 'Don't ask me, ask the
horse.'

Letter to Wilhelm Fliess, 7 July 1898, in *Aus den Anfängen der
Psychoanalyse* (Origins of Psychoanalysis, 1950) p. 275

7 *Wir sind so eingerichtet, dass wir nur den Kontrast intensiv
geniessen können, den Zustand nur sehr wenig.*

We are so made, that we can only derive intense
enjoyment from a contrast, and only very little from
a state of things.

Das Unbehagen in der Kultur (Civilization and its Discontents,
1930) ch. 2

8 *Vergleiche entscheiden nichts, das ist wahr, aber sie können
machen, dass man sich heimischer fühlt.*

Analogies decide nothing, that is true, but they can
make one feel more at home.

Neue Folge der Vorlesungen zur Einführung in die Psychoanalyse
(New Introductory Lectures on Psychoanalysis, 1933) ch. 31

9 The great question that has never been answered and
which I have not yet been able to answer, despite my
thirty years of research into the feminine soul, is 'What
does a woman want?'

Letter to Marie Bonaparte, in Ernest Jones *Sigmund Freud:
Life and Work* (1955) vol. 2, pt. 3, ch. 16

Max Frisch 1911–

10 *Diskussion mit Hanna!—über Technik (laut Hanna) als
Kniff, die Welt so einzurichten, dass wir sie nicht erleben
müssen.*

Discussion with Hanna—about technology (according
to Hanna) as the knack of so arranging the world that
we need not experience it.

Homo Faber (1957) pt. 2

Charles Frohman 1860–1915

11 Why fear death? It is the most beautiful adventure in
life.

Last words before drowning in the *Lusitania*, 7 May 1915, in
I. F. Marcosson and D. Frohman *Charles Frohman* (1916)
ch. 19. Cf. J. M. Barrie 19:9

Erich Fromm 1900–1980

12 Man's main task in life is to give birth to himself, to
become what he potentially is. The most important
product of his effort is his own personality.

Man for Himself (1947) ch. 4

13 In the nineteenth century the problem was that *God is
dead*; in the twentieth century the problem is that *man
is dead*. In the nineteenth century inhumanity meant
cruelty; in the twentieth century it means schizoid
self-alienation. The danger of the past was that men
became slaves. The danger of the future is that men
may become robots.

The Sane Society (1955) ch. 9

David Frost 1939–

14 Hello, good evening, and welcome.

Catch-phrase in 'The Frost Programme' on BBC Television,
1966 onwards

15 Seriously, though, he's doing a grand job!

Catch-phrase in 'That Was The Week That Was', on BBC
Television, 1962–3

Robert Frost 1874–1963

16 It should be of the pleasure of a poem itself to tell how
it can. The figure a poem makes. It begins in delight
and ends in wisdom. The figure is the same as for
love.

Collected Poems (1939) 'Figure a Poem Makes'

17 No tears in the writer, no tears in the reader.

Collected Poems (1939) 'Figure a Poem Makes'

18 Like a piece of ice on a hot stove the poem must ride on
its own melting. A poem may be worked over once it is
in being, but may not be worried into being.

Collected Poems (1939) 'Figure a Poem Makes'

19 They cannot scare me with their empty spaces
Between stars—on stars where no human race is.
I have it in me so much nearer home
To scare myself with my own desert places.

Further Range (1936) 'Desert Places'

20 I never dared be radical when young
For fear it would make me conservative when old.

Further Range (1936) 'Precaution'

1 Never ask of money spent
Where the spender thinks it went.
Nobody was ever meant
To remember or invent
What he did with every cent.
Further Range (1936) 'Hardship of Accounting'

2 I've given offence by saying that I'd as soon write free
verse as play tennis with the net down.
In Edward Lathem *Interviews with Robert Frost* (1966) p. 203

3 Forgive, O Lord, my little jokes on Thee
And I'll forgive Thy great big one on me.
In the Clearing (1962) 'Cluster of Faith'

4 I shall be telling this with a sigh
Somewhere ages and ages hence:
Two roads diverged in a wood, and I—
I took the one less travelled by,
And that has made all the difference.
Mountain Interval (1916) 'Road Not Taken'

5 I'd like to get away from earth awhile
And then come back to it and begin over.
May no fate wilfully misunderstand me
And half grant what I wish and snatch me away
Not to return. Earth's the right place for love:
I don't know where it's likely to go better.
I'd like to go by climbing a birch tree,
And climb black branches up a snow-white trunk
Toward heaven, till the tree could bear no more,
But dipped its top and set me down again.
That would be good both going and coming back.
One could do worse than be a swinger of birches.
Mountain Interval (1916) 'Birches'

6 Some say the world will end in fire,
Some say in ice.
From what I've tasted of desire
I hold with those who favour fire.
But if it had to perish twice,
I think I know enough of hate
To say that for destruction ice
Is also great
And would suffice.
New Hampshire (1923) 'Fire and Ice'

7 The woods are lovely, dark and deep.
But I have promises to keep,
And miles to go before I sleep,
And miles to go before I sleep.
New Hampshire (1923) 'Stopping by Woods on a Snowy Evening'

8 I'm going out to clean the pasture spring;
I'll only stop to rake the leaves away
(And wait to watch the water clear, I may):
I shan't be gone long.—You come too.
North of Boston (1914) 'The Pasture'

9 Something there is that doesn't love a wall,
That sends the frozen-ground-swell under it.
North of Boston (1914) 'Mending Wall'

10 My apple trees will never get across
And eat the cones under his pines, I tell him.
He only says, 'Good fences make good neighbours.'
North of Boston (1914) 'Mending Wall'

11 Before I built a wall I'd ask to know

What I was walling in or walling out,
And to whom I was like to give offence.
North of Boston (1914) 'Mending Wall'

12 And nothing to look backward to with pride,
And nothing to look forward to with hope.
North of Boston (1914) 'Death of the Hired Man'

13 'Home is the place where, when you have to go there,
They have to take you in.'
'I should have called it
Something you somehow haven't to deserve.'
North of Boston (1914) 'Death of the Hired Man'

14 Most of the change we think we see in life
Is due to truths being in and out of favour.
North of Boston (1914) 'Black Cottage'

15 Len says one steady pull more ought to do it.
He says the best way out is always through.
North of Boston (1914) 'Servant to Servants'

16 I've broken Anne of gathering bouquets.
It's not fair to the child. It can't be helped though:
Pressed into service means pressed out of shape.
North of Boston (1914) 'Self-Seeker'

17 Poetry is what is lost in translation. It is also what is
lost in interpretation.
In Louis Untermeyer *Robert Frost: a Backward Look* (1964)
p. 18

18 Asked . . . whether he would define poetry as 'escape'
he answered hardily: 'No. Poetry is a way of taking life
by the throat.'
Elizabeth S. Sergeant *Robert Frost: the Trial by Existence*
(1960) ch. 18

19 I have been one acquainted with the night.
West-Running Brook (1928) 'Acquainted with the Night'

20 Happiness makes up in height for what it lacks in
length.
Title of poem in *Witness Tree* (1942)

21 The land was ours before we were the land's.
She was our land more than a hundred years
Before we were her people.
Witness Tree (1942) 'Gift Outright'

22 And were an epitaph to be my story
I'd have a short one ready for my own.
I would have written of me on my stone:
I had a lover's quarrel with the world.
Witness Tree (1942) 'Lesson for Today'

23 We dance round in a ring and suppose,
But the Secret sits in the middle and knows.
Witness Tree (1942) 'The Secret Sits'

Christopher Fry 1907–

24 The dark is light enough.
Title of play (1954)

25 I travel light; as light,
That is, as a man can travel who will
Still carry his body around because
Of its sentimental value.
The Lady's not for Burning (1949) act 1

26 What after all
Is a halo? It's only one more thing to keep clean.
The Lady's not for Burning (1949) act 1

1 What is official
   Is incontestable. It undercuts
   The problematical world and sells us life
   At a discount.
      The Lady's not for Burning (1949) act 1

2 Where in this small-talking world can I find
   A longitude with no platitude?
      The Lady's not for Burning (1949) act 3

3 The moon is nothing
   But a circumambulating aphrodisiac
   Divinely subsidized to provoke the world
   Into a rising birth-rate.
      The Lady's not for Burning (1949) act 3

4 I hear
   A gay modulating anguish, rather like music.
      The Lady's not for Burning (1949) act 3

5 The Great Bear is looking so geometrical
   One would think that something or other could be
      proved.
      The Lady's not for Burning (1949) act 3

6 The best
   Thing we can do is to make wherever we're lost in
   Look as much like home as we can.
      The Lady's not for Burning (1949) act 3

7 Try thinking of love, or something.
   Amor vincit insomnia.
      A Sleep of Prisoners (1951) p. 37

8 I hope
   I've done nothing so monosyllabic as to cheat,
   A spade is never so merely a spade as the word
   Spade would imply.
      Venus Observed (1950) act 2, sc. 1

9 I tell you,
   Miss, I knows an undesirable character
   When I see one; I've been one myself for years.
      Venus Observed (1950) act 2, sc. 1

Roger Fry 1866–1934

10 Mr Fry . . . brought out a screen upon which there
    was a picture of a circus. The interviewer was puzzled
    by the long waists, bulging necks and short legs of the
    figures. 'But how much wit there is in those figures,'
    said Mr Fry. 'Art is significant deformity.'
      Virginia Woolf *Roger Fry* (1940) ch. 8

11 Bach almost persuades me to be a Christian.
      In Virginia Woolf *Roger Fry* (1940) ch. 11

R. Buckminster Fuller 1895–1983

12 Right now I am a passenger on space vehicle Earth
    zooming about the Sun at 60,000 miles per hour
    somewhere in the solar system.
      In Gene Youngblood *Expanded Cinema* (1970) p. 24

13 Either war is obsolete or men are.
      In *New Yorker* 8 Jan. 1966, p. 93

14 Here is God's purpose—
    for God, to me, it seems,
    is a verb

not a noun,
proper or improper.
   No More Secondhand God (1963) p. 28 (poem written in
   1940)

15 Now there is one outstandingly important fact
    regarding Spaceship Earth, and that is that no
    instruction book came with it.
      Operating Manual for Spaceship Earth (1969) ch. 4

Alfred Funke 1869–?

16 *Gott strafe England!*

   God punish England!
      Schwert und Myrte (Sword and Myrtle, 1914) p. 78

Sir David Maxwell Fyfe 1900–1967

See LORD KILMUIR

Will Fyffe 1885–1947

17 I belong to Glasgow
    Dear Old Glasgow town!
    But what's the matter wi' Glasgow?
    For it's going round and round.
    I'm only a common old working chap,
    As anyone can see,
    But when I get a couple of drinks on a Saturday,
    Glasgow belongs to me.
      I Belong to Glasgow (1920 song)

Rose Fyleman 1877–1957

18 There are fairies at the bottom of our garden!
      Punch 23 May 1917 'Fairies'

Zsa Zsa Gabor (Sari Gabor) 1919–

19 You mean apart from my own?
      When asked how many husbands she had had, in
      K. Edwards *I Wish I'd Said That* (1976) p. 75

20 A man in love is incomplete until he has married. Then
    he's finished.
      In *Newsweek* 28 Mar. 1960, p. 89

21 I never hated a man enough to give him diamonds
    back.
      In *Observer* 25 Aug. 1957

Norman Gaff d. 1988

22 A Mars a day helps you work, rest and play.
      Advertising slogan for Mars bar, *c*.1960 onwards

Hugh Gaitskell 1906–1963

23 I say this to you: we may lose the vote today [on
    retaining nuclear weapons] and the result may deal
    this Party a grave blow. It may not be possible to
    prevent it, but I think there are many of us who will
    not accept that this blow need be mortal, who will not
    believe that such an end is inevitable. There are some
    of us, Mr Chairman, who will fight and fight and fight
    again to save the Party we love. We will fight and

fight and fight again to bring back sanity and honesty and dignity, so that our Party with its great past may retain its glory and its greatness.

> Speech at Labour Party Conference, 5 Oct. 1960, in *Report of 59th Annual Conference* p. 201

1 It [a European federation] does mean, if this is the idea, the end of Britain as an independent European state. ... It means the end of a thousand years of history.

> Speech at Labour Party Conference, 3 Oct. 1962, in *Report of 61st Annual Conference* p. 159

J. K. Galbraith 1908–

2 These are the days when men of all social disciplines and all political faiths seek the comfortable and the accepted; when the man of controversy is looked upon as a disturbing influence; when originality is taken to be a mark of instability; and when, in minor modification of the scriptural parable, the bland lead the bland.

> *Affluent Society* (1958) ch. 1

3 Perhaps the thing most evident of all is how new and varied become the problems we must ponder when we break the nexus with the work of Ricardo and face the economics of affluence of the world in which we live. It is easy to see why the conventional wisdom resists so stoutly such a change. It is a far, far better thing to have a firm anchor in nonsense than to put out on the troubled seas of thought.

> *Affluent Society* (1958) ch. 11

4 In a community where public services have failed to keep abreast of private consumption things are very different. Here, in an atmosphere of private opulence and public squalor, the private goods have full sway.

> *Affluent Society* (1958) ch. 18. Cf. Sallust's *Catiline* 1ii. 22: *Habemus publice egestatem, privatim opulentiam.* We have public poverty and private opulence.

5 Politics is not the art of the possible. It consists in choosing between the disastrous and the unpalatable.

> Letter to President Kennedy, 2 Mar. 1962, in *Ambassador's Journal* (1969) p. 312. Cf. R. A. Butler 43:1

John Galsworthy 1867–1933

6 He [Jolyon] was afflicted by the thought that where Beauty was, nothing ever ran quite straight, which, no doubt, was why so many people looked on it as immoral.

> *In Chancery* (1920) pt. 1, ch. 13

7 I s'pose Jolyon's told you something about the young man. From all *I* can learn, he's got no business, no income, and no connection worth speaking of; but then, I know nothing—nobody tells me anything.

> *Man of Property* (1906) pt. 1, ch. 1

Ray Galton 1930– and *Alan Simpson* 1929–

8 I came in here in all good faith to help my country. I don't mind giving a reasonable amount [of blood], but a pint ... why that's very nearly an armful. I'm sorry. I'm not walking around with an empty arm for anybody.

> *The Blood Donor* (1961 television programme) in *Hancock's Half Hour* (1974) p. 113 (words spoken by Tony Hancock)

Mohandas Karamchand Gandhi 1869–1948

9 Recently I saw a film of Gandhi when he came to England in 1930. He disembarked in Southampton and on the gangway he was already overwhelmed by journalists asking questions. One of them asked, 'Mr Gandhi, what do you think of modern civilization?' And Mr Gandhi said, 'That would be a good idea.'

> E. F. Schumacher *Good Work* (1979) ch. 2

10 What difference does it make to the dead, the orphans and the homeless, whether the mad destruction is wrought under the name of totalitarianism or the holy name of liberty or democracy?

> *Non-Violence in Peace and War* (1942) vol. 1, ch. 142

11 The moment the slave resolves that he will no longer be a slave, his fetters fall. He frees himself and shows the way to others. Freedom and slavery are mental states.

> *Non-Violence in Peace and War* (1949) vol. 2, ch. 5

12 I wanted to avoid violence. Non-violence is the first article of my faith. It is also the last article of my creed.

> Speech at Shahi Bag, 18 Mar. 1922, in *Young India* 23 Mar. 1922

Greta Garbo (*Greta Lovisa Gustafsson*) 1905–1990

13 I want to be alone. .... I just want to be alone.

> *Grand Hotel* (1932 film; script by William A. Drake)

14 I tank I go home.

> On being refused a pay rise by Louis B. Mayer, in Norman Zierold *Moguls* (1969) ch. 9

Ed Gardner 1905–1963

15 Opera is when a guy gets stabbed in the back and, instead of bleeding, he sings.

> In *Duffy's Tavern* (1940s American radio programme)

John Nance Garner 1868–1967

16 The vice-presidency isn't worth a pitcher of warm piss.

> In O. C. Fisher *Cactus Jack* (1978) ch. 11

Bamber Gascoigne 1935–

17 Your starter for ten.

> Phrase often used in *University Challenge* (ITV quiz series, 1962–1987)

Noel Gay (*Richard Moxon Armitage*) 1898–1954

18 I'm leaning on a lamp-post at the corner of the street, In case a certain little lady comes by.

> *Leaning on a Lamp-Post* (1937 song; sung by George Formby in film *Father Knew Best*)

Noel Gay 1898–1954 and Ralph Butler

1 Run, rabbit, run, rabbit, run, run, run.
Run, rabbit, run, rabbit, run, run, run.
Bang, bang, bang, bang, goes the farmer's gun,
Run, rabbit, run, rabbit, run, run, run.
Run Rabbit Run! (1939 song)

Sir Eric Geddes 1875–1937

2 The Germans, if this Government is returned, are
going to pay every penny; they are going to be
squeezed as a lemon is squeezed—until the pips
squeak. My only doubt is not whether we can squeeze
hard enough, but whether there is enough juice.
Speech at Cambridge, 10 Dec. 1918, in *Cambridge Daily News*
11 Dec. 1918

Bob Geldof 1954–

3 Most people get into bands for three very simple rock
and roll reasons: to get laid, to get fame, and to get
rich.
Melody Maker 27 Aug. 1977

Bob Geldof 1954– and Midge Ure

4 Feed the world
Feed the world.
Feed the world
Let them know it's Christmas time again.
Do They Know it's Christmas? (1984 song)

King George V 1865–1936

5 After I am dead, the boy [Edward VIII] will ruin
himself in twelve months.
In Keith Middlemas and John Barnes *Baldwin* (1969) ch. 34

6 I said to your predecessor: 'You know what they're all
saying, no more coals to Newcastle, no more Hoares to
Paris.' The fellow didn't even laugh.
Remark to Anthony Eden, 23 Dec. 1935, following Samuel
Hoare's resignation as Foreign Secretary on 18 Dec. 1935, in
Earl of Avon *Facing the Dictators* (1962) pt. 2, ch. 1

7 I venture to allude to the impression which seemed
generally to prevail among their brethren across the
seas, that the Old Country must wake up if she intends
to maintain her old position of pre-eminence in her
Colonial trade against foreign competitors.
Speech at Guildhall, 5 Dec. 1901, in Harold Nicolson *King
George V* (1952) p. 73 (the speech was reprinted in 1911
with the title 'Wake up, England')

8 Bugger Bognor.
Remark said to have been made either in 1929 when the
King was informed that a deputation of leading citizens was
asking that the town should be named Bognor Regis because
of his convalescence there after a serious illness, or on his
death-bed in 1936 when one of his doctors sought to soothe
him with the remark 'Cheer up, your Majesty, you will soon
be at Bognor again.' See Kenneth Rose *King George V* (1983)
ch. 9

9 The last time I talked to the King [George V] on the
morning of his death, Monday 20th, he had *The Times*
on his table in front of him opened at the 'Imperial and

Foreign' page and I think his remark to me, 'How's the
Empire?' was prompted by some para. he had read on
this page.
Letter from Lord Wigram, 31 Jan. 1936, in J. E. Wrench
Geoffrey Dawson and Our Times (1955) ch. 28

10 Gentlemen, I am so sorry for keeping you waiting like
this. I am unable to concentrate.
Words spoken on his death-bed, reported in memorandum
by Lord Wigram, 20 Jan. 1936, in *History Today* Dec. 1986

11 I have many times asked myself whether there can be
more potent advocates of peace upon earth through the
years to come than this massed multitude of silent
witnesses to the desolation of war.
Message read at Terlincthun Cemetery, Boulogne, 13 May
1922, in *The Times* 15 May 1922

Daniel George (Daniel George Bunting)

12 O Freedom, what liberties are taken in thy name!
In Sagittarius and D. George *Perpetual Pessimist* (1963) p. 58

George Gershwin 1898–1937

See IRA GERSHWIN

Ira Gershwin 1896–1983

13 A foggy day in London Town
Had me low and had me down.
I viewed the morning with alarm,
The British Museum had lost its charm.
How long, I wondered, could this thing last?
But the age of miracles hadn't passed,
For, suddenly, I saw you there
And through foggy London town the sun was shining
everywhere.
A Foggy Day (1937 song; music by George Gershwin)

14 I got rhythm,
I got music,
I got my man
Who could ask for anything more?
I Got Rhythm (1930 song; music by George Gershwin)

15 Lady, be good!
Title of musical (1924; music by George Gershwin)

16 You like potato and I like po-tah-to,
You like tomato and I like to-mah-to;
Potato, po-tah-to, tomato, to-mah-to-
Let's call the whole thing off!
Let's Call the Whole Thing Off (1937 song; music by George
Gershwin)

17 Holding hands at midnight
'Neath a starry sky,
Nice work if you can get it,
And you can get it if you try.
Nice Work If You Can Get It (1937 song; music by George
Gershwin)

Stella Gibbons 1902–1989

18 Every year, in the fulness o' summer, when the
sukebind hangs heavy from the wains . . . 'tes the

same. And when the spring comes her hour is upon her again. 'Tes the hand of Nature and we women cannot escape it.
Cold Comfort Farm (1932) ch. 5

1 When you were very small—so small that the lightest puff of breeze blew your little crinoline skirt over your head—you had seen something nasty in the woodshed.
Cold Comfort Farm (1932) ch. 10

2 Mr Mybug, however, did ask Rennett to marry him. He said that, by god, D. H. Lawrence was right when he had said there must be a dumb, dark, dull, bitter belly-tension between a man and a woman, and how else could this be achieved save in the long monotony of marriage?
Cold Comfort Farm (1932) ch. 20

Wolcott Gibbs 1902–1958

3 Backward ran sentences until reeled the mind.
New Yorker 28 Nov. 1936 'Time ... Fortune ... Life ... Luce' (satirizing the style of Time magazine)

4 Where it will all end, knows God!
New Yorker 28 Nov. 1936 'Time ... Fortune ... Life ... Luce' (satirizing the style of Time magazine)

Kahlil Gibran 1883–1931

5 Your children are not your children.
They are the sons and daughters of Life's longing for itself.
They came through you but not from you
And though they are with you yet they belong not to you.
You may give them your love but not your thoughts,
For they have their own thoughts.
You may house their bodies but not their souls,
For their souls dwell in the house of tomorrow, which you cannot visit, not even in your dreams.
You may strive to be like them, but seek not to make them like you,
For life goes not backward nor tarries with yesterday.
You are the bows from which your children as living arrows are sent forth.
Prophet (1923) 'On Children'

6 Work is love made visible. And if you cannot work with love but only with distaste, it is better that you should leave your work and sit at the gate of the temple and take alms of those who work with joy.
Prophet (1923) 'On Work'

7 An exaggeration is a truth that has lost its temper.
Sand and Foam (1926) p. 59

Wilfrid Wilson Gibson 1878–1962

8 But we, how shall we turn to little things
And listen to the birds and winds and streams
Made holy by their dreams,
Nor feel the heart-break in the heart of things?
Whin (1918) 'Lament'

André Gide 1869–1951

9 M'est avis ... que le profit n'est pas toujours ce qui mène l'homme; qu'il y a des actions désintéressées. ... Par

désintéressé j'entends: gratuit. Et que le mal, ce que l'on appelle: le mal, peut être aussi gratuit que le bien.

I believe ... that profit is not always what motivates man; that there are disinterested actions. ... By disinterested I mean: gratuitous. And that evil acts, what people call evil, can be as gratuitous as good acts.
Les Caves du Vatican (The Vatican Cellars, 1914) bk. 4, ch. 7

10 Hugo—hélas!

Hugo—alas!
Answer when he was asked who was the greatest 19th-century poet, in Claude Martin La Maturité d'André Gide (1977) p. 502

Eric Gill 1882–1940

11 That state is a state of Slavery in which a man does what he likes to do in his spare time and in his working time that which is required of him.
Art-nonsense and Other Essays (1929) 'Slavery and Freedom'

Terry Gilliam 1940–

See GRAHAM CHAPMAN et al.

Penelope Gilliatt 1933–

12 It would be unfair to suggest that one of the most characteristic sounds of the English Sunday is the sound of Harold Hobson barking up the wrong tree.
Encore Nov.-Dec. 1959

13 Sunday, bloody Sunday.
Title of film (1971)

Allen Ginsberg 1926–

14 What if someone gave a war & Nobody came?
Life would ring the bells of Ecstasy and Forever be Itself again.
Fall of America (1972) 'Graffiti'

15 I saw the best minds of my generation destroyed by madness, starving hysterical naked,
dragging themselves through the negro streets at dawn looking for an angry fix,
angelheaded hipsters burning for the ancient heavenly connection to the starry dynamo in the machinery of the night.
Howl (1956) p. 9

George Gipp d. 1920

16 'Some time, Rock,' he said, 'when the team's up against it, when things are wrong and the breaks are beating the boys—tell them to go in there with all they've got and win just one for the Gipper.'
Knut Rockne 'Gipp the Great' in Collier's 22 Nov. 1930

Jean Giraudoux 1882–1944

17 Nous savons tous ici que le droit est la plus puissante des écoles de l'imagination. Jamais poète n'a interprété la nature aussi librement qu'un juriste la réalité.

We all know here that the law is the most powerful of schools for the imagination. No poet ever interpreted nature as freely as a lawyer interprets the truth.

La Guerre de Troie n'aura pas lieu (The Trojan War Will Not Take Place, 1935) act. 2, sc. 5

George Glass 1910–1984

1 An actor is a kind of a guy who if you ain't talking about him ain't listening.

In Bob Thomas *Brando* (1973) ch. 8 (said to be often quoted by Marlon Brando, who is cited as quoting it in *Observer* 1 Jan. 1956)

John A. Glover-Kind d. 1918

2 I do like to be beside the seaside.

Title of song (1909)

Jean-Luc Godard 1930–

3 *La photographie, c'est la vérité. Le cinéma: la vérité vingt-quatre fois par seconde.*

Photography is truth. The cinema is truth twenty-four times per second.

Le Petit Soldat (1960 film), in *Lettres Françaises* 31 Jan. 1963

4 'Movies should have a beginning, a middle and an end,' harrumphed French Film Maker Georges Franju at a symposium some years back. 'Certainly,' replied Jean-Luc Godard. 'But not necessarily in that order.'

Time 14 Sept. 1981

A. D. Godley 1856–1925

5 What is this that roareth thus?
Can it be a Motor Bus?
Yes, the smell and hideous hum
Indicat Motorem Bum! ...
How shall wretches live like us
Cincti Bis Motoribus?
Domine, defende nos
Contra hos Motores Bos!

Letter to C. R. L. Fletcher, 10 Jan 1914, in *Reliquiae* (1926) vol. 1, p. 292

Joseph Goebbels 1897–1945

6 *Ohne Butter werden wir fertig, aber nicht beispielsweise ohne Kanonen. Wenn wir einmal überfallen werden, dann können wir uns nicht mit Butter, sondern nur mit Kanonen verteidigen.*

We can manage without butter but not, for example, without guns. If we are attacked we can only defend ourselves with arms not with butter.

Speech in Berlin, 17 Jan. 1936, in *Deutsche Allgemeine Zeitung* 18 Jan. 1936. Cf. Hermann Goering

Hermann Goering 1893–1946

7 We have no butter, *meine Volksgenossen* [my countrymen], but I ask you—would you rather have butter or guns? Shall we import lard or metal ores?

Let me tell you—preparedness makes us powerful. Butter merely makes us fat.

Speech at Hamburg, 1936, in W. Frischauer *Goering* (1951) ch. 10

Ivan Goff 1910– and Ben Roberts (Benjamin Eisenberg) 1916–1984

8 Anyway, Ma, I made it. ... Top of the world!

White Heat (1949 film; last lines—spoken by James Cagney)

Isaac Goldberg 1887–1938

9 Diplomacy is to do and say
The nastiest thing in the nicest way.

Reflex Oct. 1927, p. 77

William Golding 1911–

10 Lord of the flies.

Title of novel (1954)

Emma Goldman 1869–1940

11 Anarchism, then, really, stands for the liberation of the human mind from the dominion of religion; the liberation of the human body from the dominion of property; liberation from the shackles and restraints of government.

Anarchism and Other Essays (1910) p. 68

Barry Goldwater 1909–

12 I would remind you that extremism in the defence of liberty is no vice! And let me remind you also that moderation in the pursuit of justice is no virtue!

Speech accepting the presidential nomination, 16 July 1964, in *New York Times* 17 July 1964, p. 1

Sam Goldwyn (Samuel Goldfish) 1882–1974

13 Pictures are for entertainment, messages should be delivered by Western Union.

In Arthur Marx *Goldwyn* (1976) ch. 15

14 Gentlemen, include me out.

Said on resigning from the Motion Picture Producers and Distributors of America, Oct. 1933, in Michael Freedland *The Goldwyn Touch* (1986) ch. 10

15 A verbal contract isn't worth the paper it is written on.

In Alva Johnston *The Great Goldwyn* (1937) ch. 1

16 'I can answer you in two words, "im-possible"' is almost the cornerstone of the Goldwyn legend, but Sam did not say it. It was printed late in 1925 in a humorous magazine and credited to an anonymous Potash or Perlmutter.

Alva Johnston *The Great Goldwyn* (1937) ch. 1

17 That's the way with these directors, they're always biting the hand that lays the golden egg.

In Alva Johnston *The Great Goldwyn* (1937) ch. 1

18 Any man who goes to a psychiatrist should have his head examined.

In Norman Zierold *Moguls* (1969) ch. 3

1 It is doubtful that Goldwyn made the remark attributed to him by several authors: 'The reason so many people showed up at his [Louis B. Mayer's] funeral was because they wanted to make sure he was dead.' In Hollywood one hears that sentiment attributed to other moguls at other funerals. It's a good story, and the temptation to use it is almost irresistible. Goldwyn, however, denies making the remark. He did not go to the funeral, was in fact not invited, but his son who was with him on that day says he was deeply moved despite the fact that he never liked Mayer.
> Norman Zierold *Moguls* (1969) ch. 3

2 Why should people go out and pay to see bad movies when they can stay at home and see bad television for nothing?
> In *Observer* 9 Sept. 1956

Paul Goodman 1911–1972

3 All men are creative but few are artists.
> *Growing up Absurd* (1961) ch. 9

Mack Gordon 1904–1959

4 Pardon me boy is that the Chattanooga Choo-choo,
Track twenty nine,
Boy you can gimme a shine.
I can afford to board a Chattanooga Choo-choo,
I've got my fare and just a trifle to spare.
You leave the Pennsylvania station 'bout a quarter to four,
Read a magazine and then you're in Baltimore,
Dinner in the diner nothing could be finer
Than to have your ham'n eggs in Carolina.
> *Chattanooga Choo-choo* (1941 song; music by Harry Warren)

Stuart Gorrell 1902–1963

5 Georgia, Georgia, no peace I find,
Just an old sweet song keeps Georgia on my mind.
> *Georgia on my Mind* (1930 song; music by Hoagy Carmichael)

Sir Edmund Gosse 1849–1928

6 At a lunch at the House of Lords [*c*.1906] given by Edmund Gosse ... the woolly-bearded poet, Sturge Moore ... entered late. Gosse, a naughty host, whispered in my ear, 'A sheep in sheep's clothing.'
> F. Greenslet *Under the Bridge* (1943) ch. 10. Cf. Winston Churchill 56:3

Lord Gowrie (2nd Earl of Gowrie) 1939–

7 [£1,500 a month] is not what people need for living in central London, and which I am more or less obliged to do.
> In BBC radio interview, 4 Sept. 1985, in *The Times* 5 Sept. 1985 (giving reason for resigning as Minister for the Arts)

Lew Grade (Baron Grade) 1906–

8 All my shows are great. Some of them are bad. But they are all great.
> In *Observer* 14 Sept. 1975

D. M. Graham 1911–

9 That this House will in no circumstances fight for its King and Country.
> Motion worded by Graham (the then-Librarian) for debate at the Oxford Union, 9 Feb. 1933, and passed by 275 votes to 153

Harry Graham 1874–1936

10 Weep not for little Léonie
Abducted by a French Marquis!
Though loss of honour was a wrench
Just think how it's improved her French.
> *More Ruthless Rhymes for Heartless Homes* (1930) 'Compensation'

11 Aunt Jane observed, the second time
She tumbled off a bus,
'The step is short from the Sublime
To the Ridiculous.'
> *Ruthless Rhymes for Heartless Homes* (1899) 'Equanimity'

12 Billy, in one of his nice new sashes,
Fell in the fire and was burnt to ashes;
Now, although the room grows chilly,
I haven't the heart to poke poor Billy.
> *Ruthless Rhymes for Heartless Homes* (1899) 'Tender-Heartedness'

13 O'er the rugged mountain's brow
Clara threw the twins she nursed,
And remarked, 'I wonder now
Which will reach the bottom first?'
> *Ruthless Rhymes for Heartless Homes* (1899) 'Calculating Clara'

14 'There's been an accident,' they said,
'Your servant's cut in half; he's dead!'
'Indeed!' said Mr Jones, 'and please,
Send me the half that's got my keys.'
> *Ruthless Rhymes for Heartless Homes* (1899) 'Mr Jones' (poem attributed to 'G.W.')

Kenneth Grahame 1859–1932

15 The curate faced the laurels—hesitatingly. But Aunt Maria flung herself on him. 'O Mr Hodgitts!' I heard her cry, 'you are brave! for my sake do not be rash!' He was not rash.
> *The Golden Age* (1895) 'The Burglars'

16 Monkeys, who very sensibly refrain from speech, lest they should be set to earn their livings.
> *The Golden Age* (1895) 'Lusisti Satis'

17 Believe me, my young friend, there is *nothing*—absolutely nothing—half so much worth doing as simply messing about in boats.
> *Wind in the Willows* (1908) ch. 1

18 'There's cold chicken inside it,' replied the Rat briefly; 'coldtonguecoldhamcoldbeefpickledgerkinssaladfrench-rollscresssandwidgespottedmeatgingerbeerlemonade-sodawater—'
> *Wind in the Willows* (1908) ch. 1

19 'Glorious, stirring sight!' murmured Toad, never offering to move. 'The poetry of motion! The *real* way to travel! The *only* way to travel! Here today—in next

week tomorrow! Villages skipped, towns and cities jumped—always somebody else's horizon! O bliss! O poop-poop! O my! O my!'
Wind in the Willows (1908) ch. 2

1 The clever men at Oxford
Know all that there is to be knowed.
But they none of them know one half as much
As intelligent Mr Toad!
Wind in the Willows (1908) ch. 10

Bernie Grant 1944–

2 The police were to blame for what happened on Sunday night and what they got was a bloody good hiding.
Speech as leader of Haringey Council outside Tottenham Town Hall, 8 Oct. 1985, in *The Times* 9 Oct. 1985

Ethel Watts-Mumford Grant 1878–1940

See ETHEL WATTS MUMFORD

Robert Graves 1895–1985

3 'What did the mayor do?'
'I was coming to that.'
Collected Poems (1938) 'Welsh Incident'

4 Goodbye to all that.
Title of autobiography (1929)

5 If there's no money in poetry, neither is there poetry in money.
Speech at London School of Economics, 6 Dec. 1963, in *Mammon and Black Goddess* (1965) p. 3

6 His eyes are quickened so with grief,
He can watch a grass or leaf
Every instant grow; he can
Clearly through a flint wall see,
Or watch the startled spirit flee
From the throat of a dead man.
Pier-Glass (1921) 'Lost Love'

7 As you are woman, so be lovely:
As you are lovely, so be various,
Merciful as constant, constant as various,
So be mine, as I yours for ever.
Poems (1927) 'Pygmalion to Galatea'

8 Children are dumb to say how hot the day is,
How hot the scent is of the summer rose.
Poems (1927) 'Cool Web'

9 Counting the beats,
Counting the slow heart beats,
The bleeding to death of time in slow heart beats,
Wakeful they lie.
Poems and Satires (1951) 'Counting the Beats'

10 Far away is close at hand
Close joined is far away,
Love shall come at your command
Yet will not stay.
Whipperginny (1923) 'Song of Contrariety'

Hannah Green (Joanne Greenberg)

11 I never promised you a rose garden.
Title of novel (1964)

Graham Greene 1904–

12 Catholics and Communists have committed great crimes, but at least they have not stood aside, like an established society, and been indifferent. I would rather have blood on my hands than water like Pilate.
Comedians (1966) pt. 3, ch. 4

13 Against the beautiful and the clever and the successful, one can wage a pitiless war, but not against the unattractive.
Heart of the Matter (1948) bk. 1, pt. 1, ch. 2

14 Despair is the price one pays for setting oneself an impossible aim.
Heart of the Matter (1948) bk. 1, pt. 1, ch. 2

15 He [Harris] felt the loyalty we all feel to unhappiness—the sense that that is where we really belong.
Heart of the Matter (1948) bk. 2, pt. 2, ch. 1

16 Any victim demands allegiance.
Heart of the Matter (1948) bk. 3, pt. 1, ch. 1

17 His hilarity was like a scream from a crevasse.
Heart of the Matter (1948) bk. 3, pt. 1, ch. 1

18 Our man in Havana.
Title of novel (1958)

19 There is always one moment in childhood when the door opens and lets the future in.
The Power and the Glory (1940) pt. 1, ch. 1

Oswald Greene

20 Greene and Bevan's research largely consisted of visiting pubs and asking people why they drank Guinness. Again and again they received the ... reply—they drank Guinness because it was good for them. So universal was this idea, Greene decided he need look no further for a copyline. 'Guinness' the advertisements would simply say 'is good for you.'
Brian Sibley *Book of Guinness Advertising* (1985) ch. 4

Germaine Greer 1939–

21 Human beings have an inalienable right to invent themselves; when that right is pre-empted it is called brain-washing.
The Times 1 Feb. 1986

Hubert Gregg 1914–

22 Maybe it's because I'm a Londoner
That I love London so,
Maybe it's because I'm a Londoner—
That I think of her—Wherever I go.
I get a funny feeling inside of me—
Just walking up and down,—
Maybe it's because I'm a Londoner
That I love London Town.
Maybe It's Because I'm a Londoner (1947 song)

Joyce Grenfell 1910–1979

1 George—don't do that.

> Recurring line in monologues about a nursery school, from the 1950s, in *George—Don't Do That* (1977) p. 24

2 Stately as a galleon, I sail across the floor,
Doing the Military Two-step, as in the days of yore.

> *Stately as a Galleon* (1978) p. 31

Julian Grenfell 1888–1915

3 The naked earth is warm with Spring,
And with green grass and bursting trees
Leans to the sun's kiss glorying,
And quivers in the sunny breeze;

And Life is Colour and Warmth and Light
And a striving evermore for these;
And he is dead, who will not fight;
And who dies fighting has increase.

The fighting man shall from the sun
Take warmth, and life from the glowing earth.
Speed with the light-foot winds to run,
And with the trees to newer birth.

> *The Times* 28 May 1915 'Into Battle'

Clifford Grey 1887–1941

4 If you were the only girl in the world
And I were the only boy.

> *If You Were the only Girl in the World* (song from musical *The Bing Boys* (1916); music by Nat Ayer)

Sir Edward Grey (Viscount Grey of Fallodon) 1862–1933

5 A friend came to see me on one of the evenings of the last week—he thinks it was on Monday August 3 [1914]. We were standing at a window of my room in the Foreign Office. It was getting dusk, and the lamps were being lit in the space below on which we were looking. My friend recalls that I remarked on this with the words: 'The lamps are going out all over Europe; we shall not see them lit again in our lifetime.'

> *25 Years* (1925) vol. 2, ch. 18

Mervyn Griffith-Jones 1909–1979

6 You may think that one of the ways in which you can test this book [*Lady Chatterley's Lover* by D. H. Lawrence], and test it from the most liberal outlook, is to ask yourselves the question when you have read it through: 'Would you approve of your young sons and daughters—because girls can read as well as boys—reading this book?' Is it a book you would have lying around in your own house? Is it a book you would even wish your wife or your servants to read?

> Speech for the prosecution at the Central Criminal Court, Old Bailey, 20 Oct. 1960, in *The Times* 21 Oct. 1960

Leon Griffiths

7 'Er indoors.

> Used in ITV television series *Minder* (1979 onwards) by Arthur Daley (played by George Cole) to refer to his wife

Jo Grimond (Baron Grimond) 1913–

8 In bygone days, commanders were taught that when in doubt, they should march their troops towards the sound of gunfire. I intend to march my troops towards the sound of gunfire.

> Speech at Liberal Party Annual Assembly, 14 Sept. 1963, in *Guardian* 16 Sept. 1963

Philip Guedalla 1889–1944

9 Any stigma, as the old saying is, will serve to beat a dogma.

> *Masters and Men* (1923) 'Ministers of State'

10 History repeats itself. Historians repeat each other.

> *Supers and Supermen* (1920) 'Some Historians'

11 The cheerful clatter of Sir James Barrie's cans as he went round with the milk of human kindness.

> *Supers and Supermen* (1920) 'Some Critics'

12 The work of Henry James has always seemed divisible by a simple dynastic arrangement into three reigns: James I, James II, and the Old Pretender.

> *Supers and Supermen* (1920) 'Some Critics'

R. Guidry

13 See you later, alligator,
After 'while, crocodile;
Can't you see you're in my way, now,
Don't you know you cramp my style?

> *See You Later Alligator* (1956 song)

Texas Guinan (Mary Louise Cecilia Guinan) 1884–1933

14 Fifty million Frenchmen can't be wrong.

> In *New York World–Telegram* 21 Mar. 1931, p. 25 (asserts that Guinan used the phrase at her night club at least six or seven years previously. The saying is also attributed to Jack Osterman and Mae West; it was the title of a 1927 song (see Billy Rose and Willie Raskin) and a film of 1931. The latter was inspired by Cole Porter's 1929 musical *Fifty Million Frenchmen*). Cf. Billy Rose and Willie Raskin

Nubar Gulbenkian 1896–1972

15 The best number for a dinner party is two—myself and a dam' good head waiter.

> In *Daily Telegraph* 14 Jan. 1965

Thom Gunn 1929–

16 You know I know you know I know you know.

> *Fighting Terms* (1954) 'Carnal Knowledge'

Dorothy Frances Gurney 1858–1932

17 The kiss of the sun for pardon,
The song of the birds for mirth,
One is nearer God's Heart in a garden
Than anywhere else on earth.

> *Poems* (1913) 'God's Garden'

Woody Guthrie (Woodrow Wilson Guthrie) 1912–1967

1 This land is your land, this land is my land,
From California to the New York Island.
From the redwood forest to the Gulf Stream waters
This land was made for you and me.

This Land is Your Land (1956 song)

Earl Haig 1861–1928

2 D. [the 17th Earl of Derby] is a very weak-minded
fellow I am afraid, and, like the feather pillow, bears
the marks of the last person who has sat on him!
I hear he is called in London 'genial Judas'!

Letter to Lady Haig, 14 Jan. 1918, in R. Blake Private Papers
of Douglas Haig (1952) ch. 16

3 Every position must be held to the last man: there must
be no retirement. With our backs to the wall, and
believing in the justice of our cause, each one of us
must fight on to the end. The safety of our Homes and
the Freedom of mankind alike depend upon the conduct
of each one of us at this critical moment.

Order to British troops, 12 Apr. 1918, in A. Duff Cooper Haig
(1936) vol. 2, ch. 23

Lord Hailsham (Baron Hailsham, Quintin Hogg) 1907–

4 A great party is not to be brought down because of
a scandal by a woman of easy virtue and a proved liar.

In BBC television interview on the Profumo affair, 13 June
1963, in The Times 14 June 1963

5 If the British public falls for this [the programme of
the Labour party], I think it will be stark, raving
bonkers.

In press conference at Conservative Central Office, 12 Oct.
1964, in The Times 13 Oct. 1964

J. B. S. Haldane 1892–1964

6 Now, my own suspicion is that the universe is not
only queerer than we suppose, but queerer than we
can suppose. I have read and heard many attempts at
a systematic account of it, from materialism and
theosophy to the Christian system or that of Kant, and
I have always felt that they were much too simple.
I suspect that there are more things in heaven and
earth than are dreamed of, or can be dreamed of, in
any philosophy. That is the reason why I have no
philosophy myself, and must be my excuse for
dreaming.

Possible Worlds and Other Essays (1927) 'Possible Worlds'

7 From the fact that there are 400,000 species of beetles
on this planet, but only 8,000 species of mammals, he
[Haldane] concluded that the Creator, if He exists, has
a special preference for beetles, and so we might be
more likely to meet them than any other type of animal
on a planet which would support life.

Report of lecture, 7 Apr. 1951, cited in Journal of the British
Interplanetary Society (1951) vol. 10, p. 156

H. R. Haldeman 1929–

8 Once the toothpaste is out of the tube, it is awfully
hard to get it back in.

Comment to John Wesley Dean on Watergate affair, 8 Apr.
1973, in Hearings Before the Select Committee on Presidential
Campaign Activities of US Senate: Watergate and Related
Activities (1973) vol. 4, p. 1399

Sir William Haley 1901–

9 It is a moral issue.

Heading of leading article on the Profumo affair, in The Times
11 June 1963

Henry Hall 1899–1989

10 This is Henry Hall speaking, and tonight is my guest
night.

Catch-phrase on BBC Radio's Guest Night from 1934 (see
Henry Hall's Here's to the Next Time (1955) ch. 11)

Sir Peter Hall 1930–

11 Sir Peter [Hall] has always maintained that, although
nobody appeared to want a National Theatre when it
was first promulgated, the public has consistently
supported it with cash at the box office—with
'bottoms on seats' to use his own earthy phrase.

Spectator 10 May 1980 (the phrase is often 'bums on seats')

Margaret Halsey 1910–

12 Englishwomen's shoes look as if they had been made
by someone who had often heard shoes described but
had never seen any.

With Malice Toward Some (1938) pt. 2, p. 107

13 Towards people with whom they disagree the English
gentry, or at any rate that small cross section of them
which I have seen, are tranquilly good-natured. It is
not comme il faut to establish the supremacy of an idea
by smashing in the faces of all the people who try to
contradict it. The English never smash in a face. They
merely refrain from asking it to dinner.

With Malice Toward Some (1938) pt. 3, p. 208

Oscar Hammerstein II 1895–1960

14 Climb ev'ry mountain, ford ev'ry stream
Follow ev'ry rainbow, till you find your dream!

Climb Ev'ry Mountain (1959 song; music by Richard
Rodgers)

15 June is bustin' out all over.

Title of song (1945; music by Richard Rodgers)

16 The last time I saw Paris
Her heart was warm and gay,
I heard the laughter of her heart in ev'ry street café.

The Last Time I saw Paris (1940 song; music by Jerome Kern)

17 The corn is as high as an elephant's eye,
An' it looks like it's climbin' clear up to the sky.

Oh, What a Beautiful Mornin' (1943 song; music by Richard
Rodgers)

18 Oh, what a beautiful mornin',
Oh, what a beautiful day!

I got a beautiful feelin'
Ev'rything's goin' my way.
> *Oh, What a Beautiful Mornin'* (1943 song; music by Richard Rodgers)

1 Ol' man river, dat ol' man river,
He must know sumpin', but don't say nothin',
He just keeps rollin',
He keeps on rollin' along.
> *Ol' Man River* (1927 song; music by Jerome Kern)

2 Some enchanted evening,
You may see a stranger,
You may see a stranger,
Across a crowded room.
> *Some Enchanted Evening* (1949 song; music by Richard Rodgers)

3 The hills are alive with the sound of music,
With songs they have sung for a thousand years.
The hills fill my heart with the sound of music,
My heart wants to sing ev'ry song it hears.
> *The Sound of Music* (1959 song; music by Richard Rodgers)

4 There is nothin' like a dame.
> Title of song (1949; music by Richard Rodgers)

5 You'll never walk alone.
> Title of song (1945; music by Richard Rodgers)

Christopher Hampton 1946–

6 Masturbation is the thinking man's television.
> *Philanthropist* (1970) act. 1, sc. 3

7 If I had to give a definition of capitalism I would say:
the process whereby American girls turn into American
women.
> *Savages* (1974) sc. 16

Learned Hand 1872–1961

8 A self-made man may prefer a self-made name.
> In Bosley Crowther *Lion's Share* (1957) ch. 7 (referring to
> Samuel Goldfish changing his name to Samuel Goldwyn)

Minnie Hanff 1880–1942

9 High o'er the fence leaps Sunny Jim
'Force' is the food that raises him.
> Advertising slogan (1903)

Brian Hanrahan 1949–

10 I'm not allowed to say how many planes joined the
raid [on Port Stanley in the Falkland Islands] but
I counted them all out and I counted them all back.
> Report broadcast by BBC, 1 May 1982, in *Battle for the
> Falklands* (1982) p. 21

Otto Harbach 1873–1963

11 When a lovely flame dies,
Smoke gets in your eyes.
> *Smoke Gets in your Eyes* (1933 song; music by Jerome Kern)

E. Y. 'Yip' Harburg 1898–1981

12 Once I built a railroad. Now it's done—
Brother can you spare a dime?
> *Brother Can You Spare a Dime?* (1932 song; music by Jay
> Gorney)

13 Somewhere over the rainbow
Way up high,
There's a land that I heard of
Once in a lullaby.
> *Over the Rainbow* (1939 song; music by Harold Arlen)

14 When I'm not near the girl I love,
I love the girl I'm near.
> *When I'm Not Near the Girl I Love* (1947 song; music by
> Burton Lane)

Gilbert Harding 1907–1960

15 Before he [Gilbert Harding] could go to New York he
had to get a US visa at the American consulate in
Toronto. He was called upon to fill in a long form with
many questions, including 'Is it your intention to
overthrow the Government of the United States by
force?' By the time Harding got to that one he was so
irritated that he answered: 'Sole purpose of visit.'
> W. Reyburn *Gilbert Harding* (1978) ch. 2

16 If, sir, I possessed, as you suggest, the power of
conveying unlimited sexual attraction through the
potency of my voice, I would not be reduced to
accepting a miserable pittance from the BBC for
interviewing a faded female in a damp basement.
> In S. Grenfell *Gilbert Harding by his Friends* (1961) p. 118
> (reply to Mae West's manager who asked 'Can't you sound
> a bit more sexy when you interview her?')

Warren G. Harding 1865–1923

17 America's present need is not heroics, but healing; not
nostrums but normalcy; not revolution, but
restoration.
> Speech at Boston, 14 May 1920, in Frederick E.
> Schortemeier *Rededicating America* (1920) ch. 17

Godfrey Harold Hardy 1877–1947

18 Beauty is the first test: there is no permanent place in
the world for ugly mathematics.
> *A Mathematician's Apology* (1940) p. 25

Thomas Hardy 1840–1928

19 A local thing called Christianity.
> *Dynasts* (1904) pt. 1, act 1, sc. 6

20 My argument is that War makes rattling good history;
but Peace is poor reading.
> *Dynasts* (1904) pt. 1, act 2, sc. 5

21 A lover without indiscretion is no lover at all.
> *Hand of Ethelberta* (1876) ch. 20

22 A piece of paper was found upon the floor, on which
was written, in the boy's hand, with the bit of lead
pencil that he carried: 'Done because we are too
menny.'
> *Jude the Obscure* (1896) pt. 6, ch. 2

1 The bower we shrined to Tennyson,
   Gentlemen,
   Is roof-wrecked; damps there drip upon
   Sagged seats, the creeper-nails are rust,
   The spider is sole denizen;
   Even she who voiced those rhymes is dust,
   Gentlemen!
   Late Lyrics and Earlier (1922) 'An Ancient to Ancients'

2 This is the weather the cuckoo likes,
   And so do I;
   When showers betumble the chestnut spikes,
   And nestlings fly:
   And the little brown nightingale bills his best,
   And they sit outside at 'The Travellers' Rest',
   And maids come forth sprig-muslin drest,
   And citizens dream of the south and west,
   And so do I.
   Late Lyrics and Earlier (1922) 'Weathers'

3 And meadow rivulets overflow,
   And drops on gate-bars hang in a row,
   And rooks in families homeward go,
   And so do I.
   Late Lyrics and Earlier (1922) 'Weathers'

4 Life's little ironies.
   Title of book (1894)

5 'Well, poor soul; she's helpless to hinder that or
   anything now,' answered Mother Cuxsom. 'And all her
   shining keys will be took from her, and her cupboards
   opened; and things a' didn't wish seen, anybody will
   see; and her little wishes and ways will all be as
   nothing!'
   Mayor of Casterbridge (1886) ch. 18

6 One grievous failing of Elizabeth's was her occasional
   pretty and picturesque use of dialect words—those
   terrible marks of the beast to the truly genteel.
   Mayor of Casterbridge (1886) ch. 20

7 I am the family face;
   Flesh perishes, I live on,
   Projecting trait and trace
   Through time to times anon,
   And leaping from place to place
   Over oblivion.
   Moments of Vision (1917) 'Heredity'

8 In the third-class seat sat the journeying boy
   And the roof-lamp's oily flame
   Played down on his listless form and face,
   Bewrapt past knowing to what he was going,
   Or whence he came.
   Moments of Vision (1917) 'Midnight on the Great Western'

9 Only a man harrowing clods
   In a slow silent walk
   With an old horse that stumbles and nods
   Half asleep as they stalk.

   Only thin smoke without flame
   From the heaps of couch-grass;
   Yet this will go onward the same
   Though Dynasties pass.

   Yonder a maid and her wight
   Come whispering by:

War's annals will cloud into night
Ere their story die.
   Moments of Vision (1917) 'In Time of "The Breaking of
   Nations"'

10 When the Present has latched its postern behind my
    tremulous stay,
    And the May month flaps its glad green leaves like
    wings,
    Delicate-filmed as new-spun silk, will the neighbours
    say,
    'He was a man who used to notice such things'?
    Moments of Vision (1917) 'Afterwards'

11 At once a voice outburst among
    The bleak twigs overhead
    In a full-hearted evensong
    Of joy illimited;
    An aged thrush, frail, gaunt, and small,
    In blast-beruffled plume,
    Had chosen thus to fling his soul
    Upon the growing gloom.

    So little cause for carollings
    Of such ecstatic sound
    Was written on terrestrial things
    Afar or nigh around,
    That I could think there trembled through
    His happy good-night air
    Some blessed Hope, whereof he knew
    And I was unaware.
    Poems of Past and Present (1902) 'Darkling Thrush'

12 If way to the Better there be, it exacts a full look at the
    worst.
    Poems of Past and Present (1902) 'De Profundis'

13 In a solitude of the sea
    Deep from human vanity,
    And the Pride of Life that planned her, stilly couches
    she.

    Steel chambers, late the pyres
    Of her salamandrine fires,
    Cold currents thrid, and turn to rhythmic tidal lyres.

    Over the mirrors meant
    To glass the opulent
    The sea-worm crawls—grotesque, slimed, dumb,
    indifferent.
    Satires of Circumstance (1914) 'Convergence of the Twain'

14 The Immanent Will that stirs and urges everything.
    Satires of Circumstance (1914) 'Convergence of the Twain'

15 When I set out for Lyonnesse,
    A hundred miles away,
    The rime was on the spray,
    And starlight lit my lonesomeness
    When I set out for Lyonnesse
    A hundred miles away.
    Satires of Circumstance (1914) p. 20

16 What of the faith and fire within us
    Men who march away
    Ere the barn-cocks say
    Night is growing grey,
    To hazards whence no tears can win us;
    What of the faith and fire within us
    Men who march away?
    Satires of Circumstance (1914) 'Men Who March Away'

1 'Justice' was done, and the President of the Immortals (in Aeschylean phrase) had ended his sport with Tess.

Tess of the D'Urbervilles (1891) ch. 59

2 Let me enjoy the earth no less
Because the all-enacting Might
That fashioned forth its loveliness
Had other aims than my delight.

Time's Laughing Stocks (1909) 'Let me Enjoy'

3 Yes; quaint and curious war is!
You shoot a fellow down
You'd treat if met where any bar is,
Or help to half-a-crown.

Time's Laughing Stocks (1909) 'Man he Killed'

4 Good, but not religious-good.

Under the Greenwood Tree (1872) ch. 2

5 Well, World, you have kept faith with me,
Kept faith with me;
Upon the whole you have proved to be
Much as you said you were.

Winter Words (1928) 'He Never Expected Much'

6 'Peace upon earth!' was said. We sing it,
And pay a million priests to bring it.
After two thousand years of mass
We've got as far as poison-gas.

Winter Words (1928) 'Christmas: 1924'

Maurice Evan Hare 1886–1967

7 There once was an old man who said, 'Damn!
It is borne in upon me I am
An engine that moves
In determinate grooves,
I'm not even a bus, I'm a tram.'

Limerick (1905)

Robertson Hare 1891–1979

8 Oh, calamity!

Catch-phrase, in *Yours Indubitably* (1956) p. 32

W. F. Hargreaves 1846–1919

9 I'm Burlington Bertie
I rise at ten thirty and saunter along like a toff,
I walk down the Strand with my gloves on my hand,
Then I walk down again with them off.

Burlington Bertie from Bow (1915 song)

10 I acted so tragic the house rose like magic,
The audience yelled 'You're sublime.'
They made me a present of Mornington Crescent
They threw it a brick at a time.

The Night I Appeared as Macbeth (1922 song)

Lord Harlech (David Ormsby Gore) 1918–1985

11 In the end it may well be that Britain will be honoured by historians more for the way she disposed of an empire than for the way in which she acquired it.

In *New York Times* 28 Oct. 1962, sec. 4, p. 11

Jimmy Harper, Will E. Haines, and Tommie Connor

12 The biggest aspidistra in the world.

Title of song (1938; popularized by Gracie Fields)

Frank Harris (James Thomas Harris) 1856–1931

13 Christ went deeper than I have, but I've had a wider range of experience.

In conversation with Hugh Kingsmill, in Hesketh Pearson and Malcolm Muggeridge *About Kingsmill* (1951) ch. 3

14 Sex is the gateway to life.

In Enid Bagnold *Autobiography* (1969) ch. 4

H. H. Harris

15 Bovril. . . . Prevents that sinking feeling.

Advertising slogan (1920)

Lorenz Hart 1895–1943

16 Bewitched, bothered and bewildered.

Title of song (1941; music by Richard Rodgers)

17 When love congeals
It soon reveals
The faint aroma of performing seals,
The double crossing of a pair of heels.
I wish I were in love again!

I Wish I Were in Love Again (1937 song; music by Richard Rodgers)

18 I get too hungry for dinner at eight.
I like the theatre, but never come late.
I never bother with people I hate.
That's why the lady is a tramp.

The Lady is a Tramp (1937 song; music by Richard Rodgers)

19 On the first of May
It is moving day;
Spring is here, so blow your job—
Throw your job away;
Now's the time to trust
To your wanderlust.
In the city's dust you wait.
Must you wait?
Just you wait:

In a mountain greenery
Where God paints the scenery—
Just two crazy people together;
While you love your lover, let
Blue skies be your coverlet—
When it rains we'll laugh at the weather.

Mountain Greenery (1926 song; music by Richard Rodgers)

Moss Hart 1904–1961 and George Kaufman 1889–1961

20 You can't take it with you.

Title of play (1936)

L. P. Hartley 1895–1972

1 The past is a foreign country: they do things differently there.
  The Go-Between (1953) prologue

F. W. Harvey 1888–?

2 From troubles of the world
  I turn to ducks
  Beautiful comical things.
  Ducks and Other Verses (1919) 'Ducks'

Minnie Louise Haskins 1875–1957

3 And I said to the man who stood at the gate of the year: 'Give me a light that I may tread safely into the unknown.'
  And he replied:
  'Go out into the darkness and put your hand into the Hand of God. That shall be to you better than light and safer than a known way.'
  Desert (1908) 'God Knows'

Lord Haw-Haw

See WILLIAM JOYCE

Ian Hay (John Hay Beith) 1876–1952

4 What do you mean, funny? Funny-peculiar or funny ha-ha?
  Housemaster (1938) act 3

J. Milton Hayes 1884–1940

5 There's a one-eyed yellow idol to the north of Khatmandu,
  There's a little marble cross below the town,
  There's a broken-hearted woman tends the grave of Mad Carew,
  And the Yellow God forever gazes down.
  The Green Eye of the Yellow God (1911)

Lee Hazlewood 1929–

6 These boots are made for walkin'.
  Title of song (1966)

Denis Healey 1917–

7 That part of his [Sir Geoffrey Howe's] speech was rather like being savaged by a dead sheep.
  Hansard 14 June 1978, col. 1027

8 I plan to be the Gromyko of the Labour Party.
  In *Sunday Times* 5 Feb. 1984

9 I warn you there are going to be howls of anguish from the 80,000 people who are rich enough to pay over 75% [tax] on the last slice of their income.
  Speech at Labour Party Conference, 1 Oct. 1973, in *The Times* 2 Oct. 1973

Seamus Heaney 1939–

10 Between my finger and my thumb
  The squat pen rests.
  I'll dig with it.
  Death of a Naturalist (1966) 'Digging'

11 All agog at the plasterer on his ladder
  Skimming our gable and writing our name there
  With his trowel point, letter by strange letter.
  The Haw Lantern (1987) 'Alphabets'

12 Who would connive
  in civilised outrage
  yet understand the exact
  and tribal, intimate revenge.
  North (1975) 'Punishment'

13 The famous
  Northern reticence, the tight gag of place
  And times: yes, yes. Of the 'wee six' I sing
  Where to be saved you only must save face
  And whatever you say, you say nothing.
  North (1975) 'Whatever You Say Say Nothing'

14 Is there a life before death? That's chalked up
  In Ballymurphy. Competence with pain,
  Coherent miseries, a bite and sup,
  We hug our little destiny again.
  North (1975) 'Whatever You Say Say Nothing'

15 Don't be surprised
  If I demur, for, be advised
  My passport's green.
  No glass of ours was ever raised
  To toast *The Queen.*
  Open Letter (Field Day pamphlet no. 2, 1983) p. 9 (rebuking the editors of *The Penguin Book of Contemporary British Poetry* for including his work)

Edward Heath 1916–

16 It is the unpleasant and unacceptable face of capitalism.
  Hansard 15 May 1973, col. 1243 (on the Lonrho affair)

17 The alternative is to break into the wage/price spiral by acting directly to reduce prices. This can be done by reducing those taxes which bear directly on prices and costs, such as the selective employment tax, and by taking a firm grip on public sector prices and charges such as coal, steel, gas, electricity, transport charges and postal charges. This would, at a stroke, reduce the rise in prices, increase production and reduce unemployment.
  Press release, 16 June 1970, in *The Times* 17 June 1970

Fred Heatherton

18 I've got a loverly bunch of cocoanuts,
  There they are a-standing in a row,
  Big ones, small ones, some as big as your head,
  Give 'em a twist, a flick of the wrist,
  That's what the showman said.
  I've Got a Lovely Bunch of Cocoanuts (1944 song; revised version 1948)

Robert A. Heinlein 1907–

1 'Oh, "tanstaafl". Means "There ain't no such thing as a free lunch." And isn't,' I added, pointing to a FREE LUNCH sign across room, 'or these drinks would cost half as much. Was reminding her that anything free costs twice as much in the long run or turns out worthless.'

   Moon is Harsh Mistress (1966) ch. 11

Werner Heisenberg 1901–1976

2 *Ein Fachmann ist ein Mann, der einige der gröbsten Fehler kennt, die man in dem betreffenden Fach machen kann und der sie deshalb zu vermeiden versteht.*

An expert is someone who knows some of the worst mistakes that can be made in his subject and how to avoid them.

   Der Teil und das Ganze ('The Part and the Whole', 1969) ch. 17 (translated by A. J. Pomerans in 1971 as *Physics and Beyond*)

Joseph Heller 1923–

3 There was only one catch and that was Catch-22, which specified that a concern for one's own safety in the face of dangers that were real and immediate was the process of a rational mind. Orr was crazy and could be grounded. All he had to do was ask; and as soon as he did, he would no longer be crazy and would have to fly more missions. Orr would be crazy to fly more missions and sane if he didn't, but if he was sane he had to fly them. If he flew them he was crazy and didn't have to; but if he didn't want to he was sane and had to. Yossarian was moved very deeply by the absolute simplicity of this clause of Catch-22 and let out a respectful whistle.
   'That's some catch, that Catch-22,' he observed.
   'It's the best there is,' Doc Daneeka agreed.
   Catch-22 (1961) ch. 5 (the first chapter of this novel was published as *Catch-18* in *New World Writing* (1955) No. 7—see Kiley and MacDonald '*Catch-22' Casebook* (1973) 294)

4 Some men are born mediocre, some men achieve mediocrity, and some men have mediocrity thrust upon them. With Major Major it had been all three.
   Catch-22 (1961) ch. 9. Cf. *Oxford Dictionary of Quotations* (1979) 489:14

5 Good God, how much reverence can you have for a Supreme Being who finds it necessary to include such phenomena as phlegm and tooth-decay in His divine system of creation?
   Catch-22 (1961) ch. 18

6 'You put so much stock in *winning* wars,' the grubby iniquitous old man scoffed. 'The real trick lies in *losing* wars, and in knowing which wars can be *lost*. Italy has been losing wars for centuries, and just see how splendidly we've done nonetheless. France wins wars and is in a continual state of crisis. Germany loses and prospers. Look at our own recent history. Italy won a war in Ethiopia and promptly stumbled into serious trouble. Victory gave us such insane delusions of grandeur that we helped start a world war we hadn't a chance of winning. But now that we are losing again, everything has taken a turn for the better, and we will certainly come out on top again if we succeed in being defeated.'
   Catch-22 (1961) ch. 23

Lillian Hellman 1905–1984

7 Cynicism is an unpleasant way of saying the truth.
   The Little Foxes (1939) act 1

8 I do not like subversion or disloyalty in any form and if I had ever seen any I would have considered it my duty to have reported it to the proper authorities. But to hurt innocent people whom I knew many years ago in order to save myself is to me inhuman and indecent and dishonorable. I cannot and will not cut my conscience to fit this year's fashions, even though I long ago came to the conclusion that I was not a political person and could have no comfortable place in any political group.
   Letter to John S. Wood, 19 May 1952, in *US Congress Committee Hearing on Un-American Activities* (1952) pt. 8, p. 3546

Sir Robert Helpmann 1909–1986

9 No. You see there are portions of the human anatomy which would keep swinging after the music had finished.
   In Elizabeth Salter *Helpmann* (1978) ch. 21 [reply to question on whether the fashion for nudity would extend to dance]

Ernest Hemingway 1899–1961

10 All good books are alike in that they are truer than if they had really happened and after you are finished reading one you will feel that all that happened to you and afterwards it all belongs to you: the good and the bad, the ecstasy, the remorse and sorrow, the people and the places and how the weather was. If you can get so that you can give that to people, then you are a writer.
   Esquire Dec. 1934 'Old Newsman Writes'

11 'Just kiss me.'
   She kissed him on the cheek.
   'No.'
   'Where do the noses go? I always wondered where the noses would go.'
   'Look, turn thy head' and then their mouths were tight together.
   For Whom the Bell Tolls (1940) ch. 7

12 He said, 'Maria . . . I feel as though I wanted to die when I am loving thee.'
   'Oh,' she said. 'I die each time. Do you not die?'
   'No. Almost. But did thee feel the earth move?'
   'Yes. As I died. Put thy arm around me, please.'
   For Whom the Bell Tolls (1940) ch. 13

13 All modern American literature comes from one book by Mark Twain called *Huckleberry Finn*.
   Green Hills of Africa (1935) ch. 1

14 Cowardice, as distinguished from panic, is almost always simply a lack of ability to suspend the functioning of the imagination.
   Men at War (1942)

1 If you are lucky enough to have lived in Paris as
a young man, then wherever you go for the rest of
your life, it stays with you, for Paris is a movable feast.
 Movable Feast (1964) epigraph

2 'Exactly what do you mean by "guts"?' 'I mean,'
Ernest Hemingway said, 'grace under pressure.'
 Interview with Dorothy Parker, in *New Yorker* 30 Nov. 1929

3 I started out very quiet and I beat Mr Turgenev. Then
I trained hard and I beat Mr de Maupassant. I've fought
two draws with Mr Stendhal, and I think I had an edge
in the last one. But nobody's going to get me in any
ring with Mr Tolstoy unless I'm crazy or I keep getting
better.
 New Yorker 13 May 1950

4 A man can be destroyed but not defeated.
 The Old Man and the Sea (1952) p. 103

5 The most essential gift for a good writer is a built-in,
shock-proof shit detector. This is the writer's radar and
all great writers have had it.
 Paris Review Spring 1958

6 The sun also rises.
 Title of novel (1926)

7 Switzerland is a small, steep country, much more up
and down than sideways, and is all stuck over with
large brown hotels built on the cuckoo clock style of
architecture.
 Toronto Star Weekly 4 Mar. 1922, in William White *By-line:
Ernest Hemingway* (1967) p. 18

 See also F. SCOTT FITZGERALD

Arthur W. D. Henley

8 Nobody loves a fairy when she's forty
 Title of song (1934)

O. Henry (William Sydney Porter)
1862–1910

9 Life is made up of sobs, sniffles, and smiles, with
sniffles predominating.
 Four Million (1906) 'Gift of the Magi'

10 If men knew how women pass the time when they are
alone, they'd never marry.
 Four Million (1906) 'Memoirs of a Yellow Dog'

11 It was beautiful and simple as all truly great swindles
are.
 Gentle Grafter (1908) 'Octopus Marooned'

12 Turn up the lights; I don't want to go home in the dark.
 Last words, quoting 1907 song by Harry Williams 'I'm
afraid to come home in the dark', in Charles Alphonso Smith
O. Henry Biography (1916) ch. 9

A. P. Herbert 1890–1971

13 Other people's babies—
That's my life!
Mother to dozens,
And nobody's wife.
 Ballads for Broadbrows (1930) 'Other People's Babies' (also
a 1934 song, with music by Vivian Ellis)

14 Let's find out what everyone is doing,
And then stop everyone from doing it.
 Ballads for Broadbrows (1930) 'Let's Stop Somebody from
Doing Something!'

15 As my poor father used to say
In 1863,
Once people start on all this Art
Goodbye, moralitee!
And what my father used to say
Is good enough for me.
 Ballads for Broadbrows (1930) 'Lines for a Worthy Person'

16 Holy deadlock.
 Title of novel (1934)

17 Don't tell my mother I'm living in sin,
Don't let the old folks know.
 Laughing Ann (1925) 'Don't Tell My Mother I'm Living in Sin'

18 Not huffy, or stuffy, not tiny or tall,
But fluffy, just fluffy, with no brains at all.
 Plain Jane (1927) 'I Like them Fluffy'

19 Don't let's go to the dogs tonight,
For mother will be there.
 She-Shanties (1926) 'Don't Let's Go to the Dogs Tonight'

20 The Farmer will never be happy again;
He carries his heart in his boots;
For either the rain is destroying his grain
Or the drought is destroying his roots.
 Tinker Tailor (1922) 'The Farmer'

21 This high official, all allow,
Is grossly overpaid;
There wasn't any Board, and now
There isn't any Trade.
 Tinker Tailor (1922) 'The President of the Board of Trade'

22 Nothing is wasted, nothing is in vain:
The seas roll over but the rocks remain.
 Tough at the Top (c.1949 operetta), in *A.P.H.* (1970) ch. 7

23 The Common Law of England has been laboriously built
about a mythical figure—the figure of 'The Reasonable
Man'.
 Uncommon Law (1935) 'The Reasonable Man'

24 People must not do things for fun. We are not here for
fun. There is no reference to fun in any Act of
Parliament.
 Uncommon Law (1935) 'Is it a Free Country?'

25 The critical period in matrimony is breakfast-time.
 Uncommon Law (1935) 'Is Marriage Lawful?'

26 The Englishman never enjoys himself except for a noble
purpose.
 Uncommon Law (1935) 'Fox-Hunting Fun'

27 Milord, in that case an Act of God was defined as
'something which no reasonable man could have
expected'.
 Uncommon Law (1935) 'Act of God'

Oliver Herford 1863–1935

28 'Perhaps it is only a whim,' said the Queen. The King
laughed mirthlessly. 'King Barumph has a whim of
iron!'
 Excuse it Please (1929) 'Impossible Pudding'

 See also ETHEL WATTS MUMFORD

Jerry Herman 1933–

1 Hello, Dolly, well, hello Dolly
It's so nice to have you back where you belong.
Hello, Dolly (1964 song from the musical *Hello, Dolly*)

June Hershey

2 Deep in the heart of Texas.
Title of song (1941; music by Don Swander)

Hermann Hesse 1877–1962

3 *Wenn wir einen Menschen hassen, so hassen wir in seinem Bild etwas, was in uns selber sisst. Was nicht in uns selber ist, das regt uns nicht auf.*

If you hate a person, you hate something in him that is part of yourself. What isn't part of ourselves doesn't disturb us.
Demian (1919) ch. 6

4 *Auf Kosten der Intensität also erreicht er* [der Bürger] *Erhaltung und Sicherheit, statt Gottbesessenheit erntet er Gewissensruhe, statt Lust Behagen, statt Freiheit Bequemlichkeit, statt tödlicher Glut eine angenehme Temperatur.*

The bourgeois prefers comfort to pleasure, convenience to liberty, and a pleasant temperature to the deathly inner consuming fire.
Der Steppenwolf (1927) 'Tractat vom Steppenwolf' (Treatise on the Steppenwolf)

Gordon Hewart (Viscount Hewart) 1870–1943

5 A long line of cases shows that it is not merely of some importance, but is of fundamental importance that justice should not only be done, but should manifestly and undoubtedly be seen to be done.
Rex v Sussex Justices, 9 Nov. 1923, in *Law Reports King's Bench Division* (1924) vol. 1, p. 259

Patricia Hewitt 1948–

6 It is obvious from our polling, as well as from the doorstep, that the 'London Effect' is now very noticeable. The 'loony Labour left' is taking its toll; the gays and lesbians issue is costing us dear among the pensioners, and fear of extremism and higher rates/taxes is particularly prominent in the Greater London Council area.
Letter to Frank Dobson and other Labour leaders, in *The Times* 6 Mar. 1987

Du Bose Heyward 1885–1940 and Ira Gershwin 1896–1983

7 It ain't necessarily so.
Title of song (1935; music by George Gershwin)

8 Summer time an' the livin' is easy.
Summer Time (1935 song; music by George Gershwin)

Sir Seymour Hicks 1871–1949

9 You will recognize, my boy, the first sign of old age: it is when you go out into the streets of London and realize for the first time how young the policemen look.
In C. R. D. Pulling *They Were Singing* (1952) ch. 7

Jack Higgins (Henry Patterson) 1929–

10 The eagle has landed.
Title of novel (1975)

Joe Hill 1879–1915

11 I will die like a true-blue rebel. Don't waste any time in mourning—organize.
Farewell telegram to Bill Haywood, 18 Nov. 1915, before his death by firing squad, in *Salt Lake* (Utah) *Tribune* 19 Nov. 1915

12 You will eat, bye and bye,
In that glorious land above the sky;
Work and pray, live on hay,
You'll get pie in the sky when you die.
Songs of the Workers (Industrial Workers of the World, 1911) 'Preacher and the Slave'

Pattie S. Hill 1868–1946

13 Happy birthday to you.
Title of song (1935; music by Mildred J. Hill)

Sir Edmund Hillary 1919–

14 [After the ascent of Everest] George [Lowe] met us with a mug of soup just above camp, and seeing his stalwart frame and cheerful face reminded me how fond of him I was. My comment was not specially prepared for public consumption but for George. . . . 'Well, we knocked the bastard off!' I told him and he nodded with pleasure. . . . 'Thought you must have!'
Nothing Venture (1975) ch. 10

Fred Hillebrand 1893–

15 Home James, and don't spare the horses.
Title of song (1934)

Lady Hillingdon 1857–1940

16 I am happy now that Charles calls on my bedchamber less frequently than of old. As it is, I now endure but two calls a week and when I hear his steps outside my door I lie down on my bed, close my eyes, open my legs and think of England.
Journal 1912, in J. Gathorne-Hardy *Rise and Fall of the British Nanny* (1972) ch. 3

James Hilton 1900–1954

17 Nothing really wrong with him—only anno domini, but that's the most fatal complaint of all, in the end.
Goodbye, Mr Chips (1934) ch. 1

Alfred Hitchcock 1899–1980

1 Television has brought back murder into the home—where it belongs.

In *Observer* 19 Dec. 1965

2 Actors are cattle.

In *Saturday Evening Post* 22 May 1943, p. 56

Adolf Hitler 1889–1945

3 *Die neue and diesmal blutige Erhebung—die Nacht der langen Messer, wie man sie grauenvoll bezeichnete—meinem eigenen Sinn entspräche.*

The new, and this time bloody, rising—'The Night of the Long Knives' was their ghastly name for it—was exactly what I myself desired.

Speech to the Reichstag, 13 July 1934, in Max Domarus (ed.) *Hitler: Reden und Proklamationen 1932–1945* (1962) p. 418

4 *Ich gehe mit traumwandlerischer Sicherheit den Weg, den mich die Vorsehung gehen heisst.*

I go the way that Providence dictates with the assurance of a sleepwalker.

Speech in Munich, 15 Mar. 1936, in Max Domarus (ed.) *Hitler: Reden und Proklamationen 1932–1945* (1962) p. 606

5 *Und nun steht vor uns das letzte Problem, das gelöst werden muss und gelöst werden wird! Es* [das Sudetenland] *ist die letzte territoriale Forderung, die ich Europa zu stellen habe, aber es ist die Forderung, von der ich nicht abgehe, und die ich, so Gott will, erfüllen werde.*

And now before us stands the last problem that must be solved and will be solved. It [the Sudetenland] is the last territorial claim which I have to make in Europe, but it is the claim from which I will not recede and which, God-willing, I will make good.

Speech at Berlin Sportpalast, 26 Sept. 1938, in Max Domarus (ed.) *Hitler: Reden und Proklamationen 1932–1945* (1962) p. 927

6 *In bezug auf das sudetendeutsche Problem meine Geduld jetzt zu Ende ist!*

With regard to the problem of the Sudeten Germans, my patience is now at an end!

Speech at Berlin Sportpalast, 26 Sept. 1938, in Max Domarus (ed.) *Hitler: Reden und Proklamationen 1932–1945* (1962) p. 932

7 *Brennt Paris?*

Is Paris burning?

Question, 25 Aug. 1944, in Larry Collins and Dominique Lapierre *Is Paris Burning?* (1965) ch. 5

8 *Die breite Masse eines Volkes . . . einer grossen Lüge leichter zum Opfer fällt als einer kleinen.*

The broad mass of a nation . . . will more easily fall victim to a big lie than to a small one.

Mein Kampf (My Struggle, 1925) vol. 1, ch. 10

Ralph Hodgson 1871–1962

9 Time, you old gipsy man,
Will you not stay,
Put up your caravan
Just for one day?

Poems (1917) 'Time, You Old Gipsy Man'

10 I climbed a hill as light fell short,
And rooks came home in scramble sort,
And filled the trees and flapped and fought
And sang themselves to sleep.

Poems (1917) 'Song of Honour'

11 I stood and stared; the sky was lit,
The sky was stars all over it,
I stood, I knew not why,
Without a wish, without a will,
I stood upon that silent hill
And stared into the sky until
My eyes were blind with stars and still
I stared into the sky.

Poems (1917) 'Song of Honour'

12 When stately ships are twirled and spun
Like whipping tops and help there's none
And mighty ships ten thousand ton
Go down like lumps of lead.

Poems (1917) 'Song of Honour'

13 'Twould ring the bells of Heaven
The wildest peal for years,
If Parson lost his senses
And people came to theirs,
And he and they together
Knelt down with angry prayers
For tamed and shabby tigers
And dancing dogs and bears,
And wretched, blind, pit ponies,
And little hunted hares.

Poems (1917) 'Bells of Heaven'

14 See an old unhappy bull,
Sick in soul and body both,
Slouching in the undergrowth
Of the forest beautiful,
Banished from the herd he led,
Bulls and cows a thousand head.

Poems (1917) 'The Bull'

15 Reason has moons, but moons not hers,
Lie mirror'd on her sea,
Confounding her astronomers,
But, O! delighting me.

Poems (1917) 'Reason Has Moons'

'Red' Hodgson

16 I blow through here;
The music goes 'round and around.
Whoa-ho-ho-ho-ho, and it comes up here.

Music Goes 'round and Around (1935 song; music by Edward Farley and Michael Riley)

Eric Hoffer 1902–1983

17 It is easier to love humanity as a whole than to love one's neighbour.

New York Times Magazine 15 Feb. 1959, p. 12

18 When people are free to do as they please, they usually imitate each other. Originality is deliberate and forced, and partakes of the nature of a protest.

Passionate State of Mind (1955) p. 21

Al Hoffman 1902–1960 and
Dick Manning 1912–

1 Takes two to tango.
   Title of song (1952)

Gerard Hoffnung 1925–1959

2 Standing among savage scenery, the hotel offers
   stupendous revelations. There is a French widow in
   every bedroom, affording delightful prospects.
   Speech at Oxford Union, 4 Dec. 1958 (supposedly quoting
   a letter from a Tyrolean landlord)

Lancelot Hogben 1895–1975

3 This is not the age of pamphleteers. It is the age of the
   engineers. The spark-gap is mightier than the pen.
   Democracy will not be salvaged by men who talk
   fluently, debate forcefully and quote aptly.
   Science for the Citizen (1938) epilogue

Billie Holiday (Eleanor Fagan) 1915–1959
and *Arthur Herzog Jr.* 1901–1983

4 Them that's got shall get,
   Them that's not shall lose,
   So the Bible said,
   And it still is news;
   Mama may have, papa may have,
   But God bless the child that's got his own!
   That's got his own.
   God Bless the Child (1941 song)

Stanley Holloway 1890–1982

5 Sam, Sam, pick up tha' musket.
   Pick Up Tha' Musket (1930 recorded monologue)

John H. Holmes 1879–1964

6 This, now, is the judgement of our scientific age—the
   third reaction of man upon the universe! This
   universe is not hostile, nor yet is it friendly. It is
   simply indifferent.
   The Sensible Man's View of Religion (1932) ch. 4

Lord Home (Baron Home of the Hirsel,
formerly Sir Alec Douglas-Home) 1903–

7 As far as the fourteenth earl is concerned, I suppose
   Mr [Harold] Wilson, when you come to think of it, is
   the fourteenth Mr Wilson.
   Television interview, 21 Oct. 1963, in *Daily Telegraph* 22 Oct.
   1963 (replying to question on how he was going to meet
   attacks by the Labour Party on his then position as
   a 'fourteenth Earl, a reactionary, and an out-of-date figure')

8 When I have to read economic documents I have to
   have a box of matches and start moving them into
   position to simplify and illustrate the points to myself.
   In *Observer* 16 Sept. 1962

Arthur Honegger 1892–1955

9 *Il est certain que la première qualité d'un compositeur,
   c'est d'être mort.*

   There is no doubt that the first requirement for
   a composer is to be dead.
   Je suis compositeur (I am a Composer, 1951) p. 16

Herbert Hoover 1874–1964

10 Older men declare war. But it is youth who must fight
   and die. And it is youth who must inherit the
   tribulation, the sorrow, and the triumphs that are the
   aftermath of war.
   Speech at the Republican National Convention, Chicago,
   27 June 1944, in *Addresses upon the American Road* (1946)
   p. 254.

11 Our country has deliberately undertaken a great social
   and economic experiment, noble in motive and
   far-reaching in purpose (i.e. 18th Amendment on
   Prohibition).
   Letter to Senator W. H. Borah, 23 Feb. 1928, in Claudius O.
   Johnson *Borah of Idaho* (1936) ch. 21

12 When the war closed . . . we were challenged with
   a peace-time choice between the American system of
   rugged individualism and a European philosophy of
   diametrically opposed doctrines—doctrines of
   paternalism and state socialism.
   Speech in New York City, 22 Oct. 1928, in *New Day* (1928)
   p. 154

13 Another proposal of our opponents which would
   wholly alter our American system of life is to reduce the
   protective tariff to a competitive tariff for revenue. . . .
   The grass will grow in the streets of a hundred cities,
   a thousand towns; the weeds will overrun the fields of
   millions of farms if that protection be taken away.
   Speech, 31 Oct. 1932, in *State Papers of Herbert Hoover*
   (1934) vol. 2, p. 418

Anthony Hope (Sir Anthony Hope
Hawkins) 1863–1933

14 Economy is going without something you do want in
   case you should, some day, want something you
   probably won't want.
   Dolly Dialogues (1894) no. 12

15 'You oughtn't to yield to temptation.' 'Well, somebody
   must, or the thing becomes absurd,' said I.
   Dolly Dialogues (1894) no. 14

16 'Bourgeois,' I observed, 'is an epithet which the riff-raff
   apply to what is respectable, and the aristocracy to
   what is decent.' 'But it's not a nice thing to be, all the
   same,' said Dolly, who is impervious to the most
   penetrating remark.
   Dolly Dialogues (1894) no. 17

17 I wish you would read a little poetry sometimes. Your
   ignorance cramps my conversation.
   Dolly Dialogues (1894) no. 22

18 Anthony Hope—a friend, a true friend, yet pledged
   always to his own and far more Attic interpretation of
   life—sat there [at the first night of J. M. Barrie's *Peter
   Pan* in 1904] looking primmer and drier at every

extravagance, and more and more as if, in his opinion, children should be kept in their right place. When he spoke, his comment was also far more succinct. 'Oh, for an hour of Herod!' he said.

Denis Mackail *Story of JMB* (1941) ch. 17

Bob Hope 1903–

1 A bank is a place that will lend you money if you can prove that you don't need it.

In Alan Harrington *Life in the Crystal Palace* (1959) 'The Tyranny of Farms'

Francis Hope 1938–1974

2 And scribbled lines like fallen hopes
On backs of tattered envelopes.

Instead of a Poet and Other Poems (1965) 'Instead of a Poet'

Laurence Hope (Adela Florence Nicolson) 1865–1904

3 Less than the dust, beneath thy Chariot wheel,
Less than the rust, that never stained thy Sword,
Less than the trust thou hast in me, Oh, Lord,
Even less than these!
Less than the weed, that grows beside thy door,
Less than the speed, of hours, spent far from thee,
Less than the need thou hast in life of me.
Even less am I.

Garden of Kama (1901) 'Less than the Dust'

4 Pale hands I loved beside the Shalimar,
Where are you now? Who lies beneath your spell?
. . . Pale hands, pink tipped, like lotus buds that float
On those cool waters where we used to dwell,
I would have rather felt you round my throat
Crushing out life; than waving me farewell!

Garden of Kama (1901) 'Kashmiri Song'

Zilphia Horton 1907–1957

See Anonymous 9:13

A. E. Housman 1859–1936

5 Mud's sister, not himself, adorns my legs.

Fragment of a Greek Tragedy (*Bromsgrovian* vol. 2, no. 5, 1883) in *Alfred Edward Housman*, the Housman Memorial Supplement of the Bromsgrovian (1936)

6 This great College, of this ancient University, has seen some strange sights. It has seen Wordsworth drunk and Porson sober. And here am I, a better poet than Porson, and a better scholar than Wordsworth, betwixt and between.

Speech at Trinity College, Cambridge, in G. K. Chesterton *Autobiography* (1936) ch. 12

7 If I were the Prince of Peace, I would choose a less provocative Ambassador.

In Alan Wood *Bertrand Russell: Passionate Sceptic* (1957) p. 103

8 Oh who is that young sinner with the handcuffs on his wrists?
And what has he been after that they groan and shake their fists?

And wherefore is he wearing such a conscience-stricken air?
Oh they're taking him to prison for the colour of his hair.

'Tis a shame to human nature, such a head of hair as his;
In the good old time 'twas hanging for the colour that it is;
Though hanging isn't bad enough and flaying would be fair
For the nameless and abominable colour of his hair.

Collected Poems (1939) 'Additional Poems' no. 18

9 That is indeed very good. I shall have to repeat that on the Golden Floor!

In *Daily Telegraph* 21 Feb. 1984 (said to his physician who told him a risqué story to cheer him up just before he died)

10 The Grizzly Bear is huge and wild;
He has devoured the infant child.
The infant child is not aware
He has been eaten by the bear.

Infant Innocence in *Oxford Book of Light Verse* (1938) p. 489

11 *Nous n'irons plus aux bois,*
Les lauriers sont coupés.

We'll go to the woods no more,
The laurels all are cut.

Translation of nursery rhyme in *Last Poems* (1922) introductory

12 Pass me the can, lad; there's an end of May.

Last Poems (1922) no. 9

13 May will be fine next year as like as not:
Oh, ay, but then we shall be twenty-four.

Last Poems (1922) no. 9

14 We for a certainty are not the first
Have sat in taverns while the tempest hurled
Their hopeful plans to emptiness, and cursed
Whatever brute and blackguard made the world.

Last Poems (1922) no. 9

15 The troubles of our proud and angry dust
Are from eternity, and shall not fail.
Bear them we can, and if we can we must.
Shoulder the sky, my lad, and drink your ale.

Last Poems (1922) no. 9

16 But men at whiles are sober
And think by fits and starts,
And if they think, they fasten
Their hands upon their hearts.

Last Poems (1922) no. 10

17 The laws of God, the laws of man,
He may keep that will and can;
Not I: let God and man decree
Laws for themselves and not for me;
And if my ways are not as theirs
Let them mind their own affairs.

Last Poems (1922) no. 12

18 And how am I to face the odds
Of man's bedevilment and God's?
I, a stranger and afraid
In a world I never made.

Last Poems (1922) no. 12

1 The candles burn their sockets,
The blinds let through the day,
The young man feels his pockets
And wonders what's to pay.
Last Poems (1922) no. 21

2 To think that two and two are four
And neither five nor three
The heart of man has long been sore
And long 'tis like to be.
Last Poems (1922) no. 35

3 These, in the day when heaven was falling,
The hour when earth's foundations fled,
Followed their mercenary calling
And took their wages and are dead.

Their shoulders held the sky suspended;
They stood, and earth's foundations stay;
What God abandoned, these defended,
And saved the sum of things for pay.
Last Poems (1922) no. 37

4 For nature, heartless, witless nature,
Will neither care nor know
What stranger's feet may find the meadow
And trespass there and go,
Nor ask amid the dews of morning
If they are mine or no.
Last Poems (1922) no. 40

5 Experience has taught me, when I am shaving of
a morning, to keep watch over my thoughts, because, if
a line of poetry strays into my memory, my skin bristles
so that the razor ceases to act. . . . The seat of this
sensation is the pit of the stomach.
Lecture at Cambridge, 9 May 1933, *The Name and Nature of
Poetry* (1933) p. 47

6 The rainy Pleiads wester,
Orion plunges prone,
The stroke of midnight ceases,
And I lie down alone.
More Poems (1936) no. 11

7 Life, to be sure, is nothing much to lose;
But young men think it is, and we were young.
More Poems (1936) no. 36

8 Good-night. Ensured release
Imperishable peace,
Have these for yours,
While earth's foundations stand
And sky and sea and land
And heaven endures.
More Poems (1936) no. 48 'Alta Quies'

9 Loveliest of trees, the cherry now
Is hung with bloom along the bough,
And stands about the woodland ride
Wearing white for Eastertide.

Now, of my threescore years and ten,
Twenty will not come again,
And take from seventy springs a score,
It only leaves me fifty more.

And since to look at things in bloom
Fifty springs are little room,
About the woodlands I will go
To see the cherry hung with snow.
Shropshire Lad (1896) no. 2

10 Clay lies still, but blood's a rover;
Breath's a ware that will not keep.
Up, lad: when the journey's over
There'll be time enough to sleep.
Shropshire Lad (1896) no. 4

11 And naked to the hangman's noose
The morning clocks will ring
A neck God made for other use
Than strangling in a string.
Shropshire Lad (1896) no. 9

12 When I was one-and-twenty
I heard a wise man say,
'Give crowns and pounds and guineas
But not your heart away;
Give pearls away and rubies,
But keep your fancy free.'
But I was one-and-twenty,
No use to talk to me.
Shropshire Lad (1896) no. 13

13 Oh, when I was in love with you,
Then I was clean and brave,
And miles around the wonder grew
How well I did behave.

And now the fancy passes by,
And nothing will remain,
And miles around they'll say that I
Am quite myself again.
Shropshire Lad (1896) no. 18

14 In summertime on Bredon
The bells they sound so clear;
Round both the shires they ring them
In steeples far and near,
A happy noise to hear.

Here of a Sunday morning
My love and I would lie,
And see the coloured counties,
And hear the larks so high
About us in the sky.
Shropshire Lad (1896) no. 21

15 'Come all to church, good people,'—
Oh, noisy bells, be dumb;
I hear you, I will come.
Shropshire Lad (1896) no. 21

16 The lads in their hundreds to Ludlow come in for the
fair,
There's men from the barn and the forge and the mill
and the fold,
The lads for the girls and the lads for the liquor are
there,
And there with the rest are the lads that will never
be old.
Shropshire Lad (1896) no. 23

17 Is my team ploughing,
That I was used to drive
And hear the harness jingle
When I was man alive?
Shropshire Lad (1896) no. 27

18 On Wenlock Edge the wood's in trouble;
His forest fleece the Wrekin heaves;
The wind it plies the saplings double,
And thick on Severn snow the leaves.
Shropshire Lad (1896) no. 31

1 The gale, it plies the saplings double,
It blows so hard, 'twill soon be gone:
To-day the Roman and his trouble
Are ashes under Uricon.
    Shropshire Lad (1896) no. 31

2 From far, from eve and morning
And yon twelve-winded sky,
The stuff of life to knit me
Blew hither: here am I.
    Shropshire Lad (1896) no. 32

3 Speak now, and I will answer;
How shall I help you, say;
Ere to the wind's twelve quarters
I take my endless way.
    Shropshire Lad (1896) no. 32

4 Into my heart an air that kills
From yon far country blows:
What are those blue remembered hills,
What spires, what farms are those?

That is the land of lost content,
I see it shining plain,
The happy highways where I went
And cannot come again.
    Shropshire Lad (1896) no. 40

5 And bound for the same bourn as I,
On every road I wandered by,
Trod beside me, close and dear,
The beautiful and death-struck year.
    Shropshire Lad (1896) no. 41

6 Clunton and Clunbury,
Clungunford and Clun,
Are the quietest places
Under the sun.
    Shropshire Lad (1896) no. 50, epigraph

7 With rue my heart is laden
For golden friends I had,
For many a rose-lipt maiden
And many a lightfoot lad.

By brooks too broad for leaping
The lightfoot boys are laid;
The rose-lipt girls are sleeping
In fields where roses fade.
    Shropshire Lad (1896) no. 54

8 Say, for what were hop-yards meant,
Or why was Burton built on Trent?
Oh many a peer of England brews
Livelier liquor than the Muse,
And malt does more than Milton can
To justify God's ways to man.
Ale, man, ale's the stuff to drink
For fellows whom it hurts to think.
    Shropshire Lad (1896) no. 62

9 Oh I have been to Ludlow fair
And left my necktie God knows where,
And carried half-way home, or near,
Pints and quarts of Ludlow beer:
Then the world seemed none so bad,
And I myself a sterling lad;
And down in lovely muck I've lain,
Happy till I woke again.
    Shropshire Lad (1896) no. 62

10 I tell the tale that I heard told.
Mithridates, he died old.
    Shropshire Lad (1896) no. 62

Sidney Howard

See MARGARET MITCHELL

Elbert Hubbard 1859–1915

11 Never explain—your friends do not need it and your
enemies will not believe you anyway.
    Motto Book (1907) p. 31

12 Life is just one damned thing after another.
    Philistine Dec. 1909, p. 32. The saying is often attributed to
    Frank Ward O'Malley

13 Editor: a person employed by a newspaper, whose
business it is to separate the wheat from the chaff, and
to see that the chaff is printed.
    Roycroft Dictionary (1914) p. 46

14 Little minds are interested in the extraordinary; great
minds in the commonplace.
    Thousand and One Epigrams (1911) p. 133

15 One machine can do the work of fifty ordinary men. No
machine can do the work of one extraordinary man.
    Thousand and One Epigrams (1911) p. 151

Frank McKinney ('Kin') Hubbard 1868–1930

16 Classic music is th'kind that we keep thinkin'll turn
into a tune.
    Comments of Abe Martin and His Neighbors (1923)

17 It's no disgrace t'be poor, but it might as well be.
    Short Furrows (1911) p. 42

L. Ron Hubbard 1911–1986

18 Hubbard . . . told us that writing science fiction for
about a penny a word was no way to make a living. If
you really want to make a million, he said, the
quickest way is to start your own religion.
    Sam Moscowitz recalling Hubbard speaking to the Eastern
    Science Fiction Association at Newark, New Jersey, in 1947,
    in B. Corydon and L. Ron Hubbard Jr. *L. Ron Hubbard* (1987)
    ch. 3

Howard Hughes Jr. 1905–1976

19 That man's ears make him look like a taxi-cab with
both doors open.
    In Charles Higham and Joel Greenberg *Celluloid Muse* (1969)
    p. 156 (describing Clark Gable)

Jimmy Hughes and Frank Lake

20 Bless 'em all! Bless 'em all!
The long and the short and the tall.
    Bless 'Em All (1940 song)

Langston Hughes 1902–1967

21 'It's powerful,' he said.
'What?'

'That one drop of Negro blood—because just *one* drop of black blood makes a man coloured. *One* drop—you are a Negro!'
Simple Takes a Wife (1953) p. 85

1 I, too, sing America.

I am the darker brother.
They send me to eat in the kitchen
When company comes.
But I laugh,
And eat well,
And grow strong.

Tomorrow
I'll sit at the table
When company comes
Nobody'll dare
Say to me,
'Eat in the kitchen'
Then.

Besides, they'll see how
beautiful I am
And be ashamed,—

I, too, am America.
Survey Graphic Mar. 1925, 'I, Too'

Ted Hughes 1930–

2 It took the whole of Creation
To produce my foot, my each feather:
Now I hold Creation in my foot.
Lupercal (1960) 'Hawk Roosting'

Josephine Hull ?1886–1957

3 [Josephine Hull's] stage reminiscences are not the least of her charms. 'Shakespeare,' she recalls, 'is so tiring. You never get a chance to sit down unless you're a king.'
Time 16 Nov. 1953, p. 90

Hubert Humphrey 1911–1978

4 There are not enough jails, not enough policemen, not enough courts to enforce a law not supported by the people.
Speech at Williamsburg, 1 May 1965, in *New York Times* 2 May 1965, sec. 1, p. 34

5 The right to be heard does not automatically include the right to be taken seriously.
Speech to National Student Association at Madison, 23 Aug. 1965, in *New York Times* 24 Aug. 1965, p. 12

6 And here we are, just as we ought to be, here we are, the people, here we are in a spirit of dedication, here we are the way politics ought to be in America, the politics of happiness, the politics of purpose and the politics of joy.
Speech in Washington, 27 Apr. 1968, in *New York Times* 28 Apr. 1968, p. 66

Herman Hupfeld 1894–1951

7 You must remember this, a kiss is still a kiss,
A sigh is just a sigh;

The fundamental things apply,
As time goes by.
As Time Goes By (1931 song)

Aldous Huxley 1894–1963

8 Christlike in my behaviour,
Like every good believer,
I imitate the Saviour,
And cultivate a beaver.
Antic Hay (1923) ch. 4

9 There are few who would not rather be taken in adultery than in provincialism.
Antic Hay (1923) ch. 10

10 Official dignity tends to increase in inverse ratio to the importance of the country in which the office is held.
Beyond the Mexique Bay (1934) p. 34

11 The sexophones wailed like melodious cats under the moon.
Brave New World (1932) ch. 5

12 That men do not learn very much from the lessons of history is the most important of all the lessons that history has to teach.
Collected Essays (1959) 'Case of Voluntary Ignorance'

13 The proper study of mankind is books.
Crome Yellow (1921) ch. 28

14 Too much consistency is as bad for the mind as it is for the body. Consistency is contrary to nature, contrary to life. The only completely consistent people are the dead.
Do What You Will (1929) 'Wordsworth in the Tropics'

15 The end cannot justify the means, for the simple and obvious reason that the means employed determine the nature of the ends produced.
Ends and Means (1937) ch. 1

16 So long as men worship the Caesars and Napoleons, Caesars and Napoleons will duly arise and make them miserable.
Ends and Means (1937) ch. 8

17 Chastity—the most unnatural of all the sexual perversions, he added parenthetically, out of Remy de Gourmont.
Eyeless in Gaza (1936) ch. 27

18 'Death,' said Mark Staithes. 'It's the only thing we haven't succeeded in completely vulgarizing.'
Eyeless in Gaza (1936) ch. 31

19 'Bed,' as the Italian proverb succinctly puts it, 'is the poor man's opera.'
Heaven and Hell (1956) p. 41

20 A million million spermatozoa,
All of them alive:
Out of their cataclysm but one poor Noah
Dare hope to survive.

And among that billion minus one
Might have chanced to be
Shakespeare, another Newton, a new Donne—
But the One was Me.
Leda (1920) 'Fifth Philosopher's Song'

21 Beauty for some provides escape,
Who gain a happiness in eyeing

The gorgeous buttocks of the ape
Or Autumn sunsets exquisitely dying.
Leda (1920) 'Ninth Philosopher's Song'

1 Then brim the bowl with atrabilious liquor!
We'll pledge our Empire vast across the flood:
For Blood, as all men know, than Water's thicker,
But Water's wider, thank the Lord, than Blood.
Leda (1920) 'Ninth Philosopher's Song'

2 Ragtime . . . but when the wearied Band
Swoons to a waltz, I take her hand,
And there we sit in peaceful calm,
Quietly sweating palm to palm.
Leda (1920) 'Frascati's'

3 I can sympathize with people's pains, but not with their pleasures. There is something curiously boring about somebody else's happiness.
Limbo (1920) 'Cynthia'

4 After silence, that which comes nearest to expressing the inexpressible is music.
Music at Night (1931) p. 17

5 'And besides,' he added, forgetting that several excuses are always less convincing than one, 'Lady Edward's inviting an American editor specially for my sake.'
Point Counter Point (1928) ch. 1

6 A bad book is as much of a labour to write as a good one; it comes as sincerely from the author's soul.
Point Counter Point (1928) ch. 13

7 There is no substitute for talent. Industry and all the virtues are of no avail.
Point Counter Point (1928) ch. 13

8 Brought up in an epoch when ladies apparently rolled along on wheels, Mr Quarles was peculiarly susceptible to calves.
Point Counter Point (1928) ch. 20

9 Parodies and caricatures are the most penetrating of criticisms.
Point Counter Point (1928) ch. 28

10 That all men are equal is a proposition to which, at ordinary times, no sane human being has ever given his assent.
Proper Studies (1927) 'The Idea of Equality'

11 Those who believe that they are exclusively in the right are generally those who achieve something.
Proper Studies (1927) 'Note on Dogma'

12 Facts do not cease to exist because they are ignored.
Proper Studies (1927) 'Note on Dogma'

13 Experience is not what happens to a man; it is what a man does with what happens to him.
Texts and Pretexts (1932) p. 5

14 Most human beings have an almost infinite capacity for taking things for granted.
Themes and Variations (1950) 'Variations on a Philosopher'

15 'There's only one corner of the universe you can be certain of improving, and that's your own self. Your own self,' he repeated. So you have to begin there, not outside, not on other people. That comes afterwards, when you've worked on your own corner.
Time Must Have a Stop (1945) ch. 7

Sir Julian Huxley 1887–1975

16 Operationally, God is beginning to resemble not a ruler but the last fading smile of a cosmic Cheshire cat.
Religion without Revelation (1957 edn.) ch. 3

Dolores Ibarruri ('La Pasionaria') 1895–1989

17 *Il vaut mieux mourir debout que de vivre à genoux!*

It is better to die on your feet than to live on your knees.
Speech in Paris, 3 Sept. 1936, in *L'Humanité* 4 Sept. 1936 (also attributed to Emiliano Zapata)

18 *No pasarán.*

They shall not pass.
Radio broadcast, Madrid, 19 July 1936, in *Speeches and Articles 1936–38* (1938) p. 7 (cf. Anonymous 6:25)

Henrik Ibsen 1828–1906

19 *Luftslotte,—de er så nemme at ty ind i, de. Og nemme at bygge også.*

Castles in the air—they are so easy to take refuge in. And so easy to build, too.
Bygmester Solness (The Master Builder, 1892) act 3

20 *Flertallet har aldrig retten på sin side. Aldrig, siger jeg! Det er en af disse samfundsløgne, som en fri, tænkende mand må gøre oprør imod. Hvem er det, som udgør flertallet af beboerne i et land? Er det de kloge folk, eller er det dè dumme? Jeg taenker, vi får vaere enige om, at dumme mennesker er tilstede i en ganske forskraek kelig overvældende majoritet rundt omkring på den hele vide jord. Men det kan da vel, for fanden, aldrig i evighed vaere ret, at de dumme skal herske over de kloge!*

The majority never has right on its side. Never I say! That is one of the social lies that a free, thinking man is bound to rebel against. Who makes up the majority in any given country? Is it the wise men or the fools? I think we must agree that the fools are in a terrible overwhelming majority, all the wide world over.
En Folkefiende (An Enemy of the People, 1882) act 4

21 *En skulde aldrig ha' sine bedste buxer på, når en er ude og strider for frihed og sandhed.*

You should never have your best trousers on when you go out to fight for freedom and truth.
En Folkefiende (An Enemy of the People, 1882) act 5

22 *Sagen er den, ser I, at den stærkeste mand i verden, det er han, som står mest alene.*

The thing is, you see, that the strongest man in the world is the man who stands most alone.
En Folkefiende (An Enemy of the People, 1882) act 5

23 *Mor, gi' mig solen.*

Mother, give me the sun.
Gengangere (Ghosts, 1881) act 3

24 *Men, gud sig forbarme,—sligt noget gør man da ikke!*

But good God, people don't do such things!
Hedda Gabler (1890) act 4

1 *Hvad skal manden være? Sig selv, det er mit korte svar.*

What ought a man to be? Well, my short answer is 'himself'.
Peer Gynt (1867) act 4

2 *Tar de livsløgnen fra et gennemsnitsmenneske, så tar De lykken fra ham med det samme.*

Take the life-lie away from the average man and straight away you take away his happiness.
Vildanden (The Wild Duck, 1884) act 5

Harold L. Ickes 1874–1952

3 The trouble with Senator Long ... is that he is suffering from halitosis of the intellect. That's presuming Emperor Long has an intellect.
Speech, 1935, in G. Wolfskill and J. A. Hudson *All But the People: Franklin D. Roosevelt and his Critics, 1933–39* (1969) ch. 11

4 Dewey threw his diaper into the ring.
On the Republican candidate for the presidency, in *New York Times* 12 Dec. 1939, p. 32

Eric Idle 1943–

See GRAHAM CHAPMAN *et al.*

Francis Iles (Anthony Berkeley Cox) 1893–1970

5 It was not until several weeks after he had decided to murder his wife that Dr Bickleigh took any active steps in the matter. Murder is a serious business.
Malice Aforethought (1931) p. 7

Ivan Illich 1926–

6 Man must choose whether to be rich in things or in the freedom to use them.
Deschooling Society (1971) ch. 4

7 In a consumer society there are inevitably two kinds of slaves: the prisoners of addiction and the prisoners of envy.
Tools for Conviviality (1973) ch. 3

Charles Inge 1868–1957

8 This very remarkable man
Commends a most practical plan:
You can do what you want
If you don't think you can't,
So don't think you can't think you can.
Weekend Book (1928) 'On Monsieur Coué'

William Ralph Inge (Dean Inge) 1860–1954

9 The aim of education is the knowledge not of facts but of values.
'The Training of the Reason' in A. C. Benson (ed.) *Cambridge Essays on Education* (1917) ch. 2

10 The enemies of Freedom do not argue; they shout and they shoot.
End of an Age (1948) ch. 4

11 The effect of boredom on a large scale in history is underestimated. It is a main cause of revolutions, and would soon bring to an end all the static Utopias and the farmyard civilization of the Fabians.
End of an Age (1948) ch. 6

12 To become a popular religion, it is only necessary for a superstition to enslave a philosophy.
Idea of Progress (Romanes Lecture delivered at Oxford, 27 May 1920) p. 9

13 Many people believe that they are attracted by God, or by Nature, when they are only repelled by man.
More Lay Thoughts of a Dean (1931) pt. 4, ch. 1

14 It takes in reality only one to make a quarrel. It is useless for the sheep to pass resolutions in favour of vegetarianism, while the wolf remains of a different opinion.
Outspoken Essays: First Series (1919) 'Patriotism'

15 The nations which have put mankind and posterity most in their debt have been small states—Israel, Athens, Florence, Elizabethan England.
Outspoken Essays: Second Series (1922) 'State, visible and invisible'

16 A man may build himself a throne of bayonets, but he cannot sit on it; and he cannot avow that the bayonets are meant to keep his own subjects quiet.
Philosophy of Plotinus (1923) vol. 2, lecture 22

17 Literature flourishes best when it is half a trade and half an art.
Victorian Age (Rede Lecture delivered at Cambridge, 1922) p. 49

Eugène Ionesco 1912–

18 *C'est une chose anormale de vivre.*

Living is abnormal.
Le Rhinocéros (1959) act 1

19 *Tu ne prévois les événements que lorsqu'ils sont déjà arrivés.*

You can only predict things after they have happened.
Le Rhinocéros (1959) act 3

20 *Un fonctionnaire ne plaisante pas.*

A civil servant doesn't make jokes.
Tueur sans gages (The Killer, 1958) act 1

Weldon J. Irvine

21 Young, gifted and black.
Title of song (1969; music by Nina Simone)

Christopher Isherwood 1904–1986

22 The common cormorant (or shag)
Lays eggs inside a paper bag,
You follow the idea, no doubt?
It's to keep the lightning out.

But what these unobservant birds
Have never thought of, is that herds

Of wandering bears might come with buns
And steal the bags to hold the crumbs.
Exhumations (1966) 'Common Cormorant'

1 I am a camera with its shutter open, quite passive,
recording, not thinking. Recording the man shaving at
the window opposite and the woman in the kimono
washing her hair. Some day, all this will have to be
developed, carefully printed, fixed.
Goodbye to Berlin (1939) 'Berlin Diary' Autumn 1930

2 Mr Norris changes trains.
Title of novel (1935)

See also W. H. AUDEN and CHRISTOPHER ISHERWOOD

Holbrook Jackson 1874–1948

3 A mother never realizes that her children are no
longer children.
All Manner of Folk (1912) 'On a Certain Arrangement' p. 89

4 Pedantry is the dotage of knowledge.
Anatomy of Bibliomania (1930) vol. 1, p. 150

5 As soon as an idea is accepted it is time to reject it.
Platitudes in the Making (1911) p. 13

Joe Jacobs 1896–1940

6 We was robbed!
Shouted into the microphone after Jack Sharkey beat Max
Schmeling (of whom Jacobs was manager) in the
heavyweight title fight, 21 June 1932, in Peter Heller *In This
Corner* (1975) p. 44

7 I should of stood [i.e. have stayed] in bed.
Said after he left his sick-bed in October 1935 to attend the
World Baseball Series in Detroit and he bet on the losers, in
John Lardner *Strong Cigars* (1951) p. 61

Mick Jagger 1943–
and Keith Richard (Keith Richards) 1943–

8 It's only rock 'n' roll.
Title of song (1974)

9 Ev'rywhere I hear the sound of marching, charging
feet, oh, boy,
'Cause summer's here and the time is oh, right for
fighting in the street, boy.
But what can a poor boy do
Except to sing for a rock 'n' roll band,
'Cause in sleepy London town
There's just no place for street fighting man!
Street Fighting Man (1968 song)

Henry James 1843–1916

10 The ever-importunate murmur, 'Dramatize it,
dramatize it!'
Altar of the Dead (1909 ed.) preface

11 The terrible *fluidity of self-revelation.*
Ambassadors (1909 ed.) preface

12 Live all you can; it's a mistake not to. It doesn't so
much matter what you do in particular, so long as you
have your life. If you haven't had that, what *have* you
had?
Ambassadors (1903) bk. 5, ch. 11

13 The deep well of unconscious cerebration.
The American (1909 ed.) preface

14 The historian, essentially, wants more documents than
he can really use; the dramatist only wants more
liberties than he can really take.
Aspern Papers (1909 ed.) preface

15 Summer afternoon—summer afternoon; to me those
have always been the two most beautiful words in the
English language.
In Edith Wharton *Backward Glance* (1934) ch. 10

16 He [Henry James] is said to have told his old friend Lady
Prothero, when she saw him after the first stroke, that
in the very act of falling (he was dressing at the time)
he heard in the room a voice which was distinctly, it
seemed, not his own saying: 'So here it is at last, the
distinguished thing!'
Edith Wharton *Backward Glance* (1934) ch. 14

17 To kill a human being is, after all, the least injury you
can do him.
Complete Tales (1962) vol. 1 'My Friend Bingham' (1867
short story)

18 We work in the dark—we do what we can—we give
what we have. Our doubt is our passion and our
passion is our task. The rest is the madness of art.
Complete Tales (1964) vol. 9 'Middle Years' (1893 short
story)

19 Vereker's secret, my dear man—the general intention
of his books: the string the pearls were strung on, the
buried treasure, the figure in the carpet.
Figure in the Carpet (1896) ch. 11

20 It takes a great deal of history to produce a little
literature.
Hawthorne (1879) ch. 1

21 Whatever question there may be of his [Thoreau's]
talent, there can be none, I think, of his genius. It was
a slim and crooked one; but it was eminently personal.
He was imperfect, unfinished, inartistic; he was worse
than provincial—he was parochial.
Hawthorne (1879) ch. 4

22 Cats and monkeys—monkeys and cats—all human life
is there!
Madonna of the Future (1879) vol. 1, p. 59 ('All human life is
there' was used by Maurice Smelt as an advertising slogan
for the *News of the World* in the late 1950s)

23 They have fairly faced the full, the monstrous
demonstration that Tennyson was not Tennysonian.
Middle Years (1917 autobiography) ch. 6

24 The only reason for the existence of a novel is that it
does attempt to represent life.
Partial Portraits (1888) 'Art of Fiction'

25 The only obligation to which in advance we may hold
a novel, without incurring the accusation of being
arbitrary, is that it be interesting.
Partial Portraits (1888) 'Art of Fiction'

26 Experience is never limited, and it is never complete; it
is an immense sensibility, a kind of huge spider-web of

the finest silken threads suspended in the chamber of consciousness, and catching every air-borne particle in its tissue.

Partial Portraits (1888) 'Art of Fiction'

1 What is character but the determination of incident? What is incident but the illustration of character? What is either a picture or a novel that is *not* character?

Partial Portraits (1888) 'Art of Fiction'

2 We must grant the artist his subject, his idea, his *donnée*: our criticism is applied only to what he makes of it.

Partial Portraits (1888) 'Art of Fiction'

3 I don't care anything about reasons, but I know what I like.

Portrait of a Lady (1881) vol. 2, ch. 5. Cf. Max Beerbohm 23:14

4 I didn't, of course, stay her hand—there never *is* in such cases 'time'; and I had once more the full demonstration of the fatal futility of Fact.

Spoils of Poynton (1909 ed.) preface

5 We were alone with the quiet day, and his little heart, dispossessed, had stopped.

Turn of the Screw (1898) p. 169

William James 1842–1910

6 Man, biologically considered, and whatever else he may be into the bargain, is simply the most formidable of all the beasts of prey, and, indeed, the only one that preys systematically on its own species.

Atlantic Monthly Dec. 1904, p. 845

7 I now perceive one immense omission in my Psychology,—the deepest principle of Human Nature is the *craving to be appreciated*, and I left it out altogether from the book, because I had never had it gratified till now.

Letter to his class at Radcliffe College, 6 Apr. 1896, in *Letters* (1920) vol. 2, p. 33

8 The moral flabbiness born of the exclusive worship of the bitch-goddess *success*. That—with the squalid cash interpretation put on the word success—is our national disease.

Letter to H. G. Wells, 11 Sept. 1906, in *Letters* (1920) vol. 2, p. 260

9 Real culture lives by sympathies and admirations, not by dislikes and disdains—under all misleading wrappings it pounces unerringly upon the human core.

McClure's Magazine Feb. 1908, p. 422

10 So long as antimilitarists propose no substitute for war's disciplinary function, no *moral equivalent* of war, analogous, as one might say, to the mechanical equivalent of heat, so long they fail to realize the full inwardness of the situation.

Memories and Studies (1911) 'The Moral Equivalent of War' p. 283

11 There is no more miserable human being than one in whom nothing is habitual but indecision.

Principles of Psychology (1890) vol. 1, ch. 4

12 The art of being wise is the art of knowing what to overlook.

Principles of Psychology (1890) vol. 2, ch. 22

13 The first thing to learn in intercourse with others is non-interference with their own peculiar ways of being happy, provided those ways do not assume to interfere by violence with ours.

Talks to Teachers (1899) 'What makes a Life Significant?'

14 If merely 'feeling good' could decide, drunkenness would be the supremely valid human experience.

Varieties of Religious Experience (1902) lecture 1, p. 16

15 An idea, to be suggestive, must come to the individual with the force of a revelation.

Varieties of Religious Experience (1902) lectures 4 and 5, p. 113

16 There is no worse lie than a truth misunderstood by those who hear it.

Varieties of Religious Experience (1902) lectures 14 and 15, p. 355

Randall Jarrell 1914–1965

17 One of the most obvious facts about grown-ups, to a child, is that they have forgotten what it is like to be a child.

Introduction to Christina Stead *The Man Who Loved Children* (1965) p. xxvi

Douglas Jay 1907–

18 It was Bert Amey who asked me to send him a brief rhyming North Battersea slogan [for the 1946 by-election]. I suggested: 'Fair Shares for All, is Labour's Call'; and from this by-election 'Fair Shares for All' spread in a few years round the country.

Change and Fortune (1980) ch. 7

19 For in the case of nutrition and health, just as in the case of education, the gentleman in Whitehall really does know better what is good for people than the people know themselves.

Socialist Case (1939) ch. 30

Sir James Jeans 1877–1946

20 Taking a very gloomy view of the future of the human race, let us suppose that it can only expect to survive for two thousand million years longer, a period about equal to the past age of the earth. Then, regarded as a being destined to live for three-score years and ten, humanity, although it has been born in a house seventy years old, is itself only three days old.

Eos (1928) p. 12

21 Life exists in the universe only because the carbon atom possesses certain exceptional properties.

Mysterious Universe (1930) ch. 1

22 From the intrinsic evidence of his creation, the Great Architect of the Universe now begins to appear as a pure mathematician.

Mysterious Universe (1930) ch. 5

Patrick Jenkin 1926–

23 People can clean their teeth in the dark, use the top of the stove instead of the oven, all sorts of savings, but they must use less electricity.

Radio broadcast, 15 Jan. 1974, in *The Times* 16 Jan. 1974

Rt. Revd David Jenkins (Bishop of Durham) 1925–

1 I wouldn't put it past God to arrange a virgin birth if he wanted to, but I very much doubt if he would—because it seems to be contrary to the way in which he deals with persons and brings his wonders out of natural personal relationships.

    In *Church Times* 4 May 1984

2 The withdrawal of an imported, elderly American [Ian MacGregor] to leave a reconciling opportunity for some local product is surely neither dishonourable nor improper.

    In *The Times* 22 Sept. 1984

Roy Jenkins (Baron Jenkins of Hillhead) 1920–

3 The politics of the left and centre of this country are frozen in an out-of-date mould which is bad for the political and economic health of Britain and increasingly inhibiting for those who live within the mould. Can it be broken?

    Speech to Parliamentary Press Gallery, 9 June 1980, in *The Times* 10 June 1980

Paul Jennings 1918–1989

4 I am prepared to testify on oath that on the portico pillars of one building there is a bronze office sign which simply says: ACTIVATED SLUDGE.

    Oddly Enough (1950) 'Activated Sludge'

5 Clark-Trimble arranged four hundred pieces of carpet in ascending degrees of quality, from coarse matting to priceless Chinese silk. Pieces of toast and marmalade, graded, weighed, and measured, were then dropped on each piece of carpet, and the marmalade-downwards incidence was statistically analysed. The toast fell right-side-up every time on the cheap carpet . . . and it fell marmalade-downwards every time on the Chinese silk.

    Town and Country Sept. 1949, 'Report on Resistentialism'

Jerome K. Jerome 1859–1927

6 It is always the best policy to speak the truth—unless, of course, you are an exceptionally good liar.

    The Idler Feb. 1892, p. 118

7 It is impossible to enjoy idling thoroughly unless one has plenty of work to do.

    Idle Thoughts of an Idle Fellow (1886) 'On Being Idle'

8 Love is like the measles; we all have to go through it.

    Idle Thoughts of an Idle Fellow (1886) 'On Being in Love'

9 We drink one another's healths, and spoil our own.

    Idle Thoughts of an Idle Fellow (1886) 'On Eating and Drinking'

10 The world must be getting old, I think; it dresses so very soberly now.

    Idle Thoughts of an Idle Fellow (1886) 'On Dress and Deportment'

11 I did not intend to write a funny book, at first. I did not know I was a humorist. I have never been sure about it.

In the middle ages, I should probably have gone about preaching and got myself burnt or hanged.

    My Life and Times (1926) ch. 6

12 The passing of the third floor back.

    Title of story (1907) and play (1910)

13 I want a house that has got over all its troubles; I don't want to spend the rest of my life bringing up a young and inexperienced house.

    They and I (1909) ch. 11

14 It is a most extraordinary thing, but I never read a patent medicine advertisement without being impelled to the conclusion that I am suffering from the particular disease therein dealt with in its most virulent form.

    Three Men in a Boat (1889) ch. 1

15 But there, everything has its drawbacks, as the man said when his mother-in-law died, and they came down upon him for the funeral expenses.

    Three Men in a Boat (1889) ch. 3

16 I like work: it fascinates me. I can sit and look at it for hours. I love to keep it by me: the idea of getting rid of it nearly breaks my heart.

    Three Men in a Boat (1889) ch. 15

William Jerome 1865–1932

17 Any old place I can hang my hat is home sweet home to me.

    Title of song (1901; music by Jean Schwartz)

18 You needn't try to reason,
Your excuse is out of season,
Just kiss yourself goodbye.

    Just Kiss Yourself Goodbye (1902 song; music by Jean Schwartz)

C. E. M. Joad 1891–1953

19 It all depends what you mean by . . .

    Frequent opening to replies on the BBC radio series 'The Brains Trust' (originally 'Any Questions'), 1941–8

20 My life is spent in a perpetual alternation between two rhythms, the rhythm of attracting people for fear I may be lonely, and the rhythm of trying to get rid of them because I know that I am bored.

    In *Observer* 12 Dec. 1948, p. 2

Pope John XXIII (Angelo Giuseppe Roncalli) 1881–1963

21 If civil authorities legislate for or allow anything that is contrary to that order and therefore contrary to the will of God, neither the laws made or the authorizations granted can be binding on the consciences of the citizens, since God has more right to be obeyed than man.

    Pacem in Terris (1963) p. 142

22 The social progress, order, security and peace of each country are necessarily connected with the social progress, order, security and peace of all other countries.

    Pacem in Terris (1963) p. 150

1 John XXIII said that during the first months of his pontificate he often woke during the night, thinking himself still a cardinal and worried over a difficult decision to be made, and he would say to himself: 'I'll talk it over with the Pope!' Then he would remember where he was. 'But *I'm* the Pope!' he said to himself. After which he would conclude: 'Well I'll talk it over with Our Lord!'

Henri Fesquet *Wit and Wisdom of Good Pope John* (1964) p. 59

2 Anybody can be pope; the proof of this is that I have become one.

Henri Fesquet *Wit and Wisdom of Good Pope John* (1964) p. 112

Lyndon Baines Johnson
1908–1973

3 I don't want loyalty. I want *loyalty*. I want him to kiss my ass in Macy's window at high noon and tell me it smells like roses. I want his pecker in my pocket.

In David Halberstam *Best and Brightest* (1972) ch. 20

4 It's probably better to have him [J. Edgar Hoover] inside the tent pissing out, than outside pissing in.

In David Halberstam *Best and Brightest* (1972) ch. 20

5 Jerry Ford is so dumb he can't fart and chew gum at the same time.

In Richard Reeves *A Ford, not a Lincoln* (1975) ch. 2

6 For the first time in our history, it is possible to conquer poverty.

Speech to Congress, 16 Mar. 1964, in *New York Times* 17 Mar. 1964, p. 22

7 All I have I would have given gladly not to be standing here today.

Speech to Congress, 27 Nov. 1963, in *Public Papers of the Presidents of the United States: Lyndon B. Johnson 1963–64* vol. 1, p. 8 (after the previous president, J. F. Kennedy, was assassinated)

8 We have talked long enough in this country about equal rights. We have talked for a hundred years or more. It is time now to write the next chapter, and to write it in the books of law.

Speech to Congress, 27 Nov. 1963, in *Public Papers of the Presidents of the United States: Lyndon B. Johnson 1963–64* vol. 1, p. 9

9 We hope that the world will not narrow into a neighbourhood before it has broadened into a brotherhood.

Speech at lighting of the Nation's Christmas Tree, 22 Dec. 1963, in *Public Papers of the Presidents of the United States: Lyndon B. Johnson 1963–64*, vol. 1, item 65

10 This administration today, here and now declares unconditional war on poverty in America.

State of the Union address to Congress, 8 Jan. 1964, in *Public Papers of the Presidents of the United States: Lyndon B. Johnson 1963–64* vol. 1, p. 114

11 In your time we have the opportunity to move not only toward the rich society and the powerful society, but upward to the Great Society.

Speech at University of Michigan, 22 May 1964, in *Public Papers of the Presidents of the United States: Lyndon B. Johnson 1963–64* vol. 1, p. 704

12 We Americans know, although others appear to forget, the risks of spreading conflict. We still seek no wider war.

Speech on radio and television, 4 Aug. 1964, in *Public Papers of the Presidents of the United States: Lyndon B. Johnson 1963–64* vol. 2, p. 927

13 We are not about to send American boys 9 or 10,000 miles away from home to do what Asian boys ought to be doing for themselves.

Speech at Akron University, 21 Oct. 1964, in *Public Papers of the Presidents of the United States: Lyndon B. Johnson 1963–64* vol. 2, p. 1391

14 Extremism in the pursuit of the Presidency is an unpardonable vice. Moderation in the affairs of the nation is the highest virtue.

Speech in New York, 31 Oct. 1964, in *Public Papers of the Presidents of the United States: Lyndon B. Johnson 1963–64* vol. 2, p. 1559

15 A President's hardest task is not to *do* what is right, but to *know* what is right.

State of the Union address to Congress, 4 Jan. 1965, in *Public Papers of the Presidents of the United States: Lyndon B. Johnson 1965* vol. 1, p. 9

16 I am a free man, an American, a United States Senator, and a Democrat, in that order.

Texas Quarterly Winter 1958

Philander Chase Johnson
1866–1939

17 Cheer up! the worst is yet to come!

Everybody's Magazine May 1920

Philip Johnson 1906–

18 Architecture is the art of how to waste space.

New York Times 27 Dec. 1964, p. 9E)

Hanns Johst 1890–1978

19 *Wenn ich Kultur höre ... entsichere ich meinen Browning!*

Whenever I hear the word culture ... I release the safety-catch of my Browning [pistol]!

Schlageter (1933) act 1, sc. 1. Often attributed to Hermann Goering

Al Jolson 1886–1950

20 It can be revealed for the first time that it was in San Francisco [in 1906] that Al Jolson first uttered his immortal slogan, 'You ain't heard nuttin' yet!' One night at the cafe he had just finished a song when a deafening burst of noise from a building project across the street drowned out the applause. At the top of his lungs, Jolson screamed, 'You think that's noise—you ain't heard nuttin' yet!' And he proceeded to deliver an encore which for sheer blasting power put to everlasting shame all the decibels of noise the carpenters, the brick-layers and the drillers could scare up between them.

Martin Abramson *Real Story of Al Jolson* (1950) p. 12

James Jones 1921–

1 From here to eternity.

Title of novel (1951). Cf. Rudyard Kipling 123:16

LeRoi Jones

See IMAMU AMIRI BARAKA

Erica Jong 1942–

2 The zipless fuck is the purest thing there is. And it is rarer than the unicorn. And I have never had one.

Fear of Flying (1973) ch. 1

Janis Joplin 1943–1970

3 Oh, Lord, won't you buy me a Mercedes Benz
My friends all drive Porsches,
I must make amends.

Mercedes Benz (1970 song)

4 Fourteen heart attacks and he had to die in my week. In MY week.

Said when Eisenhower's death prevented her photograph from being on the front cover of *Newsweek*, in *New Musical Express* 12 Apr. 1969

Sir Keith Joseph 1918–

5 Perhaps there is at work here a process, apparent in many situations but imperfectly understood, by which problems reproduce themselves from generation to generation. If I refer to this as a 'cycle of deprivation' I do not want to be misunderstood.

Speech in London to Pre-School Playgroups Association, 29 June 1972

James Joyce 1882–1941

6 Yes, the newspapers were right: snow was general all over Ireland. It was falling on every part of the dark central plain, on the treeless hills, falling softly upon the Bog of Allen and, farther westward, softly falling into the dark mutinous Shannon waves. It was falling, too, upon every part of the lonely churchyard on the hill where Michael Furey lay buried. It lay thickly drifted on the crooked crosses and headstones, on the spears of the little gate, on the barren thorns. His soul swooned slowly as he heard the snow falling faintly through the universe and faintly falling, like the descent of their last end, upon all the living and the dead.

Dubliners (1914) 'The Dead'

7 riverrun, past Eve and Adam's, from swerve of shore to bend of bay, brings us by a commodious vicus of recirculation back to Howth Castle and Environs.

Finnegans Wake (1939) pt. 1, p. 3

8 That ideal reader suffering from an ideal insomnia.

Finnegans Wake (1939) pt. 1, p. 120

9 The flushpots of Euston and the hanging garments of Marylebone.

Finnegans Wake (1939) pt. 1, p. 192

10 O
tell me all about
Anna Livia! I want to hear all
about Anna Livia. Well, you know Anna Livia?
Yes, of course, we all know Anna Livia. Tell me all. Tell me now.

Finnegans Wake (1939) pt. 1, p. 196

11 Tell me, tell me, tell me, elm! Night night! Telmetale of stem or stone. Beside the rivering waters of hitherandthithering waters of. Night!

Finnegans Wake (1939) pt. 1, p. 216

12 All moanday, tearsday, wailsday, thumpsday, frightday, shatterday till the fear of the Law.

Finnegans Wake (1939) pt. 2, p. 301

13 Three quarks for Muster Mark!

Finnegans Wake (1939) pt. 2, p. 383

14 The Gracehoper was always jigging ajog, hoppy on akkant of his joyicity.

Finnegans Wake (1939) pt. 3, p. 414

15 If I seen him bearing down on me now under whitespread wings like he'd come from Arkangels, I sink I'd die down over his feet, humbly dumbly, only to washup. Yes, tid. There's where. First. We pass through grass behush the bush to. Whish! A gull. Gulls. Far calls. Coming, far! End here. Us then. Finn, again! Take. Bussoftlhee, mememormee! Till thousendsthee. Lps. The keys to. Given! A way a lone a last a loved a long the

Finnegans Wake (1939) pt. 4, p. 627

16 Once upon a time and a very good time it was there was a moocow coming down along the road and this moocow that was down along the road met a nicens little boy named baby tuckoo.

A Portrait of the Artist as a Young Man (1916) ch. 1

17 The artist, like the God of the creation, remains within or behind or beyond or above his handiwork, invisible, refined out of existence, indifferent, paring his fingernails.

A Portrait of the Artist as a Young Man (1916) ch. 5

18 Ireland is the old sow that eats her farrow.

A Portrait of the Artist as a Young Man (1916) ch. 5

19 Pity is the feeling which arrests the mind in the presence of whatsoever is grave and constant in human sufferings and unites it with the human sufferer. Terror is the feeling which arrests the mind in the presence of whatsoever is grave and constant in human sufferings and unites it with the secret cause.

A Portrait of the Artist as a Young Man (1916) ch. 5

20 Welcome, O life! I go to encounter for the millionth time the reality of experience and to forge in the smithy of my soul the uncreated conscience of my race. . . . Old father, old artificer, stand me now and ever in good stead.

A Portrait of the Artist as a Young Man (1916) ch. 5

21 I will not serve that in which I no longer believe whether it call itself my home, my fatherland or my church: and I will try to express myself in some mode of

life or art as freely as I can and as wholly as I can, using for my defence the only arms I allow myself to use, silence, exile, and cunning.

A Portrait of the Artist as a Young Man (1916) ch. 5

1 Stately, plump Buck Mulligan came from the stairhead, bearing a bowl of lather on which a mirror and a razor lay crossed. A yellow dressinggown, ungirdled, was sustained gently behind him by the mild morning air. He held the bowl aloft and intoned:
—*Introibo ad altare Dei.*

Ulysses (1922) p. 1

2 The snotgreen sea. The scrotumtightening sea.

Ulysses (1922) p. 5

3 It is a symbol of Irish art. The cracked lookingglass of a servant.

Ulysses (1922) p. 7

4 When I makes tea I makes tea, as old mother Grogan said. And when I makes water I makes water. . . .
Begob, ma'am, says Mrs. Cahill, *God send you don't make them in the one pot.*

Ulysses (1922) p. 12

5 I fear those big words, Stephen said, which make us so unhappy.

Ulysses (1922) p. 31

6 History, Stephen said, is a nightmare from which I am trying to awake.

Ulysses (1922) p. 34

7 Lawn Tennyson, gentleman poet.

Ulysses (1922) p. 50

8 Mr Leopold Bloom ate with relish the inner organs of beasts and fowls. He liked thick giblet soup, nutty gizzards, a stuffed roast heart, liver slices fried with crustcrumbs, fried hencod's roes. Most of all he liked grilled mutton kidneys which gave to his palate a fine tang of faintly scented urine.

Ulysses (1922) p. 53

9 Come forth, Lazarus! And he came fifth and lost the job.

Ulysses (1922) p. 102

10 She used to say Ben Dollard had a base barreltone voice.

Ulysses (1922) p. 147

11 A man of genius makes no mistakes. His errors are volitional and are the portals of discovery.

Ulysses (1922) p. 182

12 Greater love than this, he said, no man hath that a man lay down his wife for his friend. Go thou and do likewise. Thus, or words to that effect, saith Zarathustra, sometime regius professor of French letters to the university of Oxtail.

Ulysses (1922) p. 375

13 The heaventree of stars hung with humid nightblue fruit.

Ulysses (1922) p. 651

14 He kissed me under the Moorish wall and I thought well as well him as another and then I asked him with my eyes to ask again yes and then he asked me would I yes to say yes my mountain flower and first I put my arms

around him yes and drew him down to me so he could feel my breasts all perfume yes and his heart was going like mad and yes I said yes I will Yes.

Ulysses (1922) p. 732

15 When a young man came up to him in Zurich and said, 'May I kiss the hand that wrote *Ulysses*?' Joyce replied, somewhat like King Lear, 'No, it did lots of other things too.'

Richard Ellmann *James Joyce* (1959) p. 114

William Joyce (Lord Haw-Haw)
1906–1946

16 Germany calling! Germany calling!

Habitual introduction to propaganda broadcasts to Britain during the Second World War

Jack Judge 1878–1938 and Harry Williams 1874–1924

17 It's a long way to Tipperary,
It's a long way to go;
It's a long way to Tipperary,
To the sweetest girl I know!
Goodbye, Piccadilly,
Farewell, Leicester Square,
It's a long, long way to Tipperary,
But my heart's right there!

It's a Long Way to Tipperary (1912 song)

Carl Gustav Jung 1875–1961

18 *Ein Mensch, der nicht durch die Hölle seiner Leidenschaften gegangen ist, hat sie auch nie überwunden.*

A man who has not passed through the inferno of his passions has never overcome them.

Errinerungen, Träume, Gedanken (Memories, Dreams, Reflections, 1962) ch. 9

19 *Soweit wir zu erkennen vermögen, ist es die einzige Sinn der menschlichen Existenz, ein Licht anzünden in der Finsternis des blossen Seins.*

As far as we can discern, the sole purpose of human existence is to kindle a light in the darkness of mere being.

Errinerungen, Träume, Gedanken (Memories, Dreams, Reflections, 1962) ch. 11

20 *Jede Form von Süchtigkeit ist von übel, gleichgültig, ob es sich um Alkohol oder Morphium oder Idealismus handelt.*

Every form of addiction is bad, no matter whether the narcotic be alcohol or morphine or idealism.

Errinerungen, Träume, Gedanken (Memories, Dreams, Reflections, 1962) ch. 12

21 I do not believe. . . . I know.

In L. van der Post *Jung and the Story of our Time* (1976) p. 215

22 *Wo die Liebe herrscht, da gibt es keinen Machtwillen, und wo die Macht den Vorrang hat, da fehlt die Liebe. Das eine ist der Schatten des andern.*

Where love rules, there is no will to power, and where power predominates, love is lacking. The one is the shadow of the other.

Über die Psychologie des Unbewussten (On the Psychology of the Unconscious, 1917) in *Gesammelte Werke* (1964) vol. 7, p. 58

1 *Alles, was wir an den Kindern ändern wollen, sollten wir zunächst wohl aufmerksam prüfen, ob es nicht etwas sei, was besser an uns zu ändern wäre.*

If there is anything that we wish to change in the child, we should first examine it and see whether it is not something that could better be changed in ourselves.

Vom Werden der Persönlichkeit (On the Development of Personality, 1932) in *Gesammelte Werke* (1972) vol. 17, p. 194

2 *Persönlichkeit ist höchste Verwirklichung der eingeborenen Eigenart des besonderen lebenden Wesens. Persönlichkeit ist der Tat des höchsten Lebensmutes, der absoluten Bejahung des individuell Seienden und der erfolgreichsten Anpassung an das universal Gegetene bei grösstmöglicher Freiheit der eigenen Entscheidung.*

Personality is the supreme realization of the innate individuality of a particular living being. Personality is an act of the greatest courage in the face of life, the absolute affirmation of all that constitutes the individual, and the most successful adaptation to the universal conditions of existence coupled with the greatest possible freedom of personal decision.

Vom Werden der Persönlichkeit (On the Development of Personality, 1932) in *Gesammelte Werke* (1972) vol. 17, p. 195

3 *Eine gewissermassen oberflächliche Schicht des Unbewussten ist zweifellos persönlich. Wir nennen sie das* persönliche Unbewusste. *Dieses ruht aber auf einer tieferen Schicht, welche nicht mehr persönlicher Erfahrung und Erwerbung entstammt, sondern angeboren ist. Diese tiefere Schicht ist das sogenannte* kollektive Unbewusste. *. . . Die Inhalte des persönlichen Unbewussten sind in der Hauptsache die sogenannten* gefühlsbetonten Komplexe. *. . . Die Inhalte des kollektiven Unbewussten dagegen sind die sogenannten* Archetypen.

A more or less superficial layer of the unconscious is undoubtedly personal. I call it the *personal unconscious*. But this personal unconscious rests upon a deeper layer, which does not derive from personal experience and is not a personal acquisition but is inborn. This deeper layer I call the *collective unconscious*. . . . The contents of the personal unconscious are chiefly the *feeling-toned complexes*. . . . The contents of the collective unconscious, on the other hand, are known as *archetypes*.

Eranos Jahrbuch (Eranos Yearbook, 1934) p. 180

Pauline Kael 1919–

4 The words 'Kiss Kiss Bang Bang' which I saw on an Italian movie poster, are perhaps the briefest statement imaginable of the basic appeal of movies.

Kiss Kiss Bang Bang (1968) 'Note on the Title'

5 She [Barbra Streisand in *What's Up, Doc?*] does her own shtick—the rapid, tricky New Yorkese line readings . . . but she doesn't do anything she hasn't

already done. She's playing herself—and it's awfully soon for that.

New Yorker 25 Mar. 1972, p. 122

Franz Kafka 1883–1924

6 *Jemand musste Josef K. verleumdet haben, denn ohne dass er etwas Böses getan hätte, wurde er eines Morgens verhaftet.*

Someone must have traduced Joseph K., for without having done anything wrong he was arrested one fine morning.

Der Prozess (The Trial, 1925) opening sentence

7 *Sie können einwenden, dass es ja überhaupt kein Verfahren ist, Sie haben sehr recht, denn es ist ja nur ein Verfahren, wenn ich es als solches anerkenne.*

You may object that it is not a trial at all; you are quite right, for it is only a trial if I recognize it as such.

Der Prozess (The Trial, 1925) ch. 2

8 *Es ist oft besser, in Ketten, als frei zu sein.*

It's often better to be in chains than to be free.

Der Prozess (The Trial, 1925) ch. 8

9 *Als Gregor Samsa eines Morgens aus unruhigen Träume erwachte, fand er sich in seinem Bett zu einem ungeheueren Ungeziefer verwandelt.*

As Gregor Samsa awoke one morning from uneasy dreams he found himself transformed in his bed into a gigantic insect.

Die Verwandlung (The Metamorphosis, 1915) opening sentence

Gus Kahn 1886–1941 and Raymond B. Egan 1890–1952

10 There's nothing surer,
The rich get rich and the poor get children.
In the meantime, in between time,
Ain't we got fun.

Ain't We Got Fun (1921 song; music by Richard A. Whiting)

Bert Kalmar 1884–1947, Harry Ruby 1895–1974, Arthur Sheekman 1891–1978, and Nat Perrin

11 Remember, you're fighting for this woman's honour . . . which is probably more than she ever did.

Duck Soup (1933 film; said by Groucho Marx)

12 If you can't leave in a taxi you can leave in a huff. If that's too soon, you can leave in a minute and a huff.

Duck Soup (1933 film; said by Groucho Marx)

George S. Kaufman 1889–1961

13 Satire is what closes Saturday night.

In Scott Meredith *George S. Kaufman and his Friends* (1974) ch. 6

George S. Kaufman 1889–1961 and Moss Hart 1904–1961

1 The man who came to dinner.
   Title of play (1939)

George S. Kaufman 1889–1961 and Morrie Ryskind 1895–1985

2 One morning I shot an elephant in my pajamas. How he got into my pajamas I'll never know.
   Animal Crackers (1930 film; said by Groucho Marx) in Richard J. Anobile *Hooray for Captain Spaulding* (1974) p. 168

3 DRIFTWOOD (Groucho Marx): It's all right. That's—that's in every contract. That's—that's what they call a sanity clause.
   FIORELLO (Chico Marx): You can't fool me. There ain't no Sanity Claus.
   Night at the Opera (1935 film), in Richard J. Anobile *Why a Duck?* (1971) p. 206

Gerald Kaufman 1930–

4 Our second handicap was an election manifesto which Gerald Kaufman rightly described as 'the longest suicide note in history'.
   Denis Healey *Time of My Life* (1989) ch. 23 (describing the Labour Party's *New Hope for Britain*, published in 1983)

Paul Kaufman and Mike Anthony

5 Poetry in motion.
   Title of song (1960)

Patrick Kavanagh 1905–1967

6 I hate what every poet hates in spite
   Of all the solemn talk of contemplation.
   Oh, Alexander Selkirk knew the plight
   Of being king and government and nation.
   A road, a mile of kingdom, I am king
   Of banks and stones and every blooming thing.
   Ploughman and Other Poems (1936), 'Inniskeen Road: July Evening'

7 Cassiopeia was over
   Cassidy's hanging hill,
   I looked and three whin bushes rode across
   The horizon—the Three Wise Kings.
   Soul for Sale (1947) 'Christmas Childhood'

8 Clay is the word and clay is the flesh
   Where the potato-gatherers like mechanized scarecrows move
   Along the side-fall of the hill—Maguire and his men.
   Soul for Sale (1947) 'The Great Hunger'

9 That was how his life happened.
   No mad hooves galloping in the sky,
   But the weak, washy way of true tragedy—
   A sick horse nosing around the meadow for a clean place to die.
   Soul for Sale (1947) 'The Great Hunger'

Ted Kavanagh 1892–1958

10 CECIL: After you, Claude.
   CLAUDE: No, after you, Cecil.
   Catch-phrase in *ITMA* (BBC radio programme, 1939–49)

11 Can I do you now, sir?
   Catch-phrase spoken by 'Mrs Mopp' in *ITMA* (BBC radio programme, 1939–49)

12 Don't forget the diver.
   Catch-phrase spoken by 'The Diver' in *ITMA* (BBC radio programme, 1939–49); in *ITMA 1939–1948* (1948) p. 19, Francis Worsley says: This character was a memory of the pier at New Brighton where Tommy [Handley] used to go as a child. . . . A man in a bathing suit . . . whined 'Don't forget the diver, sir.'

13 I don't mind if I do.
   Catch-phrase spoken by 'Colonel Chinstrap' in *ITMA* (BBC radio programme, 1939–49)

14 I go—I come back.
   Catch-phrase spoken by 'Ali Oop' in *ITMA* (BBC radio programme, 1939–49)

15 It's being so cheerful as keeps me going.
   Catch-phrase spoken by 'Mona Lott' in *ITMA* (BBC radio programme, 1939–49)

Helen Keller 1880–1968

16 Science may have found a cure for most evils; but it has found no remedy for the worst of them all—the apathy of human beings.
   My Religion (1927) ch. 6

Jaan Kenbrovin and John William Kellette

17 I'm forever blowing bubbles.
   Title of song (1919)

Florynce Kennedy 1916–

18 If men could get pregnant, abortion would be a sacrament.
   In *Ms.* Mar. 1973, p. 89

Jimmy Kennedy 1902–1984

19 If you go down in the woods today
   You're sure of a big surprise
   If you go down in the woods today
   You'd better go in disguise
   For every Bear that ever there was
   Will gather there for certain because,
   Today's the day the Teddy Bears have their Picnic.
   Teddy Bear's Picnic (1932 song; music by John W. Bratton)

Jimmy Kennedy 1902–1984 and Michael Carr 1904–1968

20 South of the Border—down Mexico way.
   South of the Border (1939 song)

21 We're gonna hang out the washing on the Siegfried Line.
   Title of song (1939)

Jimmy Kennedy 1902–1984 and Hugh Williams (Will Grosz)

1 Red sails in the sunset.
   Title of song (1935)

John F. Kennedy 1917–1963

2 I just received the following wire from my generous Daddy [Joseph P. Kennedy]—'Dear Jack. Don't buy a single vote more than necessary. I'll be damned if I'm going to pay for a landslide.'
   Speech in Washington, 1958, in J. F. Cutler *Honey Fitz* (1962) p. 306

3 When we got into office, the thing that surprised me most was to find that things were just as bad as we'd been saying they were.
   Speech at White House, 27 May 1961, in *New York Times* 28 May 1961, p. 39

4 Mankind must put an end to war or war will put an end to mankind.
   Speech to United Nations General Assembly, 25 Sept. 1961, in *New York Times* 26 Sept. 1961, p. 14

5 The President described the dinner [for Nobel Prizewinners] as 'probably the greatest concentration of talent and genius in this house except for perhaps those times when Thomas Jefferson ate alone.'
   New York Times 30 Apr. 1962, p. 1

6 Two thousand years ago the proudest boast was '*civis Romanus sum*'. Today, in the world of freedom the proudest boast is '*Ich bin ein Berliner*'. . . . All free men, wherever they may live, are citizens of Berlin. And, therefore, as a free man, I take pride in the words, '*Ich bin ein Berliner*'.
   Speech in West Berlin, 26 June 1963, in *New York Times* 27 June 1963, p. 12

7 When power leads man toward arrogance, poetry reminds him of his limitations. When power narrows the areas of man's concern, poetry reminds him of the richness and diversity of his existence. When power corrupts, poetry cleanses. For art establishes the basic human truths which must serve as the touchstone of our judgement.
   Speech at Amherst College, Mass., 26 Oct. 1963, in *New York Times* 27 Oct. 1963, p. 87

8 In free society art is not a weapon. . . . Artists are not engineers of the soul.
   Speech at Amherst College, Mass., 26 Oct. 1963, in *New York Times* 27 Oct. 1963, p. 87

9 It was involuntary. They sank my boat.
   Reply when asked how he became a war hero, in Arthur M. Schlesinger Jr. *A Thousand Days* (1965) ch. 4

10 We stand today on the edge of a new frontier—the frontier of the 1960s—a frontier of unknown opportunities and perils—a frontier of unfulfilled hopes and threats. Woodrow Wilson's New Freedom promised our nation a new political and economic framework. Franklin Roosevelt's New Deal promised security and succor to those in need. But the New Frontier of which I speak is not a set of promises—it is a set of challenges.

It sums up not what I intend to offer the American people, but what I intend to ask of them.
   Speech accepting Democratic nomination in Los Angeles, 15 July 1960, in *Vital Speeches* 1 Aug. 1960, p. 611

11 Let the word go forth from this time and place, to friend and foe alike, that the torch has been passed to a new generation of Americans—born in this century, tempered by war, disciplined by a hard and bitter peace, proud of our ancient heritage—and unwilling to witness or permit the slow undoing of those human rights to which this nation has always been committed, and to which we are committed today at home and around the world.
   Let every nation know, whether it wishes us well or ill, that we shall pay any price, bear any burden, meet any hardship, support any friend, oppose any foe to assure the survival and the success of liberty.
   Inaugural address, 20 Jan. 1961, in *Vital Speeches* 1 Feb. 1961, p. 226

12 If a free society cannot help the many who are poor, it cannot save the few who are rich.
   Inaugural address, 20 Jan. 1961, in *Vital Speeches* 1 Feb. 1961, p. 226

13 Let us never negotiate out of fear. But let us never fear to negotiate.
   Inaugural address, 20 Jan. 1961, in *Vital Speeches* 1 Feb. 1961, p. 227

14 All this will not be finished in the first 100 days. Nor will it be finished in the first 1,000 days, nor in the life of this Administration, nor even perhaps in our lifetime on this planet. But let us begin.
   Inaugural address, 20 Jan. 1961, in *Vital Speeches* 1 Feb. 1961, p. 227

15 Now the trumpet summons us again—not as a call to bear arms, though arms we need—not as a call to battle, though embattled we are—but a call to bear the burden of a long twilight struggle, year in and year out, 'rejoicing in hope, patient in tribulation'—a struggle against the common enemies of man: tyranny, poverty, disease and war itself.
   Inaugural address, 20 Jan. 1961, in *Vital Speeches* 1 Feb. 1961, p. 227

16 And so, my fellow Americans: ask not what your country can do for you—ask what you can do for your country. My fellow citizens of the world: ask not what America will do for you, but what together we can do for the freedom of man.
   Inaugural address, 20 Jan. 1961, in *Vital Speeches* 1 Feb. 1961, p. 227. Cf. Oliver Wendell Holmes Jr., speech at Keene, New Hampshire, 30 May 1884: 'We pause to . . . recall what our country has done for each of us and to ask ourselves what we can do for our country in return.'

17 I believe that this Nation should commit itself to achieving the goal, before this decade is out, of landing a man on the Moon and returning him safely to earth.
   Supplementary State of the Union message to Congress, 25 May 1961, in *Vital Speeches* 15 June 1961, p. 518

18 Those who make peaceful revolution impossible will make violent revolution inevitable.
   Speech at White House, 13 Mar. 1962, in *Vital Speeches* 1 Apr. 1962, p. 356

Joseph P. Kennedy 1888–1969

1 When the going gets tough, the tough get going.
In J. H. Cutler *Honey Fitz* (1962) p. 291 (also attributed to
Knute Rockne)
See also JOHN F. KENNEDY

Robert F. Kennedy 1925–1968

2 About one-fifth of the people are against everything all
the time.
Speech at University of Pennsylvania, 6 May 1964, in
Philadelphia Inquirer 7 May 1964

Jack Kerouac 1922–1969

3 John Clellon Holmes . . . and I were sitting around
trying to think up the meaning of the Lost Generation
and the subsequent Existentialism and I said, 'You
know, this is really a beat generation' and he leapt up
and said 'That's it, that's right!'
Playboy June 1959, p. 32

Jean Kerr 1923–

4 As someone pointed out recently, if you can keep your
head when all about you are losing theirs, it's just
possible you haven't grasped the situation.
Please Don't Eat the Daisies (1957) introduction. Cf. Rudyard
Kipling 126:13

5 I'm tired of all this nonsense about beauty being only
skin-deep. That's deep enough. What do you want—an
adorable pancreas?
The Snake has all the Lines (1958) p. 142

Joseph Kesselring 1902–1967

6 Arsenic and old lace.
Title of play (1941)

John Maynard Keynes (Baron Keynes) 1883–1946

7 I work for a Government I despise for ends I think
criminal.
Letter to Duncan Grant, 15 Dec. 1917, in *British Library Add.
MSS 57931* fo. 119

8 He [Clemenceau] felt about France what Pericles felt of
Athens—unique value in her, nothing else mattering;
but his theory of politics was Bismarck's. He had one
illusion—France; and one disillusion—mankind,
including Frenchmen, and his colleagues not least.
Economic Consequences of the Peace (1919) ch. 3

9 Like Odysseus, the President [Woodrow Wilson] looked
wiser when he was seated.
Economic Consequences of the Peace (1919) ch. 3

10 Lenin was right. There is no subtler, no surer means of
overturning the existing basis of society than to
debauch the currency. The process engages all the
hidden forces of economic law on the side of
destruction, and does it in a manner which not one
man in a million is able to diagnose.
Economic Consequences of the Peace (1919) ch. 6

11 A study of the history of opinion is a necessary
preliminary to the emancipation of the mind. I do not
know which makes a man more conservative—to know
nothing but the present, or nothing but the past.
End of Laissez-Faire (1926) pt. 1

12 Marxian Socialism must always remain a portent to the
historians of Opinion—how a doctrine so illogical and
so dull can have exercised so powerful and enduring an
influence over the minds of men, and, through them, the
events of history.
End of Laissez-Faire (1926) pt. 3

13 The important thing for Government is not to do things
which individuals are doing already, and to do them
a little better or a little worse; but to do those things
which at present are not done at all.
End of Laissez-Faire (1926) pt. 4

14 I think that Capitalism, wisely managed, can probably
be made more efficient for attaining economic ends
than any alternative system yet in sight, but that in
itself it is in many ways extremely objectionable.
End of Laissez-Faire (1926) pt. 5

15 How can I convey to the reader, who does not know
him, any just impression of this extraordinary figure of
our time, this syren, this goat-footed bard, this
half-human visitor to our age from the hag-ridden
magic and enchanted woods of Celtic antiquity? One
catches in his company that flavour of final
purposelessness, inner irresponsibility, existence outside
or away from our Saxon good and evil, mixed with
cunning, remorselessness, love of power, that lend
fascination, enthralment, and terror to the fair-seeming
magicians of North European folklore.
Essays in Biography (1933) 'Mr Lloyd George'

16 It is better that a man should tyrannize over his bank
balance than over his fellow-citizens.
General Theory of Employment (1936) ch. 24

17 The ideas of economists and political philosophers, both
when they are right and when they are wrong, are
more powerful than is commonly understood. Indeed
the world is ruled by little else. Practical men, who
believe themselves to be quite exempt from any
intellectual influences, are usually the slaves of some
defunct economist. Madmen in authority, who hear
voices in the air, are distilling their frenzy from some
academic scribbler of a few years back. I am sure that
the power of vested interests is vastly exaggerated
compared with the gradual encroachment of ideas. Not,
indeed, immediately, but after a certain interval; for in
the field of economic and political philosophy there are
not many who are influenced by new theories after
they are twenty-five or thirty years of age, so that the
ideas which civil servants and politicians and even
agitators apply to current events are not likely to be the
newest. But soon or late, it is ideas, not vested interests,
which are dangerous for good or evil.
General Theory of Employment (1936; 1947 ed.) ch. 24

18 I remember in my youth asking Maynard Keynes,
'What do you think happens to Mr Lloyd George when
he is alone in the room?' And Keynes replied, 'When he
is alone in the room there is nobody there.'
Lady Violet Bonham-Carter *Impact of Personality in Politics*
(Romanes Lecture, 1963) p. 6

1 But this *long run* is a misleading guide to current affairs.
In the long run we are all dead.
> *Tract on Monetary Reform* (1923) ch. 3

Nikita Khrushchev 1894–1971

2 Comrades! We must abolish the cult of the individual decisively, once and for all.
> Speech to secret session of 20th Congress of the Communist Party, 25 Feb. 1956, in *Dethronement of Stalin* (Manchester Guardian) 11 June 1956, p. 27

3 If anyone believes that our smiles involve abandonment of the teaching of Marx, Engels and Lenin he deceives himself. Those who wait for that must wait until a shrimp learns to whistle.
> Speech in Moscow, 17 Sept. 1955, in *New York Times* 18 Sept. 1955, p. 19

4 If you start throwing hedgehogs under me, I shall throw a couple of porcupines under you.
> In *New York Times* 7 Nov. 1963

5 Кто считает, что можно убаюкать рабочего хорошей реьолюционной фразой тот ошибается. ... Если же не проявлятъ заботы о росте материальных и духовных богатств, то люди сегодня послушают, завтра послушают, а потом могут сказать: что вы нам все обещаете в будущем, говорите, так сказать, о загробной жизни. Нам уже поп говорил об этом.

Anyone who believes that the worker can be lulled by fine revolutionary phrases is mistaken. . . . If no concern is shown for the growth of material and spiritual riches, the people will listen today, they will listen tomorrow, and then they may say: 'Why do you promise us everything for the future? You are talking, so to speak, about life beyond the grave. The priest has already told us about this.'
> Speech at World Youth Forum, 19 Sept. 1964, in *Pravda* 22 Sept. 1964

6 If one cannot catch the bird of paradise, better take a wet hen.
> In *Time* 6 Jan. 1958

7 We say this not only for the socialist states, who are more akin to us. We base ourselves on the idea that we must peacefully co-exist. About the capitalist States, it doesn't depend on you whether or not we exist. If you don't like us, don't accept our invitations and don't invite us to come to see you. Whether you like it or not, history is on our side. We will bury you.
> Speech to Western diplomats at reception in Moscow for Polish leader Mr Gomulka, 18 Nov. 1956, in *The Times* 19 Nov. 1956

Joyce Kilmer 1886–1918

8 I think that I shall never see
A poem lovely as a tree.
> *Trees and Other Poems* (1914) 'Trees'

9 Poems are made by fools like me,
But only God can make a tree.
> *Trees and Other Poems* (1914) 'Trees'

Lord Kilmuir (Sir David Maxwell Fyfe) 1900–1967

10 Loyalty is the Tory's secret weapon.
> In Anthony Sampson *Anatomy of Britain* (1962) ch. 6

Martin Luther King 1929–1968

11 Injustice anywhere is a threat to justice everywhere.
> Letter from Birmingham Jail, Alabama, 16 Apr. 1963, in *Atlantic Monthly* Aug. 1963, p. 78

12 I have almost reached the regrettable conclusion that the Negro's great stumbling block in the stride toward freedom is not the White Citizens Councillor or the Ku Klux Klanner but the white moderate who is more devoted to order than to justice; who prefers a negative peace which is the absence of tension to a positive peace which is the presence of justice.
> Letter from Birmingham Jail, Alabama, 16 Apr. 1963, in *Atlantic Monthly* Aug. 1963, p. 81

13 I submit to you that if a man hasn't discovered something he will die for, he isn't fit to live.
> Speech in Detroit, 23 June 1963, in J. Bishop *Days of M. L. King Jr.* (1971) ch. 4

14 I want to be the white man's brother, not his brother-in-law.
> In *New York Journal-American* 10 Sept. 1962, p. 1

15 Now, I say to you today my friends, even though we face the difficulties of today and tomorrow, I still have a dream. It is a dream deeply rooted in the American dream. I have a dream that one day this nation will rise up and live out the true meaning of its creed:—'We hold these truths to be self-evident, that all men are created equal.'
  I have a dream that one day on the red hills of Georgia the sons of former slaves and the sons of former slave owners will be able to sit down together at the table of brotherhood.
  I have a dream that one day even the state of Mississippi, a state sweltering with the people's injustice, sweltering with the heat of oppression, will be transformed into an oasis of freedom and justice.
  I have a dream that my four little children will one day live in a nation where they will not be judged by the color of their skin but by the content of their character.
> Speech at Civil Rights March in Washington, 28 Aug. 1963, in *New York Times* 29 Aug. 1963, p. 21

16 Well, I don't know what will happen now. We've been to the mountain top. I won't mind. Like anybody, I would like to have a long life. Longevity has its place. But I'm not concerned about that now. I just want to do God's will. And he's allowed me to go up to the mountain. And I've looked over, and I've seen the promised land. I may not get there with you, but I want you to know tonight that we as a people will get to the promised land. So I'm happy tonight. I'm not worried about anything. I'm not fearing any man. Mine eyes have seen the glory of the coming of the Lord.
> Speech in Memphis, 3 Apr. 1968 (the day before King was assassinated), in *New York Times* 4 Apr. 1968, p. 24

1 The ultimate measure of a man is not where he stands in moments of comfort and convenience, but where he stands at times of challenge and controversy.
  Strength to Love (1963) ch. 3

2 Nothing in all the world is more dangerous than sincere ignorance and conscientious stupidity.
  Strength to Love (1963) ch. 4

3 Jesus eloquently affirmed from the cross a higher law. He knew that the old eye-for-an-eye philosophy would leave everyone blind. He did not seek to overcome evil with evil. He overcame evil with good.
  Strength to Love (1963) ch. 4

4 The means by which we live have outdistanced the ends for which we live. Our scientific power has outrun our spiritual power. We have guided missiles and misguided men.
  Strength to Love (1963) ch. 7

5 If we assume that mankind has a right to survive, then we must find an alternative to war and destruction. In our day of space vehicles and guided ballistic missiles, the choice is either nonviolence or nonexistence.
  Strength to Love (1963) ch. 17

6 We must learn to live together as brothers or perish together as fools.
  Speech at St. Louis, 22 Mar. 1964, in *St Louis Post-Dispatch* 23 Mar. 1964

7 A riot is at bottom the language of the unheard.
  Where Do We Go From Here? (1967) ch. 4

Stoddard King 1889–1933

8 There's a long, long trail awinding
  Into the land of my dreams,
  Where the nightingales are singing
  And a white moon beams;
  There's a long, long night of waiting
  Until my dreams all come true,
  Till the day when I'll be going down
  That long, long trail with you.
  There's a Long, Long Trail (1913 song; music by Zo (Alonso) Elliott)

David Kingsley, Dennis Lyons, and Peter Lovell-Davis

9 Yesterday's men (they failed before!).
  Advertising slogan for the Labour Party (referring to the Conservatives), 1970, in David Butler and Michael Pinto-Duschinsky *British General Election of 1970* (1971) ch. 6

Hugh Kingsmill (Hugh Kingsmill Lunn) 1889–1949

10 Friends . . . are God's apology for relations.
   In Michael Holroyd *Best of Hugh Kingsmill* (1970) p. 12

11 What still alive at twenty-two,
   A clean upstanding chap like you?
   Sure, if your throat 'tis hard to slit,
   Slit your girl's, and swing for it.

Like enough, you won't be glad,
When they come to hang you, lad:
But bacon's not the only thing
That's cured by hanging from a string.
  Table of Truth (1933) 'Two Poems, after A. E. Housman', no. 1

12 'Tis Summer Time on Bredon,
   And now the farmers swear:
   The cattle rise and listen
   In valleys far and near,
   And blush at what they hear.

   But when the mists in autumn
   On Bredon top are thick,
   And happy hymns of farmers
   Go up from fold and rick,
   The cattle then are sick.
   Table of Truth (1933) 'Two Poems, after A. E. Housman', no. 2

Neil Kinnock 1942–

13 If Margaret Thatcher wins on Thursday, I warn you not to be ordinary, I warn you not to be young, I warn you not to fall ill, and I warn you not to grow old.
   Speech at Bridgend, 7 June 1983, in *Guardian* 8 June 1983

14 Mr Shultz went off his pram.
   Comment after a meeting with the US Secretary of State, in *Guardian* 15 Feb. 1984

15 I would die for my country but I could never let my country die for me.
   Speech at Labour Party Conference, 30 Sept. 1986, in *Guardian* 1 Oct. 1986

16 Why am I the first Kinnock in a thousand generations to be able to get to a university? Why is Glenys the first woman in her family in a thousand generations to be able to get to a university? Was it because all our predecessors were thick? Did they lack talent? Those people who could sing and play and write poetry? Those people who could make wonderful beautiful things with their hands? Those people who could dream dreams, see visions? Was it because they were weak, those people who could work eight hours underground and then come up and play football, weak? Does anybody really think that they didn't get what we had because they didn't have the talent or the strength or the endurance or the commitment? Of course not. It's because they didn't have a platform on which they could stand.
   Speech in party political broadcast, 21 May 1987, in *New York Times* 12 Sept. 1987, p. 1 (this speech was later plagiarized by the American politician Joe Biden)

Rudyard Kipling 1865–1936

17 But I consort with long-haired things
   In velvet collar-rolls,
   Who talk about the Aims of Art,
   And 'theories' and 'goals',
   And moo and coo with women-folk
   About their blessed souls.
   Abaft the Funnel (1909) 'In Partibus'

18 When you've shouted 'Rule Britannia', when you've sung 'God save the Queen'—

When you've finished killing Kruger with your
    mouth—
Will you kindly drop a shilling in my little tambourine
For a gentleman in *Kharki* ordered South?
He's an absent-minded beggar and his weaknesses are
    great—
But we and Paul must take him as we find him—
He is out on active service, wiping something off
    a slate—
And he's left a lot o' little things behind him!
    Absent-Minded Beggar (1899) p. 1

1 There is sorrow enough in the natural way
From men and women to fill our day;
But when we are certain of sorrow in store,
Why do we always arrange for more?
Brothers and Sisters, I bid you beware
Of giving your heart to a dog to tear.
    Actions and Reactions (1909) 'The Power of the Dog'

2 There are nine and sixty ways of constructing tribal
    lays,
And—every—single—one—of—them—is—right!
    Ballads and Barrack-Room Ballads (1893) 'In the Neolithic
    Age'

3 'What are the bugles blowin' for?' said Files-on-Parade.
'To turn you out, to turn you out,' the Colour-Sergeant
    said.
    Barrack-Room Ballads (1892) 'Danny Deever'

4 For they're hangin' Danny Deever, you can hear the
    Dead March play,
The regiment's in 'ollow square—they're hangin' him
    to-day;
They've taken of his buttons off an' cut his stripes
    away,
An' they're hangin' Danny Deever in the mornin'.
    Barrack-Room Ballads (1892) 'Danny Deever'

5 O it's Tommy this, an' Tommy that, an' 'Tommy, go
    away';
But it's 'Thank you, Mister Atkins,' when the band
    begins to play.
    Barrack-Room Ballads (1892) 'Tommy'

6 Then it's Tommy this, an' Tommy that, an 'Tommy
    'ow's yer soul?'
But it's 'Thin red line of 'eroes' when the drums begin
    to roll.
    Barrack-Room Ballads (1892) 'Tommy'

7 For it's Tommy this, an' Tommy that, an' 'Chuck him
    out, the brute!'
But it's 'Saviour of 'is country' when the guns begin to
    shoot.
    Barrack-Room Ballads (1892) 'Tommy'

8 So 'ere's *to* you, Fuzzy-Wuzzy, at your 'ome in the
    Soudan;
You're a pore benighted 'eathen but a first-class fightin'
    man;
An' 'ere's *to* you, Fuzzy-Wuzzy, with your 'ayrick 'ead
    of 'air—
You big black boundin' beggar—for you broke a British
    square!
    Barrack-Room Ballads (1892) 'Fuzzy-Wuzzy'

9 The uniform 'e wore
Was nothin' much before,
An' rather less than 'arf o' that be'ind.
    Barrack-Room Ballads (1892) 'Gunga Din'

10 Though I've belted you and flayed you,
By the livin' Gawd that made you,
You're a better man than I am, Gunga Din!
    Barrack-Room Ballads (1892) 'Gunga Din'

11 'Ave you 'eard o' the Widow at Windsor
With a hairy gold crown on 'er 'ead?
She 'as ships on the foam—she 'as millions at 'ome,
An' she pays us poor beggars in red.
    Barrack-Room Ballads (1892) 'The Widow at Windsor'

12 When you're wounded and left on Afghanistan's plains
And the women come out to cut up what remains
Just roll to your rifle and blow out your brains
An' go to your Gawd like a soldier.
    Barrack-Room Ballads (1892) 'The Young British Soldier'

13 By the old Moulmein Pagoda, lookin' eastward to the
    sea,
There's a Burma girl a-settin', and I know she thinks o'
    me;
For the wind is in the palm-trees, an' the temple-bells
    they say:
'Come you back, you British soldier; come you back to
    Mandalay!'
Come you back to Mandalay,
Where the old Flotilla lay:
Can't you 'ear their paddles chunkin' from Rangoon to
    Mandalay?
On the road to Mandalay,
Where the flyin'-fishes play,
An' the dawn comes up like thunder outer China 'crost
    the Bay!
    Barrack-Room Ballads (1892) 'Mandalay'

14 An' I seed her first a-smokin' of a whackin' white
    cheroot,
An' a-wastin' Christian kisses on an 'eathen idol's
    foot.
    Barrack-Room Ballads (1892) 'Mandalay'

15 Ship me somewheres east of Suez, where the best is like
    the worst,
Where there aren't no Ten Commandments an' a man
    can raise a thirst.
    Barrack-Room Ballads (1892) 'Mandalay'

16 We're poor little lambs who've lost our way,
Baa! Baa! Baa!
We're little black sheep who've gone astray,
Baa-aa-aa!
Gentlemen-rankers out on the spree,
Damned from here to Eternity,
God ha' mercy on such as we,
Baa! Yah! Bah!
    Barrack-Room Ballads (1892) 'Gentlemen-Rankers'

17 Oh, East is East, and West is West, and never the twain
    shall meet,
Till Earth and Sky stand presently at God's great
    Judgement Seat;
But there is neither East nor West, Border, nor Breed,
    nor Birth,
When two strong men stand face to face, tho' they
    come from the ends of earth!
    Barrack-Room Ballads (1892) 'The Ballad of East and West'

18 And the talk slid north, and the talk slid south,
With the sliding puffs from the hookah-mouth.

Four things greater than all things are,—
Women and Horses and Power and War.
Barrack-Room Ballads (1892) 'The Ballad of the King's Jest'

1 When the flush of a new-born sun fell first on Eden's
   green and gold,
   Our father Adam sat under the Tree and scratched with
   a stick in the mould;
   And the first rude sketch that the world had seen was
   joy to his mighty heart,
   Till the Devil whispered behind the leaves, 'It's pretty,
   but is it Art?'
   Barrack-Room Ballads (1892) 'The Conundrum of the
   Workshops'

2 We know that the tail must wag the dog, for the horse
   is drawn by the cart;
   But the Devil whoops, as he whooped of old: 'It's
   clever, but is it Art?'
   Barrack-Room Ballads (1892) 'The Conundrum of the
   Workshops'

3 Winds of the World, give answer! They are whimpering
   to and fro—
   And what should they know of England who only
   England know?—
   The poor little street-bred people that vapour and fume
   and brag.
   Barrack-Room Ballads (1892) 'The English Flag'

4 For the sin ye do by two and two ye must pay for one
   by one!
   Barrack-Room Ballads (1892) 'Tomlinson'

5 There be triple ways to take, of the eagle or the snake,
   Or the way of a man with a maid;
   But the sweetest way to me is a ship's upon the sea
   In the heel of the North-East Trade.
   Barrack-Room Ballads (1892) 'L'Envoi'

6 What the horses o' Kansas think to-day, the horses of
   America will think tomorrow; an' I tell *you* that when
   the horses of America rise in their might, the day o' the
   Oppressor is ended.
   The Day's Work (1898) 'A Walking Delegate'

7 The toad beneath the harrow knows
   Exactly where each tooth-point goes;
   The butterfly upon the road
   Preaches contentment to that toad.
   Departmental Ditties (1886) 'Pagett, MP'

8 A Nation spoke to a Nation,
   A Throne sent word to a Throne:
   'Daughter am I in my mother's house,
   But mistress in my own.
   The gates are mine to open,
   As the gates are mine to close,
   And I abide by my Mother's House.'
   Said our Lady of the Snows.
   Departmental Ditties (1898 US ed.) 'Our Lady of the Snows'

9 Who hath desired the Sea?—the sight of salt water
   unbounded—
   The heave and the halt and the hurl and the crash of
   the comber wind-hounded?
   The sleek-barrelled swell before storm, grey, foamless,
   enormous, and growing—
   Stark calm on the lap of the Line or the crazy-eyed
   hurricane blowing.
   The Five Nations (1903) 'The Sea and the Hills'

10 And here the sea-fogs lap and cling
   And here, each warning each,
   The sheep-bells and the ship-bells ring
   Along the hidden beach.
   The Five Nations (1903) 'Sussex'

11 God gives all men all earth to love,
   But since man's heart is small,
   Ordains for each one spot shall prove
   Belovèd over all.
   Each to his choice, and I rejoice
   The lot has fallen to me
   In a fair ground—in a fair ground—
   Yea, Sussex by the sea!
   The Five Nations (1903) 'Sussex'

12 Then ye returned to your trinkets; then ye contented
   your souls
   With the flannelled fools at the wicket or the muddied
   oafs at the goals.
   The Five Nations (1903) 'The Islanders'

13 We're foot—slog—slog—slog—sloggin' over Africa!—
   Foot—foot—foot—foot—sloggin' over Africa—
   (Boots—boots—boots—boots—movin' up and down
   again!)
   There's no discharge in the war!
   The Five Nations (1903) 'Boots' (for the last line, cf. *Oxford
   Dictionary of Quotations* (1979) 55:25)

14 An' it all goes into the laundry,
   But it never comes out in the wash,
   'Ow we're sugared about by the old men
   ('Eavy-sterned amateur old men!)
   That 'amper an' 'inder an' scold men
   For fear o' Stellenbosh!
   The Five Nations (1903) 'Stellenbosh'

15 For all we have and are,
   For all our children's fate,
   Stand up and take the war.
   The Hun is at the gate!
   For All We Have and Are (1914) p. 1

16 There is but one task for all—
   For each one life to give.
   What stands if freedom fall?
   Who dies if England live?
   For All We Have and Are (1914) p. 2

17 It is always a temptation to a rich and lazy nation,
   To puff and look important and to say:-
   'Though we know we should defeat you, we have not
   the time to meet you,
   We will therefore pay you cash to go away.'

   And that is called paying the Dane-geld;
   But we've proved it again and again,
   That if once you have paid him the Dane-geld
   You never get rid of the Dane.
   History of England (1911) 'Dane-Geld'

18 'Oh, where are you going to, all you Big Steamers,
   With England's own coal, up and down the salt seas?'
   'We are going to fetch you your bread and your butter,
   Your beef, pork, and mutton, eggs, apples, and cheese.'
   History of England (1911) 'Big Steamers'

19 Our England is a garden that is full of stately views,
   Of borders, beds and shrubberies and lawns and
   avenues,

With statues on the terraces and peacocks strutting
by;
But the Glory of the Garden lies in more than meets
the eye.
History of England (1911) 'The Glory of the Garden'

1 Our England is a garden, and such gardens are not
made
By singing:—'Oh, how beautiful!' and sitting in the
shade,
While better men than we go out and start their
working lives
At grubbing weeds from gravel paths with broken
dinner-knives.
History of England (1911) 'The Glory of the Garden'

2 Oh, Adam was a gardener, and God who made him sees
That half a proper gardener's work is done upon his
knees,
So when your work is finished, you can wash your
hands and pray
For the Glory of the Garden that it may not pass away!
And the Glory of the Garden it shall never pass away!
History of England (1911) 'The Glory of the Garden'

3 Lalun is a member of the most ancient profession in the
world.
In Black and White (1888) 'On the City Wall'

4 'We be one blood, thou and I', Mowgli answered. 'I
take my life from thee to-night. My kill shall be thy kill
if ever thou art hungry, O Kaa.'
Jungle Book (1894) 'Kaa's Hunting'

5 Brother, thy tail hangs down behind!
The Jungle Book (1894) 'Road Song of the Bandar-Log'

6 You must *not* forget the suspenders, Best Beloved.
Just So Stories (1902) 'How the Whale got his Throat'

7 Then the Whale stood up on his Tail and said, 'I'm
hungry.' And the small 'Stute Fish said in a small 'stute
voice, 'Noble and generous Cetacean, have you ever
tasted Man?' 'No,' said the Whale. 'What is it like?'
'Nice,' said the small 'Stute Fish. 'Nice but nubbly.'
Just So Stories (1902) 'How the Whale got his Throat'

8 He had his Mummy's leave to paddle, or else he would
never have done it, because he was a man of
infinite-resource-and-sagacity.
Just So Stories (1902) 'How the Whale got his Throat'

9 The Camel's hump is an ugly lump
Which well you may see at the Zoo;
But uglier yet is the hump we get
From having too little to do.
Just So Stories (1902) 'How the Camel got his Hump'

10 We get the hump—
Cameelious hump—
The hump that is black and blue!
Just So Stories (1902) 'How the Camel got his Hump'

11 The cure for this ill is not to sit still,
Or frowst with a book by the fire;
But to take a large hoe and a shovel also,
And dig till you gently perspire.
Just So Stories (1902) 'How the Camel got his Hump'

12 But there was one Elephant—a new Elephant—an
Elephant's Child—who was full of 'satiable curtiosity,
and that means he asked ever so many questions.
Just So Stories (1902) 'The Elephant's Child'

13 Then Kolokolo Bird said, with a mournful cry, 'Go to
the banks of the great grey-green, greasy Limpopo
River, all set about with fever-trees, and find out.'
Just So Stories (1902) 'The Elephant's Child'

14 Then the Elephant's Child put his head down close to
the Crocodile's musky, tusky mouth, and the Crocodile
caught him by his little nose. . . . At this, O Best
Beloved, the Elephant's Child was much annoyed, and
he said, speaking through his nose, like this, 'Led go!
You are hurtig be!'
Just So Stories (1902) 'The Elephant's Child'

15 I keep six honest serving-men
(They taught me all I knew);
Their names are What and Why and When
And How and Where and Who.
Just So Stories (1902) 'The Elephant's Child'

16 Yes, weekly from Southampton,
Great steamers, white and gold,
Go rolling down to Rio
(Roll down—roll down to Rio!).
And I'd like to roll to Rio
Some day before I'm old!
Just So Stories (1902) 'Beginning of the Armadilloes'

17 But the wildest of all the wild animals was the Cat. He
walked by himself, and all places were alike to him.
Just So Stories (1902) 'The Cat that Walked by Himself'

18 And he went back through the Wet Wild Woods,
waving his wild tail and walking by his wild lone. But
he never told anybody.
Just So Stories (1902) 'The Cat that Walked by Himself'

19 When [Max] Aitken acquired the *Daily Express* his
political views seemed to Kipling to become more and
more inconsistent, and one day Kipling asked him what
he was really up to. Aitken is supposed to have replied:
'What I want is power. Kiss 'em one day and kick 'em
the next'; and so on. 'I see,' said Kipling. 'Power
without responsibility: the prerogative of the harlot
throughout the ages.' So, many years later, when
[Stanley] Baldwin deemed it necessary to deal sharply
with such lords of the press, he obtained leave of his
cousin [Kipling] to borrow that telling phrase, which he
used to some effect on the 18th March, 1931, at . . . the
old Queen's Hall in Langham Place.
Speech by Earl Baldwin to the Kipling Society, 5 Oct. 1971,
in *Kipling Journal* Dec. 1971

20 If I were hanged on the highest hill,
Mother o' mine, O mother o' mine!
I know whose love would follow me still,
Mother o' mine, O mother o' mine!

If I were drowned in the deepest sea,
Mother o' mine, O mother o' mine!
I know whose tears would come down to me,
Mother o' mine, O mother o' mine.

If I were damned of body and soul,
I know whose prayers would make me whole,
Mother o' mine, O mother o' mine.
The Light That Failed (1891) dedication

21 The man who would be king.
Title of story (1888)

22 And the end of the fight is a tombstone white, with the
name of the late deceased,

And the epitaph drear: 'A fool lies here who tried to hustle the East.'

The Naulahka (1892) ch. 5

1 Take my word for it, the silliest woman can manage a clever man; but it takes a very clever woman to manage a fool.

Plain Tales from the Hills (1888) 'Three and—an Extra'

2 Every one is more or less mad on one point.

Plain Tales from the Hills (1888) 'On the Strength of a Likeness'

3 Of all the trees that grow so fair,
Old England to adorn,
Greater are none beneath the Sun,
Than Oak, and Ash, and Thorn.

Puck of Pook's Hill (1906) 'Tree Song'

4 England shall bide till Judgement Tide
By Oak, and Ash, and Thorn!

Puck of Pook's Hill (1906) 'Tree Song'

5 What is a woman that you forsake her,
And the hearth-fire and the home-acre,
To go with the old grey Widow-maker?

Puck of Pook's Hill (1906) 'Harp Song of the Dane Women'

6 If you wake at midnight, and hear a horse's feet,
Don't go drawing back the blind, or looking in the street,
Them that asks no questions isn't told a lie.
Watch the wall, my darling, while the Gentlemen go by!
Five and twenty ponies,
Trotting through the dark—
Brandy for the Parson,
'Baccy for the Clerk;
Laces for a lady, letters for a spy,
Watch the wall, my darling, while the Gentlemen go by!

Puck of Pook's Hill (1906) 'Smuggler's Song'

7 Land of our birth, we pledge to thee
Our love and toil in the years to be;
When we are grown and take our place,
As men and women with our race.

Puck of Pook's Hill (1906) 'Children's Song'

8 Teach us Delight in simple things,
And Mirth that has no bitter springs;
Forgiveness free of evil done,
And Love to all men 'neath the sun!

Puck of Pook's Hill (1906) 'Children's Song'

9 The tumult and the shouting dies—
The captains and the kings depart—
Still stands Thine ancient Sacrifice,
An humble and a contrite heart.
Lord God of Hosts, be with us yet,
Lest we forget—lest we forget!

Recessional, in *The Times* 17 July 1897

10 Far-called our navies melt away—
On dune and headland sinks the fire—
Lo, all our pomp of yesterday
Is one with Nineveh, and Tyre!

Recessional, in *The Times* 17 July 1897

11 If, drunk with sight of power, we loose
Wild tongues that have not Thee in awe—

Such boasting as the Gentiles use,
Or lesser breeds without the Law.

Recessional, in *Times* 17 July 1897

12 They shut the road through the woods.
Seventy years ago.
Weather and rain have undone it again,
And now you would never know
There was once a road through the woods.

Rewards and Fairies (1910) 'Way through the Woods'

13 If you can keep your head when all about you
Are losing theirs and blaming it on you;
If you can trust yourself when all men doubt you,
But make allowance for their doubting too;
If you can wait and not be tired by waiting,
Or being lied about, don't deal in lies,
Or being hated, don't give way to hating,
And yet don't look too good, nor talk too wise;
If you can dream—and not make dreams your master;
If you can think—and not make thoughts your aim,
If you can meet with Triumph and Disaster
And treat those two imposters just the same . . .

Rewards and Fairies (1910) 'If—'

14 If you can make one heap of all your winnings
And risk it on one turn of pitch-and-toss,
And lose, and start again at your beginnings
And never breathe a word about your loss . . .

Rewards and Fairies (1910) 'If—'

15 If you can talk with crowds and keep your virtue,
Or walk with Kings—nor lose the common touch,
If neither foes nor loving friends can hurt you,
If all men count with you, but none too much;
If you can fill the unforgiving minute
With sixty seconds' worth of distance run,
Yours is the Earth and everything that's in it,
And—which is more—you'll be a Man, my son!

Rewards and Fairies (1910) 'If—'

16 One man in a thousand, Solomon says,
Will stick more close than a brother.

Rewards and Fairies (1910) 'The Thousandth Man'

17 The female of the species is more deadly than the male.

Rudyard Kipling's Verse (1919) 'The Female of the Species'

18 As it will be in the future, it was at the birth of Man—
There are only four things certain since Social Progress began:—
That the Dog returns to his Vomit and the Sow returns to her Mire,
And the burnt Fool's bandaged finger goes wabbling back to the Fire.

Rudyard Kipling's Verse (1927) 'The Gods of the Copybook Headings'

19 England's on the anvil—hear the hammers ring—
Clanging from the Severn to the Tyne!
Never was a blacksmith like our Norman King—
England's being hammered, hammered, hammered into line!

Rudyard Kipling's Verse (1927) 'The Anvil'

20 Now this is the Law of the Jungle—as old and as true as the sky;
And the Wolf that shall keep it may prosper, but the Wolf that shall break it must die.

Second Jungle Book (1895) 'The Law of the Jungle'

1 Keep ye the law—be swift in all obedience—
  Clear the land of evil, drive the road and bridge the ford.
  Make ye sure to each his own
  That he reap where he hath sown;
  By the peace among our peoples let men know we serve
      the Lord!
  The Seven Seas (1896) 'A Song of the English'

2 We have fed our sea for a thousand years
  And she calls us, still unfed,
  Though there's never a wave of all her waves
  But marks our English dead:
  We have strawed our best to the weed's unrest
  To the shark and sheering gull.
  If blood be the price of admiralty,
  Lord God, we ha' paid in full!
  The Seven Seas (1896) 'The Song of the Dead'

3 And Ye take mine honour from me if Ye take away the
      sea!
  The Seven Seas (1896) 'Last Chantey'

4 The Liner she's a lady, an' she never looks nor 'eeds—
  The Man-o'-War's 'er 'usband, 'an 'e gives 'er all she
      needs;
  But, oh, the little cargo boats that sail the wet seas
      roun',
  They're just the same as you 'an me a-plyin' up and
      down!
  The Seven Seas (1896) 'The Liner She's a Lady'

5 When 'Omer smote 'is bloomin' lyre,
  He'd 'eard men sing by land an' sea;
  An' what he thought 'e might require,
  'E went an' took—the same as me!
  The Seven Seas (1896) p. 162

6 I've taken my fun where I've found it,
  An' now I must pay for my fun,
  For the more you 'ave known o' the others
  The less will you settle to one;
  An' the end of it's sittin' and thinkin',
  An' dreamin' Hell-fires to see;
  So be warned by my lot (which I know you will not),
  An' learn about women from me!
  The Seven Seas (1896) 'The Ladies'

7 An' I learned about women from 'er!
  The Seven Seas (1896) 'The Ladies'

8 When you get to a man in the case,
  They're like as a row of pins—
  For the Colonel's Lady an' Judy O'Grady
  Are sisters under their skins!
  The Seven Seas (1896) 'The Ladies'

9 The 'eathen in 'is blindness bows down to wood an'
      stone;
  'E don't obey no orders unless they is 'is own;
  'E keeps 'is side-arms awful: 'e leaves 'em all about,
  An' then comes up the Regiment an' pokes the 'eathen
      out.
  The Seven Seas (1896) 'The 'Eathen'

10 The 'eathen in 'is blindness must end where 'e began.
   But the backbone of the Army is the non-commissioned
       man!
   The Seven Seas (1896) 'The 'Eathen'

11 And only the Master shall praise us, and only the
       Master shall blame;
   And no one shall work for money, and no one shall
       work for fame,
   But each for the joy of the working, and each, in his
       separate star,
   Shall draw the Thing as he sees It for the God of Things
       as They are!
   The Seven Seas (1896) 'When Earth's Last Picture is Painted'

12 Words are, of course, the most powerful drug used by
   mankind.
   Speech, 14 Feb. 1923, in *The Times* 15 Feb. 1923

13 Mr Raymond Martin, beyond question, was born in
   a gutter, and bred in a Board-School, where they played
   marbles. He was further (I give the barest handful from
   great store) a Flopshus Cad, an Outrageous Stinker,
   a Jelly-bellied Flag-flapper (this was Stalky's
   contribution), and several other things which it is not
   seemly to put down.
   Stalky & Co. (1899) p. 214

14 Being kissed by a man who didn't wax his moustache
   was—like eating an egg without salt.
   The Story of the Gadsbys (1889) 'Poor Dear Mamma'

15 Down to Gehenna or up to the Throne,
   He travels the fastest who travels alone.
   The Story of the Gadsbys (1890) 'L'Envoi'

16 'Tisn't beauty, so to speak, nor good talk necessarily.
   It's just It. Some women'll stay in a man's memory if
   they once walked down a street.
   Traffics and Discoveries (1904) 'Mrs Bathurst'

17 It's north you may run to the rime-ringed sun,
   Or south to the blind Horn's hate;
   Or east all the way into Mississippi Bay,
   Or west to the Golden Gate.
   Twenty Poems (1918) 'The Long Trail'

18 A fool there was and he made his prayer
   (Even as you and I!)
   To a rag and a bone and a hank of hair
   (We called her the woman who did not care)
   But the fool he called her his lady fair—
   (Even as you and I!)
   The Vampire (1897) p. 1

19 Take up the White Man's burden—
   Send forth the best ye breed—
   Go, bind your sons to exile
   To serve your captives' need;
   To wait, in heavy harness,
   On fluttered folk and wild—
   Your new-caught, sullen peoples,
   Half devil and half child.
   The White Man's Burden (1899)

20 By all ye will or whisper,
   By all ye leave or do,
   The silent sullen peoples
   Shall weigh your God and you.
   The White Man's Burden (1899)

21 If any question why we died,
   Tell them, because our fathers lied.
   The Years Between (1919) 'Common Form'

Henry Kissinger 1923–

1 'We are the President's men,' he [Kissinger] would exclaim, 'and we must behave accordingly.'
M. and B. Kalb *Kissinger* (1974) ch. 7

2 There cannot be a crisis next week. My schedule is already full.
In *New York Times Magazine* 1 June 1969, p. 11

3 Power, he [Kissinger] has observed, 'is the great aphrodisiac.'
New York Times 19 Jan. 1971, p. 12

Fred Kitchen 1872–1950

4 Meredith, we're in!
Catch-phrase originating in *The Bailiff* (1907 stage sketch) —see J. P. Gallagher *Fred Karno* (1971) ch. 9, p. 90

Lord Kitchener 1850–1916

5 You are ordered abroad as a soldier of the King to help our French comrades against the invasion of a common enemy. You have to perform a task which will need your courage, your energy, your patience. Remember that the honour of the British Army depends on your individual conduct. It will be your duty not only to set an example of discipline and perfect steadiness under fire, but also to maintain the most friendly relations with those whom you are helping in this struggle. The operations in which you are engaged will, for the most part, take place in a friendly country, and you can do your own country no better service than in showing yourself in France and Belgium in the true character of a British soldier.
Be invariably courteous, considerate, and kind. Never do anything likely to injure or destroy property, and always look upon looting as a disgraceful act. You are sure to meet with a welcome and to be trusted; your conduct must justify that welcome and that trust.
Your duty cannot be done unless your health is sound. So keep constantly on your guard against any excesses. In this new experience you may find temptations both in wine and women. You must entirely resist both temptations, and, while treating all women with perfect courtesy, you should avoid any intimacy. Do your duty bravely. Fear God. Honour the King.
Message to soldiers of the British Expeditionary Force (1914), in *The Times* 19 Aug. 1914

Paul Klee 1879–1940

6 *Eine aktive Linie, die sich frei ergeht, ein Spaziergang um seiner selbst willen, ohne Ziel. Das agens ist ein Punkt, der sich verschiebt.*

An active line on a walk, moving freely without a goal. A walk for walk's sake.
Pädagogisches Skizzenbuch (Pedagogical Sketchbook, 1925) p. 6

7 *Kunst gibt nicht das Sichtbare wieder, sondern macht sichtbar.*

Art does not reproduce the visible; rather, it makes visible.
Schöpferische Konfession (Creative Credo, 1920) in *Im Zwischenreich* (1957) (Inward Vision, 1958) p. 5

Charles Knight and Kenneth Lyle

8 Here we are! here we are!! here we are again!!!
There's Pat and Mac and Tommy and Jack and Joe.
When there's trouble brewing,
When there's something doing,
Are we downhearted?
No! Let 'em all come!
Here we are! Here we are again!! (1914 song)

Frederick Knott 1916–

9 Dial 'M' for murder.
Title of play (1952)

Monsignor Ronald Knox 1888–1957

10 There once was a man who said, 'God
Must think it exceedingly odd
If he finds that this tree
Continues to be
When there's no one about in the Quad.'
In Langford Reed *Complete Limerick Book* (1924) p. 44 (This reply was written by an unknown author:
Dear Sir,
Your astonishment's odd:
I am always about in the Quad.
And that's why the tree
Will continue to be,
Since observed by
Yours faithfully,
God.)

11 The tumult and the shouting dies,
The captains and the kings depart,
And we are left with large supplies
Of cold blancmange and rhubarb tart.
In R. Eyres *In Three Tongues* (1959) p. 130 'After the Party'—a parody of Kipling 126:9

12 It is stupid of modern civilization to have given up believing in the devil, when he is the only explanation of it.
Let Dons Delight (1939) ch. 8

Arthur Koestler 1905–1983

13 The most persistent sound which reverberates through man's history is the beating of war drums.
Janus (1978) prologue

14 Man can leave the earth and land on the moon, but cannot cross from East to West Berlin. Prometheus reaches for the stars with an insane grin on his face and a totem-symbol in his hand.
Janus (1978) prologue

Jiddu Krishnamurti d. 1986

1 I maintain that Truth is a pathless land, and you cannot approach it by any path whatsoever, by any religion, by any sect.

Speech in Holland, 3 Aug. 1929, in Lilly Heber *Krishnamurti* (1931) ch. 2

Kris Kristofferson 1936– and Fred Foster

2 Freedom's just another word for nothin' left to lose, Nothin' ain't worth nothin', but it's free.

Me and Bobby McGee (1969 song)

Joseph Wood Krutch 1893–1970

3 The most serious charge which can be brought against New England is not Puritanism but February.

Twelve Seasons (1949) 'February'

4 Cats seem to go on the principle that it never does any harm to ask for what you want.

Twelve Seasons (1949) 'February'

Stanley Kubrick 1928–

5 The great nations have always acted like gangsters, and the small nations like prostitutes.

In *Guardian* 5 June 1963

Satish Kumar 1937–

6 Lead me from death to life, from falsehood to truth. Lead me from despair to hope, from fear to trust. Lead me from hate to love, from war to peace. Let peace fill our heart, our world, our universe.

Prayer for Peace (1981; adapted from the Upanishads)

Henry Labouchere 1831–1912

7 Mr Labouchere's jest about Mr Gladstone laying upon Providence the responsibility of always placing the ace of trumps up his sleeve was a good one. In one of his private letters I find the quip worded a little more pungently. 'Who cannot refrain,' he says, referring to the then Prime Minister, 'from perpetually bringing an ace down his sleeve, even when he has only to play fair to win the trick.'

A. L. Thorold *Life of Henry Labouchere* (1913) ch. 15. Cf. Earl Curzon's *Modern Parliamentary Eloquence* (1913) p. 25 'I recall a phrase of that incorrigible cynic Labouchere, alluding to Mr Gladstone's frequent appeals to a higher power, that he did not object to the old man always having a card up his sleeve, but he did object to his insinuating that the Almighty had placed it there.'

Fiorello La Guardia 1882–1947

8 When I make a mistake, it's a beaut!

In William Manners *Patience and Fortitude* (1976) p. 219 (on the appointment of Herbert O'Brien as a judge in 1936)

R. D. Laing 1927–1989

9 Schizophrenia cannot be understood without understanding despair.

The Divided Self (1960) ch. 2

10 Few books today are forgivable.

Politics of Experience (1967) introduction

11 We are effectively destroying ourselves by violence masquerading as love.

Politics of Experience (1967) ch. 3

12 The brotherhood of man is evoked by particular men according to their circumstances. But it seldom extends to all men. In the name of our freedom and our brotherhood we are prepared to blow up the other half of mankind and to be blown up in turn.

Politics of Experience (1967) ch. 4

13 Madness need not be all breakdown. It may also be break-through. It is potential liberation and renewal as well as enslavement and existential death.

Politics of Experience (1967) ch. 6

14 The experience and behaviour that gets labelled schizophrenic is a special strategy that a person invents in order to live in an unlivable situation.

Politics of Experience (1967) ch. 5

Arthur J. Lamb 1870–1928

15 She's a bird in a gilded cage.

Title of song (1900; music by Harry von Tilzer)

Constant Lambert 1905–1951

16 To put it vulgarly, the whole trouble with a folk song is that once you have played it through there is nothing much you can do except play it over again and play it rather louder.

Music Ho! (1934) ch. 3

17 The average English critic is a don *manqué*, hopelessly parochial when not exaggeratedly teutonophile, over whose desk must surely hang the motto (presumably in Gothic lettering) 'Above all no enthusiasm'.

Opera Dec. 1950

Giuseppe di Lampedusa 1896–1957

18 *Se vogliamo che tutto rimanga come è, bisogna che tutto cambi.*

If we want things to stay as they are, things will have to change.

Il Gattopardo (The Leopard, 1957) p. 33

Sir Osbert Lancaster 1908–1986

19 Today, when the passer-by is a little unnerved at being suddenly confronted with a hundred and fifty accurate reproductions of Anne Hathaway's cottage, each complete with central heating and garage, he should pause to reflect on the extraordinary fact that all over the country the latest and most scientific methods of mass-production are being utilized to turn out a stream of old oak beams, leaded window-panes and small discs of bottle-glass, all structural devices which our ancestors lost no time in abandoning as soon as an increase in wealth and knowledge enabled them to do so.

Pillar to Post (1938) 'Stockbroker's Tudor'

Bert Lance 1931–

1 Bert Lance believes he can save Uncle Sam billions if he can get the government to adopt a single motto: 'If it ain't broke, don't fix it.' He explains: 'That's the trouble with government: Fixing things that aren't broken and not fixing things that are broken.'

Nation's Business 27 May 1977

Andrew Lang 1844–1912

2 St Andrews by the Northern sea,
A haunted town it is to me!

Ballades and Verses Vain (1884) p. 79

3 They hear like ocean on a western beach
The surge and thunder of the Odyssey.

Poetical Works (1923) vol. 2, 'The Odyssey'

4 If the wild bowler thinks he bowls,
Or if the batsman thinks he's bowled,
They know not, poor misguided souls,
They too shall perish unconsoled.
I am the batsman and the bat,
I am the bowler and the ball,
The umpire, the pavilion cat,
The roller, pitch, and stumps, and all.

Poetical Works (1923) vol. 2, 'Brahma' (a parody of Emerson—see *Oxford Dictionary of Quotations* (1979) 206:17)

Julia Lang 1921–

5 Are you sitting comfortably? Then we'll begin.

Introduction to stories on *Listen with Mother*, BBC Radio programme, 1950–1982 (sometimes 'Then I'll begin')

Suzanne K. Langer 1895–1985

6 Art is the objectification of feeling, and the subjectification of nature.

Mind (1967) vol. 1, pt. 2, ch. 4

Ring Lardner 1885–1933

7 Are you lost daddy I arsked tenderly.
Shut up he explained.

The Young Immigrunts (1920) ch. 10

Philip Larkin 1922–1985

8 Rather than words comes the thought of high windows:
The sun-comprehending glass,
And beyond it, the deep blue air, that shows
Nothing, and is nowhere, and is endless.

High Windows (1974) 'High Windows'

9 Perhaps being old is having lighted rooms
Inside your head, and people in them, acting.

People you know, yet can't quite name.

High Windows (1974) 'The Old Fools'

10 Next year we are to bring the soldiers home
For lack of money, and it is all right.
Places they guarded, or kept orderly,
Must guard themselves, and keep themselves orderly.

High Windows (1974) 'Homage to a Government'

11 Next year we shall be living in a country
That brought its soldiers home for lack of money.
The statues will be standing in the same
Tree-muffled squares, and look nearly the same.
Our children will not know it's a different country.
All we can hope to leave them now is money.

High Windows (1974) 'Homage to a Government'

12 They fuck you up, your mum and dad.
They may not mean to, but they do.
They fill you with the faults they had
And add some extra, just for you.

High Windows (1974) 'This Be The Verse'

13 Man hands on misery to man.
It deepens like a coastal shelf.
Get out as early as you can,
And don't have any kids yourself.

High Windows (1974) 'This Be The Verse'

14 Sexual intercourse began
In nineteen sixty-three
(Which was rather late for me)—
Between the end of the *Chatterley* ban
And the Beatles' first LP.

High Windows (1974) 'Annus Mirabilis'

15 Hatless, I take off
My cycle-clips in awkward reverence.

The Less Deceived (1955) 'Church Going'

16 A serious house on serious earth it is,
In whose blent air all our compulsions meet,
Are recognised, and robed as destinies.

The Less Deceived (1955) 'Church Going'

17 Why should I let the toad *work*
Squat on my life?
Can't I use my wit as a pitchfork
And drive the brute off?

Six days of the week it soils
With its sickening poison—
Just for paying a few bills!
That's out of proportion.

The Less Deceived (1955) 'Toads'

18 Nothing, like something, happens anywhere.

The Less Deceived (1955) 'I Remember, I Remember'

19 Far too many [of the books entered for the 1977 Booker Prize] relied on the classic formula of a beginning, a muddle, and an end.

New Fiction no. 15, Jan. 1978

20 Deprivation is for me what daffodils were for Wordsworth.

Reply to question 'Do you think people go around feeling they haven't got out of life what life has to offer?'–*Required Writing* (1983) p. 47

21 Give me your arm, old toad;
Help me down Cemetery Road.

The Whitsun Weddings (1964) 'Toads Revisited'

1 I thought of London spread out in the sun,
Its postal districts packed like squares of wheat.
The Whitsun Weddings (1964) 'The Whitsun Weddings'

2 What are days for?
Days are where we live.
They come, they wake us
Time and time over.
They are to be happy in:
Where can we live but days?
The Whitsun Weddings (1964) 'Days'

3 Never such innocence,
Never before or since,
As changed itself to past
Without a word—the men
Leaving the gardens tidy,
The thousands of marriages
Lasting a little while longer:
Never such innocence again.
The Whitsun Weddings (1964) 'MCMXIV'

4 Don't read too much now: the dude
Who lets the girl down before
The hero arrives, the chap
Who's yellow and keeps the store,
Seem far too familiar. Get stewed:
Books are a load of crap.
The Whitsun Weddings (1964) 'Study of Reading Habits'

5 Life is first boredom, then fear.
Whether or not we use it, it goes,
And leaves what something hidden from us chose,
And age, and then the only end of age.
The Whitsun Weddings (1964) 'Dockery & Son'

6 Time has transfigured them into
Untruth. The stone fidelity
They hardly meant has come to be
Their final blazon, and to prove
Our almost-instinct almost true:
What will survive of us is love.
The Whitsun Weddings (1964) 'An Arundel Tomb'

Sir Harry Lauder 1870–1950

7 Keep right on to the end of the road,
Keep right on to the end.
Tho' the way be long, let your heart be strong.
Keep right on round the bend.
Tho' you're tired and weary,
Still journey on
Till you come to your happy abode,
Where all you love you've been dreaming of
Will be there at the end of the road.
The End of the Road (1924 song)

8 I love a lassie, a bonnie, bonnie lassie,
She's as pure as the lily in the dell.
She's as sweet as the heather, the bonnie bloomin'
heather—
Mary, ma Scotch Bluebell.
I Love a Lassie (1905 song)

9 It's nice to get up in the mornin' (but it's nicer to lie in
bed).
Title of song (1913)

10 Roamin' in the gloamin',
On the bonnie banks o' Clyde.

Roamin' in the gloamin'
Wae my lassie by my side.
Roamin' in the Gloamin' (1911 song)

Stan Laurel (*Arthur Stanley Jefferson*)
1890–1965

11 Well, here's another nice mess you've gotten me into.
Another Fine Mess (1930 film; words spoken by Oliver Hardy
in many Laurel and Hardy films: often 'another fine mess')

12 Why don't you do something to *help* me?
Drivers' Licence Sketch (1947), in J. McCabe *Comedy World of
Stan Laurel* (1974) p. 107 (words spoken by Oliver Hardy)

James Laver 1899–1975

13 The same costume will be

Indecent	...	10 years before its time	
Shameless	...	5 years " " "	
Outré (daring)	...	1 year " " "	
Smart			
Dowdy	...	1 year after its time	
Hideous	...	10 years " " "	
Ridiculous	...	20 years " " "	
Amusing	...	30 years " " "	
Quaint	...	50 years " " "	
Charming	...	70 years " " "	
Romantic	...	100 years " " "	
Beautiful	...	150 years " " "	

Taste and Fashion (1937) ch. 18

Andrew Bonar Law 1858–1923

See BONAR LAW

D. H. Lawrence 1885–1930

14 Is it the secret of the long-nosed Etruscans?
The long-nosed, sensitive-footed, subtly-smiling
Etruscans
Who made so little noise outside the cypress groves?
Birds, Beasts and Flowers (1923) 'Cypresses'

15 Men! The only animal in the world to fear!
Birds, Beasts and Flowers (1923) 'Mountain Lion'

16 A snake came to my water-trough
On a hot, hot day, and I in pyjamas for the heat,
To drink there.
Birds, Beasts and Flowers (1923) 'Snake'

17 And I thought of the albatross,
And I wished he would come back, my snake.
For he seemed to me again like a king,
Like a king in exile, uncrowned in the underworld,
Now due to be crowned again.
And so, I missed my chance with one of the lords
Of life.
And I have something to expiate:
A pettiness.
Birds, Beasts and Flowers (1923) 'Snake'

18 Curse the blasted, jelly-boned swines, the slimy, the
belly-wriggling invertebrates, the miserable sodding

rotters, the flaming sods, the snivelling, dribbling, dithering, palsied, pulse-less lot that make up England today. They've got white of egg in their veins, and their spunk is that watery it's a marvel they can breed. They *can* nothing but frog-spawn—the gibberers! God, how I hate them!

Letter to Edward Garnett, 3 July 1912, in *Collected Letters* (1962) vol. 1, p. 134

1 I like to write when I feel spiteful; it's like having a good sneeze.

Letter to Lady Cynthia Asquith, ?25 Nov. 1913, in *Collected Letters* (1962) vol. 1, p. 246

2 The dead don't die. They look on and help.

Letter to J. Middleton Murry, 2 Feb. 1923, in *Collected Letters* (1962) vol. 2, p. 736

3 The autumn always gets me badly, as it breaks into colours. I want to go south, where there is no autumn, where the cold doesn't crouch over one like a snow-leopard waiting to pounce. The heart of the North is dead, and the fingers of cold are corpse fingers.

Letter to J. Middleton Murry, 3 Oct. 1924, in *Collected Letters* (1962) vol. 2, p. 812

4 I'd like to write an essay on [Arnold] Bennett—sort of pig in clover.

Letter to Aldous Huxley, 27 Mar. 1928, in *Collected Letters* (1962) vol. 2, p. 1048

5 My God, what a clumsy *olla putrida* James Joyce is! Nothing but old fags and cabbage-stumps of quotations from the Bible and the rest, stewed in the juice of deliberate, journalistic dirty-mindedness.

Letter to Aldous and Maria Huxley, 15 Aug. 1928, in *Collected Letters* (1962) vol. 2, p. 1074

6 To the Puritan all things are impure, as somebody says.

Etruscan Places (1932) 'Cerveteri'

7 Ours is essentially a tragic age, so we refuse to take it tragically.

Lady Chatterley's Lover (1928) ch. 1

8 Some things can't be ravished. You can't ravish a tin of sardines.

Lady Chatterley's Lover (1928) ch. 8

9 John Thomas says good-night to Lady Jane, a little droopingly, but with a hopeful heart.

Lady Chatterley's Lover (1928) ch. 19

10 Now it is autumn and the falling fruit
And the long journey towards oblivion . . .
Have you built your ship of death, O have you?
O build your ship of death, for you will need it.

Last Poems (1932) 'Ship of Death'

11 Along the avenue of cypresses
All in their scarlet cloaks, and surplices
Of linen go the chanting choristers,
The priests in gold and black, the villagers.

Look! We Have Come Through! (1917) 'Giorno dei Morti'

12 Not I, not I, but the wind that blows through me!
A fine wind is blowing the new direction of Time.

Look! We Have Come Through! (1917) 'Song of a Man who has Come Through'

13 So now it is vain for the singer to burst into clamour
With the great black piano appassionato. The glamour

Of childish days is upon me, my manhood is cast
Down in the flood of remembrance, I weep like a child
for the past.

New Poems (1918) 'Piano'

14 Don't be sucked in by the su-superior,
don't swallow the culture bait,
don't drink, don't drink and get beerier and beerier,
do learn to discriminate.

Pansies (1929) 'Don'ts'

15 How beastly the bourgeois is
Especially the male of the species.

Pansies (1929) 'How Beastly the Bourgeois Is'

16 I never saw a wild thing
Sorry for itself.

Pansies (1929) 'Self-Pity'

17 For while we have sex in the mind, we truly have none
in the body.

Pansies (1929) 'Leave Sex Alone'

18 When I read Shakespeare I am struck with wonder
That such trivial people should muse and thunder
In such lovely language.

Pansies (1929) 'When I Read Shakespeare'

19 Pornography is the attempt to insult sex, to do dirt
on it.

Phoenix (1936) 'Pornography and Obscenity' ch. 3

20 The very first copy of The White Peacock that was ever sent out, I put into my mother's hands when she was dying. She looked at the outside, and then at the title-page, and then at me, with darkening eyes. And though she loved me so much, I think she doubted whether it could be much of a book, since no one more important than I had written it. Somewhere, in the helpless privacies of her being, she had wistful respect for me. But for me in the face of the world, not much. This David would never get a stone across at Goliath. And why try? Let Goliath alone! Anyway, she was beyond reading my first immortal work. It was put aside, and I never wanted to see it again. She never saw it again.

After the funeral, my father struggled through half a page, and it might as well have been Hottentot.
'And what dun they gi'e thee for that, lad?'
'Fifty pounds, father.'
'Fifty pounds!' He was dumbfounded, and looked at me with shrewd eyes, as if I were a swindler. 'Fifty pounds! An' tha's niver done a day's hard work in thy life.'

Phoenix (1936) p. 232

21 Never trust the artist. Trust the tale. The proper function of a critic is to save the tale from the artist who created it.

Studies in Classic American Literature (1923) ch. 1

22 'Be a good animal, true to your instincts,' was his motto.

White Peacock (1911) pt. 2, ch. 2

23 Don't you find it a beautiful clean thought, a world empty of people, just uninterrupted grass, and a hare sitting up?

Women in Love (1920) ch. 11

T. E. Lawrence 1885–1930

1 Many men would take the death-sentence without
a whimper to escape the life-sentence which fate
carries in her other hand.
The Mint (1955) pt. 1, ch. 4

2 The seven pillars of wisdom.
Title of book (1926). Cf. *Oxford Dictionary of Quotations*
(1979) 53:27

3 I loved you, so I drew these tides of men into my hands
and wrote my will across the sky in stars
To earn you Freedom, the seven pillared worthy house,
that your eyes might be shining for me
When we came.
The Seven Pillars of Wisdom (1926) dedication 'to S.A.'

Sir Edmund Leach 1910–

4 Far from being the basis of the good society, the
family, with its narrow privacy and tawdry secrets, is
the source of all our discontents.
BBC Reith Lectures, 1967, in *Listener* 30 Nov. 1967

Stephen Leacock 1869–1944

5 The parent who could see his boy as he really is,
would shake his head and say: 'Willie, is no good; I'll
sell him.'
Essays and Literary Studies (1916) 'Lot of a Schoolmaster'

6 Advertising may be described as the science of arresting
human intelligence long enough to get money from it.
Garden of Folly (1924) 'The Perfect Salesman'

7 I am what is called a *professor emeritus*—from the Latin
e, 'out', and *meritus*, 'so he ought to be'.
Here are my Lectures (1938) ch. 14

8 There are no handles to a horse, but the 1910 model
has a string to each side of its face for turning its head
when there is anything you want it to see.
Literary Lapses (1910) 'Reflections on Riding'

9 I detest life-insurance agents; they always argue that
I shall some day die, which is not so.
Literary Lapses (1910) 'Insurance up to Date'

10 Get your room full of good air, then shut up the
windows and keep it. It will keep for years. Anyway,
don't keep using your lungs all the time. Let them rest.
Literary Lapses (1910) 'How to Live to be 200'

11 A sportsman is a man who, every now and then, simply
has to get out and kill something. Not that he's cruel.
He wouldn't hurt a fly. It's not big enough.
My Remarkable Uncle (1942) p. 73

12 Lord Ronald said nothing; he flung himself from the
room, flung himself upon his horse and rode madly off
in all directions.
Nonsense Novels (1911) 'Gertrude the Governess'

13 A decision of the courts decided that the game of golf
may be played on Sunday, not being a game within the
view of the law, but being a form of moral effort.
Over the Footlights (1923) 'Why I Refuse to Play Golf'

14 The general idea, of course, in any first-class laundry, is
to see that no shirt or collar ever comes back twice.
Winnowed Wisdom (1926) ch. 6

Timothy Leary 1920–

15 If you take the game of life seriously, if you take your
nervous system seriously, if you take your sense
organs seriously, if you take the energy process
seriously, you must turn on, tune in and drop out.
Lecture, June 1966, in *Politics of Ecstasy* (1968) ch. 21

F. R. Leavis 1895–1978

16 It is well to start by distinguishing the few really
great—the major novelists who count in the same
way as the major poets, in the sense that they not
only change the possibilities of the art for practitioners
and readers, but that they are significant in terms of
the human awareness they promote; awareness of the
possibilities of life.
The Great Tradition (1948) ch. 1

17 The Sitwells belong to the history of publicity rather
than of poetry.
New Bearings in English Poetry (1932) ch. 2

Fran Lebowitz

18 All God's children are not beautiful. Most of God's
children are, in fact, barely presentable.
Metropolitan Life (1978) p. 6

19 There is no such thing as inner peace. There is only
nervousness or death. Any attempt to prove otherwise
constitutes unacceptable behaviour.
Metropolitan Life (1978) p. 6

20 Life is something to do when you can't get to sleep.
Metropolitan Life (1978) p. 101

21 Food is an important part of a balanced diet.
Metropolitan Life (1978) p. 110

22 Being a woman is of special interest only to aspiring
male transsexuals. To actual women, it is merely
a good excuse not to play football.
Metropolitan Life (1978) p. 144

Stanislaw Lec 1909–1966

23 Is it progress if a cannibal uses knife and fork?
Myśli Nieuczesane (Unkempt Thoughts, 1962) p. 78

John le Carré (David John Moore Cornwell) 1931–

24 The spy who came in from the cold.
Title of novel (1963)

Le Corbusier (Charles Édouard Jeanneret) 1887–1965

25 *Une maison est une machine-à-habiter.*

A house is a machine for living in.
Vers une architecture (Towards an Architecture, 1923) p. ix

Harper Lee 1926–

1 Shoot all the bluejays you want, if you can hit 'em,
but remember it's a sin to kill a mockingbird.
To Kill a Mockingbird (1960) ch. 10

Laurie Lee 1914–

2 I was set down from the carrier's cart at the age of
three; and there with a sense of bewilderment and
terror my life in the village began.
Cider with Rosie (1959) p. 9

3 Such a morning it is when love
leans through geranium windows
and calls with a cockerel's tongue.

When red-haired girls scamper like roses
over the rain-green grass,
and the sun drips honey.
Sun is my Monument (1947) 'Day of these Days'

Ernest Lehman

4 Somebody up there likes me.
Title of film (1956)

5 Sweet smell of success.
Title of book and film (1957)

Tom Lehrer 1928–

6 Life is like a sewer. What you get out of it depends on
what you put into it.
Preamble to song 'We Will All Go Together When We Go', in
An Evening Wasted with Tom Lehrer (1953 record album)

7 Plagiarize! Let no one else's work evade your eyes,
Remember why the good Lord made your eyes,
So don't shade your eyes but plagiarize, plagiarize,
plagiarize!
Lobachevski (1953 song)

8 And we will all go together when we go—
Every Hottentot and every Eskimo.
We Will All Go Together When We Go (1953 song)

Jerry Leiber 1933–
and Mike Stoller 1933–

9 You ain't nothin' but a hound dog,
Cryin' all the time.
Hound Dog (1956 song)

Fred W. Leigh d. 1924

10 There was I, waiting at the church,
Waiting at the church, waiting at the church,
When I found he'd left me in the lurch,
Lor, how it did upset me!
All at once he sent me round a note,
Here's the very note,
This is what he wrote—
'Can't get away to marry you today,
My wife won't let me!'
Waiting at the Church (*My Wife Won't Let Me*) (1906 song;
music by Henry E. Pether)

Fred W. Leigh d. 1924, Charles Collins, and Lily Morris

11 Why am I always the bridesmaid,
Never the blushing bride?
Why Am I Always the Bridesmaid? (1917 song)

Fred W. Leigh d. 1924 and George Arthurs

12 A little of what you fancy does you good.
Title of song (1915)

Curtis E. LeMay 1906–1990

13 My solution to the problem would be to tell them [the
North Vietnamese] frankly that they've got to draw in
their horns and stop their aggression, or we're going
to bomb them back into the Stone Age.
Mission with LeMay (1965) p. 565

Lenin (Vladimir Ilich Ulyanov) 1870–1924

14 We must now set about building a proletarian socialist
state in Russia.
Speech in Petrograd, 7 Nov. 1917, in *Collected Works* (1964)
vol. 26, p. 240

15 Коммунизм есть Советская власть плюс
электрификация всей страны.

Communism is Soviet power plus the electrification of
the whole country.
Report to 8th Congress, 1920, in *Collected Works* (ed. 5)
vol. 42, p. 30

16 He [George Bernard Shaw] is a good man fallen among
Fabians.
In Arthur Ransome *Six Weeks in Russia in 1919* (1919)
'Notes of Conversations with Lenin'

17 It is true that liberty is precious—so precious that it
must be rationed.
In Sidney and Beatrice Webb *Soviet Communism* (1936)
p. 1036

18 Нет. Демократия *не* тождественна с подчинением
меньшинства большинству. Демократия есть
признающее подчинение меньшинства
большинству *государство*, т.е. организация для
систематического *насилия* одного класса над
другим, одной части населения над другую.

No, Democracy is *not* identical with majority rule. No,
Democracy is a *State* which recognizes the subjection of
the minority to the majority, that is, an organization for
the systematic use of *violence* by one class against the
other, by one part of the population against another.
State and Revolution (1919) ch. 4

19 Пока есть государство, нет свободы. Когда
будет свобода не будет государства.

While the State exists, there can be no freedom. When
there is freedom there will be no State.
State and Revolution (1919) ch. 5

John Lennon 1940–1980

20 Imagine there's no heaven,
It's easy if you try,

No hell below us,
Above us only sky,
Imagine all the people
Living for today.
Imagine (1971 song)

1 Will the people in the cheaper seats clap your hands?
All the rest of you, if you'll just rattle your jewellery.
At Royal Variety Performance, 4 Nov. 1963, in R. Colman
John Winston Lennon (1984) pt. 1, ch. 11

2 Christianity will go. It will vanish and shrink. I needn't
argue about that; I'm right and I will be proved right.
We're [the Beatles are] more popular than Jesus now;
I don't know which will go first—rock 'n' roll or
Christianity.
Interview with Maureen Cleave in *Evening Standard* 4 Mar.
1966. Cf. Zelda Fitzgerald

John Lennon 1940–1980 and Paul McCartney 1942–

3 All you need is love.
Title of song (1967)

4 Back in the USSR.
Title of song (1968)

5 For I don't care too much for money,
For money can't buy me love.
Can't Buy Me Love (1964 song)

6 I heard the news today, oh boy.
Four thousand holes in Blackburn Lancashire.
And though the holes were rather small,
They had to count them all.
Now they know how many holes it takes to fill the
Albert Hall.
I'd love to turn you on.
A Day in the Life (1967 song)

7 Give peace a chance.
Title of song (1969)

8 It's been a hard day's night,
And I've been working like a dog.
A Hard Day's Night (1964 song)

9 Magical mystery tour.
Title of song and TV film (1967)

10 She loves you, yeh, yeh, yeh,
And with a love like that, you know you should be
glad.
She Loves You (1963 song)

11 Strawberry fields forever.
Title of song (1967)

12 She's got a ticket to ride, but she don't care.
Ticket to Ride (1965 song)

13 Will you still need me, will you still feed me,
When I'm sixty four?
When I'm Sixty Four (1967 song)

14 Oh I get by with a little help from my friends.
With a Little Help From My Friends (1967 song)

15 We all live in a yellow submarine, yellow submarine,
yellow submarine.
Yellow Submarine (1966 song)

16 Yesterday, all my troubles seemed so far away,
Now it looks as though they're here to stay.
Oh I believe in yesterday.
Yesterday (1965 song)

Dan Leno (George Galvin) 1860–1904

17 Ah! what is man? Wherefore does he why? Whence
did he whence? Whither is he withering?
Dan Leno Hys Booke (1901) ch. 1

Alan Jay Lerner 1918–1986

18 I'm getting married in the morning,
Ding! dong! the bells are gonna chime.
Pull out the stopper;
Let's have a whopper;
But get me to the church on time!
Get Me to the Church on Time (1956 song; music by Frederick
Loewe)

19 Why can't a woman be more like a man?
Men are so honest, so thoroughly square;
Eternally noble, historically fair;
Who, when you win, will always give your back a pat.
Why can't a woman be like that?
A Hymn to Him (1956 song; music by Frederick Loewe)

20 Ah yes! I remember it well.
I Remember it Well (1958 song; music by Frederick Loewe)

21 I've grown accustomed to the trace
Of something in the air;
Accustomed to her face.
I've Grown Accustomed to her Face (1956 song; music by
Frederick Loewe)

22 On a clear day (you can see forever).
Title of song from musical *On a Clear Day* (1965; music by
Burton Lane)

23 The rain in Spain stays mainly in the plain.
The Rain in Spain (1956 song; music by Frederick Loewe)

24 Thank heaven for little girls!
For little girls get bigger every day.
Thank Heaven for Little Girls (1958 song; music by Frederick
Loewe)

25 All I want is a room somewhere,
Far away from the cold night air,
With one enormous chair;
Oh, wouldn't it be loverly?
Wouldn't it be Loverly (1956 song; music by Frederick
Loewe)

Doris Lessing 1919–

26 There's only one real sin, and that is to persuade
oneself that the second-best is anything but the
second-best.
Golden Notebook (1962) p. 554

27 When a white man in Africa by accident looks into the
eyes of a native and sees the human being (which it is
his chief preoccupation to avoid), his sense of guilt,
which he denies, fumes up in resentment and he brings
down the whip.
The Grass is Singing (1950) ch. 8

Winifred Mary Letts 1882–1972

1 I saw the spires of Oxford
As I was passing by,
The grey spires of Oxford
Against a pearl-grey sky;
My heart was with the Oxford men
Who went abroad to die.
   Hallow-e'en (1916) 'The Spires of Oxford'

Oscar Levant 1906–1972

2 Epigram: a wisecrack that played Carnegie Hall.
   Coronet Sept. 1958

3 Underneath this flabby exterior is an enormous lack of character.
   Memoirs of an Amnesiac (1965) ch. 11

4 I don't drink liquor. I don't like it. It makes me feel good.
   Time 5 May 1958

Ros Levenstein

5 I'm only here for the beer.
   Slogan for Double Diamond beer, 1971 onwards, in Nigel Rees *Slogans* (1982) p. 11

Viscount Leverhulme (William Hesketh Lever) 1851–1925

6 Half the money I spend on advertising is wasted, and the trouble is I don't know which half.
   In David Ogilvy *Confessions of an Advertising Man* (1963) ch. 3

Ada Leverson 1865–1936

7 He [Oscar Wilde] seemed at ease and to have the look of the last gentleman in Europe.
   Letters to the Sphinx (1930) p. 34

8 You don't know a woman until you have had a letter from her.
   Tenterhooks (1912) ch. 7

Bernard Levin 1928–

9 [Tony] Benn flung himself into the Sixties technology with the enthusiasm (not to say language) of a newly enrolled Boy Scout demonstrating knot-tying to his indulgent parents.
   The Pendulum Years (1970) ch. 11

10 I have heard tell of a Professor of Economics who has a sign on the wall of his study, reading 'the future is not what it was'. The sentiment was admirable; unfortunately, the past is not getting any better either.
   Sunday Times 22 May 1977

Claude Lévi-Strauss 1908–

11 *La langue est une raison humaine qui a ses raisons, et que l'homme ne connaît pas.*

Language is a form of human reason and has its reasons which are unknown to man.
   La Pensée sauvage (The Savage Mind, 1962) ch. 9. Cf. Pascal in *Oxford Dictionary of Quotations* (1979) 369:10

Cecil Day Lewis

See C. Day-Lewis

C. S. Lewis 1898–1963

12 There is wishful thinking in Hell as well as on Earth.
   Screwtape Letters (1942) preface

13 We have trained them [men] to think of the Future as a promised land which favoured heroes attain—not as something which everyone reaches at the rate of sixty minutes an hour, whatever he does, whoever he is.
   Screwtape Letters (1942) no. 25

14 She's the sort of woman who lives for others—you can always tell the others by their hunted expression.
   Screwtape Letters (1942) no. 26

15 I remember summing up what I took to be our destiny, in conversation with my best friend at Chartres, by the formula, 'Term, holidays, term, holidays, till we leave school, and then work, work, work till we die.'
   Suprised by Joy (1955) ch. 4

John Spedan Lewis 1885–1963

16 Service to customers: never knowingly undersold.
   Slogan (*c*.1920) in *Partnership for All* (1948) ch. 29

Percy Wyndham Lewis 1882–1957

17 'The Art of Being Ruled' might be described from some points of view as an infernal Utopia. . . . An account, comprising many chapters, of the decadence occupying the trough between the two world wars introduces us to a moronic inferno of insipidity and decay (which is likewise the inferno of 'The Apes of God').
   Rude Assignment (1950) ch. 31

18 Gertrude Stein's prose-song is a cold, black suet-pudding. We can represent it as a cold suet-roll of fabulously-reptilian length. Cut it at any point, it is the same thing; the same heavy, sticky, opaque mass all through, and all along. It is weighted, projected, with a sibylline urge. It is mournful and monstrous, composed of dead and inanimate material. It is all fat, without nerve. Or the evident vitality that informs it is vegetable rather than animal. Its life is a low-grade, if tenacious one; of the sausage, by-the-yard, variety.
   Time and Western Man (1927) pt. 1, ch. 13

Sam M. Lewis 1885–1959 and Joe Young 1889–1939

19 How 'ya gonna keep 'em down on the farm (after they've seen Paree)?
   Title of song (1919; music by Walter Donaldson)

Sinclair Lewis 1885–1951

1 Our American professors like their literature clear and
cold and pure and very dead.
The American Fear of Literature (Nobel Prize Address, 12 Dec.
1930), in H. Frenz *Literature 1901–1967* (1969) p. 285

2 His name was George F. Babbitt. He was forty-six years
old now, in April, 1920, and he made nothing in
particular, neither butter nor shoes nor poetry, but he
was nimble in the calling of selling houses for more
than people could afford to pay.
Babbitt (1922) ch. 1

3 To George F. Babbitt, as to most prosperous citizens of
Zenith, his motor car was poetry and tragedy, love and
heroism. The office was his pirate ship but the car his
perilous excursion ashore.
Babbitt (1922) ch. 3

4 In other countries, art and literature are left to a lot of
shabby bums living in attics and feeding on booze and
spaghetti, but in America the successful writer or
picture-painter is indistinguishable from any other
decent business man.
Babbitt (1922) ch. 14

5 It can't happen here.
Title of novel (1935)

Robert Ley 1890–1945

6 *Kraft durch Freude.*

Strength through joy.
German Labour Front slogan, in *The Times* 30 Nov. 1933,
p. 13

Liberace (Wladziu Valentino Liberace) 1919–1987

7 He [Liberace] begins to belabour the critics
announcing that *he* doesn't mind what they say but
that poor George [his brother] 'cried all the way to the
bank'.
Collier's 17 Sept. 1954 (Cf. Liberace's *Autobiography* (1973)
ch. 2: 'When the reviews are bad I tell my staff that they can
join me as I cry all the way to the bank')

Beatrice Lillie 1894–1989

8 At one early, glittering dinner party at Buckingham
Palace, the trembling hand of a nervous waiter spilled
a spoonful of decidedly hot soup down my neck. How
could I manage to ease his mind and turn his
embarrassed apologies into a smile, except to put on
a pretended frown and say, without thinking: 'Never
darken my Dior again!'
Every Other Inch a Lady (1973) ch. 14

R. M. Lindner 1914–1956

9 Rebel without a cause . . . the hypnoanalysis of
a criminal psychopath.
Title of book (1944)

Audrey Erskine Lindop 1920–1986

10 The singer not the song.
Title of book (1953)

Howard Lindsay 1888–1968 and Russel Crouse 1893–1966

11 Call me madam.
Title of musical (1950; music by Irving Berlin)

Vachel Lindsay 1879–1931

12 Booth led boldly with his big brass drum—
(Are you washed in the blood of the Lamb?)
The Saints smiled gravely and they said: 'He's come.'
(Are you washed in the blood of the Lamb?)
Walking Lepers followed, rank on rank,
Lurching bravos from the ditches dank,
Drabs from the alleyways and drug fiends pale—
Minds still passion-ridden, soul-power frail:—
Vermin-eaten saints with moldy breath,
Unwashed legions with the ways of Death—
(Are you washed in the blood of the Lamb?)
Collected Poems (1934) 'General William Booth Enters into
Heaven' (1913)

13 Booth died blind and still by faith he trod,
Eyes still dazzled by the ways of God.
Collected Poems (1934) 'General William Booth Enters into
Heaven' (1913)

14 Then I saw the congo, creeping through the black,
Cutting through the forest with a golden track.
The Congo and Other Poems (1922) 'The Congo' (1914) pt. 1

Eric Linklater 1899–1974

15 'There won't be any revolution in America,' said
Isadore. Nikitin agreed. 'The people are all too clean.
They spend all their time changing their shirts and
washing themselves. You can't feel fierce and
revolutionary in a bathroom.'
Juan in America (1931) bk. 5, pt. 3

Art Linkletter 1912–

16 The four stages of man are infancy, childhood,
adolescence and obsolescence.
A Child's Garden of Misinformation (1965) ch. 8

Walter Lippmann 1889–1974

17 Mr Coolidge's genius for inactivity is developed to
a very high point. It is far from being an indolent
activity. It is a grim, determined, alert inactivity which
keeps Mr Coolidge occupied constantly. Nobody has
ever worked harder at inactivity, with such force of
character, with such unremitting attention to detail,
with such conscientious devotion to the task.
Inactivity is a political philosophy and a party program
with Mr Coolidge.
Men of Destiny (1927) p. 12

18 The final test of a leader is that he leaves behind him in
other men the conviction and the will to carry on.
New York Herald Tribune 14 Apr. 1945

Joan Littlewood and Charles Chilton 1914–

1 Oh what a lovely war.
   Title of stage show (1963)

Maxim Litvinov 1876–1951

2 Peace is indivisible.
   Note to the Allies, 25 Feb. 1920, in A. U. Pope *Maxim Litvinoff* (1943) p. 234

Ken Livingstone 1945–

3 The problem is that many MPs never see the London that exists beyond the wine bars and brothels of Westminster.
   The Times 19 Feb. 1987

Richard Llewellyn (Richard Dafydd Vivian Llewellyn Lloyd) 1907–1983

4 How green was my valley.
   Title of book (1939)

Jack Llewelyn-Davies 1894–1959

5 *Little Mary* [by J.M. Barrie] opened at Wyndham's Theatre on September 24th, 1903, and . . . it contained a sprinkling of lines contributed by the boys, including a remark from Jack [Llewelyn-Davies]. When stuffing himself with cakes at tea, Sylvia had warned him, 'You'll be sick tomorrow.' 'I'll be sick tonight,' replied Jack cheerily.
   Andrew Birkin *J. M. Barrie and the Lost Boys* (1979) p. 99

David Lloyd George (Earl Lloyd-George of Dwyfor) 1863–1945

6 Negotiating with de Valera . . . is like trying to pick up mercury with a fork.
   In M. J. MacManus *Eamon de Valera* (1944) ch. 6 (to which de Valera replied, 'Why doesn't he use a spoon?')

7 This [The House of Lords] is the leal and trusty mastiff which is to watch over our interests, but which runs away at the first snarl of the trade unions. . . . A mastiff? It is the right hon. Gentleman's [Mr Balfour's] poodle.
   Hansard 26 June 1907, col. 1429

8 Those are the conditions of the armistice. Thus at eleven o'clock this morning came to an end the cruellest and most terrible War that has ever scourged mankind. I hope we may say that thus, this fateful morning, came to an end all wars.
   Hansard 11 Nov. 1918, col. 2463. Cf. H. G. Wells 225:4

9 Winston was nervous before a speech, but he was not shy. L.G. said he himself was both nervous and shy. Winston would go up to his Creator and say that he would very much like to meet His Son, about Whom he had heard a great deal and, if possible, would like to call on the Holy Ghost. Winston *loved* meeting people.
   A. J. Sylvester *Diary* 2 Jan. 1937, in *Life with Lloyd George* (1975) p. 166

10 He [Ramsay MacDonald] had sufficient conscience to bother him, but not sufficient to keep him straight.
    In A. J. Sylvester *Life with Lloyd George* (1975) p. 216

11 A fully-equipped duke costs as much to keep up as two Dreadnoughts; and dukes are just as great a terror and they last longer.
    Speech at Newcastle, 9 Oct. 1909, in *The Times* 11 Oct. 1909

12 The great peaks of honour we had forgotten—Duty, Patriotism, and—clad in glittering white—the great pinnacle of Sacrifice, pointing like a rugged finger to Heaven.
    Speech at Queen's Hall, London, 19 Sept. 1914, in *The Times* 20 Sept. 1914

13 What is our task? To make Britain a fit country for heroes to live in.
    Speech at Wolverhampton, 23 Nov. 1918, in *The Times* 25 Nov. 1918

14 M. Clemenceau . . . is one of the greatest living orators, but he knows that the finest eloquence is that which gets things done and the worst is that which delays them.
    Speech at Paris Peace Conference, 18 Jan. 1919, in *The Times* 20 Jan. 1919

15 The world is becoming like a lunatic asylum run by lunatics.
    In *Observer* 8 Jan. 1933

16 What were politicians? A politician was a person with whose politics you did not agree. When you did agree, he was a statesman.
    Speech at Central Hall, Westminster, 2 July 1935, in *The Times* 3 July 1935

David Lodge 1935–

17 Literature is mostly about having sex and not much about having children. Life is the other way round.
    The British Museum is Falling Down (1965) ch. 4

Frank Loesser 1910–1969

18 See what the boys in the back room will have And tell them I'm having the same.
    Boys in the Back Room (1939 song; music by Frederick Hollander)

19 I'd love to get you On a slow boat to China, All to myself, alone.
    Slow Boat to China (1948 song)

20 Spring will be a little late this year.
    Title of song (1944)

Jack London (John Griffith London) 1876–1916

21 The call of the wild.
    Title of novel (1903)

Alice Roosevelt Longworth 1884–1980

22 [Warren] Harding was not a bad man. He was just a slob.
    Crowded Hours (1933) ch. 20

1 If you haven't got anything good to say about anyone
   come and sit by me.
   > Maxim embroidered on a cushion, in Michael Teague *Mrs L:
   > Conversations with Alice Roosevelt Longworth* (1981) p. xi

Frederick Lonsdale 1881–1954

2 'Don't keep finishing your sentences,' he said to me
   once when I was telling him something; 'I'm not
   a bloody fool.'
   > Frances Donaldson *Child of the Twenties* (1959) p. 11

Anita Loos 1893–1981

3 So this gentleman said a girl with brains ought to do
   something with them besides think.
   > *Gentlemen Prefer Blondes* (1925) ch. 1

4 Gentlemen always seem to remember blondes.
   > *Gentlemen Prefer Blondes* (1925) ch. 1

5 She said she always believed in the old addage, 'Leave
   them while you're looking good.'
   > *Gentlemen Prefer Blondes* (1925) ch. 1

6 So I really think that American gentlemen are the best
   after all, because kissing your hand may make you feel
   very very good but a diamond and safire bracelet lasts
   forever.
   > *Gentlemen Prefer Blondes* (1925) ch. 4

7 You have got to be a Queen to get away with a hat like
   that.
   > *Gentlemen Prefer Blondes* (1925) ch. 4

8 Fun is fun but no girl wants to laugh all of the time.
   > *Gentlemen Prefer Blondes* (1925) ch. 4

9 So then Dr Froyd said that all I needed was to cultivate
   a few inhibitions and get some sleep.
   > *Gentlemen Prefer Blondes* (1925) ch. 5

10 So then he said that he used to be a member of the
    choir himself, so who was he to cast the first rock at
    a girl like I.
    > *Gentlemen Prefer Blondes* (1925) ch. 5

Frederico García Lorca 1899–1936

11 *A las cinco de la tarde.*
    Eran las cinco en punto de la tarde.
    Un niño trajo la blanca sábana
    a las cinco de la tarde.

    At five in the afternoon.
    It was exactly five in the afternoon.
    A boy brought the white sheet
    at five in the afternoon.
    > *Llanto por Ignacio Sánchez Mejías* (Lament for Ignacio Sánchez
    > Mejías, 1935) 'La Cogida y la muerte'

12 *Verde que te quiero verde.*
    Verde viento.
    Verde ramas.
    El barco sobre la mar
    y el caballo en la montaña.

    Green how I love you green.
    Green wind.
    Green boughs.

The ship on the sea
and the horse on the mountain.
> *Romancero Gitano* (Gypsy Romances, 1924–1927) 'Romance
> Sonámbulo'

Konrad Lorenz 1903–1989

13 *Überhaupt ist es für den Forscher ein guter Morgensport,*
    täglich vor dem Frühstück eine Lieblingshypothese
    einzustampfen—das erhält jung.

    It is a good morning exercise for a research scientist to
    discard a pet hypothesis every day before breakfast. It
    keeps him young.
    > *Das sogennante Böse* (The So-Called Evil, 1963; translated
    > 1966 by Marjorie Latzke as *On Aggression*) ch. 2

Joe Louis 1914–1981

14 He [Billy Conn] can run, but he can't hide.
    > In *New York Herald Tribune* 9 June 1946

Terry Lovelock

15 Heineken refreshes the parts other beers cannot reach.
    > Slogan for Heineken lager, 1975 onwards, in Nigel Rees
    > *Slogans* (1982) p. 16

Robert Loveman 1864–1923

16 It isn't raining rain to me,
    It's raining violets.
    > *Gates of Silence* (1903) 'Song' (words adapted by Buddy De
    > Sylva in 1921 song *April Showers*; music by Louis Silver)

David Low 1891–1963

17 I have never met anyone who wasn't against war.
    Even Hitler and Mussolini were, according to
    themselves.
    > *New York Times Magazine* 10 Feb. 1946

Amy Lowell 1874–1925

18 And the softness of my body will be guarded by
        embrace
    By each button, hook, and lace.
    For the man who should loose me is dead,
    Fighting with the Duke in Flanders,
    In a pattern called a war.
    Christ! What are patterns for?
    > *Men, Women and Ghosts* (1916) 'Patterns'

19 I [Death] was astonished to see him in Baghdad, for
    I had an appointment with him tonight in Samarra.
    > *Sheppy* (1933) act 3

20 All books are either dreams or swords,
    You can cut, or you can drug, with words.
    > *Sword Blades and Poppy Seed* (1914) title poem

Robert Lowell 1917–1977

21 We feel the machine slipping from our hands
    As if someone else were steering;

If we see light at the end of the tunnel,
It's the light of the oncoming train.
  Day by Day (1977) 'Since 1939'. Cf. Paul Dickson

1 My eyes have seen what my hand did.
  The Dolphin (1973) 'Dolphin'

2 The aquarium is gone.
  Everywhere,
  giant finned cars nose forward like fish;
  a savage servility
  slides by on grease.
    For the Union Dead (1964) title poem

3 These are the tranquillized *Fifties*,
  and I am forty. Ought I to regret my seed-time?
  I was a fire-breathing Catholic C.O.,
  and made my manic statement,
  telling off the state and president, and then
  sat waiting sentence in the bull pen
  beside a Negro boy with curlicues
  of marijuana in his hair.
    Life Studies (1956) 'Memories of West Street and Lepke'

4 I saw the spiders marching through the air,
  Swimming from tree to tree that mildewed day
  In latter August when the hay
  Came creaking to the barn.
    Poems 1938–1949 (1950) 'Mr Edwards and the Spider'

5 This is death.
  To die and know it. This is the Black Widow, death.
    Poems 1938–1949 (1950) 'Mr Edwards and the Spider'

6 The Lord survives the rainbow of His will.
    Poems 1938–1949 (1950) 'The Quaker Graveyard in Nantucket'

L. S. Lowry 1887–1976

7 I'm a simple man, and I use simple materials.
    In Mervyn Levy *Paintings of L. S. Lowry* (1975) p. 11

Malcolm Lowry 1909–1957

8 How alike are the groans of love to those of the dying.
    Under the Volcano (1947) ch. 12

E. V. Lucas 1868–1938

9 Poor G.K.C., his day is past—
  Now God will know the truth at last.
    Mock epitaph for G. K. Chesterton, in Dudley Barker
    G. K. Chesterton (1973) ch. 16

10 There can be no defence like elaborate courtesy.
    Reading, Writing and Remembering (1932) ch. 8

11 I have noticed that the people who are late are often so
   much jollier than the people who have to wait for them.
    365 Days and One More (1926) p. 277

George Lucas 1944–

12 The Empire strikes back.
    Title of film (1980)

13 Then man your ships, and may the force be with you.
    Star Wars: from the Adventures of Luke Skywalker (1976)
    ch. 11

Clare Booth Luce 1903–

14 But if God had wanted us to think just with our
   wombs, why did He give us a brain?
    Life 16 Oct. 1970

Joanna Lumley

15 To be a judge you don't have to know about books,
   you have to be skilled at picking shrapnel out of your
   head.
    In *Observer* 17 Nov. 1985 (comment on the Booker Prize)

Sir Edwin Lutyens 1869–1944

16 I had proposed that we should lunch together at the
   Garrick Club, because I had obviously to ask father if
   he had any serious objection to the writing or the
   writer of this essay. But, when I broached the matter,
   he merely mumbled in obvious embarrassment: 'Oh,
   my!'—just as his father was used to do. Then, as the
   fish was served, he looked at me seriously over the
   rims of his two pairs of spectacles and remarked: ' The
   piece of cod passeth all understanding'!
    Robert Lutyens *Sir Edwin Lutyens* (1942) p. 74

Rosa Luxemburg 1871–1919

17 *Freiheit ist immer nur Freiheit des anders Denkenden.*

   Freedom is always and exclusively freedom for the one
   who thinks differently.
    Die Russische Revolution (The Russian Revolution, 1918)
    sec. 4

Lady Lytton (Pamela Frances Audrey, Countess of Lytton) 1874–1971

18 The first time you meet Winston [Churchill] you see
   all his faults and the rest of your life you spend in
   discovering his virtues.
    Letter to Sir Edward Marsh, Dec. 1905, in Edward Marsh
    A Number of People (1939) ch. 8

Alexander McArthur and H. Kingsley Long

19 Battles and sex are the only free diversions in slum
   life. Couple them with drink, which costs money, and
   you have the three principal outlets for that escape
   complex which is for ever working in the tenement
   dweller's subconscious mind.
    No Mean City (1935) ch. 4

Charles MacArthur 1895–1956 and Ben Hecht 1894–1964

20 The son of a bitch stole my watch!
    Front Page (1928) last line

General Douglas MacArthur 1880–1964

21 In war, indeed, there can be no substitute for victory.
    Congressional Record 19 Apr. 1951, vol. 97, pt. 3, p. 4125

1 The President of the United States ordered me to break through the Japanese lines and proceed from Corregidor to Australia for the purpose, as I understand it, of organizing the American offensive against Japan. A primary purpose of this is relief of the Philippines. I came through and I shall return.

Statement in Adelaide, 20 Mar. 1942, in *New York Times* 21 Mar. 1942, p. 1

Dame Rose Macaulay 1881–1958

2 'Take my camel, dear,' said my aunt Dot, as she climbed down from this animal on her return from High Mass.

Towers of Trebizond (1956) p. 9

General Anthony McAuliffe 1898–1975

3 Nuts!

Response to German demand to surrender at Bastogne, Belgium, 22 Dec. 1944, in *New York Times* 28 Dec. 1944, p. 4, and 30 Dec. 1944, p. 1

Sir Desmond MacCarthy 1877–1952

4 A biographer is an artist who is on oath, and anyone who knows anything about artists, knows that that is almost a contradiction in terms.

Memories (1953) 'Lytton Strachey and the Art of Biography'

5 The whole of art is an appeal to a reality which is not without us but in our minds.

Theatre (1954) 'Diction and Realism'

Joe McCarthy

6 You made me love you,
I didn't want to do it.

You Made Me Love You (1913 song; music by James V. Monaco)

Joseph McCarthy 1908–1957

7 McCarthyism is Americanism with its sleeves rolled.

Speech in Wisconsin, 1952, in Richard Rovere *Senator Joe McCarthy* (1973) p. 8

Mary McCarthy 1912–1989

8 I once said in an interview that every word she [Lillian Hellman] writes is a lie, including 'and' and 'the'.

New York Times 16 Feb. 1980, p. 12

9 When an American heiress wants to buy a man, she at once crosses the Atlantic. The only really materialistic people I have ever met have been Europeans.

On the Contrary (1961) 'America the Beautiful'

10 The immense popularity of American movies abroad demonstrates that Europe is the unfinished negative of which America is the proof.

On the Contrary (1961) 'America the Beautiful'

11 There are no new truths, but only truths that have not been recognized by those who have perceived them without noticing. A truth is something that everyone can be shown to know and to have known, as people say, all along.

On the Contrary (1961) 'Vita Activa'

12 In violence, we forget who we are.

On the Contrary (1961) 'Characters in Fiction'

13 If someone tells you he is going to make a 'realistic decision', you immediately understand that he has resolved to do something bad.

On the Contrary (1961) 'American Realist Playwrights'

Paul McCartney 1942–

14 He [John Lennon] could be a manœuvring swine, which no one ever realized.

In Hunter Davies *The Beatles* (1985) p. 469

See also JOHN LENNON

David McCord 1897–

15 By and by
God caught his eye.

Bay Window Ballads (1935) 'Remainders' (epitaph for a waiter)

Horace McCoy 1897–1955

16 They shoot horses don't they.

Title of novel (1935)

John McCrae 1872–1918

17 In Flanders fields the poppies blow
Between the crosses, row on row,
That mark our place; and in the sky
The larks, still bravely singing, fly
Scarce heard amid the guns below.

Punch 8 Dec. 1915 'In Flanders Fields'

18 To you from failing hands we throw
The torch; be yours to hold it high.
If ye break faith with us who die
We shall not sleep, though poppies grow.

Punch 8 Dec. 1915, 'In Flanders Fields'

Carson McCullers 1917–1967

19 The heart is a lonely hunter.

Title of novel (1940; taken from *The Lonely Hunter* (1896), a poem by 'Fiona Macleod' (William Sharp): 'My heart is a lonely hunter that hunts on a lonely hill')

Derek McCulloch 1897–1967

20 Goodnight, children . . . everywhere.

Children's Hour (BBC Radio programme; closing words normally spoken by 'Uncle Mac' in the 1930s and 1940s)

Hugh MacDiarmid (Christopher Murray Grieve) 1892–1978

21 I'll ha'e nae hauf-way hoose, but aye be whaur
Extremes meet—it's the only way I ken

To dodge the curst conceit o' bein' richt
That damns the vast majority o' men.
 A Drunk Man Looks at the Thistle (1926) p. 6

1 He's no a man ava',
And lacks a proper pride,
Gin less than a' the world
Can ser' him for a bride!
 A Drunk Man Looks at the Thistle (1926) p. 36

Ramsay MacDonald 1866–1937

2 Yes, tomorrow every Duchess in London will be
wanting to kiss me!
 Comment after forming the National Government, 25 Aug.
 1931, in Philip Viscount Snowden *Autobiography* (1934)
 vol. 2, p. 957

3 If God were to come to me and say 'Ramsay, would you
rather be a country gentleman than a prime minister?',
I should reply, 'Please God, a country gentleman.'
 In Harold Nicolson *Diary* 5 Oct. 1930, in *Diaries and Letters*
 (1966) p. 57

4 We hear war called murder. It is not: it is suicide.
 In *Observer* 4 May 1930

A. G. Macdonell 1889–

5 England, their England.
 Title of novel (1933)

John McEnroe 1959–

6 You cannot be serious!
 Said to tennis umpire at Wimbledon, early 1980s

7 This must be the pits.
 Comment after disagreement with Wimbledon umpire, in
 Sun 23 June 1981

Arthur McEwen d. 1907

8 'What we're after,' said Arthur McEwen, 'is the
'gee-whiz' emotion.' Pressed for further explanation,
he said: 'We run our paper so that when the reader
opens it he says: "Gee-whiz!" An issue is a failure
which doesn't make him say that.'
 Colliers 18 Feb. 1911

Roger McGough 1937–

9 Let me die a youngman's death
Not a clean & in-between-
The-sheets, holy-water death,
Not a famous-last-words
Peaceful out-of-breath death.
 'Let Me Die a Youngman's Death' in Edward Lucie Smith (ed.)
 The Liverpool Scene (1967) p. 47

10 Girls are simply the prettiest things
My cat and i believe
And we're always saddened
When it's time for them to leave

We watch them titivating
(that often takes a while)
and though they keep us waiting
My cat and i just smile

We like to see them to the door
Say how sad it couldn't last
Then my cat and i go back inside
And talk about the past.
 Watchwords (1969) 'My Cat and i'

Sir Ian MacGregor 1912–

11 People are now discovering the price of
insubordination and insurrection. And boy, are we
going to make it stick!
 Comment during the coal-miners' strike, in *Sunday Telegraph*
 10 Mar. 1985

Jimmy McGregor

12 Oh, he's football crazy, he's football mad
And the football it has robbed him o' the wee bit sense
he had.
And it would take a dozen skivvies, his clothes to wash
and scrub,
Since our Jock became a member of that terrible
football club.
 Football Crazy (1960 song)

Dennis McHarrie

13 'He died who loved to live,' they'll say,
'Unselfishly so we might have today!'
Like hell! He fought because he had to fight;
He died that's all. It was his unlucky night.
 In V. Selwyn et al *Return to Oasis* (1980) pt. 3, p. 172 'Luck'

Colin MacInnes 1914–1976

14 And I thought, 'My lord, one thing is certain, and
that's that they'll make musicals one day about the
glamour-studded 1950s.' And I thought, my heaven,
one thing is certain too, I'm miserable.
 Absolute Beginners (1959) p. 81

Claude McKay 1890–1948

15 If we must die, let it not be like hogs
Hunted and penned in an inglorious spot,
While round us bark the mad and hungry dogs,
Making their mock at our accursed lot.
If we must die, O let us nobly die,
So that our precious blood may not be shed
In vain; then even the monsters we defy
Shall be constrained to honor us though dead!
O, kinsmen! we must meet the common foe!
Though far outnumbered let us show us brave,
And for their thousand blows deal one deathblow!
What though before us lies the open grave?
Like men we'll face the murderous, cowardly pack,
Pressed to the wall, dying, but fighting back!
 Selected Poems (1953) 'If We Must Die'

Sir Compton Mackenzie 1883–1972

16 Women do not find it difficult nowadays to behave like
men, but they often find it extremely difficult to
behave like gentlemen.
 Literature in My Time (1933) ch. 22

1 You are offered a piece of bread and butter that feels like a damp handkerchief and sometimes, when cucumber is added to it, like a wet one.
   Vestal Fire (1927) bk. 1, ch. 3

Joyce McKinney 1950–

2 I loved Kirk so much, I would have skied down Mount Everest in the nude with a carnation up my nose.
   Evidence given at Epsom Magistrates' Court, 6 Dec. 1977, in *The Times* 7 Dec. 1977

Alexander Maclaren 1826–1910

3 'The Church is an anvil which has worn out many hammers', and the story of the first collision is, in essentials, the story of all.
   Expositions of Holy Scripture: Acts of the Apostles (1907) ch. 4

Alistair Maclean 1923–1987

4 Where eagles dare.
   Title of novel (1967)

Archibald MacLeish 1892–1982

5 A Poem should be palpable and mute
As a globed fruit

Dumb
As old medallions to the thumb

Silent as the sleeve-worn stone
Of casement ledges where the moss has grown—

A poem should be wordless
As the flight of birds
   Streets in the Moon (1926) 'Ars Poetica'

6 A poem should not mean
But be.
   Streets in the Moon (1926) 'Ars Poetica'

Irene Rutherford McLeod 1891–1964

7 I'm a lean dog, a keen dog, a wild dog, and lone;
I'm a rough dog, a tough dog, hunting on my own;
I'm a bad dog, a mad dog, teasing silly sheep;
I love to sit and bay at the moon, to keep fat souls from sleep.
   Songs to Save a Soul (1915) 'Lone Dog'

Marshall McLuhan 1911–1980

8 The new electronic interdependence recreates the world in the image of a global village.
   Gutenberg Galaxy (1962) p. 31

9 One matter Englishmen don't think in the least funny is their happy consciousness of possessing a deep sense of humour.
   Mechanical Bride (1951) 'The Ballet Luce'

10 The medium is the message.
   Understanding Media (1964) title of ch. 1

11 The name of a man is a numbing blow from which he never recovers.
   Understanding Media (1964) p. 32

12 The car has become an article of dress without which we feel uncertain, unclad and incomplete in the urban compound.
   Understanding Media (1964) p. 217

13 The car has become the carapace, the protective and aggressive shell, of urban and suburban man.
   Understanding Media (1964) p. 224

Ed McMahon 1923–

14 And now . . . heeeeere's Johnny!
   Introduction to Johnny Carson on NBC-TV's *Tonight* show (from 1961; also used by Jack Nicholson in the 1980 film *The Shining*)

Harold Macmillan (Lord Stockton) 1894–1986

15 He [Aneurin Bevan] enjoys prophesying the imminent fall of the capitalist system and is prepared to play a part, any part, in its burial, except that of mute.
   In Michael Foot *Aneurin Bevan* (1962) pt. 1, ch. 5

16 After a long experience of politics I have never found that there is any inhibition caused by ignorance as regards criticism.
   Hansard 11 July 1963, col. 1411

17 I was determined that no British government should be brought down by the action of two tarts.
   Comment on the Profumo affair, July 1963, in Anthony Sampson *Macmillan* (1967) p. 243

18 There ain't gonna be no war.
   Said at London press conference, 24 July 1955, after Geneva summit, in *News Chronicle* 25 July 1955

19 He [a Foreign Secretary] is forever poised between a cliché and an indiscretion.
   In *Newsweek* 30 Apr. 1956

20 Even before Mr Heath's troubles of 1972 and 1974, Mr Harold Macmillan was fond of remarking that there were three bodies no sensible man directly challenged: the Roman Catholic Church, the Brigade of Guards and the National Union of Mineworkers.
   Alan Watkins in *Observer* 22 Feb. 1981

21 The most striking of all the impressions I have formed since I left London a month ago is of the strength of this African national consciousness. In different places it takes different forms, but it is happening everywhere. The wind of change is blowing through this continent, and, whether we like it or not, this growth of national consciousness is a political fact. We must all accept it as a fact, and our national policies must take account of it.
   Speech at Cape Town, 3 Feb. 1960, *Pointing the Way* (1972) p. 475

22 Indeed, let us be frank about it: most of our people have never had it so good. Go around the country, go to the industrial towns, go to the farms, and you will see a state of prosperity such as we have never had in my lifetime—nor indeed ever in the history of this country. What is beginning to worry some of us is, Is it too good to be true?—or perhaps I should say, Is it too good to last?
   Speech at Bedford, 20 July 1957, in *The Times* 22 July 1957

1 I thought the best thing to do was to settle up these
little local difficulties, and then turn to the wider vision
of the Commonwealth.
   Statement at London airport on leaving for Commonwealth
   tour, 7 Jan. 1958, following the resignation of the
   Chancellor of the Exchequer and others, in *The Times* 8 Jan.
   1958

2 As usual the Liberals offer a mixture of sound and
original ideas. Unfortunately none of the sound ideas is
original and none of the original ideas is sound.
   Speech to London Conservatives, 7 Mar. 1961, in *The Times*
   8 Mar. 1961

3 First of all the Georgian silver goes, and then all that
nice furniture that used to be in the saloon. Then the
Canalettos go.
   Speech on privatization to the Tory Reform Group, 8 Nov.
   1985, in *The Times* 9 Nov. 1985

Louis MacNeice 1907–1963

4 Better authentic mammon than a bogus god.
   Autumn Journal (1939) p. 49

5 The sunlight on the garden
Hardens and grows cold,
We cannot cage the minute
Within its net of gold,
When all is told
We cannot beg for pardon.
   Earth Compels (1938) 'Sunlight on the Garden'

6 Our freedom as free lances
Advances towards its end;
The earth compels, upon it
Sonnets and birds descend;
And soon, my friend,
We shall have no time for dances.
   Earth Compels (1938) 'Sunlight on the Garden'

7 It's no go the merrygoround, it's no go the rickshaw,
All we want is a limousine and a ticket for the
   peepshow.
   Earth Compels (1938) 'Bagpipe Music'

8 It's no go the picture palace, it's no go the stadium,
It's no go the country cot with a pot of pink geraniums,
It's no go the Government grants, it's no go the
   elections,
Sit on your arse for fifty years and hang your hat on
   a pension.
   Earth Compels (1938) 'Bagpipe Music'

9 It's no go my honey love, it's no go my poppet;
Work your hands from day to day, the winds will blow
   the profit.
The glass is falling hour by hour, the glass will fall for
   ever,
But if you break the bloody glass you won't hold up the
   weather.
   Earth Compels (1938) 'Bagpipe Music'

10 I take a rather common-sense view of poetry. I think
that the poet is a sensitive instrument designed to
record anything which interests his mind or affects his
emotions.
   Listener 27 July 1939

11 By a high star our course is set,
Our end is Life. Put out to sea.
   London Magazine Feb. 1964 'Thalassa' (poem published
   posthumously)

12 And under the totem poles—the ancient terror—
Between the enormous fluted Ionic columns
There seeps from heavily jowled or hawk-like foreign
   faces
The guttural sorrow of the refugees.
   Plant and Phantom (1941) 'The British Museum Reading
   Room'

13 Time was away and somewhere else,
There were two glasses and two chairs
And two people with the one pulse
(Somebody stopped the moving stairs):
Time was away and somewhere else.
   Plant and Phantom (1941) 'Meeting Point'

14 So they were married—to be the more together—
And found they were never again so much together,
Divided by the morning tea,
By the evening paper,
By children and tradesmen's bills.
   Plant and Phantom (1941) 'Les Sylphides'

15 Crumbling between the fingers, under the feet,
Crumbling behind the eyes,
Their world gives way and dies
And something twangs and breaks at the end of the
   street.
   Plant and Phantom (1941) 'Débâcle'

16 Down the road someone is practising scales,
The notes like little fishes vanish with a wink of tails,
Man's heart expands to tinker with his car
For this is Sunday morning, Fate's great bazaar.
   Poems (1935) 'Sunday Morning'

17 World is crazier and more of it than we think,
Incorrigibly plural. I peel and portion
A tangerine and spit the pips and feel
The drunkenness of things being various.
   Poems (1935) 'Snow'

18 I am not yet born; O fill me
With strength against those who would freeze my
humanity, would dragoon me into a lethal automaton,
would make me a cog in a machine, a thing with
one face, a thing, and against all those
who would dissipate my entirety, would
blow me like thistledown hither and
thither or hither and thither
like water held in the
hands would spill me.
Let them not make me a stone and let them not spill
   me,
Otherwise kill me.
   Springboard (1944) 'Prayer Before Birth'

Salvador de Madariaga 1886–1978

19 Since, in the main, it is not armaments that cause
wars but wars (or the fears thereof) that cause
armaments, it follows that every nation will at every
moment strive to keep its armament in an efficient
state as required by its fear, otherwise styled security.
   Morning Without Noon (1974) pt. 1, ch. 9

Maurice Maeterlinck 1862–1949

1 *Il n'y a pas de morts.*

   There are no dead.
   L'Oiseau bleu (The Blue Bird, 1909) act 4

John Gillespie Magee 1922–1941

2 Oh! I have slipped the surly bonds of earth
   And danced the skies on laughter-silvered wings;
   Sunward I've climbed, and joined the tumbling mirth
   Of sun-split clouds—and done a hundred things
   You have not dreamed of—wheeled and soared and
      swung
   High in the sunlit silence. Hov'ring there
   I've chased the shouting wind along, and flung
   My eager craft through footless halls of air.

   Up, up the long, delirious, burning blue
   I've topped the wind-swept heights with easy grace,
   Where never lark, nor even eagle flew—
   And, while with silent lifting mind I've trod
   The high, untrespassed sanctity of space,
   Put out my hand and touched the face of God.
   In K. Rhys *More Poems from the Forces* (1943) 'High Flight'

Magnus Magnusson 1929–

3 I've started so I'll finish.
   Said when a contestant's time runs out while a question is
   being put in *Mastermind*, BBC television (1972 onwards)

Sir John Pentland Mahaffy 1839–1919

4 In Ireland the inevitable never happens and the
   unexpected constantly occurs.
   In W. B. Stanford and R. B. McDowell *Mahaffy* (1971) ch. 4

Gustav Mahler 1860–1911

5 On seeing Niagara Falls, Mahler exclaimed:
   'Fortissimo at last!'
   K. Blaukopf *Gustav Mahler* (1973) ch. 8

Derek Mahon 1941–

6 'I am just going outside and may be some time.'
   The others nod, pretending not to know.
   At the heart of the ridiculous, the sublime.
   Antarctica (1985) title poem (for the first line, cf. Captain
   Lawrence Oates)

Norman Mailer 1923–

7 Sentimentality is the emotional promiscuity of those
   who have no sentiment.
   Cannibals and Christians (1966) p. 51

8 Hip is the sophistication of the wise primitive in a giant
   jungle.
   Dissent Summer 1957, p. 281

9 Once a newspaper touches a story, the facts are lost
   forever, even to the protagonists.
   Esquire June 1960

10 The horror of the Twentieth Century was the size of
   each event, and the paucity of its reverberation.
   A Fire on the Moon (1970) pt. 1, ch. 2

11 So we think of Marilyn who was every man's love affair
   with America, Marilyn Monroe who was blonde and
   beautiful and had a sweet little rinky-dink of a voice
   and all the cleanliness of all the clean American
   backyards.
   Marilyn (1973) p. 15

12 Ultimately a hero is a man who would argue with the
   Gods, and so awakens devils to contest his vision.
   The Presidential Papers (1976) Special Preface to the 1st
   Berkeley Edition

Bernard Malamud 1914–1986

13 I think I said 'All men are Jews except they don't
   know it.' I doubt I expected anyone to take the
   statement literally. But I think it's an understandable
   statement and a metaphoric way of indicating how
   history, sooner or later, treats all men.
   Leslie and Joyce Field (ed.) *Bernard Malamud* (1975) 'An
   interview with Bernard Malamud' p. 11

14 The past exudes legend: one can't make pure clay of
   time's mud. There is no life that can be recaptured
   wholly; as it was. Which is to say that all biography is
   ultimately fiction.
   Dubin's Lives (1979) p. 20

George Leigh Mallory 1886–1924

15 Because it's there.
   Response to question 'Why do you want to climb Mount
   Everest?', in *New York Times* 18 Mar. 1923

André Malraux 1901–1976

16 *L'art est un anti-destin.*

   Art is a revolt against fate.
   Les Voix du silence (Voices of Silence, 1951) pt. 4, ch. 7

Lord Mancroft (Baron Mancroft) 1914–

17 Our soft grass and mild climate has enabled us to
   foster new sports. Racing, golf, football and
   particularly cricket—a game which the English, not
   being a spiritual people, have invented in order to give
   themselves some conception of eternity—all owe their
   development to our climate.
   Bees in Some Bonnets (1979) p. 185

Winnie Mandela 1936–

18 We are going to dismantle apartheid ourselves. That
   programme will be brought to you by the ANC.
   Together, hand in hand, with that stick of matches,
   with our necklace, we shall liberate this country.
   Speech in black townships, 14 Apr. 1986, in *Guardian*
   15 Apr. 1986

Osip Mandelstam 1891–1938

19 Perhaps my whisper was already born before my lips.
   Selected Poems (1973, trans. by D. McDuff) p. 129

Herman J. Mankiewicz 1897–1953 and Orson Welles 1915–1985

1 KATHERINE: What's Rosebud?
RAYMOND: That's what he said when he died. . . .
LOUISE: If you could have found out what Rosebud meant, I bet that would've explained everything.
THOMPSON: No, I don't think so. No. Mr Kane was a man who got everything he wanted, and then lost it. Maybe Rosebud was something he couldn't get or something he lost. Anyway, it wouldn't have explained anything. I don't think any word can explain a man's life. No, I guess Rosebud is just a piece in a jigsaw puzzle, a missing piece.
Citizen Kane (1941 film)

Joseph L. Mankiewicz 1909–

2 Fasten your seat-belts, it's going to be a bumpy night.
All About Eve (1950 film; words spoken by Bette Davis)

Thomas Mann 1875–1955

3 *Der Tod in Venedig.*
Death in Venice.
Title of novella (1912)

4 *Tatsächlich ist unser Sterben mehr eine Angelegenheit der Weiterlebenden als unserer selbst.*
It is a fact that a man's dying is more the survivor's affair than his own.
Der Zauberberg (The Magic Mountain, 1924) ch. 6, pt. 8

Katherine Mansfield (Kathleen Mansfield Beauchamp) 1888–1923

5 E. M. Forster never gets any further than warming the teapot. He's a rare fine hand at that. Feel this teapot. Is it not beautifully warm? Yes, but there ain't going to be no tea.
Journal May 1917 (1927) p. 69

6 Whenever I prepare for a journey I prepare as though for death. Should I never return, all is in order. This is what life has taught me.
Journal 29 Jan. 1922 (1927) p. 224

7 Looking back, I imagine I was always writing. Twaddle it was, too. But better far write twaddle or anything, anything, than nothing at all.
Journal 1922 (1927) p. 243

Mao Tse-Tung 1893–1976

8 Letting a hundred flowers blossom and a hundred schools of thought contend is the policy for promoting progress in the arts and the sciences and a flourishing socialist culture in our land.
Speech at Peking, 27 Feb. 1957, in *Quotations of Chairman Mao* (1966) p. 302

9 A revolution is not the same as inviting people to dinner, or writing an essay, or painting a picture. . . . A revolution is an insurrection, an act of violence by which one class overthrows another.
Report, Mar. 1927, in *Selected Works* (1954) vol. 1, p. 27

10 The atom bomb is a paper tiger which the United States reactionaries use to scare people. It looks terrible, but in fact it isn't. Of course, the atom bomb is a weapon of mass slaughter, but the outcome of a war is decided by the people, not by one or two new types of weapon.
Interview with Anne Louise Strong, Aug. 1946, in *Selected Works* (1961) vol. 4, p. 100

11 All reactionaries are paper tigers. In appearance, the reactionaries are terrifying, but in reality they are not so powerful. From a long-term point of view, it is not the reactionaries but the people who are really powerful.
Interview with Anne Louise Strong, Aug. 1946, in *Selected Works* (1961) vol. 4, p. 100

12 Politics is war without bloodshed while war is politics with bloodshed.
Lecture, 1938, in *Selected Works* (1965) vol. 2, p. 153

13 Every Communist must grasp the truth, 'Political power grows out of the barrel of a gun'.
Speech at 6th Plenary Session of 6th Central Committee, 6 Nov. 1938, in *Selected Works* (1965) vol. 2, p. 224

Edwin Markham 1852–1940

14 Bowed by the weight of centuries he leans
Upon his hoe and gazes on the ground,
The emptiness of ages in his face,
And on his back the burden of the world.
Who made him dead to rapture and despair,
A thing that grieves not and that never hopes,
Stolid and stunned, a brother to the ox?
Man with the Hoe and Other Poems (1899) 'Man with the Hoe'

15 He drew a circle that shut me out—
Heretic, rebel, a thing to flout.
But Love and I had the wit to win:
We drew a circle that took him in!
Shoes of Happiness (1915) 'Outwitted'

Dewey 'Pigmeat' Markham 1906–1981

16 Here comes the judge.
Title of song (1968; written with Dick Alen, Bob Astor, and Sarah Harvey; subsequently a catch-phrase, often in the form 'Here come de judge')

Johnny Marks 1909–1985

17 Rudolph, the Red-Nosed Reindeer
Had a very shiny nose,
And if you ever saw it,
You would even say it glows.
Rudolph, the Red-Nosed Reindeer (1949 song), based on a Robert L. May story (1939)

Don Marquis 1878–1937

18 but wotthehell wotthehell
oh i should worry and fret
death and I will coquette
there s a dance in the old dame yet
toujours gai toujours gai.
archy and mehitabel (1927) 'the song of mehitabel'

19 procrastination is the
art of keeping
up with yesterday.
archy and mehitabel (1927) 'certain maxims of archy'

1 an optimist is a guy
that has never had
much experience.
  archy and mehitabel (1927) 'certain maxims of archy'

2 I have got you out here
in the great open spaces
where cats are cats.
  archy and mehitabel (1927) 'mehitabel has an adventure'

3 but wotthehell
archy wotthehell
it s cheerio
my deario that
pulls a lady through.
  archy and mehitabel (1927) 'cheerio, my deario'

4 but wotthehell archy wotthehell
jamais triste archy jamais triste
that is my motto.
  archy and mehitabel (1927) 'mehitabel sees paris'

5 boss there is always
a comforting thought
in time of trouble when
it is not our trouble
  archy does his part (1935) 'comforting thoughts'

6 honesty is a good
thing but
it is not profitable to
its possessor
unless it is
kept under control.
  archys life of mehitabel (1933) 'archygrams'

7 did you ever
notice that when
a politician
does get an idea
he usually
gets it all wrong.
  archys life of mehitabel (1933) no. 40 'archygrams'

8 now and then
there is a person born
who is so unlucky
that he runs into accidents
which started to happen
to somebody else.
  archys life of mehitabel (1933) 'archy says'

9 Writing a book of poetry is like dropping a rose petal
down the Grand Canyon and waiting for the echo.
  In E. Anthony *O Rare Don Marquis* (1962) p. 146

10 The art of newspaper paragraphing is to stroke
a platitude until it purrs like an epigram.
  In E. Anthony *O Rare Don Marquis* (1962) p. 354

Anthony Marriott 1931–
and Alistair Foot

11 No sex please—we're British.
  Title of play (1971)

Arthur Marshall 1910–1989

12 Oh My! Bertha's got a bang on the boko. Keep a stiff
upper lip, Bertha dear. What, knocked a tooth out?
Never mind, dear, laugh it off, laugh it off; it's all part
of life's rich pageant.
  The Games Mistress (recorded monologue, 1937)

Thomas R. Marshall 1854–1925

13 What this country needs is a really good 5-cent cigar.
  In *New York Tribune* 4 Jan. 1920, pt. 7, p. 1

Dean Martin 1917–

14 You're not drunk if you can lie on the floor without
holding on.
  In Paul Dickson *Official Rules* (1978) p. 112

Holt Marvell

15 A cigarette that bears a lipstick's traces,
An airline ticket to romantic places;
And still my heart has wings
These foolish things
Remind me of you.
  These Foolish Things Remind Me of You (1935 song; music by
  Jack Strachey and Harry Link)

Chico Marx 1891–1961

16 I wasn't kissing her, I was just whispering in her
mouth.
  In Groucho Marx and Richard J. Anobile *Marx Brothers
  Scrapbook* (1973) ch. 24

Groucho Marx 1895–1977

17 From the moment I picked up your book until I laid it
down, I was convulsed with laughter. Some day
I intend reading it.
  In Hector Arce *Groucho* (1979) p. 188 (a blurb written for
  S. J. Perelman's 1928 book *Dawn Ginsberg's Revenge*)

18 I sent the club a wire stating, PLEASE ACCEPT MY
RESIGNATION. I DON'T WANT TO BELONG TO ANY CLUB THAT
WILL ACCEPT ME AS A MEMBER.
  Groucho and Me (1959) ch. 26

19 I never forget a face, but in your case I'll be glad to
make an exception.
  In Leo Rosten *People I have Loved, Known or Admired* (1970)
  'Groucho'

Queen Mary 1867–1953

20 'Well, Mr Baldwin!' Queen Mary exclaimed, stepping
briskly into the room, her hands held out before her in
a gesture of despair, '*this* is a pretty kettle of fish!'
  James Pope-Hennessy *Life of Queen Mary* (1959) pt. 4, ch. 7
  (said on 17 Nov. 1936, after Edward VIII had told her he
  was prepared to give up the throne to marry Mrs Simpson)

21 So *that's* what hay looks like.
  James Pope-Hennessy *Life of Queen Mary* (1959) pt. 4, ch. 8
  (said at Badminton House, where she was evacuated during
  the Second World War)

Eric Maschwitz 1901–1969

1 A nightingale sang in Berkeley Square.
  Title of song (1940; music by Manning Sherwin)

John Masefield 1878–1967

2 Quinquireme of Nineveh from distant Ophir
  Rowing home to haven in sunny Palestine,
  With a cargo of ivory,
  And apes and peacocks,
  Sandalwood, cedarwood, and sweet white wine.
  Ballads (1903) 'Cargoes'

3 Dirty British coaster with a salt-caked smoke stack,
  Butting through the Channel in the mad March days,
  With a cargo of Tyne coal,
  Road-rails, pig lead,
  Firewood, ironware, and cheap tin trays.
  Ballads (1903) 'Cargoes'

4 Oh some are fond of Spanish wine, and some are fond of
    French,
  And some'll swallow tay and stuff fit only for a wench.
  Ballads (1903) 'Captain Stratton's Fancy'

5 Oh some are fond of fiddles, and a song well sung,
  And some are all for music for a lilt upon the tongue;
  But mouths were made for tankards, and for sucking at
    the bung,
  Says the old bold mate of Henry Morgan.
  Ballads (1903) 'Captain Stratton's Fancy'

6 I have seen dawn and sunset on moors and windy hills,
  Coming in solemn beauty like slow old tunes of Spain.
  Ballads (1903) 'Beauty'

7 But the loveliest things of beauty God ever has showed
    to me,
  Are her voice, and her hair, and eyes, and the dear red
    curve of her lips.
  Ballads (1903) 'Beauty'

8 One road leads to London,
  One road runs to Wales,
  My road leads me seawards
  To the white dipping sails.
  Ballads (1903) 'Roadways'

9 In the dark womb where I began
  My mother's life made me a man.
  Through all the months of human birth
  Her beauty fed my common earth.
  I cannot see, nor breathe, nor stir,
  But through the death of some of her.
  Ballads and Poems (1910) 'C.L.M.'

10 Jane brought the bowl of stewing gin
  And poured the egg and lemon in,
  And whisked it up and served it out
  While bawdy questions went about.
  Jack chucked her chin, and Jim accost her
  With bits out of the 'Maid of Gloster'.
  And fifteen arms went round her waist.
  (And then men ask, Are Barmaids Chaste?)
  The Everlasting Mercy (1911) st. 26

11 And he who gives a child a treat
  Makes joy-bells ring in Heaven's street.
  And he who gives a child a home

Builds palaces in Kingdom come,
  And she who gives a baby birth
  Brings Saviour Christ again to Earth,
  For life is joy, and mind is fruit,
  And body's precious earth and root.
  The Everlasting Mercy (1911) st. 47

12 The corn that makes the holy bread
  By which the soul of man is fed,
  The holy bread, the food unpriced,
  Thy everlasting mercy, Christ.
  The Everlasting Mercy (1911) st. 86

13 Death opens unknown doors. It is most grand to die.
  Pompey The Great (1910) act 2

14 And all the way, that wild high crying,
  To cold his blood with the thought of dying.
  Reynard the Fox (1919) pt. 2, st. 49

15 The stars grew bright in the winter sky,
  The wind came keen with a tang of frost,
  The brook was troubled for new things lost,
  The copse was happy for old things found,
  The fox came home and he went to ground.
  Reynard the Fox (1919) pt. 2, st. 137

16 I must down to the seas again, to the lonely sea and the
    sky,
  And all I ask is a tall ship and a star to steer her by,
  And the wheel's kick and the wind's song and the
    white sail's shaking,
  And a grey mist on the sea's face and a grey dawn
    breaking.
  Salt-Water Ballads (1902) 'Sea Fever'

17 I must down to the seas again, for the call of the
    running tide
  Is a wild call and a clear call that may not be denied.
  Salt-Water Ballads (1902) 'Sea Fever'

18 I must down to the seas again, to the vagrant gypsy life,
  To the gull's way and the whale's way where the
    wind's like a whetted knife;
  And all I ask is a merry yarn from a laughing
    fellow-rover,
  And quiet sleep and a sweet dream when the long
    trick's over.
  Salt-Water Ballads (1902) 'Sea Fever'

19 It's a warm wind, the west wind, full of birds' cries;
  I never hear the west wind but tears are in my eyes.
  For it comes from the west lands, the old brown hills,
  And April's in the west wind, and daffodils.
  Salt-Water Ballads (1902) 'West Wind'

20 It is good to be out on the road, and going one knows
    not where,
  Going through meadow and village, one knows not
    whither nor why.
  Salt-Water Ballads (1902) 'Tewkesbury Road'

21 In this life he laughs longest who laughs last.
  Widow in Bye Street (1912) ch. 4, p. 66

Donald Mason 1913–

22 Sighted sub, sank same.
  Radio message, 28 Jan. 1942, in *New York Times* 27 Feb.
  1942 (on sinking Japanese submarine in the Atlantic region,
  the first US naval success in the war)

Sir James Mathew 1830–1908

1 In England, justice is open to all—like the Ritz Hotel.
   In R. E. Megarry *Miscellany-at-Law* (1955) p. 254

Melissa Mathison 1950–

2 E.T. phone home.
   E.T. (1982 film; directed by Steven Spielberg)

Henri Matisse 1869–1954

3 *Ce que je rêve, c'est un art d'équilibre, de pureté, de tranquillité, sans sujet inquiétant ou préoccupant, qui soit . . . un lénifiant, un calmant cérébral, quelque chose d'analogue à un bon fauteuil qui le délasse de ses fatigues physiques.*

   What I dream of is an art of balance, of purity and serenity devoid of troubling or depressing subject matter . . . a soothing, calming influence on the mind, something like a good armchair which provides relaxation from physical fatigue.
   Notes d'un peintre (Notes of a Painter, 1908) in Dominique Fourcade *Écrits et propos sur l'art* (1972) p. 30

Reginald Maudling 1917–1979

4 There comes a time in every man's life when he must make way for an older man.
   Remark after he was dropped from the Shadow Cabinet and replaced by an older man, in *Guardian* 20 Nov. 1976

W. Somerset Maugham 1874–1965

5 Hypocrisy is the most difficult and nerve-racking vice that any man can pursue; it needs an unceasing vigilance and a rare detachment of spirit. It cannot, like adultery or gluttony, be practised at spare moments; it is a whole-time job.
   Cakes and Ale (1930) ch. 1

6 This is not so strange when you reflect that from the earliest times the old have rubbed it into the young that they are wiser than they, and before the young had discovered what nonsense this was they were old too, and it profited them to carry on the imposture.
   Cakes and Ale (1930) ch. 11

7 Poor Henry [James], he's spending eternity wandering round and round a stately park and the fence is just too high for him to peep over and they're having tea just too far away for him to hear what the countess is saying.
   Cakes and Ale (1930) ch. 11

8 You can't learn too soon that the most useful thing about a principle is that it can always be sacrificed to expediency.
   Circle (1921) act 3

9 A woman will always sacrifice herself if you give her

the opportunity. It is her favourite form of self-indulgence.
   Circle (1921) act 3

10 'Dying' he [Maugham] said to me, 'is a very dull, dreary affair.' Suddenly he smiled. 'And my advice to you is to have nothing whatever to do with it,' he added.
   Robin Maugham *Escape from the Shadows* (1972) pt. 5, p. 233

11 There can be nothing so gratifying to an author as to arouse the respect and esteem of the reader. Make him laugh and he will think you a trivial fellow, but bore him in the right way and your reputation is assured.
   Gentleman in the Parlour (1930) ch. 11

12 God knows that I have never been that [anti-Semitic]; some of my best friends both in England and America are Jews.
   Letter, May 1946, in Ted Morgan *Somerset Maugham* (1980) ch. 6

13 I forget who it was that recommended men for their soul's good to do each day two things they disliked: it was a wise man, and it is a precept that I have followed scrupulously; for every day I have got up and I have gone to bed.
   Moon and Sixpence (1919) ch. 2

14 Impropriety is the soul of wit.
   Moon and Sixpence (1919) ch. 4

15 She saw shrewdly that the world is quickly bored by the recital of misfortune, and willingly avoids the sight of distress.
   Moon and Sixpence (1919) ch. 16

16 It is not true that suffering ennobles the character; happiness does that sometimes, but suffering, for the most part, makes men petty and vindictive.
   Moon and Sixpence (1919) ch. 17

17 'A woman can forgive a man for the harm he does her,' he said, 'but she can never forgive him for the sacrifices he makes on her account.'
   Moon and Sixpence (1919) ch. 41

18 Like all weak men he laid an exaggerated stress on not changing one's mind.
   Of Human Bondage (1915) ch. 39

19 People ask you for criticism, but they only want praise.
   Of Human Bondage (1915) ch. 50

20 Money is like a sixth sense without which you cannot make a complete use of the other five.
   Of Human Bondage (1915) ch. 51

21 It was such a lovely day I thought it was a pity to get up.
   Our Betters (1923) act 3

22 I would sooner read a time-table or a catalogue than nothing at all. . . . They are much more entertaining than half the novels that are written.
   Summing Up (1938) p. 92

23 The common idea that success spoils people by making them vain, egotistic and self-complacent is erroneous; on the contrary it makes them, for the most part, humble, tolerant and kind. Failure makes people bitter and cruel.
   Summing Up (1938) p. 187

1 *Lucky Jim* [by Kingsley Amis] is a remarkable novel. It has been greatly praised and widely read, but I have not noticed that any of the reviewers have remarked on its ominous significance. I am told that today rather more than 60 per cent of the men who go to the universities go on a Government grant. This is a new class that has entered upon the scene. . . . They are scum.
Sunday Times 25 Dec. 1955

2 At a dinner party one should eat wisely but not too well, and talk well but not too wisely.
Writer's Notebook (1949) p. 17 (written in 1896)

3 Few misfortunes can befall a boy which bring worse consequences than to have a really affectionate mother.
Writer's Notebook (1949) p. 27 (written in 1896)

Bill Mauldin 1921–

4 I feel like a fugitive from th' law of averages.
Up Front (1945) cartoon caption

James Maxton 1885–1946

5 All I say is, if you cannot ride two horses you have no right in the circus.
Said at Scottish Independent Labour Party Conference on being told that he could not be in two parties, in Daily Herald 12 Jan. 1931

John May

6 You're never alone with a Strand.
Slogan for Strand cigarettes, 1960, in Nigel Rees Slogans (1982) p. 108

Percy Mayfield 1920–1984

7 Hit the road, Jack.
Title of song (1961)

Charles H. Mayo 1865–1939

8 The definition of a specialist as one who 'knows more and more about less and less' is good and true.
Modern Hospital Sept. 1938, p. 69

Margaret Mead 1901–1978

9 Women want mediocre men, and men are working hard to be as mediocre as possible.
In Quote Magazine 15 June 1958

Shepherd Mead 1914–

10 How to succeed in business without really trying.
Title of book (1952)

Hughes Mearns 1875–1965

11 As I was walking up the stair
I met a man who wasn't there.
He wasn't there again today.
I wish, I wish he'd stay away.
The Psycho-ed (1910 play), in Newsweek 15 Jan. 1940

Dame Nellie Melba (Helen Porter Mitchell) 1861–1931

12 So you're going to Australia! Well, *I* made twenty thousand pounds on my tour there, but of course *that* will never be done again. Still, it's a wonderful country, and you'll have a good time. What are you going to sing? All I can say is—sing 'em muck! It's all they can understand!
Advice to Dame Clara Butt, in W. H. Ponder Clara Butt (1928) ch. 12

H. L. Mencken 1880–1956

13 Here, indeed, was his [Calvin Coolidge's] one peculiar *Fach*, his one really notable talent. He slept more than any other President, whether by day or by night. Nero fiddled, but Coolidge only snored.
American Mercury Apr. 1933

14 The saddest life is that of a political aspirant under democracy. His failure is ignominious and his success is disgraceful.
Baltimore Evening Sun 9 Dec. 1929

15 No one in this world, so far as I know—and I have searched the records for years, and employed agents to help me—has ever lost money by underestimating the intelligence of the great masses of the plain people.
Chicago Tribune 19 Sept. 1926

16 When women kiss it always reminds one of prize-fighters shaking hands.
Chrestomathy (1949) ch. 30

17 Love is the delusion that one woman differs from another.
Chrestomathy (1949) ch. 30

18 Men have a much better time of it than women. For one thing, they marry later. For another thing, they die earlier.
Chrestomathy (1949) ch. 30

19 Puritanism. The haunting fear that someone, somewhere, may be happy.
Chrestomathy (1949) ch. 30

20 Democracy is the theory that the common people know what they want, and deserve to get it good and hard.
Little Book in C major (1916) p. 19

21 Conscience: the inner voice which warns us that someone may be looking.
Little Book in C major (1916) p. 42

22 I've made it a rule never to drink by daylight and never to refuse a drink after dark.
New York Post 18 Sept. 1945

23 It is now quite lawful for a Catholic woman to avoid pregnancy by a resort to mathematics, though she is still forbidden to resort to physics and chemistry.
Notebooks (1956) 'Minority Report'

1 The capacity of human beings to bore one another seems to be vastly greater than that of any other animals. Some of their most esteemed inventions have no other apparent purpose, for example, the dinner party of more than two, the epic poem, and the science of metaphysics.
　　Notebooks (1956) 'Minority Report'

2 All successful newspapers are ceaselessly querulous and bellicose. They never defend any one or anything if they can help it; if the job is forced upon them, they tackle it by denouncing some one or something else.
　　Prejudices (1919) 1st ser., ch. 13

3 Poetry is a comforting piece of fiction set to more or less lascivious music.
　　Prejudices (1922) 3rd ser., ch. 7

4 Faith may be defined briefly as an illogical belief in the occurrence of the improbable.
　　Prejudices (1922) 3rd ser., ch. 14

5 If, after I depart this vale, you ever remember me and have thought to please my ghost, forgive some sinner and wink your eye at some homely girl.
　　Smart Set Dec. 1921

David Mercer 1928–1980

6 A suitable case for treatment.
　　Title of play (1962) in *Three TV Comedies* (1966)

Johnny Mercer 1909–1976

7 You've got to ac-cent-tchu-ate the positive
Elim-my-nate the negative
Latch on to the affirmative
Don't mess with Mister In-between.
　　Ac-cent-tchu-ate the Positive (1944 song; music by Harold Arlen)

8 We're drinking my friend,
To the end of a brief episode,
Make it one for my baby
And one more for the road.
　　One For My Baby (1943 song; music by Harold Arlen)

9 That old black magic.
　　Title of song (1942; music by Harold Arlen)

Bob Merrill

10 How much is that doggie in the window?
　　Title of song (1953)

Dixon Lanier Merritt 1879–1972

11 Oh, a wondrous bird is the pelican!
His beak holds more than his belican.
He takes in his beak
Food enough for a week.
But I'll be darned if I know how the helican.
　　Nashville Banner 22 Apr. 1913

Viola Meynell 1886–1956

12 The dust comes secretly day after day,
Lies on my ledge and dulls my shining things.
But O this dust that I shall drive away
Is flowers and Kings,
Is Solomon's temple, poets, Nineveh.
　　Verses (1919) 'Dusting'

Princess Michael of Kent 1945–

13 I don't enjoy my public obligations. I was not made to cut ribbons and kiss babies.
　　Life Nov. 1986

George Mikes 1912

14 On the Continent people have good food; in England people have good table manners.
　　How to be an Alien (1946) p. 10

15 Continental people have sex life; the English have hot-water bottles.
　　How to be an Alien (1946) p. 25

16 An Englishman, even if he is alone, forms an orderly queue of one.
　　How to be an Alien (1946) p. 44

Edna St Vincent Millay 1892–1950

17 Down, down, down into the darkness of the grave
Gently they go, the beautiful, the tender, the kind;
Quietly they go, the intelligent, the witty, the brave.
I know. But I do not approve. And I am not resigned.
　　Buck in the Snow (1928) 'Dirge Without Music'

18 My candle burns at both ends;
It will not last the night;
But ah, my foes, and oh, my friends—
It gives a lovely light.
　　A Few Figs From Thistles (1920) 'First Fig'

19 Safe upon solid rock the ugly houses stand:
Come and see my shining palace built upon the sand!
　　A Few Figs From Thistles (1920) 'Second Fig'

20 I only know that summer sang in me
A little while, that in me sings no more.
　　Harp-Weaver and Other Poems (1923) sonnet 19

21 Euclid alone
Has looked on Beauty bare. Fortunate they
Who, though once only and then but far away,
Have heard her massive sandal set on stone.
　　Harp-Weaver and Other Poems (1923) sonnet 22

22 It's not true that life is one damn thing after another—it's one damn thing over and over.
　　Letter to Arthur Davison Ficke, 24 Oct. 1930, in A. R. Macdougal *Letters of Edna St V. Millay* (1952) p. 240

23 Death devours all lovely things;
Lesbia with her sparrow
Shares the darkness—presently
Every bed is narrow.
　　Second April (1921) 'Passer Mortuus Est'

1 After all, my erstwhile dear,
My no longer cherished,
Need we say it was not love,
Now that love is perished?
> *Second April* (1921) 'Passer Mortuus Est'

2 Childhood is not from birth to a certain age and at
a certain age
The child is grown, and puts away childish things.
Childhood is the kingdom where nobody dies.
Nobody that matters, that is.
> *Wine from these Grapes* (1934) 'Childhood is the Kingdom where Nobody dies'

Alice Duer Miller 1874–1942

3 I am American bred,
I have seen much to hate here—much to forgive,
But in a world where England is finished and dead,
I do not wish to live.
> *White Cliffs* (1940) p. 70

Arthur Miller 1915–

4 I don't say he's a great man. Willy Loman never made
a lot of money. His name was never in the paper. He's
not the finest character that ever lived. But he's
a human being, and a terrible thing is happening to
him. So attention must be paid. He's not to be allowed
to fall into his grave like an old dog. Attention,
attention must be finally paid to such a person.
> *Death of a Salesman* (1949) act 1

5 Willy was a salesman. And for a salesman, there is no
rock bottom to the life. He don't put a bolt to a nut, he
don't tell you the law or give you medicine. He's a man
way out there in the blue, riding on a smile and
a shoeshine. And when they start not smiling
back—that's an earthquake. And then you get yourself
a couple of spots on your hat, and you're finished.
Nobody dast blame this man. A salesman is got to
dream, boy. It comes with the territory.
> *Death of a Salesman* (1949) 'Requiem'

6 I used . . . to keep a book in which I would talk to
myself. One of the aphorisms I wrote was, 'The
structure of a play is always the story of how the birds
came home to roost.'
> *Harper's Magazine* Aug. 1958

7 Roslyn: 'How do you find your way back in the dark?'
Gay nods, indicating the sky before them: 'Just head for
that big star straight on. The highway's under it; take
us right home.'
> *The Misfits* (1961) ch. 12

8 A good newspaper, I suppose, is a nation talking to
itself.
> In *Observer* 26 Nov. 1961

Henry Miller 1891–1980

9 Even before the music begins there is that bored look
on people's faces. A polite form of self-imposed torture,
the concert.
> *Tropic of Cancer* (1934) p. 84

10 Every man with a bellyful of the classics is an enemy to
the human race.
> *Tropic of Cancer* (1934) p. 280

Jonathan Miller 1934–

11 In fact, I'm not really a *Jew*. Just Jew-*ish*. Not the
whole hog, you know.
> *Beyond the Fringe* (1960) 'Real Class', in Alan Bennett *et al.*
> *Complete Beyond the Fringe* (1987) p. 84

Spike Milligan (Terence Alan Milligan) 1918–

12 GRYTPYPE-THYNNE: You silly twisted boy.
> *Dreaded Batter Pudding Hurler* in *The Goon Show* (BBC radio
> series) 12 Oct. 1954, in *Goon Show Scripts* (1972) p. 26

13 SEAGOON: Ying tong iddle I po.
> *Dreaded Batter Pudding Hurler* in *The Goon Show* (BBC radio
> series) 12 Oct. 1954, in *Goon Show Scripts* (1972) p. 27;
> catch-phrase also used in *The Ying Tong Song* (1956)

14 He's fallen in the water.
> Catch-phrase used by 'Little Jim' (Spike Milligan) in *The Goon
> Show* (BBC radio series, used from 1956 onwards)

15 BLUEBOTTLE: You rotten swines. I told you I'd be
deaded.
> *Hastings Flyer* in *The Goon Show* (BBC radio series) 3 Jan.
> 1956, in *Goon Show Scripts* (1972) p. 170

16 I'm walking backwards for Christmas
Across the Irish Sea.
> *I'm Walking Backwards for Christmas* (1956 song)

17 MORIARTY: Sapristi Nuckoes—do you always drink
ink?
SEAGOON: Only in the mating season.
MORIARTY: Shall we dance?
> *Napoleon's Piano* in *The Goon Show* (BBC radio series) 11 Oct.
> 1955, in *Goon Show Scripts* (1972) p. 100

18 BLUEBOTTLE: I don't like this game, let's play another
game—let's play doctor and nurses.
> *The Phantom Head-Shaver* in *The Goon Show* (BBC radio series)
> 15 Oct. 1954, in *Goon Show Scripts* (1972) p. 54 (the
> catch-phrase was often 'I do not like this game')

19 Money couldn't buy friends but you got a better class of
enemy.
> *Puckoon* (1963) ch. 6

A. J. Mills, Fred Godfrey, and Bennett Scott

20 Take me back to dear old Blighty,
Put me on the train for London town.
> *Take Me Back to Dear Old Blighty* (1916 song)

Irving Mills 1894–1985

21 It don't mean a thing
If it ain't got that swing.
> *It Don't Mean a Thing* (1932 song; music by Duke Ellington)

A. A. Milne 1882–1956

1 The more it snows
(Tiddely pom),
The more it goes
(Tiddely pom),
The more it goes
(Tiddely pom)
On snowing.
And nobody knows
(Tiddely pom),
How cold my toes
(Tiddely pom),
How cold my toes
(Tiddely pom),
Are growing.
  House at Pooh Corner (1928) ch. 1

2 Tiggers don't like honey.
  House at Pooh Corner (1928) ch. 2

3 King John was not a good man—
He had his little ways.
And sometimes no one spoke to him
For days and days and days.
  Now We Are Six (1927) 'King John's Christmas'

4 When I was young, we *always* had mornings like this.
  Toad of Toad Hall (1929) act 2, sc. 3 (Milne's dramatization of
  Kenneth Grahame's *Wind in the Willows*)

5 They're changing guard at Buckingham Palace—
Christopher Robin went down with Alice.
Alice is marrying one of the guard.
'A soldier's life is terrible hard,'
Says Alice.
  When We Were Very Young (1924) 'Buckingham Palace'

6 John had
Great Big
Waterproof
Boots on;
John had a
Great Big
Waterproof
Hat;
John had a
Great Big
Waterproof
Mackintosh—
And that
(Said John)
Is
That.
  When We Were Very Young (1924) 'Happiness'

7 James James
Morrison Morrison
Weatherby George Dupree
Took great
Care of his Mother,
Though he was only three.
James James
Said to his Mother,
'Mother,' he said, said he;
'You must never go down to the end of the town, if you
  don't go down with me.'
  When We Were Very Young (1924) 'Disobedience'

8 *What* is the matter with Mary Jane?
She's perfectly well and she hasn't a pain,
And it's lovely rice pudding for dinner again!
What *is* the matter with Mary Jane?
  When We Were Very Young (1924) 'Rice Pudding'

9 The King asked
The Queen, and
The Queen asked
The Dairymaid:
'Could we have some butter for
The Royal slice of bread?'
  When We Were Very Young (1924) 'The King's Breakfast'

10 The King said
'Butter, eh?'
And bounced out of bed.
  When We Were Very Young (1924) 'The King's Breakfast'

11 Nobody,
My darling,
Could call me
A fussy man—
BUT
I do like a little bit of butter to my bread!
  When We Were Very Young (1924) 'The King's Breakfast'

12 Little Boy kneels at the foot of the bed,
Droops on the little hands little gold head.
Hush! Hush! Whisper who dares!
Christopher Robin is saying his prayers.
  When We Were Very Young (1924) 'Vespers'

13 Isn't it funny
How a bear likes honey?
Buzz! Buzz! Buzz!
I wonder why he does?
  Winnie-the-Pooh (1926) ch. 1

14 How sweet to be a Cloud
Floating in the Blue!
It makes him very proud
To be a little cloud.
  Winnie-the-Pooh (1926) ch. 1

15 Pooh always liked a little something at eleven o'clock in
the morning, and he was very glad to see Rabbit getting
out the plates and mugs; and when Rabbit said, 'Honey
or condensed milk with your bread?' he was so excited
that he said, 'Both,' and then, so as not to seem greedy,
he added, 'But don't bother about the bread, please.'
And for a long time after that he said nothing . . . until
at last, humming to himself in a rather sticky voice, he
got up, shook Rabbit lovingly by the paw, and said that
he must be going on.
  Winnie-the-Pooh (1926) ch. 2

16 'Well,' said Owl, 'the customary procedure in such
cases is as follows.' 'What does Crustimoney
Proseedcake mean?' said Pooh. 'For I am a Bear of Very
Little Brain, and long words Bother me.'
  Winnie-the-Pooh (1926) ch. 4

17 Eeyore, the old grey Donkey, stood by the side of the
stream, and looked at himself in the water. 'Pathetic,'
he said. 'That's what it is. Pathetic.'
  Winnie-the-Pooh (1926) ch. 6

18 Cottleston, Cottleston, Cottleston Pie.
A fly can't bird, but a bird can fly.
Ask me a riddle and I reply:
'Cottleston, Cottleston, Cottleston Pie.'
  Winnie-the-Pooh (1926) ch. 6

1 Time for a little something.
Winnie-the-Pooh (1926) ch. 6

2 My spelling is Wobbly. It's good spelling but it Wobbles, and the letters get in the wrong places.
Winnie-the-Pooh (1926) ch. 6

3 On Monday, when the sun is hot
I wonder to myself a lot:
'Now is it true, or is it not,
'That what is which and which is what?'
Winnie-the-Pooh (1926) ch. 7

4 3 Cheers for Pooh!
(*For Who?*)
For Pooh—
(*Why what did he do?*)
I thought you knew;
He saved his friend from a wetting!
Winnie-the-Pooh (1926) ch. 10

Lord Milner (Alfred, Viscount Milner) 1854–1925

5 If we believe a thing to be bad, and if we have a right to prevent it, it is our duty to try to prevent it and to damn the consequences.
Speech at Glasgow, 26 Nov. 1909, in *The Times* 27 Nov. 1909

Adrian Mitchell 1932–

6 Most people ignore most poetry
because
most poetry ignores most people.
Poems (1964) p. 8

Joni Mitchell 1945–

7 I've looked at life from both sides now,
From win and lose and still somehow
It's life's illusions I recall;
I really don't know life at all.
Both Sides Now (1967 song)

8 They paved paradise
And put up a parking lot,
With a pink hotel,
A boutique, and a swinging hot spot.
Big Yellow Taxi (1970 song)

9 We are stardust,
We are golden,
And we got to get ourselves
Back to the garden.
Woodstock (1969 song)

Margaret Mitchell 1900–1949

10 Death and taxes and childbirth! There's never any convenient time for any of them.
Gone with the Wind (1936) ch. 38

11 Scarlett . . . I wish I could care what you do or where you go but I can't. . . . My dear, I don't give a damn.
Gone with the Wind (1936) ch. 57 (in Sidney Howard's script for the film version (1939) this became 'Frankly, my dear, I don't give a damn!')

12 Tomorrow, I'll think of some way to get him back. After all, tomorrow is another day.
Gone with the Wind (1936) ch. 57 (closing words)

Jessica Mitford 1917–

13 According to one of my correspondents, Jessica Mitford was overheard to remark, 'I have nothing against undertakers personally. It's just that I wouldn't want one to bury my sister.'
Saturday Review 1 Feb. 1964

Nancy Mitford 1904–1973

14 'Always be civil to the girls, you never know who they may marry' is an aphorism which has saved many an English spinster from being treated like an Indian widow.
Love in a Cold Climate (1949) pt. 1, ch. 2

15 'Twenty three and a quarter minutes past,' Uncle Matthew was saying furiously, 'in precisely six and three-quarter minutes the damned fella will be late.'
Love in a Cold Climate (1949) pt. 1, ch. 13

16 An aristocracy in a republic is like a chicken whose head has been cut off: it may run about in a lively way, but in fact it is dead.
Noblesse Oblige (1956) p. 39

17 I have only ever read one book in my life, and that is *White Fang*. It's so frightfully good I've never bothered to read another.
Pursuit of Love (1945) ch. 9

18 Uncle Matthew's four years in France and Italy between 1914 and 1918 had given him no great opinion of foreigners. 'Frogs,' he would say, 'are slightly better than Huns or Wops, but abroad is unutterably bloody and foreigners are fiends.'
Pursuit of Love (1945) ch. 15

Addison Mizner 1892–1933

See ETHEL WATTS MUMFORD

Wilson Mizner 1876–1933

19 Among his [Mizner's] philosophical maxims were 'Be nice to people on your way up because you'll meet 'em on your way down', 'Treat a whore like a lady and a lady like a whore', and 'If you steal from one author, it's plagiarism; if you steal from many, it's research'.
Alva Johnston *The Legendary Mizners* (1953) ch. 4

20 Mizner's comment on Hollywood, 'It's a trip through a sewer in a glass-bottomed boat', was converted by Mayor Jimmy Walker into 'A reformer is a guy who rides through a sewer in a glass-bottomed boat'.
Alva Johnston *The Legendary Mizners* (1953) ch. 4

Walter Mondale 1928–

See CLIFF FREEMAN

William Cosmo Monkhouse 1840–1901

1 There once was an old man of Lyme
Who married three wives at a time,
When asked 'Why a third?'
He replied, 'One's absurd!
And bigamy, Sir, is a crime!'
Nonsense Rhymes (1902)

Harold Monro 1879–1932

2 When the tea is brought at five o'clock,
And all the neat curtains are drawn with care,
The little black cat with bright green eyes
Is suddenly purring there.
Children of Love (1914) 'Milk for the Cat'

Marilyn Monroe 1926–1962

3 Asked if she really had nothing on in the [calendar] photograph, Marilyn, her blue eyes wide, purred: 'I had the radio on.'
Time 11 Aug. 1952

C. E. Montague 1867–1928

4 War hath no fury like a non-combatant.
Disenchantment (1922) ch. 16

Field-Marshal Montgomery (Viscount Montgomery of Alamein) 1887–1976

5 Rule 1, on page 1 of the book of war, is: 'Do not march on Moscow'. Various people have tried it, Napoleon and Hitler, and it is no good. That is the first rule. I do not know whether your Lordships will know Rule 2 of war. It is: 'Do not go fighting with your land armies in China.' It is a vast country, with no clearly defined objectives, and an army fighting there would be engulfed by what is known as the Ming Bing, the people's insurgents.
Hansard (Lords) 30 May 1962, col. 227

6 Far from helping these unnatural practices along, surely our task is to build a bulwark which will defy evil influences which are seeking to undermine the very foundations of our national character—defy them; do not help them. I have heard some say—and, indeed, the noble Earl said so himself—that such practices are allowed in France and in other NATO countries. We are not French, and we are not other nationals. We are British, thank God!
Hansard (Lords) 24 May 1965, col. 648 (2nd reading of Sexual Offences Bill)

George Moore 1852–1933

7 All reformers are bachelors.
Bending of the Bough (1900) act 1

8 A man travels the world in search of what he needs and returns home to find it.
Brook Kerith (1916) ch. 11

9 Had I not myself written, only half conscious of the truth, that art must be parochial in the beginning to become cosmopolitan in the end?
Hail and Farewell: Ave (1911) p. 3

10 The lot of critics is to be remembered by what they failed to understand.
Impressions and Opinions (1891) 'Balzac'

11 Our contention is . . . that acting is therefore the lowest of the arts, if it be an art at all.
Impressions and Opinions (1891) 'Mummer-Worship'

Marianne Moore 1887–1972

12 O to be a dragon,
a symbol of the power of Heaven—of silkworm size or immense; at times invisible.
Felicitous phenomenon!
O To Be a Dragon (1959) title poem

13 I, too, dislike it: there are things that are important beyond all this fiddle.
Reading it, however, with a perfect contempt for it, one discovers in it, after all, a place for the genuine.
Selected Poems (1935) 'Poetry'

14 Nor till the poets among us can be
'literalists of
the imagination'—above
insolence and triviality and can present
for inspection, imaginary gardens with real toads in them, shall we have
it.
Selected Poems (1935) 'Poetry'

15 My father used to say,
'Superior people never make long visits,
have to be shown Longfellow's grave
or the glass flowers at Harvard.'
Selected Poems (1935) 'Silence'

16 Nor was he insincere in saying, 'Make my house your inn.'
Inns are not residences.
Selected Poems (1935) 'Silence'

Larry Morey 1905–1971

17 Heigh-ho, heigh-ho,
It's off to work we go.
Heigh-Ho (1937 song; music by Frank Churchill)

18 Whistle while you work.
Title of song (1937; music by Frank Churchill)

Robin Morgan 1941–

19 Sisterhood is powerful.
Title of book (1970)

Christian Morgenstern 1871–1914

20 Es war einmal ein Lattenzaun,
mit Zwischenraum, hindurchzuschaun.
Ein Architekt, der dieses sah,
Stand eines Abends plötzlich da—
und nahm den Zwischenraum heraus
und baute draus ein grosses Haus.

One time there was a picket fence
With space to gaze from hence to thence.
An architect who saw this sight
Approached it suddenly one night,
Removed the spaces from the fence
And built of them a residence.

> Galgenlieder (Gallows Songs, 1905) 'Der Lattenzaun'; tr. Max
> Knight 1963

Christopher Morley 1890–1957

1 Life is a foreign language: all men mispronounce it.
> Thunder on the Left (1925) ch. 14

Lord Morley (John, Viscount Morley of Blackburn) 1838–1923

2 Simplicity of character is no hindrance to subtlety of intellect.
> Life of Gladstone (1903) vol. 1, p. 194

3 You have not converted a man, because you have silenced him.
> On Compromise (1874) ch. 5

Desmond Morris 1928–

4 Clearly, then, the city is not a concrete jungle, it is a human zoo.
> The Human Zoo (1969) p. 8

5 There are one hundred and ninety-three living species of monkeys and apes. One hundred and ninety-two of them are covered with hair. The exception is a naked ape self-named Homo sapiens.
> The Naked Ape (1967) p. 9

Herbert Morrison (Baron Morrison of Lambeth) 1888–1965

6 Work is the call. Work at war speed. Good-night—and go to it.
> Broadcast as Minister of Supply, 22 May 1940, in Daily
> Herald 23 May 1940

Jim Morrison 1943–1971, Ray Manzarek 1935– , Robby Krieger 1946– , and John Densmore 1945–

7 C'mon, baby, light my fire.
> Light My Fire (1967 song)

R. F. Morrison

8 Just a wee deoch-an-doris,
Just a wee yin, that's a'.
Just a wee deoch-an-doris,
Before we gang awa'.
There's a wee wifie waitin',
In a wee but-an-ben;
If you can say
'It's a braw bricht moonlicht nicht',
Ye're a' richt, ye ken.
> Just a Wee Deoch-an-Doris (1911 song; music by Whit
> Cunliffe; sung by Harry Lauder)

Dwight Morrow 1873–1931

9 The world is divided into people who do things and people who get the credit. Try, if you can, to belong to the first class. There's far less competition.
> Letter to his son, in Harold Nicolson Dwight Morrow (1935)
> ch. 3

John Mortimer 1923–

10 The shelf life of the modern hardback writer is somewhere between the milk and the yoghurt.
> In Observer 28 June 1987

11 No brilliance is needed in the law. Nothing but common sense, and relatively clean finger nails.
> Voyage Round My Father (1971) act 1

J. B. Morton ('Beachcomber') 1893–1975

12 One disadvantage of being a hog is that at any moment some blundering fool may try to make a silk purse out of your wife's ear.
> By the Way (1931) p. 282

13 Hush, hush,
Nobody cares!
Christopher Robin
Has
 Fallen
  Down-
   Stairs.
> By the Way (1931) p. 367

14 Mr Justice Cocklecarrot began the hearing of a very curious case yesterday. A Mrs Tasker is accused of continually ringing the doorbell of a Mrs Renton, and then, when the door is opened, pushing a dozen red-bearded dwarfs into the hall and leaving them there.
> Diet of Thistles (1938) pt. 7

15 The Doctor is said also to have invented an extraordinary weapon which will make war less brutal. It is described as a very powerful liquid which rots braces at a distance of a mile.
> Gallimaufry (1936) 'Bracerot'

16 The man with the false nose had gone to that bourne from which no hollingsworth returns.
> Gallimaufry (1936) 'Another True Story'

17 Dr Strabismus (Whom God Preserve) of Utrecht has patented a new invention. It is an illuminated trouser-clip for bicyclists who are using main roads at night.
> Morton's Folly (1933) p. 99

Rogers Morton 1914–1979

18 After losing five of the last six primaries, President Ford's campaign manager, Rogers Morton, was asked if he plans any change in strategy. Said Morton: 'I'm not going to rearrange the furniture on the deck of the Titanic.'
> Washington Post 16 May 1976, p. C8

Sir Oswald Mosley 1896–1980

1 I am not, and never have been, a man of the right. My position was on the left and is now in the centre of politics.

Letter in *The Times* 26 Apr. 1968

Lord Louis Mountbatten (*Viscount Mountbatten of Burma*) 1900–1979

2 I can't think of a more wonderful thanksgiving for the life I have had than that everyone should be jolly at my funeral.

In Richard Hough *Mountbatten* (1980) p. 3

3 As a military man who has given half a century of active service, I say in all sincerity that the nuclear arms race has no military purpose. Wars cannot be fought with nuclear weapons. Their existence only adds to our perils because of the illusions which they have generated.

Speech at Strasbourg, 11 May 1979, in P. Ziegler *Mountbatten* (1985) ch. 52

Lord Moynihan (*Berkeley Moynihan, Baron Moynihan*) 1865–1936

4 Lord Dawson of Penn
Has killed lots of men.
So that's why we sing
God save the King.

In Kenneth Rose *King George V* (1983) ch. 9

Robert Mugabe 1924–

5 Cricket civilizes people and creates good gentlemen. I want everyone to play cricket in Zimbabwe; I want ours to be a nation of gentlemen.

In *Sunday Times* 26 Feb. 1984

Kitty Muggeridge

6 David Frost has risen without trace.

Said *c*.1965 to Malcolm Muggeridge

Malcolm Muggeridge 1903–1990

7 An orgy looks particularly alluring seen through the mists of righteous indignation.

The Most of Malcolm Muggeridge (1966) 'Dolce Vita in a Cold Climate'

8 Once in the lobby of the Midland Hotel in Manchester when I happened to be in some public disfavour, a man came up to me, grasped my hand and observed: 'Never forget that only dead fish swim with the stream.'

Radio Times 9 July 1964

9 Good taste and humour . . . are a contradiction in terms, like a chaste whore.

Time 14 Sept. 1953

10 The orgasm has replaced the Cross as the focus of longing and the image of fulfilment.

Tread Softly (1966) p. 46

11 As has truly been said in his days as an active politician, he [Sir Anthony Eden] was not only a bore; he bored for England.

Tread Softly (1966) p. 147

Edwin Muir 1887–1959

12 And without fear the lawless roads
Ran wrong through all the land.

Journeys and Places (1937) 'Hölderlin's Journey'

Herbert J. Muller 1905–

13 Few have heard of Fra Luca Pacioli, the inventor of double-entry book-keeping; but he has probably had much more influence on human life than has Dante or Michelangelo.

Uses of the Past (1957) ch. 8

Ethel Watts Mumford 1878–1940, Oliver Herford 1863–1935, and Addison Mizner 1872–1933

14 In the midst of life we are in debt.

Altogether New Cynic's Calendar (1907)—a parody of Book of Common Prayer: see *Oxford Dictionary of Quotations* (1979) 389:12

15 God gives us our relatives—thank God we can choose our friends.

Cynic's Calendar (1903)

Lewis Mumford 1895–

16 Every generation revolts against its fathers and makes friends with its grandfathers.

The Brown Decades (1931) p. 3

17 Our national flower is the concrete cloverleaf.

Quote Magazine 8 Oct. 1961

Sir Alfred Munnings 1878–1959

18 I find myself a President of a body of men who are what I call shilly-shallying. They feel that there is something in this so-called modern art. . . . I myself would rather have—excuse me, my Lord Archbishop—a damned bad failure, a bad, dusty old picture where somebody has tried to do something, to set down something that they have seen and felt, than all this affected juggling, this following of well—shall we call it the school of Paris? . . . Anthony Blunt . . . once stood in this room with me when the King's pictures were here. And there was a Reynolds hanging there and he said, 'That Reynolds isn't as great as a Picasso.' Believe me, what an extraordinary thing for a man to say.

Speech at Royal Academy, 28 Apr. 1949, in *The Finish* (1952) ch. 22

Richard Murdoch 1907–1990 and Kenneth Horne 1900–1969

19 Have you read any good books lately?

Catch-phrase used by Richard Murdoch in radio comedy series *Much-Binding-in-the-Marsh* (started 2 Jan. 1947)

1 Good morning, sir—was there something?

> Catch-phrase used by Sam Costa in radio comedy series
> *Much-Binding-in-the-Marsh* (started 2 Jan. 1947), in
> Norman Hackforth *Solo for Horne* (1976) p. 58

C. W. Murphy and Will Letters

2 Has anybody here seen Kelly?
Kelly from the Isle of Man?

> *Has Anybody Here Seen Kelly?* (1909 song)

Ed Murphy

3 I was project manager at Edwards Airforce Base
during Colonel J. P. Stapp's experimental crash
research testing on the track at North Base. The law's
namesake was Captain Ed Murphy—a development
engineer from Wright aircraft lab. Frustration with
a strap transducer which was malfunctioning due to
an error by a lab technician in the wiring of the strain
gauge bridges caused Murphy to remark: 'If there's
any way to do it wrong, he will!' I assigned Murphy's
Law to the statement and the associated variations.

> George E. Nichols in *Listener* 16 Feb. 1984

Fred Murray

4 Ginger, you're balmy!

> Title of song (1910)

5 I'm Henery the Eighth, I am!
Henery the Eighth, I am, I am!
I got married to the widow next door,
She's been married seven times before.
Every one was a Henery,
She wouldn't have a Willie or a Sam.
I'm her eighth old man named Henery
I'm Henery the Eighth, I am!

> *I'm Henery the Eighth, I Am!* (1911 song)

Edward R. Murrow 1908–1965

6 As Ed Murrow once said about Vietnam, anyone who
isn't confused doesn't really understand the situation.

> Walter Bryan *The Improbable Irish* (1969) ch. 1

7 This—is London.

> Words used to open his broadcasts from London, 1938–45:
> see E. R. Murrow *In Search of Light* (1967) p. 7

8 He [Winston Churchill] mobilized the English language
and sent it into battle to steady his fellow countrymen
and hearten those Europeans upon whom the long dark
night of tyranny had descended.

> Broadcast, 30 Nov. 1954, in *In Search of Light* (1967) p. 276

Benito Mussolini 1883–1945

9 *Voglio partire in perfetto orario. . . . D'ora innanzi ogni
cosa deve camminare alla perfezione.*

We must leave exactly on time. . . . From now on
everything must function to perfection.

> Giorgio Pini *Mussolini* (1939) vol. 2, ch. 6, p. 251 (said to
> a station-master). Cf. HRH Infanta Eulalia of Spain *Courts
> and Countries after the War* (1925) ch. 13: 'The first benefit of
> Benito Mussolini's direction in Italy begins to be felt when
> one crosses the Italian Frontier and hears 'Il treno arriva
> all'orario' [i.e. 'the train is arriving on time']

A. J. Muste 1885–1967

10 There is no way to peace. Peace is the way.

> In *New York Times* 16 Nov. 1967, p. 46

Vladimir Nabokov 1899–1977

11 Her exotic daydreams do not prevent her from being
small-town bourgeois at heart, clinging to
conventional ideas or committing this or that
conventional violation of the conventional, adultery
being a most conventional way to rise above the
conventional.

> *Lectures on Literature* (1980) 'Madame Bovary'

12 Lolita, light of my life, fire of my loins. My sin, my soul.
Lo-lee-ta: the tip of the tongue taking a trip of three
steps down the palate to tap, at three, on the teeth. Lo.
Lee. Ta.

> *Lolita* (1955) ch. 1

13 Life is a great surprise. I do not see why death should
not be an even greater one.

> *Pale Fire* (1962) p. 225

14 The cradle rocks above an abyss, and common sense
tells us that our existence is but a brief crack of light
between two eternities of darkness.

> *Speak, Memory* (1951) ch. 1

15 I think like a genius, I write like a distinguished author,
and I speak like a child.

> *Strong Opinions* (1973) foreword

16 A work of art has no importance whatever to society. It
is only important to the individual, and only the
individual reader is important to me.

> *Strong Opinions* (1973) p. 33

Ralph Nader 1934–

17 Unsafe at any speed.

> Title of book (1965)

Sarojini Naidu 1879–1949

18 If only Bapu [Gandhi] knew the cost of setting him up
in poverty!

> In A. Campbell-Johnson *Mission with Mountbatten* (1951)
> ch. 12

Fridtjof Nansen 1861–1930

19 He [Nansen] once told me the rules by which, in his
explorations and at Geneva, his work was done. There
were three of them, and they were very simple: 'Never
stop because you are afraid—you are never so likely to
be wrong.' 'Never keep a line of retreat: it is
a wretched invention.' 'The difficult is what takes
a little time; the impossible is what takes a little
longer.'

> Philip Noel-Baker in *Listener* 14 Dec. 1939

Ogden Nash 1902–1971

20 The camel has a single hump;
The dromedary, two;

Or else the other way around,
I'm never sure. Are you?

Bad Parents' Garden of Verse (1936) 'The Camel'

1 The trouble with a kitten is
THAT
Eventually it becomes a
CAT.

The Face is Familiar (1940) 'The Kitten'

2 Oh, what a tangled web do parents weave
When they think that their children are naïve.

The Face is Familiar (1940) 'Baby, What Makes the Sky Blue'

3 Sure, deck your lower limbs in pants;
Yours are the limbs, my sweeting.
You look divine as you advance—
Have you seen yourself retreating?

The Face is Familiar (1940) 'What's the Use?'

4 The cow is of the bovine ilk;
One end is moo, the other, milk;

Free Wheeling (1931) 'The Cow'

5 A bit of talcum
Is always walcum.

Free Wheeling (1931) 'The Baby'

6 Life is not having been told that the man has just
waxed the floor.

Good Intentions (1942) 'You and Me and P. B. Shelley'

7 Beneath this slab
John Brown is stowed.
He watched the ads,
And not the road.

Good Intentions (1942) 'Lather as You Go'

8 I have a bone to pick with Fate.
Come here and tell me, girlie,
Do you think my mind is maturing late,
Or simply rotted early?

Good Intentions (1942) 'Lines on Facing Forty'

9 I test my bath before I sit,
And I'm always moved to wonderment
That what chills the finger not a bit
Is so frigid upon the fundament.

Good Intentions (1942) 'Samson Agonistes'

10 Women would rather be right than be reasonable.

Good Intentions (1942) 'Frailty, Thy Name is a Misnomer'

11 Parsley
Is gharsley.

Good Intentions (1942) 'Further Reflections on Parsley'

12 God in His wisdom made the fly
And then forgot to tell us why.

Good Intentions (1942) 'The Fly'

13 Any kiddie in school can love like a fool,
But hating, my boy, is an art.

Happy Days (1933) 'Plea for Less Malice Toward None'

14 I think that I shall never see
A billboard lovely as a tree.
Perhaps, unless the billboards fall,
I'll never see a tree at all.

Happy Days (1933) 'Song of the Open Road'. Cf. Joyce Kilmer
121:8

15 Children aren't happy with nothing to ignore,
And that's what parents were created for.

Happy Days (1933) 'The Parent'

16 One would be in less danger
From the wiles of the stranger
If one's own kin and kith
Were more fun to be with.

Hard Lines (1931) 'Family Court'

17 A girl whose cheeks are covered with paint
Has an advantage with me over one whose ain't.

Hard Lines (1931) 'Biological Reflection'

18 Candy
Is dandy
But liquor
Is quicker.

Hard Lines (1931) 'Reflections on Ice-breaking'

19 The turtle lives 'twixt plated decks
Which practically conceal its sex.
I think it clever of the turtle
In such a fix to be so fertile.

Hard Lines (1931) 'Autres Bêtes, Autres Moeurs'

20 Let us pause to consider the English,
Who when they pause to consider themselves they get
all reticently thrilled and tinglish,
Because every Englishman is convinced of one thing,
viz.:
That to be an Englishman is to belong to the most
exclusive club there is.

I'm a Stranger Here Myself (1938) 'England Expects'

21 There was a young belle of old Natchez
Whose garments were always in patchez.
When comment arose
On the state of her clothes,
She drawled, When Ah itchez, Ah scratchez.

I'm a Stranger Here Myself (1938) 'Requiem'

22 Home is heaven and orgies are vile,
But you *need* an orgy, once in a while.

Primrose Path (1935) 'Home, $99^{44}/_{100}$% Sweet Home'

23 He tells you when you've got on too much lipstick,
And helps you with your girdle when your hips stick.

Versus (1949) 'The Perfect Husband'

George Jean Nathan 1882–1958

24 The test of a real comedian is whether you laugh at
him before he opens his mouth.

American Mercury Sept. 1929

Terry Nation

25 Exterminate! Exterminate!

Said by the Daleks in BBC television series *Dr Who* from Dec.
1963, in David Whitaker and Terry Nation *Dr Who* (1964)
ch. 9

James Ball Naylor 1860–1945

26 King David and King Solomon
Led merry, merry lives,
With many, many lady friends,
And many, many wives;
But when old age crept over them—

With many, many qualms!—
King Solomon wrote the Proverbs
And King David wrote the Psalms.
  Vagrant Verse (1935) 'King David and King Solomon'

Jawaharlal Nehru 1889–1964

1 Friends and comrades, the light has gone out of our
lives and there is darkness everywhere. I do not know
what to tell you and how to say it. Our beloved leader,
Bapu as we called him, the father of the nation, is no
more.
  Broadcast, 30 Jan. 1948 (after Gandhi's assassination), in
  Richard J. Walsh *Nehru on Gandhi* (1948) ch. 6

2 Democracy and socialism are means to an end, not the
end itself.
  'Basic Approach', repr. in Vincent Shean *Nehru: the Years of
  Power* (1960) p. 294

3 Normally speaking, it may be said that the forces of
a capitalist society, if left unchecked, tend to make the
rich richer and the poor poorer and thus increase the
gap between them.
  'Basic Approach', repr. in Vincent Shean *Nehru: the Years of
  Power* (1960) p. 295

Allan Nevins 1890–1971

4 The former Allies had blundered in the past by offering
Germany too little, and offering even that too late,
until finally Nazi Germany had become a menace to all
mankind.
  In *Current History* (New York) May 1935, p. 178

Anthony Newley 1931– and Leslie Bricusse 1931–

5 Stop the world, I want to get off.
  Title of musical (1961)

Huey Newton 1942–

6 I suggested [in 1966] that we use the panther as our
symbol and call our political vehicle the Black Panther
Party. The panther is a fierce animal, but he will not
attack until he is backed into a corner; then he will
strike out.
  Revolutionary Suicide (1973) ch. 16

Vivian Nicholson 1936–

7 I want to spend, and spend, and spend.
  Said to reporters on arriving to collect her husband's football
  pools winnings of £152,000, in *Daily Herald* 28 Sept. 1961

Sir Harold Nicolson 1886–1968

8 Chamberlain (who has the mind and manner of
a clothes-brush) aims only at assuring temporary
peace at the price of ultimate defeat.
  Diary 6 June 1938, in *Diaries and Letters* (1966) p. 345

9 Attlee is a charming and intelligent man, but as
a public speaker he is, compared to Winston
[Churchill], like a village fiddler after Paganini.
  Diary 10 Nov. 1947, in *Diaries and Letters* (1968) p. 113

Reinhold Niebuhr 1892–1971

10 Man's capacity for justice makes democracy possible,
but man's inclination to injustice makes democracy
necessary.
  Children of Light and Children of Darkness (1944) foreword

11 God, give us the serenity to accept what cannot be
changed;
Give us the courage to change what should be
changed;
Give us the wisdom to distinguish one from the other.
  In Richard Wightman Fox *Reinhold Niebuhr* (1985) ch. 12
  (prayer said to have been first published in 1951)

Carl Nielsen 1865–1931

12 *Musik er liv, som dette und slukkelig.*

Music *is* life, and like it is inextinguishable.
  4th Symphony ('The Inextinguishable', 1916) preface

Martin Niemöller 1892–1984

13 When Hitler attacked the Jews I was not a Jew,
therefore, I was not concerned. And when Hitler
attacked the Catholics, I was not a Catholic, and
therefore, I was not concerned. And when Hitler
attacked the unions and the industrialists, I was not
a member of the unions and I was not concerned.
Then, Hitler attacked me and the Protestant
church—and there was nobody left to be concerned.
  In *Congressional Record* 14 Oct. 1968, p. 31636

Florence Nightingale 1820–1910

14 On December 5 [1907], Sir Douglas Dawson . . .
brought the Order [of Merit] . . . to South Street. Miss
Nightingale understood that some kindness had been
done to her, but hardly more. 'Too kind, too kind,' she
said.
  E. Cook *Life of Florence Nightingale* (1913) vol. 2, pt. 7, ch. 9

Richard Milhous Nixon 1913–

15 When the President does it, that means that it is not
illegal.
  In David Frost *I Gave Them a Sword* (1978) ch. 8

16 I brought myself down. I gave them a sword. And they
stuck it in. And they twisted it with relish. And, I guess,
if I'd been in their position, I'd have done the same
thing.
  Television interview with David Frost, 19 May 1977, in
  David Frost *I Gave Them a Sword* (1978) ch. 10

17 I leave you gentlemen now and you will now write it.
You will interpret it. That's your right. But as I leave
you I want you to know—just think how much you're
going to be missing. You won't have Nixon to kick
around any more because, gentlemen, this is my last
press conference. . . . I hope that what I have said today
will at least make television, radio, the press first
recognize the great responsibility they have to report all
the news and, second, recognize that they have a right
and a responsibility, if they're against a candidate, to
give him the shaft, but also recognize if they give him

the shaft, put one lonely reporter on the campaign who
will report what the candidate says now and then.
Thank you gentlemen, and good day.

> After losing the election for Governor of California, 5 Nov.
> 1962, in *New York Times* 8 Nov. 1962, p. 8

1 Let us begin by committing ourselves to the truth, to
see it like it is and tell it like it is, to find the truth, to
speak the truth and to live the truth. That's what we
will do.

> Nomination acceptance speech, Miami, 8 Aug. 1968, in *New
> York Times* 9 Aug. 1968, p. 20

2 Hello, Neil and Buzz. I'm talking to you by telephone
from the Oval Room at the White House, and this
certainly has to be the most historic telephone call ever
made.

> Speaking to the first men to land on the moon, 20 July 1969,
> in *New York Times* 21 July 1969, p. 2

3 This is the greatest week in the history of the world
since the Creation.

> Speech 24 July 1969, welcoming the return of the first men
> to land on the moon, in *New York Times* 25 July 1969, p. 29

4 There can be no whitewash at the White House.

> Television speech on Watergate, 30 Apr. 1973, in *New York
> Times* 1 May 1973, p. 31

5 I made my mistakes, but in all my years of public life,
I have never profited, never profited from public service.
I've earned every cent. And in all of my years in public
life I have never obstructed justice. And I think, too,
that I can say that in my years of public life that
I welcome this kind of examination because people have
got to know whether or not their President is a crook.
Well, I'm not a crook. I've earned everything I've got.

> Speech at press conference, 17 Nov. 1973, in *New York
> Times* 18 Nov. 1973, p. 62

6 This country needs good farmers, good businessmen,
good plumbers, good carpenters.

> Farewell address at White House, 9 Aug. 1974, cited in *New
> York Times* 10 Aug. 1974, p. 4

7 Pat and I have the satisfaction that every dime that
we've got is honestly ours. I should say this—that Pat
doesn't have a mink coat. But she does have
a respectable Republican cloth coat. And I always tell
her that she'd look good in anything. One other thing
I probably should tell you, because if I don't they'll
probably be saying this about me too, we did get
something—a gift—after the election. . . . It was a little
cocker-spaniel dog. . . . And our little girl—Tricia, the
6-year-old—named it Checkers. And you know the
kids love that dog and I just want to say this right now,
that regardless of what they say about it, we're going to
keep it.

> Speech on television, 23 Sept. 1952, in P. Andrews *This Man
> Nixon* (1952) p. 60

David Nobbs

8 'This one's going to be a real winner,' said C. J.
'I didn't get where I am today without knowing
a real winner when I see one.'

> *Death of Reginald Perrin* (1975) p. 9 (subsequently
> a catch-phrase in BBC television series *The Fall and Rise of
> Reginald Perrin*, 1976–80)

Milton Nobles 1847–1924

9 The villain still pursued her.

> *Phoenix* (1900) act 1, sc. 3

Albert J. Nock 1873–1945

10 It is an economic axiom as old as the hills that goods
and services can be paid for only with goods and
services.

> *Memoirs of a Superfluous Man* (1943) ch. 13

Frank Norman 1931–
and Lionel Bart 1930–

11 Fings ain't wot they used t'be.

> Title of musical (1959). *Cf.* Ted Persons 170:9

Lord Northcliffe (Alfred Charles William Harmsworth, Viscount Northcliffe) 1865–1922

12 Harmsworth had always said: 'When I want
a peerage, I shall buy it like an honest man.'

> Tom Driberg *Swaff: the Life and Times of Hannen Swaffer*
> (1974) ch. 2

Jack Norworth 1879–1959

13 Oh, shine on, shine on, harvest moon
Up in the sky.
I ain't had no lovin'
Since April, January, June, or July.

> *Shine On, Harvest Moon* (1908 song; music by Nora
> Bayes-Norworth)

14 Take me out to the ball game.

> Title of song (1908; music by Albert Von Tilzer)

Alfred Noyes 1880–1958

15 Go down to Kew in lilac-time, in lilac-time, in
lilac-time,
Go down to Kew in lilac-time (it isn't far from
London!)
And you shall wander hand in hand with love in
summer's wonderland;
Go down to Kew in lilac-time (it isn't far from
London!)

> *Poems* (1904) 'The Barrel-Organ'

16 The wind was a torrent of darkness among the gusty
trees,
The moon was a ghostly galleon tossed upon cloudy
seas,
The road was a ribbon of moonlight over the purple
moor,
And the highwayman came riding-Riding-riding-
The highwayman came riding, up to the old inn-door.

> *Forty Singing Seamen and Other Poems* (1907) 'The
> Highwayman'

17 He whistled a tune to the window, and who should be
waiting there
The landlord's black-eyed daughter,

Bess, the landlord's daughter,
Plaiting a dark red love-knot into her long black hair.
Forty Singing Seamen and Other Poems (1907) 'The Highwayman'

1 Look for me by moonlight;
Watch for me by moonlight;
I'll come to thee by moonlight, though hell should bar the way!
Forty Singing Seamen and Other Poems (1907) 'The Highwayman'

Bill Nye (Edgar Wilson Nye)

2 The late Bill Nye once said, 'I have been told that Wagner's music is better than it sounds.'
Mark Twain *Autobiography* (1924) vol. 1, p. 338

Captain Lawrence Oates 1880–1912

3 I am just going outside and may be some time.
Last words, quoted in R. F. Scott *Diary* 16–17 Mar. 1912, in *Last Expedition* (1913) p. 593

Edna O'Brien 1932–

4 August is a wicked month.
Title of novel (1965)

5 The vote, I thought, means nothing to women. We should be armed.
In Erica Jong *Fear of Flying* (1973) ch. 16

6 Oh, God, who does not exist, you hate women, otherwise you'd have made them different.
Girls in their Married Bliss (1964) ch. 10

Flann O'Brien (Brian O'Nolan or O Nuallain) 1911–1966

7 The Pooka MacPhellimey, a member of the devil class, sat in his hut in the middle of a firwood meditating on the nature of the numerals and segregating in his mind the odd ones from the even.
At Swim-Two-Birds (1939) ch. 1

8 The conclusion of your syllogism, I said lightly, is fallacious, being based upon licensed premises.
At Swim-Two-Birds (1939) ch. 1

9 A pint of plain is your only man.
At Swim-Two-Birds (1939) 'The Workman's Friend'

10 It is not that I half knew my mother. I knew half of her: the lower half—her lap, legs, feet, her hands and wrists as she bent forward.
The Hard Life (1961) p. 11

11 People who spend most of their natural lives riding iron bicycles over the rocky roadsteads of this parish get their personalities mixed up with the personalities of their bicycles as a result of the interchanging of the atoms of each of them and you would be surprised at the number of people in these parts who nearly are half people and half bicycles.
The Third Policeman (1967) p. 85

Sean O'Casey 1884–1964

12 He's an oul' butty o' mine—oh, he's a darlin' man, a daarlin' man.
Juno and the Paycock (1925) act 1

13 The whole worl's in a state o' chassis!
Juno and the Paycock (1925) act 1

14 I often looked up at the sky an' assed meself the question—what is the stars, what is the stars?
Juno and the Paycock (1925) act 1

15 Sacred Heart of the Crucified Jesus, take our hearts o' stone . . . an' give us hearts o' flesh! . . . Take away this murdherin' hate . . . an' give us Thine own eternal love!
Juno and the Paycock (1925) act 2

16 The Polis as Polis, in this city, is Null an' Void!
Juno and the Paycock (1925) act 3

17 When one has reached 81 . . . one likes to sit back and let the world turn by itself, without trying to push it.
New York Times 25 Sept. 1960, pt. 2, p. 3

18 There's no reason to bring religion into it. I think we ought to have as great a regard for religion as we can, so as to keep it out of as many things as possible.
The Plough and the Stars (1926) act 1

19 It's my rule never to lose me temper till it would be dethrimental to keep it.
The Plough and the Stars (1926) act 2

20 English literature's performing flea [P. G. Wodehouse].
In P. G. Wodehouse *Performing Flea* (1953) p. 217

Edwin O'Connor 1918–1968

21 The last hurrah.
Title of novel (1956)

Seán O'Faoláin 1900–

22 Stories, like whiskey, must be allowed to mature in the cask.
Atlantic Monthly Dec. 1956, p. 76

David Ogilvy 1911–

23 The consumer isn't a moron; she is your wife. You insult her intelligence if you assume that a mere slogan and a few vapid adjectives will persuade her to buy anything.
Confessions of an Advertising Man (1963) ch. 5

Geoffrey O'Hara 1882–1967

24 K-K-K-Katy, beautiful Katy,
You're the only g-g-g-girl that I adore;—
When the m-m-m-moon shines,
Over the cow shed,
I'll be waiting at the k-k-k-kitchen door.
K-K-K-Katy (1918 song)

John O'Hara 1905–1970

1 George [Gershwin] died on July 11, 1937, but I don't have to believe that if I don't want to.
Newsweek 15 July 1940, p. 34

Patrick O'Keefe 1872–1934

2 Say it with flowers.
Slogan for the Society of American Florists, in *Florists' Exchange* 15 Dec. 1917, p. 1268

Chauncey Olcott and George Graff Jr.

3 When Irish eyes are smiling.
Title of song (1912; music by Ernest R. Ball)

Frederick Scott Oliver 1864–1934

4 A wise politician will never grudge a genuflexion or a rapture if it is expected of him by prevalent opinion.
The Endless Adventure (1930) vol. 1, pt. 1, ch. 20

Laurence Olivier (Baron Olivier of Brighton) 1907–1989

5 Acting is a masochistic form of exhibitionism. It is not quite the occupation of an adult.
In *Time* 3 July 1978, p. 33

Frank Ward O'Malley 1875–1932

See ELBERT HUBBARD

Mary O'Malley 1941–

6 Once a Catholic always a Catholic. That's the rule.
Once a Catholic (1971) act 1, sc. 2. Cf. Angus Wilson

Eugene O'Neill 1888–1953

7 For de little stealin' dey gits you in jail soon or late. For de big stealin' dey makes you Emperor and puts you in de Hall o' Fame when you croaks.
The Emperor Jones (1921) sc. 1

8 The iceman cometh.
Title of play (1946)

9 Life is for each man a solitary cell whose walls are mirrors.
Lazarus Laughed (1927) act 2, sc. 1

10 When men make gods, there is no God!
Lazarus Laughed (1927) act 2, sc. 2

11 A long day's journey into night.
Title of play (written 1940–1; published 1956)

12 Life is perhaps most wisely regarded as a bad dream between two awakenings, and every day is a life in miniature.
Marco Millions (1928) act 2, sc. 2

13 The sea hates a coward!
Mourning becomes Electra (1931) pt. 2, act 4

14 What beastly incidents our memories insist on cherishing! . . . the ugly and disgusting . . . the beautiful things we have to keep diaries to remember!
Strange Interlude (1928) pt. 1, act 2

15 The only living life is in the past and future . . . the present is an interlude . . . strange interlude in which we call on past and future to bear witness we are living.
Strange Interlude (1928) pt. 2, act 8

16 Strange interlude! Yes, our lives are merely strange dark interludes in the electrical display of God the Father!
Strange Interlude (1928) pt. 2, act 9

Brian O'Nolan 1911–1966

See FLANN O'BRIEN

J. Robert Oppenheimer 1904–1967

17 In some sort of crude sense which no vulgarity, no humour, no overstatement can quite extinguish, the physicists have known sin; and this is a knowledge which they cannot lose.
Lecture at Massachusetts Institute of Technology, 25 Nov. 1947, in *Open Mind* (1955) ch. 5

Susie Orbach 1946–

18 Fat is a feminist issue.
Title of book (1978)

Baroness Orczy 1865–1947

19 We seek him here, we seek him there,
Those Frenchies seek him everywhere.
Is he in heaven?—Is he in hell?
That demmed, elusive Pimpernel?
The Scarlet Pimpernel (1905) ch. 12

David Ormsby Gore 1918–1985

See LORD HARLECH

José Ortega y Gasset 1883–1955

20 Yo soy yo y mi circunstancia, y si no la salvo a ella no me salvo yo.

I am I plus my surroundings and if I do not preserve the latter, I do not preserve myself.
Meditaciones del Quijote (Meditations of Quixote, 1914) in *Obras Completas* (1946) vol. 1, p. 322

21 La civilización no es otra cosa que el ensayo de reducir la fuerza a ultima ratio.

Civilization is nothing more than the effort to reduce the use of force to the last resort.
La Rebelión de las Masas (The Revolt of the Masses, 1930) in *Obras Completas* (1947) vol. 4, p. 191

Joe Orton 1933–1967

22 I'd the upbringing a nun would envy and that's the truth. Until I was fifteen I was more familiar with Africa than my own body.
Entertaining Mr Sloane (1964) act 1

1 KATH: Can he be present at the birth of his child? . . .
ED: It's all any reasonable child can expect if the dad is
present at the conception.
Entertaining Mr Sloane (1964) act 3

2 Every luxury was lavished on you—atheism,
breast-feeding, circumcision. I had to make my own
way.
Loot (1967) act 1

3 Policemen, like red squirrels, must be protected.
Loot (1967) act 1

4 Reading isn't an occupation we encourage among
police officers. We try to keep the paper work down to a
minimum.
Loot (1967) act 2

5 The kind of people who always go on about whether
a thing is in good taste invariably have very bad taste.
Transatlantic Review Spring 1967, p. 95

6 You were born with your legs apart. They'll send you
to the grave in a Y-shaped coffin.
What the Butler Saw (1969) act 1

George Orwell (Eric Blair) 1903–1950

7 Man is the only creature that consumes without
producing.
Animal Farm (1945) ch. 1

8 Four legs good, two legs bad.
Animal Farm (1945) ch. 3

9 All animals are equal but some animals are more equal
than others.
Animal Farm (1945) ch. 10

10 At 50, everyone has the face he deserves.
Last words in his notebook, 17 April 1949, in *Collected
Essays* (1968) vol. 4, p. 515

11 I'm fat, but I'm thin inside. Has it ever struck you that
there's a thin man inside every fat man, just as they say
there's a statue inside every block of stone?
Coming up For Air (1939) pt. 1, ch. 3. See also 59:12

12 [Clement] Attlee reminds me of nothing so much as
a recently dead fish, before it has had time to stiffen.
Diary 19 May 1942, in *Essays* (1968) vol. 2, p. 426

13 He was an embittered atheist (the sort of atheist who
does not so much disbelieve in God as personally dislike
Him), and took a sort of pleasure in thinking that
human affairs would never improve.
Down and Out in Paris and London (1933) ch. 30

14 Whatever is funny is subversive, every joke is
ultimately a custard pie. . . . A dirty joke is a sort of
mental rebellion.
Horizon Sept. 1941 'The Art of Donald McGill'

15 Most revolutionaries are potential Tories, because they
imagine that everything can be put right by altering the
shape of society; once that change is effected, as it
sometimes is, they see no need for any other.
Inside the Whale (1940) 'Charles Dickens'

16 Keep the aspidistra flying.
Title of novel (1936)

17 England is not the jewelled isle of Shakespeare's
much-quoted passage, nor is it the inferno depicted by

Dr Goebbels. More than either it resembles a family,
a rather stuffy Victorian family, with not many black
sheep in it but with all its cupboards bursting with
skeletons. . . . A family with the wrong members in
control—that, perhaps, is as near as one can come to
describing England in a phrase.
The Lion and the Unicorn (1941) pt. 1 'England Your England'

18 Probably the battle of Waterloo *was* won on the
playing-fields of Eton, but the opening battles of all
subsequent wars have been lost there.
The Lion and the Unicorn (1941) pt. 1 'England Your England'

19 It was a bright cold day in April, and the clocks were
striking thirteen.
Nineteen Eighty-Four (1949) pt. 1, ch. 1

20 On each landing, opposite the lift shaft, the poster with
the enormous face gazed from the wall. It was one of
those pictures which are so contrived that the eyes
follow you about when you move. BIG BROTHER IS
WATCHING YOU, the caption beneath it ran.
Nineteen Eighty-Four (1949) pt. 1, ch. 1

21 War is peace. Freedom is slavery. Ignorance is strength.
Nineteen Eighty-Four (1949) pt. 1, ch. 1

22 'Who controls the past,' ran the Party slogan, 'controls
the future: who controls the present controls the past.'
Nineteen Eighty-Four (1949) pt. 1, ch. 3

23 Freedom is the freedom to say that two plus two make
four. If that is granted, all else follows.
Nineteen Eighty-Four (1949) pt. 1, ch. 7

24 *Doublethink* means the power of holding two
contradictory beliefs in one's mind simultaneously, and
accepting both of them.
Nineteen Eighty-Four (1949) pt. 2, ch. 9

25 Power is not a means, it is an end. One does not
establish a dictatorship in order to safeguard
a revolution; one makes the revolution in order to
establish the dictatorship.
Nineteen Eighty-Four (1949) pt. 3, ch. 3

26 If you want a picture of the future, imagine a boot
stamping on a human face—for ever.
Nineteen Eighty-Four (1949) pt. 3, ch. 3

27 The Catholic and the Communist are alike in assuming
that an opponent cannot be both honest and
intelligent.
Polemic Jan. 1946 'The Prevention of Literature'

28 The quickest way of ending a war is to lose it.
Polemic May 1946 'Second Thoughts on James Burnham'

29 It is only because miners sweat their guts out that
superior persons can remain superior.
The Road to Wigan Pier (1937) ch. 2

30 A person of bourgeois origin goes through life with
some expectation of getting what he wants, within
reasonable limits. Hence the fact that in times of stress
'educated' people tend to come to the front.
The Road to Wigan Pier (1937) ch. 3

31 There can hardly be a town in the South of England
where you could throw a brick without hitting the
niece of a bishop.
The Road to Wigan Pier (1937) ch. 7

1 As with the Christian religion, the worst advertisement for Socialism is its adherents.
   The Road to Wigan Pier (1937) ch. 11

2 The typical Socialist is . . . a prim little man with a white-collar job, usually a secret teetotaller and often with vegetarian leanings, with a history of Nonconformity behind him, and, above all, with a social position which he has no intention of forfeiting.
   The Road to Wigan Pier (1937) ch. 11

3 To the ordinary working man, the sort you would meet in any pub on Saturday night, Socialism does not mean much more than better wages and shorter hours and nobody bossing you about.
   The Road to Wigan Pier (1937) ch. 11

4 The high-water mark, so to speak, of Socialist literature is W. H. Auden, a sort of gutless Kipling.
   The Road to Wigan Pier (1937) ch. 11

5 We of the sinking middle class . . . may sink without further struggles into the working class where we belong, and probably when we get there it will not be so dreadful as we feared, for, after all, we have nothing to lose but our aitches.
   The Road to Wigan Pier (1937) ch. 13

6 In our time, political speech and writing are largely the defence of the indefensible.
   Shooting an Elephant (1950) 'Politics and the English Language'

7 The great enemy of clear language is insincerity. When there is a gap between one's real and one's declared aims, one turns as it were instinctively to long words and exhausted idioms, like a cuttlefish squirting out ink.
   Shooting an Elephant (1950) 'Politics and the English Language'

8 Political language—and with variations this is true of all political parties, from Conservatives to Anarchists—is designed to make lies sound truthful and murder respectable, and to give an appearance of solidity to pure wind.
   Shooting an Elephant (1950) 'Politics and the English Language'

9 Saints should always be judged guilty until they are proved innocent.
   Shooting an Elephant (1950) 'Reflections on Gandhi'

10 To see what is in front of one's nose needs a constant struggle.
   Tribune 22 Mar. 1946, 'In Front of your Nose'

John Osborne 1929–

11 Don't clap too hard—it's a very old building.
   The Entertainer (1957) no. 7

12 Thank God we're normal, normal, normal,
   Thank God we're normal,
   Yes, this is our finest shower!
   The Entertainer (1957) no. 7

13 But I have a go, lady, don't I? I 'ave a go. I do.
   The Entertainer (1957) no. 7

14 Never believe in mirrors or newspapers.
   The Hotel in Amsterdam (1968) act 1

15 Oh heavens, how I long for a little ordinary human enthusiasm. Just enthusiasm—that's all. I want to hear a warm, thrilling voice cry out Hallelujah! Hallelujah! I'm alive!
   Look Back in Anger (1956) act 1

16 His knowledge of life and ordinary human beings is so hazy, he really deserves some sort of decoration for it—a medal inscribed 'For Vaguery in the Field'.
   Look Back in Anger (1956) act 1

17 I don't think one 'comes down' from Jimmy's university. According to him, it's not even red brick, but white tile.
   Look Back in Anger (1956) act 2, sc. 1

18 They spend their time mostly looking forward to the past.
   Look Back in Anger (1956) act 2, sc. 1

19 There aren't any good, brave causes left. If the big bang does come, and we all get killed off, it won't be in aid of the old-fashioned, grand design. It'll just be for the Brave New-nothing-very-much-thank-you. About as pointless and inglorious as stepping in front of a bus.
   Look Back in Anger (1956) act 3, sc. 1

20 This is a letter of hate. It is for you my countrymen, I mean those men of my country who have defiled it. The men with manic fingers leading the sightless, feeble, betrayed body of my country to its death. . . . I only hope it [my hate] will keep me going. I think it will. I think it may sustain me in the last few months. Till then, damn you England. You're rotting now, and quite soon you'll disappear. My hate will outrun you yet, if only for a few seconds. I wish it could be eternal.
   Tribune 18 Aug. 1961

Sir William Osler 1849–1919

21 That man can interrogate as well as observe nature, was a lesson slowly learned in his evolution.
   In *Aphorisms from his Bedside Teachings* (1961) p. 62

22 Failure to examine the throat is a glaring sin of omission, especially in children. One finger in the throat and one in the rectum makes a good diagnostician.
   In *Aphorisms from his Bedside Teachings* (1961) p. 104

23 One of the first duties of the physician is to educate the masses not to take medicine.
   In *Aphorisms from his Bedside Teachings* (1961) p. 105

24 It is strange how the memory of a man may float to posterity on what he would have himself regarded as the most trifling of his works.
   In *Aphorisms from his Bedside Teachings* (1961) p. 112

25 The desire to take medicine is perhaps the greatest feature which distinguishes man from animals.
   In H. Cushing *Life of Sir William Osler* (1925) vol. 1, ch. 14

26 My second fixed idea is the uselessness of men above sixty years of age, and the incalculable benefit it would be in commercial, political, and in professional life, if as a matter of course, men stopped work at this age.
   Speech at Johns Hopkins University, 22 Feb. 1905, in H. Cushing *Life of Sir William Osler* (1925) vol. 1, ch. 24

1 To talk of diseases is a sort of *Arabian Nights* entertainment.

> In Oliver Sacks *The Man Who Mistook his Wife for a Hat* (1985) epigraph

2 The greater the ignorance the greater the dogmatism.

> *Montreal Medical Journal* Sept. 1902, p. 696

3 The natural man has only two primal passions, to get and beget.

> *Science and Immortality* (1904) ch. 2

Peter Demianovich Ouspensky 1878–1947

4 Truths that become old become decrepit and unreliable; sometimes they may be kept going artificially for a certain time, but there is no life in them. This explains why reverting to old ideas, when people become disappointed in new ideas, does not help much. Ideas can be too old.

> *A New Model of the Universe* (ed. 2, 1934) preface

David Owen 1938–

5 We are fed up with fudging and mudging, with mush and slush. We need courage, conviction, and hard work.

> Speech to his supporters at Labour Party Conference in Blackpool, 2 Oct. 1980, in *Guardian* 3 Oct. 1980

6 The price of championing human rights is a little inconsistency at times.

> *Hansard* 30 Mar. 1977, p. 397

7 I don't care if you criticize us, agree with us or disagree with us. Just mention us, that is all we ask.

> *Observer* 28 Apr. 1985

Wilfred Owen 1893–1918

8 Above all I am not concerned with Poetry.
My subject is War, and the pity of War.
The Poetry is in the pity.
Yet these elegies are to this generation in no sense consolatory. They may be to the next. All a poet can do today is warn. That is why the true Poets must be truthful.

> *Poems* (1963 ed.) preface

9 What passing-bells for these who die as cattle?
Only the monstrous anger of the guns.
Only the stuttering rifles' rapid rattle
Can patter out their hasty orisons.
No mockeries now for them; no prayers nor bells,
Nor any voice of mourning save the choirs,—
The shrill, demented choirs of wailing shells;
And bugles calling for them from sad shires.

> What candles may be held to speed them all?
Not in the hands of boys, but in their eyes
Shall shine the holy glimmers of good-byes.
The pallor of girls' brows shall be their pall;
Their flowers the tenderness of patient minds,
And each slow dusk a drawing-down of blinds.

> *Poems* (1963 ed.) 'Anthem for Doomed Youth'

10 If you could hear, at every jolt, the blood
Come gargling from the froth-corrupted lungs,
Obscene as cancer, bitter as the cud
Of vile, incurable sores on innocent tongues,—
My friend, you would not tell with such high zest
To children ardent for some desperate glory,
The old Lie: Dulce et decorum est
Pro patria mori.

> *Poems* (1963 ed.) 'Dulce et Decorum Est'

11 Move him into the sun—
Gently its touch awoke him once,
At home, whispering of fields unsown,
Always it woke him, even in France,
Until this morning and this snow.
If anything might rouse him now
The kind old sun will know.

> *Poems* (1963 ed.) 'Futility'

12 Was it for this the clay grew tall?
—O what made fatuous sunbeams toil
To break earth's sleep at all?

> *Poems* (1963 ed.) 'Futility'

13 Red lips are not so red
As the stained stones kissed by the English dead.

> *Poems* (1963 ed.) 'Greater Love'

14 So secretly, like wrongs hushed-up, they went.
They were not ours:
We never heard to which front these were sent.

> Nor there if they yet mock what women meant
Who gave them flowers.

> *Poems* (1963 ed.) 'The Send-Off'

15 It seemed that out of battle I escaped
Down some profound dull tunnel, long since scooped
Through granites which titanic wars had groined.

> *Poems* (1963 ed.) 'Strange Meeting'

16 'Strange friend,' I said, 'here is no cause to mourn.'
'None,' said that other, 'save the undone years,
The hopelessness. Whatever hope is yours,
Was my life also; I went hunting wild
After the wildest beauty in the world.

> *Poems* (1963 ed.) 'Strange Meeting'

17 Courage was mine, and I had mystery,
Wisdom was mine, and I had mastery:
To miss the march of this retreating world
Into vain citadels that are not walled.

> *Poems* (1963 ed.) 'Strange Meeting'

18 I am the enemy you killed, my friend.
I knew you in this dark: for you so frowned
Yesterday through me as you jabbed and killed.
I parried; but my hands were loath and cold.
Let us sleep now . . .

> *Poems* (1963 ed.) 'Strange Meeting'

Oxford and Asquith, Countess of 1864–1945

See MARGOT ASQUITH

Oxford and Asquith, Earl of 1852–1928

See HERBERT HENRY ASQUITH

Vance Packard 1914–

1 The hidden persuaders.
   Title of book (1957)

William Tyler Page 1868–1942

2 I believe in the United States of America as
   a government of the people, by the people, for the
   people, whose just powers are derived from the
   consent of the governed; a democracy in a republic;
   a sovereign Nation of many sovereign States; a perfect
   Union, one and inseparable, established upon those
   principles of freedom, equality, justice, and humanity
   for which American patriots sacrificed their lives and
   fortunes. I therefore believe it is my duty to my
   country to love it, to support its Constitution, to obey
   its laws, to respect its flag, and to defend it against all
   enemies.
   American's Creed (prize-winning competition entry, 3 Apr.
   1918) in *Congressional Record* vol. 56, pt. 12 (appendix),
   p. 286

Reginald Paget 1908–

3 There is no disguise or camouflage about the Prime
   Minister. He is the original banana man, yellow
   outside and a softer yellow inside.
   Of Sir Anthony Eden in a House of Commons debate, *Hansard*
   14 Sept. 1956, col. 432

Gerald Page-Wood

4 It beats as it sweeps as it cleans.
   Advertising slogan for Hoover vacuum cleaners, devised in
   1919, in Nigel Rees *Slogans* (1982) p. 40

Revd Ian Paisley 1926–

5 I would rather be British than just.
   Remark to Bernadette Devlin, Oct. 1969, reported by *Sunday
   Times* Insight Team in *Ulster* (1972) ch. 3

Michael Palin 1943–

See GRAHAM CHAPMAN *et al.*

Norman Panama 1914–
and Melvin Frank 1913–1988

6 The pellet with the poison's in the vessel with the
   pestle. The chalice from the palace has the brew that
   is true.
   Court Jester (1955 film; words spoken—with difficulty—by
   Danny Kaye)

7 I'll take a lemonade! . . . In a dirty glass!
   Road to Utopia (1946 film; words spoken by Bob Hope)

Dame Christabel Pankhurst 1880–1958

8 Never lose your temper with the Press or the public is
   a major rule of political life.
   Unshackled (1959) ch. 5

9 We are here to claim our right as women, not only to
   be free, but to fight for freedom. That it is our right as

well as our duty. It is our privilege, as well as our pride
and our joy, to take some part in this militant
movement which, as we believe, means the
regeneration of all humanity.
   Speech in London, 23 Mar. 1911, in *Votes for Women*
   31 Mar. 1911

Emmeline Pankhurst 1858–1928

10 After all, is not a woman's life, is not her health, are
   not her limbs more valuable than panes of glass?
   There is no doubt of that, but most important of all,
   does not the breaking of glass produce more effect
   upon the Government?
   Speech on 16 Feb. 1912, in *My Own Story* (1914) p. 213

11 There is something that Governments care far more for
   than human life, and that is the security of property,
   and so it is through property that we shall strike the
   enemy. . . . Be militant each in your own way. Those of
   you who can express your militancy by going to the
   House of Commons and refusing to leave without
   satisfaction, as we did in the early days—do so. . . . And
   my last word is to the Government: I incite this meeting
   to rebellion. I say to the Government: You have not
   dared to take the leaders of Ulster for their incitement to
   rebellion. Take me if you dare.
   Speech at Albert Hall, 17 Oct. 1912, in *My Own Story*
   (1914) p. 265

Emmeline Pankhurst 1858–1928,
Dame Christabel Pankhurst 1880–1958,
and Annie Kenney 1879–1953

12 We laid our plans to begin this work at a great
   meeting to be held in the Free Trade Hall, Manchester
   [on 13 Oct. 1905] with Sir Edward Grey as the
   principal speaker. We intended to get seats in the
   gallery, directly facing the platform and we made for
   the occasion a large banner with the words 'Will the
   Liberal Party Give Votes for Women?' . . . At the last
   moment, however, we had to alter the plan because it
   was impossible to get the gallery seats we wanted.
   There was no way in which we could use our large
   banner, so . . . we cut out and made a small banner
   with the three-word inscription 'Votes for Women'.
   Thus, quite accidentally, there came into existence the
   present slogan of the suffrage movement around the
   world.
   Emmeline Pankhurst *My Own Story* (1914) ch. 3

Charlie Parker 1920–1955

13 Music is your own experience, your thoughts, your
   wisdom. If you don't live it, it won't come out of your
   horn.
   In Nat Shapiro and Nat Hentoff *Hear Me Talkin' to Ya* (1955)
   p. 358

Dorothy Parker 1893–1967

14 One more drink and I'd have been under the host.
   In Howard Teichmann *George S. Kaufman* (1972) p. 68

1 You can always tell that the crash is coming when
I start getting tender about Our Dumb Friends. Three
highballs and I think I'm St Francis of Assisi.
   Here Lies (1939) 'Just a Little One'

2 And I'll stay off Verlaine too; he was always chasing
Rimbauds.
   Here Lies (1939) 'The Little Hours'

3 I'm never going to be famous. My name will never be
writ large on the roster of Those Who Do Things.
I don't do anything. Not one single thing. I used to bite
my nails, but I don't even do that any more.
   Here Lies (1939) 'The Little Hours'

4 Sorrow is tranquillity remembered in emotion.
   Here Lies (1939) 'Sentiment'. Cf. *Oxford Dictionary of
   Quotations* (1979) 583:10

5 At intermission [in the 1933 premiere of *The Lake*],
Dorothy Parker turned to a companion and made her
famous quip: 'Katharine Hepburn runs the gamut from
A to B.'
   In G. Carey *Katharine Hepburn* (1985) ch. 6

6 The affair between Margot Asquith and Margot Asquith
will live as one of the prettiest love stories in all
literature.
   Review of Margot Asquith's *Lay Sermons* in *New Yorker*
   22 Oct. 1927, in *A Month of Saturdays* (1970) p. 10

7 And it is that word 'hummy', my darlings, that marks
the first place in 'The House at Pooh Corner' at which
Tonstant Weader fwowed up.
   New Yorker 20 Oct. 1928 (review by Dorothy Parker as
   'Constant Reader')

8 Where's the man could ease a heart like a satin gown?
   Not So Deep as a Well (1937) 'The Satin Dress'

9 By the time you say you're his,
Shivering and sighing
And he vows his passion is
Infinite, undying—
Lady, make a note of this:
One of you is lying.
   Not So Deep as a Well (1937) 'Unfortunate Coincidence'

10 Four be the things I'd been better without:
Love, curiosity, freckles, and doubt.
   Not So Deep as a Well (1937) 'Inventory'

11 Oh, life is a glorious cycle of song,
A medley of extemporanea;
And love is a thing that can never go wrong;
And I am Marie of Roumania.
   Not So Deep as a Well (1937) 'Comment'

12 Razors pain you
Rivers are damp;
Acids stain you;
And drugs cause cramp.
Guns aren't lawful;
Nooses give;
Gas smells awful;
You might as well live.
   Not So Deep as a Well (1937) 'Résumé'

13 Why is it no one ever sent me yet
One perfect limousine, do you suppose?

Ah no, it's always just my luck to get
One perfect rose.
   Not So Deep as a Well (1937) 'One Perfect Rose'

14 Men seldom make passes
At girls who wear glasses.
   Not So Deep as a Well (1937) 'News Item'

15 Woman wants monogamy;
Man delights in novelty.
Love is woman's moon and sun;
Man has other forms of fun.
Woman lives but in her lord;
Count to ten, and man is bored.
With this the gist and sum of it,
What earthly good can come of it?
   Not So Deep as a Well (1937) 'General Review of the Sex
   Situation'

16 Whose love is given over-well
Shall look on Helen's face in hell
Whilst they whose love is thin and wise
Shall see John Knox in Paradise.
   Not So Deep as a Well (1937) 'Partial Comfort'

17 Accursed from birth they be
Who seek to find monogamy,
Pursuing it from bed to bed—
I think they would be better dead.
   Not So Deep as a Well (1937) 'Reuben's Children'

18 If, with the literate, I am
Impelled to try an epigram,
I never seek to take the credit;
We all assume that Oscar said it.
   Not So Deep as a Well (1937) 'A Pig's-Eye View of Literature'

19 Drink and dance and laugh and lie,
Love, the reeling midnight through,
For tomorrow we shall die!
(But, alas, we never do.)
   Not So Deep as a Well (1937) 'The Flaw in Paganism'

20 He lies below, correct in cypress wood,
And entertains the most exclusive worms.
   Not So Deep as a Well (1937) 'Tombstones in the Starlight'

21 Scratch a lover, and find a foe.
   Not So Deep as a Well (1937) 'Ballade of a Great Weariness'

22 There's a hell of a distance between wise-cracking and
wit. Wit has truth in it; wise-cracking is simply
callisthenics with words.
   In *Paris Review* Summer 1956, p. 81

23 *House Beautiful* is play lousy.
   Review in *New Yorker* (1933), in Phyllis Hartnoll *Plays and
   Players* (1984) p. 89

24 Excuse My Dust.
   Suggested epitaph for herself (1925), in Alexander Woollcott
   While Rome Burns (1934) 'Our Mrs Parker'

25 That woman speaks eighteen languages, and can't say
No in any of them.
   In Alexander Woollcott *While Rome Burns* (1934) 'Our Mrs
   Parker'

26 And there was that wholesale libel on a Yale prom. If
all the girls attending it were laid end to end, Mrs
Parker said, she wouldn't be at all surprised.
   Alexander Woollcott *While Rome Burns* (1934) 'Our Mrs
   Parker'

1 'Good work, Mary,' our Mrs Parker wired collect [to Mrs Sherwood on the arrival of her baby]. 'We all knew you had it in you.'

Alexander Woollcott *While Rome Burns* (1934) 'Our Mrs Parker'

2 How do they know?

Reaction to the death of President Calvin Coolidge in 1933, in Malcolm Cowley *Writers at Work* 1st Series (1958) p. 65

3 As artists they're rot, but as providers they're oil wells; they gush.

Comment on lady novelists in Malcolm Cowley *Writers at Work* 1st Series (1958) p. 69

4 Hollywood money isn't money. It's congealed snow, melts in your hand, and there you are.

In Malcolm Cowley *Writers at Work* 1st Series (1958) p. 81

5 Brevity is the soul of lingerie, as the Petticoat said to the Chemise.

Caption written for *Vogue* (1916) in John Keats *You Might as well Live* (1970) p. 32. Cf. Shakespeare's *Hamlet* act 2, sc. 2: 'Brevity is the soul of wit'

6 You can lead a horticulture, but you can't make her think.

On being challenged to use 'horticulture' in a sentence, in John Keats *You Might as well Live* (1970) p. 46

7 It serves me right for putting all my eggs in one bastard.

On her abortion, in John Keats *You Might as well Live* (1970) pt. 2, ch. 3

Dorothy Parker 1893–1967, Alan Campbell 1905–1963, and Robert Carson 1910–1983

8 A star is born.

Title of film (1937)

Ross Parker 1914–1974 and Hugh Charles 1907–

9 There'll always be an England
While there's a country lane,
Wherever there's a cottage small
Beside a field of grain.

There'll always be an England (1939 song)

10 We'll meet again, don't know where,
Don't know when,
But I know we'll meet again some sunny day.

We'll Meet Again (1939 song)

C. Northcote Parkinson 1909–

11 Expenditure rises to meet income.

The Law and the Profits (1960) opening sentence

12 Work expands so as to fill the time available for its completion.

Parkinson's Law (1958) p. 4

13 It might be termed the Law of Triviality. Briefly stated, it means that the time spent on any item of the agenda will be in inverse proportion to the sum involved.

Parkinson's Law (1958) 'High Finance'

14 It is now known, however, that men enter local politics solely as a result of being unhappily married.

Parkinson's Law (1958) 'Pension Point'

'Banjo' Paterson (Andrew Barton Paterson) 1864–1941

15 Once a jolly swagman camped by a billabong,
Under the shade of a coolibah tree;
And he sang as he watched and waited till his 'Billy' boiled:
'You'll come a-waltzing, Matilda, with me.'

Waltzing Matilda (1903 song)

Alan Paton 1903–

16 Cry, the beloved country.

Title of novel (1948)

Norman Vincent Peale 1898–

17 The power of positive thinking.

Title of book (1952)

Charles S. Pearce

18 Keep that schoolgirl complexion.

Advertising slogan for Palmolive soap, from 1917, in Nigel Rees *Slogans* (1982) p. 113

Hesketh Pearson 1887–1964

19 Misquotation is, in fact, the pride and privilege of the learned. A widely-read man never quotes accurately, for the rather obvious reason that he has read too widely.

Common Misquotations (1934) Introduction

20 There is no stronger craving in the world than that of the rich for titles, except perhaps that of the titled for riches.

The Pilgrim Daughters (1961) ch. 6

Lester Pearson 1897–1972

21 The grim fact is that we prepare for war like precocious giants and for peace like retarded pygmies.

Speech in Toronto, 14 Mar. 1955

22 Not only did he [Dean Acheson] not suffer fools gladly, he did not suffer them at all.

Time 25 Oct. 1971, p. 20

Charles Péguy 1873–1914

23 *Qui ne gueule pas la vérité, quand il sait la vérité, se fait le complice des menteurs et des faussaires.*

He who does not bellow the truth when he knows the truth makes himself the accomplice of liars and forgers.

Lettre du Provincial 21 Dec. 1899, in *Basic Verities* (1943) 'Honest People'

24 *La tyrannie est toujours mieux organisée que la liberté.*

Tyranny is always better organised than freedom.

In *Basic Verities* (1943) 'War and Peace'

Vladimir Peniakoff 1897–1951

1 That night a message came on the wireless for me. It said: 'SPREAD ALARM AND DESPONDENCY'. So the time had come, I thought, Eighth Army was taking the offensive. The date was, I think, May 18th, 1942.
> *Private Army* (1950) pt. 2, ch. 5

William H. Penn

See ALBERT H. FITZ

S. J. Perelman 1904–1979

2 Crazy like a fox.
> Title of book (1944)

3 I have Bright's disease and he has mine, sobbed the panting palooka.
> *Judge* 16 Nov. 1929

S. J. Perelman 1904–1979, Will B. Johnstone, and Arthur Sheekman

4 Do you suppose I could buy back my introduction to you?
> *Monkey Business* (1931 film), in *The Four Marx Brothers in Monkey Business and Duck Soup* (1972) p. 18

5 Look at me. Worked myself up from nothing to a state of extreme poverty.
> *Monkey Business* (1931 film), in *The Four Marx Brothers in Monkey Business and Duck Soup* (1972) p. 54

Carl Perkins 1932–

6 It's one for the money,
Two for the show,
Three to get ready,
Now go, cat, go!
But don't you step on my Blue Suede Shoes.
You can do anything but lay off my Blue Suede Shoes.
> *Blue Suede Shoes* (1956 song)

Frances Perkins 1882–1965

7 Why not 'Madam Secretary', if that form is to be used at all? One is accustomed to 'madam chairman' . . . so it comes more naturally, don't you think?
> When asked how she should be addressed as the first US woman cabinet member, in *New York Times* 6 Mar. 1933, p. 14. Cf. Howard Lindsay and Russel Crouse

Juan Perón 1895–1974

8 If I had not been born Perón, I would have liked to be Perón.
> In *Observer* 21 Feb. 1960

Ted Persons

9 Things ain't what they used to be.
> Title of song (1941; music by Mercer Ellington). Cf. Frank Norman and Lionel Bart

Henri Philippe Pétain 1856–1951

10 To write one's memoirs is to speak ill of everybody except oneself.
> In *Observer* 26 May 1946

Laurence Peter 1919– and Raymond Hull

11 My analysis . . . led me to formulate *The Peter Principle*: In a Hierarchy Every Employee Tends to Rise to His Level of Incompetence.
> *The Peter Principle* (1969) ch. 1

12 In time, every post tends to be occupied by an employee who is incompetent to carry out its duties. . . . Work is accomplished by those employees who have not yet reached their level of incompetence.
> *The Peter Principle* (1969) ch. 1

13 Competence, like truth, beauty and contact lenses, is in the eye of the beholder.
> *The Peter Principle* (1969) ch. 3

Kim Philby (Harold Adrian Russell Philby) 1912–1988

14 To betray, you must first belong. I never belonged.
> In *Sunday Times* 17 Dec. 1967, p. 2

Prince Philip, Duke of Edinburgh 1921–

15 I don't think doing it [killing animals] for money makes it any more moral. I don't think a prostitute is more moral than a wife, but they are doing the same thing.
> Speech in London, 6 Dec. 1988, comparing participation in blood sports to selling slaughtered meat, in *The Times* 7 Dec. 1988

16 I never see any home cooking. All I get is fancy stuff.
> In *Observer* 28 Oct. 1962

17 If you stay here much longer you'll all be slitty-eyed.
> Remark to Edinburgh University students in Peking, 16 Oct. 1986, in *The Times* 17 Oct. 1986

18 Just at this moment we are suffering a national defeat comparable to any lost military campaign, and, what is more, it is self-inflicted. I could use any one of the several stock phrases or platitudes about this. But I prefer one I picked up during the war. It is brief and to the point: Gentlemen, I think it is about time we 'pulled our fingers out'. . . . If we want to be more prosperous we've simply got to get down to it and work for it. The rest of the world does not owe us a living.
> Speech in London, 17 Oct. 1961, in *Daily Mail* 18 Oct. 1961

19 We now look upon it [the English-Speaking Union] as including those countries which use English as an inter-Commonwealth language. I include 'pidgin-English' in this even though I am referred to in that splendid language as 'Fella belong Mrs Queen'.
> Speech to English-Speaking Union, Ottawa, 29 Oct. 1958, in *Prince Philip Speaks* (1960) pt. 2, ch. 3

Morgan Phillips 1902–1963

1 The Labour Party owes more to Methodism than to
Marxism.
>In James Callaghan *Time and Chance* (1987) ch. 1

Stephen Phillips 1864–1915

2 Behold me now
A man not old, but mellow, like good wine.
Not over-jealous, yet an eager husband.
>*Ulysses* (1902) act 3, sc. 2

Eden Phillpotts 1862–1960

3 Now old man's talk o' the days behind me;
My darter's youngest darter to mind me;
A little dreamin', a little dyin',
A little lew corner of airth to lie in.
>*Miniatures* (1942) 'Gaffer's Song'

Pablo Picasso 1881–1973

4 I paint objects as I think them, not as I see them.
>In John Golding *Cubism* (1959) p. 60

5 God is really only another artist. He invented the
giraffe, the elephant, and the cat. He has no real style.
He just goes on trying other things.
>Remark to Françoise Gilot in 1944, in Françoise Gilot and
Carlton Lake *Life With Picasso* (1964) pt. 1

6 Every positive value has its price in negative terms, and
you never see anything very great which is not, at the
same time, horrible in some respect. The genius of
Einstein leads to Hiroshima.
>Remark to Françoise Gilot in 1946, in Françoise Gilot and
Carlton Lake *Life With Picasso* (1964) pt. 2

7 We all know that Art is not truth. Art is a lie that
makes us realize truth, at least the truth that is given us
to understand.
>In Dore Ashton *Picasso on Art* (1972) 'Two statements by
Picasso'

8 Everyone wants to understand art. Why not try to
understand the song of a bird? Why does one love the
night, flowers, everything around one, without trying
to understand them? But in the case of a painting
people have to *understand*. . . . People who try to explain
pictures are usually barking up the wrong tree.
>In Dore Ashton *Picasso on Art* (1972) 'Two statements by
Picasso'

Wilfred Pickles 1904–

9 Are yer courtin'?
>Catch-phrase in *Have a Go!* (BBC radio quiz programme,
1946–67)

10 Give him the money, Barney.
>Catch-phrase in *Have a Go!* (BBC radio quiz programme,
1946–67)

Harold Pinter 1930–

11 'But what would you say your plays were *about*, Mr
Pinter?' 'The weasel under the cocktail cabinet.'
>In J. Russell Taylor *Anger and After* (1962) p. 231

12 I said to this monk, here, I said, look here, mister, he
opened the door, big door, he opened it, look here
mister, I said, I showed him these, I said, you haven't
got a pair of shoes, have you, a pair of shoes, I said,
enough to help me on my way. Look at these, they're
nearly out, I said, they're no good to me. I heard you
got a stock of shoes here. Piss off, he said to me.
>*The Caretaker* (1960) act 1

13 I can't drink Guinness from a thick mug. I only like it
out of a thin glass.
>*The Caretaker* (1960) act 1

14 If only I could get down to Sidcup! I've been waiting for
the weather to break. He's got my papers, this man
I left them with, it's got it all down there, I could prove
everything.
>*The Caretaker* (1960) act 1

Luigi Pirandello 1867–1936

15 *Sei personaggi in cerca d'autore.*

Six characters in search of an author.
>Title of play (1921)

16 *Quando i personaggi son vivi, vivi veramente davanti al loro
autore, questo non fa altro che seguirli nelle parole, nei gesti
ch'essi appunto gli propongono.*

When the characters are really alive before their
author, the latter does nothing but follow them in their
action, in their words, in the situations which they
suggest to him.
>*Sei personaggi in cerca d'autore* (Six Characters in search of an
Author, 1921) in *Three Plays* (1964) p. 64

Armand J. Piron

17 I wish I could shimmy like my sister Kate,
She shivers like the jelly on a plate.
>*Shimmy like Kate* (1919 song)

Robert Pirosh, George Seaton, and George Oppenheimer

18 (*Feeling patient's pulse*): Either he's dead, or my watch
has stopped.
>*A Day at the Races* (1937 film; line spoken by Groucho Marx)

19 Emily, I've a little confession to make. I really am
a horse doctor. But marry me, and I'll never look at any
other horse!
>*A Day at the Races* (1937 film; lines spoken by Groucho
Marx)

Robert M. Pirsig 1928–

20 Zen and the art of motorcycle maintenance.
>Title of book (1974)

Walter B. Pitkin 1878–1953

21 Life begins at forty.
>Title of book (1932)

Ruth Pitter 1897–

1 I dream
Already that I hear my lover's voice;
What music shall I have—what dying wails—
The seldom female in a world of males!
On Cats (1947) 'Kitten's Eclogue'

Sylvia Plath 1932–1963

2 Love set you going like a fat gold watch.
The midwife slapped your footsoles, and your bald cry
Took its place among the elements.
Ariel (1965) 'Morning Song'

3 Dying,
Is an art, like everything else.
I do it exceptionally well.
Encounter Oct. 1963, 'Lady Lazarus'

4 Every woman adores a Fascist,
The boot in the face, the brute
Brute heart of a brute like you.
Encounter Oct. 1963, 'Daddy'

William Plomer 1903–1973

5 They took the hill (Whose hill? What for?)
But what a climb they left to do!
Out of that bungled, unwise war
An alp of unforgiveness grew.
Collected Poems (1960) 'The Boer War'

6 On a sofa upholstered in panther skin
Mona did researches in original sin.
Collected Poems (1960) 'Mews Flat Mona'

7 A rose-red sissy half as old as time.
The Dorking Thigh (1945) 'Playboy of the Demi-World'. Cf.
Oxford Dictionary of Quotations (1979) 108:4

8 A family portrait not too stale to record
Of a pleasant old buffer, nephew to a lord,
Who believed that the bank was mightier than the
sword,
And that an umbrella might pacify barbarians abroad:
Just like an old liberal
Between the wars.
The Dorking Thigh (1945) 'Father and Son'

9 Fissures appeared in football fields
And houses in the night collapsed.
The Thames flowed backward to its source,
The last trickle seen to disappear
Swiftly, like an adder to its hole,
And here and there along the river-bed
The stranded fish gaped among empty tins,
Face downward lay the huddled suicides
Like litter that a riot leaves.
Visiting the Caves (1936) 'The Silent Sunday'

Henri Poincaré 1854–1912

10 Science is built up of facts, as a house is built of
stones; but an accumulation of facts is no more
a science than a heap of stones is a house.
Science and Hypothesis (1905) ch. 9

Georges Pompidou 1911–1974

11 A statesman is a politician who places himself at the
service of the nation. A politician is a statesman who
places the nation at his service.
In *Observer* 30 Dec. 1973

Arthur Ponsonby (first Baron Ponsonby of Shulbrede) 1871–1946

12 When war is declared, Truth is the first casualty.
Kommt der Krieg ins Land
Gibt Lügen wie Sand.

[When war enters a country
It produces lies like sand.]
Epigraphs to *Falsehood in Wartime* (1928) p. 11

Sir Karl Popper 1902–

13 We may become the makers of our fate when we have
ceased to pose as its prophets.
The Open Society and its Enemies (1945) Introduction

14 There is no history of mankind, there are only many
histories of all kinds of aspects of human life. And one of
these is the history of political power. This is elevated
into the history of the world.
The Open Society and its Enemies (1945) vol. 2, ch. 25

15 We must plan for freedom, and not only for security, if
for no other reason than that only freedom can make
security secure.
The Open Society and its Enemies (1945) vol. 2, ch. 21

16 Piecemeal social engineering resembles physical
engineering in regarding the ends as beyond the
province of technology.
Poverty of Historicism (1957) pt. 3, sect. 21

17 For this, indeed, is the true source of our
ignorance—the fact that our knowledge can only be
finite, while our ignorance must necessarily be infinite.
Lecture to British Academy, 20 Jan. 1960, in *Proceedings of
the British Academy* (1960) vol. 46, p. 69

Cole Porter 1891–1964

18 In olden days a glimpse of stocking
Was looked on as something shocking
Now, heaven knows,
Anything goes.
Anything Goes (1934 song)

19 When they begin the Beguine
It brings back the sound of music so tender,
It brings back a night of tropical splendour,
It brings back a memory ever green.
Begin the Beguine (1935 song)

20 Oh, give me land, lots of land
Under starry skies above
DON'T FENCE ME IN.
Don't Fence Me In (1934 song; revived in 1944 film
Hollywood Canteen)

21 I get no kick from champagne,
Mere alcohol doesn't thrill me at all,

So tell me why should it be true
That I get a kick out of you?
I Get a Kick Out of You (1934 song)

1 I've got you under my skin.
Title of song (1936)

2 So goodbye dear, and Amen,
Here's hoping we meet now and then,
It was great fun,
But it was just one of those things.
Just One of Those Things (1935 song)

3 Birds do it, bees do it,
Even educated fleas do it.
Let's do it, let's fall in love.
Let's Do It (1954 song; these words are not in the original
1928 version)

4 Miss Otis regrets (she's unable to lunch today).
Title of song (1934)

5 My heart belongs to Daddy.
Title of song (1938)

6 Night and day, you are the one,
Only you beneath the moon and under the sun.
Night and Day (1932 song)

7 SHE: Have you heard it's in the stars,
Next July we collide with Mars?
HE: Well, did you evah! What a swell party this is.
Well, Did You Evah? (1956 song)

8 Who wants to be a millionaire?
Title of song (1956)

9 You're the top.
Title of song (1934)

Beatrix Potter 1866–1943

10 In the time of swords and periwigs and full-skirted
coats with flowered lappets—when gentlemen wore
ruffles, and gold-laced waistcoats of paduasoy and
taffeta—there lived a tailor in Gloucester.
Tailor of Gloucester (1903) p. 9

11 The tailor replied—'Simpkin, we shall make our
fortune, but I am worn to a ravelling. Take this groat
(which is our last fourpence) and . . . with the last
penny of our fourpence buy me one penn'orth of
cherry-coloured silk. But do not lose the last penny of
the fourpence, Simpkin, or I am undone and worn to
a thread-paper, for I have NO MORE TWIST.'
Tailor of Gloucester (1903) p. 22

12 It is said that the effect of eating too much lettuce is
'soporific'.
Tale of the Flopsy Bunnies (1909) p. 9

13 Once upon a time there were four little Rabbits, and
their names were—Flopsy, Mopsy, Cottontail, and Peter.
Tale of Peter Rabbit (1902) p. 9

14 You may go into the fields or down the lane, but don't
go into Mr McGregor's garden: your Father had an
accident there; he was put in a pie by Mrs McGregor.
Tale of Peter Rabbit (1902) p. 10

15 Peter sat down to rest; he was out of breath and
trembling with fright. . . . After a time he began to

wander about, going lippity-lippity—not very fast, and
looking all round.
The Tale of Peter Rabbit (1902) p. 58

Gillie Potter (Hugh William Peel)
1887–1975

16 Good evening, England. This is Gillie Potter speaking
to you in English.
Heard at Hogsnorton (opening words of broadcasts, 6 June
1946 and 11 Nov. 1947)

Stephen Potter 1900–1969

17 A good general rule is to state that the bouquet is
better than the taste, and vice versa.
One-Upmanship (1952) ch. 14

18 *How to be one up*—how to make the other man feel that
something has gone wrong, however slightly.
Some Notes on Lifemanship (1950) p. 14

19 'Yes, but not in the South', with slight adjustments,
will do for any argument about any place, if not about
any person.
Some Notes on Lifemanship (1950) p. 43

20 The theory and practice of gamesmanship or The art of
winning games without actually cheating.
Title of book (1947)

Ezra Pound 1885–1972

21 The author's conviction on this day of New Year is
that music begins to atrophy when it departs too far
from the dance; that poetry begins to atrophy when it
gets too far from music.
ABC of Reading (1934) 'Warning'

22 Any general statement is like a cheque drawn on
a bank. Its value depends on what is there to meet it.
ABC of Reading (1934) ch. 1

23 One of the pleasures of middle age is to *find out* that one
WAS right, and that one was much righter than one
knew at say 17 or 23.
ABC of Reading (1934) ch. 1

24 Literature is news that STAYS news.
ABC of Reading (1934) ch. 2

25 Real education must ultimately be limited to one who
INSISTS on knowing, the rest is mere sheep-herding.
ABC of Reading (1934) ch. 8

26 Tching prayed on the mountain and
wrote MAKE IT NEW
on his bath tub.
Day by day make it new
cut underbrush,
pile the logs
keep it growing.
Cantos (1954) no. 53

27 Hang it all, Robert Browning,
There can be but the one 'Sordello'.
Draft of XXX Cantos (1930) no. 2

28 And even I can remember
A day when the historians left blanks in their writings,
I mean for things they didn't know.
Draft of XXX Cantos (1930) no. 13

1 Great literature is simply language charged with
   meaning to the utmost possible degree.
   How To Read (1931) pt. 2

2 For three years, out of key with his time,
   He strove to resuscitate the dead art
   Of poetry; to maintain 'the sublime'
   In the old sense. Wrong from the start—

   No, hardly, but seeing he had been born
   In a half savage country, out of date.
   Hugh Selwyn Mauberley, E. P. *Ode pour l'élection de son
   sépulcre* (1920) pt. 1

3 His true Penelope was Flaubert,
   He fished by obstinate isles;
   Observed the elegance of Circe's hair
   Rather than the mottoes on sundials.
   Hugh Selwyn Mauberley, E. P. *Ode pour l'élection de son
   sépulcre* (1920) pt. 1

4 The age demanded an image
   Of its accelerated grimace,
   Something for the modern stage,
   Not, at any rate, an Attic grace;

   Not, not certainly, the obscure reveries
   Of the inward gaze;
   Better mendacities
   Than the classics in paraphrase!
   Hugh Selwyn Mauberley, E. P. *Ode pour l'élection de son
   sépulcre* (1920) pt. 1

5 Christ follows Dionysus
   Phallic and ambrosial
   Made way for macerations;
   Caliban casts out Ariel.
   Hugh Selwyn Mauberley, E. P. *Ode pour l'élection de son
   sépulcre* (1920) pt. 1

6 There died a myriad,
   And of the best, among them,
   For an old bitch gone in the teeth,
   For a botched civilization.
   Hugh Selwyn Mauberley, E. P. *Ode pour l'élection de son
   sépulcre* (1920) pt. 1

7 The tip's a good one, as for literature
   It gives no man a sinecure.

   And no one knows, at sight, a masterpiece.
   And give up verse, my boy,
   There's nothing in it.
   Hugh Selwyn Mauberley, E. P. *Ode pour l'élection de son
   sépulcre* (1920) pt. 1

8 Poetry must be *as well written as prose.*
   Letter to Harriet Monroe, Jan. 1915, in D. D. Paige *Letters of
   Ezra Pound* (1950) p. 48

9 Artists are the antennae of the race, but the
   bullet-headed many will never learn to trust their great
   artists.
   Literary Essays (1954) 'Henry James'

10 Winter is icummen in,
    Lhude sing Goddamm,
    Raineth drop and staineth slop,

And how the wind doth ramm!
Sing: Goddamm.
   Lustra (1917) 'Ancient Music'. Cf. *Oxford Dictionary of
   Quotations* (1979) 7:18

11 The apparition of these faces in the crowd;
    Petals on a wet, black bough.
    Lustra (1916) 'In a Station of the Metro'

12 Bah! I have sung women in three cities,
    But it is all the same;
    And I will sing of the sun.
    Personae (1908) 'Cino'

13 The ant's a centaur in his dragon world.
    Pull down thy vanity, it is not man
    Made courage, or made order, or made grace,
    Pull down thy vanity, I say pull down.
    Learn of the green world what can be thy place
    In scaled invention or true artistry,
    Pull down thy vanity,
    Paquin pull down!
    The green casque has outdone your elegance.
    Pisan Cantos (1948) no. 81

14 Pull down thy vanity
    Thou art a beaten dog beneath the hail,
    A swollen magpie in a fitful sun,
    Half black half white
    Nor knowst'ou wing from tail
    Pull down thy vanity.
    Pisan Cantos (1948) no. 81

Anthony Powell 1905–

15 He fell in love with himself at first sight and it is
    a passion to which he has always remained faithful.
    Acceptance World (1955) ch. 1

16 Self-love seems so often unrequited.
    Acceptance World (1955) ch. 1

17 Dinner at the Huntercombes' possessed 'only two
    dramatic features—the wine was a farce and the food
    a tragedy'.
    Acceptance World (1955) ch. 4

18 Books do furnish a room.
    Title of novel (1971)

19 Parents—especially step-parents—are sometimes a bit
    of a disappointment to their children. They don't fufil
    the promise of their early years.
    A Buyer's Market (1952) ch. 2

20 A dance to the music of time.
    Title of a novel sequence (1951–75), after title given by
    Giovanni Pietro Bellori to a painting by Nicolas Poussin, *Le 4
    stagioni che ballano al suono del tempo*

21 Growing old is like being increasingly penalized for
    a crime you haven't committed.
    Temporary Kings (1973) ch. 1

Enoch Powell 1912–

22 All political lives, unless they are cut off in midstream
    at a happy juncture, end in failure, because that is the
    nature of politics and of human affairs.
    Joseph Chamberlain (1977) epilogue

1 History is littered with the wars which everybody knew
would never happen.
  Speech to Conservative Party Conference, 19 Oct. 1967, in
  The Times 20 Oct. 1967

2 As I look ahead, I am filled with foreboding. Like the
Roman, I seem to see 'the River Tiber foaming with
much blood'.
  Speech at Annual Meeting of West Midlands Area
  Conservative Political Centre, Birmingham, 20 Apr. 1968, in
  Observer 21 Apr. 1968

Sandy Powell 1900–1982

3 Can you hear me, mother?
  Catch-phrase: see *Can You Hear Me, Mother? Sandy Powell's
  Lifetime of Music-Hall* (1975) p. 62

Vince Powell and *Harry Driver*

4 Never mind the quality, feel the width.
  Title of ITV comedy series, 1967–9

Jacques Prévert 1900–1977

5 *C'est tellement simple, l'amour.*

Love is so simple.
  Les Enfants du Paradis (1945 film)

6 *Notre Père qui êtes aux cieux
Restez-y
Et nous nous resterons sur la terre
Qui est quelquefois si jolie.*

Our Father which art in heaven
Stay there
And we will stay on earth
Which is sometimes so pretty.
  Paroles (revised ed., 1949) 'Pater Noster'

J. B. Priestley 1894–1984

7 To say that these men paid their shillings to watch
twenty-two hirelings kick a ball is merely to say that
a violin is wood and catgut, that *Hamlet* is so much
paper and ink. For a shilling the Bruddersford United
AFC offered you Conflict and Art.
  Good Companions (1929) bk. 1, ch. 1

8 An inspector calls.
  Title of play (1947)

9 This little steamer, like all her brave and battered
sisters, is immortal. She'll go sailing proudly down the
years in the epic of Dunkirk. And our
great-grand-children, when they learn how we began
this war by snatching glory out of defeat, and then
swept on to victory, may also learn how the little
holiday steamers made an excursion to hell and came
back glorious.
  Radio broadcast, 5 June 1940, in *Listener* 13 June 1940

10 God can stand being told by Professor Ayer and
Marghanita Laski that He doesn't exist.
  In *Listener* 1 July 1965, p. 12

11 It is hard to tell where the MCC ends and the Church of
England begins.
  In *New Statesman* 20 July 1962, p. 78

V. S. Pritchett 1900–

12 The principle of procrastinated rape is said to be the
ruling one in all the great best-sellers.
  The Living Novel (1946) 'Clarissa'

13 What Chekhov saw in our failure to communicate was
something positive and precious: the private silence in
which we live, and which enables us to endure our
own solitude. We live, as his characters do, beyond any
tale we happen to enact.
  Myth Makers (1979) 'Chekhov, a doctor'

14 The detective novel is the art-for-art's-sake of our
yawning Philistinism, the classic example of
a specialized form of art removed from contact with the
life it pretends to build on.
  New Statesman 16 June 1951, 'Books in General'

Marcel Proust 1871–1922

15 *A la recherche du temps perdu.*

In search of lost time.
  Title of novel (1913–27), translated by C. K. Scott-Moncrieff
  and S. Hudson, 1922–31, as 'Remembrance of things past'

16 *Longtemps, je me suis couché de bonne heure.*

For a long time I used to go to bed early.
  Du côté de chez Swann (Swann's Way, 1913, translated 1922
  by C. K. Scott-Moncrieff, vol. 1, p. 1)

17 *Je portai à mes lèvres une cuillerée du thé où j'avais laissé
s'amollir un morceau de madeleine. . . . Et tout d'un coup le
souvenir m'est apparu. Ce goût c'était celui du petit
morceau de madeleine que le dimanche matin à Combray . . .
ma tante Léonie m'offrait après l'avoir trempé dans son
infusion de thé ou de tilleul.*

I raised to my lips a spoonful of the tea in which I had
soaked a morsel of cake. . . . And suddenly the memory
returns. The taste was that of the little crumb of
madeleine which on Sunday mornings at Combray . . .
my aunt Léonie used to give me, dipping it first in her
own cup of real or of lime-flower tea.
  Du côté de chez Swann (Swann's Way, 1913, translated 1922
  by C. K. Scott-Moncrieff, vol. 1, pp. 46 and 61)

18 *Et il ne fut plus question de Swann chez les Verdurin.*

After which there was no more talk of Swann at the
Verdurins'.
  Du côté de chez Swann (Swann's Way, 1913, translated 1922
  by C. K. Scott-Moncrieff, vol. 2, p. 99)

19 *Dire que j'ai gâché des années de ma vie, que j'ai voulu
mourir, que j'ai eu mon plus grand amour, pour une femme
qui ne me plaisait pas, qui n'était pas mon genre!*

To think that I have wasted years of my life, that I have
longed for death, that the greatest love that I have ever
known has been for a woman who did not please me,
who was not in my style!
  Du côté de chez Swann (Swann's Way, 1913, translated 1922
  by C. K. Scott-Moncrieff, vol. 2, p. 228)

20 *On devient moral dès qu'on est malheureux.*

As soon as one is unhappy one becomes moral.

A l'ombre des jeunes filles en fleurs (Within a Budding Grove, 1918, translated 1924 by C. K. Scott-Moncrieff, vol. 1, p. 290)

1 *Tout ce que nous connaissons de grand nous vient des nerveux. Ce sont eux et non pas d'autres qui ont fondé les religions et composé les chefs-d'œuvre. Jamais le monde ne saura tout ce qu'il leur doit et surtout ce qu'eux ont souffert pour le lui donner.*

All the greatest things we know have come to us from neurotics. It is they and they only who have founded religions and created great works of art. Never will the world be conscious of how much it owes to them, nor above all of what they have suffered in order to bestow their gifts on it.

Le côté de Guermantes (Guermantes Way, 1921, translated 1925 by C. K. Scott-Moncrieff, vol. 1, p. 418)

2 *Il n'y a rien comme le désir pour empêcher les choses qu'on dit d'avoir aucune ressemblance avec ce qu'on a dans la pensée.*

There is nothing like desire for preventing the thing one says from bearing any resemblance to what one has in mind.

Le côté de Guermantes (Guermantes Way, 1921, translated 1925 by C. K. Scott-Moncrieff, vol. 2, p. 60)

3 *Un artiste n'a pas besoin d'exprimer directement sa pensée dans son ouvrage pour que celui-ci en reflète la qualité; on a même pu dire que la louange la plus haute de Dieu est dans la négation de l'athée qui trouve la Création assez parfaite pour se passer d'un créateur.*

An artist has no need to express his mind directly in his work for it to express the quality of that mind; it has indeed been said that the highest praise of God consists in the denial of Him by the atheist, who finds creation so perfect that it can dispense with a creator.

Le côté de Guermantes (Guermantes Way, 1921, translated 1925 by C. K. Scott-Moncrieff, vol. 2, p. 147)

4 *Du reste, continua Mme de Cambremer, j'ai horreur des couchers de soleil, c'est romantique, c'est opéra.*

'Anyhow,' Mme de Cambremer went on, 'I have a horror of sunsets, they're so romantic, so operatic.'

Sodome et Gomorrhe (Cities of the Plain, 1922, translated by C. K. Scott-Moncrieff, vol. 1, p. 296)

5 *Une de ces dépêches dont M. de Guermantes avait spirituellement fixé le modèle: 'Impossible venir, mensonge suit'.*

One of those telegrams of which the model had been wittily invented by M. de Guermantes: 'Impossible to come, lie follows'.

Le temps retrouvé (Time Regained, 1926, translated 1931 by S. Hudson, ch. 1, p. 7). Cf. Lord Charles Beresford

6 *Les vrais paradis sont les paradis qu'on a perdus.*

The true paradises are paradises we have lost.

Le temps retrouvé (Time Regained, 1926, translated 1931 by S. Hudson, ch. 3, p. 215)

7 *Le bonheur seul est salutaire pour le corps, mais c'est le chagrin qui développe les forces de l'esprit.*

Happiness is salutary for the body but sorrow develops the powers of the spirit.

Le temps retrouvé (Time Regained, 1926, translated 1931 by S. Hudson, ch. 3, p. 259)

Olive Higgins Prouty 1882–1974

8 She [Charlotte] drew in her breath sharply as if he had touched a nerve. 'O Jerry,' she said when she could trust her voice. 'Don't let's ask for the moon! We have the stars!'

THE END

Now, Voyager (1941) ch. 29 (words spoken by Bette Davis in the 1942 film version)

John Pudney 1909–1977

9 Do not despair
For Johnny-head-in-air;
He sleeps as sound
As Johnny underground.

Fetch out no shroud
For Johnny-in-the-cloud;
And keep your tears
For him in after years.

Better by far
For Johnny-the-bright-star,
To keep your head,
And see his children fed.

Dispersal Point (1942) 'For Johnny'

Mario Puzo 1920–

10 He's a businessman. . . . I'll make him an offer he can't refuse.

The Godfather (1969) ch. 1

11 A lawyer with his briefcase can steal more than a hundred men with guns.

The Godfather (1969) ch. 1

12 Mario had called George Mandel to say he'd heard Joe [Heller] was paralysed. 'No, Mario. . . . He's got something called Guillain-Barré.' 'My God,' Mario blurted out. 'That's terrible!' A surprised George murmured, 'Hey Mario, you know about Guillain-Barré?' 'No, I never heard nothing about it,' Mario replied. 'But when they name any disease after two guys, it's got to be terrible!'

Joseph Heller *No Laughing Matter* (1986) p. 44

Q

See SIR ARTHUR QUILLER-COUCH

Salvatore Quasimodo 1901–1968

13 Poetry . . . is the revelation of a feeling that the poet believes to be interior and personal—which the reader recognizes as his own.

Speech in New York, 13 May 1960, in *New York Times* 14 May 1960, p. 47

Peter Quennell 1905–

14 He [André Gide] was very bald . . . with . . . the general look of an elderly fallen angel travelling incognito.

The Sign of the Fish (1960) ch. 2

Sir Arthur Quiller-Couch ('Q') 1863–1944

1 Literature is not an abstract science, to which exact definitions can be applied. It is an Art rather, the success of which depends on personal persuasiveness, on the author's skill to give as on ours to receive.
    Inaugural Lecture at Cambridge University, 1913, in On the Art of Writing (1916) p. 16

2 The best is the best, though a hundred judges have declared it so.
    Oxford Book of English Verse (1900) preface

3 Know you her secret none can utter?
Hers of the Book, the tripled Crown?
    Poems (1929) 'Alma Mater'

4 He that loves but half of Earth
Loves but half enough for me.
    Poems and Ballads (1896) 'The Comrade'

5 Not as we wanted it,
But as God granted it.
    Poems and Ballads (1896) 'To Bearers'

James Rado 1939–
and Gerome Ragni 1942–

6 When the moon is in the seventh house,
And Jupiter aligns with Mars,
Then peace will guide the planets,
And love will steer the stars;
This is the dawning of the age of Aquarius,
The age of Aquarius.
    Aquarius (1967 song; music by Galt MacDermot)

John Rae 1931–

7 War is, after all, the universal perversion. We are all tainted: if we cannot experience our perversion at first hand we spend our time reading war stories, the pornography of war; or seeing war films, the blue films of war; or titillating our senses with the imagination of great deeds, the masturbation of war.
    The Custard Boys (1960) ch. 13

Milton Rakove 1918–1983

8 The second law, Rakove's law of principle and politics, states that the citizen is influenced by principle in direct proportion to his distance from the political situation.
    In *Virginia Quarterly Review* (1965) vol. 41, p. 349

Sir Walter Raleigh 1861–1922

9 In Examinations those who do not wish to know ask questions of those who cannot tell.
    Laughter from a Cloud (1923) 'Some Thoughts on Examinations'

10 We could not lead a pleasant life,
And 'twould be finished soon,
If peas were eaten with the knife,
And gravy with the spoon.

Eat slowly: only men in rags
And gluttons old in sin
Mistake themselves for carpet bags
And tumble victuals in.
    Laughter from a Cloud (1923) 'Stans Puer ad Mensam'

11 I wish I loved the Human Race;
I wish I loved its silly face;
I wish I liked the way it walks;
I wish I liked the way it talks;
And when I'm introduced to one
I wish I thought *What Jolly Fun!*
    Laughter from a Cloud (1923) 'Wishes of an Elderly Man'

12 An anthology is like all the plums and orange peel picked out of a cake.
    Letter to Mrs Robert Bridges, 15 Jan. 1915, in *Letters of Sir Walter Raleigh* (1926) vol. 2, p. 411

Srinivasa Ramanujan 1887–1920

13 I remember once going to see him when he was lying ill at Putney. I had ridden in taxi-cab No. 1729, and remarked that the number (7.13.19) seemed to me rather a dull one. 'No,' he replied, 'it is a very interesting number; it is the smallest number expressible as a sum of two cubes in two different ways.'
    G. H. Hardy in *Proceedings of the London Mathematical Society* 26 May 1921, p. 57. (The two ways are $1^3 + 12^3$ and $9^3 + 10^3$)

John Crowe Ransom 1888–1974

14 Here lies a lady of beauty and high degree.
Of chills and fever she died, of fever and chills,
The delight of her husband, her aunts, an infant of three,
And of medicos marvelling sweetly on her ills.
    Chills and Fever (1924) 'Here Lies a Lady'

Arthur Ransome 1884–1967

15 Mother smiled, and read the telegram aloud: BETTER DROWNED THAN DUFFERS IF NOT DUFFERS WONT DROWN. 'Does that mean Yes?' asked Roger. 'I think so.'
    Swallows and Amazons (1930) ch. 1

Frederic Raphael 1931–

16 He glanced with disdain at the big centre table where the famous faces of the Cambridge theatre were eating a loud meal. 'So this is the city of dreaming spires,' Sheila said. 'Theoretically speaking that's Oxford,' Adam said. 'This is the city of perspiring dreams.'
    Glittering Prizes: (1976) ch. 3. Cf. *Oxford Dictionary of Quotations* (1979) 15:4

Terence Rattigan 1911–1977

17 The headmaster said you ruled them with a rod of iron. He called you the Himmler of the lower fifth.
    The Browning Version (1948) (spoken by Peter Gilbert to Andrew Crocker-Harris)

18 Let us invent a character, a nice respectable, middle-class, middle-aged, maiden lady, with time on her hands and the money to help her pass it. She enjoys

pictures, books, music, and the theatre and though to none of these arts (or rather, for consistency's sake, to none of these three arts and the one craft) does she bring much knowledge or discernment, at least, as she is apt to tell her cronies, she 'does know what she likes'. Let us call her Aunt Edna. . . . Aunt Edna is universal, and to those who may feel that all the problems of the modern theatre might be solved by her liquidation, let me add that I have no doubt at all that she is also immortal.

> Collected Plays (1953) vol. 2, preface

1 KENNETH: If you're so hot, you'd better tell me how to say she has ideas above her station.
BRIAN: Oh, yes, I forgot. It's fairly easy, old boy. Elle a des idées au-dessus de sa gare.
KENNETH: You can't do it like that. You can't say *au-dessus de sa gare*. It isn't that sort of station.

> French without Tears (1937) act 1

2 Do you know what 'le vice Anglais'—the English vice—really is? Not flagellation, not pederasty—whatever the French believe it to be. It's our refusal to admit our emotions. We think they demean us, I suppose.

> In Praise of Love (1973) act 2

3 You can be in the Horseguards and still be common, dear.

> Separate Tables (1954) 'Table Number Seven' sc. 1

Gwen Raverat 1885–1957

4 I have defined Ladies as people who did not do things themselves. Aunt Etty was most emphatically such a person.

> Period Piece (1952) ch. 7

Irving Ravetch and Harriet Frank

5 The long hot summer.

> Title of film (1958), based on stories by William Faulkner

Ted Ray (Charles Olden) 1906–1977

6 Ee, it was agony, Ivy.

> Catch-phrase in Ray's a Laugh (BBC radio programme, 1949–61)

7 He's loo-vely, Mrs Hoskin . . . he's loo . . . ooo . . . vely!

> Catch-phrase in Ray's a Laugh (BBC radio programme, 1949–61) in Raising the Laughs (1952) p. 158

Sam Rayburn 1882–1961

8 If you want to get along, go along.

> In Neil MacNeil Forge of Democracy (1963) ch. 6

Sir Herbert Read 1893–1968

9 Do not judge this movement kindly. It is not just another amusing stunt. It is defiant—the desperate act of men too profoundly convinced of the rottenness of our civilization to want to save a shred of its respectability.

> Introduction to International Surrealist Exhibition Catalogue, New Burlington Galleries, London, 11 June–4 July 1936

10 I saw him stab
And stab again
A well-killed Boche.

This is the happy warrior,
This is he. . . .

> Naked Warriors (1919) 'The Scene of War, 4. The Happy Warrior'

Nancy Reagan 1923–

11 A woman is like a teabag—only in hot water do you realise how strong she is.

> In Observer 29 Mar. 1981

Ronald Reagan 1911–

12 You can tell a lot about a fellow's character by his way of eating jellybeans.

> In New York Times 15 Jan. 1981

13 So in your discussions of the nuclear freeze proposals, I urge you to beware the temptation of pride—the temptation blithely to declare yourselves above it all and label both sides equally at fault, to ignore the facts of history and the aggressive impulses of an evil empire, to simply call the arms race a giant misunderstanding and thereby remove yourself from the struggle between right and wrong, good and evil.

> Speech to National Association of Evangelicals, 8 Mar. 1983, in New York Times 9 Mar. 1983

14 My fellow Americans, I am pleased to tell you I just signed legislation which outlaws Russia forever. The bombing begins in five minutes.

> Said during radio microphone test, 11 Aug. 1984, in New York Times 13 Aug. 1984

15 We are especially not going to tolerate these attacks from outlaw states run by the strangest collection of misfits, Looney Tunes and squalid criminals since the advent of the Third Reich.

> Speech following the hi-jack of a US plane, 8 July 1985, in New York Times 9 July 1985

16 We know that this mad dog of the Middle East has a goal of a world revolution, Muslim fundamentalist revolution, which is targeted on many of his own Arab compatriots and where we figure in that I don't know.

> Said of Col. Gadaffi of Libya at press conference, 9 Apr. 1986, in New York Times 10 Apr. 1986, p. A 22

17 Politics is supposed to be the second oldest profession. I have come to realize that it bears a very close resemblance to the first.

> At a conference in Los Angeles, 2 Mar. 1977, in Bill Adler Reagan Wit (1981) ch. 5

Erell Reaves

18 Lady of Spain, I adore you.
Right from the night I first saw you,
My heart has been yearning for you,
What else could any heart do?

> Lady of Spain (1931 song; music by Tolchard Evans)

Henry Reed 1914–1986

19 Today we have naming of parts. Yesterday,
We had daily cleaning. And tomorrow morning,

We shall have what to do after firing. But today,
Today we have naming of parts. Japonica
Glistens like coral in all of the neighbour gardens,
And today we have naming of parts.
> *A Map of Verona* (1946) 'Lessons of the War: 1, Naming of Parts'

1 They call it easing the Spring: it is perfectly easy
If you have any strength in your thumb: like the bolt,
And the breech, and the cocking-piece, and the point of balance,
Which in our case we have not got; and the almond blossom
Silent in all of the gardens and the bees going backwards and forwards,
For today we have naming of parts.
> *A Map of Verona* (1946) 'Lessons of the War: 1, Naming of Parts'

2 And the various holds and rolls and throws and breakfalls
Somehow or other I always seemed to put
In the wrong place. And as for war, my wars
Were global from the start.
> *A Map of Verona* (1946) 'Lessons of the War: 3, Unarmed Combat'

3 As we get older we do not get any younger.
Seasons return, and today I am fifty-five,
And this time last year I was fifty-four,
And this time next year I shall be sixty-two.
> *A Map of Verona* (1946) 'Chard Whitlow (Mr Eliot's Sunday Evening Postscript)'

4 It is, we believe,
Idle to hope that the simple stirrup-pump
Can extinguish hell.
> *A Map of Verona* (1946) 'Chard Whitlow (Mr Eliot's Sunday Evening Postscript)'

5 And the sooner the tea's out of the way, the sooner we can get out the gin, eh?
> *Private Life of Hilda Tablet* (1954 radio play) in *Hilda Tablet and Others: four pieces for radio* (1971) p. 60

6 DUCHESS: Of course we've all *dreamed* of reviving the *castrati*; but it's needed Hilda to take the first practical steps towards making them a reality.
REEVES: P-practical steps?
DUCHESS: Yes, thank God. She's drawn up a list of well-known singers who she thinks would benefit from . . . treatment. Some of them have been singing baritone, or even bass, for years. It's only a question of getting them to agree.
> *Private Life of Hilda Tablet* (1954 radio play) in *Hilda Tablet and Others: four pieces for radio* (1971) p. 72

John Reed 1887–1920

7 Ten days that shook the world.
> Title of book (1919)

Max Reger 1873–1916

8 *Ich sitze in dem kleinsten Zimmer in meinem Hause. Ich habe Ihre Kritik vor mir. Im nächsten Augenblick wird sie hinter mir sein.*

I am sitting in the smallest room of my house. I have your review before me. In a moment it will be behind me.
> Letter to Munich critic Rudolph Louis in response to his review in *Münchener Neueste Nachrichten*, 7 Feb. 1906, in Nicolas Slonimsky *Lexicon of Musical Invective* (1953) p. 139

Charles A. Reich 1928–

9 The greening of America.
> Title of book (1970)

Keith Reid and Gary Brooker

10 A whiter shade of pale.
> Title of song (1967) (performed by Procol Harum)

Erich Maria Remarque 1898–1970

11 All quiet on the western front.
> Title of translation of his novel *Im Westen nichts Neues* (Nothing New in the West, 1929). Cf. the title of a poem by Ethel L. Beers: *All Quiet along the Potomac* (1861)

Dr Montague John Rendall 1862–1950

12 Nation shall speak peace unto nation.
> Motto of the BBC, adapted from Micah 4:3 'Nation shall not lift up sword against nation'

James Reston 1909–

13 This is the devilish thing about foreign affairs: they are foreign and will not always conform to our whim.
> In *New York Times* 16 Dec. 1964, p. 42

14 All politics, however, are based on the indifference of the majority.
> In *New York Times* 12 June 1968, p. 46

David Reuben 1933–

15 Everything you always wanted to know about sex, but were afraid to ask.
> Title of book (1969)

Charles Revson 1906–1975

16 In the factory we make cosmetics; in the store we sell hope.
> In A. Tobias *Fire and Ice* (1976) ch. 8

Malvina Reynolds 1900–1978

17 Little boxes on the hillside,
Little boxes made of ticky-tacky,
Little boxes on the hillside,
Little boxes all the same;
There's a green one and a pink one
And a blue one and a yellow one
And they're all made out of ticky-tacky
And they all look just the same.
> *Little Boxes* (1962 song)

Quentin Reynolds 1902–1965

1 There is an old political adage which says 'If you can't lick 'em, jine 'em.'
   Wounded Don't Cry (1941) ch. 1

Cecil Rhodes 1853–1902

2 Ask any man what nationality he would prefer to be, and ninety-nine out of a hundred will tell you that they would prefer to be Englishmen.
   In Gordon Le Sueur *Cecil Rhodes* (1913) p. 40

3 Rhodes chose this time [in December 1896] to awaken his friend Albert Grey from his sleep one night in Bulawayo to ask him whether he had ever considered how fortunate he was to be alive and in good health and to have been born an Englishman, when so many millions of other human beings had no such luck.
   J. G. Lockhart and C. M. Woodhouse *Rhodes* (1963) p. 29

4 So little done, so much to do.
   Said to Lewis Michell on the day he died, in Lewis Michell *Life of Rhodes* (1910) vol. 2, ch. 39

Jean Rhys (Ella Gwendolen Rees Williams) ?1890–1979

5 The feeling of Sunday is the same everywhere, heavy, melancholy, standing still. Like when they say 'As it was in the beginning, is now, and ever shall be, world without end.'
   Voyage in the Dark (1934) ch. 4, pt. 1

Grantland Rice 1880–1954

6 All wars are planned by old men
   In council rooms apart.
   The Final Answer (1955) 'The Two Sides of War'

7 Outlined against a blue-gray October sky, the Four Horsemen rode again. In dramatic lore they were known as Famine, Pestilence, Destruction, and Death. These are only aliases. Their real names are Stuhldreher, Miller, Crowley, and Layden. They formed the crest of the South Bend cyclone before which another fighting Army football team was swept over the precipice at the Polo Grounds yesterday afternoon as 55,000 spectators peered down on the bewildering panorama spread on the green below.
   Report of football match on 18 Oct. 1924 between US Military Academy at West Point NY and University of Notre Dame, in *New York Tribune* 19 Oct. 1924

8 For when the One Great Scorer comes to mark against your name,
   He writes—not that you won or lost—but how you played the Game.
   Only the Brave (1941) 'Alumnus Football'

Tim Rice 1944–

9 Don't cry for me Argentina.
   Title of song (1976; music by Andrew Lloyd Webber)

10 Prove to me that you're no fool
   Walk across my swimming pool.
   Herod's Song (1970; music by Andrew Lloyd Webber)

Mandy Rice-Davies 1944–

11 MR BURGE: Do you know Lord Astor has made a statement to the police saying that these allegations of yours are absolutely untrue?
   MANDY RICE-DAVIES: He would, wouldn't he? (*Laughter*).
   At the trial of Stephen Ward, 29 June 1963, in *Guardian* 1 July 1963

12 An American tourist, seeing me the centre of a crowd, came up to me. 'Hello, my dear, may I have your autograph. And would you mind telling me who you are?' I hated having to say my name. For years Mandy Rice-Davies was such an embarrassment to me. It is only in recent times I have been able to say my name without a quiver of discomfort. 'Call me Lady Hamilton,' I said.
   Mandy (1980) ch. 16

Dicky Richards

13 My Goodness, My Guinness.
   Advertising slogan (1935) in B. Sibley *Book of Guinness Advertising* (1985) p. 83

Frank Richards (Charles Hamilton) 1876–1961

14 My postal-order hasn't come yet.
   Magnet (1908) vol. 1, no. 2 'The Taming of Harry'

15 Hazeldene looked from one to the other—from the well-set-up, athletic Lancashire lad, to the fat greedy owl of the Remove, and burst into a laugh.
   Magnet (1909) vol. 3, no. 72 'The Greyfriars Photographer'

16 'I—I say, you fellows—'
   'Shut up, Bunter.'
   'But—but I say—'
   'Keep that cush over his chivvy.'
   'I—I say—groo—groo—yarooh!'
   And Bunter's remarks again tailed off under the cushion.
   Magnet (1909) vol. 3, no. 85 'The Greyfriars Visitors'

I. A. Richards 1893–1979

17 It is very probable that the Hindenburg Line to which the defence of our traditions retired as a result of the onslaughts of the last century will be blown up in the near future. If this should happen a mental chaos such as man has never experienced may be expected. We shall then be thrown back . . . upon poetry. It is capable of saving us; it is a perfectly possible means of overcoming chaos.
   Science and Poetry (1926) ch. 7

Sir Ralph Richardson 1902–1983

18 'Acting,' Ralph Richardson of the Old Vic pronounced last week, 'is merely the art of keeping a large group of people from coughing.'
   New York Herald Tribune 19 May 1946, pt. 5, p. 1

Hans Richter 1843–1916

1 Your damned nonsense can I stand twice or once, but sometimes always, by God, Never.
   In *Hansard* 13 Feb. 1958, col. 574

Rainer Maria Rilke 1875–1926

2 *Kunst-Werke sind von einer unendlichen Einsamkeit und mit nichts so wenig erreichbar als mit Kritik. Nur Liebe kann sie erfassen und halten und kann gerecht sein gegen sie.*

Works of art are of an infinite solitariness, and nothing is less likely to bring us near to them than criticism. Only love can apprehend and hold them, and can be just towards them.
   Briefe an einen jungen Dichter (Letters to a Young Poet, 1929, translated by Reginald Snell, 1945) 23 Apr. 1903

3 *Und diese menschlichere Liebe (die unendlich rücksichtsvoll und leise, und gut und klar in Binden und Lösen sich vollziehen wird) wird jener ähneln, die wir ringend und mühsam vorbereiten, der Liebe, die darin besteht, dass zwei Einsamkeiten einander schützen, grenzen und grüssen.*

And this more human love (which will consummate itself infinitely thoughtfully and gently, and well and clearly in binding and loosing) will be something like that which we are preparing with struggle and toil, the love which consists in the mutual guarding, bordering and saluting of two solitudes.
   Briefe an einen jungen Dichter (Letters to a Young Poet, 1929, translated by Reginald Snell, 1945) 14 May 1904

4 *Wer hat uns also umgedreht, dass wir,*
   was wir auch tun, in jener Haltung sind
   von einem, welcher fortgeht? Wie er auf
   den letzten Hügel, der ihm ganz sein Tal
   noch einmal zeigt, sich wendet, anhält, weilt—,
   so leben wir und nehmen immer Abschied.

Who's turned us around like this, so that we always,
do what we may, retain the attitude
of someone who's departing? Just as he,
on the last hill, that shows him all his valley
for the last time, will turn and stop and linger,
we live our lives, for ever taking leave.
   Duineser Elegien (Duino Elegies, translated by J. B. Leishman and Stephen Spender, 1948) no. 8

5 *Ich für die höchste Aufgabe einer Verbindung zweier Menschen diese halte: dass einer dem andern seine Einsamkeit bewache.*

I hold this to be the highest task for a bond between two people: that each protects the solitude of the other.
   Letter to Paula Modersohn-Becker, 12 Feb. 1902, in *Gesammelte Briefe* (Collected Letters, 1904) vol. 1, p. 204

Hal Riney 1932–

6 It's morning again in America.
   Slogan for Ronald Reagan's election campaign, 1984, in *Newsweek* 6 Aug. 1984

Robert L. Ripley 1893–1949

7 Believe it or not.
   Title of syndicated newspaper feature (from 1918)

César Ritz 1850–1918

8 *Le client n'a jamais tort.*

The customer is never wrong.
   In R. Nevill and C. E. Jerningham *Piccadilly to Pall Mall* (1908) p. 94

Joan Riviere 1883–

9 Civilization and its discontents.
   Title of translation of Sigmund Freud's *Das Unbehagen in der Kultur* (1930)

Lord Robbins (Lionel Charles Robbins, Baron Robbins) 1898–1984

10 Economics is the science which studies human behaviour as a relationship between ends and scarce means which have alternative uses.
   Essay on the Nature and Significance of Economic Science (1932) ch. 1, sect. 3

Leo Robin 1900–

11 Diamonds are a girl's best friend.
   Title of song (1949; music by Jule Styne)

Leo Robin 1900– and Ralph Rainger

12 Thanks for the memory.
   Title of song (1937)

Edwin Arlington Robinson 1869–1935

13 So on we worked, and waited for the light,
   And went without meat, and cursed the bread;
   And Richard Cory, one calm summer night,
   Went home and put a bullet through his head.
   Children of the Night (1897) 'Richard Cory'

14 I shall have more to say when I am dead.
   The Three Taverns (1920) 'John Brown' (last line)

15 Miniver loved the Medici,
   Albeit he had never seen one;
   He would have sinned incessantly
   Could he have been one.
   The Town down the River (1910) 'Miniver Cheevy'

Rt. Revd John Robinson (Bishop of Woolwich) 1919–1983

16 What Lawrence is trying to do, I think, is to portray the sex relation as something sacred. . . . I think Lawrence tried to portray this relation as in a real sense an act of holy communion. For him flesh was sacramental of the spirit.
   Said as defence witness in case brought against Penguin Books for publishing *Lady Chatterley's Lover*, 27 Oct. 1960, in *The Times* 28 Oct. 1960

John D. Rockefeller 1839–1937

17 The growth of a large business is merely a survival of the fittest. . . . The American beauty rose can be produced in the splendour and fragrance which bring cheer to its beholder only by sacrificing the early buds which grow up around it.

In W. J. Ghent *Our Benevolent Feudalism* (1902) p. 29

Knute Rockne 1888–1931

See JOSEPH P. KENNEDY

Cecil Rodd

1 Stop me and buy one.

Advertising slogan for Wall's ice cream (from spring 1922) in *Wall's Magazine* Summer 1957, p. 33

Gene Roddenberry 1921–

2 Space—the final frontier. . . . These are the voyages of the starship *Enterprise*. Its five-year mission: to explore strange new worlds, to seek out new life and new civilizations, to boldly go where no man has gone before.

Introduction to *Star Trek* (television series) 1966 onwards, in James A. Lely *Star Trek* (1979) p. 32

3 Beam us up, Mr Scott.

Star Trek (television series 1966 onwards) 'Gamesters of Triskelion' (often quoted as the catch-phrase 'Beam me up, Scotty', which was not actually used in the series)

Theodore Roethke 1908–1963

4 I wake to sleep, and take my waking slow.
I feel my fate in what I cannot fear.
I learn by going where I have to go.

The Waking (1953) p. 120

Will Rogers 1879–1935

5 There is only one thing that can kill the Movies, and that is education.

Autobiography of Will Rogers (1949) ch. 6

6 The more you read and observe about this Politics thing, you got to admit that each party is worse than the other. The one that's out always looks the best.

Illiterate Digest (1924) 'Breaking into the Writing Game'

7 The Income Tax has made more Liars out of the American people than Golf has. Even when you make one out on the level, you don't know when it's through if you are a Crook or a Martyr.

Illiterate Digest (1924) 'Helping the Girls with their Income Taxes'

8 Everything is funny as long as it is happening to Somebody Else.

Illiterate Digest (1924) 'Warning to Jokers: lay off the prince'

9 Well, all I know is what I read in the papers.

New York Times 30 Sept. 1923

10 You know everybody is ignorant, only on different subjects.

In *New York Times* 31 Aug. 1924

11 You can't say civilization don't advance, however, for in every war they kill you in a new way.

New York Times 23 Dec. 1929

12 Half our life is spent trying to find something to do with the time we have rushed through life trying to save.

Letter in *New York Times* 29 Apr. 1930

13 I bet you if I had met him [Trotsky] and had a chat with him, I would have found him a very interesting and human fellow, for I never yet met a man that I didn't like.

In *Saturday Evening Post* 6 Nov. 1926

14 I don't make jokes—I just watch the government and report the facts.

In *Saturday Review* 25 Aug. 1962

15 Communism is like prohibition, it's a good idea but it won't work.

Weekly Articles (1981) vol. 3, p. 93 (first pubd. 1927)

16 Heroing is one of the shortest-lived professions there is.

Newspaper article, 15 Feb. 1925, in Paula McSpadden Grove *The Will Rogers Book* (1961) p. 193

Frederick William Rolfe ('Baron Corvo') 1860–1913

17 'There is no Holiness here,' George interrupted, in that cold, white, candent voice which was more caustic than silver nitrate and more thrilling than a scream.

Hadrian VII (1904) ch. 21

18 Pray for the repose of His soul. He was so tired.

Hadrian VII (1904) ch. 24

Angelo Giuseppe Roncalli

See POPE JOHN XXIII

Eleanor Roosevelt 1884–1962

19 No one can make you feel inferior without your consent.

In *Catholic Digest* Aug. 1960, p. 102

Franklin D. Roosevelt 1882–1945

20 It is fun to be in the same decade with you.

Cable to Winston Churchill, replying to congratulations on Roosevelt's 60th birthday, in W. S. Churchill *Hinge of Fate* (1950) ch. 4

21 These unhappy times call for the building of plans that . . . build from the bottom up . . . that put their faith once more in the forgotten man at the bottom of the economic pyramid.

Radio address, 7 Apr. 1932, in *Public Papers* (1938) vol. 1, p. 625

22 I pledge you, I pledge myself, to a new deal for the American people. Let us all here assembled constitute ourselves prophets of a new order of competence and of courage. This is more than a political campaign; it is a call to arms. Give me your help, not to win votes alone, but to win in this crusade to restore America to its own people.

Speech to Democratic Convention in Chicago, 2 July 1932, accepting nomination for presidency, in *Public Papers* (1938) vol. 1, p. 647

1 First of all, let me assert my firm belief that the only thing we have to fear is fear itself—nameless, unreasoning, unjustified terror which paralyses needed efforts to convert retreat into advance.

Inaugural address, 4 Mar. 1933, in *Public Papers* (1938) vol. 2, p. 11

2 In the field of world policy I would dedicate this Nation to the policy of the good neighbour.

Inaugural address, 4 Mar. 1933, in *Public Papers* (1938) vol. 2, p. 14

3 I have seen war. I have seen war on land and sea. I have seen blood running from the wounded. I have seen men coughing out their gassed lungs. I have seen the dead in the mud. I have seen cities destroyed. I have seen 200 limping, exhausted men come out of line—the survivors of a regiment of 1,000 that went forward 48 hours before. I have seen children starving. I have seen the agony of mothers and wives. I hate war.

Speech at Chautauqua, NY, 14 Aug. 1936, in *Public Papers* (1936) vol. 5, p. 289

4 I see one-third of a nation ill-housed, ill-clad, ill-nourished.

Second inaugural address, 20 Jan. 1937, in *Public Papers* (1941) vol. 6, p. 5

5 When peace has been broken anywhere, the peace of all countries everywhere is in danger.

'Fireside Chat' radio broadcast, 3 Sept. 1939, in *Public Papers* (1941) vol. 8, p. 461

6 I am reminded of four definitions: A Radical is a man with both feet firmly planted—in the air.
A Conservative is a man with two perfectly good legs who, however, has never learned to walk forward.
A Reactionary is a somnambulist walking backwards.
A Liberal is a man who uses his legs and his hands at the behest—at the command—of his head.

Radio address to *New York Herald Tribune* Forum, 26 Oct. 1939, in *Public Papers* (1941) vol. 8, p. 556

7 And while I am talking to you mothers and fathers, I give you one more assurance. I have said this before, but I shall say it again and again and again: Your boys are not going to be sent into any foreign wars.

Speech in Boston, 30 Oct. 1940, in *Public Papers* (1941) vol. 9, p. 517

8 We have the men—the skill—the wealth—and above all, the will. . . . We must be the great arsenal of democracy.

'Fireside Chat' radio broadcast, 29 Dec. 1940, in *Public Papers* (1941) vol. 9, p. 643

9 In the future days, which we seek to make secure, we look forward to a world founded upon four essential human freedoms. The first is freedom of speech and expression—everywhere in the world. The second is freedom of every person to worship God in his own way—everywhere in the world. The third is freedom from want—which, translated into world terms, means economic understanding which will secure to every nation a healthy peacetime life for its inhabitants—everywhere in the world. The fourth is freedom from fear—which, translated into world terms, means a world-wide reduction of armaments to such a point and in such a thorough fashion that no nation will be in a position to commit an act of physical aggression against any neighbour—anywhere in the world.

Message to Congress, 6 Jan. 1941, in *Public Papers* (1941) vol. 9, p. 672

10 Yesterday, December 7, 1941—a date which will live on in infamy—the United States of America was suddenly and deliberately attacked by naval and air forces of the Empire of Japan.

Address to Congress, 8 Dec. 1941, in *Public Papers* (1950) vol. 10, p. 514

11 The work, my friend, is peace. More than an end of this war—an end to the beginnings of all wars. Yes, an end forever to this impractical, unrealistic settlement of the differences between governments by the mass killings of peoples.

Undelivered address for Jefferson Day, 13 Apr. 1945 (the day after Roosevelt died) in *Public Papers* (1950) vol. 13, p. 615

12 The only limit to our realization of tomorrow will be our doubts of today. Let us move forward with strong and active faith.

Undelivered address for Jefferson Day, 13 Apr. 1945, final lines, in *Public Papers* (1950) vol. 13, p. 616

13 We all know that books burn—yet we have the greater knowledge that books can not be killed by fire. People die, but books never die. No man and no force can abolish memory. No man and no force can put thought in a concentration camp forever. No man and no force can take from the world the books that embody man's eternal fight against tyranny of every kind. In this war, we know, books are weapons. And it is a part of your dedication always to make them weapons for man's freedom.

'Message to the Booksellers of America' read at banquet, 6 May 1942, in *Publisher's Weekly* 9 May 1942

Theodore Roosevelt 1858–1919

14 The first requisite of a good citizen in this Republic of ours is that he shall be able and willing to pull his weight.

Speech in New York, 11 Nov. 1902, in *Addresses and Presidential Messages 1902–4* (1904) p. 85

15 A man who is good enough to shed his blood for the country is good enough to be given a square deal afterwards. More than that no man is entitled to, and less than that no man shall have.

Speech at the Lincoln Monument, Springfield, Illinois, 4 June 1903, in *Addresses and Presidential Messages 1902–4* (1904) p. 224

16 [William] McKinley has no more backbone than a chocolate éclair!

In H. T. Peck *Twenty Years of the Republic* (1906) p. 642

17 There is a homely old adage which runs: 'Speak softly and carry a big stick; you will go far.' If the American nation will speak softly, and yet build and keep at a pitch of the highest training a thoroughly efficient navy, the Monroe Doctrine will go far.

Speech at Chicago, 3 Apr. 1903, in *New York Times* 4 Apr. 1903

1 There can be no fifty-fifty Americanism in this country. There is room here for only 100 per cent. Americanism, only for those who are Americans and nothing else.

> Speech in Saratoga, 19 July 1918, in *Roosevelt Policy* (1919) vol. 3, p. 1079

2 I wish to preach, not the doctrine of ignoble ease, but the doctrine of the strenuous life.

> Speech to the Hamilton Club, Chicago, 10 Apr. 1899, in *Works*, Memorial edition (1925), vol. 15, p. 267

3 No man is justified in doing evil on the ground of expediency.

> In *Works*, Memorial edition (1925) vol. 15, p. 388 'Latitude and Longitude among Reformers'

4 The men with the muck-rakes are often indispensable to the well-being of society; but only if they know when to stop raking the muck.

> Speech in Washington, 14 Apr. 1906, in *Works*, Memorial edition (1925) vol. 18, p. 574

5 A hyphenated American is not an American at all. This is just as true of the man who puts 'native' before the hyphen as of the man who puts German or Irish or English or French before the hyphen. Americanism is a matter of the spirit and of the soul. Our allegiance must be purely to the United States. We must unsparingly condemn any man who holds any other allegiance.

> Speech in New York, 12 Oct. 1915, in *Works*, Memorial edition (1925) vol. 20, p. 457

6 There are the foolish fanatics always to be found in such a movement and always discrediting it—the men who form the lunatic fringe in all reform movements.

> *Autobiography* (1913) ch. 7, in *Works*, Memorial edition (1925) vol. 22, p. 247

7 I wish in this campaign to do . . . whatever is likely to produce the best results for the Republican ticket. I am as strong as a bull moose and you can use me to the limit.

> Letter to Mark Hanna, 27 June 1900, in *Works*, Memorial edition (1926) vol. 23, p. 162 ('Bull Moose' became the popular name of the Progressive Party)

8 One of our defects as a nation is a tendency to use what have been called 'weasel words'. When a weasel sucks eggs the meat is sucked out of the egg. If you use a 'weasel word' after another, there is nothing left of the other.

> Speech in St Louis, 31 May 1916, in *Works*, Memorial edition (1926) vol. 24, p. 483

9 Good to the last drop.

> Said to Joel Cheek in 1907 about Maxwell House coffee, and subsequently used as an advertising slogan

Arthur Rose and Douglas Furber

10 Any time you're Lambeth way,
Any evening, any day,
You'll find us all
Doin' the Lambeth Walk.

> *Lambeth Walk* (1937 song; music by Noel Gay)

Billy Rose 1899–1966

11 Me and my shadow.

> Title of song (1927; music by Al Jolson and Dave Dreyer)

Billy Rose 1899–1966 and Marty Bloom

12 Does the spearmint lose its flavour on the bedpost overnight?

> Title of song (1924; music by Ernest Breuer; revived in 1959 by Lonnie Donegan with the title 'Does your chewing-gum lose its flavour on the bedpost overnight?')

Billy Rose 1899–1966 and Willie Raskin 1896–1942

13 Fifty million Frenchmen can't be wrong.

> Title of song (1927; music by Fred Fisher). Cf. Texas Guinan

William Rose 1918–1987

14 The Russians are coming, the Russians are coming.

> Title of film (1966)

Lord Rosebery (Archibald Philip Primrose, 5th Earl of Rosebery) 1847–1929

15 There is no need for any nation, however great, leaving the Empire, because the Empire is a commonwealth of nations.

> Speech in Adelaide, Australia, 18 Jan. 1884, in Marquess of Crewe *Lord Rosebery* (1931) vol. 1, ch. 7

16 And now we cannot but observe that it is beginning to be hinted that we are a nation of amateurs.

> Rectorial Address at Glasgow University, 16 Nov. 1900, in *The Times* 17 Nov. 1900

17 I must plough my furrow alone. That is my fate, agreeable or the reverse; but before I get to the end of that furrow it is possible that I may find myself not alone.

> Speech at City of London Liberal Club, 19 July 1901, on remaining outside Liberal Party leadership, in *The Times* 20 July 1901

Ethel Rosenberg 1916–1953 and Julius Rosenberg 1918–1953

18 We are innocent, as we have proclaimed and maintained from the time of our arrest. This is the whole truth. To forsake this truth is to pay too high a price even for the priceless gift of life—for life thus purchased we could not live out in dignity and self-respect.

> Petition for executive clemency, filed 9 Jan. 1953, in Ethel Rosenberg *Death House Letters* (1953) p. 149

19 Ethel wants it made known that we are the first victims of American Fascism.

> Letter from Julius to Emanuel Bloch before their execution for espionage, 19 June 1953, in Ethel Rosenberg *Testament of Ethel and Julius Rosenberg* (1954) p. 187

Alan S. C. Ross 1907–1980

20 U and Non-U. An essay in sociological linguistics.

> Title of essay in Nancy Mitford *Noblesse Oblige* (1956), first published in *Neuphilologische Mitteilungen* (1954)

Harold Ross 1892–1951

1 Usually he [Ross] confined himself to written comments. His later famed 'What mean?' 'Who he?' and the like began to appear on manuscripts and proofs.

> Dale Kramer *Ross and The New Yorker* (1952) ch. 13

2 The *New Yorker* will be the magazine which is not edited for the old lady in Dubuque.

> In James Thurber *The Years with Ross* (1959) ch. 4

3 'I don't want you to think I'm not incoherent,' he [Ross] once rattled off to somebody in '21'.

> James Thurber *The Years with Ross* (1959) ch. 5

4 I understand the hero [of Hemingway's *A Farewell to Arms*] keeps getting in bed with women, and the war wasn't fought that way.

> In James Thurber *The Years with Ross* (1959) ch. 7

Sir Ronald Ross 1857–1932

5 This day relenting God
Hath placed within my hand
A wondrous thing; and God
Be praised. At his command,

Seeking His secret deeds
With tears and toiling breath,
I find thy cunning seeds,
O million-murdering Death.

I know this little thing
A myriad men will save,
O Death, where is thy sting?
Thy victory, O Grave?

> *Philosophies* (1910) 'In Exile' pt. 7 (describing his part in discovering the life-cycle of the malaria parasite in 1897; cf. *Oxford Dictionary of Quotations* (1979) 77:1)

Jean Rostand 1894–1977

6 *Mon pessimisme va jusqu'à suspecter la sincérité des pessimistes.*

My pessimism goes to the point of suspecting the sincerity of the pessimists.

> *Journal d'un caractère* (Journal of a Character, 1931)

7 *Être adulte, c'est être seul.*

To be adult is to be alone.

> *Pensées d'un biologiste* (Thoughts of a Biologist, 1954) p. 134

8 *On tue un homme, on est un assassin. On tue des millions d'hommes, on est conquérant. On les tue tous, on est un dieu.*

Kill a man, and you are an assassin. Kill millions of men, and you are a conqueror. Kill everyone, and you are a god.

> *Pensées d'un biologiste* (Thoughts of a Biologist, 1939) p. 116

Leo Rosten 1908–

9 The only thing I can say about W. C. Fields, whom I have admired since the day he advanced upon Baby LeRoy with an ice pick, is this: any man who hates dogs and babies can't be all bad.

> Speech at Hollywood dinner in honour of W. C. Fields, 16 Feb. 1939, in *Saturday Review* 12 June 1976

Philip Roth 1933–

10 A Jewish man with parents alive is a fifteen-year-old boy, and will remain a fifteen-year-old boy until *they die!*

> *Portnoy's Complaint* (1967) p. 111

11 Doctor, my doctor, what do you say, LET'S PUT THE ID BACK IN YID!

> *Portnoy's Complaint* (1967) p. 124

Dan Rowan 1922–1987 and Dick Martin 1923–

12 Very interesting ... but stupid.

> Catch-phrase in *Rowan and Martin's Laugh-In* (American television series, 1967–73)

Helen Rowland 1875–1950

13 A husband is what is left of a lover, after the nerve has been extracted.

> *A Guide to Men* (1922) p. 19

14 Somehow a bachelor never quite gets over the idea that he is a thing of beauty and a boy forever.

> *A Guide to Men* (1922) p. 25

15 The follies which a man regrets most, in his life, are those which he didn't commit when he had the opportunity.

> *A Guide to Men* (1922) p. 87

16 When you see what some girls marry, you realize how they must hate to work for a living.

> *Reflections of a Bachelor Girl* (1909) p. 45

Richard Rowland ?1881–1947

17 The lunatics have taken charge of the asylum.

> Comment on take-over of United Artists by Charles Chaplin, Mary Pickford, Douglas Fairbanks and D. W. Griffith, in Terry Ramsaye *A Million and One Nights* (1926) vol. 2, ch. 79

Maude Royden 1876–1956

18 The Church should go forward along the path of progress and be no longer satisfied only to represent the Conservative Party at prayer.

> Address at Queen's Hall, London, 16 July 1917, in *The Times* 17 July 1917

Naomi Royde-Smith ?1875–1964

19 I know two things about the horse
And one of them is rather coarse.

> *Weekend Book* (1928) p. 231

Paul Alfred Rubens 1875–1917

20 Oh! we don't want to lose you but we think you ought to go
For your King and your Country both need you so;
We shall want you and miss you but with all our might and main

We shall cheer you, thank you, kiss you
When you come back again.
Your King and Country Want You (1914 song)

Damon Runyon 1884–1946

1 I do see her in tough joints more than somewhat.
Collier's 22 May 1930, 'Social Error'

2 'You are snatching a hard guy when you snatch Bookie
Bob. A very hard guy, indeed. In fact,' I say, 'I hear the
softest thing about him is his front teeth.'
Collier's 26 Sept. 1931, 'Snatching of Bookie Bob'

3 I always claim the mission workers came out too early
to catch any sinners on this part of Broadway. At such
an hour the sinners are still in bed resting up from their
sinning of the night before, so they will be in good
shape for more sinning a little later on.
Collier's 28 Jan. 1933, 'The Idyll of Miss Sarah Brown'

4 'In fact,' Sam the Gonoph says, 'I long ago come to the
conclusion that all life is 6 to 5 against.'
Collier's 8 Sept. 1934, 'A Nice Price'

5 'My boy,' he says, 'always try to rub up against money,
for if you rub up against money long enough, some of it
may rub off on you.'
Cosmopolitan Aug. 1929, 'A Very Honourable Guy'

Dean Rusk 1909–

6 We're eyeball to eyeball, and I think the other fellow
just blinked.
Comment on Cuban missile crisis, 24 Oct. 1962, in *Saturday
Evening Post* 8 Dec. 1962

Bertrand Russell (*Bertrand Arthur William, third Earl Russell*) 1872–1970

7 Three passions, simple but overwhelmingly strong,
have governed my life: the longing for love, the search
for knowledge, and unbearable pity for the suffering of
mankind.
Autobiography (1967) vol. 1, prologue

8 I was told that the Chinese said they would bury me by
the Western Lake and build a shrine to my memory.
I have some slight regret that this did not happen as
I might have become a god, which would have been
very *chic* for an atheist.
Autobiography (1968) vol. 2, ch. 3

9 Men who are unhappy, like men who sleep badly, are
always proud of the fact.
Conquest of Happiness (1930) ch. 1

10 Boredom is therefore a vital problem for the moralist,
since half the sins of mankind are caused by the fear of
it.
Conquest of Happiness (1930) ch. 4

11 One of the symptoms of approaching nervous
breakdown is the belief that one's work is terribly
important, and that to take a holiday would bring all
kinds of disaster. If I were a medical man, I should
prescribe a holiday to any patient who considered his
work important.
Conquest of Happiness (1930) ch. 5

12 Envy is the basis of democracy.
Conquest of Happiness (1930) ch. 6

13 One should as a rule respect public opinion in so far as
is necessary to avoid starvation and to keep out of
prison, but anything that goes beyond this is voluntary
submission to an unnecessary tyranny, and is likely to
interfere with happiness in all kinds of ways.
Conquest of Happiness (1930) ch. 9

14 A sense of duty is useful in work, but offensive in
personal relations. People wish to be liked, not to be
endured with patient resignation.
Conquest of Happiness (1930) ch. 10

15 Of all forms of caution, caution in love is perhaps the
most fatal to true happiness.
Conquest of Happiness (1930) ch. 12

16 To be able to fill leisure intelligently is the last product
of civilization, and at present very few people have
reached this level.
Conquest of Happiness (1930) ch. 14

17 Aristotle maintained that women have fewer teeth than
men; although he was twice married, it never occurred
to him to verify this statement by examining his wives'
mouths.
Impact of Science on Society (1952) ch. 1

18 The fact that an opinion has been widely held is no
evidence whatever that it is not utterly absurd; indeed
in view of the silliness of the majority of mankind,
a widespread belief is more likely to be foolish than
sensible.
Marriage and Morals (1929) ch. 5

19 To fear love is to fear life, and those who fear life are
already three parts dead.
Marriage and Morals (1929) ch. 19

20 Mathematics may be defined as the subject in which we
never know what we are talking about, nor whether
what we are saying is true.
Mysticism and Logic (1917) ch. 4

21 Only on the firm foundation of unyielding despair, can
the soul's habitation henceforth be safely built.
Philosophical Essays (1910) no. 2

22 Mathematics, rightly viewed, possesses not only truth,
but supreme beauty—a beauty cold and austere, like
that of sculpture.
Philosophical Essays (1910) no. 4

23 It is undesirable to believe a proposition when there is
no ground whatever for supposing it is true.
Sceptical Essays (1928) 'On the Value of Scepticism'

24 The infliction of cruelty with a good conscience is
a delight to moralists. That is why they invented Hell.
Sceptical Essays (1928) 'On the Value of Scepticism'

25 Every man, wherever he goes, is encompassed by
a cloud of comforting convictions, which move with
him like flies on a summer day.
Sceptical Essays (1928) 'Dreams and Facts'

26 Machines are worshipped because they are beautiful,
and valued because they confer power; they are hated
because they are hideous, and loathed because they
impose slavery.
Sceptical Essays (1928) 'Machines and Emotions'

1 We have, in fact, two kinds of morality side by side: one which we preach but do not practise, and another which we practise but seldom preach.

    Sceptical Essays (1928) 'Eastern and Western Ideals of Happiness'

2 It is obvious that 'obscenity' is not a term capable of exact legal definition; in the practice of the Courts, it means 'anything that shocks the magistrate'.

    Sceptical Essays (1928) 'Recrudescence of Puritanism'

3 The fundamental defect of fathers, in our competitive society, is that they want their children to be a credit to them.

    Sceptical Essays (1928) 'Freedom versus Authority in Education'

4 Man is a credulous animal, and must believe *something*; in the absence of good grounds for belief, he will be satisfied with bad ones.

    Unpopular Essays (1950) 'Outline of Intellectual Rubbish' ·

5 Fear is the main source of superstition, and one of the main sources of cruelty. To conquer fear is the beginning of wisdom, in the pursuit of truth as in the endeavour after a worthy manner of life.

    Unpopular Essays (1950) 'Outline of Intellectual Rubbish'

Dora Russell (Countess Russell) 1894–1986

6 We want better reasons for having children than not knowing how to prevent them.

    Hypatia (1925) ch. 4

George William Russell

See AE

John Russell 1919–

7 Certain phrases stick in the throat, even if they offer nothing that is analytically improbable. 'A dashing Swiss officer' is one such. Another is 'the beautiful Law Courts'.

    Paris (1960) ch. 11

Ernest Rutherford (Baron Rutherford of Nelson) 1871–1937

8 I do not ... want to give the impression that the use of large machines or of elaborate techniques is always justified; sometimes it contributes merely to the sense of self-importance of the investigator, and it is always salutary to remember Rutherford's 'We haven't got the money, so we've got to think!'

    R. V. Jones in *Bulletin of the Institute of Physics* (1962) vol. 13, p. 102

9 All science is either physics or stamp collecting.

    In J. B. Birks *Rutherford at Manchester* (1962) p. 108

Gilbert Ryle 1900–1976

10 A myth is, of course, not a fairy story. It is the presentation of facts belonging to one category in the idioms appropriate to another. To explode a myth is

accordingly not to deny the facts but to re-allocate them. And this is what I am trying to do.

    Concept of Mind (1949) introduction

11 Philosophy is the replacement of category-habits by category-disciplines.

    Concept of Mind (1949) introduction

12 Such in outline is the official theory. I shall often speak of it, with deliberate abusiveness, as 'the dogma of the Ghost in the Machine'.

    Concept of Mind (1949) ch. 1 (referring to Descartes' mental-conduct concepts)

Rafael Sabatini 1875–1950

13 He was born with a gift of laughter and a sense that the world was mad. And that was all his patrimony.

    Scaramouche (1921) bk. 1, ch. 1

Oliver Sacks 1933–

14 The man who mistook his wife for a hat.

    Title of book (1985)

Victoria ('Vita') Sackville-West 1892–1962

15 The greater cats with golden eyes
Stare out between the bars.
Deserts are there, and different skies,
And night with different stars.

    King's Daughter (1929) pt. 2, no. 1 'The Greater Cats with Golden Eyes'

16 The country habit has me by the heart,
For he's bewitched for ever who has seen,
Not with his eyes but with his vision, Spring
Flow down the woods and stipple leaves with sun.

    The Land (1926) 'Winter'

Françoise Sagan 1935–

17 *Rien n'est plus affreux que le rire pour la jalousie.*

To jealousy, nothing is more frightful than laughter.

    La Chamade (1965) ch. 9

Antoine de Saint-Exupéry 1900–1944

18 *Les grandes personnes ne comprennent jamais rien toutes seules, et c'est fatigant, pour les enfants, de toujours et toujours leur donner des explications.*

Grown-ups never understand anything for themselves, and it is tiresome for children to be always and forever explaining things to them.

    Le Petit Prince (The Little Prince, 1943) ch. 1

19 *On ne voit bien qu'avec le cœur. L'essentiel est invisible pour les yeux.*

It is only with the heart that one can see rightly; what is essential is invisible to the eye.

    Le Petit Prince (The Little Prince, 1943) ch. 21

20 *L'expérience nous montre qu'aimer ce n'est point nous regarder l'un l'autre mais regarder ensemble dans la même direction.*

Life has taught us that love does not consist in gazing at each other but in looking together in the same direction.

Terre des Hommes (translated as 'Wind, Sand and Stars', 1939) ch. 8

George Saintsbury 1845–1933

1 I have never yet given a second-hand opinion of any thing, or book, or person.

Notes on a Cellar-Book (1920) 'Preliminary'

Saki (Hector Hugh Munro) 1870–1916

2 'But why should you want to shield him?' cried Egbert; 'the man is a common murderer.' 'A common murderer, possibly, but a very uncommon cook.'

Beasts and Super-Beasts (1914) 'The Blind Spot'

3 'Waldo is one of those people who would be enormously improved by death,' said Clovis.

Beasts and Super-Beasts (1914) 'The Feast of Nemesis'

4 He's simply got the instinct for being unhappy highly developed.

Chronicles of Clovis (1911) 'The Match-Maker'

5 'I think oysters are more beautiful than any religion,' he resumed presently. 'They not only forgive our unkindness to them; they justify it, they incite us to go on being perfectly horrid to them. Once they arrive at the supper-table they seem to enter thoroughly into the spirit of the thing. There's nothing in Christianity or Buddhism that quite matches the sympathetic unselfishness of an oyster.'

Chronicles of Clovis (1911) 'The Match-Maker'

6 All decent people live beyond their incomes nowadays, and those who aren't respectable live beyond other peoples'. A few gifted individuals manage to do both.

Chronicles of Clovis (1911) 'The Match-Maker'

7 The people of Crete unfortunately make more history than they can consume locally.

Chronicles of Clovis (1911) 'The Jesting of Arlington Stringham'

8 His socks compelled one's attention without losing one's respect.

Chronicles of Clovis (1911) '"Ministers of Grace"'

9 People may say what they like about the decay of Christianity; the religious system that produced green Chartreuse can never really die.

Reginald (1904) 'Reginald on Christmas Presents'

10 Every reformation must have its victims. You can't expect the fatted calf to share the enthusiasm of the angels over the prodigal's return.

Reginald (1904) 'Reginald on the Academy'

11 I always say beauty is only sin deep.

Reginald (1904) 'Reginald's Choir Treat'

12 Her frocks are built in Paris, but she wears them with a strong English accent.

Reginald (1904) 'Reginald on Worries'

13 The young have aspirations that never come to pass, the old have reminiscences of what never happened.

Reginald (1904) 'Reginald at the Carlton'

14 There may have been disillusionments in the lives of the medieval saints, but they would scarcely have been better pleased if they could have forseen that their names would be associated nowadays chiefly with racehorses and the cheaper clarets.

Reginald (1904) 'Reginald at the Carlton'

15 The cook was a good cook, as cooks go; and as good cooks go, she went.

Reginald (1904) 'Reginald on Besetting Sins'

16 Women and elephants never forget an injury.

Reginald (1904) 'Reginald on Besetting Sins'

17 The Young Turkish candidate, who had conformed to the Western custom of one wife and hardly any mistresses, stood by helplessly while his adversary's poll swelled to a triumphant majority.

Reginald in Russia (1910) 'A Young Turkish Catastrophe'

18 The death of John Pennington had left his widow in circumstances which were more straitened than ever, and the Park had receded even from her notepaper, where it had long been retained as a courtesy title on the principle that addresses are given to us to conceal our whereabouts.

Reginald in Russia (1910) 'Cross Currents'

19 But, good gracious, you've got to educate him first. You can't expect a boy to be vicious till he's been to a good school.

Reginald in Russia (1910) 'The Baker's Dozen'

20 I should be the last person to say anything against temptation, naturally, but we have a proverb down here 'in baiting a mouse-trap with cheese, always leave room for the mouse'.

The Square Egg (1924) 'The Infernal Parliament'

21 A little inaccuracy sometimes saves tons of explanation.

The Square Egg (1924) 'Clovis on the Alleged Romance of Business'

22 Children with Hyacinth's temperament don't know better as they grow older; they merely know more.

Toys of Peace and Other Papers (1919) 'Hyacinth'

23 A buzz of recognition came from the front rows of the pit, together with a craning of necks on the part of those in less favoured seats. It heralded the arrival of Sherard Blaw, the dramatist who had discovered himself, and who had given so ungrudgingly of his discovery to the world.

The Unbearable Bassington (1912) ch. 13

J. D. Salinger 1919–

24 If you really want to hear about it, the first thing you'll probably want to know is where I was born, and what my lousy childhood was like, and how my parents were occupied and all before they had me, and all that David Copperfield kind of crap, but I don't feel like going into it.

Catcher in the Rye (1951) ch. 1

25 What really knocks me out is a book that, when you're all done reading it, you wish the author that wrote it was a terrific friend of yours and you could call him up on the phone whenever you felt like it.

Catcher in the Rye (1951) ch. 3

1 Sex is something I really don't understand too hot. You never know *where* the hell you are. I keep making up these sex rules for myself, and then I break them right away.

Catcher in the Rye (1951) ch. 9

2 The only thing old Phoebe liked was when Hamlet patted this dog on the head. She thought that was funny and nice, and it was. What I'll have to do is, I'll have to read that play. The trouble with me is, I always have to read that stuff by myself. If an actor acts it out, I hardly listen. I keep worrying about whether he's going to do something phoney every minute.

Catcher in the Rye (1951) ch. 16

3 Take most people, they're crazy about cars. They worry if they get a little scratch on them, and they're always talking about how many miles they get to a gallon, and if they get a brand-new car already they start thinking about trading it in for one that's even newer. I don't even like *old* cars. I mean they don't even interest me. I'd rather have a goddam horse. A horse is at least *human*, for God's sake.

Catcher in the Rye (1951) ch. 17

4 'You know that song "If a body catch a body comin' through the rye"? I'd like—'
'It's "If a body *meet* a body coming through the rye"!' old Phoebe said. 'It's a poem. By Robert *Burns*.'
'I *know* it's a poem by Robert Burns.'
She was right, though. It *is* 'If a body meet a body coming through the rye'. I didn't know it then, though.
'I thought it was "If a body catch a body",' I said. 'Anyway, I keep picturing all these little kids playing some game in this big field of rye and all. Thousands of little kids, and nobody's around—nobody big, I mean—except me. And I'm standing on the edge of some crazy cliff. What I have to do, I have to catch everybody if they start to go over the cliff—I mean if they're running and they don't look where they're going I have to come out from somewhere and catch them. That's all I'd do all day. I'd just be the catcher in the rye and all. I know it's crazy, but that's the only thing I'd really like to be. I know it's crazy.'

Catcher in the Rye (1951) ch. 22

5 A confessional passage has probably never been written that didn't stink a little bit of the writer's pride in having given up his pride.

Seymour: an Introduction (1959) in *Raise High the Roof Beam, Carpenters and Seymour: an Introduction* (1963) p. 195

Lord Salisbury (*Robert Arthur James Gascoyne-Cecil, fifth Marquess of Salisbury*) 1893–1972

6 He is, as we all know, a man of most unusual intellectual brilliance; and he is, moreover, both brave and resolute. Those are valuable and not too common attributes in politics. But the fact remains that I believe he has adopted, especially in his relationship to the white communities of Africa, a most unhappy and an entirely wrong approach. He has been too clever by half.

Said of Iain Macleod, Colonial Secretary, in *Hansard* (House of Lords) 7 Mar. 1961, col. 307

Anthony Sampson 1926–

7 Members [of civil service orders] rise from CMG (known sometimes in Whitehall as 'Call Me God') to the KCMG ('Kindly Call Me God') to—for a select few governors and super-ambassadors—the GCMG ('God Calls Me God').

Anatomy of Britain (1962) ch. 18

Lord Samuel (Herbert Louis, first Viscount Samuel) 1870–1963

8 A library is thought in cold storage.

A Book of Quotations (1947) p. 10

9 It takes two to make a marriage a success and only one a failure.

A Book of Quotations (1947) p. 115

10 Without doubt the greatest injury of all was done by basing morals on myth. For, sooner or later, myth is recognized for what it is, and disappears. Then morality loses the foundation on which it has been built.

Romanes Lecture, 1947, p. 14

Carl Sandburg 1878–1967

11 Poetry is the opening and closing of a door, leaving those who look through to guess about what is seen during a moment.

Atlantic Monthly Mar. 1923 'Poetry Considered'

12 Poetry is the achievement of the synthesis of hyacinths and biscuits.

Atlantic Monthly Mar. 1923 'Poetry Considered'

13 Hog Butcher for the World,
Tool Maker, Stacker of Wheat,
Player with Railroads and the Nation's Freight Handler;
Stormy, husky, brawling,
City of the Big Shoulders.

Chicago Poems (1916) 'Chicago'

14 The fog comes
on little cat feet.

It sits looking
over harbor and city
on silent haunches
and then moves on.

Chicago Poems (1916) 'Fog'

15 I tell you the past is a bucket of ashes.

Cornhuskers (1918) 'Prairie'

16 When Abraham Lincoln was shovelled into the tombs, he forgot the copperheads and the assassin . . .
in the dust, in the cool tombs.

Cornhuskers (1918) 'Cool Tombs'

17 Pile the bodies high at Austerlitz and Waterloo.
Shovel them under and let me work—
I am the grass; I cover all.

Cornhuskers (1918) 'Grass'

18 I am an idealist. I don't know where I'm going but I'm on the way.

Incidentals (1907) p. 8

1 Slang is a language that rolls up its sleeves, spits on its hands and goes to work.
  In *New York Times* 13 Feb. 1959, p. 21

2 Little girl. . . . Sometime they'll give a war and nobody will come.
  The People, Yes (1936) (cf. Charlotte Keyes in *McCall's* Oct. 1966 'Suppose They Gave a War and No One Came?'; a 1970 American film was entitled 'Suppose They Gave a War and Nobody Came?')

3 Why is there always a secret singing
  When a lawyer cashes in?
  Why does a hearse horse snicker
  Hauling a lawyer away?
  Smoke and Steel (1920) 'The Lawyers Know Too Much'

Henry 'Red' Sanders

4 Sure, winning isn't everything. It's the only thing.
  In *Sports Illustrated* 26 Dec. 1955 (often attributed to Vince Lombardi)

William Sansom 1926–1976

5 A writer lives, at best, in a state of astonishment. Beneath any feeling he has of the good or the evil of the world lies a deeper one of wonder at it all. To transmit that feeling, he writes.
  Blue Skies, Brown Studies (1961) 'From a Writer's Notebook'

George Santayana 1863–1952

6 The young man who has not wept is a savage, and the old man who will not laugh is a fool.
  Dialogues in Limbo (1925) ch. 3

7 Fanaticism consists in redoubling your effort when you have forgotten your aim.
  Life of Reason (1905) vol. 1, Introduction

8 Happiness is the only sanction of life; where happiness fails, existence remains a mad and lamentable experiment.
  Life of Reason (1905) vol. 1, ch. 10

9 Progress, far from consisting in change, depends on retentiveness. . . . Those who cannot remember the past are condemned to repeat it.
  Life of Reason (1905) vol. 1, ch. 12

10 It takes patience to appreciate domestic bliss; volatile spirits prefer unhappiness.
  Life of Reason (1905) vol. 2, ch. 2

11 An artist is a dreamer consenting to dream of the actual world.
  Life of Reason (1905) vol. 4, ch. 3

12 Music is essentially useless, as life is: but both have an ideal extension which lends utility to its conditions.
  Life of Reason (1905) vol. 4, ch. 4

13 An artist may visit a museum, but only a pedant can live there.
  Life of Reason (1905) vol. 4, ch. 7

14 Nothing is really so poor and melancholy as art that is interested in itself and not in its subject.
  Life of Reason (1905) vol. 4, ch. 8

15 The truth is cruel, but it can be loved, and it makes free those who have loved it.
  Little Essays (1920) 'Ideal Immortality'

16 England is the paradise of individuality, eccentricity, heresy, anomalies, hobbies, and humours.
  Soliloquies in England (1922) 'The British Character'

17 There is no cure for birth and death save to enjoy the interval.
  Soliloquies in England (1922) 'War Shrines'

18 It is a great advantage for a system of philosophy to be substantially true.
  The Unknowable (1923) p. 4

19 For an idea ever to be fashionable is ominous, since it must afterwards be always old-fashioned.
  Winds of Doctrine (1913) ch. 2

20 Intolerance itself is a form of egoism, and to condemn egoism intolerantly is to share it.
  Winds of Doctrine (1913) ch. 4

'Sapper' (Herman Cyril MacNeile) 1888–1937

21 Hugh pulled out his cigarette-case. 'Turkish this side—Virginia that.'
  Bull-dog Drummond (1920) ch. 8

John Singer Sargent 1856–1925

22 Every time I paint a portrait I lose a friend.
  In N. Bentley and E. Esar *Treasury of Humorous Quotations* (1951)

Leslie Sarony 1897–1985

23 Ain't it grand to be blooming well dead?
  Title of song (1932)

24 I lift up my finger and I say 'tweet tweet'.
  Title of song (1929)

Nathalie Sarraute 1902–

25 Today, thanks to technical progress, the radio and television, to which we devote so many of the leisure hours once spent listening to parlour chatter and parlour music, have succeeded in lifting the manufacture of banality out of the sphere of handicraft and placed it in that of a major industry.
  Times Literary Supplement 10 June 1960

Jean-Paul Sartre 1905–1980

26 *Quand les riches se font la guerre ce sont les pauvres qui meurent.*

  When the rich wage war it's the poor who die.
  Le Diable et le bon Dieu (The Devil and the Good Lord, 1951) act 1, first tableau

27 *L'écrivain doit donc refuser de se laisser transformer en institution.*

A writer must refuse to allow himself to be transformed into an institution.

> Declaration read at Stockholm, 22 Oct. 1964, refusing the Nobel Prize, in Michel Contat and Michel Rybalka (eds.) *Les Écrits de Sartre* (1970) p. 403

1 *L'existence précède et commande l'essence.*

Existence precedes and rules essence.

> *L'Être et le néant* (Being and Nothingness, 1943) pt. 4, ch. 1

2 *Je suis condamné à être libre.*

I am condemned to be free.

> *L'Être et le néant* (Being and Nothingness, 1943) pt. 4, ch. 1

3 *L'homme est une passion inutile.*

Man is a useless passion.

> *L'Être et le néant* (Being and Nothingness, 1943) pt. 4, ch. 2

4 *Alors, c'est ça l'Enfer. Je n'aurais jamais cru. . . . Vous vous rappelez: le soufre, le bûcher, le gril. . . . Ah! quelle plaisanterie. Pas besoin de gril, l'Enfer, c'est les Autres.*

So that's what Hell is: I'd never have believed it. . . . Do you remember, brimstone, the stake, the gridiron?. . . . What a joke! No need of a gridiron, Hell is other people.

> *Huis Clos* (Closed Doors, 1944) sc. 5

5 *Il n'y a pas de bon père, c'est la règle; qu'on n'en tienne pas grief aux hommes mais au lien de paternité qui est pourri. Faire des enfants, rien de mieux; en avoir, quelle iniquité!*

There is no good father, that's the rule. Don't lay the blame on men but on the bond of paternity, which is rotten. To beget children, nothing better; to *have* them, what iniquity!

> *Les Mots* (The Words, 1964) 'Lire'

6 *Les bons pauvres ne savent pas que leur office est d'exercer notre générosité.*

The poor don't know that their function in life is to exercise our generosity.

> *Les Mots* (The Words, 1964) 'Lire'

7 *Elle [ma grand-mère] ne croyait à rien; seul, son scepticism l'empêchait d'être athée.*

She [my grandmother] believed in nothing; only her scepticism kept her from being an atheist.

> *Les Mots* (The Words, 1964) 'Lire'

8 *Comme tous les songe-creux, je confondis le désenchantement avec la vérité.*

Like all dreamers, I mistook disenchantment for truth.

> *Les Mots* (The Words, 1964) 'Écrire'

9 *Je confondis les choses avec leurs noms: c'est croire.*

I confused things with their names: that is belief.

> *Les Mots* (The Words, 1964) 'Écrire'

10 *Trois heures, c'est toujours trop tard ou trop tôt pour ce qu'on veut faire.*

Three o'clock is always too late or too early for anything you want to do.

> *La Nausée* (Nausea, 1938) 'Vendredi'

11 *Ma pensée, c'est moi: voilà pourquoi je ne peux pas m'arrêter. J'existe par ce que je pense . . . et je ne peux pas m'empêcher de penser.*

My thought is *me*: that's why I can't stop. I exist by what I think . . . and I can't prevent myself from thinking.

> *La Nausée* (Nausea, 1938) 'Lundi'

12 *Je déteste les victimes quand elles respectent leurs bourreaux.*

I hate victims who respect their executioners.

> *Les Séquestrés d'Altona* (The Condemned of Altona, 1960) act 1, sc. 1

13 *Je me méfie des incommunicables, c'est la source de toute violence.*

I distrust the incommunicable: it is the source of all violence.

> *Les Temps Modernes* July 1947, p. 106, 'Qu'est-ce que la littérature?' (What is Literature?)

Siegfried Sassoon 1886–1967

14 Soldiers are citizens of death's gray land,
Drawing no dividend from time's tomorrows.
> *Counter-Attack* (1918) 'Dreamers'

15 In the great hour of destiny they stand,
Each with his feuds, and jealousies, and sorrows.
Soldiers are sworn to action; they must win
Some flaming, fatal climax with their lives.
Soldiers are dreamers; when the guns begin
They think of firelit homes, clean beds, and wives.
> *Counter-Attack* (1918) 'Dreamers'

16 If I were fierce, and bald, and short of breath,
I'd live with scarlet Majors at the Base,
And speed glum heroes up the line to death.
You'd see me with my puffy petulant face,
Guzzling and gulping in the best hotel,
Reading the Roll of Honour. 'Poor young chap',
I'd say—'I used to know his father well;
Yes, we've lost heavily in this last scrap.'
And when the war is done and youth stone dead,
I'd toddle safely home and die—in bed.
> *Counter-Attack* (1918) 'Base Details'

17 'Good-morning; good morning!' the General said
When we met him last week on our way to the line.
Now the soldiers he smiled at are most of 'em dead,
And we're cursing his staff for incompetent swine.
'He's a cheery old card,' grunted Harry to Jack
As they slogged up to Arras with rifle and pack.

But he did for them both by his plan of attack.
> *Counter-Attack* (1918) 'The General'

18 Does it matter?—losing your legs? . . .
For people will always be kind,
And you need not show that you mind
When the others come in after hunting
To gobble their muffins and eggs.

Does it matter?—losing your sight? . . .
There's such splendid work for the blind;
And people will always be kind,
As you sit on the terrace remembering
And turning your face to the light.
> *Counter-Attack* (1918) 'Does it Matter?'

19 Who will remember, passing through this Gate,
The unheroic Dead who fed the guns?
Who shall absolve the foulness of their fate,—
Those doomed, conscripted, unvictorious ones?
> *The Heart's Journey* (1928) 'On Passing the New Menin Gate'

1 I am making this statement as an act of wilful
defiance of military authority, because I believe that
the War is being deliberately prolonged by those who
have the power to end it.
  Memoirs of an Infantry Officer (1930) pt. 10, ch. 2

2 I'd like to see a Tank come down the stalls,
Lurching to rag-time tunes, or 'Home, sweet Home',—
And there'd be no more jokes in Music-halls
To mock the riddled corpses round Bapaume.
  The Old Huntsman (1917) 'Blighters'

3 And he'd come home again to find it more
Desirable than it ever was before.
How right it seemed that he should reach the span
Of comfortable years allowed to man!
Splendid to eat and sleep and choose a wife,
Safe with his wound, a citizen of life.
He hobbled blithely through the garden gate,
And thought: 'Thank God they had to amputate!'
  The Old Huntsman (1917) 'The One-Legged Man'

4 Why do you lie with your legs ungainly huddled,
And one arm bent across your sullen cold
Exhausted face? It hurts my heart to watch you,
Deep-shadow'd from the candle's glittering gold;
And you wonder why I shake you by the shoulder;
Drowsy, you mumble and sigh and turn your head . . .
You are too young to fall asleep for ever;
And when you sleep you remind me of the dead.
  War Poems (1919) 'The Dug-Out'

5 But the past is just the same,—and War's a bloody
  game . . .
Have you forgotten yet? . . .
Look down, and swear by the slain of the War that
  you'll never forget.
  War Poems (1919) 'Aftermath'

6 Everyone suddenly burst out singing;
And I was filled with such delight
As prisoned birds must find in freedom
Winging wildly across the white
Orchards and dark green fields; on; on; and out of
  sight.

Everyone's voice was suddenly lifted,
And beauty came like the setting sun.
My heart was shaken with tears and horror
Drifted away . . . O but every one
Was a bird; and the song was wordless; the singing will
  never be done.
  War Poems (1919) 'Everyone Sang'

Erik Satie 1866–1925

7 *Ravel refuse la Légion d'Honneur, mais son œuvre
l'accepte.*

Ravel refuses the Legion of Honour, but all his music
accepts it.
  In Jean Cocteau *Le Discours d'Oxford* (1956) p. 49

Telly Savalas 1926–

8 Who loves ya, baby?
  Catch-phrase in American TV series *Kojak* (1973–8)

Dorothy L. Sayers 1893–1957

9 I admit it is better fun to punt than to be punted, and
that a desire to have all the fun is nine-tenths of the
law of chivalry.
  Gaudy Night (1935) ch. 14

10 With a gesture of submission he bowed his head and
stood gravely, the square cap dangling in his hand.
'Placetne, magistra?' 'Placet.'
  Gaudy Night (1935) ch. 23 (Lord Peter Wimsey's marriage
  proposal to Harriet Vane, and her acceptance)

11 Plain lies are dangerous: the only weapons left him [the
advertiser] are the *suggestio falsi* and the *suppressio veri*,
and his use even of these would be very much more
circumscribed if one person in ten had ever been taught
how to read. . . . Those who prefer their English sloppy
have only themselves to thank if the advertisement
writer uses his mastery of vocabulary and syntax to
mislead their weak minds. . . . The moral of all this . . .
is that we have the kind of advertising we deserve.
  Spectator 19 Nov. 1937 'The Psychology of Advertising'

12 As I grow older and older,
And totter towards the tomb,
I find that I care less and less
Who goes to bed with whom.
  'That's Why I Never Read Modern Novels', in Janet
  Hitchman *Such a Strange Lady* (1975) ch. 12

Al Scalpone

13 The family that prays together stays together.
  Slogan devised for the Roman Catholic Family Rosary
  Crusade in 1947: see Patrick Peyton *All for Her* (1967)
  p. 144

Hugh Scanlon (Baron Scanlon) 1913–

14 Of course liberty is not licence. Liberty in my view is
conforming to majority opinion.
  Television interview, 9 Aug. 1977, in *Listener* 11 Aug. 1977

Arthur Scargill 1938–

15 Parliament itself would not exist in its present form
had people not defied the law.
  Said in evidence to House of Commons Select Committee on
  Employment, 2 Apr. 1980, in *House of Commons Paper
  no. 462 of Session 1979–80* p. 55

Age Scarpelli, Luciano Vincenzoni 1926– , and Sergio Leone 1921–

16 *Il buono, il bruto, il cattivo.*

The good, the bad, and the ugly.
  Title of film (1966)

Moritz Schlick

17 The meaning of a proposition is the method of its
verification.
  Philosophical Review (1936) vol. 45, p. 341 'Meaning and
  Verification'

Artur Schnabel 1882–1951

1 The notes I handle no better than many pianists. But the pauses between the notes—ah, that is where the art resides!

In *Chicago Daily News* 11 June 1958

2 Applause is a receipt, not a note of demand.

In *Saturday Review of Literature* 29 Sept. 1951

3 I don't think there was ever a piece of music that changed a man's decision on how to vote.

My Life and Music (1961) pt. 2, ch. 8

4 When I am asked, 'What do you think of our audience?' I answer, 'I know two kinds of audiences only—one coughing, and one not coughing.'

My Life and Music (1961) pt. 2, ch. 10

Arnold Schoenberg 1874–1951

5 If it is art, it is not for the masses. 'If it is for the masses it is not art' is a topic which is rather similar to a word of yourself.

Letter to W. S. Schlamm, 1 July 1945, in Erwin Stein *Arnold Schoenberg Letters* (1964) p. 235

Budd Schulberg 1914–

6 You don't understand. I could have had class. I could have been a contender. I could have been somebody—instead of a bum, which is what I am, let's face it.

On the Waterfront (1954 film; words spoken by Marlon Brando)

7 What makes Sammy run?

Title of novel (1941)

Diane B. Schulder 1937–

8 Law is a reflection and a source of prejudice. It both enforces and suggests forms of bias.

In Robin Morgan *Sisterhood is Powerful* (1970) p. 139

E. F. Schumacher 1911–1977

9 Call a thing immoral or ugly, soul-destroying or a degradation of man, a peril to the peace of the world or to the well-being of future generations: as long as you have not shown it to be 'uneconomic' you have not really questioned its right to exist, grow, and prosper.

Small is Beautiful (1973) pt. 1, ch. 3

10 Small is beautiful. A study of economics as if people mattered.

Title of book (1973)

Albert Schweitzer 1875–1965

11 *Am Abend des dritten Tages, als wir bei Sonnenuntergang gerade durch eine Herde Nilpferde hindurchfuhren, stand urplötzlich, von mir nicht geahnt und nicht gesucht, das Wort "Ehrfurcht vor dem Leben" vor mir.*

Late on the third day, at the very moment when, at sunset, we were making our way through a herd of hippopotamuses, there flashed upon my mind, unforeseen and unsought, the phrase, 'Reverence for Life'.

Aus meinem Leben und Denken (My Life and Thought, 1933) ch. 13

12 *"Heda, kamerad," rufe ich, "willst du uns nicht ein wenig helfen?" "Ich bin ein Intellektueller und trage kein Holz," lautete die Antwort. "Hast du Glück," erwiderte ich; "auch ich wollte ein Intellektueller werden, aber es ist mir nicht gelungen."*

'Hullo! friend,' I call out, 'Won't you lend us a hand?' 'I am an intellectual and don't drag wood about,' came the answer. 'You're lucky,' I reply. 'I too wanted to become an intellectual, but I didn't succeed.'

Mitteilungen aus Lambarene (1928, tr. by C. T. Campion, 1931 as *More from the Primeval Forest*) ch. 5

13 *Die Wahrheit hat keine Stunde. Ihre Zeit ist immer und gerade dann wenn sie am unzeitgemässesten scheint.*

Truth has no special time of its own. Its hour is now—always, and indeed then most truly when it seems most unsuitable to actual circumstances.

Zwischen Wasser und Urwald (On the Edge of the Primeval Forest, 1922) ch. 11

Kurt Schwitters 1887–1948

14 *Ich bin Maler, ich nagle meine Bilder.*

I am a painter and I nail my pictures together.

Remark to Raoul Hausmann, 1918, in Raoul Hausmann *Am Anfang war Dada* (In the Beginning was Dada, 1972) p. 63

Martin Scorsese 1942– and Mardik Martin

15 You don't make up for your sins in church; you do it in the street, you do it at home. The rest is bullshit and you know it.

Mean Streets (1973 film) in Michael Bliss *Martin Scorsese and Michael Cimino* (1985) ch. 3

C. P. Scott 1846–1932

16 A newspaper is of necessity something of a monopoly, and its first duty is to shun the temptations of monopoly. Its primary office is the gathering of news. At the peril of its soul it must see that the supply is not tainted. Neither in what it gives, nor in what it does not give, nor in the mode of presentation must the unclouded face of truth suffer wrong. Comment is free, but facts are sacred.

Manchester Guardian 5 May 1921

Paul Scott 1920–1978

17 The jewel in the crown.

Title of novel (1966)

Robert Falcon Scott 1868–1912

18 Great God! this [the South Pole] is an awful place and terrible enough for us to have laboured to it without the reward of priority.

Diary, 17 Jan. 1912, in *Scott's Last Expedition* (1913) vol. 1, ch. 18

1 For God's sake look after our people.
> Diary, 29 Mar. 1912, in *Scott's Last Expedition* (1913) vol. 1, ch. 20

2 Make the boy interested in natural history if you can; it is better than games; they encourage it in some schools.
> Final letter to his wife, in *Scott's Last Expedition* (1913) vol. 1, ch. 20

3 Had we lived, I should have had a tale to tell of the hardihood, endurance, and courage of my companions which would have stirred the heart of every Englishman. These rough notes and our dead bodies must tell the tale.
> 'Message to the Public' in *Scott's Last Expedition* (1913) vol. 1, ch. 20

Florida Scott-Maxwell

4 No matter how old a mother is she watches her middle-aged children for signs of improvement.
> *Measure of my Days* (1968) p. 16

Alan Seeger 1888–1916

5 I have a rendezvous with Death
At some disputed barricade,
When Spring comes round with rustling shade
And apple blossoms fill the air.
I have a rendezvous with Death
When Spring brings back blue days and fair.
> *North American Review* Oct. 1916 'I Have a Rendezvous with Death'

Pete Seeger 1919–

6 Where have all the flowers gone?
The girls have picked them every one.
Oh, when will you ever learn?
> *Where Have all the Flowers Gone?* (1961 song)

See also ANONYMOUS 9:13

Erich Segal 1937–

7 Love means not ever having to say you're sorry.
> *Love Story* (1970) ch. 13

W. C. Sellar 1898–1951 and R. J. Yeatman 1898–1968

8 For every person who wants to teach there are approximately thirty who don't want to learn—much.
> *And Now All This* (1932) introduction

9 The Roman Conquest was, however, a *Good Thing*, since the Britons were only natives at the time.
> *1066 and All That* (1930) ch. 1

10 The conversion of England was thus effected by the landing of St Augustine in Thanet and other places, which resulted in the country being overrun by a Wave of Saints. Among these were St Ive, St Pancra, the great St Bernard (originator of the clerical collar), St Bee, St Ebb, St Neot (who invented whisky), St Kit and St Kin, and the Venomous Bead (author of The Rosary).
> *1066 and All That* (1930) ch. 3

11 Edward III had very good manners. One day at a royal dance he noticed some men-about-court mocking a lady whose garter had come off, whereupon to put her at her ease he stopped the dance and made the memorable epitaph: 'Honi soie qui mal y pense' ('Honey, your silk stocking's hanging down').
> *1066 and All That* (1930) ch. 24

12 Shortly after this the cruel Queen died and a post-mortem examination revealed the word 'CALLOUS' engraved on her heart.
> *1066 and All That* (1930) ch. 32

13 The utterly memorable Struggle between the Cavaliers (Wrong but Wromantic) and the Roundheads (Right but Repulsive).
> *1066 and All That* (1930) ch. 35

14 Charles II was always very merry and was therefore not so much a king as a Monarch.
> *1066 and All That* (1930) ch. 36

15 The National Debt is a very Good Thing and it would be dangerous to pay it off, for fear of Political Economy.
> *1066 and All That* (1930) ch. 38

16 Napoleon's armies always used to march on their stomachs shouting: 'Vive l'Intérieur!' and so moved about very slowly (*ventre-à-terre*, as the French say) thus enabling Wellington to catch them up and defeat them.
> *1066 and All That* (1930) ch. 48

17 Gladstone also invented the Education Rate by which it was possible to calculate how soon anybody could be educated, and he spent his declining years trying to guess the answer to the Irish Question; unfortunately whenever he was getting warm, the Irish secretly changed the Question.
> *1066 and All That* (1930) ch. 57

18 AMERICA was thus clearly top nation, and History came to a .
> *1066 and All That* (1930) ch. 62

19 Do not on any account attempt to write on both sides of the paper at once.
> *1066 and All That* (1930) 'Test Paper 5'

Robert W. Service 1874–1958

20 Ah! the clock is always slow;
It is later than you think.
> *Ballads of a Bohemian* (1921) 'It Is Later Than You Think'

21 When we, the Workers, all demand: 'What are WE fighting for?' . . .
Then, then we'll end that stupid crime, that devil's madness—War.
> *Ballads of a Bohemian* (1921) 'Michael'

22 This is the law of the Yukon, that only the Strong shall thrive;
That surely the Weak shall perish, and only the Fit survive.
Dissolute, damned and despairful, crippled and palsied and slain,
This is the Will of the Yukon,—Lo, how she makes it plain!
> *Songs of a Sourdough* (1907) 'The Law of the Yukon'

23 A bunch of the boys were whooping it up in the Malamute saloon;

The kid that handles the music-box was hitting
   a jag-time tune;
Back of the bar, in a solo game, sat Dangerous Dan
   McGrew,
And watching his luck was his light-o'-love, the lady
   that's known as Lou.
Songs of a Sourdough (1907) 'Shootings of Dan McGrew'

1 A promise made is a debt unpaid, and the trail has its
own stern code.
Songs of a Sourdough (1907) 'Cremation of Sam McGee'

Anne Sexton 1928–1974

2 In a dream you are never eighty.
All My Pretty Ones (1962) 'Old'

James Seymour and Rian James 1899–

3 You're going out a youngster but you've *got* to come
back a star.
42nd Street (1933 film)

Peter Shaffer 1926–

4 All my wife has ever taken from the
Mediterranean—from that whole vast intuitive
culture—are four bottles of Chianti to make into
lamps, and two china condiment donkeys labelled
Sally and Peppy.
Equus (1973) act 1, sc. 18

5 Passion, you see, can be destroyed by a doctor. It
cannot be created.
Equus (1973) act 2, sc. 35

Eileen Shanahan

6 The length of a meeting rises with the square of the
number of people present.
Attributed

Bill Shankly 1914–1981

7 Some people think football is a matter of life and
death. I don't like that attitude. I can assure them it is
much more serious than that.
In *Sunday Times* 4 Oct. 1981

Tom Sharpe 1928–

8 The South African police would leave no stone
unturned to see that nothing disturbed the even terror
of their lives.
Indecent Exposure (1973) ch. 1

9 Skullion had little use for contraceptives at the best of
times. Unnatural, he called them, and placed them in
the lower social category of things along with
elastic-sided boots and made-up bow ties. Not the sort
of attire for a gentleman.
Porterhouse Blue (1974) ch. 9

George Bernard Shaw 1856–1950

10 All great truths begin as blasphemies.
Annajanska (1919) p. 262

11 One man that has a mind and knows it can always beat
ten men who havnt and dont.
The Apple Cart (1930) act 1

12 What Englishman will give his mind to politics as long
as he can afford to keep a motor car?
The Apple Cart (1930) act 1

13 Breakages, Limited, the biggest industrial corporation
in the country.
The Apple Cart (1930) act 1

14 I never resist temptation because I have found that
things that are bad for me do not tempt me.
The Apple Cart (1930) interlude

15 Arms and the man.
Title of play (1898). Cf. Virgil in *Oxford Dictionary of
Quotations* (1979) 557:8

16 You can always tell an old soldier by the inside of his
holsters and cartridge boxes. The young ones carry
pistols and cartridges; the old ones, grub.
Arms and the Man (1898) act 1

17 Oh, you are a very poor soldier—a chocolate cream
soldier!
Arms and the Man (1898) act 1

18 I never apologize!
Arms and the Man (1898) act 3

19 Youre not a man, youre a machine.
Arms and the Man (1898) act 3

20 You see things; and you say 'Why?' But I dream things
that never were; and I say 'Why not?'
Back to Methuselah (1921) pt. 1, act 1

21 Make me a beautiful word for doing things tomorrow;
for that surely is a great and blessed invention.
Back to Methuselah (1921) pt. 1, act 1

22 I enjoy convalescence. It is the part that makes illness
worth while.
Back to Methuselah (1921) pt. 2

23 Silence is the most perfect expression of scorn.
Back to Methuselah (1921) pt. 5

24 Life is not meant to be easy, my child; but take
courage: it can be delightful.
Back to Methuselah (1921) pt. 5

25 A strange lady giving an address in Zurich wrote him
[Shaw] a proposal, thus: 'You have the greatest brain
in the world, and I have the most beautiful body; so we
ought to produce the most perfect child.' Shaw asked:
'What if the child inherits my body and your brains?'
In Hesketh Pearson *Bernard Shaw* (1942) p. 310

26 He is a barbarian, and thinks that the customs of his
tribe and island are the laws of nature.
Caesar and Cleopatra (1901) act 2 (said by Caesar of his
secretary, a Briton)

27 When a stupid man is doing something he is ashamed
of, he always declares that it is his duty.
Caesar and Cleopatra (1901) act 3

1 He who has never hoped can never despair.
   Caesar and Cleopatra (1901) act 4

2 A man of great common sense and good taste, meaning
   thereby a man without originality or moral courage.
   Notes to Caesar and Cleopatra (1901) 'Julius Caesar'

3 We have no more right to consume happiness without
   producing it than to consume wealth without
   producing it.
   Candida (1898) act 1

4 Do you think that the things people make fools of
   themselves about are any less real and true than the
   things they behave sensibly about? They are more true:
   they are the only things that are true.
   Candida (1898) act 1

5 It is easy—terribly easy—to shake a man's faith in
   himself. To take advantage of that to break a man's
   spirit is devil's work.
   Candida (1898) act 1

6 I'm only a beer teetotaller, not a champagne teetotaller.
   Candida (1898) act 3

7 The worst sin towards our fellow creatures is not to
   hate them, but to be indifferent to them: thats the
   essence of inhumanity.
   The Devil's Disciple (1901) act 2

8 Martyrdom . . . is the only way in which a man can
   become famous without ability.
   The Devil's Disciple (1901) act 3

9 I never expect a soldier to think.
   The Devil's Disciple (1901) act 3

10 SWINDON: 'What will history say?'
   BURGOYNE: 'History, sir, will tell lies as usual.'
   The Devil's Disciple (1901) act 3

11 Your friend the British soldier can stand up to anything
   except the British War Office.
   The Devil's Disciple (1901) act 3

12 There is at bottom only one genuinely scientific
   treatment for all diseases, and that is to stimulate the
   phagocytes.
   The Doctor's Dilemma (1911) act 1

13 All professions are conspiracies against the laity.
   The Doctor's Dilemma (1911) act 1

14 I don't believe in morality. I am a disciple of Bernard
   Shaw.
   The Doctor's Dilemma (1911) act 3

15 I believe in Michael Angelo, Velasquez, and
   Rembrandt; in the might of design, the mystery of
   colour, the redemption of all things by Beauty
   everlasting, and the message of Art that has made these
   hands blessed. Amen. Amen.
   The Doctor's Dilemma (1911) act 4

16 Parentage is a very important profession, but no test of
   fitness for it is ever imposed in the interest of the
   children.
   Everybody's Political What's What? (1944) ch. 9

17 A government which robs Peter to pay Paul can always
   depend on the support of Paul.
   Everybody's Political What's What? (1944) ch. 30

18 It's all that the young can do for the old, to shock them
   and keep them up to date.
   Fanny's First Play (1914) 'Induction'

19 You don't expect me to know what to say about a play
   when I don't know who the author is, do you?
   Fanny's First Play (1914) epilogue

20 If it's by a good author, it's a good play, naturally. That
   stands to reason.
   Fanny's First Play (1914) epilogue

21 Home life as we understand it is no more natural to us
   than a cage is natural to a cockatoo.
   Getting Married (1911) preface 'Hearth and Home'

22 The one point on which all women are in furious secret
   rebellion against the existing law is the saddling of the
   right to a child with the obligation to become the
   servant of a man.
   Getting Married (1911) preface 'The Right to Motherhood'

23 Physically there is nothing to distinguish human
   society from the farm-yard except that children are
   more troublesome and costly than chickens and calves,
   and that men and women are not so completely
   enslaved as farm stock.
   Getting Married (1911) preface 'The Personal Sentimental
   Basis of Monogamy'

24 What God hath joined together no man ever shall put
   asunder: God will take care of that.
   Getting Married (1911) p. 216

25 Sam wanted to make a Goldwyn writer of George
   Bernard Shaw. They discussed it over tea one day in
   London. . . . A version of the conversation was cabled
   over to Howard Dietz, Goldwyn's publicity chief;
   he compressed Shaw's words into: 'The trouble,
   Mr Goldwyn, is that you are only interested in art and
   I am only interested in money.' This was cabled back
   to London and released there. It added considerably
   to Shaw's reputation as a wit.
   Alva Johnson The Great Goldwyn (1937) ch. 3

26 I am a woman of the world, Hector; and I can assure
   you that if you will only take the trouble always to do
   the perfectly correct thing, and to say the perfectly
   correct thing, you can do just what you like.
   Heartbreak House (1919) act 1

27 Go anywhere in England where there are natural,
   wholesome, contented, and really nice English people;
   and what do you always find? That the stables are the
   real centre of the household.
   Heartbreak House (1919) act 3

28 The captain is in his bunk, drinking bottled
   ditch-water; and the crew is gambling in the forecastle.
   She will strike and sink and split. Do you think the laws
   of God will be suspended in favour of England because
   you were born in it?
   Heartbreak House (1919) act 3

29 Money is indeed the most important thing in the world;
   and all sound and successful personal and national
   morality should have this fact for its basis.
   The Irrational Knot (1905) preface

30 Reminiscences make one feel so deliciously aged and
   sad.
   The Irrational Knot (1905) ch. 14

1 A man who has no office to go to—I don't care who he is—is a trial of which you can have no conception.
The Irrational Knot (1905) ch. 18

2 An Irishman's heart is nothing but his imagination.
John Bull's Other Island (1907) act 1

3 My way of joking is to tell the truth. Its the funniest joke in the world.
John Bull's Other Island (1907) act 2

4 What really flatters a man is that you think him worth flattering.
John Bull's Other Island (1907) act 4

5 There are only two qualities in the world: efficiency and inefficiency, and only two sorts of people: the efficient and the inefficient.
John Bull's Other Island (1907) act 4

6 The greatest of evils and the worst of crimes is poverty . . . our first duty—a duty to which every other consideration should be sacrificed—is not to be poor.
Major Barbara (1907) preface

7 The universal regard for money is the one hopeful fact in our civilization, the one sound spot in our social conscience. Money is the most important thing in the world. It represents health, strength, honour, generosity and beauty as conspicuously and undeniably as the want of it represents illness, weakness, disgrace, meanness and ugliness. Not the least of its virtues is that it destroys base people as certainly as it fortifies and dignifies noble people.
Major Barbara (1907) preface

8 Cusins is a very nice fellow, certainly: nobody would ever guess that he was born in Australia.
Major Barbara (1907) act 1

9 Nobody can say a word against Greek: it stamps a man at once as an educated gentleman.
Major Barbara (1907) act 1

10 I am a Millionaire. That is my religion.
Major Barbara (1907) act 2

11 I can't talk religion to a man with bodily hunger in his eyes.
Major Barbara (1907) act 2

12 Wot prawce Selvytion nah?
Major Barbara (1907) act 2

13 Alcohol is a very necessary article. . . . It makes life bearable to millions of people who could not endure their existence if they were quite sober. It enables Parliament to do things at eleven at night that no sane person would do at eleven in the morning.
Major Barbara (1907) act 2

14 He knows nothing; and he thinks he knows everything. That points clearly to a political career.
Major Barbara (1907) act 3

15 The sixth Undershaft wrote up these words: NOTHING IS EVER DONE IN THIS WORLD UNTIL MEN ARE PREPARED TO KILL ONE ANOTHER IF IT IS NOT DONE.
Major Barbara (1907) act 3

16 Like all young men, you greatly exaggerate the difference between one young woman and another.
Major Barbara (1907) act 3

17 But a lifetime of happiness! No man alive could bear it: it would be hell on earth.
Man and Superman (1903) act 1

18 We are ashamed of everything that is real about us; ashamed of ourselves, of our relatives, of our incomes, of our accents, of our opinions, of our experience, just as we are ashamed of our naked skins.
Man and Superman (1903) act 1

19 The more things a man is ashamed of, the more respectable he is.
Man and Superman (1903) act 1

20 Vitality in a woman is a blind fury of creation. She sacrifices herself to it.
Man and Superman (1903) act 1

21 The true artist will let his wife starve, his children go barefoot, his mother drudge for his living at seventy, sooner than work at anything but his art.
Man and Superman (1903) act 1

22 Of all human struggles there is none so treacherous and remorseless as the struggle between the artist man and the mother woman.
Man and Superman (1903) act 1

23 There is no love sincerer than the love of food.
Man and Superman (1903) act 1

24 Very nice sort of place, Oxford, I should think, for people that like that sort of place. They teach you to be a gentleman there. In the Polytechnic they teach you to be an engineer or such like.
Man and Superman (1903) act 2

25 You think that you are Ann's suitor; that you are the pursuer and she the pursued; that it is your part to woo, to persuade, to prevail, to overcome. Fool: it is you who are the pursued, the marked down quarry, the destined prey.
Man and Superman (1903) act 2

26 It is a woman's business to get married as soon as possible, and a man's to keep unmarried as long as he can.
Man and Superman (1903) act 2

27 MENDOZA: I am a brigand: I live by robbing the rich.
TANNER: I am a gentleman: I live by robbing the poor.
Man and Superman (1903) act 3

28 Hell is full of musical amateurs: music is the brandy of the damned.
Man and Superman (1903) act 3

29 Englishmen never will be slaves: they are free to do whatever the Government and public opinion allow them to do.
Man and Superman (1903) act 3

30 An Englishman thinks he is moral when he is only uncomfortable.
Man and Superman (1903) act 3

31 In the arts of life man invents nothing; but in the arts of death he outdoes Nature herself, and produces by chemistry and machinery all the slaughter of plague, pestilence and famine.
Man and Superman (1903) act 3

32 In the arts of peace Man is a bungler.
Man and Superman (1903) act 3

1 As an old soldier I admit the cowardice: it's as universal
as sea sickness, and matters just as little.
Man and Superman (1903) act 3

2 When the military man approaches, the world locks up
its spoons and packs off its womankind.
Man and Superman (1903) act 3

3 What is virtue but the Trade Unionism of the married?
Man and Superman (1903) act 3

4 Those who talk most about the blessings of marriage
and the constancy of its vows are the very people who
declare that if the chain were broken and the prisoners
were left free to choose, the whole social fabric would
fly asunder. You can't have the argument both ways. If
the prisoner is happy, why lock him in? If he is not,
why pretend that he is?
Man and Superman (1903) act 3

5 Beauty is all very well at first sight; but who ever looks
at it when it has been in the house three days?
Man and Superman (1903) act 4

6 There are two tragedies in life. One is not to get your
hearts desire. The other is to get it.
Man and Superman (1903) act 4

7 Revolutions have never lightened the burden of
tyranny: they have only shifted it to another shoulder.
Man and Superman (1903) 'The Revolutionist's Handbook',
foreword

8 Do not do unto others as you would that they should do
unto you. Their tastes may not be the same.
Man and Superman (1903) 'Maxims for Revolutionists: The
Golden Rule'

9 The golden rule is that there are no golden rules.
Man and Superman (1903) 'Maxims for Revolutionists: The
Golden Rule'

10 The art of government is the organization of idolatry.
The bureaucracy consists of functionaries; the
aristocracy, of idols; the democracy, of idolaters. The
populace cannot understand the bureaucracy: it can
only worship the national idols.
Man and Superman (1903) 'Maxims for Revolutionists:
Idolatry'

11 Democracy substitutes election by the incompetent
many for appointment by the corrupt few.
Man and Superman (1903) 'Maxims for Revolutionists:
Democracy'

12 Liberty means responsibility. That is why most men
dread it.
Man and Superman (1903) 'Maxims for Revolutionists:
Liberty and Equality'

13 The vilest abortionist is he who attempts to mould
a child's character.
Man and Superman (1903) 'Maxims for Revolutionists:
Education'

14 He who can, does. He who cannot, teaches.
Man and Superman (1903) 'Maxims for Revolutionists:
Education'

15 Marriage is popular because it combines the maximum
of temptation with the maximum of opportunity.
Man and Superman (1903) 'Maxims for Revolutionists:
Marriage'

16 Titles distinguish the mediocre, embarrass the superior,
and are disgraced by the inferior.
Man and Superman (1903) 'Maxims for Revolutionists: Titles'

17 When domestic servants are treated as human beings it
is not worth while to keep them.
Man and Superman (1903) 'Maxims for Revolutionists:
Servants'

18 If you strike a child take care that you strike it in anger,
even at the risk of maiming it for life. A blow in cold
blood neither can nor should be forgiven.
Man and Superman (1903) 'Maxims for Revolutionists: How
to Beat Children'

19 Beware of the man whose god is in the skies.
Man and Superman (1903) 'Maxims for Revolutionists:
Religion'

20 Self-denial is not a virtue: it is only the effect of
prudence on rascality.
Man and Superman (1903) 'Maxims for Revolutionists:
Virtues and Vice'

21 In heaven an angel is nobody in particular.
Man and Superman (1903) 'Maxims for Revolutionists:
Greatness'

22 A moderately honest man with a moderately faithful
wife, moderate drinkers both, in a moderately healthy
house: that is the true middle class unit.
Man and Superman (1903) 'Maxims for Revolutionists:
Moderation'

23 The reasonable man adapts himself to the world: the
unreasonable one persists in trying to adapt the world
to himself. Therefore all progress depends on the
unreasonable man.
Man and Superman (1903) 'Maxims for Revolutionists:
Reason'

24 The man who listens to Reason is lost: Reason enslaves
all whose minds are not strong enough to master her.
Man and Superman (1903) 'Maxims for Revolutionists:
Reason'

25 Decency is Indecency's conspiracy of silence.
Man and Superman (1903) 'Maxims for Revolutionists:
Decency'

26 Life levels all men: death reveals the eminent.
Man and Superman (1903) 'Maxims for Revolutionists: Fame'

27 Home is the girl's prison and the woman's workhouse.
Man and Superman (1903) 'Maxims for Revolutionists:
Women in the Home'

28 Every man over forty is a scoundrel.
Man and Superman (1903) 'Maxims for Revolutionists: Stray
Sayings'

29 Youth, which is forgiven everything, forgives itself
nothing: age, which forgives itself everything, is
forgiven nothing.
Man and Superman (1903) 'Maxims for Revolutionists: Stray
Sayings'

30 Take care to get what you like or you will be forced to
like what you get.
Man and Superman (1903) 'Maxims for Revolutionists: Stray
Sayings'

31 It is dangerous to be sincere unless you are also stupid.
Man and Superman (1903) 'Maxims for Revolutionists: Stray
Sayings'

1 Beware of the man who does not return your blow: he neither forgives you nor allows you to forgive yourself.
  Man and Superman (1903) 'Maxims for Revolutionists: Stray Sayings'

2 Self-sacrifice enables us to sacrifice other people without blushing.
  Man and Superman (1903) 'Maxims for Revolutionists: Self-Sacrifice'

3 There is nothing so bad or so good that you will not find Englishmen doing it; but you will never find an Englishman in the wrong. He does everything on principle. He fights you on patriotic principles; he robs you on business principles; he enslaves you on imperial principles; he bullies you on manly principles; he supports his king on loyal principles and cuts off his king's head on republican principles.
  Man of Destiny (1898) p. 201

4 Anybody on for a game of tennis?
  Misalliance (1914) p. 25 (perhaps the origin of the phrase 'Anyone for tennis?', said to be typical of drawing-room comedies; cf. Humphrey Bogart)

5 Anarchism is a game at which the police can beat you.
  Misalliance (1914) p. 85

6 The only way for a woman to provide for herself decently is for her to be good to some man that can afford to be good to her.
  Mrs Warren's Profession (1898) act 2

7 A great devotee of the Gospel of Getting On.
  Mrs Warren's Profession (1898) act 4 (said of Miss Warren)

8 [Dancing is] a perpendicular expression of a horizontal desire.
  In *New Statesman* 23 Mar. 1962

9 Youll never have a quiet world til you knock the patriotism out of the human race.
  O'Flaherty V.C. (1919) p. 178

10 As long as I have a want, I have a reason for living. Satisfaction is death.
  Overruled (1916) p. 72

11 There is, on the whole, nothing on earth intended for innocent people so horrible as a school. To begin with, it is a prison. But it is in some respects more cruel than a prison. In a prison, for instance, you are not forced to read books written by the warders and the governor . . . and beaten or otherwise tormented if you cannot remember their utterly unmemorable contents.
  Parents and Children (1914) 'School'

12 The secret of being miserable is to have leisure to bother about whether you are happy or not. The cure for it is occupation.
  Parents and Children (1914) 'Children's Happiness'

13 A perpetual holiday is a good working definition of hell.
  Parents and Children (1914) 'Children's Happiness'

14 The fickleness of the women I love is only equalled by the infernal constancy of the women who love me.
  The Philanderer (1898) act 2

15 There is only one religion, though there are a hundred versions of it.
  Plays Pleasant and Unpleasant (1898) vol. 2, preface

16 The English have no respect for their language, and will not teach their children to speak it. They spell it so abominably that no man can teach himself what it sounds like. It is impossible for an Englishman to open his mouth without making some other Englishman hate or despise him.
  Pygmalion (1916) preface

17 Hes a gentleman: look at his boots.
  Pygmalion (1916) act 1

18 Remember that you are a human being with a soul and the divine gift of articulate speech: that your native language is the language of Shakespear and Milton and The Bible; and don't sit there crooning like a bilious pigeon.
  Pygmalion (1916) act 1

19 I don't want to talk grammar, I want to talk like a lady.
  Pygmalion (1916) act 2

20 PICKERING: Have you no morals, man?
  DOOLITTLE: Can't afford them, Governor. Neither could you if you was as poor as me.
  Pygmalion (1916) act 2

21 I'm one of the undeserving poor: that's what I am. Think of what that means to a man. It means that he's up agen middle-class morality all the time.
  Pygmalion (1916) act 2

22 My aunt died of influenza: so they said. But it's my belief they done the old woman in.
  Pygmalion (1916) act 3

23 Gin was mother's milk to her.
  Pygmalion (1916) act 3

24 FREDDY: Are you walking across the Park, Miss Doolittle? If so—
  LIZA: Walk! Not bloody likely. I am going in a taxi.
  Pygmalion (1916) act 3

25 I have to live for others and not for myself: thats middle-class morality.
  Pygmalion (1916) act 5

26 The Churches must learn humility as well as teach it.
  Saint Joan (1924) preface

27 If ever I utter an oath again may my soul be blasted to eternal damnation!
  Saint Joan (1924) sc. 2

28 A miracle, my friend, is an event which creates faith. That is the purpose and nature of miracles. . . . Frauds deceive. An event which creates faith does not deceive: therefore it is not a fraud, but a miracle.
  Saint Joan (1924) sc. 2

29 We were not fairly beaten, my lord. No Englishman is ever fairly beaten.
  Saint Joan (1924) sc. 4

30 How can what an Englishman believes be heresy? It is a contradiction in terms.
  Saint Joan (1924) sc. 4

31 Must then a Christ perish in torment in every age to save those that have no imagination?
  Saint Joan (1924) epilogue

32 With the single exception of Homer, there is no eminent writer, not even Sir Walter Scott, whom I can despise so

entirely as I despise Shakespeare when I measure my mind against his. The intensity of my impatience with him occasionally reaches such a pitch, that it would positively be a relief to me to dig him up and throw stones at him, knowing as I do how incapable he and his worshippers are of understanding any less obvious form of indignity.

> *Saturday Review* 26 Sept. 1896 (reviewing a production of *Cymbeline*)

1 Assassination is the extreme form of censorship.
> *Shewing-Up of Blanco Posnet* (1911) 'Limits to Toleration'

2 'Do you know what a pessimist is?' 'A man who thinks everybody is as nasty as himself, and hates them for it.'
> *An Unsocial Socialist* (1887) ch. 5

3 We dont bother much about dress and manners in England, because, as a nation, we dont dress well and weve no manners.
> *You Never Can Tell* (1898) act 1

4 Well, sir, you never can tell. Thats a principle in life with me, sir, if youll excuse my having such a thing, sir.
> *You Never Can Tell* (1898) act 2

5 The great advantage of a hotel is that it's a refuge from home life.
> *You Never Can Tell* (1898) act 2

6 My speciality is being right when other people are wrong.
> *You Never Can Tell* (1898) act 4

7 The younger generation is knocking at the door, and as I open it there steps spritely in the incomparable Max.
> *Saturday Review* 21 May 1898 'Valedictory' (on handing over the theatre review column to Max Beerbohm)

Sir Hartley Shawcross (Baron Shawcross) 1902–

8 'But,' said Alice, 'the question is whether you can make a word mean different things.' 'Not so,' said Humpty-Dumpty, 'the question is which is to be the master. That's all.' We are the masters at the moment, and not only at the moment, but for a very long time to come.
> *Hansard* 2 Apr. 1946, col. 1213. Cf. *Oxford Dictionary of Quotations* (1979) 135:22

Patrick Shaw-Stewart 1888–1917

9 I saw a man this morning
Who did not wish to die;
I ask and cannot answer
If otherwise wish I.
> Poem (1916) in M. Baring *Have You Anything to Declare?* (1936) p. 39

10 He [Shaw-Stewart] once asked me if I knew a certain Duke's eldest son, and when I said no, and from what I heard I didn't think we should like him if we did, he answered: 'I've yet to meet the Duke I couldn't like.'
> Edward Marsh *A Number of People* (1939) ch. 9

Gloria Shayne

11 Goodbye cruel world.
> Title of song (1961)

E. A. Sheppard

See CHARLES COLLINS

Burt Shevelove 1915–1982 and Larry Gelbart ?1928–

12 A funny thing happened on the way to the Forum.
> Title of musical (1962; music and lyrics by Stephen Sondheim)

Emanuel Shinwell (Baron Shinwell) 1884–1986

13 We know that the organised workers of the country are our friends. As for the rest, they don't matter a tinker's cuss.
> Speech to Electrical Trades Union conference at Margate, 7 May 1947, in *Manchester Guardian* 8 May 1947

Jean Sibelius 1865–1957

14 'Never pay any attention to what critics say,' he [Sibelius] proceeded, and expatiated on this theme. When I ventured to put in the remark that their articles might sometimes be of great importance, he cut me short. 'Remember,' he said, 'a statue has never been set up in honour of a critic!'
> In Bengt de Törne *Sibelius: A Close-Up* (1937) ch. 2

Walter Sickert 1860–1942

15 Nothing knits man to man, the Manchester School wisely taught, like the frequent passage from hand to hand of cash.
> *New Age* 28 July 1910 'The Language of Art'

Maurice Sigler 1901–1961 and Al Hoffman 1902–1960

16 Little man, you've had a busy day.
> Title of song (1934)

Alan Sillitoe 1928–

17 The loneliness of the long-distance runner.
> Title of novel (1959)

Frank Silver 1892–1960 and Irving Cohn 1898–1961

18 Yes! we have no bananas,
We have no bananas today.
> *Yes! We Have No Bananas* (1923 song)

Georges Simenon 1903–1989

1 *J'ai eu 10,000 femmes depuis l'âge de 13 ans et demi. Ce n'était pas du tout un vice. Je n'ai aucun vice sexuel, mais j'avais besoin de communiquer.*

I have made love to 10,000 women since I was 13½. It wasn't in any way a vice. I've no sexual vices. But I needed to communicate.
> Interview with Federico Fellini in *L'Express* 21 Feb. 1977

2 Writing is not a profession but a vocation of unhappiness.
> Interview in *Paris Review* Summer 1955

James Simmons 1933–

3 For every year of life we light
A candle on your cake
To mark the simple sort of progress
Anyone can make,
And then, to test your nerve or give
A proper view of death,
You're asked to blow each light, each year,
Out with your own breath.
> *In the Wilderness and Other Poems* (1969) 'A Birthday Poem'

Paul Simon 1942–

4 And here's to you, Mrs Robinson
Jesus loves you more than you will know.
God bless you please, Mrs Robinson
Heaven holds a place for those who pray.
> *Mrs Robinson* (1968 song; used in the film *The Graduate*)

Harold Simpson

5 Down in the forest something stirred:
It was only the note of a bird.
> *Down in the Forest* (1906 song; music by Landon Ronald)

Kirke Simpson

6 [Warren] Harding of Ohio was chosen by a group of men in a smoke-filled room early today as Republican candidate for President.
> News report, 12 June 1920

N. F. Simpson 1919–

7 Knocked down a doctor? With an ambulance? How could she? It's a contradiction in terms.
> *One Way Pendulum* (1960) act 1

Noble Sissle 1889–1975 and Eubie Blake 1883–1983

8 I'm just wild about Harry.
> Title of song (1921)

C. H. Sisson 1914–

9 Here lies a civil servant. He was civil
To everyone, and servant to the devil.
> In *The London Zoo* (1961) p. 29

Dame Edith Sitwell 1887–1964

10 Jane, Jane,
Tall as a crane,
The morning light creaks down again.
> *Bucolic Comedies* (1923) 'Aubade'

11 The fire was furry as a bear.
> *Bucolic Comedies* (1923) 'Façade: Dark Song'

12 I have often wished I had time to cultivate modesty. . . . But I am too busy thinking about myself.
> In *Observer* 30 Apr. 1950

13 Virginia Woolf, I enjoyed talking to her, but thought nothing of her writing. I considered her 'a beautiful little knitter'.
> Letter to Geoffrey Singleton, 11 July 1955, in John Lehmann and Derek Palmer (eds.) *Selected Letters* (1970)

14 Daisy and Lily,
Lazy and silly,
Walk by the shore of the wan grassy sea—
Talking once more 'neath a swan-bosomed tree.
> *Song of the Cold* (1948) 'Waltz'

15 Still falls the Rain—
Dark as the world of man, black as our loss—
Blind as the nineteen hundred and forty nails
Upon the Cross.
> *Street Songs* (1942) 'The Raids, 1940. Night and Dawn'

16 Mr [Percy Wyndham] Lewis's pictures appeared, as a very great painter said to me, to have been painted by a mailed fist in a cotton glove.
> *Taken Care Of* (1965) ch. 11

Sir Osbert Sitwell 1892–1969

17 The British Bourgeoise
Is not born,
And does not die,
But, if it is ill,
It has a frightened look in its eyes.
> *At the House of Mrs Kinfoot* (1921) p. 8

18 In reality, killing time
Is only the name for another of the multifarious ways
By which Time kills us.
> *Poems about People* (1958) 'Milordo Inglese'

19 *Educ*: during the holidays from Eton.
> Entry in *Who's Who* (1929)

'Red Skelton' (Richard Skelton) 1913–

20 Well, it only proves what they always say—give the public something they want to see, and they'll come out for it.
> Comment on crowds attending the funeral of Harry Cohn on 2 Mar. 1958, in Bob Thomas *King Cohn* (1967) 'Foreground'

B. F. Skinner 1904–1990

21 Education is what survives when what has been learned has been forgotten.
> *New Scientist* 21 May 1964

Elizabeth Smart 1913–1986

1 By Grand Central Station I sat down and wept.
   Title of book (1945). Cf. Psalm 137:1

Alfred Emanuel Smith 1873–1944

2 No sane local official who has hung up an empty
   stocking over the municipal fireplace, is going to shoot
   Santa Claus just before a hard Christmas.
   Comment on the New Deal, in *New Outlook* Dec. 1933

3 The crowning climax to the whole situation is the
   undisputed fact that William Randolph Hearst gave him
   [Ogden Mills] the kiss of death.
   Comment on Hearst's support for Smith's unsuccessful
   opponent for governor of New York State in *New York Times*
   25 Oct. 1926

4 All the ills of democracy can be cured by more
   democracy.
   Speech in Albany, 27 June 1933, in *New York Times* 28 June
   1933

Sir Cyril Smith 1928–

5 This place is the longest running farce in the West
   End.
   Comment to journalists on the House of Commons, July
   1973, in *Big Cyril* (1977) ch. 8

Dodie Smith 1896–1990

6 And so I give you our toast. From that young man
   upstairs who has had the impudence to make me
   a great-uncle, to Mother and Father on their Golden
   Wedding; through four generations of us, and to those
   who have gone, and those who are to come. To the
   family—that dear octopus from whose tentacles we
   never quite escape, nor, in our inmost hearts, ever
   quite wish to.
   Dear Octopus (1938) p. 120

7 Noble deeds and hot baths are the best cures for
   depression.
   I Capture the Castle (1949) pt. 1, ch. 3

Edgar Smith 1857–1938

8 You may tempt the upper classes
   With your villainous demi-tasses,
   But; Heaven will protect a working-girl!
   Heaven Will Protect the Working-Girl (1909 song; music by
   A. Baldwin Sloane)

F. E. Smith (*Earl of Birkenhead*) 1872–1930

9 We have the highest authority for believing that the
   meek shall inherit the Earth; though I have never
   found any particular corroboration of this aphorism in
   the records of Somerset House.
   Contemporary Personalities (1924) 'Marquess Curzon'

10 Judge Willis . . . after a long wrangle with F. E. Smith,
   whom by this time he must have come to loathe, upon
   a point of procedure asked plaintively: 'What do you

suppose I am on the Bench for, Mr Smith?' 'It is not for
me, Your Honour, to attempt to fathom the inscrutable
workings of Providence.'
   In Second Earl of Birkenhead *F. E. The Life of F. E. Smith First
   Earl of Birkenhead* (1959 ed.) ch. 9

11 JUDGE: I have read your case, Mr Smith, and I am no
   wiser now than I was when I started.
   SMITH: Possibly not, My Lord, but far better informed.
   In Second Earl of Birkenhead *F. E. The Life of F. E. Smith First
   Earl of Birkenhead* (1959 ed.) ch. 9

12 JUDGE WILLIS: You are extremely offensive, young
   man.
   F. E. SMITH: As a matter of fact, we both are, and the
   only difference between us is that I am trying to be,
   and you can't help it.
   In Second Earl of Birkenhead *Frederick Edwin Earl of
   Birkenhead* (1933) vol. 1, ch. 9

13 MR JUSTICE DARLING: And who is George Robey?
   F. E. SMITH: Mr George Robey is the Darling of the
   music halls, m'lud.
   In A. E. Wilson *The Prime Minister of Mirth* (1956) ch. 1

14 The world continues to offer glittering prizes to those
   who have stout hearts and sharp swords.
   Rectorial Address, Glasgow University, 7 Nov. 1923, in *The
   Times* 8 Nov. 1923

Ian Smith 1919–

15 Let me say again, I don't believe in black majority rule
   in Rhodesia—not in a thousand years. I believe in
   blacks and whites working together.
   Broadcast speech, 20 Mar. 1976, in *Sunday Times* 21 Mar.
   1976

Logan Pearsall Smith 1865–1946

16 Happiness is a wine of the rarest vintage, and seems
   insipid to a vulgar taste.
   Afterthoughts (1931) 'Life and Human Nature'

17 There are two things to aim at in life: first, to get what
   you want; and, after that, to enjoy it. Only the wisest of
   mankind achieve the second.
   Afterthoughts (1931) 'Life and Human Nature'

18 How awful to reflect that what people say of us is true!
   Afterthoughts (1931) 'Life and Human Nature'

19 How many of our daydreams would darken into
   nightmares if there seemed any danger of their coming
   true!
   Afterthoughts (1931) 'Life and Human Nature'

20 There are few sorrows, however poignant, in which
   a good income is of no avail.
   Afterthoughts (1931) 'Life and Human Nature'

21 An improper mind is a perpetual feast.
   Afterthoughts (1931) 'Life and Human Nature'

22 There is more felicity on the far side of baldness than
   young men can possibly imagine.
   Afterthoughts (1931) 'Age and Death'

23 What music is more enchanting than the voices of
   young people, when you can't hear what they say?
   Afterthoughts (1931) 'Age and Death'

1 The denunciation of the young is a necessary part of the hygiene of older people, and greatly assists the circulation of their blood.
  Afterthoughts (1931) 'Age and Death'

2 I cannot forgive my friends for dying; I do not find these vanishing acts of theirs at all amusing.
  Afterthoughts (1931) 'Age and Death'

3 Those who set out to serve both God and Mammon soon discover that there is no God.
  Afterthoughts (1931) 'Other People'

4 Most people sell their souls, and live with a good conscience on the proceeds.
  Afterthoughts (1931) 'Other People'

5 All Reformers, however strict their social conscience, live in houses just as big as they can pay for.
  Afterthoughts (1931) 'Other People'

6 When they come downstairs from their Ivory Towers, Idealists are very apt to walk straight into the gutter.
  Afterthoughts (1931) 'Other People'

7 Married women are kept women, and they are beginning to find it out.
  Afterthoughts (1931) 'Other People'

8 You cannot be both fashionable and first-rate.
  Afterthoughts (1931) 'In the World'

9 It is the wretchedness of being rich that you have to live with rich people.
  Afterthoughts (1931) 'In the World'

10 To suppose, as we all suppose, that we could be rich and not behave as the rich behave, is like supposing that we could drink all day and keep absolutely sober.
  Afterthoughts (1931) 'In the World'

11 The test of a vocation is the love of the drudgery it involves.
  Afterthoughts (1931) 'Art and Letters'

12 A best-seller is the gilded tomb of a mediocre talent.
  Afterthoughts (1931) 'Art and Letters'

13 People say that life is the thing, but I prefer reading.
  Afterthoughts (1931) 'Myself'

14 Thank heavens, the sun has gone in, and I don't have to go out and enjoy it.
  Afterthoughts (1931) 'Myself'

15 What I like in a good author is not what he says, but what he whispers.
  All Trivia (1933) 'Afterthoughts' pt. 5

16 Two weeks before his death, a friend asked him half-jokingly if he had discovered any meaning in life. 'Yes,' he replied, 'there is a meaning, at least for me, there is one thing that matters—to set a chime of words tinkling in the minds of a few fastidious people.'
  Cyril Connolly 'Logan Pearsall Smith', obituary notice in *New Statesman* 9 Mar. 1946

Stevie Smith (Florence Margaret Smith)
1902–1971

17 This Englishwoman is so refined
  She has no bosom and no behind.
  A Good Time was had by All (1937) 'This Englishwoman'

18 Nobody heard him, the dead man,
  But still he lay moaning:
  I was much further out than you thought
  And not waving but drowning.

  Poor chap, he always loved larking
  And now he's dead
  It must have been too cold for him his heart gave way,
  They said.

  Oh, no no no, it was too cold always
  (Still the dead one lay moaning)
  I was much too far out all my life
  And not waving but drowning.
  Not Waving but Drowning (1957) title poem

19 People who are always praising the past
  And especially the times of faith as best
  Ought to go and live in the Middle Ages
  And be burnt at the stake as witches and sages.
  Not Waving but Drowning (1957) 'The Past'

20 There you are you see, quite simple. If you cannot have your dear husband for a comfort and a delight, for a breadwinner and a crosspatch, for a sofa, chair or a hot-water bottle, one can use him as a Cross to be Borne.
  Novel on Yellow Paper (1936) p. 247

21 Oh I am a cat that likes to
  Gallop about doing good.
  Scorpion and Other Poems (1972) 'The Galloping Cat'

22 I long for the Person from Porlock
  To bring my thoughts to an end,
  I am growing impatient to see him
  I think of him as a friend.
  Selected Poems (1962) 'Thoughts about the "Person from Porlock"'

23 Private Means is dead
  God rest his soul, officers and fellow-rankers said.
  Selected Poems (1962) 'Private Means is Dead'

24 Why does my Muse only speak when she is unhappy?
  She does not, I only listen when I am unhappy
  When I am happy I live and despise writing
  For my Muse this cannot but be dispiriting.
  Selected Poems (1964) 'My Muse'

John Snagge 1904–

25 His [Snagge's] famous gaffe [in a commentary on the Boat Race] to the effect that he couldn't see who was in the lead but it was either Oxford or Cambridge he had no recollection of until he heard a recording afterwards.
  C. Dodd *Oxford and Cambridge Boat Race* (1983) ch. 14

C. P. Snow (Baron Snow of Leicester)
1905–1980

26 The official world, the corridors of power, the dilemmas of conscience and egotism—she disliked them all.
  Homecomings (1956) ch. 22

27 I believe the intellectual life of the whole of western society is increasingly being split into two polar groups. . . . Literary intellectuals at one pole—at the other scientists, and as the most representative, the physical scientists. Between the two a gulf of mutual incomprehension.

The Two Cultures and the Scientific Revolution (1959 Rede Lecture) p. 3

1 A good many times I have been present at gatherings of people who, by the standards of the traditional culture, are thought highly educated and who have with considerable gusto been expressing their incredulity at the illiteracy of scientists. Once or twice I have been provoked and have asked the company how many of them could describe the Second Law of Thermodynamics. The response was cold: it was also negative.

The Two Cultures and the Scientific Revolution (1959 Rede Lecture) p. 14

Philip Snowden (*Viscount Snowden*)
1864–1937

2 It would be desirable if every Government, when it comes to power, should have its old speeches burnt.

In C. E. Bechofer Roberts ('Ephesian') *Philip Snowden* (1929) ch. 12

3 I hope you have read the election programme of the Labour Party: It is the most fantastic and impracticable programme ever put before the electors. All the derelict industries are to be taken over by the State, and the taxpayer is to shoulder the losses. The banks and financial houses are to be placed under national ownership and control, which means, I suppose, that they are to be run by a joint committee of the Labour Party and the Trades Union Council. Your investments are to be ordered by some board, and your foreign investments are to be mobilized to finance this madcap policy. This is not Socialism. It is Bolshevism run mad.

BBC radio election broadcast, 17 Oct. 1931, in *The Times* 19 Oct. 1931

Alexander Solzhenitsyn 1918–

4 А между тем ВНУТРЕННИХ ДЕЛ вообще не осталось на нашей тесной Земле! И спасение человечества только в том, чтобы всем было дело до всего: людям Востока было бы сплошь небезразлично, что думают на Западе; людям Запада — сплошь небезразлично, что совершается на Востоке.

Meanwhile no such thing as INTERNAL AFFAIRS remains on our crowded Earth. Mankind's salvation lies exclusively in everyone's making everything his business, in the people of the East being anything but indifferent to what is thought in the West, and in the people of the West being anything but indifferent to what happens in the East.

Nobel Prize Lecture, 1970, in John W. Dunlop, Richard Haugh and Alexis Klimoff (eds.) *Aleksandr Solzhenitsyn: Critical Essays and Documentary Materials* (1974) p. 574

5 Если десятки лет за десятками лет не разрешать рассказывать то, как оно есть, — непоправимо разблуживаются человеческие мозги, и уже соотечественника понять труднее, чем марсианина.

If decade after decade the truth cannot be told, each person's mind begins to roam irretrievably. One's fellow countrymen become harder to understand than Martians.

Раковый Корпус (Cancer Ward, 1968) pt. 2, ch. 32

6 Вы сильны лишь постольку, поскольку отбираете у людей *не всё*. Но человек, у которого вы отобрали *всё* — уже не подвластен вам, он снова свободен.

You only have power over people as long as you don't take everything away from them. But when you've robbed a man of everything he's no longer in your power—he's free again.

В Кругу Первом (The First Circle, 1968) ch. 17

7 Yes, we are still the prisoners of communism, and yet, for us in Russia, communism is a dead dog, while for many people in the West it is still a living lion.

Broadcast on BBC Russian Service, in *Listener* 15 Feb. 1979

8 У нас ложь стала не просто нравственной категорией, но и государственным столпом.

In our country the lie has become not just a moral category but a pillar of the State.

1974 interview, printed in appendix to Водался Теленок ц бубом (The Oak and the Calf, 1975)

Anastasio Somoza 1925–1980

9 Indeed, you won the elections, but I won the count.

Reply to accusation of ballot-rigging, in *Guardian* 17 June 1977

Stephen Sondheim 1930–

10 Everything's coming up roses.

Title of song (1959; music by Jule Styne)

11 Send in the clowns.

Title of song (1973)

Susan Sontag 1933–

12 Interpretation is the revenge of the intellect upon art.

Evergreen Review Dec. 1964

13 Real art has the capacity to make us nervous. By reducing the work of art to its content, and then interpreting *that*, one tames the work of art. Interpretation makes art manageable, conformable.

Evergreen Review Dec. 1964

14 The camera makes everyone a tourist in other people's reality, and eventually in one's own.

New York Review of Books 18 Apr. 1974

15 A photograph is not only an image (as a painting is an image), an interpretation of the real; it is also a trace, something directly stencilled off the real, like a footprint or a death mask.

New York Review of Books 23 June 1977

16 Illness is the night-side of life, a more onerous citizenship. Everyone who is born holds dual citizenship, in the kingdom of the well and in the kingdom of the sick. Although we all prefer to use only the good passport, sooner or later each of us is obliged, at least for a spell, to identify ourselves as citizens of that other place.

New York Review of Books 26 Jan. 1978

1 The truth is that Mozart, Pascal, Boolean algebra, Shakespeare, parliamentary government, baroque churches, Newton, the emancipation of women, Kant, Marx, Balanchine ballet *et al.*, don't redeem what this particular civilization has wrought upon the world. The white race *is* the cancer of human history, it is the white race, and it alone—its ideologies and inventions—which eradicates autonomous civilizations wherever it spreads, which has upset the ecological balance of the planet, which now threatens the very existence of life itself.

Partisan Review Winter 1967, p. 57

Donald Soper (Baron Soper) 1903–

2 The quality of debate [in the House of Lords] is pretty high—and it is, I think, good evidence of life after death.

Radio interview, in Listener *17 Aug. 1978*

Charles Hamilton Sorley 1895–1915

3 When you see millions of the mouthless dead
Across your dreams in pale battalions go,
Say not soft things as other men have said,
That you'll remember. For you need not so.
Give them not praise. For, deaf, how should they know
It is not curses heaped on each gashed head?

Marlborough and Other Poems (1916) 'A Sonnet'

Henry D. Spalding d. 1990

4 I like Ike.

US button badge first used in 1947 when General Eisenhower was seen as a potential presidential nominee, in *New Republic* 27 Oct. 1947

Muriel Spark 1918–

5 Parents learn a lot from their children about coping with life.

The Comforters (1957) ch. 6

6 'I am putting old heads on your young shoulders,' Miss Brodie had told them at that time, 'and all my pupils are the crème de la crème.'

Prime of Miss Jean Brodie (1961) ch. 1

7 Give me a girl at an impressionable age, and she is mine for life.

Prime of Miss Jean Brodie (1961) ch. 1

8 One's prime is elusive. You little girls, when you grow up, must be on the alert to recognise your prime at whatever time of your life it may occur. You must live it to the full.

Prime of Miss Jean Brodie (1961) ch. 1

John Sparrow 1906–

9 That indefatigable and unsavoury engine of pollution, the dog.

Letter in The Times *30 Sept. 1975*

Countess Spencer (Raine Spencer) 1929–

10 Alas, for our towns and cities. Monstrous carbuncles of concrete have erupted in gentle Georgian Squares.

The Spencers on Spas (1983) p. 14. Cf. Prince Charles 50:2

Sir Stanley Spencer 1891–1959

11 Painting is saying "Ta" to God.

In letter from Spencer's daughter Shirin, *Observer* 7 Feb. 1988

Stephen Spender 1909–

12 Never being, but always at the edge of Being.

Poems (1933) no. 10

13 My parents kept me from children who were rough
And who threw words like stones and who wore torn clothes.

Poems (1933) no. 12

14 What I had not foreseen
Was the gradual day
Weakening the will
Leaking the brightness away.

Poems (1933) no. 13

15 Who live under the shadow of a war,
What can I do that matters?

Poems (1933) no. 17

16 The names of those who in their lives fought for life
Who wore at their hearts the fire's centre.
Born of the sun they travelled a short while towards the sun,
And left the vivid air signed with their honour.

Poems (1933) no. 23 'I think continually of those who were truly great'

17 After the first powerful plain manifesto
The black statement of pistons, without more fuss
But gliding like a queen, she leaves the station.

Poems (1933) no. 26 'The Express'

18 Now over these small hills they have built the concrete
That trails black wire:
Pylons, those pillars
Bare like nude, giant girls that have no secret.

Poems (1933) no. 28 'The Pylons'

19 Consider: only one bullet in ten thousand kills a man.
Ask: was so much expenditure justified
On the death of one so young and so silly
Stretched under the olive trees, Oh, world, Oh, death?

Stephen Spender and John Lehmann (eds.) *Poems for Spain* (1939) 'Regum Ultimo Ratio'

20 . . . their collected
Hearts wound up with love, like little watch springs.

Still Centre (1939) 'The Past Values'

1 People sometimes divide others into those you laugh at and those you laugh with. The young Auden was someone you could laugh-at-with.

  W. H. Auden (address delivered at Auden's memorial service at Christ Church Cathedral, Oxford, 27 Oct. 1973)

Oswald Spengler 1880–1936

2 *Der Sozialismus ist nichts als der Kapitalismus der Unterklasse.*

Socialism is nothing but the capitalism of the lower classes.

  Jahre der Entscheidung (The Hour of Decision, 1933) pt. 1

Steven Spielberg 1947–

3 Close encounters of the third kind.
  Title of film (1977)

Dr Benjamin Spock 1903–

4 You know more than you think you do.
  Common Sense Book of Baby and Child Care (1946) [later *Baby and Child Care*], opening words

5 To win in Vietnam, we will have to exterminate a nation.
  Dr Spock on Vietnam (1968) ch. 7

William Archibald Spooner 1844–1930

6 Mr Spooner has a habit of transferring his syllables, so that it is no unusual experience for the members of New College to hear their late Dean give out in chapel a well-known sentence in the unintelligible guise of 'Kinkering Kongs their tykles tate'.
  Echo 4 May 1892

7 A famous New College personality . . . was Warden Spooner. . . . 'You have tasted your worm,' he is reputed to have said to an undergraduate, 'you have hissed my mystery lectures, and you must leave by the first town drain.' He was also responsible for proposing a toast to 'our queer old dean'.
  Oxford University What's What (1948) p. 8 (William Hayter in *Spooner* (1977) ch. 6 maintains these sayings are apocryphal)

8 Mr Huxley assures me that it's no farther from the north coast of Spitzbergen to the North Pole than it is from Land's End to John of Gaunt.
  Julian Huxley in *SEAC* (Calcutta) 27 Feb. 1944

9 You will find as you grow older that the weight of rages will press harder and harder upon the employer.
  In William Hayter *Spooner* (1977) ch. 6

10 Poor soul, very sad; her late husband, you know, a very sad death—eaten by missionaries—poor soul!
  In William Hayter *Spooner* (1977) ch. 6

Sir Cecil Spring Rice 1859–1918

11 I vow to thee, my country—all earthly things above—
Entire and whole and perfect, the service of my love,
The love that asks no question: the love that stands the test,

That lays upon the altar the dearest and the best:
The love that never falters, the love that pays the price,
The love that makes undaunted the final sacrifice.
  Poems (1920) 'I Vow to Thee, My Country'

12 And there's another country, I've heard of long ago—
Most dear to them that love her, most great to them that know.
  Poems (1920) 'I Vow to Thee, My Country'

13 And her ways are ways of gentleness and all her paths are Peace.
  Poems (1920) 'I Vow to Thee, My Country'

14 I am the Dean of Christ Church, Sir:
There's my wife; look well at her.
She's the Broad and I'm the High;
We are the University.
  The Masque of Balliol in W. G. Hiscock (ed.) *The Balliol Rhymes* (1939) p. 29

Bruce Springsteen 1949–

15 We gotta get out while we're young,
'Cause tramps like us, baby, we were born to run.
  Born to Run (1975 song)

Sir J. C. Squire 1884–1958

16 But I'm not so think as you drunk I am.
  M. Baring et al. *One Hundred and One Ballades* (1931 'Ballade of Soporific Absorption'

17 It did not last: the Devil howling 'Ho!
Let Einstein be!' restored the status quo.
  Poems (1926) 'In continuation of Pope on Newton'.
  Cf. *Oxford Dictionary of Quotations* (1979) 378:7

Joseph Stalin (Iosif Vissarionovich Dzhugashvili) 1879–1953

18 Государство есть машина в руках господствующего класса для подавления сопротивления своих классовых противников.

The State is an instrument in the hands of the ruling class, used to break the resistance of the adversaries of that class.
  Foundations of Leninism (1924) section 4/6

19 Mr Churchill, Mr Prime Minister, how many divisions did you say the Pope had?
  At the Potsdam Conference, reported by Harry S. Truman in speech to American Association for the Advancement of Science, in *New York Times* 14 Sept. 1948, p. 24 (reporting Stalin's reaction to Churchill's statement that the Pope would not like the Communists to take over the Catholic part of Poland)

20 Вопрос о *возможности* построения социализма силами одной страны, на что должен быть дан положительный ответ.

First of all there is the question: Can Socialism *possibly* be established in one country alone by that country's unaided strength? The question must be answered in the affirmative.
  Problems of Leninism (1926) ch. 6

Charles E. Stanton 1859–1933

1 *Lafayette, nous voila!*

Lafayette, we are here.
At the tomb of Lafayette in Paris, 4 July 1917, in *New York Tribune* 6 Sept. 1917

Frank L. Stanton 1857–1927

2 Sweetes' li'l' feller,
Everybody knows;
Dunno what to call him,
But he's mighty lak' a rose!
Mighty Lak' a Rose (1901 song; music by Ethelbert Nevin)

Dame Freya Stark 1893–

3 The great and almost only comfort about being a woman is that one can always pretend to be more stupid than one is and no one is surprised.
The Valleys of the Assassins (1934) ch. 2

Enid Starkie 1897–1970

4 Unhurt people are not much good in the world.
Letter, 18 June 1943, in Joanna Richardson *Enid Starkie* (1973) pt. 6, ch. 18

Christina Stead 1902–1983

5 If all the rich people in the world divided up their money among themselves there wouldn't be enough to go round.
House of All Nations (1938) 'Credo'

6 A self-made man is one who believes in luck and sends his son to Oxford.
House of All Nations (1938) 'Credo'

Sir David Steel 1938–

7 I have the good fortune to be the first Liberal leader for over half a century who is able to say to you at the end of our annual assembly: go back to your constituencies and prepare for government.
Speech at Liberal Party Assembly, Llandudno, 18 Sept. 1981, in *The Times* 19 Sept. 1981

Lincoln Steffens 1866–1936

8 I have seen the future; and it works.
Letter to Marie Howe, 3 Apr. 1919, in *Letters* (1938) vol. 1, p. 463 (describing a visit to the Soviet Union in 1919; cf. Steffens's *Autobiography* (1931) ch. 18: 'So you've been over into Russia?' said Bernard Baruch, and I answered very literally, 'I have been over into the future, and it works')

Gertrude Stein 1874–1946

9 Hemingway ... brought the manuscript he intended sending to America. He handed it to Gertrude Stein. He had added to his stories a little story of meditations and in these he said that The Enormous Room was the greatest book he had ever read. It was then that Gertrude Stein said, Hemingway, remarks are not literature.
Autobiography of Alice B. Toklas (1933) ch. 7

10 Anyone who marries three girls from St Louis hasn't learned much.
Said of Ernest Hemingway in James R. Mellow *Charmed Circle: Gertrude Stein and Company* (1974) ch. 16

11 Anything scares me, anything scares anyone but really after all considering how dangerous everything is nothing is really very frightening.
Everybody's Autobiography (1937) ch. 2

12 It takes a lot of time to be a genius, you have to sit around so much doing nothing, really doing nothing.
Everybody's Autobiography (1937) ch. 2

13 What was the use of my having come from Oakland it was not natural to have come from there yes write about it if I like or anything if I like but not there, there is no there there.
Everybody's Autobiography (1937) ch. 4

14 Ezra Pound failed to impress her [Stein]. ... She said he was a village explainer, excellent if you were a village, but if you were not, not.
Janet Hobhouse *Everyone who was Anybody* (1975) ch. 6

15 You are so afraid of losing your moral sense that you are not willing to take it through anything more dangerous than a mud-puddle.
Fernhurst, Q.E.D., and Other Early Writings (1971) 'Q.E.D.' (1903) bk. 1

16 Pigeons on the grass alas.
Four Saints in Three Acts (1934) act 3, sc. 2

17 In the United States there is more space where nobody is than where anybody is. That is what makes America what it is.
The Geographical History of America (1936)

18 Just before she [Stein] died she asked, 'What *is* the answer?' No answer came. She laughed and said, 'In that case what is the question?' Then she died.
Donald Sutherland *Gertrude Stein, A Biography of her Work* (1951) ch. 6

19 Disillusionment in living is the finding out nobody agrees with you not those that are and were fighting with you. Disillusionment in living is the finding out nobody agrees with you not those that are fighting for you. Complete disillusionment is when you realise that no one can for they can't change.
Making of Americans (1934) ch. 5

20 Rose is a rose is a rose is a rose, is a rose.
Sacred Emily (1913) p. 187

21 You are all a lost generation.
In Ernest Hemingway *The Sun Also Rises* (1926) epigraph (Gertrude Stein heard the phrase 'a lost generation' (*une génération perdue*) from a French garage-owner: see James R. Mellow *Charmed Circle* (1974) ch. 10)

John Steinbeck 1902–1968

22 Man, unlike any other thing organic or inorganic in the universe, grows beyond his work, walks up the stairs of his concepts, emerges ahead of his accomplishments.
Grapes of Wrath (1939) ch. 14

1 I know this—a man got to do what he got to do.
Grapes of Wrath (1939) ch. 18

2 Okie use' ta mean you was from Oklahoma. Now it means you're a dirty son-of-a-bitch. Okie means you're scum. Don't mean nothing itself, it's the way they say it.
Grapes of Wrath (1939) ch. 18

Gloria Steinem 1934–

3 Now, we are becoming the men we wanted to marry.
Ms July/Aug. 1982

4 A woman without a man is like a fish without a bicycle.
Attributed

James Stephens 1882–1950

5 Women are stronger than men—they do not die of wisdom.
They are better than men because they do not seek wisdom.
They are wiser than men because they know less and understand more.
The Crock of Gold (1912) bk. 1, ch. 2

6 Finality is death. Perfection is finality.
Nothing is perfect. There are lumps in it.
The Crock of Gold (1912) bk. 1, ch. 4

7 I hear a sudden cry of pain!
There is a rabbit in a snare:
Now I hear the cry again,
But I cannot tell from where. . . .
Little one! Oh, little one!
I am searching everywhere.
Songs from the City (1915) 'The Snare'

Andrew B. Sterling 1874–1955

8 Wait till the sun shines, Nellie,
When the clouds go drifting by.
Wait till the Sun Shines, Nellie (1905 song; music by Harry von Tilzer)

Wallace Stevens 1879–1955

9 Poetry is the supreme fiction, madame.
Harmonium (1923) 'A High-Toned old Christian Woman'

10 Call the roller of big cigars,
The muscular one, and bid him whip
In kitchen cups concupiscent curds.
Let the wenches dawdle in such dress
As they are used to wear, and let the boys
Bring flowers in last month's newspapers.
Let be be finale of seem.
The only emperor is the emperor of ice-cream.
Harmonium (1923) 'The Emperor of Ice-Cream'

11 Complacencies of the peignoir, and late
Coffee and oranges in a sunny chair,
And the green freedom of a cockatoo
Upon a rug mingle to dissipate
The holy hush of ancient sacrifice.
Harmonium (1923) 'Sunday Morning, I'

12 Just as my fingers on these keys
Make music, so the self-same sounds
On my spirit make a music, too.

Music is feeling, then, not sound;
And thus it is that what I feel,
Here in this room, desiring you,

Thinking of your blue-shadowed silk,
Is music.
Harmonium (1923) 'Peter Quince at the Clavier' pt. 1

13 Beauty is momentary in the mind—
The fitful tracing of a portal;
But in the flesh it is immortal.
The body dies; the body's beauty lives.
Harmonium (1923) 'Peter Quince at the Clavier' pt. 4

14 I do not know which to prefer,
The beauty of inflections
Or the beauty of innuendoes,
The blackbird whistling
Or just after.
Harmonium (1923) ' Thirteen Ways of Looking at a Blackbird'

15 The man bent over his guitar,
A shearsman of sorts. The day was green.

They said, 'You have a blue guitar,
You do not play things as they are.'

The man replied, 'Things as they are
Are changed upon the blue guitar.'
The Man with the Blue Guitar (1937) title poem

16 They will get it straight one day at the Sorbonne.
We shall return at twilight from the lecture
Pleased that the irrational is rational.
Notes Toward a Supreme Fiction (1942) 'It must give Pleasure'

17 The poet is the priest of the invisible.
Opus Posthumous (1957) 'Adagia'

Adlai Stevenson 1900–1965

18 I suppose flattery hurts no one, that is, if he doesn't inhale.
TV broadcast, 30 Mar. 1952, in N. F. Busch *Adlai E. Stevenson* (1952) ch. 5

19 I have been thinking that I would make a proposition to my Republican friends . . . that if they will stop telling lies about the Democrats, we will stop telling the truth about them.
Speech during 1952 Presidential Campaign, in J. B. Martin *Adlai Stevenson and Illinois* (1976) ch. 8

20 We must be patient—making peace is harder than making war.
Speech to Chicago Council on Foreign Relations, 21 Mar. 1946, in *Chicago Daily News* 22 Mar. 1946

21 In America any boy may become President and I suppose it's just one of the risks he takes!
Speech in Indianapolis, 26 Sept. 1952, in *Major Campaign Speeches of Adlai E. Stevenson; 1952* (1953) p. 174

22 My definition of a free society is a society where it is safe to be unpopular.
Speech in Detroit, 7 Oct. 1952, in *Major Campaign Speeches of Adlai E. Stevenson; 1952* (1953) p. 218

1 We hear the Secretary of State [John Foster Dulles] boasting of his brinkmanship—the art of bringing us to the edge of the abyss.
> Speech in Hartford, Connecticut, 25 Feb. 1956, in *New York Times* 26 Feb. 1956, p. 64

2 She [Eleanor Roosevelt] would rather light a candle than curse the darkness, and her glow has warmed the world.
> Comment on learning of Mrs Roosevelt's death, in *New York Times* 8 Nov. 1962

3 A funny thing happened to me on the way to the White House.
> Speech in Washington, 13 Dec. 1952 (after his defeat in the Presidential election), in Alden Whitman *Portrait: Adlai E. Stevenson* (1965) ch. 1

4 Let's face it. Let's talk sense to the American people. Let's tell them the truth, that there are no gains without pains, that we are now on the eve of great decisions, not easy decisions, like resistance when you're attacked, but a long, patient, costly struggle which alone can assure triumph over the great enemies of man—war, poverty and tyranny—and the assaults upon human dignity which are the most grievous consequences of each.
> Speech of Acceptance at the Democratic National Convention, Chicago, Illinois, 26 July 1952, in *Speeches of Adlai Stevenson* (1952) p. 20

5 A hungry man is not a free man.
> Speech at Kasson, Minnesota, 6 Sept. 1952, in *Speeches of Adlai Stevenson* (1952) 'Farm Policy'

6 There is no evil in the atom; only in men's souls.
> Speech at Hartford, Connecticut, 18 Sept. 1952, in *Speeches of Adlai Stevenson* (1952) 'The Atomic Future'

7 It reminds me of the small boy who jumbled his biblical quotations and said: 'A lie is an abomination unto the Lord, and a very present help in trouble.'
> In Bill Adler *The Stevenson Wit* (1966) p. 84 (cf. Proverbs 12:22, Psalms 46:1)

Anne Stevenson 1933–

8 Blackbirds are the cellos of the deep farms.
> *Minute by Glass Minute* (1982) 'Green Mountain, Black Mountain'

Caskie Stinnett 1911–

9 A diplomat . . . is a person who can tell you to go to hell in such a way that you actually look forward to the trip.
> *Out of the Red* (1960) ch. 4

Rt. Revd Mervyn Stockwood 1913–

10 A psychiatrist is a man who goes to the Folies-Bergère and looks at the audience.
> In *Observer* 15 Oct. 1961

Tom Stoppard 1937–

11 It's not the voting that's democracy, it's the counting.
> *Jumpers* (1972) act 1

12 My problem is that I am not frightfully interested in anything, except myself. And of all forms of fiction autobiography is the most gratuitous.
> *Lord Malquist and Mr Moon* (1966) pt. 2

13 The House of Lords, an illusion to which I have never been able to subscribe—responsibility without power, the prerogative of the eunuch throughout the ages.
> *Lord Malquist and Mr Moon* (1966) pt. 6. Cf. Rudyard Kipling

14 A foreign correspondent is someone who lives in foreign parts and corresponds, usually in the form of essays containing no new facts. Otherwise he's someone who flies around from hotel to hotel and thinks that the most interesting thing about any story is the fact that he has arrived to cover it.
> *Night and Day* (1978) act 1

15 WAGNER: You don't care much for the media, do you, Ruth?
> RUTH: The media. It sounds like a convention of spiritualists.
> CARSON: Ruth has mixed feelings about reporters.
> *Night and Day* (1978) act 1

16 MILNE: No matter how imperfect things are, if you've got a free press everything is correctable, and without it everything is concealable.
> RUTH: I'm with you on the free press. It's the newspapers I can't stand.
> *Night and Day* (1978) act 1

17 We do on stage things that are supposed to happen off. Which is a kind of integrity, if you look on every exit as being an entrance somewhere else.
> *Rosencrantz and Guildenstern Are Dead* (1967) act 1

18 GUILDENSTERN: Well then—one of the Greeks, perhaps? You're familiar with the tragedies of antiquity, are you? The great homicidal classics? Matri, patri, sorori, uxori and it goes without saying—suicidal—hm? Maidens aspiring to godheads—
> ROSENCRANTZ: And vice versa.
> *Rosencrantz and Guildenstern Are Dead* (1967) act 1

19 I can do you blood and love without the rhetoric, and I can do you blood and rhetoric without the love, and I can do you all three concurrent or consecutive, but I can't do you love and rhetoric without the blood. Blood is compulsory—they're all blood, you see.
> *Rosencrantz and Guildenstern Are Dead* (1967) act 1

20 To sum up: your father, whom you love, dies, you are his heir, you come back to find that hardly was the corpse cold before his young brother popped onto his throne and into his sheets, thereby offending both legal and natural practice. Now why exactly are you behaving in this extraordinary manner?
> *Rosencrantz and Guildenstern Are Dead* (1967) act 1

21 We're *actors*—we're the opposite of people! . . . Think, in your head, *now*, think of the most . . . *private* . . . *secret* . . . *intimate* thing you have ever done secure in the knowledge of its privacy. . . . Are you thinking of it? . . . *Well, I saw you do it!*
> *Rosencrantz and Guildenstern Are Dead* (1967) act 2

22 Eternity's a terrible thought. I mean, where's it all going to end?
> *Rosencrantz and Guildenstern Are Dead* (1967) act 2

1 The bad end unhappily, the good unluckily. That is what tragedy means.

> Rosencrantz and Guildenstern Are Dead (1967) act 2. Cf. Oxford Dictionary of Quotations (1979) 573:3

2 Life is a gamble at terrible odds—if it was a bet, you wouldn't take it.

> Rosencrantz and Guildenstern Are Dead (1967) act 3

3 I doubt that art needed Ruskin any more than a moving train needs one of its passengers to shove it.

> Times Literary Supplement 3 June 1977

4 War is capitalism with the gloves off and many who go to war know it but they go to war because they don't want to be a hero.

> Travesties (1975) act 1

Lytton Strachey 1880–1932

5 [Samuel] Johnson's aesthetic judgements are almost invariably subtle, or solid, or bold; they have always some good quality to recommend them—except one: they are never right.

> Books and Characters (1922) 'Lives of the Poets'

6 The history of the Victorian Age will never be written: we know too much about it. For ignorance is the first requisite of the historian—ignorance, which simplifies and clarifies, which selects and omits, with a placid perfection unattainable by the highest art.

> Eminent Victorians (1918) preface

7 The time was out of joint, and he [Hurrell Froude] was only too delighted to have been born to set it right.

> Eminent Victorians (1918) 'Cardinal Manning' pt. 2. Cf. Oxford Dictionary of Quotations (1979) 524:4

8 Miss Nightingale, however, with all her experience of public life, never stopped to consider the question whether God might not be a Limited Monarchy. Yet her conception of God was certainly not orthodox. She felt towards Him as she might have felt towards a glorified sanitary engineer; and in some of her speculations she seems hardly to distinguish between the Deity and the Drains.

> Eminent Victorians (1918) 'Florence Nightingale' pt. 4

9 His legs, perhaps, were shorter than they should have been.

> Eminent Victorians (1918) 'Dr Arnold'

10 Asked by the chairman [of a military tribunal] the usual question: 'I understand, Mr Strachey, that you have a conscientious objection to war?' he replied (in his curious falsetto voice), 'Oh no, not at all, only to this war.' Better than this was his reply to the chairman's other stock question, which had previously never failed to embarrass the claimant. 'Tell me, Mr Strachey, what would you do if you saw a German soldier trying to violate your sister?' With an air of noble virtue: 'I would try to get between them.'

> Robert Graves Good-bye to All That (1929) ch. 23

11 Discretion is not the better part of biography.

> In Michael Holroyd Lytton Strachey vol. 1 (1967) preface

12 He [Max Beerbohm] has the most remarkable and seductive genius—and I should say about the smallest in the world.

> Letter to Clive Bell, 4 Dec. 1917, in Michael Holroyd Lytton Strachey vol. 2 (1968) pt. 1, ch. 5

13 'If this is dying,' he remarked quietly, just before falling into unconsciousness, 'then I don't think much of it.'

> Michael Holroyd Lytton Strachey vol. 2, (1968) pt. 2, ch. 6

Igor Stravinsky 1882–1971

14 Music is, by its very nature, essentially powerless to express anything at all . . . music expresses itself.

> In Esquire Dec. 1972

15 My music is best understood by children and animals.

> In Observer 8 Oct. 1961

16 A good composer does not imitate; he steals.

> In Peter Yates Twentieth Century Music (1967) pt. 1, ch. 8. Cf. T. S. Eliot 76:8, Lionel Trilling 218:1

Simeon Strunsky 1879–1948

17 People who want to understand democracy should spend less time in the library with Aristotle and more time on the buses and in the subway.

> No Mean City (1944) ch. 2

18 Famous remarks are very seldom quoted correctly.

> No Mean City (1944) ch. 38

G. A. Studdert Kennedy 1883–1929

19 Waste of Muscle, waste of Brain,
Waste of Patience, waste of Pain,
Waste of Manhood, waste of Health,
Waste of Beauty, waste of Wealth,
Waste of Blood, and waste of Tears,
Waste of youth's most precious years,
Waste of ways the saints have trod,
Waste of Glory, waste of God,
War!

> More Rough Rhymes of a Padre by 'Woodbine Willie' (1919) 'Waste'

20 When Jesus came to Golgotha they hanged Him on a tree,
They drave great nails through hands and feet, and made a Calvary.
They crowned Him with a crown of thorns, red were His wounds and deep,
For those were crude and cruel days, and human flesh was cheap.
When Jesus came to Birmingham they simply passed Him by,
They never hurt a hair of Him, they only let Him die.
For men had grown more tender and they would not give Him pain,
They only just passed down the street, and left Him in the rain.

> Peace Rhymes of a Padre (1921) 'Indifference'

Terry Sullivan

21 She sells sea-shells on the sea-shore,
The shells she sells are sea-shells, I'm sure,
For if she sells sea-shells on the sea-shore,
Then I'm sure she sells sea-shore shells.

> She Sells Sea-Shells (1908 song; music by Harry Gifford)

Arthur Hays Sulzberger 1891–

1 We [journalists] tell the public which way the cat is jumping. The public will take care of the cat.
   Time 8 May 1950

Edith Summerskill 1901–1980

2 The housewife is the Cinderella of the affluent state. . . . She is wholly dependent on the whim of an individual to give her money for the essentials of life. If she complains she is a nagger—for nagging is the repetition of unpalatable truths.
   Speech to Married Women's Association, House of Commons, 14 July 1960, in *The Times* 15 July 1960

Jacqueline Susann (Mrs Irving Mansfield) 1921–1974

3 Valley of the dolls.
   Title of novel (1966)

Hannen Swaffer 1879–1962

4 Perhaps it was about now [*c*.1902] that he [Swaffer] began to formulate a dictum which, though not always attributed to him, has often been quoted (among others, by witnesses before the first Royal Commssion on the Press): 'Freedom of the press in Britain means freedom to print such of the proprietor's prejudices as the advertisers don't object to.'
   Tom Driberg *Swaff* (1974) ch. 2

Herbert Bayard Swope 1882–1958

5 The First Duty of a newspaper is to be Accurate. If it is Accurate, it follows that it is Fair.
   Letter to *New York Herald Tribune* 16 Mar. 1958

6 He [Swope] enunciated no rules for success, but offered a sure formula for failure: *Just try to please everyone.*
   In E. J. Kahn Jr. *World of Swope* (1965) p. 7

See also BERNARD BARUCH

Eric Sykes and Max Bygraves 1922–

7 Eric Sykes had this quick ear and could tell by any inflection I put into a line how to make it a catch phrase—at one time I had more catch phrases than I could handle. I had the whole country saying things like 'I've arrived and to prove it I'm here!' 'A good idea—son' 'Bighead!' 'Dollar lolly'.
   Max Bygraves *I Wanna Tell You a Story!* (1976) p. 96 (describing catch-phrases on *Educating Archie*, 1950–3 BBC radio comedy series)

John Millington Synge 1871–1909

8 'A man who is not afraid of the sea will soon be drownded,' he said 'for he will be going out on a day he shouldn't. But we do be afraid of the sea, and we do only be drownded now and again.'
   Aran Islands (1907) pt. 2

9 'A translation is no translation,' he said, 'unless it will give you the music of a poem along with the words of it.'
   Aran Islands (1907) pt. 3

10 When I was writing 'The Shadow of the Glen', some years ago, I got more aid than any learning could have given me from a chink in the floor of the old Wicklow house where I was staying, that let me hear what was being said by the servant girls in the kitchen.
   Playboy of the Western World (1907) preface

11 Oh my grief, I've lost him surely. I've lost the only Playboy of the Western World.
   Playboy of the Western World (1907) act 3 (last lines)

Thomas Szasz 1920–

12 A child becomes an adult when he realizes that he has a right not only to be right but also to be wrong.
   The Second Sin (1973) 'Childhood'

13 Masturbation: the primary sexual activity of mankind. In the nineteenth century, it was a disease; in the twentieth, it's a cure.
   The Second Sin (1973) 'Sex'

14 Traditionally, sex has been a very private, secretive activity. Herein perhaps lies its powerful force for uniting people in a strong bond. As we make sex less secretive, we may rob it of its power to hold men and women together.
   The Second Sin (1973) 'Sex'

15 Happiness is an imaginary condition, formerly often attributed by the living to the dead, now usually attributed by adults to children, and by children to adults.
   The Second Sin (1973) 'Emotions'

16 The stupid neither forgive nor forget; the naïve forgive and forget; the wise forgive but do not forget.
   The Second Sin (1973) 'Personal Conduct'

17 Two wrongs don't make a right, but they make a good excuse.
   The Second Sin (1973) 'Social Relations'

18 If you talk to God, you are praying; if God talks to you, you have schizophrenia. If the dead talk to you, you are a spiritualist; if God talks to you, you are a schizophrenic.
   The Second Sin (1973) 'Schizophrenia'

19 Formerly, when religion was strong and science weak, men mistook magic for medicine; now, when science is strong and religion weak, men mistake medicine for magic.
   The Second Sin (1973) 'Science and Scientism'

George Szell 1897–1970

20 Conductors must give unmistakable and suggestive signals to the orchestra—not choreography to the audience.
   Newsweek 28 Jan. 1963

Albert von Szent-Györgyi 1893–1986

1 Discovery consists of seeing what everybody has seen and thinking what nobody has thought.
In Irving Good (ed.) The Scientist Speculates (1962) p. 15

Sir Rabindranath Tagore 1861–1941

2 Bigotry tries to keep truth safe in its hand
With a grip that kills it.
Fireflies (1928) p. 29

Nellie Talbot

3 Jesus wants me for a sunbeam.
Title of hymn (1921), in CSSM Choruses No. 1

S. G. Tallentyre (E. Beatrice Hall) 1868–

4 'On the Mind' [*De l'Esprit*] became not the success of the season, but one of the most famous books of the century. The men who had hated it, and had not particularly loved Helvétius, flocked round him now. Voltaire forgave him all injuries, intentional or unintentional. . . . 'I disapprove of what you say, but I will defend to the death your right to say it,' was his attitude now.
The Friends of Voltaire (1906) ch. 7 (often attributed to Voltaire but not found in his works)

Booth Tarkington 1869–1946

5 There are two things that will be believed of any man whatsoever, and one of them is that he has taken to drink.
Penrod (1914) ch. 10

A. J. P. Taylor 1906–1990

6 He [Lord Northcliffe] aspired to power instead of influence, and as a result forfeited both.
English History, 1914–1945 (1965) ch. 1

7 Communism continued to haunt Europe as a spectre—a name men gave to their own fears and blunders. But the crusade against Communism was even more imaginary than the spectre of Communism.
Origins of the Second World War (1962) ch. 2

8 A racing tipster who only reached Hitler's level of accuracy would not do well for his clients.
Origins of the Second World War (1962) ch. 7

Bert Leston Taylor 1866–1901

9 A bore is a man who, when you ask him how he is, tells you.
The So-Called Human Race (1922) p. 163

Norman Tebbit 1931–

10 We cannot ignore the price that unemployment today is exacting from the failures of the past. I have known about these things. I grew up in the Thirties with our

unemployed father. He did not riot, he got on his bike and looked for work.
Speech at Conservative Party Conference, 15 Oct. 1981, in Daily Telegraph 16 Oct. 1981

Archbishop William Temple 1881–1944

11 In place of the conception of the power-state we are led to that of the welfare-state.
Citizen and Churchman (1941) ch. 2

12 It is a mistake to suppose that God is only, or even chiefly, concerned with religion.
In R. V. C. Bodley In Search of Serenity (1955) ch. 12

13 Christianity is the most materialistic of all great religions.
Readings in St John's Gospel vol. 1 (1939) introduction

A. S. J. Tessimond 1902–1962

14 Cats, no less liquid than their shadows,
Offer no angles to the wind.
They slip, diminished, neat, through loopholes
Less than themselves.
Cats (1934) p. 20

Margaret Thatcher 1925–

15 We have to get our production and our earnings into balance. There's no easy popularity in what we are proposing, but it is fundamentally sound. Yet I believe people accept there is no real alternative.
Speech at Conservative Women's Conference, 21 May 1980, in Daily Telegraph 22 May 1980

16 A triumphant Prime Minister declared 'Rejoice, rejoice' last night. . . . 'Let us congratulate our armed forces and the Marines,' she added.
On recapture of South Georgia, 25 Apr. 1982, Daily Telegraph 26 Apr. 1982

17 In church on Sunday morning—it was a lovely morning and we haven't had many lovely days—the sun was coming through a stained glass window and falling on some flowers, falling right across the church. It just occurred to me that this was the day I was meant not to see. Then all of a sudden I thought, 'there are some of my dearest friends who are not seeing this day.'
Television interview, 15 Oct. 1984, after the Brighton bombing, in Daily Telegraph 16 Oct. 1984

18 We're going to be rather lucky to be living at a time when you get the turn of the thousand years and we really ought to set Britain's course for the next century as well as this. . . . Yes, I hope to go on and on.
Television interview, 11 May 1987, in Independent 12 May 1987

19 I don't mind how much my Ministers talk, as long as they do what I say.
In Observer 27 Jan. 1980

20 I am extraordinarily patient, provided I get my own way in the end.
In Observer 4 Apr. 1989

21 Ladies and gentlemen, I stand before you tonight in my red chiffon evening gown, my face softly made up, my fair hair gently waved . . . the Iron Lady of the Western

World! Me? A cold war warrior? Well, yes—if that is how they wish to interpret my defence of values and freedoms fundamental to our way of life.

> Speech at Finchley, 31 Jan. 1976, in *Sunday Times* 1 Feb. 1976

1 I was asked whether I was trying to restore Victorian values. I said straight out I was. And I am.

> Speech to British Jewish Community, 21 July 1983, in M. McFadyean & M. Renn *Thatcher's Reign* (1984) p. 114

2 We shall not be diverted from our course. To those waiting with bated breath for that favourite media catch-phrase, the U-turn, I have only this to say. 'You turn if you want; the lady's not for turning.'

> Speech at Conservative Party Conference in Brighton, 10 Oct. 1980, in *The Times* 11 Oct. 1980

3 Let me make one thing absolutely clear. The National Health Service is safe with us.

> Speech at Conservative party Conference, 8 Oct. 1982, in *The Times* 9 Oct. 1982

4 The Prime Minister [Mrs Thatcher] said yesterday that she liked Mr Gorbachev—'we can do business together'—and that she was cautiously optimistic for detente and world peace in the new year.

> *The Times* 18 Dec. 1984

5 We must try to find ways to starve the terrorist and the hijacker of the oxygen of publicity on which they depend.

> Speech to American Bar Association in London, 15 July 1985, in *The Times* 16 July 1985

6 No one would remember the Good Samaritan if he'd only had good intentions. He had money as well.

> Television interview, 6 Jan. 1986, in *The Times* 12 Jan. 1986

7 Mrs Margaret Thatcher informed the world with regal panache yesterday that her daughter-in-law had given birth to a son. 'We have become a grandmother,' the Prime Minister said.

> *The Times* 4 Mar. 1989

8 There is no such thing as Society. There are individual men and women, and there are families.

> *Woman's Own* 31 Oct. 1987

Sam Theard and Fleecie Moore

9 Let the good times roll.

> Title of song (1946)

Diane Thomas

10 Romancing the stone.

> Title of film (1984)

Dylan Thomas 1914–1953

11 One Christmas was so much like another, in those years around the sea-town corner now and out of all sound except the distant speaking of the voices I sometimes hear a moment before sleep, that I can never remember whether it snowed for six days and six nights when I was twelve or whether it snowed for twelve days and twelve nights when I was six.

> *A Child's Christmas in Wales* (1954) p. 5

12 Years and years and years ago, when I was a boy, when there were wolves in Wales, and birds the colour of red-flannel petticoats whisked past the harp-shaped hills, when we sang and wallowed all night and day in caves that smelt like Sunday afternoons in damp front farmhouse parlours, and we chased, with the jawbones of deacons, the English and the bears, before the motor car, before the wheel, before the duchess-faced horse, when we rode the daft and happy hills bareback, it snowed and it snowed.

> *A Child's Christmas in Wales* (1954) p. 11

13 Do not go gentle into that good night,
Old age should burn and rave at close of day;
Rage, rage against the dying of the light.

> *Collected poems* (1952) 'Do Not Go Gentle into that Good Night'

14 After the first death, there is no other.

> *Deaths and Entrances* (1946) 'A Refusal to Mourn the Death, by Fire, of a Child in London'

15 It was my thirtieth year to heaven
Woke to my hearing from harbour and neighbour wood
And the mussel pooled and the heron
Priested shore.
The morning beckon.

> *Deaths and Entrances* (1946) 'Poem in October'

16 Pale rain over the dwindling harbour
And over the sea wet church the size of a snail
With its horns through mist and the castle
Brown as owls
But all the gardens
Of spring and summer were blooming in the tall vales
Beyond the border and under the lark full cloud.
There could I marvel
My birthday
Away but the weather turned around.

> *Deaths and Entrances* (1946) 'Poem in October'

17 Now as I was young and easy under the apple boughs
About the lilting house and happy as the grass was green.

> *Deaths and Entrances* (1946) 'Fern Hill'

18 Oh as I was young and easy in the mercy of his means,
Time held me green and dying
Though I sang in my chains like the sea.

> *Deaths and Entrances* (1946) 'Fern Hill'

19 The land of my fathers [Wales]. My fathers can have it.

> In *Adam* Dec. 1953

20 The force that through the green fuse drives the flower
Drives my green age; that blasts the roots of trees
Is my destroyer.
And I am dumb to tell the crooked rose
My youth is bent by the same wintry fever.

> *18 Poems* (1934) 'The Force that through the Green Fuse drives the Flower'

21 Light breaks where no sun shines;
Where no sea runs, the waters of the heart
Push in their tides.

> *18 Poems* (1934) 'Light Breaks Where No Sun Shines'

22 Dylan talked copiously, then stopped. 'Somebody's boring me,' he said, 'I think it's me.'

> Rayner Heppenstall *Four Absentees* (1960) ch. 16

1 Dylan himself once defined an alcoholic as a man you don't like who drinks as much as you do.

    Constantine Fitzgibbon *Life of Dylan Thomas* (1965) ch. 6

2 Portrait of the artist as a young dog.

    Title of book (1940); cf. James Joyce's *Portrait of the Artist as a Young Man* (1916)

3 Too many of the artists of Wales spend too much time talking about the position of the artists of Wales. There is only one position for an artist anywhere: and that is, upright.

    Quite Early One Morning (1954) pt. 2 'Wales and the Artist'

4 The hand that signed the paper felled a city;
Five sovereign fingers taxed the breath,
Doubled the globe of dead and halved a country;
These five kings did a king to death.

    25 Poems (1936) 'The Hand that Signed the Paper Felled a City'

5 The hand that signed the treaty bred a fever,
And famine grew, and locusts came;
Great is the hand that holds dominion over
Man by a scribbled name.

    25 Poems (1936) 'The Hand That Signed the Paper Felled a City'

6 Though they go mad they shall be sane,
Though they sink through the sea they shall rise again;
Though lovers be lost love shall not;
And death shall have no dominion.

    25 Poems (1936) 'And Death Shall Have No Dominion'. Cf. Romans 6:9

7 To begin at the beginning: It is spring, moonless night in the small town, starless and bible-black, the cobblestreets silent and the hunched courters'-and-rabbits' wood limping invisible down to the sloeblack, slow, black, crowblack, fishingboat-bobbing sea.

    Under Milk Wood (1954) p. 1

8 MR PRITCHARD: I must dust the blinds and then I must raise them.
MRS OGMORE-PRITCHARD: And before you let the sun in, mind it wipes its shoes.

    Under Milk Wood (1954) p. 16

9 Alone until she dies, Bessie Bighead, hired help, born in the workhouse, smelling of the cowshed, snores bass and gruff on a couch of straw in a loft in Salt Lake Farm and picks a posy of daisies in Sunday Meadow to put on the grave of Gomer Owen who kissed her once by the pig-sty when she wasn't looking and never kissed her again although she was looking all the time.

    Under Milk Wood (1954) p. 19

10 Me, Polly Garter, under the washing line, giving the breast in the garden to my bonny new baby. Nothing grows in our garden, only washing. And babies. And where's their fathers live, my love? Over the hills and far away. You're looking up at me now. I know what you're thinking, you poor little milky creature. You're thinking, you're no better than you should be, Polly, and that's good enough for me. Oh, isn't life a terrible thing, thank God?

    Under Milk Wood (1954) p. 30

11 MAE ROSE COTTAGE: I'm fast. I'm a bad lot. God will strike me dead. I'm seventeen. I'll go to hell.
SECOND VOICE: She tells the goats.

MAE ROSE COTTAGE: You just wait. I'll sin till I blow up!
SECOND VOICE: She lies deep, waiting for the worst to happen; the goats champ and sneer.

    Under Milk Wood (1954) p. 78

Edward Thomas 1878–1917

12 Out in the dark over the snow
The fallow fawns invisible go
With the fallow doe;
And the winds blow
Fast as the stars are slow.

    Last Poems (1918) 'Out in the Dark'

13 If I should ever by chance grow rich
I'll buy Codham, Cockridden, and Childerditch,
Roses, Pyrgo, and Lapwater,
And let them all to my elder daughter.

    Poems (1917) 'If I Should Ever By Chance'

14 The past is the only dead thing that smells sweet.

    Poems (1917) 'Early One Morning'

15 Yes; I remember Adlestrop—
The name, because one afternoon
Of heat the express-train drew up there
Unwontedly. It was late June.

    Poems (1917) 'Adlestrop'

16 As well as any bloom upon a flower
I like the dust on the nettles, never lost
Except to prove the sweetness of a shower.

    Poems (1917) 'Tall Nettles'

17 I have come to the borders of sleep,
The unfathomable deep
Forest where all must lose
Their way, however straight
Or winding, soon or late;
They can not choose.

    Poems (1917) 'Lights Out'

Gwyn Thomas 1913–

18 There are still parts of Wales where the only concession to gaiety is a striped shroud.

    Punch 18 June 1958

Francis Thompson 1859–1907

19 Wake! for the Ruddy Ball has taken flight
That scatters the slow Wicket of the Night;
And the swift Batsman of the Dawn has driven
Against the Star-spiked Rails a fiery smite.

    'Wake! for the Ruddy Ball has Taken Flight' (parody of Edward Fitzgerald) in J. C. Squire *Apes and Parrots* (1929) p. 173

20 The fairest things have fleetest end,
Their scent survives their close:
But the rose's scent is bitterness
To him that loved the rose!

    Poems (1913) vol. 1 'Daisy'

21 She went her unremembering way,
She went and left in me
The pang of all the partings gone,
And partings yet to be.

She left me marvelling why my soul
Was sad that she was glad;
At all the sadness in the sweet,
The sweetness in the sad.
  Poems (1913) vol. 1 'Daisy'

1 Nothing begins, and nothing ends,
That is not paid with moan;
For we are born in other's pain,
And perish in our own.
  Poems (1913) vol. 1 'Daisy'

2 Summer set lip to earth's bosom bare,
And left the flushed print in a poppy there.
  Poems (1913) vol. 1 'The Poppy'

3 The sleep-flower sways in the wheat its head,
Heavy with dreams, as that with bread:
The goodly grain and the sun-flushed sleeper
The reaper reaps, and Time the reaper.

I hang 'mid men my needless head,
And my fruit is dreams, as theirs is bread:
The goodly men and the sun-hazed sleeper
Time shall reap, but after the reaper
The world shall glean of me, me the sleeper.
  Poems (1913) vol. 1 'The Poppy'

4 Look for me in the nurseries of heaven.
  Poems (1913) vol. 1 'To My Godchild Francis M.W.M.'

5 I fled Him, down the nights and down the days;
I fled Him, down the arches of the years;
I fled Him, down the labyrinthine ways
Of my own mind; and in the mist of tears
I hid from Him, and under running laughter.
  Poems (1913) vol. 1 'Hound of Heaven' pt. 1

6 But with unhurrying chase,
And unperturbèd pace,
Deliberate speed, majestic instancy,
They beat—and a Voice beat
More instant than the Feet—
All things betray thee, who betrayest Me.
  Poems (1913) vol. 1 'Hound of Heaven' pt. 1

7 For, though I knew His love Who followèd,
Yet was I sore adread
Lest, having Him, I must have naught beside.
  Poems (1913) vol. 1 'Hound of Heaven' pt. 2

8 Fear wist not to evade, as Love wist to pursue.
  Poems (1913) vol. 1 'Hound of Heaven' pt. 2

9 I said to Dawn: Be sudden—to Eve:
Be soon.
  Poems (1913) vol. 1 'Hound of Heaven' pt. 2

10 To all swift things for swiftness did I sue;
Clung to the whistling mane of every wind.
  Poems (1913) vol. 1 'Hound of Heaven' pt. 2

11 Still with unhurrying chase,
And unperturbèd pace,
Deliberate speed, majestic instancy,
Came on the following Feet,
And a Voice above their beat—
'Naught shelters thee, who wilt not shelter Me.'
  Poems (1913) vol. 1 'Hound of Heaven' pt. 2

12 I was heavy with the even,
When she lit her glimmering tapers
Round the day's dead sanctities.
  Poems (1913) vol. 1 'Hound of Heaven' pt. 3

13 My harness piece by piece Thou hast hewn from me,
And smitten me to my knee.
  Poems (1913) vol. 1 'Hound of Heaven' pt. 4

14 Yea, faileth now even dream
The dreamer, and the lute the lutanist;
Even the linked fantasies, in whose blossomy twist
I swung the earth a trinket at my wrist.
  Poems (1913) vol. 1 'Hound of Heaven' pt. 4

15 Ah! must—
Designer infinite!—
Ah! must Thou char the wood ere Thou canst limm
  with it?
  Poems (1913) vol. 1 'Hound of Heaven' pt. 4

16 Such is: what is to be?
The pulp so bitter, how shall taste the rind?
  Poems (1913) vol. 1 'Hound of Heaven' pt. 4

17 Yet ever and anon a trumpet sounds
From the hid battlements of Eternity;
Those shaken mists a space unsettle, then
Round the half-glimpsèd turrets slowly wash again.
  Poems (1913) vol. 1 'Hound of Heaven' pt. 4

18 Now of that long pursuit
Comes on at hand the bruit;
That Voice is round me like a bursting sea:
'And is thy earth so marred,
Shattered in shard on shard?
Lo, all things fly thee, for thou fliest Me!'
  Poems (1913) vol. 1 'Hound of Heaven' pt. 5

19 All which I took from thee I did but take,
Not for thy harms,
But just that thou might'st seek it in My arms.
  Poems (1913) vol. 1 'Hound of Heaven' pt. 5

20 Halts by me that footfall:
Is my gloom, after all,
Shade of His hand, outstretched caressingly?
'Ah, fondest, blindest, weakest,
I am He whom thou seekest!
Thou dravest love from thee, who dravest Me.'
  Poems (1913) vol. 1 'Hound of Heaven' pt. 5

21 And thou—what needest with thy tribe's black tents
Who hast the red pavilion of my heart?
  Poems (1913) vol. 1 'Arab Love-Song'

22 It is little I repair to the matches of the Southron folk,
Though my own red roses there may blow;
It is little I repair to the matches of the Southron folk,
Though the red roses crest the caps I know.
For the field is full of shades as I near the shadowy
  coast,
And a ghostly batsman plays to the bowling of a ghost,
And I look through my tears on a soundless-clapping
  host
As the run-stealers flicker to and fro,
To and fro:—
O my Hornby and my Barlow long ago!
  Poems (1913) vol. 1 'At Lord's'

23 There is no expeditious road
To pack and label men for God,

And save them by the barrel-load.
Some may perchance, with strange surprise,
Have blundered into Paradise.
> *Poems* (1913) vol. 1 'Epilogue to "A Judgement in Heaven"'

1 Go, songs, for ended is our brief, sweet play;
Go, children of swift joy and tardy sorrow:
And some are sung, and that was yesterday,
And some unsung, and that may be to-morrow.
> *Poems* (1913) vol. 1 'Envoy'

2 Ah, for a heart less native to high Heaven,
A hooded eye, for jesses and restraint,
Or for a will accipitrine to pursue!
> *Poems* (1913) vol. 2 'Dread of Height'

3 Spring is come home with her world-wandering feet,
And all things are made young with young desires.
> *Poems* (1913) vol. 2 'From the Night of Forebeing'

4 Let even the slug-abed snail upon the thorn
Put forth a conscious horn!
> *Poems* (1913) vol. 2 'From the Night of Forebeing'

5 And, while she feels the heavens lie bare,
She only talks about her hair.
> *Poems* (1913) vol. 2 'The Way of a Maid'

6 Pontifical Death, that doth the crevasse bridge
To the steep and trifid God.
> *Poems* (1913) vol. 2 'An Anthem of Earth'

7 And all man's Babylons strive but to impart
The grandeurs of his Babylonian heart.
> *Poems* (1913) vol. 2 'The Heart' no. 2

8 What heart could have thought you?—
Past our devisal
(O filigree petal!)
Fashioned so purely,
Fragilely, surely,
From what Paradisal
Imagineless metal,
Too costly for cost?
> *Poems* (1913) vol. 2 'To a Snowflake'

9 Insculped and embossed,
With His hammer of wind,
And His graver of frost.
> *Poems* (1913) vol. 2 'To a Snowflake'

10 O world invisible, we view thee,
O world intangible, we touch thee,
O world unknowable, we know thee,
Inapprehensible, we clutch thee!
> *Poems* (1913) vol. 2 'The Kingdom of God'

11 The angels keep their ancient places;—
Turn but a stone, and start a wing!
'Tis ye, 'tis your estrangèd faces,
That miss the many-splendoured thing.

But (when so sad thou canst not sadder)
Cry;—and upon thy so sore loss
Shall shine the traffic of Jacob's ladder
Pitched betwixt Heaven and Charing Cross.

Yea, in the night, my Soul, my daughter,
Cry,—clinging Heaven by the hems;
And lo, Christ walking on the water
Not of Gennesareth, but Thames!
> *Poems* (1913) vol. 2 'The Kingdom of God'

Hunter S. Thompson 1939–

12 Fear and loathing in Las Vegas.
> Title of two articles in *Rolling Stone* 11 and 25 Nov. 1971
> (under the pseudonym 'Raoul Duke')

Lord Thomson (Roy Herbert Thomson, Baron Thomson of Fleet) 1894–1976

13 It is just like having a licence to print your own money.
> On the profitability of commercial television in Britain, in
> R. Braddon *Roy Thomson* (1965) ch. 32

Jeremy Thorpe 1929–

14 Greater love hath no man than this, that he lay down
his friends for his life.
> Comment on Harold Macmillan sacking many of his Cabinet,
> 13 July 1962 , in D. E. Butler and Anthony King *General
> Election of 1964* (1965) ch. 1

James Thurber 1894–1961

15 I suppose that the high-water mark of my youth in
Columbus, Ohio, was the night the bed fell on my
father.
> *My Life and Hard Times* (1933) ch. 1

16 Her own mother lived the latter years of her life in the
horrible suspicion that electricity was dripping invisibly
all over the house.
> *My Life and Hard Times* (1933) ch. 2

17 All right, have it your own way—you heard a seal
bark!
> Cartoon caption in *New Yorker* 30 Jan. 1932

18 That's my first wife up there and this is the *present* Mrs
Harris.
> Cartoon caption in *New Yorker* 16 Mar. 1933

19 The war between men and women.
> Title of series of cartoons in *New Yorker* 20 Jan.–28 Apr.
> 1934

20 It's a naïve domestic Burgundy without any breeding,
but I think you'll be amused by its presumption.
> Cartoon caption in *New Yorker* 27 Mar. 1937

21 Well, if I called the wrong number, why did you answer
the phone?
> Cartoon caption in *New Yorker* 5 June 1937

22 There is no safety in numbers, or in anything else.
> *New Yorker* 4 Feb. 1939 'The Fairly Intelligent Fly'

23 Early to rise and early to bed makes a male healthy and
wealthy and dead.
> *New Yorker* 18 Feb. 1939 'The Shrike and the Chipmunks'

24 It's our *own* story *exactly*! He bold as a hawk, she soft
as the dawn.
> Cartoon caption in *New Yorker* 25 Feb. 1939

25 Then, with that faint fleeting smile playing about his
lips, he faced the firing squad; erect and motionless,
proud and disdainful, Walter Mitty, the undefeated,
inscrutable to the last.
> *New Yorker* 18 Mar. 1939 'The Secret Life of Walter Mitty'

1 You might as well fall flat on your face as lean over too far backward.
  New Yorker 29 Apr. 1939 'The Bear Who Let It Alone'

2 You can fool too many of the people too much of the time.
  New Yorker 29 Apr. 1939 'The Owl who was God'

3 'Humour,' he said, 'is emotional chaos remembered in tranquillity.'
  In *New York Post* 29 Feb. 1960. Cf. *Oxford Dictionary of Quotations* (1979) 583:10

Paul Tillich 1886–1965

4 Neurosis is the way of avoiding non-being by avoiding being.
  The Courage To Be (1952) pt. 2, ch. 3

5 He who knows about depth knows about God.
  The Shaking of the Foundations (1948) ch. 7

Dion Titheradge

6 And her mother came too!
  Title of song (1921; music by Ivor Novello)

Alvin Toffler 1928–

7 Future shock.
  Title of book (1970)

J. R. R. Tolkien 1892–1973

8 In a hole in the ground there lived a hobbit. Not a nasty, dirty, wet hole, filled with the ends of worms and an oozy smell, nor yet a dry, bare, sandy hole with nothing in it to sit down on or to eat: it was a hobbit-hole, and that means comfort.
  The Hobbit (1937) ch. 1

9 One Ring to rule them all, One Ring to find them
  One Ring to bring them all and in the darkness bind them.
  Lord of the Rings, pt. 1 *The Fellowship of the Ring* (1954) epigraph

Nicholas Tomalin

10 The only qualities for real success in journalism are ratlike cunning, a plausible manner and a little literary ability. . . . The capacity to steal other people's ideas and phrases—that one about ratlike cunning was invented by my colleague Murray Sayle—is also invaluable.
  Sunday Times Magazine 26 Oct. 1969

Barry Took and Marty Feldman

11 Hello, I'm Julian and this is my friend, Sandy.
  Catch-phrase in *Round the Horne* (BBC radio series, 1965–8)

Sue Townsend

12 The secret diary of Adrian Mole aged 13¾.
  Title of book (1982)

Pete Townshend 1945–

13 Hope I die before I get old.
  My Generation (1965 song)

Polly Toynbee 1946–

14 Feminism is the most revolutionary idea there has ever been. Equality for women demands a change in the human psyche more profound than anything Marx dreamed of. It means valuing parenthood as much as we value banking.
  Guardian 19 Jan. 1987

Sir Herbert Beerbohm Tree 1852–1917

15 To a man who was staggering in the street under the weight of a grandfather clock. 'My poor fellow, why not carry a watch?'
  Hesketh Pearson *Beerbohm Tree* (1956) ch. 12

16 His own note books inform us that a gramophone company asked him for a testimonial, and he replied that he never gave testimonials to objects of merchandise. The company begged him to favour their special case, since his own voice had been reproduced by this means. So he wrote the following: 'Sirs, I have tested your machine. It adds a new terror to life and makes death a long-felt want.' He was asked to amend this, as the public might misconstrue it; but he answered that it was not open to misconstruction. 'The immortalism must stand,' said he; but it was not used as an advertisement by the company.
  Hesketh Pearson *Beerbohm Tree* (1956) ch. 19

17 He [Israel Zangwill] is an old bore. Even the grave yawns for him.
  In Max Beerbohm *Herbert Beerbohm Tree* (1920) appendix 4

18 He [Beerbohm Tree] approved cheerfully enough of everything until he came to the collection of damsels that had been dragged into the theatre as ladies in waiting to the queen. He looked at them in pained and prolonged dissatisfaction and then said what we have all wanted to say of the extra-women in nearly every throne-room and ball-room and school-room scene since the theatre began. 'Ladies,' said Tree, peering at them plaintively through his monocle, 'just a little more virginity, if you don't mind.'
  Alexander Woollcott *Shouts and Murmurs* (1923) 'Capsule Criticism'

Herbert Trench 1865–1923

19 Come, let us make love deathless, thou and I.
  Deirdre Lived and Other Poems (1901) 'Come, let us make love deathless'

G. M. Trevelyan 1876–1962

20 Disinterested intellectual curiosity is the life-blood of real civilization.
  English Social History (1942) introduction

21 It [education] has produced a vast population able to read but unable to distinguish what is worth reading, an easy prey to sensations and cheap appeals.
  English Social History (1942) ch. 18

Lionel Trilling 1905–1975

1 Immature artists imitate. Mature artists steal.
   In *Esquire* Sept. 1962. Cf. Igor Stravinsky 210:16

Tommy Trinder 1909–1989

2 Overpaid, overfed, oversexed, and over here.
   Describing American troops in Britain during World War II,
   in *Sunday Times* 4 Jan. 1976

Leon Trotsky (*Lev Davidovich Bronstein*) 1879–1940

3 Old age is the most unexpected of all things that
   happen to a man.
   Diary in Exile (1959) 8 May 1935

4 Цивилизация сделала крестьянина своим вьючным
   ослом. Буржуазия в конце концов изменила лишь
   форму вьюка.

   Civilization has made the peasantry its pack animal.
   The bourgeoisie in the long run only changed the form
   of the pack.
   History of the Russian Revolution (1933) vol. 3, ch. 1

5 Вы — жалкие единицы, вы — банкроты, ваша роль
   сыграна, отправляйтесь туда, где вам отныне
   надлежит быть: в сорную корзину истории!

   You [the Mensheviks] are pitiful isolated individuals;
   you are bankrupts; your role is played out. Go where
   you belong from now on—into the dustbin of history!
   History of the Russian Revolution (1933) vol. 3, ch. 10

6 Where force is necessary, there it must be applied
   boldly, decisively and completely. But one must know
   the limitations of force; one must know when to blend
   force with a manœuvre, a blow with an agreement.
   What Next? (1932) ch. 14

Harry S Truman 1884–1972

7 I never give them [the public] hell. I just tell the truth,
   and they think it is hell.
   In *Look* 3 Apr. 1956

8 I used to have a saying that applies here, and I note
   that some people have picked it up: 'If you can't stand
   the heat, get out of the kitchen.'
   Mr Citizen (1960) ch. 15 (see also Harry Vaughan)

9 A politician is a man who understands government,
   and it takes a politician to run a government.
   A statesman is a politician who's been dead 10 or 15
   years.
   In *New York World Telegram and Sun* 12 Apr. 1958

10 It's a recession when your neighbour loses his job; it's
   a depression when you lose yours.
   In *Observer* 13 Apr. 1958

11 All the President is, is a glorified public relations man
   who spends his time flattering, kissing and kicking
   people to get them to do what they are supposed to do
   anyway.
   Letter to his sister, 14 Nov. 1947, in *Off the Record: the
   Private Papers of Harry S. Truman* (1980) p. 119

12 I didn't fire him [General MacArthur] because he was
   a dumb son of a bitch, although he was, but that's not
   against the law for generals. If it was, half to
   three-quarters of them would be in jail.
   In Merle Miller *Plain Speaking* (1974) ch. 24

13 When the decision is up before you—and on my desk I
   have a motto which says 'The buck stops here'—the
   decision has to be made.
   Speech at National War College, 19 Dec. 1952, in *Public
   Papers 1952–53* (1966) p. 1094

14 Wherever you have an efficient government you have
   a dictatorship.
   Lecture at Columbia University, 28 Apr. 1959, in *Truman
   Speaks* (1960) p. 51

Barbara W. Tuchman 1912–1989

15 Dead battles, like dead generals, hold the military
   mind in their dead grip and Germans, no less than
   other peoples, prepare for the last war.
   August 1914 (1962) ch. 2

16 No more distressing moment can ever face a British
   government than that which requires it to come to
   a hard, fast and specific decision.
   August 1914 (1962) ch. 9

17 For one August in its history Paris was French—and
   silent.
   August 1914 (1962) ch. 20

Sophie Tucker 1884–1966

18 From birth to 18 a girl needs good parents. From 18
   to 35, she needs good looks. From 35 to 55, good
   personality. From 55 on, she needs good cash. I'm
   saving my money.
   In Michael Freedland *Sophie* (1978) p. 214

Walter James Redfern Turner 1889–1946

19 When I was but thirteen or so
   I went into a golden land,
   Chimborazo, Cotopaxi
   Took me by the hand.
   The Hunter and Other Poems (1916) 'Romance'

Mark Twain (*Samuel Langhorne Clemens*) 1835–1910

20 'The Adventures of Tom Sawyer' . . . was made by Mr
   Mark Twain, and he told the truth, mainly. There was
   things which he stretched, but mainly he told the
   truth.
   The Adventures of Huckleberry Finn (1884) ch. 1

21 There was some books. . . . One was 'Pilgrim's
   Progress', about a man that left his family it didn't say
   why. I read considerable in it now and then. The
   statements was interesting, but tough. Another was
   'Friendship's Offering', full of beautiful stuff and poetry;
   but I didn't read the poetry.
   The Adventures of Huckleberry Finn (1884) ch. 17

1 All kings is mostly rapscallions.
The Adventures of Huckleberry Finn (1884) ch. 23

2 Hain't we got all the fools in town on our side? and ain't that a big enough majority in any town?
The Adventures of Huckleberry Finn (1884) ch. 26

3 If there was two birds setting on a fence, he would bet you which one would fly first.
The Celebrated Jumping Frog (1867) p. 10

4 I don't see no p'ints about that frog that's any better'n any other frog.
The Celebrated Jumping Frog (1867) p. 16

5 An experienced, industrious, ambitious, and quite often picturesque liar.
Century Magazine Dec. 1885 'Private History of a Campaign that Failed'

6 Be virtuous and you will be eccentric.
A Curious Dream (1872) 'Mental Photographs'

7 Soap and education are not as sudden as a massacre, but they are more deadly in the long run.
A Curious Dream (1872) 'Facts concerning the Recent Resignation'

8 Barring that natural expression of villainy which we all have, the man looked honest enough.
A Curious Dream (1872) 'A Mysterious Visit'

9 Truth is the most valuable thing we have. Let us economize it.
Following the Equator (1897) ch. 7

10 It is by the goodness of God that in our country we have those three unspeakably precious things: freedom of speech, freedom of conscience, and the prudence never to practise either of them.
Following the Equator (1897) ch. 20

11 'Classic.' A book which people praise and don't read.
Following the Equator (1897) ch. 25. Cf. Twain's speech to the 19th Century Club in New York, 20 Nov. 1900, in *Speeches* (1910) p. 194: 'It's a classic, just as Professor [Caleb] Winchester says, and it meets his definition of a classic—something that everybody wants to have read and nobody wants to read.'

12 Man is the Only Animal that Blushes. Or needs to.
Following the Equator (1897) ch. 27

13 Let us be thankful for the fools. But for them the rest of us could not succeed.
Following the Equator (1897) ch. 28

14 There are several good protections against temptations, but the surest is cowardice.
Following the Equator (1897) ch. 36

15 By trying we can easily learn to endure adversity. Another man's, I mean.
Following the Equator (1897) ch. 39

16 It takes your enemy and your friend, working together, to hurt you to the heart: the one to slander you and the other to get the news to you.
Following the Equator (1897) ch. 45

17 I must have a prodigious quantity of mind; it takes me as much as a week, sometimes, to make it up.
The Innocents Abroad (1869) ch. 7

18 They spell it Vinci and pronounce it Vinchy; foreigners always spell better than they pronounce.
The Innocents Abroad (1869) ch. 19

19 I do not want Michael Angelo for breakfast—for luncheon—for dinner—for tea—for supper—for between meals.
The Innocents Abroad (1869) ch. 27

20 Lump the whole thing! say that the Creator made Italy from designs by Michael Angelo!
The Innocents Abroad (1869) ch. 27

21 That joke was lost on the foreigner—guides cannot master the subtleties of the American joke.
The Innocents Abroad (1869) ch. 27

22 If you've got a nice *fresh* corpse, fetch him out!
The Innocents Abroad (1869) ch. 27

23 The report of my death was an exaggeration.
New York Journal 2 June 1897 (correcting newspaper reports which erroneously said that he was ill or dead, confusing him with his cousin, James Ross Clemens, who had been seriously ill in London)

24 He [Thomas Carlyle] said it in a moment of excitement, when chasing Americans out of his backyard with brickbats. They used to go there and worship. At bottom he was probably fond of them, but he was always able to conceal it.
New York World 10 Dec. 1899, 'Mark Twain's Christmas Book'

25 What a good thing Adam had. When he said a good thing he knew nobody had said it before.
Notebooks (1935) p. 67

26 Familiarity breeds contempt—and children.
Notebooks (1935) p. 237

27 Good breeding consists in concealing how much we think of ourselves and how little we think of the other person.
Notebooks (1935) p. 345

28 Adam was but human—this explains it all. He did not want the apple for the apple's sake; he wanted it only because it was forbidden.
Pudd'nhead Wilson (1894) ch. 2

29 Whoever has lived long enough to find out what life is, knows how deep a debt of gratitude we owe to Adam, the first great benefactor of our race. He brought death into the world.
Pudd'nhead Wilson (1894) ch. 3

30 Training is everything. The peach was once a bitter almond; cauliflower is nothing but cabbage with a college education.
Pudd'nhead Wilson (1894) ch. 5

31 One of the most striking differences between a cat and a lie is that a cat has only nine lives.
Pudd'nhead Wilson (1894) ch. 7

32 When angry, count four; when very angry, swear.
Pudd'nhead Wilson (1894) ch. 10

33 As to the Adjective: when in doubt, strike it out.
Pudd'nhead Wilson (1894) ch. 11

34 Put all your eggs in the one basket, and—WATCH THAT BASKET.
Pudd'nhead Wilson (1894) ch. 15

1 Few things are harder to put up with than the annoyance of a good example.
   Pudd'nhead Wilson (1894) ch. 19

2 It were not best that we should all think alike; it is difference of opinion that makes horse-races.
   Pudd'nhead Wilson (1894) ch. 19

3 There is a sumptuous variety about the New England weather that compels the stranger's admiration—and regret. The weather is always doing something there; always attending strictly to business; always getting up new designs and trying them on the people to see how they will go. But it gets through more business in spring than in any other season. In the spring I have counted one hundred and thirty-six different kinds of weather inside of four-and-twenty hours.
   Speech to New England Society in New York, 22 Dec. 1876, in *Speeches* (1910) p. 59

4 There's plenty of boys that will come hankering and grovelling around you when you've got an apple, and beg the core off of you; but when they've got one, and you beg for the core and remind them how you give them a core one time, they say thank you 'most to death, but there ain't-a-going to be no core.
   Tom Sawyer Abroad (1894) ch. 1

5 There ain't no way to find out why a snorer can't hear himself snore.
   Tom Sawyer Abroad (1894) ch. 10

6 The cross of the Legion of Honour has been conferred upon me. However, few escape that distinction.
   A Tramp Abroad (1880) ch. 8

7 All you need in this life is ignorance and confidence; then success is sure.
   Letter to Mrs Foote, 2 Dec. 1887, in B. DeCasseres *When Huck Finn Went Highbrow* (1934) p. 7

Kenneth Tynan 1927–1980

8 Forty years ago he [Noel Coward] was Slightly in *Peter Pan,* and you might say that he has been wholly in *Peter Pan* ever since.
   Curtains (1961) pt. 1, p. 59

9 What, when drunk, one sees in other women, one sees in Garbo sober.
   Curtains (1961) pt. 2, p. 347

10 A critic is a man who knows the way but can't drive the car.
   In *New York Times Magazine* 9 Jan. 1966, p. 27

11 A good drama critic is one who perceives what is happening in the theatre of his time. A great drama critic also perceives what is *not* happening.
   Tynan Right and Left (1967) foreword

Miguel de Unamuno 1864–1937

12 *La vida es duda,*
   y la fe sin la duda es sólo muerte.

   Life is doubt,
   And faith without doubt is nothing but death.
   Poésias (1907) 'Salmo II'

13 *Cúrate de la affeccion de preocuparte cómo aparezías a los demás. Cuídate sólo de cómo aparezías Dios, cuídate de la idea que de ti Dios tenga.*

   Cure yourself of the condition of bothering about how you look to other people. Concern yourself only with how you appear to God, with the idea that God has of you.
   Vida de Don Quixote y Sancho (Life of Don Quixote and Sancho, 1905) pt. 1

John Updike 1932–

14 One out of three hundred and twelve Americans is a bore, for instance, and a healthy male adult bore consumes each year one and a half times his own weight in other people's patience.
   Assorted Prose (1965) 'Confessions of a Wild Bore'

15 The difficulty with humorists is that they will mix what they believe with what they don't; whichever seems likelier to win an effect.
   Rabbit, Run (1960) p. 160

Sir Peter Ustinov 1921–

16 I was irrevocably betrothed to laughter, the sound of which has always seemed to me the most civilized music in the world.
   Dear Me (1977) ch. 3

17 Contrary to general belief, I do not believe that friends are necessarily the people you like best, they are merely the people who got there first.
   Dear Me (1977) ch. 5

18 Laughter would be bereaved if snobbery died.
   In *Observer* 13 Mar. 1955

19 If Botticelli were alive today he'd be working for *Vogue.*
   In *Observer* 21 Oct. 1962

20 As for being a General, well at the age of four with paper hats and wooden swords we're all Generals. Only some of us never grow out of it.
   Romanoff and Juliet (1956) act 1

21 A diplomat these days is nothing but a head-waiter who's allowed to sit down occasionally.
   Romanoff and Juliet (1956) act 1

Paul Valéry 1871–1945

22 *Un poème n'est jamais achevé—c'est toujours un accident qui le termine, c'est-à-dire qui le donne au public.*

   A poem is never finished; it's always an accident that puts a stop to it—i.e. gives it to the public.
   Littérature (1930) p. 46

23 *Il faut n'appeler Science: que l'ensemble des recettes qui réussissent toujours.—Tout le reste est littérature.*

   'Science' means simply the aggregate of all the recipes that are always successful. All the rest is literature.
   Moralités (1932) p. 41

24 *Dieu créa l'homme, et ne le trouvant pas assez seul, il lui donne une compagne pour lui faire mieux sentir sa solitude.*

God created man and, finding him not sufficiently alone, gave him a companion to make him feel his solitude more keenly.
Tel Quel 1 (1941) 'Moralités'

1 La politique est l'art d'empêcher les gens de se mêler de ce qui les regarde.

Politics is the art of preventing people from taking part in affairs which properly concern them.
Tel Quel 2 (1943) 'Rhumbs'

Paul Vance and Lee Pockriss

2 Itsy bitsy teenie weenie, yellow polkadot bikini.
Title of song (1960)

Vivien van Damm ?1889–1960

3 I did not coin the slogan 'We Never Closed' [for the Windmill Theatre in London]. It was merely a statement of fact.
Tonight and Every Night (1952) ch. 18

Laurens van der Post 1906–

4 Human beings are perhaps never more frightening than when they are convinced beyond doubt that they are right.
Lost World of the Kalahari (1958) ch. 3

Bartolomeo Vanzetti 1888–1927

5 If it had not been for these thing, I might have live out my life talking at street corners to scorning men. I might have die, unmarked, unknown, a failure. Now we are not a failure. This is our career and our triumph. Never in our full life could we hope to do such work for tolerance, for joostice, for man's onderstanding of man as now we do by accident.
     Our words—our lives—our pains—nothing! The taking of our lives—lives of a good shoemaker and a poor fish-peddler—all! That last moment belongs to us—that agony is our triumph.
Statement after being sentenced, 9 Apr. 1927, in M. D. Frankfurter and G. Jackson Letters of Sacco and Vanzetti (1928) preface

6 Sacco's name will live in the hearts of the people and in their gratitude when Katzmann's and yours bones will be dispersed by time, when your name, his name, your laws, institutions, and your false god are but a deem rememoring of a cursed past in which man was wolf to the man.
Note by Vanzetti of what he wanted to say at his trial, 9 Apr. 1927, in M. D. Frankfurter and G. Jackson Letters of Sacco and Vanzetti (1928) p. 380

Harry Vaughan

7 If you can't stand the heat, get out of the kitchen.
In Time 28 Apr. 1952 (often used by Harry S. Truman, q.v.)

Ralph Vaughan Williams 1872–1958

8 I don't know whether I like it [the 4th symphony], but it's what I meant.
In Christopher Headington Bodley Head History of Western Music (1974) p. 293

9 On arrival on a visit to the United States, Ralph Vaughan Williams was met by a crowd of reporters. One of them seized him by the arm and said, 'Tell me, Dr Vaughan Williams, what do you think about music?' The old man peered quizzically into his face and made the solemn pronouncement: 'It's a Rum Go!'
Leslie Ayr The Wit of Music (1966) p. 43

Thorstein Veblen 1857–1929

10 Conspicuous consumption of valuable goods is a means of reputability to the gentleman of leisure.
Theory of the Leisure Class (1899) ch. 4

11 So it is something of a homiletical commonplace to say that the outcome of any serious research can only be to make two questions grow where one question grew before.
University of California Chronicle (1908) vol. 10, no. 4, 'Evolution of the Scientific Point of View'

Gore Vidal 1925–

12 It is not enough to succeed. Others must fail.
In G. Irvine Antipanegyric for Tom Driberg 8 Dec. 1976, p. 2

13 It is the spirit of the age to believe that any fact, no matter how suspect, is superior to any imaginative exercise, no matter how true.
Encounter Dec. 1967, 'French Letters: Theories of the New Novel'

14 A triumph of the embalmer's art.
In Observer 26 Apr. 1981 (describing Ronald Reagan)

15 I'm all for bringing back the birch, but only between consenting adults.
In Sunday Times Magazine 16 Sept. 1973

16 Whenever a friend succeeds, a little something in me dies.
In Sunday Times Magazine 16 Sept. 1973

17 American writers want to be not good but great; and so are neither.
Two Sisters (1970) p. 65

King Vidor 1895–1982

18 Take it from me, marriage isn't a word ... it's a sentence!
The Crowd (1928 film)

José Antonio Viera Gallo 1943–

19 El socialismo puede llegar solo en bicicleta.

Socialism can only arrive by bicycle.
Said when Assistant Secretary of Justice in Chilean Government, in Ivan Illich Energy and Equity (1974) p. 11

John Wain 1925–

1 Poetry is to prose as dancing is to walking.
   BBC radio broadcast, 13 Jan. 1976

Jerry Wald 1911–1962 and Richard Macaulay

2 Naughty but nice.
   Title of film (1939)

Prince of Wales

See PRINCE CHARLES

Arthur Waley 1889–1966

3 What is hard today is to censor one's own thoughts—
   To sit by and see the blind man
   On the sightless horse, riding into the bottomless
   abyss.
   Censorship

Edgar Wallace 1875–1932

4 What is a highbrow? He is a man who has found
   something more interesting than women.
   New York Times 24 Jan. 1932, sec. 8, p. 6

5 Dreamin' of thee! Dreamin' of thee!
   Writ in Barracks (1900) 'T. A. in Love' (popularised in 1930
   broadcast by Cyril Fletcher)

George Wallace 1919–

6 Segregation now, segregation tomorrow and
   segregation forever!
   Inaugural speech as Governor of Alabama, Jan. 1963, in
   Birmingham World 19 Jan. 1963

Henry Wallace 1888–1965

7 The century on which we are entering—the century
   which will come out of this war—can be and must be
   the century of the common man.
   Speech, 8 May 1942, in *Vital Speeches* (1942) vol. 8, p. 483

Graham Wallas 1858–1932

8 The little girl had the making of a poet in her who,
   being told to be sure of her meaning before she spoke,
   said, 'How can I know what I think till I see what
   I say?'
   Art of Thought (1926) ch. 4. Cf. E. M. Forster 83:9

Sir Hugh Walpole 1884–1941

9 'Tisn't life that matters! 'Tis the courage you bring to
   it.
   Fortitude (1913) bk.1, ch. 1

Andy Warhol 1927–1987

10 It's the place where my prediction from the sixties
   finally came true: 'In the future everyone will be
   famous for fifteen minutes.' I'm bored with that line.
   I never use it anymore. My new line is, 'In fifteen
   minutes everybody will be famous.'
   Andy Warhol's Exposures (1979) 'Studio 54'

11 Being good in business is the most fascinating kind of
   art.
   In *Observer* 1 Mar. 1987

12 An artist is someone who produces things that people
   don't need to have but that he—for some
   reason—thinks it would be a good idea to give them.
   Philosophy of Andy Warhol (From A to B and Back Again)
   (1975) ch. 10

Jack Warner (Horace Waters) 1895–1981

13 Mind my bike!
   Catch-phrase used in the BBC radio series *Garrison Theatre*,
   1939 onwards, in D. Parker *Radio: the Great Years* (1977)
   p. 94

Ned Washington

14 Hi diddle dee dee (an actor's life for me).
   Title of song (1940; music by Leigh Harline)

15 When you wish upon a star.
   Title of song (1940; music by Leigh Harline)

Sir William Watson 1858–1935

16 April, April,
   Laugh thy girlish laughter;
   Then, the moment after,
   Weep thy girlish tears!
   Poems (1905) vol. 1, 'Song'

17 These and a thousand tricks and ways and traits
   I noted as of Demos at their root,
   And foreign to the staid, conservative
   Came-over-with-the Conqueror type of mind.
   Poems (1905) vol. 1, 'A Study in Contrasts'

Evelyn Waugh 1903–1966

18 Brideshead revisited.
   Title of novel (1945)

19 A shriller note could now be heard rising from Sir
   Alastair's rooms; any who have heard that sound will
   shrink at the recollection of it; it is the sound of English
   county families baying for broken glass.
   Decline and Fall (1928) 'Prelude'. Cf. Hilaire Belloc 25:9

20 I expect you'll be becoming a schoolmaster, sir. That's
   what most of the gentlemen does, sir, that gets sent
   down for indecent behaviour.
   Decline and Fall (1928) 'Prelude'

21 'We class schools, you see, into four grades: Leading
   School, First-rate School, Good School, and School.
   Frankly,' said Mr Levy, 'School is pretty bad.'
   Decline and Fall (1928) pt. 1, ch. 1

22 For generations the British bourgeoisie have spoken of
   themselves as gentlemen, and by that they have meant,
   among other things, a self-respecting scorn of irregular

perquisites. It is the quality that distinguishes the gentleman from both the artist and the aristocrat.

Decline and Fall (1928) pt. 1, ch. 6

1 'I often think,' he continued, 'that we can trace almost all the disasters of English history to the influence of Wales!'

Decline and Fall (1928) pt. 1, ch. 8

2 I haven't been to sleep for over a year. That's why I go to bed early. One needs more rest if one doesn't sleep.

Decline and Fall (1928) pt. 2, ch. 3

3 Apparently he has been reading a series of articles by a popular bishop and has discovered that there is a species of person called a 'Modern Churchman' who draws the full salary of a beneficed clergyman and need not commit himself to any religious belief.

Decline and Fall (1928) pt. 2, ch. 4

4 I came to the conclusion many years ago that almost all crime is due to the repressed desire for aesthetic expression.

Decline and Fall (1928) pt. 3, ch. 1

5 Any one who has been to an English public school will always feel comparatively at home in prison. It is the people brought up in the gay intimacy of the slums, Paul learned, who find prison so soul-destroying.

Decline and Fall (1928) pt. 3, ch. 4

6 Punctuality is the virtue of the bored.

Michael Davie (ed.) *Diaries of Evelyn Waugh* (1976) 'Irregular Notes 1960–65', 26 Mar. 1962

7 Randolph Churchill went into hospital . . . to have a lung removed. It was announced that the trouble was not 'malignant'. Seeing Ed Stanley in White's, on my way to Rome, I remarked that it was a typical triumph of modern science to find the only part of Randolph that was not malignant and remove it.

Michael Davie (ed.) *Diaries of Evelyn Waugh* (1976) 'Irregular Notes 1960–65', Mar. 1964

8 You never find an Englishman among the under-dogs—except in England, of course.

The Loved One (1948) ch. 1

9 In the dying world I come from quotation is a national vice. No one would think of making an after-dinner speech without the help of poetry. It used to be the classics, now it's lyric verse.

The Loved One (1948) ch. 9

10 Manners are especially the need of the plain. The pretty can get away with anything.

In *Observer* 15 Apr. 1962

11 'The Beast stands for strong mutually antagonistic governments everywhere,' he [Lord Copper] said. 'Self-sufficiency at home, self-assertion abroad.'

Scoop (1938) bk. 1, ch. 1

12 Mr Salter's side of the conversation was limited to expressions of assent. When Lord Copper was right, he said, 'Definitely, Lord Copper'; when he was wrong, 'Up to a point'.

Scoop (1938) bk. 1, ch. 1

13 'He [Boot]'s supposed to have a particularly high-class style: 'Feather-footed through the plashy fen passes the

questing vole' . . . would that be it?' 'Yes,' said the Managing Editor. 'That must be good style.'

Scoop (1938) bk. 1, ch. 1

14 News is what a chap who doesn't care much about anything wants to read. And it's only news until he's read it. After that it's dead.

Scoop (1938) bk. 1, ch. 5

15 'I will not stand for being called a woman in my own house,' she [Mrs Earl Russell Jackson] said.

Scoop (1938) bk. 2, ch. 1

16 Other nations use 'force'; we Britons alone use 'Might'.

Scoop (1938) bk. 2, ch. 5

17 All this fuss about sleeping together. For physical pleasure I'd sooner go to my dentist any day.

Vile Bodies (1930) ch. 6

18 Lady Peabury was in the morning room reading a novel; early training gave a guilty spice to this recreation, for she had been brought up to believe that to read a novel before luncheon was one of the gravest sins it was possible for a gentlewoman to commit.

Work Suspended (1942) 'An Englishman's Home'

19 The trouble with the Conservative Party is that it has not turned the clock back a single second.

Attributed

Frederick Weatherly 1848–1929

20 Where are the boys of the old Brigade,
Who fought with us side by side?

The Old Brigade

21 Roses are flowering in Picardy,
But there's never a rose like you.

Roses of Picardy (1916 song)

Beatrice Webb 1858–1943

22 If I ever felt inclined to be timid as I was going into a room full of people, I would say to myself, 'You're the cleverest member of one of the cleverest families in the cleverest class of the cleverest nation in the world, why should you be frightened?'

In Bertrand Russell *Autobiography* (1967) vol. 1, ch. 4

See also SIDNEY WEBB AND BEATRICE WEBB

Geoffrey Webb and *Edward J. Mason*

23 An everyday story of country folk.

Introduction to *The Archers* (BBC radio serial, 1950 onwards)

Jim Webb 1946–

24 Up, up and away.

Title of song (1967)

Sidney Webb (*Baron Passfield*) 1859–1947

25 First let me insist on what our opponents habitually ignore, and indeed, what they seem intellectually incapable of understanding, namely the inevitable gradualness of our scheme of change.

> Presidential address at Labour Party Conference in London, 26 June 1923, in *Report* (1923) p. 178

Sidney Webb (Baron Passfield) 1859–1947 and Beatrice Webb 1858–1943

1 Sidney would remark, 'I know just what Beatrice is saying at this moment. She is saying, "as Sidney always says, marriage is the waste-paper basket of the emotions."'

> Bertrand Russell *Autobiography* (1967) vol. 1, ch. 4

Simone Weil 1909–1943

2 What a country calls its vital economic interests are not the things which enable its citizens to live, but the things which enable it to make war. Gasoline is much more likely than wheat to be a cause of international conflict.

> In W. H. Auden *A Certain World* (1971) p. 384

3 *La culture est un instrument manié par des professeurs pour fabriquer des professeurs qui à leur tour fabriqueront des professeurs.*

Culture is an instrument wielded by professors, to manufacture professors, who when their turn comes will manufacture professors.

> *L'Enracinement* (The Need for Roots, 1949) 'Déracinement ouvrier'

4 *Tous les Péchés sont des tentatives pour combler des vides.*

All sins are attempts to fill voids.

> *La Pesanteur et la grâce* (Gravity and Grace, 1948) p. 27

Johnny Weissmuller 1904–1984

5 I didn't have to act in 'Tarzan, the Ape Man'—just said, 'Me Tarzan, you Jane.'

> *Photoplay Magazine* June 1932 (the words 'Me Tarzan, you Jane' do not occur in the 1932 film)

Thomas Earle Welby 1881–1933

6 'Turbot, Sir,' said the waiter, placing before me two fishbones, two eyeballs, and a bit of black mackintosh.

> *The Dinner Knell* (1932) 'Birmingham or Crewe?'

Fay Weldon 1931–

7 Natalie had left the wives and joined the women.

> *Heart of the Country* (1987) p. 51

8 The life and loves of a she-devil.

> Title of novel (1984)

Colin Welland 1934–

9 The British are coming.

> Speech accepting an Oscar for his *Chariots of Fire* screenplay, 30 Mar. 1982, in *Sight & Sound* Summer 1982

Orson Welles 1915–1985

10 To his associate, Richard Wilson ... Orson [Welles] then declared, 'This [the RKO studio] is the biggest electric train set any boy ever had!'

> Peter Noble *The Fabulous Orson Welles* (1956) ch. 7

11 In Italy for thirty years under the Borgias they had warfare, terror, murder, bloodshed—they produced Michelangelo, Leonardo da Vinci and the Renaissance. In Switzerland they had brotherly love, five hundred years of democracy and peace and what did that produce ... ? The cuckoo clock.

> *The Third Man* (1949 film; words added by Welles to the script, in Graham Greene and Carol Reed *The Third Man* (1969) p. 114

H. G. Wells 1866–1946

12 If Max [Beaverbrook] gets to Heaven he won't last long. He will be chucked out for trying to pull off a merger between Heaven and Hell ... after having secured a controlling interest in key subsidiary companies in both places, of course.

> In A. J. P. Taylor *Beaverbrook* (1972) ch. 8

13 The thing his [Henry James's] novel is *about* is always there. It is like a church lit but without a congregation to distract you, with every light and line focussed on the high altar. And on the altar, very reverently placed, intensely there, is a dead kitten, an egg-shell, a bit of string.

> *Boon* (1915) ch. 4

14 It is leviathan retrieving pebbles. It is a magnificent but painful hippopotamus resolved at any cost, even at the cost of its dignity, upon picking up a pea which has got into a corner of its den. Most things, it insists, are beyond it, but it can, at any rate modestly, and with an artistic singleness of mind, pick up that pea.

> *Boon* (1915) ch. 4 (on Henry James)

15 He [James Holroyd] was a practical electrician but fond of whisky, a heavy, red-haired brute with irregular teeth. He doubted the existence of the Deity but accepted Carnot's cycle, and he had read Shakespeare and found him weak in chemistry.

> *Complete Short Stories* (1927) 'Lord of the Dynamos'

16 But Nunez advanced with the confident steps of a youth who enters upon life. All the old stories of the lost valley and the Country of the Blind had come back to his mind, and through his thoughts ran this old proverb, as if it were a refrain—In the Country of the Blind the One-Eyed Man is King.

> *The Country of the Blind* (1904; revised 1939) p. 52

17 'Sesquippledan,' he would say. 'Sesquippledan verboojuice.'

> *History of Mr Polly* (1909) ch. 1, pt. 5

18 'I'm a Norfan, both sides,' he would explain, with the air of one who had seen trouble.

> *Kipps* (1905) bk. 1, ch. 6, pt. 1

19 'I expect,' he said, 'I was thinking jest what a Rum Go everything is. I expect it was something like that.'

> *Kipps* (1905) bk. 3, ch. 3, pt. 8

1 The Social Contract is nothing more or less than a vast conspiracy of human beings to lie to and humbug themselves and one another for the general Good. Lies are the mortar that bind the savage individual man into the social masonry.

Love and Mr Lewisham (1900) ch. 23

2 Human history becomes more and more a race between education and catastrophe.

Outline of History (1920) vol. 2, ch. 41, pt. 4

3 The shape of things to come.

Title of book (1933)

4 The war that will end war.

Title of book (1914). Cf. David Lloyd-George 138:8

5 Moral indignation is jealousy with a halo.

The Wife of Sir Isaac Harman (1914) ch. 9, sect. 2

6 In England we have come to rely upon a comfortable time-lag of fifty years or a century intervening between the perception that something ought to be done and a serious attempt to do it.

The Work, Wealth and Happiness of Mankind (1931) ch. 2

Arnold Wesker 1932–

7 And then I saw the menu, stained with tea and beautifully written by a foreign hand, and on top it said—God I hated that old man—it said 'Chips with everything'. Chips with every damn thing. You breed babies and you eat chips with everything.

Chips with Everything (1962) act 1, sc. 2

Mae West 1892–1980

8 It's better to be looked over than overlooked.

Belle of the Nineties (1934 film)

9 A man in the house is worth two in the street.

Belle of the Nineties (1934 film)

10 You ought to get out of those wet clothes and into a dry Martini.

Every Day's a Holiday (1937 film). A similar line is spoken by Robert Benchley in the 1942 film *The Major and the Minor*, written by Charles Brackett and Billy Wilder. Cf. 7:12

11 I always say, keep a diary and some day it'll keep you.

Every Day's a Holiday (1937 film)

12 Beulah, peel me a grape.

I'm No Angel (1933 film)

13 I've been things and seen places.

I'm No Angel (1933 film)

14 When I'm good, I'm very, very good, but when I'm bad, I'm better.

I'm No Angel (1933 film)

15 It's not the men in my life that counts—it's the life in my men.

I'm No Angel (1933 film)

16 Give a man a free hand and he'll try to put it all over you.

Klondike Annie (1936 film)

17 Between two evils, I always pick the one I never tried before.

Klondike Annie (1936 film)

18 I've been in *Who's Who*, and I know what's what, but it'll be the first time I ever made the dictionary.

Letter to the RAF, early 1940s, on having an inflatable life jacket named after her, in Fergus Cashin *Mae West* (1981) ch. 9

19 'Goodness, what beautiful diamonds!'
'Goodness had nothing to do with it, dearie.'

Night After Night (1932 film)

20 Is that a gun in your pocket, or are you just glad to see me?

In Joseph Weintraub *Peel Me a Grape* (1975) p. 47

21 I used to be Snow White . . . but I drifted.

In Joseph Weintraub *Peel Me a Grape* (1975) p. 47

22 Why don't you come up sometime, and see me? I'm home every evening.

She Done Him Wrong (1933 film; often misquoted as 'Come up and see me sometime', which became Mae West's catch-phrase)

Dame Rebecca West (Cicily Isabel Fairfield) 1892–1983

23 Journalism—an ability to meet the challenge of filling the space.

New York Herald Tribune 22 Apr. 1956, sec. 6, p. 2

24 He [Michael Arlen] is every other inch a gentleman.

In Victoria Glendinning *Rebecca West* (1987) pt. 3, ch. 5

25 God forbid that any book should be banned. The practice is as indefensible as infanticide.

The Strange Necessity (1928) 'The Tosh Horse'

26 Just how difficult it is to write biography can be reckoned by anybody who sits down and considers just how many people know the truth about his or her love affairs.

Vogue 1 Nov. 1952

Edith Wharton 1862–1937

27 She sang, of course, 'M'ama!' and not 'he loves me', since an unalterable and unquestioned law of the musical world required that the German text of French operas sung by Swedish artists should be translated into Italian for the clearer understanding of English-speaking audiences.

Age of Innocence (1920) bk. 1, ch. 1

28 She keeps on being Queenly in her own room with the door shut.

The House of Mirth (1905) bk. 2, ch. 1

29 Another unsettling element in modern art is that common symptom of immaturity, the dread of doing what has been done before.

The Writing of Fiction (1925) ch. 1

30 Mrs Ballinger is one of the ladies who pursue Culture in bands, as though it were dangerous to meet it alone.

Xingu and Other Stories (1916) 'Xingu'

E. B. White 1899–1985

1 MOTHER: It's broccoli, dear.
CHILD: I say it's spinach, and I say the hell with it.
New Yorker 8 Dec. 1928 (cartoon caption)

2 Democracy is the recurrent suspicion that more than half of the people are right more than half of the time.
New Yorker 3 July 1944

3 Commuter—one who spends his life
In riding to and from his wife;
A man who shaves and takes a train,
And then rides back to shave again.
Poems and Sketches (1982) 'The Commuter'

T. H. White 1906–1964

4 The Victorians had not been anxious to go away for the weekend. The Edwardians, on the contrary, were nomadic.
Farewell Victoria (1933) pt. 4

5 The once and future king.
Title of novel (1958)

Alfred North Whitehead 1861–1947

6 Life is an offensive, directed against the repetitious mechanism of the Universe.
Adventures of Ideas (1933) pt. 1, ch. 5

7 It is more important that a proposition be interesting than that it be true. This statement is almost a tautology. For the energy of operation of a proposition in an occasion of experience is its interest, and is its importance. But of course a true proposition is more apt to be interesting than a false one.
Adventures of Ideas (1933) pt. 4, ch. 16

8 There are no whole truths; all truths are half-truths. It is trying to treat them as whole truths that plays the devil.
Dialogues (1954) prologue

9 Intelligence is quickness to apprehend as distinct from ability, which is capacity to act wisely on the thing apprehended.
Dialogues (1954) 15 Dec. 1939

10 What is morality in any given time or place? It is what the majority then and there happen to like, and immorality is what they dislike.
Dialogues (1954) 30 Aug. 1941

11 Art is the imposing of a pattern on experience, and our aesthetic enjoyment is recognition of the pattern.
Dialogues (1954) 10 June 1943

12 Civilization advances by extending the number of important operations which we can perform without thinking about them.
Introduction to Mathematics (1911) ch. 5

13. The safest general characterization of the European philosophical tradition is that it consists of a series of footnotes to Plato.
Process and Reality (1929) pt. 2, ch. 1

Bertrand Whitehead

14 Drinka Pinta Milka Day.
Slogan for the British Milk Marketing Board, 1958

Katharine Whitehorn 1926–

15 No nice men are good at getting taxis.
Observer 1977

16 Hats divide generally into three classes: offensive hats, defensive hats, and shrapnel.
Shouts and Murmurs (1963) 'Hats'

17 I wouldn't say when you've seen one Western you've . seen the lot; but when you've seen the lot you get the feeling you've seen one.
Sunday Best (1976) 'Decoding the West'

George Whiting

18 My blue heaven.
Title of song (1927; music by Walter Donaldson)

19 When you're all dressed up and have no place to go.
Title of song (1912; music by Newton Harding)

Gough Whitlam 1916–

20 Well may he say 'God Save the Queen'. But after this nothing will save the Governor-General. . . . Maintain your rage and your enthusiasm through the campaign for the election now to be held and until polling day.
Speech in Canberra, 11 Nov. 1975, in *The Times* 12 Nov. 1975

Charlotte Whitton 1896–1975

21 Whatever women do they must do twice as well as men to be thought half as good. Luckily, this is not difficult.
In *Canada Month* June 1963

William H. Whyte 1917–

22 This book is about the organization man. . . . I can think of no other way to describe the people I am talking about. They are not the workers, nor are they the white-collar people in the usual, clerk sense of the word. These people only work for the Organization. The ones I am talking about *belong* to it as well.
The Organization Man (1956) ch. 1

Anna Wickham (Edith Alice Mary Harper) 1884–1947

23 It is well within the order of things
That man should listen when his mate sings;
But the true male never yet walked
Who liked to listen when his mate talked.
The Contemplative Quarry (1915) 'The Affinity'

Richard Wilbur 1921–

24 We milk the cow of the world, and as we do
We whisper in her ear, 'You are not true.'
Ceremony and Other Poems (1950) 'Epistemology'

Billy Wilder (Samuel Wilder) 1906–

1 Hindsight is always twenty-twenty.
   In J. R. Columbo *Wit and Wisdom of the Moviemakers* (1979) ch. 7

Billy Wilder 1906–
and I. A. L. Diamond

2 GERRY: We can't get married at all. . . . I'm a man.
   OSGOOD: Well, nobody's perfect.
   Some Like It Hot (1959 film; closing words)

Thornton Wilder 1897–1975

3 Marriage is a bribe to make a housekeeper think she's a householder.
   Merchant of Yonkers (1939) act 1

4 The fights are the best part of married life. The rest is merely so-so.
   Merchant of Yonkers (1939) act 2

5 Literature is the orchestration of platitudes.
   In *Time* 12 Jan. 1953

Kaiser Wilhelm II 1859–1941

6 We have . . . fought for our place in the sun and have won it. It will be my business to see that we retain this place in the sun unchallenged, so that the rays of that sun may exert a fructifying influence upon our foreign trade and traffic.
   Speech in Hamburg, 18 June 1901, in *The Times* 20 June 1901

Geoffrey Willans 1911–1958 and Ronald Searle 1920–

7 The only good things about skool are the BOYS wizz who are noble brave fearless etc. although you hav various swots, bulies, cissies, milksops, greedy guts and oiks with whom i am forced to mingle hem-hem.
   Down With Skool! (1953) p. 7

8 This is wot it is like when we go back on the skool trane. There are lots of new bugs and all there maters blub they hav every reason if they knew what they were going to. For us old lags however it is just another stretch same as any other and no remision for good conduc. We kno what it will be like at the other end Headmaster beaming skool bus ratle off leaving trail of tuck boxes peason smugling in a box of flat 50 cigs fotherington-tomas left in the lugage rack and new bugs stand as if amazed.
   How To Be Topp (1954) ch. 1

9 There is no better xsample of a goody-goody than fotherington-tomas in the world in space. You kno he is the one who sa Hullo Clouds Hullo Sky and skip about like a girly.
   How To Be Topp (1954) ch. 4

10 Still xmas is a good time with all those presents and good food and i hope it will never die out or at any rate not until i am grown up and hav to pay for it all.
   How To Be Topp (1954) ch. 11

Harry Williams 1874–1924

11 I'm afraid to come home in the dark.
   Title of song (1907; music by Egbert van Alstyne)

Kenneth Williams 1926–1988

12 The nice thing about quotes is that they give us a nodding acquaintance with the originator which is often socially impressive.
   Acid Drops (1980) preface

Tennessee Williams (Thomas Lanier Williams) 1911–1983

13 We have to distrust each other. It's our only defence against betrayal.
   Camino Real (1953) block 10

14 We're all of us guinea pigs in the laboratory of God. Humanity is just a work in progress.
   Camino Real (1953) block 12

15 What is the victory of a cat on a hot tin roof?—I wish I knew. . . . Just staying on it, I guess, as long as she can.
   Cat on a Hot Tin Roof (1955) act 1

16 BRICK: Well, they say nature hates a vacuum, Big Daddy.
   BIG DADDY: That's what they say, but sometimes I think that a vacuum is a hell of a lot better than some of the stuff that nature replaces it with.
   Cat on a Hot Tin Roof (1955) act 2. Cf. *Oxford Dictionary of Quotations* (1979) 403:27

17 Mendacity is a system that we live in. Liquor is one way out an' death's the other.
   Cat on a Hot Tin Roof (1955) act 2

18 I didn't go to the moon, I went much further—for time is the longest distance between two places.
   The Glass Menagerie (1945) p. 123

19 We're all of us sentenced to solitary confinement inside our own skins, for life!
   Orpheus Descending (1958) act 2, sc. 1

20 Turn that off! I won't be looked at in this merciless glare!
   A Streetcar Named Desire (1947) sc. 1

21 I have always depended on the kindness of strangers.
   A Streetcar Named Desire (1947) sc. 11 (Blanche's final words)

William Carlos Williams 1883–1963

22 I will teach you my townspeople
   how to perform a funeral
   for you have it over a troop
   of artists—
   unless one should scour the world—
   you have the ground sense necessary.
   Book of Poems Al Que Quiere! (1917) 'Tract'

23 Minds like beds always made up,
   (more stony than a shore)
   unwilling or unable.
   Paterson (1946) bk. 1, preface

1 so much depends
upon

a red wheel
barrow

glazed with rain
water

beside the white
chickens.

    Spring and All (1923) 'The Red Wheelbarrow'

2 Is it any better in Heaven, my friend Ford,
Than you found it in Provence?

    The Wedge (1944) 'To Ford Madox Ford in Heaven'

Ted Willis (Edward Henry Willis, Baron Willis of Chislehurst) 1918–

3 Evening, all.

    Opening words spoken by Jack Warner as Sergeant Dixon in
    Dixon of Dock Green (BBC television series, 1956–76)

Wendell Willkie 1892–1944

4 The constitution does not provide for first and second
class citizens.

    An American Programme (1944) ch. 2

5 Freedom is an indivisible word. If we want to enjoy it,
and fight for it, we must be prepared to extend it to
everyone, whether they are rich or poor, whether they
agree with us or not, no matter what their race or the
colour of their skin.

    One World (1943) ch. 13

Angus Wilson 1913–

6 'God knows how you Protestants can be expected to
have any sense of direction,' she said. 'It's different
with us, I haven't been to mass for years, I've got
every mortal sin on my conscience, but I know when
I'm doing wrong. I'm still a Catholic, it's there,
nothing can take it away from me.' 'Of course,
duckie,' said Jeremy . . . 'once a Catholic always
a Catholic.'

    The Wrong Set (1949) p. 168. Cf. Mary O'Malley

Charles E. Wilson 1890–1961

7 For years I thought what was good for our country
was good for General Motors and vice versa. The
difference did not exist. Our company is too big. It
goes with the welfare of the country. Our contribution
to the nation is quite considerable.

    Testimony to the Senate Armed Services Committee on his
    proposed nomination to be Secretary of Defence, 15 Jan.
    1953, in *New York Times* 24 Feb. 1953, p. 8

Edmund Wilson 1895–1972

8 Of all the great Victorian writers, he [Dickens] was
probably the most antagonistic to the Victorian age
itself.

    The Wound and the Bow (1941) 'Dickens: the Two Scrooges'

Harold Wilson (Baron Wilson of Rievaulx) 1916–

9 Traders and financiers all over the world had been
listening to the Chancellor. For months he had said
that if he could not stop the wage claims, the country
was 'facing disaster'. . . . Rightly or wrongly these
people believed him. For them, 5th September—the
day that the Trades Union Congress unanimously
rejected the policy of wage restraint—marked the end
of an era. And all these financiers, all the little gnomes
in Zurich and the other financial centres about whom
we keep on hearing, started to make their dispositions
in regard to sterling.

    Hansard 12 Nov. 1956, col. 578

10 The Smethwick Conservatives can have the satisfaction
of having topped the poll, and of having sent here as
their Member one who, until a further General Election
restores him to oblivion, will serve his term here as
a Parliamentary leper.

    Hansard 3 Nov. 1964, col. 71

11 My hon. Friends know that if one buys land on which
there is a slag heap 120 ft. high and it costs £100,000
to remove that slag, that is not land speculation in the
sense that we condemn it. It is land reclamation.

    Hansard 4 Apr. 1974, col. 1441

12 If I had the choice between smoked salmon and tinned
salmon, I'd have it tinned. With vinegar.

    In *Observer* 11 Nov. 1962

13 The Monarchy is a labour-intensive industry.

    In *Observer* 13 Feb. 1977

14 Harold Wilson . . . was unable to remember when he
first uttered his dictum to the effect that: A week is
a long time in politics. . . . Inquiries among political
journalists led to the conclusion that in its present form
the phrase was probably first uttered at a meeting
between Wilson and the Parliamentary lobby in the
wake of the Sterling crisis shortly after he first took
office as Prime Minister in 1964. However, Robert
Carvel . . . recalled Wilson at a Labour Party conference
in 1960 saying 'Forty-eight hours is a long time in
politics.'

    Nigel Rees *Sayings of the Century* (1984) p. 149

15 This Party [the Labour Party] is a moral crusade or it is
nothing.

    Speech at Labour Party Conference, 1 Oct. 1962, in *The
    Times* 2 Oct. 1962

16 The Prime Ministers [at the Lagos Conference,
9–12 Jan. 1966] noted the statement by the British
Prime Minister that on the expert advice available to
him the cumulative effects of the economic and
financial sanctions might well bring the rebellion to an
end within a matter of weeks rather than months.

    The Times 13 Jan. 1966

17 From now the pound abroad is worth 14 per cent or so
less in terms of other currencies. It does not mean, of
course, that the pound here in Britain, in your pocket
or purse or in your bank, has been devalued.

    Ministerial broadcast, 19 Nov. 1967, in *The Times* 20 Nov.
    1967

18 Everyone wanted more wage increases, he [Mr Wilson]
said, believing that prices would remain stable; but

one man's wage increase was another man's price increase.

> Speech at Blackburn, 8 Jan. 1970, in *The Times* 9 Jan. 1970

McLandburgh Wilson 1892–

1 'Twixt the optimist and pessimist
The difference is droll:
The optimist sees the doughnut
But the pessimist sees the hole.

> *Optimist and Pessimist*

Sandy Wilson 1924–

2 It's never too late to have a fling,
For Autumn is just as nice as Spring,
And it's never too late to fall in love.

> *It's Never too Late to Fall in Love* (1953 song)

Woodrow Wilson 1856–1924

3 It must be a peace without victory. . . . Only a peace between equals can last. Only a peace the very principle of which is equality and a common participation in a common benefit.

> Speech to US Senate, 22 Jan. 1917, in *Messages and Papers* (1924) vol. 1, p. 352

4 Sometimes people call me an idealist. Well, that is the way I know I am an American. America, my fellow citizens—I do not say it in disaparagement of any other great people—America is the only idealistic Nation in the world.

> Speech at Sioux Falls, South Dakota, 8 Sept. 1919, in *Messages and Papers* (1924) vol. 2, p. 822

5 Once lead this people into war and they will forget there ever was such a thing as tolerance.

> In John Dos Passos *Mr Wilson's War* (1917) pt. 3, ch. 12

6 We have stood apart, studiously neutral.

> Speech to Congress, 7 Dec. 1915, in *New York Times* 8 Dec. 1915, p. 4

7 America can not be an ostrich with its head in the sand.

> Speech at Des Moines, 1 Feb. 1916, in *New York Times* 2 Feb. 1916, p. 1

8 A little group of wilful men representing no opinion but their own, have rendered the Great Government of the United States helpless and contemptible.

> Statement, 4 Mar. 1917, after a successful filibuster against Wilson's bill to arm American merchant ships, in *New York Times* 5 Mar. 1917, p. 1

9 Liberty has never come from the government. Liberty has always come from the subjects of government. The history of liberty is the history of resistance. The history of liberty is a history of the limitation of governmental power, not the increase of it.

> Speech to New York Press Club in New York, 9 Sept. 1912, in *Papers of Woodrow Wilson* (1978) vol. 25, p. 124

10 No nation is fit to sit in judgement upon any other nation.

> Speech in New York, 20 Apr. 1915, in *Selected Addresses* (1918) p. 79

11 There is such a thing as a man being too proud to fight; there is such a thing as a nation being so right that it does not need to convince others by force that it is right.

> Speech in Philadelphia, 10 May 1915, in *Selected Addresses* (1918) p. 88

12 Armed neutrality is ineffectual enough at best.

> Speech to Congress, 2 Apr. 1917, in *Selected Addresses* (1918) p. 190

13 The world must be made safe for democracy. Its peace must be planted upon the tested foundations of political liberty.

> Speech to Congress, 2 Apr. 1917, in *Selected Addresses* (1918) p. 195

14 The right is more precious than peace.

> Speech to Congress, 2 Apr. 1917, in *Selected Addresses* (1918) p. 197

15 The programme of the world's peace . . . is this: 1. Open covenants of peace, openly arrived at, after which there shall be no private international understandings of any kind but diplomacy shall proceed always frankly and in the public view.

> Speech to Congress, 8 Jan. 1918, in *Selected Addresses* (1918) p. 247

Robb Wilton 1881–1957

16 The day war broke out.

> Catch-phrase, from *c.*1940

Arthur Wimperis 1874–1953

17 I've gotter motter
Always merry and bright!
Look around and you will find
Every cloud is silver-lined;
The sun will shine
Altho' the sky's a grey one;
I've often said to meself, I've said,
'Cheer up, curly you'll soon be dead!
A short life and a gay one!'

> *My Motter* (1909 song; music by Lionel Monckton and Howard Talbot)

Owen Wister 1860–1938

18 Therefore Trampas spoke. 'You bet, you son-of-a—'
The Virginian's pistol came out, and . . . he issued his orders to the man Trampas:—'When you call me that, *smile!*'

> *The Virginian* (1902) ch. 2

Ludwig Wittgenstein 1889–1951

19 If there were a verb meaning 'to behave falsely', it would not have any significant first person, present indicative.

> *Philosophical Investigations* (1953) pt. 2, sec. 10

20 *Was sich überhaupt sagen lässt, lässt sich klar sagen; und wovon man nicht reden kann, darüber muss man schweigen.*

What can be said at all can be said clearly; and whereof one cannot speak thereof one must be silent.

> *Tractatus Logico-Philosophicus* (1922) preface

21 *Die Welt ist alles, was der Fall ist.*

The world is everything that is the case.
Tractatus Logico-Philosophicus (1922) p. 30

1 *Die Logik muss für sich selber sorgen.*

Logic must take care of itself.
Tractatus Logico-Philosophicus (1922) p. 126

2 *Die Grenzen meiner Sprache bedeuten die Grenzen meiner Welt.*

The limits of my language mean the limits of my world.
Tractatus Logico-Philosophicus (1922) p. 148

3 *Die Welt des Glücklichen ist eine andere als die des Unglücklichen.*

The world of the happy is quite different from that of the unhappy.
Tractatus Logico-Philosophicus (1922) p. 184

P. G. *Wodehouse* 1881–1975

4 Chumps always make the best husbands. When you marry, Sally, grab a chump. Tap his forehead first, and if it rings solid, don't hesitate. All the unhappy marriages come from the husbands having brains. What good are brains to a man? They only unsettle him.
The Adventures of Sally (1920) ch. 10

5 It is never difficult to distinguish between a Scotsman with a grievance and a ray of sunshine.
Blandings Castle and Elsewhere (1935) 'The Custody of the Pumpkin'

6 At this point in the proceedings there was another ring at the front door. Jeeves shimmered out and came back with a telegram.
Carry On, Jeeves! (1925) 'Jeeves Takes Charge'

7 He spoke with a certain what-is-it in his voice, and I could see that, if not actually disgruntled, he was far from being gruntled, so I tactfully changed the subject.
The Code of the Woosters (1938) ch. 1

8 Slice him where you like, a hellhound is always a hellhound.
The Code of the Woosters (1938) ch. 1

9 It is no use telling me that there are bad aunts and good aunts. At the core, they are all alike. Sooner or later, out pops the cloven hoof.
The Code of the Woosters (1938) ch. 2

10 Roderick Spode? Big chap with a small moustache and the sort of eye that can open an oyster at sixty paces?
The Code of the Woosters (1938) ch. 2

11 To my daughter Leonora without whose never-failing sympathy and encouragement this book would have been finished in half the time.
The Heart of a Goof (1926) dedication

12 The lunches of fifty-seven years had caused his chest to slip down into the mezzanine floor.
The Heart of a Goof (1926) 'Chester Forgets Himself'

13 I turned to Aunt Agatha, whose demeanour was now rather like that of one who, picking daisies on the railway, has just caught the down express in the small of the back.
The Inimitable Jeeves (1923) ch. 4

14 Sir Roderick Glossop, Honoria's father, is always called a nerve specialist, because it sounds better, but everybody knows that he's really a sort of janitor to the looney-bin.
The Inimitable Jeeves (1923) ch. 7

15 As a rule, you see, I'm not lugged into Family Rows. On the occasions when Aunt is calling to Aunt like mastodons bellowing across primeval swamps and Uncle James's letter about Cousin Mabel's peculiar behaviour is being shot round the family circle ('Please read this carefully and send it on to Jane'), the clan has a tendency to ignore me. It's one of the advantages I get from being a bachelor—and, according to my nearest and dearest, practically a half-witted bachelor at that.
The Inimitable Jeeves (1923) ch. 16

16 It was my Uncle George who discovered that alcohol was a food well in advance of medical thought.
The Inimitable Jeeves (1923) ch. 16

17 It is a good rule in life never to apologize. The right sort of people do not want apologies, and the wrong sort take a mean advantage of them.
The Man Upstairs (1914) title story

18 She fitted into my biggest armchair as if it had been built round her by someone who knew they were wearing armchairs tight about the hips that season.
My Man Jeeves (1919) 'Jeeves and the Unbidden Guest'

19 What with excellent browsing and sluicing and cheery conversation and what-not, the afternoon passed quite happily.
My Man Jeeves (1919) 'Jeeves and the Unbidden Guest'

20 'What ho!' I said.
'What ho!' said Motty.
'What ho! What ho!'
'What ho! What ho! What ho!'
After that it seemed rather difficult to go on with the conversation.
My Man Jeeves (1919) 'Jeeves and the Unbidden Guest'

21 I spent the afternoon musing on Life. If you come to think of it, what a queer thing Life is! So unlike anything else, don't you know, if you see what I mean.
My Man Jeeves (1919) 'Rallying Round Old George'

22 Ice formed on the butler's upper slopes.
Pigs Have Wings (1952) ch. 5

23 The Right Hon. was a tubby little chap who looked as if he had been poured into his clothes and had forgotten to say 'When!'.
Very Good, Jeeves (1930) 'Jeeves and the Impending Doom'

Humbert *Wolfe* 1886–1940

24 You cannot hope
to bribe or twist,
thank God! the
British journalist.

But, seeing what
the man will do
unbribed, there's
no occasion to.
The Uncelestial City (1930) 'Over the Fire'

Thomas Wolfe 1900–1938

1 Most of the time we think we're sick, it's all in the mind.
    Look Homeward, Angel (1929) pt. 1, ch. 1

2 'Where they got you stationed now, Luke?' said Harry Tugman peering up snoutily from a mug of coffee. 'At the p-p-p-present time in Norfolk at the Navy base,' Luke answered, 'm-m-making the world safe for hypocrisy.'
    Look Homeward, Angel (1929) pt. 3, ch. 36

3 You can't go home again.
    Title of novel (1940)

Tom Wolfe 1931–

4 The bonfire of the vanities.
    Title of novel (1987)

Woodbine Willie

See G. A. STUDDERT KENNEDY

Lt.-Commander Thomas Woodroofe 1899–1978

5 At the present moment, the whole Fleet's lit up. When I say 'lit up', I mean lit up by fairy lamps.
    Radio broadcast, 20 May 1937

Harry Woods

6 Oh we ain't got a barrel of money,
    Maybe we're ragged and funny,
    But we'll travel along
    Singin' a song,
    Side by side.
      Side by Side (1927 song)

7 When the red, red, robin comes bob, bob, bobbin' along.
    Title of song (1926)

Virginia Woolf 1882–1941

8 Righteous indignation . . . is misplaced if we agree with the lady's maid that high birth is a form of congenital insanity, that the sufferer merely inherits diseases of his ancestors, and endures them, for the most part very stoically, in one of those comfortably padded lunatic asylums which are known, euphemistically, as the stately homes of England.
    The Common Reader (1925) 'Lady Dorothy Nevill'. Cf. *Oxford Dictionary of Quotations* (1979) 244:21

9 We are nauseated by the sight of trivial personalities decomposing in the eternity of print.
    The Common Reader (1925) 'The Modern Essay'

10 Each had his past shut in him like the leaves of a book known to him by heart; and his friends could only read the title.
    Jacob's Room (1922) ch. 5

11 Never did I read such tosh [as James Joyce's *Ulysses*]. As for the first two chapters we will let them pass, but the 3rd 4th 5th 6th—merely the scratching of pimples on the body of the bootboy at Claridges.
    Letter to Lytton Strachey, 24 Apr. 1922, in *Letters* (1976) vol. 2, p. 551

12 A woman must have money and a room of her own if she is to write fiction.
    A Room of One's Own (1929) ch. 1

13 Women have served all these centuries as looking-glasses possessing the magic and delicious power of reflecting the figure of a man at twice its natural size.
    A Room of One's Own (1929) ch. 2

14 Literature is strewn with the wreckage of men who have minded beyond reason the opinions of others.
    A Room of One's Own (1929) ch. 3

15 So that is marriage, Lily thought, a man and a woman looking at a girl throwing a ball.
    To the Lighthouse (1927) pt. 1, ch. 13

16 Things have dropped from me. I have outlived certain desires; I have lost friends, some by death—Percival—others through sheer inability to cross the street.
    The Waves (1931) p. 202

Alexander Woollcott 1887–1943

17 A broker is a man who takes your fortune and runs it into a shoestring.
    In Samuel Hopkins Adams *Alexander Woollcott* (1945) ch. 15

18 I have no need of your God-damned sympathy. I only wish to be entertained by some of your grosser reminiscences.
    Letter to Rex O'Malley, 1942, in Samuel Hopkins Adams *Alexander Woollcott* (1945) ch. 34

19 She [Dorothy Parker] is so odd a blend of Little Nell and Lady Macbeth. It is not so much the familiar phenomenon of a hand of steel in a velvet glove as a lacy sleeve with a bottle of vitriol concealed in its folds.
    While Rome Burns (1934) 'Our Mrs Parker'

20 All the things I really like to do are either illegal, immoral, or fattening.
    In R. E. Drennan *Wit's End* (1973)

Frank Lloyd Wright 1867–1959

21 The necessities were going by default to save the luxuries until I hardly knew which were necessities and which luxuries.
    Autobiography (1945) bk. 2, p. 108

22 The physician can bury his mistakes, but the architect can only advise his client to plant vines—so they should go as far as possible from home to build their first buildings.
    New York Times 4 Oct. 1953, sec. 6, p. 47

Woodrow Wyatt (Baron Wyatt) 1919–

23 A man falls in love through his eyes, a woman through her ears.
    To the Point (1981) p. 107

Laurie Wyman

1 Left hand down a bit!
   The Navy Lark (BBC radio series, 1959–77)

George Wyndham 1863–1913

2 Over the construction of Dreadnoughts. . . . What the people said was, 'We want eight, and we won't wait.'
   Speech in Wigan, 27 Mar. 1909, in *The Times* 29 Mar. 1909

Tammy Wynette (Wynette Pugh) 1942– and Billy Sherrill

3 Stand by your man.
   Title of song (1968)

R. J. Yeatman 1898–1968

See W. C. SELLAR AND R. J. YEATMAN

W. B. Yeats 1865–1939

4 I think it better that at times like these
   We poets keep our mouths shut, for in truth
   We have no gift to set a statesman right;
   He's had enough of meddling who can please
   A young girl in the indolence of her youth
   Or an old man upon a winter's night.
   'A Reason for Keeping Silent' in Edith Wharton (ed.) *The Book of the Homeless* (1916) p. 45

5 We had fed the heart on fantasies,
   The heart's grown brutal from the fare,
   More substance in our enmities
   Than in our love; Oh, honey-bees
   Come build in the empty house of the stare.
   The Cat and the Moon (1924) 'Meditations in Time of Civil War 6: The Stare's Nest by my Window'

6 Out-worn heart, in a time out-worn,
   Come clear of the nets of wrong and right;
   Laugh, heart, again in the gray twilight;
   Sigh, heart, again in the dew of morn.
   The Celtic Twilight (1893) 'Into the Twilight'

7 When you are old and grey and full of sleep,
   And nodding by the fire, take down this book
   And slowly read and dream of the soft look
   Your eyes had once, and of their shadows deep.

   How many loved your moments of glad grace,
   And loved your beauty with love false or true,
   But one man loved the pilgrim soul in you,
   And loved the sorrows of your changing face.
   And bending down beside the glowing bars
   Murmur, a little sad, 'From us fled Love.
   He paced upon the mountains far above,
   And hid his face amid a crowd of stars.'
   The Countess Kathleen (1892) 'When You Are Old'

8 A pity beyond all telling,
   Is hid in the heart of love.
   The Countess Kathleen (1892) 'The Pity of Love'

9 I will arise and go now, and go to Innisfree,
   And a small cabin build there, of clay and wattles made;
   Nine bean rows will I have there, a hive for the honey bee,
   And live alone in the bee-loud glade.

   And I shall have some peace there, for peace comes dropping slow,
   Dropping from the veils of the morning to where the cricket sings;
   There midnight's all a glimmer, and noon a purple glow,
   And evening full of the linnet's wings.

   I will arise and go now, for always night and day
   I hear lake water lapping with low sounds by the shore;
   While I stand on the roadway or on the pavements gray,
   I hear it in the deep heart's core.
   The Countess Kathleen (1892) 'The Lake Isle of Innisfree'

10 We make out of the quarrel with others, rhetoric, but of the quarrel with ourselves, poetry.
   Essays (1924) 'Anima Hominis' sec. 5

11 Why, what could she have done being what she is?
   Was there another Troy for her to burn?
   The Green Helmet and Other Poems (1910) 'No Second Troy'

12 The fascination of what's difficult
   Has dried the sap out of my veins, and rent
   Spontaneous joy and natural content
   Out of my heart.
   The Green Helmet and Other Poems (1910) 'The Fascination of What's Difficult'

13 But where's the wild dog that has praised his fleas?
   The Green Helmet and Other Poems (1910) 'To a Poet, Who would have Me Praise certain bad Poets, Imitators of His and of Mine'

14 When I was young,
   I had not given a penny for a song
   Did not the poet sing it with such airs,
   That one believed he had a sword upstairs.
   The Green Helmet and Other Poems (1910) 'All Things can Tempt Me'

15 Where, where but here have Pride and Truth,
   That long to give themselves for wage,
   To shake their wicked sides at youth
   Restraining reckless middle age?
   The Green Helmet and Other Poems (1912) 'On hearing that the Students of our New University have joined the Agitation against Immoral Literature'

16 I said 'a line will take us hours maybe,
   Yet if it does not seem a moment's thought
   Our stitching and unstitching has been naught.'
   In the Seven Woods (1903) 'Adam's Curse'

17 The land of faery,
   Where nobody gets old and godly and grave,
   Where nobody gets old and crafty and wise,
   Where nobody gets old and bitter of tongue.
   The Land of Heart's Desire (1894) p. 12

18 Land of Heart's Desire,
   Where beauty has no ebb, decay no flood,
   But joy is wisdom, Time an endless song.
   The Land of Heart's Desire (1894) p. 36

1 Measurement began our might:
Forms a stark Egyptian thought,
Forms that gentler Phidias wrought.
Michaelangelo left a proof
On the Sistine Chapel roof,
Where but half-awakened Adam
Can disturb globe-trotting Madam
Till her bowels are in heat,
Proof that there's a purpose set
Before the secret working mind:
Profane perfection of mankind.
Last Poems (1939) 'Under Ben Bulben' pt. 4

2 Irish poets, learn your trade,
Sing whatever is well made,
Scorn the sort now growing up
All out of shape from toe to top,
Their unremembering hearts and heads
Base-born products of base beds.
Sing the peasantry, and then
Hard-riding country gentlemen,
The holiness of monks, and after
Porter-drinkers' randy laughter.
Last Poems (1939) 'Under Ben Bulben' pt. 5

3 Cast your mind on other days
That we in coming days may be
Still the indomitable Irishry.
Last Poems (1939) 'Under Ben Bulben' pt. 5

4 Under bare Ben Bulben's head
In Drumcliffe churchyard Yeats is laid.
An ancestor was rector there
Long years ago, a church stands near,
By the road an ancient cross.
No marble, no conventional phrase;
On limestone quarried near the spot
By his command these words are cut:
   Cast a cold eye
   On life, on death.
   Horseman pass by!
Last Poems (1939) 'Under Ben Bulben' pt. 6

5 Pythagoras planned it. Why did the people stare?
His numbers, though they moved or seemed to move
In marble or in bronze, lacked character.
But boys and girls, pale from the imagined love
Of solitary beds, knew what they were,
That passion could bring character enough,
And pressed at midnight in some public place
Live lips upon a plummet-measured face.

No! Greater than Pythagoras, for the men
That with a mallet or a chisel modelled these
Calculations that look but casual flesh, put down
All Asiatic vague immensities,
And not the banks of oars that swam upon
The many-headed foam at Salamis.
Europe put off that foam when Phidias
Gave women dreams and dreams their looking glass.
Last Poems (1939) 'The Statues'

6 When Pearse summoned Cuchulain to his side
What stalked through the Post Office? What intellect,
What calculation, number, measurement, replied?
We Irish, born into that ancient sect
But thrown upon this filthy modern tide
And by its formless spawning, fury wrecked,

Climb to our proper dark, that we may trace
The lineaments of a plummet-measured face.
Last Poems (1939) 'The Statues'

7 Our master Caesar is in the tent
Where the maps are spread,
His eyes fixed upon nothing,
A hand under his head.
Like a long-legged fly upon the stream
His mind moves upon silence.
Last Poems (1939) 'Long-Legged Fly'

8 Now that my ladder's gone
I must lie down where all ladders start
In the foul rag and bone shop of the heart.
Last Poems (1939) 'The Circus Animals' Desertion' pt. 3

9 I have met them at close of day
Coming with vivid faces
From counter or desk among grey
Eighteenth-century houses.
I have passed with a nod of the head
Or polite meaningless words,
Or have lingered awhile and said
Polite meaningless words,
And thought before I had done
Of a mocking tale or a gibe
To please a companion
Around the fire at the club,
Being certain that they and I
But lived where motley is worn:
All changed, changed utterly:
A terrible beauty is born.
Michael Robartes and the Dancer (1920) 'Easter, 1916'

10 Too long a sacrifice
Can make a stone of the heart.
O when may it suffice?
Michael Robartes and the Dancer (1920) 'Easter, 1916'

11 I write it out in a verse—
MacDonagh and MacBride
And Connolly and Pearse
Now and in time to be,
Wherever green is worn,
Are changed, changed utterly:
A terrible beauty is born.
Michael Robartes and the Dancer (1920) 'Easter, 1916'

12 Turning and turning in the widening gyre
The falcon cannot hear the falconer;
Things fall apart; the centre cannot hold;
Mere anarchy is loosed upon the world,
The blood-dimmed tide is loosed, and everywhere
The ceremony of innocence is drowned;
The best lack all conviction, while the worst
Are full of passionate intensity.
Michael Robartes and the Dancer (1920) 'The Second Coming'

13 The darkness drops again but now I know
That twenty centuries of stony sleep
Were vexed to nightmare by a rocking cradle,
And what rough beast, its hour come round at last,
Slouches towards Bethlehem to be born?
Michael Robartes and the Dancer (1920) 'The Second Coming'

14 An intellectual hatred is the worst,
So let her think opinions are accursed.
Have I not seen the loveliest woman born
Out of the mouth of Plenty's horn,

Because of her opinionated mind
Barter that horn and every good
By quiet natures understood
For an old bellows full of angry wind?
> *Michael Robartes and the Dancer* (1920) 'A Prayer for My Daughter'

1 The ghost of Roger Casement
Is beating on the door.
> *New Poems* (1938) 'The Ghost of Roger Casement'

2 Think where man's glory most begins and ends
And say my glory was I had such friends.
> *New Poems* (1938) 'The Municipal Gallery Re-visited'

3 You think it horrible that lust and rage
Should dance attendance upon my old age;
They were not such a plague when I was young;
What else have I to spur me into song?
> *New Poems* (1938) 'The Spur'

4 I thought no more was needed
Youth to prolong
Than dumb-bell and foil
To keep the body young.
Oh, who could have foretold
That the heart grows old?
> *Nine Poems* (1918) 'A Song'

5 That is no country for old men. The young
In one another's arms, birds in the trees—
Those dying generations—at their song,
The salmon-falls, the mackerel-crowded seas,
Fish flesh or fowl, commend all summer long
Whatever is begotten born and dies.
Caught in that sensual music all neglect
Monuments of unageing intellect.
> *October Blast* (1927) 'Sailing to Byzantium'

6 An aged man is but a paltry thing,
A tattered coat upon a stick, unless
Soul clap its hands and sing, and louder sing
For every tatter in its mortal dress.
> *October Blast* (1927) 'Sailing to Byzantium'

7 And therefore I have sailed the seas and come
To the holy city of Byzantium.
> *October Blast* (1927) 'Sailing to Byzantium'

8 O body swayed to music, O brightening glance
How can we know the dancer from the dance?
> *October Blast* (1927) 'Among School Children'

9 The Light of Lights
Looks always on the motive, not the deed,
The Shadow of Shadows on the deed alone.
> *Poems* (1895) 'The Countess Cathleen' act 3

10 The years like great black oxen tread the world,
And God the herdsman goads them on behind,
And I am broken by their passing feet.
> *Poems* (1895) 'The Countess Cathleen' act 4

11 Red Rose, proud Rose, sad Rose of all my days!
Come near me, while I sing the ancient ways.
> *Poems* (1895) 'To the Rose upon the Rood of Time'

12 Rose of all Roses, Rose of all the World!
> *Poems* (1895) 'The Rose of Battle'

13 Down by the salley gardens my love and I did meet;
She passed the salley gardens with little snow-white feet.

She bid me take love easy, as the leaves grow on the tree;
But I, being young and foolish, with her would not agree.
In a field by the river my love and I did stand,
And on my leaning shoulder she laid her snow-white hand.
She bid me take life easy, as the grass grows on the weirs;
But I was young and foolish, and now am full of tears.
> *Poems* (1895) 'Down by the Salley Gardens'

14 In dreams begins responsibility.
> *Responsibilities* (1914) epigraph

15 Was it for this the wild geese spread
The grey wing upon every tide;
For this that all that blood was shed,
For this Edward Fitzgerald died,
And Robert Emmet and Wolfe Tone,
All that delirium of the brave;
Romantic Ireland's dead and gone,
It's with O'Leary in the grave.
> *Responsibilities* (1914) 'September, 1913'

16 I made my song a coat
Covered with embroideries
Out of old mythologies
From heel to throat;
But the fools caught it,
Wore it in the world's eye
As though they'd wrought it.
Song, let them take it
For there's more enterprise
In walking naked.
> *Responsibilities* (1914) 'A Coat'

17 A woman of so shining loveliness
That men threshed corn at midnight by a tress,
A little stolen tress.
> *The Secret Rose* (1897) 'To the Secret Rose'

18 When shall the stars be blown about the sky,
Like the sparks blown out of a smithy, and die?
Surely thine hour has come, thy great wind blows,
Far off, most secret, and inviolate Rose?
> *The Secret Rose* (1897) 'To the Secret Rose'

19 Bald heads forgetful of their sins,
Old, learned, respectable bald heads
Edit and annotate the lines
That young men, tossing on their beds,
Rhymed out in love's despair
To flatter beauty's ignorant ear.

All shuffle there; all cough in ink;
All wear the carpet with their shoes;
All think what other people think;
All know the man their neighbour knows.
Lord, what would they say
Did their Catullus walk that way?
> *Selected Poems* (1929) 'The Scholars'

20 Does the imagination dwell the most
Upon a woman won or woman lost?
If on the lost, admit you turned aside
From a great labyrinth out of pride.
> *The Tower* (1928) 'The Tower' pt. 2

21 A sudden blow: the great wings beating still
Above the staggering girl, her thighs caressed

By the dark webs, her nape caught in his bill,
He holds her helpless breast upon his breast.

How can those terrified vague fingers push
The feathered glory from her loosening thighs?
> *The Tower* (1928) 'Leda and the Swan'

1 A shudder in the loins engenders there
The broken wall, the burning roof and tower
And Agamemnon dead.
> *The Tower* (1928) 'Leda and the Swan'

2 Never to have lived is best, ancient writers say;
Never to have drawn the breath of life, never to have
  looked into the eye of day;
The second best's a gay goodnight and quickly turn
  away.
> *The Tower* (1928) 'From *Oedipus at Colonus*'

3 I mourn for that most lonely thing; and yet God's will
  be done,
I knew a phoenix in my youth so let them have their
  day.
> *The Wild Swans at Coole* (1917) 'His Phoenix'

4 I see a schoolboy when I think of him
With face and nose pressed to a sweet-shop window,
For certainly he sank into his grave
His senses and his heart unsatisfied,
And made—being poor, ailing and ignorant,
Shut out from all the luxury of the world,
The ill-bred son of a livery stable-keeper—
Luxuriant song.
> *The Wild Swans at Coole* (1917) 'Ego Dominus Tuus' [of
> Keats]

5 Nor law, nor duty bade me fight,
Nor public man, nor angry crowds,
A lonely impulse of delight
Drove to this tumult in the clouds;
I balanced all, brought all to mind,
The years to come seemed waste of breath,
A waste of breath the years behind
In balance with this life, this death.
> *The Wild Swans at Coole* (1919) 'An Irish Airman Foresees his
> Death'

6 And pluck till time and times are done,
The silver apples of the moon,
The golden apples of the sun.
> *The Wind Among the Reeds* (1899) 'Song of Wandering
> Aengus'

7 Had I the heavens' embroidered cloths,
Enwrought with golden and silver light,
The blue and the dim and the dark cloths
Of night and light and the half light,
I would spread the cloths under your feet:
But I, being poor, have only my dreams;
I have spread my dreams under your feet;
Tread softly because you tread on my dreams.
> *The Wind Among the Reeds* (1899) 'Aedh Wishes for the
> Cloths of Heaven'

8 The light of evening, Lissadell,
Great windows open to the south,
Two girls in silk kimonos, both
Beautiful, one a gazelle.
> *The Winding Stair* (1929) 'In Memory of Eva Gore Booth and
> Con Markiewicz'

9 The innocent and the beautiful
Have no enemy but time.
> *The Winding Stair* (1929) 'In Memory of Eva Gore Booth and
> Con Markiewicz'

10 Nor dread nor hope attend
A dying animal;
A man awaits his end
Dreading and hoping all.
> *The Winding Stair* (1929) 'Death'

11 He knows death to the bone—
Man has created death.
> *The Winding Stair* (1929) 'Death'

12 What lively lad most pleasured me
Of all that with me lay?
I answer that I gave my soul
And loved in misery,
But had great pleasure with a lad
That I loved bodily.

Flinging from his arms I laughed
To think his passion such
He fancied that I gave a soul
Did but our bodies touch,
And laughed upon his breast to think
Beast gave beast as much.
> *The Winding Stair* (1929) 'A Woman Young and Old' pt. 9

13 We were the last romantics—chose for theme
Traditional sanctity and loveliness;
Whatever's written in what poets name
The book of the people; whatever most can bless
The mind of man or elevate a rhyme;
But all is changed, that high horse riderless,
Though mounted in that saddle Homer rode
Where the swan drifts upon a darkening flood.
> *The Winding Stair and Other Poems* (1933) 'Coole and
> Ballylee, 1931'

14 A woman can be proud and stiff
When on love intent;
But Love has pitched his mansion in
The place of excrement;
For nothing can be sole or whole
That has not been rent.
> *The Winding Stair and Other Poems* (1933) 'Crazy Jane Talks
> with the Bishop'

15 A starlit or a moonlit dome disdains
All that man is;
All mere complexities,
The fury and the mire of human veins.
> *Words for Music Perhaps and Other Poems* (1932) 'Byzantium'

16 Those images that yet
Fresh images beget,
That dolphin-torn, that gong-tormented sea.
> *Words for Music Perhaps and Other Poems* (1932) 'Byzantium'

17 While on the shop and street I gazed
My body of a sudden blazed;
And twenty minutes more or less
It seemed, so great my happiness,
That I was blessèd and could bless.
> *Words for Music Perhaps and Other Poems* (1932) 'Vacillation'

18 The intellect of man is forced to choose
Perfection of the life, or of the work,

And if it take the second must refuse
A heavenly mansion, raging in the dark.
> Words for Music Perhaps and Other Poems (1932) 'Coole Park and Ballylee, 1932'

1 Only God, my dear,
Could love you for yourself alone
And not your yellow hair.
> Words for Music Perhaps and Other Poems (1932) 'Anne Gregory'

2 Swift has sailed into his rest;
Savage indignation there
Cannot lacerate his breast.
Imitate him if you dare,
World-besotted traveller; he
Served human liberty.
> Words for Music Perhaps and Other Poems (1932) 'Swift's Epitaph'

3 Out of Ireland have we come.
Great hatred, little room,
Maimed us at the start.
I carry from my mother's womb
A fanatic heart.
> Words for Music Perhaps and Other Poems (1932) 'Remorse for Intemperate Speech'

4 What were all the world's alarms
To mighty Paris when he found
Sleep upon a golden bed
That first night in Helen's arms?
> Words for Music Perhaps and Other Poems (1932) 'Lullaby'

Jack Yellen 1892–1958

5 Happy days are here again!
The skies above are clear again.
Let us sing a song of cheer again,
Happy days are here again!
> Happy Days Are Here Again (1929 song; music by Milton Ager)

6 I'm the last of the red-hot mamas.
> Title of song (1928; popularized by Sophie Tucker)

Michael Young 1915–

7 The rise of the meritocracy 1870–2033.
> Title of book (1958)

Waldemar Young et al.

8 We have ways of making men talk.
> Lives of a Bengal Lancer (1935 film; the words became a catch-phrase as 'We have ways of making you talk')

Darryl F. Zanuck 1902–1979

9 For God's sake don't say yes until I've finished talking.
> In Philip French The Movie Moguls (1969) ch. 5

Emiliano Zapata 1879–1919

10 *Muchos de ellos, por complacer a tiranos, por un puñado de monedas, o por cohecho o soborno, están derramando la sangre de sus hermanos.*

Many of them, so as to curry favour with tyrants, for a fistful of coins, or through bribery or corruption, are shedding the blood of their brothers.
> Plan de Ayala 28 Nov. 1911, para. 10 (referring to the maderistas who, in Zapata's view, had betrayed the revolutionary cause)

Frank Zappa 1940–

11 Rock journalism is people who can't write interviewing people who can't talk for people who can't read.
> In Linda Botts Loose Talk (1980) p. 177

Robert Zemeckis 1952–
and Bob Gale 1952–

12 Back to the future.
> Title of film (1985)

Ronald L. Ziegler 1939–

13 Reminded of the President's previous statements that the White House was not involved [in the Watergate affair], Ziegler said that Mr Nixon's latest statement 'is the Operative White House Position . . . and all previous statements are inoperative.'
> Boston Globe 18 Apr. 1973

Grigori Zinoviev 1883–1936

14 Armed warfare must be preceded by a struggle against the inclinations to compromise which are embedded among the majority of British workmen, against the ideas of evolution and peaceful extermination of capitalism. Only then will it be possible to count upon complete success of an armed insurrection.
> Letter to the British Communist Party, 15 Sept. 1924, in The Times 25 Oct. 1924 (the 'Zinoviev Letter', said by some to be a forgery: see Listener 17 Sept. 1987)

Index

Index

agree (*cont.*):
  When you did a., he was   LLOY 138:16
agreeable: as a. as optimism   BENN 28:12
agreement: a. signed last night
     CHAM 48:13
agrees: nobody a. with you   STEIN 207:19
ahead: If you want to get a.   ANON 6:24
a-hold: And always keep a. of Nurse
     BELL 24:10
aid: entitled to claim the a.   CHUR 54:9
Aids: A. pandemic is a classic own-goal
     ANNE 5:8
  misbehaving will not catch A.   CURR 64:6
aim: have forgotten your a.   SANT 190:7
  oneself an impossible a.   GREE 93:14
  things is a. at in life   SMITH 202:17
  You ask, what is our a.   CHUR 54:8
aimer: *qu'a. ce n'est point nous*   SAIN 187:20
aims: Had other a. than my delight
     HARDY 98:2
ain't: a. a fit night out   FIEL 79:16
  a.-a-going to be no core   TWAIN 220:4
  A. it all a bleedin shame   ANON 8:8
  A. we got fun   KAHN 117:10
  It a. necessarily so   HEYW 102:7
  There a. gonna be no war   MACM 143:18
  There a. no Sanity Claus   KAUF 118:3
  You a. heard nuttin' yet   JOLS 114:20
air: a. as inexperienced people   CONR 59:24
  a. a voice without a face   AUDEN 15:8
  burning fills the startled A.   BELL 26:6
  Clear the a.   ELIOT 75:2
  conscience-stricken a.   HOUS 105:8
  Dust in the a. suspended   ELIOT 74:18
  feet firmly planted—in the a.   ROOS 183:6
  His happy good-night a.   HARDY 97:11
  Into my heart an a. that kills
     HOUS 107:4
  I take the a. there willingly   BECK 21:12
  since the day of the a.   BALD 17:8
  The a. is full of our cries   BECK 21:25
  This is the death of a.   ELIOT 74:18
  vans to beat the a.   ELIOT 73:17
  your room full of good a.   LEAC 133:10
airconditioning: with respectability and a.
     BAR 18:9
airing: The toothbrush too is a.   BETJ 32:5
airline: a. ticket to romantic places
     MARV 147:15
airmen: out to the British a.   CHUR 54:12
airports: a. almost deserted   AUDEN 12:20
airs: poet sing it with such a.   YEATS 232:14
aitches: nothing to lose but our a.
     ORW 165:5
Alamein: Before A. we never had a victory
     CHUR 55:20
à la mode: It began *à.*   DOBS 68:2
alarm: I viewed the morning with a.
     GERS 89:13
  SPREAD A. AND DESPONDENCY   PEN 170:1
alarms: What were all the world's a.
     YEATS 236:4
alas: A. but cannot help   AUDEN 15:10
  A., Time stays, *we* go   DOBS 68:4
  a.! we return   FORS 83:12
  And some, a., with Kate   AUDEN 14:6
  But, a., we never do   PARK 168:19
  Hugo—a.   GIDE 90:10
  Pigeons on the grass a.   STEIN 207:16
albatross: And I thought of the a.
     LAWR 131:17
Albert: Frankie and A. were lovers
     ANON 6:10
  takes to fill the A. Hall   LENN 135:6

Albert (*cont.*):
  Went there with young A.   EDGAR 71:20
alcohol: a. doesn't thrill me   PORT 172:21
  A. is a very necessary article
     SHAW 197:13
  a. produces a delightful   BENN 28:10
  a. was a food well in advance
     WOD 230:16
  have taken more out of a.   CHUR 53:5
  narcotic be a. or morphine   JUNG 116:20
alcoholic: a. as a man you don't like
     THOM 214:1
alcoholism: smoking and a.   CURR 64:7
Aldershot: burnish'd by A. sun   BETJ 32:1
ale: a.'s the stuff to drink   HOUS 107:8
  drink your a.   HOUS 105:15
Alexander: A.'s ragtime band   BERL 29:13
alibi: He always has an a.   ELIOT 75:4
Alice: Christopher Robin went down
  with A.   MILNE 153:5
alien: a. people clutching   ELIOT 73:15
alike: a. are the groans of love
     LOWRY 140:8
  think a.   TWAIN 220:2
alive: God is not dead but a. and working
     ANON 6:13
  hills are a. with the sound   HAMM 96:3
  how it feels to be a.   BARZ 20:10
  If Botticelli were a. today   UST 220:19
  Is that he is no longer a.   BENT 29:4
  Is that thing a.   BERR 30:14
  Not while I'm a. 'e aint   BEVIN 33:13
  that Lord Jones was a.   CHES 52:14
  What still a. at twenty-two   KING 122:11
  When I was a man a.   HOUS 106:17
all: A. before my little room   BROO 40:10
  a. depends what you mean   JOAD 113:19
  A. God's children are not   LEB 133:18
  a. go together when we go   LEHR 134:8
  A. human beings are born   ANON 9:1
  a. human life is there   JAMES 111:22
  A. I need to make a comedy   CHAP 49:8
  a. life is 6 to 5 against   RUNY 186:4
  A. men are creative   GOOD 92:3
  A. men are equal   FORS 83:15
  a. men are rapists   FREN 85:4
  A. my shows are great   GRADE 92:8
  A. quiet on the western front
     REM 179:11
  A. the President's men   BERN 30:12
  A. the way with LBJ   ANON 5:10
  a. things fly thee   THOM 215:18
  And a. shall be well   ELIOT 74:23
  Evening, a.   WILL 228:3
  Fair Shares for A.   JAY 112:11
  fool a. of the people   ADAMS 1:19
  From a. that terror teaches   CHES 51:18
  slum you've seen them a.   AGNEW 2:21
allegiance: Any victim demands a.
     GREE 93:16
  which you have pledged a.   BALD 16:19
alley: I think we are in rats' a.   ELIOT 76:20
alleys: a. in London do not present
     DOYLE 69:6
alliance: A., n. In international   BIER 33:22
  rapture there is a family a.   BELL 23:31
Allies: A. had blundered   NEV 160:4
alligator: See you later, a.   GUID 94:13
allow: would a. such a conventional
     BARR 19:29
all-powerful: a. to be impotent   CHUR 54:5
all-round: was a wonderful a. man
     BEER 22:20

alone: a. against smiling enemies
     BOWEN 37:14
  a. in the room there   KEYN 120:18
  a. you leave it to a torrent   CHES 51:14
  And I lie down a.   HOUS 106:6
  dangerous to meet it a.   WHAR 225:30
  fastest who travels a.   KIPL 127:15
  I want to be a.   GARBO 88:13
  must plough my furrow a.   ROS 184:17
  not good for man to be a.   BARR 19:27
  not sufficiently a.   VALÉ 220:24
  One is always a.   ELIOT 73:20
  To be adult is to be a.   ROST 185:7
  We live, as we dream— a.   CONR 59:20
  were a. with the quiet day   JAMES 112:5
  You'll never walk a.   HAMM 96:5
  You're never a. with a Strand   MAY 150:6
along: He keeps on rollin' a.   HAMM 96:1
  If you want to get along, go a.
     RAYB 178:8
alp: An a. of unforgiveness grew
     PLOM 172:5
Alps: beneath some snow-deep A.
     ELIOT 73:10
also: The sun a. rises   HEM 101:6
altar: a. the dearest   SPR 206:11
  And on the a., very reverently
     WELLS 224:13
  high a. on the move   BOWEN 37:8
alterations: carried on as usual during a.
     CHUR 53:8
alternation: a. between two rhythms
     JOAD 113:20
alternative: a. to war and destruction
     KING 122:5
  Considering the a.   CHEV 52:15
  there is no real a.   THAT 212:15
alternatives: exhausted all other a.
     EBAN 71:17
  have to decide between a.   BONH 36:2
always: a. another one walking   ELIOT 77:4
  a. at the edge of Being   SPEN 205:12
  a. depended on the kindness   WILL 227:21
  a. had mornings like this   MILNE 153:4
  A. merry and bright   WIMP 229:17
  a. night and day   YEATS 232:9
  best way out is a. through   FROST 86:15
  soul it is a. three o'clock   FITZ 80:17
  There is a. a forgotten thing   CHES 50:10
am: Where I a., I don't know   BECK 21:14
amateur: 'Eavy-sterned a. old men
     KIPL 124:14
amateurs: disease that afflicts a.   CHES 51:3
  Hell is full of musical a.   SHAW 197:28
  that we are a nation of a.   ROS 184:16
amaze: these cogitations still a.   ELIOT 76:3
amazement: And to her a. she discovered
     EWART 78:2
Amazon: She was an A. Her whole
     BLAN 34:23
ambassador: A. in Berlin handed
     CHAM 48:15
  choose a less provocative A.   HOUS 105:7
ambiguity: Seven types of a.   EMPS 77:16
ambition: A., n. An overmastering
     BIER 33:23
  the lilies of a.   DOUG 68:9
ambitions: a. are lawful except those
     CONR 60:1
  deceives with whispering a.   ELIOT 73:12
ambitious: on a much less a. project
     ANON 6:13
ambrosial: Phallic and a.   POUND 174:5

ambulance: down a doctor? With an a.
SIMP 201:7
âme: *les aventures de son â.* FRAN 84:16
amends: I must make a. JOPL 115:3
America: A. can not be an ostrich
WILS 229:7
A. is the only idealistic WILS 229:4
A. is the way parents obey EDW 72:7
A.'s present need is not HARD 96:17
A. there are two classes BENC 27:1
A. was thus clearly top SELL 194:18
A. will think tomorrow KIPL 124:6
arts in A. are a gigantic racket
BEEC 22:10
God bless A. BERL 29:15
I, too, sing A. HUGH 108:1
It's morning again in A. RINEY 181:6
next to of course god a. i CUMM 63:15
restore A. to its own people ROOS 182:22
The greening of A. REICH 179:9
what A. will do for you KENN 119:16
what makes A. what it is STEIN 207:17
which A. is the proof MCC 141:10
American: about to send A. boys
JOHN 114:13
acts in A. lives FITZ 80:22
A hyphenated A. is not ROOS 184:5
A. as cherry pie BROWN 41:8
A. Express ANON 5:11
A. gentlemen are the best LOOS 139:6
A. heiress wants to buy MCC 141:9
A. literature comes from HEM 100:13
A. people is business COOL 60:15
A. system of life HOOV 104:13
A. system of rugged individualism
HOOV 104:12
A. white man to find BALD 16:16
A. who had spoken disparagingly
BURNS 42:15
A. women shoot the hippopotamus
FORS 83:5
A. writers want to be not VIDAL 221:17
I am a free man, an A. JOHN 114:16
I am A. bred MILL 152:3
idea I'm knocking the A. CAP 46:12
imported, elderly A. JENK 113:2
justice and the A. way ANON 6:8
process whereby A. girls HAMP 96:7
rooted in the A. dream KING 121:15
root of the A. Negro problem BALD 16:16
The A. beauty rose ROCK 181:17
Americanism: can be no fifty-fifty A.
ROOS 184:1
McCarthyism is A. with its sleeves
MCC 141:7
Americans: A. have a perfect right
BEER 23:13
new generation of A. KENN 119:11
twelve A. is a bore UPD 220:14
Amis: [by Kingsley A.] MAUG 150:1
ammunition: Praise the Lord and pass
the a. FORGY 83:1
amor: A. vincit insomnia FRY 87:7
amour: *C'est tellement simple, l'a.*
PRÉV 175:5
Il y a l'a. bien sûr ANOU 9:19
Vous savez bien que l'a. ANOU 9:20
amours: *Et nos a., faut-il qu'il* APOL 9:22
amputate: Thank God they had to a.
SASS 192:3
amuse: A talent to a. COW 61:17
amusing: am generally rather a.
BEER 22:24

amusing (*cont.*):
besides being very a. BUTL 43:14
analogies: A. decide nothing FREUD 85:8
analysis: writings of Marx whose a.
BENN 27:10
anarchism: A. is a game SHAW 199:5
A., then, really GOLD 91:11
anarchist: set up a small a. community
BENN 27:20
anarchy: a. is loosed upon the world
YEATS 233:12
Anatomie: *Die A. ist das Schicksal*
FREUD 85:5
anatomy: A. is destiny FREUD 85:5
portions of the human a. HELP 100:9
ANC: brought to you by the A.
MAND 145:18
ancestors: all classes, our a. CHES 51:13
a. lost no time in abandoning
LANC 129:19
anchor: a. in nonsense GALB 88:3
ancient: burning for the a. heavenly
GINS 90:15
In a. shadows and twilights AE 2:18
while I sing the a. ways YEATS 234:11
and: including 'a.' MCC 141:8
Andrea: A. del Sarto appears BEER 22:27
Andromache: kissed his sad A. goodbye
CORN 61:9
angel: a. travelling incognito QUEN 176:14
enough for an a. to pass FIRB 80:2
In heaven an a. is nobody SHAW 198:21
angelheaded: a. hipsters burning
GINS 90:15
angels: A. can fly because they CHES 51:15
a. keep their ancient places THOM 216:11
a. over the prodigal's SAKI 188:10
a. play only Bach in praising God
BARTH 20:2
Hark! the herald a. sing BEEC 22:11
treefull of a. at Peckham Rye BENÉT 27:9
anger: a. of men who have no opinions
CHES 51:4
life of telegrams and a. FORS 83:16
Look Back in A. OSB 165:15
monstrous a. of the guns OWEN 166:9
Anglais: le vice A. RATT 178:2
angles: Offer no a. to the wind TESS 212:14
Anglo-Irish: A. slurred BOWEN 37:15
Anglo-Irishman: He was an A.
BEHAN 23:21
Anglo-Saxons: public-school men or even
of A. FORS 83:2
angry: a. if any one gives me BUTL 44:3
Knelt down with a. prayers
HODG 103:13
known as the A. Young Man FEAR 78:15
looking for an a. fix GINS 90:15
were a. and poor and happy CHES 51:23
when very a., swear TWAIN 219:32
anguish: A gay modulating a. FRY 87:4
going to be howls of a. HEAL 99:9
animal: A dying a. YEATS 235:10
a. ever invented anything CHES 50:4
a. on a planet which would HALD 95:7
Bang! Now the a. DE L 66:19
Be a good a., true LAWR 132:22
Only A. that Blushes TWAIN 219:12
The only a. in the world LAWR 131:15
animals: All a., except man BUTL 44:6
a. are equal but some animals
ORW 164:9
distinguishes man from a. OSLER 165:25
The a. will not look AUDEN 15:10

ankle socks: women who wear a.
BENN 27:21
Ann: A., Ann DE L 66:13
Anna: A. Livia! I want to hear all
JOYCE 115:10
annals: War's a. will cloud into night
HARDY 97:9
annihilating: means for a. itself
BORN 36:11
anno: only a. domini HILT 102:17
annotate: Edit and a. the lines
YEATS 234:19
annoyance: a. of a good example
TWAIN 220:1
another: a. nice mess you've gotten
LAUR 131:11
tomorrow is a. day MITC 154:12
answer: A. to the Great Question
ADAMS 1:14
a. to the Irish Question SELL 194:14
a. yes without having asked
CAMUS 45:20
asked, 'What *is* the a.?' STEIN 207:14
Please a. my question BEER 23:18
short a. is 'himself' IBSEN 110:1
Speak now, and I will a. HOUS 107:3
The a., my friend, is blowin' DYLAN 71:4
way to a pertinent a. BRON 39:14
why did you a. the phone THUR 216:21
answered: They a., as they took
BELL 24:12
ant: a.'s a centaur in his dragon
POUND 174:13
antagonistic: a. governments everywhere
WAUGH 223:11
a. to the Victorian age WILS 228:8
antennae: Artists are the a. POUND 174:9
anthology: a. is like all the plums
RAL 177:12
anthropology: most familiar facts of a.
FRAZ 84:17
anti-christ: against the a. of Communism
BUCH 42:1
anti-clerical: understand a. things so well
BELL 25:1
anti-destin: *L'art est un a.* MALR 145:16
antimilitarists: a. propose no substitute
JAMES 112:10
anti-Semitic: I have never been that [a.]
MAUG 149:12
anvil: England's on the a. KIPL 126:19
The Church is an a. MACL 143:3
any: a. man who hates dogs ROST 185:9
A. old iron, any old iron COLL 58:4
anybody: A. can be pope JOHN 114:2
A. can Win, unless there ADE 2:10
a. could become President DARR 64:14
Has a. here seen Kelly MURP 158:2
Is there a. there DE L 66:8
anyone: never said 'Tennis, a.?' BOGA 35:12
anything: A. goes PORT 172:18
course of true a. never does run smooth
BUTL 43:11
I can do a. better than you BERL 29:14
Remembering him like a. CHES 51:21
Who could ask for a. more GERS 89:14
anyway: Whose life is it a. CLARK 56:8
anywhere: a. in the world ROOS 183:9
apart: In council rooms a. RICE 180:6
things being a. YEATS 233:12
We have stood a., studiously WILS 229:6
You mean a. from my own GABOR 87:19

apartheid: We are going to dismantle a.
                                             MAND 145:18
apathy: a. of human beings   KELL 118:16
ape: naked a. self-named *Homo*
                                             MORR 156:5
The gorgeous buttocks of the a.
                                             HUXL 108:21
their manners from the A.   BELL 24:6
apes: And a. and peacocks   MAS 148:2
aphrodisiac: But a circumambulating a.
                                             FRY 87:3
Power 'is the great a.'   KISS 128:3
Aphrodite: Blonde A. rose up excited
                                             AUDEN 15:11
Apollo: A young A., golden-haired
                                             CORN 61:7
apologies: people do not want a.
                                             WOD 230:17
apologize: I never a.   SHAW 195:18
Never a.   FISH 80:9
rule in life never to a.   WOD 230:17
apology: An a. for the Devil   BUTL 43:25
God's a. for relations   KING 122:10
appeal: basic a. of movies   KAEL 117:4
appear: Blessed Cecilia, a. in visions
                                             AUDEN 15:12
with how you a. to God   UNAM 220:13
appearance: a. leaves the world   BRAD 38:7
applause: A. is a receipt, not   SCHN 193:2
A., n. The echo of a platitude   BIER 33:24
apple: a. falling towards England
                                             AUDEN 14:9
a. for the apple's sake   TWAIN 219:28
a. trees will never get   FROST 86:10
easy under the a. boughs   THOM 213:17
when you've got an a.   TWAIN 220:4
apples: On moon-washed a. of wonder
                                             DRIN 70:4
The silver a. of the moon   YEATS 235:6
applications: And a. for situations
                                             AUDEN 14:22
apply: The fundamental things a.
                                             HUPF 108:7
You know my methods. A. them
                                             DOYLE 69:23
appointment: a. by the corrupt few
                                             SHAW 198:11
I had an a. with him   LOW 139:19
we have kept our a.   BECK 21:22
appreciated: *craving to be a.*   JAMES 112:7
appreciation: developing his faculty of a.
                                             CECIL 48:4
total dependence on the a.   CONN 58:18
apprehend: Intelligence is quickness to a.
                                             WHIT 226:9
apprehension: passionate a. of form
                                             BELL 23:29
apprentice: become an a. once more
                                             BEAV 21:1
apprenticeship: cannot be any a. for
freedom   BAR 18:8
approve: a. of your young sons   GRIF 94:6
But I do not a.   MILL 151:17
apricot: And the a. tree   CAUS 47:17
April: And A.'s in the west wind
                                             MAS 148:19
April, A.   WATS 222:16
A. is the cruellest month   ELIOT 76:13
bright cold day in A.   ORW 164:19
aquarium: The a. is gone   LOW 140:2
Aquarius: the age of A.   RADO 177:6
Arab: his own A. compatriots   REAG 178:16
Arabia: with the spell of far A.   DE L 66:7

Arabs: ragged little street A.   DOYLE 69:24
Arbeit: *A. macht frei.*   ANON 5:12
archbishop: a. had come to see me
                                             BURG 42:10
Archer: [Jeffrey A.'s book]   BANK 18:6
Mary A. in the witness box   CAUL 47:16
arches: down the a. of the years
                                             THOM 215:5
Underneath the A.   FLAN 81:2
archetypes: are known as *a.*   JUNG 117:3
architect: An a. who saw this sight
                                             MORG 155:20
a. can only advise   WRIG 231:22
Great A. of the Universe   JEANS 112:22
architecture: a. a certain inhumanity
                                             CLARK 56:9
A. is the art   JOHN 114:18
A., of all the arts   DIMN 67:14
cuckoo clock style of a.   HEM 101:7
fall of English a.   BETJ 31:13
left leg, it's modern a.   BANK 18:5
New styles of a.   AUDEN 15:3
ardent: children a. for some desperate
                                             OWEN 166:10
are: sees things as they a.   BIER 34:4
so very indubitably a.   BEER 22:19
argent: *d'a. et de grosses armées*   ANOU 9:18
Argentina: Don't cry for me A.   RICE 180:9
argue: don't want to a. about it
                                             AGATE 2:20
hero is a man who would a.   MAIL 145:12
argument: a. is that War makes rattling
                                             HARDY 96:20
once in the use of an a.   BENN 28:11
arias: Clear a. of light thrilling   DAY-L 65:10
arise: a. and make them miserable
                                             HUXL 108:16
I will a. and go now   YEATS 232:9
aristocracy: a. in a republic is like
                                             MITF 154:16
a. to what is decent   HOPE 104:16
while a. means government   CHES 51:9
aristocrat: both the artist and the a.
                                             WAUGH 222:22
Aristotle: A. maintained that women
                                             RUSS 186:17
Arkangels: like he'd come from A.
                                             JOYCE 115:15
arm: Give me your a., old toad
                                             LARK 130:21
skin from the a.   ELIOT 75:2
armaments: a. that cause wars
                                             MAD 144:19
reduction of a.   ROOS 183:9
armchair: a. which provides relaxation
                                             MAT 149:3
armchairs: a. tight about the hips
                                             WOD 230:18
armed: A. neutrality is ineffectual
                                             WILS 229:12
A. warfare must be preceded   ZIN 236:14
women. We should be a.   O'BR 162:5
armées: *d'argent et de grosses a.*   ANOU 9:18
Armenteers: Mademoiselle from A.
                                             ANON 7:20
armful: that's very nearly an a.   GALT 88:8
armies: interested in a. and fleets
                                             AUDEN 12:18
plenty of money and large a.   ANOU 9:18
stronger than all the a.   ANON 8:17
armistice: conditions of the a.   LLOY 138:8
it is an a. for twenty years   FOCH 82:7
arms: A. and the man   SHAW 195:15

arms (*cont.*):
a. around him yes and drew
                                             JOYCE 116:14
a. went round her waist   MAS 148:10
But in my a. till break of day
                                             AUDEN 13:7
defend ourselves with a.   GOEB 91:6
In one another's a.   YEATS 234:5
might'st seek it in My a.   THOM 215:19
simply call the a.   REAG 178:13
world in a. is not spending   EIS 73:7
army: A. is the non-commissioned
                                             KIPL 127:10
contemptible little a.   ANON 6:9
honour of the British A.   KITC 128:5
aroma: a. of performing seals   HART 98:17
around: but the weather turned a.
                                             THOM 213:16
arranging: knack of so a. the world
                                             FRIS 85:10
arrest: a. of attention   BELL 26.12
But neither a. nor movement   ELIOT 74:5
arrested: was a. one fine morning
                                             KAFKA 117:6
arrive: to a. where we started   ELIOT 74:20
arrived: a. and to prove it I'm   SYKES 211:7
that he has a. to cover it   STOP 209:14
arrows: living a. are sent forth   GIBR 90:5
ars: *A. gratia artis.*   DIETZ 67:12
arse: politician is an a. upon   CUMM 64:1
sit on your a. for fifty years   MACN 144:8
arsenal: great a. of democracy   ROOS 183:8
arsenic: A. and old lace   KESS 120:6
art: are only interested in a.   SHAW 196:25
A. and Religion   BELL 23:31
A. distils sensation   BARZ 20:11
A. does not reproduce   KLEE 128:7
A. for art's sake   DIETZ 67:12
a.-for-art's-sake   PRIT 175:14
a. has no importance   NAB 158:16
a. has something to do   BELL 26:12
a. has the capacity   SONT 204:13
A. is a lie that makes   PIC 171:7
a. is an appeal to a reality   MACC 141:5
A. is a revolt against fate   MALR 145:16
A. is born of humiliation   AUDEN 15:15
A. is meant to disturb   BRAQ 38:16
A. is significant deformity   FRY 87:10
A. is something which is designed
                                             BARN 18:19
a. is that common symptom
                                             WHAR 225:29
A. is the imposing   WHIT 226:11
A. is the objectification   LANG 130:6
a. is the only thing   BOWEN 37:9
A. is vice   DEGAS 65:16
a. must be parochial   MOORE 155:9
a. needed Ruskin any more   STOP 210:3
a. of balance   MAT 149:3
a. of being wise   JAMES 112:12
a. of keeping a large group   RICH 180:18
A. of the Possible   BUTL 43:1
a. should carry its justification
                                             CONR 59:26
a. student wears coloured   BRAT 38:18
A. that has made these   SHAW 196:15
a. that is interested   SANT 190:14
at anything but his a.   SHAW 197:21
A triumph of the embalmer's a.
                                             VIDAL 221:14
But hating, my boy, is an a.
                                             NASH 159:13
compassion of the healer's a.   ELIOT 74:12
element of a. in their being   CHES 51:3

attention: a. in the midst of distraction
                                    BELL 26:12
  give their entire a. to it   BENN 28:16
  So a. must be paid   MILL 152:4
  socks compelled one's a.   SAKI 188:8
attentive: a. when she was in process
                                    FITZ 80:23
attire: sort of a. for a gentleman
                                    SHAR 195:9
attitude: enchantingly wavering a.
                                    FITZ 80:23
Attlee: A. is a charming and intelligent
                                    NIC 160:9
  A. reminds me of nothing   ORW 164:12
  [Clement A. is] a modest   CHUR 53:6
  Mr A., whom Churchill once   CHUR 56:3
  opened [Clement] A. got out   CHUR 53:4
attracted: that they are a. by God
                                    INGE 110:13
attracting: rhythm of a. people for fear
                                    JOAD 113:20
attraction: sexual a. through the potency
                                    HARD 96:16
attractive: if they are in the least a.
                                    CAMP 45:13
attribute: moral a. of a Scotsman
                                    BARR 19:23
attribution: a. of false motive   BALD 17:4
auctioneer: A., n. The man who proclaims
                                    BIER 33:25
audace: Le tact dans l'a. c'est   COCT 57:3
audacity: a. is knowing how far   COCT 57:3
Auden: A., a sort of gutless   ORW 165:4
  A. was someone you could   SPEN 206:1
audience: Folies-Bergère and looks at
  the a.   STOC 209:10
audiences: know two kinds of a. only
                                    SCHN 193:4
August: A. for the people   AUDEN 14:16
  A. in its history Paris   TUCH 218:17
  A. is a wicked month   O'BR 162:4
  In latter A. when the hay   LOW 140:4
aunt: A. like mastodons bellowing
                                    WOD 230:15
  Her A. was off to the Theatre   BELL 24:15
  Her A., who, from her Earliest
                                    BELL 24:14
  therefore when her A. returned
                                    BELL 24:16
aunts: bad a. and good a.   WOD 230:9
  Where his a., who are not   CHES 52:12
austere: beauty cold and a.   RUSS 186:22
Austerlitz: high at A. and Waterloo
                                    SAND 189:17
Australia: So you're going to A.
                                    MELBA 150:12
  that he was born in A.   SHAW 197:8
Australians: A. wouldn't give a XXXX
                                    ANON 5:13
Austria: A. is going to the war   CHES 51:17
authentic: a. mammon than a bogus
                                    MACN 144:4
author: a. is not what he says
                                    SMITH 203:15
  a. that wrote it was   SAL 188:25
  a. was executed for murdering
                                    BARR 19:3
  characters in search of an a.   PIR 171:15
  don't know who the a. is   SHAW 196:19
  If it's by a good a.   SHAW 196:20
  on the a.'s skill to give   QUIL 177:1
  really alive before their a.   PIR 171:16
  sincerely from the a.'s soul   HUXL 109:6

authoritarian: triumph of an a. state
                                    CLARK 56:9
authorities: a. whom we do not control
                                    CONN 59:16
  reported it to the proper a.   HELL 100:8
authority: And the lie of A.   AUDEN 13:9
  I don't like a., at least   BENS 28:20
  system can rest solely on a.   AYER 16:3
autobiography: a. is an obituary in serial
                                    CRISP 63:3
  a. is the most gratuitous   STOP 209:12
  Every artist writes his own a. ELLIS 77:13
automatic: smoothes her hair with a.
  hand   ELIOT 77:2
automobile: And fix up his a.   CLAR 56:11
  l'a. est aujourd'hui l'équivalent BART 20:4
autres: l'Enfer, c'est les A.   SART 191:4
autumn: a. always gets me badly
                                    LAWR 132:3
  a. and the falling fruit   LAWR 132:10
  a. arrives in the early   BOWEN 37:5
  A. sunsets exquisitely   HUXL 108:21
avail: virtues are of no a.   HUXL 109:7
aventures: a. de son âme au milieu
                                    FRAN 84:16
average: a. guy who could carry
                                    CROS 63:7
avoid: subject and how to a. them
                                    HEIS 100:2
avoiding: non-being by a. being TILL 217:4
avoids: a. the sight of distress
                                    MAUG 149:15
awaits: A man a. his end   YEATS 235:10
awakenings: bad dream between two a.
                                    O'NEI 163:12
aware: insignificant and is a.   BECK 21:8
  The infant child is not a.   HOUS 105:10
awareness: a. of the possibilities
                                    LEAV 133:16
  positive signs of his a.   BLUNT 35:4
away: Up, up and a.   WEBB 223:24
awe: a. and dread   FRAZ 84:17
awful: a. place and terrible   SCOTT 193:18
  a. to reflect that what   SMITH 202:18
  nobody goes, it's a.   BECK 21:18
  The a. things that rabbits do   ANON 8:6
awfully: will be an a. big adventure
                                    BARR 19:9
awoke: a. one morning from uneasy
                                    KAFKA 117:9
  Gently its touch a. him once
                                    OWEN 166:11
axes: no a. are being ground   BROUN 41:4
Axis: under-belly of the A.   CHUR 54:14

B

Babbitt: B. He was forty-six   LEWIS 137:2
babies: breed b. and you eat chips
                                    WESK 225:7
  cut ribbons and kiss b.   MICH 151:13
  hates dogs and b.   ROST 185:9
  milk into b.   CHUR 53:14
  Other people's b.   HERB 101:13
baby: A B. in an ox's stall   BETJ 31:4
  b. laughed for the first   BARR 19:7
  bats with b. faces   ELIOT 77:5
  Burn, b., burn   ANON 5:21
  garden to my bonny new b.
                                    THOM 214:10
  Make it one for my b.   MERC 151:8

baby (cont.):
  Who loves ya, b.   SAV 192:8
Babylonian: The grandeurs of his B. heart
                                    THOM 216:7
Bach: angels play only B.   BARTH 20:2
  B. almost persuades me   FRY 87:11
bachelor: b. never quite gets over
                                    ROWL 185:14
  facts that you are a b.   DOYLE 69:17
  half-witted b.   WOD 230:15
bachelors: All reformers are b.
                                    MOORE 155:7
back: always give your b. a pat
                                    LERN 135:19
  at my b. from time to time   ELIOT 76:23
  B. in the USSR   LENN 135:4
  B. to the future   ZEM 236:12
  B. to the garden   MITC 154:9
  b. upon the window-panes   ELIOT 75:14
  boys in the b. room   LOES 138:18
  boys in the b. rooms   BEAV 21:5
  gets stabbed in the b.   GARD 88:15
  I counted them all b.   HANR 96:10
  I have a beast on my b.   DOUG 68:12
  safe to go b. in the water   ANON 7:7
  The Empire strikes b.   LUCAS 140:12
  when the eyes and b.   ELIOT 76:24
  Winston is b.   ANON 9:16
  you b. where you belong   HERM 102:1
backbone: b. of the Army is the
  non-commissioned   KIPL 127:10
  McKinley has no more b.   ROOS 183:16
backhand: your wonderful b. drive
                                    BETJ 32:8
backing: I'm b. Britain   ANON 6:26
backs: On b. of tattered envelopes
                                    HOPE 105:2
backward: B. ran sentences until reeled
                                    GIBBS 90:3
  For life goes not b.   GIBR 90:5
  Leaned b. with a lipless grin   ELIOT 75:8
  lean over too far b.   THUR 217:1
  look b. to with pride   FROST 86:12
backwards: I'm walking b. for Christmas
                                    MILL 152:16
backyards: all the clean American b.
                                    MAIL 145:11
bacon: But b.'s not the only thing
                                    KING 122:11
  When their lordships asked B.
                                    BENT 28:23
bad: babies can't be all b.   ROST 185:9
  b. against the worse   DAY-L 65:11
  b. as we'd been saying   KENN 119:3
  b. aunts and good aunts   WOD 230:9
  b. book is as much   HUXL 109:6
  b. for me do not tempt   SHAW 195:14
  b. movies when they can   GOLD 92:2
  b. publicity   BEHAN 23:28
  b. taste is better   BENN 28:7
  B. women never take   BROO 41:1
  believe a thing to be b.   MILN 154:5
  consistency is as b. for the mind
                                    HUXL 108:14
  feeling is b. form   FORS 83:3
  Four legs good, two legs b.   ORW 164:8
  he is b. enough as it is   CAMP 45:6
  her badness when she's b.   BARR 19:19
  I call you b., my little child BELL 24:5
  I'm a b. lot   THOM 214:11
  it's not too b. at all   CHEV 52:15
  She was not really b. at heart
                                    BELL 24:20
  Some of them are b.   GRADE 92:8

bad (*cont.*):
so much b. in the best of us   ANON 8:18
The b. end unhappily   STOP 210:1
The good, the b., and the ugly
   SCAR 192:16
they will come to a b. end   BEER 23:8
told how b. things are   CHUR 54:13
when I'm b., I'm better   WEST 225:14
world seemed none so b.   HOUS 107:9
badly: government by the b. educated
   CHES 51:9
it is worth doing b.   CHES 52:9
badness: b. of her badness when
   BARR 19:19
Baghdad: astonished to see him in B.
   LOW 139:19
bags: carry other people's b.   BRAC 38:1
Bailey: Won't you come home Bill B.
   CANN 46:10
baiting: b. a mouse-trap with cheese
   SAKI 188:20
baked: millionaires love a b.   FIRB 80:3
Baker: B. Street irregulars   DOYLE 69:24
balance: dream of is an art of b.   MAT 149:3
bald: [André Gide] was very b.
   QUEN 176:14
B. heads forgetful   YEATS 234:19
Can't act. Slightly b.   ANON 5:24
two b. men over a comb   BORG 36:10
baldness: felicity on the far side of b.
   SMITH 202:22
Baldwin: Mr B. denouncing sanctions
   BEAV 21:2
never hears of B. nowadays   CHUR 53:16
Baldwins: two Mr B. on the stage
   BEAV 21:2
ball: at a girl throwing a b.   WOOLF 231:15
Ruddy B. has taken   THOM 214:19
Take me out to the b. game
   NORW 161:14
ballet: unearthly b. of bloodless   BRAD 38:7
ball-floor: Dance on this b. thin and wan
   BLUN 34:25
Balliol: B. made me, B. fed me   BELL 26:2
God be with you, B. men   BELL 26:2
balls: And a thousand lost golf b.
   ELIOT 76:5
Ballymurphy: That's chalked up In B.
   HEAN 99:14
balmy: Ginger, you're b.   MURR 158:4
Baltimore: magazine and then you're in B.
   GORD 92:4
ban: B. the bomb   ANON 5:14
banality: b. out of the sphere   SARR 190:25
word-and-thought-defying b. *of evil*
   AREN 10:4
banana: original b. man   PAGET 167:3
bananas: Yes! we have no b.   SILV 200:18
band: It's the best b. in the land
   BERL 29:13
rock 'n' roll b.   JAGG 111:9
twilight! importunate b.   BETJ 32:3
when the b. begins   KIPL 123:5
when the wearied B.   HUXL 109:2
bands: people get into b. for three
   GELD 89:3
who pursue Culture in b.   WHAR 225:30
bang: A bigger b. for a buck   ANON 5:19
b., goes the farmer's gun   GAY 89:1
B.! Now the animal   DE L 66:19
Bertha's got a b. on the boko
   MARS 147:12
If the big b. does come   OSB 165:19
Not with a b. but a whimper   ELIOT 75:12

bang (*cont.*):
The words 'Kiss Kiss B.B.'   KAEL 117:4
banished: B. from the herd he led
   HODG 103:14
banishment: b. of its properly elected
   CAIR 44:19
bank: all the way to the b.   LIB 137:7
b. compared with founding   BREC 39:1
b. is a place that will   HOPE 105:1
b. was mightier   PLOM 172:8
should tyrannize over his b.   KEYN 120:16
Bankhead: B. barged down the Nile
   BROWN 41:11
banking: much as we value b.
   TOYN 217:14
bankrupts: you are b.; your role
   TROT 218:5
banks: b. and stones   KAV 118:6
b. of the great grey-green   KIPL 125:13
thanks, letters from b.   AUDEN 14:22
banned: that any book should be b.
   WEST 225:25
Bapu: B. as we called him   NEHRU 160:1
bar: treat if met where any b.   HARDY 98:3
Barabbas: crowd will always save B.
   COCT 57:5
barbarian: He is a b., and thinks
   SHAW 195:26
barbarians: The B. are coming today
   CAV 48:1
barbarism: methods of b. in South Africa
   CAMP 45:16
bard: this goat-footed b.   KEYN 120:15
bare: B. like nude, giant girls   SPEN 205:18
Under b. Ben Bulben's head   YEATS 233:4
bareback: daft and happy hills b.
   THOM 213:12
barged: Bankhead b. down the Nile
   BROWN 41:11
baritone: have been singing b.   REED 179:6
bark: you heard a seal b.   THUR 216:17
barking: sound of Harold Hobson b.
   GILL 90:12
Barlow: O my Hornby and my B. long ago
   THOM 215:22
barmaids: Are B. Chaste   MAS 148:10
barn: from the b. and the forge
   HOUS 106:16
barn-cocks: Ere the b. say   HARDY 97:16
Barney: Give him the money, B.
   PICK 171:10
barrel: decompose in a b. of porter
   DONL 68:7
Oh we ain't got a b. of money
   WOODS 231:6
out of the b. of a gun   MAO T 146:13
barreltone: Ben Dollard had a base b.
   JOYCE 116:10
barricade: At some disputed b.   SEEG 194:5
Barrie: *Little Mary* [by J.M. B.]   LLEW 138:5
clatter of Sir James B.'s cans   GUED 94:11
barring: B. that natural expression
   TWAIN 219:8
Barrymore: No B. would allow such
a conventional   BARR 19:29
bars: Between their silver b.   FLEC 81:14
barter: mental or physical b.   AUDEN 14:3
Barumph: King B. has a whim of iron
   HERF 101:28
base: b. people as certainly   SHAW 197:7
had a b. barreltone voice   JOYCE 116:10
basement: faded female in a damp b.
   HARD 96:16
basest: b. of all things   FAUL 78:12

basically: b. he's an underachiever
   ALLEN 3:16
basin: Stare, stare in the b.   AUDEN 12:17
basket: both come from the same b.
   CONR 59:29
WATCH THAT B.   TWAIN 219:34
bason: b. and a hose thing   ASHF 10:18
bastard: putting all my eggs in one b.
   PARK 169:7
we knocked the b. off   HILL 102:14
bastards: Don't let the b. grind you down
   ANON 7:27
bataille: *La France a perdu une b.*   DE G 65:19
bath: b. room said Bernard it   ASHF 10:18
conifers, sound of the b.   BETJ 32:2
I test my b. before I sit   NASH 159:9
on his b. tub   POUND 173:26
who watched the b. water   ABSE 1:4
bathroom: church as he goes to the b.
   BLYT 35:7
man in the b. cupboard   EWART 78:2
revolutionary in a b.   LINK 137:15
bats: b. with baby faces   ELIOT 77:5
batsman: B. of the Dawn has driven
   THOM 214:19
I am the b. and the bat   LANG 130:4
battalions: your dreams in pale b. go
   SORL 205:3
Battery: Bronx is up but the B.'s
   COMD 58:7
battle: b. depends the survival   CHUR 54:11
B., n. A method of untying   BIER 33:26
b. of Waterloo *was* won   ORW 164:18
France has lost a b.   DE G 65:19
that out of b. I escaped   OWEN 166:15
battlements: came and perched on b.
   BEER 23:16
From the hid b. of Eternity   THOM 215:17
battles: B. and sex are the only
   MCAR 140:19
Dead b., like dead generals   TUCH 218:15
opening b.   ORW 164:18
battleship: Get me a b.   BENC 26:23
battu: *mais de s'être bien b.*   COUB 61:12
bawdy: While b. questions went about
   MAS 148:10
bay: keeping feelings at b.   BROO 41:2
steamer breaking from the b.
   AUDEN 14:18
baying: county families b. for broken
   WAUGH 222:19
bayonet: b. is a weapon with a worker
   ANON 5:15
bayonets: build himself a throne of b.
   INGE 110:15
bazaar: morning, Fate's great b.
   MACN 144:16
BBC: B. for interviewing   HARD 96:16
has demanded that the B.   CRIT 63:5
be: But b.   MACL 143:6
Let b. be finale of seem   STEV 208:10
Such is: what is to b.   THOM 215:16
beach: Along the hidden b.   KIPL 124:10
low voice: 'On the b.'   CHES 51:5
walk upon the b.   ELIOT 75:19
beaches: enough for lazing upon b.
   BETJ 31:8
We shall fight on the b.   CHUR 54:10
Beachy Head: Birmingham by way of B.
   CHES 50:22
beam: B. us up, Mr Scott   RODD 182:3
bean: Nine b. rows will I have   YEATS 232:9

bean (*cont.*):
The home of the b. and the cod
BOSS 36:12
beanz: B. meanz Heinz   DRAKE 70:3
bear: B. is looking so geometrical   FRY 87:5
B. of Very Little Brain   MILNE 153:16
B. them we can, and if   HOUS 105:15
Cannot b. very much reality ELIOT 74:4
Grizzly B. is huge   HOUS 105:10
so b. ourselves   CHUR 54:11
The fire was furry as a b.   SITW 201:11
Their habits from the B.   BELL 24:6
bearable: b. to millions of people
SHAW 197:13
beard: has a fringe and a b.   BRAT 38:18
bearer: b. of this letter   ASHF 11:1
bearing: b. down on me now under
JOYCE 115:15
bears: And dancing dogs and b.
HODG 103:13
b. might come with buns   ISH 110:22
Teddy B. have their Picnic   KENN 118:19
beast: And what rough b.   YEATS 233:13
b. and the monk   FORS 83:17
B. gave beast as much   YEATS 235:12
B. stands for strong mutually
WAUGH 223:11
b. to the truly genteel   HARDY 97:6
I have a b. on my back   DOUG 68:12
night out for man or b.   FIEL 79:16
people call this b. to mind BELL 24:9
was Beauty killed the B.   CREE 62:17
beastly: b. incidents our memories
O'NEI 163:14
has been b. to the Bank   CRIT 63:5
How b. the bourgeois   LAWR 132:15
let's be b. to the Germans   COW 61:16
beat: reading the B. novels   CAP 46:14
really a b. generation   KER 120:3
So we b. on, boats against   FITZ 80:21
The b. goes on   BONO 36:4
They beat—and a Voice b.   THOM 215:6
beaten: have won but to be well b.
COUB 61:12
I was b. up by Quakers   ALLEN 4:8
No Englishman is ever fairly b.
SHAW 199:29
beating: b. of war drums   KOES 128:13
Is b. on the door   YEATS 234:1
beatings: dread of b.   BETJ 32:10
Beatles: And the B.' first LP   LARK 130:14
[the B. are] more popular   LENN 135:2
beats: B. like a fatalistic drum   ELIOT 75:21
Counting the slow heart b.   GRAV 93:9
It b. as it sweeps as it cleans   PAG 167:4
Beattock: Pulling up B., a steady climb
AUDEN 14:21
beaut: make a mistake, it's a b.   LA G 129:8
beautiful: Against the b. and the clever
GREE 93:13
Another is 'the b. Law Courts'
RUSS 187:7
b. and simple as all truly   HENRY 101:11
B. comical things   HARV 99:2
b. I am   HUGH 108:1
B., one a gazelle   YEATS 235:8
b. stuff and poetry   TWAIN 218:21
b. things we have to keep   O'NEI 163:14
b. word for doing things tomorrow
SHAW 195:21
Black is b.   ANON 5:20
find it a b. clean thought   LAWR 132:23
God's children are not b.   LEB 133:18
her 'a b. little knitter'   SITW 201:13

beautiful (*cont.*):
more b. than any religion   SAKI 188:5
most b. adventure   FROH 85:11
Of the forest b.   HODG 103:14
'Oh, how b.!' and sitting   KIPL 125:1
Oh, what a b. mornin'   HAMM 95:18
Small is b.   SCH 193:10
The b. and damned   FITZ 80:13
The b. and death-struck year
HOUS 107:5
The entirely b.   AUDEN 13:7
The innocent and the b.   YEATS 235:9
worshipped because they are b.
RUSS 186:26
beauty: American b. rose can   ROCK 181:17
A terrible b. is born   YEATS 233:9
B. and the lust for learning   BEER 23:11
b. being only skin-deep   KERR 120:5
b. came like the setting sun   SASS 192:6
B. crieth in an attic   BUTL 44:2
B. for some provides escape   HUXL 108:21
B. is all very well at first   SHAW 198:5
B. is momentary in the mind
STEV 208:13
B. is the first test   HARDY 96:18
b. lives though lilies   FLEC 81:6
B.'s conquest of your face   AUDEN 14:11
B. she was statue cold   FLEC 81:17
B. took from those   DE L 66:12
body's b. lives   STEV 208:13
But b. vanishes; beauty passes
DE L 66:10
For such B., so descending   BELL 25:20
Has looked on B. bare   MILL 151:21
Her b. fed my common earth   MAS 148:9
It was B. killed the Beast   CREE 62:17
loveliest things of b.   MAS 148:7
say b. is only sin deep   SAKI 188:11
Say, is there b. yet to find   BROO 40:15
So is the b. Of an agéd face   CAMP 45:4
The b. of inflections   STEV 208:14
thing of b. and a boy   ROWL 185:14
thought that where B. was   GALS 88:6
'Tisn't b., so to speak   KIPL 127:16
truth, but supreme b.   RUSS 186:22
Where b. has no ebb   YEATS 232:18
why talk of b.   CUMM 63:15
wildest b. in the world   OWEN 166:16
beaver: And cultivate a b.   HUXL 108:8
Beaverbrook: [B.] gets to Heaven he won't
WELLS 224:12
B. is so pleased   BAXT 20:15
mind was that of Lord B.   ATTL 12:9
because: B. I do not hope to turn again
ELIOT 73:16
B. it's there   MALL 145:15
B. these wings are no longer   ELIOT 73:17
B. We're here   ANON 9:10
Done b. we are too menny   HARDY 96:22
beckon: The morning b.   THOM 213:15
becoming: b. the men we wanted
STEI 208:3
bed: And bounced out of b.   MILNE 153:10
'B.,' as the Italian proverb   HUXL 108:19
b. fell on my father   THUR 216:15
b. with me and she said 'no'   ALLEN 4:3
b. with my catamite when   BURG 42:10
Every b. is narrow   MILL 151:23
getting in b. with women   ROSS 185:4
[have stayed] in b.   JAC 111:7
I'd love to remain in b.   BERL 29:16
I toward thy b.   FLEC 81:11
it's nicer to lie in b.   LAUD 131:9
kneels at the foot of the b.   MILNE 153:12

bed (*cont.*):
Lying in b. would   CHES 52:5
mind is not a b. to be made   AGATE 2:20
Now can we go to b.   COPE 61:1
Out on the lawn I lie in b.   AUDEN 14:10
Pursuing it from b. to bed   PARK 168:17
stay in b. all day   BENC 26:16
That's why I go to b. early   WAUGH 223:2
Up to b.   DE L 66:14
used to go to b. early   PROU 175:16
Who goes to b. with whom   SAY 192:12
bedevilment: Of man's b. and God's
HOUS 105:18
bedpost: lose its flavour on the b.
ROSE 184:12
bedroom: b. as long as you don't
CAMP 45:7
French widow in every b.   HOFF 104:2
Stranger, unless with b. eyes
AUDEN 12:14
The view from my b. of moss-dappled
BETJ 32:2
beds: Minds like b. always made up
WILL 227:23
Of solitary b., knew what   YEATS 233:5
bedside: I was at the b. making   BENN 28:2
bee: butterfly, sting like a b.   ALI 3:9
honeysuckle, I am the b.   FITZ 80:11
Beecham's Pills: B. are just the thing
BEEC 22:11
beef: Boiled b. and carrots   COLL 58:3
Where's the b.   FREE 85:2
beefsteak: b. and put some red blood
CAMP 45:6
beefy: As b. ATS   BETJ 31:18
bee-loud: And live alone in the b. glade
YEATS 232:9
been: I've b. things and seen places
WEST 225:13
beer: I'm only a b. teetotaller   SHAW 196:6
I'm only here for the b.   LEV 136:5
Pints and quarts of Ludlow b.
HOUS 107:9
Beerbohm: [Max B.] has the most
STR 210:12
beers: parts other b. cannot reach
LOV 139:15
bees: Birds do it, b. do it   PORT 173:3
Beethoven: Roll over, B.   BERRY 30:13
the greatest composers since B.   BUCK 42:4
beetles: species of b. on this planet
HALD 95:7
before: B. I built a wall I'd ask   FROST 86:11
B. we were her people   FROST 86:11
B. you can call him a man   DYLAN 71:4
doing what has been done b.
WHAR 225:29
beg: b. in the streets   FRAN 84:15
We cannot b. for pardon   MACN 144:5
beget: passions, to get and b.   OSLER 166:3
To b. children   SART 191:5
beggar: You big black boundin' b.
KIPL 123:8
begin: back to it and b. over   FROST 86:5
But let us b.   KENN 119:14
To b. at the beginning   THOM 214:7
When they b. the Beguine   PORT 172:19
beginning: begin at the b.   THOM 214:7
classic formula of a b.   LARK 130:19
end is to make a b.   ELIOT 74:21
even the b. of the end   CHUR 53:17
In my b. is my end   ELIOT 74:8
In the b. was the Word   ELIOT 75:7
Is a new b., a raid   ELIOT 74:13

bewache: *andern seine Einsamkeit b.*
RILKE 181:5

beware: B. of rudely crossing it
AUDEN 12:14
B. of the man who does not SHAW 199:1
B. of the man whose god SHAW 198:19
Sisters, I bid you b. KIPL 123:1

bewildered: Bewitched, bothered and b.
HART 98:16
unprincipled to the utterly b. CAPP 46:17

bewitched: B., bothered and bewildered
HART 98:16
b. for ever who has seen SACK 187:16

bewrapt: B. past knowing to what
HARDY 97:8

beyond: b. the obvious facts DOYLE 69:17
But is there anything B. BROO 40:6

bias: suggests forms of b. SCH 193:8

biases: critic is a bundle of b. BALL 17:22
It b. the judgement DOYLE 69:26

Bible: So the B. said HOL 104:4

bible-black: town, starless and b.
THOM 214:7

bicicleta: *puede llegar solo en b.* VIER 221:19

Bickleigh: murder his wife that Dr B.
ILES 110:5

bicycle: like a fish without a b. STEI 208:4
Socialism can only arrive by b.
VIER 221:19
so is a b. repair kit CONN 58:13
Tomorrow the b. races AUDEN 15:9

bicycles: b. over the rocky roadsteads
O'BR 162:11

bicyclists: illuminated trouser-clip for b.
MORT 156:17

bid: She b. me take love easy YEATS 234:13

big: B. BROTHER IS WATCHING
ORW 164:20
b. enough to take away FORD 82:16
B. ones, small ones HEAT 99:18
carry a b. stick ROOS 183:17
he was too b. for them BULM 42:6
I am b. It's the pictures BRAC 37:21
live in houses just as b. SMITH 203:5
victim to a b. lie HITL 103:8
Who's afraid of the b. bad wolf
CHUR 53:2
Your feet's too b. BENS 28:19
You used to be b. BRAC 37:21

bigamy: And b., Sir, is a crime
MONK 155:1
B. is having one husband ANON 5:18

bigger: A b. bang for a buck ANON 5:19
girls get b. every day LERN 135:24
The b. they are FITZ 81:1

biggest: b. electric train set WELL 224:10
b. industrial corporation SHAW 195:13
The b. aspidistra in the world
HARP 98:12

bighead: 'B.!' 'Dollar lolly' SYKES 211:7

bigotry: B. may be roughly defined
CHES 51:4
B. tries to keep truth TAG 212:2

bijoux: *jamais de b. artistiques* COL 57:17

bike: b. and looked for work TEBB 212:10
Mind my b. WARN 222:13

bikini: yellow polkadot b. VANCE 221:2

bill: her nape caught in his b.
YEATS 234:21

billabong: swagman camped by a b.
PAT 169:15

billboard: A b. lovely as a tree
NASH 159:14

billion: And among that b. minus one
HUXL 108:20

bills: By children and tradesmen's b.
MACN 144:14
Just for paying a few b. LARK 130:17
nightingale b. his best HARDY 97:2
Receipted b. and invitations
AUDEN 14:22

Billy: B., in one of his nice GRAH 92:12

bind: are the mortar that b. WELLS 225:1
darkness b. them TOLK 217:9
Go, b. your sons to exile KIPL 127:19

biographer: b. is an artist MACC 141:4

biography: b. is ultimately fiction
MAL 145:14
B. should be written BALF 17:20
But B. is about Chaps BENT 28:24
how difficult it is to write b. WEST 225:26
not the better part of b. STR 210:11
The Art of B. BENI 28:24

birch: bringing back the b. VIDAL 221:15

birches: than be a swinger of b. FROST 86:5

bird: b. can fly MILNE 153:18
b. that thinks two notes DAV 65:1
I know why the caged b. sings ANG 5:6
It's a b.! It's a plane ANON 6:8
It was only the note of a b. SIMP 201:5
like a b. on the wing BOUL 37:3
Like the first b. FARJ 78:7
She's a b. in a gilded cage LAMB 129:15
Was a b.; and the song was SASS 192:6

birds: And listen to the b. GIBS 90:8
b. came home to roost MILL 152:6
B. do it, bees do it PORT 173:3
B. in their little nests agree BELL 25:10
b. in the trees YEATS 234:5
b. must find in freedom SASS 192:6
b., wild flowers BALD 17:11
two b. setting on a fence TWAIN 219:3

Birkenhead: B. is very clever but
sometimes ASQ 11:17

Birmingham: B. by way of Beachy Head
CHES 50:22
When Jesus came to B. they
STUD 210:20

birth: And with the trees to newer b.
GREN 94:3
at the b. of his child ORTON 164:1
B., and copulation, and death ELIOT 76:9
B. or Death ELIOT 73:15
cure for b. and death SANT 190:17
give b. astride of a grave BECK 21:24
Rainbow gave thee b. DAV 65:3
task in life is to give b. FROMM 85:12
There was a B., certainly ELIOT 73:15

birthday: afternoon of my eighty-first b.
BURG 42:10
Happy b. to you HILL 102:13
is it my b. or am I dying ASTOR 12:1
marvel My b. Away THOM 213:16

birth-rate: Into a rising b. FRY 87:3

biscuits: synthesis of hyacinths and b.
SAND 189:12

bisexuality: On b.: It immediately doubles
ALLEN 3:20

bishop: articles by a popular b.
WAUGH 223:3
b. was feeling rather sea-sick
DOUG 68:14
blonde to make a b. kick CHAN 49:3
hitting the niece of a b. ORW 164:31
The sun like a B.'s bottom ASQ 11:20

Bismarck: theory of politics was B.'s
KEYN 120:8

bit: b. in the corner you can't BENN 27:18

bitch: old b. gone in the teeth
POUND 174:6
was a dumb son of a b. TRUM 218:12

bitch-goddess: worship of the b. *success*
JAMES 112:8

bite: miseries, a b. and sup HEAN 99:14

bites: But if a man b. a dog BOGA 35:13

biting: b. the hand that lays GOLD 91:17

bits: have swallowed their b. BETJ 31:9
Look at it, it's all in b. AYCK 16:1

bitter: Failure makes people b.
MAUG 149:23

bitterness: But the rose's scent is b.
THOM 214:20
must have no hatred or b. CAV 48:3

black: bit of b. mackintosh WELBY 224:6
b. as our loss SITW 201:15
b. blood makes a man coloured
HUGH 107:21
b. face and a different EDW 72:6
B. is beautiful ANON 5:20
b. majority rule in Rhodesia
SMITH 202:15
b. people in this country CARM 46:19
climb b. branches up FROST 86:5
last night two b. owls BEER 23:16
rings b. Cyprus FLEC 81:19
slow, b., crowblack THOM 214:7
so long as it's b. FORD 82:19
That old b. magic MERC 151:9
The hump that is b. and blue
KIPL 125:10
vehicle the B. Panther Party NEWT 160:6
Young, gifted and b. IRV 110:21

blackbird: B. has spoken FARJ 78:7
Bye bye b. DIXON 67:17
The b. whistling STEV 208:14

blackbirds: B. are the cellos STEV 209:8

Blackburn: Four thousand holes in B.
LENN 135:6

black-eyed: The landlord's b. daughter
NOYES 161:17

blackguard: A b. whose faulty vision
BIER 34:4

Blackpool: seaside place called B.
EDGAR 71:20

Black Power: B. is one of the most
legitimate CARM 46:19

blacksmith: b. like our Norman King
KIPL 126:19

Black Widow: This is the B., death
LOW 140:5

blade: b. struck the water a full COKE 57:14

Blake: B. saw a treefull of angels
BENÉT 27:9

blame: Bad women never take the b.
BROO 41:1
b. Marx for what was done BENN 27:11
b. on men but on the bond SART 191:5
It's the poor wot gets the b. ANON 8:8
The police were to b. GRANT 93:2

blancmange: Of cold b. and rhubarb tart
KNOX 128:11

bland: b. lead the bland GALB 88:2

blanket: right side of the b. ASHF 11:1

blankets: Of b.; grainy wood BROO 39:19

blasphemies: All great truths begin as b.
SHAW 195:10

blast-beruffled: In b. plume HARDY 97:11

blasts: that b. the roots of trees
                                    THOM 213:20
blazed: My body of a sudden b.
                                    YEATS 235:17
blazing: At that Mother got proper b.
                                    EDGAR 72:1
blazon: Their final b., and to prove
                                    LARK 131:6
bleedin: Ain't it all a b. shame   ANON 8:8
bleeding: Beneath the b. hands we feel
                                    ELIOT 74:12
  b. to death of time   GRAV 93:9
  instead of b., he sings   GARD 88:15
blend: b. of cold chalk soup   AMIS 4:16
blent: b. air all our compulsions
                                    LARK 130:16
bless: B. 'em all! Bless 'em all
                                    HUGH 107:20
  was blessèd and could b.   YEATS 235:17
  whatever most can b.   YEATS 235:13
blessed: B. Cecilia, appear in visions
                                    AUDEN 15:12
  Some b. Hope, whereof he knew
                                    HARDY 97:11
blessing: b. or the greatest curse
                                    BARR 19:12
  boon and a b. to men   ANON 8:21
  he has one matchless b.   EDW 72:8
  simple b. of a rainbow   ABSE 1:3
  Thou have paid thy utmost b.   DE L 66:12
blighted: Saying 'Farewell, b. love.'
                                    ANON 8:8
blighty: Take me back to dear old B.
                                    MILLS 152:20
blind: And old Maeonides the b.   FLEC 81:22
  And wretched, b., pit ponies
                                    HODG 103:13
  b. side of the heart   CHES 50:10
  Country of the B. the One-Eyed
                                    WELLS 224:16
  eyes were b. with stars   HODG 103:11
  religion without science is b.   EINS 73:5
  splendid work for the b.   SASS 191:18
  though b., throbbing between
                                    ELIOT 76:24
  To sit by and see the b. man
                                    WALEY 222:3
blindness: 'eathen in 'is b.   KIPL 127:9
blinds: dusk a drawing-down of b.
                                    OWEN 166:9
  I must dust the b.   THOM 214:8
  The b. let through the day   HOUS 106:1
blinked: other fellow just b.   RUSK 186:6
bliss: appreciate domestic b.   SANT 190:10
  Gives promise of pneumatic b.   ELIOT 75:9
blitz: b. of a boy is Timothy   CAUS 47:18
blizzard: willingly to his death in a b.
                                    ATK 12:5
blonde: B. Aphrodite rose up excited
                                    AUDEN 15:11
  b. to make a bishop kick   CHAN 49:3
  Monroe was b. and beautiful
                                    MAIL 145:11
blondes: Gentlemen Prefer B.   LOOS 139:3
  seem to remember b.   LOOS 139:4
blood: at every jolt, the b.   OWEN 166:10
  beefsteak and put some red b.   CAMP 45:6
  b. and love without the rhetoric
                                    STOP 209:19
  b. be the price of admiralty   KIPL 127:2
  b. of their brothers   ZAP 236:10
  b. running from the wounded
                                    ROOS 183:3

blood (cont.):
  b.'s a rover   HOUS 106:10
  For B., as all men know   HUXL 109:1
  I would rather have b.   GREE 93:12
  nothing to offer but b.   CHUR 54:7
  poison the whole b.   EMPS 77:15
  that all that b. was shed   YEATS 234:15
  That one drop of Negro b.   HUGH 107:21
  there's b. upon her gown   FLEC 81:17
  Tiber foaming with much b.   POW 175:2
  washed in the b. of the Lamb
                                    LIND 137:12
  We be one b., thou   KIPL 125:4
blood-dimmed: The b. tide is loosed
                                    YEATS 233:12
bloodless: unearthly ballet of b. BRAD 38:7
bloodshed: b. while war is politics
                                    MAO T 146:12
bloody: And sang within the b. wood
                                    ELIOT 75:5
  got was a b. good hiding   GRANT 93:2
  Not b. likely   SHAW 199:24
  Sunday, b. Sunday   GILL 90:13
bloom: As well as any b. upon a flower
                                    THOM 214:16
  B. ate with relish   JOYCE 116:8
  Just now the lilac is in b.   BROO 40:10
  look at things in b.   HOUS 106:9
  risk of spoiling its b.   CONR 59:18
  sort of b. on a woman   BARR 19:20
  with b. along the bough   HOUS 106:9
bloomed: stallions, b. that spring
                                    CRANE 62:14
blooming: grand to be b. well dead
                                    SAR 190:23
  stones and every b. thing   KAV 118:6
blossom: almond b.   REED 179:1
  b. seethed and departed   BETJ 32:5
blossomed: B. Sarah   BERR 30:14
blots: absence b. people out   BOWEN 37:7
blow: A b. in cold blood neither
                                    SHAW 198:18
  A sudden b.: the great wings
                                    YEATS 234:21
  b. from which he never   MCL 143:11
  B. out, you bugles   BROO 40:3
  b. up the other half   LAING 129:12
  could not b. his nose   CONN 59:6
  does not return your b.   SHAW 199:1
  For the hardest b. of all   BERL 29:16
  I'll sin till I b. up   THOM 214:11
  Spring is here, so b. your job   HART 98:19
blowin': b. in the wind   DYLAN 71:4
blowing: And thoughts go b. through
                                    BROO 40:9
  b. of a nose   FORS 83:21
  by b. up the world   ADAMS 2:7
  I'm forever b. bubbles   KENB 118:17
blows: From yon far country b.
                                    HOUS 107:4
  It b. so hard, 'twill soon   HOUS 107:1
blub: b. they hav every reason   WILL 227:8
blue: b. films of war   RAE 177:7
  B. skies be your coverlet   HART 98:19
  brings back b. days and fair   SEEG 194:5
  deep b. air   LARK 130:8
  Floating in the B.   MILNE 153:14
  In his b. gardens   FITZ 80:19
  lay off my B. Suede Shoes   PERK 170:6
  My b. heaven   WHIT 226:18
  those b. remembered hills   HOUS 107:4
  University Statutes bound in b.
                                    BETJ 32:11
  Where the b. of the night   CROS 63:8

bluebirds: b. over the white cliffs
                                    BURT 42:18
blunder: At so grotesque a b.   BENT 29:7
blundered: Have b. into Paradise
                                    THOM 215:23
Blunt: Anthony B.   MUNN 157:18
blush: And b. at what they hear
                                    KING 122:12
blushes: Animal that B.   TWAIN 219:12
blushing: other people without b.
                                    SHAW 199:2
board: Everything goes by the b.
                                    FAUL 78:11
  There wasn't any B., and now
                                    HERB 101:21
boards: I sit upon her B.   DENN 67:3
boast: How many people can b.   BECK 21:22
boat: bonnie b., like a bird   BOUL 37:3
  involuntary. They sank my b.
                                    KENN 119:9
boats: b. against the current   FITZ 80:21
  b. began to near the winning-post
                                    COKE 57:14
  simply messing about in b.   GRAH 92:17
bob: red, robin comes b.   WOODS 231:7
Boche: A well-killed B.   READ 178:10
bodies: b. high at Austerlitz   SAND 189:17
  b. no sensible man directly
                                    MACM 143:20
  Did but our b. touch   YEATS 235:12
  their b. but not their souls   GIBR 90:5
  with well-developed b.   FORS 83:2
bodily: That I loved b.   YEATS 235:12
body: b. but sorrow develops   PROU 176:7
  b. from the dominion   GOLD 91:11
  b. I would throw it out   BECK 21:13
  b.'s precious earth   MAS 148:11
  inherits my b. and your brains
                                    SHAW 195:25
  mind as it is for the b.   HUXL 108:14
  My b. of a sudden blazed   YEATS 235:17
  O b. swayed to music   YEATS 234:8
  Sick in soul and b. both   HODG 103:14
  Still carry his b. around   FRY 86:25
  The b. dies   STEV 208:13
  truly have none in the b.   LAWR 132:17
  who had one b. and one heart
                                    DOUG 68:11
  with Africa than my own b.
                                    ORTON 163:22
Bog: upon the B. of Allen   JOYCE 115:6
Bognor: Bugger B.   GEOR 89:8
bogus: authentic mammon than a b. god
                                    MACN 144:4
bohreens: Bells are booming down the b.
                                    BETJ 32:6
boiled: B. beef and carrots   COLL 58:3
  parliamentarian is a bag of b. sweets
                                    CRIT 63:4
boko: Bertha's got a bang on the b.
                                    MARS 147:12
bold: He b. as a hawk, she soft
                                    THUR 216:24
  with one b. stare   ELIOT 77:1
boldly: b. go where no man has
                                    RODD 182:2
Bolshevism: It is B. run mad   SNOW 204:3
bolt: your thumb: like the b.   REED 179:1
bomb: Ban the b.   ANON 5:14
  b. them back into the Stone
                                    LEMAY 134:1
  defence against the atom b.   ANON 5:16
bombed: I'm glad we've been b.   ELIZ 77:9

bombed (*cont.*):
protect him from being b.   BALD 17:7
bomber: b. will always get through
        BALD 17:7
bombing: b. begins in five minutes
        REAG 178:14
bombs: Come, friendly b.   BETJ 31:1
bon: *b. critique est celui qui*   FRAN 84:16
Bonar Law: Unknown Prime Minister [B.]
        ASQ 11:12
bond: b. between two people   RILKE 181:5
bonds: have slipped the surly b.
        MAGEE 145:2
bone: b. to pick with graveyards
        BECK 21:12
He knows death to the b.   YEATS 235:11
rag and a b. and a hank   KIPL 127:18
rag and b. shop   YEATS 233:8
take the muscle from b.   ELIOT 75:2
boneless: years to see the b. wonder
        CHUR 54:4
bones: dead men lost their b.   ELIOT 76:20
bonfire: The b. of the vanities   WOLFE 231:4
bonheur: *b. seul est salutaire pour*
        PROU 176:7
bonhomie: Overcame his natural *b.*
        BENT 29:3
bonjour: *B. tristesse*   ELUA 77:14
bonkers: will be stark, raving b.   HAIL 95:5
bonnet: In her latest new b.   DOBS 68:2
bonnie: b. boat, like a bird   BOUL 37:3
bonny: Belbroughton Road is b.   BETJ 32:5
book: A b. which people praise
        TWAIN 219:11
any b. should be banned   WEST 225:25
bad b. without showing   AUDEN 13:18
b. becomes a substitute   BURG 42:12
b. is as much of a labour   HUXL 109:6
b. known to him by heart   WOOLF 231:10
b. until I laid it down   MARX 147:17
b. was published I carried   BARR 19:16
b. which somehow sold   BOOR 36:6
b. you would have lying   GRIF 94:6
do not throw this b. about   BELL 24:4
encouragement this b.   WOD 230:11
Hers of the B., the tripled   QUIL 177:3
knocks me out is a b.   SAL 188:25
read one b. in my life   MITF 154:17
take down this b.   YEATS 232:7
when he can read the b.   BEVAN 33:3
write a b. about it   BRAB 37:20
book-keeping: inventor of double-entry b.
        MULL 157:13
books: b. are alike in that they   HEM 100:10
B. are a load of crap   LARK 131:4
b. are either dreams   LOW 139:20
b. are undeservedly forgotten
        AUDEN 13:17
B. are where things   BARN 18:20
b. at the British Museum   BUTL 44:3
b. can not be killed   ROOS 183:13
B. do furnish a room   POW 174:18
B. from Boots' and country   BETJ 32:9
B. make sense of life   BARN 18:20
B. say: she did this   BARN 18:20
b. written by the warders   SHAW 199:11
don't have to know about b.
        LUML 140:15
Few b. today are forgivable
        LAING 129:10
God has written all the b.   BUTL 43:25
Have you read any good b.   MURD 157:19
his b. were read   BELL 25:16
I do not like b.   BUTL 44:3

books (*cont.*):
Long b., when read   FORS 83:11
my b. had been any worse   CHAN 49:6
only b. that influence   FORS 84:8
read b. of quotations   CHUR 55:11
study of mankind is b.   HUXL 108:13
The more b. we read   CONN 59:7
write it in the b. of law   JOHN 114:8
boom: groaning as the guns b.   CHES 51:17
booming: Bells are b. down the bohreens
        BETJ 32:6
boon: b. and a blessing to men   ANON 8:21
boot: imagine a b. stamping   ORW 164:26
The b. in the face, the brute
        PLATH 172:4
bootboy: b. at Claridges   WOOLF 231:11
Booth: B. died blind and still   LIND 137:13
B. led boldly   LIND 137:12
boots: before truth has got his b.   CALL 45:2
Books from B.' and country   BETJ 32:9
b. and made-up bow ties   SHAR 195:9
b.—movin' up and down again
        KIPL 124:13
He carries his heart in his b.
        HERB 101:20
Hes a gentleman: look at his b.
        SHAW 199:17
school without any b.   BULM 42:6
Their b. are heavy on the floor
        AUDEN 14:14
their heart is in their b.   CHES 50:17
These b. are made for walkin'   HAZL 99:6
booze: with b. until he's fifty   FAUL 78:14
boozes: man who "b." by the company
        BURT 42:17
Border: Night Mail crossing the B.
        AUDEN 14:21
borders: I have come to the b. of sleep
        THOM 214:17
bore: A b. is a man   TAYL 212:9
b. him in the right way   MAUG 149:11
B., n. A person who talks   BIER 33:27
b. one another seems   MENC 151:1
[Israel Zangwill] is an old b.   TREE 217:11
twelve Americans is a b.   UPD 220:14
was not only a b.   MUGG 157:11
bored: And said,'I feel a little b.'   CHES 52:2
because I know that I am b.   JOAD 113:20
begins there is that b. look   MILL 152:9
Ever to confess you're b.   BERR 30:17
he b. for England   MUGG 157:11
virtue of the b.   WAUGH 223:6
world is quickly b.   MAUG 149:15
boredom: B. is therefore a vital
        RUSS 186:10
b. on a large scale   INGE 110:11
Life is first b., then fear   LARK 131:5
Borgias: B. they had warfare   WELL 224:11
last night with the B.   BEER 22:18
boring: b. about somebody else's
        HUXL 109:3
Life, friends, is b.   BERR 30:16
Somebody's b. me   THOM 213:22
born: already b. before my lips
        MAND 145:19
Art is b. of humiliation   AUDEN 15:15
A star is b.   PARK 169:8
A terrible beauty is b.   YEATS 233:9
be b. is the best for man   AUDEN 14:8
been b. to set it right   STR 210:7
b. an Englishman and remained
        BEHAN 23:20
b. falls into a dream like   CONR 59:24
b. in 1896 and my parents   ACK 1:10

born (*cont.*):
b. in a house seventy years
        JEANS 112:20
B. of the sun they travelled   SPEN 205:16
B. on the fourth of July   COHAN 57:13
b. with a gift of laughter   SAB 187:13
b. with your legs apart   ORTON 164:6
British Bourgeoise Is not b.   SITW 201:17
England because you were b.
        SHAW 196:28
ever b. in a conference   FITZ 80:14
For we are b. in other's pain
        THOM 215:1
human beings are b. free   ANON 9:1
I am not yet b.; O fill me   MACN 144:18
I've been b., and once   ELIOT 76:9
lad that's b. to be king   BOUL 37:3
One is not b. a woman   DE B 65:12
seeing he had been b.   POUND 174:2
that he was b. in Australia   SHAW 197:8
Then surely I was b.   CHES 52:10
They are b. three thousand   DEL 67:1
towards Bethlehem to be b.
        YEATS 233:13
We all are b. mad   BECK 21:23
we extol thee who are b.   BENS 28:21
we were b. to run   SPR 206:15
borne: b. back ceaselessly   FITZ 80:21
It is b. in upon me I am   HARE 98:7
borrow: well enough to b. from   BIER 33:19
boshaft: *aber b. ist er nicht*   EINS 72:13
bosom: She has no b. and no behind
        SMITH 203:17
Thou hast not felt thy b. keep   DAV 65:4
boss: b. there is always   MARQ 147:5
bossing: shorter hours and nobody b.
        ORW 165:3
Boston: And this is good old B.   BOSS 36:12
botanize: Hardy went down to b.
        CHES 52:6
botch: I am a sundial, and I make a b.
        BELL 25:23
bother: I never b. with people I hate
        HART 98:18
long words B. me   MILNE 153:16
bothered: Bewitched, b. and bewildered
        HART 98:16
Botticelli: B. were alive today he'd
        UST 220:19
bottle: chair or a hot-water b.
        SMITH 203:20
bottles: English have hot-water b.   MIKES 151:15
put new wine into old b.   ATTL 12:8
bottom: at the b. of our garden   FYL 87:18
forgotten man at the b.   ROOS 182:21
The sun like a Bishop's b.   ASQ 11:20
Which will reach the b. first   GRAH 92:13
bottoms: b. of my trousers rolled
        ELIOT 75:19
b. on seats   HALL 95:11
bough: Petals on a wet, black b.
        POUND 174:1
with bloom along the b.   HOUS 106:9
boughs: easy under the apple b.
        THOM 213:17
than ever on orchard b.   DRIN 70:4
bought: when I've just b. some   BREC 39:7
boum: 'B.' is the sound as far   FORS 83:21

bound: And b. for the same bourn
HOUS 107:5
bounds: wider shall thy b. be set
BENS 28:21
bouquet: b. is better than the taste
POTT 173:17
bouquets: broken Anne of gathering b.
FROST 86:16
bourgeois: b. always bounces up
CONN 59:5
'B.,' I observed
HOPE 104:16
b. origin goes through
ORW 164:30
b. prefers comfort to pleasure
HESSE 102:4
How beastly the b.
LAWR 132:15
small-town b. at heart
NAB 158:11
bourgeoise: The British B.
SITW 201:17
bourgeoisie: b. have spoken of themselves
WAUGH 222:22
The b. in the long run
TROT 218:4
The discreet charm of the b.
BUÑ 42:7
bourn: And bound for the same b.
HOUS 107:5
bourne: b. from which no hollingsworth
MORT 156:16
bourreaux: elles respectent leurs b.
SART 191:12
boutique: hour ago from this very b.
CHAP 49:13
Bovril: B. . . . Prevents that
HARR 98:15
made into B. when she dies
ASQ 11:14
bow: elastic-sided boots and made-up b.
ties
SHAR 195:9
What of the b.
DOYLE 70:2
bowed: B. by the weight of centuries
MARK 146:14
bowels: Have molten b.; your vision
BOTT 36:14
Till her b. are in heat
YEATS 233:1
bower: The b. we shrined to Tennyson
HARDY 97:1
bowl: b. aloft and intoned
JOYCE 116:1
b. with atrabilious
HUXL 109:1
Life is just a b. of cherries
BROWN 41:12
bowler: I am the b. and the ball
LANG 130:4
bows: b. from which your children
GIBR 90:5
box: documents I have to have a b.
HOME 104:8
with cash at the b. office
HALL 95:11
boxes: Little b. all the same
REYN 179:17
boy: A b. brought the white sheet
LORCA 139:11
And I were the only b.
GREY 94:4
Being read to by a b.
ELIOT 73:11
b. [Edward VIII] will ruin
GEOR 89:5
b. is that the Chattanooga
GORD 92:4
b. may become President
STEV 208:21
B. Scout demonstrating
LEVIN 136:9
b. somebody ought to have
CAMP 45:5
But what can a poor b. do
JAGG 111:9
electric train set any b.
WELL 224:10
fifteen-year-old b.
ROTH 185:10
I am the Yankee Doodle B.
COHAN 57:13
Mad about the b.
COW 62:3
misfortunes can befall a b.
MAUG 150:3
O are you the b.
CAUS 47:17
parent who could see his b.
LEAC 133:5
seat sat the journeying b.
HARDY 97:8
thing of beauty and a b.
ROWL 185:14
you like your blueeyed b.
CUMM 63:16
You silly twisted b.
MILL 152:12

boyhood: In the lost b. of Judas
AE 2:18
boys: b. are not going
ROOS 183:7
b. are still there
BAR 20:8
b. in the back rooms
BEAV 21:5
b. in the back room will
LOES 138:18
b. of the old Brigade
WEAT 223:20
B. shout
DAV 65:2
b. were whooping
SERV 194:23
Not in the hands of b.
OWEN 166:9
send American b. 9 or 10
JOHN 114:13
The lightfoot b. are laid
HOUS 107:7
Till the b. come Home
FORD 82:20
were b. when I was a boy
BELL 25:26
brace: b. ourselves to our duty CHUR 54:11
braces: powerful liquid which rots b.
MORT 156:15
Bradford: hat on a B. millionaire
ELIOT 77:1
Bradshaw: The vocabulary of 'B.'
DOYLE 69:30
brain: Bear of Very Little B.
MILNE 153:16
b. attic stocked with all
DOYLE 69:5
B., n. An apparatus
BIER 34:1
dry b. in a dry season
ELIOT 73:13
My b.? It's my second favourite
ALLEN 4:7
through which the b. explores
DOUG 68:12
why did He give us a b.
LUCE 140:14
brains: b. of a Minerva
BARR 19:26
gentleman said a girl with b.
LOOS 139:3
inherits my body and your b.
SHAW 195:25
rifle and blow out your b.
KIPL 123:12
sometimes his b. go to his head
ASQ 11:17
What good are b. to a man
WOD 230:4
with no b. at all
HERB 101:18
brain-washing: pre-empted it is called b.
GREER 93:21
branches: black b. up a snow-white
FROST 86:5
brandy: B. for the Parson
KIPL 126:6
b. of the damned
SHAW 197:28
brass: facts when you come to b. tacks
ELIOT 76:9
brassière: Art is not a b.
BARN 18:19
b. is the French
BARN 18:19
brave: All that delirium of the b.
YEATS 234:15
b. causes left
OSB 165:19
heard her cry, 'you are b.'
GRAH 92:15
Then I was clean and b.
HOUS 106:13
braw: b. bricht moonlicht nicht
MORR 156:8
bread: b. and butter that feels MACK 143:1
cursed the b.
ROB 181:13
don't bother about the b.
MILNE 153:15
In eating B. he made no Crumbs
BELL 24:21
The holy b., the food unpriced
MAS 148:12
To eat dusty b.
BOGAN 35:11
your b. and your butter
KIPL 124:18
break: b. a man's spirit is devil's
SHAW 196:5
b. the bloody glass you
MACN 144:9
Crack and sometimes b.
ELIOT 74:6
Never give a sucker an even b.
FIEL 79:11
then I b. them right away
SAL 189:1
To b. earth's sleep at all
OWEN 166:12
Breakages: B., Limited, the biggest
SHAW 195:13

breakdown: approaching nervous b.
RUSS 186:11
Madness need not be all b. LAING 129:13
breakers: like b. cliffward leaping
CRANE 62:14
breakfalls: rolls and throws and b.
REED 179:2
breakfast: embarrassment and b.
BARN 18:17
teatime, clears her b.
ELIOT 76:18
That B., Dinner, Lunch, and Tea
BELL 24:13
want Michael Angelo for b.
TWAIN 219:19
breakfast-time: period in matrimony is b.
HERB 101:25
breaking: You're b. my heart
BERN 30:9
breaks: be there when it b.
CAMP 45:8
Light b. where no sun shines
THOM 213:21
break-through: It may also be b.
LAING 129:13
breast: helpless b. upon his breast
YEATS 234:21
laughed upon his b. to think
YEATS 235:12
breastless: And b. creatures underground
ELIOT 75:8
breasts: b. all perfume yes
JOYCE 116:14
Twye was soaping her b.
EWART 78:2
with wrinkled female b.
ELIOT 76:24
breath: B.'s a ware that will not keep
HOUS 106:10
Out with your own b.
SIMM 201:3
breathless: B., we flung us
BROO 39:18
Bredon: In summertime on B. HOUS 106:14
'Tis Summer Time on B.
KING 122:12
breed: it's a marvel they can b.
LAWR 131:18
breeding: b. consists in concealing
TWAIN 219:27
Burgundy without any b.
THUR 216:20
cruellest month, b.
ELIOT 76:13
breeds: Chaos often b. life
ADAMS 2:3
Or lesser b. without the Law KIPL 126:11
breeze: And quivers in the sunny b.
GREN 94:3
comes forth in every b.
DAV 65:4
brevity: B. is the soul of lingerie
PARK 169:5
brew: has the b. that is true
PAN 167:6
bribe: b. or twist
WOLFE 230:24
b. to make a housekeeper
WILD 227:3
bribes: How many b. he had taken
BENT 28:23
bricht: It's a braw b. moonlicht
MORR 156:8
brick: b. without hitting
ORW 164:31
paved with yellow b.
BAUM 20:12
They threw it a b. at a time
HARG 98:10
brickbats: his backyard with b.
TWAIN 219:24
bricks: That carries the b. to Lewley
BETJ 32:7
bride: all jealousy to the b.
BARR 19:1
Can ser' him for a b.
MACD 142:1
My b. to be he murmered
ASHF 11:4
Never the blushing b.
LEIGH 134:11
Brideshead: B. revisited
WAUGH 222:18
bridesmaid: Why am I always the b.
LEIGH 134:11
bridge: Champagne, and B.
BELL 25:19

bridge (cont.):
Come shooting through the b.
                                        BETJ 31:18
might be going a b. too far   BROW 41:14
See her on the b. at midnight   ANON 8:8
bridges: build b. and throw railroads
                                        BROUN 41:6
poor to sleep under b.   FRAN 84:15
brief: end of a b. episode   MERC 151:8
briefest: b. statement imaginable
                                        KAEL 117:4
brigade: boys of the old B.   WEAT 223:20
B. of Guards   MACM 143:20
fire b. and the fire   CHUR 54:3
brigand: I am a b.: I live by robbing
                                        SHAW 197:27
brigands: b. demand your money or
                                        BUTL 43:13
Briggs: Matilda B. . . . was a ship
                                        DOYLE 69:7
bright: Always merry and b.   WIMP 229:17
B.'s disease and he has   PER 170:3
brightness: Leaking the b. away
                                        SPEN 205:14
brilliance: b. is needed in the law
                                        MORT 156:11
brilliant: far less b. pen than mine
                                        BEER 23:4
sound like a b. drawing-room DE VR 67:5
The dullard's envy of b.   BEER 23:8
brim: b. the bowl with atrabilious
                                        HUXL 109:1
bring: difficult is it to b. it home
                                        DOYLE 69:4
'Tis the courage you b.   WALP 222:9
bringing: B. the cheque and the postal
                                        AUDEN 14:21
b. up a young and inexperienced
                                        JER 113:13
brings: he b. down the whip   LESS 135:27
brink: We walked to the b.   DULL 70:10
brinkmanship: boasting of his b.
                                        STEV 209:1
Britain: Battle of B. is about to begin
                                        CHUR 54:11
B. a fit country for heroes   LLOY 138:13
B. as an independent European
                                        GAIT 88:1
B. has lost an empire   ACH 1:8
B. needs is a new social   CALL 45:15
B. will be honoured   HARL 98:11
B. would fight on alone   CHUR 53:13
I'm backing B.   ANON 6:26
Britannia: you've shouted 'Rule B.'
                                        KIPL 122:18
British: B. have the distinction   ATTL 12:8
B. nation is unique   CHUR 54:13
B. people have taken   CHUR 53:8
I would rather be B. than just   PAIS 167:5
majority of B. workmen   ZIN 236:14
No sex please— we're B.   MARR 147:11
The B. are coming   WELL 224:9
those who aren't B.   BARN 18:17
We are B., thank God   MONT 155:6
you B. soldier   KIPL 123:13
you broke a B. square   KIPL 123:8
Britishers: Which the B. won't wear
                                        COW 62:4
British Museum: at the B. and at Mudie's
                                        BUTL 44:3
B. had lost   GERS 89:13
I found [the B.]   BEER 22:20
Britons: B. were only natives   SELL 194:9
we B. alone use 'Might'   WAUGH 223:16

broad: B. of Church   BETJ 31:17
By brooks too b. for leaping   HOUS 107:7
She's the B. and I'm the High
                                        SPR 206:14
broadcasters: important to be left to the b.
                                        BENN 27:13
broadcasting: B. is really too important
                                        BENN 27:13
broadened: has b. into a brotherhood
                                        JOHN 114:9
Broadway: Give my regards to B.
                                        COHAN 57:11
sinners on this part of B.   RUNY 186:3
broccoli: It's b., dear   WHITE 226:1
broke: If it ain't b., don't   LANCE 130:1
broken: baying for b. glass   WAUGH 222:19
b. Anne of gathering bouquets
                                        FROST 86:16
b. by their passing feet   YEATS 234:10
b. the lock and splintered   AUDEN 14:14
Don't tell me peace has b.   BREC 39:7
He liked the Sound of B. Glass BELL 25:9
mould. Can it be b.   JENK 113:3
peace has been b. anywhere   ROOS 183:5
whose tongues were all b.   DYLAN 71:6
broken-hearted: b. woman tends the
grave   HAYES 99:5
broker: b. is a man who takes
                                        WOOL 231:17
Bronx: B. is up but the Battery's
                                        COMD 58:7
bronze: B. cloud   FREE 85:3
Stone, b., stone   ELIOT 76:12
brook: b. was troubled for new
                                        MAS 148:15
Fish say, in the Eternal B.   BROO 40:8
brooks: By b. too broad for leaping
                                        HOUS 107:7
The b. were frozen   AUDEN 12:20
brothels: bars and b. of Westminster
                                        LIV 138:3
brother: be the white man's b.   KING 121:14
BIG B. IS WATCHING YOU   ORW 164:20
B. can you spare a dime   HARB 96:12
B., thy tail hangs down behind
                                        KIPL 125:5
I am the darker b.   HUGH 108:1
My B., good morning   BELL 26:8
stick more close than a b.   KIPL 126:16
Strong b. in God and last   BELL 25:13
brotherhood: b. of man is evoked
                                        LAING 129:12
has broadened into a b.   JOHN 114:9
brother-in-law: man's brother, not his b.
                                        KING 121:14
brotherly: Switzerland they had b. love
                                        WELL 224:11
brothers: together as b. or perish
                                        KING 122:6
brought: government should be b. down
                                        MACM 143:17
great party is not to be b.   HAIL 95:4
He b. death into the world   TWAIN 219:29
brow: hope to meet my Maker b. to b.
                                        CORN 61:6
Slowly her white b. among   FREE 85:3
brown: b. fog of a winter dawn
                                        ELIOT 76:17
old b. hills   MAS 148:19
quick b. fox jumps over   ANON 8:5
strong b. god   ELIOT 74:7
Browning: Hang it all, Robert B.
                                        POUND 173:27

Browning (cont.):
safety-catch of my B.   JOHST 114:19
brows: The pallor of girls' b.   OWEN 166:9
browsing: b. and sluicing and cheery
                                        WOD 230:19
Bruce: would have made Adam and B.
                                        BRY 41:16
Bruckner: [by B.]   BEEC 22:3
bruit: Dont meurt le b. parmi le vent
                                        APOL 9:23
brush: And never b. their hair   BELL 24:6
brutal: grown b. from the fare YEATS 232:5
brute: b. and blackguard made
                                        HOUS 105:14
B. heart of a brute like you   PLATH 172:4
should be treated as a b.   EDW 72:6
brutes: Exterminate all the b.   CONR 59:21
bubbles: I'm forever blowing b.
                                        KENB 118:17
buck: A bigger bang for a b.   ANON 5:19
day they pass the b.   AYRES 16:5
The b. stops here   TRUM 218:13
bucket: past is a b. of ashes   SAND 189:15
Buckingham: They're changing guard
at B.   MILNE 153:5
Buffalo Bill: B.'s defunct   CUMM 63:16
bugger: B. Bognor   GEOR 89:8
buggers: b. can't be choosers
                                        BOWRA 37:17
bugler: Is to hear the b. call   BERL 29:16
bugles: are the b. blowin'   KIPL 123:3
Blow out, you b.   BROO 40:3
b. calling for them from   OWEN 166:9
bugs: lugage rack and new b.   WILL 227:8
build: And so easy to b.   IBSEN 109:19
b. from the bottom up   ROOS 182:21
b. their first buildings   WRIG 231:22
building: it's a very old b.   OSB 165:11
built: Before I b. a wall I'd   FROST 86:11
frocks are b. in Paris   SAKI 188:12
It is not what they b.   FENT 79:1
bull: b. by both horns he kissed ASHF 11:4
b. moose and you can use   ROOS 184:7
See an old unhappy b.   HODG 103:14
bullet: b. in thousand kills   SPEN 205:19
b. may just as well have   COLL 58:6
Faster than a speeding b.   ANON 6:8
put a b. through his head   ROB 181:13
bullets: With b. made of platinum
                                        BELL 24:8
bullshit: The rest is b. and you
                                        SCOR 193:15
bum: Indicat Motorem B.   GODL 91:5
instead of a b.   SCH 193:6
bumpy: it's going to be a b.   MANK 146:2
bums: b. on seats   HALL 95:11
bunch: b. of the boys were whooping
                                        SERV 194:23
none better left on the b.   BUTL 43:21
bungler: arts of peace Man is a b.
                                        SHAW 197:32
bunk: History is more or less b.
                                        FORD 82:18
bunny: I am a b. rabbit   AYRES 16:5
buns: bears might come with b.   ISH 110:22
Bunter: Shut up, B.   RICH 180:16
burden: b. of responsibility   EDW 72:8
I lay down my b.   EDW 72:8
sometimes break, under the b. ELIOT 74:6
Take up the White Man's b.   KIPL 127:19
bureaucrats: Guidelines for b.   BOREN 36:7
Burgundies: B. is that I hate them
                                        AMIS 4:16

burgundy: B. without any breeding
                                            THUR 216:20
burial: any part, in its b.   MACM 143:15
buried: B. beneath some snow-deep Alps
                                            ELIOT 73:10
Burlington: I'm B. Bertie   HARG 98:9
Burma: B. girl a-settin'   KIPL 123:13
burn: age should b. and rave THOM 213:13
  another Troy for her to b.   YEATS 232:11
  B., baby, burn   ANON 5:21
  Hurry! We b.   DAY-L 65:8
burned: Matilda, and the House, were B.
                                            BELL 24:16
burning: A smell of b. fills   BELL 26:6
  b. of the leaves   BINY 34:16
  b. roof and tower   YEATS 235:1
  hipsters b. for the ancient   GINS 90:15
  Is Paris b.   HITL 103:7
  Keep the Home-fires b.   FORD 82:20
  Lady's not for B.   FRY 86:25
burnish'd: b. by Aldershot sun BETJ 32:1
burnished: like a b. throne   ELIOT 76:18
Burns: it's a poem by Robert B. SAL 189:4
burnt: ash the b. roses leave   ELIOT 74:18
  b. at the stake as witches   SMITH 203:19
  got myself b. or hanged   JER 113:11
burnt-out: The b. ends of smoky days
                                            ELIOT 75:20
burst: suddenly b. out singing SASS 192:6
bursting: round me like a b. sea
                                            THOM 215:18
Burton: Or why was B. built on Trent
                                            HOUS 107:8
bury: b. my body in Sussex grass
                                            BENÉT 27:8
  B. my heart at Wounded Knee
                                            BENÉT 27:8
  The physician can b.   WRIG 231:22
  want one to b. my sister   MITF 154:13
  We will b. you   KHR 121:7
bus: Can it be a Motor B.   GODL 91:5
  he missed the b.   CHAM 48:16
  I'm not even a b., I'm a tram HARE 98:7
  She tumbled off a b.   GRAH 92:11
  stepping in front of a b.   OSB 165:19
buses: more time on the b.   STR 210:17
business: American people is b. COOL 60:15
  any other decent b. man   LEWIS 137:4
  B. carried on as usual   CHUR 53:8
  b. is the most fascinating   WARH 222:11
  b. without really trying   MEAD 150:10
  had attended b. college   ADE 2:9
  It is the b. of the wealthy man BELL 25:7
  Liberty is always unfinished b.
                                            ANON 7:15
  making everything his b.   SOLZ 204:4
  Murder is a serious b.   ILES 110:5
  no b. like show business   BERL 30:1
  That's no b. That's social   BRAC 38:1
  The growth of a large b.   ROCK 181:17
  we can do b. together   THAT 213:4
  woman's b. to get married   SHAW 197:26
businessman: He's a b.   PUZO 176:10
businessmen: My message to the b.
                                            CURR 64:6
bust: Uncorseted, her friendly b. ELIOT 75:9
bustin': June is b. out all over HAMM 95:15
busy: But I am too b. thinking SITW 201:12
  Little man, you've had a b. day
                                            SIGL 200:16
but: And If and Perhaps and B. ELIOT 74:1
butcher: b. but his mother was ASHF 11:1
  Hog B. for the World   SAND 189:13

butchers: become policemen or b.
                                            CONN 58:15
butler: on the b.'s upper slopes
                                            WOD 230:22
  The b. did it   ANON 5:22
butlers: In my opinion, B. ought
                                            BELL 24:17
butter: B., eh   MILNE 153:10
  Can you tell Stork from b.   ANON 5:25
  Could we have some b.   MILNE 153:9
  like a little bit of b.   MILNE 153:11
  rather have b. or guns   GOER 91:7
  We can manage without b.   GOEB 91:6
butterfly: Float like a b.   ALI 3:9
  The b. upon the road   KIPL 124:7
buttocks: The gorgeous b. of the ape
                                            HUXL 108:21
button: By each b., hook, and lace
                                            LOW 139:18
  job of sewing on a b.   BROUN 41:6
buttons: b. off an' cut his stripes
                                            KIPL 123:4
butty: He's an oul' b. o' mine
                                            O'CAS 162:12
buy: b. a single vote more   KENN 119:2
  b. back my introduction   PER 170:4
  b. it like an honest man   NORT 161:12
  Stop me and b. one   RODD 182:1
  won't you b. me a Mercedes JOPL 115:3
buys: public b. its opinions   BUTL 43:29
buzz: B.! Buzz! Buzz   MILNE 153:13
by: B. and b. God caught   MCC 141:15
bye: B. bye blackbird   DIXON 67:17
Byron: B.!—he would be all forgotten
                                            BEER 23:19
Byronic: think all poets were B. COPE 60:20
Byzantium: And the Soldan of B.
                                            CHES 51:16
  To the holy city of B.   YEATS 234:7

C

cab: Get me a c.   BENC 26:23
cabbage: c. with a college education
                                            TWAIN 219:30
cabin: small c. build there   YEATS 232:9
Cabinet: another to mislead the C.
                                            ASQ 11:10
  C. ministers are educated   BENN 28:18
Cabots: Lowells talk to the C.   BOSS 36:12
cad: Flopshus C., an Outrageous
                                            KIPL 127:13
cadence: reverent c. and subtle psalm
                                            AUDEN 15:11
Cadogan: One-eighty-nine C. Square
                                            BETJ 32:9
Caesar: Our master C. is in the tent
                                            YEATS 233:7
Caesars: worship the C. and Napoleons
                                            HUXL 108:16
café: heart in ev'ry street c.   HAMM 95:16
cage: He keeps a lady in a c.   CHES 50:16
  natural to us than a c.   SHAW 196:21
  We cannot c. the minute   MACN 144:5
caged: I know why the c. bird sings
                                            ANG 5:6
cake: had soaked a morsel of c.
                                            PROU 175:17
  peel picked out of a c.   RAL 177:12
calamities: C. are of two kinds BIER 34:2
calamity: Oh, c.   HARE 98:8

calculating: Party is a desiccated c.
  machine   BEVAN 32:15
calculations: C. that look but casual
                                            YEATS 233:5
calf: c. to share the enthusiasm
                                            SAKI 188:10
  The lion and the c. shall   ALLEN 3:17
Caliban: C. casts out Ariel   POUND 174:5
California: C. is a fine place to live
                                            ALLEN 3:11
  From C. to the New York Island
                                            GUTH 95:1
call: All, is Labour's C.   JAY 112:18
  C. me Lady Hamilton   RIC 180:12
  C. me madam   LIND 137:11
  C. no man foe, but never   BENS 28:22
  c. of the running tide   MAS 148:17
  do you c. that a rose   AYCK 16:1
  Dunno what to c. him   STAN 207:2
  Let's c. the whole thing off   GERS 89:16
  May I c. you 338   COW 62:1
  The c. of the wild   LOND 138:21
  When you c. me that   WIST 229:18
  Whitehall as 'C. Me God'   SAMP 189:7
  Work is the c.   MORR 156:6
called: if I c. the wrong number
                                            THUR 216:21
calling: Followed their mercenary c.
                                            HOUS 106:3
  Germany c.! Germany calling
                                            JOYCE 116:16
callisthenics: simply c. with words
                                            PARK 168:22
callous: the word 'c.' engraved
                                            SELL 194:12
calls: If anybody c.   BENT 29:1
calm: c. on the lap of the Line   KIPL 124:9
  there we sit in peaceful c.   HUXL 109:2
calves: peculiarly susceptible to c.
                                            HUXL 109:8
Camberley: Into nine-o'clock C. BETJ 32:3
Cambridge: C. ladies who live in furnished
                                            CUMM 63:17
  C. theatre were eating   RAPH 177:16
  dons from C. or junior   AMIS 4:16
  For C. people rarely smile   BROO 40:13
  gently back at Oxford or C.   BEER 22:23
Cambridgeshire: And C., of all England
                                            BROO 40:13
came: I c. through and I shall   MAC 141:1
cameelious: C. hump   KIPL 125:10
camel: c. is a horse designed   ANON 5:23
  Take my c., dear   MAC 141:2
  The c. has a single hump   NASH 158:20
  The C.'s hump is an ugly lump
                                            KIPL 125:9
camera: c. makes everyone a tourist
                                            SONT 204:14
  I am a c. with its shutter   ISH 111:1
campaigning: years organizing and c.
                                            BROD 39:12
can: C. I do you now, sir   KAV 118:11
  C. you tell Stork from butter   ANON 5:25
  Gizza job . . . . I c. do that   BLEA 34:24
  He who c., does   SHAW 198:14
  Pass me the c., lad   HOUS 105:12
  talent which does what it c.   BAR 18:13
Canadian: [Definition of a C.:] BERT 30:19
canal: swimming along in the old c.
                                            BETJ 32:7
Canalettos: Then the C. go   MACM 144:3
cancer: c. of human history   SONT 205:1
  Obscene as c., bitter   OWEN 166:10

chase (cont.):
Still with unhurrying c.   THOM 215:11
chasing: c. Americans out   TWAIN 219:24
he was always c. Rimbauds   PARK 168:2
chasm: There exists a great c.   BERL 30:4
chassis: worl's in a state o' c.   O'CAS 162:13
chaste: like a c. whore   MUGG 157:9
men ask, Are Barmaids C.   MAS 148:10
chastity: C.—the most unnatural
  HUXL 108:17
chat: [Trotsky] and had a c.   ROG 182:13
Chattanooga: Pardon me boy is that the C.
  GORD 92:4
Chatterley: Between the end of the C. ban
  LARK 130:14
test this book [Lady C.'s]   GRIF 94:6
cheap: how potent c. music is   COW 62:7
cheaper: c. seats clap your hands
  LENN 135:1
c. to do this than to keep   BUTL 43:29
cheat: so monosyllabic as to c.   FRY 87:8
The sweet c. gone   DE L 66:11
cheating: games without actually c.
  POTT 173:20
period of c. between   BIER 34:12
Checkers: named it C. And you know
  NIXON 161:7
cheeks: A girl whose c. are covered
  NASH 159:17
cheer: C. up, curly you'll soon
  WIMP 229:17
C. up! the worst is yet to come
  JOHN 114:17
cheerful: so c. as keeps me going
  KAV 118:15
cheeriness: Oh! Chintzy, Chintzy c.
  BETJ 31:14
cheering: had no need for c. dreams
  CHUR 55:18
with the great cause of c.   BENN 28:5
cheerio: it s c.   MARQ 147:3
cheers: 3 C. for Pooh   MILNE 154:4
Two c. for Democracy   FORS 84:6
cheese: eggs, apples, and c.   KIPL 124:18
has 246 varieties of c.   DE G 66:1
like some valley c.   AUDEN 13:14
no such thing as a bad c.   FAD 78:5
cheesed: humanity soon had me c. off
  BENN 28:1
chefs-d'œuvre: au milieu des c.   FRAN 84:16
Chekhov: C. saw in our failure   PRIT 175:13
chemistry: c. and machinery all
  SHAW 197:31
cheque: Bringing the c. and the postal
  AUDEN 14:21
statement is like a c.   POUND 173:22
cherished: My no longer c.   MILL 152:1
cheroot: whackin' white c.   KIPL 123:14
cherries: Life is just a bowl of c.
  BROWN 41:12
cherry: as American as c. pie   BROWN 41:8
Loveliest of trees, the c. now   HOUS 106:9
Cheshire: cosmic C. cat   HUXL 109:16
chess-players: c. do   CHES 51:11
chest: c. to slip down   WOD 230:12
Chesterton: That dared attack my C.
  BELL 26:4
chestnut: showers betumble the c.
  HARDY 97:2
chew: fart and c. gum   JOHN 114:5
chewing: Was c. little bits of String
  BELL 24:11
chewing gum: so much c. for the eyes
  ANON 8:12

Chianti: are four bottles of C.   SHAF 195:4
chic: very c. for an atheist   RUSS 186:8
chicken: republic is like a c.   MITF 154:16
Some c.   CHUR 53:13
chickens: beside the white c.   WILL 228:1
chicks: have been a crowd of c.   AYRES 16:7
chief: The C. Defect of Henry King
  BELL 24:11
child: at the birth of his c.   ORTON 164:1
Become a C. on earth for me   BETJ 31:4
But God bless the c. that's   HOL 104:4
c. becomes an adult when   SZASZ 211:12
C.! do not throw this book   BELL 24:4
c. if I were a young Macaulay
  BARB 18:12
c. inherits my body   SHAW 195:25
c. of seven or eight years   BLUNT 35:5
c. take care that you strike   SHAW 198:18
Every time a c. says   BARR 19:8
find I am to have his c.   BURG 42:11
He has devoured the infant c.
  HOUS 105:10
I call you bad, my little c.   BELL 24:5
illegitimate c. of Karl Marx   ATTL 12:12
I speak like a c.   NAB 158:15
It's not fair to the c.   FROST 86:16
Proves the c. ephemeral   AUDEN 13:7
She was an aggravating c.   BELL 24:20
The nicest c. I ever knew   BELL 24:21
what it is like to be a c.   JARR 112:17
when I see a c.'s eyes gleam   BELL 24:22
wish to change in the c.   JUNG 117:1
Wretched C. expires   BELL 24:13
childbirth: Death and taxes and c.
  MITC 154:10
childhood: c., adolescence and
obsolescence   LINK 137:16
C. is not from birth   MILL 152:2
moment in c. when the door   GREE 93:19
what my lousy c. was   SAL 188:24
Where c. had strayed   AE 2:18
childish: puts away c. things   MILL 152:2
children: all our lives raising c.
  EDGAR 72:1
And c. listen   BERL 30:3
best understood by c.   STR 210:15
better reasons for having c.   RUSS 187:6
breeds contempt—and c.   TWAIN 219:26
By c. and tradesmen's bills   MACN 144:14
by c. to adults   SZASZ 211:15
c. ardent for some desperate
  OWEN 166:10
C. are dumb to say how   GRAV 93:8
C. are no longer children   JACK 111:3
C. aren't happy with   NASH 159:15
c. for signs of improvement   SCOT 194:4
C. have never been very   BALD 16:20
c. to be a credit to them   RUSS 187:3
c. to be always and forever   SAIN 187:18
c. will not know   LARK 130:11
C. with Hyacinth's temperament
  SAKI 188:22
disappointment to their c.   POW 174:19
except that c. are more troublesome
  SHAW 196:23
first class, and with c.   BENC 27:1
generally hate people and c.   CAMP 45:12
God's c. are not beautiful   LEB 133:18
Goodnight, c. . . . . everywhere
  MCC 141:20
hands of young c.   DYLAN 71:6
he reappears in your c.   CONN 59:5
I have seen c. starving   ROOS 183:3

children (cont.):
in the interest of the c.   SHAW 196:16
learn a lot from their c.   SPARK 205:5
little c. died in the streets   AUDEN 12:18
not much about having c.   LODGE 138:17
parents kept me from c.   SPEN 205:13
rich and the poor get c.   KAHN 117:10
sleepless c.'s hearts are glad   BETJ 31:4
teach their c. to speak it   SHAW 199:16
that c. produce adults   DE VR 67:7
that their c. are naïve   NASH 159:2
The labouring c. can look out
  CLEG 56:15
To beget c., nothing better   SART 191:5
violations committed by c.   BOWEN 37:10
way parents obey their c.   EDW 72:7
Your c. are not your children   GIBR 90:5
Chile: earthquake in C.   COCK 57:2
chills: Of c. and fever she died   RANS 177:14
chilly: although the room grows c.
  GRAH 92:12
Chimborazo: C., Cotopaxi   TURN 218:19
chime: c. of words tinkling   SMITH 203:16
chimes: c. ring out with a carol
  BOND 35:19
China: C. is not the powerful nation
  BRAD 38:10
On a slow boat to C.   LOES 138:19
Till C. and Africa meet   AUDEN 12:16
up like thunder outer C.   KIPL 123:13
your land armies in C.   MONT 155:5
Chinamen: With C., but not with me
  BELL 25:10
Chinese: C. said they would bury
  RUSS 186:8
The C. wouldn't dare   COW 62:4
chintzy: Oh! Chintzy, C. cheeriness
  BETJ 31:14
chips: C. with everything   WESK 225:7
chisel: That with a mallet or a c.
  YEATS 233:5
chivalry: nine-tenths of the law of c.
  SAY 192:9
chocolate: c. cream soldier   SHAW 195:17
choir: joined the c. invisible   CHAP 49:13
choirs: demented c. of wailing shells
  OWEN 166:9
choose: As those who c.   BROW 41:13
c. to be a plumber   EINS 73:4
c. to run for President   COOL 60:16
man is forced to c.   YEATS 235:18
must c. whether to be rich   ILL 110:6
They can not c.   THOM 214:17
choosers: buggers can't be c.   BOWRA 37:17
chooses: "boozes" by the company he c.
  BURT 42:19
choosing: c. between the disastrous
  GALB 88:5
chord: play the c. of C major   BEEC 22:6
chords: c. of summer sustained
  DAY-L 65:10
choreography: not c. to the audience
  SZELL 211:20
choristers: Of linen go the chanting c.
  LAWR 132:11
choses: les c. avec leurs noms   SART 191:9
Christ: And lo, C. walking on the water
  THOM 216:11
C. follows Dionysus   POUND 174:5
C. perish in torment   SHAW 199:31
C. was betrayed   AE 2:18
C. went deeper than I have   HARR 98:13
C. were coming this afternoon   CART 47:4

Christian: But the souls of C. peoples
CHES 51:20
C. ideal has not been tried   CHES 52:8
C. people who wouldn't   CURR 64:6
C. religion doubted   BUTL 44:5
C. teaching at the time   BENN 27:11
persuades me to be a C.   FRY 87:11
Christianity: A local thing called C.
HARDY 96:19
C. is the most materialistic   TEMP 212:13
C., of course ... but why   BALF 17:17
C. will go   LENN 135:2
from C. and journalism   BALF 17:17
Christlike: C. in my behaviour HUXL 108:8
Christmas: C.-morning bells   BETJ 31:4
C. was so much like another
THOM 213:11
Claus just before a hard C.   SMITH 202:2
I'm dreaming of a white C.   BERL 30:3
I'm walking backwards for C.
MILL 152:16
Let them know it's C. time   GELD 89:4
Christopher: C. Robin has fallen
MORT 156:13
C. Robin is saying his prayers
MILNE 153:12
C. Robin went down with Alice
MILNE 153:5
chuck: C. it, Smith   CHES 51:20
chumps: C. always make the best
WOD 230:4
c., you may be quite sure   BENN 28:15
church: Broad of C.   BETJ 31:17
C. can feed and sleep   ELIOT 75:6
c. he currently did not   AMIS 4:20
C. is an anvil which has   MACL 143:3
c. lit but without a congregation
WELLS 224:13
C. should go forward along   ROYD 185:18
c. stands near   YEATS 233:4
Come all to c., good people   HOUS 106:15
get me to the c. on time   LERN 135:18
he goes to c. as he goes   BLYT 35:7
make up for your sins in c.   SCOR 193:15
Stands the C. clock   BROO 40:15
The C.'s Restoration   BETJ 31:15
Waiting at the c., waiting   LEIGH 134:10
wet c. the size of a snail   THOM 213:16
churches: C. must learn humility
SHAW 199:26
Churchill: C. but the mind was ATTL 12:9
C. on top of the wave has   BEAV 21:7
[C.] was a young man   BALF 17:19
[C.] you see all his faults   LYTT 140:18
compared to Winston [C.]   NIC 160:9
Randolph C. went into hospital
WAUGH 223:7
think Winston C. wants war
BEVAN 32:18
[Winston C.] is a man   BEVAN 32:13
[Winston C.] mobilized   MURR 158:8
churchman: As for the British c. BLYT 35:7
person called a 'Modern C.'
WAUGH 223:3
Church of England: ends and the C. begins
PRIE 175:11
churchyard: In Drumcliffe c. Yeats is laid
YEATS 233:4
chute: *Vivre est une c. horizontale.*
COCT 57:7
cigar: really good 5-cent c.   MARS 147:13
cigarette: c. that bears a lipstick's
MARV 147:15

cigars: Call the roller of big c. STEV 208:10
Cinderella: The housewife is the C.
SUMM 211:2
cinema: The c. is truth 24 times GOD 91:3
circle: He drew a c. that shut me out
MARK 146:15
Round and round the c.   ELIOT 74:16
circulation: assists the c. of their blood
SMITH 203:1
c. I could only entertain   ASQ 11:13
circumambulating: But a c. aphrodisiac
FRY 87:3
circumstance: escape from c. to ecstasy
BELL 23:31
circus: celebrated Barnum's c. CHUR 54:4
have no right in the c.   MAXT 150:5
citadels: Where from c. on high
AUDEN 14:11
cities: streets of a hundred c. HOOV 104:13
citizen: c. in this Republic   ROOS 183:14
his wound, a c. of life   SASS 192:3
I am a c. of the world   EINS 73:1
that the c. is influenced   RAK 177:8
To the c. or the police   AUDEN 13:9
citizens: c. dream of the south HARDY 97:2
c. of death's gray land   SASS 191:14
c. of that other place   SONT 204:16
first and second class c.   WILL 228:4
citizenship: who is born holds dual c.
SONT 204:16
city: A big hard-boiled c.   CHAN 49:5
c. is not a concrete jungle   MORR 156:4
C. is the centre   CHAM 48:7
c. of dreaming spires   RAPH 177:16
C. of the Big Shoulders   SAND 189:13
this c., is Null an' Void   O'CAS 162:16
Unreal C.   ELIOT 76:17
civil: A c. servant doesn't make jokes
ION 110:20
Always be c. to the girls   MITF 154:14
Here lies a c. servant   SISS 201:9
civilised: c. outrage   HEAN 99:12
civilization: authenticating sign of c.
BIER 34:10
can't say c. don't advance   ROG 182:11
C. advances by extending   WHIT 226:12
C. and its discontents   RIV 181:9
C. and profits go hand in hand
COOL 60:14
C. has made the peasantry   TROT 218:4
C. is nothing more   ORT 163:21
c. of one epoch becomes   CONN 59:11
farmyard c. of the Fabians   INGE 110:11
For a botched c.   POUND 174:6
hopeful fact in our c.   SHAW 197:7
last product of c.   RUSS 186:16
life-blood of real c.   TREV 217:20
rottenness of our c.   READ 178:9
survival of Christian c.   CHUR 54:11
you think of modern c.   GAND 88:9
civilized: most c. music in the world
UST 220:16
civil servants: wonderfully gifted c.
CLARK 56:9
Civil Service: C. is profoundly deferential
CROS 63:9
claim: c. which I have to make HITL 103:5
entitled to c. the aid of all   CHUR 54:9
clairvoyante: Madame Sosostris, famous c.
ELIOT 76:16
clap: believe, c. your hands   BARR 19:10
Don't c. too hard   OSB 165:11
people in the cheaper seats c.   LENN 135:1

clap (*cont.*):
Soul c. its hands   YEATS 234:6
Clara: C. threw the twins she nursed
GRAH 92:13
clarets: racehorses and the cheaper c.
SAKI 188:14
Claridges: body of the bootboy at C.
WOOLF 231:11
class: got a better c. of enemy MILL 152:19
I could have had c.   SCH 193:6
passes, c. distinction   BETJ 32:9
This is a new c.   MAUG 150:1
true middle c. unit   SHAW 198:22
use of *violence* by one c.   LENIN 134:18
violence by which one c.   MAO T 140.9
while there is a lower c.   DEBS 65:14
classes: c. which need sanctuary
BALD 17:11
divisible into two great c.   BEER 22:17
there are two c. of travel   BENC 27:1
classic: 'C.' A book which people
TWAIN 219:11
C. music is th'kind   HUBB 107:16
classics: bellyful of the c.   MILL 152:10
Than the c. in paraphrase   POUND 174:4
clatter: c. of Sir James Barrie's GUED 94:11
Claude: After you, C.   KAV 118:10
clause: what they call a sanity c.
KAUF 118:3
claws: been a pair of ragged c. ELIOT 75:16
right place to use his c.   CHUR 56:2
clay: c. and wattles made   YEATS 232:9
C. is the word and clay   KAV 118:8
C. lies still, but blood's   HOUS 106:10
make pure c. of time's mud   MAL 145:14
this the c. grew tall   OWEN 166:12
Clayhanger: C. trilogy *is* good BENN 28:2
clean: c. the pasture spring   FROST 86:8
c. the sky   ELIOT 75:2
for a c. place to die   KAV 118:9
Not a c. & in-between-   MCG 142:9
one more thing to keep c.   FRY 86:26
Then I was c. and brave   HOUS 106:13
cleaning: We had daily c. And tomorrow
REED 178:19
cleanness: swimmers into c. leaping
BROO 40:1
cleans: It beats as it sweeps as it c.
PAG 167:4
clear: C. arias of light thrilling DAY-L 65:10
C. the air   ELIOT 75:2
climbin' c. up to the sky   HAMM 95:17
enemy of c. language is insincerity
ORW 165:7
literature c. and cold   LEWIS 137:1
On a c. day   LERN 135:22
The bells they sound so c.   HOUS 106:14
clearing-house: c. of the world CHAM 48:7
clearly: C. through a flint wall GRAV 93:6
Clemenceau: [C.] felt about France what
KEYN 120:8
C. is one of the greatest   LLOY 138:14
Cleopatra: Nile last night as C.
BROWN 41:11
clercs: *La trahison des c.*   BENDA 27:5
clergyman: beneficed c.   WAUGH 223:3
clerk: 'Baccy for the C.   KIPL 126:6
small house agent's c.   ELIOT 77:1
clever: c. and the successful   GREE 93:13
c. enough to get all   CHES 52:13
c. ones learn Latin   CHUR 55:8
c. people round me here   CAMP 45:10
has been too c. by half   SAL 189:6
It's c., but is it Art   KIPL 124:2

colonel: C.'s Lady an' Judy O'Grady
    KIPL 127:8
colony: status of a fuzzy wuzzy c.
    CAIR 44:19
colors: c. dont quite match   ASHF 10:17
colour: c. of children's pee   AMIS 4:16
  c. that of a tea-tray painter   BLUNT 35:5
  have the Model T in any c.   FORD 82:19
  Her c. comes and goes   DOBS 68:3
  I know the c. rose   ABSE 1:2
  Life is C. and Warmth   GREN 94:3
  mystery of c.   SHAW 196:15
  prison for the c. of his hair   HOUS 105:8
  problem of the c. line   DUB 70:8
  'twas hanging for the c.   HOUS 105:8
coloured: And see the c. counties
    HOUS 106:14
  black blood makes a man c.
    HUGH 107:21
colourless: C. green ideas sleep furiously
    CHOM 52:19
  some c. movement of atoms   BRAD 38:7
colours: With c. that never fade
    BOND 35:19
Columbus: mark of my youth in C.
    THUR 216:15
columnists: political c. say   ADAMS 1:17
columns: enormous fluted Ionic c.
    MACN 144:12
comb: two bald men over a c.   BORG 36:10
combat: *le triomphe mais le c.*   COUB 61:12
come: believe in the life to c.   BECK 21:11
  Christmas-morning bells say 'C.'
    BETJ 31:4
  C. all to church   HOUS 106:15
  c. back till it's over   COHAN 57:12
  C., friendly bombs   BETJ 31:1
  C. mothers and fathers   DYLAN 71:14
  C. on down   CROW 63:11
  C. then, let us go forward   CHUR 54:9
  c. to thee by moonlight   NOYES 162:1
  c. to the end of a perfect   BOND 35:19
  c. up sometime   WEST 225:22
  C. with me to the Casbah   BOYER 37:19
  C. you back to Mandalay   KIPL 123:13
  I go— I c. back   KAV 118:14
  In the room the women c. and go
    ELIOT 75:14
  No! Let 'em all c.   KNIG 128:8
  Out of Ireland have we c.   YEATS 236:3
  sailed the seas and c. To the holy city
    YEATS 234:7
  The shape of things to c.   WELLS 225:3
  they'll c. out for it   SKEL 201:20
  war and nobody will c.   SAND 190:2
  When you c. back again   RUB 185:20
  worst is yet to c.   JOHN 114:17
comedian: test of a real c.   NATH 159:24
comedy: brilliant drawing-room c.
    DE VR 67:5
  make a c. is a park   CHAP 49:8
comes: c. as sincerely from   HUXL 109:6
  it c. up here   HODG 103:16
  nobody c., nobody goes   BECK 21:18
  no shirt or collar ever c. back
    LEAC 133:14
  then just as it c.   BETJ 31:12
cometh: The iceman c.   O'NEI 163:8
comfort: bourgeois prefers c. to pleasure
    HESSE 102:4
  c. about being a woman   STARK 207:3
  I tell you naught for your c.   CHES 50:8

comfort (*cont.*):
  moments of c. and convenience
    KING 122:1
  That c. cruel men   CHES 51:18
  that means c.   TOLK 217:8
  your dear husband for a c.   SMITH 203:20
comfortable: be baith grand and c.
    BARR 19:5
  c. and the accepted   GALB 88:2
  into something more c.   EST 78:1
  Progress is a c. disease   CUMM 64:2
comfortably: Are you sitting c.   LANG 130:5
comforting: cloud of c. convictions
    RUSS 186:25
  c. thought   MARQ 147:5
comical: Beautiful c. things   HARV 99:2
comin': C. in on a wing and a pray'r
    ADAM 2:8
coming: A cold c. we had of it   ELIOT 73:14
  be c. for us that night   BALD 16:18
  Everything's c. up roses   SOND 204:10
  good both going and c.   FROST 86:5
  I was c. to that   GRAV 93:3
  The Barbarians are c. today   CAV 48:1
  The British are c.   WELL 224:9
  The Russians are c.   ROSE 184:14
  We'll be over, we're c. over
    COHAN 57:12
command: Are beyond your c.
    DYLAN 71:14
  Love shall come at your c.   GRAV 93:10
comment: C. is free, but facts
    SCOTT 193:16
  C. *voulez-vous gouverner*   DE G 66:1
commit: c. when he had the opportunity
    ROWL 185:15
committed: c. suicide 25 years after
    BEAV 21:6
  I've c. adultery   CART 47:6
  You have c. every crime   CHUR 53:10
committee: C.—a group of men who
  individually   ALLEN 3:13
  horse designed by a c.   ANON 5:23
common: century of the c. man
    WALL 222:7
  c. interest   ATK 12:4
  C. Law of England has been   HERB 101:23
  find no c. denominator   AUDEN 14:5
  happiness of the c. man   BEV 33:10
  Horseguards and still be c.   RATT 178:3
  I'm only a c. old working chap
    FYFFE 87:17
  man is a c. murderer   SAKI 188:2
  nor lose the c. touch   KIPL 126:15
  Nothing but c. sense   MORT 156:11
  The c. cormorant   ISH 110:22
  The c. man, I think   BEVIN 33:14
commonplace: featureless and c. a crime
    DOYLE 69:4
  great minds in the c.   HUBB 107:14
  The most c. crime is often   DOYLE 69:28
commonwealth: because the Empire is a c.
    ROS 184:15
  C. and its Empire lasts   CHUR 54:11
communicate: But I needed to c.   SIM 201:1
  c. was something positive   PRIT 175:13
communication: the c. Of the dead
    ELIOT 74:17
communion: sense an act of holy c.
    ROB 181:16
  weeks of perfect c.   AUDEN 15:9
communism: about capitalism and c.
    BAR 20:9
  against the anti-Christ of C.   BUCH 42:1

communism (*cont.*):
  C. continued to haunt Europe
    TAYL 212:7
  c. is a dead dog   SOLZ 204:7
  C. is like prohibition   ROG 182:15
  C. is Soviet power plus   LENIN 134:15
  [Russian C. is] the illegitimate child
    ATTL 12:12
Communist: The Catholic and the C.
    ORW 164:27
communists: Catholics and C. have
  committed   GREE 93:12
community: a c. of thought   ADAMS 2:4
  set up a small anarchist c.   BENN 27:20
commuter: C.—one who spends his life
    WHITE 226:3
compact: C. of ancient tales, and port
    BELL 26:5
companion: gave him a c. to make
    VALÉ 220:24
company: "boozes" by the c. he chooses
    BURT 42:17
  When c. comes   HUGH 108:1
compassion: sharp c. of the healer
    ELIOT 74:12
compel: c. an agonizing reappraisal
    DULL 70:11
competence: C., like truth, beauty
    PETER 170:13
  C. with pain   HEAN 99:14
complacencies: C. of the peignoir, and late
    STEV 208:11
complain: Never c. and never explain
    BALD 17:4
complaining: triple-towered sky, the
  dove c.   DAY-L 65:7
complaint: that's the most fatal c.
    HILT 102:17
completely: something c. different
    CHAP 49:11
completing: C. the charm   ELIOT 74:16
completion: time available for its c.
    PARK 169:12
complexes: chiefly the *feeling-toned* c.
    JUNG 117:3
complexion: different c. or slightly flatter
    CONR 59:19
  Keep that schoolgirl c.   PEAR 169:18
complexities: All mere c.   YEATS 235:15
complicated: A c. gesture learned from
    BOLT 35:16
compliment: rather a c. to be called an
  agnostic   DARR 64:15
composer: c. on leaving the theatre
    BEEC 22:6
  good c. does not imitate   STR 210:16
  requirement for a c. is to be dead
    HON 104:9
composers: greatest c. since Beethoven
    BUCK 42:4
composing: C. mortals with immortal fire
    AUDEN 15:12
compromise: inclinations to c. which are
  embedded   ZIN 236:14
compulsions: whose blent air all our c.
    LARK 130:16
compulsory: Blood is c.—they're all
    STOP 209:19
computer: foul things up requires a c.
    ANON 8:24
comrade: surprise us with a lady C.
    BRAC 37:23
conceal: c. our whereabouts   SAKI 188:1
  people have something to c.   CONN 58:18

conceal (*cont.*):
was always able to c. it   TWAIN 219:24
concealable: without it everything is c.
STOP 209:16
concealing: c. how much we think
TWAIN 219:27
conceit: curst c. o' bein' richt
MACD 141:21
concentrate: I am unable to c.   GEOR 89:10
concentration: c. of talent and genius
KENN 119:5
conception: dad is present at the c.
ORTON 164:1
some c. of how men   FORS 83:7
concepts: up the stairs of his c.   STEI 207:22
concern: Since our c. was speech
ELIOT 74:19
concerned: I am not c. with Poetry
OWEN 166:8
concert: At the c. I make them   BEEC 22:12
self-imposed torture, the c.   MILL 152:9
concession: where the only c. to gaiety
THOM 214:18
conclusion: The c. of your syllogism
O'BR 162:8
conclusions: sufficient c. from insufficient
BUTL 43:18
concrete: city is not a c. jungle
MORR 156:4
flower is the c. cloverleaf   MUMF 157:17
Hurries down the c. station   BETJ 31:7
Monstrous carbuncles of c.   SPEN 205:10
they have built the c.   SPEN 205:18
condemn: c. egoism intolerantly
SANT 190:20
c. recourse to war   BRIA 39:10
nor the years c.   BINY 34:18
condemned: I am c. to be free   SART 191:2
past are c. to repeat it   SANT 190:9
They c. millions of first-class   BEVAN 33:7
condition: A c. of complete simplicity
ELIOT 74:23
conditions: c. of tyranny it is far   AREN 10:3
get better living c.   BAR 20:9
universal c. of existence   JUNG 117:2
conductor: greatest c. in this country
BEEC 22:5
conductors: C. must give unmistakable
SZELL 211:20
these third-rate foreign c.   BEEC 22:15
cones: eat the c. under his pines
FROST 86:10
conference: naked into the c. chamber
BEVAN 33:1
was ever born in a c.   FITZ 80:14
conferred: Legion of Honour has been c.
TWAIN 220:6
confession: after the sweetness of c.
FIRB 80:4
confessional: c. passage has probably
SAL 189:5
confide: c. in those who are better
CAMUS 46:2
confidence: ignorance and c.   TWAIN 220:7
confier: *la c. à des militaires*   CLEM 56:16
confinement: c. inside our own skins
WILL 227:19
confions: *c. rarement à ceux qui*
CAMUS 46:2
conflict: cause of international c.
WEIL 224:2
human c. was so much owed
CHUR 54:12
offered you C. and Art   PRIE 175:7

conflict (*cont.*):
risks of spreading c.   JOHN 114:12
We are in an armed c.   EDEN 71:18
conflicts: solution of all disputes or c.
BRIA 39:10
conform: not always c. to our whim
REST 179:13
confound: c. strangeness with mystery
DOYLE 69:28
confounding: C. her astronomers
HODG 103:15
confused: anyone who isn't c. doesn't
really understand   MURR 158:6
congeals: When love c.   HART 98:17
congo: Then I saw the c., creeping
LIND 137:14
congratulate: c. our armed forces
THAT 212:16
conifers: The scent of the c.   BETJ 32:2
Conn: [Billy C.] can run   LOUIS 139:14
connect: Only c.   FORS 83:17
connected: necessarily c. with the social
progress   JOHN 113:22
connection: heavenly c. to the starry
GINS 90:15
connive: Who would c.   HEAN 99:12
conquer: How shall we c.? Like a wind
FLEC 81:22
possible to c. poverty   JOHN 114:6
To c. fear is the beginning   RUSS 187:5
conqueror: you are a c.   ROST 185:8
conquest: Beauty's c. of your face
AUDEN 14:11
The c. of the earth   CONR 59:19
conscience: C. is thoroughly well-bred
BUTL 43:12
C.: the inner voice   MENC 150:21
cruelty with a good c.   RUSS 186:24
freedom of c.   TWAIN 219:10
good c. on the proceeds   SMITH 203:4
had sufficient c. to bother   LLOY 138:10
happiness or a quiet c.   BERL 30:6
sound spot in our social c.   SHAW 197:7
uncreated c. of my race   JOYCE 115:20
will not cut my c.   HELL 100:8
consciences: c. of the citizens   JOHN 113:21
conscience-stricken: wearing such a c. air
HOUS 105:8
consciousness: c. of possessing a deep
MCL 143:9
forces operating through human c.
BURR 42:16
consent: inferior without your c.
ROOS 182:19
consenting: only between c. adults
VIDAL 221:15
consequences: prevent it and to damn
the c.   MILN 154:5
renounce war for its c.   FOSD 84:13
conservatism: c. is based upon the idea
CHES 51:14
conservative: A C. is a man with two
ROOS 183:6
C., n. A statesman   BIER 34:3
c. on the day after   AREN 10:5
C. Party at prayer   ROYD 185:18
most c. man in this world   BEVIN 33:15
stomach is nothing if not c.   BUTL 43:20
trouble with the C. Party   WAUGH 223:19
which makes a man more c.   KEYN 120:11
would make me c. when old
FROST 85:20
Conservatives: Life's better with the C.
ANON 7:17

considering: C. the alternative   CHEV 52:15
consistency: c. is as bad for the mind
HUXL 108:14
consistent: c. people are the dead
HUXL 108:14
conspicuous: C. consumption   VEBL 221:10
Vega c. overhead   AUDEN 14:10
conspiracies: are c. against the laity
SHAW 196:13
conspiracy: c. of human beings to lie
WELLS 225:1
Indecency's c. of silence   SHAW 198:25
constancy: c. of the women who love
SHAW 199:14
constant: c. in human sufferings
JOYCE 115:19
constellations: c. of feeling   DOUG 68:12
constituencies: c. and prepare for
government   STEEL 207:7
constitution: c. does not provide
WILL 228:4
nightmare is over. Our C. works
FORD 82:14
constructed: defences of peace must be c.
ANON 6:16
consume: more history than they can c.
SAKI 188:7
consumer: c. society there are inevitably
ILL 110:7
The c. isn't a moron   OGIL 162:23
consumes: that c. without producing
ORW 164:7
consuming: deathly inner c. fire
HESSE 102:4
consumption: Conspicuous c. of valuable
goods   VEBL 221:10
keep abreast of private c.   GALB 88:4
contemplation: grasped by action, not
by c.   BRON 39:13
Has left for c.   BETJ 31:15
Of all the solemn talk of c.   KAV 118:6
contempt: Familiarity breeds c.
TWAIN 219:26
contemptible: French's c. little army
ANON 6:9
contender: I could have been a c.
SCH 193:6
content: C. in the tight hot cell
BOGAN 35:11
That is the land of lost c.   HOUS 107:4
their skin but by the c.   KING 121:15
contentment: Preaches c. to that toad
KIPL 124:7
contest: not the victory but the c.
COUB 61:12
continent: On the C. people have good
food   MIKES 151:14
Thou knowest of no strange c.   DAV 65:4
continental: C. people have sex life
MIKES 151:15
continentally: Learn to think c.   CHAM 48:8
continents: nations and three separate c.
DOYLE 69:21
contingent: c. and the unforeseen
FISH 80:5
contraception: fast word about oral c.
ALLEN 4:3
contraceptives: Skullion had little use for c.
SHAR 195:9
contract: c. into which men enter
CHUR 53:21
c. now needs to be re-negotiated
BENN 27:14

country (cont.):
one day this c. of ours COW 61:14
past is a foreign c. HART 99:1
security and peace of each c. JOHN 113:22
Switzerland is a small, steep c. HEM 101:7
That is no c. for old men YEATS 234:5
The trouble with this c. ADAMS 1:19
This c. needs good farmers NIXON 161:6
what was good for our c. WILS 228:7
While there's a c. lane PARK 169:9
you can do for your c. KENN 119:16
countryman: c. must have praise BLYT 35:8
countryside: smiling and beautiful c. DOYLE 69:6
county: English c. families baying WAUGH 222:19
cœur: voit bien qu'avec le c. SAIN 187:19
courage: act of the greatest c. JUNG 117:2
C. is the thing BARR 19:15
c. to change what should NIEB 160:11
C. was mine, and I had mystery OWEN 166:17
c. you bring to it WALP 222:9
originality or moral c. SHAW 196:2
piety, c.—they exist FORS 84:1
spirit of gallantry and c. COW 61:14
Than C. of Heart or Holiness BELL 26:1
course: c. of true anything never BUTL 43:11
forgot his c. FLEC 81:20
served to him c. by c. CHUR 54:6
court: C. him, elude him BLUN 34:25
The C. is shaking FARJ 78:8
courteous: Be invariably c., considerate KITC 128:5
courtesy: c. title on the principle SAKI 188:18
defence like elaborate c. LUCAS 140:10
That the Grace of God is in C. BELL 26:1
courtin': Are yer c. PICK 171:9
courtmartialled: I was c. in my absence BEHAN 23:23
courts: not enough c. to enforce HUMP 108:4
covenants: Open c. of peace WILS 229:15
coverlet: Blue skies be your c. HART 98:19
cow: isn't grass to graze a c. BETJ 31:1
Over the c. shed O'HARA 162:24
The c. is of the bovine ilk NASH 159:4
this than to keep a c. BUTL 43:29
We milk the c. of the world WILB 226:24
coward: [Noel C.] was Slightly TYNAN 220:8
The sea hates a c. O'NEI 163:13
cowardice: C., as distinguished from HEM 100:14
soldier I admit the c. SHAW 198:1
surest is c. TWAIN 219:14
were guilty of Noel C. DE VR 67:5
cows: Bulls and c. a thousand head HODG 103:14
cowshed: smelling of the c. THOM 214:9
cowslip: C. and shad-blow CRANE 62:14
crack: And the c. in the tea-cup opens AUDEN 12:17
C. and sometimes break ELIOT 74:6
crackle: Snap! C.! Pop ANON 8:10
cradle: c. rocks above an abyss NAB 158:14
from the c. to the grave CHUR 56:1
nightmare by a rocking c. YEATS 233:13
craftsmen: was the work not of c. CLARK 56:9

cramps: ignorance c. my conversation HOPE 104:17
crane: Tall as a c. SITW 201:10
crank: apprenticeship as a c. BROUN 41:5
crap: Copperfield kind of c. SAL 188:24
crash: c. is coming when I start PARK 168:1
craving: c. in the world PEAR 169:20
c. to be appreciated JAMES 112:7
crawls: The sea-worm c.—grotesque HARDY 97:13
crazed: c. with the spell of far DE L 66:7
crazier: World is c. and more MACN 144:17
crazy: C. like a fox PER 170:2
Just two c. people together HART 98:19
creaking: Came c. to the barn LOW 140:4
creaks: The morning light c. down SITW 201:10
creation: His divine system of c. HELL 100:5
intrinsic evidence of his c. JEANS 112:22
It took the whole of C. HUGH 108:2
who finds c. so perfect PROU 176:3
woman is a blind fury of c. SHAW 197:20
world since the C. NIXON 161:3
création: une grande c. d'époque BART 20:4
creative: are c. but few are artists GOOD 92:3
C. writers are always greater FORS 84:9
creator: can dispense with a c. PROU 176:3
concluded that the C. HALD 95:7
C. made Italy TWAIN 219:20
creature: Let the living c. lie AUDEN 13:7
only c. that consumes ORW 164:7
creatures: And breastless c. underground ELIOT 75:8
credit: I never seek to take the c. PARK 168:18
In science the c. goes DARW 64:16
people who get the c. MORR 156:9
their children to be a c. RUSS 187:3
credulities: upwards on the miseries or c. CONR 60:1
credulous: Man is a c. animal RUSS 187:4
creed: last article of my c. GAND 88:12
true meaning of its c. KING 121:15
creep: c. again, leap again DE L 66:19
creeper-nails: Sagged seats, the c. are rust HARDY 97:1
creeps: it c. like a rat BOWEN 37:13
crème: all my pupils are the c. SPARK 205:6
Crete: people of C. unfortunately make more SAKI 188:7
crevasse: like a scream from a c. GREE 93:17
crew: Set the c. laughing FLEC 81:20
cricket: C. civilizes people MUG 157:5
football and particularly c. MANC 145:17
morning to where the c. sings YEATS 232:9
Cricklewood: Midland, bound for C. BETJ 31:19
cried: c. all the way LIB 137:7
c. the little children AUDEN 12:18
he c. out twice, a cry CONR 59:22
cries: The air is full of our c. BECK 21:25
crime: c. is due to the repressed WAUGH 223:4
c. is often the most mysterious DOYLE 69:28
c. you haven't committed POW 174:21
featureless and commonplace a c. DOYLE 69:4

crime (cont.):
have committed every c. CHUR 53:10
lamentable catalogue of human c. CHUR 54:8
Napoleon of c. DOYLE 69:16
Napoleon of C. ELIOT 75:4
we'll end that stupid c. SERV 194:21
crimes: have committed great c. GREE 93:12
worst of c. is poverty SHAW 197:6
criminal: despise for ends I think c. KEYN 120:7
while there is a c. element DEBS 65:14
criminals: Looney Tunes and squalid c. REAG 178:15
crises: c. that seemed intolerable ATK 12:3
crisis: cannot be a c. next week KISS 128:2
C.? What C.? CALL 45:3
critic: A great drama c. also TYNAN 220:11
c. is a bundle of biases BALL 17:22
c. is a man who knows TYNAN 220:10
c. is to save the tale LAWR 132:21
English c. is a don manqué LAMB 129:17
function of the c. BELL 24:1
good c. is he who relates FRAN 84:16
set up in honour of a c. SIB 200:14
critical: at this c. moment HAIG 95:3
c. period in matrimony HERB 101:25
criticism: c. by the few than a subject BROWN 41:10
c. is applied only to what JAMES 112:2
c. this past summer ALGR 3:8
ignorance as regards c. MACM 143:16
near to them than c. RILKE 181:2
People ask you for c. MAUG 149:19
two because it permits c. FORS 84:6
criticisms: most penetrating of c. HUXL 109:9
criticize: And don't c. DYLAN 71:14
I don't care if you c. OWEN 166:7
critics: C. are biased BALL 17:22
c. is to be remembered MOORE 155:10
that there are true c. ALGR 3:8
critique: Le bon c. est celui qui FRAN 84:16
crocodile: After 'while, c. GUID 94:13
C. caught him KIPL 125:14
croire: avec leurs noms: c'est c. SART 191:9
Cromwell: bit of a ruin that C. BEDF 21:26
C. said to the Long Parliament AMERY 4:12
crook: their President is a c. NIXON 161:5
you are a C. or a Martyr ROG 182:7
crooked: are as c. as corkscrews AUDEN 14:8
The c. be made straight ELIOT 74:16
crooning: c. like a bilious pigeon SHAW 199:18
cross: By the road an ancient c. YEATS 233:4
cling to the old rugged c. BENN 27:17
C. as the focus of longing MUGG 157:10
c. of the Legion of Honour TWAIN 220:6
C. to be Borne SMITH 203:20
King's C. FARJ 78:8
The c. be uncrossed ELIOT 74:16
There's a little marble c. HAYES 99:5
through sheer inability to c. the road WOOLF 231:16
crosses: Between the c., row on row MCCR 141:17
clinging to their c. CHES 51:19
crossing: double c. of a pair of heels HART 98:17

crossness: c. and dirt succeed where
                                    FORS 83:10
crossroads: mankind faces a c.   ALLEN 3:21
crowblack: c., fishingboat-bobbing
                                    THOM 214:7
crowd: c. flowed over London Bridge
                                    ELIOT 76:17
  c. will always save   COCT 57:5
  have been a c. of chicks   AYRES 16:7
crowded: Across a c. room   HAMM 96:2
crowing: cock c. on its own dunghill
                                    ALD 3:4
crown: c. of thorns *and* the thirty
                                    BEVAN 32:16
  exchange it some day for a c.
                                    BENN 27:17
  hairy gold c. on 'er 'ead   KIPL 123:11
  Out of his C.   FARJ 78:8
  The jewel in the c.   SCOTT 193:17
crowned: Into the c. knot of fire
                                    ELIOT 74:23
crowns: Give c. and pounds and guineas
                                    HOUS 106:12
croyait: *était un fou qui se c.*   COCT 57:8
cru: *étonné quand il est c.*   DE G 66:2
crucified: choose who is to be c.   COCT 57:5
  therefore the c.   BONH 36:3
crucify: It's God they ought to c. CART 47:8
cruel: Goodbye c. world   SHAY 200:11
  Not that he's c.   LEAC 133:11
  That comfort c. men   CHES 51:18
  The truth is c.   SANT 190:15
cruellest: April is the c. month   ELIOT 76:13
  c. and most terrible War   LLOY 138:8
cruelty: c. with a good conscience
                                    RUSS 186:24
  inhumanity meant c.   FROMM 85:13
  main sources of c.   RUSS 187:5
crumbling: C. between the fingers
                                    MACN 144:15
crumbs: bags to hold the c.   ISH 110:22
  In eating Bread he made no C.
                                    BELL 24:21
crumpets: Over buttered scones and c.
                                    ELIOT 73:10
crusade: c. against Communism was
                                    TAYL 212:7
  moral c. or it is nothing WILS 228:15
crushing: C. out life   HOPE 105:4
cry: C., the beloved country   PATON 169:16
  Don't c. for me Argentina RICE 180:9
  Forgot the c. of gulls   ELIOT 77:3
  I hear a sudden c. of pain STEP 208:7
  your bald c.   PLATH 172:2
crying: that wild high c.   MAS 148:14
crystal: Why read the c. when   BEVAN 33:3
cubes: c. in two different ways   RAM 177:13
Cuchulain: When Pearse summoned C.
                                    YEATS 233:6
cuckoo: And hear the pleasant c.   DAV 65:1
  A rainbow and a c.'s song   DAV 64:20
  c. clock style   HEM 101:7
  The c. clock   WELL 224:11
  This is the weather the c. HARDY 97:2
cucumber: when c. is added to it
                                    MACK 143:1
cud: bitter as the c.   OWEN 166:10
cult: After all, what's a c.   ALTM 4:11
  c. of the individual   KHR 121:2
cultivate: And c. a beaver   HUXL 108:8
  c. a few inhibitions   LOOS 139:9
  which dictators may c.   BEV 33:9

culturally: behind economically or c.
                                    DUBČ 70:5
culture: C. is an instrument wielded
                                    WEIL 224:3
  c. is no better   AUDEN 15:6
  c. lives by sympathies   JAMES 112:9
  C. may even be described   ELIOT 75:3
  c. that a poet can earn   AUDEN 13:15
  don't swallow the c. bait LAWR 132:14
  whole vast intuitive c.   SHAF 195:4
  who pursue C. in bands   WHAR 225:30
  word c.   JOHST 114:19
cultured: intelligentsia and the c.
                                    BERD 29:10
cunning: exile, and c.   JOYCE 115:21
  History has many c. passages
                                    ELIOT 73:12
cupboards: her c. opened   HARDY 97:5
curate: c. at home as something   FIRB 80:1
  c. who has strayed by mistake
                                    AUDEN 14:1
  The c. faced the laurels   GRAH 92:15
  To sit upon the c.'s knee CHES 51:22
curates: C., long dust, will come and go
                                    BROO 40:12
curb: snaffle and the c.   CAMP 45:11
curds: kitchen cups concupiscent c.
                                    STEV 208:10
cure: But I wish that they could c.
                                    AYRES 16:8
  c. for birth and death   SANT 190:17
  c. for it is occupation   SHAW 199:12
  c. for this ill is not   KIPL 125:11
  found a c. for most evils KELL 118:16
  no C. for this Disease   BELL 24:12
  twentieth, it's a c.   SZASZ 211:13
cured: be c. by more democracy
                                    SMITH 202:4
cures: best c. for depression   SMITH 202:7
curiosity: intellectual c. is the life-blood
                                    TREV 217:20
  Love, c., freckles, and doubt PARK 168:10
curious: c. incident of the dog   DOYLE 69:14
  Yes; quaint and c. war   HARDY 98:3
currency: than to debauch the c.
                                    KEYN 120:10
current: boats against the c.   FITZ 80:21
currents: Cold c. thrid   HARDY 97:13
curse: And the c. be ended   ELIOT 74:16
  blessing or the greatest c. BARR 19:12
  c. to this country in time CHUR 55:2
curses: c. heaped on each gashed
                                    SORL 205:3
cursing: c. his staff for incompetent
                                    SASS 191:17
curtain: And so I face the final c. ANKA 5:7
  iron c. has descended   CHUR 53:15
  sensuous c.   BRAD 38:7
curtains: c. are drawn with care
                                    MONRO 155:2
  Nottingham lace of the c. BETJ 30:21
curtiosity: 'satiable c.   KIPL 125:12
curve: dear red c. of her lips   MAS 148:7
custard: joke is ultimately a c. pie
                                    ORW 164:14
custom: c. of one wife and hardly
                                    SAKI 188:17
customer: c. is never wrong   RITZ 181:8
customs: thinks that the c.   SHAW 195:26
cut: c. my conscience to fit   HELL 100:8
  Was c. out of the grass   CHES 50:7
  You can c., or you can drug LOW 139:20
cutting: c. edge of the mind   BRON 39:13

cutting (*cont.*):
  interest is that of c. each other's throat
                                    ATK 12:4
cuttlefish: like a c. squirting out ORW 165:7
cycle: c. of deprivation   JOS 115:5
cycle-clips: My c. in awkward reverence
                                    LARK 130:15
cynic: C., n. A blackguard whose   BIER 34:4
cynical: c. and entirely undemocratic
                                    CAIR 44:19
cynicism: C. is an unpleasant way
                                    HELL 100:7
cypress: little noise outside the c.
                                    LAWR 131:14
cypresses: Along the avenue of c.
                                    LAWR 132:11
Cyprus: black C. with a lake   FLEC 81:19
Cyril: Nice one, C.   ANON 7:29
Czechoslovakia: C. and in the matters
                                    CHUR 54:6
  far away country [C.]   CHAM 48:12

D

dad: child can expect if the d.   ORTON 164:1
  that married dear old d.   DILL 67:13
dada: encountered the mama of d.
                                    FAD 78:6
Daddy: D. sat up very late working
                                    BENC 27:2
  My heart belongs to D.   PORT 173:5
daffodils: d. were for Wordsworth
                                    LARK 130:20
daily: D. the steamers sidle up
                                    AUDEN 14:16
daintily: D. alights Elaine   BETJ 31:7
dairymaid: Queen asked The D.
                                    MILNE 153:9
daisies: d. in Sunday Meadow   THOM 214:9
  picking d. on the railway WOD 230:13
  would be pushing up the d. CHAP 49:13
Daisy: D. and Lily   SITW 201:14
dallied: But I dillied and d.   COLL 58:2
Dalton: resignation of Hugh D.
                                    BIRCH 34:19
damage: which might d. his career
                                    BARR 19:23
dame: There is nothin' like a d.
                                    HAMM 96:4
damn: D. it all, you can't have
                                    BEVAN 32:16
  d. the consequences   MILN 154:5
  d. you England   OSB 165:20
  D. you, Jack   BONE 36:1
  old man who said, 'D.'   HARE 98:7
  public doesn't give a d.   BEEC 22:1
  true that life is one d. thing MILL 151:22
damnation: be blasted to eternal d.
                                    SHAW 199:27
  From sleep and from d.   CHES 51:18
damned: better than any d. foreigner
                                    BEEC 22:5
  brandy of the d.   SHAW 197:28
  D. from here to Eternity   KIPL 123:19
  If I were d. of body and soul KIPL 125:20
  Life is just one d. thing HUBB 107:12
  stink of the d. dead niggers ASQ 11:20
  The beautiful and d.   FITZ 80:13
damns: d. the vast majority o'
                                    MACD 141:21
damp: d. souls of housemaids   ELIOT 76:1
  female in a d. basement   HARDY 96:16

damps: d. there drip upon — HARDY 97:1
dance: A d. to the music of time
                                              POW 174:20
  And spectral d., before — BROO 40:12
  d. attendance upon my old — YEATS 234:3
  Dance, dance, d., little lady — COW 61:15
  Dance, d., dance till you drop
                                              AUDEN 14:8
  d., for the figure is easy — AUDEN 14:8
  d. in the old dame yet — MARQ 146:18
  D. on this ball-floor thin — BLUN 34:25
  dancer from the d. — YEATS 234:8
  d. round in a ring — FROST 86:23
  D. then wherever you may — CART 47:7
  D. till the stars come — AUDEN 14:8
  departs too far from the d.
                                              POUND 173:21
  Each d. the others would — DE L 66:16
  from the car park the d. — BETJ 32:3
  point, there the d. — ELIOT 74:5
  Shall we d. — MILL 152:17
  we d. at the Golf Club — BETJ 32:2
danced: didn't he d. his did — CUMM 63:13
  I d. in the morning — CART 47:7
dancer: know the d. from the dance
                                              YEATS 234:8
dancers: d. are all gone under — ELIOT 74:10
dances: Slightly bald. Also d. — ANON 5:24
  We shall have no time for d.
                                              MACN 144:6
dancing: And d. dogs and bears
                                              HODG 103:13
  [D. is] a perpendicular expression
                                              SHAW 199:8
  prose as d. is to walking — WAIN 222:1
dandy: Candy Is d. — NASH 159:18
  I'm a Yankee Doodle D. — COHAN 57:13
Dane: You never get rid of the D.
                                              KIPL 124:17
Dane-geld: called paying the D.
                                              KIPL 124:17
danger: d. of their coming true
                                              SMITH 202:19
  The d. of the future — FROMM 85:13
  The d. of the past — FROMM 85:13
dangereux: n'est plus d. qu'une idée
                                              ALAIN 3:1
dangerous: are d. for good or evil
                                              KEYN 120:17
  considering how d. everything is
                                              STEIN 207:11
  d. than sincere ignorance — KING 122:2
  d. to be sincere unless — SHAW 198:31
  more d. than a mud-puddle — STEIN 207:15
  more d. than an idea — ALAIN 3:1
  sat D. Dan McGrew — SERV 194:23
  were d. to meet it alone — WHAR 225:30
dapper: d. from your napper — COLL 58:4
dare: Do I d. to eat a peach — ELIOT 75:19
  Nobody'll d. — HUGH 108:1
  Take me if you d. — PANK 167:11
  Where eagles d. — MACL 143:4
dares: Who d. wins — ANON 9:14
dark: clock has stopped in the d.
                                              ELIOT 74:15
  come home in the d. — WILL 227:11
  d. age made more sinister — CHUR 54:11
  d. and deep — FROST 86:7
  D. as the world of man — SITW 201:15
  d. night of the soul — FITZ 80:17
  day of his death was a d. — AUDEN 12:20
  I knew you in this d. — OWEN 166:18
  In the nightmare of the d. — AUDEN 13:3

dark (cont.):
  O d. dark dark — ELIOT 74:11
  Out in the d. over the snow
                                              THOM 214:12
  raging in the d. — YEATS 235:18
  refuse a drink after d. — MENC 150:22
  The d. is light enough — FRY 86:24
  These are not d. days — CHUR 53:11
  They all go into the d. — ELIOT 74:11
  through the spaces of the d. — ELIOT 75:21
  want to go home in the d. — HENRY 101:12
  We work in the d. — JAMES 111:18
darken: Never d. my Dior again — LILL 137:8
darkening: swan drifts upon a d.
                                              YEATS 235:13
darker: d. to the lighter — DUB 70:8
  I am the d. brother — HUGH 108:1
  speak of d. days — CHUR 53:11
darkness: between two eternities of d.
                                              NAB 158:14
  candle than curse the d. — STEV 209:2
  d. among the gusty trees — NOYES 161:16
  d. and put your hand — HASK 99:3
  d. drops again but now — YEATS 233:13
  d. of mere being — JUNG 116:19
  Shares the d.—presently — MILL 151:23
  there is d. everywhere — NEHRU 160:1
darlin': oh, he's a d. man — O'CAS 162:12
darling: Robey is the D. of the music
                                              SMITH 202:13
  Yes, my d. daughter — ANON 7:25
  Yes, my d. daughter — DE L 66:20
dashing: A d. Swiss officer — RUSS 187:7
date: d. which will live — ROOS 183:10
  keep them up to d. — SHAW 196:18
  savage country, out of d. — POUND 174:2
daughter: all to my elder d. — THOM 214:13
  And on her d. — ELIOT 76:23
  D. am I in my mother's house — KIPL 124:8
  Don't put your d. on the stage — COW 62:5
  father would wish his d. — ANON 8:20
  The landlord's black-eyed d.
                                              NOYES 161:17
  Translated D., come down — AUDEN 15:12
  Yes, my darling d. — ANON 7:25
  Yes, my darling d. — DE L 66:20
daughters: Your sons and your d.
                                              DYLAN 71:14
David: King D. and King Solomon
                                              NAYL 159:26
Davy: Sir Humphrey D. — BENT 29:2
dawn: brown fog of a winter d. — ELIOT 76:17
  d. and sunset on moors — MAS 148:6
  d. comes up like thunder — KIPL 123:13
  D. is my brother — BELL 26:8
  D. shall over Lethe break — BELL 25:20
  gray d. of the morning after — ADE 2:13
  grey d. breaking — MAS 148:16
  I said to D.: Be sudden—to Eve
                                              THOM 215:9
  see by the d.'s early — CUMM 63:15
  she soft as the d. — THUR 216:24
  through night hooting at d. — BEER 23:16
dawning: d. of the age of Aquarius
                                              RADO 177:6
Dawson: Lord D. of Penn — MOYN 157:4
  not been for that fool D. — ASQ 11:16
day: A long d.'s journey into night
                                              O'NEI 163:11
  And I work all d. — CHAP 49:10
  bright cold d. in April — ORW 164:19
  d. after the revolution — AREN 10:5
  d. I was meant not to see — THAT 212:17
  d. of his death was a dark — AUDEN 12:20

day (cont.):
  d. of small nations has — CHAM 48:9
  d. when heaven was falling — HOUS 106:3
  end of a perfect d. — BOND 35:19
  Every d., in every way — COUÉ 61:13
  every d. is a life — O'NEI 163:12
  Go ahead, make my d. — FINK 79:18
  I have met them at close of d.
                                              YEATS 233:9
  left alone with our d. — AUDEN 15:10
  not a second on the d. — COOK 60:7
  Oh, what a beautiful d. — HAMM 95:18
  Round the d.'s dead sanctities
                                              THOM 215:12
  The blinds let through the d. — HOUS 106:1
  The d. war broke out — WILT 229:16
daydreams: d. do not prevent her from
                                              NAB 158:11
  d. would darken into nightmares
                                              SMITH 202:19
daylight: never to drink by d. — MENC 150:22
days: And the d. grow short — AND 4:21
  Cast your mind on other d. — YEATS 233:3
  D. are where we live — LARK 131:2
  d. of yore — GREN 94:2
  good old d. were a myth — ATK 12:3
  Half to remember d. — FLEC 81:16
  Happy d. are here again — YELL 236:5
  In other d. — DE L 66:12
  in the first 100 d. — KENN 119:14
  itself only three d. old — JEANS 112:20
  let us speak of darker d. — CHUR 53:11
  Ten d. that shook the world — REED 179:7
  The burnt-out ends of smoky d.
                                              ELIOT 75:20
  The d. go by, I remain — APOL 9:22
dazzled: Eyes still d. by the ways
                                              LIND 137:13
dead: A d. sinner revised — BIER 34:14
  After that it's d. — WAUGH 223:14
  already three parts d. — RUSS 186:19
  be blooming well d. — SAR 190:23
  Better red than d. — ANON 5:7
  Chile. Not many d. — COCK 57:2
  cold and pure and very d. — LEWIS 137:1
  composer is to be d. — HON 104:9
  consistent people are the d. — HUXL 108:14
  curly you'll soon be d. — WIMP 229:17
  d. fish swim with the stream
                                              MUGG 157:8
  d. had no speech — ELIOT 74:17
  d. is tongued with fire — ELIOT 74:17
  d. men lost their bones — ELIOT 76:20
  D. religions do not produce — BREN 39:9
  d. sound on the final stroke — ELIOT 76:17
  d. that's what's wrong — CHAP 49:13
  d. thing that smells sweet — THOM 214:14
  d. to rapture and despair — MARK 146:14
  democracy of the d. — CHES 51:13
  difference does it make to the d.
                                              GAND 88:10
  Droops to sink among the D. — BELL 25:20
  Either he's d. — PIR 171:18
  Fame is a food that d. men — DOBS 68:1
  For being d. — BENT 29:4
  From the throat of a d. man — GRAV 93:6
  gathered flowers are d. — FLEC 81:12
  God is not d. but alive — ANON 6:13
  healthy and wealthy and d. — THUR 216:23
  he is d. who will not fight — GREN 94:3
  her d. across the sea — BINY 34:17
  If the d. talk to you — SZASZ 211:18
  Is d. and dumb and done — DE L 66:16
  kissed by the English d. — OWEN 166:13

dead (*cont.*):
like d. generals	TUCH 218:15
Lilacs out of the d. land	ELIOT 76:13
make sure he was d.	GOLD 92:1
millions of the mouthless d.	SORL 205:3
Mistah Kurtz— he d.	CONR 59:23
more to say when I am d.	ROB 181:14
move in a world of the d.	FORS 83:7
over the rich D.	BROO 40:3
Phoenician, a fortnight d.	ELIOT 77:3
Private Means is d.	SMITH 203:23
quick, and the d.	DEWAR 67:8
Remember me when I am d.	DOUG 68:10
rough notes and our d.	SCOTT 194:3
saying 'Lord Jones D.'	CHES 52:14
servant's cut in half; he's d.	GRAH 92:14
shakes a d. geranium	ELIOT 75:21
somewhere that falls down d.	BARR 19:8
stars are d.	AUDEN 15:10
strove to resuscitate the d.	POUND 174:2
The d. don't die	LAWR 132:2
their wages and are d.	HOUS 106:3
There are no d.	MAFT 145:1
The very d. of winter	ELIOT 73:14
they would be better d.	PARK 168:17
unheroic D. who fed the guns	SASS 191:19
When I am d., I hope it	BELL 25:16
Where d. men meet, on lips	BUTL 43:4
you remind me of the d.	SASS 192:4
deaded: I told you I'd be d.	MILL 152:15
deadener: habit is a great d.	BECK 21:25
deadlock: Holy d.	HERB 101:16
deadly: more d. than the male	KIPL 126:17
they are more d.	TWAIN 219:7
Deadwood: Tucson and D. and Lost Mule	BENÉT 27:7
deaf: d., how should they know	SORL 205:3
deal: be given a square d.	ROOS 183:15
D. around me	ALGR 3:8
modest man who has a good d.	CHUR 53:6
new d. for the American	ROOS 182:22
was a faith-healer of D.	ANON 8:19
dealing: d. with estate workers	DOUG 68:17
dean: D. of Christ Church	SPR 206:14
The sly shade of a Rural D.	BROO 40:12
dear: D. 338171	COW 62:1
D. One is mine as mirrors	AUDEN 14:7
death: After the first d.	THOM 213:14
And d. shall have no dominion	THOM 214:6
And d., who had the soldier	DOUG 68:11
A proper view of d.	SIMM 201:3
Birth, and copulation, and d.	ELIOT 76:9
Birth or D.	ELIOT 73:15
Black Widow, d.	LOW 140:5
bleeding to d. of time	GRAV 93:9
brought d. into the world	TWAIN 219:29
d. and I will coquette	MARQ 146:18
D. and taxes and childbirth	MITC 154:10
d. could scarcely be bettered	BENN 28:2
D. destroys a man	FORS 83:18
D. devours all lovely things	MILL 151:23
d. in a blizzard to try	ATK 12:5
D. in Venice	MANN 146:3
[D. is] nature's way	ANON 5:28
d. is one of the few things	ALLEN 3:23
d. of one so young	SPEN 205:19
D. opens unknown doors	MAS 148:13
d. reveals the eminent	SHAW 198:26
'D.,' said Mark Staithes	HUXL 108:18

death (*cont.*):
defend to the d. your right	TALL 212:4
doubt is nothing but d.	UNAM 220:12
enormously improved by d.	SAKI 188:3
fear d.	FROH 85:11
Finality is d. Perfection	STEP 208:6
friend and enemy is but D.	BROO 40:1
heroes up the line to d.	SASS 191:16
idea of D. saves him	FORS 83:18
I do not see why d. should	NAB 158:13
I have a rendezvous with D.	SEEG 194:5
I should be glad of another d.	ELIOT 73:15
I signed my d. warrant	COLL 58:6
Is there a life before d.	HEAN 99:14
Lead me from d. to life	KUMAR 129:6
maid is like d. by drowning	FERB 79:3
Man has created d.	YEATS 235:11
my d. was an exaggeration	TWAIN 219:23
no cure for birth and d.	SANT 190:17
O D., where is thy sting	ROSS 185:5
O D., where is thy sting-a-ling	ANON 8:1
[Ogden Mills] the kiss of d.	SMITH 202:3
O million-murdering D.	ROSS 185:5
one way out an' d.'s	WILL 227:17
On life, on d.	YEATS 233:4
only nervousness of d.	LEB 133:19
Peaceful out-of-breath d.	MCG 142:9
Pledges them that D. is ending	BELL 25:20
Pontifical D., that doth	THOM 216:6
prepare as though for d.	MANS 146:6
Satisfaction is d.	SHAW 199:10
seen visible, D.'s artifact	ABSE 1:3
suicide 25 years after his d.	BEAV 21:6
Swarm over, D.	BETJ 31:1
terror to life and makes d.	TREE 217:16
that I have longed for d.	PROU 175:19
The d. of hope and despair	ELIOT 74:18
The nearest thing to d. in life	ANON 7:26
The only possible d.	DUB 70:7
This is the d. of air	ELIOT 74:18
thought d. had undone so many	ELIOT 76:17
through the d. of some of her	MAS 148:9
until the arrival of d.	BERNE 30:10
was much possessed by d.	ELIOT 75:8
you know, a very sad d.	SPOO 206:10
you're frightened of d.	DONL 68:6
deathless: let us make love d.	TREN 217:19
deathly: d. inner consuming fire	HESSE 102:4
death-sentence: d. without a whimper	LAWR 133:1
death-struck: The beautiful and d. year	HOUS 107:5
debate: d. forcefully and quote	HOGB 104:3
The quality of d.	SOPER 205:2
debt: A promise made is a d.	SERV 195:1
d. of gratitude we owe	TWAIN 219:29
midst of life we are in d.	MUMF 157:14
The National D. is a very	SELL 194:15
decade: d. after decade the truth	SOLZ 204:5
fun to be in the same d.	ROOS 182:20
decay: D. with imprecision	ELIOT 74:6
has no ebb, d. no flood	YEATS 232:18
deceitfulness: Cat of such d. and suavity	ELIOT 75:4
deceive: creates faith does not d.	SHAW 199.28
deceived: Let us not be d.	BAR 20:7

deceives: d. with whispering ambitions	ELIOT 73:12
December: From May to D.	AND 4:21
might have roses in D.	BARR 19:13
decency: D. is Indecency's conspiracy	SHAW 198:25
decent: aristocracy to what is d.	HOPE 104:16
d. people live beyond	SAKI 188:6
Here were d. godless people	ELIOT 76:5
decerated: d. dark red as I have somber	ASHF 10:18
decide: d. between alternatives	BONH 36:2
You'll have to d.	DYLAN 71:15
decided: d. only to be undecided	CHUR 54:5
decision: d. has to be made	TRUM 218:13
fast and specific d.	TUCH 218:16
freedom of personal d.	JUNG 117:2
make a 'realistic d.'	MCC 141:13
monologue is not a d.	ATTL 12:10
questions of will or d.	CHOM 52:18
decisions: on the eve of great d.	STEV 209:4
deck: d. put on its leaves again	FLEC 81:21
declaration: There has been no d. of war	EDEN 71:18
declarations: And timid lovers' d.	AUDEN 14:22
declare: contracting powers solemnly d.	BRIA 39:10
d. before you all	ELIZ 77:7
declared: hundred judges have d.	QUIL 177:2
decline: d. utterly to be impartial	CHUR 54:3
went into a bit of a d.	ADAMS 1:15
decompose: d. in a barrel of porter	DONL 68:7
decomposing: d. in the eternity of print	WOOLF 231:9
decoration: some sort of d. for it	OSB 165:16
decorative: be d. and to do right	FIRB 79:19
decorum: The old Lie: Dulce et d. est	OWEN 166:10
deductions: features from which d.	DOYLE 69:28
dee: Hi diddle dee d.	WASH 222:14
deed: motive, not the d.	YEATS 234:9
right d. for the wrong	ELIOT 75:1
time the d. took place	ELIOT 75:4
deep: A gentle motion with the d.	DAV 65:4
are lovely, dark and d.	FROST 86:7
D. from human vanity	HARDY 97:13
D. in the heart of Texas	HERS 102:2
d. is the silence	DRIN 70:4
d. peace of the double-bed	CAMP 45:9
Oh, d. in my heart	ANON 9:13
say beauty is only sin d.	SAKI 188:11
deepens: It d. like a coastal shelf	LARK 130:13
deeper: Christ went d. than I have	HARR 98:13
This d. layer I call	JUNG 117:3
Deever: Danny D. in the mornin'	KIPL 123:4
defeat: Alamein we never had a d.	CHUR 55:20
d. comparable to any lost	PHIL 170:18
d. is an orphan	CIANO 56:7
In d.: defiance	CHUR 55:16
In d. unbeatable	CHUR 53:3

defeat (cont.):
we know we should d. you   KIPL 124:17
defeated: be destroyed but not d.
                                    HEM 101:4
History to the d.   AUDEN 15:10
we succeed in being d.   HELL 100:6
defect: The Chief D. of Henry King
                                    BELL 24:11
defence: best d. against the atom
                                    ANON 5:16
d. against the anti-Christ   BUCH 42:1
d. like elaborate courtesy   LUCAS 140:10
d. of England you no longer   BALD 17:8
d. of the indefensible   ORW 165:6
extremism in the d. of liberty
                                    GOLD 91:12
only d. against betrayal   WILL 227:13
The only d. is in offence   BALD 17:7
defences: d. of peace must be constructed
                                    ANON 6:16
defend: d. any one or anything
                                    MENC 151:2
d. ourselves with arms   GOEB 91:6
D. the bad against the worse
                                    DAY-L 65:11
I will d. to the death   TALL 212:4
we shall d. our island   CHUR 54:10
defiance: In defeat: d.   CHUR 55:16
d. of military authority   SASS 192:1
defiant: It is d.   READ 178:9
definition: capable of exact legal d.
                                    RUSS 187:2
d. is the enclosing a wilderness
                                    BUTL 43:27
d. of a free society   STEV 208:22
d. of a specialist as one   MAYO 150:8
d. of capitalism I would   HAMP 96:7
good working d. of hell   SHAW 199:13
deflowered: At last you are d.   COW 62:10
deformity: Art is significant d.   FRY 87:10
degree: d. of independence still   EINS 73:4
dei: Introibo ad altare D   JOYCE 116:1
deity: between the D. and the Drains
                                    STR 210:8
D. but accepted Carnot's   WELLS 224:15
delegate: When in trouble, d.   BOREN 36:7
deleted: Expletive d.   ANON 6:7
Delia: D., if S-E-X ever rears   AYCK 15:19
deliberate: D. speed, majestic instancy
                                    THOM 215:6
Originality is d. and forced   HOFF 103:18
delicate-filmed: D. as new-spun silk
                                    HARDY 97:10
delight: A lonely impulse of d.   YEATS 235:5
And I was filled with such d.   SASS 192:6
begins in d. and ends   FROST 85:16
Had other aims than my d.   HARDY 98:2
I most d. in Me   CAMP 45:10
leaping light for your d.   AUDEN 14:12
Moved to d. by the melody   AUDEN 15:11
Teach us D. in simple things   KIPL 126:8
The d. of her husband   RANS 177:14
Till to d.   DE L 66:12
visions for a simple human d.
                                    BARB 18:10
delighted: literature is to be d. CECIL 48:4
delightful: affording d. prospects
                                    HOFF 104:2
alcohol produces a d. social   BENN 28:10
really d. sensation   FERB 79:3
take courage: it can be d.   SHAW 195:24
delighting: But, O! d. me   HODG 103:15
delirium: All that d. of the brave
                                    YEATS 234:15

deliver: D. us, good Lord   CHES 51:18
Del Monte: The man from D. says 'Yes'
                                    ANON 7:23
deluge: d. subsides and the waters
                                    CHUR 54:2
delusion: d. that one woman   MENC 150:17
delusions: gave us such insane d.
                                    HELL 100:6
demand: not a note of d.   SCHN 193:2
demean: We think they d. us   RATT 178:2
demesne: Is private pagus or d.
                                    AUDEN 12:14
demeure: Les jours s'en vont, je d.
                                    APOL 9:22
democracies: d. it is the only sacred
                                    FRAN 84:14
democracy: can be cured by more d.
                                    SMITH 202:4
capacity for justice makes d.   NIEB 160:10
D. and proper drains   BETJ 32:9
D. and socialism are means   NEHRU 160:2
d. by universal suffrage   BENN 27:14
D. is a State which recognizes
                                    LENIN 134:18
d. is that it has tolerated   BEVAN 33:2
D. is the name we give   FLERS 82:4
D. is the recurrent suspicion
                                    WHITE 226:2
D. is the theory   MENC 150:20
d. is the worst form   CHUR 55:3
D. means government by discussion
                                    ATTL 12:13
D. means government by the
uneducated   CHES 51:9
D. resumed her reign   BELL 25:19
d. should spend less time   STR 210:17
D. substitutes election   SHAW 198:11
D. tells us not to neglect   CHES 51:13
D. will not be salvaged   HOGB 104:3
d. would have rallied   BALD 17:10
Envy is the basis of d.   RUSS 186:12
great arsenal of d.   ROOS 183:8
It is the d. of the dead   CHES 51:13
little less d. to save   ATK 12:2
must be made safe for d.   WILS 229:13
no d. can afford   BEV 33:9
political aspirant under d.   MENC 150:14
puts in the place of d.   FOSD 84:13
So Two cheers for D.   FORS 84:6
voting that's d.   STOP 209:11
Democrat: D., in that order   JOHN 114:16
démocratie: D. est le nom que nous
                                    MARQ 82:4
démocraties: dans les d. elle est FRAN 84:14
democrats: d. object to men being
                                    CHES 51:13
telling lies about the D.   STEV 208:19
demur: If I d., for, be advised   HEAN 99:15
denial: d. of Him by the atheist
                                    PROU 176:3
denied: call that may not be d.   MAS 148:17
denizen: The spider is sole d.   HARDY 97:1
denominator: I can find no common d.
                                    AUDEN 14:5
denouncing: d. some one or something
                                    MENC 151:2
dentist: sooner go to my d. any day
                                    WAUGH 223:17
denunciation: d. of the young is
a necessary   SMITH 203:1
deoch-an-doris: Just a wee d.   MORR 156:8
depart: D., I say, and let us   AMERY 4:12
departing: someone who's d.   RILKE 181:4

department: fair sex is your d.   DOYLE 69:18
dépêches: Une de ces d. dont M   PROU 176:5
depended: always d. on the kindness
                                    WILL 227:21
dependence: d. on the appreciation
                                    CONN 58:18
depends: It all d. what you mean
                                    JOAD 113:19
so much d.   WILL 228:1
That d. on the tip   BRAC 38:1
deposit: d. in my name at a Swiss
                                    ALLEN 3:19
depression: are the best cures for d.
                                    SMITH 202:7
it's a d. when you lose   TRUM 218:10
deprivation: D. is for me what daffodils
                                    LARK 130:20
this as a 'cycle of d.'   JOS 115:5
depth: about d. knows about God
                                    TILL 217:5
Derby: [the 17th Earl of D.]   HAIG 95:2
descended: iron curtain has d.   CHUR 53:15
désenchantement: confondis le d. avec la
vérité   SART 191:8
desert: scare myself with my own d.
                                    FROST 85:19
The d. sighs in the bed   AUDEN 12:17
Zuleika, on a d. island   BEER 23:7
deserts: D. are there, and different
                                    SACK 187:15
In the d. of the heart   AUDEN 13:4
It's my d.; I'm a second   BARR 19:2
deserve: d. to get it good and hard
                                    MENC 150:20
war, but only d. it   CHUR 55:19
you somehow haven't to d.   FROST 86:13
deserves: everyone has the face he d.
                                    ORW 164:10
déshabille: on dirait qu'elle se d. COL 57:16
desiccated: Party is a d. calculating
machine   BEVAN 32:15
design: might of d.   SHAW 196:15
designed: horse d. by a committee
                                    ANON 5:23
designer: D. infinite   THOM 215:15
designing: Say I am d. St Paul's   BENT 29:1
désir: d. pour empêcher les choses
                                    PROU 176:2
desirable: D. than it ever was before
                                    SASS 192:3
desire: d. for preventing the thing
                                    PROU 176:2
d. on the part   BUTL 43:19
d. to be vilified by enemies   BIER 33:23
d. to have all the fun   SAY 192:9
d. to take medicine   OSLER 165:25
From what I've tasted of d.   FROST 86:6
Land of Heart's D.   YEATS 232:18
Memory and d., stirring   ELIOT 76:13
Yea, naught for your d.   CHES 50:8
desired: You who d. so much   CRANE 62:16
desires: d. of the heart   AUDEN 14:8
desireus: d. of being the correct ASHF 11:1
desiring: admire without d.   BRAD 38:4
desk: From counter or d. among grey
                                    YEATS 233:9
Turn upward from the d.   ELIOT 76:24
desolation: witnesses to the d. of war
                                    GEOR 89:11
despair: A minor form of d.   BIER 34:11
d. and utter hopelessness   ALLEN 3:21
D. is the price one pays   GREE 93:14
Do not d.   PUDN 176:9

despair (*cont.*):
  foundation of unyielding d.   RUSS 186:21
  Lead me from d. to hope   KUMAR 129:6
  never hoped can never d.   SHAW 196:1
  or the quality of his d.   CONN 59:3
  Rhymed out in love's d.   YEATS 234:19
  The death of hope and d.   ELIOT 74:18
  without understanding d.   LAING 129:9
desperate: ardent for some d. glory
          OWEN 166:10
  d. act of men too profoundly   READ 178:9
despise: d. Shakespeare when I measure
          SHAW 199:32
  Government I d. for ends   KEYN 120:7
despised: d. by the rest of society
          BHAI 38:18
despondency: SPREAD ALARM AND D.
          PEN 170:1
despondently: Sprouting d. at area gates
          ELIOT 76:1
destined: d. to live for three-score
          JEANS 112:20
destinies: development of human d.
          FISH 80:5
  recognised, and robed as d.   LARK 130:16
destiny: Anatomy is d.   FREUD 85:5
  d. can determine how   DE B 65:12
  D., n. A tyrant's authority   BIER 34:15
  I were walking with d.   CHUR 55:18
  We hug our little d. again   HEAN 99:14
destroy: D. him as you will   CONN 59:5
  necessary to d. the town   ANON 7:2
  When you d. a blade of grass   BOTT 36:13
  Whom the gods wish to d.   CONN 58:16
destroyed: be d. but not defeated
          HEM 101:4
  can be d. by a doctor   SHAF 195:5
  generation d. by madness   GINS 90:15
destroyer: Is my d.   THOM 213:20
destroying: d. ourselves by violence
          LAING 129:11
destroys: Death d. a man   FORS 83:18
destruction: by a brief fit of d.   BORN 36:11
  To say that for d. ice   FROST 86:6
  whether the mad d.   GAND 88:10
destructive: d. element submit yourself
          CONR 59:24
detachment: vigilance and a rare d.
          MAUG 149:5
detected: d. only once in the use
          BENN 28:11
detection: D. is, or ought   DOYLE 69:19
detective: d. novel is the art-for-art's-sake
          PRIT 175:14
detector: shock-proof shit d.   HEM 101:5
detente: d. and world peace   THAT 213:4
deteriorating: With shabby equipment
  always d.   ELIOT 74:13
determination: character but the d. of
  incident   JAMES 112:1
determine: means employed d. the nature
          HUXL 108:15
dethrimental: temper till it would be d.
          O'CAS 162:19
de Valera: Negotiating with d.   LLOY 138:6
development: d. of human destinies
          FISH 80:5
devil: An apology for the D.   BUTL 43:25
  But the D. whoops   KIPL 124:2
  D. whispered behind   KIPL 124:1
  last: the D. howling   SQUI 206:17
  man's spirit is d.'s work   SHAW 196:5
  that d.'s madness—War   SERV 194:21
  The D., having nothing else   BELL 25:17

devil (*cont.*):
  The d.'s walking parody   CHES 52:10
  up believing in the d.   KNOX 128:12
devils: And down on the d. we shot
          ASQ 11:20
  d. to contest his vision   MAIL 145:12
devoid: entirely d. of interest   DOYLE 69:3
Devon: 'Twas D., glorious D.   BOUL 37:2
devoured: He has d. the infant child
          HOUS 105:10
devours: Death d. all lovely things
          MILL 151:23
dew: again in the d. of morn   YEATS 232:6
  drenched with d.   DE L 66:6
Dewey: D. threw his diaper   ICKES 110:4
  [Thomas D.] is just about the nastiest
          DYKS 71:3
dews: Nor ask amid the d. of morning
          HOUS 106:4
diagnostician: rectum makes a good d.
          OSLER 165:22
dial: D. 'M' for murder   KNOTT 128:9
dialect: picturesque use of d.   HARDY 97:6
  To purify the d. of the tribe   ELIOT 74:19
diametrically: d. opposed doctrines
          HOOV 104:12
diamond: d. and safire bracelet   LOOS 139:6
diamonds: D. are a girl's best friend
          ROBIN 181:11
  Goodness, what beautiful d.   WEST 225:19
  man enough to give him d.   GABOR 87:21
Diana: It's awf'lly bad luck on D.
          BETJ 31:9
diaper: threw his d. into the ring
          ICKES 110:4
diaries: keep d. to remember   O'NEI 163:14
diary: d. and some day it'll keep
          WEST 225:11
  life of every man is a d.   BARR 19:4
  secret d. of Adrian Mole   TOWN 217:12
dice: [God] does not play d.   EINS 72:14
Dickens: D. as children but it never
          BENN 28:1
  he [D.] was probably   WILS 228:8
dictated: We will not be d. to   CHES 50:24
dictation: at d. speed what he knew
          AMIS 4:18
dictator: the German d.   CHUR 54:6
dictators: D. ride to and fro upon tigers
          CHUR 55:21
  which d. may cultivate   BEV 33:9
dictatorship: government you have a d.
          TRUM 218:14
  order to establish the d.   ORW 164:25
dictatorships: d. it puts in the place
          FOSD 84:13
dictionary: time I ever made the d.
          WEST 225:18
did: d. for them both   SASS 191:17
didn't: D. she do well   FORS 84:10
die: better to d. on your feet   IBAR 109:17
  clean place to d.   KAV 118:9
  d. for my country   KINN 122:15
  D.? I should say not   BARR 19:29
  d. like a true-blue rebel   HILL 102:11
  d. will be an awfully big adventure
          BARR 19:9
  Don't d. of ignorance   ANON 6:3
  fifteen-year-old boy until *they d.*
          ROTH 185:10
  he had to d. in MY week   JOPL 115:4
  Hope I d. before I get old   TOWN 217:13
  I d. each time   HEM 100:12
  If I should d., think only   BROO 40:5

die (*cont.*):
  If we must d., let it not   MCKAY 142:15
  It is most grand to d.   MAS 148:13
  Let me d. a youngman's death
          MCG 142:9
  Live and let d.   FLEM 82:3
  not that I'm afraid to d.   ALLEN 3:14
  Old soldiers never d.   FOLEY 82:8
  People d., but books never   ROOS 183:13
  pie in the sky when you d.   HILL 102:12
  something he will d. for   KING 121:13
  these who d. as cattle   OWEN 166:9
  they d. earlier   MENC 150:18
  they do not d. of wisdom   STEP 208:5
  they only let Him d.   STUD 210:20
  To d. and know it   LOW 140:5
  war it's the poor who d.   SART 190:26
  We must love one another or d.
          AUDEN 13:9
  Who did not wish to d.   SHAW 200:9
  Who went abroad to d.   LETTS 136:1
  work, work till we d.   LEWIS 136:15
  you asked this man to d.   AUDEN 15:7
  youth who must fight and d.
          HOOV 104:10
died: d. if it had not been   ASQ 11:16
  d. to save their country   CHES 50:6
  foolish ideas have d.   FITZ 80:14
  He d. who loved to live   MCH 142:13
  If any question why we d.   KIPL 127:21
  Mithridates, he d. old   HOUS 107:10
  Mother d. today. Or perhaps
          CAMUS 46:4
  There d. a myriad   POUND 174:6
dies: begotten born and d.   YEATS 234:5
  d. fighting has increase   GREN 94:3
  into Bovril when she d.   ASQ 11:14
  kingdom where nobody d.   MILL 152:2
  little something in me d.   VIDAL 221:16
  When a lovely flame d.   HARB 96:11
  Who d. if England live   KIPL 124:15
diet: part of a balanced d.   LEB 133:2
Dieu: *D. est avec tout le monde*   ANOU 9:18
  D. pour la rendre responsable   DUH 70:9
  le bon D. who drives it   CHR 53:1
  tue tous, on est un d.   ROST 185:8
difference: And that has made all the d.
          FROST 86:4
  d. between accidental limitations
          AUDEN 13:16
  d. between our talents   DE B 65:13
  d. does it make to the dead   GAND 88:10
  d. within the sexes   COMP 58:11
  greatly exaggerate the d.   SHAW 197:16
  it is d. of opinion   TWAIN 220:2
differences: unrealistic settlement of the d.
          ROOS 183:11
different: had thought they were d.
          ELIOT 73:15
  only on d. subjects   ROG 182:10
  something completely d.   CHAP 49:11
  They are d. from you   FITZ 80:19
  will not know it's a d. country
          LARK 130:11
  you'd have made them d.   O'BR 162:6
differently: one who thinks d.   LUX 140:17
  they do things d. there   HART 99:1
differs: delusion that one woman d.
          MENC 150:17
difficult: at present, must be d.   ELIOT 76:11
  d. is what takes a little time   NANS 158:19
  It has been found d.   CHES 52:8
  Luckily, this is not d.   WHIT 226:21

difficult (*cont.*):
The fascination of what's d.
YEATS 232:12
difficulties: these little local d.   MACM 144:1
difficulty: quits the memory with a d.
BEEC 22:9
dig: D. for Victory   DORM 68:8
d. him up and throw stones
SHAW 199:32
d. till you gently perspire   KIPL 125:11
I'll d. with it   HEAN 99:10
digestions: Few radicals have good d.
BUTL 43:20
digging: d. in the garden   ASHF 10:16
dignify: Dared d. the labor   CRANE 62:16
dignité: *égaux en d. et en droits*   ANON 9:1
dignity: d. and greatness and peace
COW 61:14
equal in d. and rights   ANON 9:1
Official d. tends to increase HUXL 108:10
dillied: But I d. and dallied   COLL 58:2
dilly-dally: Don't d. on the way COLL 58:2
dime: Brother can you spare a d.
HARB 96:12
d. that we've got is honestly
NIXON 161:7
dine: going to d. with some men BENT 29:1
dined: d. last night   BEER 22:18
more d. against than dining
BOWRA 37:18
ding: D.! dong! the bells   LERN 135:18
dining: d. with the Borgias   BEER 22:18
more dined against than d. BOWRA 37:18
dinky: Hinky, d., parley-voo   ANON 7:20
dinner: D. in the diner nothing GORD 92:4
I get too hungry for d.   HART 98:18
refrain from asking it to d. HALS 95:13
The best number for a d.   GULB 94:15
The man who came to d.   KAUF 118:1
dinner-knives: gravel paths with broken d.
KIPL 125:1
diodes: terrible pain in all the d.
ADAMS 1:13
Dior: Never darken my D. again LILL 137:8
diplomacy: D. is to do and say   GOLD 91:9
d. shall proceed always   WILS 229:15
diplomat: A d.   STIN 209:9
d. these days is nothing   UST 220:21
dipping: age o'ercargoed, d. deep
FLEC 81:19
direction: With no d. home   DYLAN 71:8
dirt: d. succeed where sweetness
FORS 83:10
first four years the d.   CRISP 63:1
insult sex, to do d. on it   LAWR 132:19
dirty: give pornography a d. name
BARN 18:16
In a d. glass   PAN 167:7
Is sex d.   ALLEN 3:15
'Jug Jug' to d. ears   ELIOT 76:19
you d. rat   CAGN 44:14
Dirty Dick: At D.'s and Sloppy Joe's
AUDEN 14:6
dirty-mindedness: deliberate,
journalistic d.   LAWR 132:5
disadvantage: d. of being a hog
MORT 156:12
disagree: agree with us or d. with us
OWEN 166:7
disappeared: He d. in the dead of winter
AUDEN 12:20
disappointed: Sir! you have d. us
BELL 24:18
disappointing: he'll be the least d. BAR 20:6

disappointment: d. to their children
POW 174:19
disapprove: I d. of what you say
TALL 212:4
disaster: meet with Triumph and D.
KIPL 126:13
disasters: d. of English history
WAUGH 223:1
d. of the world are due   CONN 59:11
disastrous: d. and the unpalatable
GALB 88:5
war is as d. as to lose   CHR 52:20
discard: scientist to d. a pet hypothesis
LOR 139:13
discharge: There's no d. in the war
KIPL 124:13
disciple: am a d. of Bernard Shaw
SHAW 196:14
Discobolus: D. standeth and turneth
BUTL 44:2
discontents: Civilization and its d. RIV 181:9
source of all our d.   LEACH 133:4
discount: sells us life At a d.   FRY 87:1
discover: d. that I had no talent BENC 27:4
d. that there is no God   SMITH 203:3
discovered: dramatist who had d.
SAKI 188:23
discovering: process of d. who we are
AUDEN 13:16
discovery: are the portals of d.
JOYCE 116:11
D. consists of seeing what   SZEN 212:1
his d. to the world   SAKI 188:23
Medicinal d.   AYRES 16:8
discreet: The d. charm of the bourgeoisie
BUÑ 42:7
discretion: D. is not the better part
STR 210:11
discriminate: do learn to d.   LAWR 132:14
discussion: means government by d.
ATTL 12:13
disease: But when they name any d.
PUZO 176:12
d. that afflicts amateurs   CHES 51:3
from the particular d.   JER 113:14
I have Bright's d.   PER 170:3
nineteenth century, it was a d.
SZASZ 211:13
our national d.   JAMES 112:8
sexually transmitted d.   ANON 7:16
There is no Cure for this D. BELL 24:12
diseases: d. is a sort of *Arabian* OSLER 166:1
scientific treatment for all d.
SHAW 196:12
sneezes spread d.   ANON 5:27
disenchantment: I mistook d. for truth
SART 191:8
disgrace: Intellectual d.   AUDEN 13:3
It's no d. t'be poor   HUBB 107:17
Its private life is a d.   ANON 8:6
disgruntled: if not actually d. WOD 230:7
disgusting: murder of men is d. EINS 72:12
dishonoured: To stain the stiff d. shroud
ELIOT 75:5
disillusion: France; and one d. KEYN 120:8
disillusionment: D. in living is the finding
STEIN 207:19
disillusionments: d. in the lives SAKI 188:14
disinterested: that there are d. actions
GIDE 90:9
dislike: d. it   MOORE 155:13
I d. what I fancy I feel   ANON 8:19
know whether I like or d.   FORS 83:19

disliked: day two things they d.
MAUG 149:13
disloyalty: not like subversion or d.
HELL 100:8
dismantle: d. apartheid ourselves
MAND 145:18
dismount: which they dare not d.
CHUR 55:21
disorder: put back in d. by authorities
CONN 59:16
dispensation: ease here, in the old d.
ELIOT 73:15
dispiriting: Muse this cannot but be d.
SMITH 203:24
disposed: way she d. of an empire
HARL 98:11
dispossessed: his little heart, d.
JAMES 112:5
disputes: d. or conflicts of whatever
BRIA 39:10
dissipated: still keep looking so d.
BENC 26:18
dissociation: d. of sensibility set
ELIOT 76:10
dissolution: at home? A lingering d.
BECK 21:9
distains: A starlit or a moonlit dome d.
YEATS 235:15
distance: d. from the political situation
RAK 177:8
longest d. between two places
WILL 227:18
distempered: That questions the d. part
ELIOT 74:12
distils: Art d. sensation and embodies
BARZ 20:11
distinction: British have the d.   ATTL 12:8
d. at this dangerous moment BELL 26:11
D. between the Ashes   DOYLE 69:20
few escape that d.   TWAIN 220:6
see you were a man of d.   FIEL 79:6
distinguish: d. human society from
SHAW 196:23
Give us the wisdom to d.   NIEB 160:11
distinguished: d. thing   JAMES 111:16
I write like a d. author   NAB 158:15
distortion: d. of the Marxist idea
BENN 27:11
distortions: d. of ingrown virginity
AUDEN 15:2
distraction: attention in the midst of d.
BELL 26:12
distress: avoids the sight of d.
MAUG 149:15
distressing: d. moment can ever face
TUCH 218:16
distrust: I d. the incommunicable
SART 191:11
We have to d. each other   WILL 227:13
disturb: Art is meant to d.   BRAQ 38:16
part of ourselves doesn't d. HESSE 102:3
disturbing: upon as a d. influence
GALB 88:2
diver: Don't forget the d.   KAV 118:12
divided: D. by the morning tea
MACN 144:14
dividend: d. from time's tomorrows
SASS 191:14
divine: You look d. as you advance
NASH 159:3
divinely: D. subsidized to provoke   FRY 87:3
divisible: d. into two great classes
BEER 22:17

divisions: d. did you say the Pope
STAL 206:19
divorced: Demand to be d. CHES 52:12
my fault that we got d. ALLEN 4:2
Dixon: D. . . . tried to flail his features
AMIS 4:17
do: Can I d. you now, sir KAV 118:11
Didn't she d. well FORS 84:10
Diplomacy is to d. and say GOLD 91:9
d. anything she hasn't KAEL 117:5
D. evil in return AUDEN 13:8
D. I dare to eat a peach ELIOT 75:19
D. not do unto others SHAW 198:8
D. not expect again a phoenix
DAY-L 65:7
D. not fold, spindle ANON 6:1
d. something to *help* me LAUR 131:12
d. the perfectly correct SHAW 196:26
d. the right deed ELIOT 75:1
d. those things KEYN 120:13
D. what thou wilt shall CROW 63:10
Goodness had nothing to d. WEST 225:19
Let's d. it, let's fall PORT 173:3
long as they d. what I say THAT 212:19
not d. things themselves RAV 178:4
So little done, so much to d. RHOD 180:4
wild extremes I could d. or die DURY 71:2
Doc: cards with a man called D. ALGR 3:6
What's up, D. AVERY 15:17
doctor: can be destroyed by a d.
SHAF 195:5
I really am a horse d. PIR 171:19
Knocked down a d. SIMP 201:7
my d., what do you say ROTH 185:11
doctors: We d. know CUMM 64:3
doctrine: d. of ignoble ease ROOS 184:2
how a d. so illogical KEYN 120:12
doctrines: diametrically opposed d.
HOOV 104:12
documents: d. I have to have a box
HOME 104:8
dodo: The D. never had a chance
CUPPY 64:5
doe: With the fallow d. THOM 214:12
dog: beaten d. beneath the hail
POUND 174:14
been working like a d. LENN 135:8
But if a man bites a d. BOGA 35:13
But where's the wild d. YEATS 232:13
d. and I just want to say NIXON 161:7
D. returns to his Vomit KIPL 126:18
engine of pollution, the d. SPAR 205:9
great pleasure of a d. BUTL 43:26
I'm a lean d., a keen dog MCL 143:7
jumps over the lazy d. ANON 8:5
mad d. of the Middle East REAG 178:16
your heart to a d. to tear KIPL 123:1
doggie: that d. in the window
MERR 151:10
dogma: d. of the Ghost RYLE 187:12
will serve to beat a d. GUED 94:9
dogmatism: ignorance the greater the d.
OSLER 166:2
dogs: All the d. of Europe bark AUDEN 13:3
And dancing d. and bears HODG 103:13
D. bark, School's out DAV 65:2
d. go on with their doggy AUDEN 13:9
hates d. and babies can't ROST 185:9
keep parrots or puppy d. CAMP 45:12
let's go to the d. tonight HERB 101:19
Mad d. and Englishmen COW 62:4
really kind to d. BEER 23:10

doileys: Beg pardon, I'm soiling the d.
BETJ 31:12
doing: he's d. a grand job FROST 85:15
dollar: D. lolly SYKES 211:7
dolls: Valley of the d. SUS 211:3
Dolly: Hello, D., well, hello Dolly
HERM 102:1
dolphin-torn: That d., that
gong-tormented YEATS 235:16
dome: moonlit d. distains YEATS 235:15
domestic: naïve d. Burgundy without
THUR 216:20
respectable d. establishment BENN 27:19
dominate: seeking to d. the world
BRAD 38:10
domination: d. of Prussia is wholly
ASQ 11:11
Soviet d. of Eastern Europe FORD 82:15
domine: D., defende nos GODL 91:5
dominion: And death shall have no d.
THOM 214:6
from the d. of religion GOLD 91:11
hand that holds d. THOM 214:5
domino: 'falling d.' principle EIS 73:8
don: *c'est avant tout le d.* ANOU 9:20
D. different from those BELL 26:5
Remote and ineffectual D. BELL 26:4
done: belief they d. the old woman in
SHAW 199:22
D. because we are too HARDY 96:22
d. very well out of the war BALD 17:5
have d. being what she is YEATS 232:11
he d. her wrong ANON 6:10
Is dead and dumb and d. DE L 66:19
Nothing to be d. BECK 21:15
ought never to have d. BEVIN 33:16
Something should be d. EDW 72:9
donkeys: d. labelled Sally and Peppy
SHAF 195:4
Donne: another Newton, a new D.
HUXL 108:20
dons: D. admirable! Dons of Might
BELL 26:5
technology d. from Cambridge AMIS 4:16
don't: And d. criticize DYLAN 71:14
And d. go near the water DE L 66:20
But d. go near the water ANON 7:25
D. ask a man to drink and drive
ANON 6:2
D. ask me, ask the horse FREUD 85:6
D. die of ignorance ANON 6:3
d. do it in the street CAMP 45:7
D. follow leaders DYLAN 71:13
D. forget the diver KAV 118:12
D. panic ADAMS 1:11
d. spare the horses HILL 102:15
D. tell my mother I'm living
HERB 101:17
D. think twice, it's all right DYLAN 71:5
d. think you can't think INGE 110:8
George—d. do that GREN 94:1
doodle: A Yankee D., do or die
COHAN 57:13
Doolittle: across the Park, Miss D.
SHAW 199:24
door: childhood when the d. GREE 93:19
Converses at the d. apart ELIOT 75:5
generation is knocking at the d.
SHAW 200:7
Is beating on the d. YEATS 234:1
lock and splintered the d. AUDEN 14:14
On the wrong side of the d. CHES 50:10
own room with the d. shut WHAR 225:28

door (*cont.*):
that grows beside thy d. HOPE 105:3
Towards the d. we never opened
ELIOT 74:3
We like to see them to the d. MCG 142:10
doorbell: d. of a Mrs Renton MORT 156:14
doors: Death opens unknown d.
MAS 148:13
In Little Girls is slamming D. BELL 24:19
taxi-cab with both d. open HUGH 107:19
doorstep: Leave your worry on the d.
FIEL 79:9
Dorchester: Safe in the D. Hotel BETJ 31:4
Dorset: vault for funeral Monday D.
BEER 23:17
dotage: Pedantry is the d. of knowledge
JACK 111:4
double: about a joke with a d. BARK 18:15
it plies the saplings d. HOUS 106:18
double-bed: d. after the hurly-burly
CAMP 45:9
doubled: D. the globe of dead THOM 214:4
doubles: It immediately d. ALLEN 3:20
doublethink: D. means the power
ORW 164:24
doubt: And troubled with religious d.
CHES 51:22
d. is our passion and our JAMES 111:18
freckles, and d. PARK 168:10
Life is d. UNAM 220:12
Oh! let us never, never d. BELL 25:6
trust yourself when all men d. you
KIPL 126:13
When in d., mumble BOREN 36:7
when in d., strike it out TWAIN 219:33
doubted: Christian religion d. BUTL 44:5
doubts: will be our d. of today ROOS 183:12
doughnut: The optimist sees the d.
WILS 229:1
Douglas-Home: he [Alec D.] CONN 59:1
dove: d. complaining DAY-L 65:7
Dover: chalk cliffs of D. BALD 17:8
white cliffs of D. BURT 42:15
down: Come on d. CROW 63:11
D. and Out in Paris ORW 164:4
D. by the salley gardens YEATS 234:13
d., down into the darkness MILL 151:17
d. express in the small WOD 230:13
'd.' from Jimmy's university OSB 165:17
D. in the forest something SIMP 201:4
D. the passage which we ELIOT 74:3
D. these mean streets CHAN 49:1
D. to Gehenna or up KIPL 127:15
Had me low and had me d. GERS 89:13
meet 'em on your way d. MIZN 154:19
must d. to the seas again MAS 148:16
downhearted: Are we d. KNIG 128:8
We are not d. CHAM 48:10
Downing Street: from Germany to D.
peace CHAM 48:14
[10 D.] is an inconvenient ASQ 11:13
dozed: d. off into a stupor when
BENC 26:17
dozen: d. dirty and ragged little
DOYLE 69:24
dozens: Mother to d. HERB 101:13
dragging: d. themselves through
GINS 90:15
dragon: O to be a d. MOORE 155:12
dragon-green: The d., the luminous
FLEC 81:13

drain: leave by the first town d.
SPOO 206:7

drained: Empire are irresistibly d.
DOYLE 69:25

drains: between the Deity and the D.
STR 210:8
Democracy and proper d. BETJ 32:9

drama: d. critic also perceives
TYNAN 220:11

dramatist: d. only wants more liberties
JAMES 111:14
d. who had discovered himself
SAKI 188:23

dramatize: ever-importunate murmur, 'D.
it' JAMES 111:10

dravest: Thou d. love from thee
THOM 215:20

drawbacks: everything has its d.
JER 113:15

drawing: d. sufficient conclusions
BUTL 43:18
The d. is on the level BLUNT 35:5

drawing room: was flowing through my d.
EDEN 71:19

drawing-room: brilliant d. comedy
DE VR 67:5

dread: d. of doing what has WHAR 225:29
d. with which the untutored FRAZ 84:17
Nor d. nor hope attend YEATS 235:1
That is why most men d. it SHAW 198:12
The d. of beatings BETJ 32:10

dreadful: d. martyrdom must run
AUDEN 13:6

Dreadnoughts: construction of D.
WYND 232:2
much to keep up as two D. LLOY 138:11

dream: And slowly read and d.
YEATS 232:7
A salesman is got to d. MILL 152:5
born falls into a d. CONR 59:24
But I d. things that never SHAW 195:20
citizens d. of the south HARDY 97:2
d. between two awakenings O'NEI 163:12
d. of the days when work CHES 51:23
d. that I am home again FLEC 81:16
I d. my dreams away FLAN 81:2
If you can d.—and not make KIPL 126:13
I have a d. that one day KING 121:15
In a d. you are never eighty SEXT 195:2
It was a d. I had last week COPE 61:3
quiet sleep and a sweet d. MAS 148:18
till you find your d. HAMM 95:14
To follow the d. CONR 59:24
True to the d. I am dreaming COW 62:9
We live, as we d.—alone CONR 59:20
Where we used to sit and d. ARMS 10:7
Yea, faileth now even d. THOM 215:14

dreamed: heaven and earth than are d.
HALD 95:6

dreamer: An artist is a d. consenting
SANT 190:11

dreamers: Like all d., I mistook SART 191:8
Soldiers are d. SASS 191:15

dreamin': A little d., a little dyin'
PHIL 171:3
D. of thee! Dreamin' of thee WALL 222:5

dreaming: d. on the verge of strife
CORN 61:7
I'm d. of a white Christmas BERL 30:3
must be my excuse for d. HALD 95:6

dreams: are either d. or swords
LOW 139:20
city of perspiring d. RAPH 177:16

dreams (cont.):
d. happy as her day BROO 40:5
d. he found himself transformed
KAFKA 117:9
d. their looking glass YEATS 233:5
Facts are better than d. CHUR 55:18
forgotten scream for help in d. CAN 46:9
Heavy with d. THOM 215:3
I have spread my d. under YEATS 235:7
In d. begins responsibility YEATS 234:14
Into the land of my d. KING 122:8
Made holy by their d. GIBS 90:8
Noon of my d., O noon FLEC 81:17
we who lived by honest d. DAY-L 65:11

dreamt: I d. I went to Manderley
DU M 70:12

dress: car has become an article of d.
MCL 143:12
Please adjust your d. CHUR 55:6
we dont d. well and weve SHAW 200:3
white d. after the sweetness FIRB 80:4

dressed: All d. in his best EDGAR 71:20
D. in style, brand new tile COLL 58:4
d. up and have no place WHIT 226:19

dresser: Slept under the d. BENT 29:5

dressers: kitchen d. of this life BENN 27:18

dresses: d. so very soberly now JER 113:10

dried: A little life with d. tubers
ELIOT 76:13
d. the sap out of my veins YEATS 232:12

drift: adamant for d. CHUR 54:5
thus d. toward unparalleled EINS 73:2

drifted: Snow White . . . but I d.
WEST 225:21

drifting: When the clouds go d. STER 208:8

drink: Ale, man, ale's the stuff to d.
HOUS 107:8
Couple them with d. MCAR 140:19
Don't ask a man to d. and drive
ANON 6:2
d. all day and keep absolutely
SMITH 203:10
D. and dance and laugh and lie
PARK 168:19
d. and get beerier LAWR 132:14
d. and I'd have been under PARK 167:14
d. by daylight MENC 150:22
d. he was drinking was BENC 27:3
d. one another's healths JER 113:9
d. to the spirit of gallantry COW 61:14
d. your ale HOUS 105:15
drunkenness—or so good as d.
CHES 50:4
intelligence to buy a d. CUMM 63:14
One reason why I don't d. ASTOR 11:21
or sleep or d. again DE L 66:19
Shall sit and d. with me BELL 25:26
She drove me to d. FIEL 79:13
that he has taken to d. TARK 212:5
your husband I would d. it ASTOR 11:23

drinka: D. Pinta Milka Day WHIT 226:14

drinks: couple of d. on a Saturday
FYFFE 87:17
man you don't like who d. THOM 214:1

drip: damps there d. upon HARDY 97:1

dripping: that electricity was d.
THUR 216:16

drive: And d. the brute off LARK 130:17
Don't ask a man to drink and d.
ANON 6:2
That I was used to d. HOUS 106:17
way but can't d. the car TYNAN 220:10

driven: pure as the d. slush BANK 18:2

driver: he was in the d.'s seat BEAV 21:4

drives: D. my green age THOM 213:20
it is *le bon Dieu* who d. CHR 53:1

droite: *ma d. recule, situation* FOCH 82:6

droits: *égaux en dignité et en d.* ANON 9:1

dromedary: The d., two NASH 158:20

droop: D. in a hundred A.B.C.'s
ELIOT 73:10

droopingly: Lady Jane, a little d.
LAWR 132:9

droops: D. on the little hands
MILNE 153:12
D. to sink among the Dead BELL 25:20

drop: dance till you d. AUDEN 14:8
Good to the last d. ROOS 184:9
never said 'D. the gun, Louie'
BOGA 35:12
That one d. of Negro blood HUGH 107:21
tune in and d. out LEARY 133:15

dropped: Things have d. from me
WOOLF 231:16

dropping: like d. a rose petal MARQ 147:9
peace comes d. slow YEATS 232:9

drops: d. on gate-bars hang HARDY 97:3

drought: d. is destroying his roots
HERB 101:20

drove: d. to the club in the late BETJ 32:3
She d. me to drink FIEL 79:13

drown: Inns d. your empty selves
BELL 25:24

drownded: no wrecks and nobody d.
EDGAR 71:20
sea will soon be d. SYNGE 211:8

drowned: ceremony of innocence is d.
YEATS 233:12
D. THAN DUFFERS IF NOT RANS 177:15
were d. in the deepest sea KIPL 125:20

drowning: And not waving but d.
SMITH 203:18
old maid is like death by d. FERB 79:3

drudgery: vocation is the love of the d.
SMITH 203:11

drug: or you can d., with words
LOW 139:20
powerful d. used by mankind
KIPL 127:12

drugs: And d. cause cramp PARK 168:12
Sex and d. and rock and roll DURY 71:1

drum: Beats like a fatalistic d. ELIOT 75:21

drummer: any kin to the snare d.
FREB 84:19

drumming: Down in the valley d.
AUDEN 14:13

drums: beating of war d. KOES 128:13
when the d. begin to roll KIPL 123:6

drunk: d. with sight of power KIPL 126:11
not so think as you d. SQUI 206:16
when d., one sees in other TYNAN 220:9
Wordsworth d. and Porson sober
HOUS 105:6
You're not d. if you can lie MART 147:14

drunkard: The rolling English d. made
CHES 50:22

drunkenness: d. would be the supremely
JAMES 112:14
invented anything so bad as d.
CHES 50:4
The d. of things being various
MACN 144:17

dry: clothes and into a d. Martini
WEST 225:10
old man in a d. month ELIOT 73:11
Thoughts of a d. brain ELIOT 73:13

Dublin: served in all the pubs in D.
DONL 68:7
When I came back to D. BEHAN 23:23
Dubuque: old lady in D. ROSS 185:2
duchess: tomorrow every D. in London
MACD 142:2
duck: Honey, I just forgot to d. DEMP 67:2
ducks: I turn to d. HARV 99:2
duda: *La vida es d.* UNAM 220:12
dude: Don't read too much now: the d.
LARK 131:4
duffers: BETTER DROWNED THAN D.
RANS 177:15
dugs: old man with wrinkled d. ELIOT 77:1
duke: meet the D. I couldn't like
SHAW 200:10
dukes: drawing room full of d. AUDEN 14:1
d. are just as great a terror LLOY 138:11
dulce: The old Lie: D. et decorum est
OWEN 166:10
dull: I am always deadly d. BEER 22:24
dullard: d.'s envy of brilliant BEER 23:8
dumb: Children are d. to say GRAV 93:8
D. As old medallions MACL 143:5
d. to tell the crooked THOM 213:20
Ford is so d. he can't fart JOHN 114:5
Is dead and d. and done DE L 66:19
Oh, noisy bells, be d. HOUS 106:15
tender our Our D. Friends PARK 168:1
was a d. son of a bitch TRUM 218:12
dumb-bell: Than d. and foil YEATS 234:4
dump: What a d. COFF 57:9
dungeon: life-sentence in the d. of self
CONN 59:14
dunghill: cock crowing on its own d.
ALD 3:4
Dunkirk: years in the epic of D. PRIE 175:9
Dunn: Hunter D., Miss J BETJ 32:1
Miss Joan Hunter D. BETJ 32:4
Dupree: Weatherby George D. MILNE 153:7
durch: *Vorsprung d. Technik.* ANON 9:3
dure: *ça d. ce que ça dure* DE G 65:17
dust: d. comes secretly day after
MEYN 151:12
D. inbreathed was a house ELIOT 74:18
D. in the air suspended ELIOT 74:18
d., in the cool tombs SAND 189:16
d. the blinds and then THOM 214:8
d. upon the paper eye DOUG 68:11
Excuse My D. PARK 168:24
fear in a handful of d. ELIOT 76:15
In the city's d. you wait HART 98:19
Less than the d. HOPE 105:3
like the d. on the nettles THOM 214:16
our proud and angry d. HOUS 105:15
rich earth a richer d. BROO 40:5
voiced those rhymes is d. HARDY 97:1
dustbin: into the d. of history TROT 218:5
duty: declares that it is his d. SHAW 195:27
do his d. faithfully BLUNT 35:4
do your D. BAD 16:9
Do your d. bravely KITC 128:5
d. is useful in work RUSS 186:14
D. of a newspaper SWOPE 211:5
d. to have reported it HELL 100:8
d. to my country to love PAGE 167:2
it is our d. to try MILN 154:5
Nor law, nor d. bade me fight
YEATS 235:5
dwarfs: dozen red-bearded d. MORT 156:14
dyin': little dreamin', a little d. PHIL 171:3
dying: achieve it through not d. ALLEN 4:1

dying (cont.):
A d. animal YEATS 235:10
against the d. of the light THOM 213:13
But I'm d. now and done BETJ 31:8
D., Is an art PLATH 172:3
'D.' he [Maugham] said MAUG 149:10
d. is more the survivor's MANN 146:4
forgive my friends for d. SMITH 203:2
'If this is d.,' he remarked STR 210:13
my birthday or am I d. ASTOR 12:1
shall I have—what d. wails PITT 172:1
sunsets exquisitely d. HUXL 108:21
Though we yawned like d. cod
ASQ 11:20
time my father was d. DENN 28:2
with the thought of d. MAS 148:14
dynamo: starry d. in the machinery
GINS 90:15
dynasties: Though D. pass HARDY 97:9

E

each: mermaids singing, e. to each
ELIOT 75:19
eagle: e. or the snake KIPL 124:5
Fate is not an e. BOWEN 37:13
The e. has landed HIGG 102:10
eagles: e. and the trumpets ELIOT 73:10
Where e. dare MACL 143:4
ear: A stench in the e. BIER 34:10
e. with facility and quits BEEC 22:9
have an e. for her music DAY-L 65:10
penetrated into the e. of man FORS 83:13
purse out of your wife's e. MORT 156:12
We whisper in her e. WILB 226:24
earl: e. and a knight of the garter
ATTL 12:6
fourteenth e. is concerned HOME 104:7
early: E. to rise and early THUR 216:23
I used to go to bed e. PROU 175:16
earn: poet can e. much more money
AUDEN 13:15
set to e. their livings GRAH 92:16
earned: e. everything I've got NIXON 161:5
ears: And e. like errant wings CHES 52:10
E. like bombs and teeth CAUS 47:18
e. make him look like HUGH 107:19
e. yielding like swinging DOUG 68:12
'Jug Jug' to dirty e. ELIOT 76:19
woman through her e. WYATT 231:23
earth: advocates of peace upon e.
GEOR 89:11
And e. is but a star FLEC 81:7
And I danced on the e. CART 47:7
And is thy e. so marred THOM 215:18
And we will stay on e. PRÉV 175:6
are the scum of the e. CHES 50:20
between the e. and skies CAMP 45:14
did thee feel the e. move HEM 100:12
E. and everything that's KIPL 126:15
E. and Sky stand presently KIPL 123:17
e. a richer dust concealed BROO 40:5
e. a trinket at my wrist THOM 215:14
E. in forgetful snow, feeding ELIOT 76:13
e. is warm with Spring GREN 94:3
E., receive an honoured guest
AUDEN 13:2
E.'s the right place FROST 86:5
e. than are dreamed of HALD 95:6
He that loves but half of E. QUIL 177:4
Let me enjoy the e. no less HARDY 98:2
like to get away from e. FROST 86:5

earth (cont.):
meek shall inherit the E. SMITH 202:9
serious house on serious e. LARK 130:16
Than anywhere else on e. GURN 94:17
The conquest of the e. CONR 59:19
The e. compels, upon it MACN 144:6
vehicle E. zooming about FULL 87:12
While e.'s foundations stand HOUS 106:8
earthly: all e. things above SPR 206:11
earthquake: Small e. in Chile COCK 57:2
ease: doctrine of ignoble e. ROOS 184:2
gold and heart's first e. DAY-L 65:7
man could e. a heart like PARK 168:8
easier: e. to fight for one's principles
ADLER 2:15
e. to love humanity HOFF 103:17
e. to make war CLEM 56:18
It will be e. for you CHIL 52:17
tyranny it is far e. to act AREN 10:3
easily: will more e. fall victim HITL 103:8
easing: They call it e. the Spring
REED 179:1
east: e. all the way into Mississippi
KIPL 127:17
E. is East, and West KIPL 123:17
feel I can look the E. ELIZ 77:9
me somewheres e. of Suez KIPL 123:15
tried to hustle the E. KIPL 125:22
Eastern: Full of E. promise ANON 6:11
Soviet domination of E. FORD 82:15
Eastertide: Wearing white for E.
HOUS 106:9
easy: Life is not meant to be e.
SHAW 195:24
She bid me take love e. YEATS 234:13
so e. to take refuge IBSEN 109:19
terribly e.—to shake a man's
SHAW 196:5
time an' the livin' is e. HEYW 102:8
woman of e. virtue HAIL 95:4
young and e. under the apple
THOM 213:17
eat: dare to e. a peach ELIOT 75:19
E. or sleep or drink again DE L 66:19
E. slowly: only men in rags RAL 177:10
e. the cones under FROST 86:10
e. wisely but not too well MAUG 150:2
I'll try to e., but I cannot ADE 2:13
me to e. in the kitchen HUGH 108:1
You will e., bye and bye HILL 102:12
eaten: e. by missionaries SPOO 206:10
He has been e. by the bear HOUS 105:10
'eathen: e. in 'is blindness KIPL 127:9
eating: e. or opening a window
AUDEN 13:5
E. people is wrong FLAN 81:5
Venice is like e. an entire CAP 46:15
eccentric: Be virtuous and you will be e.
TWAIN 219:6
ecclesiologist: A keen e. BETJ 31:17
echo: e. in a Marabar cave FORS 83:21
Footfalls e. in the memory ELIOT 74:3
rose-garden. My words e. ELIOT 74:3
The e. of a platitude BIER 33:24
waiting for the e. MARQ 147:9
éclair: backbone than a chocolate é.
ROOS 183:16
eclipses: e. and predominates DOYLE 68:18
ecological: e. balance of the planet
SONT 205:1
economic: attaining e. ends KEYN 120:14
e. documents I have HOME 104:8
e. interests are not WEIL 224:2

economic (*cont.*):
e. law on the side of destruction
KEYN 120:10
e. understanding   ROOS 183:9
social and e. experiment   HOOV 104:11
economical: being e. with the truth
ARMS 10:11
economically: behind e. or culturally
DUBČ 70:5
economics: E. and art are strangers
CATH 47:13
E. is the science   ROBB 181:10
face the e. of affluence   GALB 88:3
study of e. as if people   SCH 193:10
economists: e. and political philosophers
KEYN 120:17
economize: Let us e. it   TWAIN 219:9
economy: E. is going without something
HOPE 104:14
e. right in five years   BENN 27:16
fear of Political E.   SELL 194:15
Principles of Political E.   BENT 29:3
écrivain: L'é. doit donc refuser   SART 190:27
ecstasy: bells of E. and Forever   GINS 90:14
from circumstance to e.   BELL 23:31
ecstatic: Of such e. sound   HARDY 97:11
Eden: [Anthony E.] is the best   BUTL 43:2
E. submitted a long-winded   CHUR 55:6
on E.'s green and gold   KIPL 124:1
[Sir Anthony E.] was not only a bore
MUGG 157:11
edge: always at the e.   SPEN 205:12
e. of the abyss   STEV 209:1
Edinburgh: travels north to E.   BEAV 21:2
edit: E. and annotate the lines
YEATS 234:19
editor: E.: a person employed   HUBB 107:13
Edna: Aunt E. is universal   RATT 177:18
educate: physician is to e.   OSLER 165:23
educated: Cabinet ministers are e.
BENN 28:18
'e.' people tend to come   ORW 164:30
once as an e. gentleman   SHAW 197:9
thought highly e.   SNOW 204:1
education: best kind of e.   BUCH 41:18
between e. and catastrophe   WELLS 225:2
cabbage with a college e.   TWAIN 219:30
[e.] has produced a vast   TREV 217:21
e. is the knowledge not of facts
INGE 110:9
E. is what survives when   SKIN 201:21
e. must ultimately be limited
POUND 173:25
E., n. That which discloses   BIER 34:5
e. or of absence of self-control
BEVAN 32:15
Gladstone also invented the E.
SELL 194:17
just as in the case of e.   JAY 112:19
Movies, and that is e.   ROG 182:5
Soap and e. are not   TWAIN 219:7
What poor e. I have received   BOTT 37:1
Edward: E. III had very good manners
SELL 194:11
E. the Confessor   BENT 29:5
[E. VIII] will ruin himself   GEOR 89:5
Edwardians: The E., on the contrary
WHITE 226:4
Eeyore: E., the old grey Donkey
MILNE 153:17
effect: e. upon the Government
PANK 167:10
seems likelier to win an e.   UPD 220:15

effective: e. if you can stop people talking
ATTL 12:13
efficiency: e. and inefficiency   SHAW 197:5
efficient: e. government you have
TRUM 218:14
effort: e. is his own personality
FROMM 85:12
e. nor the failure tires   EMPS 77:15
e. when you have forgotten   SANT 190:7
effusive: The e. welcome of the pier
AUDEN 14:16
égalité: majestueuse é. des lois   FRAN 84:15
égaux: libres et é. en dignité   ANON 9:1
egg: And lay one more bloody e.
AYRES 16:7
Go to work on an e.   ANON 6:15
like eating an e. without   KIPL 127:14
Wall St. lays an e.   ANON 9:5
way of making another e.   BUTL 43:16
eggs: all my e. in one bastard   PARK 169:7
Lays e. inside a paper bag   ISH 110:22
your e. in the one basket   TWAIN 219:34
egoism: itself is a form of e.   SANT 190:20
egotist: E., n. A person of low   BIER 34:6
Ehrfurcht: "E. vor dem Leben" vor mir
SCHW 193:11
Eichmann: [E.] was summing up
AREN 10:4
eight: We want e., and we   WYND 232:2
eighth: I'm Henery the E., I am
MURR 158:5
eighty: In a dream you are never e.
SEXT 195:2
ein: E. Reich, ein Volk, ein Führer   ANON 6:4
Nor can anyone understand E.
ANON 6:22
eine: I'll have e. kleine Pause   FERR 79:4
eingerichtet: Wir sind so e., dass wir
FREUD 85:7
Einsamkeit: andern seine E. bewache
RILKE 181:5
Einsamkeiten: zwei E. einander schützen
RILKE 181:3
Einstein: E. leads to Hiroshima   PIC 171:6
Let E. be   SQUI 206:17
einzurichten: Kniff, die Welt so e.
FRIS 85:10
either: E. war is obsolete or men
FULL 87:13
elderly: e. American [Ian MacGregor]
JENK 113:2
Mr Salteena was an e. man   ASHF 10:15
elders: at listening to their e.   BALD 16:20
eldritch: e. light of sundown   DAY-L 65:7
election: Democracy substitutes e.
SHAW 198:1
e. from my point of view   BALD 17:10
e. now to be held   WHIT 226:20
e. programme of the Labour   SNOW 204:3
elections: E. are won   ADAMS 1:20
it's no go the e.   MACN 144:8
you won the e.   SOM 204:9
Electra: Mourning becomes E.   O'NEI 163:13
electric: biggest e. train set   WELL 224:10
tried to mend the E. Light   BELL 25:7
electrical: dark interludes in the e. display
O'NEI 163:16
electrician: The E. is no longer there
BELL 26:6
was a practical e.   WELLS 224:15
electricity: e. was dripping invisibly
THUR 216:16
they must use less e.   JENK 112:23

electrification: Soviet power plus the e.
LENIN 134:15
electronic: e. interdependence recreates
MCL 143:8
elegance: casque has outdone your e.
POUND 174:13
Has she e.? Has she fragrance
CAUL 47:16
Observed the e. of Circe's hair
POUND 174:3
elegant: It's so e.   ELIOT 76:21
Most intelligent, very e.   BUCK 42:3
My e. car   BELL 26:10
elegies: e. are to this generation
OWEN 166:8
Elektra: [Strauss's E.]   BEEC 22:6
elementary: 'E.,' said he   DOYLE 69:15
elements: Took its place among the e.
PLATH 172:2
elephant: E.'s Child   KIPL 125:12
high as an e.'s eye   HAMM 95:17
shot an e. in my pajamas   KAUF 118:2
elephants: Women and e. never forget
SAKI 188:16
elevate: The mind of man or e. a rhyme
YEATS 235:13
eleven: e. o'clock in the morning
CHAN 49:2
heard from them by e. o'clock
CHAM 48:15
second e. sort of chap   BARR 19:2
Elgar: Dear old E.—he is furious
BEEC 22:13
eliminated: you have e. the impossible
DOYLE 69:22
Eliot: How unpleasant to meet Mr E.
ELIOT 74:1
Elizabeth: grievous failing of E.'s
HARDY 97:6
elm: tell me, e.! Night night   JOYCE 115:11
elopement: e. would be preferable   ADE 2:12
worked a love-story or an e.   DOYLE 69:19
eloquence: e. is that which gets things
LLOY 138:14
else: happening to Somebody E.   ROG 182:8
that I am not someone e.   ALLEN 3:25
elsewhere: Altogether e.   AUDEN 14:23
elude: Court him, e. him, reel   BLUN 34:25
elusive: One's prime is e.   SPARK 205:8
That demmed, e. Pimpernel
ORCZY 163:19
Elysium: Keep alive our lost E.   BETJ 31:7
emancipation: preliminary to the e. of the
mind   KEYN 120:11
emancipator: whim so does every e.
BROUN 41:5
embalmer: A triumph of the e.'s art
VIDAL 221:14
embarrassment: land of e. and breakfast
BARN 18:17
embittered: He was an e. atheist
ORW 164:13
embroidered: Had I the heavens' e. cloths
YEATS 235:7
embroideries: Covered with e.
YEATS 234:16
emeralds: E. is paved with yellow
BAUM 20:12
emergency: e. following upon another
FISH 80:5
emeritus: called a professor e.   LEAC 133:7
Emily: least sought for: E., hear
CRANE 62:16

eminent: death reveals the e.   SHAW 198:26
Emmet: And Robert E. and Wolfe Tone
                                                     YEATS 234:15
emotion: degree of my aesthetic e.
                                                       BELL 24:1
  dependable international e.   ALSOP 4:10
  e. in the form of art   ELIOT 76:7
  e. is immediately evoked   ELIOT 76:7
  not a turning loose of e.   ELIOT 76:6
  tranquillity remembered in e.   PARK 168:4
emotional: Sentimentality is the e.
  promiscuity   MAIL 145:7
emotions: have personality and e.
                                                     ELIOT 76:6
  refusal to admit our e.   RATT 178:2
  waste-paper basket of the e.   WEBB 224:1
  world of the e.   COL 57:15
emperor: E. and puts you in de Hall
                                                     O'NEI 163:7
  E. himself can actually   BREC 39:5
  e. of ice-cream   STEV 208:10
  looking for the sacred E.   BRAM 38:13
  That's presuming E. Long   ICKES 110:3
emphasis: Is underlined for e.   ELIOT 75:9
empire: Britain has lost an e.   ACH 1:8
  E. is a commonwealth   ROS 184:15
  E. lasts for a thousand   CHUR 54:11
  idlers of the E. are irresistibly
                                                     DOYLE 69:25
  impulses of an evil e.   REAG 178:13
  liquidation of the British E.   CHUR 53:18
  our E. beyond the seas   CHUR 54:10
  pledge our E. vast across   HUXL 109:1
  remark to me, 'How's the E.?'   GEOR 89:9
  The E. strikes back   LUCAS 140:12
  way she disposed of an e.   HARL 98:11
empires: e. of the future   CHUR 55:14
  The day of E. has come   CHAM 48:9
employee: Hierarchy Every E. Tends to
  Rise   PETER 170:11
employer: harder upon the e.   SPOO 206:9
employers: e. of past generations
                                                     BALD 17:15
employment: happily known as gainful e.
                                                       ACH 1:7
  To give e. to the artisan   BELL 25:7
emptiness: And all the little e. of love
                                                     BROO 40:1
  Panic and e.   FORS 83:14
  The e. of ages in his face   MARK 146:14
  Their hopeful plans to e.   HOUS 105:14
empty: Bring on the e. horses   CURT 64:8
  e. taxi arrived at 10 Downing   CHUR 53:4
  me with their e. spaces   FROST 85:19
enchanted: Some e. evening   HAMM 96:2
enchantments: last e. of the Middle Age
                                                     BEER 23:6
enclosing: definition is the e. a wilderness
                                                     BUTL 43:27
encompassed: e. by a cloud of comforting
                                                     RUSS 186:25
encounter: I go to e. for the millionth
                                                     JOYCE 115:20
encounters: Close e. of the third kind
                                                     SPIE 206:3
encourage: they e. it in some schools
                                                     SCOTT 194:2
encouragement: e. this book would have
                                                     WOD 230:11
encouraging: E. her to join the public
                                                     AYCK 15:21
end: And now the e. is near   ANKA 5:7
  beginning is often the e.   ELIOT 74:21

end (cont.):
  came to an e. all wars   LLOY 138:8
  e. cannot justify the means   HUXL 108:15
  e. forever to this   ROOS 183:11
  e. is to make a beginning   ELIOT 74:21
  e. of a thousand years   GAIT 88:1
  e. of it's sittin'   KIPL 127:6
  e. of the beginning   CHUR 53:17
  great e. comes slowly   DUB 70:7
  In my beginning is my e.   ELIOT 74:8
  Keep right on to the e.   LAUD 131:7
  middle and an e.   GOD 91:4
  Our e. is Life. Put out to sea
                                                     MACN 144:11
  patience is now at an e.   HITL 103:6
  The bad e. unhappily   STOP 210:1
  The e. is where we start from
                                                     ELIOT 74:21
  there's an e. of May   HOUS 105:12
  The war that will e. war   WELLS 225:4
  Where it will all e., knows God
                                                     GIBBS 90:4
  where's it all going to e.   STOP 209:22
  who have the power to e.   SASS 192:1
  world will e. in fire   FROST 86:6
endeavours: e. are unlucky explorers
                                                     DOUG 68:9
ended: And the curse be e.   ELIOT 74:16
  But he e. PM   ATTL 12:6
  had e. his sport with Tess   HARDY 98:1
  The song is e.   BERL 29:18
ending: e. a war is to lose it   ORW 164:28
endless: I take my e. way   HOUS 107:3
  nowhere, and is e.   LARK 130:8
ends: delight and e. in wisdom
                                                     FROST 85:16
  determine the nature of the e.
                                                     HUXL 108:15
  e. and scarce means   ROBB 181:10
  e. as beyond the province   POPP 172:16
  e. I think criminal   KEYN 120:7
  MCC e. and the Church of England
                                                     PRIE 175:11
  Out to the undiscovered e.   BELL 26:3
  The burnt-out e. of smoky days
                                                     ELIOT 75:20
endure: easily learn to e. adversity
                                                     TWAIN 219:15
  man will not merely e.   FAUL 78:13
endured: not to be e. with patient
                                                     RUSS 186:14
enemies: against the common e. of man
                                                     KENN 119:15
  alone against smiling e.   BOWEN 37:14
  desire to be vilified by e.   BIER 33:23
  e. of Freedom do not argue   INGE 110:10
  e. will not believe you   HUBB 107:11
enemy: classics is an e. to the human
                                                     MILL 152:10
  e. if you want to save   BALD 17:7
  e. of good art   CONN 58:17
  e. of thought and the friend   CONR 59:27
  friend and e. is but Death   BROO 40:1
  got a better class of e.   MILL 152:19
  Have no e. but time   YEATS 235:9
  I am the e. you killed   OWEN 166:18
  Sir, no man's e., forgiving all
                                                     AUDEN 15:2
  sometimes his own worst e.   BEVIN 33:13
  then there's life, its e.   ANOU 9:19
  with the wrong e.   BRAD 38:10
  written by an acute e.   BALF 17:20
  your e. and your friend   TWAIN 219:16
enfants: Faire des e., rien de   SART 191:5

enfants (cont.):
  pour les e., de toujours   SAIN 187:18
Enfer: l'E., c'est les Autres   SART 191:4
enforce: e. a law not supported
                                                     HUMP 108:4
engaged: e. to Miss Joan Hunter   BETJ 32:4
Engels: teaching of Marx, E. and Lenin
                                                     KHR 121:3
engine: An e. that moves   HARE 98:7
  tremendous from her great e.
                                                     AUDEN 15:11
  unsavoury e. of pollution   SPAR 205:9
  when the human e. waits   ELIOT 76:24
  you'll be a Really Useful E.   AWDRY 15:18
engineer: be an e. or such like
                                                     SHAW 197:24
engineering: Piecemeal social e. resembles
                                                     POPP 172:16
engineers: Artists are not e.   KENN 119:8
  It is the age of the e.   HOGB 104:3
England: And get me to E. once again
                                                     BROO 40:13
  apple falling towards E.   AUDEN 14:9
  E. is a garden   KIPL 124:19
  E. is finished and dead   MILL 152:3
  E. is not the jewelled isle   ORW 164:17
  E. is the paradise of individuality
                                                     SANT 190:16
  E. mourns for her dead   BINY 34:17
  E. shall bide till Judgement   KIPL 126:4
  E.'s on the anvil   KIPL 126:19
  E., their England   MACD 142:5
  E. who only England know   KIPL 124:3
  E. will have her neck wrung   CHUR 53:13
  Establishment which we call E.
                                                     DENN 67:3
  Florence, Elizabethan E.   INGE 110:15
  For E.'s the one land, I know
                                                     BROO 40:13
  Good evening, E.   POTT 173:16
  Gott strafe E.!   FUNKE 87:16
  have lost the last of E.   BELL 25:24
  History is now and E.   ELIOT 74:22
  In E., justice is open to all   MATH 149:1
  in E. people have good table manners
                                                     MIKES 151:14
  lot that make up E. today   LAWR 131:18
  my legs and think of E.   HILL 102:16
  Noon strikes on E.   FLEC 81:17
  Oh many a peer of E. brews   HOUS 107:8
  Speak for E.   AMERY 4:13
  stately homos of E.   CRISP 63:2
  suspended in favour of E.   SHAW 196:28
  That is for ever E.   BROO 40:5
  The bow was made in E.   DOYLE 70:2
  There'll always be an E.   PARK 169:9
  think of the defence of E.   BALD 17:8
  thoughts by E. given   BROO 40:5
  Till then, damn you E.   OSB 165:20
  Who dies if E. live   KIPL 124:16
  With E.'s own coal   KIPL 124:18
  You that love E., who have   DAY-L 65:10
English: An E. unofficial rose   BROO 40:11
  breathing E. air   BROO 40:5
  But I was taught E.   CHUR 55:8
  But marks our E. dead   KIPL 127:2
  E. and the bears   THOM 213:12
  E. gentry   HALS 95:13
  E. have hot-water bottles   MIKES 151:15
  E. have no respect   SHAW 199:16
  E. never smash in a face   HALS 95:13
  E. sloppy have only themselves
                                                     SAY 192:11
  E. up with which I will   CHUR 55:15

English (*cont.*):
E. vice   RATT 178:2
E. without an accent now   BENC 26:13
game which the E.   MANC 145:17
if he went among the E.   BARR 19:21
mobilized the E. language   MURR 158:8
pause to consider the E.   NASH 159:20
Potter speaking to you in E.   POTT 173:16
really nice E. people   SHAW 196:27
stones kissed by the E. dead
                                         OWEN 166:13
Student of our sweet E. tongue
                                         FLEC 81:23
The E. may not like music   BEEC 22:8
The wood of E. bows   DOYLE 70:2
words in the E. language   JAMES 111:15
Englishman: An E., even if he is alone
                                        MIKES 151:16
born an E. and remained   BEHAN 23:20
E. among the under-dogs   WAUGH 223:8
E. believes be heresy   SHAW 199:30
E. hate or despise him   SHAW 199:16
E. is to belong   NASH 159:20
E. never enjoys himself   HERB 101:26
E. thinks he is moral when   SHAW 197:30
E. will give his mind   SHAW 195:12
find an E. in the wrong   SHAW 199:3
have been born an E.   RHOD 180:3
No E. is ever fairly beaten   SHAW 199:29
that the E. can't feel   FORS 83:3
Englishmen: E. detest a siesta   COW 62:4
E. act better than Frenchmen   BENN 28:6
E. don't think in the least funny
                                         MCL 143:9
E. never will be slaves   SHAW 197:29
Mad dogs and E.   COW 62:4
they would prefer to be E.   RHOD 180:2
English-speaking: understanding of E.
audiences   WHAR 225:27
Englishwoman: This E. is so refined
                                       SMITH 203:17
Englishwomen: E.'s shoes look as if they
                                        HALS 95:12
Frenchwomen better than E.   BENN 28:6
enhanced: e. meaning in memorable
                                        BARZ 20:11
enigma: mystery inside an e.   CHUR 55:4
Resolving the e. of the fever   ELIOT 74:12
enjoy: business of life is to e. it   BUTL 44:6
e. it   SMITH 202:17
have to go out and e. it   SMITH 203:14
His duty is to e. himself   CECIL 48:4
I e. convalescence   SHAW 195:22
Let me e. the earth no less   HARDY 98:2
enjoyment: aesthetic e. is recognition
                                        WHIT 226:11
intense e. from a contrast   FREUD 85:7
enjoys: The Englishman never e. himself
                                        HERB 101:26
enmities: More substance in our e.
                                        YEATS 232:5
ennemie: *il y a la vie, son e.*   ANOU 9:19
enormous: At the far end of the e. room
                                        AUDEN 14:19
With one e. chair   LERN 135:25
enough: e. in the world for everyone's
                                        BUCH 42:2
e. people to make a minority   ALTM 4:11
It is not e. to succeed   VIDAL 221:12
patriotism is not e.   CAV 48:3
The dark is light e.   FRY 86:24
wouldn't be e. to go round   STEAD 207:5
enslaved: completely e. as farm stock
                                        SHAW 196:23

ensured: Good-night. E. release
                                        HOUS 106:8
enterprise: For there's more e.
                                        YEATS 234:16
regeneration of industry and e.
                                        CHAR 50:1
starship E.   RODD 182:2
entertain: could only e. my Liberal
                                        ASQ 11:13
entertained: e. by some of your grosser
                                        WOOL 231:18
entertaining: e. than half the novels
                                        MAUG 149:22
entertainment: Pictures are for e.
                                        GOLD 91:13
sort of *Arabian Nights* e.   OSLER 166:1
entertains: e. the most exclusive worms
                                        PARK 168:20
enthusiasm: Above all no e.   LAMB 129:17
little ordinary human e.   OSB 165:15
that e. moves the world   BALF 17:21
enthusiasts: e. can be trusted to speak
                                        BALF 17:21
entirely: The e. beautiful   AUDEN 13:7
entitled: than that no man is e.
                                        ROOS 183:15
entrance: every exit as being an e.
                                        STOP 209:17
entrust: matter to e. to military
                                        CLEM 56:16
envelopes: On backs of tattered e.
                                        HOPE 105:2
envy: E. is the basis of democracy
                                        RUSS 186:12
into the mind, do not e. me   DOUG 68:12
prisoners of e.   ILL 110:7
enwrought: E. with golden and silver
                                        YEATS 235:7
Ep: E.'s statues are junk   ANON 6:22
ephemeral: lacking which any story is e.
                                        FAUL 78:12
Proves the child e.   AUDEN 13:7
epic: e. poem, and the science   MENC 151:1
epigram: E.: a wisecrack that played
                                        LEV 136:2
Impelled to try an e.   PARK 168:18
until it purrs like an e.   MARQ 147:10
episode: To the end of a brief e.
                                        MERC 151:8
epitaph: And were an e. to be my story
                                        FROST 86:22
epithet: e. which the riff-raff   HOPE 104:16
epoch: e. when ladies apparently
                                        HUXL 109:8
Epstein: E.'s sculptures   ANON 8:20
equal: All animals are e.   ORW 164:9
All men are e.—all men   FORS 83:3
all men are e. is a proposition
                                        HUXL 109:10
compel us to be e. upstairs   BARR 19:1
country about e. rights   JOHN 114:8
free and e. in dignity   ANON 9:1
equality: E. for women   TOYN 217:14
e. in the servants' hall   BARR 19:1
'E.,' I spoke the word   DYLAN 71:12
majestic e. of the law   FRAN 84:15
not e. or fairness   BERL 30:6
equals: Only a peace between e.   WILS 229:3
equipment: e. always deteriorating
                                        ELIOT 74:13
eradicate: e. from my heart a deep
                                        BEVAN 33:7
err: e. is human but to really   ANON 8:24

err (*cont.*):
To e. With her   ANON 9:17
errors: e. of those who think   BID 33:18
His e. are volitional   JOYCE 116:11
erstwhile: After all, my e. dear   MILL 152:1
escape: Beauty for some provides e.
                                        HUXL 108:21
e. complex   MCAR 140:19
e. from emotion   ELIOT 76:6
few e. that distinction   TWAIN 220:6
tentacles we never quite e.   SMITH 202:6
we women cannot e.   GIBB 89:18
escaped: that out of battle I e.
                                        OWEN 166:15
Eskimo: Every Hottentot and every E.
                                        LEHR 134:8
essay: e. on the life-history   BARB 18:11
essence: Existence precedes and rules e.
                                        SART 191:1
The e. of war is violence   FISH 80:6
essential: what is e. is invisible
                                        SAIN 187:19
established: like an e. society   GREE 93:12
establishment: E. which we call England
                                        DENN 67:3
estate: used to dealing with e. workers
                                        DOUG 68:17
état: *un renforcement de l'É.*   CAMUS 46:6
eternal: e. Footman hold my coat
                                        ELIOT 75:17
himself and her of an e. tie   AUDEN 14:9
I wish it could be e.   OSB 165:20
justice is e. publicity   BENN 28:13
eternities: between two e. of darkness
                                        NAB 158:14
eternity: Are from e., and shall not
                                        HOUS 105:15
Damned from here to E.   KIPL 123:16
decomposing in the e. of print
                                        WOOLF 231:9
E.'s a terrible thought   STOP 209:22
From here to e.   JONES 115:1
some conception of e.   MANC 145:17
Ethel: E. patted her hair and looked
                                        ASHF 11:2
E. wants it made known   ROS 184:19
muttered E. this is so sudden   ASHF 11:4
etherized: Like a patient e. upon a table
                                        ELIOT 75:13
Ethiopia: E. and promptly stumbled
                                        HELL 100:6
Eton: during the holidays from E.
                                        SITW 201:19
feelings on leaving E.   CONN 59:2
playing-fields of E.   ORW 164:18
Spiritually I was at E.   BETJ 32:12
étonne: *É.-moi.*   DIAG 67:9
étonné: *é. quand il est cru sur*   DE G 66:2
Etruscans: secret of the long-nosed E.
                                        LAWR 131:14
Ettie: E. [Lady Desborough]   ASQ 11:14
Etty: E. was most emphatically   RAV 178:4
Euclid: E. alone   MILL 151:21
fifth proposition of E.   DOYLE 69:19
eunuch: between a e. and a snigger
                                        FIRB 80:1
prerogative of the e.   STOP 209:13
eunuchs: A seraglio of e.   FOOT 82:10
Europe: All the dogs of E. bark   AUDEN 13:3
alterations on the map of E.   CHUR 53:8
are going out all over E.   GREY 94:5
E. is the unfinished negative   MCC 141:10
E. may be free   CHUR 54:11
large tracts of E.   CHUR 54:10

Europe (*cont.*):
   last gentleman in E.   LEV 136:7
   smaller nationalities of E.   ASQ 11:11
   The whole map of E. has   CHUR 54:2
   wisest woman in E.   ELIOT 76:16
European: individualism and a E.
   philosophy   HOOV 104:12
   involved in a E. war   BEAV 21:3
Euston: flushpots of E. and the hanging
     JOYCE 115:9
   three in E. waiting-room   CORN 61:9
evah: Well, did you e.   PORT 173:7
eve: at e. our fancies blow   FLEC 81:22
   Be sudden—to E.   THOM 215:9
   From far, from e. and morning
     HOUS 107:2
   past E. and Adam's   JOYCE 115:7
   The fallen sons of E.   CHES 50:18
   When Adam and E. were dispossessed
     BOUL 37:2
even: E. less am I   HOPE 105:3
   e. terror of their lives   SHAR 195:8
   I was heavy with the e.   THOM 215:12
événements: *Tu ne prévois les é. que*
     ION 110:19
evening: Any e., any day   ROSE 184:10
   E., all   WILL 228:3
   e. full of the linnet's   YEATS 232:9
   e. is spread out against   ELIOT 75:13
   e. that the first hour of spring
     BOWEN 37:5
   Hello, good e., and welcome
     FROST 85:14
   into the corners of the e.   ELIOT 75:14
   shadow at e. rising   ELIOT 76:15
   Softly along the road of e.   DE L 66:6
   Some enchanted e.   HAMM 96:2
   The light of e., Lissadell   YEATS 235:8
   The winter e. settles down   ELIOT 75:20
evensong: In a full-hearted e.   HARDY 97:11
events: e., mostly unimportant   BIER 34:8
Everest: down Mount E. in the nude
     MCK 143:2
ever-importunate: The e. murmur
     JAMES 111:10
everlasting: Thy e. mercy, Christ
     MAS 148:12
every: candidates appeal to 'E. intelligent
   voter'   ADAMS 1:17
   columnists say 'E. thinking man'
     ADAMS 1:17
   e. day I have got up   MAUG 149:13
   E. day, in e. way   COUÉ 61:13
everybody: E. wants to get inta the act
     DUR 70:15
   You know e. is ignorant   ROG 182:10
everyday: An e. story of country folk
     WEBB 223:23
everyone: e. must know that a *short*
     EDW 72:5
   E. suddenly burst out singing   SASS 192:6
   future e. will be famous   WARH 222:10
   Kill e., and you are a god   ROST 185:8
everything: Almost e. has been tried
     BENN 27:12
   E. exists, nothing has value   FORS 84:1
   E. goes by the board   FAUL 78:11
   e. in its place and nothing   BEVAN 32:14
   E. is funny as long as it   ROG 182:8
   E. must be like something   FORS 83:4
   E.'s coming up roses   SOND 204:10
   E. you always wanted   REUB 179:15
   I'm not young enough to know e.
     BARR 18:22

everything (*cont.*):
   it said 'Chips with e.'   WESK 225:7
   Life, the Universe and E.   ADAMS 1:14
   when you've robbed a man of e.
     SOLZ 204:6
   world is e. that is the case   WITT 229:21
everywhere: expression—e. in the world
     ROOS 183:9
evidence: e. of life after death   SOPER 205:2
   e. of the lack of proper   BEVAN 32:15
   intrinsic e. of his creation   JEANS 112:22
evil: Clear the land of e.   KIPL 127:1
   don't think that he's e.   ALLEN 3:16
   e. on the ground of expediency
     ROOS 184:3
   He overcame e. with good   KING 122:3
   impulses of an e. empire   REAG 178:13
   it is a necessary e.   BRAD 38:6
   root of all e.   BUTL 43:5
   supernatural source of e.   CONR 60:3
   There is no e. in the atom   STEV 209:6
   Those to whom e. is done   AUDEN 13:8
   what people call e.   GIDE 90:9
   word-and-thought-defying *banality of e.*
     AREN 10:4
evils: Between two e., I always
     WEST 225:17
   enamoured of existing e.   BIER 34:3
   e. and the worst of crimes   SHAW 197:6
   found a cure for most e.   KELL 118:16
evolution: e. and peaceful extermination
     ZIN 236:14
ev'rything: E.'s goin' my way   HAMM 95:18
ev'rywhere: E. I hear the sound
     JAGG 111:9
exact: e. science, and should   DOYLE 69:19
   understand the e. and tribal   HEAN 99:7
exaggerate: e. the difference between
     SHAW 197:16
exaggerated: e. stress on not changing
     MAUG 149:18
exaggeration: e. is a truth that has
     GIBR 90:7
   report of my death was an e.
     TWAIN 219:23
examinations: In E. those who do not wish
     RAL 177:9
example: annoyance of a good e.
     TWAIN 220:1
exams: rigorous judging e.   COOK 60:10
exception: I'll be glad to make an e.
     MARX 147:19
exceptional: possesses certain e. properties
     JEANS 112:21
excesses: your guard against any e.
     KITC 128:5
exchange: And e. it some day for a crown
     BENN 27:17
   e. of one Nuisance   ELLIS 77:12
excited: Blonde Aphrodite rose up e.
     AUDEN 15:11
exciting: films. They are too e.   BERR 30:18
exclusively: e. in the right are generally
     HUXL 109:11
excrement: The place of e.   YEATS 235:14
excursion: e. to hell and came back
     PRIE 175:9
   his perilous e. ashore   LEWIS 137:3
excuse: E. me while I slip   EST 78:1
   E. My Dust   PARK 168:24
   e. not to play football   LEB 133:22
   must be my e. for dreaming   HALD 95:6
   they make a good e.   SZASZ 211:17
   Your e. is out of season   JER 113:18

excuses: e. are always less convincing
     HUXL 109:5
execute: e. him, expropriate him
     CONN 59:5
execution: fascination of a public e.
     FOOT 82:9
executioners: victims who respect their e.
     SART 191:12
executive: e. expression of human
     BRIT 39:11
executives: e. Would never want to
   tamper   AUDEN 13:1
exercise: e. for a research scientist
     LOR 139:13
exhaustion: The e. of weaning, the liar's
     AUDEN 15:2
exhibitionism: masochistic form of e.
     OLIV 163:5
exile: silence, e., and cunning
     JOYCE 115:21
exist: have a perfect right to e.   BEER 23:13
   I e. by what I think   SART 191:11
   impression that we e.   BECK 21:21
   Laski that He doesn't e.   PRIE 175:10
   questioned its right to e.   SCH 193:9
   they e., but are identical   FORS 84:1
   war would e. between us   CHAM 48:15
   who does not e., you hate   O'BR 162:6
existence: e. is but a brief crack
     NAB 158:14
   E. precedes and rules essence   SART 191:1
   e. remains a mad and lamentable
     SANT 190:8
   human e. is to kindle   JUNG 116:19
   may have the e. of mankind   ADAMS 2:7
   that He tolerates their e.   BUTL 43:6
   Their e. only adds   MOUN 157:3
   universal conditions of e.   JUNG 117:2
   very e. of life itself   SONT 205:1
existential: enslavement and e. death
     LAING 129:13
Existenz: *Sinn der menschlichen E.*
     JUNG 116:19
exists: And no one e. alone   AUDEN 13:9
   Everything e., nothing   FORS 84:1
   e. a great chasm between   BERL 30:4
exit: e. as being an entrance   STOP 209:17
ex-parrot: THIS IS AN E.   CHAP 49:13
expect: Do not e. again a phoenix hour
     DAY-L 65:7
   e. a boy to be vicious   SAKI 188:19
   e. if the dad is present   ORTON 164:1
   That is what you may e.   DOYLE 69:10
expectations: our talents and our e.
     DE B 65:13
   revolution of rising e.   CLEV 56:19
expected: I too awaited the e. guest
     ELIOT 77:1
expects: e. the Spanish Inquisition
     CHAP 49:14
expediency: always be sacrificed to e.
     MAUG 149:2
   evil on the ground of e.   ROOS 184:3
expedition: come back, abandoning the e.
     DOUG 68:9
expenditure: Ask: was so much e. justified
     SPEN 205:19
   E. rises to meet income   PARK 169:11
expense: behalf, and at your e.   COOK 60:9
   repay the trouble and e.   BELL 24:7
expensive: extremely e. it is to be poor
     BALD 17:1

experience: all my thirty years' e.
CARR 47:2
benefit of much e.
BENN 27:12
E. is never limited
JAMES 111:26
E. is not what happens
HUXL 109:13
E. isn't interesting till
BOWEN 37:4
e. of life has been drawn
BEER 23:12
e. of women that extends
DOYLE 69:21
had a wider range of e.
HARR 98:13
imposing of a pattern on e.
WHIT 226:11
man of no e.
CURZ 64:9
Music is your own e.
PARK 167:13
never had much e.
MARQ 147:1
point of trying every e.
BAX 20:14
world that we need not e.
FRIS 85:10
experienced: An e., industrious
TWAIN 219:5
experiment: mad and lamentable e.
SANT 190:8
social and economic e.
HOOV 104:11
expert: e. is someone who knows
HEIS 100:2
expires: Wretched Child e.
BELL 24:13
explain: e. why it didn't happen
CHUR 53:7
Never complain and never e.
BALD 17:4
Never e.
FISH 80:9
Never e.
HUBB 107:11
one could never e.
BARZ 20:10
People who try to e. pictures
PIC 171:8
explained: Shut up he e.
LARD 130:7
explainer: said he was a village e.
STEIN 207:14
explaining: forever e. things to them
SAIN 187:18
explanation: fuss and with no e.
BLYT 35:7
sometimes saves tons of e.
SAKI 188:21
when he is the only e.
KNOX 128:12
explanations: loathe entering upon e.
BARR 19:6
expletive: E. deleted
ANON 6:7
exploding: poets e. like bombs
AUDEN 15:9
exploit: I'm sure you'd never e. one
COPE 61:1
exploitation: continue as forms of
mutual e.
AUDEN 14:3
exploration: We shall not cease from e.
ELIOT 74:20
explore: e. strange new worlds
RODD 182:2
explorers: endeavours are unlucky e.
DOUG 68:9
exploring: And the end of all our e.
ELIOT 74:20
exposure: e. of the under-belly
CHUR 54:14
express: essentially powerless to e.
STR 210:14
E. declares that Great Britain
BEAV 21:3
e. myself in some mode
JOYCE 115:21
He must not e. great joy
FORS 83:3
just caught the down e.
WOD 230:13
expressing: e. the inexpressible
HUXL 109:4
expression: desire for aesthetic e.
WAUGH 223:4
most perfect e. of scorn
SHAW 195:23
express-train: Of heat the e. drew up there
THOM 214:15
exquisitely: Or Autumn sunsets e. dying
HUXL 108:21
extend: prepared to e. it to everyone
WILL 228:5
extension: e. of the franchise
CHES 51:13
e. which lends utility
SANT 190:12

extérieure: *politique e., je fais*
CLEM 56:17
exterior: Underneath this flabby e.
LEV 136:3
exterminate: E. all the brutes
CONR 59:21
E.! E!
NAT 159:25
will have to e. a nation
SPOCK 206:5
extinct: e. and that was all
CUPPY 64:5
extinction: The other, to total e.
ALLEN 3:21
extol: e. thee who are born
BENS 28:21
extra: And add some e., just for you
LARK 130:12
extraordinary: are interested in the e.
HUBB 107:14
can do the work of one e.
HUBB 107:15
extremes: E. meet—it's the only way I ken
MACD 141:21
I could lean to wild e.
DURY 71:2
extremism: e. and higher rates/taxes
HEW 102:6
e. in the defence of liberty
GOLD 91:12
E. in the pursuit of the Presidency
JOHN 114:14
eye: *Cast a cold e.*
YEATS 233:4
dust upon the paper e.
DOUG 68:11
e. of the beholder
PETER 170:13
e. of the storm
BELL 26:12
e. that can open an oyster
WOD 230:10
friend one must close one e.
DOUG 68:13
God caught his e.
MCC 141:15
high as an elephant's e.
HAMM 95:17
looked into the e. of day
YEATS 235:2
more important than the e.
BRON 39:13
There's no malice in me e.
AYRES 16:8
this than meets the e.
BANK 18:3
Wore it in the world's e.
YEATS 234:16
eyeball: We're e. to eyeball
RUSK 186:6
eyebrows: with e. made of platinum
FORS 83:5
eye-for-an-eye: e. philosophy
KING 122:3
eyeing: Who gain a happiness in e.
HUXL 108:21
eyelids: When she raises her e.
COL 57:16
eyes: And each man fixed his e.
ELIOT 76:17
And their e. are burning
AUDEN 14:14
bodily hunger in his e.
SHAW 197:11
chewing gum for the e.
ANON 8:12
close my e., open my legs
HILL 102:16
close your e. before you
AYCK 15:19
Crumbling behind the e.
MACN 144:15
e. are quickened
GRAV 93:6
e. as wide as a football-pool
CAUS 47:18
e. follow you about when
ORW 164:20
e. have seen what my hand
LOW 140:1
e. is deeper than all noses
CUMM 63:18
e. might be shining
LAWR 133:3
E. still dazzled
LIND 137:13
e. to ask again yes
JOYCE 116:14
e. were blind with stars
HODG 103:11
frightened look in its e.
SITW 201:17
Gasp and Stretch one's E.
BELL 24:14
good Lord made your e.
LEHR 134:7
If at times my e. are lenses
DOUG 68:12
love through his e.
WYATT 231:23
My e. are bleared, my coppers
ADE 2:13
Or was it his bees-winged e.
BETJ 30:21
Smoke gets in your e.
HARB 96:11
They rape us with their e.
FREN 85:4
When Irish e. are smiling
OLC 163:3
when the e. and back
ELIOT 76:24
Your e. had once
YEATS 232:7

Fabians: civilization of the F.
INGE 110:11
good man fallen among F.
LENIN 134:16
façade: f. of the National Gallery
CHAR 50:2
face: Accustomed to her f.
LERN 135:21
A f. peered. All the grey night
DE L 66:11
And hid his f. amid a crowd
YEATS 232:7
And so I f. the final curtain
ANKA 5:7
Beauty's conquest of your f.
AUDEN 14:11
black f. and a different religion
EDW 72:6
dont quite match your f.
ASHF 10:17
Exhausted f.? It hurts
SASS 192:4
f. and promising himself
AMIS 4:17
f. looks like a wedding-cake
AUDEN 15:14
f. which gave a clearer
DOYLE 69:21
flat on your f. as lean
THUR 217:1
hand and touched the f. of God
MAGEE 145:2
has the f. he deserves
ORW 164:10
have the f. of a Venus
BARR 19:26
his listless form and f.
HARDY 97:8
I am the family f.
HARDY 97:7
I never forget a f.
MARX 147:19
I wish I loved its silly f.
RAL 177:11
only f. I like to see
CAMP 45:10
plummet-measured f.
YEATS 233:6
saved you only must save f.
HEAN 99:13
smash in a f.
HALS 95:13
smile on the f. of the tiger
ANON 8:4
stamping on a human f.
ORW 164:26
Stares from every human f.
AUDEN 13:3
strong men stand f. to face
KIPL 123:17
The rabbit has a charming f.
ANON 8:6
To get very red in the f.
BENT 28:23
unacceptable f. of capitalism
HEATH 99:16
we looked it in the f.
DULL 70:10
faced: he f. the firing squad
THUR 216:25
faces: baby f. in the violet
ELIOT 77:5
Coming with vivid f.
YEATS 233:9
Private f. in public places
AUDEN 15:1
public f. in private places
AUDEN 15:1
these f. in the crowd
POUND 174:11
facility: penetrates the ear with f.
BEEC 22:9
fact: any f., no matter how suspect
VIDAL 221:13
fatal futility of F.
JAMES 112:4
only one great f.
FISH 80:5
factory: f. we make cosmetics
REVS 179:16
facts: beyond the obvious f.
DOYLE 69:17
consists in ignoring f.
ADAMS 2:6
F. are better than dreams
CHUR 55:18
f. are lost forever
MAIL 145:9
f. are sacred
SCOTT 193:16
f. but to re-allocate them
RYLE 187:10
F. do not cease to exist
HUXL 109:12
f. when you come to brass
ELIOT 76:9
if the f. had been put
BEVIN 33:14
not of f. but of values
INGE 110:9
obvious f. about grown-ups
JARR 112:17
Science is built up of f.
POIN 172:10
will give you all the f.
AUDEN 14:15
fade: In fields where roses f.
HOUS 107:7
They simply f. away
FOLEY 82:8
faded: interviewing a f. female
HARD 96:16
fades: Until she f. away
CHES 50:17
fading: the last f. smile
HUXL 109:16

faery: The land of f.   YEATS 232:17
fail: succeed. Others must f.   VIDAL 221:12
  was sure I should not f.   CHUR 55:18
  We shall not f. or falter   CHUR 53:9
  we shall not flag or f.   CHUR 54:10
failed: f. to inspire sympathy   BEER 23:10
  Light That F.   KIPL 125:20
  remembered by what they f.
                              MOORE 155:10
  they f. before   KING 122:9
failing: f. of Elizabeth's   HARDY 97:6
  To you from f. hands we throw
                              MCCR 141:18
failure: end in f.   POW 174:22
  F. makes people bitter   MAUG 149:23
  formula for f.   SWOPE 211:6
  His f. is ignominious   MENC 150:14
  not the effort nor the f.   EMPS 77:15
  Now we are not a f.   VANZ 221:5
  success and only one a f.   SAM 189:9
  there's no success like f.   DYLAN 71:9
faintly: F., faintlier afar   FREE 85:3
fair: f. and floral air   FLEC 81:17
  f. sex is your department   DOYLE 69:18
  F. Shares for All   JAY 112:18
  flaying would be f.   HOUS 105:8
  In a f. ground   KIPL 124:11
  it follows that it is F.   SWOPE 211:5
  It's not f. to the child   FROST 86:16
  Ludlow come in for the f.   HOUS 106:16
  noble, historically f.   LERN 135:19
  remained at 'set f.'   BENN 28:3
fairest: f. things have fleetest   THOM 214:20
fairies: Do you believe in f.   BARR 19:10
  f. at the bottom of our   FYL 87:18
  I don't believe in f.   BARR 19:8
  was the beginning of f.   BARR 19:7
fairly: dealt f. with their men   BALD 17:15
  Englishman is ever f. beaten
                              SHAW 199:29
fairness: equality or f. or justice   BERL 30:6
fairy: loves a f. when she's forty
                              HENL 101:8
  myth is, of course, not a f. story
                              RYLE 187:10
  there is a little f. somewhere   BARR 19:8
faith: creates f. does not deceive
                              SHAW 199:28
  f. chiefly in the sense   AMIS 4:20
  F. may be defined briefly   MENC 151:4
  f. without doubt is nothing   UNAM 220:12
  first article of my f.   GAND 88:12
  If ye break f. with us who die
                              MCCR 141:18
  regaining f. in Mother Church   FITZ 80:23
  shake a man's f.   SHAW 196:5
  sudden explosions of f.   BREN 39:9
  What of the f. and fire   HARDY 97:16
  with strong and active f.   ROOS 183:12
  you have kept f.   HARDY 98:5
faithful: f. if they are in the least attractive
                              CAMP 45:13
  f. soul would walk   CARB 46:18
faith-healer: was a f. of Deal   ANON 8:19
faithless: Human on my f. arm
                              AUDEN 13:7
falcon: f. cannot hear the falconer
                              YEATS 233:12
falconer: The falcon cannot hear the f.
                              YEATS 233:12
Falklands: The F. thing [the F. War of
  1982]   BORG 36:10
fall: easily f. victim to a big lie   HITL 103:8

fall (*cont.*):
  f. flat on your face   THUR 217:1
  further they have to f.   FITZ 81:1
  hard rain's a gonna f.   DYLAN 71:6
  I meditated on the F.   BETJ 31:6
  Life is a horizontal f.   COCT 57:7
  Things f. apart   YEATS 233:12
  too late to f. in love   WILS 229:2
fallacious: I said lightly, is f.   O'BR 162:8
fallen: F. in the cause of the free
                              BINY 34:17
  good man f. among Fabians
                              LENIN 134:16
  He's f. in the water   MILL 152:14
  scribbled lines like f. hopes   HOPE 105:2
falling: apple f. towards England
                              AUDEN 14:9
  'f. domino' principle   EIS 73:8
  You'll find your fortune f.   BURKE 42:13
falls: F. the Shadow   ELIOT 75:11
false: interesting than a f. one   WHIT 226:7
falsely: meaning 'to behave f.'   WITT 229:11
falter: fail or f.   CHUR 53:9
falters: The love that never f.   SPR 206:11
Famagusta: For F. and the hidden sun
                              FLEC 81:19
fame: F. is a food that dead   DOBS 68:1
  no one shall work for f.   KIPL 127:11
  Physicians of the Utmost F.   BELL 24:12
familiar: Seem far too f. Get stewed
                              LARK 131:4
familiarity: F. breeds contempt
                              TWAIN 219:26
families: Mothers of large f.   BELL 24:7
  there are f.   THAT 213:8
family: f. that prays together   SCAL 192:13
  f., with its narrow   LEACH 133:4
  f. with the wrong members   ORW 164:17
  I am the f. face   HARDY 97:7
  I don't like the f. Stein   ANON 6:22
  man that left his f.   TWAIN 218:21
  not lugged into F. Rows   WOD 230:15
  To the f.—that dear octopus
                              SMITH 202:6
famous: become f. without ability
                              SHAW 196:8
  by that time I was too f.   BENC 27:4
  everyone will be f. for fifteen minutes
                              WARH 222:10
  F. remarks are very seldom   STR 210:18
  f. seaside place called   EDGAR 71:20
  I'm never going to be f.   PARK 168:3
  minutes everybody will be f.
                              WARH 222:10
fanatic: A f. heart   YEATS 236:3
  A f. is a great leader   BROUN 41:5
fanaticism: F. consists in redoubling
                              SANT 190:7
fanatics: f. always to be found   ROOS 184:6
fancies: That falls at eve our f. blow
                              FLEC 81:22
fancy: All I get is f. stuff   PHIL 170:16
  And now the f. passes   HOUS 106:13
  But keep your f. free   HOUS 106:12
  I dislike what I f. I feel   ANON 8:19
  what you f. does you good   LEIGH 134:12
fantasies: Even the linked f.   THOM 215:14
  We had fed the heart on f.   YEATS 232:5
fantasy: of course far more than a f.
                              FORS 83:10
far: audacity is knowing how f.   COCT 57:3
  be going a bridge too f.   BROW 41:14
  F. away is close at hand   GRAV 93:10
  f. end of the enormous   AUDEN 14:19

far (*cont.*):
  It is a f., far better   GALB 88:3
  much too f. out all my life   SMITH 203:18
  stick; you will go f.   ROOS 183:17
far away: quarrel in a f. country
                              CHAM 48:12
farce: longest running f. in the West
                              SMITH 202:5
  theatre of f.   BENT 29:8
  wine was a f. and the food   POW 174:17
fare: f. and just a trifle to spare   GORD 92:4
farewell: F., Leicester Square   JUDGE 116:17
  F., my friends. I am going   DUNC 70:13
  F. sadness   ELUA 77:14
  Saying 'F., blighted love.'   ANON 8.8
  So f. then   ANON 8:11
  than waving me f.   HOPE 105:4
farm: gonna work on Maggie's F.
                              DYLAN 71:10
  keep 'em down on the f.   LEWIS 136:19
farmer: F. will never be happy
                              HERB 101:20
farmers: This country needs good f.
                              NIXON 161:6
  Three jolly F.   DE L 66:16
farms: cellos of the deep f.   STEV 209:8
  f. if that protection   HOOV 104:13
  What spires, what f. are those
                              HOUS 107:4
farmyard: I might have been a f. hen
                              AYRES 16:7
far-reaching: noble in motive and f.
                              HOOV 104:11
farrow: old sow that eats her f.
                              JOYCE 115:18
fart: dumb he can't f. and chew
                              JOHN 114:5
farther: f. down our particular   FORS 84:8
fascinates: I like work: it f. me   JER 113:16
fascinating: most f. kind of art
                              WARH 222:11
fascination: f. of a public execution
                              FOOT 82:9
  The f. of what's difficult   YEATS 232:12
Fascism: victims of American F.
                              ROS 184:19
Fascist: Every woman adores a F.
                              PLATH 172:4
fashion: worn-out poetical f.   ELIOT 74:9
fashionable: both f. and first-rate
                              SMITH 203:8
  ever to be f. is ominous   SANT 190:19
fashioned: That f. forth its loveliness
                              HARDY 98:2
fashions: conscience to fit this year's f.
                              HELL 100:8
fast: f. word about oral contraception
                              ALLEN 4:3
  I'm f. I'm a bad lot   THOM 214:11
fasten: And if they think, they f.
                              HOUS 105:16
  F. your seat-belts   MANK 146:2
faster: F. than a speeding bullet   ANON 6:8
fastest: f. who travels alone   KIPL 127:15
fastidious: minds of a few f.   SMITH 203:16
fat: Butter merely makes us f.   GOER 91:7
  f. greedy owl of the Remove   RICH 180:15
  F. is a feminist issue   ORB 163:18
  f. lady sings   COOK 60:8
  f. white woman whom nobody
                              CORN 61:8
  Imprisoned in every f. man a thin
                              CONN 59:12

fat (*cont.*):

incredibly f. or incredibly thin   BARR 19:17

It is all f., without nerve   LEWIS 136:18
Outside every f. man there   AMIS 4:19
thin man inside every f.   ORW 164:11

fatal: f. futility of Fact   JAMES 112:4
most f. complaint of all   HILT 102:17
most f. to true happiness   RUSS 186:15

fatalistic: Beats like a f. drum   ELIOT 75:21

fate: Art is a revolt against f.   MALR 145:16
f. in what I cannot fear   ROET 182:4
F. is not an eagle   BOWEN 37:13
F.'s great bazaar   MACN 144:16
f. wilfully misunderstand   FROST 86:5
F. wrote her [Queen Caroline]   BEER 23:2
For all our children's f.   KIPL 124:15
foulness of their f.   SASS 191:19
I have a bone to pick with F.   NASH 159:8
makers of our f.   POPP 172:13

fat-head: F. poet that nobody reads   CHES 51:8

father: As my poor f. used to say   HERB 101:15

even if he is our f.   CHES 51:13
f. gave me some advice   FITZ 80:18
f. of the nation   NEHRU 160:1
f. spent the first year   BREC 38:19
f. was the distinction   BOHR 35:14
f. would wish his daughter   ANON 8:20
Lloyd George knows my f.   ANON 7:18
night the bed fell on my f.   THUR 216:15
Our F. which art in heaven   PRÉV 175:6
There is no good f.   SART 191:5
time my f. was dying   BENN 28:2
your F. had an accident   POTT 173:14
your f., whom you love   STOP 209:20

fatherhood: Mirrors and f. are abominable   BORG 36:9

fathers: And where's their f. live   THOM 214:10

Come mothers and f.   DYLAN 71:14
fundamental defect of f.   RUSS 187:3
My f. can have it   THOM 213:19
revolts against its f.   MUMF 157:16
talking to you mothers and f.   ROOS 183:7
Tell them, because our f. lied   KIPL 127:21
Victory has a hundred f.   CIANO 56:7

fathom: f. the inscrutable workings   SMITH 202:10

fatigue: relaxation from physical f.   MAT 149:3

fattening: immoral, or f.   WOOL 231:20

Faulkner: F., and Steinbeck   ALGR 3:8

faults: f. of the age come from   BALF 17:17
They fill you with f.   LARK 130:12
you see all his f.   LYTT 140:18

fauteuil: *f. qui le délasse de ses*   MAT 149:3

favour: being in and out of f.   FROST 86:14
I hold with those who f. fire   FROST 86:6

favourite: It's my second f. organ   ALLEN 4:7
people and their f. islands   AUDEN 14:16

fawns: The fallow f. invisible go   THOM 214:12

fear: direction of our f.   BERR 30:15
fate in what I cannot fear   ROET 182:4
F. and loathing in Las Vegas   THOM 216:12
F. God   KITC 128:5
F. is the main source   RUSS 187:5
f. it would make me conservative   FROST 85:20

fear (*cont.*):

f. love is to fear life   RUSS 186:19
f. of finding something worse   BELL 24:10
f. of life become publishers   CONN 58:15
F. wist not to evade   THOM 215:8
fourth is freedom from f.   ROOS 183:9
I f. those big words   JOYCE 116:5
Life is first boredom, then f.   LARK 131:5
never f. to negotiate   KENN 119:13
only thing we have to f.   ROOS 183:1
people for f. I may be lonely   JOAD 113:20
show you f. in a handful   ELIOT 76:15
state as required by its f.   MAD 144:19
The haunting f. that someone   MENC 150:19
till the f. of the Law   JOYCE 115:12
Why f. death   FROH 85:11
without f. the lawless roads   MUIR 157:12

feast: mind is a perpetual f.   SMITH 202:21
Paris is a movable f.   HEM 101:1

feather: To produce my foot, my each f.   HUGH 108:2

feathered: f. glory from her loosening   YEATS 234:21

feather-footed: F. through the plashy   WAUGH 223:13

featureless: more f. and commonplace a crime   DOYLE 69:4

features: f. from which deductions   DOYLE 69:28

February: not Puritanism but F.   KRUT 129:3

fed: f. your hunger like   CRANE 62:16

feed: Church can f. and sleep   ELIOT 75:6
F. the world   GELD 89:4
will you still f. me   LENN 135:13

feel: Englishman can't f.   FORS 83:3
f. fierce and revolutionary   LINK 137:15
f. like a fugitive from   MAUL 150:4
f. the earth move   HEM 100:12
f. the heart-break   GIBS 90:8
f. the machine slipping   LOW 139:21
f. with Norman that I have   AYCK 16:2
I dislike what I fancy I f.   ANON 8:19
I don't f. like going into it   SAL 188:24
I f. as I always have   BENC 26:20
It makes me f. good   LEV 136:4
make one f. more at home   FREUD 85:8

feelin': I got a beautiful f.   HAMM 95:18

feeling: constellations of f.   DOUG 68:12
f. of Sunday is the same   RHYS 180:5
f. that the poet believes   QUAS 176:13
If merely 'f. good'   JAMES 112:14
I get a funny f. inside of me   GREGG 93:22
mess of imprecision of f.   ELIOT 74:13
Music is f., then, not sound   STEV 208:12
Prevents that sinking f.   HARR 98:15
school that f. is bad form   FORS 83:3

feelings: keeping f. at bay   BROO 41:2

feeling-toned: chiefly the *f.* complexes   JUNG 117:3

fees: they took their F.   BELL 24:12

feet: And palms before my f.   CHES 52:11
better to die on your f.   IBAR 109:17
broken by their passing f.   YEATS 234:10
Came on the following F.   THOM 215:11
his eyes before his f.   ELIOT 76:17
Just direct your f.   FIEL 79:9
marching, charging f.   JAGG 111:9
on little cat f.   SAND 189:14
Radical is a man with both f.   ROOS 183:6
stranger's f. may find the meadow   HOUS 106:4

feet (*cont.*):

wash their f. in soda   ELIOT 76:23
with little snow-white f.   YEATS 234:13
Your f.'s too big   BENS 28:19

felicitous: F. phenomenon   MOORE 155:12

felicity: f. on the far side of baldness   SMITH 202:22

fell: bed f. on my father   THUR 216:15

fella: F. belong Mrs Queen   PHIL 170:19

felled: that signed the paper f.   THOM 214:4

feller: Sweetes' li'l' f.   STAN 207:2

fellow: other f. just blinked   RUSK 186:6

fellows: For f. whom it hurts to think   HOUS 107:8

I—I say, you f.   RICH 180:16

felt: f. towards Him as she might   STR 210:8
rather f. you round my throat   HOPE 105:4
Thou hast not f. thy bosom keep   DAV 65:4

female: faded f. in a damp basement   HARD 96:16
f. in a world of males   PITT 172:1
f. of the species is more   KIPL 126:17
f. will appear in society   DE B 65:12
f. worker is the slave   CONN 59:17
vindictiveness of the f.   CONN 59:9

feminism: F. is the most revolutionary   TOYN 217:14

feminist: Fat is a f. issue   ORB 163:18

femme: *f. qui ne me plaisait pas*   PROU 175:19

On ne naît pas f.   DE B 65:12

fen: plashy f. passes the questing   WAUGH 223:13

fence: DON'T F. ME IN   PORT 172:20
jonquils by sunny garden f.   BETJ 32:5
One time there was a picket f.   MORG 155:20
stately park and the f.   MAUG 149:7
two birds setting on a f.   TWAIN 219:3

fences: f. make good neighbours   FROST 86:10

Fermanagh: steeples of F. and Tyrone   CHUR 54:2

fertile: In such a fix to be so f.   NASH 159:19

fester: that f. are not springlike   ABSE 1:2

fetch: *fresh* corpse, f. him out   TWAIN 219:22

fetters: his f. fall   GAND 88:11

fever: enigma of the f. chart   ELIOT 74:12
Of chills and f. she died   RANS 177:14
signed the treaty bred a f.   THOM 214:5

fevers: Time and f. burn away   AUDEN 13:7

fever-trees: all set about with f.   KIPL 125:13

few: criticism by the f.   BROWN 41:10
death is one of the f.   ALLEN 3:23
F. thought he was even   ATTL 12:6
f. who would not rather   HUXL 108:9
owed by so many to so f.   CHUR 54:12

fiancée: discerning young man his f.   ANON 8:20

fickleness: f. of the women I love   SHAW 199:14

fiction: biography is ultimately f.   MAL 145:14
f. autobiography   STOP 209:12
f. is a necessity   CHES 50:11
f. set to more or less   MENC 151:3
one form of continuous f.   BEVAN 33:8
Poetry is the supreme f.   STEV 208:9

fiddle: important beyond all this f.   MOORE 155:13
tune played on an old f.   BUTL 44:9

fiddler: village f. after Paganini   NIC 160:9
fiddles: Oh some are fond of f.   MAS 148:5
fiddlin': they were f. and small
                                    EDGAR 71:20
fidelity: Untruth. The stone f.   LARK 131:6
field: Beside a f. of grain   PARK 169:9
   corner of a foreign f.   BROO 40:5
   f. by the river my love   YEATS 234:13
   f. is full of shades   THOM 215:22
   For Vaguery in the F.   OSB 165:16
   Never in the f. of human   CHUR 54:12
fields: f. and in the streets   CHUR 54:10
   f. of millions of farms   HOOV 104:13
   Here lies W. C. F.   FIEL 79:15
   In f. where roses fade   HOUS 107:7
   Strawberry f. forever   LENN 135:11
   whispering of f. unsown   OWEN 166:11
fiends: bloody and foreigners are f.
                                    MITF 154:18
fifteen: always f. years older   BAR 20:5
   famous for f. minutes   WARH 222:10
   f. minutes everybody will   WARH 222:10
fifth: came f. and lost the job   JOYCE 116:9
fifties: These are the tranquillized F.
                                    LOW 140:3
fifty: F. million Frenchmen can't
                                    ROSE 184:13
   It only leaves me f. more   HOUS 106:9
   with booze until he's f.   FAUL 78:14
fifty-fifty: f. Americanism   ROOS 184:1
fight: bade me f. had told me so   EWER 78:3
   cease when men refuse to f.   ANON 9:6
   dead, who will not f.   GREN 94:3
   f. and fight and fight   GAIT 87:23
   f. for freedom and truth   IBSEN 109:21
   f. for its King and Country   GRAH 92:9
   f. for one's principles   ADLER 2:15
   man being too proud to f.   WILS 229:11
   must f. on to the end   HAIG 95:3
   Nor law, nor duty bade me f.
                                    YEATS 235:5
   shall f. on the beaches   CHUR 54:10
   that Britain would f.   CHUR 53:13
   thought it wrong to f.   BELL 25:22
   youth who must f. and die   HOOV 104:10
fighting: And who dies f. has increase
                                    GREN 94:3
   between two periods of f.   BIER 34:12
   f. back   MCKAY 142:15
   f. Blenheim all over again   BEVAN 32:18
   f. for this woman's honour   KALM 117:11
   right for f. in the street   JAGG 111:9
   The f. man shall from the sun   GREN 94:3
   those that are f. for you   STEIN 207:19
   What are WE f. for   SERV 194:21
fights: f. are the best part   WILD 227:4
figs: And f. grew upon thorn   CHES 52:10
figure: f. in the carpet   JAMES 111:19
   f. of Juno   BARR 19:26
   Not even a public f.   CURZ 64:9
   The f. a poem makes   FROST 85:16
   The f. is the same   FROST 85:16
figures: other f. in it   ELIOT 73:20
   wit there is in those f.   FRY 87:10
Files-on-Parade: said F.   KIPL 123:3
fill: f. you with the faults   LARK 130:12
   I am not yet born; O f. me   MACN 144:18
   Sleep your f.— but when   BELL 25:20
filling: challenge of f. the space
                                    WEST 225:23
films: I seldom go to f. They   BERR 30:18
filth: so is f.   FORS 84:1
final: And so I face the f. curtain   ANKA 5:7

final *(cont.)*:
   dead sound on the f.   ELIOT 76:17
   This is my f. word   BEAV 21:1
finality: Perfection is f.   STEP 208:6
financiers: And all these f.   WILS 228:9
Finchley: F. tried to mend the Electric
                                    BELL 25:7
find: beginning to f. it out   SMITH 203:7
   f. a friend one must close   DOUG 68:13
   f. out what everyone   HERB 101:14
   f. out why a snorer can't   TWAIN 220:5
   f. the truth, to speak   NIXON 161:1
   returns home to f. it   MOORE 155:8
   Scratch a lover, and f. a foe   PARK 168:21
   Someday I'll f. you   COW 62:9
   till you f. your dream   HAMM 95:14
   We always f. something   BECK 21:21
   You will f. no new places   CAV 48:2
finds: War always f. a way   BREC 39:6
fine: A f. romance with no kisses   FIEL 79:7
   California is a f. place   ALLEN 3:11
   f. sense of the ridiculous   ALBEE 3:3
   May will be f. next year   HOUS 105:13
finer: diner nothing could be f.   GORD 92:4
finest: This was their f. hour   CHUR 54:11
finger: Between my f. and my thumb
                                    HEAN 99:10
   chills the f. not a bit   NASH 159:9
   f. do you want on the trigger   ANON 9:15
   f. goes wabbling back   KIPL 126:18
   f. in the throat and one   OSLER 165:22
   It's f. lickin' good   ANON 7:8
   lift up my f. and I say   SAR 190:24
   like a rugged f. to Heaven   LLOY 138:12
fingernails: indifferent, paring his f.
                                    JOYCE 115:17
fingers: Crumbling between the f.
                                    MACN 144:15
   Just as my f. on these keys   STEV 208:12
   Let your f. do the walking   ANON 7:14
   sovereign f. taxed the breath
                                    THOM 214:4
   those terrified vague f.   YEATS 234:21
   time we 'pulled our f. out'   PHIL 170:18
fings: F. ain't wot they used t'be
                                    NORM 161:11
finish: I've started so I'll f.   MAGN 145:3
   Nice guys. F. last   DUR 70:16
   start together and f.   BEEC 22:1
   that you f. it   BENN 28:9
   tools and we will f. the job   CHUR 53:9
finished: A poem is never f.   VALÉ 220:22
   f. in the first 100 days   KENN 119:14
   married. Then he's f.   GABOR 87:20
   world where England is f.   MILL 152:3
   would have been f. in half   WOD 230:11
finishing: keep f. your sentences
                                    LONS 139:2
finite: knowledge can only be f.
                                    POPP 172:17
finned: f. cars forward like   LOW 140:2
fiords: probably pining for the f.
                                    CHAP 49:13
fire: And nodding by the f.   YEATS 232:7
   C'mon, baby, light my f.   MORR 156:7
   Cyprus with a lake of f.   FLEC 81:19
   deathly inner consuming f.   HESSE 102:4
   every time She shouted 'F.'   BELL 24:16
   f. and the rose are one   ELIOT 74:23
   f. and was burnt to ashes   GRAH 92:12
   fire brigade and the f.   CHUR 54:3
   f. next time   ANON 6:12
   f. of my loins   NAB 158:12
   F. your little gun   DE L 66:19

fire *(cont.)*:
   I didn't f. him [General]   TRUM 218:12
   Into the crowned knot of f.   ELIOT 74:23
   The f. next time   BALD 16:15
   The f. was furry as a bear   SITW 201:11
   wabbling back to the F.   KIPL 126:18
   What of the faith and f.   HARDY 97:16
   with f. beyond the language   ELIOT 74:17
   with those who favour f.   FROST 86:6
   world will end in f.   FROST 86:6
fired: ever got f. for buying IBM   ANON 7:28
fireplace: stocking over the municipal f.
                                    SMITH 202:2
fires: Of her salamandrine f.   HARDY 97:13
firing: have what to do after f.   REED 178:19
   he faced the f. squad   THUR 216:25
first: After the f. death   THOM 213:14
   After the f. four years   CRISP 63:1
   any significant f. person   WITT 229:11
   be done for the f. time   CORN 61:11
   certainty are not the f.   HOUS 105:14
   f. and second class citizens   WILL 228:4
   f. message of India   FORS 84:2
   f. requirement for a composer   HON 104:9
   f. requirement of a statesman   ACH 1:6
   f. sign of old age   HICKS 102:9
   f. team and who just miss   BRON 39:16
   f. ten million years were   ADAMS 1:15
   First things f., second   CONR 60:6
   know the place for the f.   ELIOT 74:20
   Like the f. bird   FARJ 78:7
   Like the f. morning   FARJ 78:7
   Non-violence is the f. article   GAND 88:12
   people who got there f.   UST 220:17
   team we have Who's on f.   ABB 1:1
first class: f., and with children   BENC 27:1
first-rate: A test of a f. work   BENN 28:9
   fashionable and f.   SMITH 203:8
firwood: f. meditating on the nature
                                    O'BR 162:7
fish: cars nose forward like f.   LOW 140:2
   coal and surrounded by f.   BEVAN 32:17
   f. gaped among empty tins   PLOM 172:9
   F. say, they have   BROO 40:6
   f. swim with the stream   MUGG 157:8
   like a f. without a bicycle   STEI 208:4
   much as a recently dead f.   ORW 164:12
   pretty kettle of f.   MARY 147:20
   There's a f. that *talks*   DE L 66:13
fishbones: placing before me two f.
                                    WELBY 224:6
fished: f. down their throats   BETJ 31:9
fishes: invasion. So are the f.   CHUR 55:5
   When f. flew and forests walked
                                    CHES 52:10
fishingboat: crowblack, f.-bobbing sea
                                    THOM 214:7
fish-knives: Phone for the f., Norman
                                    BETJ 31:11
fissures: F. appeared in football fields
                                    PLOM 172:9
fist: mailed f. in a cotton glove   SITW 201:16
fistful: f. of coins   ZAP 236:10
fists: groan and shake their f.   HOUS 105:8
fit: ain't a f. night out   FIEL 79:16
   Britain a f. country   LLOY 138:13
   It isn't f. for humans now   BETJ 31:1
   only the F. survive   SERV 194:22
fitness: no test of f.   SHAW 196:16
fits: And think by f. and starts
                                    HOUS 105:14
   frightened them all into f.   BETJ 31:9
fittest: survival of the f.   ROCK 181:17

fitting: f. that we should have buried
ASQ 11:12
Fitzgerald: For this Edward F. died
YEATS 234:15
five: At f. in the afternoon   LORCA 139:11
be only f. Kings left   FAR 78:9
economy right in f. years   BENN 27:16
F. go off in a caravan   BLYT 35:9
f. kings did a king   THOM 214:4
The bombing begins in f. minutes
REAG 178:14
fivepence: We have saved f.   BECK 21:10
fix: ain't broke, don't f. it   LANCE 130:1
And f. up his automobile   CLAR 56:11
looking for an angry f.   GINS 90:15
fixed: f. point in a changing   DOYLE 69:11
His eyes f. upon nothing   YEATS 233:7
flag: f. to which you have pledged
BALD 16:19
German f. will be hauled   BEAT 20:17
we shall not f. or fail   CHUR 54:10
flagellation: Not f., not pederasty
RATT 178:2
flag-flapper: Jelly-bellied F.   KIPL 127:13
flags: f. straining in the night-blasts
CHES 51:17
flame: roof-lamp's oily f.   HARDY 97:8
tongues of f. are in-folded   ELIOT 74:23
When a lovely f. dies   HARB 96:11
Flanders: In F. fields the poppies blow
MCCR 141:17
flannel: wear white f. trousers   ELIOT 75:19
flannelled: f. fools at the wicket
KIPL 124:12
flapped: filled the trees and f.   HODG 103:10
flare: The f. was up in the gymn   BETJ 32:7
flash: f. through the flowery   CHES 51:8
flatten: His hide is sure to f. 'em   BELL 24:8
flatter: To f. beauty's ignorant ear
YEATS 234:19
flattering: who spends his time f.
TRUM 218:11
you think him worth f.   SHAW 197:4
flattery: out of ten to tout for f.   COLL 58:5
suppose f. hurts no one   STEV 208:18
Flaubert: His true Penelope was F.
POUND 174:3
flaunt: when you got it, f. it   BROO 41:3
flavour: lose its f. on the bedpost
ROSE 184:12
flaying: f. would be fair   HOUS 105:8
flea: literature's performing f.   O'CAS 162:20
fleas: Even educated f. do it   PORT 173:3
f. that tease in the High   BELL 25:15
that has praised his f.   YEATS 232:13
fled: I f. Him, down the nights   THOM 215:5
flee: Or watch the startled spirit f.
GRAV 93:6
fleece: forest f. the Wrekin heaves
HOUS 106:18
fleet: f. of stars is anchored   FLEC 81:18
whole F.'s lit up   WOOD 231:5
fleetest: The fairest things have f. end
THOM 214:20
flesh: an' give us hearts o' f.   O'CAS 162:15
F. of her flesh they were   BINY 34:17
F. perishes, I live   HARDY 97:7
For him f. was sacramental   ROB 181:16
In that land of f. and bone   AUDEN 14:11
Neither f. nor fleshless   ELIOT 74:5
that look but casual f.   YEATS 233:5
word and clay is the f.   KAV 118:8
flew: f. between me and the sun   BLUN 35:2

flexible: Access—your f. friend   ANON 5:9
flick: f. of the wrist   HEAT 99:18
flicker: moment of my greatness f.
ELIOT 75:17
flies: like f. on a summer day   RUSS 186:25
Lord of the f.   GOLD 91:10
on his skin the swart f.   DOUG 68:11
fliest: fly thee, for thou f. Me   THOM 215:18
fling: Had chosen thus to f. his soul
HARDY 97:11
flinging: F. from his arms I laughed
YEATS 235:12
flints: soul would walk the f.   CARB 46:18
float: F. like a butterfly   ALI 3:9
floating: F. in the Blue   MILNE 153:14
flood: Empire vast across the f.   HUXL 109:1
flooded: STREETS F.   BENC 26:14
floor: lie on the f. without holding on
MART 147:14
passing of the third f.   JFR 113:12
sail across the f.   GREN 94:2
floors: across the f. of silent   ELIOT 75:16
flop: f. than the organization   BAEZ 16:10
Flopsy: F., Mopsy, Cottontail   POTT 173:13
floraisons: *f. mois des métamorphoses*
ARAG 10:2
floral: f. air and the love   FLEC 81:17
florid: Let the f. music praise   AUDEN 14:11
flotilla: Where the old F. lay   KIPL 123:13
flow: F. down the woods and stipple
SACK 187:16
flower: f. is the concrete cloverleaf
MUMF 157:17
green fuse drives the f.   THOM 213:20
Pride is a f. that's free   COW 62:2
flowerings: O month of f.   ARAG 10:2
flowers: f. the tenderness of patient
OWEN 166:9
gathered f. are dead   FLEC 81:12
her f. to love, her ways   BROO 40:5
Letting a hundred f. blossom
MAO T 146:8
Say it with f.   O'KEE 163:2
Where have all the f. gone   SEEG 194:6
Who gave them f.   OWEN 166:14
flowery: you flash through the f.   CHES 51:8
flowing: if the Suez Canal was f.
EDEN 71:19
fluffy: But f., just fluffy   HERB 101:19
fluidity: *f. of self-revelation*   JAMES 111:11
solid for f., all-powerful   CHUR 54:5
flung: f. us on the windy hill   BROO 39:18
he f. himself from   LEAC 133:12
flush: f. to suffuse his face   AMIS 4:17
flushing: f. runneth from windows
BETJ 32:5
flushpots: f. of Euston and the hanging
JOYCE 115:9
flute: The f. and the trumpet   AUDEN 14:11
flutter: F. and bear him up   BETJ 31:3
fly: A f. can't bird, but a bird   MILNE 153:14
all things f. thee   THOM 215:18
And nestlings f.   HARDY 97:2
Angels can f. because   CHES 51:15
God in His wisdom made the f.
NASH 159:12
He wouldn't hurt a f.   LEAC 133:11
long-legged f. upon the stream
YEATS 233:7
Oh! never f. conceals a hook   BROO 40:8
flyin'-fishes: Where the f. play   KIPL 123:13
flying: F. Scotsman is no less   BEAV 21:2
Keep the aspidistra f.   ORW 164:16

flying (*cont.*):
men in their f. machines   DAV 64:19
foam: off that f. when Phidias   YEATS 233:5
foe: Call no man f., but never   BENS 28:22
f. was folly and his weapon   ANON 6:21
Scratch a lover, and find a f.
PARK 168:21
foes: judge of a man by his f.   CONR 59:25
fog: brown f. of a winter dawn   ELIOT 76:17
The f. comes   SAND 189:14
yellow f. that rubs its back   ELIOT 75:14
foggy: A f. day in London Town
GERS 89:13
fold: Do not f., spindle   ANON 6:1
F. your clothes up neat   DE L 66:20
mill and the f.   HOUS 106:16
folded: To undo the f. lie   AUDEN 13:9
folds: spring has kept in its f.   ARAG 10:2
Folies-Bergère: F. and looks at the
audience   STOC 209:10
folk: All music is f. music   ARMS 10:8
f. that live in Liverpool   CHES 50:17
trouble with a f. song   LAMB 129:16
folk-dancing: excepting incest and f.
BAX 20:14
folklore: magicians of North European f.
KEYN 120:15
folks: Don't let the old f. know
HERB 101:17
follies: f. which a man regrets
ROWL 185:15
follow: contrived that the eyes f.
ORW 164:20
Don't f. leaders   DYLAN 71:13
expect to see when I f.   DOYLE 69:10
F. ev'ry rainbow, till   HAMM 95:14
My old man said, 'F. the van'   COLL 58:2
So, f. me, follow   FLAN 81:4
follows: Impossible to come, lie f.
PROU 176:5
folly: foe was f. and his weapon   ANON 6:21
human f. like the back   AUDEN 12:18
lovely woman stoops to f.   ELIOT 77:2
fonctionnaire: *Un f. ne plaisante pas*
ION 110:20
fond: He was extremely f. of sums
BELL 24:21
was probably f. of them   TWAIN 219:24
food: And the sweet sticky f.   AYRES 16:6
Continent people have good f.
MIKES 151:14
discovered that alcohol was a f.
WOD 230:16
Fame is a f. that dead   DOBS 68:1
farce and the f. a tragedy   POW 174:17
F. comes first, then morals   BREC 38:22
F. enough for a week   MERR 151:11
F. is an important part   LEB 133:21
f. that raises him   HANFF 96:9
lays out f. in tins   ELIOT 76:24
problem is f.   DONL 68:6
sincerer than the love of f.   SHAW 197:23
fool: clever woman to manage a f.
KIPL 126:1
f. all of the people all   ADAMS 1:19
f. lies here who tried   KIPL 125:22
f.'s excuse for failure   BIER 34:15
f. there was and he made   KIPL 127:18
f. too many of the people   THUR 217:2
f. us with how fast they   AUDEN 15:6
I'm not a bloody f.   LONS 139:12
make a f. of himself too   BUTL 43:26
Prove to me that you're no f.
RICE 180:10

found (*cont.*):
I f. it, I found it — ABSE 1:4
tragedy of a man who has f. — BARR 19:24
foundation: f. of unyielding despair — RUSS 186:21
foundations: The hour when earth's f. fled — HOUS 106:3
While earth's f. stand — HOUS 106:8
founding: compared with f. a bank — BREC 39:1
fountain: Let the healing f. start — AUDEN 13:4
founts: f. falling in the Courts — CHES 51:16
four: count f. — TWAIN 219:32
first f. years the dirt — CRISP 63:1
f. essential human freedoms — ROOS 183:9
F. Horsemen rode again — RICE 180:7
F. legs good, two legs bad — ORW 164:8
f. with paper hats — UST 220:20
looking over a f. leaf clover — DIXON 67:18
that two plus two make f. — ORW 164:23
four-footed: On all f. things — CHES 52:10
fourteenth: f. Mr Wilson — HOME 104:7
fourth: f. time that infernal noise — EDW 72:4
fourth-rate: f. country and I don't — CHAR 50:1
fox: Better than that of the f. — BLUNT 35:6
brown f. jumps over — ANON 8:5
Crazy like a f. — PER 170:2
f. came home and he went — MAS 148:15
They've shot our f. — BIRCH 34:19
foxes: second to the f. — BERL 30:4
foxholes: There are no atheists in the f. — CUMM 64:4
frag: *f. das Pferd* — FREUD 85:6
fragments: f. I have shored against — ELIOT 77:6
Live in f. no longer — FORS 83:17
fragrance: Has she elegance? Has she f.? — CAUL 47:16
frame: Are all the Human F. requires — BELL 24:13
France: Always it woke him, even in F. — OWEN 166:11
en F., est rétrospective — ARON 10:12
felt about F. what Pericles — KEYN 120:8
F. and Belgium in the true — KITC 128:5
F. and Germany remain apart — DULL 70:11
F. has lost a battle — DE G 65:19
F. is adequately secured — ASQ 11:11
F. will declare — EINS 73:1
F. wins wars — HELL 100:6
Political thought, in F., is retrospective — ARON 10:12
We shall fight in F. — CHUR 54:10
franchise: extension of the f. — CHES 51:13
Francis: highballs and I think I'm St F. — PARK 168:1
frank: f. words in our respective — COOK 60:9
Frankie: F. and Albert were lovers — ANON 6:10
frankness: views with an appalling f. — BALD 17:10
fraternize: I beckon you to f. — AUDEN 12:14
fraud: therefore it is not a f. — SHAW 199:28
frauds: then all great men are f. — LAW 35:18
freckles: Love, curiosity, f. — PARK 168:10
free: A hungry man is not a f. man — STEV 209:5
A man is either f. — BAR 18:8
born f. and equal in dignity — ANON 9:1
chains than to be f. — KAFKA 117:8

free (*cont.*):
Fallen in the cause of the f. — BINY 34:17
f. as they want — BALD 17:2
f. society is a society — STEV 208:22
f. society in — BEV 33:11
F. speech, free passes — BETJ 32:9
F. speech is about as good — BROUN 41:4
he's f. again — SOLZ 204:6
I am a f. man, an American — JOHN 114:16
I am condemned to be f. — SART 191:2
man a f. hand and he'll — WEST 225:16
Mother of the F. — BENS 28:21
prison, I am not f. — DEBS 65:14
such thing as a f. lunch — HEIN 100:1
The best things in life are f. — DE SY 67:4
they are f. to do whatever — SHAW 197:29
truth which makes men f. — AGAR 2:19
Was he f. — AUDEN 13:11
When people are f. to do — HOFF 103:18
worth nothin', but it's f. — KRIS 129:2
write f. verse — FROST 86:2
freedom: And the green f. of a cockatoo — STEV 208:11
any apprenticeship for f. — BAR 18:8
better organised than f. — PÉGUY 169:24
can do for the f. of man — KENN 119:16
F. and slavery are mental — GAND 88:11
F. is always and exclusively — LUX 140:17
F. is an indivisible word — WILL 228:5
f. is reserved — COLL 58:1
F. is slavery — ORW 164:21
F. is something people take — BALD 17:2
F. is the freedom to say — ORW 164:23
F. of mankind alike depend — HAIG 95:3
f. of personal decision — JUNG 117:2
f. of speech, freedom — TWAIN 219:10
F. of the press in Britain — SWAF 211:4
F.'s just another word — KRIS 129:2
go out to fight for f. — IBSEN 109:21
I gave my life for f. — EWER 78:3
O F., what liberties — GEOR 89:12
Our f. as free lances — MACN 144:6
The enemies of F. do not — INGE 110:10
there can be no f. — LENIN 134:19
things or in the f. — ILL 110:6
We must plan for f. — POPP 172:15
What stands if f. fall — KIPL 124:16
freedoms: four essential human f. — ROOS 183:9
freely: nature as f. as a lawyer — GIR 90:17
freemason: F., and an asthmatic — DOYLE 69:17
freemasonry: kind of bitter f. — BEER 23:9
freer: f., and more loving — BALD 16:17
f. society — BERD 29:10
frees: He f. himself and shows — GAND 88:11
freeze: those who would f. my humanity — MACN 144:18
freezes: Yours till Hell f. — FISH 80:7
frei: *Arbeit macht f.* — ANON 5:12
freiheit: *F. ist immer nur Freiheit* — LUX 140:17
French: F. for life-jacket — BARN 18:19
F. letters to the university — JOYCE 116:12
F. without Tears — RATT 178:1
German text of F. operas — WHAR 225:27
how it's improved her F. — GRAH 92:10
No more Latin, no more F. — ANON 7:30
Paris was F.—and silent — TUCH 218:17
some are fond of F. — MAS 148:4
The only tribute a F. translator — BEER 22:25
There is a F. widow — HOFF 104:2

French (*cont.*):
We are not F., and we — MONT 155:6
Frenchies: Those F. seek him everywhere — ORCZY 163:19
Frenchmen: Englishmen act better than F. — BENN 28:6
Fifty million F. can't be wrong — GUIN 94:14
Fifty million F. can't be wrong — ROSE 184:13
Frenchwomen: F. better than Englishwomen — BENN 28:6
fresh: F. from the Lord — FARJ 78:7
got a nice f. corpse — TWAIN 219:22
noted for f. air and fun — EDGAR 71:20
Freud: trouble with [Sigmund] F. — DODD 68:5
friend: A f. in power is a friend lost — ADAMS 2:2
country and betraying my f. — FORS 84:5
Diamonds are a girl's best f. — ROBIN 181:11
enemy of thought and the f. — CONR 59:27
f. and enemy is but Death — BROO 40:1
f. of yours and you could — SAL 188:25
I think of him as a f. — SMITH 203:22
lay down his wife for his f. — JOYCE 116:12
much-loved and elegant f. — CHAR 50:2
my f., is blowin' — DYLAN 71:4
O f. unseen, unborn, unknown — FLEC 81:23
One f. in a lifetime — ADAMS 2:4
portrait I lose a f. — SARG 190:22
Strange f. — OWEN 166:16
The soul of a f. we've made — BOND 35:19
To find a f. one must close — DOUG 68:13
Whenever a f. succeeds — VIDAL 221:16
your enemy and your f. — TWAIN 219:16
friendly: nor yet is it f. — HOLM 104:6
friends: And the dear f. have to part — BOND 35:19
closest f. won't tell — ANON 6:5
country are our f. — SHIN 200:13
don't trust him, we are f. — BREC 39:4
down his f. for his life — THOR 216:14
foes as well as by his f. — CONR 59:25
forgive my f. for dying — SMITH 203:2
For golden f. I had — HOUS 107:5
F. . . . are God's apology — KING 122:10
f. are necessarily — UST 220:17
f. who are not seeing this — THAT 212:17
f. with its grandfathers — MUMF 157:16
glory was I had such f. — YEATS 234:2
God we can choose our f. — MUMF 157:15
have really no absent f. — BOWEN 37:7
his f. could only — WOOLF 231:10
I have lost f., some — WOOLF 231:16
laughter and the love of f. — BELL 26:3
little help from my f. — LENN 135:14
made ridiculous by f. — BIER 33:23
Money couldn't buy f. — MILL 152:19
My f. all drive Porsches — JOPL 115:3
some of my best f. both — MAUG 149:12
win f. and influence people — CARN 47:1
your f. do not need it — HUBB 107:11
friendship: f. called slight when — BIER 33:19
F. needs a certain parallelism — ADAMS 2:4
frighten: street and f. the horses — CAMP 45:7
frightened: And f. them all into fits — BETJ 31:9
It has a f. look in its eyes — SITW 201:17
then you're f. of death — DONL 68:6
why should you be f. — WEBB 223:22

frightening: f. than when they are
  convinced   VAN D 221:4
  nothing is really very f.   STEIN 207:11
fringe: lunatic f. in all reform ROOS 184:6
frivolity: precious is f.   FORS 83:6
frocks: Her f. are built in Paris SAKI 188:12
frog: f. that's any better'n TWAIN 219:4
Frogs: 'F.,' he would say   MITF 154:18
frog-spawn: They *can* nothing but f.
                                 LAWR 131:18
from: F. far, from eve and morning
                                 HOUS 107:2
  F. here to eternity   JONES 115:1
  F. Russia with love   FLEM 82:2
  F. what I've tasted of desire FROST 86:6
  Neither f. nor towards   ELIOT 74:5
fromage: *quarante-six variétés de f.*
                                 DE G 66:1
front: All quiet on the western f.
                                 REM 179:11
  which f. these were sent   OWEN 166:14
frontier: on the edge of a new f.
                                 KENN 119:10
  Space—the final f.   RODD 182:2
  That is where our f. lies   BALD 17:8
  The f. of my Person goes   AUDEN 12:14
frontiers: old f. are gone   BALD 17:8
Frost: F. has risen without trace
                                 MUGG 157:6
Froude: [Hurrell F.] was only too delighted
                                 STR 210:7
frowned: It is not true to say I f. CHES 52:2
  this dark: for you so f.   OWEN 166:18
frowning: f. at one another across
                                 COOP 60:18
frowst: Or f. with a book by the fire
                                 KIPL 125:11
Froyd: F. said that all I needed LOOS 139:9
frozen: f. in an out-of-date mould
                                 JENK 113:3
frozen-ground-swell: That sends the f.
  under it   FROST 86:9
fruit: And my f. is dreams   THOM 215:3
  plucking the f. of memory   CONR 59:18
  veranda, and the f.   AUDEN 14:18
  with humid nightblue f.   JOYCE 116:13
frying-pan: In the f.   DE L 66:13
fuck: They f. you up, your mum
                                 LARK 130:12
  zipless f. is the purest   JONG 115:2
fudging: up with f. and mudging
                                 OWEN 166:5
fugitive: feel like a f. from th' law
                                 MAUL 150:4
fugues: if he had written f. BUTL 43:22
fühlt: *man sich heimischer f.* FREUD 85:8
Führer: *Ein Reich, ein Volk, ein F.*
                                 ANON 6:4
fulfilment: longing and the image of f.
                                 MUGG 157:10
full: Are f. of passionate intensity
                                 YEATS 233:12
  F. of Eastern promise   ANON 6:11
  Lord God, we ha' paid in f.   KIPL 127:2
  this life if, f. of care   DAV 65:5
full-hearted: In a f. evensong HARDY 97:11
fun: Ain't we got f.   KAHN 117:10
  And certainly damps the f.   COW 62:11
  f. enough for far into the night BETJ 31:8
  f. I ever had without laughing ALLEN 4:4
  F. is fun but no girl wants   LOOS 139:8
  f. to be in the same decade   ROOS 182:20
  f. to punt than to be punted   SAY 192:9

fun (*cont.*):
  f. where I've found it   KIPL 127:6
  Gladstone read Homer for f.   CHUR 55:10
  It was great f.   PORT 173:2
  I wish I thought *What Jolly F.!*
                                 RAL 177:11
  must not do things for f.   HERB 101:24
  noted for fresh air and f.   EDGAR 71:20
  Oh, what f.   DE L 66:19
  What on earth was all the f. for?
                                 BETJ 31:8
function: everything must f. to perfection
                                 MUSS 158:9
  f. in life is to exercise   SART 191:6
fundament: Is so frigid upon the f.
                                 NASH 159:9
fundamental: The f. things apply
                                 HUPF 108:7
funeral: f. expenses   JER 113:15
  f. was because they wanted   GOLD 92:1
  how to perform a f.   WILL 227:22
  should be jolly at my f.   MOUN 157:2
  vault for f. Monday Dorset   BEER 23:17
funny: Everything is f. as long ROG 182:8
  f. thing happened   SHEV 200:12
  f. thing happened to me   STEV 209:3
  Isn't it f.   MILNE 153:13
  What do you mean, f.   HAY 99:4
  Whatever is f. is subversive   ORW 164:14
funny-peculiar: F. or funny ha-ha
                                 HAY 99:4
fur: On some other f.   ANON 9:17
furiously: Colourless green ideas sleep f.
                                 CHOM 52:19
furnaces: Your worship is your f.
                                 BOTT 36:14
furnish: Books do f. a room   POW 174:18
furnish'd: F. and burnish'd by Aldershot
                                 BETJ 32:1
furniture: f. that he is likely DOYLE 69:5
  f. that used   MACM 144:3
  rearrange the f.   MORT 156:18
furrow: plough my f. alone   ROS 184:17
furry: The fire was f. as a bear SITW 201:11
furs: hot water; f. to touch   BROO 39:19
further: f. out than you thought
                                 SMITH 203:18
  f. they have to fall   FITZ 81:1
fury: blind f. of creation   SHAW 197:20
  f. and the mire of human   YEATS 235:15
  f. like a non-combatant   MONT 155:4
  f. like a woman looking   CONN 59:8
fuse: green f. drives the flower
                                 THOM 213:20
fuss: f. about sleeping together
                                 WAUGH 223:17
  f. and with no explanation   BLYT 35:7
fussy: A f. man   MILNE 153:11
  Now I'm not a f. woman   AYRES 16:8
futility: fatal f. of Fact   JAMES 112:4
future: Back to the f.   ZEM 236:12
  controls the f.   ORW 164:22
  door opens and lets the f.   GREE 93:19
  F. as a promised land   LEWIS 136:13
  f. everyone will be famous   WARH 222:10
  f. is not what it was   LEVIN 136:10
  F., n. That period   BIER 34:7
  f. of the human race   JEANS 112:20
  F. shock   TOFF 217:7
  orgastic f. that year   FITZ 80:21
  perhaps present in time f.   ELIOT 74:2
  seen the f.   STEF 207:8
  The danger of the f.   FROMM 85:13
  The empires of the f.   CHUR 55:14

future (*cont.*):
  The once and f. king   WHITE 226:5
  want a picture of the f.   ORW 164:26
Fuzzy-Wuzzy: F., at your 'ome KIPL 123:8
fwowed: which Tonstant Weader f. up
                                 PARK 168:7
Fyfe: Is David Patrick Maxwell F.
                                 ANON 7:26

G

gable: Skimming our g. and writing
                                 HEAN 99:11
Gaels: For the great G. of Ireland
                                 CHES 50:9
gag: tight g. of place   HEAN 99:13
gaiety: concession to g. is a striped
                                 THOM 214:18
gaily: G. into Ruislip Gardens BETJ 31:7
gainful: known as g. employment ACH 1:7
gains: are no g. without pains STEV 209:4
gale: The g., it plies the saplings
                                 HOUS 107:1
gallant: died a very g. gentleman ATK 12:5
gallantry: g. and courage that made
                                 COW 61:14
galleon: Stately as a g., I sail GREN 94:2
  The moon was a ghostly g.
                                 NOYES 161:16
gallop: G. about doing good   SMITH 203:21
  withdrawn and watch them g.
                                 DURY 71:2
galloping: No mad hooves g. in the sky
                                 KAV 118:9
gallows: The g. in my garden   CHES 52:3
gamble: g. at terrible odds   STOP 210:2
game: g. at which the police   SHAW 199:5
  g. at which two can play   BEER 23:18
  g. of life seriously   LEARY 133:15
  g. within the view   LEAC 133:13
  how you played the G.   RICE 180:8
  I don't like this g.   MILL 152:18
  Take me out to the ball g.   NORW 161:14
games: children's g. from the beginning
                                 CHES 51:7
  dread of g.   BETJ 32:10
  G. people play   BERNE 30:11
  it is better than g.   SCOTT 194:2
gamesmanship: g. or The art of winning
                                 POTT 173:20
gamut: Katharine Hepburn runs the g.
                                 PARK 168:5
Gandhi: [G.] knew the cost of setting
                                 NAIDU 158:18
gang: g. at Forty-Second Street
                                 COHAN 57:11
gangsters: have always acted like g.
                                 KUBR 129:5
gaol: Woman's place was in the g.
                                 BRAH 38:11
Garbo: one sees in G. sober   TYNAN 220:9
garden: And in that g., black   BROO 40:12
  at the bottom of our g.   FYL 87:18
  Back to the g.   MITC 154:9
  g. and I am parshial   ASHF 10:16
  Glory of the G.   KIPL 125:2
  In a g. shady this holy lady   AUDEN 15:11
  I never promised you a rose g.
                                 GREEN 93:11
  Lean on a g. urn   ELIOT 76:2
  nearer God's Heart in a g.   GURN 94:17
  Of the g. hard by Heaven   BOUL 37:2

garden (*cont.*):
Our England is a g.   KIPL 124:19
The gallows in my g.   CHES 52:3
The sunlight on the g.   MACN 144:5
who in his g. watching   AUDEN 14:9
Garden City: G. Café with its murals
    BETJ 31:6
gardener: Oh, Adam was a g.   KIPL 125:2
Will come the G. in white   FLEC 81:12
gardens: all of the neighbour g.
    REED 178:19
But all the g.   THOM 213:16
g. with real toads in them
    MOORE 155:14
In his blue g., men   FITZ 80:19
Leaving the g. tidy   LARK 131:3
time in the g. of the West   CONN 59:3
gare: idées au-dessus de sa g.   RATT 178:1
gargling: g. from the froth-corrupted
    OWEN 166:10
garments: g. were always in patchez
    NASH 159:21
garter: An earl and a knight of the g.
    ATTL 12:6
Polly G., under the washing line
    THOM 214:10
gas: G. smells awful   PARK 168:12
The g. was on in the Institute   BETJ 32:7
gas-masks: trenches and trying on g.
    CHAM 48:12
gasoline: G. is much more likely
    WEIL 224:2
gasp: G. and Stretch one's Eyes   BELL 24:14
gate: g. where they're turning
    AUDEN 14:14
stood at the g. of the year   HASK 99:3
gate-bars: And drops on g. hang in a row
    HARDY 97:3
gates: despondently at area g.   ELIOT 76:1
g. to the glorious   FORS 83:12
gateway: Sex is the g. to life   HARR 98:14
gathering: broken Anne of g. bouquets
    FROST 86:16
Gatsby: G. believed in the green   FITZ 80:21
gay: A g. modulating anguish   FRY 87:4
g. goodnight and quickly   YEATS 235:2
He has a g. appeal   COW 62:3
Her heart was warm and g.   HAMM 95:16
gays: g. and lesbians issue   HEW 102:6
gazed: shop and street I g.   YEATS 235:17
gazes: Yellow God forever g.   HAYES 99:5
gazing: does not consist in g.   SAIN 187:20
Geduld: *meine G. jetzt zu Ende ist*
    HITL 103:6
geese: Like g. about the sky   AUDEN 12:16
this the wild g. spread   YEATS 234:15
gee-whiz: is the 'g.' emotion   MCEW 142:8
Gehenna: Down to G. or up to the Throne
    KIPL 127:15
gems: He's torn the g.   FARJ 78:8
General Motors: country was good for G.
    WILS 228:7
generals: against the law for g.
    TRUM 218:12
wooden swords we're all G.   UST 220:20
generation: elegies are to this g.
    OWEN 166:8
g. is knocking at the door   SHAW 200:7
g. revolts against   MUMF 157:16
minds of my g. destroyed   GINS 90:15
reproduce themselves from g.   JOS 115:5
this is really a beat g.   KER 120:3
You are all a lost g.   STEIN 207:21

generations: Those dying g.—at their song
    YEATS 234:5
generosity: life is to exercise our g.
    SART 191:6
genial: called in London 'g. Judas'
    HAIG 95:2
geniessen: *den Kontrast intensiv g.*
    FREUD 85:7
genitals: would only stare at his g.
    ABSE 1:4
you're breaking their g.   BERN 30:9
genius: G. . . . has been defined   BUTL 43:24
G. is one per cent inspiration   EDIS 72:2
g. makes no mistakes   JOYCE 116:11
g. of Einstein leads   PIC 171:6
g. of its scientists   EIS 73:7
g. which does what it must   BAR 18:13
g. who had not to pay   BEER 22:16
instantly recognizes g.   DOYLE 70:1
I think like a g.   NAB 158:15
lot of time to be a g.   STEIN 207:12
Only an organizing g.   BEVAN 32:17
remarkable and seductive g.   STR 210:12
geniuses: G. are the luckiest   AUDEN 14:17
gent: gentleman is to a g.   BALD 17:13
genteel: marks of the beast to the truly g.
    HARDY 97:6
Gentiles: Such boasting as the G. use
    KIPL 126:11
gentle: A g. motion with the deep
    DAV 65:4
g. into that good night   THOM 213:16
gentleman: died a very gallant g.   ATK 12:5
every other inch a g.   WEST 225:24
g. from both the artist   WAUGH 222:2
g. in Whitehall really   JAY 112:19
g. with iron-grey whiskers   BEER 23:19
Hes a g.: look at his boots   SHAW 199:17
I am a g.: I live by robbing   SHAW 197:27
I am not quite a g.   ASHF 10:16
intelligentsia what a g. is to a gent
    BALD 17:13
last g. in Europe   LEV 136:7
once as an educated g.   SHAW 197:9
sort of attire for a g.   SHAR 195:9
They teach you to be a g.   SHAW 197:24
gentlemen: behave like a g.   MACK 142:16
G. always seem to remember   LOOS 139:4
G. do not take soup   CURZ 64:10
G. Prefer Blondes   LOOS 139:3
people and creates good g.   MUG 157:5
Three jolly g.   DE L 66:14
what most of the g. does   WAUGH 222:20
while the G. go by   KIPL 126:6
gentlemen-rankers: G. out on the spree
    KIPL 123:16
gentlewoman: possible for a g. to commit
    WAUGH 223:18
gentleness: ways of g.   SPR 206:13
gently: G. they go, the beautiful
    MILL 151:17
gentry: disagree the English g.   HALS 95:13
genuine: place for the g.   MOORE 155:13
geography: G. is about Maps   BENT 28:24
Is different from G.   BENT 28:24
geometrical: The Great Bear is looking
so g.   FRY 87:5
George: And later by G. the Fourth
    COW 62:12
G.—don't do that   GREN 94:1
G. the Third   BENT 29:7
Georgia: G. the sons of former slaves
    KING 121:15

Georgia (*cont.*):
song keeps G. on my mind   GORR 92:5
Georgian: erupted in gentle G. Squares
    SPEN 205:10
the G. silver goes   MACM 144:3
geranium: As a madman shakes a dead g.
    ELIOT 75:21
leans through g. windows   LEE 134:3
German: been that the G. dictator
    CHUR 54:6
G. Emperor on August 19th   ANON 6:9
G. flag will be hauled   BEAT 20:17
G. soldier trying to violate   STR 210:10
G. text of French operas   WHAR 225:27
talk with the G. Chancellor   CHAM 48:13
Germans: let's be beastly to the G.
    COW 61:16
The G., if this Government   GEDD 89:2
their dead grip and G.   TUCH 218:15
They're G. Don't mention   CLEE 56:13
Germany: country is at war with G.
    CHAM 48:15
G. calling! Germany calling
    JOYCE 116:16
G. had become a menace   NEV 160:4
G. loses and prospers   HELL 100:6
G. to Downing Street peace   CHAM 48:14
G. was rearming   BALD 17:10
G. will claim me   EINS 73:1
if France and G. remain apart
    DULL 70:11
I went first to G.   COOK 60:9
germs: g. in your handkerchief   ANON 5:27
Gershwin: George [G.] died on July 11
    O'HARA 163:1
Gert: G.'s writings are punk   ANON 6:22
Gestapo: G. and all the odious apparatus
    CHUR 54:10
gesture: Morality's a g.   BOLT 35:16
get: And you can g. it if you try
    GERS 89:17
g. and beget   OSLER 166:3
g. by with a little help   LENN 135:14
g. laid, to get fame   GELD 89:3
g. me to the church   LERN 135:18
G. out as early as you can   LARK 130:13
g. out of these wet clothes   ANON 7:12
g. out while we're young   SPR 206:15
g. what you like or you   SHAW 198:30
g. what you want   SMITH 202:17
g. where I am today without
    NOBBS 161:8
got to g. up this morning   BERL 29:16
governments had better g.   EIS 73:9
He'd have to g. under   CLAR 56:11
If you want to g. ahead   ANON 6:24
If you want to g. along   RAYB 178:8
It's nice to g. up   LAUD 131:9
I want to g. off   NEWL 160:5
getting: devotee of the Gospel of G. On
    SHAW 199:7
ghastly: G. good taste   BETJ 31:13
ghetto: wouldn't go into g. areas
    AGNEW 2:21
ghost: G. in the Machine   RYLE 187:1
g. of a crazy younger son   COW 62:13
The g. of Roger Casement   YEATS 234:1
thought to please my g.   MENC 151:5
ghostly: g. batsman plays   THOM 215:22
giant: one g. leap for mankind   ARMS 10:10
giants: g. and for peace like retarded
    PEAR 169:21
giblet: He liked thick g. soup   JOYCE 116:8

Gide: [André G.] was very bald
QUEN 176:14

gift: g. for a good writer HEM 101:5
g. of oneself ANOU 9:20
your g. survived it all AUDEN 13:1
gifted: Young, g. and black IRV 110:21
gigantic: footprints of a g. hound
DOYLE 69:12
his bed into a g. insect KAFKA 117:9
shadows pass g. on the sand FLEC 81:8
Gilbert: [W. S. G.'s] foe was folly
ANON 6:21
gilded: She's a bird in a g. cage
LAMB 129:15
gin: g. joints in all the towns EPST 77:17
G. less than a' the world MACD 142:1
G. was mother's milk to her
SHAW 199:23
sooner we can get out the g. REED 179:5
Ginger: G., you're balmy MURR 158:4
gingerbread: Off the g. COW 62:11
Gipper: win just one for the G. GIPP 90:16
gipsy: Time, you old g. man HODG 103:9
giraffes: G.!— a People CAMP 45:14
girders: Rumbling under blackened g.
BETJ 31:19
girdle: g. when your hips stick
NASH 159:23
girl: Above the staggering g. YEATS 234:21
A pretty g. is like a melody BERL 29:17
at a g. throwing a ball WOOLF 231:15
big mountainous sports g. BETJ 32:8
Diamonds are a g.'s best ROBIN 181:11
first rock at a g. LOOS 139:10
g. at an impressionable age SPARK 205:7
g. had the making WALL 222:8
g. in the indolence YEATS 232:4
g. needs good parents TUCK 218:18
g. next door AUDEN 14:21
g. wants to laugh all LOOS 139:8
g. whose cheeks are covered
NASH 159:17
g. with brains ought LOOS 139:3
just like the g. that married DILL 67:13
only g. in the world GREY 94:4
policeman and a pretty g. CHAP 49:8
Poor little rich g. COW 62:6
Sex and the single g. BROWN 41:9
The naughtiest g. in the school
BLYT 35:10
To the sweetest g. I know JUDGE 116:17
When I'm not near the g. HARB 96:14
your eye at some homely g. MENC 151:5
girlish: Laugh thy g. laughter WATS 222:16
girls: Always be civil to the g. MITF 154:14
And g. in slacks remember Dad
BETJ 31:4
are like g. and roses DE G 65:17
At g. who wear glasses PARK 168:14
G. are simply the prettiest MCG 142:10
G. scream DAV 65:2
g. that have no secret SPEN 205:18
g. turn into American women
HAMP 96:7
In Little G. is slamming Doors
BELL 24:19
marries three g. from St Louis
STEIN 207:10
men and g. came and went FITZ 80:19
see what some g. marry ROWL 185:16
The lads for the g. HOUS 106:16
The rose-lipt g. are sleeping HOUS 107:7
girly: skip about like a g. WILL 227:9

gist: With this the g. and sum of it
PARK 168:15
give: g. a war and nobody will SAND 190:2
G. crowns and pounds HOUS 106:12
G. him the money, Barney PICK 171:10
G. me a girl at an impressionable age
SPARK 205:7
G. me a light HASK 99:3
G. me a no-nonsense AUDEN 13:13
G. me the man who will surrender
BARB 18:10
G. my regards to Broadway
COHAN 57:11
g. the public something they want
SKEL 201:20
G. us the tools and we CHUR 53:9
g. you anything but love FIEL 79:8
I couldn't g. it up BENC 27:4
would be a good idea to g. WARH 222:12
given: that anybody can be g. BALD 17:2
who had g. so ungrudgingly SAKI 188:23
gizza: G. job . . . . I can do BLEA 34:24
G.K.C.: Poor G., his day is past
LUCAS 140:9
glacier: The g. knocks in the cupboard
AUDEN 12:17
glad: g. green leaves like wings
HARDY 97:10
gladness when she's g. BARR 19:19
I'm g. tomorrow's Thursday AYRES 16:5
I'm g. we've been bombed ELIZ 77:9
or are you just g. to see WEST 225:20
Was sad that she was g. THOM 214:21
you know you should be g. LENN 135:10
glade: alone in the bee-loud g. YEATS 232:9
gladly: g. not to be standing here
JOHN 114:7
gladness: g. of her gladness when
BARR 19:19
Gladstone: G. also invented the Education
SELL 194:17
G. laying upon Providence LAB 129:7
Mr G. read Homer for fun CHUR 55:10
glamour: g. Of childish days LAWR 132:13
glance: O brightening g. YEATS 234:8
glare: at in this merciless g. WILL 227:20
To protect you from the g. COW 62:4
Glasgow: G. belongs to me FYFFE 87:17
G. Empire Saturday night DODD 68:5
G. to do some work BUCH 41:19
glass: families baying for broken g.
WAUGH 222:19
g. is falling hour by hour MACN 144:9
g. produce more effect PANK 167:10
hate you through the g. BLUN 34:25
In a dirty g. PAN 167:7
like it out of a thin g. PINT 171:13
No g. of ours was ever raised
HEAN 99:15
sewer in a g.-bottomed boat MIZN 154:20
Sound of Broken G. BELL 25:9
The sun-comprehending g. LARK 130:8
To g. the opulent HARDY 97:13
glasses: At girls who wear g. PARK 168:14
with plenty of looking g. ASHF 10:20
gleam: They g. there for you and me
DE SY 67:4
gleams: light g. an instant BECK 21:24
gliding: But g. like a queen SPEN 205:5
glimmers: holy g. of good-byes
OWEN 166:9
glittering: g. prizes to those SMITH 202:14
gloamin': Roamin' in the g. LAUD 131:10

global: image of a g. village MCL 143:8
Were g. from the start REED 179:2
globe-trotting: Can disturb g. Madam
YEATS 233:1
gloire: Je vais à la g. DUNC 70:13
gloom: Upon the growing g. HARDY 97:11
glorious: g. and the unknown FORS 83:3
In that g. land above the sky
HILL 102:12
leaves the world more g. BRAD 38:7
Mud! Mud! G. mud FLAN 81:4
glory: ardent for some desperate g.
OWEN 166:10
g. of rulers or of races BEV 33:10
G. of the Garden lies KIPL 124:19
g. was I had such friends YEATS 234:2
I am going to g. DUNC 70:13
Land of Hope and G. BENS 28:21
That the g. of this world BRAD 38:7
What price g. AND 5:1
Glossop: Sir Roderick G., Honoria's
WOD 230:14
Gloucester: there lived a tailor in G.
POTT 173:10
glove: mailed fist in a cotton g.
SITW 201:16
velvet g. as a lacy sleeve WOOL 231:19
gloves: About people in g. and such
CHES 51:8
capitalism with the g. off STOP 210:4
down the Strand with my g. HARG 98:9
through the fields in g. CORN 61:8
glow: g. in the heart CONR 60:4
her g. has warmed STEV 209:2
Star captains g. FLEC 81:18
glowing: life from the g. earth GREN 94:3
glow-worm: believe that I am a g.
CHUR 56:5
Glücklichen: G. ist eine andere als
WITT 230:3
glue: g. that holds Government
FORD 82:13
gluttons: And g. old in sin RAL 177:10
Glyn: With Elinor G. ANON 9:17
gnomes: little g. in Zurich WILS 228:9
gnostics: For one of those g. BORG 36:9
gnu: I'm a g. FLAN 81:3
go: better 'ole, g. to it BAIR 16:12
boldly g. where no man RODD 182:12
But I have a g., lady OSB 165:13
Do not pass g. DARR 64:13
Five g. off in a caravan BLYT 35:9
get along, g. along RAYB 178:8
G. ahead, make my day FINK 79:18
G. down like lumps of lead HODG 103:12
g. home and sleep quietly CHAM 48:14
Good-night—and g. to it MORR 156:6
G. out into the darkness HASK 99:3
g. the way that Providence HITL 103:4
G. together like a horse CAHN 44:15
go together when we g. LEHR 134:8
G. to jail DARR 64:13
G. to work on an egg ANON 6:15
have no place to g. WHIT 226:19
Here we g., here we go ANON 6:20
hope to g. on and on THAT 212:18
I can't g. on, I'll go BECK 21:14
I g.— I come back KAV 118:14
Inspiring prospects. Let's g. BECK 21:17
In the name of God, g. AMERY 4:12
let us g. forward together CHUR 54:9
Let us g. then, you ELIOT 75:13
mean streets a man must g. CHAN 49:1

go (*cont.*):

pronouncement: 'It's a Rum G.!'
         VAUG 221:9
They all g. into the dark   ELIOT 74:11
thinking jest what a Rum G.
         WELLS 224:19
Victoria Station and g.   BEVIN 33:17
We'll g. to the woods no more
         HOUS 105:11
we think you ought to g.   RUB 185:20
will arise and g. now   YEATS 232:9
goal: moving freely without a g.
         KLEE 128:6
goals: And 'theories' and 'g.'   KIPL 122:17
muddied oafs at the g.   KIPL 124:12
goat: sort of fleecy hairy g.   BELL 25:4
goats: g. champ and sneer   THOM 214:11
goblins: The g. were right   FORS 83:14
god: about depth knows about G.
         TILL 217:5
A Jewish G.   BROW 41:13
And the Cabots talk only to G.
         BOSS 36:12
A neck G. made for other   HOUS 106:11
A thick skin is a gift from G.   ADEN 2:14
brown g.   ELIOT 74:7
But as G. granted it   QUIL 177:5
But O my G., what a relief   BARR 19:27
But only G. can make a tree   KILM 121:9
discover that there is no G.   SMITH 203:3
every cliché except 'G. is Love'
         CHUR 55:6
G. be thanked Who has matched
         BROO 40:1
G. be with you, Balliol men   BELL 26:2
G. bless America   BERL 29:15
G. bless the child that's   HOL 104:4
G. Calls Me God   SAMP 189:7
G. cannot alter the past   BUTL 43:6
G. can stand being told   PRIE 175:10
G. caught his eye   MCC 141:15
G. created man   VALÉ 220:24
[G.] does not play dice   EINS 72:14
G. gave Noah the rainbow   ANON 6:12
G. gave us memory   BARR 19:13
G. gives all men all earth   KIPL 124:11
G. gives us our relatives   MUMF 157:15
G. had wanted us to think   LUCE 140:14
G. has any validity   BALD 16:17
G. has been replaced   BAR 18:9
G. has more right   JOHN 113:21
G. has written all the books   BUTL 43:25
G. hath joined together   SHAW 196:24
G. in human form   BONH 36:3
G. is a little tribal G.   BURR 42:16
G. is beginning to resemble   HUXL 109:16
G. is not dead but alive   ANON 6:13
G. is on everyone's side   ANOU 9:18
G. is really only another artist   PIC 171:5
G. is subtle but he is not   EINS 72:13
G. might not be a Limited   STR 210:8
G. Must think it exceedingly odd
         KNOX 128:10
G. punish England   FUNKE 87:16
G. rest his soul, officers   SMITH 203:23
G. si Love   FORS 84:2
G. that He has spared me   BELL 24:23
G. to arrange a virgin   JENK 113:1
G. to let Carlyle and Mrs   BUTL 43:14
G. to make it responsible   DUH 70:9
G., who does not exist   O'BR 162:6
G. who made thee mighty   BENS 28:21
G. will know the truth   LUCAS 140:9
G. works in a mysterious way   ELIOT 75:6

god (*cont.*):

G. works in mysterious ways   AND 5:3
G. would give me some clear   ALLEN 3:19
G. would have made Adam   BRY 41:16
Had G. on his side   DYLAN 71:15
hand into the Hand of G.   HASK 99:3
Here is G.'s purpose   FULL 87:14
honest G.'s the noblest   BUTL 43:8
How do you know you're ... G.
         BARN 18:21
How odd Of G.   EWER 78:4
if G. talks to you   SZASZ 211:18
In the name of G., go   AMERY 4:12
It's G. they ought to crucify   CART 47:8
laboratory of G.   WILL 227:14
make gods, there is no G.   O'NEI 163:10
might have become a g.   RUSS 186:8
Not I: let G. and man decree
         HOUS 105:17
Not only is there no G.   ALLEN 3:18
only Bach in praising G.   BARTH 20:2
Only G., my dear   YEATS 236:1
Painting is saying "Ta" to G.
         SPEN 205:11
problem was that G. *is dead*
         FROMM 85:13
Strong brother in G.   BELL 25:13
suppose that G. is only   TEMP 212:12
Thank G. we're normal   OSB 165:12
Thanks to G., I am still   BUÑ 42:8
they are attracted by G.   INGE 110:13
This day relenting G.   ROSS 185:5
To justify G.'s ways to man   HOUS 107:8
To the steep and trifld G.   THOM 216:6
turns out that there is a G.   ALLEN 3:16
What G. abandoned, these   HOUS 106:3
when you've sung 'G. save   KIPL 122:18
Where G. paints the scenery   HART 98:19
Where it will all end, knows G.
         GIBBS 90:4
whose g. is in the skies   SHAW 198:19
with how you appear to G.   UNAM 220:13
you are a g.   ROST 185:8
godheads: Maidens aspiring to g.
         STOP 209:18
godless: decent g. people   ELIOT 76:5
Godot: We're waiting for G.   BECK 21:17
gods: g. that made the gods   CHES 50:7
g. wish to destroy they   CONN 58:16
machine for making g.   BERG 29:12
not know much about g.   ELIOT 74:7
people clutching their g.   ELIOT 73:15
there are innumerable g.   BURR 42:16
what the g. had given him   BEER 22:16
When men make g.   O'NEI 163:10
Goebbels: inferno depicted by Dr G.
         ORW 164:17
goes: All g. if courage goes   BARR 19:15
nobody g., it's awful   BECK 21:18
The beat g. on   BONO 36:4
going: are g. out all over Europe
         GREY 94:5
certain they are still g.   BIRK 34:21
cheerful as keeps me g.   KAV 118:15
Economy is g. without something
         HOPE 104:14
g. down of the sun   BINY 34:18
g. out a youngster   SEYM 195:3
g. to be your next president   CART 47:5
good both g. and coming   FROST 86:5
I am g. to glory   DUNC 70:13
I learn by g. where I have   ROET 182:4
Safe shall be my g.   BROO 40:2
When the g. gets tough   KENN 120:1

gold: g. with plenty of looking glasses
         ASHF 10:20
Meets the g. of the day   CROS 63:8
rain of g. and heart's   DAY-L 65:7
rarer gifts than g.   BROO 40:3
golden: For g. friends I had   HOUS 107:7
g. rule is that there   SHAW 198:9
hand that lays the g. egg   GOLD 91:17
I went into a g. land   TURN 218:19
Miles and miles of g. moss   AUDEN 14:23
Or west to the G. Gate   KIPL 127:17
Red hair she had and g. skin   BETJ 31:5
repeat that on the G. Floor   HOUS 105:9
The g. apples of the sun   YEATS 235:6
through the forest with a g.   LIND 137:14
We are g.   MITC 154:9
Goldwyn: Mr G., is that you   SHAW 196:25
golf: American people than G. has
         ROG 182:7
And a thousand lost g. balls   ELIOT 76:5
g. may be played on Sunday
         LEAC 133:13
too young to take up g.   ADAMS 1:18
golf-links: The g. lie so near the mill
         CLEG 56:15
Golgotha: G. they hanged Him
         STUD 210:20
gongs: g. groaning as the guns CHES 51:17
struck regularly, like g.   COW 62:8
gong-tormented: That dolphin-torn, that g.
sea   YEATS 235:16
good: And this is g. old Boston BOSS 36:12
another for the general G.   WELLS 225:1
be not g. but great   VIDAL 221:17
be thought half as g.   WHIT 226:21
bloody g. hiding   GRANT 93:2
every age 'the g. old days'   ATK 12:3
Gallop about doing g.   SMITH 203:21
God-willing, I will make g.   HITL 103:5
g. both going and coming   FROST 86:5
G., but not religious-good   HARDY 98:4
g. cooks go   SAKI 188:15
g. critic is he who relates   FRAN 84:16
G. evening, England   POTT 173:16
G. fences make good neighbours
         FROST 86:10
g. for our country was   WILS 228:7
G. government could never   CAMP 45:17
G. taste and humour   MUGG 157:9
g. taste invariably have   ORTON 164:5
G. taste is better than bad   BENN 28:7
G. *Thing*, since   SELL 194:9
g. to be out on the road   MAS 148:20
g. to say about anyone   LONG 139:1
g. to some man that can   SHAW 199:6
G. to the last drop   ROOS 184:9
g. unluckily   STOP 210:1
G. women always think it   BROO 41:1
Guinness ... is g. for you   GREE 93:20
have never had it so g.   MACM 143:22
Hello, g. evening, and welcome
         FROST 85:14
If it's by a g. author   SHAW 196:20
Is g. enough for me   HERB 101:15
It's *finger lickin'* g.   ANON 7:8
know better what is g.   JAY 112:19
know when I am having a g. time
         ASTOR 11:21
Lady, be g.   GERS 89:15
Let the g. times roll   THEA 213:9
like is not necessarily g.   BELL 24:2
makes rattling g. history   HARDY 96:20
Men have never been g.   BARTH 20:1

good (*cont.*):
much g. in the worst of us   ANON 8:18
or so g. as drink   CHES 50:4
people are not much g.   STAR 207:4
policy of the g. neighbour   ROOS 183:2
simply say 'is g. for you'   GREE 93:20
stars and isles where g. men rest
                                         FLEC 81:6
that's g. enough for me   THOM 214:10
That would be a g. idea   GAND 88:9
The g., the bad, and the ugly
                                         SCAR 192:16
those who go about doing g.   CREI 62:18
What earthly g. can come of it
                                         PARK 168:15
what you fancy does you g.
                                         LEIGH 134:12
When he said a g. thing   TWAIN 219:25
When I'm g., I'm very   WEST 225:14
goodbye: G., moralitee   HERB 101:15
G., Piccadilly   JUDGE 116:17
G. to all that   GRAV 93:4
he did not say g.   BARR 19:3
Just kiss yourself g.   JER 113:18
kissed his sad Andromache g.   CORN 61:9
So g. dear, and Amen   PORT 173:2
That's all. G.   AYRES 16:8
good-day: G. sadness   ELUA 77:14
good-humoured: g. boy   BEER 22:22
goodness: And g. only knowses
                                         CHES 50:19
G. had nothing to do   WEST 225:19
My G., My Guinness   RICH 180:13
good night: Has smiled and said 'G.'
                                         BELL 25:18
goodnight: gay g. and quickly turn
                                         YEATS 235:2
G., children . . . everywhere   MCC 141:20
good-night: G. Ensured release
                                         HOUS 106:8
His happy g. air   HARDY 97:11
Thomas says g. to Lady Jane   LAWR 132:9
goods: both parties run out of g.
                                         AUDEN 14:3
consumption of valuable g.   VEBL 221:10
g. and services can   NOCK 161:10
private g. have full sway   GALB 88:4
goodwill: In peace: g.   CHUR 55:16
goody-goody: g. than fotherington-tomas
                                         WILL 227:9
Gorbachev: she liked Mr G.   THAT 213:4
gorgeous: The g. buttocks of the ape
                                         HUXL 108:21
gospel: G. of Getting On   SHAW 199:7
gossip: For pines are g. pines   FLEC 81:15
g. from all the nations   AUDEN 14:22
got: man g. to do what   STEI 208:1
when you g. it   BROO 41:3
you've g. to come back a star
                                         SEYM 195:3
gotcha: G.   ANON 6:14
Gothic: great G. cathedrals   BART 20:4
gothiques: *grandes cathédrales g.*   BART 20:4
Gott: G. strafe England!   FUNKE 87:16
Gotto: its name is Ainsley G.   ERWIN 77:22
Gourmont: out of Remy de G.   HUXL 108:17
gouverner: *Comment voulez-vous g. un pays*
                                         DE G 66:1
govern: Go out and g. New South Wales
                                         BELL 24:18
How can you g. a country   DE G 66:1
government: America as a g. of the people
                                         PAGE 167:2
be desirable if every G.   SNOW 204:2

government (*cont.*):
constituencies and prepare for g.
                                         STEEL 207:7
Democracy means g. by discussion
                                         ATTL 12:13
forms of G. have been tried   CHUR 55:3
glue that holds G.   FORD 82:13
G. and public opinion allow
                                         SHAW 197:29
g. by the people themselves   CAMP 45:17
G. feels in its inside   BENN 28:15
G. I despise for ends   KEYN 120:7
g. in peace and in war   BEV 33:10
G. is big enough to give   FORD 82:16
G. is not to do things   KEYN 120:13
g. is the organization   SHAW 198:10
g. should be brought down
                                         MACM 143:17
g. than that which requires   TUCH 218:16
g. which robs Peter   SHAW 196:17
g. you have a dictatorship   TRUM 218:14
great Republic is a G.   FORD 82:14
I just watch the g.   ROG 182:14
It's no go the G. grants   MACN 144:8
king and g. and nation   KAV 118:6
means g. by the uneducated   CHES 51:9
more effect upon the G.   PANK 167:10
never come from the g.   WILS 229:9
overthrow the G. of the United
                                         HARD 96:15
pleased to be in the G.   BAXT 20:15
politician to run a g.   TRUM 218:9
shackles and restraints of g.   GOLD 91:11
too much in forms of g.   BAR 20:9
worst form of G.   CHUR 55:3
governments: g. had better get out   EIS 73:9
Governor-General: nothing will save
the G.   WHIT 226:20
gown: Or sail in amply billowing g.
                                         BELL 26:5
red chiffon evening g.   THAT 212:21
there's blood upon her g.   FLEC 81:17
grab: G. your coat, and get your hat
                                         FIEL 79:9
grace: g. last night two black   BEER 23:16
G. of God is in Courtesy   BELL 26:1
g. of Terpsichore   BARR 19:26
g. under pressure   HEM 101:2
He had at least the g.   BENT 28:23
the g. of a boy   BETJ 32:1
with what g. he throws   FLEC 81:10
gracehoper: G. was always jigging ajog
                                         JOYCE 115:14
grades: into four g.: Leading School
                                         WAUGH 222:21
gradient: The g.'s against her
                                         AUDEN 14:21
gradual: Was the g. day   SPEN 205:14
gradualness: g. of our scheme of change
                                         WEBB 223:25
Grafton: G. Gallery to look   BLUNT 35:5
grain: rain is destroying his g.   HERB 101:20
grammar: I don't want to talk g.
                                         SHAW 199:19
grammatical: 'g.' cannot be identified
                                         CHOM 52:19
gramophone: And puts a record on the g.
                                         ELIOT 77:2
g. company asked him   TREE 217:16
grand: baith g. and comfortable   BARR 19:5
doing a g. job   FROST 85:15
G. Central Station I sat   SMART 202:1
g. little lad was young   EDGAR 71:20
g. to be blooming well dead   SAR 190:23

grand (*cont.*):
It is most g. to die   MAS 148:13
rose petal down the G.   MARQ 147:9
grandeur: *g. en eux ne font pas de*
                                         CAMUS 45:15
grandeurs: The g. of his Babylonian heart
                                         THOM 216:7
grandfather: weight of a g. clock
                                         TREE 217:17
grandfathers: makes friends with its g.
                                         MUMF 157:16
grandmother: We have become a g.
                                         THAT 213:7
granites: g. which titanic wars had
                                         OWEN 166:15
grant: g. what I wish and snatch
                                         FROST 86:5
universities go on a Government g.
                                         MAUG 150:1
Grantchester: The lovely hamlet G.
                                         BROO 40:13
granted: But as God g. it   QUIL 177:5
taking things for g.   HUXL 109:14
grape: Beulah, peel me a g.   WEST 225:12
grapes: Always eat g. downwards
                                         BUTL 43:21
sour g. and ashes without   ASHF 11:3
grasped: haven't g. the situation
                                         KERR 120:4
grass: g. grows on the weirs   YEATS 234:13
g. is soft as the breast   CORN 61:8
green g. and bursting trees   GREN 94:3
happy as the g. was green   THOM 213:17
He can watch a g. or leaf   GRAV 93:6
I am the g.; I cover all   SAND 189:17
just uninterrupted g.   LAWR 132:23
kissed the lovely g.   BROO 39:18
Pigeons on the g. alas   STEIN 207:16
The g. will grow   HOOV 104:13
Was cut out of the g.   CHES 50:7
When you destroy a blade of g.
                                         BOTT 36:13
grassy: shore of the wan g. sea
                                         SITW 201:14
gratitude: G., like love, is never
                                         ALSOP 4:10
gratuitous: autobiography is the most g.
                                         STOP 209:12
disinterested I mean: g.   GIDE 90:9
grave: about life beyond the g.   KHR 121:5
before us lies the open g.   MCKAY 142:15
birth astride of a g.   BECK 21:24
Even the g. yawns   TREE 217:17
from the cradle to the g.   CHUR 56:1
g. and constant in human   JOYCE 115:19
g. in a Y-shaped coffin   ORTON 164:6
g. of Gomer Owen who   THOM 214:9
his g. like an old dog   MILL 152:4
It's with O'Leary in the g.   YEATS 234:13
tends the g. of Mad Carew   HAYES 99:5
Thoughtful children, and the g.
                                         AUDEN 13:7
Thy victory, O G.   ROSS 185:5
graver: And His g. of frost   THOM 216:9
graveyards: no bone to pick with g.
                                         BECK 21:12
gravy: And g. with the spoon   RAL 177:10
It's the rich wot gets the g.   ANON 8:8
grease: slides by on g.   LOW 140:2
great: All my shows are g.   GRADE 92:8
distinguishing the few really g.
                                         LEAV 133:16
forgive Thy g. big one on me   FROST 86:3
G. Architect   JEANS 112:22

great (cont.):
G. Bear is looking so geometrical
FRY 87:5
g. end comes slowly DUB 70:7
G. hatred, little room YEATS 236:3
G. is the hand that holds THOM 214:5
g. lies about his wooden FLEC 81:20
g. life if you don't weaken BUCH 41:19
g. minds in the commonplace
HUBB 107:14
g. party is not to be brought HAIL 95:4
If I am a g. man, then LAW 35:18
Is also g. FROST 86:6
streets where the g. men go FLEC 81:17
The g. illusion ANG 5:5
these are g. days CHUR 53:11
time close to g. minds BUCH 41:18
upward to the G. Society JOHN 114:11
want to be not good but g. VIDAL 221:17
Great Britain: G. was going to make war
BETH 30:20
G. will not be involved BEAV 21:3
greater: always g. than the causes
FORS 84:9
G. love than this JOYCE 116:12
g. the ignorance the greater OSLER 166:2
greatest: g. composers since Beethoven
BUCK 42:4
I'm the g. ALI 3:10
greatness: g. within them do not go
CAMUS 45:19
moment of my g. flicker ELIOT 75:17
greed: enough for everyone's g. BUCH 42:2
Greek: can say a word against G.
SHAW 197:9
G. as a treat CHUR 55:8
G. divine-human form BONH 36:3
G. one then is my hero ABSE 1:4
Greeks: The G. had a word for it
AKINS 2:23
green: believed in the g. light FITZ 80:21
Colourless g. ideas sleep CHOM 52:19
evermore no g. life shoots BOTT 36:13
G. how I love you green LORCA 139:12
happy as the grass was g. THOM 213:17
How g. was my valley LLEW 138:4
that through the g. fuse THOM 213:20
The day was g. STEV 208:15
The g. plant groweth CHES 50:10
There's a g. one and a pink one
REYN 179:17
Wherever g. is worn YEATS 233:11
greenery: In a mountain g. HART 98:19
greenfly: sure there weren't any g.
AYCK 16:1
greening: The g. of America REICH 179:9
greens: And healing g., leaves ABSE 1:2
Grenzen: G. meiner Sprache bedeuten
WITT 230:2
grey: g. and full of sleep YEATS 232:7
little g. cells CHR 52:21
Night is growing g. HARDY 97:16
The g. wing upon every tide
YEATS 234:15
Griddlebone: I might mention G. ELIOT 75:4
grief: are quickened so with g. GRAV 93:6
griefs: isolation and the busy g.
AUDEN 13:1
grievance: Scotsman with a g. WOD 230:5
grieves: g. not and that never hopes
MARK 146:14
grimace: Of its accelerated g. POUND 174:4
grin: backward with a lipless g. ELIOT 75:8

grin (cont.):
g. on his face and a totem-symbol
KOES 128:14
grind: don't let the bastards g. you down
ANON 7:27
grip: With a g. that kills it TAG 212:2
Grishkin: G. is nice: her Russian eye
ELIOT 75:9
grisly: g. gang who work your wicked
CHUR 53:10
grizzly: The G. Bear is huge and wild
HOUS 105:10
groan: g. and shake their fists HOUS 105:8
groans: alike are the g. of love
LOWRY 140:8
grocer: God made the wicked G.
CHES 50:15
groined: which titanic wars had g.
OWEN 166:15
Gromyko: G. of the Labour Party
HEAL 99:8
groom: even if he is our g. CHES 51:13
grooves: In determinate g. HARE 98:7
grope: Whose buildings g. the sky
AUDEN 13:9
grosser: your g. reminiscences
WOOL 231:18
Groucho: G. tendency ANON 7:6
Je suis Marxiste—tendance G. ANON 7:6
ground: G. control to Major Tom
BOWIE 37:16
Off the g. DE L 66:16
proposition when there is no g.
RUSS 186:23
ride in a hole in the g. COMD 58:7
group: g. of men who individually
ALLEN 3:13
grow: Every instant g.; he can GRAV 93:6
few people who g. up CHES 51:7
g. where one question grew VEBL 221:11
never g. out of it UST 220:20
They shall g. not old BINY 34:18
growing: keep it g. POUND 173:26
grown: are g. and take our place
KIPL 126:7
I've g. accustomed to the trace
LERN 135:21
grown-ups: G. never understand
SAIN 187:18
obvious facts about g. JARR 112:17
grows: Nothing g. in our garden
THOM 214:10
growth: g. of a large business ROCK 181:17
grub: old ones, g. SHAW 195:16
grubs: And Paradisal g. are found
BROO 40:8
grudge: politician will never g. OLIV 163:4
gruntled: he was far from being g.
WOD 230:7
guarantee: one can g. success in war
CHUR 55:19
guard: changing g. at Buckingham
MILNE 153:5
g. against the acquisition EIS 73:6
Must g. themselves LARK 130:10
guarding: consists in the mutual g.
RILKE 181:3
guerre: faire la g. que la paix CLEM 56:18
g. ce sont les pauvres SART 190:26
La g., c'est une chose CLEM 56:16
guess: g. that he was born SHAW 197:8
guessing: G. so much and so much
CHES 51:8

guest: Earth, receive an honoured g.
AUDEN 13:2
I too awaited the expected g. ELIOT 77:1
tonight is my g. night HALL 95:10
guests: classes: hosts and g. BEER 22:17
guided: g. missiles and misguided
KING 122:4
guides: g. cannot master the subtleties
TWAIN 219:21
G. us by vanities ELIOT 73:12
guile: packed with g. BROO 40:13
Guillain-Barré: got something called G.
PUZO 176:12
guilt: his sense of g. LESS 135:27
guilty: g. of several monographs
DOYLE 69:20
g. until they are proved innocent
ORW 165:9
Mortal, g., but to me AUDEN 13:7
were g. of Noel Cowardice DE VR 67:5
guinea: g. pigs in the laboratory
WILL 227:14
guineas: Give crowns and pounds and g.
HOUS 106:12
Guinness: drink G. from a thick mug
PINT 171:13
G. . . . is good for you GREE 93:20
My Goodness, My G. RICH 180:13
guitar: Are changed upon the blue g.
STEV 208:15
gulf: Between the two a g. SNOW 203:27
redwood forest to the G. GUTH 95:1
gulls: Forgot the cry of g. ELIOT 77:3
gum: chew g. at the same time
JOHN 114:5
gun: barrel of a g. MAO T 146:13
Every g. that is made EIS 73:7
Fire your little g. DE L 66:16
goes the farmer's g. GAY 89:1
I have no g., but I can spit AUDEN 12:14
never said 'Drop the g., Louie'
BOGA 35:12
that a g. in your pocket WEST 225:20
gun-boat: situation is send a g.
BEVAN 32:18
gunfire: towards the sound of g. GRIM 94:8
Gunga: better man than I am, G. Din
KIPL 123:10
guns: for example, without g. GOEB 91:6
groaning as the g. boom CHES 51:17
G. aren't lawful PARK 168:12
rather have butter or g. GOER 91:7
saw g. and sharp swords DYLAN 71:6
Scarce heard amid the g. below
MCCR 141:17
than a hundred men with g.
PUZO 176:11
unheroic Dead who fed the g.
SASS 191:19
when the g. begin SASS 191:15
when the g. begin to shoot KIPL 123:7
gush: they're oil wells; they g. PARK 169:3
gut: Menschen aber waren nie g. BARTH 20:1
gutless: sort of g. Kipling ORW 165:4
guts: g. to betray my country FORS 84:5
what do you mean by "g." HEM 101:2
gutter: so I lay down in the g. BURT 42:17
walk straight into the g. SMITH 203:6
guttural: The g. sorrow of the refugees
MACN 144:12
guy: actor is a kind of a g. GLASS 91:1
g. who could carry a tune CROS 63:7
guys: Nice g. Finish last DUR 70:16

gymn: The flare was up in the g. BETJ 32:7
gypsy: vagrant g. life MAS 148:18
gyre: turning in the widening g.
  YEATS 233:12

H

habit: But h. is a great deadener
  BECK 21:25
habitation: can the soul's h. henceforth
  RUSS 186:21
habit-forming: Cocaine h.? Of course not
  BANK 18:4
habitual: nothing is h. but indecision
  JAMES 112:11
had: all knew you h. it in you PARK 169:1
Haig: [Earl H.'s] Private Papers BEAV 21:6
hail: beaten dog beneath the h.
  POUND 174:14
hair: And never brush their h. BELL 24:6
  And not your yellow h. YEATS 236:1
  colour of his h. HOUS 105:8
  drew her long black h. ELIOT 77:5
  grainy wood; live h. BROO 39:19
  h. with automatic hand ELIOT 77:2
  her voice, and her h. MAS 148:7
  into her long black h. NOYES 161:17
  never hurt a h. of Him STUD 210:20
  part my h. behind ELIOT 75:19
  patted her h. and looked ASHF 11:2
  She only talks about her h. THOM 216:5
  such a head of h. HOUS 105:8
  sunlight in your h. ELIOT 76:2
half: H. dead and half alive BETJ 31:14
  H. devil and half child KIPL 127:19
  h. grant what I wish FROST 86:5
  H. to forget the wandering FLEC 81:16
  has been too clever by h. SAL 189:6
  have been finished in h. the time
  WOD 230:11
  He that loves but h. of Earth QUIL 177:4
  I don't know which h. LEV 136:6
  I knew h. of her O'BR 162:10
  Send me the h. that's got GRAH 92:14
half-a-crown: Or help to h. HARDY 98:3
half-men: h., and their dirty BROO 40:1
half-truths: all truths are h. WHIT 226:8
half-way: A lie can be h. around
  CALL 45:2
halitosis: h. of the intellect ICKES 110:3
hall: [H.] has always maintained
  HALL 95:11
  Meet her in the h. COW 62:13
  than the pram in the h. CONN 58:17
  The Absolute across the h. BELL 26:5
hallelujah: thrilling voice cry out H.
  OSB 165:15
halo: indignation is jealousy with a h.
  WELLS 225:5
  Is a h.? It's only one more FRY 86:26
halts: h. by me that footfall THOM 215:20
Hamilton: Alexander H. . . . he left a
  precious legacy CHAM 48:8
  Call me Lady H. RIC 180:12
Hamlet: H. is so much paper PRIE 175:7
  H. patted this dog SAL 189:2
  I am not Prince H. ELIOT 75:18
hammer: who proclaims with a h.
  BIER 33:25
  With His h. of wind THOM 216:9

hammers: anvil—hear the h. ring
  KIPL 126:19
  which has worn out many h.
  MACL 143:3
ham'n eggs: have your h. in Carolina
  GORD 92:4
Ha'nacker: Sally is gone from H. Hill
  BELL 25:14
hand: adorable tennis-girl's h. BETJ 32:3
  A h. under his head YEATS 233:7
  biting the h. that lays GOLD 91:17
  darkness and put your h. HASK 99:3
  eyes have seen what my h. LOW 140:1
  from h. to hand of cash SICK 200:15
  Give a man a free h. WEST 225:16
  hair with automatic h. ELIOT 77:2
  h. and touched the face MAGEE 145:2
  h. in hand with love NOYES 161:15
  h. that holds dominion THOM 214:5
  h. that signed the paper THOM 214:4
  Hath placed within my h. ROSS 185:5
  If you can't lend your h. DYLAN 71:14
  laid her snow-white h. YEATS 234:13
  Left h. down a bit WYMAN 232:1
  My h. in yours CRANE 62:14
  rare fine h. MANS 146:5
  The h. is the cutting edge BRON 39:13
  Took me by the h. TURN 218:19
  waltz, I take her h. HUXL 109:2
handbag: hitting it with her h. CRIT 63:5
handclasp: Out where the h.'s a little
  CHAP 49:9
handcuffs: young sinner with the h.
  HOUS 105:8
handful: fear in a h. of dust ELIOT 76:15
handicraft: out of the sphere of h.
  SARR 190:25
handkerchief: feels like a damp h.
  MACK 143:1
  h. binding her hair CONN 59:15
  on the state of the h. industry CONN 59:6
  tie and display h. CHAN 49:2
  Trap the germs in your h. ANON 5:27
handles: no h. to a horse LEAC 133:8
hands: Beneath the bleeding h. we feel
  ELIOT 74:12
  h. could lay hold BENÉT 27:9
  h. I have built her up AYCK 15:21
  h. I loved beside the Shalimar
  HOPE 104:5
  h. of young children DYLAN 71:6
  h. that do dishes ANON 6:17
  h. that hold the aces BETJ 31:2
  has such small h. CUMM 63:18
  Holding h. at midnight GERS 89:17
  its h. and goes to work SAND 190:1
  my h. were loath OWEN 166:18
  prize-fighters shaking h. MENC 150:16
  Soul clap its h. and sing YEATS 234:6
  Their h. upon their hearts HOUS 105:16
  Work your h. from day to MACN 144:9
handsome: Hi! h. hunting man DE L 66:19
hang: H. it all, Robert Browning
  POUND 173:27
  h. my hat is home sweet JER 113:17
  H. your clothes on a hickory DE L 66:20
  [Patrick Gray] h. there EHRL 72:10
  When they come to h. you, lad
  KING 122:11
  will not h. myself today CHES 52:3
hanged: got myself burnt or h. JER 113:11
  h. on the highest hill KIPL 125:20

hangin': they're h. Danny Deever
  KIPL 123:4
hanging: Cassidy's h. hill KAV 118:7
  h. for the colour HOUS 105:8
  h. garments of Marylebone JOYCE 115:9
  h. isn't bad enough HOUS 105:8
hangman: And naked to the h.'s noose
  HOUS 106:11
hank: rag and a bone and a h. KIPL 127:18
hansom: And was helped to a h. outside
  BETJ 30:21
happen: are supposed to h. off STOP 209:17
  don't know what will h. now
  KING 121:16
  everybody knew would never h.
  POW 175:1
  foretell what is going to h. CHUR 53:7
  It can't h. here LEWIS 137:5
  which started to h. MARQ 147:8
happened: funny thing h. on the way
  SHEV 200:12
  h. to you and afterwards HEM 100:10
  things after they have h. ION 110:19
happening: A way of h., a mouth
  AUDEN 13:1
  perceives what is *not* h. TYNAN 220:11
happens: be there when it h. ALLEN 3:14
  Experience is not what h. HUXL 109:13
  judgement. It h. every day CAMUS 46:3
  Nothing h., nobody comes BECK 21:18
  something, h. anywhere LARK 130:18
happiness: about somebody else's h.
  HUXL 109:3
  away you take away his h. IBSEN 110:2
  But a lifetime of h. SHAW 197:17
  H. is an imaginary condition
  SZASZ 211:15
  H. is a wine of the rarest SMITH 202:16
  H. is salutary for the body PROU 176:7
  H. is the only sanction SANT 190:8
  H. is to admire without BRAD 38:4
  H. makes up in height FROST 86:20
  h. of the common man BEV 33:10
  h. or a quiet conscience BERL 30:6
  It seemed, so great my h. YEATS 235:17
  more right to consume h. SHAW 196:3
  most fatal to true h. RUSS 186:15
  our h. is assured BIER 34:7
  politics of h. HUMP 108:6
  Who gain a h. in eyeing HUXL 108:21
happy: A h. noise to hear HOUS 106:14
  Farmer will never be h. HERB 101:20
  H. birthday to you HILL 102:13
  H. days are here again YELL 236:5
  h. home with his wife EDW 72:8
  H. the hare at morning AUDEN 15:16
  H. till I woke again HOUS 107:9
  His h. good-night air HARDY 97:11
  house and h. as the grass THOM 213:17
  I only wanted to make you h.
  AYCK 15:22
  peculiar ways of being h. JAMES 112:13
  remote from the h. AUDEN 12:15
  See the h. moron ANON 8:7
  somewhere, may be h. MENC 150:19
  The h. highways where I went
  HOUS 107:4
  The world of the h. WITT 230:3
  They are to be h. LARK 131:2
  This is the h. warrior READ 178:10
  Was he h. AUDEN 13:11
  were angry and poor and h. CHES 51:23
  whether you are h. or not SHAW 199:12

harbour: Pale rain over the dwindling h.
                                                    THOM 213:16
hard: ask the h. question   AUDEN 15:5
   A very h. guy, indeed   RUNY 186:2
   h. rain's a gonna fall   DYLAN 71:6
   it is awfully h. to get   HALD 95:8
   It's been a h. day's night   LENN 135:8
   soldier's life is terrible h.   MILNE 153:5
hardback: modern h. writer   MORT 156:10
hard-boiled: h. city with no more
   personality   CHAN 49:5
harder: We're number two. We try h.
                                                    ANON 9:9
hardest: President's h. task   JOHN 114:15
hard-faced: are a lot of h. men   BALD 17:5
Harding: H. of Ohio was chosen
                                                    SIMP 201:6
   H. was not a bad man   LONG 138:22
hardships: his comrades, beset by h.
                                                    ATK 12:5
Hardy: H. went down to botanize
                                                    CHES 52:6
hare: Happy the h. at morning
                                                    AUDEN 15:16
   h. sitting up   LAWR 132:23
   I like the hunting of the h.   BLUNT 35:6
   that Caught the Pubic H.   BEHAN 23:22
hares: And little hunted h.   HODG 103:13
hark: H. the herald angels sing   ANON 6:18
   H.! the herald angels sing   BEEC 22:11
harlot: prerogative of the h.   KIPL 125:19
Harlow: H. kept calling Margot   ASQ 11:15
harm: forgive a man for the h.
                                                    MAUG 149:17
   h. as those who go about   CREI 62:18
   h. to ask for what you   KRUT 129:4
harms: Not for thy h.   THOM 215:19
harness: And hear the h. jingle
                                                    HOUS 106:17
   h. piece by piece Thou   THOM 215:13
harpsichord: [The h.] sounds   BEEC 22:2
Harris: Frank H. . . . said   BALF 17:17
   this is the *present* Mrs H.   THUR 216:18
Harrison: George H. are the greatest
                                                    BUCK 42:4
harrow: H. the house of the dead
                                                    AUDEN 15:3
   worthy to pass into H.   CHUR 55:7
harrowing: Only a man h. clods
                                                    HARDY 97:9
Harry: I'm just wild about H.   SISS 201:8
Harvard: or the glass flowers at H.
                                                    MOORE 155:15
harvest: Oh, shine on, shine on, h. moon
                                                    NORW 161:13
hassen: *Wenn wir einen Menschen h.*
                                                    HESSE 102:3
hat: get ahead, get a h.   ANON 6:24
   hang my h. is home sweet   JER 113:17
   h. at a private view   EDW 72:5
   He can't think without his h.   BECK 21:19
   mistook his wife for a h.   SACKS 187:14
   Queen to get away with a h.   LOOS 139:7
   silk h. on a Bradford   ELIOT 77:1
   The sun has got his h. on   BUTL 43:3
hate: away this murdherin' h.
                                                    O'CAS 162:15
   bother with people I h.   HART 98:18
   creatures is not to h. them   SHAW 196:7
   Each sequestered in its h.   AUDEN 13:3
   h. to get up in the morning   BERL 29:16
   h. victims who respect   SART 191:12
   h. what every poet hates   KAV 118:6

hate (*cont.*):
   h. will outrun you yet   OSB 165:20
   h. you through the glass   BLUN 34:25
   have seen much to h. here   MILL 152:3
   how I h. them   LAWR 131:18
   If you h. a person   HESSE 102:3
   I h. inaccuracy   BUTL 44:1
   I think I know enough of h.   FROST 86:6
   Lead me from h. to love   KUMAR 129:6
   The man you love to h.   ANON 7:24
   This is a letter of h.   OSB 165:20
   you h. women, otherwise   O'BR 162:6
hated: never h. a man enough
                                                    GABOR 87:21
   they are h. because they   RUSS 186:26
hates: any man who h. dogs   ROST 185:9
   h. them for it   SHAW 200:2
   H. you 'cause your feet's   BENS 28:19
   The sea h. a coward   O'NEI 163:13
Hathaway: reproductions of Anne H.'s
   cottage   LANC 129:19
hating: But h., my boy, is an art
                                                    NASH 159:13
   special reason for h. school   BEER 22:22
hatless: H., I take off   LARK 130:15
hatred: h. for the Tory Party   BEVAN 33:7
   have no h. or bitterness   CAV 48:3
   intellectual h. is the worst   YEATS 233:14
   undying h. it arouses   FOSD 84:13
hatreds: systematic organization of h.
                                                    ADAMS 2:1
hats: H. divide generally   WHIT 226:16
hauf-way: I'll ha'e nae h. hoose
                                                    MACD 141:21
hauled: German flag will be h.   BEAT 20:17
hauling: H. a lawyer away   SAND 190:3
haunches: on silent h.   SAND 189:14
haunted: A h. town it is to me   LANG 130:2
haunts: That h. you night and day
                                                    BERL 29:17
Havana: Our man in H.   GREE 93:18
have: But I h. a go, lady   OSB 165:13
   h. nothing whatever   MAUG 149:10
   h. to believe that if   O'HARA 163:1
   I h. to tell you now   CHAM 48:15
   long as you h. your life   JAMES 111:12
   Mama may h., papa may have
                                                    HOL 104:4
   something they must h.   BOWEN 37:11
   They h. to take you in   FROST 86:13
   when you h. to go there   FROST 86:13
hawk: He bold as a h.   THUR 216:24
hay: So *that's* what h. looks like
                                                    MARY 147:21
   Work and pray, live on h.   HILL 102:12
hazards: h. whence no tears can
                                                    HARDY 97:16
hazy: ordinary human beings is so h.
                                                    OSB 165:16
he: H. would, wouldn't h.?   RIC 180:11
   'Who h.?' and the like   ROSS 185:1
head: at the command—of his h.
                                                    ROOS 183:6
   ever rears its ugly h.   AYCK 15:19
   h. for that big star straight   MILL 152:7
   h. when all about you   KERR 120:4
   h. when there is anything   LEAC 133:8
   heaped on each gashed h.   SORL 205:3
   his brains go to his h.   ASQ 11:17
   If you can keep your h.   KIPL 126:13
   I hang 'mid men my needless h.
                                                    THOM 215:3
   Lady, when your lovely h.   BELL 25:20

head (*cont.*):
   Lay your sleeping h., my love
                                                    AUDEN 13:7
   monstrous h. and sickening cry
                                                    CHES 52:10
   psychiatrist should have his h.
                                                    GOLD 91:18
   some as big as your h.   HEAT 99:18
   such a h. of hair   HOUS 105:8
   To keep your h.   PUDN 176:9
headmaster: H. beaming skool bus ratle
                                                    WILL 227:8
   h. said you ruled them   RATT 177:17
headmasters: H. have powers   CHUR 55:9
headpiece: H. filled with straw. Alas
                                                    ELIOT 75:10
head-waiter: h. who's allowed to sit
                                                    UST 220:21
healer: compassion of the h.'s art
                                                    ELIOT 74:12
healing: And h. greens, leaves   ABSE 1:2
   not heroics, but h.   HARD 96:17
heals: Time wounds all h.   BREC 38:20
health: case of nutrition and h.   JAY 112:19
   character is the h. of his wife
                                                    CONN 59:13
   His h., his honour   BLUN 35:1
   When you have both it's h.   DONL 68:6
healths: drink one another's h.   JER 113:9
healthy: all h. instinct for it   BUTL 43:28
   h. and wealthy and dead   THUR 216:23
   H. citizens are the greatest   CHUR 53:14
   h. stomach is nothing if   BUTL 43:20
heap: h. of all your winnings   KIPL 126:14
hear: And h. the harness jingle
                                                    HOUS 106:17
   And h. the larks so high   HOUS 106:14
   can't h. what they say   SMITH 202:23
   Can you h. me, mother   POW 175:3
   Come on and h.   BERL 29:13
   h. like ocean on a western   LANG 130:3
   h. the pleasant cuckoo   DAV 65:1
   h. what was being said   SYNGE 211:10
   If you could h.   OWEN 166:10
   I h. A gay modulating anguish   FRY 87:4
   I h. a sudden cry of pain   STEP 208:7
   I h. you, I will come   HOUS 106:15
   read music but can't h.   BEEC 21:27
   really want to h. about it   SAL 188:24
   Whenever I h. the word   JOHST 114:19
   which men prefer not to h.   AGAR 2:19
   who do not wish to h. it   BUTL 43:12
heard: ain't h. nuttin' yet   JOLS 114:20
   Have you h. it's in the stars   PORT 173:7
   h. one side of the case   BUTL 43:25
   h. shoes described   HALS 95:12
   should certainly have h.   AUDEN 13:11
   you h. a seal bark   THUR 216:17
hearing: assails our sense of h.   ELLIS 77:12
   Woke to my h. from harbour
                                                    THOM 213:15
Hearst: William Randolph H. gave him
                                                    SMITH 202:3
heart: A fanatic h.   YEATS 236:3
   An Irishman's h. is nothing   SHAW 197:2
   blind side of the h.   CHES 50:10
   bone shop of the h.   YEATS 233:8
   book known to him by h.   WOOLF 231:10
   Brute h. of a brute like you   PLATH 172:4
   Bury my h. at Wounded Knee
                                                    BENÉT 27:8
   But my h.'s right there   JUDGE 116:17
   But not your h. away   HOUS 106:12
   But since man's h. is small   KIPL 124:11

heart (cont.):
Can make a stone of the h.   YEATS 233:10
Can mean to a tired h.   BOND 35:19
country begins in the h.   CATH 47:14
Deep in the h. of Texas   HERS 102:2
ease a h. like a satin gown   PARK 168:8
engraved on her h.   SELL 194:12
gold and h.'s first ease   DAY-L 65:7
grandeurs of his Babylonian h.
                                 THOM 216:7
h. are as crooked   AUDEN 14:8
h. attacks and he had   JOPL 115:4
heart-break in the h.   GIBS 90:8
h. could have thought you   THOM 216:8
h. expands to tinker   MACN 144:16
h. less native to high   THOM 216:2
h. may think it knows better
                                 BOWEN 37:7
H. of Darkness   CONR 59:19
h. of man has long been   HOUS 106:2
h. of the ridiculous   MAHON 145:6
h. that one can see rightly   SAIN 187:19
h. to poke poor Billy   GRAH 92:12
h. wants to sing ev'ry   HAMM 96:3
h. was shaken with tears   SASS 192:6
He carries his h. in his boots
                                 HERB 101:20
Her h. was warm and gay   HAMM 95:16
his little h.   JAMES 112:5
In the deserts of the h.   AUDEN 13:4
Into my h. an air that kills   HOUS 107:4
I said to H.   BELL 26:7
It hurts my h. to watch   SASS 192:4
it in the deep h.'s core   YEATS 232:9
Land of H.'s Desire   YEATS 232:18
laughing h.'s long peace   BROO 40:1
laughter of her h.   HAMM 95:16
let your h. be strong   LAUD 131:7
My h. belongs to Daddy   PORT 173:5
My h. was with the Oxford men
                                 LETTS 136:1
occasional h. attack   BENC 26:20
Oh, deep in my h.   ANON 9:13
Out of my h.   YEATS 232:12
Out-worn h., in a time out-worn
                                 YEATS 232:6
red pavilion of my h.   THOM 215:21
That the h. grows old   YEATS 234:4
The h. is a lonely hunter   MCC 141:19
The hills fill my h.   HAMM 96:3
verities and truths of the h.   FAUL 78:12
waters of the h.   THOM 213:21
We had fed the h. on fantasies
                                 YEATS 232:5
What else could any h. do   REAV 178:18
who had one body and one h.
                                 DOUG 68:11
With rue my h. is laden   HOUS 107:7
You're breaking my h.   BERN 30:9
You're my h.'s desire   ARMS 10:7
heart-break: feel the h. in the heart
                                 GIBS 90:8
hearth-fire: And the h. and the home-acre
                                 KIPL 126:5
heartless: For nature, h., witless nature
                                 HOUS 106:4
hearts: H. wound up with love
                                 SPEN 205:20
not to get your h. desire   SHAW 198:6
Their hands upon their h.   HOUS 105:16
tight hot cell of their h.   BOGAN 35:11
undevoted h.   FORS 83:2
While your h. are yearning   FORD 82:20
Who sing to find your h.   FLEC 81:6

heat: If you can't stand the h.   TRUM 218:8
If you can't stand the h.   VAUG 221:7
heathen: But Higgins is a H.   CHES 52:12
heather: bonnie bloomin' h.   LAUD 131:8
heaven: A lawyer's dream of h.   BUTL 43:9
And h. endures   HOUS 106:8
And I came down from h.   CART 47:7
betwixt H. and Charing Cross
                                 THOM 216:11
Cry,—clinging H. by the hems
                                 THOM 216:11
day when h. was falling   HOUS 106:3
gets to H. he won't last   WELLS 224:12
h. for a man like Adolf   BUCH 42:1
H. holds a place for those   SIMON 201:4
H. out of unbelievable Hell   COW 61:14
H. will protect a working-girl
                                 SMITH 202:8
Hell, and H. how high   BENÉT 27:9
Imagine there's no h.   LENN 134:20
In h. an angel is nobody in particular
                                 SHAW 198:21
Is he in h.?—Is he in hell?   ORCZY 163:19
Is it any better in H.   WILL 228:2
It was my thirtieth year to h.
                                 THOM 213:15
joy-bells ring in H.'s street   MAS 148:11
more things in h. and earth   HALD 95:6
My blue h.   WHIT 226:18
nurseries of h.   THOM 215:4
Of the garden hard by H.   BOUL 37:2
Pennies from h.   BURKE 42:13
that H. of all their wish   BROO 40:8
Toward h., till the tree   FROST 86:5
'Twould ring the bells of H.   HODG 103:13
under an English h.   BROO 40:5
heavenly: A h. mansion, raging
                                 YEATS 235:18
ancient h. connection   GINS 90:15
heavens: h.' embroidered cloths
                                 YEATS 235:7
she feels the h. lie bare   THOM 216:5
heaves: forest fleece the Wrekin h.
                                 HOUS 106:18
heavy: I was h. with the even
                                 THOM 215:12
Hebrides: seas colder than the H.
                                 FLEC 81:18
Hector: ago H. took off his plume
                                 CORN 61:9
hedgehogs: personality belongs to the h.
                                 BERL 30:4
start throwing h. under me   KHR 121:4
heels: crossing of a pair of h. HART 98:17
nipping the h. of Hemingway   ALGR 3:8
heigh-ho: H., heigh-ho   MOREY 155:17
height: h. for what it lacks   FROST 86:20
not think up to the h.   CHES 52:7
heimischer: dass man sich h. fühlt
                                 FREUD 85:8
Heineken: H. refreshes the parts other
                                 LOV 139:15
Heinz: Beanz meanz H.   DRAKE 70:3
heiress: When an American h. wants
                                 MCC 141:9
Helen: Shall look on H.'s face in hell
                                 PARK 168:16
That first night in H.'s arms   YEATS 236:4
hell: Blake knew how deep is H.
                                 BENÉT 27:9
Can extinguish h.   REED 179:4
give them [the public] h.   TRUM 218:7
H. go ting-a-ling-a-ling   ANON 8:1

hell (cont.):
h. in such a way that you   STIN 209:9
H. is full of musical amateurs
                                 SHAW 197:20
H. is oneself   ELIOT 73:20
H. is other people   SART 191:4
H., madam, is to love no more
                                 BERN 30:8
interests of H.   FORS 83:10
I say the h. with it   WHITE 226:1
Is he in heaven?—Is he in h.?
                                 ORCZY 163:19
it would be h. on earth   SHAW 197:17
made an excursion to h.   PRIE 175:9
merger between Heaven and H.
                                 WELLS 224:12
out of unbelievable H.   COW 61:14
seventeen. I'll go to h.   THOM 214:11
They go to h. like lambs   CHES 50:17
though h. should bar the way
                                 NOYES 162:1
What is h.   ELIOT 73:20
why they invented H.   RUSS 186:24
wicked as Lord George H.   BEER 23:5
wishful thinking in H.   LEWIS 136:12
working definition of h.   SHAW 199:13
Yours till H. freezes   FISH 80:7
hell-fires: An' dreamin' H. to see
                                 KIPL 127:6
hellhound: h. is always a hellhound
                                 WOD 230:8
Hellman: she [Lillian H.] writes MCC 141:8
hello: H., Dolly   HERM 102:1
H., good evening, and welcome
                                 FROST 85:14
help: cannot h. nor pardon   AUDEN 15:10
Give me your h., not   ROOS 182:22
h. and support of the woman   EDW 72:8
'h. me, heaven,' she prayed   FIRB 79:19
How shall I h. you, say   HOUS 107:3
Like whipping tops and h.   HODG 103:12
little h. from my friends   LENN 135:14
Or h. to half-a-crown   HARDY 98:3
scream for h. in dreams   CAN 46:9
very present h. in trouble   STEV 209:7
you can't h. it   SMITH 202:12
you do something to h. me   LAUR 131:1
helpless: h. to hinder that or anything
                                 HARDY 97:5
helps: Mars a day h. you work   GAFF 87:22
hem-hem: am forced to mingle h.
                                 WILL 227:7
Hemingway: nipping the heels of H.
                                 ALGR 3:8
hen: better take a wet h.   KHR 121:6
have been a farmyard h.   AYRES 16:7
h. is only an egg's way   BUTL 43:16
Henery: I'm H. the Eighth, I am
                                 MURR 158:5
Hepburn: H. runs the gamut from
                                 PARK 168:5
herald: Hark! the h. angels sing
                                 BEEC 22:11
herd: Banished from the h. he led
                                 HODG 103:14
herds: H. of reindeer move across
                                 AUDEN 14:23
herdsman: h. goads them on behind
                                 YEATS 234:10
here: And h.'s to you, Mrs Robinson
                                 SIMON 201:4
buck stops h.   TRUM 218:13
From h. to eternity   JONES 115:1
H. comes the judge   MARK 146:16

here (*cont.*):

H. I am, an old man	ELIOT 73:11
H.'s looking at you, kid	EPST 77:19
H. we are	KNIG 128:8
H. we go, here we go	ANON 6:20
H. *we go round the prickly pear*	
	ELIOT 75:11
H. were decent godless	ELIOT 76:5
I'm only h. for the beer	LEV 136:5
It can't happen h.	LEWIS 137:5
Lafayette, we are h.	STAN 207:1
We're h. Because We're h.	ANON 9:10
We're h. because we're queer	
	BEHAN 23:27

heresies: Religions are kept alive by h.
    BREN 39:9
heresy: Englishman believes be h.
    SHAW 199:30
heretic: H., rebel, a thing to flout
    MARK 146:15
  oppressor or a h.   CAMUS 46:7
heritage: And we have come into our h.
    BROO 40:4
hero: Greek one then is my h. ABSE 1:4
  h. is a man who would argue
    MAIL 145:12

I understand the h.	ROSS 185:4
Show me a h. and I will	FITZ 80:15
they don't want to be a h.	STOP 210:4

Herod: hour of H. HOPE 104:18
heroes: And its h. were made AE 2:18

Britain a fit country for h.	LLOY 138:13
h. up the line to death	SASS 191:16
land that has no h.	BREC 39:2
land that needs h.	BREC 39:2

heroic: I'm not the h. type ALLEN 4:8
heroics: present need is not h. HARD 96:17
heroing: H. is one of the shortest-lived
    ROG 182:16
heroism: thing as splendour or h.
    FORS 83:14
heron: mussel pooled and the h.
    THOM 213:15
Herr: German Foreign Minister, H.
    COOK 60:9
Herrgott: *Raffiniert ist der H.*
    EINS 72:13
hers: H. of the Book, the tripled QUIL 177:3
herself: playing h. KAEL 117:5
Herzog: thought Moses H. BELL 26:9
heure: *Vienne la nuit, sonne l'h.*
    APOL 9:22
hey: H.! big spender FIEL 79:6
  H.! Mr Tambourine Man DYLAN 71:11
hi: H. diddle dee dee WASH 222:14
hick: Sticks nix h. pix ANON 8:13
hickory: Hang your clothes on a h. limb
    DE L 66:20
hid: h. his face amid a crowd YEATS 232:7
  I h. from Him, and under THOM 215:5
hidden: For Famagusta and the h. sun
    FLEC 81:19
  The h. persuaders PACK 167:1
hide: can run, but he can't h.
    LOUIS 139:14
  h. of a rhinoceros BARR 19:26
  His h. is sure to flatten 'em BELL 24:8
hiding: got was a bloody good h.
    GRANT 93:2
hier: *Ou peut-être h., je ne* CAMUS 46:4
hierarchy: H. Every Employee Tends
    PETER 170:11
high: And hear the larks so h.
    HOUS 106:14
  By a h. star our course is set
    MACN 144:11

high (*cont.*):

Every man who is h. up	BARR 19:25
h. altar on the move	BOWEN 37:8
h. as an elephant's eye	HAMM 95:17
h. birth is a form of congenital insanity	
	WOOLF 231:8
h. contracting powers solemnly	
	BRIA 39:10
H. o'er the fence leaps	HANFF 96:9
hold my house in the h. wood	
	BELL 25:26
She's the Broad and I'm the H.	
	SPR 206:14
window at h. noon	JOHN 114:3

highballs: Three h. and I think I'm
    PARK 168:1
highbrow: What is a h.? He is a man
    WALL 222:4
higher: And find my own the h. CORN 61:6
  I am capable of h. things FORS 83:6
highest: nation is the h. virtue
    JOHN 114:14
high-mindedness: joss-sticks and
  honourable h. BRAM 38:15
high-tech: h. approach if you demolished
    CHAR 50:2
high-water: h. mark of my youth
    THUR 216:15
  The h. mark, so to speak ORW 165:4
highway: The h.'s under it MILL 152:7
  travelled each and ev'ry h. ANKA 5:7
highwayman: The h. came riding
    NOYES 161:16
highways: The happy h. where I went
    HOUS 107:4
hijacker: h. of the oxygen THAT 213:5
hilarity: h. was like a scream from
    GREE 93:17
Hilda: it's needed H. REED 179:6
hill: are all gone under the h. ELIOT 74:10

Cassidy's hanging h.	KAV 118:7
flung us on the windy h.	BROO 39:18
h. as light fell short	HODG 103:10
on the last h., that shows	RILKE 181:4
They took the h.	PLOM 172:5

hills: h. are alive with the sound
    HAMM 96:3

h. fill my heart	HAMM 96:3
h. of the South Country	BELL 25:25
those blue remembered h.	HOUS 107:4
we shall fight in the h.	CHUR 54:10

Himmler: He called you the H. RATT 177:17
himself: His opinion of h. BENN 28:3
  interested in h. than in me BIER 34:6
  my short answer is 'h.' IBSEN 110:1
Hindenburg: H. Line to which the defence
    RICH 180:17
hinder: she's helpless to h. HARDY 97:5
hind-legs: standing a sheep on its h.
    BEER 23:15
hindsight: H. is always twenty-twenty
    WILD 227:1
hinky: H., dinky, parley-voo ANON 7:20
hinter: *Augenblick wird sie h. mir sein*
    REGER 179:8
hip: H. is the sophistication MAIL 145:8
Hippo: Lord H. suffered fearful loss
    BELL 25:8
hippopotamus: h. resolved at any cost
    WELLS 224:14
  I shoot the H. BELL 24:8
  shoot the h. with eyebrows FORS 83:5
  The h.'s day ELIOT 75:6

hips: armchairs tight about the h.
    WOD 230:18
  your girdle when your h. NASH 159:23
hipsters: angelheaded h. burning
    GINS 90:15
hired: they h. the money COOL 60:12
Hiroshima: Einstein leads to H. PIC 171:6
historian: first requisite of the h. STR 210:6
  h. must have a third quality FORS 83:7
  one safe rule for the h. FISH 80:5
  The h., essentially JAMES 111:14
historians: h. can BUTL 43:6
  h. left blanks POUND 173:28
  H. repeat each other GUED 94:10
  honoured by h. more for the way
    HARL 98:11
  men who are not h. behave FORS 83:7
history: A people without h. ELIOT 74:22
  cancer of human h. SONT 205:1
  disasters of English h. WAUGH 223:1
  discerned in h. a plot FISH 80:5
  from the lessons of h. HUXL 108:12
  good h. HARDY 96:20
  greatest week in the h. NIXON 161:3
  h. becomes more and more WELLS 225:2
  H. came SELL 194:18
  H. has many cunning passages
    ELIOT 73:12
  H. is a combination of reality COCT 57:6
  h. is a pattern ELIOT 74:22
  H. is littered POW 175:1
  H. is more or less bunk FORD 82:18
  H. is now and England ELIOT 74:22
  h. is on our side KHR 121:7
  H., n. An account BIER 34:8
  h. of art is the history BUTL 43:23
  h. of every country begins CATH 47:14
  H. repeats itself GUED 94:10
  H., Stephen said JOYCE 116:6
  H. teaches us that men EBAN 71:17
  h. than they can consume SAKI 188:7
  h. to produce a little literature
    JAMES 111:20
  H. to the defeated AUDEN 15:10
  h. we make today FORD 82:18
  H. will absolve me CAST 47:12
  into the dustbin of h. TROT 218:5
  longest suicide note in h. KAUF 118:4
  memorable in the h. of our race
    CHUR 53:11
  natural h. if you can SCOTT 194:2
  Thames is liquid h. BURNS 42:15
  There is no h. of mankind POPP 172:14
  thousand years of h. GAIT 88:1
  What will h. say SHAW 196:10
history-making: Man is a h. creature
    AUDEN 14:4
hit: H. the road, Jack MAYF 150:7
Hitler: Even H. and Mussolini LOW 139:17
  German Chancellor, Herr H. CHAM 48:13
  H. attacked the Jews NIEM 160:13
  H. knows that he will have CHUR 54:11
  H.'s level of accuracy TAYL 212:8
  H. swept out of his Berlin ANON 7:4
  H. thought he might get CHAM 48:16
  man like Adolf H. BUCH 42:1
  one voice would say to H. CHUR 53:10
hitting: h. a jag-time tune SERV 194:23
hive: h. for the honey bee YEATS 232:9
ho: 'What h.!' I said WOD 230:20
Hoares: no more H. to Paris GEOR 89:6
hobbit: ground there lived a h. TOLK 217:8

Hobson: sound of Harold H. barking
GILL 90:12
hock: at a weak h. and seltzer   BETJ 30:21
Hodgitts: 'O Mr H.!' I heard her
GRAH 92:15
hog: disadvantage of being a h.
MORT 156:12
Not the whole h.   MILL 152:11
hogs: let it not be like h.   MCKAY 142:15
hoisted: h. again without permission
BEAT 20:17
hold: centre cannot h.   YEATS 233:12
h. with those who favour   FROST 86:6
holds: h. and rolls and throws   REED 179:2
hole: h. with nothing in it   TOLK 217:8
ride in a h. in the ground   COMD 58:7
holes: h. in Blackburn Lancashire
LENN 135:6
holiday: h. is a good working definition
SHAW 199:13
h. to any patient who considered
RUSS 186:11
holidays: *Educ*: during the h. from Eton
SITW 201:19
Term, h., term   LEWIS 136:15
holiness: Than Courage of Heart or H.
BELL 26:1
There is no H. here   ROLFE 182:17
hollingsworth: bourne from which no h.
MORT 156:16
hollow: Down to the h.   FLAN 81:4
We are the h. men   ELIOT 75:10
Hollywood: H. is a place where people
ALLEN 3:12
H. money isn't money   PARK 169:4
invited to H.   CHAN 49:6
Holroyd: [James H.]   WELLS 224:15
holy: H. deadlock   HERB 101:16
In a h. place   CAMP 45:4
totalitarianism or the h. name
GAND 88:10
Holy Ghost: like to call on the H.
LLOY 138:9
home: A house is not a h.   ADLER 2:17
can't find your way h.   COLL 58:2
dream that I am h.   FLEC 81:16
E.T. phone h.   MATH 149:2
h. again to find it more   SASS 192:3
h. discovers that he has   DOUG 68:16
H. is heaven and orgies   NASH 159:22
H. is the girl's prison   SHAW 198:27
H. is the place where   FROST 86:13
H. James, and don't spare   HILL 102:15
H. life as we understand   SHAW 196:21
I can hang my hat is h.   JER 113:17
I tank I go h.   GARBO 88:14
Look as much like h. as we can   FRY 87:6
[Lord H.] is used to dealing   DOUG 68:17
make one feel more at h.   FREUD 85:8
me so much nearer h.   FROST 85:19
murder into the h.   HITC 103:1
My h. policy   CLEM 56:17
My h. sweet home   BERL 29:15
never see any h. cooking   PHIL 170:16
street, you do it at h.   SCOR 193:15
that it's a refuge from h.   SHAW 200:5
The h. of the bean and the cod
BOSS 36:12
They dream of H.   FORD 82:20
Till the boys come H.   FORD 82:20
want to go h. in the dark   HENRY 101:12
what is it to be at h.   BECK 21:9
With no direction h.   DYLAN 71:8

home *(cont.)*:
You can't go h. again   WOLFE 231:3
you come h. Bill Bailey   CANN 46:10
home-acre: And the hearth-fire and the h.
KIPL 126:5
home-fires: Keep the H. burning
FORD 82:20
homeless: orphans and the h.   GAND 88:10
Homer: Gladstone read H. for fun
CHUR 55:10
mounted in that saddle H. rode
YEATS 235:13
homes: h. and first beginning   BELL 26:3
The Stately H. of England   COW 62:11
They think of firelit h.   SASS 191:15
homeward: And rooks in families h. go
HARDY 97:3
H., and brings the sailor   ELIOT 76:24
homicidal: The great h. classics
STOP 209:18
homme: *h. politique ne croit jamais*
DE G 66:2
L'h. est une passion inutile.   SART 191:3
homo: naked ape self-named H.
MORR 156:5
homos: stately h. of England   CRISP 63:2
homosexuality: h. were the normal way
BRY 41:16
honest: both h. and intelligent   ORW 164:27
h. God's the noblest work   BUTL 43:8
man looked h. enough   TWAIN 219:8
shall buy it like an h. man   NORT 161:12
She was poor but she was h.   ANON 8:8
That we who lived by h. dreams
DAY-L 65:11
honesty: h. is a good thing   MARQ 147:6
honey: And is there h. still for tea
BROO 40:15
hive for the h. bee   YEATS 232:9
H. or condensed milk   MILNE 153:15
H., your silk stocking's   SELL 194:11
How a bear likes h.   MILNE 153:13
sun drips h.   LEE 134:3
Tiggers don't like h.   MILNE 153:2
honey-bees: Than in our love; Oh, h.
YEATS 232:5
honeysuckle: h., I am the bee   FITZ 80:11
honi: H. soie qui mal y pense   SELL 194:11
honour: air signed with their h.
SPEN 205:16
Fear God. H. the King   KITC 128:5
fighting for this woman's h.
KALM 117:11
h. from me if Ye take away   KIPL 127:3
H. has come back   BROO 40:4
h. of the British Army   KITC 128:5
h. we had forgotten   LLOY 138:12
Let us h. if we can   AUDEN 15:4
Of h. and the sword   CHES 51:18
peace with h.   CHAM 48:14
set up in h. of a critic   SIB 200:14
Though loss of h. was a wrench
GRAH 92:10
honourably: h. ineligible for the struggle
CONN 59:1
honoured: will be h. by historians
HARL 98:11
honours: good card to play for H.
BENN 28:18
Honours List: H. and you can instantly
BENN 28:15
hoof: out pops the cloven h.   WOD 230:9
hookah-mouth: sliding puffs from the h.
KIPL 123:18

hooray: Hip hip hip h.   BUTL 43:3
hoot: literary mornings with its h.
AUDEN 14:18
hooter: because the h. hoots   CHES 50:17
hooting: h. at dawn flew away   BEER 23:16
Hoover: [J. Edgar H.] inside the tent
JOHN 114:4
hooves: No mad h. galloping in the sky
KAV 118:9
hope: H., politeness, the blowing
FORS 83:21
h. that the simple stirrup-pump
REED 179:4
h. that the world will   JOHN 114:9
I h. to go on and on   THAT 212:18
Land of H. and Glory   BENS 28:21
Lead me from despair to h.   KUMAR 129:6
look forward to with h.   FROST 86:12
Nor dread nor h. attend   YEATS 235:10
Some blessed H., whereof   HARDY 97:11
store we sell h.   REVS 179:16
The death of h. and despair   ELIOT 74:18
Whatever h. is yours   OWEN 166:16
hoped: never h. can never despair
SHAW 196:1
hopelessness: despair and utter h.
ALLEN 3:21
The h. Whatever hope is yours
OWEN 166:16
hopes: h. of its children   EIS 73:7
scribbled lines like fallen h.   HOPE 105:2
hoping: Here's h. we meet now and then
PORT 173:2
hop-yards: Say, for what were h. meant
HOUS 107:8
horizon: always somebody else's h.
GRAH 92:19
The h.— the Three Wise Kings
KAV 118:7
horizontal: But the h. one   AUDEN 15:4
Life is a h. fall   COCT 57:7
perpendicular expression of a h.
SHAW 199:8
horn: mouth of Plenty's h.   YEATS 233:14
Put forth a conscious h.   THOM 216:4
won't come out of your h.   PARK 167:13
Hornby: O my H. and my Barlow long ago
THOM 215:22
horns: Memories are hunting h.   APOL 9:23
sound of h. and motors   ELIOT 76:23
horrible: h. and the miserable   ALLEN 4:6
h. in some respect   PIC 171:6
horror: h. of the Twentieth Century
MAIL 145:10
I have a h. of sunsets   PROU 176:4
imagination there is no h.   DOYLE 69:27
The h.! The h.!   CONR 59:22
horse: A h. is at least *human*   SAL 189:3
are no handles to a h.   LEAC 133:8
But where's the bloody h.   CAMP 45:11
By putting money on a h.   BELL 25:8
camel is a h. designed   ANON 5:23
Don't ask me, ask the h.   FREUD 85:6
Go together like a h.   CAHN 44:15
heard no h. sing a song   ARMS 10:8
h. is drawn by the cart   KIPL 124:2
h. nosing around the meadow   KAV 118:9
h. on the mountain   LORCA 139:12
h. that stumbles and nods   HARDY 97:9
I know two things about the h.
ROYD 185:19
lies about his wooden h.   FLEC 81:20
life and the torturer's h.   AUDEN 13:6

horse (cont.):
never look at any other h.   PIR 171:19
On the sightless h.   WALEY 222:3
that high h. riderless   YEATS 235:13
Why does a hearse h. snicker
                                   SAND 190:3
Horseguards: H. and still be common
                                   RATT 178:3
horseman: H. pass by!   YEATS 233:4
horsemen: Four H. rode again   RICE 180:7
horse-races: opinion that makes h.
                                  TWAIN 220:2
horses: Bring on the empty h.   CURT 64:8
don't spare the h.   HILL 102:15
h. o' Kansas think to-day   KIPL 124:6
if you cannot ride two h.   MAXT 150:5
oakleaves, h.' heels   ELIOT 76:12
street and frighten the h.   CAMP 45:7
They shoot h. don't they   MCCOY 141:16
Women and H. and Power and War
                                  KIPL 123:18
horticulture: You can lead a h. PARK 169:6
hose: tip up bason and a h.   ASHF 10:18
Hoskin: He's loo-vely, Mrs H.   RAY 178:7
host: have been under the h.   PARK 167:14
The h. with someone indistinct
                                  ELIOT 75:5
hostile: This universe is not h. HOLM 104:6
hostilities: others by their h.   BOWEN 37:6
hosts: h. and guests   BEER 22:17
hot: cat on a h. tin roof   WILL 227:5
h. the scent   GRAV 93:8
Noble deeds and h. baths   SMITH 202:7
only in h. water do you   REAG 178:11
Rosy and round and h.   ASQ 11:20
The long h. summer   RAV 178:5
hotel: h. is that it's a refuge SHAW 200:5
h. offers stupendous   HOFF 104:2
hotels: h. built on the cuckoo clock style
                                  HEM 101:7
Hottentot: Every H. and every Eskimo
                                  LEHR 134:8
hound: footprints of a gigantic h.
                                 DOYLE 69:12
H. that Caught the Pubic   BEHAN 23:22
You ain't nothin' but a h. dog LEIB 134:9
hour: At the violet h.   ELIOT 76:24
expect again a phoenix h.   DAY-L 65:7
Fools! For I also had my h.   CHES 52:11
Have known the lightning's h.
                                  DAY-L 65:9
h. of destiny they stand   SASS 191:15
h. of Herod   HOPE 104:18
h. when earth's foundations   HOUS 106:3
its h. come round at last   YEATS 233:13
matched us with His h.   BROO 40:1
night come, ring out the h.   APOL 9:22
spring comes her h.   GIBB 89:18
Surely this h. has come   YEATS 234:8
this h. and this trial   CHUR 55:18
This was their finest h.   CHUR 54:11
hours: better wages and shorter h.
                                  ORW 165:3
h. is a long time in politics   WILS 228:14
h. I've put into that woman   AYCK 15:21
Mary Woolnoth kept the h.   ELIOT 76:17
than the speed, of h.   HOPE 105:3
house: A h. is a machine for living
                                  LE C 133:25
A h. is not a home   ADLER 2:17
called a woman in my own h.
                                 WAUGH 223:15
Dust inbreathed was a h.   ELIOT 74:18
dwell in the h. of tomorrow   GIBR 90:5

house (cont.):
Harrow the h. of the dead   AUDEN 15:3
hold my h. in the high wood   BELL 25:26
H. Beautiful is play lousy   PARK 168:23
h. is built of stones   POIN 172:10
H. of Lords is the British   BENN 27:15
h. their bodies but not   GIBR 90:5
H. will in no circumstances   GRAH 92:9
h. with three poor staircases ASQ 11:13
it has been born in a h.   JEANS 112:20
Make my h. your inn   MOORE 155:16
man in the h. is worth two   WEST 225:9
moon is in the seventh h.   RADO 177:6
serious h. on serious earth   LARK 130:16
small h. agent's clerk   ELIOT 77:1
The H. at Pooh Corner   PARK 168:7
The H. of Lords, an illusion   STOP 209:13
tragic the h. rose like magic HARG 98:10
voice in her elected H.   DENN 67:3
young and inexperienced h.   JER 113:13
household: real centre of the h.
                                  SHAW 196:27
householder: housekeeper think she's a h.
                                  WILD 227:3
housekeeper: bribe to make a h.
                                  WILD 227:3
housemaids: damp souls of h.   ELIOT 76:1
houses: h. are all gone under ELIOT 74:10
It is not the h.   FENT 79:1
live in h. just as big   SMITH 203:5
housewife: h. is the Cinderella
                                 SUMM 211:2
housework: need to do any h. at all
                                 CRISP 63:1
how: And H. and Where and Who
                                  KIPL 125:15
H. about you   FREED 85:1
H. can I tell what I think   FORS 83:9
H. can you govern a country   DE G 66:1
H. does it feel   DYLAN 71:8
H. do they know   PARK 169:2
H. many roads must a man   DYLAN 71:4
H. much is that doggie   MERR 151:10
H.'s the Empire?   GEOR 89:9
H. shall we conquer   FLEC 81:22
H. to succeed in business   MEAD 150:10
H. to win friends and influence
                                  CARN 47:1
Howe: [Sir Geoffrey H.'s] speech HEAL 99:7
howl: I hear a famisht h.   BERR 30:14
howls: h. of anguish from   HEAL 99:9
Howth: H. Castle and Environs
                                 JOYCE 115:7
Huckleberry: Mark Twain called H. Finn
                                  HEM 100:13
hues: thee all her lovely h.   DAV 65:3
huff: taxi you can leave in a h.
                                 KALM 117:12
huffy: Not h., or stuffy   HERB 101:18
hug: We h. our little destiny again
                                 HEAN 99:14
huge: Bear is h. and wild   HOUS 105:10
Hügel: den letzten H., der ihm RILKE 181:4
Hugo: H.—alas   GIDE 90:10
H. was a madman who thought
                                 COCT 57:8
hullo: H. Clouds Hullo Sky   WILL 227:9
hum: Yes, the smell and hideous h.
                                 GODL 91:5
humains: Tous les êtres h. naissent
                                  ANON 9:1
human: All h. beings are born   ANON 9:1
all h. life is there   JAMES 111:22
Always h. beings will live   DUB 70:7

human (cont.):
apathy of h. beings   KELL 118:16
bombs could end the h.   BENN 27:10
But he's a h. being   MILL 152:4
classics is an enemy to the h.
                                  MILL 152:10
expression of h. immaturity   BRIT 39:11
field of h. conflict was   CHUR 54:12
future of the h. race   JEANS 112:20
horse is at least h.   SAL 189:3
H. beings are perhaps never VAN D 221:4
h. beings have an almost   HUXL 109:14
H. beings have an inalienable
                                 GREER 93:21
h. but to really foul   ANON 8:24
H. kind Cannot bear   ELIOT 74:4
H. Nature is the craving   JAMES 112:7
H. on my faithless arm   AUDEN 13:7
h. race commit suicide   ADAMS 2:7
h. race has today the means   BORN 36:11
importance of the h. factor   CHAR 49:15
it is a h. zoo   MORR 156:4
I wish I loved the H. Race   RAL 177:11
measles of the h. race   EINS 72:11
on stars where no h. race   FROST 85:19
ordinary h. enthusiasm   OSB 165:15
own-goal scored by the h.   ANNE 5:8
people are only h.   COMP 58:9
robot may not injure a h.   ASIM 11:5
servants are treated as h.   SHAW 198:17
shame to h. nature   HOUS 105:8
simplification of the h. character
                                 FORS 83:10
socialism would not lose its h. face
                                  DUBČ 70:5
The h. race   CHES 51:7
humanity: deeper needs of h.   BENN 27:10
'H.' and all such abstracts   CAMP 45:12
H. i love you   CUMM 63:14
H. is just a work in progress WILL 227:14
It is easier to love h.   HOFF 103:17
regeneration of all h.   PANK 167:9
three-score years and ten, h.
                                 JEANS 112:20
unremitting h. soon had me cheesed
                                  BENN 28:1
humans: It isn't fit for h. now BETJ 31:1
humbled: maintains that I am h.
                                 CORN 61:6
humblest: h. hour is when he compares
                                 BARR 19:4
humbugs: most artists and all h.
                                 CONN 58:19
humiliated: capable of being h.
                                 AUDEN 15:15
humiliation: Art is born of h. AUDEN 15:15
humility: learn h. as well as teach
                                 SHAW 199:26
hummy: it is that word 'h.'   PARK 168:7
humorists: h. is that they will mix
                                  UPD 220:15
humour: Good taste and h.   MUGG 157:9
h. and irony is generally   BUTL 43:15
'H.,' he said   THUR 217:3
no sense of h.   ALBEE 3:3
possessing a deep sense of h. MCL 143:9
hump: But uglier yet is the h. we get
                                  KIPL 125:9
The camel has a single h.   NASH 158:20
We get the h.   KIPL 125:10
Hun: The H. is at the gate   KIPL 124:15
hundred: Droop in a h. A.B.C.'s
                                 ELIOT 73:10
h. flowers blossom   MAO T 146:8

hundred-horse-power: comes Winston
  with his h.   BALD 17:12
hundreds: lads in their h. to Ludlow
      HOUS 106:16
hung: h. with bloom along HOUS 106:9
hunger: H. allows no choice AUDEN 13:9
  theft from those who h.   EIS 73:7
  with bodily h. in his eyes SHAW 197:11
hungry: A h. man is not a free man
      STEV 209:5
  h. for dinner at eight   HART 98:18
  tigers are getting h.   CHUR 55:21
Huns: better than H. or Wops MITF 154:18
hunted: And little h. hares HODG 103:13
  H. and penned in an inglorious
      MCKAY 142:15
  others by their h. expression
      LEWIS 136:14
hunter: heart is a lonely h.   MCC 141:19
  The H.'s waking thoughts AUDEN 15:16
hunting: Hi! handsome h. man DE L 66:19
  I like the h. of the hare BLUNT 35:6
  life also; I went h. wild OWEN 166:16
hurly-burly: h. of the chaise-longue
      CAMP 45:9
hurrah: The last h.   O'CON 162:21
hurricane: crazy-eyed h. blowing
      KIPL 124:9
hurry: H. up please it's time ELIOT 76:22
  H.! We burn   DAY-L 65:8
  multitude of young men in a h.
      CORN 61:10
  So who's in a h.   BENC 27:3
hurt: has done the lover mortal h.
      DOUG 68:11
  h. you to the heart TWAIN 219:16
  The wish to h., the momentary
      BRON 39:15
hurtig: Led go! You are h. KIPL 125:14
hurting: once it has stopped h.
      BOWEN 37:9
hurts: For fellows whom it h. HOUS 107:8
husband: having one h. too many
      ANON 5:18
  h. for a comfort SMITH 203:20
  h. is a whole-time job BENN 28:16
  h. is what is left ROWL 185:13
  over-jealous, yet an eager h. PHIL 171:2
  words 'My h. and I' ELIZ 77:8
  your h. I would drink it ASTOR 11:23
  your own h. that took you BEHAN 23:26
husbands: always make the best h.
      WOD 230:4
hush: have said 'h.' just once CAMP 45:5
  H., hush   MORT 156:13
  H.! Hush! Whisper who dares
      MILNE 153:12
hushed-up: secretly, like wrongs h.
      OWEN 166:14
hustle: who tried to h. the East KIPL 125:22
hutch: Sitting in me h.   AYRES 16:5
hyacinths: synthesis of h. and biscuits
      SAND 189:12
hygiene: h. of older people SMITH 203:1
hymn: A lass was singing a h. BETJ 32:7
hymns: And happy h. of farmers
      KING 122:12
  Sing on, with h. uproarious BETJ 31:16
hyphen: before the h. ROOS 184:5
hyphenated: h. American is not an
  American   ROOS 184:5
hypocrisy: H. is the most difficult
      MAUG 149:5

hypocrisy (cont.):
  m-m-making the world safe for h.
      WOLFE 231:2
hypothesis: scientist to discard a pet h.
      LOR 139:13
Hyssopps: H. of the Glen so you see
      ASHF 11:1
hysterical: starving h. naked GINS 90:15

I

I: I am a camera   ISH 111:1
  I am a free man, an American
      JOHN 114:16
  I am a passenger on space FULL 87:12
  I am the family face HARDY 97:7
  I, a stranger and afraid HOUS 105:18
  I don't mind if I do KAV 118:13
  I go—I come back KAV 118:14
  I got rhythm GERS 89:14
  I grow old . . . I grow old ELIOT 75:19
  I only wanted to make you happy
      AYCK 15:22
  I should do so DOYLE 69:29
  It is I   DE L 66:18
  I tank I go home GARBO 88:14
  I, this incessant snow DE L 66:18
  I, too, am America HUGH 108:1
  I travel light; as light FRY 86:25
  I want to be alone GARBO 88:13
  I will show you fear ELIOT 76:15
  Thou a person becomes I BUBER 41:17
  words 'My husband and I' ELIZ 77:8
IBM: got fired for buying I. ANON 7:28
ice: always skating on thin i. CAMP 45:8
  I. formed on the butler's WOD 230:22
  i. on a hot stove the poem FROST 85:18
  lies to i. a wedding cake ASQ 11:18
  Some say in i. FROST 86:6
  To say that for destruction i. FROST 86:6
ice-cream: emperor is the emperor of i.
      STEV 208:10
iceman: The i. cometh O'NEI 163:8
id: PUT THE I. BACK IN YID ROTH 185:11
idea: A good i.—son SYKES 211:7
  An i., to be suggestive JAMES 112:15
  Between the i. ELIOT 75:11
  good i. but it won't work ROG 182:15
  good i. to give them WARH 222:12
  i. ever to be fashionable SANT 190:19
  i. is accepted it is time JACK 111:5
  i. of Death saves FORS 83:18
  i. was ever born in a conference
      FITZ 80:14
  i. whose time has come ANON 8:17
  i. within a wall of words BUTL 43:27
  I hate the i. of causes FORS 84:5
  more dangerous than an i. ALAIN 3:1
  respect for the i. of God DUH 70:9
  That would be a good i. GAND 88:9
  whom the i. first occurs DARW 64:16
ideal: Christian i. has not been tried
      CHES 52:8
  i. reader suffering from JOYCE 115:8
  Youth would be an i. state ASQ 11:9
idealism: alcohol or morphine or i.
      JUNG 116:20
idealist: I am an i. I don't know
      SAND 189:18
  Sometimes people call me an i.
      WILS 229:4
idealistic: America is the only i. WILS 229:4

idealists: I. are very apt to walk
      SMITH 203:6
ideals: i. of a nation by its advertisements
      DOUG 68:15
ideas: has i. above her station RATT 178:1
  I. can be too old OUSP 166:4
  instead of genuine i. BENT 29:9
  it is i., not vested interests KEYN 120:17
  sound and original i. MACM 144:2
  steal other people's i. TOM 217:10
idée: plus dangereux qu'une i. ALAIN 3:1
  respecte trop l'i. de Dieu DUH 70:9
idées: i. au-dessus de sa gare RATT 178:1
identical: they exist, but are i. FORS 84:1
identified: 'He's i.,' said the first BENN 28:5
idioms: i. appropriate to another
      RYLE 187:10
  words and exhausted i. ORW 165:7
idle: I. to hope that the simple REED 179:4
idleness: i. and impotent stupidity
      BLUNT 35:5
idlers: loungers and i. of the Empire
      DOYLE 69:25
idling: impossible to enjoy i. JER 113:7
idol: i. to the north of Khatmandu
      HAYES 99:5
idolatry: organization of i. SHAW 198:10
if: And I. and Perhaps and But ELIOT 74:1
  i. I had to choose FORS 84:5
  I. it moves, salute it ANON 6:23
  I. you've seen one city AGNEW 2:21
  I. you want to get ahead ANON 6:24
  I. you were the only girl GREY 94:4
ignoble: doctrine of i. ease ROOS 184:2
ignorance: dangerous than sincere i.
      KING 122:2
  Don't die of i. ANON 6:3
  i. and failing to realise CURR 64:7
  I. is an evil weed BEV 33:9
  I. is strength ORW 164:21
  i. is the first requisite STR 210:6
  i. the greater the dogmatism
      OSLER 166:2
  inhibition caused by i. MACM 143:16
  life is i. and confidence TWAIN 220:7
  while our i. must necessarily
      POPP 172:17
  Your i. cramps my conversation
      HOPE 104:17
ignorant: know everybody is i. ROG 182:10
  where many i. men are sure DARR 64:15
ignore: happy with nothing to i.
      NASH 159:15
  Most people i. most poetry MITC 154:6
ignored: exist because they are i.
      HUXL 109:12
Ike: I like I. SPAL 205:4
ill: But, if it is i. SITW 201:17
  Government is dangerously i.
      BENN 28:15
ill-bred: i. son of a livery stable-keeper
      YEATS 235:4
illegal: like to do are either i. WOOL 231:20
  means that it is not i. NIXON 160:15
illegitimate: i. child of Karl Marx
      ATTL 12:12
illegitimi: Nil carborundum i. ANON 7:27
ill-housed: one-third of a nation i.
      ROOS 183:4
illimited: Of joy i. HARDY 97:11
illiteracy: at the i. of scientists SNOW 204:1
illness: I. is the night-side SONT 204:16

illness (*cont.*):
  part that makes i. worth while
                                          SHAW 195:22
ill-nourished: ill-clad, i.   ROOS 183:4
ills: i. of democracy can   SMITH 202:4
  marvelling sweetly on her i.   RANS 177:14
illuminated: i. trouser-clip for bicyclists
                                          MORT 156:17
illusion: He had one i.   KEYN 120:8
  The great i.   ANG 5:5
  visible universe was an i.   BORG 36:9
illusions: It's life's i. I recall MITC 154:7
  perils because of the i.   MOUN 157:3
illustrate: simplify and i. the points
                                          HOME 104:8
illustration: i. of character   JAMES 112:1
I'm: I. backing Britain   ANON 6:26
  I. in charge   FORS 84:12
  I. the greatest   ALI 3:10
image: A photograph is not only an i.
                                          SONT 204:15
  c'est l'i. de la passion   BART 20:3
  consommée dans son i.   BART 20:4
  i. if not in usage   BART 20:4
  i. of myself which I try   AUDEN 14:2
  public wants is the i.   BART 20:3
  The age demanded an i.   POUND 174:4
images: Fresh i. beget   YEATS 235:16
imaginary: Happiness is an i. condition
                                          SZASZ 211:15
imagination: Does the i. dwell the most
                                          YEATS 234:20
  functioning of the i.   HEM 100:14
  heart is nothing but his i.   SHAW 197:2
  lie in logic, not in i.   CHES 51:11
  literalists of the i.   MOORE 155:14
  no i. there is no horror   DOYLE 69:27
  save those that have no i.   SHAW 199:31
  schools for the i.   GIR 90:17
imaginative: superior to any i.
                                          VIDAL 221:13
imagine: I. there's no heaven   LENN 134:20
  young men can possibly i.   SMITH 202:22
imbecility: Moderation in war is i.
                                          FISH 80:6
imitate: composer does not i.   STR 210:16
  I i. the Saviour   HUXL 108:8
  I. him if you dare   YEATS 236:2
  Immature artists i.   TRIL 218:1
  never failed to i. them   BALD 16:20
  poets i.   ELIOT 76:8
  they usually i. each other   HOFF 103:18
imitation: i. of a semi-house-trained
                                          FOOT 82:11
immanent: I. Will that stirs   HARDY 97:14
immature: I. poets imitate   ELIOT 76:8
immaturity: expression of human i.
                                          BRIT 39:11
  that common symptom of i.
                                          WHAR 225:29
immense: Last night at twelve I felt i.
                                          ADE 2:13
immensities: All Asiatic vague i.
                                          YEATS 233:5
immoral: i., or fattening   WOOL 231:20
  people looked on it as i.   GALS 88:6
immorality: i. is what they dislike
                                          WHIT 226:10
immortal: No subject for i. verse
                                          DAY-L 65:11
immortalism: The i. must stand
                                          TREE 217:16
immortality: achieve i. through my work
                                          ALLEN 4:1

immortality (*cont.*):
  milk's leap toward i.   FAD 78:5
  that millions long for i.   ERTZ 77:21
  they gave, their i.   BROO 40:3
immortals: President of the I.   HARDY 98:1
impartial: decline utterly to be i.
                                          CHUR 54:3
impatience: i. with him occasionally
                                          SHAW 199:32
imperial: Her i. standards fly   AUDEN 14:11
imperially: Learn to think I.   CHAM 48:8
imperishable: I. peace   HOUS 106:8
impertinent: ask an i. question   BRON 39:14
importance: i. of the country   HUXL 108:10
important: Broadcasting is really too i.
                                          BENN 27:13
  i. thing in life is not   COUB 61:12
  i. things a man has   BUTL 43:10
  infinitely the most i.   DOYLE 69:2
  Money is indeed the most i.
                                          SHAW 196:29
  Personal relations are the i.   FORS 83:16
  The most i. product   FROMM 85:12
  think that the most i.   BREN 39:8
imported: The withdrawal of an i.
                                          JENK 113:2
imposing: Art is the i. of a pattern
                                          WHIT 226:11
impossibility: i. of circulation I could
                                          ASQ 11:13
im-possible: answer you in two
  words, "i."   GOLD 91:16
impossible: have eliminated the i.
                                          DOYLE 69:22
  i. he is very probably wrong   CLAR 56:10
  i. is what takes   NANS 158:19
  i. to carry the heavy burden   EDW 72:8
  I. to come, lie follows   PROU 176:5
  i. to enjoy idling thoroughly   JER 113:7
  setting oneself an i. aim   GREE 93:14
imposters: those two i. just the same
                                          KIPL 126:13
impotent: all-powerful to be i.   CHUR 54:5
  idleness and i. stupidity   BLUNT 35:5
imprecision: Decay with i.   ELIOT 74:6
  mess of i. of feeling   ELIOT 74:13
impresses: i. me most about America
                                          EDW 72:7
impression: i. that we exist   BECK 21:21
impressionable: Give me a girl at an i.
                                          SPARK 205:7
impressive: i. sights in the world
                                          BARR 19:22
imprisoned: I. in every fat man a thin
                                          CONN 59:12
improbable: occurrence of the i.
                                          MENC 151:4
  whatever remains, *however i.*
                                          DOYLE 69:22
improper: An i. mind is a perpetual feast
                                          SMITH 202:21
  i. thoughts about their neighbours
                                          BRAD 38:2
  proper or i.   FULL 87:14
impropriety: I. is the soul of wit
                                          MAUG 149:14
improved: enormously i. by death
                                          SAKI 188:3
improvement: children for signs of i.
                                          SCOT 194:4
improving: you can be certain of i.
                                          HUXL 109:15
impure: Puritan all things are i.
                                          LAWR 132:6

in: being i. and out of favour   FROST 86:14
  be i. town tonight   ANON 8:2
  I. my beginning is my end   ELIOT 74:8
  Meredith, we're i.   KITC 128:4
inability: i. to cross the street
                                          WOOLF 231:16
inaccuracy: i. sometimes saves tons
                                          SAKI 188:21
  mind lying, but I hate i.   BUTL 44:1
inactivity: Coolidge's genius for i.
                                          LIPP 137:17
inarticulate: raid on the i.   ELIOT 74:13
in-between: Don't mess with Mister I.
                                          MERC 151:7
inborn: acquisition but is i.   JUNG 117:3
inbreathed: Dust i. was a house
                                          ELIOT 74:18
incest: excepting i. and folk-dancing
                                          BAX 20:14
inch: other i. a gentleman   WEST 225:24
inches: Some thirty i. from my nose
                                          AUDEN 12:14
incident: determination of i.   JAMES 112:1
  To the curious i.   DOYLE 69:14
incite: i. this meeting to rebellion
                                          PANK 167:11
inclined: I am i. to think   DOYLE 69:29
include: Gentlemen, i. me out   GOLD 91:14
incognito: fallen angel travelling i.
                                          QUEN 176:14
incoherent: you to think I'm not i.
                                          ROSS 185:3
income: Expenditure rises to meet i.
                                          PARK 169:11
  good i. is of no avail   SMITH 202:20
  I. Tax has made more Liars   ROG 182:7
  last slice of their i.   HEAL 99:9
  organism to live beyond its i.   BUTL 43:19
incomes: beyond their i. nowadays
                                          SAKI 188:6
incommunicable: I distrust the i.
                                          SART 191:13
incomparable: steps spritely in the i. Max
                                          SHAW 200:7
incompetence: Rise to His Level of I.
                                          PETER 170:11
incompetent: i. to carry out its duties
                                          PETER 170:12
incomplete: A man in love is i. until
                                          GABOR 87:20
  i. in the urban compound   MCL 143:12
inconsistency: human rights is a little i.
                                          OWEN 166:6
incontestable: Is i. It undercuts   FRY 87:1
inconvenience: i. is only an adventure
                                          CHES 50:3
inconvenient: A cause may be i.
                                          BENN 28:14
  i. house with three   ASQ 11:13
increase: And who dies fighting has i.
                                          GREN 94:3
  dignity tends to i. in inverse
                                          HUXL 108:10
  wage i. was another man's   WILS 228:18
indebted: thing I'm i. to her   FIEL 79:13
indecency: Decency is I.'s conspiracy
                                          SHAW 198:25
indecent: sent down for i. behaviour
                                          WAUGH 222:20
indecision: nothing is habitual but i.
                                          JAMES 112:11
indefensible: largely the defence of the i.
                                          ORW 165:6

independence: that modest degree of i.
EINS 73:4
independent: end of Britain as an i.
GAIT 88:1
index: i. of a man's character CONN 59:13
India: first message of I. FORS 84:2
Indian: not sailed in I. Seas DAV 65:4
treated like an I. widow MITF 154:14
Indians: Cooper killing off the I.
BALD 16:19
that the I. are you BALD 16:19
indicative: first person, present i.
WITT 229:19
indifference: i. of the majority REST 179:14
indifferent: be i. to them SHAW 196:7
established society, and been i.
GREE 93:12
friendly. It is simply i. HOLM 104:6
i. to what is thought SOLZ 204:4
well-meaning man of i. judgement
BEAV 21:2
indignation: mists of righteous i.
MUGG 157:7
Moral i. is jealousy WELLS 225:5
Righteous i. WOOLF 231:8
Savage i. there YEATS 236:2
indignity: He has spared me the i.
BELL 24:23
indiscretion: A lover without i. is no
HARDY 96:21
between a cliché and an i. MACM 143:19
indistinct: The host with someone i.
ELIOT 75:5
individual: abolish the cult of the i.
KHR 121:2
I. beauty from AUDEN 13:7
i. reader is important NAB 158:16
that constitutes the i. JUNG 117:2
There are i. men and women THAT 213:8
individualism: rugged i. and a European
HOOV 104:12
individuality: England is the paradise of i.
SANT 190:16
realization of the innate i. JUNG 117:2
without i. have no taste BENN 28:7
indivisible: Freedom is an i. word
WILL 228:5
Peace is i. LITV 138:2
indolence: A young girl in the i.
YEATS 232:4
indolent: i. expression and an undulating
BELL 25:4
indomitable: Still the i. Irishry YEATS 233:3
indoors: 'Er i. GRIF 94:7
indubitably: They so very i. *are*, you know
BEER 22:19
indulge: I. in loud unseemly jape BELL 24:6
that I i. them privately DENN 67:3
industrial: biggest i. corporation
SHAW 195:13
i. strategy for the period BENN 27:12
it in that of a major i. SARR 190:25
labour-intensive i. WILS 228:13
regeneration of i. and enterprise
CHAR 50:1
ineffectual: Remote and i. Don BELL 26:4
inefficiency: efficiency and i. SHAW 197:5
ineligible: honourably i. for the struggle
CONN 59:1
inevitable: i. gradualness of our scheme
WEBB 223:25
In Ireland the i. never MAH 145:4

inexactitude: risk of terminological i.
CHUR 53:21
inexperienced: young and i. house
JER 113:13
inexpressible: expressing the i. is music
HUXL 109:4
inextinguishable: like it is i. NIEL 160:12
infamy: will live on in i. ROOS 183:10
infancy: stages of man are i. LINK 137:16
infant: i. mind even was bitter BARB 18:12
What's a mixed i.? BEHAN 23:24
infanticide: indefensible as i. WEST 225:25
inferior: are disgraced by the i.
SHAW 198:16
i. without your consent ROOS 182:19
infernal: fourth time that i. noise EDW 72:4
inferno: i. depicted by Dr Goebbels
ORW 164:17
i. of his passions has JUNG 116:18
i. of insipidity and decay LEWIS 136:17
moronic i. had caught BELL 26:10
infinite: i. capacity for taking HUXL 109:14
must necessarily be i. POPP 172:17
infinite-resource-and-sagacity: man of i.
KIPL 125:8
infinitive: that when I split an i. CHAN 49:4
inflections: The beauty of i. STEV 208:14
infliction: i. of cruelty with a good
RUSS 186:24
influence: acquisition of unwarranted i.
EIS 73:6
How to win friends and i. CARN 47:1
i. on human life than has MULL 157:13
i. over the minds of men KEYN 120:12
only books that i. FORS 84:8
power instead of i. TAYL 212:6
influenced: that the citizen is i. RAK 177:8
influenza: can call it i. if ye like BENN 28:4
My aunt died of i. SHAW 199:22
in-folded: tongues of flame are i.
ELIOT 74:23
inform: i. the reader but to protect ACH 1:9
informally: Quite i. COW 62:12
information: knowledge we have lost in i.
ELIOT 76:4
informed: far better i. SMITH 202:11
ingenious: i. machine for turning
DIN 67:16
inglorious: About as pointless and i.
OSB 165:19
inhale: if he doesn't i. STEV 208:18
inherit: must i. the tribulation
HOOV 104:10
inhibition: i. caused by ignorance
MACM 143:16
inhibitions: was to cultivate a few i.
LOOS 139:9
inhumanity: i. meant cruelty
FROMM 85:13
thats the essence of i. SHAW 196:7
injury: least i. you can do him
JAMES 111:17
injustice: I. anywhere is a threat
KING 121:11
i. makes democracy necessary
NIEB 160:10
That's social i. BRAC 38:1
ink: all cough in i. YEATS 234:19
do you always drink i. MILL 152:17
that the i. had not faded BARR 19:16
inmate: i. in a long term institution
DURY 71:2
inn: Do you remember an I. BELL 25:15

Innisfree: go now, and go to I. YEATS 232:9
innocence: Everyone insists on his i.
CAMUS 46:1
Never such i. LARK 131:3
The ceremony of i. is drowned
YEATS 233:12
innocent: But to hurt i. people HELL 100:8
Chacun exige d'être i. CAMUS 46:1
The i. and the beautiful YEATS 235:9
until they are proved i. ORW 165:9
We are i., as we have proclaimed
ROS 184:18
inns: And go to i. to dine CHES 50:15
From the towns all I. have BELL 25:24
I. are not residences MOORE 155:16
innuendoes: the beauty of i. STEV 208:14
inoperative: previous statements are i.
ZIEG 236:13
Inquisition: Nobody expects the Spanish I.
CHAP 49:1
teaching at the time of the I. BENN 27:11
insanity: form of congenital i.
WOOLF 231:8
inscrutable: undefeated, i. to the last
THUR 216:25
insculped: I. and embossed THOM 216:9
insect: bed into a gigantic i. KAFKA 117:9
insects: life-history of i. BARB 18:11
inside: i. the tent pissing out JOHN 114:4
insignificance: And of the utmost i.
CURZ 64:9
insignificant: i. and is aware of it
BECK 21:8
insincere: Nor was he i. in saying
MOORE 155:16
insincerity: clear language is i. ORW 165:7
i. of purpose to spend BRAM 38:13
i. possible between two BAUM 20:13
insipid: i. to a vulgar taste SMITH 202:16
insists: one who i. on knowing
POUND 173:25
insomnia: Amor vincit i. FRY 87:7
suffering from an ideal i. JOYCE 115:8
inspect: i. new stock or to visit
AUDEN 14:22
inspector: An i. calls PRIE 175:8
inspiration: Genius is one per cent i.
EDIS 72:2
inspired: that I i. the nation CHUR 56:2
instability: taken to be a mark of i.
GALB 88:2
instalment: serial form with the last i.
CRISP 63:3
instant: light gleams an i. BECK 21:24
instinct: all healthy i. BUTL 43:28
his i. told him BUTL 44:8
i. for being unhappy highly SAKI 188:4
what we believe upon i. BRAD 38:5
instincts: animal, true to your i.
LAWR 132:22
institute: I., Legion and Social BETJ 31:2
The gas was on in the I. BETJ 32:7
institution: inmate in a long term i.
DURY 71:2
i. without hitting it CRIT 63:5
transformed into an i. SART 190:27
institutions: i. that has been unaltered
CHUR 54:2
instruction: no i. book FULL 87:15
instrument: poet is a sensitive i.
MACN 144:10
public and learning the i. BUTL 43:7
The State is an i. STAL 206:18

instruments: What i. we have agree
AUDEN 12:20
insubordination: price of i. and
insurrection MACG 142:11
insuccesso: *vuole riconoscere l'i.* CIANO 56:7
insufferable: Oxford that has made me i.
BEER 22:22
insufficient: sufficient conclusions from i.
premises BUTL 43:18
insult: do not consider it an i. DARR 64:15
insurance: i. for all classes CHUR 56:1
insurrection: A revolution is an i.
MAO T 146:9
insubordination and i. MACG 142:11
success of an armed i. ZIN 236:14
integrity: i. of their quarrel CHUR 54:2
Which is a kind of i. STOP 209:17
intellect: from halitosis of the i. ICKES 110:3
hindrance to subtlety of i. MORL 156:2
i. of man is forced YEATS 235:18
Monuments of unageing i. YEATS 234:5
revenge of the i. upon art SONT 204:12
intellectual: An i. hatred is the worst
YEATS 233:14
i. and artistic personality BERL 30:4
i. curiosity is the life-blood TREV 217:20
I. disgrace AUDEN 13:3
i. is someone whose mind CAMUS 45:18
i. life of the whole SNOW 203:27
'I.' suggests straight away AUDEN 14:20
wanted to become an i. SCHW 193:12
intellectuals: characterize themselves as i.
AGNEW 2:22
intellectuel: *I. = celui qui se dédouble*
CAMUS 45:18
intelligence: I. is quickness to apprehend
WHIT 226:9
i. is the ability to hold FITZ 80:16
science of arresting human i. LEAC 133:6
underestimating the i. MENC 150:15
intelligent: As i. Mr Toad GRAH 93:1
cannot be both honest and i.
ORW 164:27
i. are to the intelligentsia BALD 17:13
i. readers soon discover BALL 17:22
Most i., very elegant BUCK 42:3
So i. ELIOT 76:21
intelligently: able to fill leisure i.
RUSS 186:16
intelligentsia: i. and the cultured classes
BERD 29:10
i. what a gentleman BALD 17:13
intend: Some day I i. reading MARX 147:17
intense: i. enjoyment from a contrast
FREUD 85:7
intensity: Are full of passionate i.
YEATS 233:12
intensiv: *Kontrast i. geniessen* FREUD 85:7
intention: i. to overthrow the Government
HARD 96:15
intentions: if he'd only had good i.
THAT 213:6
interdit: *qui i. au riche comme* FRAN 84:15
interest: common i. is that of cutting
ATK 12:4
not entirely devoid of i. DOYLE 69:3
secured a controlling i. WELLS 224:12
interested: i. in art and I am only
SHAW 196:25
wasn't particularly i. BENC 26:17
whatever he is most i. in BARR 19:18
you're i. in the arts AYCK 15:20

interesting: Experience isn't i. till
BOWEN 37:4
have anything i. to say CAP 46:14
i. thing about any story STOP 209:14
something more i. than women
WALL 222:4
that a proposition be i. WHIT 226:7
that it be i. JAMES 111:25
To see that I. Play BELL 24:15
Very i. . . . but stupid ROWAN 185:12
interests: character in the i. of Hell
FORS 83:10
interfere: i. by violence with ours
JAMES 112:13
intérieure: *Politique i., je fais la* CLEM 56:17
interior: poet believes to be i. QUAS 176:13
interlude: present is an i. O'NEI 163:15
interludes: dark i. in the electrical
O'NEI 163:16
internal: I. AFFAIRS remains SOLZ 204:4
i. combustion engine BEVAN 32:15
international: dependable i. emotion
ALSOP 4:10
interpretation: also what is lost in i.
FROST 86:17
I. is the revenge SONT 204:12
I. makes art manageable SONT 204:13
interpreter: i. can do no more BEEC 22:7
interprets: lawyer i. the truth GIR 90:17
interrogate: can i. as well as observe
OSLER 165:21
interstellar: The vacant i. spaces
ELIOT 74:11
interval: death save to enjoy the i.
SANT 190:17
interviewing: BBC for i. a faded female
HARD 96:16
i. people who can't talk ZAPPA 236:11
intimacy: gay i. of the slums WAUGH 223:5
you should avoid any i. KITC 128:5
intimate: i. when he is rich or famous
BIER 33:19
tribal, i. revenge HEAN 99:12
intolerable: crises that seemed i. ATK 12:3
Curing the i. neutral itch AUDEN 15:2
still with the i. wrestle ELIOT 74:9
intolerance: I. itself is a form of egoism
SANT 190:20
intractable: sullen, untamed and i.
ELIOT 74:7
introduced: And when I'm i. to one
RAL 177:11
introduction: I could buy back my i.
PER 170:4
introibo: *I. ad altare Dei* JOYCE 116:1
invasion: *l'i. promise de longue* CHUR 55:5
long-promised i. CHUR 55:5
invent: inalienable right to i. GREER 93:21
To remember or i. FROST 86:1
invented: i. for the sole purpose
CUPPY 64:5
No animal ever i. anything CHES 50:4
Truth exists; only lies are i. BRAQ 38:17
invention: great and blessed i.
SHAW 195:21
Marriage is a wonderful i. CONN 58:13
invents: arts of life man i. SHAW 197:31
inverse: agenda will be in i. PARK 169:13
increase in i. ratio to the importance
HUXL 108:10
inversion: But will his negative i.
AUDEN 15:2
inverted: i. Victorianism FORS 83:10

investigator: self-importance of the i.
RUTH 187:8
investment: i. for any community
CHUR 53:14
invisible: man who has no i. means
BUCH 41:20
O world i., we view thee THOM 216:10
priest of the i. STEV 208:17
what is essential is i. SAIN 187:19
invitations: i. and don't invite us
KHR 121:7
Receipted bills and i. AUDEN 14:22
involuntary: It was i. They sank my boat
KENN 119:9
involved: not be i. in a European BEAV 21:3
inwardness: full i. of the situation
JAMES 112:10
Iowa: I. mistake each other ALLEN 3:12
Ireland: For the great Gaels of I. CHES 50:9
I. has her madness AUDEN 13:1
I. hurt you into poetry AUDEN 13:1
I. is the old sow that eats JOYCE 115:18
I. the inevitable never happens
◄ MAH 145:4
Out of I. have we come YEATS 236:3
Romantic I.'s dead and YEATS 234:15
was general all over I. JOYCE 115:6
what I have got for I. COLL 58:6
words 'I.' and 'island' BOWEN 37:15
Irish: Across the I. Sea MILL 152:16
guess the answer to the I. Question
SELL 194:17
I. poets, learn your trade YEATS 233:2
Let the I. vessel lie AUDEN 13:2
symbol of I. art JOYCE 116:3
We I., born into that ancient
YEATS 233:6
When I. eyes are smiling OLC 163:3
Irishman: I.'s heart is nothing SHAW 197:2
Irishry: Still the indomitable I. YEATS 233:3
iron: Adriatic an i. curtain CHUR 53:15
Any old i., an old iron COLL 58:6
Barumph has a whim of i. HERF 101:28
I. Lady of the Western THAT 212:21
ruled them with a rod of i. RATT 177:17
The i. lady ANON 6:28
ironies: Life's little i. HARDY 97:4
irony: most perfect humour and i.
BUTL 43:15
irrational: i. is rational STEV 208:16
irregulars: Baker Street i. DOYLE 69:24
irresistibly: Empire are i. drained
DOYLE 69:25
irresolute: resolved to be i. CHUR 54:5
is: I. Paris burning HITL 103:7
I. your journey *really* necessary
ANON 7:1
island: i. is made mainly of coal
BEVAN 32:17
i. or a large part of it CHUR 54:10
'i.' to be synonymous BOWEN 37:15
Look, stranger, at this i. AUDEN 14:12
The i., the veranda AUDEN 14:18
this i. or lose the war CHUR 54:11
islands: their favourite i. AUDEN 14:16
isles: stars and i. where good FLEC 81:6
isolation: i. and the busy griefs
AUDEN 13:1
robbed of the i. FORS 83:17
issue: Fat is a feminist i. ORB 163:18
It *is* a moral i. HALEY 95:9
make an i. of my womanhood
BRAC 37:23

it: I. *is* a moral issue   HALEY 95:9
It's just I. Some women'll   KIPL 127:16
Italian: I. for the clearer understanding
                                          WHAR 225:27
Italy: I. for thirty years under WELL 224:11
I. from designs by Michael Angelo
                                          TWAIN 219:20
I. has been losing wars   HELL 100:6
traveller who has gone to I.   FORS 84:4
itch: intolerable neutral i.   AUDEN 15:2
it's: I. for you-hoo   ANON 7:3
I. that man again   ANON 7:4
itself: Ecstasy and Forever be I. GINS 90:14
i. and not in its subject   SANT 190:14
itsy: I. bitsy teenie weenie   VANCE 221:2
ivory: downstairs from their I. Towers
                                          SMITH 203:6
Ivy: Ee, it was agony, I.   RAY 178:6

J

jabbed: me as you j. and killed
                                          OWEN 166:18
Jack: Damn you, J.   BONE 36:1
jacket: short j. is always worn   EDW 72:5
jack-knife: Just a j. has Macbeath, dear
                                          BREC 38:21
Jacob: traffic of J.'s ladder   THOM 216:11
jail: Go to j. Go directly   DARR 64:13
stealin' dey gits you in j.   O'NEI 163:7
jails: There are not enough j.   HUMP 108:4
jake: j. then you're frightened   DONL 68:6
jalousie: *que le rire pour la j.* SAGAN 187:17
jamais: j. triste archy jamais triste
                                          MARQ 147:4
James: [Henry J.'s] novel   WELLS 224:13
Home J., and don't spare   HILL 102:15
J. I, James II   GUED 94:12
J. James   MILNE 153:7
Poor Henry [J.], he's spending
                                          MAUG 149:7
Jane: Aunt J. observed, the second
                                          GRAH 92:11
good-night to Lady J.   LAWR 132:9
J., Jane   SITW 201:10
Me Tarzan, you J.   WEIS 224:5
janitor: j. to the looney-bin   WOD 230:14
Japan: forces of the Empire of J.
                                          ROOS 183:10
Japanese: J. action with prudence
                                          CHUR 53:12
The J. don't care   COW 62:4
jape: Indulge in loud unseemly j. BELL 24:6
japonica: J. Glistens like coral   REED 178:19
jargon: language, we have j.   BENT 29:9
j'attaque: *situation excellente, j.* FOCH 82:6
jaw-jaw: j. is always better   CHUR 55:12
jealous: Not over-j.   PHIL 171:2
jealousy: indignation is j. with a halo
                                          WELLS 225:5
J. is no more than feeling   BOWEN 37:14
j. to the bride and good   BARR 19:11
To j., nothing is more   SAGAN 187:17
jeans: wears dirty j.   BRAT 38:18
Jeeves: J. shimmered out and came
                                          WOD 230:6
Jefferies: I prefer Richard J. to Swedenborg
                                          BARB 18:10
Jefferson: when Thomas J. ate alone
                                          KENN 119:5

Jellicoe: J. was the only man on either
                                          CHUR 56:6
jelly: She shivers like the j.   PIRON 171:17
jellybeans: by his way of eating j.
                                          REAG 178:12
Jesus: J. came to Birmingham   STUD 210:20
J. for what was done   BENN 27:11
J. is there only for others   BONH 36:3
J. loves you more   SIMON 201:4
J. wants me for a sunbeam   TALB 212:3
Jolson is greater than J.   FITZ 80:24
more popular than J. now   LENN 135:2
teachings of J.   BENN 27:10
jeunes filles: *les j. et comme les roses*
                                          DE G 65:17
Jew: declare that I am a J.   EINS 73:1
I'm not really a J.   MILL 152:11
jewel: me in 'J. in the Crown'   ASHC 10:14
The j. in the crown   SCOTT 193:17
jewellery: Don't ever wear artistic j.
                                          COL 57:17
you'll just rattle your j.   LENN 135:1
jewels: j. make women either incredibly
                                          BARR 19:17
Jewish: A J. God   BROW 41:13
J. man with parents alive   ROTH 185:10
national home for the J.   BALF 17:16
Jew-*ish*: really a *Jew*. Just J. MILL 152:11
Jews: But spurn the J.   BROW 41:13
England and America are J.
                                          MAUG 149:12
Hitler attacked the J.   NIEM 160:13
J. except they don't know   MAL 145:13
J. in any other country   BALF 17:16
To choose The J.   EWER 78:4
jigsaw: just a piece in a j.   MANK 146:1
Jim: fence leaps Sunny J.   HANFF 96:9
I'm worried about J.   ANON 6:27
jine: can't lick 'em, j. 'em   REYN 180:1
jingle: hear the harness j.   HOUS 106:17
job: came fifth and lost the j.   JOYCE 116:9
Gizza j..... I can do that   BLEA 34:24
here, so blow your j.   HART 98:19
he's doing a grand j.   FROST 85:15
husband is a whole-time j.   BENN 28:16
it is a whole-time j.   MAUG 149:5
neighbour loses his j.   TRUM 218:10
we will finish the j.   CHUR 53:9
John: from Land's End to J. of Gaunt
                                          SPOO 206:8
J. had   MILNE 153:6
Spiritually I was at Eton, J.   BETJ 32:12
Johnny: And now ... heeeeere's J.
                                          MCM 143:14
Johnny-head-in-air: For J.   PUDN 176:9
Johnson: J.'s aesthetic judgements
                                          STR 210:5
joie: *j. venait toujours après*   APOL 9:22
joined: Close j. is far away   GRAV 93:10
joint: minute you walked in the j. FIEL 79:6
joints: gin j. in all the towns   EPST 77:17
tough j. more than somewhat
                                          RUNY 186:1
joke: every j. is ultimately   ORW 164:14
It's our only j.   BARR 19:25
Its the funniest j.   SHAW 197:3
j. with a double meaning   BARK 18:14
subtleties of the American j.
                                          TWAIN 219:21
jokes: A civil servant doesn't make j.
                                          ION 110:20
I don't make j.—I just   ROG 182:14
my little j. on Thee   FROST 86:3

jokes (*cont.*):
no more j. in Music-halls   SASS 192:2
joking: j. is to tell the truth   SHAW 197:3
jolly: should be j. at my funeral
                                          MOUN 157:2
Three j. Farmers   DE L 66:16
Three j. gentlemen   DE L 66:14
Jolson: J. is greater than Jesus   FITZ 80:24
Jolyon: [J.] was afflicted by the thought
                                          GALS 88:9
Jones: saying 'Lord J. Dead'   CHES 52:14
jonquils: land-locked pools of j. BETJ 32:5
Joseph: Someone must have traduced J.
                                          KAFKA 117:6
Josephine: Not tonight, J.   DAVID 64:18
joss-sticks: j. and honourable
high-mindedness   BRAM 38:15
journalism: but why j.   BALF 17:17
from Christianity and j.   BALF 17:17
J.—an ability to meet   WEST 225:23
j. are ratlike cunning   TOM 217:10
j. is people who can't   ZAPPA 236:11
J. largely consists in saying   CHES 52:14
j. what will be read once   CONN 58:14
journalist: British j.   WOLFE 230:24
journalists: J. say a thing that they
                                          BENN 28:17
journey: A long day's j. into night
                                          O'NEI 163:11
For a j., and such a long   ELIOT 73:14
I prepare for a j.   MANS 146:6
Is your j. *really* necessary   ANON 7:1
j. seem like to those   BARN 18:17
long j. towards oblivion   LAWR 132:10
On a j. North   COW 62:12
Up, lad: when the j.'s over   HOUS 106:10
journeying: third-class seat sat the j. boy
                                          HARDY 97:8
jours: *Les j. s'en vont, je demeure* APOL 9:22
joy: But j. is wisdom, Time   YEATS 232:18
I know of no j.   FIRB 80:4
J. always comes after pain   APOL 9:22
j. from girl and boy   AUDEN 14:2
j. of the working   KIPL 127:11
j. that the day has brought   BOND 35:19
must not express great j.   FORS 83:3
Of j. illimited   HARDY 97:11
politics of j.   HUMP 108:4
Strength through j.   LEY 137:6
Joyce: clumsy *olla putrida* James J.
                                          LAWR 132:5
go for a Proust or a J.   COBB 57:1
joyicity: hoppy on akkant of his j.
                                          JOYCE 115:14
Judas: called in London 'genial J.'
                                          HAIG 95:2
In the lost boyhood of J.   AE 2:18
Whether J. Iscariot   DYLAN 71:15
judge: Here comes the j.   MARK 146:16
I could have been a j.   COOK 60:10
j. of a man by his foes   CONR 59:25
j. this movement kindly   READ 178:9
j. you don't have to know   LUML 140:15
judgement: at God's great J. Seat
                                          KIPL 123:17
England shall bide till J. Tide   KIPL 126:4
It biases the j.   DOYLE 69:26
j. of our scientific age   HOLM 104:6
nation is fit to sit in j.   WILS 229:10
judgements: Johnson's aesthetic j.
                                          STR 210:5
judges: j. have declared it   QUIL 177:2
She threw me in front of the J.
                                          BETJ 31:10

judging: had the Latin for the j.
COOK 60:10
Judy: actually did say was 'J.'   CAGN 44:14
jug: 'J. Jug' to dirty ears   ELIOT 76:19
jugement: *N'attendez pas le j. dernier*
CAMUS 46:3
Juin: *sans nuage et J. poignardé*   ARAG 10:2
Julia: missed the point completely, J.
ELIOT 73:19
Julian: J. and this is my friend, Sandy
TOOK 217:11
Julias: Now the J., Maeves and Maureens
BETJ 32:6
July: Born on the fourth of J.   COHAN 57:13
January, June, or J.   NORW 161:13
Next J. we collide with Mars   PORT 173:7
jump: what Trojan 'orses will j.
BEVIN 33:12
jumps: fox j. over the lazy dog   ANON 8:5
June: I like *New York* in J.   FREED 85:1
J. is bustin' out all over   HAMM 95:15
May without cloud and J.   ARAG 10:2
Unwontedly. It was late J.   THOM 214:15
jungle: not a concrete j.   MORR 156:4
primitive in a giant j.   MAIL 145:8
this is the Law of the J.   KIPL 126:20
junior: Cambridge or j. television
producers   AMIS 4:16
juniper-tree: leopards sat under a j.
ELIOT 73:18
junk: Ep's statues are j.   ANON 6:22
just: J. a wee deoch-an-doris   MORR 156:8
j. going outside and may   MAHON 145:6
j. going outside and may   OATES 162:3
J. like that!   COOP 60:19
j. one of those things   PORT 173:2
J. when you thought it was   ANON 7:7
J. you wait   HART 98:19
rather be British than j.   PAIS 167:5
The scrupulous and the j.   CONR 60:2
justice: j. and the American way   ANON 6:8
j. is open to all   MATH 149:1
j. makes democracy possible   NIEB 160:10
j. should not only be done   HEW 102:5
'J.' was done   HARDY 98:1
or j. or human happiness   BERL 30:6
price of j. is eternal   BENN 28:13
pursuit of j. is no virtue   GOLD 91:12
threat to j. everywhere   KING 121:11
justification: art should carry its j.
CONR 59:26
justify: The end cannot j. the means
HUXL 108:15
To j. God's ways to man   HOUS 107:8
justifying: j. his position at whatever
AMERY 4:14

K

Kaiser: put the kibosh on the K.   ELL 77:10
Kansas: horses o' K. think   KIPL 124:6
Karajan: [Herbert von K. is]   BEEC 22:4
Kate: And some, alas, with K.   AUDEN 14:6
Kathaleen: K. Ní Houlihan, your road's
CARB 46:18
Katy: K-K-K-Katy, beautiful K.
O'HARA 162:24
Keats: *Prancing Nigger*, Blunden, K.
BETJ 32:11
keep: But k. your fancy free   HOUS 106:12
diary and some day it'll k.   WEST 225:11

keep *(cont.)*:
He may k. that will and can
HOUS 105:17
k. 'em down on the farm   LEWIS 136:19
k. fat souls from sleep   MCL 143:7
K. on truckin'   CRUMB 63:12
K. right on to the end   LAUD 131:7
K. that schoolgirl complexion
PEAR 169:18
K. the aspidistra flying   ORW 164:16
K. the Home-fires burning   FORD 82:20
K. violence in the mind   ALD 3:5
K. ye the law   KIPL 127:1
k. your head when all about   KIPL 126:13
To k. your head   PUDN 174:9
ware that will not k.   HOUS 106:10
worth while to k. them   SHAW 198:17
keeping: art of k.   MARQ 146:19
I am so sorry for k. you   GEOR 89:10
merely the art of k.   RICH 180:18
usefully in k. feelings at bay   BROO 41:2
keeps: And gave it us for k.   AYRES 16:8
cheerful as k. me going   KAV 118:15
He just k. rollin'   HAMM 96:1
Kelly: K. from the Isle of Man   MURP 158:2
Kempis: Oscar Wilde to Thomas à K.
BARB 18:10
Kensal Green: Paradise by way of K.
CHES 50:23
kept: must be k. in their place
AWDRY 15:18
'That I k. my word,' he said   DE L 66:9
Kerouac: can write, not even Mr K.
CAP 46:14
kettle: pretty k. of fish   MARY 147:20
Kew: down to K. in lilac-time
NOYES 161:15
key: k. is Russian national   CHUR 55:4
looking for the k.   BENN 27:18
out of k. with his time   POUND 174:2
keys: And all her shining k.   HARDY 97:5
half that's got my k.   GRAH 92:14
kharki: gentleman in K. ordered South
KIPL 122:18
Khatmandu: idol to the north of K.
HAYES 99:5
kibosh: put the k. on the Kaiser   ELL 77:10
kick: k. a hole in a stained   CHAN 49:3
k. around any more   NIXON 160:17
Kiss 'em one day and k.   KIPL 125:19
That I get a k. out of you   PORT 172:21
kicking: k. his something something
CHUR 53:19
kissing and k. people   TRUM 218:11
kid: Here's looking at you, k.   EPST 77:19
kiddies: k. have crumpled the serviettes
BETJ 31:11
kidnapped: k. and they snap into action
ALLEN 3:26
kidneys: k. which gave to his palate
JOYCE 116:8
kids: And don't have any k. yourself
LARK 130:13
k. playing some game   SAL 189:4
many k. have you killed   ANON 7:11
kill: get out and k. something   LEAC 133:11
K. a man, and you   ROST 185:8
K. millions of men   ROST 185:8
k. more women and children   BALD 17:7
k. shall be thy kill   KIPL 125:4
MEN ARE PREPARED TO K.   SHAW 197:15
Otherwise he.   MACN 144:18
sin to k. a mockingbird   LEE 134:1
that can k. the Movies   ROG 182:5

kill *(cont.)*:
they k. you in a new way   ROG 182:11
To k. a human being   JAMES 111:17
killed: Beauty k. the Beast   CREE 62:17
Has k. lots of men   MOYN 157:4
how many kids have you k.   ANON 7:11
I am the enemy you k.   OWEN 166:18
me as you jabbed and k.   OWEN 166:18
The effort very nearly k. her   BELL 24:14
who k. him   BELL 25:22
killer: For here the lover and k.
DOUG 68:11
killing: In reality, k. time   SITW 201:18
killings: mass k. of peoples   ROOS 183:11
kills: Into my heart an air that k.
HOUS 107:4
With a grip that k. it   TAG 212:2
kilometres: Peeling off the k.   CONN 59:15
kimonos: Two girls in silk k.   YEATS 235:8
kin: k. to the snare drummer   FREB 84:19
kind: been very k. to me here   CAV 48:3
encounters of the third k.   SPIE 206:3
For people will always be k.   SASS 191:18
Human k.   ELIOT 74:4
k. of a people do they   CHUR 53:12
Too kind, too k.   NIGH 160:14
kindle: existence is to k. a light
JUNG 116:19
kindliness: cool k. of sheets   BROO 39:19
kindly: K. Call Me God   SAMP 189:7
Sally is gone that was so k.   BELL 25:14
kindness: depended on the k. of strangers
WILL 227:21
with the milk of human k.   GUED 94:11
king: chance to sit down unless you're
a k.   HULL 108:3
duty as K. and Emperor   EDW 72:8
fight for its K. and Country   GRAH 92:9
K. and Country need you   FIELD 79:5
k. and government and nation
KAV 118:6
K. and your Country both   RUB 185:20
K. [George V] told me   ASQ 11:16
K. John was not a good man
MILNE 153:3
K.'s Cross   FARJ 78:8
K.'s life is moving peacefully   DAWS 65:6
K.'s Moll Reno'd in Wolsey's   ANON 7:9
lad that's born to be k.   BOUL 37:3
Like a k. in exile   LAWR 131:17
mile of kingdom, I am k.   KAV 118:6
Mrs Simpson's pinched our k.   ANON 6:18
much a k. as a Monarch   SELL 194:14
Northcliffe has sent for the K.   ANON 6:19
One-Eyed Man is K.   WELLS 224:16
self-dedication of the K. himself
BLUNT 35:4
The Chief Defect of Henry K.   BELL 24:11
The K. asked   MILNE 153:9
The man who would be k.   KIPL 125:21
The once and future k.   WHITE 226:5
kingdom: A road, a mile of k., I am king
KAV 118:6
k. of the well   SONT 204:16
k. where nobody dies   MILL 152:2
kingdoms: our places, these K.   ELIOT 73:15
kings: All k. is mostly rapscallions
TWAIN 219:1
godly k. had built her   FLEC 81:17
The captains and the k. depart
KIPL 126:9
there will be only five K.   FAR 78:9
These five k. did a king   THOM 214:4
walk with K.   KIPL 126:15

kinkering: K. Kongs their tykles
       SPOO 206:6
Kinnock: first K. in a thousand
 generations   KINN 122:16
Kipling: sort of gutless K. ORW 165:4
kiss: cut ribbons and k. babies MICH 151:13
 I want him to k. my ass JOHN 114:3
 Just k. yourself goodbye JER 113:18
 K. 'em one day and kick KIPL 125:19
 k. is still a kiss   HUPF 108:7
 k. of death   SMITH 202:3
 Leans to the sun's k. glorying GREN 94:3
 rough male k.   BROO 39:19
 thank you, k. you RUB 185:20
 The k. of the sun for pardon GURN 94:17
 When women k. it always MENC 150:16
 will be wanting to k. me MACD 142:2
 words 'K. Kiss Bang Bang' KAEL 117:4
kissed: Hasn't been k. for forty years
       ANON 7:20
 k. by a man who didn't wax KIPL 127:14
 k. his sad Andromache goodbye
       CORN 61:9
 k. the lovely grass BROO 39:18
 wasn't looking and never k. THOM 214:9
kisses: A fine romance with no k. FIEL 79:7
 k. on an 'eathen idol's KIPL 123:14
kissing: I wasn't k. her, I was
       MARX 147:16
 I wonder who's k. her now ADAMS 1:16
 k. and kicking people TRUM 218:11
Kissinger: Power, he [K.] has observed
       KISS 128:3
kit-bag: troubles in your old k. KISS 128:3
kitchen: get out of the k. TRUM 218:8
 get out of the k. VAUG 221:7
 servant girls in the k. SYNGE 211:10
 They send me to eat in the k.
       HUGH 108:1
Kitchener: K. is a great poster ASQ 11:6
kith: If one's own kin and k. NASH 159:16
kitten: dead k., an egg-shell WELLS 224:13
 The trouble with a k. NASH 159:1
kleinsten: k. Zimmer in meinem Hause
       REGER 179:8
knack: k. of so arranging FRIS 85:10
knee: And smitten me to my k.
       THOM 215:13
 Picture you upon my k. CAES 44:12
knees: than to live on your k. IBAR 109:17
 work is done upon his k. KIPL 125:2
knew: all k. you had it in you PARK 169:1
 blessed Hope, whereof he k.
       HARDY 97:11
 k. practically everything BENC 26:17
 k. that the lower classes CURZ 64:11
knife: If peas were eaten with the k.
       RAL 177:10
 progress if a cannibal uses k. LEC 133:23
 wind's like a whetted k. MAS 148:18
Kniff: als K., die Welt so einzurichten
       FRIS 85:10
knight: An earl and a k. of the garter
       ATTL 12:6
knit: The stuff of life to k. me HOUS 107:2
knits: Nothing k. man to man SICK 200:15
knitter: beautiful little k. SITW 201:13
knives: Night of the Long K. HITL 103:3
knock: Don't k. masturbation ALLEN 4:5
knocked: It is what they k. down
       FENT 79:1
 K. down a doctor SIMP 201:7
 we k. the bastard off HILL 102:14

knocking: K. on the moonlit door
       DE L 66:8
 k. the American system CAP 46:12
knot: Into the crowned k. of fire
       ELIOT 74:23
 So the k. be unknotted ELIOT 74:16
 teeth a political k. BIER 33:26
know: because I wish to k. ASTOR 11:21
 Eh? K. what I mean CHAP 49:12
 enough to k. everything BARR 18:22
 He must k. sumpin' HAMM 96:1
 How do they k.   PARK 169:2
 How do you k. you're . . . God
       BARN 18:21
 I do not believe. . . . I k. JUNG 116:21
 I Don't K. is on third ABB 1:1
 I don't k. where I'm going SAND 189:18
 I k. nothing whatever DOYLE 69:17
 I k. two things about the horse
       ROYD 185:19
 I k. what I like   BEER 23:14
 I k. what I like   JAMES 112:3
 I k. why the caged bird sings ANG 5:6
 I think I k. enough of hate FROST 86:6
 K. all that there is GRAH 93:1
 k. anything about music BEER 23:14
 k. ask questions of those RAL 177:9
 k. a woman until you have LEV 136:8
 k. better than anybody AGATE 2:20
 k. I know you know I know GUNN 94:16
 k. is what I read ROG 182:9
 k. less and understand more STEP 208:5
 k. more than you think SPOCK 206:4
 k. such a frightful lot CHES 51:8
 k. that summer sang MILL 151:20
 k. the man their neighbour
       YEATS 234:19
 k. the place for the first time ELIOT 74:20
 k. what is right   JOHN 114:15
 k. what I think till WALL 222:8
 k. what they have said CHUR 54:1
 k. what we are talking RUSS 186:20
 not k. much about gods ELIOT 74:7
 Not many people k. CAINE 44:18
 She knows, you k. BAKER 16:13
 The kind old sun will k. OWEN 166:11
 they k. enough who know ADAMS 2:5
 they merely k. more SAKI 188:22
 things they didn't k. POUND 173:28
 wanted to k. about sex REUB 179:15
 We Americans k., although JOHN 114:12
 Where I am, I don't k. BECK 21:14
 Whitehall really does k. JAY 112:19
 You k. my methods. Apply them
       DOYLE 69:23
 you k. you should be glad LENN 135:10
knowing: Bewrapt past k. to what
       HARDY 97:8
 For lust of k. what should FLEC 81:9
 one who INSISTS on k. POUND 173:25
knowingly: He asked him k. . . . . nudge
       CHAP 49:12
 never k. undersold LEWIS 136:16
knowledge: After such k., what
 forgiveness   ELIOT 73:12
 k. we have lost in information
       ELIOT 76:4
 our k. can only be finite POPP 172:17
 Pedantry is the dotage of k. JACK 111:4
 search for k.   RUSS 186:7
 wisdom we have lost in k. ELIOT 76:4
known: k. for his well-knownness
       BOOR 36:5

known (cont.):
 more than they have k. BROO 40:9
 safer than a k. way HASK 99:3
knows: He k. death to the bone
       YEATS 235:11
 He k. nothing   SHAW 197:14
 k. an undesirable character FRY 87:9
 k. not whither nor why MAS 148:20
 man who k. the way TYNAN 220:10
 She k., you know BAKER 16:13
 sits in the middle and k. FROST 86:23
 specialist as one who 'k. MAYO 150:8
 that has a mind and k. it SHAW 195:11
 What one k. is, in youth ADAMS 2:5
 you k. of a better 'ole BAIR 16:12
Knox: Shall see John K. in Paradise
       PARK 168:16
kongs: guise of 'Kinkering K.' SPOO 206:6
Kontrast: wir nur den K. intensiv
       FREUD 85:7
Krieg: Kommt der K. ins Land PONS 172:12
kritik: Ich habe Ihre K. vor mir REGER 179:8
 wenig erreichbar als mit K. RILKE 181:2
Kruger: killing K. with your mouth
       KIPL 122:18
Ku: K. Klux Klanner KING 121:12
kultur: Wenn ich K. höre JOHST 114:19
Kurtz: Mistah K.— he dead CONR 59:23

L

laboratory: guinea pigs in the l. of God
       WILL 227:14
labour: be the Gromyko of the L. Party
       HEAL 99:8
 Don't let L. ruin it ANON 7:17
 election programme of the L. Party
       SNOW 204:3
 interests of capital and l. ATK 12:4
 L. isn't working ANON 7:10
 L. Party is a desiccated BEVAN 32:15
 L. Party owes more to Methodism
       PHIL 171:1
 much of a l. to write HUXL 109:6
 programme of the L. party HAIL 95:5
 Shares for All, is L.'s Call JAY 112:18
 [the L. Party] is a moral crusade
       WILS 228:15
 The 'loony L. left' HEW 102:6
 [the poor] have to l. FRAN 84:15
labour-intensive: The Monarchy is a l.
 industry   WILS 228:13
labyrinth: From a great l. YEATS 234:20
labyrinthine: I fled Him, down the l. ways
       THOM 215:5
lace: Arsenic and old l. KESS 120:6
lacerate: Cannot l. his breast YEATS 236:2
lack: best l. all conviction YEATS 233:12
 l. of ability to suspend HEM 100:14
lacks: what it l. in length FROST 86:20
lacy: glove as a l. sleeve WOOL 231:9
lad: A grand little l. was young
       EDGAR 71:20
 And I myself a sterling l. HOUS 107:9
 And many a lightfoot l. HOUS 107:7
 Carry the l. that's born BOUL 37:3
 great pleasure with a l. YEATS 235:12
 lively l. most pleasured me YEATS 235:12
ladder: Now that my l.'s gone YEATS 233:8
 plasterer on his l. HEAN 99:11
laden: With rue my heart is l. HOUS 107:7
ladies: I am parshial to l. ASHF 10:16

law (cont.):
 l. is the most powerful — GIR 90:17
 L. of the Jungle — KIPL 126:20
 l. of the Yukon — SERV 194:22
 lesser breeds without the L. — KIPL 126:11
 majestic equality of the l. — FRAN 84:15
 Nor l., nor duty bade me — YEATS 235:5
 people not defied the l. — SCAR 192:15
 The Common L. of England — HERB 101:23
 till the fear of the L. — JOYCE 115:12
 write it in the books of l. — JOHN 114:8
Law Courts: Another is 'the beautiful L.'
 — RUSS 187:7
lawful: l. for a Catholic woman
 — MENC 150:23
lawn: Out on the l. I lie in bed
 — AUDEN 14:10
Lawrence: L. tried to portray this
 — ROB 181:16
 L. was right when he had — GIBB 90:2
laws: island are the l. of nature
 — SHAW 195:26
 L. for themselves and not — HOUS 105:17
 l. made or the authorizations
 — JOHN 113:21
 l. of God will be suspended — SHAW 196:28
 their l., and their codes — FREN 85:4
 The l. of God, the laws of man
 — HOUS 105:17
lawyer: A l.'s dream of heaven — BUTL 43:9
 freely as a l. interprets — GIR 90:17
 l. with his briefcase can — PUZO 176:11
 When a l. cashes in — SAND 190:3
lay: And l. one more bloody egg
 — AYRES 16:7
 I l. down my burden — EDW 72:8
 l. down his friends — THOR 216:14
 l. down his wife — JOYCE 116:12
 L. your sleeping head, my love
 — AUDEN 13:7
layer: l. I call the collective — JUNG 117:3
 less superficial l. — JUNG 117:3
lays: constructing tribal l. — KIPL 123:2
 hand that l. the golden — GOLD 91:17
 l. out food in tins — ELIOT 76:24
Lazarus: Come forth, L. — JOYCE 116:9
lazy: jumps over the l. dog — ANON 8:5
 L. and silly — SITW 201:14
LBJ: All the way with L. — ANON 5:10
 L., how many kids have — ANON 7:11
lead: couldn't see who was in the l.
 — SNAG 203:25
 Go down like lumps of l. — HODG 103:12
 L. me from death to life — KUMAR 129:6
 l. you all in the dance — CART 47:7
 You can l. a horticulture — PARK 169:6
leaden: Because if I use l. ones — BELL 24:8
 With l. age o'ercargoed — FLEC 81:19
leader: A fanatic is a great l. — BROUN 41:5
 A political l. must keep looking — BAR 20:8
 I'll be l., you can march — CAST 47:11
 l. for the Labour Party — BEVAN 32:15
 One realm, one people, one l. — ANON 6:4
 Our beloved l., Bapu — NEHRU 160:1
 Take me to your l. — ANON 8:15
 The final test of a l. — LIPP 137:18
leaders: Don't follow l. — DYLAN 71:13
 l. of a revolution — CONR 60:2
leaf: does a wise man hide a l. — CHES 51:5
 He can watch a grass or l. — GRAV 93:6
lean: L. on a garden urn — ELIOT 76:2
 l. over too far backward — THUR 217:1
 l. to wild extremes I could — DURY 71:2
leaning: l. on a lamp-post — GAY 88:18

leaning (cont.):
 L. together — ELIOT 75:10
leap: creep again, l. again — DE L 66:19
 milk's l. toward immortality — FAD 78:5
 one giant l. for mankind — ARMS 10:10
leaping: And l. from place to place
 — HARDY 97:7
 By brooks too broad for l. — HOUS 107:7
 l. light for your delight — AUDEN 14:12
 swimmers into cleanness l. — BROO 40:1
leaps: It moves in mighty l. — AYRES 16:8
 o'er the fence l. Sunny Jim — HANFF 96:9
leapt: l. straight past the common cold
 — AYRES 16:8
learn: Churches must l. humility
 — SHAW 199:26
 Irish poets, l. your trade — YEATS 233:2
 l. a lot from their children — SPARK 205:5
 l. by going where I have — ROET 182:4
 L. to think Imperially — CHAM 48:8
 Oh, when will you ever l. — SEEG 194:6
 thirty who don't want to l. — SELL 194:8
learned: An' I l. about women from 'er
 — KIPL 127:7
 been l. has been forgotten — SKIN 201:21
 from St Louis hasn't l. — STEIN 207:10
 privilege of the l. — PEAR 169:19
learning: And sleep—and l. of a sort
 — BELL 26:5
 Beauty and the lust for l. — BEER 23:11
 public and l. the instrument — BUTL 43:7
leave: always l. room for the mouse
 — SAKI 188:20
 By all ye l. or do — KIPL 127:20
 for ever taking l. — RILKE 181:4
 L. him alone — FARJ 78:8
 l. in a taxi you can leave — KALM 117:12
 L. them while you're looking good
 — LOOS 139:5
 L. your worry on the doorstep — FIEL 79:9
 repeat his past nor l. — AUDEN 14:4
 you l. them as they are — CHES 51:14
 you must l. — SPOO 206:7
leaves: burning of the l. — BINY 34:16
 glad green l. like wings — HARDY 97:10
 only stop to rake the l. — FROST 86:8
 thick on Severn snow the l. — HOUS 106:18
 whole deck put on its l. — FLEC 81:21
 woods and stipple l. — SACK 187:16
Leben: Wort "Ehrfurcht vor dem L."
 — SCHW 193:11
lecture: And to l. rooms is forced
 — CHES 52:12
 at twilight from the l. — STEV 208:16
lectures: have hissed my mystery l.
 — SPOO 206:7
led: L. go — KIPL 125:14
ledger: floor and smudge the l. — BETJ 31:19
left: be l. to the politicians — DE G 66:3
 L. hand down a bit — WYMAN 232:1
 l. Him in the rain — STUD 210:20
 l. thee all her lovely — DAV 65:3
 l. the wives and joined — WELD 224:7
 nobody l. to be concerned — NIEM 160:13
 position was on the l. — MOSL 157:1
 The 'loony Labour l.' — HEW 102:6
 we that are l. grow old — BINY 34:18
leg: extending your left l. — BANK 18:5
legal: exact l. definition — RUSS 187:2
legend: The past exudes l. — MAL 145:14
legion: L. and Social Club — BETJ 31:2
 Ravel refuses the L. of Honour
 — SATIE 192:7

legion (cont.):
 The cross of the L. of Honour
 — TWAIN 220:6
legs: Four l. good, two legs bad — ORW 164:8
 haricot vein in one of my l. — BUTL 44:9
 His l., perhaps, were shorter — STR 210:9
 losing your l. — SASS 191:18
 not himself, adorns my l. — HOUS 105:5
 The strongest l. in Pontefract — BETJ 31:5
 two perfectly good l. — ROOS 183:6
 were born with your l. apart
 — ORTON 164:6
Leicester: Farewell, L. Square
 — JUDGE 116:17
Leidenschaften: seiner L. gegangen ist
 — JUNG 116:18
leisure: fill l. intelligently — RUSS 186:16
 gentleman of l. — VEBL 221:10
 miserable is to have l. — SHAW 199:12
lemon: squeezed as a l. is squeezed
 — GEDD 89:2
lemonade: I'll take a l. — PAN 167:7
Len: L. says one steady pull — FROST 86:15
lend: If you can't l. your hand
 — DYLAN 71:14
 not well enough to l. — BIER 33:19
 words would hardly l. — DOYLE 69:30
lend-lease: assistance called L. — CHUR 55:1
length: l. of a meeting rises — SHAN 199:6
 what it lacks in l. — FROST 86:20
Lenin: L. was right — KEYN 120:10
 Marx, Engels and L. — KHR 121:3
Lennon: [John L.] could be — MCC 141:14
 John L., Paul McCartney — BUCK 42:4
lenses: beauty and contact l. — PETER 170:13
 If at times my eyes are l. — DOUG 68:12
Léonie: aunt L. used to give me
 — PROU 175:17
 Weep not for little L. — GRAH 92:10
leopards: l. sat under a juniper-tree
 — ELIOT 73:18
leper: here as a Parliamentary l.
 — WILS 228:10
Lesbia: L. with her sparrow — MILL 151:23
lesbians: gays and l. issue — HEW 102:6
less: l. in this than meets — BANK 18:3
 l. than no man — ROOS 183:15
 L. than the dust, beneath — HOPE 105:3
 more and more about l. — MAYO 150:8
lesson: l. of the fearsome — AREN 10:4
lessons: l. of history — HUXL 108:12
lest: l. they should be set — GRAH 92:16
let: get out of the way and l. — EIS 73:9
 L. him twist slowly — EHRL 72:10
 L. me enjoy the earth no less
 — HARDY 98:2
 L. the florid music praise — AUDEN 14:11
 l. their liquid siftings — ELIOT 75:5
 L. them know it's Christmas — GELD 89:4
 L. the train take the strain — ANON 7:13
 L. us go then, you and I — ELIOT 75:13
 L. your fingers do the walking
 — ANON 7:14
 Not I: l. God and man decree
 — HOUS 105:17
Lethe: Dawn shall over L. break
 — BELL 25:20
let's: L. all go down the Strand — CAST 47:11
 L. do it, l. fall in love — PORT 173:3
letter: l. by strange letter — HEAN 99:11
 until you have had a l. — LEV 136:8
letters: l. for the rich, letters — AUDEN 14:21
 l. get in the wrong places — MILNE 154:2
 L. of thanks, letters from — AUDEN 14:22

letters (cont.):
l. to *The Times* about   BEER 23:19
lettuce: too much l. is 'soporific'
    POTT 173:12
level: their l. of incompetence
    PETER 170:12
leviathan: l. retrieving pebbles
    WELLS 224:14
liar: exceptionally good l.   JER 113:6
l. is he who makes   BUTL 44:8
quite often picturesque l.   TWAIN 219:5
still a l.   CORN 61:6
They only answered 'Little L.!'
    BELL 24:16
virtue and a proved l.   HAIL 95:4
liars: himself the accomplice of l.
    PÉGUY 169:23
Income Tax has made more L.
    ROG 182:7
liberal: A L. is a man who uses   ROOS 183:6
could only entertain my L.   ASQ 11:13
distinguished from the L.   BIER 34:3
Just like an old l.   PLOM 172:8
l. is a man who tells other   BAR 18:7
liberals: l. can understand everything
    BRUCE 41:15
L. offer a mixture of sound   MACM 144:2
liberate: we shall l. this country
    MAND 145:18
liberates: Work l.   ANON 5:12
liberation: l. of the human mind from
    GOLD 91:11
rescue and the l. of the old   CHUR 54:10
liberties: dramatist only wants more l.
    JAMES 111:14
what l. are taken in thy   GEOR 89:12
liberty: can be no effective l.   BELL 24:2
convenience to l.   HESSE 102:4
course l. is not licence   SCAN 192:14
defence of l. is no vice   GOLD 91:12
foundations of political l.   WILS 229:13
L. has never come from   WILS 229:9
L. is always unfinished   ANON 7:15
L. is liberty, not equality   BERL 30:6
L. means responsibility   SHAW 198:12
or the holy name of l.   GAND 88:10
Served human l.   YEATS 236:2
survival and the success of l.
    KENN 119:11
true that l. is precious   LENIN 134:17
voices of l. be mute   CUMM 63:15
library: A l. is thought in cold storage
    SAM 189:8
join the public l.   AYCK 15:21
l. of any literary man   BUTL 44:3
Like one of his l. books   AYCK 16:2
lumber room of his l.   DOYLE 69:5
spend less time in the l.   STR 210:17
libre: *Je suis condemné à être l.*   SART 191:2
libres: *naissent l. et égaux en*   ANON 9:1
licence: course liberty is not l.   SCAN 192:14
l. to print your own money
    THOM 216:13
Licht: *ein L. anzünden in der*   JUNG 116:19
lick: If you can't l. 'em   REYN 180:1
licorice: In the l. fields at Pontefract
    BETJ 31:5
lid: l. of the sardine tin   BENN 27:18
lie: And I l. down alone   HOUS 106:6
And the l. of Authority   AUDEN 13:9
Art is a l. that makes   PIC 171:7
between a cat and a l.   TWAIN 219:31
fall victim to a big l.   HITL 103:8

lie (cont.):
Impossible to come, l. follows
    PROU 176:5
It is possible to l.   ADLER 2:16
l. can be half-way around   CALL 45:2
l. down where all ladders   YEATS 233:8
L. follows by post   BER 29:11
l. has become not just   SOLZ 204:8
l. is an abomination unto   STEV 209:7
l. than a truth misunderstood
    JAMES 112:16
l. with your legs ungainly   SASS 192:4
My love and I would l.   HOUS 106:14
not l. easy at Winchelsea   BENÉT 27:8
old L.: Dulce et decorum   OWEN 166:10
writes is a l., including   MCC 141:8
Liebe: *Nur L. kann sie erfassen*   RILKE 181:2
Und diese menschlichere L.   RILKE 181:3
Wo die L. herrscht   JUNG 116:22
lied: because our fathers l.   KIPL 127:21
But it l.   BELL 26:7
lies: combination of reality and l.
    COCT 57:6
From l. of tongue and pen   CHES 51:18
great l. about his wooden   FLEC 81:20
He l. below, correct   PARK 168:20
Here l. a most beautiful lady   DE L 66:10
It produces l. like sand   PONS 172:12
l. about the Democrats   STEV 208:19
L. are the mortar   WELLS 225:1
l. it lives on   FOSD 84:13
L. on my ledge and dulls   MEYN 151:12
l. sound truthful and murder   ORW 165:8
Matilda told such Dreadful L.   BELL 24:14
only l. are invented   BRAQ 38:17
Plain l. are dangerous   SAY 192:11
white l. to ice a wedding   ASQ 11:18
Who l. beneath your spell   HOPE 105:4
will tell l. as usual   SHAW 196:10
life: about l. beyond the grave   KHR 121:5
actor's l. for me   WASH 222:14
A little l. with dried tubers   ELIOT 76:13
all human l. is there   JAMES 111:22
all l. is 6 to 5 against   RUNY 186:4
And then there's l.   ANOU 9:19
And the Pride of L.   HARDY 97:13
A short l. and a gay one   WIMP 229:17
attempt to represent l.   JAMES 111:24
believe in l.   DUB 70:7
believe in the l. to come   BECK 21:11
believe that since my l. began
    COW 61:17
broader and fuller l.   DUB 70:7
business of l. is to enjoy it   BUTL 44:6
change we think we see in l.
    FROST 86:14
children about coping with l.
    SPARK 205:5
Crushing out l.   HOPE 105:4
doctrine of the strenuous l.   ROOS 184:2
don't talk to me about L.   ADAMS 1:12
drawn the breath of l.   YEATS 235:2
fear love is to fear l.   RUSS 186:19
football is a matter of l.   SHAN 195:7
For each one l. to give   KIPL 124:16
For l. is joy, and mind   MAS 148:11
gave my l. for freedom   EWER 78:3
good evidence of l. after death
    SOPER 205:2
great l. if you don't weaken   BUCH 41:19
his friends for his l.   THOR 216:14
I feel that l.—is divided   ALLEN 4:6
In balance with this l.   YEATS 235:5
I really don't know l. at all   MITC 154:7

life (cont.):
isn't l. a terrible thing   THOM 214:10
it's the l. in my men   WEST 225:15
Lead me from death to l.   KUMAR 129:6
L. begins at forty   PITK 171:21
L. exists in the universe   JEANS 112:21
L., friends, is boring   BERR 30:16
l. goes not backward   GIBR 90:5
l. had been but a preparation
    CHUR 55:18
L. has taught us that love   SAIN 187:20
l. in the village began   LEE 134:2
L. is a foreign language   MORL 156:1
L. is a gamble at terrible odds   STOP 210:2
l. is a glorious cycle   PARK 168:11
L. is a great surprise   NAB 158:13
L. is a horizontal fall   COCT 57:7
L. is a maze in which we   CONN 59:10
L. is an offensive   WHIT 226:6
L. is a sexually transmitted   ANON 7:16
L. is Colour and Warmth   GREN 94:3
L. is doubt   UNAM 220:12
L. is first boredom, then fear   LARK 131:5
L. is for each man a solitary   O'NEI 163:9
l. is in the past and future   O'NEI 163:15
L. is just a bowl of cherries   BROWN 41:12
L. is just one damned thing   HUBB 107:12
L. is like a sewer   LEHR 134:6
L. is like playing a violin   BUTL 43:7
L. is made up of sobs   HENRY 101:9
l. is mainly a process   BERNE 30:10
L. is not having been told   NASH 159:6
L. is not meant to be easy   SHAW 195:24
L. is one long process   BUTL 43:17
L. is perhaps most wisely   O'NEI 163:12
L. is something to do when   LEB 133:20
l. is spent in a perpetual   JOAD 113:20
L. is the art of drawing   BUTL 43:18
L. is the other way round   LODGE 138:17
L. is too short to stuff   CONR 60:5
L. is very nice, but l.   ANOU 9:21
l. is washed   BARZ 20:10
l. is where things aren't   BARN 18:20
L. levels all men   SHAW 198:26
l. of every man is a diary   BARR 19:4
l. of the modern hardback   MORT 156:10
L. says: she did this   BARN 18:20
L.'s better with the Conservatives
    ANON 7:17
l. seems to have no plots   COMP 58:12
L.'s little ironies   HARDY 97:4
l. talking at street corners   VANZ 221:5
L., the Universe and   ADAMS 1:14
L., to be sure, is nothing   HOUS 106:7
l. was coming to consist   AMIS 4:18
L. we have lost in living   ELIOT 76:4
l. will be sour grapes   ASHF 11:3
L. would ring the bells   GINS 90:14
L., you know, is rather   BENN 27:18
long as you have your l.   JAMES 111:12
measured out my l. with coffee
    ELIOT 75:15
midst of l. we are in debt   MUMF 157:14
more a way of l.   ANON 7:32
much too far out all my l.   SMITH 203:18
Music *is* l., and like it   NIEL 160:12
my experience of l. has   BEER 23:12
nature, contrary to l.   HUXL 108:14
nearest thing to death in l.   ANON 7:26
not lead a pleasant l.   RAL 177:10
On l., on death.   YEATS 233:4
only sanction of l.   SANT 190:1
Our end is L. Put out to sea
    MACN 144:11

life (*cont.*):

outer l. of telegrams	FORS 83:16
part of l.'s rich pageant	MARS 147:12
People say that l. is the thing	
	SMITH 203:13
Perfection of the l.	YEATS 235:18
priceless gift of l.	ROS 184:18
problematical world and sells us l.	
	FRY 87:1
queer thing L.	WOD 230:21
Reverence for L.	SCHW 193:11
Sex is the gateway to l.	HARR 98:14
sons and daughters of L.'s	GIBR 90:5
struggle of l.	CONN 59:1
taking l. by the throat	FROST 86:18
terror to l. and makes death	TREE 217:16
That was how his l. happened	KAV 118:9
The l. and loves of a she-devil	
	WELD 224:8
there a l. before death	HEAN 99:14
'Tisn't l. that matters	WALP 222:9
University of L.	BOTT 37:1
Was my l. also	OWEN 166:16
What is this l. if	DAV 65:5
which makes l. worth living	ELIOT 75:3
which would support l.	HALD 95:7
Whose l. is it anyway	CLARK 56:8
you all that my whole l.	ELIZ 77:7
your money or your l.	BUTL 43:13

life-blood: l. of real civilization TREV 217:20

life-insurance: I detest l. agents LEAC 133:9

life-jacket: *brassière* is the French for l.
BARN 18:19

life-lie: l. away from the average
IBSEN 110:2

life-sentence: l. in the dungeon of self
CONN 59:14

l. which fate carries	LAWR 133:1

lifetime: But a l. of happiness SHAW 197:17

lit again in our l.	GREY 94:5

light: against the dying of the l.

	THOM 213:13
C'mon, baby, l. my fire	MORR 156:7
Colour and Warmth and L.	GREN 94:3
eldritch l. of sundown	DAY-L 65:7
faces in the violet l.	ELIOT 77:5
I l. my lamp in the evening	BELL 25:25
kindle a l. in the darkness	JUNG 116:19
l. and the half light	YEATS 235:7
l. at the end of the tunnel	DICK 67:10
l. at the end of the tunnel	LOW 139:21
l. between two eternities	NAB 158:14
L. breaks where no sun shines	
	THOM 213:21
l. gleams an instant	BECK 21:24
l. has gone out of our	NEHRU 160:1
l. of my life, fire	NAB 158:12
L. That Failed	KIPL 125:20
me a l. that I may tread	HASK 99:3
mend the Electric L.	BELL 25:7
Of L. and Mrs Humphry Ward	CHES 52:2
sweetness and l. failed	FORS 83:10
The dark is l. enough	FRY 86:24
The l. of evening, Lissadell	YEATS 235:8
The L. of Lights	YEATS 234:9
turning your face to the l.	SASS 191:18
waited for the l.	ROB 181:13
was far faster than l.	BULL 42:5
while the l. fails	ELIOT 74:22

lighter: darker to the l. races DUB 70:8

lightfoot: And many a l. lad HOUS 107:7

The l. boys are laid	HOUS 107:7

light-house: Keeping a l. with his eyes
CAMP 45:14

lightly: they take themselves l.	CHES 51:15

lightning: Have known the l.'s hour

	DAY-L 65:9
It's to keep the l. out	ISH 110:22

lights: Turn up the l.; I don't

	HENRY 101:12
lignes: *dans les l. du plafond*	ELUA 77:14

like: can do just what you l. SHAW 196:26

Duke I couldn't l.	SHAW 200:10
forced to l. what you get	SHAW 198:30
How shall we conquer? L. a wind	
	FLEC 81:22
I know what I l.	BEER 23:14
I know what I l.	JAMES 112:3
I l. Ike	SPAL 205:4
I l. the hunting of the hare	BLUNT 35:6
Just l. that!	COOP 60:19
L. a complete unknown	DYLAN 71:8
l. a little bit of butter	MILNE 153:11
L. a rolling stone	DYLAN 71:8
l. it [the 4th symphony]	VAUG 221:8
l. potato and I like po-tah-to	GERS 89:16
l. the girl that married	DILL 67:13
l. to be beside the seaside	GLOV 91:2
l. to do are either illegal	WOOL 231:20
l. to get away from earth	FROST 86:5
l. who drinks as much	THOM 214:1
man that I didn't l.	ROG 182:13
people you l. best	UST 220:17
that what we l. is not	BELL 24:2
those whom I l. or admire	AUDEN 14:5
was l. to give offence	FROST 86:11
what it is l. to be a child	JARR 112:17
whether I l. or dislike them	FORS 83:19
You're going to l. this	DAN 64:12

liked: I wish I l. the way it walks

	RAL 177:11
I would have l.	PERÓN 170:8
People wish to be l.	RUSS 186:14

likely: Walk! Not bloody l. SHAW 199:24

likes: does know what she l.	RATT 177:18
Somebody up there l. me	LEHM 134:4

lilac: forget the l. and the roses ARAG 10:2

Just now the l. is in bloom	BROO 40:10

lilacs: L. out of the dead land, mixing

	ELIOT 76:13

lilac-time: Go down to Kew in l.

	NOYES 161:15
lilas: *jamais les l. ni les roses*	ARAG 10:2

lilies: beauty lives though l. FLEC 81:6

l. of ambition	DOUG 68:9

lilting: l. house and happy THOM 213:17

lily: It trembles to a l. DOBS 68:3

morning glows the l.	FLEC 81:10

limb: clothes on a hickory l. DE L 66:20

limbs: And if these poor l. die BROO 40:2

l. that fester are not	ABSE 1:2
Yours are the l., my sweeting	
	NASH 159:3

limelight: politicians take in their l.

	BELL 24:22
They do not sit in the l.	BEAV 21:5

limestone: On l. quarried near the spot

	YEATS 233:4

limit: l. to our realization ROOS 183:12

limitation: l. of governmental power

	WILS 229:9

limitations: difference between accidental l.

	AUDEN 13:16
must know the l. of force	TROT 218:6

limited: nervous and terse, but l.

	DOYLE 69:30

limits: l. of my language mean WITT 230:2

limm: wood ere Thou canst l. THOM 215:15

limousine: l. and a ticket MACN 144:7

One perfect l., do you suppose	
	PARK 168:13

Limpopo: greasy L. River, all set

	KIPL 125:13

Lincoln: I am a Ford, not a L. FORD 82:17

L. was shovelled	SAND 189:16

line: An active l. on a walk KLEE 128:6

hammered into l.	KIPL 126:19
l. will take us hours maybe	
	YEATS 232:16
season-ticket on the l.	AMERY 4:14

lineage: We Poets of the proud old l.

	FLEC 81:6

lineaments: l. of a plummet-measured

	YEATS 233:6

liner: The L. she's a lady KIPL 127:4

lines: Edit and annotate the l.

	YEATS 234:19
l. of the ceiling	ELUA 77:14
scribbled l. like fallen	HOPE 105:2

lingerie: Brevity is the soul of l. PARK 169:5

lingering: A l. dissolution BECK 21:9

lingers: melody l. on BERL 29:18

linnet: behind with my old cock l.

	COLL 58:2

lion: l. and the calf shall lie ALLEN 3:17

l. the right place to use	CHUR 56:2
that had the l.'s heart	CHUR 56:2

lions: l. to the roaring slaughter

	CUMM 63:15
To feed ruddy L.? Not me	EDGAR 72:1

lipless: Leaned backward with a l. grin
ELIOT 75:8

lippity-lippity: wander about, going l.

	POTT 173:15

lips: already born before my l.

	MAND 145:19
l. are not yet unsealed	BALD 17:9
l. upon a plummet-measured	
	YEATS 233:5
on l. of living men	BUTL 43:4
Red l. are not so red	OWEN 166:13

lipstick: cigarette that bears a l.'s

	MARV 147:15
you've got on too much l.	NASH 159:23

liqueurs: chocolate l. in one go CAP 46:15

liquid: And let their l. siftings ELIOT 75:6

less l. than their shadows	TESS 212:14
l. which rots braces	MORT 156:15
Thames is l. history	BURNS 42:15

liquidation: preside over the l. CHUR 53:18

liquor: bowl with atrabilious l. HUXL 109:1

But l. Is quicker	NASH 159:18
I don't drink l. I don't	LEV 136:4
lads for the l.	HOUS 106:16
L. is one way out an'	WILL 227:4
Livelier l. than the Muse	HOUS 107:8
We drank our l. straight	AUDEN 14:6

listen: acts it out, I hardly l. SAL 189:2

l. to the birds and winds	GIBS 90:8
l. when his mate sings	WICK 226:23
only l. when I am unhappy	
	SMITH 203:24
Stop-look-and-l.	ANON 8:14
when you wish him to l.	BIER 33:27

listener: same applies to the l. BEEC 22:7

listening: good at l. to their elders

	BALD 16:20
L. to a speech by Chamberlain	
	BEVAN 32:14
talking about him ain't l.	GLASS 91:1

listless: on his l. form and face   HARDY 97:8
lit: l. again in our lifetime   GREY 94:5
  stared; the sky was l.   HODG 103:11
  whole Fleet's l. up   WOOD 231:5
literalists: l. of the imagination
                                    MOORE 155:14
literary: beloved by l. pundits   CONN 58:19
  Like an unsuccessful l. man   BELL 25:4
  L. intellectuals at one   SNOW 203:27
  smallest library of any l.   BUTL 44:3
  The l. mornings with its hoot
                                    AUDEN 14:18
literate: If, with the l., I am   PARK 168:18
literature: All modern American l.
                                    HEM 100:13
  All the rest is l.   VALÉ 220:23
  L. flourishes best when   INGE 110:17
  L. is a luxury   CHES 50:11
  L. is mostly about having sex
                                    LODGE 138:17
  L. is news that STAYS news
                                    POUND 173:24
  L. is not an abstract science   QUIL 177:1
  l. is simply language charged
                                    POUND 174:1
  L. is strewn with the wreckage
                                    WOOLF 231:14
  L. is the art of writing   CONN 58:14
  L. is the orchestration   WILD 227:5
  l. is to be delighted   CECIL 48:4
  L.'s always a good card   BENN 28:18
  possible to gain a chair of l.   ALGR 3:8
  produce a little l.   JAMES 111:20
  professors like their l. clear   LEWIS 137:1
  remarks are not l.   STEIN 207:9
  tip's a good one, as for l.   POUND 174:7
littérature: *Tout le reste est l.*   VALÉ 220:23
little: For politics and l. else   CAMP 45:15
  From having too l. to do   KIPL 125:9
  Great hatred, l. room   YEATS 236:3
  Life's l. ironies   HARDY 97:4
  L. boxes on the hillside   REYN 179:17
  L. Boy kneels at the foot   MILNE 153:12
  L. man, you've had a busy   SIGL 200:16
  L. minds are interested   HUBB 107:14
  l. of what you fancy does   LEIGH 134:12
  L. one! Oh, little one   STEP 208:7
  l. things are infinitely   DOYLE 69:2
  Pooh always liked a l. something
                                    MILNE 153:15
  shall we turn to l. things   GIBS 90:8
  So l. done, so much to do   RHOD 180:4
  Thank heaven for l. girls   LERN 135:24
  These l. grey cells   CHR 52:21
  these l. local difficulties   MACM 144:1
littleness: always ruined by the l.
                                    BREC 39:5
  For the long l. of life   CORN 61:7
live: As you l., believe in life   DUB 70:7
  enable its citizens to l.   WEIL 224:2
  Flesh perishes, I l.   HARDY 97:7
  he isn't fit to l.   KING 121:13
  I do not wish to l.   MILL 152:3
  If you don't l. it   PARK 167:13
  L. all you can   JAMES 111:12
  L. and let die   FLEM 82:3
  l. for a time close   BUCH 41:18
  l. for others and not   SHAW 199:25
  l. in a yellow submarine   LENN 135:15
  L. in fragments no longer   FORS 83:17
  l. in houses just as big   SMITH 203:5
  l. our lives   CART 47:4
  l. this long [100 years]   BLAKE 34:22

live (*cont.*):
  l. together as brothers   KING 122:6
  l. under the shadow   SPEN 205:15
  l. with a good conscience   SMITH 203:4
  Long L. Free Quebec   DE G 65:18
  must l. it to the full   SPARK 205:8
  one's principles than to l.   ADLER 2:15
  rich that you have to l.   SMITH 203:9
  Sacco's name will l.   VANZ 221:6
  than to l. on your knees   IBAR 109:17
  To l. is like to love   BUTL 43:28
  We l., as we dream—alone   CONR 59:20
  which will l. on in infamy   ROOS 183:10
  You might as well l.   PARK 168:12
lived: Had we l., I should have
                                    SCOTT 194:3
  I've l. a life that's full   ANKA 5:7
  Never to have l. is best   YEATS 235:2
livelier: L. liquor than the Muse
                                    HOUS 107:8
Liverpool: The folk that live in L.
                                    CHES 50:17
livery: The ill-bred son of a l.   YEATS 235:4
lives: Careless talk costs l.   ANON 5:26
  cat has only nine l.   TWAIN 219:31
  Led merry, merry l.   NAYL 159:26
  second acts in American l.   FITZ 80:22
  The taking of our l.   VANZ 221:5
  we live our l., for ever   RILKE 181:4
livin': Summer time an' the l. is easy
                                    HEYW 102:8
living: language of the l.   ELIOT 74:17
  Life we have lost in l.   ELIOT 76:4
  L. and partly living   ELIOT 74:24
  L. for today   LENN 134:20
  l. in central London   GOWR 92:7
  L. is abnormal   ION 110:18
  man to find a way of l.   BALD 16:16
  must hate to work for a l.   ROWL 185:16
  reason for l.   SHAW 199:10
  West it is still a l. lion   SOLZ 204:7
  world does not owe us a l.   PHIL 170:18
llama: L. is a woolly sort   BELL 25:4
Lloyd George: L. arrived at his proper
                                    BENN 28:11
  [L.] did not seem to care   BEAV 21:4
  L. knows my father   ANON 7:18
  Minister [L.] has resigned   ANON 6:19
load: 'l.' with manly pride   BURT 42:17
loan: Norman that I have him on l.
                                    AYCK 16:2
loath: hands were l. and cold   OWEN 166:18
loathe: l. entering upon explanations
                                    BARR 19:6
loathing: Fear and l. in Las Vegas
                                    THOM 216:12
lobby: into the l. against us   BALD 17:9
local: A l. thing called Christianity
                                    HARDY 96:19
  little l. difficulties   MACM 144:1
  l., but prized elsewhere   AUDEN 13:14
lock: broken the l. and splintered
                                    AUDEN 14:14
  happy, why l. him   SHAW 198:4
locked: L. and frozen in each eye
                                    AUDEN 13:3
locks: until his l. grew grey   CARB 46:18
locusts: And famine grew, and l. came
                                    THOM 214:5
logic: any sense attacking l.   CHES 51:11
  It is the l. of our times   DAY-L 65:11
  L. must take care of itself   WITT 230:1
loin: *jusqu'où on peut aller trop l.*   COCT 57:3
loins: fire of my l.   NAB 158:12

lois: *majestueuse égalité des l.*   FRAN 84:15
Lolita: L., light of my life   NAB 158:12
Loman: L. never made a lot   MILL 152:4
London: A crowd flowed over L. Bridge
                                    ELIOT 76:17
  A foggy day in L. Town   GERS 89:13
  As he gazed at the L. skies   BETJ 30:21
  'Cause in sleepy L. town   JAGG 111:9
  City of L. remains   CHAM 48:7
  it isn't far from L.   NOYES 161:15
  it travels south to L.   BEAV 21:2
  living in central L.   GOWR 92:7
  L. and realize   HICKS 102:9
  L. Pride has been handed   COW 62:2
  L. spread out in the sun   LARK 131:1
  L., that great cesspool   DOYLE 69:25
  L. to Paris in 25 hours   DAV 64:19
  L. with one voice would   CHUR 53:10
  many MPs never see the L.   LIV 138:3
  me on the train for L.   MILLS 152:20
  One road leads to L.   MAS 148:8
  roar of L.'s traffic   ANON 8:2
  That I love L.   GREGG 93:22
  that the 'L. Effect'   HEW 102:6
  This—is L.   MURR 158:7
  vilest alleys in L.   DOYLE 69:6
  Yankee Doodle came to L.   COHAN 57:13
Londoner: Maybe it's because I'm a L.
                                    GREGG 93:22
lone: walking by his wild l.   KIPL 125:18
loneliness: l. of the long-distance
                                    SILL 200:17
lonely: A l. impulse of delight   YEATS 235:5
  l. sea and the sky   MAS 148:16
  mine as mirrors are l.   AUDEN 14:7
  people for fear I may be l.   JOAD 113:20
  The heart is a l. hunter   MCC 141:19
lonesomeness: And starlight lit my l.
                                    HARDY 97:15
long: And I. 'tis like to be   HOUS 106:2
  because time is l.   DUB 70:7
  But it's a l., long while   AND 4:21
  For the l. littleness of life   CORN 61:7
  How l., I wondered   GERS 89:13
  It's a l. way to Tipperary   JUDGE 116:17
  keep on saying it l. enough   BENN 28:17
  Life is one l. process   BUTL 43:17
  l. and the short   HUGH 107:20
  L. books, when read   FORS 83:11
  l. for the Person from   SMITH 203:22
  l. run we are all dead   KEYN 121:1
  l. time I used to go   PROU 175:16
  Night of the L. Knives   HITL 103:3
  The l. hot summer   RAV 178:5
  The l. summer   FAUL 78:10
  Too l. a sacrifice   YEATS 233:10
  too l. without a war here   BREC 39:3
  trouble with Senator L.   ICKES 110:3
  was gonna live this l.   BLAKE 34:22
  week is a l. time in politics
                                    WILS 228:14
longed: that I have l. for death
                                    PROU 175:19
longer: what takes a little l.   NANS 158:19
longest: laughs l. who laughs last
                                    MAS 148:21
  l. running farce   SMITH 202:5
  l. suicide note in history   KAUF 118:4
longevity: L. has its place   KING 121:16
Longfellow: have to be shown L.'s grave
                                    MOORE 155:15
long-haired: But I consort with l. things
                                    KIPL 122:17

love (cont.):

predominates, l. is lacking   JUNG 116:22
right place for l.   FROST 86:5
salley gardens my l.   YEATS 234:13
save the Party we l.   GAIT 87:23
school can l. like a fool   NASH 159:13
She bid me take l. easy   YEATS 234:13
Such a morning it is when l.   LEE 134:3
support of the woman I l.   EDW 72:8
than to l. one's neighbour   HOFF 103:17
that doesn't l. a wall   FROST 86:9
that the greatest l.   PROU 175:19
The man you l. to hate   ANON 7:24
There is l. of course   ANOU 9:19
They l. the Good   BROO 40:14
Thine own eternal l.   O'CAS 162:15
thing in the world is l.   BREN 39:8
time you hear your l. song   CAHN 44:16
too late to fall in l.   WILS 229:2
Try thinking of l.   FRY 87:7
Use him as though you l. him
    BLUN 34:25
violence masquerading as l.
    LAING 129:11
We must l. one another or die
    AUDEN 13:9
What will survive of us is l.   LARK 131:6
When l. congeals   HART 98:17
Where l. rules, there   JUNG 116:22
While you l. your lover, let   HART 98:19
Whose l. is given over-well   PARK 168:16
wilder shores of l.   BLAN 34:23
words, 'God si L.'   FORS 84:2
Work is l. made visible   GIBR 90:6
You made me l. you   MCC 141:6
loved: And l. in misery   YEATS 235:12
better to have l. and lost   BUTL 44:10
I l. you, so I drew these   LAWR 133:3
it can be l.   SANT 190:15
I wish I l. the Human Race   RAL 177:11
l. your moments of glad   YEATS 232:7
love-knot: l. into her long black
    NOYES 161:17
loveliest: L. of trees, the cherry now
    HOUS 106:9
l. things of beauty God   MAS 148:7
world the l. and the best   BELL 25:18
loveliness: A woman of so shining l.
    YEATS 234:17
I am weak from your l.   BETJ 32:1
That fashioned forth its l.   HARDY 98:2
lovely: And down in l. muck I've lain
    HOUS 107:9
And left thee all her l. hues   DAV 65:3
As you are woman, so be l.   GRAV 93:7
It gives a l. light   MILL 151:18
It was the l. moon—she lifted   FREE 85:3
Look thy last on all things l.   DE L 66:12
L. and willing every afternoon
    AUDEN 14:18
l. day I thought it was   MAUG 149:21
l. woman stoops to folly   ELIOT 77:2
Oh what a l. war   LITT 138:1
The woods are l.   FROST 86:7
lover: has done the l. mortal hurt
    DOUG 68:11
l. and killer are mingled   DOUG 68:11
l.'s quarrel with the world   FROST 86:22
l. without indiscretion   HARDY 96:21
Scratch a l., and find a foe   PARK 168:21
what is left of a l.   ROWL 185:13
woman looking for a new l.   CONN 59:8
loverly: Oh, wouldn't it be l.   LERN 135:25

lovers: Almighty l. in the Spring
    CHES 50:10
And timid l.' declarations   AUDEN 14:22
Frankie and Albert were l.   ANON 6:10
l. be lost love shall not   THOM 214:6
l. find their peace   FLEC 81:7
L. of 'Humanity'   CAMP 45:12
loves: And our l., must I remember
    APOL 9:22
He that l. but half of Earth   QUIL 177:4
She l. you, yeh, yeh, yeh   LENN 135:10
The life and l. of a she-devil   WELD 224:8
white woman whom nobody l.
    CORN 61:8
Who l. ya, baby   SAV 192:8
love-story: l. or an elopement   DOYLE 69:19
lovin': I ain't had no l.   NORW 161:13
loving: freer, and more l.   BALD 16:17
low: Had me l. and had me   GERS 89:13
Seem to murmur sweet and l.   ARMS 10:7
with l. sounds by the shore   YEATS 232:9
lowbrow: was the first militant l.   BERL 30:5
Lowells: L. talk to the Cabots   BOSS 36:12
lower: capitalism of the l. classes
    SPEN 206:2
never knew that the l. classes
    CURZ 64:11
they are l. than vermin   BEVAN 33:7
loyal: Lousy but l.   ANON 7:19
loyalty: I want l. I want him   JOHN 114:3
L. is the Tory's secret weapon
    KILM 121:10
l. we all feel to unhappiness   GREE 93:15
luck: always just my l. to get   PARK 168:13
'Cause with a bit of l.   AYRES 16:5
I had the l. to be called   CHUR 56:2
It's awf'lly bad l. on Diana   BETJ 31:9
l. and sends his son   STEAD 207:6
l. was his light-o'-love   SERV 194:23
luckiest: Geniuses are the l. of mortals
    AUDEN 14:17
Ludlow: L. come in for the fair
    HOUS 106:16
Oh I have been to L. fair   HOUS 107:9
Lüge: L. leichter zum Opfer fällt   HITL 103:8
Lügen: Gibt L. wie Sand   PONS 172:12
lullaby: Once in a l.   HARB 96:13
lumber: l. room of his library   DOYLE 69:5
lumberjack: I'm a l.   CHAP 49:10
lump: L. the whole thing   TWAIN 219:20
lumps: Go down like l. of lead
    HODG 103:12
There are l. in it   STEP 208:6
lunacy: fit of complete l.   BORN 36:11
lunatic: l. asylums which are known
    WOOLF 231:8
l. fringe in all reform   ROOS 184:6
themselves are all in l. asylums
    CHES 51:10
lunatics: lunatic asylum run by l.
    LLOY 138:15
l. have taken charge   ROWL 185:17
lunch: she's unable to l. today   PORT 173:4
such thing as a free l.   HEIN 100:1
took the cork out of my l.   FIEL 79:10
luncheon: do not take soup at l.
    CURZ 64:10
read a novel before l.   WAUGH 223:18
lunches: l. of fifty-seven years   WOD 230:12
lungs: froth-corrupted l.   OWEN 166:10
gold and l. of bronze   BELL 26:5
using your l. all the time   LEAC 133:10
lurch: Tho' rather in the l.   COW 62:13

lurching: L. to rag-time tunes   SASS 192:2
lust: horrible that l. and rage   YEATS 234:3
lot of women with l.   CART 47:6
l. for learning   BEER 23:11
l. of knowing what should   FLEC 81:9
lutanist: lute the l.   THOM 215:14
lutte: l. elle-même vers les sommets
    CAMUS 46:8
luxuriant: L. song   YEATS 235:4
luxuries: necessities and which l.
    WRIG 231:21
luxury: all the l. of the world   YEATS 235:4
Literature is a l.   CHES 50:11
l. was lavished on you   ORTON 164:2
lying: done as easily l. down   ALLEN 3:23
I do not mind l.   BUTL 44:1
L. in bed would be an altogether
    CHES 52:5
One of you is l.   PARK 168:9
smallest amount of l.   BUTL 44:8
Lyme: There once was an old man of L.
    MONK 155:1
Lyonnesse: When I set out for L.
    HARDY 97:15
lyre: 'Omer smote 'is bloomin' l.   KIPL 127:5
lyres: turn to rhythmic tidal l.
    HARDY 97:13
lyric: now it's l. verse   WAUGH 223:9

M

Ma: Anyway, M., I made it   GOFF 91:8
MacArthur: didn't fire him [General M.]
    TRUM 218:12
Macaulay: If I were a young M.   BARB 18:12
Macavity: M., Macavity, there's no
    ELIOT 75:4
Macbeth: Little Nell and Lady M.
    WOOL 231:19
Macdonald: boneless wonder [Ramsay M.]
    CHUR 54:4
[Ramsay M.] had sufficient conscience
    LLOY 138:10
macerations: Made way for m.
    POUND 174:5
Macheath: Just a jack-knife has M., dear
    BREC 38:21
machine: A house is a m. for living
    LE C 133:25
Ghost in the M.   RYLE 187:12
I have tested your m.   TREE 217:16
ingenious m. for turning   DIN 67:16
m. can do the work of fifty   HUBB 107:15
m. for making gods   BERG 29:12
Unpassioned beauty of a great m.
    BROO 39:19
We feel the m. slipping   LOW 139:21
Youre not a man, youre a m.
    SHAW 195:19
machinery: dynamo in the m. of the night
    GINS 90:15
machines: M. are worshipped   RUSS 186:26
M. for making more machines
    BOTT 36:14
m. or of elaborate techniques
    RUTH 187:8
men in their flying m.   DAV 64:19
macht: Arbeit m. frei   ANON 5:12
die M. den Vorrang hat   JUNG 116:22
mackintosh: bit of black m.   WELBY 224:6
Macy: ass in M.'s window   JOHN 114:3

mad: Are the men that God made m.
 CHES 50:9
 born m. BECK 21:23
 go m. they shall be sane THOM 214:6
 How m. I am, sad I am BETJ 32:1
 M. about the boy COW 62:3
 M. at you 'cause your feet's BENS 28:19
 m. dog of the Middle East REAG 178:16
 M. dogs and Englishmen COW 62:4
 or less m. on one point KIPL 126:2
 Poets do not go m. CHES 51:11
 sense that the world was m. SAB 187:13
madam: Call me m. LIND 137:11
 Why not 'M. Secretary' PERK 170:7
made: has m. all the difference FROST 86:4
 m. by someone who had often
 HALS 95:12
 mind is not a bed to be m. AGATE 2:20
 We are so m., that we can FREUD 85:7
 You m. me love you MCC 141:6
madeleine: m. which on Sunday mornings
 PROU 175:17
mademoiselle: M. from Armenteers
 ANON 7:20
madman: As a m. shakes a dead geranium
 ELIOT 75:21
 Hugo was a m. who thought COCT 57:8
madmen: M. in authority, who hear
 KEYN 120:17
madness: generation destroyed by m.
 GINS 90:15
 has her m. and her weather AUDEN 13:1
 M. need not be all breakdown
 LAING 129:13
 The rest is the m. of art JAMES 111:18
Maeonides: old M. the blind FLEC 81:22
Maggie: work on M.'s Farm no more
 DYLAN 71:10
magic: has succeeded where m.
 BRON 39:17
 house rose like m. HARG 98:10
 mistake medicine for m. SZASZ 211:19
 That old black m. MERC 151:9
magical: M. mystery tour LENN 135:9
 purely m. object BART 20:4
magique: un objet parfaitement m.
 BART 20:4
magistrate: anything that shocks the m.
 RUSS 187:2
 The M. gave his opinion EDGAR 72:1
magnanimity: In victory: m. CHUR 55:16
magnificent: inconvenient, but it's m.
 BENN 28:14
 m. men in their flying DAV 64:19
magpie: A swollen m. in a fitful sun
 POUND 174:14
Maguire: M. and his men KAV 118:8
Mahler: M. exclaimed MAHL 145:5
Mai: M. qui fut sans nuage et ARAG 10:2
maid: lady's m. that high birth
 WOOLF 231:8
 Yonder a m. and her wight HARDY 97:9
maiden: For many a rose-lipt m.
 HOUS 107:7
maidens: M. aspiring to godheads
 STOP 209:18
maids: m. come forth sprig-muslin
 HARDY 97:2
mail: Night M. crossing the Border
 AUDEN 14:21
maimed: M. us at the start YEATS 236:3
maiming: risk of m. it for life SHAW 198:18

maintenance: art of motorcycle m.
 PIRS 171:20
maison: m. est une machine-à-habiter
 LE C 133:25
majestic: face of the m. equality
 FRAN 84:15
majestueuse: travailler devant la m. égalité
 FRAN 84:15
Major: Ground control to M. Tom
 BOWIE 37:16
majority: big enough m. in any town
 TWAIN 219:2
 conforming to m. opinion SCAN 192:14
 indifference of the m. REST 179:14
 m. never has right IBSEN 109:20
 m. then and there happen WHIT 226:10
 minority to the m. LENIN 134:18
 rule the m. are wrong DEBS 65:15
make: Go ahead, m. my day FINK 79:18
 M. do and mend ANON 7:21
 M. love not war ANON 7:22
 m. two questions grow where
 VEBL 221:11
 m. way for an older man MAUD 149:4
 m. wherever we're lost FRY 87:6
 sometimes, to m. it up TWAIN 219:17
 than a Scotsman on the m. BARR 19:22
 wrote M. IT NEW POUND 173:26
 You cannot m. him out at all BELL 25:5
maker: meet my M. brow to brow
 CORN 61:6
 prepared to meet my M. CHUR 55:13
 The M. of the stars and sea BETJ 31:4
makes: Happiness m. up in height
 FROST 86:20
making: cesspit of their own m. AND 5:4
 egg's way of m. another egg BUTL 43:16
 m-m-m. the world safe WOLFE 231:2
 We have ways of m. men talk
 YOUNG 236:8
Malamute: whooping it up in the M.
 SERV 194:23
male: Especially the m. of the species
 LAWR 132:15
 more deadly than the m. KIPL 126:17
 rough m. kiss BROO 39:19
 true m. never yet walked WICK 226:23
 weapon of the m. CONN 59:9
malenky: Then I read a m. bit out
 BURG 42:9
malentendu: c'est d'être admiré par m.
 COCT 57:4
malheureux: moral dès qu'on est m.
 PROU 175:20
malice: There's no m. in me eye
 AYRES 16:8
malicious: God is subtle but he is not m.
 EINS 72:13
malignant: was not m. and remove it
 WAUGH 223:7
mallet: m. or a chisel modelled
 YEATS 233:5
malt: m. does more than Milton
 HOUS 107:8
mama: encountered the m. of dada
 FAD 78:6
 M. may have, papa may have HOL 104:4
maman: m. est morte CAMUS 46:4
mamas: I'm the last of the red-hot m.
 YELL 236:6
mammals: 8,000 species of m. HALD 95:7
mammon: authentic m. than a bogus
 MACN 144:4

man: All animals, except m. BUTL 44:6
 A m. not old, but mellow PHIL 171:2
 A m. who's untrue to his wife
 AUDEN 14:20
 A moderately honest m. SHAW 198:22
 A pint of plain is your only m.
 O'BR 162:9
 Arms and the m. SHAW 195:15
 artist m. and the mother SHAW 197:22
 Beware of the m. whose god
 SHAW 198:19
 blood makes a m. coloured HUGH 107:21
 boldly go where no m. RODD 182:2
 But if a m. bites a dog BOGA 35:13
 century of the common m. WALL 222:7
 everyone has sat except a m. CUMM 64:1
 get to a m. in the case KIPL 127:8
 God created m. VALÉ 220:24
 God, the laws of m. HOUS 105:17
 good for m. to be alone BARR 19:27
 have you ever tasted M. KIPL 125:7
 He's no a m. ava' MACD 142:1
 He was her m., but he done ANON 6:10
 How many roads must a m. DYLAN 71:4
 I am a free m., an American
 JOHN 114:16
 I got my m. GERS 89:14
 I'm a m. WILD 227:2
 I met a m. who wasn't there
 MEAR 150:11
 I never hated a m. enough GABOR 87:21
 I saw a m. this morning SHAW 200:9
 It's that m. again ANON 7:4
 less than that no m. ROOS 183:15
 m. a free hand and he'll WEST 225:16
 m. and a woman looking WOOLF 231:15
 M., biologically considered JAMES 112:6
 m. by standing a sheep BEER 23:15
 m. can interrogate as well OSLER 165:21
 M. can leave the earth KOES 128:14
 m. could ease a heart like PARK 168:8
 M. delights in novelty PARK 168:15
 m. does with what happens HUXL 109:13
 m. ever shall put asunder SHAW 196:24
 m. falls in love through WYATT 231:23
 m. fixed his eyes before ELIOT 76:17
 m. from Del Monte says ANON 7:23
 m. got to do what he got STEI 208:1
 M. hands on misery to man LARK 130:13
 M. has created death YEATS 235:11
 m. in love is incomplete GABOR 87:20
 m. in the house is worth WEST 225:9
 M. is a credulous animal RUSS 187:4
 M. is a history-making creature
 AUDEN 14:4
 M. is a useless passion SART 191:3
 m. is either free BAR 18:8
 m. is that you think him SHAW 197:4
 M. is the Only Animal TWAIN 219:12
 M. is the only creature ORW 164:7
 m. more dined against BOWRA 37:18
 M. must choose whether ILL 110:6
 m. of genius who had not BEER 22:16
 m. over forty is a scoundrel SHAW 198:28
 m. shouldn't fool with booze FAUL 78:14
 m. suffering from BEVAN 32:13
 M., unlike any other thing STEI 207:22
 m. who "boozes" BURT 42:17
 m. who goes to a psychiatrist
 GOLD 91:18
 m. who has no office SHAW 197:1
 m. who has not passed through
 JUNG 116:18

man (*cont.*):
  m. who is high up loves   BARR 19:25
  m. who is not afraid   SYNGE 211:8
  m. who listens to Reason   SHAW 198:24
  m. who mistook his wife   SACKS 187:14
  m. who should loose me   LOW 139:18
  m. who used to notice such
                                  HARDY 97:10
  m. will not merely endure   FAUL 78:13
  m. without originality   SHAW 196:2
  nastiest little m.   DYKS 71:3
  night out for m. or beast   FIEL 79:16
  noblest work of m.   BUTL 43:8
  Of m.'s bedevilment and God's
                                  HOUS 105:18
  Ol' m. river, dat ol' man   HAMM 96:1
  One m. in a thousand   KIPL 126:16
  one small step for a m.   ARMS 10:10
  Or an old m. upon a winter's
                                  YEATS 232:4
  Our m. in Havana   GREE 93:18
  problem is that *m. is dead*   FROMM 85:13
  reflecting the figure of a m.
                                  WOOLF 231:13
  right to be obeyed than m.   JOHN 113:21
  Stand by your m.   WYN 232:3
  street fighting m.   JAGG 111:9
  streets a m. must go   CHAN 49:1
  the m. for others   BONH 36:3
  The m. who came to dinner   KAUF 118:1
  The m. who would be king   KIPL 125:21
  The m. you love to hate   ANON 7:24
  Then m. your ships   LUCAS 140:13
  The Reasonable M.   HERB 101:23
  The significance of m.   BECK 21:8
  things that happen to a m.   TROT 218:3
  This very remarkable m.   INGE 110:8
  thy vanity, it is not m.   POUND 174:13
  To justify God's ways to m.   HOUS 107:8
  tragedy of a m. who has found
                                  BARR 19:24
  Ulcer M. on 4 Ulcer Pay   EARLY 71:16
  were a m. of distinction   FIEL 79:6
  what is m.? Wherefore   LENO 135:17
  What ought a m. to be   IBSEN 110:1
  When I was m. alive   HOUS 106:17
  when the m. of controversy   GALB 88:2
  without a m. is like a fish   STEI 208:4
  woman be more like a m.   LERN 135:19
  Women who love the same m.   BEER 23:9
  you'll be a M., my son   KIPL 126:15
  Youre not a m., youre a machine
                                  SHAW 195:19
manage: m. without butter but not
                                  GOEB 91:6
management: m. doesn't seem to
  understand   CHAR 49:15
manager: No m. ever got fired   ANON 7:28
Mandalay: Come you back to M.
                                  KIPL 123:13
Mandarin: called this style the M.
                                  CONN 58:19
Manderley: night I dreamt I went to M.
                                  DU M 70:12
mane: whistling m. of every wind
                                  THOM 215:10
manhood: upon me, my m. is cast
                                  LAWR 132:13
manifestly: m. and undoubtedly be seen
                                  HEW 102:5
manifesto: first powerful plain m.
                                  SPEN 205:17
man-in-the-street: Of the sensual m.
                                  AUDEN 13:9

man-in-the-street (*cont.*):
  To the m., who, I'm sorry   AUDEN 14:20
mankind: have put m. and posterity
                                  INGE 110:15
  have the existence of m.   ADAMS 2:7
  Homes and the Freedom of m.   HAIG 95:3
  m. faces a crossroads   ALLEN 3:21
  m. is divisible into two   BEER 22:17
  M. must put an end to war   KENN 119:4
  silliness of the majority of m.
                                  RUSS 186:18
  suffering of m.   RUSS 186:7
  the other half of m.   LAING 129:12
  The proper study of m. is books
                                  HUXL 108:13
  There is no history of m.   POPP 172:14
manner: All m. of thing shall be well
                                  ELIOT 74:23
  this extraordinary m.   STOP 209:20
manners: dont dress well and weve no m.
                                  SHAW 200:3
  Edward III had very good m.   SELL 194:11
  M. are especially the need
                                  WAUGH 223:10
  people have good table m.   MIKES 151:14
  Who take their m. from the Ape
                                  BELL 24:6
manœuvring: could be a m. swine
                                  MCC 141:14
man-o'-war: The M.'s 'er 'usband
                                  KIPL 127:4
mansion: A heavenly m., raging
                                  YEATS 235:18
  But Love has pitched his m.
                                  YEATS 235:14
mantled: M. in mist, remote from
                                  AUDEN 12:15
manufacture: m. professors   WEIL 224:3
manufactures: m. therefore is a secondary
                                  CHAM 48:7
manure: becomes the m. of the next
                                  CONN 59:11
many: adulation by the m.   BROWN 41:10
  m. a good tune played   BUTL 44:9
  Not m. people know   CAINE 44:18
  owed by so m. to so few   CHUR 54:12
many-splendoured: That miss the m.
  thing   THOM 216:11
map: m. of Europe has been changed
                                  CHUR 54:2
maps: Geography is about M.   BENT 28:24
  Where the m. are spread   YEATS 233:7
Marabar: echo in a M. cave is not
                                  FORS 83:21
marble: Glowed on the m.   ELIOT 76:18
  m. cross below the town   HAYES 99:5
march: Do not m. on Moscow   MONT 155:5
  m. my troops towards   GRIM 94:8
  m. of this retreating world   OWEN 166:17
  m. on their stomachs shouting
                                  SELL 194:16
  Men who m. away   HARDY 97:16
  you can m. behind   CAST 47:11
marched: Ten thousand women m.
  through   CHES 50:24
marching: hear the sound of m.
                                  JAGG 111:9
Margery: Some went upstairs with M.
                                  AUDEN 14:6
margin: m. this innocent virgin
                                  AUDEN 15:11
Maria: M. flung herself on him
                                  GRAH 92:15

Marie: And I am M. of Roumania
                                  PARK 168:11
marijuana: m. in his hair   LOW 140:3
Marilyn: M. who was every man's
                                  MAIL 145:11
Marines: armed forces and the M.
                                  THAT 212:16
marionettes: though the m. are men
                                  BENT 29:8
mark: Great Scorer comes to m.   RICE 180:8
Market Harborough: Am in M. Where
  ought   CHES 50:5
markets: m. by the sea shut fast FLEC 81:7
marks: bears the m. of the last HAIG 95:2
  m. of the beast   HARDY 97:6
marmalade-downwards: m. incidence was
  statistically   JENN 113:5
Marquis: Abducted by a French M.
                                  GRAH 92:10
marriage: long monotony of m.   GIBB 90:2
  Love and m., love and m.   CAHN 44:15
  M. always demands the finest
                                  BAUM 20:13
  m. and the constancy   SHAW 198:4
  m. a success and only one   SAM 189:9
  M. is a bribe to make   WILD 227:3
  M. is a wonderful invention   CONN 58:13
  m. is not that adults produce DE VR 67:7
  m. isn't a word   VIDOR 221:18
  M. is popular because it   SHAW 198:15
  m. is the waste-paper basket   WEBB 224:1
  M., n. The state or condition BIER 34:9
  So that is m., Lily thought
                                  WOOLF 231:15
marriages: m. come from the husbands
                                  WOD 230:4
  The thousands of m.   LARK 131:3
married: although he was twice m.
                                  RUSS 186:17
  are the best part of m.   WILD 227:4
  aunts, who are not m.   CHES 52:12
  I m. beneath me, all women do
                                  ASTOR 11:22
  I'm getting m. in the morning
                                  LERN 135:18
  incomplete until he has m.   GABOR 87:20
  M. women are kept women   SMITH 203:7
  my parents were m.   ACK 1:10
  So they were m.   MACN 144:14
  Trade Unionism of the m.   SHAW 198:3
  We can't get m. at all   WILD 227:2
  woman's business to get m.
                                  SHAW 197:26
marries: m. three girls from St Louis
                                  STEIN 207:10
marry: alone, they'd never m.
                                  HENRY 101:10
  But m. me, and I'll never   PIR 171:19
  Carlyle and Mrs Carlyle m.   BUTL 43:14
  get away to m. you today   LEIGH 134:10
  know who they may m.   MITF 154:14
  men we wanted to m.   STEI 208:3
  one thing, they m. later   MENC 150:18
  see what some girls m.   ROWL 185:16
  You don't m. it legitimately   DEGAS 65:16
Mars: M. a day helps you work   GAFF 87:22
  Next July we collide with M.   PORT 173:7
Martini: clothes and into a dry M.
                                  ANON 7:12
  clothes and into a dry M.   WEST 225:10
  like a medium Vodka dry M.   FLEM 82:1
Martinis: M. did the work for me ADE 2:13
martyr: you are a Crook or a M. ROG 182:7

martyrdom: M. . . . is the only way
               SHAW 196:8
   That even the dreadful m.   AUDEN 13:6
marvel: There could I m.   THOM 213:16
   They m. more and more   BELL 24:9
marvelling: She left me m. why my soul
              THOM 214:21
Marx: abandonment of the teaching of M.
              KHR 121:3
   anything M. dreamed   TOYN 217:14
   Karl M. and Catherine   ATTL 12:12
   M. whose analysis seems   BENN 27:10
   wholly wrong to blame M.   BENN 27:11
Marxism: Methodism than to M.
              PHIL 171:1
Marxist: I am a M.—of the Groucho
              ANON 7:6
   The distortion of the M. idea   BENN 27:11
Marxiste: *Je suis M.—tendance Groucho*
              ANON 7:6
Mary Jane: *What* is the matter with M.
              MILNE 153:8
Marylebone: hanging garments of M.
              JOYCE 115:9
Masefield: To M. something more
              BEER 22:21
masochism: A spirit of national m.
              AGNEW 2:22
masochistic: m. form of exhibitionism
              OLIV 163:5
masonry: man into the social m.
              WELLS 225:1
mass: After two thousand years of m.
              HARDY 98:6
   I go to M. every day   BELL 24:23
   Move between the fields to M.   BETJ 32:6
   The broad m. of a nation   HITL 103:8
massacre: are not as sudden as a m.
              TWAIN 219:7
masses: for the m. it is not art   SCH 193:5
mass-production: m. are being utilized
              LANC 129:19
mast: m. burst open with a rose
              FLEC 81:21
master: community consisting of a m.
              BIER 34:9
   M. shall praise us   KIPL 127:11
   not make dreams your m.   KIPL 126:13
   or can be m. of money   BEV 33:11
masterpiece: one knows, at sight, a m.
              POUND 174:7
   writer is to produce a m.   CONN 59:7
masterpieces: adventures of his soul
   among m.   FRAN 84:16
masters: are the m. at the moment
              SHAW 200:8
   Old M.   AUDEN 13:5
mastery: Wisdom was mine, and I had m.
              OWEN 166:17
mastiff: m. which is to watch over
              LLOY 138:7
mastodons: calling to Aunt like m.
              WOD 230:15
masturbation: Don't knock m.   ALLEN 4:5
   M. is the thinking man's   HAMP 96:6
   m. of war   RAE 177:7
   M.: the primary sexual   SZASZ 211:13
match: dont quite m. your face   ASHF 10:17
matched: has m. us with His hour
              BROO 40:1
matches: with that stick of m.
              MAND 145:18

matchless: he has one m. blessing
              EDW 72:8
mate: should listen when his m.
              WICK 226:23
materialistic: Christianity is the most m.
              TEMP 212:13
   m. people I have ever met   MCC 141:9
materials: I use simple m.   LOWRY 140:7
mathematical: Moriarty of m. celebrity
              DOYLE 69:16
mathematician: appear as a pure m.
              JEANS 112:22
mathematicians: M. go mad, and cashiers
              CHES 51:11
mathematics: M. may be defined
              RUSS 186:20
   M., rightly viewed   RUSS 186:22
   pregnancy by a resort to m.
              MENC 150:23
   world for ugly m.   HARDY 96:18
Matilda: M., and the House, were Burned
              BELL 24:16
   M. told such Dreadful Lies   BELL 24:14
   You'll come a-waltzing, M.   PAT 169:15
mating: Only in the m. season   MILL 152:17
matrimony: m. is breakfast-time
              HERB 101:25
matter: But what's the m. wi' Glasgow
              FYFFE 87:17
   Does it m.   SASS 191:18
   don't m. a tinker's cuss   SHIN 200:13
   What is the m. with Mary Jane
              MILNE 153:8
mattered: m. more than they should
              BOLD 35:15
mattering: m. once it has stopped
              BOWEN 37:9
matters: m. just as little   SHAW 198:1
   What can I do that m.   SPEN 205:15
mature: allowed to m. in the cask
              O'FAO 162:22
   imitate; m. poets steal   ELIOT 76:8
   M. artists steal   TRIL 218:1
   m. enough for offspring   DE VR 67:7
Maugham: he [M.] said to me
              MAUG 149:10
Max: incomparable M.   SHAW 200:7
Maxim: The M. Gun, and they have not
              BELL 25:2
maximum: m. of temptation   SHAW 198:15
may: From M. to December   AND 4:21
   M. month flaps its glad   HARDY 97:10
   M. will be fine next year   HOUS 105:13
   M. without cloud and June   ARAG 10:2
   On the first of M.   HART 98:19
   outside and m. be some time
              MAHON 145:6
   outside and m. be some time
              OATES 162:3
   there's an end of M.   HOUS 105:12
maybe: M. it's because I'm a Londoner
              GREGG 93:22
Mayer: [Louis B. M.'s] funeral   GOLD 92:1
mayor: finally married the M.   BAXT 20:15
   What did the m. do   GRAV 93:3
maze: Life is a m. in which we   CONN 59:10
mazy: A merry road, a m. road   CHES 50:22
MCC: M. ends and the Church   PRIE 175:11
McCarthyism: M. is Americanism
              MCC 141:7
McCartney: Paul M. and George Harrison
              BUCK 42:4

McGregor: go into Mr M.'s garden
              POTT 173:14
McGrew: sat Dangerous Dan M.
              SERV 194:23
McKinley: M. has no more backbone
              ROOS 183:16
me: For you but not for m.   ANON 8:1
   I most delight in M.   CAMP 45:10
   interested in himself than in m.
              BIER 34:6
   M. and my shadow   ROSE 184:11
   M. Tarzan, you Jane   WEIS 224:5
   where's the rest of m.   BELL 24:3
meadow: And m. rivulets overflow
              HARDY 97:3
   m. for a clean place   KAV 118:9
   stranger's feet may find the m.
              HOUS 106:4
meadows: Deep m. yet, for to forget
              BROO 40:15
meals: supper—for between m.
              TWAIN 219:8
mean: A poem should not m.   MACL 143:6
   Down these m. streets   CHAN 49:1
   It all depends what you m.   JOAD 113:19
   It don't m. a thing   MILLS 152:21
   What m.?   ROSS 185:1
meaner: opponent motives m.   BARR 19:14
meaning: enhanced m. in memorable
              BARZ 20:11
   Is there a m. to music   COPL 61:3
   language charged with m.   POUND 174:1
meaningful: with 'm.' or 'significant'
              CHOM 52:19
meaningless: cryptic as to be almost m.
              ANON 8:22
   Polite m. words   YEATS 233:9
meanings: words and m.   ELIOT 74:9
means: invisible m. of support   BUCH 41:20
   m. employed determine   HUXL 108:15
   m. think that the most   BREN 39:8
   mercy of his m.   THOM 213:18
   Private M. is dead   SMITH 203:23
meant: it's what I m.   VAUG 221:8
measles: It is the m. of the human
              EINS 72:11
   Love is like the m.   JER 113:8
measure: m. of a man is not where
              KING 122:1
measured: m. out my life with coffee
              ELIOT 75:15
measurement: M. began our might
              YEATS 233:1
meat: And went without m.   ROB 181:13
   I have no stomach for such m.
              DOBS 68:1
   m. no woman in London will   CAMP 45:6
   opinions as it buys its m.   BUTL 43:29
Meccah: some to M. turn to pray
              FLEC 81:11
mechanized: potato-gatherers like m.
   scarecrows   KAV 118:8
medal: a m. inscribed   OSB 165:16
medals: m. and ribbons   BELL 26:11
media: don't care much for the m.
              STOP 209:15
medical: food well in advance of m.
              WOD 230:16
Medici: Miniver loved the M.   ROB 181:15
medicinal: M. discovery   AYRES 16:8
medicine: masses not to take m.
              OSLER 165:23
   m. advertisement without   JER 113:14

medicine (*cont*.):
  men mistake m. for magic   SZASZ 211:19
  The desire to take m.   OSLER 165:25
Medicine Hat: The plumed war-bonnet
  of M.   BENÉT 27:7
medicos: m. marvelling sweetly
   RANS 177:14
mediocre: Some men are born m.
   HELL 100:4
  Titles distinguish the m.   SHAW 198:16
  Women want m. men   MEAD 150:9
mediocrity: M. knows nothing higher
   DOYLE 70:1
meditating: middle of a firwood m.
   O'BR 162:7
Mediterranean: encircling movement in
  the M.   CHUR 54:14
  ever taken from the M.   SHAF 195:4
medium: m. because nothing's well done
   ACE 1:5
  The m. is the message   MCL 143:10
medley: A m. of extemporanea
   PARK 168:11
meek: m. shall inherit the Earth
   SMITH 202:9
meet: m. my Maker brow to brow
   CORN 61:6
  m. the Duke I couldn't   SHAW 200:10
  We'll m. again, don't know   PARK 169:10
  Yet m. we shall, and part   BUTL 43:4
meetings: M. that do not come off
   BOWEN 37:12
meets: this than m. the eye   BANK 18:3
meilleurs: *ceux qui sont m. que nous*
   CAMUS 46:2
mellow: m., like good wine   PHIL 171:2
Mellstock: lie in M. churchyard now
   BETJ 31:2
melodious: wailed like m. cats under
   HUXL 108:11
melodrama: senses of the word, a m.
   AUDEN 15:13
melody: A pretty girl is like a m.
   BERL 29:17
  m. lingers on   BERL 29:18
  Moved to delight by the m. AUDEN 15:11
melting: must ride on its own m.
   FROST 85:18
melts: snow, m. in your hand   PARK 169:4
member: WILL ACCEPT ME AS A M.
   MARX 147:18
memoirs: m. is to speak ill of everybody
   PÉT 170:10
memorable: enhanced meaning in m. form
   BARZ 20:11
memorandum: m. is written not to inform
   ACH 1:9
memories: beastly incidents our m.
   O'NEI 163:14
  m. are card-indexes consulted
   CONN 59:16
  M. are hunting horns   APOL 9:23
memory: And suddenly the m. returns
   PROU 175:17
  Footfalls echo in the m.   ELIOT 74:3
  It brings back a m. ever green
   PORT 172:19
  M. and desire, stirring   ELIOT 76:13
  m. of a Macaulay   BARR 19:26
  m. of a man may float   OSLER 165:24
  Midnight shakes the m.   ELIOT 75:21
  no force can abolish m.   ROOS 183:13
  plucking the fruit of m.   CONR 59:18
  poetry strays into my m.   HOUS 106:5

memory (*cont*.):
  said that God gave us m.   BARR 19:13
  Thanks for the m.   ROBIN 181:12
  women'll stay in a man's m.   KIPL 127:16
men: All m. are creative   GOOD 92:3
  All m. are equal   FORS 83:15
  all m. are rapists   FREN 85:4
  blue sky and the m.   FORS 84:4
  boon and a blessing to m.   ANON 8:21
  But m. at whiles are sober   HOUS 105:16
  can make a crowd of m.   BEER 23:15
  cease when m. refuse to fight   ANON 9:6
  do twice as well as m.   WHIT 226:21
  Either war is obsolete or m.   FULL 87:13
  going to dine with some m.   BENT 29:1
  If m. could get pregnant   KENN 118:18
  inspire sympathy in m.   BEER 23:10
  Maguire and his m.   KAV 118:8
  many kinds of awful m.   COPE 61:2
  m. alone are quite capable   CONR 60:3
  m. and girls came   FITZ 80:19
  m. and women are not   SHAW 196:23
  m. are equal is a proposition
   HUXL 109:10
  m. are good at getting taxis   WHIT 226:15
  M. are so honest   LERN 135:19
  m. are working hard   MEAD 150:9
  M. build bridges and throw   BROUN 41:6
  m. do not learn very much   HUXL 108:12
  m. from the barn   HOUS 106:16
  M. have a much better time
   MENC 150:18
  M. have never been good   BARTH 20:1
  m. in my life that counts   WEST 225:15
  m. knew how women pass
   HENRY 101:10
  M. seldom make passes   PARK 168:14
  M.! The only animal   LAWR 131:15
  m. we wanted to marry   STEI 208:3
  M. who are unhappy   RUSS 186:9
  M. who march away   HARDY 97:16
  m. worship the Caesars   HUXL 108:16
  Older m. declare war   HOOV 104:10
  salvaged by m. who talk   HOGB 104:3
  Some m. are born mediocre   HELL 100:4
  stronger than m.   STEP 208:5
  teaches us that m. and nations
   EBAN 71:17
  ten m. who havnt and dont
   SHAW 195:11
  The true m. of action   AUDEN 14:1
  The war between m. and women
   THUR 216:19
  We are the hollow m.   ELIOT 75:10
  We are the stuffed m.   ELIOT 75:10
  We have the m.—the skill   ROOS 183:8
  When m. make gods   O'NEI 163:10
  work of fifty ordinary m.   HUBB 107:15
menace: against the m. of aggression
   ASQ 11:11
mend: Make do and m.   ANON 7:21
mendacities: Better m.   POUND 174:4
mendacity: M. is a system that we live
   WILL 227:17
mendier: *de m. dans les rues et*   FRAN 84:15
Mensch: *Unaufrichtigkeit zwischen M.*
   BAUM 20:13
Menschen: *Die M. aber waren nie gut*
   BARTH 20:1
mensonge: *alliage de réel et de m.*   COCT 57:6
  Impossible venir, m. suit   PROU 176:5
mental: Freedom and slavery are m. states
   GAND 88:11
mention: Don't m. the war   CLEE 56:13

mention (*cont*.):
  Just m. us, that is all   OWEN 166:7
mentioned: years ago no one m. it
   CHAN 49:7
menu: And then I saw the m.   WESK 225:7
Mercedes: won't you buy me a M.
   JOPL 115:3
mercenary: Followed their m. calling
   HOUS 106:3
merciful: M. as constant, constant
   GRAV 93:7
merciless: looked at in this m. glare
   WILL 227:20
mercury: m. sank in the mouth
   AUDEN 12:20
  pick up m. with a fork   LLOY 138:6
mercy: m. of his means   THOM 213:18
  Thy everlasting m., Christ   MAS 148:12
Meredith: M. climbed towards   CHES 52:6
  M., we're in   KITC 128:4
merger: m. between Heaven and Hell
   WELLS 224:12
meritocracy: rise of the m.   YOUNG 236:7
mermaids: have heard the m. singing
   ELIOT 75:19
merry: Always m. and bright   WIMP 229:17
  A m. road, a mazy road   CHES 50:22
  For all their wars are m.   CHES 50:9
merrygoround: It's no go the m.
   MACN 144:7
mess: here's another nice m.   LAUR 131:11
  m. of imprecision of feeling   ELIOT 74:13
  m. with Mister In-between   MERC 151:7
  what we can make of the m.   ELIOT 74:14
  who has made an awful m.   BURR 42:16
message: first m. of India   FORS 84:2
  The medium is the m.   MCL 143:10
messages: m. should be delivered
   GOLD 91:13
  sending of general m.   DOYLE 69:30
  you get m. of sympathy   AYCK 15:20
Messer: *die Nacht der langen M.*   HITL 103:3
messing: simply m. about in boats
   GRAH 92:17
met: m. a man that I didn't like
   ROG 182:13
metamorphoses: flowerings, month of m.
   ARAG 10:2
métamorphoses: *floraisons mois des m.*
   ARAG 10:2
metaphor: all m. is poetry   CHES 50:12
metaphysics: M. is the finding of bad
   BRAD 38:5
  science of m.   MENC 151:1
meters: Watch the parkin' m.   DYLAN 71:13
Methodism: more to M. than to Marxism
   PHIL 171:1
methods: You know my m. Apply them
   DOYLE 69:23
Mexico: South of the Border—down M.
  way   KENN 118:20
mezzanine: down into the m. floor
   WOD 230:12
Michael Angelo: Enter M. Andrea del
  Sarto   BEER 22:27
  Italy from designs by M.   TWAIN 219:20
  not want M. for breakfast   TWAIN 219:19
Michelangelo: Talking of M.   ELIOT 75:14
  they produced M.   WELL 224:11
Michelin: she with the M. beside me
   CONN 59:15
microbe: The M. is so very small   BELL 25:5
middle: beginning, a m. and an end
   GOD 91:4

middle (*cont.*):

dead centre of m. age	ADAMS 1:18
pleasures of m. age	POUND 173:23
sinking m. class	ORW 165:5
sits in the m. and knows	FROST 86:23
stay in the m. of the road	BEVAN 33:5

Middle Age: enchantments of the M.

BEER 23:6

middle-aged: watches her m. children

SCOT 194:4

middle class: The M. was quite prepared

BELL 24:18

middle-class: m. morality all the time

SHAW 199:21

thats m. morality	SHAW 199:25

Middle East: this mad dog of the M.

REAG 178:16

Middlesex: Elysium—rural M. again

BETJ 31:7

midge: lightly skims the m.   BETJ 31:18

Midlands: When I am living in the M.

BELL 25:25

midnight: Holding hands at m.   GERS 89:17

Love, the reeling m. through

PARK 168:19

m. in some public place	YEATS 233:5
M. shakes the memory	ELIOT 75:21
See her on the bridge at m.	ANON 8:8
There m.'s all a glimmer	YEATS 232:9
troubled m. and the noon	ELIOT 76:3

midst: m. of life we are in debt

MUMF 157:14

midwife: m. slapped your footsoles

PLATH 172:2

mieux: *je vais de m. en mieux*   COUÉ 61:13

might: Because the all-enacting M.

HARDY 98:2

Britons alone use 'M.'   WAUGH 223:16

mightier: believed that the bank was m.

PLOM 172:8

make thee m. yet	BENS 28:21

spark-gap is m. than the pen

HOGB 104:3

mighty: And m. ships ten thousand ton

HODG 103:12

But he's m. lak' a rose	STAN 207:2
God who made thee m.	BENS 28:21
stop the m. roar of London's	ANON 8:2

miles: 10,000 m. away from home

JOHN 114:13

60,000 m. per hour somewhere

FULL 87:12

And m. around the wonder grew

HOUS 106:13

And m. to go before I sleep   FROST 86:7

militaires: *pour la confier à des m.*

CLEM 56:16

militant: m. each in your own way

PANK 167:11

this m. movement	PANK 167:9
was the first m. lowbrow	BERL 30:5

military: arms race has no m. purpose

MOUN 157:3

Doing the M. Two-step	GREN 94:2
hold the m. mind	TUCH 218:15
matter to entrust to m.	CLEM 56:16

When the m. man approaches

SHAW 198:2

military-industrial: by the m. complex

EIS 73:6

milk: Gin was mother's m. to her

SHAW 199:23

M. and then just as it	BETJ 31:12
m. and the yoghurt	MORT 156:10

milk (*cont.*):

m. is more likely	BUTL 43:29
m. of human kindness	GUED 94:11
m. the cow of the world	WILB 226:24

One end is moo, the other, m.

NASH 159:4

putting m. into babies   CHUR 53:14

mill: golf-links lie so near the m.

CLEG 56:15

John Stuart M.	BENT 29:3
m. and the fold	HOUS 106:16
old m. by the stream	ARMS 10:7

Under the m., under the mill

BROO 40:15

million: A m. million spermatozoa

HUXL 108:20

Fifty m. Frenchmen can't	GUIN 94:14
Fifty m. Frenchmen can't	ROSE 184:13
really want to make a m.	HUBB 107:18
The first ten m. years	ADAMS 1:15

millionaire: And an old-fashioned m.

FISH 80:10

As a silk hat on a Bradford m.   ELIOT 77:1

I am a M. That is my religion

SHAW 197:10

Who wants to be a m.   PORT 173:8

millionaires: All m. love a baked apple

FIRB 80:3

full of rascals, m.   BENN 28:15

millions: Kill m. of men, and you

ROST 185:8

m. long for immortality	ERTZ 77:21
m. of the mouthless dead	SORL 205:3

Milton: And malt does more than M. can

HOUS 107:8

mind: are the empires of the m.

CHUR 55:14

Before the secret working m.

YEATS 233:1

Came-over-with-the Conqueror type
of m.   WATS 222:17

Cast your m. on other days   YEATS 233:3

Come back into my m.   BELL 25:25

consistency is as bad for the m.

HUXL 108:14

contradictory beliefs in one's m.

ORW 164:24

cutting edge of the m.	BRON 39:13
give his m. to politics	SHAW 195:12
His m. moves upon silence	YEATS 233:3
I do not m. lying	BUTL 44:1
I don't m. if I do	KAV 118:13
If I am out of my m.	BELL 26:9

improper m. is a perpetual SMITH 202:21

it's all in the m.	WOLFE 231:1
joy, and m. is fruit	MAS 148:11
keeps Georgia on my m.	GORR 92:5
Keep violence in the m.	ALD 3:5

Let them m. their own affairs

HOUS 105:17

m. and body to do	BAD 16:9

m. and knows it can always

SHAW 195:11

m. begins to roam irretrievably

SOLZ 204:5

m. from the dominion	GOLD 91:11
m. is not a bed to be made	AGATE 2:20
M. my bike	WARN 222:13
m. of man or elevate	YEATS 235:13
Mr Churchill but the m.	ATTL 12:9
my m. is maturing late	NASH 159:8
Of my own m.	THOM 215:5

on not changing one's m.   MAUG 149:18

prodigious quantity of m.   TWAIN 219:17

mind (*cont.*):

resemblance to what one has in m.

PROU 176:2

sentences until reeled the m.   GIBBS 90:3

someone whose m. watches

CAMUS 45:18

urge the m. to aftersight   ELIOT 74:19

while we have sex in the m.

LAWR 132:17

youngest darter to m. me   PHIL 171:3

minded: wreckage of men who have m.

WOOLF 231:14

minds: best m. of my generation

GINS 90:15

close to m.	BUCH 41:18
fairly developed m.	FORS 83:2

great m. in the commonplace

HUBB 107:14

have comfortable m.	CUMM 63:17
Little m. are interested	HUBB 107:14

M. like beds always made up

WILL 227:23

m. of a few fastidious	SMITH 203:16
mislead their weak m.	SAY 192:11
pervert climbs into the m.	BRON 39:15
since wars begin in the m.	ANON 6:16
Women never have young m.	DEL 67:1

mine: If they are m. or no   HOUS 106:4

M. is the only voice	CAMP 45:10
she is m. for life	SPARK 205:7

So be m., as I yours for ever   GRAV 93:7

miner: so I became a m. instead

COOK 60:10

miners: m. sweat their guts out

ORW 164:29

Mineworkers: National Union of M.

MACM 143:20

Ming Bing: what is known as the M.

MONT 155:5

miniature: every day is a life in m.

O'NEI 163:12

minimum: with the m. of fuss   BLYT 35:7

mining: snakeskin-titles of m.-claims

BENÉT 27:7

minister: been said that this M.   BAIL 16:11

M. in order to preside   CHUR 53:18

Yes, M.   CROS 63:9

ministers: mind how much my M. talk

THAT 212:19

Miniver: M. loved the Medici   ROB 181:15

mink: doesn't have a m. coat   NIXON 161:7

The trick of wearing m.   BALM 18:1

minority: enough people to make a m.

ALTM 4:11

m. to the majority	LENIN 134:18
The m. are right	DEBS 65:15

mint: pockets the mark of the m.

CHES 51:23

minute: leave in a m. and a huff

KALM 117:12

The m. you walked in the joint FIEL 79:6

minutes: And twenty m. more or less

YEATS 235:17

be famous for fifteen m.	WARH 222:10
going to say in twenty m.	BRAB 37:20
hundred and seventeen m.	BENN 28:11
m. the damned fella will	MITF 154:15

Mirabeau: M. Bridge flows the Seine

APOL 9:22

Sous le pont M. coule la Seine   APOL 9:22

miracle: not a fraud, but a m.

SHAW 199:28

miracles: But the age of m. hadn't

GERS 89:13

Miranda: remember an Inn, M.   BELL 25:15
mire: Sow returns to her M.   KIPL 126:18
mirror: bevelled edge of a sunlit m.
  ABSE 1:3
mirror'd: Lie m. on her sea   HODG 103:15
mirrors: believe in m. or newspapers
  OSB 165:14
  cell whose walls are m.   O'NEI 163:9
  mine as m. are lonely   AUDEN 14:7
  M. and fatherhood   BORG 36:9
  Over the m. meant   HARDY 97:13
  The m. of the sea are strewn   FLEC 81:14
mirth: M. that has no bitter springs
  KIPL 126:8
  The song of the birds for m.   GURN 94:17
miscarriages: pregnancies and at least
  four m.   BEEC 22:3
miserable: arise and make them m.
  HUXL 108:16
  certain too, I'm m.   MAC 142:14
  horrible and the m.   ALLEN 4:6
  make only two people m.   BUTL 43:14
  m. human being than one   JAMES 112:11
  m. is to have leisure   SHAW 199:12
miseries: Coherent m., a bite and sup
  HEAN 99:14
  m. or credulities of mankind   CONR 60:1
misery: Man hands on m. to man
  LARK 130:13
misfits: strangest collection of m.
  REAG 178:15
misfortune: bored by the recital of m.
  MAUG 149:15
  m. to ourselves, and good   BIER 34:2
misfortunes: m. can befall a boy
  MAUG 150:3
misguided: guided missiles and m. men
  KING 122:4
mishtake: Shome m., shurely   ANON 8:9
mislead: one to m. the public   ASQ 11:10
misplaced: rise of m. power exists   EIS 73:6
mispronounce: language: all men m. it
  MORL 156:1
misquotation: M. is, in fact, the pride
  PEAR 169:19
missed: he m. the bus   CHAM 48:16
  m. the point completely   ELIOT 73:19
missing: M. so much and so much
  CORN 61:8
mission: Its five-year m.   RODD 182:2
  m. workers came out too   RUNY 186:3
missionaries: sad death—eaten by m.
  SPOO 206:10
Mississippi: day even the state of M.
  KING 121:15
  east all the way into M.   KIPL 127:17
  What have you in the M.   BURNS 42:15
Miss T: That whatever M. eats   DE L 66:15
mist: White the m. along the grass
  BETJ 32:6
mistake: always made a new m. instead
  COPE 61:2
  capital m. to theorize   DOYLE 69:26
  When I make a m., it's a beaut
  LA G 129:8
mistaken: unless I am m., is our client
  DOYLE 69:8
mistakes: genius makes no m.
  JOYCE 116:11
  m. that can be made   HEIS 100:2
  nothing that make no m.   CONR 59:28
mistook: man who m. his wife
  SACKS 187:14

mistress: But m. in my own   KIPL 124:8
  m. and two slaves   BIER 34:9
mistresses: wife and hardly any m.
  SAKI 188:17
mists: And low the m. of evening lie
  BETJ 31:18
  But when the m. in autumn   KING 122:12
  m. of righteous indignation   MUGG 157:7
  shaken m. a space unsettle   THOM 215:17
misunderstand: May no fate wilfully m.
  me   FROST 86:5
misunderstood: admired through being m.
  COCT 57:4
  I do not want to be m.   JOS 115:5
  worse lie than a truth m.   JAMES 112:16
Mithridates: M., he died old   HOUS 107:10
Mitty: Walter M., the undefeated
  THUR 216:25
mixed: What's a m. infant   BEHAN 23:24
moan: That is not paid with m.
  THOM 215:1
moanday: All m., tearsday, wailsday
  JOYCE 115:12
mock: m. the riddled corpses   SASS 192:2
  yet m. what women meant   OWEN 166:14
mockeries: No m. now for them
  OWEN 166:9
mocking: Of a m. tale or a gibe
  YEATS 233:9
mockingbird: it's a sin to kill a m.
  LEE 134:1
models: they have no other m.   BALD 16:20
Model T: have the M. in any colour
  FORD 82:19
moderately: m. honest man with
  a moderately   SHAW 198:22
moderation: M. in the affairs   JOHN 114:14
  m. in the pursuit of justice   GOLD 91:12
  M. in war is imbecility   FISH 80:6
modern: called a 'M. Churchman'
  WAUGH 223:3
  it's m. architecture   BANK 18:5
  this so-called m. art   MUNN 157:18
modest: I was a m., good-humoured
  BEER 22:22
  m. man who has a good   CHUR 53:6
modesty: had time to cultivate m.
  SITW 201:12
modulating: A gay m. anguish, rather
  FRY 87:4
moi: Pretentious? M.?   CLEE 56:14
mois: m. des floraisons   ARAG 10:2
Mole: secret diary of Adrian M.
  TOWN 217:12
moll: King's M. Reno'd in Wolsey's
  ANON 7:9
Mom: at a place called M.'s   ALGR 3:6
moment: m. in childhood when
  GREE 93:19
  m. of my greatness flicker   ELIOT 75:17
  m. the slave resolves   GAND 88:11
  phoenix m.   DAY-L 65:8
  That last m. belongs to us   VANZ 221:5
momentary: Beauty is m. in the mind
  STEV 208:13
moments: timeless m.   ELIOT 74:22
Mona: M. did researches in original
  PLOM 172:6
monarch: so much a king as a M.
  SELL 194:14
monarchy: might not be a Limited M.
  STR 210:8
  M. is a labour-intensive   WILS 228:13

Monday: On M., when the sun is hot
  MILNE 154:3
monde: m. des émotions qu'on nomme
  COL 57:15
responsable d'un m. aussi absurde
  DUH 70:9
monedas: por un puñado de m.   ZAP 236:10
money: am only interested in m.
  SHAW 196:25
  arms is not spending m.   EIS 73:7
  demand your m. or your life   BUTL 43:13
  earn much more m. writing
  AUDEN 13:15
  enough to get all that m.   CHES 52:13
  For lack of m., and it   LARK 130:10
  For m. can't buy me love   LENN 135:5
  Give him the m., Barney   PICK 171:10
  He had m. as well   THAT 213:6
  Her voice is full of m.   FITZ 80:20
  his m., and his religious   BUTL 43:10
  Hollywood m. isn't money   PARK 169:4
  I'm saving my m.   TUCK 218:18
  It's one for the m.   PERK 170:6
  leave them now is m.   LARK 130:11
  licence to print your own m.
  THOM 216:13
  m. among themselves there   STEAD 207:5
  m. and large armies   ANOU 9:18
  m. by underestimating   MENC 150:15
  M. couldn't buy friends   MILL 152:19
  M. doesn't talk, it swears   DYLAN 71:7
  M. gives me pleasure all   BELL 25:21
  m. if you can prove   HOPE 105:1
  M. is better than poverty   ALLEN 3:24
  M. is indeed the most important
  SHAW 196:29
  M. is like a sixth sense   MAUG 149:20
  m. I spend on advertising   LEV 136:6
  M. is the most important   SHAW 197:7
  M., it turned out   BALD 16:14
  must have m. and a room   WOOLF 231:12
  Never ask of m. spent   FROST 86:1
  no one shall work for m.   KIPL 127:11
  Oh we ain't got a barrel of m.
  WOODS 231:6
  or can be master of m.   BEV 33:11
  poor know that it is m.   BREN 39:8
  Take the m. and run   ALLEN 3:22
  there's no m. in poetry   GRAV 93:5
  The want of m. is so quite   BUTL 43:5
  they hired the m.   COOL 60:12
  try to rub up against m.   RUNY 186:5
  We haven't got the m.   RUTH 187:8
  what to do with their m.   BAR 18:7
  when you don't have any m.   DONL 68:6
monk: beast and the m.   FORS 83:17
  I said to this m.   PINT 171:12
monkey: m. when the organ grinder
  BEVAN 33:4
  surest way to make a m.   BENC 26:21
monkeys: Cats and m.—monkeys
  JAMES 111:22
  M., who very sensibly refrain
  GRAH 92:16
monks: The holiness of m., and after
  YEATS 233:2
monogamy: too many. M. is the same
  ANON 5:18
  Who seek to find m.   PARK 168:17
monographs: been guilty of several m.
  DOYLE 69:20
monologue: m. is not a decision   ATTL 12:10

monopoly: shun the temptations of m.
SCOTT 193:16

monosyllabic: nothing so m. as to cheat
FRY 87:8

monotony: long m. of marriage   GIBB 90:2

Monroe: M. Doctrine will go   ROOS 183:17

monster: pity this busy m., manunkind
CUMM 64:2

monsters: then even the m. we defy
MCKAY 142:15

monstrous: m. carbuncle on the face
CHAR 50:2

month: [£1,500 a m.] is not   GOWR 92:7
April is the cruellest m.   ELIOT 76:13
old man in a dry m.   ELIOT 73:11
O m. of flowerings   ARAG 10:2

months: weeks rather than m.   WILS 228:16

Montparnasse: I shall not rest quiet in M.
BENÉT 27:8

Montreal: Stowed away in a M. lumber
room   BUTL 44:2

monument: Their only m. the asphalt
road   ELIOT 76:5

monuments: M. of unageing intellect
YEATS 234:5

moo: And m. and coo with women-folk
KIPL 122:17
One end is m., the other, milk
NASH 159:4

moocow: m. coming down along
JOYCE 115:16

moon: And a white m. beams   KING 122:8
And I danced in the m.   CART 47:7
A ship, an isle, a sickle m.   FLEC 81:14
Don't let's ask for the m.   PROU 176:8
I didn't go to the m.   WILL 227:18
It was the lovely m.—she lifted
FREE 85:3
melodious cats under the m.
HUXL 108:11
moment when the m. was blood
CHES 52:10
M. and returning him safely
KENN 119:17
m. and under the sun   PORT 173:6
m. is in the seventh house   RADO 177:6
m. shone bright on Mrs   ELIOT 76:23
m. was a ghostly galleon   NOYES 161:16
shine on, harvest m.   NORW 161:13
Slowly, silently, now the m.   DE L 66:7
The m. belongs to everyone   DE SY 67:4
The m. is nothing   FRY 87:3
The M. on the one hand   BELL 26:8
The silver apples of the m.   YEATS 235:6
Tryst with the m.   DRIN 70:4

moonlight: Look for me by m.   NOYES 162:1
M. behind you   COW 62:9
road was a ribbon of m.   NOYES 161:16

moonlit: A starlit or a m. dome distains
YEATS 235:15
Knocking on the m. door   DE L 66:8

moons: Reason has m., but moons
HODG 103:15

moon-washed: On m. apples of wonder
DRIN 70:4

Moorish: M. wall and I thought well
JOYCE 116:14

moorland: Past cotton-grass and m.
AUDEN 14:21

moors: seen dawn and sunset on m.
MAS 148:6

moose: strong as a bull m.   ROOS 184:7

moral: afraid of losing your m. sense
STEIN 207:15
being a form of m. effort   LEAC 133:13
Englishman thinks he is m.   SHAW 197:30
It *is* a m. issue   HALEY 95:9
m. category but a pillar   SOLZ 204:8
m. crusade or it   WILS 228:15
m. flabbiness born   JAMES 112:8
M. indignation is jealousy   WELLS 225:5
m. system can rest solely   AYER 16:3
prostitute is more m. than a wife
PHIL 170:15
unhappy one becomes m.   PROU 175:20

moralising: blow his nose without m.
CONN 59:6

moralist: vital problem for the m.
RUSS 186:10

moralists: conscience is a delight to m.
RUSS 186:24

moralitee: Goodbye, m.   HERB 101:15

morality: I don't believe in m.
SHAW 196:14
kinds of m. side by side   RUSS 187:1
m. in any given time   WHIT 226:10
m. loses the foundation   SAM 189:10
m. should have this fact   SHAW 196:29
M.'s *not* practical   BOLT 35:16
thats middle-class m.   SHAW 199:25
up agen middle-class m.   SHAW 199:21

morals: done by basing m. on myth
SAM 189:10
Food comes first, then m.   BREC 38:22
Have you no m., man   SHAW 199:20

more: joints m. than somewhat
RUNY 186:1
m. people should see me   ASHC 10:14
m. things a man is ashamed
SHAW 197:19
m. things in heaven   HALD 95:6
M. will mean worse   AMIS 4:15
some animals are m. equal   ORW 164:9
The m. it snows   MILNE 153:1
To Masefield something m.   BEER 22:21
which is probably m.   KALM 117:11
wink wink, say no m.   CHAP 49:12

Moriarty: M. of mathematical celebrity
DOYLE 69:16

mornin': Oh, what a beautiful m.
HAMM 95:18

morning: arrives in the early m.
BOWEN 37:5
Good m., sir—was there   MURD 158:1
gray dawn of the m. after   ADE 2:13
hate to get up in the m.   BERL 29:16
I danced in the m.   CART 47:7
It's m. again in America   RINEY 181:6
I viewed the m. with alarm   GERS 89:13
Like the first m.   FARJ 78:7
m. glows the lily   FLEC 81:10
M. has broken   FARJ 78:7
m. I had another talk   CHAM 48:13
Praise for the m.   FARJ 78:7
shadow at m. striding   ELIOT 76:15
Such a m. it is when love   LEE 134:3
sun and in the m.   BINY 34:18
The m. light creaks down again
SITW 201:10
they take you in the m.   BALD 16:18
was arrested one fine m.   KAFKA 117:6
You've got to get up this m.   BERL 29:16

mornings: The literary m. with its hoot
AUDEN 14:18
we *always* had m. like   MILNE 153:4

Mornington: made me a present of M.
HARG 98:10

Morocco: Dictionary, we're M. bound
BURKE 42:14

moron: I wish I were a m.   ANON 8:7
See the happy m.   ANON 8:7
The consumer isn't a m.   OGIL 162:23

moronic: m. inferno had caught up
BELL 26:10

morphine: alcohol or m. or idealism
JUNG 116:20

Morris: [William M.]   BEER 22:20

mort: *compositeur, c'est d'être m.*   HON 104:9

mortal: every tatter in its m.   YEATS 234:6
M., guilty, but to me   AUDEN 13:7

mortals: Composing m. with immortal
AUDEN 15:12
luckiest of m. because   AUDEN 14:17

mortar: Lies are the m. that bind
WELLS 225:1

mortgaged: And frequently m. to the hilt
COW 62:11

morts: *Il n'y a pas de m.*   MAET 145:1

Moscow: Do not march on M.   MONT 155:5
M. to surprise us   BRAC 37:23

moss: Miles and miles of golden m.
AUDEN 14:23
m. or a caterpillar   BARB 18:10

most: m. people vote against   ADAMS 1:20
That [sex] was the m. fun   ALLEN 4:4

mother: And her m. came too   TITH 217:6
At that M. got proper blazing
EDGAR 72:1
Can you hear me, m.   POW 175:3
Care of his M.   MILNE 153:7
Don't tell my m. I'm living   HERB 101:17
For m. will be there   HERB 101:19
Gin was m.'s milk to her   SHAW 199:23
Glory, M. of the Free   BENS 28:21
man and the m. woman   SHAW 197:22
M. died today   CAMUS 46:4
M., give me the sun   IBSEN 109:23
m. is she watches her middle-aged
SCOT 194:4
M. knows best   FERB 79:2
m. lived the latter years   THUR 216:16
M. may I go and bathe   ANON 7.25
M. may I go out to swim   DE L 66:20
m. never realizes   JACK 111:3
M. to dozens   HERB 101:14
m. was a decent family   ASHF 11:1
My m., drunk or sober   CHES 50:13
My m.'s life made me a man   MAS 148:9
my m. taught me as a boy   BERR 30:17
My M. used to say   AYCK 15:19
really affectionate m.   MAUG 150:3
that I half knew my m.   O'BR 162:10
universal m.   CHES 52:9

mother-in-law: man said when his m.
died   JER 113:14
savage contemplates his m.   FRAZ 84:17

mother-naked: And m. and
ageless-ancient   DAY-L 65:8

mothers: Come m. and fathers
DYLAN 71:14
M. of large families   BELL 24:7
talking to you m. and fathers
ROOS 183:7

moths: m. among the whisperings
FITZ 80:19

motion: A gentle m. with the deep
DAV 65:4
Between the m.   ELIOT 75:11

motion (cont.):
Poetry in m.   KAUF 118:5
poetry of m.   GRAH 92:19
motive: attribution of false m.   BALD 17:4
Looks always on the m.   YEATS 234:9
motives: m. meaner than your own
                                BARR 19:14
motorcycle: art of m. maintenance
                                PIRS 171:20
motoribus: Cincti Bis M.   GODL 91:5
motors: The sound of horns and m.
                                ELIOT 76:23
motto: is criticism's m.   FORS 84:7
that is my m.   MARQ 147:4
The scouts' m. is founded   BAD 16:9
mottoes: Rather than the m. on sundials
                                POUND 174:3
mould: frozen in an out-of-date m.
                                JENK 113:3
m. a child's character   SHAW 198:13
moulded: m. by their admirations
                                BOWEN 37:6
Moulmein: By the old M. Pagoda
                                KIPL 123:13
mount: rejected the Sermon on the M.
                                BRAD 38:9
mountain: And the river jumps over
the m.   AUDEN 12:16
Climb ev'ry m., ford ev'ry   HAMM 95:14
In a m. greenery   HART 98:19
O'er the rugged m.'s brow   GRAH 92:13
We've been to the m. top   KING 121:16
mountainous: great big m. sports girl
                                BETJ 32:8
mountains: He paced upon the m. far
above   YEATS 232:7
mounting: view there is m. chaos
                                CALL 45:3
mourn: here is no cause to m.
                                OWEN 166:16
mourning: M. becomes Electra
                                O'NEI 163:13
voice of m.   OWEN 166:9
waste any time in m.   HILL 102:11
mourns: England m. for her dead
                                BINY 34:17
mouse: leave room for the m.   SAKI 188:20
wainscot and the m.   ELIOT 74:18
moustache: m. and the sort of eye
                                WOD 230:10
who didn't wax his m.   KIPL 127:14
mouth: A way of happening, a m.
                                AUDEN 13:1
before he opens his m.   NATH 159:24
just whispering in her m.   MARX 147:16
keeping your m. shut   EINS 73:3
m. too wide when he talks   FORS 83:3
m. without making some   SHAW 199:16
mouths: examining his wives' m.
                                RUSS 186:17
m. were made for tankards   MAS 148:5
We poets keep our m. shut   YEATS 232:4
move: high altar on the m.   BOWEN 37:8
Let us m. forward   ROOS 183:12
M. him into the sun   OWEN 166:11
m. in a world of the dead   FORS 83:7
moved: We shall not be m.   ANON 9:11
movement: But neither arrest nor m.
                                ELIOT 74:5
intelligent may begin a m.   CONR 60:2
m. of clouds in benediction   DAY-L 65:10
moves: His mind m. upon silence
                                YEATS 233:7
If it m., salute it   ANON 6:23

moves (cont.):
It m. in mighty leaps   AYRES 16:8
movies: basic appeal of m.   KAEL 117:4
M. should have a beginning   GOD 91:4
pay to see bad m.   GOLD 92:2
that can kill the M.   ROG 182:5
moving: It is m. day   HART 98:19
King's life is m. peacefully   DAWS 65:6
Somebody stopped the m. stairs
                                MACN 144:13
Mozart: en famille they play M.
                                BARTH 20:2
M. and Salieri we see   BAR 18:13
The truth is that M.   SONT 205:1
MPs: M. never see the London   LIV 138:3
much: conflict was so m. owed
                                CHUR 54:12
Guessing so much and so m.   CHES 51:8
Missing so m. and so much   CORN 61:8
M. as you said you were   HARDY 98:5
seem m. for them   COMP 58:9
So little done, so m. to do   RHOD 180:4
muck: can say is— sing 'em m.
                                MELBA 150:12
in lovely m. I've lain   HOUS 107:9
muck-rakes: m. are often indispensable
                                ROOS 184:4
mud: m. against a wall may   BLUNT 35:5
M.! Mud! Glorious mud   FLAN 81:4
M.'s sister, not himself   HOUS 105:5
pure clay of time's m.   MAL 145:14
universe with m.   FORS 83:10
muddied: wicket or the m. oafs KIPL 124:12
mudging: up with fudging and m.
                                OWEN 166:5
Mudie's: British Museum and at M.
                                BUTL 44:3
mug: Guinness from a thick m. PINT 171:13
Mulligan: plump Buck M. came from
                                JOYCE 116:1
multitude: m. of silent witnesses
                                GEOR 89:11
multitudes: Weeping, weeping m.
                                ELIOT 73:10
mum: fuck you up, your m. and dad
                                LARK 130:12
mumble: When in doubt, m.   BOREN 36:7
Mungojerrie: I might mention M.
                                ELIOT 75:4
municipal: vast m. fire station CHAR 50:2
murals: Garden City Café with its m.
                                BETJ 31:6
murder: brought back m. into the home
                                HITC 103:1
Dial 'M' for m.   KNOTT 128:9
even to m., for the truth   ADLER 2:16
lies sound truthful and m.   ORW 165:8
m. his wife that Dr Bickleigh ILES 110:5
M. is a serious business   ILES 110:5
m. of men is disgusting   EINS 72:12
We hear war called m.   MACD 142:4
murderer: man is a common m.   SAKI 188:2
murdering: executed for m. his publisher
                                BARR 19:3
murmur: Seem to m. sweet and low
                                ARMS 10:7
The ever-importunate m.   JAMES 111:10
Murphy: M.'s Law to the statement
                                MURP 158:3
muscle: take the m. from bone ELIOT 75:2
muse: Livelier liquor than the M.
                                HOUS 107:8
M. only speak when she   SMITH 203:24

museum: An artist may visit a m.
                                SANT 190:13
mush: with m. and slush   OWEN 166:5
mushroom: too short to stuff a m.
                                CONR 60:5
music: A dance to the m. of time
                                POW 174:20
alive with the sound of m.   HAMM 96:3
all his m. accepts it   SATIE 192:7
All m. is folk music   ARMS 10:8
anguish, rather like m.   FRY 87:4
anything about m. really   BEER 23:14
Caught in that sensual m.   YEATS 234:5
Classic m. is th'kind   HUBB 107:16
Darling of the m. halls   SMITH 202:13
English may not like m.   BEEC 22:8
Extraordinary how potent cheap m.
                                COW 62:7
Even before the m. begins   MILL 152:9
have an ear for her m.   DAY-L 65:10
I got m.   GERS 89:14
inexpressible is m.   HUXL 109:4
Is there a meaning to m.   COPL 61:4
keep swinging after the m.   HELP 100:9
me the most civilized m.   UST 220:16
more or less lascivious m.   MENC 151:3
m. begins to atrophy when
                                POUND 173:21
m. expresses itself   STR 210:14
m. for a lilt upon   MAS 148:5
m. goes 'round and around
                                HODG 103:16
m. is best understood   STR 210:15
M. is essentially useless   SANT 190:12
M. is feeling, then, not sound
                                STEV 208:12
M. is life, and like it   NIEL 160:12
m. is more enchanting   SMITH 202:23
m. is that which penetrates   BEEC 22:9
m. is the brandy   SHAW 197:28
M. is your own experience   PARK 167:13
m. of a poem   SYNGE 211:9
m. per se means nothing   BEEC 22:7
m. that changed a man's   SCHN 193:3
O body swayed to m.   YEATS 234:8
read m. but can't hear   BEEC 21:27
sound of m. so tender   PORT 172:19
The m. [the scherzo of Beethoven's 5th
Symphony]   FORS 83:14
what do you think about m.   VAUG 221:9
What m. shall I have   PITT 172:1
whisper m. on those strings ELIOT 77:5
musical: kind of m. Malcolm Sargent
                                BEEC 22:4
musicals: m. one day about the
glamour-studded   MAC 142:14
musician: poet and not a m.   BUTL 43:22
musicians: M. did not like the piece
                                BEEC 22:6
To all m., appear and inspire
                                AUDEN 15:12
musicologist: m. is a man who can read
                                BEEC 21:27
musket: Sam, Sam, pick up tha' m.
                                HOLL 104:5
musky: close to the Crocodile's m.
                                KIPL 125:14
müssen: wir sie nicht erleben m. FRIS 85:10
Mussolini: Even Hitler and M. were
                                LOW 139:17
must: I m. have no hatred   CAV 48:3
m. and the talent   BAR 18:13
mute: except that of m.   MACM 143:15

mutilate: spindle or m. in any way
ANON 6:1
mutilated: My elegant car . . . was m.
BELL 26:10
mutual: consists in the m. guarding
RILKE 181:3
forms of m. exploitation   AUDEN 14:3
my: M. Goodness, M. Guinness
RICH 180:13
myriad: A m. men will save   ROSS 185:5
There died a m.   POUND 174:6
myself: Am quite m. again   HOUS 106:13
find I'm talking to m.   BARN 18:21
mysterious: crime is often the most m.
DOYLE 69:28
God works in a m. way   ELIOT 75:6
mystery: Courage was mine, and I had m.
OWEN 166:17
Magical m. tour   LENN 135:9
m. inside an enigma   CHUR 55:4
m. of the atom and rejected   BRAD 38:9
strangeness with m.   DOYLE 69:28
myth: A m. is, of course   RYLE 187:10
by basing morals on m.   SAM 189:10
curveship lend a m. to God   CRANE 62:15
good old days were a m.   ATK 12:3

N

Nacht: *die N. der langen Messer*   HITL 103:3
nagging: n. is the repetition   SUMM 211:2
nail: painter and I n. my pictures
SCHW 193:14
nails: I used to bite my n.   PARK 168:3
nineteen hundred and forty n.
SITW 201:15
relatively clean finger n.   MORT 156:11
naissent: *humains n. libres et égaux*
ANON 9:1
naît: *On ne n. pas femme*   DE B 65:12
naïve: n. domestic Burgundy   THUR 216:20
n. forgive and forget   SZASZ 211:16
naked: And n. to the hangman's noose
HOUS 106:11
ashamed of our n. skins   SHAW 197:18
In walking n.   YEATS 234:16
n. ape self-named *Homo*   MORR 156:5
orchid she rode quite n.   AUDEN 15:11
Secretary n. into the conference
BEVAN 33:1
starving hysterical n.   GINS 90:15
name: gable and writing our n.
HEAN 99:11
holy n. of liberty   GAND 88:10
its n. is Ainsley Gotto   ERWIN 77:22
liberties are taken in thy n.   GEOR 89:12
long as you spell my n.   COHAN 57:10
mark against your n.   RICE 180:8
may prefer a self-made n.   HAND 96:8
n. any disease after two   PUZO 176:12
n. at the top of the page   CHUR 55:7
n. of a man is a numbing blow
MCL 143:11
n. of totalitarianism   GAND 88:10
n. we give the people   FLERS 82:4
paper which bears his n.   CHAM 48:13
yet can't quite n.   LARK 130:9
nameless: n. and abominable colour
HOUS 105:8
names: love with American n.   BENÉT 27:7

names (*cont.*):
n. of those who in their lives
SPEN 205:16
n. would be associated   SAKI 188:14
things with their n.   SART 191:9
naming: Today we have n. of parts
REED 178:19
nape: her n. caught in his bill
YEATS 234:21
Napoleon: N. of crime   DOYLE 69:16
N. of Crime   ELIOT 75:4
N.'s armies always used   SELL 194:16
Napoleons: worship the Caesars and N.
HUXL 108:16
narcotic: n. be alcohol or morphine
JUNG 116:20
narrow: Every bed is n.   MILL 151:23
n. into a neighbourhood   JOHN 114:9
nastiest: n. little man I've ever   DYKS 71:3
n. thing in the nicest way   GOLD 91:9
nasty: everybody is as n. as himself
SHAW 200:2
something n. in the woodshed   GIBB 90:1
Natchez: young belle of old N.
NASH 159:21
nation: A N. spoke to a Nation   KIPL 124:8
as a n., we don't dress well   SHAW 200:3
at the service of the n.   POMP 172:11
British n. is unique   CHUR 54:13
dream that one day this n.   KING 121:15
have to exterminate a n.   SPOCK 206:5
I want ours to be a n.   MUG 157:5
king and government and n.   KAV 118:6
Let every n. know, whether   KENN 119:11
mass of a n.   HITL 103:8
n. by its advertisements   DOUG 68:15
n. is fit to sit in judgement   WILS 229:10
n. is quite considerable   WILS 228:7
n. is the highest   JOHN 114:14
N. of many sovereign States   PAGE 167:2
N. shall speak peace unto   REND 179:12
n. talking to itself   MILL 152:8
one-third of a n. ill-housed   ROOS 183:4
temptation to a rich and lazy n.
KIPL 124:17
that I inspired the n.   CHUR 56:2
was thus clearly top n.   SELL 194:18
we are a n. of amateurs   ROS 184:16
what our N. stands for   BETJ 32:9
national: N. Debt is a very Good
SELL 194:15
n. home for the Jewish   BALF 17:16
N. Theatre   HALL 95:11
our n. disease   JAMES 112:8
That key is Russian n. interest
CHUR 55:4
National Gallery: elegant façade of the N.
CHAR 50:2
National Health: N. Service is safe
THAT 213:3
nationalism: N. is an infantile sickness
EINS 72:11
N. is a silly cock crowing   ALD 3:4
nationalities: smaller n. of Europe
ASQ 11:11
nationality: Ask any man what n.
RHOD 180:2
nationals: we are not other n.   MONT 155:6
nations: And the living n. wait
AUDEN 13:3
gossip from all the n.   AUDEN 14:22
men and n. behave wisely   EBAN 71:17
n. have always acted like   KUBR 129:5

nations (*cont.*):
n. which have put mankind   INGE 110:15
Other n. use 'force'   WAUGH 223:16
The day of small n. has   CHAM 48:9
native: n. and sees the human being
LESS 135:27
'n.' before the hyphen   ROOS 184:5
natives: Britons were only n.   SELL 194:9
natural: n. man has only two primal
OSLER 166:3
n. to have come from there   STEIN 207:13
n. to us than a cage   SHAW 196:21
nature: Consistency is contrary to n.
HUXL 108:14
[Death is] n.'s way   ANON 5:28
For n., heartless, witless   HOUS 106:4
interpreted n. as freely   GIR 90:17
interrogate as well as observe n.
OSLER 165:21
N. and we women cannot   GIBB 89:18
n. not by force   BRON 39:17
n. of a protest   HOFF 103:18
necessary limitations of our n.
AUDEN 13:16
no spell to cast on n.   BRON 39:17
refined and sensitive n.   DOYLE 69:21
that n. replaces it with   WILL 227:16
naught: I must have n. beside   THOM 215:7
I tell you n. for your comfort   CHES 50:8
N. broken save this body   BROO 40:1
naughtiest: The n. girl in the school
BLYT 35:10
naughty: N. but nice   WALD 222:2
Oh wasn't it n. of Smudges   BETJ 31:10
naval: me about n. tradition   CHUR 53:20
navel: water rise above his n.   ABSE 1:4
navies: Far-called our n. melt away
KIPL 126:10
navy: put at the head of the N.   CARS 47:3
They expect the n.   CHUR 53:8
thoroughly efficient n.   ROOS 183:17
nay: And Mr Hall's n. was nay   BENT 29:6
Nazi: odious apparatus of N. rule
CHUR 54:10
near: When I'm not n. the girl   HARB 96:14
nearer: n. God's Heart in a garden
GURN 94:17
nearest: n. to expressing the inexpressible
HUXL 109:4
The n. thing to death in life   ANON 7:26
neat: I was n., clean, shaved   CHAN 49:2
n. and adequately tall   CHES 52:3
You look n.   COLL 58:4
necessarily: It ain't n. so   HEYW 102:7
necessary: everything in it is a n. evil
BRAD 38:6
into the war is the n. art   DULL 70:10
Is your journey *really* n.   ANON 7:1
n. limitations of our nature   AUDEN 13:16
n. to destroy the town   ANON 7:2
necessities: were n. and which luxuries
WRIG 231:21
necessity: luxury; fiction is a n.
CHES 50:11
neck: A n. God made for other use
HOUS 106:11
Some chicken! Some n.   CHUR 53:13
necklace: with our n., we shall
MAND 145:18
necks: comes and wrings our n.
AYRES 16:7
necktie: And left my n. God knows where
HOUS 107:9
need: All you n. is love   LENN 135:3

Nineveh (*cont.*):
Is Solomon's temple, poets, N.
    MEYN 151:12
N. from distant Ophir   MAS 148:2
nipping: n. the heels of Hemingway
    ALGR 3:8
nix: Sticks n. hick pix   ANON 8:13
no: A man who says n.   CAMUS 46:5
can't say N.   PARK 168:25
he's got n. business   GALS 88:7
land of the omnipotent N.   BOLD 35:15
n. go the merrygoround   MACN 144:7
N.! I am not Prince Hamlet   ELIOT 75:18
n. instruction book came   FULL 87:15
N. manager ever got fired   ANON 7:28
n. more coals to Newcastle   GEOR 89:6
N. more Latin, no more French
    ANON 7:30
n. plain women on television
    FORD 82:12
n. real alternative   THAT 212:15
N. sex please—we're British
    MARR 147:11
n. such thing as a *bad* cheese   FAD 78:5
n. such thing as a free lunch   HEIN 100:1
n. such thing as Society   THAT 213:8
n. such thing as splendour   FORS 83:14
N. tears in the writer   FROST 85:17
Oh, n. man knows   DE L 66:5
There is n. such thing   FAUL 78:14
Ulster says n.   ANON 9:2
Noah: cataclysm but one poor N.
    HUXL 108:20
God gave N. the rainbow sign
    ANON 6:12
N. he often said   CHES 50:14
noble: dignifies n. people   SHAW 197:7
Eternally n., historically   LERN 135:19
except for a n. purpose   HERB 101:26
N. deeds and hot baths   SMITH 202:7
nobleness: And N. walks in our ways
again   BROO 40:4
noblest: God's the n. work of man
    BUTL 43:8
nobody: And n. knows   MILNE 153:1
And n.'s wife   HERB 101:13
n. comes, nobody goes   BECK 21:18
n. gets old and godly   YEATS 232:17
N. speaks the truth when   BOWEN 37:11
n. tells me anything   GALS 88:7
N. was ever meant   FROST 86:1
someone gave a war & N.   GINS 90:14
war and n. will come   SAND 190:2
Well, n.'s perfect   WILD 227:2
What n. is sure about   BELL 25:6
wrecks and n. drownded   EDGAR 71:20
nod: Old N., the shepherd, goes   DE L 66:6
passed with a n. of the head   YEATS 233:9
no-encouragement: read an expression
of n.   BRAM 38:14
noise: absolutely love the n.   BEEC 22:8
A happy n. to hear   HOUS 106:14
fourth time that infernal n.   EDW 72:4
most sublime n.   FORS 83:13
N., n. A stench   BIER 34:10
n. outside the cypress   LAWR 131:14
noisy: Oh, n. bells, be dumb   HOUS 106:15
nom: *Démocratie est le n. que*   FLERS 82:4
nomadic: on the contrary, were n.
    WHITE 226:4
noms: *choses avec leurs n.*   SART 191:9
non: *Un homme qui dit n.*   CAMUS 46:5
non-being: avoiding n. by avoiding being
    TILL 217:4

non-combatant: War hath no fury like
a n.   MONT 155:4
non-commissioned: backbone of the Army
is the n.   KIPL 127:10
nonconformity: history of N.   ORW 165:2
none: n. of them know one half   GRAH 93:1
some have charm for n.   BARR 19:20
nonexistence: either nonviolence or n.
    KING 122:5
non-fiction: make use of her n.   AYCK 15:21
non-interference: n. with their own
peculiar   JAMES 112:13
nonsense: anchor in n. than to put
    GALB 88:3
had discovered what n.   MAUG 149:6
n. can I stand twice   RICH 181:1
n. which was knocked out   BEER 22:23
nonsensical: are equally n.   CHOM 52:19
non-u: U and N. An essay in sociological
    ROSS 184:20
nonviolence: either n. or nonexistence
    KING 122:5
non-violence: N. is the first article
    GAND 88:12
organization of n.   BAEZ 16:10
noon: Is sayin' nearly n.   AYRES 16:7
midnight and the n.'s repose   ELIOT 76:3
n. and tell me it smells   JOHN 114:3
n. a purple glow   YEATS 232:9
N. strikes on England   FLEC 81:17
noose: And naked to the hangman's n.
    HOUS 106:11
I tie the n. on in a knowing   CHES 52:3
nooses: N. give   PARK 168:12
norfan: I'm a N., both sides   WELLS 224:18
Norfolk: bear him up the N. sky   BETJ 31:3
normal: homosexuality were the n. way
    BRY 41:16
n. child and not as a prodigy   BARB 18:12
Thank God we're n.   OSB 165:12
normalcy: nostrums but n.   HARD 96:17
Norman: blacksmith like our N. King
    KIPL 126:19
I always feel with N.   AYCK 16:2
Phone for the fish-knives, N.   BETJ 31:11
Norris: Mr N. changes trains   ISH 111:2
north: heart of the N. is dead   LAWR 132:3
N.-East Trade   KIPL 124:5
n. you may run to the rime-ringed
    KIPL 127:17
Northcliffe: has resigned and N. has
    ANON 6:19
[Lord N.]   TAYL 212:6
northern: N. reticence, the tight
    HEAN 99:13
Norwegian: N. Blue   CHAP 49:13
nose: caught him by his little n.
    KIPL 125:14
Do not run up your n. dead   BALD 17:3
Had a very shiny n.   MARKS 146:17
his n. without moralising   CONN 59:6
man with the false n.   MORT 156:16
Some thirty inches from my n.
    AUDEN 12:14
what is in front of one's n.   ORW 165:10
what lies under one's n.   AUDEN 13:20
with a carnation up my n.   MCK 143:2
noselessness: The N. of Man   CHES 50:19
noses: They haven't got no n.   CHES 50:18
Where do the n. go   HEM 100:11
nostalgia: N. isn't what it used   ANON 7:31
nostrums: not n. but normalcy
    HARD 96:17

not: gladly n. to be standing   JOHN 114:7
if you were not, n.   STEIN 207:14
I say 'Why n.?'   SHAW 195:20
n. entirely devoid of interest   DOYLE 69:3
N. huffy, or stuffy   HERB 101:18
n. I, but the wind   LAWR 132:12
N. many people know that   CAINE 44:18
n. necessarily in that order   GOD 91:4
N. so much a programme   ANON 7:32
N. tonight, Josephine   DAVID 64:18
n. what we were formerly   BLUN 35:1
N. while I'm alive 'e   BEVIN 33:13
N. with a bang but a whimper
    ELIOT 75:12
they have n.   BELL 25:2
note: It was only the n. of a bird
    SIMP 201:5
once he sent me round a n.
    LEIGH 134:10
suicide n. in history   KAUF 118:4
noted: I n. as of Demos at their root
    WATS 222:17
n. for fresh air and fun   EDGAR 71:20
notes: bedside making copious n.
    BENN 28:2
n. and our dead bodies   SCOTT 194:3
n. I handle no better   SCHN 193:1
n. like little fishes vanish   MACN 144:16
n. tremendous from her   AUDEN 15:11
nothin': just another word for n.
    KRIS 129:2
N. ain't worth nothin'   KRIS 129:2
There is n. like a dame   HAMM 96:4
You ain't n. but a hound dog   LEIB 134:9
nothing: absolutely n.—half so much
    GRAH 92:17
Analogies decide n.   FREUD 85:8
And n. will remain   HOUS 106:13
diner n. could be finer   GORD 92:4
Fact, n. to laugh at at all   EDGAR 71:20
For n. can be sole or whole
    YEATS 235:14
Goodness had n. to do   WEST 225:19
I have n. to say   CAGE 44:13
It follows that n. should   CORN 61:11
moral crusade or it is n.   WILS 228:15
n. but as a group decide   ALLEN 3:13
n. ever ran quite straight   GALS 88:6
N. happens, nobody comes   BECK 21:18
n. has value   FORS 84:1
n. in his long career   ANON 9:12
N. IS EVER DONE IN THIS WORLD
    SHAW 197:15
N. is more dangerous   ALAIN 3:1
N. is wasted, nothing   HERB 101:22
N., like something   LARK 130:18
n. on in the [calendar]   MONR 155:3
nothing, really doing n.   STEIN 207:12
n. that make no mistakes   CONR 59:28
N. to be done   BECK 21:15
n. to look backward   FROST 86:12
n. to lose but our aitches   ORW 165:5
people of whom we know n.   CHAM 48:12
remembering n. but the blue sky
    FORS 84:3
The moon is n.   FRY 87:3
There's n. surer   KAHN 117:10
under there is n. but sleep   DRIN 70:4
ways will be all as n.   HARDY 97:5
Worked myself up from n.   PER 170:5
you know, she was n.   AYCK 15:21
notice: used to n. such things
    HARDY 97:10

Nottingham: N. lace of the curtains
BETJ 30:21
nought: N. but vast Sorrow DE L 66:11
noun: not a n. FULL 87:14
novel: advance we may hold a n.
JAMES 111:25
either a picture or a n. JAMES 112:1
n. before luncheon WAUGH 223:18
n. is *about* WELLS 224:13
n. is that it does attempt JAMES 111:24
n. tells a story FORS 83:8
novelist: No poet or n. wishes
AUDEN 13:19
novelists: major n. who count LEAV 133:16
novels: entertaining than half the n.
MAUG 149:22
reading the Beat n. CAP 46:14
now: History is n. and England
ELIOT 74:22
n. for something completely CHAP 49:11
N. is the time for the burning BINY 34:16
nubbly: 'Stute Fish. 'Nice but n.'
KIPL 125:7
nuclear: n. arms race has no military
MOUN 157:3
n. freeze proposals REAG 178:13
nude: n. with a carnation MCK 143:2
nudge: nudge n., snap snap CHAP 49:12
nuggets: Nuts and n. in the window
BETJ 31:19
nuisance: exchange of one N. ELLIS 77:12
squalid n. in time of war CHUR 55:2
nuit: *Vienne la n., sonne l'heure* APOL 9:22
null: this city, is N. an' Void O'CAS 162:16
NUM: against the Pope or the N.
BALD 17:3
number: if I called the wrong n.
THUR 216:21
n. for a dinner party GULB 94:15
n. of the question '1' CHUR 55:7
very interesting n. RAM 177:13
We're n. two. We try harder ANON 9:9
with the square of the n. of people
SHAN 195:6
numbers: His n., though they moved
YEATS 233:5
There is no safety in n. THUR 216:22
numerals: on the nature of the n.
O'BR 162:7
nun: An extremely rowdy N. COW 62:13
I'd the upbringing a n. ORTON 163:22
nurse: And always keep a-hold of N.
BELL 24:10
nurseries: Look for me in the n. of heaven
THOM 215:4
nurses: let's play doctor and n.
MILL 152:18
nutrition: case of n. and health JAY 112:19
nuts: N.! MCAU 141:3
N. and nuggets in the window
BETJ 31:19
nuttin': ain't heard n. yet JOLS 114:20

O

O: O bliss GRAH 92:19
O dark dark dark ELIOT 74:11
O Death, where is thy ANON 8:1
O O O O that Shakespeherian
ELIOT 76:21

oafish: And o. louts remember Mum
BETJ 31:4
oafs: muddied o. at the goals KIPL 124:12
oak: stream of old o. beams LANC 129:19
Than O., and Ash, and Thorn KIPL 126:3
oakleaves: o., horses' heels ELIOT 76:12
oar: o. was dipping COKE 57:14
oars: banks of o. that swam YEATS 233:5
Oates: O. of the Inniskilling ATK 12:5
oath: artist who is on o. MACC 141:4
o. again may my soul SHAW 199:27
obedience: be swift in all o. KIPL 127:1
obey: o. the orders given it ASIM 11:5
parents o. their children EDW 72:7
obeyed: God has more right to be o.
JOHN 113:21
obituary: autobiography is an o. in serial
CRISP 63:3
publicity except your own o.
BEHAN 23:28
object: o. that it is not a trial KAFKA 117:7
o. to people looking BIRK 34:21
The o. of art is actually ANOU 9:21
objectification: Art is the o. of feeling
LANG 130:6
objectionable: it is doubtless o. ANON 8:22
many ways extremely o. KEYN 120:14
objective: finding an 'o. correlative'
ELIOT 76:7
objet: *L'art a pour o. de lui* ANOU 9:21
obligation: o. to become the servant
SHAW 196:22
oblivion: long journey towards o.
LAWR 132:10
Over o. HARDY 97:7
obscene: O. as cancer, bitter as the cud
OWEN 166:10
obscenity: 'o.' is not a term capable
RUSS 187:2
observe: interrogate as well as o. nature
OSLER 165:21
You see, but you do not o. DOYLE 68:19
observer: Is a keen o. of life AUDEN 14:20
obsolescence: adolescence and o.
LINK 137:16
obsolete: Either war is o. or men
FULL 87:13
obstacle: o. to professional writing
BENC 26:19
obvious: o. facts about grown-ups
JARR 112:17
occasional: o. heart attack BENC 26:20
occupation: The cure for it is o.
SHAW 199:12
occupied: o. her time most usefully
BROO 41:2
occurred: Ought never to have o.
BENT 29:7
occurrence: o. of the improbable
MENC 151:4
ocean: didn't think much to the O.
EDGAR 71:20
I'll love you till the o. AUDEN 12:16
o.'s margin this innocent AUDEN 15:11
They hear like o. on a western
LANG 130:3
oceans: To the o. white with foam
BERL 29:15
o'clock: soul it is always three o.
FITZ 80:17
octopus: that dear o. from whose
SMITH 202:6
odd: But not so o. BROW 41:13

odd (*cont.*):
How o. EWER 78:4
It's a very o. thing DE L 66:15
Must think it exceedingly o. KNOX 128:10
o. about women who wear BENN 27:21
odds: And how am I to face the o.
HOUS 105:18
gamble at terrible o. STOP 210:2
o. are five to six DICK 67:10
ode: I intended an O. DOBS 68:2
O. on a Grecian Urn FAUL 78:11
odium: He lived in the o. BENT 29:2
Odysseus: Like O., the President
KEYN 120:9
Odyssey: surge and thunder of the O.
LANG 130:3
o'ercargoed: With leaden age o. FLEC 81:19
offence: whom I was like to give o.
FROST 86:11
offending: o. both legal and natural
STOP 209:20
offensive: Life is an o., directed WHIT 227:6
someone else is being o. BROO 41:1
You are extremely o. SMITH 202:12
offer: nothing to o. but blood CHUR 54:7
o. he can't refuse PUZO 176:10
office: A man who has no o. SHAW 197:1
country in which the o. HUXL 108:10
o. that Benchley and Dorothy
BENC 26:24
o. was his pirate ship LEWIS 137:3
officers: o. and fellow-rankers
SMITH 203:23
official: O. dignity tends to increase
HUXL 108:10
o. who has hung up an empty
SMITH 202:2
The o. world, the corridors SNOW 203:26
This high o., all allow HERB 101:21
What is o. FRY 87:1
offspring: mature enough for o. DE VR 67:7
O'Grady: Colonel's Lady an' Judy O.
KIPL 127:8
oiks: o. with whom i am forced WILL 227:2
oil: providers they're o. wells PARK 169:3
Okie: O. means you're scum STEI 208:2
old: All wars are planned by o. men
RICE 180:6
Any o. iron, any old iron COLL 58:4
Ash on an o. man's sleeve ELIOT 74:18
attendance upon my o. age YEATS 234:3
boys of the o. Brigade WEAT 223:20
country for o. men YEATS 234:5
don't even like o. cars SAL 189:3
Don't let the o. folks know HERB 101:17
first sign of o. age HICKS 102:9
grow o. simultaneously CONN 59:11
Hope I die before I get o. TOWN 217:13
Ideas can be too o. OUSP 166:4
I grow o. .... I grow o. ELIOT 75:19
lads that will never be o. HOUS 106:16
me conservative when o. FROST 85:20
Mithridates, he died o. HOUS 107:10
now am not too o. BLUN 35:1
o. age crept over them NAYL 159:26
o. age is always fifteen BAR 20:5
O. age is the most unexpected
TROT 218:3
o. and grey and full YEATS 232:7
o. bold mate of Henry Morgan
MAS 148:5
O. Country must wake up GEOR 89:7
o. have reminiscences SAKI 188:13
o. have rubbed it MAUG 149:6

order (cont.):
  o. of competence   ROOS 182:22
  o., security and peace   JOHN 113:22
  when o. breeds habit   ADAMS 2:3
orderly: keep themselves o.   LARK 130:10
ordinary: calmly before the o. folk
                                         BEVIN 33:14
I warn you not to be o.   KINN 122:13
organ: direction to point that o.
                                         AUDEN 13:20
  my second favourite o.   ALLEN 4:7
  o. to enlarge her prayer   AUDEN 15:11
organ grinder: monkey when the o.
                                         BEVAN 33:4
organism: o. to live beyond its income
                                         BUTL 43:19
organization: book is about the o. man
                                   WHYTE 226:22
government is the o. of idolatry
                                   SHAW 198:10
  systematic o. of hatreds   ADAMS 2:1
  than the o. of non-violence   BAEZ 16:10
organize: any time in mourning—o.
                                      HILL 102:11
organizing: o. and campaigning
                                    BROD 39:12
organs: o. of beasts and fowls   JOYCE 116:8
orgasm: o. has replaced the Cross
                                    MUGG 157:10
orgastic: o. future that year   FITZ 80:21
orgies: Home is heaven and o. are vile
                                  NASH 159:22
orgy: But you need an o.   NASH 159:22
  o. looks particularly alluring
                                     MUGG 157:7
original: o. ideas is sound   MACM 144:2
  o. is unfaithful   BORG 36:8
originality: O. is deliberate and forced
                                   HOFF 103:18
  when o. is taken   GALB 88:2
  without o. or moral courage SHAW 196:2
Orion: O. plunges prone   HOUS 106:6
orisons: Can patter out their hasty o.
                                    OWEN 166:9
orphan: defeat is an o.   CIANO 56:7
orphans: o. and the homeless GAND 88:10
orthodoxy: 'o.' not only no longer
                                    CHES 51:1
Orwell: [George O.] could not   CONN 59:6
Oscar: We all assume that O. said it
                                  PARK 168:18
ostrich: America can not be an o.
                                    WILS 229:7
other: death, there is no o.   THOM 213:14
  did lots of o. things too   JOYCE 116:15
  every o. inch a gentleman   WEST 225:24
  have one without the o.   CAHN 44:15
  Hell is o. people   SART 191:4
  like o. people's authority   BENS 28:20
  not on o. people   HUXL 109:15
  o. people in the world   CALL 45:3
  O. voices, other rooms   CAP 46:16
others: Jesus is there only for o. BONH 36:3
  o. by their hunted expression
                                     LEWIS 136:14
  O. must fail   VIDAL 221:12
otherwise: admire him would wish o.
                                    ANON 9:12
Otis: Miss O. regrets   PORT 173:4
oublierai: n'o. jamais les lilas ni   ARAG 10:2
ought: do what Asian boys o.   JOHN 114:13
  meritus, 'so he o. to be'   LEAC 133:7
  o. never to have done it   BEVIN 33:16
  Where o. I to be   CHES 50:5

our: O. man in Havana   GREE 93:18
ours: The land was o. before we
                                     FROST 86:21
ourselves: better be changed in o.
                                     JUNG 117:1
out: best way o. is always   FROST 86:15
  can say he is o. of touch   DOUG 68:17
  Gentlemen, include me o.   GOLD 91:14
  get o. of the kitchen   TRUM 218:8
  I counted them all o.   HANR 96:10
  o. always looks the best   ROG 182:6
  O. of Africa   DIN 67:15
  O. where the handclasp's   CHAP 49:9
outcast: universal in sympathy and an o.
                                    BARN 18:18
outcome: o. of a war is decided
                                    MAO T 146:10
outdistanced: o. the ends for which we
                                    KING 122:4
outer: o. life of telegrams   FORS 83:16
Outer Mongolia: British O. for retired
                                    BENN 27:15
outlast: last for ever, o. the sea   CONR 60:4
outlaw: o. states run by the strangest
                                    REAG 178:15
outlaws: legislation which o. Russia
                                    REAG 178:14
outlived: I have o. certain desires
                                   WOOLF 231:16
outrage: civilised o.   HEAN 99:12
outside: just going o. and may
                                   MAHON 145:6
  just going o. and may   OATES 162:3
  O. every fat man there was   AMIS 4:19
  than o. pissing in   JOHN 114:4
out-worn: O. heart, in a time out-worn
                                    YEATS 232:6
Ovaltineys: We are the O.   ANON 9:7
oven: stove instead of the o.   JENK 112:23
over: Cassiopeia was o.   KAV 118:7
  come back till it's o.   COHAN 57:12
  oversexed, and o. here   TRIN 218:2
  O. there, over there   COHAN 57:12
  try to put it all o. you   WEST 225:16
overcame: O. his natural bonhomie
                                     BENT 29:3
overcome: his passions has never o.
                                   JUNG 116:18
We shall o.   ANON 9:13
overflow: And meadow rivulets o.
                                    HARDY 97:3
overlook: art of knowing what to o.
                                   JAMES 112:12
overlooked: be looked over than o.
                                   WEST 225:8
That I o. before   DIXON 67:18
overpaid: Is grossly o.   HERB 101:21
  O., overfed, oversexed   TRIN 218:2
overpraised: are usually o.   FORS 83:11
oversexed: o., and over here   TRIN 218:2
overthrow: intention to o. the Government
                                    HARD 96:15
owed: much o. by so many   CHUR 54:12
owl: greedy o. of the Remove   RICH 180:15
  O., and the Waverley pen   ANON 8:21
  'Well,' said O.   MILNE 153:16
owls: o. came and perched   BEER 23:16
own: child that's got his o.   HOL 104:4
  money and a room of her o.
                                     WOOLF 231:12
  provided I get my o. way   THAT 212:20
own-goal: o. scored by the human
                                    ANNE 5:8

ox: brother to the o.   MARK 146:14
  [Lady Desborough] is an o.   ASQ 11:14
oxen: years like great black o.
                                     YEATS 234:10
Oxford: airing in this new North O.
                                    BETJ 32:5
  back at O. or Cambridge   BEER 22:23
  England, noon on O. town   FLEC 81:17
  exercise that right in O.   BEER 23:13
  It is O. that has made   BEER 22:22
  lead but it was either O.   SNAG 203:25
  My heart was with the O. men
                                    LETTS 136:1
  nice sort of place, O.   SHAW 197:24
  sends his son to O.   STEAD 207:6
  The clever men at O.   GRAH 93:1
  Theoretically speaking that's O.
                                    RAPH 177:16
oxygen: hijacker of the o. of publicity
                                    THAT 213:5
oyster: open an o. at sixty paces
                                    WOD 230:10
  o. shell on top   AUDEN 15:11
oysters: o. are more beautiful   SAKI 188:5

P

paces: open an oyster at sixty p.
                                    WOD 230:10
pacific: side except by p. means BRIA 39:10
pacifist: I am an absolute p.   EINS 72:12
pack: p. up your troubles   ASAF 10:13
  peasantry its p. animal   TROT 218:4
  To p. and label men for God
                                    THOM 215:23
  With a wicked p. of cards   ELIOT 76:16
packed: districts p. like squares LARK 131:1
padri: vittoria trova cento p.   CIANO 56:7
paga: Non si p., non si p.   FO 82:5
Paganini: village fiddler after P. NIC 160:9
page: name at the top of the p. CHUR 55:7
pageant: part of life's rich p.   MARS 147:12
pagus: Is private p. or demesne
                                    AUDEN 12:14
paid: Lord God, we ha' p. in full KIPL 127:2
  p. his subjects   BROO 40:4
  So attention must be p.   MILL 152:4
pain: Although p. isn't real   ANON 8:19
  Competence with p.   HEAN 99:14
  forget the wandering and p. FLEC 81:16
  For we are born in other's p.
                                    THOM 215:1
  Joy always comes after p.   APOL 9:22
  momentary intoxication with p.
                                    BRON 39:15
  terrible p. in all the diodes ADAMS 1:13
  well and she hasn't a p.   MILNE 153:8
pains: no gains without p.   STEV 209:4
  sympathize with people's p. HUXL 109:3
  took infinite p. over it   BENN 28:2
paint: cheeks are covered with p.
                                    NASH 159:17
  p. a portrait I lose   SARG 190:22
  p. it   ANON 6:23
  p. objects as I think them PIC 171:4
painted: has p. this perfect day
                                    BOND 35:19
  p. by a mailed fist   SITW 201:16
  so young as they are p.   BEER 22:28
  They're p. to the eyes   DOBS 68:3

painter: colour that of a tea-tray p.
                             BLUNT 35:5
  p. and I nail my pictures   SCHW 193:14
painting: P. is saying "Ta" to God
                             SPEN 205:11
  p. people have to *understand*   PIC 171:8
paints: Where God p. the scenery
                             HART 98:19
pair: been a p. of ragged claws ELIOT 75:16
paix: *faire la guerre que la p.* CLEM 56:18
  n'est pas un traité de p.   FOCH 82:7
pajamas: shot an elephant in my p.
                           KAUF 118:2
palace: chalice from the p.   PAN 167:6
  p. built upon the sand   MILL 151:19
palate: steps down the p. to tap
                           NAB 158:12
pale: A whiter shade of p.   REID 179:10
  P. hands I loved beside   HOPE 105:4
  that it's beyond the p.   COW 62:8
Palestine: home to haven in sunny P.
                          MAS 148:2
  P. of a national home   BALF 17:16
pall: When that began to p. BENT 29:5
pallor: p. of girls' brows shall OWEN 166:9
palm: Quietly sweating p. to p. HUXL 109:2
palms: And p. before my feet CHES 52:11
  p. on the staircase   BETJ 30:21
palpable: A Poem should be p. and mute
                        MACL 143:5
paltry: An aged man is but a p. thing
                       YEATS 234:6
Pam: P., you great big mountainous
                         BETJ 32:8
pamphleteers: This is not the age of p.
                      HOGB 104:3
pancreas: you want— an adorable p.
                      KERR 120:5
panders: It p. to instincts already
                      BENN 27:19
Pandora: If you open that P.'s Box
                    BEVIN 33:12
pang: p. of all the partings THOM 214:21
panic: distinguished from p. HEM 100:14
  Don't p.   ADAMS 1:11
  P. and emptiness   FORS 83:14
panther: Black P. Party   NEWT 160:6
  The p. is a fierce animal NEWT 160:6
pants: your lower limbs in p. NASH 159:3
paper: age of four with p. hats UST 220:20
  All reactionaries are p. tigers
                    MAO T 146:11
  contract isn't worth the p. GOLD 91:15
  I ran the p. [*Daily Express*] BEAV 20:18
  just for a scrap of p.   BETH 30:20
  on both sides of the p. SELL 194:19
  p. which bears his name CHAM 48:13
  p. work down to a minimum
                     ORTON 164:4
  personality than a p. cup CHAN 49:5
  signed the p. felled   THOM 214:4
  The atom bomb is a p. tiger
                    MAO T 146:10
papers: He's got my p., this man
                    PINT 171:14
  what I read in the p.   ROG 182:9
paradisal: From what P. THOM 216:8
paradise: cannot catch the bird of p.
                      KHR 121:6
  Have blundered into P. THOM 215:23
  P. by way of Kensal Green CHES 50:23
  p. of individuality   SANT 190:16
  They paved p.   MITC 154:8

paradises: p. are paradises we have
                      PROU 176:6
paradox: go on in strange p. CHUR 54:5
paragraphing: p. is to stroke a platitude
                    MARQ 147:10
parallelism: needs a certain p. of life
                    ADAMS 2:4
pardon: cannot help nor p. AUDEN 15:10
  P. me boy is that the Chattanooga
                    GORD 92:4
  The kiss of the sun for p. GURN 94:17
parent: p. who could see his boy
                    LEAC 133:5
parentage: P. is a very important
  profession   SHAW 196:16
parenthood: p. as much as we value
                    TOYN 217:14
parents: A Jewish man with p. alive
                    ROTH 185:10
  America is the way p. obey EDW 72:7
  girl needs good p.   TUCK 218:18
  how my p. were occupied SAL 188:24
  my p. were married   ACK 1:10
  P.—especially step-parents POW 174:19
  p. finally realize   ALLEN 3:26
  p. kept me from children SPEN 205:13
  P. learn a lot from SPARK 205:5
  what a tangled web do p. NASH 159:2
  what p. were created for NASH 159:15
Paris: call it the school of P. MUNN 157:18
  Down and Out in P. ORW 164:13
  flew from London to P. DAV 64:19
  frocks are built in P. SAKI 188:12
  Is P. burning   HITL 103:7
  its history P. was French TUCH 218:17
  no more Hoares to P. GEOR 89:6
  P. is a movable feast HEM 101:1
  pictures sent over from P. BLUNT 35:5
  The last time I saw P. HAMM 95:16
  To mighty P.   YEATS 236:4
parish: The p. of rich women AUDEN 13:1
park: make a comedy is a p. CHAP 49:8
Parker: [Dorothy P.] is so odd a blend
                    WOOL 231:19
  P. shared in the Metropolitan
                    BENC 26:24
parkin': Watch the p. meters DYLAN 71:13
parking: And put up a p. lot MITC 154:8
parley-voo: Hinky, dinky, p. ANON 7:20
parliament: [p.] are a lot of hard-faced
                    BALD 17:5
  P. itself would not exist SCAR 192:15
  P. to do things at eleven SHAW 197:13
parliamentarian: p. is a bag of boiled
  sweets   CRIT 63:4
parliamentary: term here as a P. leper
                  WILS 228:10
parochial: worse than provincial—he
  was p.   JAMES 111:21
  that art must be p. MOORE 155:9
parodies: P. and caricatures HUXL 109:9
parody: The devil's walking p. CHES 52:10
parried: I p.; but my hands were
                    OWEN 166:18
parrot: p. what I purchased CHAP 49:13
parrots: keep p. or puppy dogs CAMP 45:12
parshial: garden and I am p. to ladies
                    ASHF 10:16
parsley: P. Is gharsley NASH 159:11
parson: And after him the p. ran
                    CHES 50:22
  If P. lost his senses HODG 103:13

part: p. in affairs which properly
                    VALÉ 221:1
  p. of life's rich pageant MARS 147:12
  p. of ourselves doesn't HESSE 102:3
  p. of the solution CLEA 56:12
  p. of the universe   BECK 21:8
  p. that makes illness worth SHAW 195:22
  prepared to play a p. MACM 143:15
  Shall I p. my hair behind ELIOT 75:19
  that it is your p. to woo SHAW 197:25
  Yet meet we shall, and p. BUTL 43:4
parties: both p. run out of goods
                    AUDEN 14:3
partings: The pang of all the p. gone
                    THOM 214:21
partly: Living and p. living ELIOT 74:24
parts: naming of p.   REED 178:19
  refreshes the p. other beers LOV 139:15
party: dinner p. of more than two
                    MENC 151:1
  p. is not to be brought down HAIL 95:4
  p. is worse than the other ROG 182:6
  P. line is that there DJIL 67:19
  save the P. we love GAIT 87:23
  The p.'s over   COMD 58:8
pasarán: *No p.*   IBAR 109:18
pass: Do not p. go   DARR 64:13
  Horseman p. by!   YEATS 233:4
  Lord and p. the ammunition FORGY 83:1
  P. me the can, lad HOUS 105:12
  p. out into adventure FORS 83:12
  pay us, p. us; but do CHES 51:24
  They shall not p.   ANON 6:25
  They shall not p. IBAR 109:18
passage: Down the p. which we did
                    ELIOT 74:3
  p. from hand to hand SICK 200:15
passages: History has many cunning p.
                    ELIOT 73:12
passageways: With smell of steaks in p.
                    ELIOT 75:20
passed: just p. down the street
                    STUD 210:20
  That p. the time   BECK 21:20
passenger: I am a p. on space vehicle
                    FULL 87:12
passengers: train needs one of its p.
                    STOP 210:3
passeront: *Ils ne p. pas* ANON 6:25
passes: Men seldom make p. PARK 168:14
passing: The p. of the third floor back
                    JER 113:12
passing-bells: p. for these who die
                    OWEN 166:9
passion: *c'est l'image de la p.* BART 20:3
  connect the prose and the p. FORS 83:17
  Man is a useless p. SART 191:3
  our p. is our task JAMES 111:18
  p. could bring character YEATS 233:5
  passion, not p. itself BART 20:3
  p. to which he has always remained
  faithful   POW 174:15
  P., you see, can be destroyed SHAF 195:5
  To think his p. such YEATS 235:12
passionate: Are full of p. intensity
                    YEATS 233:12
  p. apprehension of form BELL 23:29
passions: inferno of his p. JUNG 116:13
  Three p., simple but overwhelmingly
                    RUSS 186:7
passport: My p.'s green HEAN 99:15
past: always praising the p. SMITH 203:19
  And talk about the p. MCG 142:10

past (*cont.*):

As changed itself to p.	LARK 131:3
ceaselessly into the p.	FITZ 80:21
looking forward to the p.	OSB 165:18
or nothing but the p.	KEYN 120:11
p. is a bucket of ashes	SAND 189:15
p. is a foreign country	HART 99:1
p. is just the same	SASS 192:5
p. is not getting any better	LEVIN 136:10
p. is the only dead thing	THOM 214:14
p. shut in him like	WOOLF 231:10
present controls the p.	ORW 164:22
rather absurd about the p.	BEER 23:3
remember the p. are condemned	
	SANT 190:9
repeat his p. nor leave	AUDEN 14:4
The danger of the p. was	FROMM 85:13
The p. exudes legend	MAL 145:14
Time present and time p.	ELIOT 74:2

pasture: clean the p. spring   FROST 86:8
paternalism: p. and state socialism
               HOOV 104:12
paternity: men but on the bond of p.
               SART 191:5
path: bedroom of moss-dappled p.
               BETJ 32:2

down our particular p.	FORS 84:8
it by any p. whatsoever	KRIS 129:1
One p. leads to despair	ALLEN 3:21

pathetic: That's what it is. P.   MILNE 153:17
pathos: P., piety, courage   FORS 84:1
paths: all her p. are Peace   SPR 206:13
patience: my p. is now at an end
               HITL 103:6

P., n. A minor form	BIER 34:11
p. to appreciate domestic	SANT 190:10
weight in other people's p.	UPD 220:14

patient: I am extraordinarily p.
               THAT 212:20

p. etherized upon a table	ELIOT 75:13

patois: broken-down p.   CHAN 49:4
patria: Pro p. mori   OWEN 166:10
patrimony: And that was all his p.
               SAB 187:13
patriot: no p. would think of saying
               CHES 50:13
patriotism: P. is a lively sense   ALD 3:4

realize that p. is not enough	CAV 48:3
world til you knock the p.	SHAW 199:9

patted: Ethel p. her hair   ASHF 11:2
pattern: history is a p.   ELIOT 74:22
   imposing of a p. on experience
               WHIT 226:11

In a p. called a war	LOW 139:18
predetermined by	FISH 80:5
The dance's p.	AUDEN 14:8

paucity: p. of its reverberation   MAIL 145:10
paupières: *Quand elle lève ses p.*   COL 57:16
pause: I'll have eine kleine P.   FERR 79:4

There was a p.— just long	FIRB 80:2

pauses: p. between the notes   SCHN 193:1
pauvres: *la guerre ce sont les p.*   SART 190:26
   [*les p.*] *y doivent travailler*   FRAN 84:15
   p. ne savent pas que leur   SART 191:6
pavement: Stand on the highest p.
               ELIOT 76:2
pavements: roadway or on the p.
               YEATS 232:9
pavilion: red p. of my heart   THOM 215:21
paving: Over the p.   ELIOT 76:12
pawn: when you're hard up you p.
               CUMM 63:14
pay: And wonders what's to p.   HOUS 106:1
   genius who had not to p.   BEER 22:16

pay (*cont.*):

hav to p. for it all	WILL 227:10
must p. for one by one	KIPL 124:4
Not a penny off the p.	COOK 60:7
p. a million priests	HARDY 98:6
Smile at us, p. us, pass us	CHES 51:24
sum of things for p.	HOUS 106:3
that we shall p. any price	KENN 119:11
Ulcer Man on 4 Ulcer P.	EARLY 71:16
We won't p., we won't pay	FO 82:5

paying: called p. the Dane-geld KIPL 124:17
pays: p. us poor beggars in red KIPL 123:11
   voulez-vous gouverner un p.   DE G 66:1
pea: p. which has got   WELLS 224:14
peace: advocates of p. upon earth
               GEOR 89:11

believe it is p. for our time	CHAM 48:14
deep p. of the double-bed	CAMP 45:9
Downing Street p. with honour	
	CHAM 48:14
even lovers find their p.	FLEC 81:7
Georgia, Georgia, no p. I find	GORR 92:5
Give p. a chance	LENN 135:7
Imperishable p.	HOUS 106:8
In p.: goodwill	CHUR 55:16
I were the Prince of P.	HOUS 105:7
Let p. fill our heart	KUMAR 129:6
make war than to make p.	CLEM 56:18
more precious than p.	WILS 229:14
my friend, is p.	ROOS 183:11
Nation shall speak p. unto	REND 179:12
not a p. treaty	FOCH 82:7
Only a p. between equals	WILS 229:3
Open covenants of p.	WILS 229:15
p. among our peoples	KIPL 127:1
p. and what did that produce	
	WELL 224:11
p. at the price of ultimate	NIC 160:8
p. comes dropping slow	YEATS 232:9
p. is harder than making	STEV 208:20
P. is indivisible	LITV 138:2
P. is nothing but slovenliness	BREC 39:3
P. is poor reading	HARDY 96:20
P. is the way	MUSTE 158:10
p. Man is a bungler	SHAW 197:32
p. must be constructed	ANON 6:16
P., n. In international	BIER 34:12
p. of all countries everywhere	
	ROOS 183:5
P. on earth and mercy mild	BEEC 22:11
P. upon earth	HARDY 98:6
precocious giants and for p.	PEAR 169:21
security and p. of each country	
	JOHN 113:22
such thing as inner p.	LEB 133:19
take chances for p.	DULL 70:10
tell me p. has broken out	BREC 39:7
Then p. will guide the planets	
	RADO 177:6
think that people want p.	EIS 73:9
this country in time of p.	CHUR 55:2
War is p.	ORW 164:21
When there was p., he was	
	AUDEN 13:10

peaceful: p. extermination of capitalism
               ZIN 236:14
peacefully: moving p. towards its close
               DAWS 65:6
   summer sustained p.   DAY-L 65:10
peace-time: p. choice between the
   American   HOOV 104:12
peach: Do I dare to eat a p.   ELIOT 75:19
   The p. was once a bitter   TWAIN 219:30

peacock: very first copy of The White P.
               LAWR 132:20
peacocks: on the terraces and p.
               KIPL 124:19
peal: The wildest p. for years HODG 103:13
pear: *Here we go round the prickly p.*
               ELIOT 75:11
pearls: Give p. away and rubies
               HOUS 106:12
   string the p. were strung   JAMES 111:19
pearly: And he shows them p. white
               BREC 38:21
Pearse: P. summoned Cuchulain
               YEATS 233:6
peas: p. were eaten with the knife
               RAL 177:10
peasantry: Sing the p., and then
               YEATS 233:2
pebble: does a wise man hide a p.
               CHES 51:5
pebbles: leviathan retrieving p.
               WELLS 224:14
péchés: *P. sont des tentatives*   WEIL 224:1
pecker: want his p. in my pocket
               JOHN 114:3
Peckham: treeful of angels at P.
               BENÉT 27:9
pedant: only a p. can live   SANT 190:13
pedantry: P. is the dotage of knowledge
               JACK 111:4
peddler: be a plumber or a p.   EINS 73:4
pederasty: Not flagellation, not p.
               RATT 178:2
pedestal: place my wife under a p.
               ALLEN 4:2
pedestrians: only two classes of p.
               DEWAR 67:8
pee: colour of children's p.   AMIS 4:16
peel: Beulah, p. me a grape   WEST 225:12
   plums and orange p.   RAL 177:12
peeling: P. off the kilometres   CONN 59:15
peep: Nevermore to p. again   DE L 66:19
peeps: p. at it to make sure   BARR 19:16
peepshow: ticket for the p.   MACN 144:7
peer: Oh many a p. of England brews
               HOUS 107:8
peerage: When I want a p.   NORT 161:12
peignoir: Complacencies of the p.
               STEV 208:11
peine: *venait toujours après la p.*   APOL 9:22
pelican: Oh, a wondrous bird is the p.
               MERR 151:11
pellet: p. with the poison's   PAN 167:6
pellets: And then me spray of p.
               AYRES 16:7
pen: far less brilliant p.   BEER 23:4

From lies of tongue and p.	CHES 51:18
mightier than the p.	HOGB 104:3
The squat p. rests	HEAN 99:10
Waverley p.	ANON 8:21

pencil: p. long enough to draw CHES 52:5
Penelope: His true P. was Flaubert
               POUND 174:3
penetrating: most p. of criticisms
               HUXL 109:9
penitence: p. condemns to silence
               BRAD 38:3
pennies: P. from heaven   BURKE 42:13
Pennsylvania: P. station 'bout a quarter
               GORD 92:4
penny: I had not given a p. for a song
               YEATS 232:14
   Not a p. off the pay   COOK 60:7

pensée: *Ma p., c'est moi* SART 191:11
pension: hang your hat on a p.
　　MACN 144:8
people: alien p. clutching ELIOT 73:15
And p. came to theirs HODG 103:13
A p. without history ELIOT 74:22
Before we were her p. FROST 86:21
between p. of whom we know nothing
　　CHAM 48:12
can fool all of the p. ADAMS 1:19
For p. will always be kind SASS 191:18
government by the p. CAMP 45:17
government of the p. PAGE 167:2
half p. and half bicycles O'BR 162:11
Hell is other p. SART 191:4
Here the p. rule FORD 82:14
I love *p.* CAMP 45:12
I never bother with p. I hate HART 98:18
kind of a p. do they think CHUR 53:12
Most p. ignore most poetry MITC 154:6
Most p. sell their souls SMITH 203:4
name we give the p. FLERS 82:4
new p. takes the land CHES 52:1
Not many p. know CAINE 44:18
One realm, one p., one leader ANON 6:4
outside, not on other p. HUXL 109:15
p. and their favourite AUDEN 14:16
p. are free to do as they HOFF 103:18
p. are only human COMP 58:9
p. are right more than half WHITE 226:2
P. can clean their teeth JENK 112:23
p. don't do such things IBSEN 109:24
p. get into bands for three GELD 89:3
p. know what they want MENC 150:20
P. must not do things HERB 101:24
P. say that life SMITH 203:13
p. too much of the time THUR 217:2
p. want peace so much EIS 73:9
p. we followed a policy DUBČ 70:5
P. who are always praising
　　SMITH 203:19
p. who are late are often LUCAS 140:11
p. who are really powerful MAO T 146:11
p. who do things and people
　　MORR 156:9
p. who get the credit MORR 156:9
p. who got there first UST 220:17
p. will get to the promised KING 121:16
P. you know, yet can't LARK 130:9
Power to the p. ANON 8:3
sake look after our p. SCOTT 194:1
study of economics as if p. SCH 193:10
Top p. take *The Times* ANON 8:25
we are the p. of England CHES 51:24
were decent godless p. ELIOT 76:5
we're the opposite of p. STOP 209:21
what is good for p. JAY 112:19
what p. say of us is true SMITH 202:18
Peoria: It will play in P. ANON 7:5
perceived: P. the scene, and foretold
　　ELIOT 77:1
percentage: It's a reasonable p. BECK 21:16
perception: p. that something ought
　　WELLS 225:6
perdu: *A la recherche du temps p.*
　　PROU 175:15
France n'a pas p. la guerre DE G 65:19
père: *Il n'y a pas de bon p.* SART 191:5
Notre P. qui êtes aux cieux PRÉV 175:6
perfect: come to the end of a p. day
　　BOND 35:19
Nothing is p. STEP 208:6
Well, nobody's p. WILD 227:2

perfection: everything must function to p.
　　MUSS 158:9
P., of a kind, was what AUDEN 12:18
P. of the life, or of the work
　　YEATS 235:18
p. unattainable STR 210:6
perfectly: p. formed one kept COOP 60:18
perform: operations which we can p.
　　WHIT 226:12
performing: English literature's p. flea
　　O'CAS 162:20
The faint aroma of p. seals HART 98:17
perhaps: And If and P. and But ELIOT 74:1
Pericles: France what P. felt of Athens
　　KEYN 120:8
perils: And spotted the p. beneath
　　AYRES 16:6
p. because of the illusions MOUN 157:3
period: critical p. in matrimony
　　HERB 101:25
p. of cheating between BIER 34:12
p. of silence on your part ATTL 12:11
p. would need a far less BEER 23:4
periphrastic: p. study in a worn-out
　　ELIOT 74:9
perish: But if it had to p. twice FROST 86:6
Must then a Christ p. SHAW 199:31
or p. together as fools KING 122:6
slip, slide, p. ELIOT 74:6
They too shall p. unconsoled LANG 130:4
permanent: *Theory of P. Adolescence*
　　CONN 59:2
there is no p. place HARDY 96:18
permeated: p. with the odour of joss-sticks
　　BRAM 38:15
Perón: If I had not been born P.
　　PERÓN 170:8
perpendicular: [Dancing is] a p. expression
　　SHAW 199:8
perpetual: An improper mind is a p. feast
　　SMITH 202:21
perquisites: self-respecting scorn of
irregular p. WAUGH 222:22
persist: p. to the threshold CORN 61:10
person: I long for the P. from Porlock
　　SMITH 203:22
The frontier of my P. goes AUDEN 12:14
To us he is no more a p. AUDEN 12:19
personaggi: *Sei p. in cerca d'autore*
　　PIR 171:15
personal: it the p. *unconscious* JUNG 117:3
P. relations are the important
　　FORS 83:16
personality: From 35 to 55, good p.
　　TUCK 218:18
his effort is his own p. FROMM 85:12
P. is the supreme realization JUNG 117:2
who have p. and emotions ELIOT 76:6
perspiration: ninety-nine per cent p.
　　EDIS 72:2
perspire: And dig till you gently p.
　　KIPL 125:11
perspiring: city of p. dreams RAPH 177:16
persuade: that is to p. oneself LESS 135:26
persuaders: The hidden p. PACK 167:1
persuades: p. me to be a Christian
　　FRY 87:11
persuasiveness: depends on personal p.
　　QUIL 177:1
pertinent: way to a p. answer BRON 39:14
perversion: universal p. RAE 177:7
perversions: unnatural of all the sexual p.
　　HUXL 108:17

pervert: p. climbs into the minds
　　BRON 39:15
pessimism: p. goes to the point ROST 185:6
P., when you get used BENN 28:12
pessimist: But the p. sees the hole
　　WILS 229:1
Do you know what a p. SHAW 200:2
p. fears this is true CAB 44:11
pessimists: p. abandon themselves
　　BENN 28:12
sincerity of the p. ROST 185:6
pestle: vessel with the p. PAN 167:6
pet: And kept it for a p. BELL 25:3
petal: rose p. down the Grand MARQ 147:9
petals: P. on a wet, black bough
　　POUND 174:11
she'd peel all the p. AYCK 16:1
Peter: Cottontail, and P. POTT 173:13
formulate *The P. Principle* PETER 170:11
government which robs P. SHAW 196:17
Peter Pan: has been wholly in P.
　　TYNAN 220:8
petrified: suffering from p. adolescence
　　BEVAN 32:13
pettiness: to expiate A p. LAWR 131:17
petty: makes men p. and vindictive
　　MAUG 149:16
peuple: *que nous donnons au p.* FLERS 82:4
pews: Talk about the p. and steeples
　　CHES 51:20
Pferd: *Weiss ich, frag das P.* FREUD 85:6
phagocytes: stimulate the p. SHAW 196:12
phallic: P. and ambrosial POUND 174:5
Ph.D.: back it up with a P. ALGR 3:8
phenomenon: Felicitous p. MOORE 155:12
Phidias: Forms that gentler P. wrought
　　YEATS 233:1
Philadelphia: I went to P., but it was
　　FIEL 79:12
rather be living in P. FIEL 79:15
Philippines: In the P., there are lovely
　　COW 62:4
this is relief of the P. MAC 141:1
philistinism: art-for-art's-sake of our
yawning P. PRIT 175:14
philosophers: economists and political p.
　　KEYN 120:17
philosophical: European p. tradition
　　WHIT 226:13
philosophy: advantage for a system of p.
　　SANT 190:18
European p. of diametrically
　　HOOV 104:12
p. and a party program LIPP 137:17
P. is the replacement RYLE 187:11
superstition to enslave a p. INGE 110:12
why I have no p. myself HALD 95:6
Phlebas: P. the Phoenician ELIOT 77:3
phlegm: p. and tooth-decay HELL 100:5
phobias: Tell us your p. and we
　　BENC 26:22
Phoenician: Phlebas the P., a fortnight
　　ELIOT 77:3
phoenix: Do not expect again a p. hour
　　DAY-L 65:7
p. in my youth so let them YEATS 235:3
p. moment DAY-L 65:8
phone: E.T. p. home MATH 149:2
P. for the fish-knives, Norman
　　BETJ 31:11
p. whenever you felt like SAL 188:25
why did you answer the p. THUR 216:21

phoney: something p. every minute
            SAL 189:2
photograph: A p. is not only an image
            SONT 204:15
photographs: interested in . . . p.?
            CHAP 49:12
photography: P. is truth   GOD 91:3
Phyllida: But P., my Phyllida   DOBS 68:3
physical: are so lightly called p. COL 57:15
   For p. pleasure I'd sooner WAUGH 223:17
physician: p. can bury his mistakes
            WRIG 231:22
   p. is to educate the masses OSLER 165:23
physicians: P. of the Utmost Fame
            BELL 24:12
physicists: p. have known sin OPP 163:17
physics: resort to p. and chemistry
            MENC 150:23
   science is either p. or stamp RUTH 187:9
physiques: *nomme, à la légère*, p. COL 57:15
pianists: no better than many p.
            SCHN 193:1
piano: great black p. appassionato
            LAWR 132:13
   when I sat down at the p. CAPL 46:11
Picardy: Roses are flowering in P.
            WEAT 223:21
Picasso: isn't as great as a P. MUNN 157:18
   P. coming down the street CHUR 53:19
Piccadilly: Goodbye, P.   JUDGE 116:17
pick: I always p. the one WEST 225:17
   Sam, Sam, p. up tha' musket
            HOLL 104:5
picked: have p. them every one SEEG 194:6
pickle: had been weaned on a p.
            ANON 8:23
Pickwick: The P., the Owl ANON 8:21
picnic: Teddy Bears have their P.
            KENN 118:19
picture: Every p. tells a story ANON 6:6
   express in a p.   BELL 23:29
   It's no go the p. palace MACN 144:8
   p. is worth ten thousand BARN 18:15
   p. or a novel that is *not* JAMES 112:1
   P. you upon my knee CAES 44:12
picture-painter: successful writer or p.
            LEWIS 137:4
pictures: It's the p. that got small
            BRAC 37:21
   Of cutting all the p. out BELL 24:4
   painter and I nail my p. SCHW 193:14
   People who try to explain p. PIC 171:8
   P. are for entertainment GOLD 91:13
   You used to be in p. BRAC 37:21
picturesque: quite often p. liar
            TWAIN 219:5
pie: p. by Mrs McGregor POTT 173:14
   p. in the sky when you HILL 102:12
pier: The effusive welcome of the p.
            AUDEN 14:16
piercing: man, it's too p. FREB 84:18
piety: Pathos, p., courage FORS 84:1
piffle: are as p. before the wind ASHF 10:21
pig: p. came up an' lay down BURT 42:17
   p. got up and slowly walked BURT 42:17
   sort of p. in clover LAWR 132:4
pigeon: crooning like a bilious p.
            SHAW 199:18
pigeons: P. on the grass alas STEIN 207:16
pig-sty: p. when she wasn't looking
            THOM 214:9
Pilate: hands than water like P.
            GREE 93:12

pile: P. the bodies high at Austerlitz
            SAND 189:17
   p. the logs   POUND 173:26
pilgrim: loved the p. soul in you
            YEATS 232:7
pilgrimage: with songs beguile your p.
            FLEC 81:6
pilgrims: love you land of the p.
            CUMM 63:15
Pilgrim's Progress: One was 'P.', about
   a man   TWAIN 218:21
pillar: category but a p. of the State
            SOLZ 204:8
pillars: Pylons, those p. SPEN 205:18
   The seven p. of wisdom LAWR 133:2
pillow: like the feather p. HAIG 95:2
Pimpernel: That demmed, elusive P.
            ORCZY 163:19
pimples: merely the scratching of p.
            WOOLF 231:11
pin: If I sit on a p. ANON 8:19
pinafore: His stockings or his p. BELL 24:21
pinched: Mrs Simpson's p. our king
            ANON 6:18
pines: cones under his p. FROST 86:10
   p. are gossip pines FLEC 81:15
pining: probably p. for the fiords
            CHAP 49:13
pink: With a p. hotel MITC 154:8
pinkly: p. bursts the spray BETJ 32:5
pinko-grey: white races are really p.
            FORS 83:20
pins: They're like as a row of p. KIPL 127:8
pint: amount [of blood], but a p. GALT 88:8
   A p. of plain is your only man
            O'BR 162:9
pinta: Drinka P. Milka Day WHIT 226:14
pints: P. and quarts of Ludlow beer
            HOUS 107:9
pious: p. but Mr Salteena was ASHF 10:19
pipe: p. might fall out if FORS 83:3
Pippa: at a window. P. passes BEER 22:27
pips: until the p. squeak GEDD 89:2
piss: P. off, he said to me PINT 171:12
   worth a pitcher of warm p. GARN 88:16
pissing: inside the tent p. out JOHN 114:4
pistols: The young ones carry p.
            SHAW 195:16
pit: And wretched, blind, p. ponies
            HODG 103:13
   p. of the stomach HOUS 106:5
pitch-and-toss: And risk it on one turn
   of p.   KIPL 126:14
pitched: But Love has p. his mansion
            YEATS 235:14
pitcher: isn't worth a p. of warm
            GARN 88:16
pitchfork: Can't I use my wit as a p.
            LARK 130:17
pits: This must be the p. MCEN 142:7
pittance: p. from the BBC for interviewing
            HARD 96:16
pity: And the seas of p. lie AUDEN 13:3
   A p. beyond all telling YEATS 232:8
   p. for the suffering RUSS 186:7
   P. is the feeling JOYCE 115:19
   The Poetry is in the p. OWEN 166:8
   thought it was a p. to get up
            MAUG 149:21
pix: Sticks nix hick p. ANON 8:13
place: And leaping from p. to place
            HARDY 97:7
   clean p. to die KAV 118:9

place (*cont.*):
   everything in its p. BEVAN 32:14
   Home is the p. where FROST 86:13
   In p. of strife CAST 47:10
   know the p. for the first ELIOT 74:20
   must be kept in their p. AWDRY 15:18
   p. for street fighting JAGG 111:9
   p. in any political group HELL 100:8
   p. in the sun and have WILH 227:6
   p. in the world for ugly HARDY 96:18
   p. where a story ended ELIOT 74:18
   p. where optimism most ELLIS 77:11
   right p. for love FROST 86:5
   sleepy and there is no p. DYLAN 71:11
   tight gag of p. HEAN 99:13
   To know their p., and not BELL 24:17
   up and have no p. to go WHIT 226:19
places: all p. were alike KIPL 125:17
   Are the quietest p. HOUS 107:6
   distance between two p. WILL 227:18
   I've been things and seen p. WEST 225:13
   P. they guarded, or kept LARK 130:10
   We returned to our p. ELIOT 73:15
   You will find no new p. CAV 48:2
placetne: P., magistra SAY 192:10
plafond: *inscrite dans les lignes du p.*
            ELUA 77:14
plagiarism: from one author, it's p.
            MIZN 154:19
plagiarize: P.! Let no one else's work
            LEHR 134:7
plague: such a p. when I was young
            YEATS 234:3
plain: A pint of p. is your only man
            O'BR 162:9
   especially the need of the p.
            WAUGH 223:10
   how she makes it p. SERV 194:22
   I see it shining p. HOUS 107:4
   no p. women on television FORD 82:12
   stays mainly in the p. LERN 135:23
plan: both by his p. of attack SASS 191:17
   Commends a most practical p. INGE 110:8
plane: It's a p. ANON 6:8
   p. trees going sha-sha-sha CONN 59:15
planet: species of beetles on this p.
            HALD 95:7
plans: hopeful p. to emptiness
            HOUS 105:14
   p. are always ruined BREC 39:5
planted: p. another one down BOUL 37:2
plants: come and talk to the p. CHAR 49:16
plashy: Feather-footed through the p. fen
            WAUGH 223:13
plasterer: at the p. on his ladder
            HEAN 99:11
plates: they have hats like p. COW 62:4
platform: p. on which they could
            KINN 122:16
platinum: With bullets made of p.
            BELL 24:8
   with eyebrows made of p. FORS 83:5
platitude: A longitude with no p. FRY 87:2
   Applause, n. The echo of a p. BIER 33:24
   p. is simply a truth repeated BALD 17:6
   stroke a p. until it purrs MARQ 147:10
platitudes: orchestration of p. WILD 227:5
Plato: series of footnotes to P. WHIT 226:13
play: And watch the men at p. CLEG 56:15
   author, it's a good p. SHAW 196:20
   But when I started to p. CAPL 46:11
   concert I make them p. BEEC 22:12
   Games people p. BERNE 30:11
   House Beautiful is p. lousy PARK 168:23

political: All p. lives, unless they
                                                      POW 174:22
  clearly to a p. career   SHAW 197:14
  comfortable place in any p.   HELL 100:8
  fear of P. Economy   SELL 194:15
  history of p. power   POPP 172:14
  old p. adage which says   REYN 180:1
  p. aspirant under democracy
                                      MENC 150:14
  p. columnists say   ADAMS 1:17
  P. language   ORW 165:8
  p. leader must keep looking   BAR 20:8
  p. person and could have   HELL 100:8
  P. power grows out   MAO T 146:13
  p. speech and writing   ORW 165:6
  P. thought, in France   ARON 10:12
politician: A p. is a statesman   POMP 172:11
  p. does get an idea   MARQ 147:7
  p. is a man who understands
                                      TRUM 218:9
  p. is an arse upon   CUMM 64:1
  p. never believes what   DE G 66:2
  p. was a person with whose   LLOY 138:16
  p. will never grudge   OLIV 163:4
  who wishes to become a p.   CHUR 53:7
politicians: matter to be left to the p.
                                      DE G 66:3
  not the p. and statesmen   AUDEN 14:1
  p. take in their limelight   BELL 24:22
  too many p. who believe   ADAMS 1:19
politics: All p., however, are based
                                      REST 179:14
  For p. and little else beside   CAMP 45:15
  In international p.   BIER 33:22
  In p., there is no use   CHAM 48:6
  law of principle and p.   RAK 177:8
  observe about this P. thing   ROG 182:6
  P. and the fate of mankind   CAMUS 45:19
  p. are too serious a matter   DE G 66:3
  P. are usually the executive   BRIT 39:11
  P., as a practice   ADAMS 2:1
  p. consists in ignoring   ADAMS 2:6
  P. is not the art   GALB 88:5
  P. is supposed   REAG 178:17
  P. is the art of preventing   VALÉ 221:1
  P. is the Art of the Possible   BUTL 43:1
  P. is war without bloodshed
                                      MAO T 146:12
  p. of happiness   HUMP 108:6
  p. of purpose   HUMP 108:6
  p. of the left and centre   JENK 113:3
  p. ought to be in America   HUMP 108:6
  p. solely as a result   PARK 169:14
  p. that you are much exposed   BALD 17:4
  presented as 'realist p.'   BERD 29:10
  purpose and the p. of joy   HUMP 108:6
  week is a long time in p.   WILS 228:14
  will give his mind to p.   SHAW 195:12
politique: Comme un homme p. ne croit
                                      DE G 66:2
  La pensée p., en France   ARON 10:12
  p. est l'art d'empêcher   VALÉ 221:1
  p. et le sort des hommes   CAMUS 45:19
  P. intérieure, je fais   CLEM 56:17
pollution: unsavoury engine of p.
                                      SPAR 205:9
Polly: P. Garter, under the washing
                                      THOM 214:10
Poltague: Went off to tempt My Lady P.
                                      BELL 25:17
polyphiloprogenitive: P.   ELIOT 75:7
polytechnic: In the P. they teach you
                                      SHAW 197:24

pomp: Lo, all our p. of yesterday
                                      KIPL 126:10
pond: have their Stream and P.   BROO 40:6
ponder: When in charge, p.   BOREN 36:7
ponies: And wretched, blind, pit p.
                                      HODG 103:13
  Five and twenty p.   KIPL 126:6
  p. have swallowed   BETJ 31:9
Pontefract: In the licorice fields at P.
                                      BETJ 31:5
ponts: de coucher sous les p.   FRAN 84:15
poodle: Gentleman's [Mr Balfour's] p.
                                      LLOY 138:7
Pooh: P. always liked a little   MILNE 153:15
  3 Cheers for P.   MILNE 154:4
Pooka: The P. MacPhellimey   O'BR 162:7
pool: Gentle and brown, above the p.
                                      BROO 40:15
  Walk across my swimming p.   RICE 180:10
poor: being p., have only my dreams
                                      YEATS 235:7
  But what can a p. boy do   JAGG 111:9
  expensive it is to be p.   BALD 17:1
  help the many who are p.   KENN 119:12
  if you was as p. as me   SHAW 199:20
  It's no disgrace t'be p.   HUBB 107:17
  It's the p. wot gets the blame   ANON 8:8
  live by robbing the p.   SHAW 197:27
  object is p. or obscure   BIER 33:19
  one of the undeserving p.   SHAW 199:21
  Peace is p. reading   HARDY 96:20
  p. don't know   SART 191:6
  p. get children   KAHN 117:10
  P. little rich girl   COW 62:6
  p. man's opera   HUXL 108:19
  rich richer and the p.   NEHRU 160:3
  sacrificed—is not to be p.   SHAW 197:6
  She was p. but she was honest   ANON 8:8
  [the p.] have to labour   FRAN 84:15
  The p. know that it is money   BREN 39:8
  war is the p. who die   SART 190:26
pop: p. my cork for every guy   FIEL 79:6
  Snap! Crackle! P.!   ANON 8:10
popcorn: Everything else is mere p.
                                      BELL 26:11
pope: against the P. or the NUM
                                      BALD 17:3
  Anybody can be p.   JOHN 114:2
  But I'm the P.   JOHN 114:1
  divisions did you say the P.   STAL 206:19
poppies: In Flanders fields the p. blow
                                      MCCR 141:17
poppy: flushed print in a p.   THOM 215:2
population: p. able to read but unable
                                      TREV 217:21
porcupines: couple of p. under you
                                      KHR 121:4
Porlock: I long for the Person from P.
                                      SMITH 203:22
pornographic: impotent stupidity, a p.
  show   BLUNT 35:5
pornography: P. is the attempt to insult
  sex   LAWR 132:19
  p. of war   RAE 177:7
  show to give p. a dirty   BARN 18:16
Porsches: My friends all drive P.
                                      JOPL 115:3
Porson: better poet than P.   HOUS 105:6
port: ancient tales, and p.   BELL 26:5
portal: fitful tracing of a p.   STEV 208:13
porter: decompose in a barrel of p.
                                      DONL 68:7

porter (cont.):
  Mrs P. in the spring   ELIOT 76:23
portions: p. of the human anatomy
                                      HELP 100:9
portrait: paint a p. I lose a friend
                                      SARG 190:22
  p. not too stale to record   PLOM 172:8
  P. of the artist as a young dog
                                      THOM 214:2
  P. of the Artist as a Young Man
                                      JOYCE 115:16
position: Its human p.   AUDEN 13:5
  My p. was on the left   MOSL 157:1
  p. must be held   HAIG 95:3
  p. of pre-eminence in her   GEOR 89:7
positive: ac-cent-tchu-ate the p.
                                      MERC 151:7
  p. peace which is the presence
                                      KING 121:12
  p. value has its price   PIC 171:6
  that he gave more p. signs   BLUNT 35:4
  The power of p. thinking   PEALE 169:17
possessed: I p., as you suggest   HARD 96:16
  Webster was much p. by death
                                      ELIOT 75:8
possession: p. of a book becomes
                                      BURG 42:12
possibilities: awareness of the p.
                                      LEAV 133:16
possible: It is p. to lie, and even
                                      ADLER 2:16
  not the art of the p.   GALB 88:5
  Politics is the Art of the P.   BUTL 43:1
  p. he is almost certainly   CLAR 56:10
  p. to conquer poverty   JOHN 114:6
  p. to gain a chair of literature   ALGR 3:8
  world is the best of all p.   BRAD 38:6
Possum: said the Honourable P.
                                      BERR 30:18
post: Lie follows by p.   BER 29:11
  p. tends to be occupied   PETER 170:12
postal: Bringing the cheque and the p.
                                      AUDEN 14:21
  p. districts packed like   LARK 131:1
postal-order: My p. hasn't come yet
                                      RICH 180:14
poster: Kitchener is a great p.   ASQ 11:6
posterity: decided to write for p.   ADE 2:11
  have put mankind and p.   INGE 110:15
  P. is as likely to be wrong   BROUN 41:7
  p. on what he would have   OSLER 165:24
postern: p. behind my tremulous
                                      HARDY 97:10
Post-Impressionist: P. pictures sent over
  from   BLUNT 35:5
postman: The p. always rings twice
                                      CAIN 44:17
post office: stalked through the P.
                                      YEATS 233:6
pot: make them in the one p.   JOYCE 116:4
potato: You like p. and I like po-tah-to
                                      GERS 89:16
potatoes: yesterday's mashed p.   FIEL 79:7
potato-gatherers: p. like mechanized
  scarecrows   KAV 118:8
potency: through the p. of my voice
                                      HARD 96:16
potent: how p. cheap music   COW 62:7
  p. advocates of peace upon   GEOR 89:11
potential: p. for the disastrous rise EIS 73:6
potentially: become what he p. is
                                      FROMM 85:12
Potter: This is Gillie P. speaking
                                      POTT 173:16

Pouilly Fuissé: glasses of Chablis or P.
        AMIS 4:16
pounces: p. unerringly upon   JAMES 112:9
pound: P. failed to impress her
        STEIN 207:14
  p. here in Britain   WILS 228:17
pounds: Fifty p.! An' tha's niver
        LAWR 132:20
  Give crowns and p. and guineas
        HOUS 106:12
poured: P. forth her song in perfect
        AUDEN 15:11
  p. into his clothes   WOD 230:23
poverty: anything to do with p. CURR 64:7
  Money is better than p.   ALLEN 3:24
  possible to conquer p.   JOHN 114:6
  p. knows how extremely   BALD 17:1
  setting him up in p.   NAIDU 158:18
  state of extreme p.   PER 170:5
  unconditional war on p.   JOHN 114:10
  worst of crimes is p.   SHAW 197:6
power: A friend in p. is a friend lost
        ADAMS 2:2
  because they confer p.   RUSS 186:26
  because we had p.   BENÉT 27:6
  corridors of p.   SNOW 203:26
  disastrous rise of misplaced p. EIS 73:6
  Horses and P. and War KIPL 123:18
  limitation of governmental p. WILS 229:9
  p. grows out of the barrel MAO T 146:13
  P., he [Kissinger] has   KISS 128:3
  p. instead of influence   TAYL 212:6
  P. is not a means   ORW 164:25
  p. of conveying unlimited HARD 96:16
  p. of vested interests   KEYN 120:17
  p. on earth that can protect BALD 17:7
  p. over people as long   SOLZ 204:6
  p.-state   TEMP 212:11
  p. to hold men and women together
        SZASZ 211:14
  P. to the people   ANON 8:3
  p. which stands on Privilege BELL 25:19
  P. without responsibility KIPL 125:19
  responsibility without p. STOP 209:13
  Send to us p. and light   AUDEN 15:2
  shares p. much more widely BENN 27:14
  symbol of the p. of Heaven
        MOORE 155:12
  The certainty of p.   DAY-L 65:9
  The p. of positive thinking PEALE 169:17
  unleashed p. of the atom   EINS 73:2
  War knows no p.   BROO 40:2
  when it comes to p.   SNOW 204:2
  When p. corrupts   KENN 119:7
  where p. predominates   JUNG 116:22
  who have the p. to end it SASS 192:1
powerful: be a p. person yourself
        CORN 61:10
  most p. of schools   GIR 90:17
  rich society and the p.   JOHN 114:11
  Sisterhood is p.   MORG 155:19
powerless: p. to *express* anything
        STR 210:14
powers: contracting p. solemnly declare
        BRIA 39:10
  Headmasters have p.   CHUR 55:9
  prostitute all their p.   FORS 83:6
practical: Commends a most p. plan
        INGE 110:8
  Morality's *not* p.   BOLT 35:16
practise: prudence never to p.
        TWAIN 219:10
  we preach but do not p. RUSS 187:1

practised: at seeing it p.   BUTL 44:5
practising: art than he can by p. it
        AUDEN 13:15
prairies: From the mountains to the p.
        BERL 29:15
praise: countryman must have p.
        BLYT 35:8
  Let the florid music p.   AUDEN 14:11
  people p. and don't read TWAIN 219:11
  P. for the singing   FARJ 78:7
  p. of God consists   PROU 176:3
  P. the Lord and pass   FORGY 83:1
  Teach the free man how to p.
        AUDEN 13:4
  they only want p.   MAUG 149:19
  things thou wouldst p.   DE L 66:12
  whom must the p. be given BEAV 21:5
praising: advantage of doing one's p.
        BUTL 44:7
  when I am p. anyone BEER 22:24
  who are always p. the past
        SMITH 203:19
pram: Mr Shultz went off his p.
        KINN 122:14
  than the p. in the hall CONN 58:17
prawce: Wot p. Selvytion nah
        SHAW 197:12
pray: place for those who p. SIMON 201:4
  P. for the repose   ROLFE 182:18
  p. to Him I find I'm talking BARN 18:21
  some to Meccah turn to p. FLEC 81:11
  Work and p., live on hay HILL 102:12
prayer: Conservative Party at p.
        ROYD 185:18
  The wish for p. is a prayer BERN 30:7
  which characterizes p.   BELL 26:12
prayers: Bernard always had a few p.
        ASHF 10:19
  Knelt down with angry p. HODG 103:13
  p. would make me whole KIPL 125:20
  Robin is saying his p. MILNE 153:12
pray'r: Comin' in on a wing and a p.
        ADAM 2:8
prays: family that p. together stays
        SCAL 192:13
preach: p. but do not practise RUSS 187:1
preaching: p. and got myself burnt
        JER 113:11
precedent: dangerous p.   CORN 61:11
precedes: Existence p. and rules essence
        SART 191:1
precious: how p. is frivolity FORS 83:6
  so p. that it must be rationed
        LENIN 134:17
  The right is more p. than peace
        WILS 229:14
predict: p. things after they have
        ION 110:19
predominates: eyes she eclipses and p.
        DOYLE 68:18
predominating: with sniffles p.
        HENRY 101:9
pre-eminence: p. in her Colonial trade
        GEOR 89:7
pre-empted: p. it is called brain-washing
        GREER 93:21
prefer: I do not know which to p.
        STEV 208:14
  I p. reading   SMITH 203:13
  may p. a self-made name HAND 96:8
  Or would you p.   ANON 9:17
  which men p. not to hear AGAR 2:19
preference: special p. for beetles HALD 95:7

pregnancies: p. and at least four
  miscarriages   BEEC 22:3
pregnancy: p. by a resort to mathematics
        MENC 150:23
pregnant: If men could get p. KENN 118:18
prejudice: P., n. A vagrant opinion
        BIER 34:13
  p. the civil and religious BALF 17:16
  reflection and a source of p. SCH 193:8
prejudices: p. as the advertisers don't
        SWAF 211:4
  their own and a critic's p. BALL 17:22
premises: based upon licensed p.
        O'BR 162:8
preparation: p. for this hour and this
        CHUR 55:18
prepare: constituencies and p. for
  government   STEEL 207:7
  p. for war like precocious PEAR 169:21
prepared: am p. to meet my Maker
        CHUR 55:13
  BE P., which means   BAD 16:9
  P. TO KILL ONE ANOTHER SHAW 197:15
  world is not yet p.   DOYLE 69:7
prerogative: p. of the eunuch throughout
        STOP 209:13
  p. of the harlot throughout KIPL 125:19
present: know nothing but the p.
        KEYN 120:11
  p. controls the past   ORW 164:22
  P. has latched its postern HARDY 97:10
  p. is an interlude   O'NEI 163:15
  p. of Mornington Crescent HARG 98:10
  Time p. and time past   ELIOT 74:2
presents: if it were not for the p. ADE 2:12
  p. and good food and i WILL 227:10
preserve: P. it as your chiefest BELL 24:4
  p.'s full of stones   BETJ 31:12
  Whom God P.   MORT 156:17
preside: p. over the liquidation CHUR 53:18
presidency: P. is an unpardonable
        JOHN 114:14
  p. so much that he'll spend BROD 39:12
president: All the P. is, is a glorified
        TRUM 218:11
  All the P.'s men   BERN 30:12
  America any boy may become P.
        STEV 208:21
  anybody could become P. DARR 64:14
  going to be your next p. CART 47:5
  more than any other P. MENC 150:13
  not choose to run for P. COOL 60:16
  not their P. is a crook NIXON 161:5
  P. of the Immortals   HARDY 98:1
  P.'s hardest task is not JOHN 114:15
  We are the P.'s men   KISS 128:1
  When the P. does it NIXON 160:15
press: Freedom of the p. SWAF 211:4
  racket is back in its p. BETJ 32:1
  with you on the free p. STOP 209:14
pressed: P. into service means pressed
        FROST 86:16
pressure: Hemingway said, 'grace
  under p.'   HEM 101:2
presumption: you'll be amused by its p.
        THUR 216:20
pretend: I do not p. to know where
        DARR 64:15
  p. to be more stupid STARK 207:3
  We shall not p. that there ANON 9:12
  why p. that he is   SHAW 198:4
Pretender: James II, and the Old P.
        GUED 94:12

pretentious: And Harry says, 'P.? *Moi?*'
    CLEE 56:14
pretty: A p. girl is like a melody BERL 29:17
  It's p., but is it Art KIPL 124:1
  policeman and a p. girl CHAP 49:8
  The p. can get away WAUGH 223:10
  Which is sometimes so p. PRÉV 175:6
prevail: not merely endure, he will p.
    FAUL 78:13
prevent: knowing how to p. them
    RUSS 187:6
  we have a right to p. it MILN 154:5
prevented: could not have been p.
    BEVIN 33:14
preventing: nothing like desire for p.
    PROU 176:2
  Politics is the art of p. VALÉ 221:1
prévois: *p. les événements que lorsqu'ils*
    ION 110:19
prey: p. to sensations and cheap
    TREV 217:21
preys: p. systematically JAMES 112:6
price: Despair is the p. one pays
    GREE 93:14
  increase was another man's p.
    WILS 228:18
  love that pays the p. SPR 206:11
  p. of championing human OWEN 166:6
  p. of insubordination MACG 142:11
  p. of justice is eternal BENN 28:13
  What p. glory AND 5:1
prices: acting directly to reduce p.
    HEATH 99:17
prickly: *Here we go round the p. pear*
    ELIOT 75:11
pride: beware the temptation of p.
    REAG 178:13
  great labyrinth out of p. YEATS 234:20
  having given up his p. SAL 189:5
  here have P. and Truth YEATS 232:15
  London P. has been handed COW 62:2
  look backward to with p. FROST 86:12
  P. of Life that planned HARDY 97:13
  The poet's inward p. DAY-L 65:9
priest: p. of the invisible STEV 208:17
priests: And pay a million p. HARDY 98:6
  associate with a lot of p. BELL 25:1
  p. were infinitely more FITZ 80:23
  The p. in gold and black LAWR 132:11
primal: has only two p. passions
    OSLER 166:3
primary: p. object of a student CECIL 48:4
prime: One's p. is elusive SPARK 205:8
Prime Minister: best P. we have BUTL 43:2
  camouflage about the P. PAGET 167:3
  country gentleman than a p.
    MACD 142:3
  P. [Lloyd George] has ANON 6:19
  The next P. but three BELL 24:18
  triumphant P. declared THAT 212:16
  Unknown P. ASQ 11:12
  would have become P. before CONN 59:1
Prime Ministers: P. have never yet been
    CHUR 55:9
  wild flowers, and P. BALD 17:11
primeval: mastodons bellowing across p.
    WOD 230:15
primitive: wise p. in a giant jungle
    MAIL 145:8
prince: Advise the p. ELIOT 75:18
  I were the P. of Peace HOUS 105:7
princes: admit p. to the corridors
    DOUG 68:12

principle: He does everything on p.
    SHAW 199:3
  law of p. and politics RAK 177:8
  p. of Human Nature JAMES 112:7
  the 'falling domino' p. EIS 73:8
  useful thing about a p. MAUG 149:8
principles: instead of p., slogans BENT 29:9
  one's p. than to live ADLER 2:15
  upon those p. of freedom PAGE 167:2
print: eternity of p. WOOLF 231:9
  licence to p. your own money
    THOM 216:13
  p. such of the proprietor's SWAF 211:4
  seeing our names in p. CHES 51:23
printemps: *p. dans ses plis a gardé*
    ARAG 10:2
printing: p. press is either BARR 19:12
printless: On lissom, clerical, p. toe
    BROO 40:12
priorities: language of p. is the religion
    BEVAN 33:6
priority: without the reward of p.
    SCOTT 193:18
prison: begin with, it is a p. SHAW 199:11
  comparatively at home in p.
    WAUGH 223:5
  Home is the girl's p. SHAW 198:27
  In the p. of his days AUDEN 13:4
  p. for the colour HOUS 105:8
  there is a soul in p. DEBS 65:14
prisoner: If the p. is happy SHAW 198:4
prisoners: p. of addiction ILL 110:7
  still the p. of communism SOLZ 204:7
privacy: narrow p. and tawdry secrets
    LEACH 133:4
private: his p. parts, his money BUTL 43:10
  Its p. life is a disgrace ANON 8:6
  P. faces in public places AUDEN 15:1
  P. Means is dead SMITH 203:23
  p. opulence and public GALB 88:4
  with a silk hat at a p. view EDW 72:5
privilege: power which stands on P.
    BELL 25:19
privy: nor a p., nor a seal BAIL 16:11
prized: local, but p. elsewhere
    AUDEN 13:14
prize-fighters: one of p. shaking hands
    MENC 150:16
prizes: offer glittering p. SMITH 202:14
  p. at the flower show BRON 39:16
problem: or you're part of the p.
    CLEA 56:12
  p. is food DONL 68:6
  p. of the colour line DUB 70:8
  p. of the twentieth century DUB 70:8
  quite a three-pipe p. DOYLE 69:1
  that they can't see the p. CHES 52:4
problematical: The p. world and sells us
  life FRY 87:1
problems: p. reproduce themselves
    JOS 115:5
proceeds: good conscience on the p.
    SMITH 203:4
process: attentive when she was in p.
    FITZ 80:23
  p. whereby American girls HAMP 96:7
proclaims: p. with a hammer BIER 33:25
procrastination: p. is the art MARQ 146:19
prodigal: angels over the p.'s SAKI 188:10
prodigious: have a p. quantity of mind
    TWAIN 219:17
prodigy: normal child and not as a p.
    BARB 18:12

producers: or junior television p. AMIS 4:16
produces: artist is someone who p.
    WARH 222:12
producing: that consumes without p.
    ORW 164:7
product: p. of the untalented CAPP 46:17
production: p. and reduce unemployment
    HEATH 99:17
profanation: From sale and p. CHES 51:18
profane: P. perfection of mankind
    YEATS 233:1
profession: ancient p. in the world
    KIPL 125:3
  be the second oldest p. REAG 178:17
  not a p. but a vocation SIM 201:2
  very important p. SHAW 196:16
professions: p. are conspiracies against
    SHAW 196:13
  shortest-lived p. there ROG 182:16
professor: called a p. emeritus LEAC 133:7
professors: instrument wielded by p.
    WEIL 224:3
  p. like their literature LEWIS 137:1
profit: And the p. and loss ELIOT 77:3
  p. is not always what motivates
    GIDE 90:9
profitable: it is not p. MARQ 147:6
profited: p. from public service
    NIXON 161:5
profits: Civilization and p. go COOL 60:14
profound: Down some p. dull tunnel
    OWEN 166:15
  p. truths recognized BOHR 35:14
programme: Not so much a p. ANON 7:32
progress: beings will live and p. DUB 70:7
  certain since Social P. began KIPL 126:18
  p. depends on the unreasonable man
    SHAW 198:23
  P., far from consisting SANT 190:9
  p. if a cannibal uses knife LEC 133:3
  p. in the arts MAO T 146:8
  P. is a comfortable disease CUMM 64:2
  p. is based upon a universal BUTL 43:19
  'P.' is the exchange ELLIS 77:12
  P. through technology ANON 9:3
  The social p., order JOHN 113:22
  They spoke of P. spiring round
    CHES 52:2
  To mark the simple sort of p. SIMM 201:3
  To swell a p. ELIOT 75:18
prohibition: Communism is like p.
    ROG 182:15
project: much less ambitious p. ANON 6:13
projected: They stay as they were p.
    BOWEN 37:12
projections: Merely p. There is nothing
    ELIOT 73:20
proletarian: p. socialist state in Russia
    LENIN 134:14
prolong: Youth to p. YEATS 234:4
prolonged: p. by those who have
    SASS 192:1
Prometheus: P. reaches for the stars
    KOES 128:14
promiscuity: Sentimentality is the
  emotional p. MAIL 145:7
promise: Full of Eastern p. ANON 6:11
  Gives p. of pneumatic bliss ELIOT 75:9
  p. made is a debt unpaid SERV 195:1
  p. of a refined and sensitive DOYLE 69:21
  p. of their early years POW 174:19
  was a young man of p. BALF 17:19

promised: I never p. you a rose garden
    GREEN 93:11
  I've seen the p. land   KING 121:16
  think of the Future as a p.   LEWIS 136:13
promises: But I have p. to keep FROST 86:7
  he is a young man of p.   BALF 17:19
  Vote for the man who p.   BAR 20:6
promising: destroy they first call p.
    CONN 58:16
prone: Orion plunges p.   HOUS 106:6
pronounce: p. a judgment   BECK 21:8
  spell better than they p. TWAIN 219:18
proof: p. of God's omnipotence DE VR 67:6
  which America is the p.   MCC 141:10
proofs: p. and tell him or her CHAN 49:4
propaganda: purely for p. BEAV 20:18
proper: and lacks a p. pride MACD 142:1
  p. or improper   FULL 87:14
  p. study of mankind   HUXL 108:13
properties: certain exceptional p.
    JEANS 112:21
property: from the dominion of p.
    GOLD 91:11
  own p. at the resurrection BUTL 43:9
  p. that we shall strike PANK 167:11
  Thieves respect p.   CHES 51:6
prophets: ceased to pose as its p.
    POPP 172:13
proportion: That's out of p. LARK 130:17
proposition: all men are equal is a p.
    HUXL 109:10
  into the fifth p. of Euclid DOYLE 69:19
  p. be interesting   WHIT 226:7
  p. is the method   SCHL 192:17
  undesirable to believe a p. RUSS 186:23
propriety: p. of some persons seems
    BRAD 38:2
prose: *as well written as p.*
    POUND 174:8
  Poetry is to p. as dancing WAIN 222:1
  p. and the passion   FORS 83:17
prose-song: Stein's p. is a cold
    LEWIS 136:18
prospects: affording delightful p.
    HOFF 104:2
prosper: in which our affairs p. BIER 34:7
prosperity: p. arrived at in a single
    BUTL 44:4
prostitute: can p. all their powers
    FORS 83:6
  p. is more moral   PHIL 170:15
prostitutes: small nations like p.
    KUBR 129:5
protect: Heaven will p. a working
    SMITH 202:8
  inform the reader but to p. ACH 1:9
  p. its own existence   ASIM 11:5
protected: squirrels, must be p.
    ORTON 164:3
protection: millions of farms if that p.
    HOOV 104:13
protections: p. against temptations
    TWAIN 219:14
protects: p. the solitude RILKE 181:5
protest: partakes of the nature of a p.
    HOFF 103:18
Protestant: A P. with a horse BEHAN 23:21
  attacked me and the P. church
    NIEM 160:13
Protestants: P. can be expected to have
    WILS 228:6
proud: are always p. of the fact
    RUSS 186:9

proud (*cont.*):
  A woman can be p. and stiff
    YEATS 235:14
  It makes him very p. MILNE 153:14
  man being too p. to fight WILS 229:11
  p. of seeing our names CHES 51:23
Proust: go for a P. or a Joyce COBB 57:1
prove: I could p. everything PINT 171:14
  I've arrived and to p. SYKES 211:7
  you money if you can p. HOPE 105:1
proved: something or other could be p.
    FRY 87:5
  virtue and a p. liar   HAIL 95:4
  whole you have p.   HARDY 98:5
Provence: Than you found it in P.
    WILL 228:2
Proverbs: King Solomon wrote the P.
    NAYL 159:26
providence: I go the way that P. dictates
    HITL 103:4
  inscrutable workings of P. SMITH 202:10
  p. to kill you before you BUTL 43:21
provident: They are p. instead
    BOGAN 35:11
providers: as p. they're oil wells
    PARK 169:3
provincial: he was worse than p.
    JAMES 111:21
provincialism: adultery than in p.
    HUXL 108:9
provocative: choose a less p. Ambassador
    HOUS 105:7
provoke: subsidized to p. the world
    FRY 87:3
prudence: effect of p. on rascality
    SHAW 198:20
  p. never to practise TWAIN 219:10
prudent: stage, a p. Mr Baldwin BEAV 21:2
prunus: p. and forsythia across BETJ 32:5
Prussia: military domination of P.
    ASQ 11:11
psalm: reverent cadence and subtle p.
    AUDEN 15:11
Psalms: And King David wrote the P.
    NAYL 159:26
psychiatrist: Any man who goes to a p.
    GOLD 91:18
  p. is a man who goes STOC 209:10
psychical: For P. Research COW 62:13
psychology: p. of human relationships
    BERNE 30:11
pub: any p. on Saturday night ORW 165:3
  wasn't a p. open in the city
    BEHAN 23:26
  Will someone take me to a p. CHES 52:2
pubic: Caught the P. Hare BEHAN 23:22
public: British p. falls for this HAIL 95:5
  Ce que le p. réclame BART 20:3
  describe holding p. office ACH 1:7
  gives it to the p.   VALÉ 220:22
  glorified p. relations TRUM 218:11
  I and the p. know   AUDEN 13:8
  now quit altogether p. EDW 72:8
  one to mislead the p. ASQ 11:10
  opulence and p. squalor GALB 88:4
  Private faces in p. places AUDEN 15:1
  p. buys its opinions BUTL 43:29
  p. school will always feel WAUGH 223:5
  p. something they want SKEL 201:20
  p. wants is the image BART 20:3
  p. will take care of the cat SULZ 211:1
  researchers into P. Opinion AUDEN 13:10
  solo in p. and learning BUTL 43:7
  The p. doesn't give a damn BEEC 22:1

public (*cont.*):
  whatever the Government and p.
  opinion   SHAW 197:29
  yourself and have no p. CONN 59:4
publicity: hijacker of the oxygen of p.
    THAT 213:5
  justice is eternal p. BENN 28:13
  p. except your own obituary
    BEHAN 23:28
  p. rather than of poetry LEAV 133:17
  qualities which create p. ATTL 12:7
publics: can impose on their p. BENN 28:7
public-school: p. men or even of
  Anglo-Saxons   FORS 83:2
published: after my first book was p.
    BARR 19:16
publisher: executed for murdering his p.
    BARR 19:3
publishers: fear of life become p.
    CONN 58:15
  Turned Down by numerous P. ADE 2:11
pubs: all the p. in Dublin DONL 68:7
pudding: Take away that p. CHUR 56:4
puddle: dangerous than a mud-p.
    STEIN 207:15
puffed: P. its sulphur to the sunset
    BETJ 31:19
pull: Len says one steady p. more
    FROST 86:15
  P. down thy vanity POUND 174:13
  willing to p. his weight ROOS 183:14
pulls: p. a lady through MARQ 147:3
pulp: The p. so bitter, how shall
    THOM 215:16
pulse: And two people with the one p.
    MACN 144:13
  p. in the eternal mind BROO 40:5
puñado: *por un p. de monedas* ZAP 236:10
punctuality: P. is the virtue of the bored
    WAUGH 223:6
punctures: And it p. my skin ANON 8:19
punk: Gert's writings are p. ANON 6:22
punt: it is better fun to p. SAY 192:9
pupils: p. are the crème de la SPARK 205:6
purchased: life thus p. we could
    ROS 184:18
pure: appear as a p. mathematician
    JEANS 112:22
  cold and p. and very dead LEWIS 137:1
  I'm as p. as the driven slush BANK 18:2
  p. as the lily in the dell LAUD 131:8
purest: zipless fuck is the p. thing
    JONG 115:2
purify: To p. the dialect of the tribe
    ELIOT 74:19
puritan: P. all things are impure
    LAWR 132:6
puritanism: England is not P. but
  February   KRUT 129:3
  P. The haunting fear MENC 150:19
purple: His P. Robe   FARJ 78:8
  noon a p. glow   YEATS 232:9
purpose: Here is God's p. FULL 87:14
  himself except for a noble p. HERB 101:26
  politics of p. and the politics HUMP 108:6
  Proof that there's a p. set YEATS 233:1
  p. of human existence JUNG 116:19
  Sole p. of visit   HARD 96:15
purring: Is suddenly p. there MONRO 155:2
purrs: until it p. like an epigram
    MARQ 147:10
pursue: those who p. many ends BERL 30:4
  who p. Culture in bands WHAR 225:30

pursued: it is you who are the p.
　　　　　　　　　　　　　　SHAW 197:25
　The villain still p. her　　　NOBL 161:9
pursuit: moderation in the p. of justice
　　　　　　　　　　　　　　GOLD 91:12
　Now of that long p.　　　THOM 215:18
　p. of the Presidency　　　JOHN 114:14
push: without trying to p. it　O'CAS 162:17
put: Our end is Life. P. out to sea
　　　　　　　　　　　　　　MACN 144:11
　p. out on the troubled　　　GALB 88:3
　what p. me up to it　　　BEVIN 33:16
　with which I will not p.　　CHUR 55:15
putting: way of p. it　　　ELIOT 74:9
pygmies: peace like retarded p.
　　　　　　　　　　　　　　PEAR 169:21
pyjamas: I in p. for the heat　LAWR 131:16
pylons: P., those pillars　SPEN 205:18
pyramid: bottom of the economic p.
　　　　　　　　　　　　　　ROOS 182:21
Pyrenees: that tease in the High P.
　　　　　　　　　　　　　　BELL 25:15
pyres: Steel chambers, late the p.
　　　　　　　　　　　　　　HARDY 97:13
Pythagoras: P. planned it　YEATS 233:5
python: sheep in the stare of a p.
　　　　　　　　　　　　　　BANK 18:6
　Who bought a P. from a man　BELL 25:3

Q

quad: no one about in the Q.　KNOX 128:10
quaint: Yes; q. and curious war
　　　　　　　　　　　　　　HARDY 98:3
Quakers: I was beaten up by Q.　ALLEN 4:8
qualification: q. for being put　CARS 47:3
qualities: only two q. in the world
　　　　　　　　　　　　　　SHAW 197:5
　q. which create publicity　ATTL 12:7
quality: have a third q. as well　FORS 83:7
　Never mind the q.　　　POW 175:4
quantity: prodigious q. of mind
　　　　　　　　　　　　　　TWAIN 219:17
quarks: Three q. for Muster Mark
　　　　　　　　　　　　　　JOYCE 115:13
quarrel: lover's q. with the world
　　　　　　　　　　　　　　FROST 86:22
　out of the q. with others　YEATS 232:10
　q. in a far away country　CHAM 48:12
　reality only one to make a q.
　　　　　　　　　　　　　　INGE 110:14
quarters: Ere to the wind's twelve q.
　　　　　　　　　　　　　　HOUS 107:3
quay: Who would wait on the q.
　　　　　　　　　　　　　　CAUS 47:17
Quebec: Long Live Free Q.　DE G 65:18
Queen: Fella belong Mrs Q.　PHIL 170:19
　Q. to get away with a hat　LOOS 139:7
　To toast *The Q.*　　　HEAN 99:15
queenly: Q. in her own room　WHAR 225:28
queer: toast to 'our q. old dean'
　　　　　　　　　　　　　　SPOO 206:7
　We're here because we're q.
　　　　　　　　　　　　　　BEHAN 23:27
　what a q. thing Life is　WOD 230:21
queerer: universe is not only q.　HALD 95:6
questing: fen passes the q. vole
　　　　　　　　　　　　　　WAUGH 223:13
question: ask an impertinent q.
　　　　　　　　　　　　　　BRON 39:14
　down the number of the q.　CHUR 55:7

question (*cont.*):
　having asked any clear q.　CAMUS 45:20
　If any q. why we died　KIPL 127:21
　questions grow where one q.
　　　　　　　　　　　　　　VEBL 221:11
　q. that has never been　FREUD 85:9
　secretly changed the Q.　SELL 194:17
　that case what is the q.　STEIN 207:18
　The q. is absurd　　　AUDEN 13:11
　To ask the hard q. is simple　AUDEN 15:5
questions: no q. isn't told a lie　KIPL 126:6
　not wish to know ask q.　RAL 177:9
　q. and form a clear opinion　BONH 36:2
　q. of will or decision　CHOM 52:18
　that all q. are open　BELL 24:2
　That q. the distempered part　ELIOT 74:12
queue: forms an orderly q. of one
　　　　　　　　　　　　　　MIKES 151:16
quick: Come! q. as you can　DE L 66:13
　q., and the dead　　　DEWAR 67:8
　q. brown fox jumps over　ANON 8:5
quickened: His eyes are q. so with grief
　　　　　　　　　　　　　　GRAV 93:6
quicker: liquor Is q.　　NASH 159:18
quickest: q. way is to start your own
　religion　　　　　　　HUBB 107:18
quiet: All q. on the western front
　　　　　　　　　　　　　　REM 179:11
　q. world til you knock　SHAW 199:9
　were alone with the q. day　JAMES 112:5
quietest: Are the q. places　HOUS 107:6
quietly: Q. sweating palm to palm
　　　　　　　　　　　　　　HUXL 109:2
　Q. they go, the intelligent　MILL 151:17
quinquireme: Q. of Nineveh　MAS 148:2
quinsy: weaning, the liar's q.　AUDEN 15:2
quit: q. altogether public affairs　EDW 72:8
quite: not q. a gentleman　ASHF 10:16
quivers: And q. in the sunny breeze
　　　　　　　　　　　　　　GREN 94:3
quotation: q. is a national vice
　　　　　　　　　　　　　　WAUGH 223:9
quotations: read books of q.　CHUR 55:11
　q. from the Bible　　　LAWR 132:5
quote: debate forcefully and q. aptly
　　　　　　　　　　　　　　HOGB 104:3
　monkey of a man is to q.　BENC 26:21
quoted: remarks are very seldom q.
　correctly　　　　　　STR 210:18
quotes: man never q. accurately
　　　　　　　　　　　　　　PEAR 169:19
　nice thing about q.　　WILL 227:12

R

rabbit: I am a bunny r.　　AYRES 16:5
　Run, r., run　　　　　GAY 89:1
　The r. has a charming face　ANON 8:6
　There is a r. in a snare　STEP 208:7
rabbits: there were four little R.
　　　　　　　　　　　　　　POTT 173:13
race: As men and women with our r.
　　　　　　　　　　　　　　KIPL 126:7
　flag as the r. wore on　COKE 57:14
　r. between education　WELLS 225:2
　r. or the colour　　　WILL 228:5
　r. relations in our time　CARM 46:19
racehorses: r. and the cheaper clarets
　　　　　　　　　　　　　　SAKI 188:14
races: darker to the lighter r.　DUB 70:8
　r. are really pinko-grey　FORS 83:20

racing: r. tipster who only reached
　　　　　　　　　　　　　　TAYL 212:8
racist: r. institutions and values
　　　　　　　　　　　　　　CARM 46:19
rack: left in the lugage r.　WILL 227:8
racket: Once in the r. you're always
　　　　　　　　　　　　　　CAP 46:13
　r. is back in its press　BETJ 32:1
　r. run by unscrupulous　BEEC 22:10
radar: r. and all great writers　HEM 101:5
radiance: strain of this trial—a r.
　　　　　　　　　　　　　　CAUL 47:16
radical: I never dared be r. when young
　　　　　　　　　　　　　　FROST 85:20
　R. is a man with both feet　ROOS 183:6
　r. revolutionary will become　AREN 10:5
radicals: one of these goddam r.　CAP 46:12
　r. have good digestions　BUTL 43:20
radio: I had the r. on　MONR 155:3
　r. and television　　　SARR 190:25
raffiniert: *R. ist der Herrgott*　EINS 72:13
rafters: stars come down with the r.
　　　　　　　　　　　　　　AUDEN 14:8
rag: foul r. and bone shop　YEATS 233:8
　r. and a bone and a hank　KIPL 127:18
　That Shakespearian r.　BUCK 42:3
　that Shakesperian R.　ELIOT 76:21
rage: horrible that lust and r.　YEATS 234:3
　Maintain your r.　　　WHIT 226:20
　r. against the dying　THOM 213:13
rages: weight of r. will press harder
　　　　　　　　　　　　　　SPOO 206:9
ragged: been a pair of r. claws　ELIOT 75:16
　rushed a dozen dirty and r.　DOYLE 69:24
raging: r. in the dark　YEATS 235:18
ragtime: Alexander's r. band　BERL 29:13
　R . . . but when the wearied Band
　　　　　　　　　　　　　　HUXL 109:2
raid: r. on the inarticulate　ELIOT 74:13
railroad: Once I built a r.　HARB 96:12
railroads: build bridges and throw r.
　　　　　　　　　　　　　　BROUN 41:6
railway: picking daisies on the r.
　　　　　　　　　　　　　　WOD 230:13
　various r. termini　　FORS 83:12
rain: boy, waiting for r.　ELIOT 73:11
　Dull roots with spring r.　ELIOT 76:13
　hard r.'s a gonna fall　DYLAN 71:6
　left Him in the r.　　STUD 210:20
　nobody, not even the r.　CUMM 63:18
　r. in Spain stays mainly　LERN 135:23
　r. is destroying his grain　HERB 101:20
　r. over the dwindling harbour
　　　　　　　　　　　　　　THOM 213:16
　Singin' in the r.　　　FREED 84:20
　Still falls the R.　　　SITW 201:15
　Sudden the r. of gold　DAY-L 65:7
　wedding-cake left out in the r.
　　　　　　　　　　　　　　AUDEN 15:14
rainbow: A r. and a cuckoo's song
　　　　　　　　　　　　　　DAV 64:20
　Follow ev'ry r.　　　HAMM 95:14
　God gave Noah the r. sign　ANON 6:12
　It was the R. gave thee birth　DAV 65:3
　simple blessing of a r.　ABSE 1:3
　Somewhere over the r.　HARB 96:13
　The Lord survives the r.　LOW 140:6
rain-green: over the r. grass　LEE 134:3
raining: It isn't r. rain to me　LOV 139:16
rains: Every time it rains, it r.　BURKE 42:13
rainy: The r. Pleiads wester　HOUS 106:6
raised: No glass of ours was ever r.
　　　　　　　　　　　　　　HEAN 99:15

raises: 'Force' is the food that r. him
                                    HANFF 96:9
rake: stop to r. the leaves   FROST 86:8
raking: when to stop r. the muck
                                    ROOS 184:4
Ramsay: R., would you rather be
                                    MACD 142:3
Ramsbottom: And Mr and Mrs R.
                                    EDGAR 71:20
ran: I r. the paper [*Daily Express*]
                                    BEAV 20:18
  nothing ever r. quite straight   GALS 88:6
ranches: r. of isolation   AUDEN 13:1
randy: Porter-drinkers' r. laughter
                                    YEATS 233:2
  R.—where—where's the rest   BELL 24:3
range: wider r. of experience   HARR 98:13
Rangoon: chunkin' from R. to Mandalay
                                    KIPL 123:13
rape: legitimately, you r. it   DEGAS 65:16
  r. is said to be the ruling   PRIT 175:12
  They r. us with their eyes   FREN 85:4
rapidly: R. again'   DYLAN 71:14
  Yes, but not so r.   BECK 21:20
rapists: all men are r.   FREN 85:4
rapscallions: All kings is mostly r.
                                    TWAIN 219:1
rapture: r. there is a family alliance
                                    BELL 23:31
rare: how r., how precious   FORS 83:6
  r. in our pockets the mark   CHES 51:23
rarer: r. than the unicorn   JONG 115:2
rascality: effect of prudence on r.
                                    SHAW 198:20
rascals: Honours List is full of r.
                                    BENN 28:15
rash: He was not r.   GRAH 92:15
  r. my dear your colors   ASHF 10:17
rat: giant r. of Sumatra   DOYLE 69:7
  it creeps like a r.   BOWEN 37:13
  Mmm, you dirty r.   CAGN 44:14
rather: I would r. have blood   GREE 93:12
  would you r. be a country   MACD 142:3
ratio: inverse r. to the importance
                                    HUXL 108:10
rational: make life more r.   AYER 16:4
  that the irrational is r.   STEV 208:16
ratlike: success in journalism are r.
                                    TOM 217:10
rattle: Shake, r. and roll   CALH 44:20
  stuttering rifles' rapid r.   OWEN 166:9
rave: Old age should burn and r.
                                    THOM 213:13
Ravel: R. refuses the Legion   SATIE 192:7
ravish: can't r. a tin of sardines
                                    LAWR 132:8
raw: R. towns that we believe   AUDEN 13:1
ray: grievance and a r. of sunshine
                                    WOD 230:5
razor: mirror and a r. lay crossed
                                    JOYCE 116:1
  that the r. ceases to act   HOUS 106:5
razors: R. pain you   PARK 168:12
reach: parts other beers cannot r.
                                    LOV 139:15
reaction: third r. of man upon HOLM 104:6
reactionaries: All r. are paper tigers
                                    MAO T 146:11
reactionary: R. is a somnambulist walking
                                    ROOS 183:6
read: bothered to r. another   MITF 154:17
  countenance this person r.   BRAM 38:14
  Don't r. too much now   LARK 131:4

read (*cont.*):
  ever been taught how to r.   SAY 192:11
  his books were r.   BELL 25:16
  I r., much of the night   ELIOT 76:14
  journalism what will be r.   CONN 58:14
  man who can r. music   BEEC 21:27
  never having r. either   COBB 57:1
  only news until he's r. it   WAUGH 223:14
  people praise and don't r.   TWAIN 219:11
  people who can't r.   ZAPPA 236:11
  r. and dream of the soft   YEATS 232:7
  r. any good books lately   MURD 157:19
  R. out my words at night   FLEC 81:23
  r. that stuff by myself   SAL 189:2
  r. the crystal when   BEVAN 33:3
  she cannot r.   AUDEN 15:16
  that he has r. too widely   PEAR 169:19
  vast population able to r.   TREV 217:21
  what I r. in the papers   ROG 182:9
reader: no tears in the r.   FROST 85:17
  only the individual r.   NAB 158:16
  r. recognizes as his own   QUAS 176:13
  r. wishes to convince others   FORS 83:11
  That ideal r. suffering   JOYCE 115:8
readers: biased, and so are r.   BALL 17:22
  so many of my r. belong   CHES 51:7
reading: becomes a substitute for r.
                                    BURG 42:12
  Peace is poor r.   HARDY 96:20
  R. isn't an occupation we   ORTON 164:4
  thing, but I prefer r.   SMITH 203:13
reads: Fat-head poet that nobody r.
                                    CHES 51:8
ready: r. for my close-up now   BRAC 37:22
  those for which we are r.   FORS 84:8
real: directly stencilled off the r.
                                    SONT 204:15
  everything that is r. about us
                                    SHAW 197:18
  r. and true than the things   SHAW 196:4
  R. life seems to have no   COMP 58:12
  The r. way to travel   GRAH 92:19
  washed in the speechless r.   BARZ 20:10
realist: presented as 'r. politics' BERD 29:10
realistic: make a 'r. decision'   MCC 141:13
reality: And the r.   ELIOT 75:11
  art is an appeal to a r.   MACC 141:5
  Cannot bear very much r.   ELIOT 74:4
  combination of r. and lies   COCT 57:6
  sense of ultimate r.   BELL 23:30
  tourist in other people's r.   SONT 204:14
realization: limit to our r. of tomorrow
                                    ROOS 183:12
  r. of the innate individuality JUNG 117:2
re-allocate: deny the facts but to r.
                                    RYLE 187:10
really: you'll be a R. Useful Engine
                                    AWDRY 15:18
realm: One r., one people, one leader
                                    ANON 6:4
reap: Time shall r., but after   THOM 215:3
reaping: without looking up, 'r.'
                                    BOTT 36:15
reappears: he r. in your children
                                    CONN 59:5
reappraisal: compel an agonizing r.
                                    DULL 70:11
rearming: said that Germany was r.
                                    BALD 17:10
rearrange: r. the furniture   MORT 156:18
rears: S-E-X ever r. its ugly head
                                    AYCK 15:19
reason: all r. is against it   BUTL 43:28
  I have a r. for living   SHAW 199:10

reason (*cont.*):
  Language is a form of human r.
                                    LÉV 136:11
  r. can convince us of those   BELL 24:2
  R. enslaves all whose   SHAW 198:24
  r. for the existence of a novel
                                    JAMES 111:24
  R. has moons, but moons   HODG 103:15
  r. so many people showed   GOLD 92:1
  r. why he should be treated   EDW 72:6
  r. why I don't drink   ASTOR 11:21
  r. why we should be anything   ASQ 11:8
  right deed for the wrong r.   ELIOT 75:1
  You needn't try to r.   JER 113:18
reasonable: figure of 'The R. Man'
                                    HERB 101:23
  It's a r. percentage   BECK 21:16
  rather be right than be r.   NASH 159:10
  r. man adapts himself   SHAW 198:23
  r. man could have expected   HERB 101:27
reasons: care anything about r.
                                    JAMES 112:3
  r. for having children   RUSS 187:6
  r. for what we believe   BRAD 38:5
  simple rock and roll r.   GELD 89:3
reassures: disturb, science r.   BRAQ 38:16
rebel: R. without a cause   LIND 137:9
  true-blue r.   HILL 102:11
  What is a r.? A man who says no
                                    CAMUS 46:5
rebellion: incite this meeting to r.
                                    PANK 167:11
  might well bring the r.   WILS 228:16
  r. against the existing law   SHAW 196:22
recall: r. he would be willing   BRAD 38:3
receipt: Applause is a r.   SCHN 193:2
received: undertaking has been r.
                                    CHAM 48:15
recession: r. when your neighbour
                                    TRUM 218:10
recherche: A la r. du temps perdu
                                    PROU 175:15
recipes: r. that are always successful
                                    VALÉ 220:23
reciting: r. the Athanasian Creed
                                    AUDEN 13:13
reckless: r. Mr Baldwin   BEAV 21:2
reclaimed: man r. his own property
                                    BUTL 43:9
reclamation: condemn it. It is land r.
                                    WILS 228:11
recognition: aesthetic enjoyment is r.
                                    WHIT 226:11
  r. of another's resemblance   BIER 33:20
recognize: only a trial if I r.   KAFKA 117:7
record: kind of r. seemed vital   COPE 61:3
  r. of sin than does   DOYLE 69:6
  r. on the gramophone   ELIOT 77:2
recover: r. it from all his forefathers
                                    BUTL 43:9
recovers: from which he never r.
                                    MCL 143:11
rector: An ancestor was r. there
                                    YEATS 233:4
rectum: r. makes a good diagnostician
                                    OSLER 165:22
red: Better r. than dead   ANON 5:17
  it's not even r. brick   OSB 165:17
  R. hair she had and golden   BETJ 31:5
  r. house in a red mahogany   BETJ 31:3
  R. lips are not so red   OWEN 166:13
  r. wheel barrow   WILL 228:1
  Their r. it never dies   DOBS 68:3
  When the r., red, robin   WOODS 231:7

redeemed: Is not r. from time   ELIOT 74:22
redemption: r. of all things   SHAW 196:15
red-haired: r. girls scamper like roses
LEE 134:3
red-hot: I'm the last of the r. mamas
YELL 236:6
reduced: I would not be r. to accepting
HARD 96:16
redwood: r. forest to the Gulf Stream
GUTH 95:1
reeled: sentences until r. the mind
GIBBS 90:3
reference: no r. to fun in any Act
HERB 101:24
refined: Good looking, so r.   FIEL 79:6
r. and sensitive nature   DOYLE 69:21
r. out of existence   JOYCE 115:17
This Englishwoman is so r.   SMITH 203:17
reflecting: r. the figure of a man
WOOLF 231:13
reform: lunatic fringe in all r.   ROOS 184:6
reformation: r. must have its victims
SAKI 188:10
reformer: r. is a guy who rides through
MIZN 154:20
reformers: All r. are bachelors
MOORE 155:7
All R., however strict   SMITH 203:5
refrain: R. from the unholy pleasure
BELL 24:4
sensibly r. from speech   GRAH 92:16
They merely r. from asking   HALS 95:13
refreshes: Heineken r. the parts   LOV 139:15
refuge: so easy to take r. in   IBSEN 109:19
that it's a r. from home   SHAW 200:5
refugees: The guttural sorrow of the r.
MACN 144:12
refusal: r. to admit our emotions
RATT 178:2
refuse: daylight and never to r.
MENC 150:22
men r. to fight   ANON 9:6
offer he can't r.   PUZO 176:10
regard: r. for religion as we can
O'CAS 162:18
regarder: r. ensemble dans la même
SAIN 187:20
regards: Give my r. to Broadway
COHAN 57:11
regeneration: r. of all humanity
PANK 167:9
Regent: who revelled with the R.
BEER 23:5
regiment: R. an' pokes the 'eathen
KIPL 127:9
regret: My one r. in life   ALLEN 3:25
r. in the theatre   BARR 19:28
regrets: follies which a man r.
ROWL 185:15
Miss Otis r.   PORT 173:4
rehearsal: r. I let the orchestra   BEEC 22:12
rehearse: obvious reluctance to r.
BEEC 22:14
Reich: *Ein R., ein Volk, ein Führer*
ANON 6:4
reindeer: Herds of r. move across
AUDEN 14:23
Rudolph, the Red-Nosed R.
MARKS 146:17
reject: accepted it is time to r. it
JACK 111:5
r. me on account   BELL 24:23

rejoice: Prime Minister declared 'R., r.'
THAT 212:16
relate: r. everything to a single   BERL 30:4
relation: r. of the darker   DUB 70:8
relations: are God's apology for r.
KING 122:10
offensive in personal r.   RUSS 186:14
Personal r. are the important   FORS 83:16
relationships: psychology of human r.
BERNE 30:11
r. begin and most of them continue
AUDEN 14:3
relative: In a r. way   BULL 42:5
Success is r.   ELIOT 74:14
relatives: God gives us our r.   MUMF 157:15
relativity: If my theory of r. is proven
EINS 73:1
relaxation: r. from physical fatigue
MAT 149:3
release: Good-night. Ensured r.
HOUS 106:8
I r. the safety-catch   JOHST 114:19
we have found r. there   BROO 40:1
relegation: r. to the status of a fuzzy
CAIR 44:19
relenting: This day r. God   ROSS 185:5
reliable: r. walls of youth collapse
FORS 83:14
relief: But O my God, what a r.   BARR 19:27
religion: Art and R. are, then   BELL 23:31
Christian r. doubted   BUTL 44:5
concerned with r.   TEMP 212:12
face and a different r.   EDW 72:6
from the dominion of r.   GOLD 91:11
me on account of my r.   BELL 24:23
Millionaire. That is my r.   SHAW 197:10
more beautiful than any r.   SAKI 188:5
priorities is the r. of Socialism
BEVAN 33:6
reason to bring r. into it   O'CAS 162:18
R. and art spring from   CATH 47:13
r. is whatever he is most   BARR 19:18
r. to a man with bodily   SHAW 197:11
r. without science   EINS 73:5
science is strong and r.   SZASZ 211:19
Science without r. is lame   EINS 73:5
start your own r.   HUBB 107:18
There is only one r.   SHAW 199:15
To become a popular r.   INGE 110:12
religions: materialistic of all great r.
TEMP 212:13
r. and created great works   PROU 176:1
R. are kept alive by heresies   BREN 39:9
religious: aesthetic and r. rapture
BELL 23:31
himself to any r. belief   WAUGH 223:3
his r. opinions   BUTL 43:10
r. system that produced   SAKI 188:9
religious-good: Good, but not r.
HARDY 98:4
reluctance: r. to rehearse on a morning
BEEC 22:14
remain: roll over but the rocks r.
HERB 101:22
The days go by, I r.   APOL 9:22
We all are born mad. Some r.
BECK 21:23
remained: born an Englishman and r.
BEHAN 23:20
remains: whatever r., *however improbable*
DOYLE 69:22
remarkable: This very r. man   INGE 110:8
remarks: r. are not literature   STEIN 207:9

remarks (*cont.*):
r. are very seldom quoted   STR 210:18
remedy: r. for the worst of them
KELL 118:16
remember: Ah yes! I r. it well   LERN 135:20
always seem to r. blondes   LOOS 139:4
And even I can r.   POUND 173:28
Do you r. an Inn   BELL 25:15
r. days that have gone by   FLEC 81:16
R. me when I am dead   DOUG 68:10
R. no man's foot can pass   BOTT 36:13
r. the Good Samaritan if   THAT 213:6
r. the past are condemned   SANT 190:9
To r. or invent   FROST 86:1
We will r. them   BINY 34:18
Who will r., passing through
SASS 191:19
Yes; I r. Adlestrop   THOM 214:15
You must r. this, a kiss   HUPF 108:7
remembered: critics is to be r.
MOORE 155:10
none are undeservedly r.   AUDEN 13:17
tranquillity r. in emotion   PARK 168:4
What are those blue r. hills   HOUS 107:4
remembering: R. him like anything
CHES 51:21
r. nothing but the blue sky   FORS 84:4
remembrance: Down in the flood of r.
LAWR 132:13
remind: R. me of you   MARV 147:15
reminiscences: old have r. of what
SAKI 188:13
R. make one feel so deliciously
SHAW 196:30
some of your grosser r.   WOOL 231:18
r-e-m-o-r-s-e: R.! Those dry Martinis
ADE 2:13
remote: R. and ineffectual Don   BELL 26:4
Remove: fat greedy owl of the R.
RICH 180:15
renaissance: Wake in her warm nest of r.
DAY-L 65:8
rendezvous: I have a r. with Death
SEEG 194:5
Reno'd: Moll R. in Wolsey's Home
ANON 7:9
renounce: recourse to war and r. it
BRIA 39:10
r. war for its consequences   FOSD 84:13
renowned: r. both far and wide
CAMP 45:15
rent: That has not been r.   YEATS 235:14
They r. out my room   ALLEN 3:26
repair: r. to the matches   THOM 215:22
repeal: about the R. of the Corn
BEER 23:19
repeat: interesting till it begins to r.
BOWEN 37:4
past are condemned to r.   SANT 190:9
r. his past nor leave it   AUDEN 14:4
r. that on the Golden Floor   HOUS 105:9
would be willing to r.   BRAD 38:3
repelled: they are only r. by man
INGE 110:13
repetition: nagging is the r.   SUMM 211:2
repetitious: r. mechanism of the Universe
WHIT 226:6
replacement: r. of category-habits
RYLE 187:11
report: r. of my death was an
exaggeration   TWAIN 219:23
r. what the candidate says   NIXON 160:17
reporters: mixed feelings about r.
STOP 209:15

repose: midnight and the noon's r.
ELIOT 76:3

represent: causes that they r.   FORS 84:9
  does attempt to r. life   JAMES 111:24
representative: indignity of being your r.
BELL 24:23

repressed: r. desire for aesthetic
WAUGH 223:4
  r. sadists are supposed   CONN 58:15
reproduce: r. themselves from generation
JOS 115:5
republic: Only Love the Beloved R.
FORS 84:6
  R. is a Government of laws   FORD 82:14
  r. is like a chicken   MITF 154:16
republican: king's head on r. principles
SHAW 199:3
  proposition to my R. friends   STEV 208:19
  results for the R. ticket   ROOS 184:7
reputation: it wrecks a woman's r.
COL 57:17
  your r. is assured   MAUG 149:11
require: he thought 'e might r.   KIPL 127:5
requirement: first r. for a composer
HON 104:9
  first r. of a statesman   ACH 1:6
requisite: first r. of the historian   STR 210:6
rescue: r. and the liberation   CHUR 54:10
research: steal from many, it's r.
MIZN 154:19
researchers: r. into Public Opinion
AUDEN 13:10
researches: Mona did r. in original sin
PLOM 172:6
resemblance: recognition of another's r.
BIER 33:20
  r. to what one has in mind   PROU 176:2
resemble: r. not a ruler   HUXL 109:16
resented: Who r. it   COW 62:13
residence: And built of them a r.
MORG 155:20
residences: Inns are not r.   MOORE 155:16
resigned: approve. And I am not r.
MILL 151:17
  has r. and Northcliffe   ANON 6:19
  r. to the way they have   CATH 47:15
resistance: liberty is the history of r.
WILS 229:9
  r. of the adversaries   STAL 206:18
resolution: In war: r. In defeat   CHUR 55:16
resolved: r. to be irresolute   CHUR 54:5
resolving: R. the enigma of the fever
ELIOT 74:12
resonance: r. of his solitude   CONN 59:3
resources: inner r., because I am heavy
BERR 30:17
respect: r. for the idea of God   DUH 70:9
  r. public opinion   RUSS 186:13
  Thieves r. property   CHES 51:6
  who r. their executioners   SART 191:12
  without losing one's r.   SAKI 188:8
respectability: r. and airconditioning
BAR 18:9
  save a shred of its r.   READ 178:9
respectable: more r. he is   SHAW 197:19
  r. live beyond other peoples'   SAKI 188:6
  riff-raff apply to what is r.   HOPE 104:16
respecte: r. trop l'idée de Dieu   DUH 70:9
respective: words in our r. languages
COOK 60:9
respects: To pay us his r.   AYRES 16:7
respiration: said it was artificial r.
BURG 42:11

respond: they r. I find   CHAR 49:16
responsable: la rendre r. d'un monde
DUH 70:9
responsibility: collective r.   ALD 3:4
  heavy burden of r.   EDW 72:8
  In dreams begins r.   YEATS 234:14
  Liberty means r.   SHAW 198:12
  Power without r.   KIPL 125:19
  r. without power, the prerogative
STOP 209:13
  writer's only r. is to his art   FAUL 78:11
responsible: idea of God to make it r.
DUH 70:9
  r. for this work of development
BEAV 21:5
rest: eyes before you see the r.   AYCK 15:19
  r. if one doesn't sleep   WAUGH 223:2
  r. is mere sheep-herding   POUND 173:25
  r. quiet in Montparnasse   BENET 27:8
  To talk about the r. of us   ANON 8:18
  where's the r. of me   BELL 24:3
resting: r. up from their sinning
RUNY 186:3
restoration: not revolution, but r.
HARD 96:17
  The Church's R.   BETJ 31:15
restraint: r. with which they write
CAMP 45:11
restricted: R. to What Precisely   ELIOT 74:1
rests: Bereft of life it r.   CHAP 49:13
resurrection: own property at the r.
BUTL 43:9
resuscitate: He strove to r. the dead art
POUND 174:2
retain: r. the ability to function   FITZ 80:16
retainer: The Old R. night and day
BELL 24:17
reticence: Northern r., the tight
HEAN 99:13
retired: British Outer Mongolia for r.
BENN 27:15
retirement: there must be no r.   HAIG 95:3
retreat: convert r. into advance
ROOS 183:1
  Never keep a line of r.   NANS 158:19
retreating: Have you seen yourself r.
NASH 159:3
retrospective: r. or utopian   ARON 10:12
return: alas! we r.   FORS 83:12
  r. at twilight from   STEV 208:19
  Should I never r.   MANS 146:6
  through and I shall r.   MAC 141:1
  who does not r. your blow   SHAW 199:1
returned: And r. on the previous night
BULL 42:5
reveal: they r. the sardines   BENN 27:18
revelation: with the force of a r.
JAMES 112:15
revelations: stupendous r.   HOFF 104:2
revelled: who r. with the Regent   BEER 23:5
revenge: r. of the intellect   SONT 204:12
  tribal, intimate r.   HEAN 99:12
revenue: competitive tariff for r.
HOOV 104:13
reverberation: paucity of its r.   MAIL 145:10
reverence: My cycle-clips in awkward r.
LARK 130:15
  phrase, 'R. for Life'   SCHW 193:11
  r. can you have for a Supreme
HELL 100:5
reverting: explains why r. to old ideas
OUSP 166:4

review: have your r. before me
REGER 179:8
  r. a bad book without showing
AUDEN 13:18
revisited: Brideshead R.   WAUGH 222:18
revivals: art is the history of r.   BUTL 43:23
reviving: dreamed of r. the castrati
REED 179:6
revolt: Art is a r. against fate   MALR 145:16
révolté: Qu'est-ce qu'un homme r.
CAMUS 46:5
revolution: A r. is an insurrection
MAO T 146:9
  catalyst that sparks the r.   DURY 71:2
  leaders of a r.   CONR 60:2
  not r., but restoration   HARD 96:17
  on the day after the r.   AREN 10:5
  order to safeguard a r.   ORW 164:25
  peaceful r. impossible   KENN 119:18
  r. of rising expectations   CLEV 56:19
revolutionaries: r. are potential Tories
ORW 164:15
revolutionary: Feminism is the most r.
TOYN 217:14
  fierce and r. in a bathroom   LINK 137:15
  r. ends as an oppressor   CAMUS 46:7
  r. phrases is mistaken   KHR 121:5
  r. will become a conservative   AREN 10:5
revolutionized: it has already r.   ACE 1:5
révolutionnaire: r. finit en oppresseur
CAMUS 46:7
revolutions: It is a main cause of r.
INGE 110:11
  r. have ended in a reinforcement
CAMUS 46:6
  R. have never lightened   SHAW 198:7
reward: without the r. of priority
SCOTT 193:18
Reynolds: R. isn't as great   MUNN 157:18
rhetoric: love without the r.   STOP 209:19
  quarrel with others, r.   YEATS 232:11
Rhine: you think of the R.   BALD 17:8
rhinoceros: hide of a r.   BARR 19:26
Rhodes: R. had not enabled them
BEER 23:13
rhubarb: Of cold blancmange and r. tart
KNOX 128:11
rhyme: man or elevate a r.   YEATS 235:13
  still more tired of R.   BELL 25:21
rhymes: voiced those r. is dust   HARDY 97:1
rhyming: r. North Battersea slogan
JAY 112:18
rhythm: I got r.   GERS 89:14
  r., a predetermined pattern   FISH 80:5
  r. of attracting people   JOAD 113:20
rhythmic: turn to r. tidal lyres
HARDY 97:13
ribbon: changing a typewriter r.
BENC 26:19
  road was a r. of moonlight   NOYES 161:16
  soldier's r. on a tunic   ABSE 1:3
ribbons: cut r. and kiss babies   MICH 151:13
  medals and r.   BELL 26:11
Ribstone: Right as a R. Pippin   BELL 26:7
Ricardo: R. and face the economics
GALB 88:3
rice: r. pudding for dinner again   MILNE 153:8
rich: behave as the r. behave
SMITH 203:10
  Do you sincerely want to be r.
CORN 61:5
  ever by chance grow r.   THOM 214:13
  If I ever become a r. man   BELL 25:26

rich (*cont.*):
  intimate when he is r.   BIER 33:19
  It's the r. wot gets the gravy   ANON 8:8
  live by robbing the r.   SHAW 197:27
  orchestra is playing to the r.
          AUDEN 14:19
  Poor little r. girl   COW 62:6
  r. are the scum   CHES 50:20
  r. enough to pay over 75%   HEAL 99:9
  r. get rich and the poor   KAHN 117:10
  r. people in the world   STEAD 207:5
  r. richer and the poor   NEHRU 160:3
  r. society and the powerful   JOHN 114:11
  r. that you have to live   SMITH 203:9
  r. wage war it's the poor   SART 190:26
  save the few who are r.   KENN 119:12
  tell you about the very r.   FITZ 80:12
  that of the r. for titles   PEAR 169:20
  whether to be r. in things   ILL 110:6
  which forbids the r.   FRAN 84:15
riche: *qui interdit au r. comme*   FRAN 84:15
riches: material and spiritual r.   KHR 121:5
  that of the titled for r.   PEAR 169:20
richesse: *la r. est chose sacrée*   FRAN 84:14
rid: r. of them because I know
          JOAD 113:20
  time we got r. of Him   BALD 16:17
riddle: Ask me a r. and I reply
          MILNE 153:18
  It is a r. wrapped   CHUR 55:4
  The r. of the sands   CHIL 52:16
ride: Just to r. the ponies   COHAN 57:13
  r. two horses you have   MAXT 150:5
  She's got a ticket to r.   LENN 135:12
  Sweet to r. forth at evening   FLEC 81:8
  Who went for a r. on a tiger   ANON 8:4
rides: r. back to shave again   WHITE 226:3
ridiculous: At the heart of the r.
          MAHON 145:6
  fine sense of the r.   ALBEE 3:3
  r. by friends when dead   BIER 33:23
  To the R.   GRAH 92:11
riding: r. at breakneck speed towards
          BLAN 34:23
  The highwayman came r.   NOYES 161:16
rien: *R. n'est plus dangereux*   ALAIN 3:1
riff-raff: epithet which the r.   HOPE 104:16
rifle: r. and blow out your brains
          KIPL 123:12
Riga: There was a young lady of R.
          ANON 8:4
right: are exclusively in the r.   HUXL 109:11
  be r. than be reasonable   NASH 159:10
  claim our r. as women   PANK 167:9
  decorative and to do r.   FIRB 79:19
  defend to the death your r.   TALL 212:4
  Don't think twice, it's all r.   DYLAN 71:5
  do the r. deed   ELIOT 75:1
  doubt that they are r.   VAN D 221:4
  Earth's the r. place   FROST 86:5
  every single one of them is r.   KIPL 123:2
  find out that one WAS r.   POUND 173:23
  half of the people are r.   WHITE 226:2
  has more r. to be obeyed   JOHN 113:21
  have been, a man of the r.   MOSL 157:1
  have no r. in the circus   MAXT 150:5
  it's all r. with me   BELL 26:9
  Jack— I'm all r.   BONE 36:1
  My country, r. or wrong   CHES 50:13
  my r. is retreating   FOCH 82:6
  no longer means being r.   CHES 51:1
  not to *do* what is r.   JOHN 114:5
  Only if it's done r.   ALLEN 3:15
  questioned its r. to exist   SCH 193:9

right (*cont.*):
  R. as a Ribstone Pippin   BELL 26:7
  r. but also to be wrong   SZASZ 211:12
  R. but Repulsive   SELL 194:13
  r. for fighting   JAGG 111:9
  r. is more precious   WILS 229:14
  r. side of the blanket   ASHF 11:1
  r. that it does not need   WILS 229:11
  r. to a child   SHAW 196:22
  r. to be heard does not   HUMP 108:5
  r. to be taken seriously   HUMP 108:5
  r. to consume happiness   SHAW 196:3
  r. to invent themselves   GREER 93:21
  speciality is being r.   SHAW 200:6
  The majority never has r.   IBSEN 109:20
  they are never r.   STR 210:5
  wrongs don't make a r.   SZASZ 211:17
righteous: have seen the r. forsaken
          BLUN 35:1
  R. indignation   WOOLF 231:8
righter: r. than one knew at say
          POUND 173:23
rights: country about equal r.   JOHN 114:8
  equal in dignity and r.   ANON 9:1
  r. is a little inconsistency   OWEN 166:6
  r. to which this nation   KENN 119:11
  until the r. of the smaller   ASQ 11:11
right-side-up: The toast fell r.   JENN 113:5
rigorous: My God, what a r. exam
          COOK 60:10
rigour: They're noted for their r.
          COOK 60:10
Rimbauds: he was always chasing R.
          PARK 168:2
rime: The r. was on the spray
          HARDY 97:15
Rime Intrinsica: R., Fontmell Magna
          BETJ 31:2
rind: how shall taste the r.   THOM 215:16
ring: his diaper into the r.   ICKES 110:4
  night come, r. out the hour   APOL 9:22
  One R. to rule them all   TOLK 217:9
  r. with Mr Tolstoy unless   HEM 101:3
  round in a r. and suppose   FROST 86:23
  'Twould r. the bells of Heaven
          HODG 103:13
  rings: r. black Cyprus   FLEC 81:19
  The postman always r. twice   CAIN 44:17
rinky-dink: r. of a voice and all
          MAIL 145:11
Rio: Go rolling down to R.   KIPL 125:16
riot: He did not r., he got   TEBB 212:10
  r. is at bottom the language   KING 122:7
ripens: But not when it r. in a tumour
          ABSE 1:2
rire: *le r. pour la jalousie*   SAGAN 187:17
rise: Every Employee Tends to R.
          PETER 170:11
  r. at ten thirty and saunter   HARG 98:9
  r. of misplaced power exists   EIS 73:6
  r. of the meritocracy   YOUNG 236:7
risen: Frost has r. without trace
          MUGG 157:6
rises: The sun also r.   HEM 101:6
rising: Into a r. birth-rate   FRY 87:3
  revolution of r. expectations   CLEV 56:19
  your shadow at evening r.   ELIOT 76:15
risks: one of the r. he takes   STEV 208:21
  r. of spreading conflict   JOHN 114:12
Ritz: like the R. Hotel   MATH 149:1
rivalry: thought, a r. of aim   ADAMS 2:4
river: field by the r. my love   YEATS 234:13
  I think that the r.   ELIOT 74:7
  laughs the immortal r. still   BROO 40:15

river (*cont.*):
  Ol' man r., dat ol' man river   HAMM 96:1
  O Sleepless as the r. under   CRANE 62:15
  r. jumps over the mountain
          AUDEN 12:16
riverrun: r., past Eve and Adam's
          JOYCE 115:7
rivers: R. are damp   PARK 168:12
rivulets: And meadow r. overflow
          HARDY 97:3
road: And not the r.   NASH 159:7
  And one more for the r.   MERC 151:8
  A r., a mile of kingdom   KAV 118:6
  Golden R. to Samarkand   FLEC 81:8
  good to be out on the r.   MAS 148:20
  hard the r. may be   CHUR 54:8
  Hit the r., Jack   MAYF 150:7
  look ahead up the white r.   ELIOT 77:4
  middle of the r.   BEVAN 33:5
  monument the asphalt r.   ELIOT 76:5
  One r. leads to London   MAS 148:8
  On every r. I wandered   HOUS 107:5
  r. in dangerous circumstances
          BALD 17:14
  r. through the woods   KIPL 126:12
  r. to the City of Emeralds   BAUM 20:12
  r. was a ribbon of moonlight
          NOYES 161:16
  rolling English r.   CHES 50:22
  Softly along the r. of evening   DE L 66:6
  There is no expeditious r.   THOM 215:23
  Your old r.   DYLAN 71:14
  your r.'s a thorny way   CARB 46:18
roads: And without fear the lawless r.
          MUIR 157:12
  By r. 'not adopted'   BETJ 32:3
  How many r. must a man   DYLAN 71:4
  two r. by which men escape   BELL 23:31
  Two r. diverged in a wood   FROST 86:4
roadway: r. or on the pavements
          YEATS 232:9
roam: love, her ways to r.   BROO 40:5
  person's mind begins to r.   SOLZ 204:5
roamin': R. in the gloamin'   LAUD 131:10
roar: called upon to give the r.   CHUR 56:2
  mighty r. of London's traffic   ANON 8:2
roareth: What is this that r. thus
          GODL 91:5
roaring: But R. Bill   BELL 25:22
rob: If a writer has to r.   FAUL 78:11
robbed: We was r.   JAC 111:6
robbing: r. a bank compared   BREC 39:1
robe: His Purple R.   FARJ 78:8
Robey: R. is the Darling   SMITH 202:13
robin: r. comes bob, bob   WOODS 231:7
Robinson: And here's to you, Mrs R.
          SIMON 201:4
robot: r. may not injure   ASIM 11:5
Robotics: Rules of R.   ASIM 11:5
robots: that men may become r.
          FROMM 85:13
robs: government which r. Peter
          SHAW 196:17
rock: cast the first r. at a girl   LOOS 139:10
  r. around the clock   DE KN 66:4
  R. journalism is people   ZAPPA 236:11
  Sex and drugs and r. and roll   DURY 71:1
rocket: every r. fired signifies   EIS 73:7
rock 'n' roll: It's only r.   JAGG 111:8
  r. or Christianity   LENN 135:2
rocks: roll over but the r. remain
          HERB 101:22
  throwing r. at the stork   BREC 38:19
rocky: iron bicycles over the r.   O'BR 162:11

rode: r. madly off in all directions
    LEAC 133:12
  R. their horses   DE L 66:14
role: has not yet found a r.   ACH 1:8
roll: Let the good times r.   THEA 213:9
  R. over, Beethoven   BERRY 30:13
  seas r. over but the rocks   HERB 101:22
  Sex and drugs and rock and r.
    DURY 71:1
  Shake, rattle and r.   CALH 44:20
rolled: apparently r. along on wheels
    HUXL 109:8
  bottoms of my trousers r.   ELIOT 75:19
roller: The r., pitch, and stumps
    LANG 130:4
rollin': He keeps on r. along   HAMM 96:1
rolling: Go r. down to Rio   KIPL 125:16
  Like a r. stone   DYLAN 71:8
  r. English drunkard made   CHES 50:22
Roman: R. came to Rye or out   CHES 50:22
  R. ever was able to say   BEER 22:18
  The R. Conquest was   SELL 194:9
  Thundered out on the R. air
    AUDEN 15:11
  To-day the R. and his trouble
    HOUS 107:1
romance: A fine r. with no kisses FIEL 79:7
romancing: R. the stone   THOM 213:10
romantic: An airline ticket to r. places
    MARV 147:15
  R. Ireland's dead and gone YEATS 234:15
  The r. lie in the brain   AUDEN 13:9
  they're so r., so operatic   PROU 176:4
romanticism: attempted to tinge it with r.
    DOYLE 69:19
romantics: We were the last r.
    YEATS 235:13
Rome: For R. so near us   DAY-L 65:8
Ronald: Lord R. said nothing   LEAC 133:12
roof: cat on a hot tin r.   WILL 227:15
  He has restored the r.   BETJ 31:16
  on a corrugated tin r.   BEEC 22:2
roof-lamp: And the r.'s oily flame
    HARDY 97:8
roof-wrecked: Is r.; damps there drip upon
    HARDY 97:1
rooks: And r. in families homeward go
    HARDY 97:3
  r. came home in scramble HODG 103:10
room: Across a crowded r.   HAMM 96:2
  All before my little r.   BROO 40:10
  All I want is a r. somewhere LERN 135:25
  although the r. grows chilly GRAH 92:12
  A r. with a view   FORS 84:3
  Books do furnish a r.   POW 174:18
  end of the enormous r.   AUDEN 14:19
  Fifty springs are little r.   HOUS 106:9
  Here in this r., desiring you STEV 208:12
  In the r. the women come and go
    ELIOT 75:14
  just entering the r.   BROUN 41:5
  men in a smoke-filled r.   SIMP 201:6
  money and a r. of her own
    WOOLF 231:12
  R. at the top   BRAI 38:12
  sitting in the smallest r.   REGER 179:8
rooms: boys in the back r.   BEAV 21:5
  old is having lighted r.   LARK 130:9
  Other voices, other r.   CAP 46:16
Roosevelt: [Eleanor R.] would STEV 209:2
  [President R.] devised   CHUR 55:1
  R.'s New Deal promised KENN 119:10
  R. told me that he was   CHUR 55:17

Roosevelt (cont.):
  will give to President R.   CHUR 53:9
roost: birds came home to r.   MILL 152:6
root: money is the r. of all evil BUTL 43:5
  r. of the American Negro   BALD 16:16
rooting: are r. for Gary Cooper BALD 16:19
roots: drought is destroying his r.
    HERB 101:20
  Dull r. with spring rain   ELIOT 76:13
  You poison England at her r. BOTT 36:13
rosary: every day. This is a r.   BELL 24:23
rose: An English unofficial r.   BROO 40:11
  But he's mighty lak' a r.   STAN 207:2
  But R. crossed the road   DOBS 68:2
  fire and the r. are one   ELIOT 74:23
  His supplication to the r.   FLEC 81:10
  If you gave Ruth a r.   AYCK 16:1
  I know the colour r.   ABSE 1:2
  inviolate R.   YEATS 234:18
  I r. politely in the club   CHES 52:2
  It wavers to a r.   DOBS 68:3
  mast burst open with a r.   FLEC 81:21
  One perfect r.   PARK 168:13
  promised you a r. garden GREEN 93:11
  R. is a rose is a rose   STEIN 207:20
  R. of all Roses, Rose   YEATS 234:12
  r.'s scent is bitterness   THOM 214:20
  Roves back the r.   DE L 66:5
  sad R. of all my days   YEATS 234:11
  scent is of the summer r.   GRAV 93:8
  tell the crooked r.   THOM 213:20
  The American beauty r.   ROCK 181:17
Rosebud: R. is just a piece   MANK 146:1
rose-garden: Into the r.   ELIOT 74:3
rose-lipt: For many a r. maiden
    HOUS 107:7
rose-red: A r. sissy half as old as time
    PLOM 172:7
roses: all the ash the burnt r.   ELIOT 74:18
  Everything's coming up r. SOND 204:10
  forget the lilac and the r.   ARAG 10:2
  girls and r.   DE G 65:17
  In fields where r. fade   HOUS 107:7
  jamais les lilas ni les r.   ARAG 10:2
  might have r. in December BARR 19:13
  own red r. there may blow THOM 215:22
  R. are flowering in Picardy WEAT 223:21
  smells like r.   JOHN 114:3
rosy: R. and round and hot   ASQ 11:20
rot: As artists they're r.   PARK 169:3
rots: liquid which r. braces   MORT 156:15
rotted: Or simply r. early   NASH 159:8
rotten: You r. swines   MILL 152:15
rottenness: r. of our civilization
    READ 178:9
rough: And what r. beast, its hour
    YEATS 233:13
  r. male kiss   BROO 39:19
round: For it's going r. and round
    FYFFE 87:17
  music goes 'r. and around HODG 103:16
  Rosy and r. and hot   ASQ 11:20
  R. and round the circle   ELIOT 74:16
  R. both the shires they   HOUS 106:14
  R. up the usual suspects   EPST 77:20
roundabouts: lost upon the r.   CHAL 48:5
Roundheads: R. (Right but Repulsive)
    SELL 194:13
rouse: If anything might r. him now
    OWEN 166:11
Rousseau: R. was the first militant
    BERL 30:5
rover: blood's a r.   HOUS 106:10
row: are a-standing in a r.   HEAT 99:18

Rowe: R.'s Rule   DICK 67:10
rowed: All r. fast   COKE 57:14
rows: not lugged into Family R.
    WOD 230:15
royal: The R. slice of bread MILNE 153:9
rub: if you r. up against money
    RUNY 186:5
rubies: Give pearls away and r.
    HOUS 106:12
ruddy: R. Ball has taken   THOM 214:19
rude: Because a manner r. and wild
    BELL 24:5
  But only rather r. and wild BELL 24:20
Rudolph: R., the Red-Nosed Reindeer
    MARKS 146:17
rue: With r. my heart is laden HOUS 107:7
rugged: cling to the old r. cross
    BENN 27:17
  system of r. individualism HOOV 104:12
ruin: r. himself in twelve months
    GEOR 89:5
  r. that Cromwell knock'd BEDF 21:26
ruined: always r. by the littleness
    BREC 39:5
ruins: have shored against my r.
    ELIOT 77:6
Ruislip: Gaily into R. Gardens BETJ 31:7
rule: major r. of political life PANK 167:8
  One Ring to r. them all   TOLK 217:9
  Rowe's R.   DICK 67:10
  r. in life never to apologize WOD 230:17
  safe r. for the historian   FISH 80:5
ruled: 'The Art of Being R.' might
    LEWIS 136:17
ruler: r. but the last fading   HUXL 109:8
rulers: are brought about by r. BIER 34:8
Rules: fundamental R. of Robotics
    ASIM 11:5
  golden r. for an orchestra BEEC 22:1
  people wouldn't obey the r. BENN 27:20
  simple little r. and few   BELL 25:3
  there are no golden r.   SHAW 198:9
ruling: hands of the r. class STAL 206:10
rum: It's a R. Go   VAUG 221:9
  r., sodomy and the lash   CHUR 53:20
  thinking jest what a R. Go WELLS 224:19
run: choose to r. for President COOL 60:16
  He [Billy Conn] can r.   LOUIS 139:14
  R., rabbit, run   GAY 89:1
  r. up your nose dead against BALD 17:3
  Take the money and r.   ALLEN 3:22
  They get r. down   BEVAN 33:5
  we were born to r.   SPR 206:15
  What makes Sammy r.   SCH 193:7
runic: r. tales to sigh or sing FLEC 81:15
runner: long-distance r.   SILL 200:17
runs: r. away at the first snarl LLOY 138:7
run-stealers: As the r. flicker to and fro
    THOM 215:22
rupture: getting r. or something DONL 68:6
rush: r. through the fields   CHES 51:8
rushed: with the time we have r.
    ROG 182:12
Ruskin: doubt that art needed R.
    STOP 210:3
  young Macaulay or R.   BARB 18:12
Russia: developed in R. was as great
    BENN 27:11
  From R. with love   FLEM 82:2
  outlaws R. forever   REAG 178:14
  proletarian socialist state in R.
    LENIN 134:13
  you the action of R.   CHUR 55:4

Russian: Grishkin is nice: her R. eye
ELIOT 75:9
Russians: The R. are coming   ROSE 184:14
rust: creeper-nails are r.   HARDY 97:1
  Less than the r., that never   HOPE 105:3
rustic: A swear-word in a r. slum
BEER 22:21
Ruth: If you gave R. a rose   AYCK 16:1
ruthless: r. if he is a good one   FAUL 78:11
  You must be r., relentless   FISH 80:8
rye: Before the Roman came to R.
CHES 50:22
  be the catcher in the r.   SAL 189:4

S

Sacco: S.'s name will live   VANZ 221:6
sack: S. the lot   FISH 80:8
sacrament: abortion would be a s.
KENN 118:18
sacramental: flesh was s. of the spirit
ROB 181:16
sacred: facts are s.   SCOTT 193:16
  The Convent of the S. Heart   ELIOT 75:5
  wealth is a s. thing   FRAN 84:14
sacrée: *richesse est chose s.*   FRAN 84:14
sacrifice: A woman will always s.
MAUG 149:9
  great pinnacle of S.   LLOY 138:12
  Self-sacrifice enables us to s.   SHAW 199:2
  Still stands Thine ancient s.   KIPL 126:9
  The holy hush of ancient s.   STEV 208:1
  Too long a s.   YEATS 233:10
  undaunted the final s.   SPR 206:11
sacrificed: always be s. to expediency
MAUG 149:8
sacrifices: s. he makes on her account
MAUG 149:17
sad: And all their songs are s.   CHES 50:9
  deliciously aged and s.   SHAW 196:30
  her sadness when she's s.   BARR 19:19
  s. subject for any publicity   ATTL 12:7
  something s. about the boy   COW 62:3
  The sweetness in the s.   THOM 214:21
saddest: s. life is that of a political
MENC 150:14
sadists: As repressed s. are supposed
CONN 58:15
sadness: At all the s. in the sweet
THOM 214:21
  Farewell s.   ELUA 77:14
  Good-day s.   ELUA 77:14
  s. of her sadness when   BARR 19:19
safe: be made s. for democracy
WILS 229:13
  it is s. to be unpopular   STEV 208:22
  National Health Service is s.   THAT 213:3
  S. shall be my going   BROO 40:2
  S. though all safety's   BROO 40:2
  s. to go back in the water   ANON 7:7
  S. upon solid rock   MILL 151:19
  S. with his wound   SASS 192:3
  woman in London will be s.   CAMP 45:6
  world s. for hypocrisy   WOLFE 231:2
safer: s. than a known way   HASK 99:3
safety: 'S. first' does not mean   BALD 17:14
  strike against the public s.   COOL 60:13
  There is no s. in numbers   THUR 216:22
  The s. of our Homes   HAIG 95:3
safety–catch: release the s. of my
  Browning   JOHST 114:19

sagged: S. seats, the creeper-nails
HARDY 97:1
said: at all can be s. clearly   WITT 229:20
  I hope it may be s.   BELL 25:16
  nobody had s. it before   TWAIN 219:25
  s. by the servant girls   SYNGE 211:10
  s. to the man who stood   HASK 99:3
  There is a great deal to be s.   BENT 29:4
sail: I s. across the floor   GREN 94:2
  Or s. in amply billowing gown   BELL 26:5
sailed: hast not s. in Indian Seas   DAV 65:4
  have s. the seas and come   YEATS 234:7
sailing: s. proudly down the years
PRIE 175:9
sailor: brings the s. home from sea
ELIOT 76:24
sailors: 'Onward,' the s. cry   BOUL 37:3
sails: Red s. in the sunset   KENN 119:1
  To the white dipping s.   MAS 148:8
saint: S., n. A dead sinner   BIER 34:14
Saint Mary Woolnoth: To where S. kept
  the hours   ELIOT 76:17
saints: lives of the medieval s.   SAKI 188:14
  overrun by a Wave of S.   SELL 194:10
  S. should always be judged   ORW 165:9
  We are not s., but we have   BECK 21:22
sake: for my s. do not be rash   GRAH 92:15
salamandrine: Of her s. fires   HARDY 97:13
Salamis: The many-headed foam at S.
YEATS 233:5
sale: From s. and profanation   CHES 51:18
salesman: A s. is got to dream   MILL 152:5
  Death of a S.   MILL 152:4
Salieri: In Mozart and S. we see   BAR 18:13
salley: by the s. gardens my love
YEATS 234:13
  s. gardens with little   YEATS 234:13
Sally: S. is gone that was so kindly
BELL 25:14
salmon: And the s. sing in the street
AUDEN 12:16
  smoked s. and tinned s.   WILS 228:12
Salteena: S. was an elderly man
ASHF 10:15
  S. was not very addicted   ASHF 10:19
salute: If it moves, s. it   ANON 6:23
salvaged: Democracy will not be s. by men
HOGB 104:3
salvation: s. lies exclusively   SOLZ 204:4
Sam: nephew of my Uncle S.'s
COHAN 57:13
  Play it again, S.   EPST 77:18
  Sam, S., pick up tha' musket   HOLL 104:5
  wouldn't have a Willie or a S.
MURR 158:5
Samaritan: would remember the Good S.
THAT 213:6
Samarkand: Along the Golden Road to S.
FLEC 81:8
Samarra: with him tonight in S.
LOW 139:19
same: are doing the s. thing   PHIL 170:15
  I'm having the s.   LOES 138:18
  s. the whole world over   ANON 8:8
  Sighted sub, sank s.   MASON 148:22
  Yet this will go onward the s.
HARDY 97:9
Sammy: What makes S. run   SCH 193:7
sanction: Happiness is the only s. of life
SANT 190:8
sanctions: s. might well bring   WILS 228:16
sanctities: Round the day's dead s.
THOM 215:12

sanctity: untrespassed s. of space
MAGEE 145:2
sanctuary: three classes which need s.
BALD 17:11
sand: It produces lies like s.   PONS 172:12
  palace built upon the s.   MILL 151:19
  pass gigantic on the s.   FLEC 81:8
  with its head in the s.   WILS 229:7
sandal: massive s. set on stone   MILL 151:21
sandalwood: S., cedarwood, and sweet
MAS 148:2
sands: are as various as the s.   FORS 83:2
  The riddle of the s.   CHIL 52:16
Sandy: this is my friend, S.   TOOK 217:11
sane: go mad they shall be s.   THOM 214:6
  no s. human being has ever
HUXL 109:10
  s. person would do at eleven
SHAW 197:13
sang: And s. themselves to sleep
HODG 103:10
  s. as he watched and waited   PAT 169:15
  s. in my chains like   THOM 213:18
sanitary: glorified s. engineer   STR 210:8
sanity: what they call a s. clause
KAUF 118:3
sank: certainly he s. into his grave
YEATS 235:4
  Sighted sub, s. same   MASON 148:22
Santa Claus: arrival of death, or S.
BERNE 30:10
  going to shoot S.   SMITH 202:2
sap: Has dried the s. out   YEATS 232:12
sapient: The s. sutlers of the Lord
ELIOT 75:7
saplings: it plies the s. double   HOUS 106:18
sapristi: S. Nuckoes   MILL 152:17
Sarah: Blossomed S.   BERR 30:14
sardines: can't ravish a tin of s.
LAWR 132:8
  like opening a tin of s.   BENN 27:18
Sargent: kind of musical Malcolm S.
BEEC 22:4
sashes: one of his nice new s.   GRAH 92:12
sat: everyone has s. except a man
CUMM 64:1
  last person who has s.   HAIG 95:2
  s. too long here   AMERY 4:12
  Station I s. down and wept   SMART 202:1
  when I s. down at the piano   CAPL 46:11
'satiable: was full of s. curtiosity
KIPL 125:12
satin: ease a heart like a s.   PARK 168:8
satire: S. is what closes Saturday
KAUF 117:13
satiric: have the s. temperament
BEER 22:24
satisfaction: S. is death   SHAW 199:10
satisfactory: putting it—not very s.
ELIOT 74:9
Saturday: date on S. night   ALLEN 3:20
  played the Glasgow Empire S.   DODD 68:5
  Satire is what closes S. night
KAUF 117:13
sausage: s., by-the-yard   LEWIS 136:18
savage: s. contemplates his mother-in-law
FRAZ 84:17
  Standing among s. scenery   HOFF 104:2
  who has not wept is a s.   SANT 190:6
savaged: being s. by a dead sheep
HEAL 99:7
save: And s. them by the barrel-load
THOM 215:23

save (cont.):
 destroy the town to s.   ANON 7:2
 exist in order to s. us   DE VR 67:6
 little less democracy to s.   ATK 12:2
 saved you only must s. face   HEAN 99:13
 s. the Governor-General   WHIT 226:20
 s. the Party we love   GAIT 87:23
 s. those that have no imagination
                                           SHAW 199:31
 s. your world you asked   AUDEN 15:7
 through life trying to s.   ROG 182:12
 will always s. Barabbas   COCT 57:5
saved: could have s. sixpence   BECK 21:10
 One of the thieves was s.   BECK 21:16
 s. his friend from a wetting   MILNE 154:4
 s. you only must save face   HEAN 99:13
 they only s. the world   CHES 50:6
saves: idea of Death s. him   FORS 83:18
 sometimes s. tons of explanation
                                           SAKI 188:21
saving: It is capable of s. us   RICH 180:17
savings: oven, all sorts of s.   JENK 112:23
saviour: I imitate the S.   HUXL 108:8
 it's 'S. of 'is country'   KIPL 123:7
saw: I s. you do it   STOP 209:21
 s. guns and sharp swords   DYLAN 71:6
 s. ten thousand talkers   DYLAN 71:6
 s. the skull beneath   ELIOT 75:8
Sawyer: The Adventures of Tom S.
                                           TWAIN 218:20
Saxon: from our S. good and evil
                                           KEYN 120:15
say: disapprove of what you s.   TALL 212:4
 don't care what you s.   COHAN 57:10
 don't s. nothin'   HAMM 96:1
 having to s. you're sorry   SEGAL 194:7
 I have nothing to s.   CAGE 44:13
 I s., you fellows   RICH 180:16
 I s. the hell with it   WHITE 226:1
 Journalists s. a thing   BENN 28:17
 long as they do what I s.   THAT 212:19
 more to s. when I am dead   ROB 181:14
 S. it with flowers   O'KEE 163:2
 s. no more   CHAP 49:12
 s. the perfectly correct   SHAW 196:26
 s. what you are going to s.   BRAB 37:20
 Some s. the world will end   FROST 86:6
 think till I see what I s.   WALL 222:8
 We must not s.   BERR 30:16
 what they are going to s.   CHUR 54:1
 you s. nothing   HEAN 99:13
saying: I am s. it   CAGE 44:13
 s. it long enough   BENN 28:17
Sayle: my colleague Murray S.   TOM 217:10
says: author is not what he s.
                                           SMITH 203:15
scaffold: s. he said goodbye   BARR 19:3
scales: someone is practising s.
                                           MACN 144:16
scandal: s. by a woman of easy virtue
                                           HAIL 95:4
scare: s. me with their empty   FROST 85:19
 s. myself with my own desert
                                           FROST 85:19
scarecrows: potato-gatherers like
 mechanized s.   KAV 118:8
scares: Anything s. me, anything
                                           STEIN 207:11
scarlet: His sins were s.   BELL 25:16
 Only the s. soldiers, dear   AUDEN 14:13
scene: start a s. or two   ELIOT 75:18
scenery: Standing among savage s.
                                           HOFF 104:2
 Where God paints the s.   HART 98:19

scent: How hot the s.   GRAV 93:8
 s. comes forth   DAV 65:4
 Their s. survives their close
                                           THOM 214:20
 The s. of the conifers   BETJ 32:2
scepticism: s. kept her from being
                                           SART 191:7
sceptre: He's thrown his S.   FARJ 78:8
schedule: My s. is already full   KISS 128:2
Schicksal: Die Anatomie ist das S.
                                           FREUD 85:5
schizoid: means s. self-alienation
                                           FROMM 85:13
schizophrenia: S. cannot be understood
                                           LAING 129:9
schizophrenic: s. is a special strategy
                                           LAING 129:14
 talks to you, you are a s.   SZASZ 211:18
scholar: better s. than Wordsworth
                                           HOUS 105:6
 scientist or s. or teacher   EINS 73:4
scholarship: slender indications of s.
                                           CHUR 55:7
school: he's been to a good s.   SAKI 188:19
 people so horrible as a s.   SHAW 199:11
 s. is all put gently back   BEER 22:23
 S. is pretty bad   WAUGH 222:21
 S.'s out   DAV 65:2
 s. that feeling is bad   FORS 83:3
 s. without any boots it   BULM 42:6
 special reason for hating s.   BEER 22:22
 The naughtiest girl in the s.   BLYT 35:10
 till we leave s.   LEWIS 136:15
schoolboy: I see a s. when I think of him
                                           YEATS 235:4
 s. who wipes his fingers   BLUNT 35:5
schoolchildren: What all s. learn
                                           AUDEN 13:8
schoolgirl: Keep that s. complexion
                                           PEAR 169:18
schoolmaster: you'll be becoming a s.
                                           WAUGH 222:20
schools: encourage it in some s.
                                           SCOTT 194:2
 s. for the imagination   GIR 90:17
 s. of thought contend   MAO T 146:8
 We class s., you see   WAUGH 222:21
schreit: s. im Traum um Hilfe   CAN 46:9
science: human s. is at a loss   CHOM 52:18
 ought to be, an exact s.   DOYLE 69:19
 religion without s. is blind   EINS 73:5
 S. is built up of facts   POIN 172:10
 s. is either physics   RUTH 187:9
 s. is strong and religion   SZASZ 211:19
 S. may have found a cure   KELL 118:16
 s. may have the existence   ADAMS 2:7
 'S.' means simply the aggregate
                                           VALÉ 220:23
 s. of arresting human intelligence
                                           LEAC 133:6
 s. reassures   BRAQ 38:16
 s. the credit goes to the man
                                           DARW 64:16
 S. without religion is lame   EINS 73:5
 That is the essence of s.   BRON 39:14
 This is why s. has succeeded   BRON 39:17
 typical triumph of modern s.
                                           WAUGH 223:7
scientific: judgement of our s. age
                                           HOLM 104:6
 s. power has outrun our   KING 122:4
scientist: research s. to discard   LOR 139:13
 s. says that something   CLAR 56:10

scientists: at the illiteracy of s.   SNOW 204:1
 myself in the company of s.   AUDEN 14:1
 representative, the physical s.
                                           SNOW 203:27
scold: only will he not s. you   BUTL 43:26
scones: afternoon tea-cakes and s.
                                           BETJ 31:12
 Over buttered s. and crumpets
                                           ELIOT 73:10
score: from seventy springs a s.
                                           HOUS 106:9
scorer: S. comes to mark against
                                           RICE 180:8
scorn: perfect expression of s.   SHAW 195:23
 S. the sort now growing up   YEATS 233:2
Scot: S. summed it all up very   BAX 20:14
Scotch: Mary, ma S. Bluebell   LAUD 131:8
 working on a case of S.   BENC 27:2
Scotland: S., land of the omnipotent No
                                           BOLD 35:15
Scotsman: moral attribute of a S.
                                           BARR 19:23
 S. of your ability let   BARR 19:21
 S. with a grievance   WOD 230:5
 The Flying S. is no less   BEAV 21:2
 world than a S. on the make   BARR 19:22
Scott: Beam us up, Mr S.   RODD 182:3
scoundrel: Every man over forty is a s.
                                           SHAW 198:28
scouts: s.' motto is founded   BAD 16:9
scramble: And rooks came home in s. sort
                                           HODG 103:10
scrap: just for a s. of paper   BETH 30:20
scratch: S. a lover, and find a foe
                                           PARK 168:21
scratches: S. its innocent behind
                                           AUDEN 13:6
scratchin': S. in the sun   AYRES 16:7
scratching: s. of pimples on the body
                                           WOOLF 231:11
scream: s. from a crevasse   GREE 93:17
screw: Turn of the S.   JAMES 112:5
scribbled: And s. lines like fallen hopes
                                           HOPE 105:2
 Man by a s. name   THOM 214:5
scrotumtightening: The snotgreen sea. The
 s. sea   JOYCE 116:2
scrupulous: The s. and the just   CONR 60:2
sculpture: austere, like that of s.
                                           RUSS 186:22
scum: are the s. of the earth   CHES 50:20
 Okie means you're s.   STEI 208:2
 They are s.   MAUG 150:1
scuttling: S. across the floors   ELIOT 75:16
sea: And the s. rises higher   CHES 50:8
 are all gone under the s.   ELIOT 74:10
 deep s. keep you up   CONR 59:24
 her dead across the s.   BINY 34:17
 if Ye take away the s.   KIPL 127:3
 In a solitude of the s.   HARDY 97:13
 Lie mirror'd on her s.   HODG 103:15
 my chains like the s.   THOM 213:18
 Over the s. to Skye   BOUL 37:3
 ride slowly towards the s.   CHES 52:1
 round me like a bursting s.   THOM 215:18
 sailor home from s.   ELIOT 76:24
 s. for a thousand years   KIPL 127:2
 s. will soon be drownded   SYNGE 211:8
 serpent-haunted s.   FLEC 81:13
 snotgreen s.   JOYCE 116:2
 that gong-tormented s.   YEATS 235:16
 that I am very much at s.   CARS 47:3
 The mirrors of the s.   FLEC 81:14

sea (*cont.*):
  The s. hates a coward   O'NEI 163:13
  The swaying sound of the s.
                        AUDEN 14:12
  Where no s. runs, the waters
                        THOM 213:21
  Who hath desired the S.   KIPL 124:9
  Within a walk of the s.   BELL 25:26
sea-fogs: And here the s. lap and cling
                        KIPL 124:10
seal: heard a s. bark   THUR 216:17
  Minister [the Lord Privy S.]   BAIL 16:11
  S. thy sense in deathly slumber
                        DE L 66:12
search: characters in s. of an author
                        PIR 171:15
  In s. of lost time   PROU 175:15
  s. for knowledge   RUSS 186:7
  travels the world in s.   MOORE 155:8
searching: I am s. everywhere   STEP 208:7
seas: floors of silent s.   ELIOT 75:16
  I must down to the s. again   MAS 148:16
  mackerel-crowded s.   YEATS 234:5
  new places, no other s.   CAV 40:8
  not sailed in Indian S.   DAV 65:4
  sailed the s. and come   YEATS 234:7
  s. roll over but the rocks   HERB 101:22
  these out to s. colder   FLEC 81:18
  troubled s. of thought   GALB 88:3
sea-shells: She sells s. on the sea-shore
                        SULL 210:21
sea-sick: bishop was feeling rather s.
                        DOUG 68:14
seaside: I do like to be beside the s.
                        GLOV 91:2
  s. place called Blackpool   EDGAR 71:20
season: dry brain in a dry s.   ELIOT 73:13
  Your excuse is out of s.   JER 113:18
seasons: S. return, and today   REED 179:3
season-ticket: has held a s. on the line
                        AMERY 4:14
seat: s. of this sensation   HOUS 106:5
  third-class s. sat the journeying
                        HARDY 97:8
seat-belts: Fasten your s., it's going
                        MANK 146:2
seated: looked wiser when he was s.
                        KEYN 120:9
seats: Sagged s., the creeper-nails
                        HARDY 97:1
  with 'bottoms on s.'   HALL 95:11
seawards: My road leads me s.   MAS 148:8
sea-worm: The s. crawls   HARDY 97:13
secluded: afternoon, in a s. chapel
                        ELIOT 74:22
second: first and s. class citizens
                        WILL 228:4
  happens to be a S. Entry   ADE 2:10
  I'm a s. eleven sort   BARR 19:2
  not a s. on the day   COOK 60:7
  s. acts in American lives   FITZ 80:22
  s. oldest profession   REAG 178:17
  s. things never   CONR 60:6
  s. time in our history   CHAM 48:14
  s. time you hear your love   CAHN 44:16
  struck the water a full s.   COKE 57:14
  The s. best is a formal order   AUDEN 14:8
  truth 24 times per s.   GOD 91:3
second-best: anything but the s.
                        LESS 135:26
second-hand: s. opinion of any thing
                        SAIN 188:1
second-rate: many s. ones of our own
                        BEEC 22:15

secret: giant girls that have no s.
                        SPEN 205:18
  Know you her s. none can utter
                        QUIL 177:3
  s. diary of Adrian Mole   TOWN 217:12
  s. of the long-nosed Etruscans
                        LAWR 131:14
  S. sits in the middle   FROST 86:23
  Vereker's s., my dear man   JAMES 111:19
secretary: Why not 'Madam S.'   PERK 170:7
secretive: As we make sex less s.
                        SZASZ 211:14
secretly: S. armed against all death's
                        BROO 40:2
  So s., like wrongs hushed-up
                        OWEN 166:14
secrets: narrow privacy and tawdry s.
                        LEACH 133:4
secure: And love is not s.   CHES 50:10
security: freedom can make s. secure
                        POPP 172:15
  otherwise styled s.   MAD 144:19
  s. and peace of each country
                        JOHN 113:22
see: And s. the coloured counties
                        HOUS 106:14
  are you just glad to s.   WEST 225:20
  Besides, they'll s. how   HUGH 108:1
  heart that one can s.   SAIN 187:19
  I'll s. you again   COW 61:18
  I'll s. you later   BARR 19:3
  I think that I shall never s.   KILM 121:8
  I think that I shall never s.   NASH 159:14
  Nice to s. you—to see you, nice
                        FORS 84:11
  not as I s. them   PIC 171:4
  Oh shall I s. the Thames again
                        BETJ 31:18
  s. a belt without hitting   ASQ 11:19
  S. an old unhappy bull   HODG 103:14
  s. it often since you've   AUDEN 14:18
  S. the happy moron   ANON 8:7
  s. what is in front   ORW 165:10
  s. who was in the lead   SNAG 203:25
  S. you later, alligator   GUID 94:13
  takes little talent to s.   AUDEN 13:20
  then can he s. clearly   BARN 18:18
  think till I s. what I say   WALL 222:8
  through a flint wall s.   GRAV 93:6
  what I think till I s.   FORS 83:9
  You s., but you do not observe
                        DOYLE 68:19
  You s. things; and you say   SHAW 195:20
seeds: I find thy cunning s.   ROSS 185:5
seed-time: Ought I to regret my s.
                        LOW 140:3
seeing: at s. it practised   BUTL 44:5
  Discovery consists of s.   SZEN 212:1
  friends who are not s.   THAT 212:17
seek: s. not to make them like   GIBR 90:5
  s. what is happily known   ACH 1:7
  We s. him here, we seek   ORCZY 163:19
  We still s. no wider war   JOHN 114:12
seekest: I am He whom thou s.
                        THOM 215:20
seems: s. that I have spent   AYER 16:4
seen: fine things to be s.   CHES 50:23
  I have s. the future   STEF 207:8
  manifestly and undoubtedly be s.
                        HEW 102:5
  s. one Western you've seen   WHIT 226:17
  s. the righteous forsaken   BLUN 35:1
  s. war on land and sea   ROOS 183:3

seen (*cont.*):
  you've s. one city slum   AGNEW 2:21
sees: one s. in other women   TYNAN 220:9
segregation: S. now, segregation
  tomorrow   WALL 222:6
Seine: Mirabeau Bridge flows the S.
                        APOL 9:22
  pont Mirabeau coule la S.   APOL 9:22
self: life-sentence in the dungeon of s.
                        CONN 59:14
  public and have no s.   CONN 59:4
  that's your own s.   HUXL 109:15
self-alienation: schizoid s.   FROMM 85:13
self-assertion: Self-sufficiency at home, s.
  abroad   WAUGH 223:11
self-control: education or of absence of s.
                        BEVAN 32:15
self-denial: S. is not a virtue   SHAW 198:20
self-importance: s. of the investigator
                        RUTH 187:8
self-indulgence: her favourite form of s.
                        MAUG 149:9
self-love: S. seems so often unrequited
                        POW 174:16
self-made: s. man is one who believes
                        STEAD 207:6
  s. man may prefer a self-made
                        HAND 96:8
self-revelation: The terrible *fluidity of s.*
                        JAMES 111:11
self-sacrifice: S. enables us to sacrifice
                        SHAW 199:2
self-sufficiency: S. at home, self-assertion
                        WAUGH 223:11
Selkirk: Alexander S. knew the plight
                        KAV 118:6
sell: I'll s. him   LEAC 133:5
selling: because it was s. well   BOOR 36:6
  nimble in the calling of s.   LEWIS 137:2
  writers are always s.   DID 67:11
sells: problematical world and s. us life
                        FRY 87:1
seltzer: He sipped at a weak hock and s.
                        BETJ 30:21
selvytion: Wot prawce S. nah
                        SHAW 197:12
semi-house-trained: imitation of a s.
  polecat   FOOT 82:11
senator: United States S.   JOHN 114:16
senators: respectable s. burst   AUDEN 12:18
send: S. in the clowns   SOND 204:11
  S. me the half that's got   GRAH 92:14
  s. me to eat in the kitchen   HUGH 108:1
  situation is s. a gun-boat   BEVAN 32:18
sending: s. of general messages
                        DOYLE 69:30
sends: s. his son to Oxford   STEAD 207:6
  s. the frozen-ground-swell   FROST 86:9
sensation: Art distils s. and embodies
                        BARZ 20:11
  really delightful s.   FERB 79:3
  seat of this s. is the pit   HOUS 106:5
sense: common s. and good taste
                        SHAW 196:2
  fine s. of the ridiculous   ALBEE 3:3
  ground s. necessary   WILL 227:22
  Money is like a sixth s.   MAUG 149:20
  s. that that is where   GREE 93:15
  s. to the American people   STEV 209:4
senses: If Parson lost his s.   HODG 103:13
  s. and his heart unsatisfied   YEATS 235:4
  s. know that absence   BOWEN 37:7
sensibility: century a dissociation of s.
                        ELIOT 76:10

sensibility (cont.):
　it is an immense s.　　　　　　JAMES 111:26
sensible: No opera plot can be s.
　　　　　　　　　　　　　　AUDEN 15:13
sensitive: more s. one is　　　　BEER 22:26
sensual: Of the s. man-in-the-street
　　　　　　　　　　　　　　AUDEN 13:9
　that s. music all neglect　　　YEATS 234:5
sentence: it's a s.　　　　　　VIDOR 221:18
　ordinary British s.　　　　　CHUR 55:8
sentenced: courtmartialled in my absence
　and s.　　　　　　　　　　BEHAN 23:23
　s. to solitary confinement　　WILL 227:19
sentences: Backward ran s. until reeled
　　　　　　　　　　　　　　GIBBS 90:3
　keep finishing your s.　　　　LONS 139:2
sentiment: those who have no s.
　　　　　　　　　　　　　　MAIL 145:7
sentimental: Of its s. value　　FRY 86:25
sentimentality: S. is the emotional
　promiscuity　　　　　　　MAIL 145:7
separate: s. the wheat from the chaff
　　　　　　　　　　　　　　HUBB 107:13
September: When you reach S.　AND 4:21
sequestered: Each s. in its hate AUDEN 13:3
seraglio: A s. of eunuchs　　　FOOT 82:10
serene: that unhoped s.　　　　BROO 40:3
serenity: s. to accept what cannot
　　　　　　　　　　　　　　NIEB 160:11
serial: autobiography is an obituary in s.
　　　　　　　　　　　　　　CRISP 63:3
serious: It's nice to meet s. people
　　　　　　　　　　　　　　COPE 61:1
　much more s.　　　　　　　SHAN 195:7
　Murder is a s. business　　　ILES 110:5
　s. house on serious earth　　LARK 130:16
　that politics are too s.　　　DE G 66:3
　too s. a matter to entrust　　CLEM 56:16
　You cannot be s.　　　　　　MCEN 142:6
seriously: right to be taken s.　HUMP 108:5
　S., though, he's doing　　　FROST 85:15
　take the game of life s.　　　LEARY 133:15
sermon: rejected the S. on the Mount
　　　　　　　　　　　　　　BRAD 38:9
serpent-haunted: s. sea　　　　FLEC 81:13
servant: obligation to become the s.
　　　　　　　　　　　　　　SHAW 196:22
　Our ugly comic s.; and then you
　　　　　　　　　　　　　　AUDEN 14:18
　s. girls in the kitchen　　　SYNGE 211:10
　s. to the devil　　　　　　　SISS 201:9
　Your s.'s cut in half　　　　GRAH 92:14
servants: equality in the s.'hall　BARR 19:1
　s. are treated as human　　　SHAW 198:17
　wish your wife or your s.　　GRIF 94:6
serve: s. both God and Mammon
　　　　　　　　　　　　　　SMITH 203:3
　s. that in which I no longer
　　　　　　　　　　　　　　JOYCE 115:21
　To s. your captives' need　　KIPL 127:19
served: have things daintily s.　BETJ 31:11
　s. to him course by course　　CHUR 54:6
　which I thought s. him　　　CHUR 55:10
service: places the nation at his s.
　　　　　　　　　　　　　　POMP 172:11
　Pressed into s. means pressed
　　　　　　　　　　　　　　FROST 86:16
　s. of our great Imperial　　　ELIZ 77:7
services: goods and s. can be paid for
　　　　　　　　　　　　　　NOCK 161:10
serviettes: kiddies have crumpled the s.
　　　　　　　　　　　　　　BETJ 31:11
servility: savage s.　　　　　　LOW 140:2

serving-men: I keep six honest s.
　　　　　　　　　　　　　　KIPL 125:15
sesquippledan: S. verboojuice
　　　　　　　　　　　　　　WELLS 224:17
set: s. down from the carrier's　LEE 134:2
　She s. out one day　　　　　BULL 42:5
settlement: s. of the differences between
　　　　　　　　　　　　　　ROOS 183:11
settles: war s. nothing　　　　CHR 52:20
seul: Être adulte, c'est être s.　ROST 185:7
seven: s. pillared worthy house
　　　　　　　　　　　　　　LAWR 133:3
　S. types of ambiguity　　　EMPS 77:16
　The s. pillars of wisdom　　LAWR 133:2
seventy: S. minutes had passed before
　　　　　　　　　　　　　　BENN 28:11
　take from s. springs　　　　HOUS 106:9
several: s. excuses are always less
　　　　　　　　　　　　　　HUXL 109:5
Severn: from the S. to the Tyne
　　　　　　　　　　　　　　KIPL 126:19
　thick on S. snow the leaves　HOUS 106:18
sewer: Life is like a s.　　　　LEHR 134:6
　through a s. in a glass　　　MIZN 154:20
sewing: remarked brightly, 's.?'
　　　　　　　　　　　　　　BOTT 36:15
　s. on a button is beyond　　BROUN 41:6
sex: attempt to insult s.　　　LAWR 132:19
　Battles and s.　　　　　　　MCAR 140:19
　Continental people have s. life
　　　　　　　　　　　　　　MIKES 151:15
　fair s. is your department　　DOYLE 69:18
　Is s. dirty　　　　　　　　ALLEN 3:15
　It's s. with someone I love　ALLEN 4:5
　No s. please—we're British　MARR 147:11
　practically conceal its s.　　NASH 159:19
　predominates the whole of her s.
　　　　　　　　　　　　　　DOYLE 68:18
　S. and drugs and rock and roll
　　　　　　　　　　　　　　DURY 71:1
　s. and not much about having
　　　　　　　　　　　　　　LODGE 138:17
　S. and the single girl　　　BROWN 41:9
　s. has been a very private　SZASZ 211:14
　S. is the gateway to life　　HARR 98:14
　s. rears its ugly 'ead　　　　ALL 4:9
　s. relation as something　　ROB 181:16
　[s.] was the most fun　　　ALLEN 4:4
　these s. rules for myself　　SAL 189:1
　wanted to know about s.　　REUB 179:15
　was exactly like s.　　　　　BALD 16:14
　we have s. in the mind　　　LAWR 132:17
　women are a s. by themselves BEER 23:1
　you have money, it's s.　　　DONL 68:6
S-E-X: if S. ever rears its ugly　AYCK 15:19
sexes: within the s. than between
　　　　　　　　　　　　　　COMP 58:11
sexophones: s. wailed like melodious
　　　　　　　　　　　　　　HUXL 108:11
sexual: all the s. perversions　HUXL 108:17
　I've no s. vices　　　　　　SIM 201:1
　primary s. activity　　　　SZASZ 211:13
　S. intercourse began　　　LARK 130:14
　unlimited s. attraction　　HARD 96:16
sexually: s. transmitted disease ANON 7:16
sex-war: s. thoughtlessness　　CONN 59:9
shabby: For tamed and s. tigers
　　　　　　　　　　　　　　HODG 103:13
　s. equipment always deteriorating
　　　　　　　　　　　　　　ELIOT 74:13
shackles: s. and restraints of government
　　　　　　　　　　　　　　GOLD 91:11

shad-blow: Cowslip and s., flaked like
　　　　　　　　　　　　　　CRANE 62:14
shade: A whiter s. of pale　　REID 179:10
　s. of a coolibah tree　　　　PAT 169:15
　s. your eyes but plagiarize　LEHR 134:7
　The sly s. of a Rural Dean　BROO 40:12
shadow: Falls the S.　　　　　ELIOT 75:11
　Me and my s.　　　　　　　ROSE 184:11
　s. at evening rising　　　　ELIOT 76:15
　s. at morning striding　　　ELIOT 76:15
　S. of Shadows on the deed　YEATS 234:9
　The one is the s.　　　　　JUNG 116:22
　Who live under the s. of a war
　　　　　　　　　　　　　　SPEN 205:15
shadows: In ancient s. and twilights
　　　　　　　　　　　　　　AE 2:18
　less liquid than their s.　　TESS 212:14
　s. pass gigantic　　　　　　FLEC 81:8
shag: cormorant (or s.)　　　ISH 110:22
shake: S., rattle and roll　　　CALH 44:20
　s. their wicked sides　　　　YEATS 232:15
shaken: S. and not stirred　　FLEM 82:1
shakes: As a madman s. a dead geranium
　　　　　　　　　　　　　　ELIOT 75:21
　Midnight s. the memory　　ELIOT 75:21
Shakespeare: entirely as I despise S.
　　　　　　　　　　　　　　SHAW 199:32
　S. and found him weak　　WELLS 224:15
　S., another Newton　　　　HUXL 108:20
　S. I am struck with wonder LAWR 132:18
　S. is not to translate　　　BEER 22:25
　S. remained more a theme　BROWN 41:10
　'S.,' she recalls　　　　　　HULL 108:3
　souls most fed with S.'s　　CHES 51:21
Shakespearian: That S. rag　BUCK 42:3
Shakespeherian: O O O O that S. Rag
　　　　　　　　　　　　　　ELIOT 76:21
shaking: s. them to make certain
　　　　　　　　　　　　　　BIRK 34:21
　The Court is s.　　　　　　FARJ 78:8
Shalimar: hands I loved beside the S.
　　　　　　　　　　　　　　HOPE 105:4
shame: Ain't it all a bleedin s.　ANON 8:8
　s. on you　　　　　　　　ARMS 10:9
　'Tis a s. to human nature　HOUS 105:8
　who have known s.　　　　BROO 40:1
Shannon: dark mutinous S. waves
　　　　　　　　　　　　　　JOYCE 115:6
shape: All out of s. from toe to top
　　　　　　　　　　　　　　YEATS 233:2
　it has no s.　　　　　　　　ANOU 9:21
　means pressed out of s.　　FROST 86:16
　The s. of things to come　　WELLS 225:3
shapely: it's s. and its name　ERWIN 77:22
shard: Shattered in s. on shard
　　　　　　　　　　　　　　THOM 215:18
shares: Fair S. for All　　　　JAY 112:18
shark: s. has pretty teeth　　BREC 38:21
sharp: s. compassion of the healer's
　　　　　　　　　　　　　　ELIOT 74:12
shaved: s. and sober　　　　　CHAN 49:2
shaves: A man who s.　　　　WHITE 226:3
Shaw: disciple of Bernard S.　SHAW 196:14
　[George Bernard S.] is a good man
　　　　　　　　　　　　　　LENIN 134:16
　Mr S. is　　　　　　　　　CHES 51:12
　S. a beefsteak and put　　CAMP 45:6
she: S. sells sea-shells　　　　SULL 210:21
　s. who voiced those rhymes HARDY 97:1
shearsman: A s. of sorts　　　STEV 208:15
sheath: s. the sword which we have
　　　　　　　　　　　　　　ASQ 11:11

shed: s. his blood for the country
ROOS 183:15
she-devil: The life and loves of a s.
WELD 224:8
sheep: being savaged by a dead s.
HEAL 99:7
   black s. who've gone astray KIPL 123:16
   s. in sheep's clothing CHUR 56:3
   s. in sheep's clothing GOSSE 92:6
   s. in the stare of a python BANK 18:6
   s. to pass resolutions INGE 110:14
   standing a s. on its hind-legs BEER 23:15
sheep-bells: The s. and the ship-bells ring
KIPL 124:10
sheep-herding: rest is mere s.
POUND 173:25
sheet: A boy brought the white s.
LORCA 139:11
sheets: cool kindliness of s. BROO 39:19
shell: protective and aggressive s.
MCL 143:13
   underneath that gloomy s. ANON 7:26
shells: demented choirs of wailing s.
OWEN 166:9
shelter: To s. me from the cold BELL 25:26
shelters: Naught s. thee, who wilt
THOM 215:11
shepherd: Old Nod, the s., goes DE L 66:6
sherry: And s. in the cupboard BETJ 32:11
shifted: s. it to another shoulder
SHAW 198:7
shilling: s. the Bruddersford United
PRIE 175:7
shilling life: s. will give you all
AUDEN 14:15
shimmered: Jeeves s. out and came
WOD 230:6
shimmy: s. like my sister Kate
PIRON 171:17
shine: Boy you can gimme a s. GORD 92:4
   s. on, harvest moon NORW 161:13
   S. on, shine AUDEN 14:11
   that's where I s. BENC 26:15
shines: Light breaks where no sun s.
THOM 213:21
   When the m-m-m-moon s.
O'HARA 162:24
shining: A woman of so s. loveliness
YEATS 234:17
   dead; look s. AUDEN 15:3
   dulls my s. things MEYN 151:12
   I see it s. plain HOUS 107:4
   London town the sun was s. GERS 89:13
   s. keys will be took from HARDY 97:5
   street in all his s. ABSE 1:4
   Through the dark cloud s. FORD 82:20
ship: built your s. of death LAWR 132:10
   It was so old a s. FLEC 81:21
   S. me somewheres east KIPL 123:15
   tall s. and a star MAS 148:16
   The s. on the sea LORCA 139:12
ship-bells: The sheep-bells and the s. ring
KIPL 124:10
ships: And mighty s. ten thousand ton
HODG 103:12
   s. and stars and isles FLEC 81:6
   s. sail like swans asleep FLEC 81:19
   stately s. are twirled HODG 103:12
   Then man your s. LUCAS 140:13
   wrong with our bloody s. BEAT 20:16
Shiraz: wine of S. into urine DIN 67:16
shires: calling for them from sad s.
OWEN 166:9

shires (*cont.*):
   Round both the s. they ring
HOUS 106:14
shirt: s. or collar ever comes LEAC 133:14
shit: shock-proof s. detector HEM 101:5
shivers: s. like the jelly PIRON 171:17
shock: Future s. TOFF 217:7
   Neither the sudden s. CHUR 53:9
   s. around the age of 5 BALD 16:19
   s. them and keep them SHAW 196:18
   The s. of the new DUNL 70:14
shocking: Was looked on as something s.
PORT 172:18
shock-proof: s. shit detector HEM 101:5
shocks: that s. the magistrate RUSS 187:3
shoe: In its s. FARJ 78:8
shoemaker: lives of a good s. VANZ 221:5
shoes: Englishwomen's s. look HALS 95:12
   got a stock of s. here PINT 171:12
   mind it wipes its s. THOM 214:8
   step on my Blue Suede S. PERK 170:6
shoestring: fortune and runs it into a s.
WOOL 231:17
shome: S. mishtake, shurely ANON 8:9
shone: star, that once had s. FLEC 81:7
shook: Ten days that s. the world
REED 179:7
shoot: could s. me in my absence
BEHAN 23:23
   I s. the Hippopotamus BELL 24:8
   They s. horses don't they MCCOY 141:16
   they shout and they s. INGE 110:10
   They up and s. themselves BROO 40:14
   women s. the hippopotamus FORS 83:5
   You s. a fellow down HARDY 98:3
shop: bone s. of the heart YEATS 233:8
   s. and street I gazed YEATS 235:17
   The s. at the corner AUDEN 14:21
shops: might shun the awful s. CHES 50:15
shore: s. of the wan grassy sea
SITW 201:14
   with low sounds by the s. YEATS 232:9
shored: have s. against my ruins
ELIOT 77:6
shores: wilder s. of love BLAN 34:23
short: And the days grow s. AND 4:21
   A s. life and a gay one WIMP 229:17
   be but a s. time tonight BALD 17:9
   Life is too s. to stuff CONR 60:5
   s. and the tall HUGH 107:20
   s. one ready for my own FROST 86:22
   step is s. from the Sublime GRAH 92:11
   who was s. and stout CHES 51:22
shorter: were s. than they should
STR 210:9
shorts: zephyr and khaki s. girl BETJ 32:8
shot: A long s., Watson DOYLE 69:13
   s. an elephant in my pajamas
KAUF 118:2
   They've s. our fox BIRCH 34:19
shoulder: shifted it to another s.
SHAW 198:7
   s. all the time to see BAR 20:8
   s. she laid her snow-white YEATS 234:13
   S. the sky, my lad HOUS 105:15
shoulders: City of the Big S. SAND 189:13
   s. held the sky suspended HOUS 106:3
shout: s. and bang and roar BELL 26:5
   There was a s. about my ears
CHES 52:11
   they s. and they shoot INGE 110:10
shouting: chased the s. wind MAGEE 145:2
   The tumult and the s. dies KIPL 126:9
   The tumult and the s. dies KNOX 128:11

shoved: s. aside in favour of things
BROUN 41:4
shovel: S. them under and let me work
SAND 189:17
shovelling: S. white steam over her
AUDEN 14:21
show: I will s. you fear ELIOT 76:15
   S. me a hero and I will FITZ 80:15
   s. to give pornography BARN 18:16
   There's no business like s. BERL 30:1
shower: Yes, this is our finest s.
OSB 165:12
showers: s. betumble the chestnut
HARDY 97:2
showing: review a bad book without s.
AUDEN 13:18
showman: That's what the s. said
HEAT 99:18
shows: All my s. are great GRADE 92:8
   And he s. them pearly white BREC 38:21
shrapnel: picking s. out of your head
LUML 140:15
shrill: It's too s., man FREB 84:18
shrimp: until a s. learns to whistle
KHR 121:3
shrine: build a s. to my memory
RUSS 186:8
shrined: The bower we s. to Tennyson
HARDY 97:1
shroud: Fetch out no s. PUDN 176:9
   gaiety is a striped s. THOM 214:18
   stiff dishonoured s. ELIOT 75:5
shtick: does her own s. KAEL 117:5
shudder: s. in the loins engenders
YEATS 235:1
shuffle: All s. there; all cough in ink
YEATS 234:19
Shultz: Mr S. went off his pram
KINN 122:14
shurely: Shome mishtake, s. ANON 8:9
shut: Each had his past s. WOOLF 231:10
   great markets by the sea s. FLEC 81:7
   S. up he explained LARD 130:7
sick: I'll be s. tonight LLEW 138:5
   kingdom of the s. SONT 204:16
   Oh, Mummy, I'm s. with disgust
BETJ 31:10
   s. hearts that honour could BROO 40:1
   s. horse nosing around KAV 118:9
   S. in soul and body both HODG 103:14
   The cattle then are s. KING 122:12
   time we think we're s. WOLFE 231:1
sickle: A ship, an isle, a s. moon
FLEC 81:14
sickness: Nationalism is an infantile s.
EINS 72:11
   universal as sea s. SHAW 198:1
Sid: Tell S. ANON 8:16
Sidcup: I could get down to S. PINT 171:14
side: S. by side WOODS 231:6
   s. with plenty of money ANOU 9:18
   This s. the tomb DAV 64:20
side-fall: Along the s. of the hill KAV 118:8
sides: I'm a Norfan, both s. WELLS 224:18
   looked at life from both s. MITC 154:7
   on both s. of the paper SELL 194:19
sideways: more up and down than s.
HEM 101:7
Siegfried: out the washing on the S.
KENN 118:21
siesta: But Englishmen detest a s. COW 62:4
siftings: And let their liquid s. fall
ELIOT 75:5

sigh: A s. is just a sigh   HUPF 108:7
  full of runic tales to s.   FLEC 81:15
  telling this with a s.   FROST 86:4
sighs: S., short and infrequent   ELIOT 76:17
sight: And he keeps it out of s.   BREC 38:21
  losing your s.   SASS 191:18
sighted: S. sub, sank same   MASON 148:22
sightless: On the s. horse, riding
    WALEY 222:3
sights: Her s. and sounds   BROO 40:5
  s. in the world   BARR 19:22
sign: would give me some clear s.
    ALLEN 3:19
signalling: thin one is wildly s.   CONN 59:12
signals: suggestive s. to the orchestra
    SZELL 211:20
signed: hand that s. the paper   THOM 214:4
  morning I s. my death warrant
    COLL 58:6
  s. legislation which outlaws   REAG 178:14
significance: s. of man   BECK 21:8
significant: Art is s. deformity   FRY 87:10
  would follow that 's. form'   BELL 23:30
signs: positive s. of his awareness
    BLUNT 35:4
silence: activities and a period of s.
    ATTL 12:11
  After s., that which comes   HUXL 109:4
  deep is the s.   DRIN 70:4
  His mind moves upon s.   YEATS 233:7
  Indecency's conspiracy of s.
    SHAW 198:25
  penitence condemns to s.   BRAD 38:3
  private s. in which we live   PRIT 175:13
  s., exile, and cunning   JOYCE 115:21
  S. is the most perfect expression
    SHAW 195:23
  through the s. beat the bells   FLEC 81:8
silenced: because you have s. him
    MORL 156:3
silent: And s. be   AUDEN 14:12
  floors of s. seas   ELIOT 75:16
  In a slow s. walk   HARDY 97:9
  I stood upon that s. hill   HODG 103:11
  multitude of s. witnesses   GEOR 89:11
  Paris was French—and s.   TUCH 218:17
  S. as the sleeve-worn stone   MACL 143:5
  thereof one must be s.   WITT 229:20
  The s. sullen peoples   KIPL 127:20
  The *t* is s., as in *Harlow*   ASQ 11:15
silently: S. and very fast   AUDEN 14:23
  Slowly, s., now the moon   DE L 66:17
silk: Delicate-filmed as new-spun s.
    HARDY 97:10
  s. hat on a Bradford millionaire
    ELIOT 77:1
  s. purse out of your wife's   MORT 156:12
  your blue-shadowed s.   STEV 208:12
silkworm: power of Heaven—of s.
    MOORE 155:12
silliest: s. woman can manage a clever
    KIPL 126:1
silliness: s. of the majority of mankind
    RUSS 186:18
silly: They are s. things   AWDRY 15:18
  You s. twisted boy   MILL 152:12
  You were s. like us   AUDEN 13:1
silver: all the Georgian s.   MACM 144:3
  Between their s. bars   FLEC 81:14
  There's a s. lining   FORD 82:20
  The s. apples of the moon   YEATS 235:6
  thirty pieces of s.   BEVAN 32:16
  Walks the night in her s.   DE L 66:17

silver (*cont.*):
  With the s. penny   CAUS 47:17
simple: I'm a s. man, and I use
    LOWRY 140:7
  It was beautiful and s.   HENRY 101:11
  Love is so s.   PRÉV 175:5
  To ask the hard question is s.
    AUDEN 15:5
simplicity: A condition of complete s.
    ELIOT 74:23
  S. of character is no hindrance
    MORL 156:2
simplification: s. of the human character
    FORS 83:10
simplify: And s. me when I'm dead
    DOUG 68:10
  s. and illustrate the points   HOME 104:8
Simpson: Mrs S.'s pinched our king
    ANON 6:18
sin: beauty is only s. deep   SAKI 188:11
  I'll s. till I blow up   THOM 214:11
  lips were shaped for s.   BETJ 31:5
  more dreadful record of s.   DOYLE 69:6
  mother I'm living in s.   HERB 101:17
  My s., my soul   NAB 158:12
  physicists have known s.   OPP 163:17
  researches in original s.   PLOM 172:6
  s. tends to be addictive   AUDEN 13:12
  s. towards our fellow creatures
    SHAW 196:7
  s. ye do by two and two   KIPL 124:4
  There's only one real s.   LESS 135:26
  what did he say about s.   COOL 60:11
  Would you like to s.   ANON 9:17
sincere: It is dangerous to be s.
    SHAW 198:31
sincerely: comes as s. from the author
    HUXL 109:6
  Do you s. want to be rich   CORN 61:5
sincerity: s. of the pessimists   ROST 185:6
  test of your s.   BENN 28:9
sinecure: It gives no man a s.
    POUND 174:7
sing: And I will s. of the sun
    POUND 174:12
  heart wants to s. ev'ry song   HAMM 96:3
  I, too, s. America   HUGH 108:1
  Lhude s. Goddamm   POUND 174:10
  never heard no horse s.   ARMS 10:8
  second best to s. them   BELL 25:11
  s. 'em muck   MELBA 150:12
  s. for a rock 'n' roll   JAGG 111:9
  s. to find your hearts   FLEC 81:6
  S. whatever is well made   YEATS 233:2
  Soul clap its hands and s.   YEATS 234:6
  think that they will s.   ELIOT 75:19
  was said. We s. it   HARDY 98:6
  while I s. the ancient ways   YEATS 234:11
singer: The s. not the song   LIND 137:10
singers: s. who she thinks would
    REED 179:6
singin': S. in the rain   FREED 84:20
singing: Everyone suddenly burst out s.
    SASS 192:6
  heard the mermaids s.   ELIOT 75:19
  s. will never be done   SASS 192:6
  Why is there always a secret s.
    SAND 190:3
single: Sex and the s. girl   BROWN 41:9
singles: s. we played after tea   BETJ 32:1
sings: instead of bleeding, he s.   GARD 88:15
  that in me s. no more   MILL 151:20
singularity: S. is almost invariably
    DOYLE 69:4

sink: s. through the sea they   THOM 214:6
sinking: Prevents that s. feeling
    HARR 98:15
sinned: He would have s. incessantly
    ROB 181:15
  The people s. against   COMP 58:10
sinner: A dead s. revised   BIER 34:14
  forgive some s. and wink   MENC 151:5
  s. with the handcuffs   HOUS 105:8
sinners: s. on this part of Broadway
    RUNY 186:3
sinning: resting up from their s.
    RUNY 186:3
sins: heads forgetful of their s.
    YEATS 234:19
  His s. were scarlet   BELL 25:16
  since half the s. of mankind   RUSS 186:10
  s. are attempts to fill   WEIL 224:4
  s. it was possible   WAUGH 223:18
  up for your s. in church   SCOR 193:15
sipped: s. at a weak hock and seltzer
    BETJ 30:21
sissy: rose-red s. half as old as time
    PLOM 172:7
sister: Mud's s., not himself   HOUS 105:5
  my S. good night   BELL 26:8
  trying to violate your s.   STR 210:10
  want one to bury my s.   MITF 154:13
sisterhood: S. is powerful   MORG 155:19
sisters: Are s. under their skins   KIPL 127:8
Sistine: On the S. Chapel roof   YEATS 233:1
Sisyphus: imagine that S. is happy
    CAMUS 46:8
sit: And they s. outside   HARDY 97:2
  anyone come and s. by me   LONG 139:1
  Fancy having to s. it out   BUTL 43:22
  head-waiter who's allowed to s.
    UST 220:21
  I can s. and look at it   JER 113:16
  s. back and let the world   O'CAS 162:17
  s. down unless you're   HULL 108:3
  s. out front and watch   BARR 19:28
  Teach us to s. still   ELIOT 73:17
  we s. in peaceful calm   HUXL 109:2
  we used to s. and dream   ARMS 10:7
  you have to s. around   STEIN 207:12
sits: It s. looking   SAND 189:14
  Secret s. in the middle   FROST 86:23
sitting: Are you s. comfortably   LANG 130:5
  He struts s. down   DYKS 71:3
  I do most of my work s.   BENC 26:15
  S. in me hutch   AYRES 16:5
situation: retreating, s. excellent
    FOCH 82:6
  s. *excellente, j'attaque*   FOCH 82:6
  s. of our youth is not   BALD 16:20
situations: And applications for s.
    AUDEN 14:22
Sitwell: [Edith S.] looked like   BOWEN 37:8
Sitwells: S. belong to the history
    LEAV 133:17
six: Now We Are S.   MILNE 153:3
  S. o'clock   ELIOT 75:20
sixpence: nothing above s.   BEVAN 32:14
  saved s.   BECK 21:10
sixty: rate of s. minutes an hour
    LEWIS 136:13
  s. seconds' worth of distance   KIPL 126:15
  uselessness of men above s.
    OSLER 165:26
  When I'm s. four   LENN 135:13
size: Twentieth Century was the s.
    MAIL 145:10

skating: always s. on thin ice   CAMP 45:8
skeletons: sounds like two s. copulating
                                              BEEC 22:2
skied: s. down Mount Everest   MCK 143:2
skies: The s. above are clear again
                                               YELL 236:5
  whose god is in the s.   SHAW 198:19
skimming: S. our gable and writing
                                                HEAN 99:11
skin: And it punctures my s.   ANON 8:19
  A thick s. is a gift from God   ADEN 2:14
  I've got you under my s.   PORT 173:1
  my s. bristles   HOUS 106:5
  s. but by the content   KING 121:15
  s. the swart flies move   DOUG 68:11
  skull beneath the s.   ELIOT 75:8
  take the s. from the arm   ELIOT 75:2
skins: Are sisters under their s.   KIPL 127:8
  classes had such white s.   CURZ 64:11
  confinement inside our own s.
                                               WILL 227:19
skip: s. about like a girly   WILL 227:9
skipping: they all went s. about   BARR 19:7
skool: only good things about s.
                                                WILL 227:7
skull: s. beneath the skin   ELIOT 75:8
sky: And s. and sea and land   HOUS 106:8
  And yon twelve-winded s.   HOUS 107:2
  clean the s.   ELIOT 75:2
  climbin' clear up to the s.   HAMM 95:17
  Clouds Hullo S. and skip   WILL 227:9
  shoulders held the s. suspended
                                                HOUS 106:3
  Shoulder the s., my lad   HOUS 105:15
  s. an' assed meself   O'CAS 162:14
  s. and the men and women   FORS 84:4
  s. grows darker yet   CHES 50:8
  spread out against the s.   ELIOT 75:14
  The s. was stars all over it   HODG 103:11
  The triple-towered s.   DAY-L 65:7
  This northern s.   DE L 66:18
  Up in the s.   NORW 161:13
Skye: Over the sea to S.   BOUL 37:3
slab: Beneath this s.   NASH 159:7
slacks: And girls in s. remember Dad
                                                BETJ 31:4
slag: there is a s. heap 120 ft   WILS 228:11
slain: swear by the s.   SASS 192:5
slamming: In Little Girls is s. Doors
                                                BELL 24:19
slander: one to s. you   TWAIN 219:16
slang: All s. is metaphor   CHES 50:12
  S. is a language that rolls   SAND 190:1
slap: You can't just s. these   BENN 28:2
slate: s. after spitting on them   BLUNT 35:5
  wiping something off a s.   KIPL 122:18
slaughter: machinery all the s. of plague
                                                SHAW 197:31
slave: s. of capitalist   CONN 59:17
  The moment the s. resolves   GAND 88:11
slavery: because they impose s.
                                                RUSS 186:26
  Freedom and s. are mental   GAND 88:11
  s. in the extreme acceptance   CHUR 53:21
  state is a state of S.   GILL 90:11
slaves: Englishmen never will be s.
                                                SHAW 197:29
  inevitably two kinds of s.   ILL 110:7
  mistress and two s.   BIER 34:9
  was that men became s.   FROMM 85:13
sleep: And miles to go before I s.
                                                FROST 86:7
  And sang themselves to s.   HODG 103:10

sleep (cont.):
  And s.—and learning of a sort   BELL 26:5
  been to s. for over a year   WAUGH 223:2
  calf won't get much s.   ALLEN 3:17
  Church can feed and s.   ELIOT 75:6
  come to the borders of s.   THOM 214:17
  Eat or s. or drink again   DE L 66:19
  From s. and from damnation   CHES 51:18
  green ideas s. furiously   CHOM 52:19
  grey and full of s.   YEATS 232:7
  hear a moment before s.   THOM 213:11
  I s. all night   CHAP 49:10
  Is passed in s.; at night   ELIOT 75:6
  I wake to s., and take   ROET 182:4
  Let us s. now   OWEN 166:11
  like men who s. badly   RUSS 186:9
  Never s. with a woman   ALGR 3:6
  poor to s. under bridges   FRAN 84:15
  recommend you to go home and s.
                                                CHAM 48:14
  s. and a sweet dream when   MAS 148:18
  S. upon a golden bed   YEATS 236:4
  s. you remind me   SASS 192:4
  S. your fill   BELL 25:20
  The Big S.   CHAN 49:2
  there is nothing but s.   DRIN 70:4
  time enough to s.   HOUS 106:10
  To break earth's s. at all   OWEN 166:12
  twenty centuries of stony s.
                                                YEATS 233:13
  We shall not s.   MCCR 141:18
  when you can't get to s.   LEB 133:20
sleeper: sun-flushed s.   THOM 215:3
sleep-flower: s. sways in the wheat
                                                THOM 215:3
sleeping: fuss about s. together
                                                WAUGH 223:17
  Lay your s. head, my love   AUDEN 13:7
  The rose-lipt girls are s.   HOUS 107:7
  wakened us from s.   BROO 40:1
sleepless: O S. as the river under thee
                                                CRANE 62:15
sleeps: He s. as sound   PUDN 176:9
sleepwalker: with the assurance of a s.
                                                HITL 103:4
sleepy: 'Cause in s. London town
                                                JAGG 111:9
  s. and there is no place   DYLAN 71:11
sleeve: Ash on an old man's s.   ELIOT 74:18
  bringing an ace down his s.   LAB 129:7
  s. with a bottle of vitriol   WOOL 231:19
sleeves: Americanism with its s.   MCC 141:7
  language that rolls up its s.   SAND 190:1
sleigh: To hear s. bells in the snow
                                                BERL 30:3
slender: s. indications of scholarship
                                                CHUR 55:7
slept: He s. in the hall   BENT 29:5
  He s. more than any other   MENC 150:13
  s. soundly and had no need   CHUR 55:18
slice: S. him where you like   WOD 230:8
slide: slip, s., perish   ELIOT 74:6
slight: friendship called s.   BIER 33:19
Slightly: he [Noel Coward] was S.
                                                TYNAN 220:8
slime: Is wetter water, slimier s.   BROO 40:7
slip: Excuse me while I s.   EST 78:1
  tension, s., slide   ELIOT 74:6
  They s., diminished   TESS 212:14
slipped: s. the surly bonds of earth
                                                MAGEE 145:2
slippered: A s. Hesper; and there
                                                BROO 40:11

slitty-eyed: longer you'll all be s.
                                                PHIL 170:17
slob: He was just a s.   LONG 138:22
slogan: rhyming North Battersea s.
                                                JAY 112:18
  s. and a few vapid adjectives   OGIL 162:23
slogans: instead of principles, s.   BENT 29:9
slogged: s. up to Arras with rifle
                                                SASS 191:17
slopes: on the butler's upper s.   WOD 230:22
Sloppy Joe: At Dirty Dick's and S.'s
                                                AUDEN 14:6
slouches: S. towards Bethlehem
                                                YEATS 233:13
slouching: S. in the undergrowth
                                                HODG 103:14
Slough: bombs, and fall on S.   BETJ 31:1
slovenliness: Peace is nothing but s.
                                                BREC 39:3
slow: Ah! the clock is always s.
                                                SERV 194:20
  In a s. silent walk   HARDY 97:9
  On a s. boat to China   LOES 138:19
  sloeblack, s., black   THOM 214:7
  was drinking was s. poison   BENC 27:3
  way of telling you to s. down   ANON 5:28
slowly: angel to pass, flying s.   FIRB 80:2
  great end comes s.   DUB 70:7
  pig got up and s. walked   BURT 42:17
  s. in the wind   EHRL 72:10
  S., silently, now the moon   DE L 66:17
sludge: simply says: ACTIVATED S.
                                                JENN 113:4
sluicing: excellent browsing and s.
                                                WOD 230:19
slum: A swear-word in a rustic s.
                                                BEER 22:21
  free diversions in s. life   MCAR 140:19
  you've seen one city s.   AGNEW 2:21
slumber: Seal thy sense in deathly s.
                                                DE L 66:12
slums: gay intimacy of the s.   WAUGH 223:5
slush: I'm as pure as the driven s.
                                                BANK 18:2
  with mush and s.   OWEN 166:5
sly: The s. shade of a Rural Dean
                                                BROO 40:12
small: day of s. nations has   CHAM 48:9
  pictures that got s.   BRAC 37:21
  s., but perfectly formed   COOP 60:18
  S. is beautiful   SCH 193:10
  That's one s. step for a man   ARMS 10:10
  The Microbe is so very s.   BELL 25:5
smallest: about the s. in the world
                                                STR 210:12
  Advice, n. The s. current coin   BIER 33:21
  s. amount of lying go   BUTL 44:8
  s. room of my house   REGER 179:8
small-talking: this s. world can I find
                                                FRY 87:2
smarter: who thought themselves s.
                                                ATTL 12:6
smash: English never s. in a face
                                                HALS 95:13
  This great society is going s.   AUDEN 15:6
smell: s. by the ferocity   ELLIS 77:12
  s. of burning fills   BELL 26:6
  s. of steaks in passageways   ELIOT 75:20
  The good s. of old clothes   BROO 39:19
  Yes, the s. and hideous hum   GODL 91:5
smells: dead thing that s. sweet
                                                THOM 214:14
  pine-woody, evergreen s.   BETJ 32:3

soleil: *horreur des couchers de s.* PROU 176:4
solemn: more s. of our number said
  BETJ 32:12
  s. beauty like slow old MAS 148:6
solicitor: s., a Freemason DOYLE 69:17
solid: Safe upon s. rock the ugly
  MILL 151:19
  s. for fluidity, all-powerful CHUR 54:5
solidity: appearance of s. to pure wind
  ORW 165:8
solitary: sentenced to s. confinement
  WILL 227:19
solitude: endure our own s. PRIT 175:13
  In a s. of the sea HARDY 97:13
  make him feel his s. VALÉ 220:24
  resonance of his s. CONN 59:3
  Soldiers, this s. DE L 66:18
  that each protects the s. RILKE 181:5
solitudes: saluting of two s. RILKE 181:3
Solomon: Is S.'s temple, poets, Nineveh
  MEYN 151:12
  King David and King S. NAYL 159:26
  One man in a thousand, S. says
  KIPL 126:16
solution: s. for the problem of habitual
  BENC 26:16
  that they can't see the s. CHES 52:4
  you're either part of the s. CLEA 56:12
somber: decorated dark red as I have s.
  ASHF 10:18
sombre: s. picture presented BERNE 30:10
some: S. chicken CHUR 53:13
  S. enchanted evening HAMM 96:2
  S. men are born mediocre HELL 100:4
  S. say the world will end FROST 86:6
somebody: I could have been s. SCH 193:6
  S. up there likes me LEHM 134:4
someday: S. I'll find you COW 62:9
somehow: you s. haven't to deserve
  FROST 86:13
someone: S. must have traduced Joseph
  KAFKA 117:6
something: Everything must be like s.
  FORS 83:4
  Good morning, sir—was there s.
  MURD 158:1
  s. nasty in the woodshed GIBB 90:1
  s. or other could be proved FRY 87:5
  S. should be done to get EDW 72:9
  S. there is that doesn't FROST 86:9
  S. you somehow haven't FROST 86:13
  Time for a little s. MILNE 154:1
  When there's s. doing KNIG 128:8
  you say s. about me COHAN 57:10
sometime: Why don't you come up s.
  WEST 225:22
somewhat: tough joints more than s.
  RUNY 186:1
somewhere: S. over the rainbow
  HARB 96:13
somnambulist: A Reactionary is a s.
  ROOS 183:6
son: good idea—s. SYKES 211:7
  his little s. should cry CORN 61:9
  s. of a bitch stole MAC 140:20
  you'll be a Man, my s. KIPL 126:15
song: A rainbow and a cuckoo's s.
  DAV 64:20
  given a penny for a s. YEATS 232:14
  have I to spur me into s. YEATS 234:3
  I made my s. a coat YEATS 234:16
  Luxuriant s. YEATS 235:4
  old sweet s. keeps Georgia GORR 92:5

song (*cont.*):
  play a s. for me DYLAN 71:11
  Poured forth her s. in perfect
  AUDEN 15:11
  s. was wordless SASS 192:6
  s. well sung MAS 148:5
  that thinks two notes a s. DAV 65:1
  The singer not the s. LIND 137:10
  The s. is ended BERL 29:18
  The s. of the birds for mirth GURN 94:17
  Time an endless s. YEATS 232:18
  time you hear your love s. CAHN 44:16
  wants to sing ev'ry s. HAMM 96:3
songe-creux: *Comme tous les s.* SART 191:8
songs: all trades, to make s. BELL 25:11
  And all their s. are sad CHES 50:9
  s. beguile your pilgrimage FLEC 81:6
  s., for ended is our brief THOM 216:1
  s. they have sung HAMM 96:3
  their dirty s. BROO 40:1
sonne: *Vienne la nuit, s. l'heure* APOL 9:22
sonnet: And it turned to a S. DOBS 68:2
sonnets: S. and birds descend MACN 144:6
sons: approve of your young s. GRIF 94:6
  further s. to their name EDGAR 72:1
  s. acclaim your glorious CUMM 63:15
  s. and daughters of Life's GIBR 90:5
  The fallen s. of Eve CHES 50:18
  Your s. and your daughters
  DYLAN 71:14
soon: Be s. THOM 215:9
  curly you'll s. be dead WIMP 229:17
  I'd as s. write free verse FROST 86:2
  it's awfully s. KAEL 117:5
  s. as one is unhappy one PROU 175:20
sophism: more precisely, a s. BORG 36:9
sophistication: s. of the wise primitive
  MAIL 145:8
soporific: too much lettuce is 's.'
  POTT 173:12
Sordello: There can be but the one 'S.'
  POUND 173:27
sordid: s. thing sound like a brilliant
  DE VR 67:5
sore: man has long been s. HOUS 106:2
sores: s. on innocent tongues OWEN 166:10
sorrow: Nought but vast S. was there
  DE L 66:11
  salutary for the body but s. PROU 176:7
  s., and the triumphs HOOV 104:10
  s. enough in the natural KIPL 123:1
  S. is tranquillity remembered PARK 168:4
sorrows: s. of your changing face
  YEATS 232:7
  There are few s., however SMITH 202:20
  The world's great s. were born AE 2:18
sorry: having to say you're s. SEGAL 194:7
  S. for itself LAWR 132:4
  s. for keeping you waiting GEOR 89:10
  Very s. can't come BER 29:11
  who, I'm s. to say AUDEN 14:20
sort: And sleep—and learning of a s.
  BELL 26:5
sorts: only two s. of people SHAW 197:5
so-so: The rest is merely s. WILD 227:4
Sosostris: Madame S., famous clairvoyante
  ELIOT 76:16
Soudan: at your 'ome in the S. KIPL 123:8
soul: By which the s. of man is fed
  MAS 148:12
  He fancied that I gave a s. YEATS 235:10
  his s. among masterpieces FRAN 84:16
  most surely, on the s. DIMN 67:14
  night of the s. it is always FITZ 80:17

soul (*cont.*):
  oath again may my s. SHAW 199:27
  repose of His s. ROLFE 182:18
  Sick in s. and body both HODG 103:14
  sincerely from the author's s. HUXL 109:6
  S. clap its hands and sing YEATS 234:6
  there is a s. in prison DEBS 65:14
  The s. of a friend we've made
  BOND 35:19
souls: bodies but not their s. GIBR 90:5
  damp s. of housemaids ELIOT 76:1
  only in men's s. STEV 209:6
  people sell their s. SMITH 203:4
  s. most fed with Shakespeare's
  CHES 51:21
  s. of Christian peoples CHES 51:20
sound: alive with the s. of music
  HAMM 96:3
  hear the s. of marching JAGG 111:9
  it is sheer s. BEEC 22:7
  Music is feeling, then, not s. STEV 208:12
  s. ideas is original MACM 144:2
  S. of Broken Glass BELL 25:9
  s. of English county families
  WAUGH 222:19
  s. of Harold Hobson GILL 90:12
  s. which reverberates through
  KOES 128:13
  s. which so thrills AUDEN 14:13
  The s. of surprise BALL 17:23
  Whose s. dies on the wind APOL 9:23
sounds: music is better than it s. NYE 162:2
soup: not take s. at luncheon CURZ 64:10
sour: life will be s. grapes ASHF 11:3
sous: *S. le pont Mirabeau coule* APOL 9:22
south: citizens dream of the s. HARDY 97:2
  go s. in the winter ELIOT 76:14
  great hills of the S. BELL 25:25
  I want to go s., where LAWR 132:3
  more seriously down S. CURR 64:7
  not in the S. POTT 173:19
  Or s. to the blind Horn's hate
  KIPL 127:17
  S. of England where you ORW 164:31
  S. of the Border KENN 118:20
South Africa: methods of barbarism in S.
  CAMP 45:16
  S., renowned both far and wide
  CAMP 45:15
South African: S. police would leave no
  SHAR 195:8
Southampton: Yes, weekly from S.
  KIPL 125:16
South Pole: [the S.] is an awful
  SCOTT 193:18
Southron: matches of the S. folk
  THOM 215:22
souvenirs: *Les s. sont cors de chasse*
  APOL 9:23
sovereign: power and light, a s. touch
  AUDEN 15:2
Soviet: S. domination of Eastern
  FORD 82:15
  S. power plus the electrification
  LENIN 134:15
sow: his Vomit and the S. KIPL 126:18
  Ireland is the old s. JOYCE 115:18
space: beyond S. and Time BROO 40:7
  challenge of filling the s. WEST 225:23
  how to waste s. JOHN 114:18
  passenger on s. vehicle FULL 87:12
  S.—the final frontier RODD 182:2
  s. where nobody is STEIN 207:17

spaces: And through the s. of the dark
                 ELIOT 75:21
  It is the s. between   FENT 79:1
  me with their empty s.   FROST 85:19
  Removed the s.   MORG 155:20
  vacant interstellar s.   ELIOT 74:11
spaceship: fact regarding S. Earth
                 FULL 87:15
spade: s. is never so merely   FRY 87:8
Spain: Lady of S., I adore you REAV 178:18
  The rain in S. stays mainly LERN 135:23
Spanish: expects the S. Inquisition
                 CHAP 49:14
  some are fond of S. wine   MAS 148:4
spanner: their throats with a s. BETJ 31:9
spare: Brother can you s. a dime
                 HARB 96:12
  don't s. the horses   HILL 102:15
  s. time and in his working GILL 90:11
spared: has s. me the indignity BELL 24:23
spark-gap: The s. is mightier HOGB 104:3
sparks: s. blown out of a smithy
                 YEATS 234:18
speak: He must s. in calm BEVAN 32:15
  I s. like a child   NAB 158:15
  let us s. of darker days   CHUR 53:11
  Nation shall s. peace   REND 179:12
  one's memoirs is to s. ill PÉT 170:10
  S. for England   AMERY 4:13
  S. now, and I will answer HOUS 107:3
  S. softly and carry   ROOS 183:17
  s. thereof one must   WITT 229:20
  Think before you s.   FORS 84:7
speaker: public s.   NIC 160:9
speaking: their watches when I am s.
                 BIRK 34:21
  This *is* Henry Hall s.   HALL 95:10
  when they are s.   CHUR 54:1
spearmint: s. lose its flavour ROSE 184:12
special: s. kind of artist   COOM 60:17
  We are all s. cases   CAMUS 46:1
specialism: his s. is omniscience
                 DOYLE 69:9
specialist: definition of a s. as one
                 MAYO 150:8
specialists: All other men are s. DOYLE 69:9
speciality: s. is being right when
                 SHAW 200:6
species: female of the s. KIPL 126:17
  s. of beetles on this planet HALD 95:7
  systematically on its own s. JAMES 112:6
specimens: s., the lilies of ambition
                 DOUG 68:9
spectators: be anything more than s.
                 ASQ 11:8
spectre: haunt Europe as a s. TAYL 212:7
speculation: not land s. in the sense
                 WILS 228:11
speech: divine gift of articulate s.
                 SHAW 199:18
  freedom of s. and expression ROOS 183:9
  freedom of s., freedom TWAIN 219:10
  sensibly refrain from s. GRAH 92:16
  Since our concern was s. ELIOT 74:19
  s. in the slack moments BROUN 41:4
  s. without the help   WAUGH 223:9
  what the dead had no s. ELIOT 74:17
speeches: From all the easy s. CHES 51:18
  have its old s. burnt   SNOW 204:2
speechless: washed in the s. real
                 BARZ 20:10
speed: candles may be held to s.
                 OWEN 166:9

speed (*cont.*):
  Less than the s., of hours HOPE 105:3
  S., bonnie boat, like   BOUL 37:3
  s. glum heroes up the line SASS 191:16
  s. towards the wilder shores BLAN 34:23
  S. with the light-foot   GREN 94:3
  Unsafe at any s.   NADER 158:17
  Work at war s.   MORR 156:6
speeding: Faster than a s. bullet ANON 6:8
spell: foreigners always s. better
                 TWAIN 219:18
  no s. to cast on nature BRON 39:17
  Who lies beneath your s. HOPE 105:4
  with the s. of far Arabia DE L 66:7
  you s. my name right COHAN 57:10
spelling: My s. is Wobbly MILNE 154:2
spend: I want to s., and spend NICH 160:7
  s. a little time with me FIEL 79:6
spender: A real big s.   FIEL 79:6
  Where the s. thinks it went FROST 86:1
spending: arms is not s. money alone
                 EIS 73:7
spent: Never ask of money s. FROST 86:1
spermatozoa: A million million s.
                 HUXL 108:20
spider: The s. is sole denizen HARDY 97:1
spiders: s. marching through LOW 140:4
spider-web: kind of huge s. JAMES 111:26
spill: stone and let them not s.
                 MACN 144:18
spin: Sob as you s.   AUDEN 12:15
spinach: I say it's s., and I say WHITE 226:1
spindle: s. or mutilate   ANON 6:1
spinster: s. from being treated like
                 MITF 154:14
spires: city of dreaming s. RAPH 177:16
  I saw the s. of Oxford LETTS 136:1
  What s., what farms are those
                 HOUS 107:4
spirit: break a man's s. SHAW 196:5
  develops the powers of the s. PROU 176:7
  Or watch the startled s. flee GRAV 93:6
  s. of her spirit   BINY 34:17
  s. of national masochism AGNEW 2:22
  was sacramental of the s. ROB 181:16
spirits: S. of well-shot woodcock BETJ 31:3
spiritual: has outrun our s. power
                 KING 122:4
  not being a s. people MANC 145:17
spiritualist: talk to you, you are a s.
                 SZASZ 211:18
spiritualists: like a convention of s.
                 STOP 209:15
spiritually: S. I was at Eton, John
                 BETJ 32:12
spit: I have no gun, but I can s.
                 AUDEN 12:14
spiteful: write when I feel s. LAWR 132:1
splendid: men with S. Hearts may go
                 BROO 40:13
  s. in the morning glows FLEC 81:10
  S. to eat and sleep   SASS 192:3
  With few but with how s. stars
                 FLEC 81:14
splendour: show of some fuller s.
                 BRAD 38:7
  such thing as s. or heroism FORS 83:14
splintered: lock and s. the door
                 AUDEN 14:14
splinters: bombs and teeth like s.
                 CAUS 47:18
split: when I s. an infinitive CHAN 49:4
spoil: healths, and s. our own JER 113:9

spoke: And sometimes no one s. to him
                 MILNE 153:3
spoken: possible to the s. one CONN 58:19
  s. to like this before   CARR 47:2
  s. with greater regret BALD 17:9
  that never have s. yet CHES 51:24
spontaneous: S. joy and natural content
                 YEATS 232:12
spoons: my life with coffee s. ELIOT 75:15
  world locks up its s. SHAW 198:2
sport: had ended his s. with Tess
                 HARDY 98:1
sportsman: A s. is a man LEAC 133:11
spot: corner, some untidy s. AUDEN 13:6
  each one s. shall prove KIPL 124:11
  penned in an inglorious s. MCKAY 142:15
  sumpshous s. all done up in gold
                 ASHF 10:20
Sprache: *Die Grenzen meiner S. bedeuten*
                 WITT 230:2
spray: And then me s. of pellets
                 AYRES 16:7
  pinkly bursts the s.   BETJ 32:5
  The rime was on the s. HARDY 97:15
spread: S. ALARM AND DESPONDENCY
                 PEN 170:1
  s. my dreams under YEATS 235:7
spreading: risks of s. conflict JOHN 114:12
sprig-muslin: And maids come forth s.
  drest   HARDY 97:2
spring: clean the pasture s. FROST 86:8
  first hour of s. strikes BOWEN 37:5
  It is s., moonless night THOM 214:7
  Mrs Porter in the s. ELIOT 76:23
  naked earth is warm with S. GREN 94:3
  S. breaks through again COW 61:18
  s. comes her hour is upon GIBB 89:18
  S. comes round with rustling SEEG 194:5
  s. has kept in its folds ARAG 10:2
  S. is come home with her THOM 216:3
  S. is here, so blow your job HART 98:19
  s. summer autumn winter CUMM 63:13
  s. than in any other season TWAIN 220:3
  S. will be a little late LOES 138:20
  They call it easing the S. REED 179:1
  with his vision, S. SACK 187:16
springing: Praise for them, s. FARJ 78:7
springlike: that fester are not s. ABSE 1:2
springs: from seventy s. a score
                 HOUS 106:9
sprouting: S. despondently at area gates
                 ELIOT 76:1
spun: ships are twirled and s. HODG 103:12
spunk: their s. is that watery LAWR 131:18
spur: have I to s. me into song
                 YEATS 234:3
spurn: But s. the Jews BROW 41:13
spy: s. who came in from LE C 133:24
squad: s. took up their positions CHIL 52:17
squalid: he was a s. nuisance CHUR 55:2
squalor: opulence and public s. GALB 88:4
square: given a s. deal afterwards
                 ROOS 183:3
  like this on the public s. CAV 48:1
  so thoroughly s.   LERN 135:19
  s. of the number of people SHAN 195:6
squares: districts packed like s. LARK 131:1
  Tree-muffled s., and look LARK 130:11
squat: s., and packed with guile
                 BROO 40:13
squawking: And the seven stars go s.
                 AUDEN 12:16
squeak: s. of a boot   FORS 83:21

steeples (*cont.*):
  s. of Fermanagh and Tyrone   CHUR 54:2
  Talk about the pews and s.   CHES 51:20
steer: ugly 'ead it's time to s.   ALL 4:9
Stein: I don't like the family S.   ANON 6:22
  S.'s prose-song is a cold   LEWIS 136:18
Steinbeck: Faulkner, and S.   ALGR 3:8
Stellenbosh: For fear o' S.   KIPL 124:14
stench: A s. in the ear   BIER 34:10
stenographers: then went off to become s.
    CHES 50:24
step: Light of s. and heart was she
    DE L 66:10
  one small s. for a man   ARMS 10:10
  s. is short from the Sublime   GRAH 92:11
  s. on my Blue Suede Shoes   PERK 170:6
step-parents: Parents — especially s.
    POW 174:19
steps: s. spritely in the incomparable
    SHAW 200:7
sterling: And I myself a s. lad   HOUS 107:9
sterner: rather speak of s. days   CHUR 53:11
Stettin: S. in the Baltic to Trieste
    CHUR 53:15
stewed: Seem far too familiar. Get s.
    LARK 131:4
stick: carry a big s.   ROOS 183:17
  going to make it s.   MACG 142:11
  phrases s. in the throat   RUSS 187:7
  s. more close than a brother   KIPL 126:16
  s. with an 'orse's 'ead   EDGAR 71:20
  tattered coat upon a s.   YEATS 234:6
sticks: S. nix hick pix   ANON 8:13
sticky: himself in a rather s. voice
    MILNE 153:15
stiff: A woman can be proud and s.
    YEATS 235:14
  stain the s. dishonoured   ELIOT 75:5
stiffen: before it has had time to s.
    ORW 164:12
stigma: Any s., as the old saying
    GUED 94:9
still: Clay lies s., but blood's   HOUS 106:10
  If you s. have to ask   ARMS 10:9
  S. falls the Rain   SITW 201:15
  s. it is not we   CHES 52:1
  s. point of the turning   ELIOT 74:5
stiller: s. than ever on orchard   DRIN 70:4
stillness: A s. which characterizes
    BELL 26:12
  s. in the midst of chaos   BELL 26:12
  that s. ultimately best   CRANE 62:16
stilly: planned her, s. couches she
    HARDY 97:13
stimulant: s. handy in case I see   FIEL 79:14
stimulate: s. the phagocytes   SHAW 196:12
sting: O Death, where is thy s.   ROSS 185:5
  s. like a bee   ALI 3:9
sting-a-ling-a-ling: O Death, where is
  thy s.   ANON 8:1
stink: s. of the damned dead niggers
    ASQ 11:20
stinker: Outrageous S.   KIPL 127:13
stirred: forest something s.   SIMP 201:5
  Shaken and not s.   FLEM 82:1
stirrup-pump: Idle to hope that the
  simple s.   REED 179:4
stirs: Will that s. and urges   HARDY 97:14
stitching: s. and unstitching has
    YEATS 232:16
St James: The ladies of S.'s   DOBS 68:3
St Louis: girls from S. hasn't learned
    STEIN 207:10
  S. team we have Who's   ABB 1:1

stocking: In olden days a glimpse of s.
    PORT 172:18
  s. over the municipal fireplace
    SMITH 202:2
  your silk s.'s hanging   SELL 194:11
stolen: They have s. his wits away
    DE L 66:7
stolid: S. and stunned, a brother
    MARK 146:14
stomach: burst s. like a cave   DOUG 68:11
  I have no s. for such meat   DOBS 68:1
  sensation is the pit of the s.   HOUS 106:5
  s. is nothing if not conservative
    BUTL 43:20
stomachs: used to march on their s.
    SELL 194:16
stone: bomb them back into the S. Age
    LEMAY 134:13
  Can make a s. of the heart   YEATS 233:10
  Like a rolling s.   DYLAN 71:8
  massive sandal set on s.   MILL 151:21
  Romancing the s.   THOM 213:10
  s. and let them not spill   MACN 144:18
  S., bronze, stone   ELIOT 76:12
  s. unturned to see   SHAR 195:8
  take our hearts o' s.   O'CAS 162:15
  take the s. from stone   ELIOT 75:2
  Turn but a s., and start   THOM 216:11
  written of me on my s.   FROST 86:22
stones: house is built of s.   POIN 172:10
  s. and every blooming   KAV 118:6
  s. kissed by the English   OWEN 166:13
stony: more s. than a shore   WILL 227:23
stood: I s. and stared   HODG 103:11
  s. [i.e. have stayed]   JAC 111:7
stop: again we s. the mighty   ANON 8:2
  if you can s. people talking   ATTL 12:13
  s. because you are afraid   NANS 158:19
  s. everyone from doing   HERB 101:14
  S.-look-and-listen   ANON 8:14
  S. me and buy one   RODD 182:1
  S. the world, I want to get off
    NEWL 160:5
  s. to rake the leaves away   FROST 86:8
stopper: Pull out the s.   LERN 135:18
stops: says 'The buck s. here'   TRUM 218:13
storage: A library is thought in cold s.
    SAM 189:8
store: in the s. we sell hope   REVS 179:16
stories: love s. in all literature   PARK 168:6
  S., like whiskey, must   O'FAO 162:22
stork: Can you tell S. from butter
    ANON 5:25
  throwing rocks at the s.   BREC 38:19
storm: sleek-barrelled swell before s.
    KIPL 124:9
story: And were an epitaph to be my s.
    FROST 86:22
  Ere their s. die   HARDY 97:9
  Every picture tells a s.   ANON 6:6
  he means to write one s.   BARR 19:4
  It's our *own* s. *exactly*   THUR 216:24
  Marks the place where a s.   ELIOT 74:18
  newspaper touches a s.   MAIL 145:9
  novel tells a s.   FORS 83:8
  s. for which the world   DOYLE 69:7
  s. is ephemeral and doomed   FAUL 78:12
stout: who was short and s.   CHES 51:22
stove: Her s., and lays out food
    ELIOT 76:24
  ice on a hot s. the poem   FROST 85:18
  s. instead of the oven   JENK 112:23

stowed: S. away in a Montreal lumber
    BUTL 44:2
St Pancras: Towers of S. Station
    BEEC 22:13
St Paul's: Say I am designing S.   BENT 29:1
Strabismus: Dr S.   MORT 156:17
strafe: *Gott s. England!*   FUNKE 87:16
straight: nothing ever ran quite s.
    GALS 88:6
  s. one day at the Sorbonne   STEV 208:16
  The crooked be made s.   ELIOT 74:16
strain: Let the train take the s.   ANON 7:13
  Words s.   ELIOT 74:6
Strand: Let's all go down the S.   CAST 47:11
  S. with my gloves   HARG 98:9
  You're never alone with a S.   MAY 150:6
strange: knowest of no s. continent
    DAV 65:4
  s. dark interludes   O'NEI 163:16
  'S. friend,' I said   OWEN 166:16
  s. interlude in which we   O'NEI 163:15
strangeness: confound s. with mystery
    DOYLE 69:28
stranger: From the wiles of the s.
    NASH 159:16
  I, a s. and afraid   HOUS 105:18
  Look, s., at this island now   AUDEN 14:12
  never love a s.   BENS 28:22
  S., unless with bedroom eyes
    AUDEN 12:14
  You may see a s.   HAMM 96:2
strangers: depended on the kindness of s.
    WILL 227:21
  Economics and art are s.   CATH 47:13
strangling: Than s. in a string
    HOUS 106:11
Strasser: Major S. has been shot
    EPST 77:20
straw: Headpiece filled with s. Alas
    ELIOT 75:10
  Of the s. for a bedding   BELL 25:15
strawberry: S. fields forever   LENN 135:11
strayed: shabby curate who has s.
    AUDEN 14:1
stream: dead fish swim with the s.
    MUGG 157:8
  have their S. and Pond   BROO 40:6
  long-legged fly upon the s.   YEATS 233:7
  mountain, ford ev'ry s.   HAMM 95:14
  old mill by the s.   ARMS 10:7
street: at the corner of the s.   GAY 88:18
  fighting in the s.   JAGG 111:9
  it in the s. and frighten   CAMP 45:7
  out my life talking at s.   VANZ 221:5
  Picasso coming down the s.   CHUR 53:19
  place for s. fighting man   JAGG 111:9
  shop and s. I gazed   YEATS 235:17
  To the sunny side of the s.   FIEL 79:9
  worth two in the s.   WEST 225:9
  you do it in the s.   SCOR 193:15
street-bred: s. people that vapour
    KIPL 124:3
streets: children died in the s.   AUDEN 12:18
  fields and in the s.   CHUR 54:10
  mean s. a man must go   CHAN 49:1
  s. at dawn looking   GINS 90:15
  S. FLOODED   BENC 26:14
  s. of a hundred cities   HOOV 104:13
  s. on a Sunday morning   BEHAN 23:26
  s. that no longer exist   FENT 79:1
  s. where the great men   FLEC 81:17
strength: S. through joy   LEY 137:6
  that country's unaided s.   STAL 206:20

strength (cont.):
together with our united s.　　CHUR 54:9
triumphant conviction of s.　　CONR 60:4
strenuous: doctrine of the s. life
　　ROOS 184:2
stretched: was things which he s.
　　TWAIN 218:20
striding: Your shadow at morning s.
　　ELIOT 76:15
strife: In place of s.　　CAST 47:10
strike: If you strike a child take care
　　SHAW 198:18
s. against the public safety　　COOL 60:13
when in doubt, s. it out　　TWAIN 219:33
strikes: The Empire s. back　　LUCAS 140:12
string: egg-shell, a bit of s.　　WELLS 224:13
Than strangling in a s.　　HOUS 106:11
Was chewing little bits of S.　　BELL 24:11
strings: whisper music on those s.
　　ELIOT 77:5
striped: gaiety is a s. shroud　　THOM 214:18
striving: s. evermore for these　　GREN 94:3
stroke: none so fast as s.　　COKE 57:14
paragraphing is to s. a platitude
　　MARQ 147:10
The s. of midnight ceases　　HOUS 106:6
strong: Is a s. brown god　　ELIOT 74:7
only the S. shall thrive　　SERV 194:22
S. brother in God and last　　BELL 25:13
S. gongs groaning　　CHES 51:17
s. people that they can　　BONH 36:2
those who think they are s.　　BID 33:18
you realise how s. she　　REAG 178:11
stronger: thing s. than all the armies
　　ANON 8:17
Women are s. than men　　STEP 208:5
strongest: s. man in the world
　　IBSEN 109:22
struck: Certain women should be s.
　　COW 62:8
structure: s. of a play is always　　MILL 152:6
s. of the ordinary British　　CHUR 55:8
struggle: burden of a long twilight s.
　　KENN 119:15
But today the s.　　AUDEN 15:9
ineligible for the s. of life　　CONN 59:1
needs a constant s.　　ORW 165:10
s. against the inclinations　　ZIN 236:14
s. between the artist man　　SHAW 197:22
s. everybody is engaged　　BAR 20:9
s. itself towards the heights　　CAMUS 46:8
would carry on the s.　　CHUR 54:10
struts: He s. sitting down　　DYKS 71:3
stuck: all s. over　　HEM 101:7
And they s. it in　　NIXON 160:16
student: S. of our sweet English tongue
　　FLEC 81:23
s. wears coloured socks　　BRAT 38:18
studio: [the RKO s.] is the biggest
　　WELL 224:10
studiously: We have stood apart, s.
neutral　　WILS 229:6
study: periphrastic s. in a worn-out
　　ELIOT 74:9
proper s. of mankind　　HUXL 108:13
stuff: Ale, man, ale's the s. to drink
　　HOUS 107:8
short to s. a mushroom　　CONR 60:5
s. of which tyrants　　BEAV 21:7
The s. of life to knit me　　HOUS 107:2
stuffed: We are the s. men　　ELIOT 75:10
stuffy: Not huffy, or s., not tiny
　　HERB 101:18

stumbles: With an old horse that s.
　　HARDY 97:9
stunt: just another amusing s.　　READ 178:9
stupendous: hotel offers s. revelations
　　HOFF 104:2
stupid: always pretend to be more s.
　　STARK 207:3
be s. enough to want it　　CHES 52:13
s. man is doing something　SHAW 195:27
s. neither forgive　　SZASZ 211:16
unless you are also s.　　SHAW 198:31
Very interesting . . . but s.
　　ROWAN 185:12
stupidity: idleness and impotent s.
　　BLUNT 35:5
ignorance and conscientious s.
　　KING 122:2
stupor: just dozed off into a s.　　BENC 26:17
style: He has no real s.　　PIC 171:5
particularly high-class s.　　WAUGH 223:13
this s. the Mandarin style　　CONN 58:19
who was not in my s.　　PROU 175:19
suavity: such deceitfulness and s.
　　ELIOT 75:4
sub: Sighted s., sank same　　MASON 148:22
subject: grant the artist his s.　JAMES 112:2
I should be a sad s.　　ATTL 12:7
itself and not in its s.　　SANT 190:14
My s. is War, and the pity　　OWEN 166:8
No s. for immortal verse　　DAY-L 65:11
subjectification: s. of nature　　LANG 130:6
subjects: from the s. of government
　　WILS 229:9
sublime: audience yelled 'You're s.'
　　HARG 98:10
Of poetry; to maintain 'the s.'
　　POUND 174:2
ridiculous, the s.　　MAHON 145:6
Symphony is the most s. noise
　　FORS 83:13
The step is short from the S.　GRAH 92:11
submit: destructive element s.　　CONR 59:24
subsidized: Divinely s. to provoke　FRY 87:3
substitute: becomes a s. for reading
　　BURG 42:12
can be no s. for victory　　MAC 140:21
There is no s. for talent　　HUXL 109:7
substitutes: Ours is the age of s.　BENT 29:9
subtle: s. but he is not malicious
　　EINS 72:13
subtleties: s. of the American joke
　　TWAIN 219:21
subtlety: hindrance to s. of intellect
　　MORL 156:2
suburban: urban and s. man　　MCL 143:13
suburbs: s. on summer evenings
　　AUDEN 15:9
subversion: s. or disloyalty　　HELL 100:8
subversive: Whatever is funny is s.
　　ORW 164:14
succeed: enough to s.　　VIDAL 221:12
How to s. in business　　MEAD 150:10
rest of us could not s.　　TWAIN 219:13
we s. in being defeated　　HELL 100:6
succeeds: Whenever a friend s.
　　VIDAL 221:16
success: bitch-goddess s.　　JAMES 112:8
can guarantee s. in war　　CHUR 55:19
confidence; then s. is sure　TWAIN 220:7
For an actress to be a s.　　BARR 19:26
his s. is disgraceful　　MENC 150:14
If A is a s. in life　　EINS 73:3
interested in, and yours is S.　BARR 19:18

success (cont.):
marriage a s.　　SAM 189:9
S. is relative　　ELIOT 74:14
s. spoils people by making　MAUG 149:23
Sweet smell of s.　　LEHM 134:5
there's no s. like failure　　DYLAN 71:9
successful: clever and the s.　　GREE 93:13
most s. adaptation　　JUNG 117:2
s. writer or picture-painter　LEWIS 137:4
Süchtigkeit: Form von S. ist von übel
　　JUNG 116:20
sucker: Never give a s. an even break
　　FIEL 79:11
sucking: s. at the bung　　MAS 148:5
sudden: I said to Dawn: Be s.—to Eve
　　THOM 215:9
muttered Ethel this is so s.　　ASHF 11:4
S. the rain of gold　　DAY-L 65:7
suddenly: For, s., I saw you there
　　GERS 89:13
Sudeten: problem of the S. Germans
　　HITL 103:6
Sudetenland: [the S.] is the last　HITL 103:5
suet-pudding: prose-song is a cold, black s.
　　LEWIS 136:18
Suez: somewheres east of S.　　KIPL 123:15
S. Canal was flowing through
　　EDEN 71:19
suffer: be prepared to s. for it　BENN 28:14
he did not s. them　　PEAR 169:22
sufferer: unites it with the human s.
　　JOYCE 115:19
suffering: About s. they were never wrong
　　AUDEN 13:5
If he sees s., privation　　BEVAN 32:15
pity for the s. of mankind　　RUSS 186:7
s. ennobles the character　　MAUG 149:16
s. from halitosis　　ICKES 110:3
s. from the particular　　JER 113:14
sufferings: constant in human s.
　　JOYCE 115:19
suffice: And would s.　　FROST 86:6
O when may it s.　　YEATS 233:10
sufficient: s. to keep him straight
　　LLOY 138:10
suffragettes: The s. were triumphant
　　BRAH 38:11
sugared: s. about by the old men
　　KIPL 124:14
suggestive: An idea, to be s.　JAMES 112:15
suicide: human race commit s.　　ADAMS 2:7
It is not: it is s.　　MACD 142:4
It is s. to be abroad　　BECK 21:9
longest s. note in history　　KAUF 118:4
s. 25 years after his death　　BEAV 21:6
suicides: downward lay the huddled s.
　　PLOM 172:9
suitable: A s. case for treatment
　　MERC 151:6
suitor: think that you are Ann's s.
　　SHAW 197:25
sukebind: when the s. hangs heavy
　　GIBB 89:18
sullen: s., untamed and intractable
　　ELIOT 74:7
The silent s. peoples　　KIPL 127:20
sulphur: Puffed its s. to the sunset
　　BETJ 31:19
sum: s. of things for pay　　HOUS 106:3
To s. up　　STOP 209:20
Sumatra: with the giant rat of S.
　　DOYLE 69:7
summer: fulness o' s.　　GIBB 89:18

sweetest: s. way to me is a ship's
                              KIPL 124:5
  To the s. girl I know   JUDGE 116:17
sweetness: after the s. of confession
                              FIRB 80:4
  succeed where s. and light   FORS 83:10
  The s. in the sad   THOM 214:21
sweets: parliamentarian is a bag of
  boiled s.   CRIT 63:4
sweet-shop: pressed to a s. window
                            YEATS 235:4
swell: deep sea s.   ELIOT 77:3
  his best; quite a s.   EDGAR 71:20
  To s. a progress, start   ELIOT 75:18
  What a s. party this is   PORT 173:7
swift: S. has sailed into his rest
                         YEATS 236:2
  s. things for swiftness THOM 215:10
swim: Mother may I go out to s.
                          DE L 66:20
swimmers: s. into cleanness leaping
                         BROO 40:1
swimming: S. from tree to tree LOW 140:4
swindles: simple as all truly great s.
                       HENRY 101:11
swine: could be a manœuvring s.
                       MCC 141:14
swines: rotten s.   MILL 152:15
swing: If it ain't got that s. MILLS 152:21
  s. for it   KING 122:11
swinger: than be a s. of birches FROST 86:5
swinging: A boutique, and a s. hot spot
                       MITC 154:8
  my ears yielding like s. doors
                       DOUG 68:12
  s. after the music had   HELP 100:9
swings: roundabouts we pulls up on the s.
                       CHAL 48:5
swirling: s. about in a human cesspit
                       AND 5:4
Swiss: A dashing S. officer RUSS 187:7
  deposit in my name at a S. ALLEN 3:19
  way a S. waiter talks   CHAN 49:4
Switzerland: S. is a small, steep country
                       HEM 101:7
  S. they had brotherly love WELL 224:11
swoons: S. to a waltz, I take her hand
                      HUXL 109:2
sword: believed he had a s. upstairs
                     YEATS 232:14
  I gave them a s.   NIXON 160:16
  Of honour and the s.   CHES 51:18
  shall never sheath the s. ASQ 11:11
  that never stained thy S. HOPE 105:3
sword-pen: against this I raise my s.
                       BURG 42:9
swords: are either dreams or s. LOW 139:20
  saw guns and sharp s. DYLAN 71:6
swore: S. not at all   BENT 29:6
swots: although you hav various s.
                       WILL 227:7
syllogism: The conclusion of your s.
                       O'BR 162:8
symbol: It is a s. of Irish art JOYCE 116:3
sympathize: s. with people's pains
                       HUXL 109:3
sympathy: boys a little tea and s. AND 5:2
  need of your God-damned s.
                      WOOL 231:18
  you get messages of s. AYCK 15:20
symphony: drastically cutting his A flat s.
                      BEEC 22:13
  Fancy a s. by Wordsworth BUTL 43:22

symphony (cont.):
  S. is the most sublime FORS 83:13
synthesis: s. of hyacinths and biscuits
                       SAND 189:12
system: His divine s. of creation HELL 100:5
  Mendacity is a s.   WILL 227:17
  somewhere in the solar s. FULL 87:12
  wholly alter our American s.
                     HOOV 104:13
systematic: s. organization of hatreds
                       ADAMS 2:1

T

t: The *t* is silent   ASQ 11:15
ta: Painting is saying "T." to God
                       SPEN 205:11
table: his victuals from the t. CHUR 54:6
  I'll sit at the t.   HUGH 108:1
  patient etherized upon a t. ELIOT 75:13
tact: t. *dans l'audace c'est* COCT 57:3
tactful: t. in audacity is knowing
                       COCT 57:3
tail: At such a little t. behind BELL 24:9
  t. must wag the dog   KIPL 124:2
  thy t. hangs down behind KIPL 125:5
tailor: lived a t. in Gloucester POTT 173:10
tails: Brushin' off my t. BERL 30:2
take: God will t. care   SHAW 196:24
  T. away that pudding   CHUR 56:4
  t. everything away from SOLZ 204:6
  t. from seventy springs HOUS 106:9
  T. me back to dear old Blighty
                     MILLS 152:20
  T. me out to the ball game NORW 161:14
  T. me to your leader   ANON 8:15
  T. the money and run ALLEN 3:22
  they t. themselves lightly CHES 51:15
  they t. you in the morning BALD 16:18
  Will someone t. me to a pub CHES 52:2
  You can't t. it with you HART 98:20
taken: quite surprised to be t. DE G 66:2
  right to be t. seriously HUMP 108:5
  t. charge of the asylum ROWL 185:17
  t. more out of alcohol CHUR 53:5
takes: T. two to tango HOFF 104:1
taking: t. things for granted HUXL 109:14
  way of t. life   FROST 86:18
talcum: A bit of t.   NASH 159:5
tale: any t. we happen to enact
                       PRIT 175:13
  I should have had a t. SCOTT 194:3
  t. that I heard told HOUS 107:10
  This most tremendous t. of all BETJ 31:4
  Trust the t.   LAWR 132:21
talent: A t. to amuse COW 61:17
  gilded tomb of a mediocre t.
                     SMITH 203:12
  greatest concentration of t. KENN 119:5
  his one really notable t. MENC 150:13
  I had no t. for writing BENC 27:4
  no substitute for t. HUXL 109:7
  t. instantly recognizes DOYLE 70:1
  t. to see clearly what AUDEN 13:20
  what it must and the t. BAR 18:13
talents: t. and our expectations DE B 65:13
tales: runic t. to sigh or sing FLEC 81:15
  T., marvellous tales   FLEC 81:6
talk: And the Cabots t. only to God
                       BOSS 36:12
  And the t. slid north KIPL 123:18
  by men who t. fluently HOGB 104:3

talk (cont.):
  Careless t. costs lives ANON 5:26
  come and t. to the plants CHAR 49:16
  If you t. to God, you SZASZ 211:18
  interviewing people who can't t.
                      ZAPPA 236:11
  I want to t. like a lady SHAW 199:19
  Money doesn't t., it swears DYLAN 71:7
  much my Ministers t. THAT 212:19
  nor good t. necessarily KIPL 127:16
  possible to t. to the unborn BARZ 20:10
  solemn t. of contemplation KAV 118:6
  t. about capitalism   BAR 20:9
  T. about the pews and steeples
                      CHES 51:20
  t. it over with Our Lord -JOHN 114:1
  t. of Swann at the Verdurins'
                      PROU 175:18
  t. on 'Sex and Civics' BETJ 31:6
  t. well but not too wisely MAUG 150:2
  t. with crowds and keep KIPL 126:15
  t. with the German Chancellor
                      CHAM 48:13
  To t. about the rest of us ANON 8:18
  We have ways of making men t.
                      YOUNG 236:8
talked: listen when his mate t.
                      WICK 226:23
talkers: thousand t. whose tongues
                      DYLAN 71:6
talking: I find I'm t. to myself BARN 18:21
  more money writing or t. AUDEN 13:15
  nation t. to itself   MILL 152:8
  never know what we are t. RUSS 186:20
  soon leaves off t.   BUTL 43:12
  T. of Michelangelo   ELIOT 75:14
  t. to you by telephone NIXON 161:2
  until I've finished t. ZAN 236:9
  was myself t. to myself BENC 26:17
talks: A person who t. when you
                      BIER 33:27
  She only t. about her hair THOM 216:5
tall: neat and adequately t. CHES 52:3
  short and the t.   HUGH 107:20
  T. as a crane   SITW 201:10
  t. ship and a star to steer MAS 148:16
  this the clay grew t. OWEN 166:12
Tallulah: T. [Bankhead] is always skating
                      CAMP 45:8
tambourine: Mr T. Man, play a song
                      DYLAN 71:11
tamed: For t. and shabby tigers
                      HODG 103:13
tames: one t. the work of art SONT 204:13
tamper: Would never want to t.
                      AUDEN 13:1
tangled: t. web do parents weave
                      NASH 159:2
tango: Takes two to t. HOFF 104:1
tank: T. come down the stalls SASS 192:2
Tanqueray: The Second Mrs T. BELL 24:15
tanstaafl: Oh, "t.". Means HEIN 100:1
tapers: When she lit her glimmering t.
                      THOM 215:12
tar: wine that tasted of the t. BELL 25:15
tariff: competitive t. for revenue
                      HOOV 104:13
tarnished: neither t. nor afraid CHAN 49:1
tart: t. who has finally married BAXT 20:15
tarts: by the action of two t. MACM 143:17
Tarzan: Me T., you Jane WEIS 224:5
task: President's hardest t. JOHN 114:15
  t. in life is to give birth FROMM 85:12
  There is but one t. for all KIPL 124:16

taste: A person of low t.   BIER 34:6
bouquet is better than the t.   POTT 173:17
common sense and good t.   SHAW 196:2
Ghastly good t., or a depressing
                         BETJ 31:13
Good t. and humour   MUGG 157:9
individuality have no t.   BENN 28:7
invariably have very bad t.   ORTON 164:5
taste is better than bad t.   BENN 28:7
together by a sense of t.   BALL 17:22
tasted: From what I've t. of desire
                         FROST 86:6
tastes: t. may not be the same   SHAW 198:8
tatter: t. in its mortal dress   YEATS 234:6
tattered: A t. coat upon a stick, unless
                         YEATS 234:6
tavern: has merely opened a t.   DOUG 68:16
taverns: t. while the tempest hurled
                         HOUS 105:14
tax: [t.] on the last slice   HEAL 99:9
taxes: Death and t. and childbirth
                         MITC 154:10
taxi: An empty t. arrived   CHUR 53:4
Like a t. throbbing waiting   ELIOT 76:24
you can't leave in a t.   KALM 117:12
taxi-cab: t. with both doors open
                         HUGH 107:19
taxis: are good at getting t.   WHIT 226:15
taxpayer: t. is to shoulder the losses
                         SNOW 204:3
tay: t. and stuff fit only   MAS 148:4
Tchaikovsky: tell T. the news   BERRY 30:13
tea: I'm going to be no t.   MANS 146:5
I makes t. I makes tea   JOYCE 116:4
little t. and sympathy   AND 5:2
Lunch, and T.   BELL 24:13
T., although an Oriental   CHES 50:21
t. for two and two   CAES 44:12
t. in which I had soaked   PROU 175:17
t. is brought at five o'clock
                         MONRO 155:2
t.'s out of the way   REED 179:5
there honey still for t.   BROO 40:15
there no Latin word for T.   BELL 25:12
this is coffee, I want t.   ARM 10:6
teabag: woman is like a t.   REAG 178:11
tea-cakes: With afternoon t. and scones
                         BETJ 31:12
teach: humility as well as t.   SHAW 199:26
T. the free man how to praise
                         AUDEN 13:4
t. there are approximately   SELL 194:8
T. us to care and not to care   ELIOT 73:17
t. you to be a gentleman   SHAW 197:24
teaches: From all that terror t.   CHES 51:18
He who cannot, t.   SHAW 198:14
tea-cup: And the crack in the t. opens
                         AUDEN 12:17
team: Is my t. ploughing   HOUS 106:17
tears: And keep your t.   PUDN 176:9
mist of t.   THOM 215:5
No t. in the writer   FROST 85:17
now am full of t.   YEATS 234:13
t. and sweat   CHUR 54:7
t. on a soundless-clapping   THOM 215:22
t. would come down to me   KIPL 125:20
To hazards whence no t.   HARDY 97:16
wind but t. are in my eyes   MAS 148:19
tease: t. in the High Pyrenees   BELL 25:15
tea-shops: Emperor in the low-class t.
                         BRAM 38:13
teatime: The typist home at t.   ELIOT 76:24

tea-tray: colour that of a t. painter
                         BLUNT 35:5
Tebbit: [Norman T.] rises   FOOT 82:11
Technik: *Diskussion mit Hanna!*—*über T.*
                         FRIS 85:10
Vorsprung durch T.   ANON 9:3
techniques: machines or of elaborate t.
                         RUTH 187:8
technology: beyond the province of t.
                         POPP 172:16
Discussion with Hanna—about t.
                         FRIS 85:10
Progress through t.   ANON 9:3
t. dons from Cambridge   AMIS 4:16
t. with the enthusiasm   LEVIN 136:9
tedding: And the t. and the spreading
                         BELL 25:15
teenie: Itsy bitsy t. weenie   VANCE 221:2
teeth: about him is his front t.   RUNY 186:2
I'd looked after me t.   AYRES 16:6
old bitch gone in the t.   POUND 174:6
People can clean their t.   JENK 112:23
shark has pretty t.   BREC 38:21
that women have fewer t.   RUSS 186:17
untying with the t.   BIER 33:26
teetotaller: I'm only a beer t.   SHAW 196:6
t. and often with vegetarian   ORW 165:2
telegram: t. to my wife in London
                         CHES 50:5
telegrams: life of t. and anger   FORS 83:16
telephone: historic t. call ever made
                         NIXON 161:2
television: are no plain women on t.
                         FORD 82:12
junior t. producers   AMIS 4:16
radio and t.   SARR 190:25
see bad t. for nothing   GOLD 92:2
sentences: 'What's on t.?'   ACE 1:5
T. has brought back murder   HITC 103:1
t. programmes are so much   ANON 8:12
thinking man's t.   HAMP 96:6
tell: closest friends won't t.   ANON 6:5
How can I t. what I think   FORS 83:9
I t. you   FRY 87:9
not t. with such high zest   OWEN 166:10
poem itself to t.   FROST 85:16
t. a lot about a fellow's   REAG 178:12
t. an old soldier   SHAW 195:16
T. me all   JOYCE 115:10
Tell me, t. me, tell me   JOYCE 115:11
T. Sid   ANON 8:16
t. Tchaikovsky   BERRY 30:13
T. them, because our fathers   KIPL 127:21
T. them I came, and no   DE L 66:9
t. them of us and say   EDM 72:3
T. us your phobias and we   BENC 26:22
t. you naught   CHES 50:8
those who cannot t.   RAL 177:9
you never can t.   SHAW 200:4
telling: A pity beyond all t.   YEATS 232:8
I shall be t. this with a sigh   FROST 86:4
tells: ask him how he is, t. you   TAYL 212:9
temper: Never lose your t.   PANK 167:8
t. till it would be dethrimental
                         O'CAS 162:19
truth that has lost its t.   GIBR 90:7
temperature: t. to the deathly inner
                         HESSE 102:4
tempered: this century, t. by war
                         KENN 119:11
tempest: taverns while the t.   HOUS 105:14
temps: *A la recherche du t. perdu*
                         PROU 175:15

tempt: are bad for me do not t.
                         SHAW 195:14
T. me no more   DAY-L 65:9
t. My Lady Poltagrue   BELL 25:17
temptation: combines the maximum of t.
                         SHAW 198:15
oughtn't to yield to t.   HOPE 104:15
t. because I have found   SHAW 195:14
t. is the greatest treason   ELIOT 75:1
t. to a rich and lazy nation   KIPL 124:17
temptations: protections against t.
                         TWAIN 219:14
t. both in wine and women   KITC 128:5
ten: Church clock at t.   BROO 40:15
It will probably take t.   BENN 27:16
T. Commandments an' a man
                         KIPL 123:15
T. days that shook the world   REED 179:7
Your starter for t.   GASC 88:17
tenants: T. of the house   ELIOT 73:13
tendance: *Je suis Marxiste*—t. Groucho
                         ANON 7:6
tendency: Groucho t.   ANON 7:6
tennis: Anybody on for a game of t.
                         SHAW 199:4
I never said 'T., anyone?'   BOGA 35:12
play t. with the net down   FROST 86:2
Tennyson: Lawn T., gentleman poet
                         JOYCE 116:7
[T.] could not think up   CHES 52:7
T. was not Tennysonian   JAMES 111:23
The bower we shrined to T.   HARDY 97:1
tension: Under the t., slip   ELIOT 74:6
tent: inside the t. pissing   JOHN 114:4
Our master Caesar is in the t.
                         YEATS 233:7
tentacles: dear octopus from whose t.
                         SMITH 202:6
term: T., holidays, t.   LEWIS 136:15
terminated: be t. when one or both
                         AUDEN 14:3
terminological: risk of t. inexactitude
                         CHUR 53:21
terrestrial: Was written on t. things
                         HARDY 97:11
terrible: A t. beauty is born   YEATS 233:9
isn't life a t. thing   THOM 214:10
it's got to be t.   PUZO 176:12
made them so t. to Helen   FORS 83:14
t. pain in all the diodes   ADAMS 1:13
that t. football club   MCGR 142:12
words T. Vaudeville   ACE 1:5
terrified: those t. vague fingers push
                         YEATS 234:21
territory: It comes with the t.   MILL 152:5
terror: adds a new t. to life   TREE 217:16
From all that t. teaches   CHES 51:18
nothing disturbed the even t.   SHAR 195:8
T. is the feeling   JOYCE 115:19
t. which paralyses needed   ROOS 183:1
victory in spite of all t.   CHUR 54:8
terrorist: t. and the hijacker   THAT 213:5
t. and the policeman both   CONR 59:29
Tess: had ended his sport with T.
                         HARDY 98:1
test: Beauty is the first t.   HARDY 96:18
t. of a first-rate intelligence   FITZ 80:16
t. of a leader   LIPP 137:14
t. of a vocation   SMITH 203:11
testament: Have you your t.   BEHAN 23:25
Texas: Deep in the heart of T.   HERS 102:2
Thames: Into the T.   FARJ 78:8
Not of Gennesareth, but T.   THOM 216:11

to-day: T. the Roman and his trouble
HOUS 107:1
toddle: t. safely home and die SASS 191:16
toe: clerical, printless t. BROO 40:12
toes: How cold my t. MILNE 153:1
  t. you will have trodden on CORN 61:10
toff: saunter along like a t. HARG 98:9
toffees: All the t. I chewed AYRES 16:6
together: May never come t. again
DAV 64:20
  never again so much t. MACN 144:14
toil: t., tears and sweat CHUR 54:7
Tokay: T. And sherry in the cupboard
BETJ 32:11
told: like to be t. the worst CHUR 54:13
  what we were formerly t. BLUN 35:1
tolerance: was such a thing as t.
WILS 229:5
tolerated: democracy is that it has t.
BEVAN 33:2
tolerates: that He t. their existence
BUTL 43:6
Tolstoy: any ring with Mr T. HEM 101:3
Tom: Ground control to Major T.
BOWIE 37:16
tomato: t. and I like to-mah-to GERS 89:16
tomatoes: like a couple of hot t. FIEL 79:7
tomb: This side the t. DAV 64:20
  t. of a mediocre talent SMITH 203:12
tombs: dust, in the cool t. SAND 189:16
  towers and t. and statues FLEC 81:17
tombstone: fight is a t. white KIPL 125:22
tomes: Deep cargoes of gigantic t.
BELL 26:5
Tommy: O it's T. this, an' Tommy
KIPL 123:5
tomorrow: cleaning. And t. morning
REED 178:19
  dwell in the house of t. GIBR 90:5
  For t. we shall die PARK 168:19
  Leave t. behind COW 61:15
  today—in next week t. GRAH 92:19
  t. every Duchess in London MACD 142:2
  T. for the young the poets AUDEN 15:9
  T. I'll sit at the table HUGH 108:1
  t. is another day MITC 154:12
  t. will be our doubts ROOS 183:12
  word for doing things t. SHAW 195:21
to-morrow: t. we will run faster FITZ 80:21
tomorrows: dividend from time's t.
SASS 191:14
  For your t. these gave EDM 72:3
ton: mighty ships ten thousand t.
HODG 103:12
Tone: And Robert Emmet and Wolfe T.
YEATS 234:1
tones: t. as dry and level AUDEN 15:8
tongue: From lies of t. and pen CHES 51:18
  our sweet English t. FLEC 81:23
  picked a pocket with his t. BIER 33:25
  t. into the corners ELIOT 75:14
  t. taking a trip of three NAB 158:12
  would not yield to the t. BIER 33:26
tongued: dead is t. with fire beyond
ELIOT 74:17
tongues: t. of flame are in-folded
ELIOT 74:23
  t. that have not Thee KIPL 126:11
  whose t. were all broken DYLAN 71:6
tonic: wicked as a ginless t. COPE 60:20
tonight: in town t. ANON 8:2
  Not t., Josephine DAVID 64:18
  t. is my guest night HALL 95:10

too: Done because we are t. HARDY 96:22
  golf and t. old to rush ADAMS 1:18
  Three o'clock is always t. SART 191:10
  T. kind, too kind NIGH 160:14
  t. young to take up golf ADAMS 1:18
took: 'E went an' t.—the same as me
KIPL 127:5
  which I t. from thee THOM 215:19
tools: t. and we will finish CHUR 53:9
toothbrush: t. too is airing in this
BETJ 32:5
tooth-decay: t. in His divine system
HELL 100:5
toothpaste: t. is out of the tube HALD 95:8
tooth-point: Exactly where each t. goes
KIPL 124:7
top: Room at the t. BRAI 38:12
  T. of the world GOFF 91:8
  T. people take *The Times* ANON 8:25
  You're the t. PORT 173:9
top hat: T. I'm puttin' on my t. BERL 30:2
tops: whipping t. and help HODG 103:12
torch: The t.; be yours to hold
MCCR 141:18
  t. has been passed KENN 119:11
torchlight: T. crimson on the copper
CHES 51:17
Tories: revolutionaries are potential T.
ORW 164:15
torrent: leave it to a t. of change
CHES 51:14
torture: form of self-imposed t. MILL 152:9
  So does t. AUDEN 13:13
torturer: life and the t.'s horse AUDEN 13:6
Tory: burning hatred for the T. BEVAN 33:7
  T.'s secret weapon KILM 121:10
tosh: Never did I read such t.
WOOLF 231:11
totalitarianism: name of t. or the holy
GAND 88:10
totem: And under the t. poles
MACN 144:12
totem-symbol: grin on his face and a t.
KOES 128:14
totter: And t. towards the tomb SAY 192:12
touch: keep in t. with us BEEC 22:14
tough: t. get going KENN 120:1
toujours: t. gai toujours gai MARQ 146:18
tour: Magical mystery t. LENN 135:9
tourist: camera makes everyone a t.
SONT 204:14
  t. the last enchantments BEER 23:6
tournament: We in the t.— you against
me BETJ 32:1
tous: T. les êtres humains naissent ANON 9:1
  T. les jours, à tous points COUÉ 61:13
tout: ten to t. for flattery COLL 58:5
toward: T. heaven, till the tree FROST 86:5
towards: Neither from nor t. ELIOT 74:5
towering: height of his own t. style
CHES 52:7
towers: t. and tombs and statues
FLEC 81:17
town: A haunted t. it is to me LANG 130:2
  air to be *in t.* tonight ANON 8:2
  All over t. BURKE 42:13
  anyone lived in a pretty how t.
CUMM 63:13
  destroy the t. to save ANON 7:2
  down to the end of the t. MILNE 153:7
  Enormous through the Sacred T.
BELL 26:5
  enough majority in any t. TWAIN 219:2

town (*cont.*):
  helluva t. COMD 58:7
  means our own dear t. to us COW 62:2
  night in the small t. THOM 214:7
  The t. will follow you CAV 48:2
towns: t. all Inns have been driven
BELL 25:24
  t. in all the world EPST 77:17
townspeople: I will teach you my t.
WILL 227:22
toy: eyes gleam over a new t. BELL 24:22
trace: Frost has risen without t.
MUGG 157:6
  it is also a t. SONT 204:15
  Projecting trait and t. HARDY 97:3
  t. almost all the disasters WAUGH 223:1
track: T. twenty nine GORD 92:4
trade: half a t. and half an art INGE 110:17
  Irish poets, learn your t. YEATS 233:2
  pre-eminence in her Colonial t.
GEOR 89:7
  There isn't any T. HERB 101:21
  T. Unionism of the married SHAW 198:3
trades: It is the best of all t. BELL 25:11
trade unionist: T. when you want to
change BEVIN 33:15
trade unions: first snarl of the t.
LLOY 138:7
tradition: T. may be defined CHES 51:13
  We don't want t. FORD 82:18
traduced: Someone must have t. Joseph
KAFKA 117:6
Trafalgar Square: T. and started again
CHAR 50:2
traffic: mighty roar of London's t.
ANON 8:2
tragedies: There are two t. in life
SHAW 198:6
  with the t. of antiquity STOP 209:18
tragedy: farce and the food a t. POW 174:17
  I will write you a t. FITZ 80:15
  most tremendous t. BEER 23:2
  That is what t. means STOP 210:1
  t. for a poet COCT 57:4
  t. of a man who has found BARR 19:24
  washy way of true t. KAV 118:9
tragic: acted so t. the house HARG 98:10
  essentially a t. age LAWR 132:7
trahison: *La t. des clercs* BENDA 27:5
trail: long, long t. awinding KING 122:8
  t. has its own stern code SERV 195:1
train: electric t. set any boy WELL 224:10
  headlight of an oncoming t. DICK 67:10
  Let the t. take the strain ANON 7:13
  Runs the red electric t. BETJ 31:7
  t. and tram alternate go BETJ 31:19
  t. for London town MILLS 152:20
  t. needs one of its passengers STOP 210:3
  t. of events has carried AMERY 4:14
  Trust the t., Mademoiselle CHR 53:1
  who shaves and takes a t. WHITE 226:3
  will pack, and take a t. BROO 40:13
training: T. is everything TWAIN 219:30
trains: through the fields in t. CHES 51:8
trait: Projecting t. and trace HARDY 97:3
traité: *n'est pas un t. de paix* FOCH 82:7
traités: *Les t., voyez-vous* DE G 65:17
tram: I'm not even a bus, I'm a t.
HARE 98:7
  train and t. alternate BETJ 31:19
tramp: That's why the lady is a t.
HART 98:18
trance: off this traveller's t. DAY-L 65:8

tranquillity: chaos remembered in t.
                        THUR 217:3
  Sorrow is t. remembered   PARK 168:4
tranquillized: These are the t. *Fifties*
                        LOW 140:3
transform: those who t. the world
                        AUDEN 14:1
transformed: dreams he found himself t.
                        KAFKA 117:9
  t. into an institution   SART 190:27
translate: Shakespeare is not to t.
                        BEER 22:25
translated: T. Daughter, come down
                        AUDEN 15:12
translation: A t. is no translation
                        SYNGE 211:9
  Poetry is what is lost in t. FROST 86:17
  unfaithful to the t.   BORG 36:8
translations: T. (like wives)   CAMP 45:13
transmit: To t. that feeling   SANS 190:5
transsexuals: only to aspiring male t.
                        LEB 133:22
Tranter Reuben: While T.   BETJ 31:2
trap: baiting a mouse-t.   SAKI 188:20
traum: *schreit im T. um Hilfe* CAN 46:9
travailler: *t. devant la majestueuse*
                        FRAN 84:15
travel: classes of t.   BENC 27:1
  I t. light; as light   FRY 86:25
  man can t. who will   FRY 86:25
  The *real* way to t.   GRAH 92:19
  t. in the direction   BERR 30:15
travelled: care which way he t. BEAV 21:4
  I took the one less t.   FROST 86:4
  t. each and ev'ry highway ANKA 5:7
traveller: t. who has gone to Italy
                        FORS 84:4
  World-besotted t.   YEATS 236:2
Travellers: sit outside at 'The T.'
                        HARDY 97:2
travelling: been t. round the world
                        COOK 60:9
travels: t. the fastest who travels
                        KIPL 127:15
  t. the world in search MOORE 155:8
trays: cheap tin t.   MAS 148:3
tread: me a light that I may t. HASK 99:3
  Tread softly because you t. YEATS 235:7
treason: temptation is the greatest t.
                        ELIOT 75:1
treasure: it as your chiefest t. BELL 24:4
treat: And he who gives a child a t.
                        MAS 148:11
  Talk about a t.   COLL 58:4
  t. if met where any bar HARDY 98:3
treaties: T., you see, are like girls
                        DE G 65:17
treatment: benefit from . . . t. REED 179:6
  scientific t. for all diseases SHAW 196:12
  suitable case for t.   MERC 151:6
treaty: not a peace t.   FOCH 82:7
  signed the t. bred a fever THOM 214:5
tree: A billboard lovely as a t. NASH 159:14
  A-hanging on the t.   CART 47:8
  A poem lovely as a t.   KILM 121:8
  by climbing a birch t.   FROST 86:5
  If he finds that this t.   KNOX 128:10
trees: And with the t. to newer birth
                        GREN 94:3
  darkness among the gusty t.
                        NOYES 161:16
  green grass and bursting t. GREN 94:3

trees (*cont.*):
  Loveliest of t., the cherry now
                        HOUS 106:9
  My apple t. will never get FROST 86:10
  t. and flapped and fought HODG 103:10
  t. because they seem more CATH 47:15
  t. that grow so fair   KIPL 126:3
tree-tops: Where the t. glisten BERL 30:3
trembled: could think there t. through
                        HARDY 97:11
trembles: It t. to a lily   DOBS 68:3
tremulous: postern behind my t. stay
                        HARDY 97:10
trenches: t. and trying on gas-masks
                        CHAM 48:12
Trent: Or why was Burton built on T.
                        HOUS 107:8
trespass: And t. there and go HOUS 106:4
  cannot t. with impunity AUDEN 13:16
tress: A little stolen t.   YEATS 234:17
trial: object that it is not a t. KAFKA 117:7
  this hour and this t.   CHUR 55:18
  t. of which you can have SHAW 197:1
trials: t. of vigilance and exertion
                        CHUR 53:9
tribal: constructing t. lays KIPL 123:2
  t. God who has made   BURR 42:16
  t., intimate revenge   HEAN 99:12
tribe: To purify the dialect of the t.
                        ELIOT 74:19
  with thy t.'s black tents THOM 215:21
tribulation: who must inherit the t.
                        HOOV 104:10
tribute: t. a French translator BEER 22:25
trick: A T. that everyone abhors
                        BELL 24:19
  dream when the long t.'s MAS 148:18
  play fair to win the t.   LAB 129:7
  t. lies in *losing* wars   HELL 100:6
  t. of wearing mink   BALM 18:1
tricks: These and a thousand t.
                        WATS 222:17
tried: been t. and found wanting
                        CHES 52:8
  has been t. at least once BENN 27:12
  pick the one I never t. WEST 225:17
Trieste: Stettin in the Baltic to T.
                        CHUR 53:15
trifling: most t. of his works OSLER 165:24
trigger: finger do you want on the t.
                        ANON 9:15
triggers: stuck to our starboard t.
                        ASQ 11:20
trilogy: Clayhanger t. is good BENN 28:2
trinket: I swung the earth a t.
                        THOM 215:14
trinkets: ye returned to your t. KIPL 124:12
triomphe: *point le t. mais le combat*
                        COUB 61:12
trip: look forward to the t. STIN 209:9
  t. through a sewer   MIZN 154:20
triple: There be t. ways to take KIPL 124:5
tripled: Hers of the Book, the t. Crown
                        QUIL 177:3
triple-towered: The t. sky DAY-L 65:7
tristesse: *Adieu t.*   ELUA 77:14
  Bonjour t.   ELUA 77:14
triumph: A t. of the embalmer's art
                        VIDAL 221:14
  meet with T. and Disaster KIPL 126:13
  our career and our t.   VANZ 221:5
  t. of modern science WAUGH 223:7
triumphs: t. that are the aftermath
                        HOOV 104:10

trivial: t. people should muse LAWR 132:18
  t. personalities decomposing
                        WOOLF 231:9
trivialities: t. where opposites BOHR 35:14
trod: T. beside me, close and dear
                        HOUS 107:5
trois: *T. heures, c'est toujours* SART 191:10
Trojan: T. 'orses will jump out BEVIN 33:12
troops: I intend to march my t. GRIM 94:8
tropical: night of t. splendour PORT 172:19
Trotsky: [T.] and had a chat ROG 182:13
trotting: T. through the dark KIPL 126:6
trouble: The t. with Senator Long
                        ICKES 110:3
  time of t. when   MARQ 147:5
  To-day the Roman and his t.
                        HOUS 107:1
  t. of all kinds and keeping BUTL 43:24
  t. with [Sigmund] Freud DODD 68:5
  t. with this country ADAMS 1:19
  very present help in t. STEV 209:7
  Wenlock Edge the wood's in t.
                        HOUS 106:9
  When in t., delegate   BOREN 36:7
  When there's t. brewing KNIG 128:8
  You have to take t.   BENN 28:2
troubled: And t. with religious doubt
                        CHES 51:22
  put out on the t. seas   GALB 88:3
  t. midnight and the noon's ELIOT 76:3
troubles: all my t. seemed so far
                        LENN 135:16
  From t. of the world   HARV 99:2
  has got over all its t.   JER 113:13
  sleep with a woman whose t. ALGR 3:6
  t. of our proud and angry HOUS 105:15
  your t. in your old kit-bag ASAF 10:13
trouser-clip: illuminated t. for bicyclists
                        MORT 156:17
trousers: bottoms of my t. rolled
                        ELIOT 75:19
  t. on when you go out IBSEN 109:21
  wear white flannel t.   ELIOT 75:19
trowel: With his t. point, letter HEAN 99:11
Troy: another T. for her to burn
                        YEATS 232:11
truce: no t. or parley with you CHUR 53:10
truckin: Keep on t.'   CRUMB 63:12
trucks: lot to learn about t. AWDRY 15:18
  t. along the lines below BETJ 31:19
true: And is it t.? And is it true BETJ 31:4
  believe is not necessarily t. BELL 24:2
  be substantially t.   SANT 190:18
  course of t. anything   BUTL 43:11
  danger of their coming t. SMITH 202:19
  her ear, 'You are not t.' WILB 226:24
  long enough it will be t. BENN 28:17
  no matter how t.   VIDAL 221:13
  Of t. wood, of yew wood DOYLE 70:2
  only things that are t. SHAW 196:4
  people say of us is t. SMITH 202:18
  pessimist fears this is t. CAB 44:11
  supposing it is t.   RUSS 186:23
  t. men of action in our AUDEN 14:1
  t. proposition is more apt WHIT 226:7
  what we are saying is t. RUSS 186:20
true-blue: die like a t. rebel HILL 102:11
truer: t. than if they had really
                        HEM 100:10
trumpet: The flute and the t. AUDEN 14:11
  Yet ever and anon a t. sounds
                        THOM 215:17

trumpets: are the eagles and the t. ELIOT 73:10

trunk: branches up a snow-white t. FROST 86:5
So large a t. before BELL 24:9

trust: Because I don't t. him BREC 39:4
can't t. the 'specials' COLL 58:2
Never t. the artist LAWR 132:21
T. the train, Mademoiselle CHR 53:1
t. thou hast in me HOPE 105:3
t. yourself when all men KIPL 126:13

trusted: it is not to be t. BROD 39:12

truth: An exaggeration is a t. GIBR 90:7
Art is not t. PIC 171:7
Bigotry tries to keep t. TAG 212:2
decade after decade the t. SOLZ 204:5
economical with the t. ARMS 10:11
fable becomes the t. COCT 57:6
here have Pride and T. YEATS 232:15
I just tell the t. TRUM 218:7
improbable, must be the t. DOYLE 69:22
joking is to tell the t. SHAW 197:3
lawyer interprets the t. GIR 90:17
Let's tell them the t. STEV 209:4
mainly he told the t. TWAIN 218:20
mistook disenchantment for t. SART 191:8
murder, for the t. ADLER 2:16
never ending battle for t. ANON 6:8
Nobody speaks the t. when BOWEN 37:11
Now God will know the t. LUCAS 140:9
opposite is also a profound t. BOHR 35:14
Photography is t. GOD 91:3
platitude is simply a t. BALD 17:6
policy to speak the t. JER 113:6
possesses not only t. RUSS 186:22
Strict Regard for T. BELL 24:14
telling the t. about them STEV 208:19
than a t. misunderstood JAMES 112:16
that T. is a pathless land KRIS 129:1
The t. is cruel, but it SANT 190:15
truer than the t. ANOU 9:21
trusted to speak the t. BALF 17:21
t. about his or her love WEST 225:26
truth and to live the t. NIXON 161:1
T. exists BRAQ 38:17
t. has got his boots on CALL 45:2
T. has no special time SCHW 193:13
t. is often a terrible weapon ADLER 2:16
t. is something that everyone MCC 141:11
T. is the first casualty PONS 172:12
T. is the glue that holds FORD 82:13
T. is the most valuable TWAIN 219:9
t. is to pay too high ROS 184:18
t. when he knows the t. PÉGUY 169:23
t. which makes men free AGAR 2:19
unpleasant way of saying the t. HELL 100:7

truthful: true Poets must be t. OWEN 166:8

truths: between the two sorts of t. BOHR 35:14
repetition of unpalatable t. SUMM 211:2
There are no new t. MCC 141:11
There are no whole t. WHIT 226:8
t. begin as blasphemies SHAW 195:10
t. being in and out FROST 86:14
T. that become old become OUSP 166:4
t. which must serve KENN 119:7
t. without a recogniton BELL 24:2
verities and t. of the heart FAUL 78:12

try: *Just t. to please everyone* SWOPE 211:6

try (*cont.*):
T. thinking of love FRY 87:7
t. to get between them STR 210:10
We're number two. We t. harder ANON 9:9

trying: business without really t. MEAD 150:10
He just goes on t. other PIC 171:5
I am t. to be SMITH 202:12
t. every experience once BAX 20:14
t. we can easily learn TWAIN 219:15

tryst: T. with the moon, and deep DRIN 70:4

tube: toothpaste is out of the t. HALD 95:8

tubers: A little life with dried t. ELIOT 76:13

tuckets: Then the t., then the trumpets CHES 51:17

tuckoo: little boy named baby t. JOYCE 115:16

Tucson: T. and Deadwood and Lost BENÉT 27:7

tue: *On t. un homme, on est* ROST 185:8

tulips: Here t. bloom as they are told BROO 40:11
Tiptoe through the t. DUBIN 70:6

tumble: And t. victuals in RAL 177:10

tumour: But not when it ripens in a t. ABSE 1:2

tumult: Drove to this t. in the clouds YEATS 235:5
The t. and the shouting dies KIPL 126:9
The t. and the shouting dies KNOX 128:11

tune: good t. played on an old BUTL 44:9
guy who could carry a t. CROS 63:7
thinkin'll turn into a t. HUBB 107:16
t. in and drop out LEARY 133:15
t. is catching and will AUDEN 14:8
we complain about the t. BEVAN 33:4

tunes: beauty like slow old t. MAS 148:6

tunic: soldier's ribbon on a t. ABSE 1:3

tunnel: Down some profound dull t. OWEN 166:15
light at the end of the t. DICK 67:10
light at the end of the t. LOW 139:21

tuppence: t. for your old watch chain COLL 58:4

turbot: 'T., Sir,' said the waiter WELBY 224:6

Turkish: T. this side SAPP 190:21

turn: Because I do not hope to t. ELIOT 73:16
goodnight and quickly t. YEATS 235:2
I t. to ducks HARV 99:2
To t. you out, to turn KIPL 123:3
T. that off WILL 227:20
T. up the lights HENRY 101:12
you must t. on, tune in LEARY 133:15

turned: t. us around like this RILKE 181:4

turning: And t. your face to the light SASS 191:18
gate where they're t. AUDEN 14:14
lady's not for t. THAT 213:2
point of the t. world ELIOT 74:5
some advice I've been t. FITZ 80:18
t. before we have learnt CONN 59:17
t. in the widening gyre YEATS 233:12
t. the tide of world war CHUR 54:12

turnip: candle in that great t. CHUR 53:16

turophile: t. no such thing as a *bad* FAD 78:5

turtle: t. lives 'twixt plated NASH 159:19

tusky: Crocodile's musky t. mouth KIPL 125:14

TV: T.—a clever contraction ACE 1:5

twaddle: But better far write t. MANS 146:7

twain: never the t. shall meet KIPL 123:17

twangs: t. and breaks at the end MACN 144:15

tweet: and I say 't. t.' SAR 190:24

twelve: At t. noon, the natives swoon COW 62:4
ruin himself in t. months GEOR 89:5

twelve-winded: And yon t. sky HOUS 107:2

twentieth: The problem of the t. century DUB 70:8
twentieth century BEVAN 32:18

twenty: armistice for t. years FOCH 82:7
chord of C major t. times BEEC 22:6
It means t. things BENN 28:8
t. minutes you ought BRAB 37:20
T. will not come again HOUS 106:9

twenty-four: then we shall be t. HOUS 105:13

twenty-twenty: Hindsight is always t. WILD 227:1

twice: But if it had to perish t. FROST 86:6
Don't think t., it's all right DYLAN 71:5
nonsense can I stand t. or once RICH 181:1
something that will be read t. CONN 58:14
The postman always rings t. CAIN 44:17
t. as often as any other COKE 57:6
t. as well as men WHIT 226:21

twigs: The bleak t. overhead HARDY 97:11

twilight: again in the gray t. YEATS 232:6
full Surrey t. BETJ 32:3
In a t. dim with rose DE L 66:6

twilights: In ancient shadows and t. AE 2:18

twins: Clara threw the t. she nursed GRAH 92:13

twirled: ships are t. and spun HODG 103:12

twist: Give 'em a t., a flick HEAT 99:18
I have NO MORE t. POTT 173:11
Let him t. slowly EHRL 72:10

twisted: And they t. it with relish NIXON 160:16

two: Between t. evils, I always WEST 225:17
game at which t. can play BEER 23:18
Just tea for t. and two CAES 44:12
making in all, t. BIER 34:9
Takes t. to tango HOFF 104:1
To think that t. and two HOUS 106:2
T. cheers for Democracy FORS 84:6
t. classes of pedestrians DEWAR 67:8
T. for a woman BEEC 22:11
t. glasses and two chairs MACN 144:13
t. people miserable instead BUTL 43:14
t. things about the horse ROYD 185:19
t. things that will TARK 212:5
t. things they disliked MAUG 149:13
worth t. in the street WEST 225:9

Twye: T. was soaping her breasts EWART 78:2

Tyne: from the Severn to the T. KIPL 126:19

types: Seven t. of ambiguity EMPS 77:16

typewriter: changing a t. ribbon BENC 26:19

typing: writing at all— it's t. CAP 46:14

typist: The t. home at teatime ELIOT 76:24

tyrannize: t. over his bank balance KEYN 120:16

tyranny: against a monstrous t.   CHUR 54:8
  conditions of t. it is far easier   AREN 10:3
  lightened the burden of t.   SHAW 198:7
  long dark night of t.   MURR 158:8
  submission to an unnecessary t.
                           RUSS 186:13
  T. is always better organised
                          PÉGUY 169:24
tyrant: A t.'s authority for crime
                          BIER 34:15
tyrants: curry favour with t.   ZAP 236:10
  stuff of which t.   BEAV 21:7
Tyre: Is one with Nineveh, and T.
                          KIPL 126:10
  which men still call T.   FLEC 81:19
Tyrone: steeples of Fermanagh and T.
                          CHUR 54:2

U

U: U and Non-U   ROSS 184:20
ugly: Once sex rears its u. 'ead   ALL 4:9
  The good, the bad, and the u.
                          SCAR 192:16
  upon solid rock the u.   MILL 151:19
  world for u. mathematics   HARDY 96:18
ulcer: I am an 8 U. Man on 4 Ulcer
                          EARLY 71:16
Ulster: The betrayal of U.   CAIR 44:19
  U. says no   ANON 9:2
Ulysses: hand that wrote U.   JOYCE 116:15
  touching on one aspect of U.   FORS 83:10
umbrella: Be sure that your u.
                          BURKE 42:13
  u. might pacify barbarians   PLOM 172:8
umbrellas: who possess u.   FORS 83:15
umpire: The u., the pavilion cat
                          LANG 130:4
unable: I am u. to concentrate   GEOR 89:10
unacceptable: u. face of capitalism
                          HEATH 99:16
unaltered: u. in the cataclysm   CHUR 54:2
unattractive: not against the u.   GREE 93:13
Unaufrichtigkeit: U. zwischen Mensch
                          BAUM 20:13
unaware: And I was u.   HARDY 97:11
unbearable: unbeatable: in victory u.
                          CHUR 53:3
unbeatable: In defeat u.   CHUR 53:3
unbeautiful: u. and have comfortable
                          CUMM 63:17
unborn: possible to talk to the u.
                          BARZ 20:10
unbribed: man will do u.   WOLFE 230:24
uncomfortable: moral when he is only u.
                          SHAW 197:30
uncommon: very u. cook   SAKI 188:2
unconditional: u. war on poverty in
  America   JOHN 114:10
unconscious: call it the *personal u.*
                          JUNG 117:3
  call the *collective u.*   JUNG 117:3
  irony is generally quite u.   BUTL 43:15
  The deep well of u. cerebration
                         JAMES 111:13
uncorseted: U., her friendly bust
                          ELIOT 75:9
uncrossed: The cross be u.   ELIOT 74:16
undaunted: u. by odds, unwearied
                          CHUR 54:12

undecided: decided only to be u.
                          CHUR 54:5
under: get out and get u.   CLAR 56:11
  I'd have been u. the host   PARK 167:14
  I've got you u. my skin   PORT 173:1
  U. Mirabeau Bridge flows   APOL 9:22
underachiever: that basically he's an u.
                          ALLEN 3:16
under-belly: exposure of the u. of the Axis
                          CHUR 54:14
undercuts: Is incontestable. It u.   FRY 87:1
under-dogs: Englishman among the u.
                          WAUGH 223:8
underestimating: money by u. the
  intelligence   MENC 150:15
undergraduates: U. owe their happiness
  chiefly   BEER 22:23
underground: And breastless creatures u.
                          ELIOT 75:8
undergrowth: Slouching in the u.
                          HODG 103:14
underlined: Is u. for emphasis   ELIOT 75:9
underneath: Though u. that gloomy shell
                          ANON 7:26
  U. the Arches   FLAN 81:2
  U. this flabby exterior   LEV 136:3
undersold: never knowingly u.
                          LEWIS 136:16
understand: confused doesn't really u.
                          MURR 158:6
  Everyone wants to u. art   PIC 171:8
  Grown-ups never u. anything
                          SAIN 187:18
  It's all they can u.   MELBA 150:12
  Nor can anyone u. Ein   ANON 6:22
  people who don't u. them   BRUCE 41:15
  really don't u. too hot   SAL 189:1
  The shire for Men who U.   BROO 40:13
  think I u. people very well   FORS 83:19
  u. what is happening   CHAM 48:10
  What you can't u.   DYLAN 71:14
  yet u. the exact   HEAN 99:12
understanding: cod passeth all u.
                          LUTY 140:16
  foolish their lack of u.   BIER 34:5
  not by force but by u.   BRON 39:17
understood: how well they u.   AUDEN 13:5
  music is best u. by children   STR 210:15
  u. this liking for war   BENN 27:19
undertakers: nothing against u. personally
                          MITF 154:13
undertaking: no such u. has been received
                          CHAM 48:15
undeserving: I'm one of the u. poor
                          SHAW 199:21
undesirable: Miss, I knows an u. character
                          FRY 87:9
  u. to believe a proposition   RUSS 186:23
undeveloped: u. hearts   FORS 83:2
undo: To u. the folded lie   AUDEN 13:9
undone: not thought death had u.
                          ELIOT 76:17
undressing: it is as if she is u.   COL 57:16
undulating: indolent expression and an u.
                          BELL 25:4
uneasy: one morning from u. dreams
                          KAFKA 117:9
uneconomic: shown it to be 'u.'   SCH 193:9
uneducated: government by the u.
                          CHES 51:9
  u. man to read books   CHUR 55:11
unemotional: same cold and u. manner
                          DOYLE 69:19

unemployment: production and reduce u.
                          HEATH 99:17
  u. today is exacting from   TEBB 212:10
unexpected: Old age is the most u.
                          TROT 218:3
  u. constantly occurs   MAH 145:4
unfaithful: u. to the translation   BORG 36:8
unfathomable: The u. deep   THOM 214:17
unfinished: Liberty is always u. business
                          ANON 7:15
unforeseen: contingent and the u.
                          FISH 80:5
unforgiveness: An alp of u. grew
                          PLOM 172:5
unforgiving: If you can fill the u. minute
                          KIPL 126:15
unhappily: result of being u. married
                          PARK 169:14
  The bad end u., the good   STOP 210:1
unhappiness: loyalty we all feel to u.
                          GREE 93:15
  profession but a vocation of u.   SIM 201:2
  U. is best defined   DE B 65:13
  volatile spirits prefer u.   SANT 190:10
unhappy: As soon as one is u. one
                          PROU 175:20
  different from that of the u.   WITT 230:3
  instinct for being u.   SAKI 188:4
  Men who are u.   RUSS 186:9
  only speak when she is u.   SMITH 203:24
  See an old u. bull   HODG 103:14
  U. the land that has no   BREC 39:2
  U. the land that needs   BREC 39:2
  which make us so u.   JOYCE 116:5
unhealthy: unscrupulous men for u.
                          BEEC 22:10
unheard: language of the u.   KING 122:7
unholy: Refrain from the u. pleasure
                          BELL 24:4
unhurt: U. people are not much good
                          STAR 207:4
unicorn: it is rarer than the u.   JONG 115:2
uniform: The u. 'e wore   KIPL 123:9
uninterested: can exist is an u. person
                          CHES 51:2
uninteresting: earth as an u. subject
                          CHES 51:2
unions: there would have been no u.
                          BALD 17:15
  u. and the industrialists   NIEM 160:13
unique: The British nation is u.
                          CHUR 54:13
unite: black people in this country to u.
                          CARM 46:19
United States: including the U.   CHUR 54:11
  must be purely to the U.   ROOS 184:5
  U. by force   HARD 96:15
  U. helpless and contemptible   WILS 229:8
universal: adaptation to the u. conditions
                          JUNG 117:2
  it's as u. as sea sickness   SHAW 198:1
  The writer must be u.   BARN 18:18
universe: cover the u. with mud
                          FORS 83:10
  essential function of the u.   BERG 29:12
  good u. next door   CUMM 64:3
  Great Architect of the U.   JEANS 112:22
  Life exists in the u. only   JEANS 112:21
  our world, our u.   KUMAR 129:6
  repetitious mechanism of the U.
                          WHIT 226:6
  that part of the u.   BECK 21:8
  This u. is not hostile   HOLM 104:6

universe (*cont.*):
U. and Everything   ADAMS 1:14
u. from one tiny part   BENÉT 27:9
u. is not only queerer   HALD 95:6
u. you can be certain   HUXL 109:15
visible u. was an illusion   BORG 36:9
universities: u. go on a Government grant
                                     MAUG 150:1
university: be able to get to a u.
                                     KINN 122:16
benefiting from u. training   AMIS 4:15
French letters to the u.   JOYCE 116:12
from Jimmy's u.   OSB 165:17
gained in the U. of Life   BOTT 37:1
We are the U.   SPR 206:14
unkempt: U. about those hedges blows
                                     BROO 40:11
unkind: That are sodden and u.   BELL 25:25
unknotted: So the knot be u.   ELIOT 74:16
unknown: buried the U. Prime Minister
                                     ASQ 11:12
glorious and the u.   FORS 83:12
Like a complete u.   DYLAN 71:8
O friend unseen, unborn, u.   FLEC 81:23
side of the U. Soldier   ASQ 11:12
tread safely into the u.   HASK 99:3
unleashed: u. power of the atom has
                                     EINS 73:2
unlike: So u. anything else   WOD 230:21
unlimited: conveying u. sexual attraction
                                     HARD 96:16
unlivable: live in an u. situation
                                     LAING 129:14
unluckily: the good u.   STOP 210:1
unlucky: It was his u. night   MCH 142:13
who is so u.   MARQ 147:8
unmarried: keep u. as long as he can
                                     SHAW 197:26
unmemorable: their utterly u. contents
                                     SHAW 199:11
unnatural: most u. of all the sexual
                                     HUXL 108:17
U., he called them   SHAR 195:9
unnecessary: said at once 'The U. War'
                                     CHUR 55:17
unnerved: As Cook is a little u. BETJ 31:11
unofficial: An English u. rose   BROO 40:11
It is the u. force   DOYLE 69:24
unpalatable: disastrous and the u.
                                     GALB 88:5
unparalleled: drift toward u. catastrophe
                                     EINS 73:2
unpardonable: Presidency is an u. vice
                                     JOHN 114:14
unpicked: their climate, still u. DOUG 68:9
unpleasant: Cynicism is an u. way
                                     HELL 100:7
How u. to meet Mr Eliot   ELIOT 74:1
unpopular: I was not u. there   BEER 22:22
where it is safe to be u.   STEV 208:22
unprepared: Magnificently u.   CORN 61:7
unprincipled: sold by the u.   CAPP 46:17
unravelled: must all be u. from within
                                     CHR 52:21
unreal: U. City   ELIOT 76:17
unreality: u. of the fable becomes
                                     COCT 57:6
unreasonable: progress depends on the u.
                                     SHAW 198:23
unregulated: And there the u. sun
                                     BROO 40:11
unremembering: She went her u. way
                                     THOM 214:21
Their u. hearts and heads   YEATS 233:2

unremitting: u. humanity soon had me
                                     BENN 28:1
unrequited: Self-love seems so often u.
                                     POW 174:16
unsafe: U. at any speed   NADER 158:17
unscrupulous: by u. men for unhealthy
                                     BEEC 22:10
unseen: O friend u., unborn, unknown
                                     FLEC 81:23
unselfish: u. and unsordid financial
                                     CHUR 55:1
unselfishly: U. so we might have today
                                     MCH 142:13
unselfishness: sympathetic u. of an oyster
                                     SAKI 188:5
unsettle: They only u. him   WOD 230:4
unsuccessful: Like an u. literary man
                                     BELL 25:4
unsung: And some u., and that may
                                     THOM 216:1
untalented: product of the u.   CAPP 46:17
untamed: u. and intractable   ELIOT 74:7
untidy: corner, some u. spot   AUDEN 13:6
until: u. the pips squeak   GEDD 89:2
untilled: And all the u. air between
                                     AUDEN 12:14
untried: difficult; and left u.   CHES 52:8
untrue: A man who's u. to his wife
                                     AUDEN 14:20
untruth: transfigured them into U.
                                     LARK 131:6
untutored: with which the u. savage
                                     FRAZ 84:17
untying: u. with the teeth a political
                                     BIER 33:26
unvictorious: u. ones   SASS 191:19
unwarranted: acquisition of u. influence
                                     EIS 73:6
unwearied: u. in their constant challenge
                                     CHUR 54:12
unyielding: foundation of u. despair
                                     RUSS 186:21
up: English u. with which   CHUR 55:15
U., lad: when the journey's
                                     HOUS 106:10
U., up and away   WEBB 223:24
was wrong, 'U. to a point'
                                     WAUGH 223:12
upbringing: u. a nun would envy
                                     ORTON 163:22
uplands: forward into broad, sunlit u.
                                     CHUR 54:11
light thrilling over her u.   DAY-L 65:10
uplift: u. and self-confidence   BARN 18:19
upper: Like many of the U. Class BELL 25:9
To prove the u. classes   COW 62:11
upside: Is u. down   BURKE 42:13
upstairs: compel us to be equal u.
                                     BARR 19:1
Some went u. with Margery   AUDEN 14:6
upstanding: A clean u. chap like you
                                     KING 122:11
upward: u. to the Great Society
                                     JOHN 114:11
urban: Being u., squat, and packed
                                     BROO 40:13
incomplete in the u.   MCL 143:12
urge: u. the mind to aftersight   ELIOT 74:19
urgency: u. in our outlook   CHAR 50:1
urges: Will that stirs and u.   HARDY 97:14
Uricon: Are ashes under U.   HOUS 107:1
urine: tang of faintly scented u.
                                     JOYCE 116:8

urine (*cont.*):
wine of Shiraz into u.   DIN 67:16
urn: Lean on a garden u.   ELIOT 76:2
usage: consumed in image if not in u.
                                     BART 20:4
sinon dans son u.   BART 20:4
use: must u. less electricity   JENK 112:23
No u. to talk to me   HOUS 106:12
picturesque u. of dialect words
                                     HARDY 97:6
U. him as though you love him
                                     BLUN 34:25
What's the u. of worrying   ASAF 10:13
used: accept that I may well be u. AND 5:3
Fings ain't wot they u. t'be
                                     NORM 161:11
man who u. to notice such   HARDY 97:10
Things ain't what they u.   PERS 170:9
You u. to be in pictures   BRAC 37:21
useful: Really U. Engine   AWDRY 15:18
u. thing about a principle   MAUG 149:8
u. to Him in this respect   BUTL 43:6
useless: Man is a u. passion   SART 191:3
Music is essentially u.   SANT 190:12
uselessness: u. of men above sixty years
                                     OSLER 165:26
using: I've been u. it for years BANK 18:4
USSR: Back in the U.   LENN 135:4
usual: as u. during alterations   CHUR 53:8
utility: extension which lends u.
                                     SANT 190:12
Utopia: view as an infernal U.
                                     LEWIS 136:17
utopian: retrospective or u.   ARON 10:12
utopias: Life is moving towards u.
                                     BERD 29:10
U. and the farmyard civilization
                                     INGE 110:11
U. are realizable   BERD 29:10
utopique: *est rétrospective ou u.* ARON 10:12
utter: her secret none can u.   QUIL 177:3
u. and get rid of the element   CHES 51:3
U-turn: U., I have only this   THAT 213:2

V

vacancy: In chaos of v. shone   DE L 66:11
vacant: v. interstellar spaces   ELIOT 74:11
vacuum: v. is a hell of a lot better
                                     WILL 227:16
vagrant: A v. opinion without visible
                                     BIER 34:13
vaguery: inscribed 'For V. in the Field'
                                     OSB 165:16
vain: nothing is in v.   HERB 101:22
v. citadels that are not   OWEN 166:17
vaincu: *v. mais de s'être bien* COUB 61:12
vais: *Je v. à la gloire*   DUNC 70:13
vales: blooming in the tall v.   THOM 213:16
valid: supremely v. human experience
                                     JAMES 112:14
valley: Down in the v. drumming
                                     AUDEN 14:13
How green was my v.   LLEW 138:4
v. of its saying where   AUDEN 13:1
V. of the dolls   SUS 211:3
valuable: Truth is the most v. thing
                                     TWAIN 219:9
v. than panes of glass   PANK 167:10
value: exists, nothing has v.   FORS 84:1
Its v. depends on what   POUND 173:22
Of its sentimental v.   FRY 86:25

virtues: spend in discovering his v.
LYTT 140:18
v. are of no avail HUXL 109:7
virtuous: Be v. and you will be eccentric
TWAIN 219:6
visible: Art does not reproduce the v.
KLEE 128:7
Work is love made v. GIBR 90:6
vision: blackguard whose faulty v.
BIER 34:4
devils to contest his v. MAIL 145:12
Have molten bowels; your v. BOTT 36:14
single central v. BERL 30:4
v. of her will probably CAUL 47:16
visions: Blessed Cecilia, appear in v.
AUDEN 15:12
visit: inspect new stock or to v.
AUDEN 14:22
Sole purpose of v. HARD 96:15
which you cannot v. GIBR 90:5
visits: Superior people never make long v.
MOORE 155:15
vitality: The lower one's v. BEER 22:26
V. in a woman is a blind SHAW 197:20
vitriol: sleeve with a bottle of v.
WOOL 231:19
vittoria: La v. trova cento padri CIANO 56:7
vive: V. Le Québec Libre DE G 65:18
vivid: v. air signed SPEN 205:16
vivre: C'est une chose anormale de v.
ION 110:18
V. est une chute horizontale COCT 57:7
vocabulary: The v. of 'Bradshaw'
DOYLE 69:30
vocation: test of a v. is the love
SMITH 203:11
v. of unhappiness SIM 201:2
Vodka: medium V. dry Martini FLEM 82:1
Vogue: he'd be working for V. UST 220:19
voice: All I have is a v. AUDEN 13:9
Are her v., and her hair MAS 148:7
At once a v. outburst among
HARDY 97:11
Her v. is full of money FITZ 80:20
His v. rose to a sharp BELL 24:3
inner v. which warns MENC 150:21
Mine is the only v. I care CAMP 45:10
Out of the air a v. without AUDEN 15:8
that I hear my lover's v. PITT 172:1
through the potency of my v.
HARD 96:16
v. but because he has FAUL 78:13
v. was suddenly lifted SASS 192:6
v. we heard was ATTL 12:9
v. which was more caustic ROLFE 182:17
voiced: she who v. those rhymes
HARDY 97:1
voices: Other v., other rooms CAP 46:16
v. of young people SMITH 202:23
voids: are attempts to fill v. WEIL 224:4
volatile: v. spirits prefer unhappiness
SANT 190:10
vole: passes the questing v. WAUGH 223:13
voler: dans les rues et de v. FRAN 84:15
volitional: His errors are v. JOYCE 116:11
Volk: Ein Reich, ein V., ein Führer
ANON 6:4
volume: v. as it is with what BARR 19:4
vomit: Dog returns to his V. KIPL 126:18
Vorsprung: V. durch Technik ANON 9:3
vote: because most people v. ADAMS 1:20
Don't buy a single v. KENN 119:2
I never v. for anybody FIEL 79:17

vote (cont.):
man's decision on how to v. SCHN 193:3
The v., I thought O'BR 162:5
V. early. Vote often ANON 9:4
V. for the man who promises BAR 20:6
voter: Every intelligent v. ADAMS 1:17
votes: inscription 'V. for Women'
PANK 167:12
v. to the most obscure CHES 51:13
voting: v. that's democracy STOP 209:11
vow: As if a wedding v. DYLAN 71:12
I v. to thee, my country SPR 206:11
vowel: nice ear for v. sounds BOWEN 37:15
voyages: v. of the starship Enterprise
RODD 182:2
vrai: plus vrai que le v. ANOU 9:21
vulgar: let the v. stuff alone BELL 25:12
seems insipid to a v. SMITH 202:16
vulgarizing: succeeded in completely v.
HUXL 108:18

W

wage: It is to w. war, by sea CHUR 54:8
I w. war CLEM 56:17
policy of w. restraint WILS 228:9
w. increase was another WILS 228:18
wage/price: w. spiral by acting directly
HEATH 99:17
wages: And took their w. and are dead
HOUS 106:3
w. and shorter hours ORW 165:3
Wagner: W.'s music is better NYE 162:2
Wahrheit: Die W. hat keine Stunde
SCHW 193:13
wail: voice rose to a sharp w. BELL 24:3
wailed: sexophones w. like melodious
HUXL 108:11
wains: hangs heavy from the w.
GIBB 89:18
wainscot: The wall, the w. and the mouse
ELIOT 74:18
wait: eight, and we won't w. WYND 232:2
Must you w. HART 98:19
Tomorrow, just you w. and see
BURT 42:18
w. and not be tired KIPL 126:13
w. for the last judgement CAMUS 46:3
W. till the sun shines, Nellie STER 208:8
w. to watch the water clear FROST 86:8
w. until a shrimp learns KHR 121:3
We had better w. and see ASQ 11:7
who have to w. for them LUCAS 140:11
waiter: dam' good head w. GULB 94:15
waiting: There was I, w. at the church
LEIGH 134:10
though they keep us w. MCG 142:10
w. at the k-k-k-kitchen O'HARA 162:24
w. for rain ELIOT 73:11
w. for the long-promised CHUR 55:5
We're w. for Godot BECK 21:17
What are we all w. for CAV 48:1
waits: Someone w. for me CROS 63:8
wake: Old Country must w. GEOR 89:7
They come, they w. us LARK 131:2
W.! for the Ruddy Ball THOM 214:19
W. in her warm nest DAY-L 65:8
W. up, England GEOR 89:7
wakeful: W. they lie GRAV 93:9
wakened: w. us from sleeping BROO 40:1
wakes: And w. a vague unpunctual star
BROO 40:11

waking: take my w. slow ROET 182:4
Wales: govern New South W. BELL 24:18
influence of W. WAUGH 223:1
land of my fathers [W.] THOM 213:19
One road runs to W. MAS 148:8
position of the artists of W. THOM 214:3
there were wolves in W. THOM 213:12
W. where the only concession
THOM 214:18
walk: An active line on a w. KLEE 128:6
A w. for walk's sake KLEE 128:6
A w. on the wild side ALGR 3:7
before we have learnt to w. CONN 59:10
Idealists are very apt to w. SMITH 203:6
In a slow silent w. HARDY 97:9
Or w. with Kings KIPL 126:15
W. across my swimming pool
RICE 180:10
w. through the fields CORN 61:8
w. upon the beach ELIOT 75:19
Within a w. of the sea BELL 25:26
You'll never w. alone HAMM 96:5
walked: He w. by himself KIPL 125:17
pig got up and slowly w. BURT 42:17
w. to the brink and we DULL 70:10
walkin': These boots are made for w.
HAZL 99:6
walking: act of w. round BEER 22:20
I'm w. backwards for Christmas
MILL 152:16
I were w. with destiny CHUR 55:18
Let your fingers do the w. ANON 7:14
opening a window or just w. AUDEN 13:5
prose as dancing is to w. WAIN 222:1
walks: The w. by the lake AUDEN 15:9
Who is the third who w. ELIOT 77:4
Yet in my W. it seems to me BELL 26:1
wall: Before I built a w. I'd FROST 86:11
that doesn't love a w. FROST 86:9
The broken w., the burning YEATS 235:1
The w., the wainscot ELIOT 74:18
turneth his face to the w. BUTL 44:2
Watch the w., my darling KIPL 126:6
walled: citadels that are not w.
OWEN 166:17
walling: was w. in or walling out
FROST 86:11
wallow: And there let us w. FLAN 81:4
walls: reliable w. of youth collapse
FORS 83:14
w. of that antique station BEER 23:6
Wall St.: W. lays an egg ANON 9:5
waltz: Swoons to a w., I take HUXL 109:2
waltzing: You'll come a-w., Matilda
PAT 169:15
wander: May w. like a river AUDEN 14:12
wandering: Half to forget the w. and pain
FLEC 81:16
wanderlust: To your w. HART 98:19
want: All I w. is a room somewhere
LERN 135:25
As long as I have a w. SHAW 199:10
believe that if I don't w. O'HARA 163:1
be stupid enough to w. it CHES 52:13
I didn't w. to do it MCC 141:8
I w. to be alone GARBO 88:13
public something they w. SKEL 201:20
something you probably won't w.
HOPE 104:14
The w. of money BUTL 43:5
third is freedom from w. ROOS 183:9
We w. eight, and we won't WYND 232:2
What does a woman w. FREUD 85:9

want (*cont.*):
You can do what you w.   INGE 110:8
wanted: I only w. to make you happy
                              AYCK 15:22
Not as we w. it   QUIL 177:5
w. to make sure he was   GOLD 92:1
wanting: been tried and found w.
                              CHES 52:8
wants: Everybody w. to get inta the act
                              DUR 70:15

war: After each w. there   ATK 12:2
against w.   LOW 139:17
are the aftermath of w.   HOOV 104:10
at all, only to *this* w.   STR 210:10
because I believe that the W. SASS 192:1
been no declaration of w.   EDEN 71:18
big w., by a brief fit   BORN 36:11
Britain was going to make w.
                              BETH 30:20
brought to the verge of w.   DULL 70:10
can wage a pitiless w.   GREE 93:13
cruellest and most terrible W. LLOY 138:8
desolation of w.   GEOR 89:11
Don't mention the w.   CLEE 56:13
Either w. is obsolete   FULL 87:13
ending a w. is to lose it   ORW 164:28
essence of w. is violence   FISH 80:6
except the British W. Office SHAW 196:11
give a w. and nobody will   SAND 190:2
gone too long without a w.   BREC 39:3
great protection against w.   BEVIN 33:14
guarantee success in w.   CHUR 55:19
harder than making w.   STEV 208:20
has been a w. yet   BEVIN 33:14
Horses and Power and W.   KIPL 123:18
involved in a European w.   BEAV 21:3
involve us in the wrong w.   BRAD 38:10
In w.: resolution   CHUR 55:16
In w., whichever side may   CHAM 48:11
It is easier to make w.   CLEM 56:18
lose the w. in an afternoon   CHUR 56:6
Make love not w.   ANON 7:22
midst of a cold w.   BAR 20:7
moral equivalent of w.   JAMES 112:10
mothers and wives. I hate w. ROOS 183:3
must take chances in w.   DULL 70:10
My argument is that W.   HARDY 96:20
My subject is W.   OWEN 166:8
nuisance in time of w.   CHUR 55:2
Oh what a lovely w.   LITT 138:1
Older men declare w.   HOOV 104:10
once 'The Unnecessary W.'   CHUR 55:17
only w. creates order   BREC 39:3
Out of that bungled, unwise w.
                              PLOM 172:5
recourse to w. and renounce   BRIA 39:10
rich wage w. it's the poor   SART 190:26
someone gave a w. & Nobody   GINS 90:14
state of w. would exist   CHAM 48:15
still seek no wider w.   JOHN 114:12
than an end of this w.   ROOS 183:11
that devil's madness—W.   SERV 194:21
that 'w. is war'   CAMP 45:16
that w. settles *nothing*   CHR 52:20
The day w. broke out   WILT 229:16
There ain't gonna be no w.
                              MACM 143:18
The w. between men and women
                              THUR 216:19
The w. that will end war   WELLS 225:4
unconditional w. on poverty
                              JOHN 114:10
understood this liking for w. BENN 27:19
under the shadow of a w.   SPEN 205:15

war (*cont.*):
very well out of the w.   BALD 17:5
W. always finds a way   BREC 39:6
w. and they will forget   WILS 229:5
w. for its consequences   FOSD 84:13
W. hath no fury like a non-combatant
                              MONT 155:4
W. is, after all, the universal RAE 177:7
W. is capitalism   STOP 210:4
W. is peace   ORW 164:21
W. is too serious a matter   CLEM 56:16
W. knows no power   BROO 40:2
w. like precocious giants   PEAR 169:21
W.'s a bloody game   SASS 192:5
W.'s annals will cloud   HARDY 97:9
w. should ever come between   BON 35:17
w. they kill you in a new   ROG 182:11
w. wasn't fought that way   ROSS 185:4
w. we hadn't a chance   HELL 100:6
W. will cease when men refuse
                              ANON 9:6
w. will put an end to mankind
                              KENN 119:4
w. with atom bombs could   BENN 27:10
w. with one another again   CHAM 48:13
waste of God, W.   STUD 210:19
way to win an atomic w.   BRAD 38:8
We hear w. called murder   MACD 142:4
When is a w. not a war   CAMP 45:16
when there was w.   AUDEN 13:10
When w. enters a country   PONS 172:12
When w. is declared   PONS 172:12
which enable it to make w.   WEIL 224:2
Winston Churchill wants w.
                              BEVAN 32:18
without bloodshed while w.
                              MAO T 146:12
Work at w. speed   MORR 156:6
Yes; quaint and curious w.   HARDY 98:3
Ward: Of Light and Mrs Humphry W.
                              CHES 52:2
ware: w. that will not keep HOUS 106:10
warfare: Armed w. must be preceded
                              ZIN 236:14
Borgias they had w.   WELL 224:11
warm: earth is w. with Spring GREN 94:3
Her heart was w. and gay   HAMM 95:16
pitcher of w. piss   GARN 88:16
Wake in her w. nest   DAY-L 65:8
Winter kept us w., covering   ELIOT 76:13
warmed: her glow has w.   STEV 209:2
warming: further than w. the teapot
                              MANS 146:5
warmth: Colour and W. and Light
                              GREN 94:3
warn: poet can do today is w. OWEN 166:8
w. you not to be ordinary   KINN 122:13
warning: w. to all persons BALD 17:14
warnings: w. over the last six years
                              CHUR 55:18
warrior: Me? A cold war w. THAT 212:21
This is the happy w.   READ 178:10
wars: All w. are planned by old men
                              RICE 180:6
And as for war, my w.   REED 179:2
armaments that cause w.   MAD 144:19
beginnings of all w.   ROOS 183:11
Between the w.   PLOM 172:8
For all their w. are merry   CHES 50:9
littered with the w.   POW 175:1
sent into any foreign w.   ROOS 183:7
trick lies in *losing* w.   HELL 100:6
w. begin in the minds   ANON 6:16
W. cannot be fought   MOUN 157:3

wars (*cont.*):
which titanic w. had groined
                              OWEN 166:15
warship: every w. launched EIS 73:7
war-war: always better than to w.
                              CHUR 55:12
was: That was the week that w.
                              BIRD 34:20
W. he free   AUDEN 13:11
wash: can w. your hands and pray
                              KIPL 125:2
never comes out in the w.   KIPL 124:14
w. their feet in soda water   ELIOT 76:23
w. the wind   ELIOT 75:2
washed: W. by the rivers, blest BROO 40:5
w. in the blood   LIND 137:12
w. in the speechless   BARZ 20:10
washing: under the w. line THOM 214:10
w. on the Siegfried Line   KENN 118:21
washy: w. way of true tragedy KAV 118:9
waste: come seemed w. of breath
                              YEATS 235:5
w. all our lives raising   EDGAR 72:1
w. any time in mourning   HILL 102:11
W. of Muscle, waste of Brain
                              STUD 210:19
w. remains and kills   EMPS 77:15
What a w., what a waste   DURY 71:2
wasted: he has not w. his time FORS 83:1
Nothing is w., nothing   HERB 101:22
that it was all w. effort   AYER 16:4
youth is w. on the young   CAHN 44:16
waste-paper: marriage is the w. basket
                              WEBB 224:1
watch: done much better by a w.
                              BELL 25:23
going like a fat gold w.   PLATH 172:2
He can w. a grass or leaf   GRAV 93:6
like little w. springs   SPEN 205:20
never sit out front and w.   BARR 19:28
or my w. has stopped   PIR 171:11
The son of a bitch stole my w.
                              MAC 140:20
wait to w. the water clear   FROST 86:8
W. for me by moonlight   NOYES 162:1
W. THAT BASKET   TWAIN 219:34
W. the parkin' meters   DYLAN 71:13
why not carry a w.   TREE 217:15
withdrawn and w. them gallop
                              DURY 71:2
watched: beautiful, I w. in vain FLEC 81:21
He w. the ads   NASH 159:7
watches: someone whose mind w.
                              CAMUS 45:18
their w. when I am speaking   BIRK 34:21
watching: BIG BROTHER IS W. YOU
                              ORW 164:20
water: And don't go near the w.
                              DE L 66:20
And wait to watch the w.   FROST 86:8
benison of hot w.   BROO 39:19
But don't go near the w.   ANON 7:25
Christ walking on the w.   THOM 216:11
don't care where the w.   CHES 50:14
drank rapidly a glass of w.   CUMM 63:15
hands than w. like Pilate   GREE 93:12
He's fallen in the w.   MILL 152:14
Is wetter w., slimier slime   BROO 40:7
makes w. I makes water   JOYCE 116:4
No more w., the fire next time
                              ANON 6:12
Oh, is the w. sweet and cool BROO 40:15
replied that there was w.   BURNS 42:15
safe to go back in the w.   ANON 7:7

water (*cont.*):
struck the w. a full second	COKE 57:14
surrounded by w. took	BOWEN 37:15
than W.'s thicker	HUXL 109:1

Waterloo: high at Austerlitz and W.
SAND 189:17
Probably the battle of W.   ORW 164:18
waterproof: W. Boots on   MILNE 153:6
waters: Across the waste of w.
BETJ 31:18
And the w. as they flow   ARMS 10:7
hitherandthithering w.   JOYCE 115:11
On those cool w. where we   HOPE 105:4
w. of the heart   THOM 213:21
Watson: A long shot, W.; a very
DOYLE 69:13
Good old W.   DOYLE 69:11
wattles: clay and w. made   YEATS 232:9
wave: Churchill on top of the w. BEAV 21:7
overrun by a W. of Saints   SELL 194:10
w. follows upon wave   FISH 80:5
wavering: enchantingly w. attitude
FITZ 80:23
Waverley: W. pen   ANON 8:21
wavers: It w. to a rose   DOBS 68:3
waves: The w., they were fiddlin'
EDGAR 71:20
waving: And not w. but drowning
SMITH 203:18
than w. me farewell   HOPE 105:4
waxed: man has just w. the floor
NASH 159:6
way: All the w. with LBJ   ANON 5:10
every w., I am getting   COUÉ 61:13
Ev'rything's goin' my w.   HAMM 95:18
get you out of the w.   CORN 61:10
going but I'm on the w.   SAND 189:18
happened on the w. to the Forum
SHEV 200:12
have it your own w.   THUR 216:17
I did it my way   ANKA 3:17
I had to make my own w.   ORTON 164:2
I take my endless w.   HOUS 107:3
It's a long w. to Tipperary   JUDGE 116:17
it's the w. they say it   STEI 208:2
knows the w. but can't drive
TYNAN 220:10
more a w. of life   ANON 7:32
nice to people on your w.   MIZN 154:19
Or the w. of a man with a maid
KIPL 124:5
Poetry is a w. of taking   FROST 86:18
provided I get my own w.   THAT 212:20
shows the w. to others   GAND 88:11
Their w., however straight   THOM 214:17
There is no w. to peace   MUSTE 158:10
they kill you in a new w.   ROG 182:11
This is the w. the world ends
ELIOT 75:12
unpleasant w. of saying the truth
HELL 100:7
War always finds a w.   BREC 39:6
was a w. of putting it   ELIOT 74:9
washy w. of true tragedy   KAV 118:9
w. he travelled providing   BEAV 21:4
w. of telling you to slow   ANON 5:28
w. she disposed   HARL 98:11
w. to the Better there be   HARDY 97:12
w. to the White House   STEV 209:3
W. up high   HARB 96:13
ways: And if my w. are not as theirs
HOUS 105:17
To justify God's w. to man   HOUS 107:8
w. deep and the weather   ELIOT 73:14

ways (*cont.*):
w. will all be as nothing	HARDY 97:5

We have w. of making men talk
YOUNG 236:8
we: slogan 'W. Never Closed'   VAN D 221:3
still it is not w.   CHES 52:1
W. are the hollow men   ELIOT 75:10
W. are the Ovaltineys   ANON 9:7
W. are the stuffed men   ELIOT 75:10
W. have become a grandmother
THAT 213:7
W. shall not be moved   ANON 9:11
W. shall not pretend   ANON 9:12
W. shall overcome   ANON 9:13
W. was robbed   JAC 111:6
weak: But the w., washy way   KAV 118:9
surely the W. shall perish   SERV 194:22
The w. have one weapon   BID 33:18
w. always have to decide   BONH 36:2
w. from your loveliness   BETJ 32:1
w. men he laid an exaggerated
MAUG 149:18
weaken: great life if you don't w.
BUCH 41:19
we shall not w. or tire   CHUR 53:9
weak-minded: very w. fellow I am
HAIG 95:2
weakness: oh! w. of joy   BETJ 32:1
wealth: w. is a sacred thing   FRAN 84:14
w. without producing it   SHAW 196:3
wealthy: business of the w.   BELL 25:7
weaned: had been w. on a pickle
ANON 8:23
weapon: art is not a w.   KENN 119:8
bayonet is a w. with a worker ANON 5:15
folly and his w. wit   ANON 6:21
Loyalty is the Tory's secret w.
KILM 121:10
Our chief w. is surprise   CHAP 49:14
terrible w. of aggression   ADLER 2:16
weak have one w.   BID 33:18
weapons: fought with nuclear w.
MOUN 157:3
we know, books are w.   ROOS 183:13
wearied: Ragtime ... but when the w.
Band   HUXL 109:2
wearing: w. armchairs tight about
WOD 230:18
w. such a conscience-stricken
HOUS 105:8
W. white for Eastertide   HOUS 105:8
wears: she w. them   SAKI 188:12
weary: Age shall not w. them BINY 34:18
weasel: If you use a 'w. word' ROOS 184:8
w. took the cork out   FIEL 79:10
w. under the cocktail cabinet
PINT 171:11
weather: but the w. turned around
THOM 213:16
her madness and her w.   AUDEN 13:1
places and how the w. was   HEM 100:10
rains we'll laugh at the w.   HART 98:19
The ways deep and the w. sharp
ELIOT 73:14
waiting for the w. to break   PINT 171:14
W. and rain have undone   KIPL 126:12
w. inside of four-and-twenty
TWAIN 220:3
w. the cuckoo likes   HARDY 97:2
w. when good fellows get   BURT 42:17
you won't hold up the w.   MACN 144:9
weave: w. the sunlight   ELIOT 76:2
Webb: When Captain W. the Dawley man
BETJ 32:7

webs: By the dark w., her nape
YEATS 234:21
Webster: Like W.'s Dictionary BURKE 42:14
W. was much possessed by death
ELIOT 75:8
wedding: As if a w. vow   DYLAN 71:12
white lies to ice a w. cake   ASQ 11:18
wedding-cake: my face looks like a w.
AUDEN 15:14
wee: Just a w. deoch-an-doris MORR 156:8
Of the 'w. six' I sing   HEAN 99:13
weed: Ignorance is an evil w. BEV 33:9
Less than the w., that grows HOPE 105:3
weeds: than mundane w. are there
BROO 40:8
w. from gravel paths   KIPL 125:1
w. will overrun the fields   HOOV 104:13
week: he had to die in MY w.   JOPL 115:4
takes me as much as a w.   TWAIN 219:17
That was the w. that was   BIRD 34:20
w. in the history   NIXON 161:3
w. is a long time in politics WILS 228:14
weekend: anxious to go away for the w.
WHITE 226:4
The w. starts here   ANON 9:8
weekends: getting a plumber on w.
ALLEN 3:18
weeks: w. rather than months WILS 228:16
weep: But she would w. to see today
DOUG 68:11
I w. like a child   LAWR 132:13
W. not for little Léonie   GRAH 92:10
W. thy girlish tears   WATS 222:16
weeping: W., weeping multitudes
ELIOT 73:10
weigh: Shall w. your God and you
KIPL 127:20
weight: w. of rages will press SPOO 206:9
willing to pull his w.   ROOS 183:14
welcome: Hello, good evening, and w.
FROST 85:14
on your part would be w.   ATTL 12:11
The effusive w. of the pier   AUDEN 14:16
W., O life! I go to encounter
JOYCE 115:20
welfare: w.-state   TEMP 212:11
with the w. of the country   WILS 228:7
well: And all shall be w.   ELIOT 74:23
Didn't she [*or* he *or* they] do w.
FORS 84:10
He does himself extremely w.   ANON 7:26
How w. I did behave   HOUS 106:13
I do it exceptionally w.   PLATH 172:3
talk w. but not too   MAUG 150:2
w. of unconscious cerebration
JAMES 111:13
well-bred: Conscience is thoroughly w.
BUTL 43:12
well-content: Sweet Stay-at-Home,
sweet W.   DAV 65:4
well-developed: into it with w. bodies
FORS 83:2
well-knownness: who is known for his w.
BOOR 36:5
well-meaning: w. man of indifferent
judgement   BEAV 21:2
wells: at evening from the w. FLEC 81:8
Welsh: about in the W. jungle BANK 18:6
Welt: *Die W. ist alles, was der* WITT 229:21
die W. so einzurichten   FRIS 85:10
wench: stuff fit only for a w. MAS 148:4
Wenlock: W. Edge the wood's in trouble
HOUS 106:18

wept: has not w. is a savage   SANT 190:6
  Station I sat down and w.   SMART 202:1
were: w. we led all that way   ELIOT 73:15
we're: W. here   ANON 9:10
  W. number two. We try harder
                                   ANON 9:9
west: another one down in the w.
                                   BOUL 37:2
  gardens of the W.   CONN 59:3
  Or w. to the Golden Gate   KIPL 127:17
  running farce in the W. End
                                   SMITH 202:5
  That's where the W. begins   CHAP 49:9
  This lady of the W. Country   DE L 66:10
  warm wind, the w. wind   MAS 148:19
  W. of these out to seas   FLEC 81:18
wester: The rainy Pleiads w.   HOUS 106:6
western: All quiet on the w. front
                                   REM 179:11
  be delivered by W. Union   GOLD 91:13
  Playboy of the W. World   SYNGE 211:11
  when you've seen one W.   WHIT 226:17
Westminster: bars and brothels of W.
                                   LIV 138:3
wet: Let's get out of these w.   ANON 7:12
  w. clothes and into a dry   WEST 225:10
wetting: He saved his friend from a w.
                                   MILNE 154:4
Weygand: General W. called   CHUR 54:11
what: are W. and Why and When
                                   KIPL 125:15
  But w. can a poor boy do   JAGG 111:9
  His later famed 'W. mean?'   ROSS 185:1
  I know what's w.   WEST 225:18
  luckiest of mortals because w.
                                   AUDEN 14:17
  Oh, w. a beautiful mornin'   HAMM 95:18
  Restricted to W. Precisely   ELIOT 74:1
  W. a dump   COFF 57:9
  W. a waste, what a waste   DURY 71:2
  W. does a woman want   FREUD 85:9
  'W. ho!' I said   WOD 230:20
  W. if someone gave a war   GINS 90:14
  W. is hell   ELIOT 73:20
  W. is man, when you come   DIN 67:16
  W. is she a-doin' of   ANON 8:8
  w. is which   MILNE 154:3
  W. of the bow   DOYLE 70:2
  W. of the faith and fire   HARDY 97:16
  W. one knows is, in youth   ADAMS 2:5
  W.'s up, Doc   AVERY 15:17
  W. we call the beginning   ELIOT 74:21
  w. we can make of the mess   ELIOT 74:14
  w. you may expect to see   DOYLE 69:10
what's: W. on second, I Don't   ABB 1:1
  W. on television   ACE 1:5
wheat: it is to separate the w.   HUBB 107:13
  sleep-flower sways in the w.   THOM 215:3
  w. to be a cause of international
                                   WEIL 224:2
wheel: beneath thy Chariot w.   HOPE 105:3
  w.'s kick and the wind's   MAS 148:16
wheels: apparently rolled along on w.
                                   HUXL 109:8
when: had forgotten to say 'W.!'
                                   WOD 230:23
  Oh, w. will you ever learn   SEEG 194:6
  w. a guy gets stabbed   GARD 88:15
  W. a lovely flame dies   HARB 96:11
  W. I am dead, I hope it   BELL 25:16
  W. I'm not near the girl   HARB 96:14
  w. in doubt, strike it out   TWAIN 219:33
  W. there was peace   AUDEN 13:10

when (cont.):
  W. you call me that   WIST 229:18
  W. you go home, tell them   EDM 72:3
  w. you got it, flaunt it   BROO 41:3
  w. you have eliminated   DOYLE 69:22
whence: Or w. he came   HARDY 97:8
  W. did he whence   LENO 135:17
whenever: W. I hear the word culture
                                   JOHST 114:19
where: But w.'s the bloody horse
                                   CAMP 45:11
  W. are the eagles   ELIOT 73:10
  W. have all the flowers gone   SEEG 194:6
  W. it will all end, knows God   GIBBS 90:4
  W. there is no imagination   DOYLE 69:27
  w.'s the rest of me   BELL 24:3
whereabouts: conceal our w.   SAKI 188:18
wherefore: W. does he why   LENO 135:17
wherever: Dance then w. you may
                                   CART 47:7
  make w. we're lost   FRY 87:6
which: W. will reach the bottom first
                                   GRAH 92:13
while: But it's a long, long w.   AND 4:21
  w. there is a lower class   DEBS 65:14
whim: Barumph has a w. of iron
                                   HERF 101:28
  conviction begins as a w.   BROUN 41:5
  strangest w. has seized me   CHES 52:3
  tempted by a private w.   BELL 25:17
whimper: Not with a bang but a w.
                                   ELIOT 75:12
whin: I looked and three w. bushes
                                   KAV 118:7
whip: he brings down the w.   LESS 135:27
whipping: Like w. tops   HODG 103:12
Whips: Chamber selected by the W.
                                   FOOT 82:10
whiskers: gentleman with iron-grey w.
                                   BEER 23:19
whiskey: bad w. Some whiskeys
                                   FAUL 78:14
  Stories, like w.   O'FAO 162:22
whisper: Hush! Hush! W. who dares
                                   MILNE 153:12
  We w. in her ear   WILB 226:24
  w. music on those strings   ELIOT 75:5
  w. to the tourist last   BEER 23:6
  w. was already born before
                                   MAND 145:19
whispering: Come w. by   HARDY 97:9
  deceives with w. ambitions   ELIOT 73:12
  was just w. in her mouth   MARX 147:16
whisperings: w. and the champagne
                                   FITZ 80:19
whispers: he says, but what he w.
                                   SMITH 203:15
  w. through the grass all   BROO 40:12
whist: w. upon w. upon w. drive
                                   BETJ 31:2
whistle: until a shrimp learns to w.
                                   KHR 121:3
  W. while you work   MOREY 155:18
whistled: w. a tune to the window
                                   NOYES 161:17
whistling: The blackbird w.   STEV 208:14
white: be the w. man's brother
                                   KING 121:14
  bluebirds over the w. cliffs   BURT 42:18
  come the Gardener in w.   FLEC 81:12
  cool w. dress after   FIRB 80:4
  I'm dreaming of a w. Christmas
                                   BERL 30:3
  Klux Klanner but the w.   KING 121:12

white (cont.):
  look ahead up the w. road   ELIOT 77:4
  necessity of the American w.   BALD 16:16
  Slowly her w. brow among   FREE 85:3
  so-called w. races   FORS 83:20
  Take up the W. Man's burden
                                   KIPL 127:19
  Their w. it stays for ever   DOBS 68:3
  Tyin' up my w. tie   BERL 30:2
  Wearing w. for Eastertide   HOUS 106:9
  wear w. flannel trousers   ELIOT 75:19
  W. as an orchid she rode   AUDEN 15:11
  w. lies to ice a wedding   ASQ 11:18
  w. man in Africa by accident
                                   LESS 135:27
  w. race is the cancer   SONT 205:1
white-collar: little man with a w. job
                                   ORW 165:2
  nor are they the w. people
                                   WHYTE 226:22
Whitehall: gentleman in W. really does
  know   JAY 112:19
White Horse: The W. of the White Horse
  Vale   CHES 50:7
White House: me on the way to the W.
                                   STEV 209:3
  no whitewash at the W.   NIXON 161:4
  Operative W. Position   ZIEG 236:13
  Oval Room at the W.   NIXON 161:2
whiter: A w. shade of pale   REID 179:10
whitewash: no w. at the White House
                                   NIXON 161:4
whither: W. is he withering   LENO 135:17
Whitman: daintily dressed Walt W.
                                   CHES 52:6
  Walt W.   CRANE 62:14
whizzing: W. them over the net   BETJ 32:8
who: W. dares wins   ANON 9:14
  W. he   ROSS 185:1
whole: For nothing can be sole or w.
                                   YEATS 235:14
  shall be the w. of the Law   CROW 63:10
  w. worl's in a state   O'CAS 162:13
wholly: w. in Peter Pan ever since
                                   TYNAN 220:8
whom: W. are you   ADE 2:9
whooping: w. it up in the Malamute
                                   SERV 194:23
whopper: Let's have a w.   LERN 135:18
whore: like a chaste w.   MUGG 157:9
  Treat a w. like a lady   MIZN 154:19
who's: So w. in a hurry   BENC 27:3
  team we have W. on first   ABB 1:1
  W. afraid of Virginia Woolf   ALBEE 3:2
whose: W. finger do you want   ANON 9:15
  W. life is it anyway   CLARK 56:8
whoso: W. maintains that I am   CORN 61:6
Who's Who: I've been in W.   WEST 225:18
why: W. fear death   FROH 85:11
  you say 'W.?'   SHAW 195:20
wicked: August is a w. month   O'BR 162:4
  gang who work your w. will
                                   CHUR 53:10
  With a w. pack of cards   ELIOT 76:16
wickedness: quite capable of every w.
                                   CONR 60:3
wicket: at the w. or the muddied
                                   KIPL 124:13
  slow W. of the Night   THOM 214:19
widely: opinion has been w.   RUSS 186:18
widening: turning in the w. gyre
                                   YEATS 233:12
wider: But Water's w., thank   HUXL 109:3
  W. still and wider shall   BENS 28:21

X

Y

Z